# The
# Complete
# Entertainment
# Discography

BOOKS BY BRIAN RUST

*London Musical Theatre, 1894–1954*
*King Joe Oliver* (with Walter C. Allen)
*Recorded Jazz: A Critical Guide* (with Rex Harris)
*Jazz Records, 1897–1942* (two volumes)
*The Victor Master Book, Volume 2, 1925–1936*
*The Dance Bands*
*British Dance Bands: A Discography, 1912–1939*
*The Complete Dance Band Discography* (in preparation)

# The Complete Entertainment Discography

from the mid-1890s to 1942

## BRIAN RUST

with

Allen G. Debus

ARLINGTON HOUSE    New Rochelle, N. Y.

*Library of Congress Catalog Card Number 73-13239*

MANUFACTURED IN THE UNITED STATES OF AMERICA

**Library of Congress Cataloging in Publication Data**

Rust, Brian A    L    1922-
   The complete entertainment discography, from the mid-1890's to 1942.

   1.  Music, Popular (Songs, etc.)--Discography.
2.  Vaudeville--Discography.  I.  Debus, Allen G., joint author.  II.  Title.
ML156.4.P6R88          016.7899'12          73-13239
ISBN 0-87000-150-7

This book bears the title THE COMPLETE ENTERTAINMENT DISCOGRAPHY.  In its
pages will be found listed all the known records, with the fullest available   information on their numbers, dates of recording, location, and so on, of artists of
the years between the beginning of commercial recording in the mid-1890s and 1942,
when the ban on recording imposed by James C. Petrillo of the American  Federation
of Musicians brought all such recording to a halt for over two years.

All artists ?  No, not quite that; a work of such a scope would call  for
a series of massive encyclopaedic works beyond the means of all but the wealthiest
collectors and enthusiasts.  So where and how have we drawn the line ?  We decided
that jazz and blues musicians, entertainers though they undoubtedly are, should be
excluded, as volumes on their recordings already exist.  Similarly, discographical
works on the commercial dance bands, American and British, are in preparation,  or
actually exist.  (This accounts for the exclusion from this book of names such  as
Ethel Waters, Lee Wiley, Rudy Vallee, Will Osborne, Carl Ravazza, Bob Crosby,  and
Maxine Sullivan).  Artists whose fame spread through their records, and who in this
medium were truly prolific, such as Billy Murray, Irving Kaufman, Edward M. Favor,
Henry Burr and Ada Jones, seem to us to deserve a volume each.

We are left with the minstrel pioneers, the vaudevillians, the film stars
and radio personalities, and the straight actors and actresses - some of whom even
lifted their voices in song, some with delightful results that leave us wishing we
had more, others rather less successfully, but with undeniably interesting results
- and these are the subjects of the hundreds of chapters in this book.   A further
qualification is that they should be artists of American birth, or of such stature
that they are as well-known in America as in their own countries, hence we can see
in this book biographies and details of the records of not only American  citizens
such as Bing Crosby, Edwin Booth, Jessie Bartlett Davis and Dinah Shore, but  Noël
Coward, Beatrice Lillie, Maurice Chevalier, Conrad Veidt, Raquel Meller and   Bert
Williams.

In his introduction to the selection of tunes in his show CAVALCADE,  Sir
Noël Coward comments about those songs that in many cases, "the voices that    sang
them will never sing again."  This, alas, is true of many of the stars whose  work
is listed here; others are delighting us now as they did when they made these  recordings long years ago. We believe this is as complete an entertainment  discography as can be compiled within the date-limits we have set; and we offer it as a
token of gratitude to the personalities who, through the invention of the   phonograph and gramophone, will never die, but who will continue to give us pleasure as

often as we choose to ask them.

BRIAN RUST.
ALLEN G. DEBUS.

June, 1973.

## ACKNOWLEDGMENTS

Although we have devoted a number of years to the compilation of the Complete Entertainment Discography, without the willing assistance and sustaining keenness of many authorities the book might well have taken many years more.   We should therefore like to express our sincerest thanks to the following friends who gave  up a great deal of time to obtaining exact details, often at a moment's notice, on many tricky subjects :- Paul Charosh; Chris Ellis (EMI Records); Ted Fagan; Derek  Lewis (BBC Gramophone Librarian); Geoff Milne (Decca Records); Mrs. G. Platford (EMI); the staff of THE GRAMOPHONE and its Managing Editor, Anthony C. Pollard; Quentin  Riggs; Patrick Saul (Director of the British Institute of Recorded Sound); Dudley  Scholte; Mrs. Maureen Spratt (EMI); and we must also acknowledge our indebtedness to  various periodicals and books for small crumbs and large helpings of invaluable detail.  The vastness of John Parker's WHO'S WHO IN THE THEATRE was a treasure-chest of material; without Leslie Halliwell's THE FILMGOER'S COMPANION, we could not have shown much of the detail of the careers of movie stars; Abel Green and Joe Laurie, Jr.'s SHOW  BIZ provided much otherwise unobtainable background information; and the files   of  THE GRAMOPHONE, with its monthly reviews of records issued since April, 1923, gave us an accurate picture of exactly what was on many records of which we had never seen  any copies at all.  We relied considerably also on the catalogues, supplements and other publicity material issued by record companies, extant and extinct : RCA Victor; CBS; Decca; Vocalion; Brunswick; Gennett, and many others; and we must not forget what we owe to Jim Walsh for his contributions to HOBBIES over more than thirty years,   and to Larry F. Kiner, whose discographies of stars such as Ruth Etting, Sophie  Tucker, Harry Richman and others were the scaffolding on which we built our own edifice.

## AUTHORS'  NOTE

As this book is an index to the artists in itself, there is no index to be found at the back; instead, the reader will find there a list of the abbreviations in use throughout the text, of both makes of record and instruments.

William "Bud" Abbott : b. Asbury Park, N.J., 1895. Parents were in circus troupe; Abbott joined the Navy at 15, and was later a box-office clerk. Lou Costello : b. Patterson, N.Y., 1908. Began work as hat salesman, then became a boxer, and stunt man for MGM. Abbott and Costello teamed up in 1930 in Brooklyn, doing seven years in burlesque theatres. They appeared on Kate Smith's radio shows in 1938 and with Carmen Miranda on stage in STREETS OF PARIS (Broadhurst, N.Y., June 19, 1939). In 1940 they began filming, and made many comedy films before splitting up in 1957. These included NIGHT IN THE TROPICS; BUCK PRIVATES; HOLD THAT GHOST; RIO RITA; AB-BOTT AND COSTELLO MEET FRANKENSTEIN; ABBOTT AND COSTELLO MEET CAPTAIN KIDD; ABBOTT AND COSTELLO IN HOLLYWOOD; ABBOTT AND COSTELLO IN THE FOREIGN LEGION, and one that flopped - their own production, DANCE WITH ME, HENRY. Costello appeared alone in THE BRIDE OF CANDY ROCK in 1958, and died on March 3, 1959.

With The Sportmen Quartet, and O/Lou Bring.
                                      Hollywood, December 8, 1941.

PBS-061962-1  Laugh, Laugh, Laugh - Part 1      Vic 27737, LPV-580, LSA-3086,
                                                HMV BD-1009
PBS-061963-1  Laugh, Laugh, Laugh - Part 2      As above

Also made children's records for Castle, Decca and Enterprise after 1942.

## HARRY AKST

Famed as the composer of such very successful songs as DINAH, and as accompanist to the late Al Jolson during the latter years of his life, Harry Akst made some sides as pianist in small instrumental groups or as one of a piano duo.

WIEDOEFT-WADSWORTH QUARTET : Rudy Wiedoeft-Wheeler Wadsworth-as/Harry Akst-J. Russel Robinson-p.                          New York, March 1, 1920.

B-23814-2  The Crocodile                        Vic 18663
B-23815-1-2-3  Lone Star                        Rejected

Piano duets with Frank Banta.           New York, May 8, 1920.

 79167-2  Typhoon                               Col A-2953
 79168-   I'll Always Keep A Corner In My Heart  Rejected
          For Tennessee

                                      New York, June 2, 1920.

 79214-1  Ding Toes (Intro. Cuddle Up)          Col A-2953

Piano duet with Ferdie Grofe, featured with Paul Whiteman and his Orchestra.
                                      New York, March 16, 1921.

B-25006-2  Down Around The 'Sip 'Sip 'Sippi Shore  Vic 18744, HMV B-1254

Piano duets with Frank Banta.           New York, June 13, 1922.

 80395-   A Bunch Of Keys                       Col rejected
 80396-   Blue-Eyed Blues                       -

## OLGA MEDOLAGO ALBANI

Vocal, acc. by own piano.               New York, April 25, 1929.

BVE-633  Mirame asi                             Vic test
BVE-634  Why Do I Love You ? ("Show Boat")      -

   Acc. by O/Robles.                    New York, June 13, 1929.

BVE-53835-   Mirame asi                         Vic 46339
BVE-53837-1-2  Mi pobre Reja                    Rejected
   NOTE:- Matrix BVE-53836 is not by Countess Albani, though made at this session.

New York, June 14, 1929.

BVE-53841-    De mal corazon (Mean To Me)              Vic 46352
BVE-53842-    No puedo digar de quererte (Can't Help    -
                Lovin' Dat Man) ("Show Boat")

New York, June 21, 1929.

BVE-53837-    Mi pobre Reja                            Vic 46339
BVE-53859-1-2  Porque te amo yo ? (Why Do I Love    Rejected
                You ?) ("Show Boat")

New York, June 28, 1929.

BVE-53893-    El Cantar de las Cantares (Where Is   Vic 46388
                The Song Of Songs For Me ?)

New York, July 2, 1929.

BVE-53896-    Torna otra vez, amor mio                 Vic 46358

New York, July 18, 1929.

BVE-55140-1-2  Dime por Dios                          Vic rejected

New York, October 24, 1929.

BVE-57022-    La Huerfanita                            Vic 46552
BVE-57023-    La Cancion del Olvido                     -

New York, October 31, 1929.

BVE-57053-1-2  Tu                                      Vic rejected

New York, November 7, 1929.

BVE-57069-1-2  Guajiras                               Vic rejected

  Acc. by O/Leonard Joy.           New York, December 3, 1929.

BVE-438      The Way Of Dreams                         Vic test

  Acc. by O/Robles.                New York, December 27, 1929.

BVE-57958-    Uno para el otro (You Were Meant For  Vic 46668
                Me)
BVE-57959-    Pisa Callandito (Tip-Toe Thru' The        -
                Tulips)
BVE-57960-1-2  Felices dias                           Rejected

  Acc. by O/Leonard Joy.           New York, December 31, 1929.

BVE-57968-1-2-3-4  I'll See You Again ("Bitter    Vic rejected
                Sweet")
BVE-57969-1-2-3  Zigeuner ("Bitter Sweet")              -

New York, January 7, 1930.

BVE-57968-8  I'll See You Again ("Bitter Sweet")   Vic 22313
BVE-57981-2  It's You I Love                           -

Vocalist with The High Hatters/Leonard Joy.
                                New York, February 13, 1930.

BVE-58570-1  In My Little Hope Chest                Vic 22322, HMV B-5853

  Acc. by O/Victor Young.          New York, August 9, 1932.

BX-12159-A  Why Do I Love You ? (w/Frank Munn)     Br 20117, 114

Vocal, acc. by O/Charles A. Prince (?)      New York, August 16, 1916.

46963-    When The Black Sheep Comes Home              Col A-2081

New York, August 17, 1916.

46970-    Turn Back The Universe And Give Me          Col rejected
          Yesterday

New York, August 21, 1916.

46976-    I Never Knew (w/Julia Jordan) ("Canary    Col rejected
          Cottage")

New York, October 16, 1916.

47069-2   I Never Knew (w/Nanette Flack) ("Canary   Col A-2126
          Cottage")

## AMOS 'N' ANDY

See Charles Correll.

## EDDIE "ROCHESTER" ANDERSON

"Gravel-voiced" negro comedian, b. 1905; long associated with Jack Benny. Many films
  including THANKS FOR THE MEMORY; BUCK BENNY RIDES AGAIN; BIRTH OF THE BLUES;  KISS
  THE BOYS GOODBYE; STAR-SPANGLED RHYTHM; TALES OF MANHATTAN;  CABIN  IN  THE  SKY;
  STORMY WEATHER; WHAT'S BUZZIN', COUSIN ?; BROADWAY RHYTHM; I LOVE A BANDLEADER.

Vocal, acc. by orchestra.                   Los Angeles, March 15, 1940.

LA-2180-A  If Money Grew On Trees               Col 36185
LA-2181-A  Waitin' For Jane                     -
LA-2182-A  Let's Scuffle                        Col 35442, DB-1936
LA-2183-A  My ! My ! (Film "Buck Benny Rides Again")   -          -

## THE  ANDREWS SISTERS

LaVerne (1915-1967), Maxene (1917) and Patti (1920) Andrews were all born in  Minneapolis, winning a talent contest in the Orpheum Theatre there while still in their
teens.  They made their debut in New York, singing with Leon Belasco's  Orchestra,
and while they were entertaining in the Hotel Edison, Jack Kapp, who was the chief
of Decca Records at that time, heard them, recorded them and brought them    world-
wide fame until they broke up the act in 1953 (although they reformed   briefly in
1956).  They made many films (STAGE-DOOR CANTEEN; THE ROAD TO UTOPIA; IN THE NAVY;
ARGENTINE NIGHTS; WHAT'S COOKIN' ?; FOLLOW THE BOYS; THE ROAD TO RIO), entertained
troops during World War II, and appeared at the London Palladium in 1950.

Vocalists with Leon Belasco and his Orchestra.
                                   New York, March 18, 1937.

B-20840-   There's A Lull In My Life - vPA         Br 7872
B-20841-   Wake Up And Live - vLA-MA-PA            -
B-20842-   Turn Off The Moon - vPA                 Br 7863
B-20843-   Jammin' - vLA-MA-PA                     -

   Acc. by O/Vic Schoen.          New York, October 18, 1937.

62686-A  Why Talk About Love ?                   Dec 1496, Br 02541
62687-A  Just A Simple Melody                     -          -

New York, November 24, 1937.

62810-A  Nice Work If You Can Get It             Dec 1562, Br 02552
62811-A  Bei mir bist du schoen                   -  7-3  -   LA-8728, AH-21

New York, February 21, 1938.

| | | |
|---|---|---|
| 63300-A | Joseph, Joseph | Dec 1691, 23605, Br 02654 |
| 63301-A | Ti-Pi-Tin | Dec 1703, Br 02592 |

New York, February 22, 1938.

| | | |
|---|---|---|
| 63314-A | Shortenin' Bread | Dec 1744, Br 02582 |
| 63315-A | It's Easier Said Than Done | Dec 1691, Br 02610 |
| 63316-A | Where Have We Met Before ? | Dec 1703, Br 02592 |
| 63317-A | OoooOH Boom ! | Dec 1744, Br 02582 |

New York, June 4, 1938.

| | | |
|---|---|---|
| 63911-A | Says My Heart | Dec 1875, Br 02629 |
| 63912-C | Oh ! Ma-Ma ! | Dec 1859, Br 02610 |
| 63913-A | Pagan Love Song | - Br 02643 |
| 63914-A | I Married An Angel | Dec 1912, Br 03368 |
| 63915-A | Oh ! Faithless Maid | Dec 1875, Br 02629 |
| 63916-B | From The Land Of The Sky-Blue Water | Dec 1912, Br 02643 |
| 63917- | Ferdinand The Bull | Rejected |

Acc. by Jimmy Dorsey and his Orchestra. New York, July 27, 1938.

| | | |
|---|---|---|
| 64350-A | Tu-Li-Tulip Time | Dec 1974, Br 02654 |
| 64352-A | Sha-Sha | - Br 02665 |

NOTE:- Other titles from this session have vocal refrains by June Richmond, Jimmy Dorsey's regular singer at the time.

Acc. by studio orchestra.    New York, August 6, 1938.

| | | |
|---|---|---|
| 64423- | Love Is Where You Find It | Dec 2016, Br 02837 |
| 64424-A | When A Prince Of A Fella Meets A Cinderella | - Br 02665 |
| 64425- | A Jitterbug's Lullaby - Part 1 | Rejected |
| 64426- | A Jitterbug's Lullaby - Part 2 | - |
| 64427- | One-Two-Three O'Leary | Br 02837 |

New York, September 8, 1938.

| | | |
|---|---|---|
| 64670-A | Lullaby To A Jitterbug | Dec 2082, Br 02696 |
| 64671-A | Pross-Tchai (Goodbye) | - - |

Acc. by Jimmy Dorsey and his Orchestra, with Ray McKinley-v.
New York, November 21, 1938.

| | | |
|---|---|---|
| 64757-A | Hold Tight, Hold Tight | Dec 2214, 23606, Br 02717, AH-21 |
| 64758-A | Billy Boy - vRM | - - |

Acc. by Woody Herman and his Orchestra. New York, January 24, 1939.

| | | |
|---|---|---|
| 64942-A | Begin The Beguine | Dec rejected |
| 64943-A | Long Time No See | - |

Acc. by Bob Crosby's Bobcats.    New York, February 6, 1939.

| | | |
|---|---|---|
| 64988-A | Begin The Beguine | Dec 2290, Br 02752 |
| 64990-A | Long Time No See | - - |

NOTE:- Other titles from this session have no vocal work at all.

Acc. by studio orchestra.    New York, March 31, 1939.

| | | |
|---|---|---|
| 65326-B | You Don't Know How Much You Can Suffer | Dec 2414, Br 02811 |
| 65327-A | Rock, Rock, Rock-a-Bye Baby | - - |

New York, May 3, 1939.

| | | |
|---|---|---|
| 65531-A | The Beer Barrel Polka (Roll Out The Barrel) | Dec 2462, 23609, Br 02769, AH-21 |
| 65532-A | Well, All Right | - - - |

New York, September 15, 1939.

```
66591-A  The Jumping Jive (Jim-Jam-Jump)        Dec 2756, Br 02874
66592-A  Chico's Love Song                         -     Br 02966
```

Acc. by Joe Venuti and his Orchestra, with Bing Crosby-v.
New York, September 20, 1939.

```
66632-A  Ciribiribin (They're So In Love)       Dec 2800, Br 02881, Coral CSP-91
66633-B  Yodelin' Jive                             -          -           -
```

Acc. by studio orchestra.          New York, November 9, 1939.

```
66498-A  Oh, Johnny ! Oh, Johnny ! Oh !         Dec 2840, Br 02874, 05782,AH-21
66499-A  South American Way                        -     Br 03157
```

New York, February 7, 1940.

```
67180-A  Say "Si, Si" (Para vigo me voy)        Dec 3013, Br 02996
67181-   Let's Have Another One                    -     Br 02966
67182-A-B  I Love You Much Too Much             Rejected
```

New York, February 21, 1940.

```
67225-A  The Woodpecker Song                    Dec 3065, Br 02996
67226-   Down By The O-Hi-O                        -     Br 03011
```

New York, March 23, 1940.

```
67383-   Rhumboogie                             Dec 3097, Br 03070
67384-   Tuxedo Junction                           -     Br 03011
```

New York, April 23, 1940.

```
67613-   The Cockeyed Mayor Of Kaunakakai       Dec 3245, Br 03070
67614-   Let's Pack Our Things And Trek            -
```

Los Angeles, July 7, 1940.

```
DLA-2039-A  Oh, He Loves Me (Film "Argentine Nights")Dec 3310, Br 03116
DLA-2040-A-B  Hit The Road (Film "Argentine Nights")  Rejected
DLA-2041-A  I Want My Mama (Mama eu quero)          Dec 3310, Br 03104
```

Los Angeles, July 15, 1940.

```
DLA-2054-  Sweet Molly Malone                   Dec 3440
DLA-2055-  Ferry-Boat Serenade (La Piccinina)   Dec 3328, Br 03082
DLA-2056-B  Hit The Road (Film "Argentine Nights")   -     Br 03116
```

New York, August 3, 1940.

```
67960-A  Johnny Peddler (I Got)                 Dec 3553, Br 03104
67961-   Beat Me, Daddy, Eight To The Bar       Dec 23607, Br 03082, AH-21
```

New York, August 28, 1940.

```
68019-A  Pennsylvania 6-5000                    Dec 3375, Br 03089
68020-   Beat Me, Daddy, Eight To The Bar          -
68021-   My Love Went Without Water             Dec SA-1873 (S. Africa only)
```

New York, September 5, 1940.

```
68046-   Mean To Me                             Dec 3440, Br 04197
68047-   Sweet Molly Malone                        -     Br 04198
68048-A  I Love You Much Too Much                     Br 03089
```

New York, November 14, 1940.

```
68351-A  I'll Be With You In Apple Blossom Time  Dec 3622, Br 03174, 05782, AH-21
68352-A  Scrub Me, Mama, With A Boogie Beat      Dec 3553, Br 03157
```

                                        Los Angeles, January 2, 1941.

DLA-2324-A  You're A Lucky Fellow, Mr. Smith    Dec 3599, Br 03195
            (Film "Buck Privates")
DLA-2325-   Bounce Me, Brother, With A Solid Four Dec 3598, Br 03147
            (Film "Buck Privates")
DLA-2326-   Boogie Woogie Bugle Boy (Film "Buck       -         -
            Privates")

                                        Los Angeles, January 7, 1941.

DLA-2356-A  I, Yi, Yi, Yi, Yi (I Like You Very    Dec 3622, Br 03195
            Much)
DLA-2357-A  Yes, My Darling Daughter              Dec 3599, Br 03174, AH-21

                                        New York, March 18, 1941.

68827-A  Aurora                             Dec 3732, Br 03213
68828-A  Music Makers                            -         -
68829-A  Lonesome Mama                                     Br 03416

                                        Los Angeles, May 21, 1941.

DLA-2395-A  Daddy                              Dec 3821, Br 03215, 04834
DLA-2396-A  Sleepy Serenade                        -         -
DLA-2397-A-B  Sonny Boy                        Rejected

                                        Los Angeles, May 29, 1941.

DLA-2425-A-B  Helena                           Rejected
DLA-2426-   Sonny Boy                          Dec 3871, Br 04197, Ah-21
DLA-2427-   Gimme Some Skin, My Friend             -
DLA-2428-A-B  Hula-Ba-Luau                     Rejected

                                        New York, July 28, 1941.

69568-A  Jealous                            Dec 4019, Br 03268
69569-A  For All We Know                    Dec 4094, Br 03290

                                        New York, July 30, 1941.

69578-   Honey                              Dec 4008, Br 03274
69579-   The Nickel Serenade                Dec 3960, Br 03254
69580-A  Jack Of All Trades                 Dec 4097, Br 03298

                                        New York, July 31, 1941.

69587-   The Booglie Wooglie Piggy          Dec 3960, Br 03254
69588-   I Wish I Had A Dime (For Ev'ry Time I  Dec 3966, Br 03257
         Missed You)

                                        New York, August 4, 1941.

69606-   Why Don't We Do This More Often ?  Dec 3966, Br 03257
69607-   Elmer's Tune                       Dec 4008, Br 03274

                                        New York, September 10, 1941.

69738-A  Rancho Pillow                      Dec 4019, Br 03268
69739-   At Sonya's Cafe (Shikker Izzer Trinkan Dec 18312
         Mizzer)

                                        New York, September 26, 1941.

69770-A-B  What To Do                       Dec rejected
69771-A-B  Elmer's Tune                          -

                                        New York, October 18, 1941.

69831-   Any Bonds Today ?                  Dec 4044

New York, November 15, 1941.

| | | |
|---|---|---|
| 69946-A | The Shrine Of St. Cecilia | Dec 4097, Br 03298 |
| 69947- | Chattanooga Choo-Choo | Dec 4094, Br 03290 |
| 69948-A | Tica-Ti Tica-Ta | Br 03337 |

New York, December 27, 1941.

| | | |
|---|---|---|
| 70108-A | I'll Be With You | Dec 4153, Br 03458 |
| 70109-A-B | What To Do | Rejected |
| 70110- | He Said - She Said | Dec 4153 |

Los Angeles, January 26, 1942.

| | | |
|---|---|---|
| DLA-2848- | Boolee Boolee Boon (Toy Balloon) | Dec 18319 |
| DLA-2849-B | A Zoot Suit (For My Sunday Gal) | Dec 4182, Br 03353 |
| DLA-2850-A | What To Do | - Br 03458 |

Los Angeles, April 4, 1942.

| | | |
|---|---|---|
| DLA-2972-A | Three Little Sisters | Dec 18319, Br 03353 |
| DLA-2973-B | Don't Sit Under The Apple Tree | Dec 18312, Br 03337 |

Los Angeles, April 23, 1942.

| | | |
|---|---|---|
| DLA-2978- | That's The Moon, My Son | Br 03402 |
| DLA-2979- | When Johnny Comes Marching Home | Dec 18533, Br 04198 |
| DLA-2980- | Six Jerks In A Jeep | Rejected |

Los Angeles, May 28, 1942.

| | | |
|---|---|---|
| DLA-3002-A-B | You're Just A Flower From An Old Bouquet | Rejected |
| DLA-3003- | Pennsylvania Polka | Dec 23608, Br 03368, AH-21 |
| DLA-3004-A | I've Got A Gal In Kalamazoo | Rejected |

New York, July 17, 1942.

| | | |
|---|---|---|
| 71103- | I've Got A Gal In Kalamazoo | Dec 18464, Br 03414 |
| 71104- | The Humming Bird | - |
| 71105- | Strip Polka | Dec 18470, Br 03402 |

New York, July 22, 1942.

| | | |
|---|---|---|
| 71151- | East Of The Rockies | Dec 18533 |
| 71152-B | Mister Five-By-Five | Dec 18470, Br 03416 |
| 71153- | Massachusetts | Dec 18497, Br 03414 |
| 71154- | Here Comes The Navy | - |

## HAROLD ARLEN

B. Buffalo, N.Y.; r.n. Harold Arluck; father a cantor. Sang in choir; played piano and sang with a band called The Buffalodians, then went into vaudeville as a solo act. Noticed by Vincent Youmans, who obtained a part for him in GREAT DAY, singing GET HAPPY. To Hollywood, 1932; wrote many hit songs for films during the next two decades (LET'S FALL IN LOVE, THE WIZARD OF OZ, BLOOMER GIRL, ST. LOUIS WOMAN among them).

Vocalist with the Buffalodians.                  New York, July, 1926.

| | | |
|---|---|---|
| 6648-2-3 | Baby Face | Ban 1776, Bwy 1027, Do 3749, 21193, NML 1178, Or 684, Pm 20469, Pur 11469, Re 8087, Sil 2770, Apex 8524, Imp 1684, LS 24043, Mic 22127, Starr 10184 |
| 6649-1-3 | How Many Times ? | Ban 1778, Bwy 1027, Do 3797, 21184, Or 670, Pm 20469, Pur 11469, Re 8088, Sil 2765, Apex 8555, Imp 1713, LS 24043, Mic 22124, Savana 1592, Starr 10185 |

Vocal, acc. by own piano.                    New York, July 23, 1928.

BVE-129    I Can't Give You Anything But Love      Vic test

Vocalist with Henry Busse and his Orchestra.
                                        New York, August 26, 1929.

BVE-55807-1-2-3  Since I Found You                Vic rejected

Vocalist with Red Nichols and his Five Pennies.
                                        New York, November 6, 1930.

E-35214-A  Linda                              Br 4982, 6844

Vocalist with Benny Goodman and his Orchestra.
                                        New York, November 7, 1930.

E-35342-   Linda                              Mt M-12024

Vocalist with Red Nichols and his Five Pennies.
                                        New York, December 10, 1930.

E-35735-A  How Come You Do Me Like You Do ?      Br 6149, 01180

                                        New York, January 16, 1931.

E-35167-A  You Said It                        Br 6029, 6842
E-35168-A  Sweet And Hot                         -    6711, 4872, 01300

                                        New York, February 19, 1931.

E-36108-A  Things I Never Knew Till Now       Br 6068
E-36109-A  Teardrops And Kisses               Br 6070, Spt S-2191
E-36110-A  Were You Sincere ?                    -        -

Vocalist with Joe Venuti's Blue Four.    New York, June 10, 1931.

404940-B  Pardon Me, Pretty Baby               OK 41506, Cl 5358-C, Har 1346-H,
                                              VT 2422-V, Par R-993
404941-B  Little Girl                         Col 2488-D, Par R-1003, Ar 4827
   NOTE:- Columbia 2488-D shows the matrix number as 151655-1, but the performance is
   identical to the issues bearing the OKeh matrix number and take.

Vocalist with Joe Venuti's Rhythm Boys.  New York, September 10, 1931.

151790-1  There's No Other Girl               Col 2535-D, Par R-1287
151791-1  Now That I Need You, You're Gone        -

Vocalist with Leo Reisman and his Orchestra.
                                        New York, January 19, 1932.

BVE-71257-1  Steppin' Into Love                Vic 22913

                                        New York, February 28, 1933.

BS-75329-1  Stormy Weather                     Vic 24262, 24716, LPV-565,
                                              HMV B-6349

                                        New York, May 2, 1933.

BS-76072-1  Happy As The Day Is Long           Vic 24315, HMV B-6378

                                        New York, July 11, 1933.

BS-76622-1  Smoke Rings                        Vic 24358, HMV B-6403

Vocal, acc. by self and Maurice Ellis-p.  New York, August 23, 1933.

BS-77531-1  Lazy Bones                         Vic rejected
BS-77532-1  Shame On You                          -

Vocal, acc. by O/Ray Sinatra.                New York, November 1, 1933.

| BS-78375-1 | Let's Fall In Love | Vic 24467 |
| BS-78376-1 | This Is Only The Beginning | - |

Acc. by Arthur Schutt-p.                New York, February 6, 1934.

| BS-81701-1 | Ill Wind (You're Blowing Me No Good) | Vic 24569 |
| BS-81702-1 | As Long As I Live | |
| BS-81703-1 | Here Goes (A Fool) | Rejected |

Vocalist with Eddy Duchin and his Orchestra.
                                New York, February 28, 1934.

| BS-81755-1 | Ill Wind (You're Blowing Me No Good) | Vic 24579, HMV B-6501 |
| BS-81756-1 | As Long As I Live | -          - |

Vocalist with Leo Reisman and his Orchestra.
                                New York, July 27, 1934.

| B-15462- | You're A Builder Upper Upper ("Life Begins At 8.40") | Br 6941 |
| B-15463- | I Knew Him When | Rejected |
| B-15464- | Fun To Be Fooled ("Life Begins At 8.40") | Br 6942 |
| B-15465- | What Can You Say In A Love Song ? | Br 6941 |
| B-15466- | Shoein' The Mare | Br 6942 |

## JULIA ARTHUR

B. Hamilton, Ontario, May 3, 1869; professional at 14; toured U.S.A. before she was 20, very successfully in many Shakespeare roles. London debut 1895 (Lyceum, revival of BECKET, with Sir Henry Irving); returned to U.S.A. with this company, first star role there as Clorinda in A LADY OF QUALITY, Detroit, October 4, 1897. Many further successes in straight drama; retired, 1899-1911; filmed THE COMMON CAUSE, 1918; toured as Joan in ST. JOAN (Shaw), 1924. Died 1950.
Speech, acc. by Mark Andrews-pipe organ. Camden, N. J., July 22, 1927.

| BVE-39539-1-2 | Crossing The Bar (Tennyson) | Rejected |
| BVE-39540-1-2 | Lead, Kindly Light (John H. Newman) | - |
| BVE-39541-1 | Battle Hymn Of The Republic (Howe) | - |
| BVE-39542-1 | America (Smith - Carey) | Vic 4020 |

Camden, N. J., August 8, 1927.

| BVE-39541-3 | Battle Hymn Of The Republic (Howe) | Vic 4020 |
| BVE-39542-3-4 | America (Smith - Carey) | Rejected |
| BVE-39557-1-2 | The Son Of God Goes Forth To War | - |
| BVE-39558-1-2 | O Little Town Of Bethlehem | - |

## ADELE ASTAIRE

B. Omaha, Neb., September 10, 1898; r.n. Adele Austerlitz. Debut New York, 1911, in vaudeville; not seen again until 1916, touring in U.S.A. and Canada with Fred, her brother. They appeared in many musicals in New York, 1917-1923; London debut, STOP FLIRTING (Shaftesbury Theatre, May 30, 1923); toured England; returned to New York to star in LADY, BE GOOD (Liberty, December 1, 1924); opened same show in London (Empire Theatre, April 14, 1926); more success in FUNNY FACE (Alvin, New York, November 22, 1927; Prince's, London, November 8, 1928). The Astaires appeared in the short-lived SMILES (Ziegfeld, N.Y., November, 1930) and the hit THE BAND WAGON (New Amsterdam, June 3, 1931); after this, Adele married Lord Charles Cavendish, ending her stage career and partnership with her brother. See also Fred Astaire.
Vocal duet with George Vollaire, acc. by Empire Theatre Orchestra/Jacques Heuvel.
                                London, April 27, 1926.

| WA-3214-1 | So Am I | Col 3979, ME MES-7036 |

Vocal duets with Bernard Clifton, acc. by novelty orchestra (sic)/Julian Jones.
                                London, November 29, 1928.

| WA-8169-1 | 'S Wonderful | Col 5175, ME MES-7037 |
| WA-8171-1 | He Loves And She Loves | -          - |

Brother of Adele Astaire; b. Omaha, Neb., May 10, 1900.  Debut in Paterson, N.J., in
vaudeville; teamed with sister and made repeated successes in New York and London,
and on tour in the U.S.A., Canada and the U.K. (see Adele Astaire); on her retirement and marriage in 1932, Fred continued alone, in  GAY DIVORCE at the Ethel Barrymore Theatre, November 29, 1932.  He appeared in this at the Palace, London,  on
November 2, 1933, having begun his career as a film-star the same year with  DANC-
ING LADY, FLYING DOWN TO RIO and the film version of GAY DIVORCE.  From 1934 until
1939. he partnered **Ginger Rogers in the series of musical films** that typify  those
years perhaps more than anything else(e.g., FLYING DOWN TO RIO; ROBERTA; TOP  HAT;
FOLLOW THE FLEET; SWING TIME; SHALL WE DANCE ?; DAMSEL IN DISTRESS;  THE STORY  OF
VERNON AND IRENE CASTLE, and, as a come-back in 1949, THE BERKLEYS OF BROADWAY).He
made HOLIDAY INN and BLUE SKIES with Bing Crosby in 1942 and 1946, and many  more,
both musical comedy and straight, the latter beginning in 1959 with ON THE BEACH,a
macabre story about the effects of global nuclear warfare !

Vocal duets with Adele Astaire, acc. by O/George W. Byng.
                                        Hayes, Middlesex, October 18, 1923.

| | | |
|---|---|---|
| Bb-3618-3 | The Whichness Of The Whatness ("Stop | HMV B-1719, ME MES-7037 |
| Bb-3619-2 | Oh Gee ! Oh Gosh !              Flirting") | -        - |

  Acc. by George Gershwin-p.              London, April 19, 1926.

| | | |
|---|---|---|
| WA-3183-1 | Hang On To Me ("Lady, Be Good") | Col 3970, ME MES-7036 |
| WA-3184-1 | Fascinating Rhythm ("Lady, Be Good") | Col 3969   - |

                                        London, April 20, 1926.

| | | |
|---|---|---|
| WA-3185-4 | The Half Of It Dearie Blues (solo)  ("Lady Be Good") | Col 3969, ME MES-7036 |
| WA-3186-2 | I'd Rather Charleston ("Lady Be Good") | Col 3970   - |

  Acc. by novelty orchestra (sic)/Julian Jones.
                                        London, November 26, 1928.

| | | |
|---|---|---|
| WA-8145-1 | Funny Face ("Funny Face") | Col 5174, ME MES-7037 |
| WA-8146-1 | The Babbitt And The Bromide ("Funny Face") | -        - |

Vocal, acc. by novelty orchestra (sic)/Julian Jones.
                                        London, November 29, 1928.

| | | |
|---|---|---|
| WA-8170-1 | High Hat ("Funny Face") | Col 5173, ME  MES-7037 |

                                        London, December 4, 1928.

| | | |
|---|---|---|
| WA-8185-3 | My One And Only ("Funny Face") | Col 5173, ME  MES-7037 |

  Acc. by Al Starita and his Boy Friends. London, April 5, 1929.

| | | |
|---|---|---|
| WA-8808-2 | Not My Girl | Col 5355, ME MES-7036 |
| WA-8809-2 | Louisiana | -        - |

  Acc. by small orchestra.              London, March 26, 1930.

| | | |
|---|---|---|
| WA-10227-1 | Puttin' On The Ritz (Film "Blue Skies") | Col DB-96, DB-2207, FB-1257, ME MES-7036 |
| WA-10228-2 | Crazy Feet | As above |

Vocalist with Leo Reisman and his Orchestra. (The second chorus of the first  number
  is sung in German).                   New York, June 30, 1931.

| | | |
|---|---|---|
| BS-69994-1 | I Love Louisa ("The Band Wagon") | Vic 22755 |
| BS-69995-1 | New Sun In The Sky ("The Band Wagon") | - |

                                        New York, September 28, 1931.

| | | |
|---|---|---|
| BS-70259-1 | White Heat ("The Band Wagon") | Vic 22836 |

New York, October 19, 1931.

BS-70292-1  Hoops (w/Adele Astaire)              Vic 22836, LPV-565, HMV B-6419

New York, November 22, 1932.

BS-73977-1  Night And Day ("The Gay Divorce")   Vic 24193, HMV B-6398, BD-5761
BS-73978-1  I've Got You On My Mind ("The Gay Divorce")-        -            -

New York, February 28, 1933.

BS-75330-1  Maybe I Love You Too Much           Vic 24262

New York, May 2, 1933.

BS-76074-1  My Temptation                       Vic 24312
BS-76075-1  The Gold Diggers' Song (We're In The  Vic 24315, LPV-565, HMV B-6376
              Money)

Acc. by studio orchestra.              New York, May 23, 1933.

265121-4  Night And Day ("The Gay Divorce")     Col DB-1215, FB-1255, ME MES-7036
265122-3  After You - Who ? ("The Gay Divorce")    -           -            -

Vocalist with Leo Reisman and his Orchestra.
                                       New York, July 11, 1933.

BS-76623-1  Heart Of Stone                      Vic 24358, HMV B-6403

Acc. by studio orchestra.              London, December 12, 1933.

CA-14212-2  Flying Down To Rio (Film "Flying Down  Col DB-1329, FB-1256, 2912-D,
                                                   ME MES-7036
CA-14213-2  Music Makes Me                      As above

Acc. by Leo Reisman and his Orchestra. New York, June 26, 1935.

B-17732-1  Cheek To Cheek (Film "Top Hat")      Br 7486, RL-296, Col DB-1825,
                                                FLM-13103
B-17733-1  No Strings (Film "Top Hat")          Br 7486, RL-296

Acc. by Johnny Green and his Orchestra. New York, June 27, 1935.

B-17735-1  Isn't This A Lovely Day ? (Film "Top  Br 7487, RL-297
             Hat")
B-17736-2  Top Hat, White Tie And Tails (Film       -         -      Col DB-1825
             "Top Hat")

Acc. by Leo Reisman and his Orchestra.  New York, July 15, 1935.

B-17810-1  The Piccolino (Film "Top Hat")       Br 7488, RL-298

Acc. by Johnny Green and his Orchestra. Los Angeles, January 24, 1936.

LA-1088-A-B  Let's Face The Music And Dance (Film  Br rejected
               "Follow  The Fleet")                  -
LA-1089-A-B  I'm Putting All My Eggs In One Basket
               (Film "Follow The Fleet")

Los Angeles, January 30, 1936.

LA-1088-C  Let's Face The Music And Dance (Film   Br 7608, Col DB-1633
             "Follow The Fleet")
LA-1089-C  I'm Putting All My Eggs In One Basket  Br 7609, Col DB-1634
             (Film "Follow The Fleet")
LA-1093-B  We Saw The Sea (Film "Follow The Fleet")  -           -
LA-1094-A  I'm Building Up To An Awful Let-Down   Br 7610, Col DB-1635
LA-1095-A  Let Yourself Go(Film "Follow The Fleet")Br 7608, Col DB-1633
LA-1096-A  I'd Rather Lead A Band (Film "Follow   Br 7610, Col DB-1635
             The Fleet")

Los Angeles, July 26, 1936.

```
LA-1133-A-B-C  A Fine Romance (Film "Swing Time")   Rejected
LA-1134-A  The Way You Look Tonight (Film "Swing     Br 7717, 02384, Voc 502,
           Time")                                    Col DB-1828
LA-1135-B  Never Gonna Dance (Film "Swing Time")     Br 7718, 02385, Voc 501
LA-1136-D  Pick Yourself Up (Film "Swing Time")      Br 7717, 02384      -
```

Los Angeles, July 28, 1936.

```
LA-1133-D  A Fine Romance (Film "Swing Time")        Br 7716, 02383, Voc 500,
                                                     Col DB-1828, Epic FLM-13103
LA-1137-A  Bojangles Of Harlem (Film "Swing Time")   Br 7718, 02385, Voc 500
```

Los Angeles, March 14, 1937.

```
LA-1272-D  They Can't Take That Away From Me (Film   Br 7855, 02426, Col 3164-D,
           "Shall We Dance ?")                        DB-1827
```

Los Angeles, March 18, 1937.

```
LA-1273-D  They All Laughed (Film "Shall We          Br 7856, 02426, Col 3165-D
           Dance ?")
```

Los Angeles, March 19, 1937.

```
LA-1274-D  (I've Got) Beginner's Luck (Film "Shall   Br 7855, 02484, Col 3164-D
           We Dance ?")
LA-1275-C  Let's Call The Whole Thing Off (Film      Br 7857, 02425, Col 3166-D,
           "Shall We Dance ?")                        DB-1827, Epic FLM-13103
```

Los Angeles, March 21, 1937.

```
LA-1276-D  Shall We Dance ? (Film "Shall We          Br 7859, 02425, Col 3166-D
           Dance ?")
LA-1277-B  Slap That Bass (Film "Shall We Dance ?")  Br 7856, 02484, Col 3165-D,
                                                     Epic FLM-13103
```

Acc. by Ray Noble and his Orchestra.    Los Angeles, October 17, 1937.

```
LA-1465-A  A Foggy Day (Film "Damsel In Distress")   Br 7982, 02532, Col DB-1826,
                                                     Epic FLM-13103
LA-1466-B  Things Are Looking Up (Film "Damsel In    Br 7983, 02533
           Distress")
```

Los Angeles, October 19, 1937.

```
LA-1467-C  Nice Work If You Can Get It (Film         Br 7983, 02533, Col DB-1826,
           "Damsel In Distress")                      Epic FLM-13103
LA-1468-A  I Can't Be Bothered Now (Film "Damsel     Br 7982, 02532, Epic FLM-13103
           In Distress")
```

Los Angeles, March 24, 1938.

```
LA-1608-A  Change Partners (Film "Carefree")         Br 8189, Col DB-1809,
                                                     Epic FLM-13103
LA-1609-B  I Used To Be Color Blind (Film            Br 8189, Col DB-1809
           Carefree")
```

Los Angeles, March 26, 1938.

```
LA-1610-A  The Yam (Film "Carefree")                 Br 8190, Col DB-1810
LA-1611-A  The Yam Step Explained (dialogue with     -            -
           Ray Noble)
```

Acc. by Benny Goodman and his Orchestra/Benny Goodman Sextet.
                              Los Angeles, May 9, 1940.
```
26807-A  Who Cares (So Long As You Care For Me)   Col 35517, DB-1943
         ("Of Thee I Sing")-BG6
26809-A  Just Like Taking Candy From A Baby           -            -
```

Acc. by O/Perry Botkin.                    Los Angeles, September 22, 1940.

LA-2357-A  Love Of My Life (Film "Second Chorus")  Col 35815, C-173, DB-2018
LA-2358-A  Poor Mister Chisholm (Film "Second     Col 35852, C-166, DB-2014
           Chorus")
LA-2359-A  Me And The Ghost Upstairs (Film "Second Col 35815, C-173, DB-2018
           Chorus")
LA-2360-A  (I Ain't Hep To That Step But I'll) Dig Col 35852, C-166, DB-2014
           It (Film "Second Chorus")

Acc. by Harry Sosnik and his Orchestra. New York, September 10, 1941.

69734-A  So Near And Yet So Far (Film "You'll     Dec 18187, Br 03287
         Never Get Rich")
69735-A  Dream Dancing (Film "You'll Never Get    Dec 18188, Br 03288
         Rich")
69736-A  Since I Kissed My Baby Goodbye (w/the    Dec 18187, Br 03287
         Delta Rhythm Boys) (Film "You'll Never Get Rich")
69737-A  The Wedding Cake Walk (w/the Delta       Dec 18188, Br 03288
         Rhythm Boys)

Acc. by Bob Crosby and his Orchestra.  Los Angeles, May 27, 1942.

DLA-2996-A  I'll Capture Your Heart (w/Bing Crosby Dec 18427, Br 03385
            and Margaret Lenheart) (Film "Holiday Inn")
DLA-2997-A  You're Easy To Dance With (Film        Dec 18428, Br 03386
            "Holiday Inn")
DLA-3000-A  I Can't Tell A Lie (Film "Holiday Inn")    -              -
DLA-3000-B  I Can't Tell A Lie (Film "Holiday Inn")          Dec Y-5793 (Australia)

## ROY ATWELL

Comedian who starred in ALONE AT LAST at the New York Shubert Theatre,  opening  on
   October 14, 1915, in which he sang and later recorded a number he wrote himself.B.
   Syracuse, N.Y., 1879; d. New York City, February 6, 1962.

Vocal, acc. by O/Charles A. Prince.    New York, December 20, 1915.

46288-1  Some Little Bug Is Going To Find You    Col A-1926
         ("Alone At Last")
46289-1  It's An Awful Thing Not To Know Where You Are -

## AUNT  JEMIMA

Vaudeville star of the twenties (r.n. Tess Gardella) who specialized in near-blues -
   though she was white - and died in 1950.

Vocal, acc. by own piano.                  New York, May 9, 1922.

         Georgia                           Vic test (un-numbered)
         Got To Cool My Doggies Now        -

                                    New York, May 25, 1922.

         Georgia                           Vic test (un-numbered)
         If You Don't Believe I Love You   -

                                    New York, August 24, 1923.

         My Sweetie Went Away              Vic test (un-numbered)

                                    Richmond, Ind., October 17, 1924.

12053, -A-B-C  There'll Be Some Changes Made    Gnt rejected
12054, -A-B  It Had To Be You                   -

                                    New York, June 21, 1927.

         I Want To Be In Dixie             Vic test (un-numbered)
         Takes A Better Man                -

Acc. by small orchestra.                    New York, February 14, 1928.

145641-3  Can't Help Lovin' Dat Man                    Col 1304-D, 4917
145642-3  Didn't I Tell You (That You'd Come Back ?)            -

## GENE AUSTIN

B. Shreveport, La., 1900; wanted stage career from childhood, ran away from home  at
15 and joined a circus as odd-job man. Volunteered for the Army at 16, served as a
member of the expedition to Mexico, released on parental objection.  Rejoined Army
on the day of U.S. entry into World War I, served in France as bugler.   Released,
1919; attended Baltimore University; formed dance band, played piano.  Teamed with
Roy Bergere as vaudeville act, 1923; went solo, 1924.  Began long series of Victor
records that had huge international success; one of the pioneers of "crooning" and
an early radio personality (sub-titled "The Voice of the Southland" after  he  had
made a great success with his record of that song).  Visited London privately 1958
(and made a guest appearance on television); died 1972.  Composer of several  very
popular songs (e.g., WHEN MY SUGAR WALKS DOWN THE STREET, HOW COME YOU DO ME  LIKE
YOU DO ? and LONESOME ROAD), and claimed to have sold a total of 86,000,000 discs!

Vocal duets with Roy Bergere, acc. by as-sw/p duet, one being his own.
                              New York, April, 1924.

  12985    A Thousand Miles From Here            Voc 14821, Gmn 7004

  Acc. by t/p.                              New York, May, 1924.

  13165    All Day Long                          Voc 14821, Gmn 7004

Vocalist with The Ambassadors/Louis Katzman.
                              New York, October, 1924.

  13883    Choo Choo (Gotta Hurry Home)          Voc 14916, X-9523

Vocal duets with George Reneau ("The Blue Ridge Duo"), acc. by h/g.
                              New York, c. October, 1924.

              Arkansas Traveler - Breakdown        Ed 51422, Amb 4936
              Little Brown Jug                          -      Amb 4973
              You Will Never Miss Your Mother Until  Ed 51498, Amb 4961
                She Is Gone
              Life's Railway To Heaven                  -      Amb 4968
              Turkey In The Straw                  Ed 51502, Amb 4977
              Susie Ann                                -      Amb 4978
              Lonesome Road Blues                  Ed 51515, Amb 4975
              Blue Ridge Blues                         -      Amb 4976
              Got The Railroad Blues               Ed 51611, Amb 5058

Vocal duet with Aileen Stanley, acc. by O/Nat Shilkret.
                              New York, January 30, 1925.

B-31792-1  When My Sugar Walks Down The Street    Vic 19585, HMV B-2006

Vocal duet with Carson Robison, acc. by the latter's guitar.
                              New York, February 4, 1925.

B-31905-2  Way Down Home                          Vic 19637

Vocal, acc. by O/Nat Shilkret.             New York, February 19, 1925.

B-31974-2  The Only, Only One For Me              Vic 19599
B-31976-2  I Never Knew How Much I Loved You            -
  NOTE:- Matrix B-31975 is a violin solo by Fritz Kreisler !

  Acc. by vn/g/u.                          New York, March 12, 1925.

B-32091-1-2-3  What A Life (When No-One Loves You) Rejected
B-32092-2  Yearning (Just For You)                Vic 19625
B-32093-3  No Wonder (I Love You)                       -

Acc. by May Singhi Breen-u.          New York, March 19, 1925.

B-32225-3  What A Life (When No-One Loves You)     Vic 19677

Vocalist with the International Novelty Orchestra/Nat Shilkret.
                                    New York, April 2, 1925.

B-32285-1-2-3-4  The Flapper Wife                Vic rejected

                                    New York, April 3, 1925.

B-32285-7  The Flapper Wife                      Vic 19638

Vocal, acc. by Nat Shilkret-p/May Singhi Breen-u.
                                    New York, April 15, 1925.

B-32431-1-2-3  Let It Rain                       Vic rejected

Vocalist with the International Novelty Orchestra/Nat Shilkret.
                                    New York, April 15, 1925.

B-32433-1  Joanna                                Vic 19649

                                    New York, April 16, 1925.

B-32437-2  Nora Lee                              Vic 19649

Vocal, acc. by Charles Stewart-h/Harry Lash-u.
                                    New York, April 16, 1925.

B-32439-1-2-3  Does My Sweetie Do - And How !    Vic rejected
B-32440-1-2-3  I Had A Sweet Mama, But She's Turned    -
               Sour Now

  Acc. by Billy Carpenter-u-"jazz effects" (sic) or Nat Shilkret-p/May Singhi Breen-
u as noted.                         New York, April 24, 1925.

BVE-32431-7  Let It Rain - pNS/uMSB              Vic 19677
BVE-32469-3  Yes, Sir ! That's My Baby - uBC    Vic 19656
BVE-32470-1  Everything Is Hotsy-Totsy Now - uBC     -

  Acc. by O/Nat Shilkret.          New York, November 25, 1925.

BVE-34100-4  Save Your Sorrow (For Tomorrow)     Vic 19857

                                    New York, November 27, 1925.

BVE-34103-1-2  Five Foot Two, Eyes Of Blue       Rejected
BVE-34104-2  I Never Knew                        Vic 19864

  Acc. by Lou Raderman-vn/Jack Shilkret-p.
                                    New York, December 2, 1925.

BVE-34111-3  My Bundle Of Love                   Vic 20030, HMV B-2359

  Acc. by Dave Franklin-p/May Singhi Breen-u.
                                    New York, December 11, 1925.

BVE-34103-3  Five Foot Two, Eyes Of Blue         Vic 19899
BVE-34139-2  Sleepy-Time Gal                         -

  Acc. by Del Staigers-c/Lou Raderman-vn/Dave Franklin-p.
                                    New York, December 21, 1925.

BVE-34170-3  Nobody's Business                   Vic 19950, HMV B-2350
BVE-34171-2  Sweet Child (I'm Wild About You)    Vic 19928, HMV B-2293

Acc. by small orchestra/Rosario Bourdon, or by Rosario Bourdon-p and O/Joseph Pasternack.                                      Camden, N. J., January 28, 1926.

BVE-34506-2  Behind The Clouds (There's Crowds And  Vic 19968, HMV B-2345
                 Crowds Of Sunbeams) - O/RB
BVE-34507-1-2-3  Tamiami Trail  - pRB/O/JP          Rejected

Acc. by Clement Barone-f/ —— Witzman-vn/William Carola-g, as shown.
                                              Camden, N. J., February 10, 1926.

BVE-33695-4  When The Moon Shines Down Upon The  Vic 20673 (as BILL COLLINS)
                 Mountain - f/g
BVE-33696-1-2-3-4  A Boy's Best Friend Is His    Rejected
                 Mother - vn/g

Acc. by vn/vc/p.                              New York, April 29, 1926.

BVE-35353-2  Ya Gotta Know How To Love           Vic 20044, HMV B-2350
BVE-35354-1  Bye-Bye, Blackbird                    -       HMV B-2345

Acc. by Frank Banta-p.                        Camden, N. J., June 11, 1926.

BVE-35485-2  But I Do - You Know I Do            Vic 20084, HMV B-2349
BVE-35486-2  Here I Am                           Vic 20107
BVE-35487-2  Tamiami Trail                       Vic 20084, HMV B-2349

Acc. by Murray Kellner-vn/Jack Shilkret-p.
                                              New York, August 12, 1926.

BVE-36042-1  For My Sweetheart                   Vic 20143
BVE-36043-1  Me Too                                -       HMV B-2359

Acc. by O/Nat Shilkret, or pNS.  New York, December 1, 1926.

BVE-36989-1  Tonight You Belong To Me           Vic 20371, HMV B-2442
BVE-36990-1  It Made You Happy When You Made Me  Rejected
                 Cry - pNS

Acc. by Jack Shilkret-p, Art Fowler-u or Abel Baer-p.
                                              New York, December 3, 1926.

BVE-36990-   It Made You Happy When You Made Me  Vic 20371, HMV B-2442
                 Cry - pJS
BVE-36994-3  Everything's Made For Love - uAF    Vic 20478, HMV B-2455
BVE-36995-1  I've Got The Girl - pAB             Vic 20397, HMV B-2422

                                              New York, December 31, 1926.

BVE-37500-1-2  I've Grown So Lonesome Thinking Of  Rejected
                 You - pAB
BVE-37501-1  Sunday - pAB                        Vic 20411, HMV B-2432

                                              New York, January 4, 1927.

BVE-37500-3  I've Grown So Lonesome, Thinking Of  Vic LPV-557, LSA-3075
                 You - pAB
BVE-37500-4  I've Grown So Lonesome, Thinking Of  Vic 20411
                 You - pAB
Acc. by O/Nat Shilkret.          New York, March 15, 1927.

BVE-38171-3  Ain't She Sweet ?                   Vic 20568. LPV-545, LSA-3077,
                                                 RD-7903, HMV B-2488
BVE-38172-2  Forgive Me                          Vic 20561

Acc. by Abel Baer-p.             New York, March 16, 1927.

BVE-38174-3  Someday, Sweetheart                 Vic 20561
BVE-38175-2  What Do I Care What Somebody Said ?  Vic 20568, HMV B-2488

Acc. by O/Nat Shilkret (the piano heard on the first side is played by the composer, Peter de Rose).                    New York, March 17, 1927.

BVE-38178-3  Muddy Water                          Vic 20569, HMV B-2529

                                        New York, March 18, 1927.

BVE-38182-1-2  Nesting Time                       Rejected
BVE-38183-2  My Idea Of Heaven                    Vic 20569, HMV B-2515
BVE-38185-1-2  Song Of The Wanderer               Rejected
   NOTE:- Matrix BVE-38184 is by the Hilo Hawaiian Orchestra, with Johnny Marvin,qv.

Acc. by Abel Baer-p, with ---- Witzman-vn/vc/g as shown.
                                        New York, May 26, 1927.

BVE-38788-   Yesterday - vn/vc/p                  Vic 20730, HMV B-2564
BVE-38789-   Mountaineer Song (Cindy) - vn/p/g    Vic 20673 (as BILL COLLINS)
BVE-38790-   One Sweet Letter From You - pAB      Vic 20730

Acc. by O/Nat Shilkret.                  New York, September 14, 1927.

BVE-39177-   My Melancholy Baby                   Vic 21015, 24640, LPM-2490
BVE-39178-   Are You Happy ?                      Vic 20977, HMV B-2642
BVE-39179-   My Blue Heaven                       Vic 20964, 24573, LPM-2490,
                                                  HMV B-2644

Vocalist with Nat Shilkret and the Victor Orchestra, or acc. by small orchestra/NS.
                                        New York, September 15, 1927.

BVE-39181-2  Nothin' - NS&VO                      Vic 21080, HMV B-5429
BVE-39183-   There's A Cradle In Caroline - O/NS  Vic 21015
BVE-39184-1-2  The Man I Love - O/NS              Rejected
   NOTE:- Matrix BVE-39182 is a hillbilly title by Ernest Stoneman, on this date.

                                        New York, September 16, 1927.

BVE-39188-2  The Lonesome Road - O/NS             Vic 21098, HMV B-3018
BVE-39189-   The Sweetheart Of Sigma Chi - O/NS   Vic 20977, HMV B-2642
BVE-39190-   Are You Thinking Of Me Tonight ?-O/NS Vic 20964, 24573, HMV B-2644

Acc. by small orchestra including Abel Baer on one of the two pianos.
                                        New York, March 27, 1928.

BVE-43506-1  Tomorrow                             Vic 21329
BVE-43507-2  So Tired                             -

Acc. by vn/p/g.                         New York, March 28, 1928.

BVE-43512-1  I Wish I Had Died In My Cradle       Vic 21833, HMV B-3294
             (Before I Grew Up To Love You)

Acc. by O/Nat Shilkret.                  New York, March 30, 1928.

BVE-43521-1-2-3  The Voice Of The Southland       Vic rejected
BVE-43522-1-2-3  In My Bouquet Of Memories        -

Viola Klaiss-pipe organ added; Bob McGimsey-whistling where shown.
                                        Camden, N. J., April 2, 1928.

BVE-42584-3  Ramona                               Vic 21334, 24573, LPM-2490
BVE-42585-3  Girl Of My Dreams - wBM              -         HMV B-2852

Klaiss and McGimsey omitted.            New York, April 13, 1928.

BVE-43521-6  The Voice Of The Southland           Vic 21714, HMV B-2904
BVE-43522-6  In My Bouquet Of Memories            Vic 21374, HMV B-2789

                                        New York, April 16, 1928.

BVE-43635-2  Without You, Sweetheart              Vic 21374

Vocalist with the All-Star Orchestra.     New York, May 1, 1928.

BVE-43689-1-2-3  Alexander's Ragtime Band          Vic rejected

Vocal, acc. by O/Nat Shilkret.            New York, May 29, 1928.

BVE-45184-2  Just Like A Melody Out Of The Sky   Vic 21454, HMV B-2803
BVE-45185-1  Old Pals Are The Best Pals After All  Vic 21545
BVE-45186-2  I Can't Do Without You              Vic 21454, HMV B-2803

  Acc. by studio orchestra.               New York, June 6, 1928.

BVE-45562-2  St. Louis Blues                    Vic 21714, LPM-2490
BVE-45563-1  Then Came The Dawn                 Vic 21564, HMV B-2854

  Acc. by O/Nat Shilkret, with Sigmund Krumgold-pipe organ and A. Cibelli-g,  where
  shown.                                  Camden, N. J., June 26, 1928.

BVE-45296-2  Memories - SK                      Vic 22518
BVE-45297-3  Jeannine (I Dream Of Lilac Time)-gAC  Vic 21564, LPV-523, LSA-3078,
                                                    HMV B-2854
BVE-45298-1  Memories Of France - gAC           Vic 21545

  Krumgold and Cibelli omitted.           New York, July 3, 1928.

BVE-45682-1-2-3  My Sorority Sweetheart           Vic rejected

                                          New York, November 7, 1928.

BVE-48134-3  Sonny Boy                          Vic 21779
BVE-48135-3  She's Funny That Way               -

                                          New York, November 23, 1928.

BVE-49203-3  I Can't Give You Anything But Love  Vic 21798

                                          New York, November 27, 1928.

BVE-49152-1-2-3  I'm Crazy Over You             Rejected
BVE-49208-2  I Wonder If You Miss Me Tonight ?  Vic 21798, HMV B-2953

Vocalist with Ben Pollack and his Park Central Hotel Orchestra.
                                          New York, December 3, 1928.

BVE-49221-2  Sentimental Baby                   Vic 21827

Vocal, acc. by O/Nat Shilkret, with Bob McGimsey-whistling where shown.
                                          New York, December 10, 1928.

BVE-48445-3  Dream Girl Of Pi K.A.              Vic 21916
BVE-48446-2  My Sorority Sweetheart - wBM       -
BVE-48447-2  Carolina Moon                      Vic 21833, HMV B-2995

                                          New York, January 15, 1929.

BVE-49646-1-2  Weary River                      Vic rejected
BVE-49647-1  On Riverside Drive                 -
BVE-49648-1-2  The Song I Love                  -

                                          New York, January 24, 1929.

BVE-49646-4  Weary River                        Vic 21856, HMV B-2995
BVE-49648-4  The Song I Love                    -

  Acc. by O/Leonard Joy, with Ed Smalle and Dick Robertson where shown.
                                          New York, February 23, 1929.

BVE-49988-2  That's What I Call Heaven          Vic 21893, HMV B-3063
BVE-49989-3  Wedding Bells (Are Breaking Up That  -              -
             Old Gang Of Mine) - ES-DR

Acc. by O/Nat Shilkret.                    New York, March 13, 1929.

BVE-50936-2  A Garden In The Rain              Vic 21915
BVE-50937-3  Dream Mother                      -         HMV B-3077

                                           New York, April 3, 1929.

BVE-51602-1  Why Can't You ?                   Vic 21952, HMV B-3113
BVE-51603-2  Little Pal                        -         -

                                           New York, May 1, 1929.

BVE-51674-1-2-3  Peace Of Mind                 Vic rejected
BVE-51675-1-2-3  The One In The World          -

   Acc. by O/Leonard Joy.                  New York, June 26, 1929.

BVE-53586-3  I've Got A Feeling I'm Falling    Vic 22033, LPM-2490, HMV B-3117
BVE-53587-3  Maybe - Who Knows ?               -                          -

                                           New York, July 30, 1929.

BVE-51674-5  Peace Of Mind                     Vic 22068, HMV B-3201
BVE-53968-3  Ain't Misbehavin'                 -         LPM-2490, HMV B-3185

   Acc. by studio orchestra, with Bob McGimsey-whistling, where shown.
                                New York, September 19, 1929.

BVE-56137-   Please Come Back To Me - wBM      Vic 22128, HMV B-3255
BVE-56138-   How Am I To Know ?                -         -

   Acc. by O/Nat Shilkret.                 New York, October 24, 1929.

BVE-57118-1-2-3  All That I'm Asking Is Sympathy  Vic rejected
BVE-57119-1-2  Georgia Pines                   -

                                           New York, November 7, 1929.

BVE-57118-5  All That I'm Asking Is Sympathy   Vic 22223, HMV B-3297
BVE-57119-3-4-5  Georgia Pines                 Rejected

   Acc. by O/Leonard Joy, with Fats Waller-p where shown.
                                New York, November 25, 1929.

BVE-57170-1  My Fate Is In Your Hands - pFW    Vic 22223, HMV B-3297

                                           New York, January 24, 1930.

BVE-58519-2  Let Me Sing And I'm Happy         Vic 22341, HMV B-3502
BVE-58520-1  To My Mammy                       -         -

   Acc. by O/Jack Shilkret, with Harry Brooks-p.
                                New York, January 28, 1930.

BVE-58529-2  After You've Gone                 Vic 22299, 24640, LPM-2490
BVE-58530-3  St. James' Infirmary              -                    - BB B-6863

   Acc. by O/Leonard Joy.                  New York, April 15, 1930.

BVE-59698-2  Under A Texas Moon                Vic 22416
BVE-59699-2  Nobody Cares If I'm Blue          Vic 22518, HMV B-3690

                                           New York, May 2, 1930.

BVE-62215-2  Telling It To The Daisies (But It  Vic 22416
               Never Gets Back To You)
BVE-62216-1-2-3  Absence Makes The Heart Grow   Rejected
               Fonder (For Somebody Else)

New York, May 8, 1930.

BVE-62216-4-5  Absence Makes The Heart Grow Fonder Vic rejected
               (For Somebody Else)

New York, June 9, 1930.

BVE-62216-8  Absence Makes The Heart Grow Fonder   Vic 22451
             (For Somebody Else)
BVE-62271-3  Rollin' Down The River                    -        HMV B-3572

New York, July 15, 1930.

BVE-62347-1-2-3-4  I Didn't Have The Heart To      Rejected
                   Break Your Heart
BVE-62348-3  When They Changed My Name To A Number Vic 22490
BVE-62349-2  For Sweethearts Only                     -

  Acc. by O/Nat Shilkret.            New York, September 4, 1930.

BVE-63622-2  If I Could Be With You One Hour     Vic 22527, LPM-2490
             Tonight
BVE-63623-2  This Side Of Paradise                    -

New York, September 5, 1930.

BVE-63130-2  Alabama Lullaby                     Vic 22539
BVE-63131-1  A Vision Of Virginia                    -

  Acc. by O/Leonard Joy.             New York, December 29, 1930.

BVE-67740-1  You're Driving Me Crazy             Vic 22601, HMV B-3762
BVE-67741-3  Crying Myself To Sleep                  -          -

New York, December 30, 1930.

BVE-67744-1-2-3  You're The One I Care For       Vic rejected
BVE-67745-1-2-3  She's Not Worth Your Tears          -

New York, February 5, 1931.

BVE-64861-1-2  And Then Your Lips Met Mine       Rejected
BVE-64862-2  When Your Lover Has Gone            Vic 22635, LPM-2490, HMV B-3903
BVE-64863-1  Please Don't Talk About Me When I'm Gone -        -       HMV B-3936
             (acc. by Dave Franklin-p/g/sb only)

  Acc. by Mike Ships-cl/Dave Franklin-p/Carl Kress-g only where noted.
                                     New York, April 21, 1931.

BVE-53044-1  Now You're In My Arms               Vic 22687
BVE-53045-1  If You Should Ever Need Me              -
BVE-53046-1-2  You Don't Know What You're Doin' - Rejected
             cl/p/g only

  Acc. by O/Nat Shilkret.            New York, June 11, 1931.

BVE-69928-1  I'm Thru' With Love                 Vic 22739, HMV B-3922
BVE-69929-1  Without That Gal !                      -          -

New York, August 19, 1931.

BS-70175-1  Mood Indigo                          Vic 22797, 22891
BS-70176-1-2  Star Dust                          Rejected
  NOTE:- Victor 22797 was never issued.

GENE AUSTIN AND HIS ORCHESTRA : Studio band with Gene Austin-v.
New York, August 20, 1931.

| | | | |
|---|---|---|---|
| 10777- | Who Am I ? | **Re**jected | |
| 10778-3 | What Is It ? | | Dec F-2619 |
| 10779- | Maybe It's The Moon | Per | |
| 10780-2 | How's Your Uncle ? | | Dec F-2619 |

New York, September 2, 1931.

10777-    Who Am I ?
10793-1-2-3  If I Didn't Have You            Rejected
10794-1-2-3  In A Dream                      -

New York, September 3, 1931.

10796-2  Guilty                             Ban 32285, Per 15526, Rom 1721,
                                            Ace 351014, Do 51014, Mt 91211,
                                            Roy 391211, Sunset 251014,
                                            Imp 2617
10797-1-2  Blue Kentucky Moon               As above except Imp 2617

Vocal, acc. by O/Nat Shilkret.    New York, September 3, 1931.

BS-70176-3  Star Dust                       Vic 22797 (not issued)

New York, September 9, 1931.

BS-70222-1  Love Letters In The Sand        Vic 22806, HMV B-3997
BS-70223-1  Blue Kentucky Moon              -

GENE AUSTIN AND HIS ORCHESTRA : Studio band/Lou Gold, with Gene Austin-v.
New York, September 17, 1931.

10793-7  If I Didn't Have You               Ban 32281, Per 15521, Rom 1716,
                                            Apex 41419, Do 51012, Mt 91205,
                                            Sterling 91205, 291205, Imp 2627
10794-6  In A Dream                         As above except Imp 2627

GENE  AUSTIN AND HIT OF THE WEEK ORCHESTRA : Studio band/Bert Hirsch, with Gene  Austin-v.                            New York, October, 1931.

117-X  Now That You're Gone                 HoW L-3

Vocal, acc. by studio orchestra.    New York, October 17, 1931.

10896-3  A Faded Summer Love                Ban 32291, Or 2355, Per 12760,
                                            Rom 1729, Apex 41441, Roy/Ster-
                                            ling 91227
10897-1  Goodnight, Sweetheart              As above

GENE AUSTIN AND HIS ORCHESTRA : Ben Pollack and his Orchestra with Gene Austin-v.
New York, November 10, 1931.

10977-1  Lies                               Ban 32325, Or 2380, Per 15542,
                                            Rom 1752, Ace 351024, Do 51024,
                                            Mt/Roy/Sterling 91235
10978-3  I'm Sorry, Dear                    As above

Vocal, acc. by small orchestra, with Bob McGimsey-whistling.
New York, November 24, 1931.

11019-4  The Lonesome Road                  Per 12790
11020-  When The Roll Is Called By The Fireside  Rejected

Acc. by a section of the Dorsey Brothers' Orchestra.
                                          New York, October 26, 1932.

12511-2  A Ghost Of A Chance                   Ban 32729, Mt M-12658, Or 2673,
                                               Per 12901, Rom 2046, Dec F-3332
12512-1  Just A Little Home For The Old Folks  Ban 32614, Cq 8081, Mt M-12529,
                                               Or 2595, Per 12862, Dec F-3332
12513-2  A Little Street Where Old Friends Meet  As above, but Dec F-3392
12514-2  When I Was A Boy From The Mountains (And  Ban 32729, Mt M-12658, Or 2673,
                                               Per 12901, Rom 2046, Dec F-3392

Acc. by instrumental group/Irving Mills, playing own piano acc.
                                          New York, September 21, 1933.

BS-77977-1  Nobody's Sweetheart Now            Vic rejected
BS-77978-1-2  I Had A Good Gal                   -
BS-77979-1-2  New Orleans                        -
BS-77980-1-2  My Blue Heaven                     -

Acc. by own p/Otto "Coco" Heimal-g/Candy Candido-sb.
                                          New York, November 29, 1933.

14400-1  Dear Old Southland                     Rejected
14401-1  Jam House Blues                        -
14402-1  Did You Ever See A Dream Walking ?     Ban 32920, Cq 8260, Mt M-12864,
                                               Or 2808, Per 12963, Rom 2181
14403-1  Build A Little Home                    As above, plus Dec F-3933

                                          New York, December 22, 1933.

14400-2-3  Dear Old Southland                   Ban 33172, Mt M-13139, Or 2974,
                                               Per 13044, Rom 2384, Dec F-3933
14401-2-3  Jam House Blues                      As above, except Dec F-3933

Acc. by small orchestra.             New York, December 29, 1933.

14486-1  Easter Parade                          Ban 32935, Mt M-12878, Or 2816,
                                               Per 12968, Rom 2189,
                                               Epic LN-24441
14487-1  Everything I Have Is Yours             Ban 32935, Cq 8263, Mt M-12878,
                                               Or 2816, Per 12968, Rom 2189,
                                               Rex 8110, Epic LN-24301

                                   Hollywood, April 26, 1934.

PBS-1349-1  Ridin' Around In The Rain           Vic test

Acc. by own p/Otto "Coco" Heimal-g/ —— Townsend-sb.
                                   Hollywood, May 9, 1934.

PBS-1349-3  Ridin' Around In The Rain           Vic 24663
PBS-1356-1-2  The Tiny Little Finger On Your Hand  Rejected

Acc. by small orchestra.             Hollywood, June 6, 1934.

PBS-79236-3  All I Do Is Dream Of You           Vic 24663, LPM-2490, X LVA-1007

Acc. by own p/ —— Anderson-g/ —— Townsend-sb.
                                   Hollywood, September 6, 1934.

PBS-79341-2  Blue Sky Avenue                    Vic 24725
PBS-79342-2  When The Roll Is Called By The Fireside  -

Acc. by Bobby van Eps-p/Otto "Coco" Heimal-g/Darryl Harper-sb where shown.
                                   Los Angeles, July 21, 1936.

DLA-447-  If I Had My Way - sbDH                Dec rejected
DLA-448-  I Cried For You - sbDH                 -
DLA-449-  I Hear You Knocking                    -
DLA-450-  Rootin' Tootin' Shootin' Man From Texas  --

Acc. by O/Victor Young.                         Los Angeles, August 9, 1936.

| DLA-546- | I Cried For You | Dec 926, DL-8433, F-6091 |
| DLA-547-A | If I Had My Way | -        -        F-6162 |
| DLA-548- | When I'm With You | Dec 904, F-6091 |
| DLA-549-A | Until Today | -    F-6162 |

Los Angeles, November 13, 1937.

| DLA-1058- | The Thrill Of A Lifetime | Dec 1578 |
| DLA-1059-A | Marie | -        Pan 25997 |

Acc. by own p/Otto "Coco" Heimal-g/Candy Candido-sb.
Los Angeles, November 18, 1937.

| DLA-1096-A | Dear Old Southland | Dec 1656, Pan 26027 |
| DLA-1097-A | China Boy | - |
| DLA-1097-B | China Boy | Dec DL-8433 |
| DLA-1097-C | China Boy | Pan 26027 |

Acc. by O/Victor Young.                         Los Angeles, December 21, 1937.

| DLA-1128- | Down Where The Trade Winds Blow | Dec 3102 |
| DLA-1129- | Paradise Isle | - |

**New York, May 10, 1938.**

| 63735-A | Music, Maestro, Please | Dec 1832, DL-8433, Pan 25997 |
| 63736- | I'm In A Mellow Mood | -        - |

Acc. by Fats Waller-elo/Albert Casey-g/Cedric Wallace-sb.
New York, February 27, 1939.

| BS-033993-1 | Sweet Sue | RFW 1, Swaggie LP-1243 |
| BS-033994-1 | I Can't Give You Anything But Love | -        - |

Acc. by studio orchestra.                       New York, November 10, 1941.

| 69957-A | Forgive Me | Dec 4175, DL-8433 |
| 69958- | Tonight You Belong To Me | Dec 3939    - |
| 69959-A | If I Could Be With You One Hour Tonight | Dec 4175    - Coral 60050 |
| 69960-A | Carolina Moon | Dec 3939 |
| 69960-B-C | Carolina Moon | -        - |

New York, May 11, 1942.

| 70730- | Yesterday | Dec 4333 |
| 70731- | Jeannine (I Dream Of Lilac Time) | Dec 4354, DL-8433 |
| 70732- | Ramona | -        - Coral 60050 |
| 70733- | My Blue Heaven | Dec 4333    - |

## VAN  AVERY

The "Original Rastus" was a black-face vaudeville comedian of the early years of the
twentieth century.

New York, c. December 21, 1914.

| 3480 | Happy, That's All | Ed 50234, Amb 2587 |
|  | Just Plain Dog | Amb 1840 |

## AVON COMEDY FOUR

One of the most famous vaudeville singing comedy teams of its time (1916-1924),  the
Avon Comedy Four consisted of Irving Kaufman (later to become famous as a vocalist
on countless records of all makes, in humorous and sentimental style alike), Harry
Goodwin, Charles Dale and Joe Smith (the last pair remained together as a team for
nearly half a century outside their appearances with the Avons, creating the char-

acter "Dr. Kronkheit"). The Victor catalogues of those days remarked that    they
were well-known "in every city where there is a Keith's theatre."

Vocal quartet, acc. by O/Rosario Bourdon.

Camden, N. J., June 7, 1916.

B-17812-2  Yaaka Hula Hickey Dula                Vic 18081
B-17814-2  My Mother's Rosary                     -
  NOTE:- Matrix B-17813 is a 'cello solo by Hans Kindler !

Camden, N. J., June 9, 1916.

B-17812-3-4  Yaaka Hula Hickey Dula             Vic rejected
C-17831-1-2-3  The Professor's Birthday            -
C-17832-1-2  Ginsberg's Stump Speech              -

Camden, N. J., June 12, 1916.

B-17843-2  You're A Dangerous Girl              Vic 18088
B-17844-3  I'm Going 'Way Back Home And Have A    -
             Wonderful Time

Camden, N. J., July 26, 1916.

B-18165-1  On A Summer Night                    Vic 18129

Camden, N. J., July 31, 1916.

C-17831-5  The Professor's Birthday             Vic 35606
C-17832-3-4  Ginsberg's Stump Speech            Rejected
B-18166-2  Gila, Galah, Galoo                   Vic 18125
B-18167-1  Songs Of Yesterday                   Vic 18126

Camden, N. J., August 3, 1916.

B-18173-2  'Way Out Yonder In The Golden West   Vic 18133
B-18174-3  When The Black Sheep Returns To The  Vic 18126
             Fold
C-18175-1-2  Cohen's Wedding                    Rejected
C-18176-1-2  Hungarian Restaurant Scene           -

  Acc. by O/Theodore Levy.          Camden, N. J., November 8, 1916.

C-18175-3-4-5  Cohen's Wedding                  Rejected
C-18176-3  Hungarian Restaurant Scene           Vic 35602

Camden, N. J., November 10, 1916.

C-17832-5  Ginsberg's Stump Speech              Vic 35606
C-18175-7  Cohen's Wedding                      Vic 35602

  Acc. by orchestra.                New York, c. November, 1916.

  2342-1  The Sweetest Melody Of All            Em 7138
          Gila, Gala, Galoo                     Em 7119
          Songs Of Yesterday                    Em 7134

Camden, N. J., August 8, 1917.

C-20604-1-2-3  Songs Of Ye Nut                  Vic rejected
C-20605-1-2-3  Clancy's Minstrels                 -
C-20606-1-2-3  Amateur Night                      -

New York, September 13, 1917.

77332-1-2-3  When I Get Back To Loveland And You Rejected
77333-2  I'm Crazy Over Every Girl In France    Col A-2399

New York, October 22, 1917.

| | | |
|---|---|---|
| 77332-6 | When I Get Back To Loveland And You | Col A-2433 |
| 77434-2-3 | You're Just As Dear To Me As Dixie Was To Lee | - |

New York, January 2, 1919.

| | | |
|---|---|---|
| 78240-3 | Come On, Papa | Col A-2692 |
| 78241-1 | Oh What A Time For The Girlies When The Boys Come Marching Home | - |

Camden, N. J., October 28, 1924.

| | | |
|---|---|---|
| C-20605-4 | Clancy's Minstrels | Vic 35750 |
| C-30981-3 | The New School Teacher | - |

## BABY ROSE-MARIE

B. 1925; one of the first genuine child performers to hit the big-time on radio, and still seen occasionally on television.

Vocal, acc. by Harry Gray-p.          New York, January 29, 1930.

| | | |
|---|---|---|
| BVE-448 | I've Got My Eye On You/He's So Unusual/ Nobody's Using It Now | Vic test |

Acc. by Fletcher Henderson and his Orchestra.
                                       New York, March 10, 1932.

| | | |
|---|---|---|
| BS-71940-1 | Say That You Were Teasing Me | Vic 22960 |
| BS-71941-1 | Take A Picture Of The Moon | - |

Acc. by O/E. E. Oberstein.          New York, November 22, 1932.

| | | |
|---|---|---|
| BS-73986-1 | In The Dim, Dim Dawning | Vic 24196 |
| BS-73987-1 | That's All That Matters To Me | - |

Acc. by O/Victor Young.          New York, April 22, 1933.

| | | |
|---|---|---|
| B-13272-A | My Bluebird's Singing The Blues | Br 6570, 01546, Mt M-12852 |
| B-13273-A | Come Out - Come Out - Wherever You Are | -          -          - |

ROSE-MARIE : Vocal, acc. by small orchestra.
                                       New York, April 1, 1938.

| | | |
|---|---|---|
| BS-021869-1 | When The Sun Bids The Moon Goodnight | BB B-7530 |
| BS-021870-1 | I Got A Guy | BB B-7515 |
| BS-021871-1 | Let's Break The Good News | BB B-7530 |
| BS-021872-1 | You Better Change Your Tune | BB B-7544, HMV BD-568 |
| BS-021873-1 | It's Raining Sunshine | - |
| BS-021874-1 | This Time It's Real | BB B-7515, HMV BD-568 |

Rose-Marie also made some LPs as a fully-grown artist during the fifties and sixties.

## FRANK BACON

B. 1864; stage debut in 1889 in FOUR NIGHTS IN A BAR-ROOM; after some years spent in San Francisco, went east and worked in New York from 1906 to 1918, during which he wrote LIGHTNIN', with Winchell Smith, playing the part of Bill Jones in this for an outstanding success (1,291 performances, opening August 26, 1918 at the Gaiety). He had a quaint personality and expressed honest humour, both of which are evident in the only records he is known to have made, a few months before his death in 1922.

Monologues.                              New York, July, 1921.

| | | |
|---|---|---|
| 7799 | The Bee Story | Voc 14224 |
| 7801 | In The Reno Divorce Court | - |

New York, July, 1921.

7872    Me And Grant                              Voc 14245

New York, August, 1921.

7926    Lightnin' Bill Jones's Escape From The    Voc 14245
          Indians

## MILDRED BAILEY

B. Mildred Rinker, Tekoa, near Seattle, Wash., February 27, 1907.  Began work as  a
song-plugger about the time her brother, Al Rinker, and Bing Crosby joined   Paul
Whiteman's orchestra; after touring the West Coast with the Fanchon and Marco revue and singing solo on radio station KMTR, she sent a "demo-disc" to Paul Whiteman, who signed her to sing with his band from 1931 to 1933. Married to jazz xyl-
ophonist Kenneth "Red" Norvo, 1933-1945; sang with Ben Bernie, Willard Robison;in
temporary retirement, 1936; sang with husband's band, 1936-1939, then briefly  on
radio with Benny Goodman.  From 1940 until her death on December 12, 1951 in  New
York, she was working solo in Cafe Society and Blue Angel in New York, and in the
Blue Note in Chicago.

Vocalist with Eddie Lang's Orchestra.    New York, October 5, 1929.

403031-A  What Kind O' Man Is You ?              Par R-840, CBS C3L-22,BPG-62098

Vocalist with Jimmie Noone's Apex Club Orchestra.
                                         Chicago, January 12, 1931.

C-7300-   He's Not Worth Your Tears             Voc 1580
C-7301-   Trav'lin' All Alone                    -

Vocal, acc. by the Casa Loma Orchestra.   New York, September 15, 1931.

E-37158-  Blues In My Heart                      Br 6190
E-37159-  You Call It Madness (But I Call It Love)Br 6184
E-37160-  When It's Sleepy-Time Down South       Br 6190, 01210
E-37161-  Wrap Your Troubles In Dreams           Br 6184    -

Vocalist with Paul Whiteman and his Orchestra.
                                         Chicago, October 4, 1931.

BS-70611-1  When It's Sleepy-Time Down South (w/  Vic 22828, HMV B-6107
              The King's Jesters)
BS-70612-1  Can't You See ?                       -

                                         Chicago, October 6, 1931.

BS-70619-1  My Goodbye To You                     Vic 22876

Vocal, acc. by small O/Matt Malneck.     Chicago, November 24, 1931.

BS-70623-2  Too Late                              Vic 22874, BB B-7873, HMV B-4084
                                                  B-8847
BS-70624-1  Georgia On My Mind                    Vic 22891, BB B-6945, HMV B-4110
BS-70625-2  Concentratin'                         Vic 22880    -

                                         Chicago, November 28, 1931.

BS-70630-1  Home                                  Vic 2287., BB B-7763, HMV B-4084
BS-70631-1  Lies                                  Vic 22880

Vocalist with Paul Whiteman and his Orchestra.
                                         Chicago, November 30, 1931.

BS-70633-1  'Leven Pounds Of Heaven               Vic 22883

                                         Chicago, December 1, 1931.

BS-70636-1  All Of Me                             Vic 22879

Vocal, acc. by O/Matt Malneck.          New York, March 1, 1932.

BS-71906-1  Dear Old Mother Dixie (w/chorus)      Vic 24137, BB B-7873, HMV B-8841

Vocalist with Paul Whiteman and his Orchestra.
                                        New York, March 2, 1932.

CS-71907-1  Hot-Cha Medley (MB sings a chorus of   Vic 36050
            THERE I GO DREAMING AGAIN)

Vocal, acc. by O/Leonard Joy.           New York, March 3, 1932.

BS-71910-1  Stop The Sun, Stop The Moon (My Man's  Vic 22942, LPV-555, LPV-570,
            Gone)                                  DPM-2027, BB B-7763, HMV B-4193
BS-71911-1  Strangers                              Vic 22942           -

Vocalist with Paul Whiteman and his Orchestra.
                                        New York, August 11, 1932.

BS-73190-1  I'll Never Be The Same                 Vic 24088
BS-73191-1  We Just Couldn't Say Goodbye           -

Vocal, acc. by O/Matt Malneck.          New York, August 18, 1932.

BS-73304-1  Rockin' Chair                          Vic 24117, LPV-555, LPV-570,
                                                   DPM-2027, BB B-6945
BS-73305-1  Love Me Tonight                        Vic 24117

  Acc. by the Dorsey Brothers' Orchestra. New York, April 8, 1933.

B-13208-A  Is That Religion ?                      Br 6558, 01544, CBS C3L-22,
                                                   BPG-62098
B-13209-A  Harlem Lullaby                          As above

                                        New York, June 6, 1933.

B-13427-A  There's A Cabin In The Pines            Br 6587, 01564, CBS C3L-22,
                                                   BPG-62098
B-13428-A  Lazy Bones                              Br 6587, 01564

                                        New York, September 5, 1933.

B-13955-A  Shoutin' In That Amen Corner            Br 6655, 01593, CBS C3L-22,
                                                   BPG-62098
B-13956-A  Snowball                                Br 6655, 01593

                                        New York, October 17, 1933.

B-14157-A  But I Can't Make A Man                  Br 7542, 01617
B-14159-A  Give Me Liberty Or Give Me Love         Br 6680, 01631, CBS C3L-22,
                                                   BPG-62098
B-14160-A  Doin' The Uptown Lowdown                Br 6680, 01631

Vocalist with the Casa Loma Orchestra.    New York, October 28, 1933.

B-14199-A  Heat Wave                               Br 6679, 01868

Vocalist with Benny Goodman and his Orchestra.
                                        New York, February 2, 1934.

152702-2  Junk Man                                 Col 2892-D
152702-3  Junk Man                                 -       CB-730, CBS C3L-22,
                                                   BPG-62098, Tpl/Sentry 4003
152703-2  Ol' Pappy                                As above
152704-2  Emaline                                  Col 2907-D, CB-759, CBS C3L-22,
                                                   BPG-62098, Jay 10, JCl 528

MILDRED BAILEY AND HER SWING BAND.        New York, September 20, 1935.

```
18090-1  I'd Love To Take Orders From You    Voc 3056, Br 02121, Col 33SX-1511
18091-1  I'd Rather Listen To Your Eyes       -              -
18092-1  Someday, Sweetheart                  Voc 3057, Br 02106, CBS C3L-22,
                                                BPG-62098
18093-1  When Day Is Done                     As above
```

MILDRED BAILEY AND HER ALLEY CATS.        New York, December 6, 1935.

```
60201-A  Willow Tree                          Dec 18108, Par R-2201, GEP-8600,
                                                CBS C3L-22, BPG-62098
60202-A  Honeysuckle Rose                     As above
60203-A  Squeeze Me                           Dec 18109, Par R-2257, GEP-8600,
                                                CBS C3L-22, BPG-62098
60204-A  Down-Hearted Blues                   As above
```

Vocalist with Red Norvo and his Orchestra.
                                          New York, August 26, 1936.

```
B-19749-1  It All Begins And Ends With You       Br 7732, Voc S-36
B-19750-1  A Porter's Love Song To A Chambermaid  Br 7744, Voc S-32
B-19752-1  Picture Me Without You                Br 7732, Voc S-36
```

                                          New York, October 19, 1936.

```
B-20092-1  It Can Happen To You                 Br 7761, Voc S-43
B-20093-1  Now That Summer Is Gone              Br 7767      -
B-20094-   It's Love I'm After                  Rejected
B-20095-1  Peter Piper                          Br 7767
```

MILDRED BAILEY AND HER ORCHESTRA.        New York, November 9, 1936.

```
20217-1  For Sentimental Reasons              Voc 3367, S-51
20218-1  It's Love I'm After                   -       -
20219-1  'Long About Midnight                 Voc 3378, S-42, CBS C3L-22,
                                                BPG-62098
20220-1  More Than You Know                   Voc 3378, S-42, Col 33SX-1511
```

Vocalist with Red Norvo and his Orchestra.
                                          Chicago, January 8, 1937.

```
C-1733-2  A Thousand Dreams Of You            Br 7815, Voc S-59
C-1734-2  Smoke Dreams                          -       - CBS C3L-22,
                                                BPG-62099
C-1735-2  Slummin' On Park Avenue             Br 7813, Voc S-102
C-1736-1  I've Got My Love To Keep Me Warm    CBS C3L-22, BPG-62099
C-1736-2  I've Got My Love To Keep Me Warm    Br 7813, Voc S-102
```

MILDRED BAILEY AND HER ORCHESTRA.        Chicago, January 19, 1937.

```
C-1751-2  My Last Affair                      Voc 3449, S-115
C-1752-1  Trust In Me                           -       S-67
C-1753-1  Where Are You ?                     Voc 3456, S-84
C-1754-2  You're Laughing At Me                 -       S-100
```

                                          Chicago, March 23, 1937.

```
C-1857-1  Never In A Million Years            Voc 3508, S-100
C-1858-2  There's A Lull In My Life             -
C-1859-1-2  Rockin' Chair                     Voc 3553, S-88, Col 35943,
                                                CBS C3L-22, BPG-62099
C-1860-1  Little Joe                          Voc 3553, S-88
```

                                          New York,  June 29, 1937.
```
21332-1  If You Should Ever Leave             Voc 3615, S-148
21333-1  The Moon Got In My Eyes              Voc 3626, S-119
21334-1  Heaven Help This Heart Of Mine       CBS C3L-22, BPG-62099
21334-2  Heaven Help This Heart Of Mine       Voc 3615, S-115
21335-1  It's The Natural Thing To Do         Voc 3626, S-119
```

Vocalist with Red Norvo and his Orchestra.
                                    New York, July 9, 1937.

B-21374-    Everyone's Wrong But Me              Br 7928
B-21375-    Posin'                               -
B-21376-2   The Morning After                    Br 7932, Voc S-108

                                    Los Angeles, September 22, 1937.

LA-1440-A   Tears In My Heart                    Br 7970, Voc S-132
LA-1441-A   Worried Over You                     -        -

MILDRED BAILEY AND HER ORCHESTRA.    Los Angeles, September 27, 1937.

LA-1444-A   Bob White (Whatcha Gonna Swing Tonight?)Voc 3712, CBS C3L-22,   BPG-62099
LA-1445-A   Just A Stone's Throw From Heaven     -        S-161
LA-1446-A   Loving You                           Voc 3758   -
LA-1447-A   Right Or Wrong                       -

                                    New York, January 10, 1938.

22265-2     I See Your Face Before Me            Voc 3931
22266-2     Thanks For The Memory                -        S-148, CBS C3L-22,
                                                 BPG-62099
22267-2     From The Land Of Sky-Blue Water      Voc 3932, S-138   -  BPG-62099
22268-1     Lover, Come Back To Me               -        -        -- BPG-62100

Vocalist with Red Norvo and his Orchestra.
                                    New York, January 21, 1938.

B-22322-1   Always And Always                    Br 8069, Voc S-156, CBS C3L-22,
                                                 BPG-62099
B-22323-1   I Was Doing All Right                Br 8068
B-22324-2   It's Wonderful                       Br 8069
B-22325-1   Love Is Here To Stay                 Br 8068

                                    New York, February 10, 1938.

B-22406-2   More Than Ever                       Br 8085, Voc S-142
B-22407-2   The Week-End Of A Private Secretary  Br 8088        -        CBS C3L-22,
                                                 BPG-62099
B-22408-1   Please Be Kind                       Br 8088, Voc S-156

                                    New York, February 23, 1938.

B-22460-2   There's A Boy In Harlem              Br 8089

MILDRED BAILEY AND HER ORCHESTRA.    New York, March 14, 1938.

22564-1     Bewildered                           Voc 4036
22565-1     I Can't Face The Music (Without Singin' Voc 4016, S-157
            The Blues)
22566-1     Don't Be That Way                    - Cq 9022 -   CBS C3L-22,
                                                 BPG-62099
22567-1     At Your Beck And Call                Voc 4036, Cq 9047

                                    New York, April 19, 1938.

22754-1     Says My Heart                        Br 8135, Par R-2552
22755-1-2   I Let A Song Go Out Of My Heart      Voc 4083, Cq 8046, Par R-2568

                                    New York, April 21, 1938.

22767-1-2   Moonshine Over Kentucky              Voc 4109
22768-1     Rock It For Me                       Voc 4083, Par R-2568
22769-1-2   After Dinner Speech                  Br 8171
22770-1     If You Were In My Place              Voc 4109

Vocalist with Red Norvo and his Orchestra.
                                    New York, May 2, 1938.

B-22840-2  Day Dreamin' (All Night Long)          Br 8145
B-22841-2  A Cigarette And A Silhouette            Br 8171
B-22842-2  (I've Been) Savin' Myself For You       Br 8145
B-22843-1  You Leave Me Breathless                 Br 8135, Par R-2552

MILDRED BAILEY AND HER ORCHESTRA.      New York, May 9, 1938.

22905-1    Washboard Blues                         Voc 4139
22906-1    My Melancholy Baby                      Voc 4474, Par R-2622
22907-1    Round The Old Deserted Farm             Voc 4139
22908-1    The Lonesome Road                       Voc 4474, Par R-2622

                                    New York, June 29, 1938.

23178-1    So Help Me                              Voc 4253
23179-2    Small Fry                               Voc 4224, Cq 9052, Par R-2595
23180-1    As Long As You Live You'll Be Dead If   Voc 4253
             You Die
23181-1    Born To Swing                           Voc 4224, Par R-2595

Vocalist with Red Norvo and his Orchestra.
                                    New York, June 30, 1938.

B-23182-2  Put Your Heart In A Song                Br 8182
B-23183-1  Wigwammin'                              Br 8194
B-23184-1  The Sunny Side Of Things                Br 8182
B-23185-1  How Can I Thank You ?                   Br 8194

                                    New York, July 26, 1938.

B-23293-2  Garden Of The Moon                      Br 8202

MILDRED BAILEY AND HER ORCHESTRA.      New York, July 28, 1938.

23299-1    Now It Can Be Told                      Voc 4282
23300-1    Jump, Jump's Here                       Br 8202
23301-1-2  I Haven't Changed A Thing               Voc 4282
23302-2    Love Is Where You Find It               Voc 4345, Cq 9106, Par R-2633
23303-2    I Used To Be Color-Blind                  -        -        Par R-2610

Vocalist with Red Norvo and his Orchestra.
                                    New York, September 12, 1938.

B-23454-   This Is Madness                         Br 8230
B-23455-   Who Blew Out The Flame ?                  -

MILDRED BAILEY AND HER ORCHESTRA.      New York, September 14, 1938.

23463-1    With You On My Mind                     Rejected
23464-1    My Reverie                              Voc 4408, Cq 9107
23465-1    What Have You Got That Gets Me ?          -        -        Par R-2610
23466-1    Old Folks                               Voc 4432, CBS C3L-22, BPG-62100

                                    New York, September 29, 1938.

23516-1    St. Louis Blues                         CBS C3L-22, BPG-62099
23516-3    St. Louis Blues                         Voc 4801, Cq 9217, Par R-2685
23519-1    Have You Forgotten So Soon ?            Voc 4432

                                    New York, December 8, 1938.

23810-1    They Say                                Voc 4548, Par R-2633
23811-2    Blame It On My Last Affair              Voc 4632, Par R-2659
23812-1    I Go For That                           Voc 4548

New York, January 28, 1939.

| | | |
|---|---|---|
| 23986-2 | I Cried For You | Voc 4619, Cq 9185, Par R-2675 |
| 23987-2 | Begin The Beguine | - | - |
| 23988-1 | What Shall I Say ? | Voc 4632, Par R-2659 |

Vocalist with Red Norvo and his Orchestra.

New York, February 8, 1939.

| | | |
|---|---|---|
| 24091- | I Get Along Without You Very Well | Voc 4648, Cq 9177 |
| 24092- | Kiss Me With Your Eyes | - |
| 24093-2 | Cuckoo In The Clock | Voc 4698, Cq 9186 |

New York, February 27, 1939.

| | | |
|---|---|---|
| 24177-1 | There'll Never Be Another You | Voc 4738, Par R-2706 |

MILDRED BAILEY AND HER ORCHESTRA.          New York, February 28, 1939.

| | | |
|---|---|---|
| 24178-1 | It's Slumbertime Along The Swanee | Voc 4708, Cq 9215 |
| 24179-1 | 'Tain't What You Do (It's The Way That You Do It) | - |
| 24180-1 | Love Is A Necessary Thing | Voc 4749 |
| 24181-1 | Down-Hearted Blues | Voc 4800 |
| 24182-1 | I Can Read Between The Lines | Voc 4749 |

MILDRED BAILEY AND HER OXFORD GREYS.          New York, March 16, 1939.

| | | |
|---|---|---|
| 24228-1 | There'll Be Some Changes Made | Voc 5268, Col 35943, CBS C3L-22, BPG-62100 |
| 24229-1 | Barrelhouse Music | Voc 4802, Par R-2692  - BPG-62099 |
| 24230-1 | Arkansas Blues | Voc 4801, Cq 9217, Par R-2685, CBS C3L-22, BPG-62099 |
| 24231-1-2 | Gulf Coast Blues | Voc 4800 -    - |
| 24232-1 | You Don't Know My Mind Blues | Voc 4802, Par R-2692, CBS C3L-22, BPG-62100 |
| 24233-1 | Prisoner Of Love | Voc 5268, CBS C3L-22, BPG-62099 |

NOTE:- Only one take of 24231 is included in the LP sets.

Vocalist with Red Norvo and his Orchestra.

New York, April 6, 1939.

| | | |
|---|---|---|
| 24345-C | Three Little Fishies (Itty Bitty Poo) | Voc 4785, Cq 9174 |

MILDRED BAILEY AND HER ORCHESTRA.          New York, April 24, 1939.

| | | |
|---|---|---|
| 24627-1 | That Sly Old Gentleman (From Featherbed Lane) | Voc 4815 |
| 24628-1 | Tit Willow | Voc 4845 |
| 24629-1 | The Lamp Is Low | - |
| 24630-1 | And The Angels Sing | Voc 4815 |

New York, June 14, 1939.

| | | |
|---|---|---|
| 24763-A | It Seems Like Old Times | Voc 4939 |
| 24764-A | Guess I'll Go Back Home (This Summer) | Voc 4966 |
| 24765-A | Moon Love | Voc 4939 |
| 24766-A | I'm Forever Blowing Bubbles | Voc 5086 |

New York, June 27, 1939.

| | | |
|---|---|---|
| 24820-A | The Little Man Who Wasn't There | Voc 4966 |
| 24821-A | (I Don't Stand) A Ghost Of A Chance (With You) | Voc 5086, CBS C3L-22, BPG-62100 |
| 24822-A | You're The Moment In My Life | Voc 5006, Par R-2720 |
| 24823-A | You And Your Love | - | - |

New York, September 21, 1939.

| 25372-1 | Don't Dally With The Devil (w/The Charioteers) | Voc 5209 |
| 25373-1 | Ain't That Good News ? (w/The Chariot-eers) | Rejected |
| 25374-1 | Sometimes I Feel Like A Motherless Child (w/The Charioteers) | Voc 5209 |

Vocalist with Benny Goodman and his Orchestra.

New York, October 20, 1939.

| 26194-A | Make With The Kisses | Col 35313 |
| 26195-A | Heaven In My Arms (Music In My Heart) | Col 35308 |
| 26196-A | I Thought About You | Col 35313, CBS C3L-22, BPG-62100 |

New York, October 24, 1939.

| 26201-A | Faithful Forever | Col 35289 |
| 26203-A | That Lucky Fellow | Col 35308 |
| 26204-A | Bluebirds In The Moonlight | Col 35289 |

Vocal, acc. by the Alec Wilder Octet.    New York, November 3, 1939.

| 25710-1 | Nobody Knows The Trouble I Seen | Col 35348 |
| 25711-1 | Swing Low, Sweet Chariot | Rejected |
| 25712-1 | All The Things You Are | Voc 5277 |
| 25713-1 | Hold On | Col 35348, CBS C3L-22, BPG-62100 |

Vocalist with Benny Goodman and his Orchestra.

New York, November 22, 1939.

| 26287-A | Darn That Dream | Col 35331, CBS C3L-22, BPG-62100 |
| 26288-A | Peace, Brother ! | -    -    - |

Vocal, acc. by the Alec Wilder Octet.    New York, November 30, 1939.

| 26258-A | Blue Rain | Voc 5277 |
| 26259-A | I've Gone Off The Deep End | Voc 5236 |
| 26260-A | I Shoulda Stood In Bed | - |

Acc. by orchestra, including oboist Reggie Merrill, who speaks on the side shown.
New York, January 15, 1940.

| 26413-A | Wham (Re-Bop-Boom-Bam) - vRM | Col 35370 |
| 26414-A | Little High Chairman | - |
| 26415-A | Easy To Love | Col 35921 |

New York, January 25, 1940.

| 26460-A-B | Give Me Time | Col 35626 |
| 26461-A | They Can't Take That Away From Me | Rejected |
| 26462-A | A Bee Gezindt | Col 35409 |
| 26463-A | After All I've Been To You | - |
| 26464-A | Don't Take Your Love From Me | Col 35921 |
| 26464-B | Don't Take Your Love From Me | Col DO-2226 (Australia only) |

New York, April 2, 1940.

| 26696-A | Fools Rush In | Col 35463, CBS C3L-22, BPG-62100 |
| 26697-A | From Another World | - |
| 26698-A | I'm Nobody's Baby | Col 35626, CBS C3L-22, BPG-62100 |

New York, May 15, 1940.

| 27302-1 | How Can I Ever Be Alone ? | Col 35532 |
| 27303-1 | Tennessee Fish Fry | - |
| 27304-1 | I'll Prsy For You | Col 35589 |
| 27305-1 | Blue And Broken-Hearted | - |

Acc. by g/sb and the Delta Rhythm Boys-v quartet.
                            New York, February 24, 1941.

68712-A  When That Man Is Dead And Gone          Dec 3661
68713-A  Jenny                                       -

                            New York, March 14, 1941.

68819-A  Georgia On My Mind                      Dec 3691, 27919
68820-A  Rockin' Chair                           Dec 3755, 27918, Br 03198
68821-A  Sometimes I'm Happy                        -      -       -
68822-A  I'm Afraid Of Myself                    Dec 3691

Acc. by Herman Chittison-p/Dave Barbour-g/Frenchy Covetti-sb/Jimmy Hoskins-d, with
the Delta Rhythm Boys-v quartet, where shown.
                            New York, June 13, 1941.

69361-A  Everything Depends On You - vDRB         Dec 3888
69362-A  Lover, Come Back To Me                   Dec 3953, Br 80109
69363-A  All Too Soon                             Dec 3888

Acc. by Herman Chittison-p.        New York, June 24, 1941.

69412-A  It's So Peaceful In The Country - vDRB   Dec 3953, Br 80109

Acc. by Harry Sosnik's Orchestra.    New York, February 12, 1942.

70310-A  Sometimes                               Dec 4252, Br 03325
70311-A  Wherever You Are                           -      -
70312-A  I Think Of You                          Dec 4267
70313-A  More Than You Know                         --      27919

Vocalist with Red Norvo and his Orchestra.
                            New York, March 5, 1942.

32565-1-2  Arthur Mirray Taught Me Dancing In A   Col 36557, CBS C3L-22, BPG-62100
           Hurry

NOTE:- All Brunswick issues from sessions involving Red Norvo appear under his name,
and all Vocalions under Mildred Bailey's. Missing matrix numbers are of sides  by
other artists, or which have no vocal work at all.

## BELLE BAKER

B. New York, 1895; became a very prominent vaudeville entertainer and  a  character-
comedienne par excellence during the 1920s; appeared in London with great  success
in cabaret and music-halls 1934-1935; occasionally in films. D. Los Angeles, April
28, 1957.


Vocal, acc. by orchestra.          New York, c. November, 1919.

67961    Poor Little Butterfly Is A Fly Gal Now  Pathe 22208
67962    I Love Him                                 -
67970    Dave Haimelach's Fidel                  PA 49114, 17025, 03655

68005    Eli, Eli                                PA 49114, 03580, Per 11163

Acc. by The Virginians (small jazz-type band).
                            New York, August 27, 1923.

B-28511-1  I've Got The Yes ! We Have No Bananas  Vic 19135, HMV B-1720
           Blues
B-28512-4  Jubilee Blues                            -

Acc. by studio orchestra.          New York, September 5, 1923.

B-28533-1-2-3-4  Why Should I Blame It On You ?   Vic rejected
B-28534-1-2-3  I Cried For You                       -

New York, September 21, 1923.

B-28534-4-5-6  I Cried For You                    Vic rejected
B-28584-1-2-3-4  Dirty Hands ! Dirty Face !       -

New York, June 30, 1924.

B-30338-1-2  You Can't Tell                       Vic rejected
B-30339-1-2-3  Nat'an (For What Are You Waitin',  -
               Nat'an ?)

Camden, N. J., August 28, 1924.

B-30730-1-2-3-4  Follow The Swallow               Rejected
B-30731-2  Hard-Hearted Hannah                    Vic 19436
B-30732-3  Sweet Little You                       -

New York, February 19, 1925.

B-31981-2  Those Panama Mamas (Are Ruining Me)    Vic 19609
B-31982-3  My Kid                                 Vic 19605

  Acc. by O/Nat Shilkret.        New York, October 13, 1925.

CVE-33566-2  Eli, Eli                             Vic 35762
CVE-33567-1  My Yiddishe Momme                    -

New York, November 25, 1925.

BVE-33899-1-2-3  Pretending                       Vic rejected

  Acc. by Peter Eisenburg-vn/Leroy Shield-p.
                                 New York, December 11, 1925.

BVE-33899-4-5-6  Pretending                       Vic rejected

  Acc. by studio orchestra.      New York, November, 1927.

E-24957/8  Baby Your Mother (Like She Babied You) Br 3706
E-24960/2  There Must Be Somebody Else            -

New York, February, 1928.

E-26326/7  One More Night                         Br 3815, 3788
E-26328/9  There Must Be A Silver Lining          -      -

New York, October 19, 1928.

E-28439-  My Man                                  Br 4086
E-28440-  That's How I Feel About You             -

New York, April, 1929.

E-29554-  I'll Always Be In Love With You         Br 4313, 5030
E-29555-  Old-Fashioned Lady                      -

New York, May, 1929.

E-29661-  Underneath The Russian Moon             Br 4343
E-29662-  My Sin                                  -

Los Angeles, October, 1929.

LAE-614-  (I'm A Dreamer) Aren't We All ?         Br 4550
LAE-615-  If I Had A Talking Picture Of You       -
LAE-616-  I'm Walking With The Moonbeams          Br 4558
          (Talking To The Stars)
LAE-617-  Take Everything But You                 -

New York, c. December, 1929.

Wanting You                                    Br 4624
Love (Your Magic Spell Is Everywhere)          -

New York, early February, 1930.

E-32018-  Cryin' For The Carolines              Br 4714
E-32019-  (The One I Love) Just Can't Be Bothered    -
          With Me

New York, April, 1930.

E-32584-  Sing, You Sinners                     Br 4765
E-32585-  You Brought A New Kind Of Love To Me       -

New York, c. May, 1930.

E-33072-  I'm Needin' You                       Br 4843
E-33073-  Cheer Up, Good Times Are Comin'            -

New York, c. October 22, 1930.

E-34955-  Sweetheart Of My Student Days         Br 4962
E-34956-  Laughing At Life                           -

New York, early February, 1931.

E-36027-  You're The One I Care For             Br 6051
E-36028-  Overnight                                  -

Acc. by O/Victor Young (who probably directed some, if not all the sessions   shown
on this page).                       New York, August, 1931.

XE-37030-  David Hamelech                       Br 20101, 0104
XE-37031-  Eili, Eili                                -        -

New York, July 21, 1932.

B-12097-  If You Were Only Mine                 Br rejected

New York, August 24, 1932.

B-12228-  As Long As Love Lives On              Br 6369, Dec F-3191
B-12229-  In A Shanty In Old Shanty Town             -        -

Acc. by O/Carroll Gibbons.           London, January 30, 1935.

OEA-746-1-2  Stay As Sweet As You Are           Rejected
OEA-747-3   The Continental                     HMV B-8288, BD-233
OEA-748-2   Blue Moon                           HMV B-8294

London, February 12, 1935.

OEA-779-1  Wish Me Good Luck - Kiss Me Goodbye  HMV B-8295
OEA-780-1  Swing High, Swing Low                     -
OEA-781-2  Old Mammy Mine                       HMV B-8294

London, February 13, 1935.

OEA-746-3  Stay As Sweet As You Are             HMV B-8288, BD-233

London, April 16, 1935.

OEA-2011-  Roadway To Romance                   HMV BD-320
OEA-2012-  Mrs. Goldberg's Bridge Party (w/vn-vc-     -
           p only)

Acc. by Gene Kardos and his Orchestra. New York, December 21, 1937.

B-22218-1  Bei mir bist du schön (Means That        Br 8042, 02560
             You're Grand)
B-22219-2  You're A Sweetheart                          -        -

Acc. by studio orchestra.              New York, c. 1940.

        Atlas                                  Gala 1006
        Mad About The Boy                         -
        Eili, Eili                             Gala 1007
        My Yiddishe Mama                          -
        Flying Tony                            Gala 1008
        Guisberg From Scotland Yard               -

## JOSEPHINE BAKER

B. St. Louis, 1903; made greatest success at the Champs-Elysees Music Hall in Paris,
France, September, 1925, in REVUE NEGRE (famous dance in skirt made of bananas !);
settled in Paris, became extremely popular there as cabaret and revue artist, even
appearing in a production of Offenbach's operette LA BELLE CREOLE; appeared   with
Maurice Chevalier, 1939; joined French Women's Air Force on outbreak of World  War
II, joined Resistance Movement after fall of France; after war she took over  Cha-
teau Milandes in Dordogne as home for refugee children; ran it with husband  (conductor Jo Bouillon, m. June 3, 1947); returned to stage in Paris (Olympia Theatre,
1966) and in the French production of HELLO, DOLLY in 1968.

Vocal, acc. by studio orchestra.       Paris, c. September, 1926.

        That Certain Feeling                   Od      , Par R-3232
        I Wonder Where My Baby Is Tonight ?             -

Acc. by unknown ukulele.               Paris, c. September, 1926.

        Feeling Kind Of Blue                   Od      , Par R-3233
        You Are The Only One For Me                     -

Acc. by Melodic-Jazz du Casino de Paris, dir. Edmond Mahieux.
                            Paris, July, 1930.

WL-2508-1  La Petite Tonkinoise               Col DF-229, 33SCX-6264
WL-2509-1  Suppose !                          Col         DB-401 -
WL-2510-1  Pretty Little Baby                              -
WL-2511-2  J'ai deux amours                   Col DF-229        -
WL-2512-1  Voulez-vous de la canne a sucre ?  Col DF-228
WL-2513-1  Dis-moi Josephine                  Col DF-229

Acc. by her own orchestra.             Paris, November, 1932.

CL-4081-1  Si j'etais blanche                 Col DF-1070
CL-4082-1  Sans amour                         Col DF-1071
CL-4083-1  Les Mots d'amour                   Col DF-1070
CL-4084-1  Ram-Pam-Pam (w/Pils and Tabet)     Col DF-1071

Acc. by studio orchestra.              Paris, February, 1933.

CL-4218-4  Sans amour                         Col DF-1180
CL-4219-1  Si j'etais blanche                      -        DB-1175

                            Paris, March, 1933.

CL-4264-1  Madiana                            Col DF-1192, DB-1175
CL-4265-1  Les Mots d'amour                        -

Acc. by le Jazz du Poste-Parisien, dir. by Al Romans.
                            Paris, November, 1934.

CL-5099-1  C'est lui (Film "Zouzou")          Col DF-1623
CL-5100-1  Haiti (Film "Zouzou")                   -

Acc. by the Comedian Harmonists (male voice sextet), acc. by Erwin Bootz-p.
Paris, August, 1935.

| CL-5462-1 | Sous le ciel d'Afrique | Col DF-1814 |
| CL-5463-1 | Espabilate | - |

Acc. by O/John Ellsworth.                  Paris, October, 1936.

| CL-5919-1 | Partir sur un bateau tout blanc | Col DF-2027 |
| CL-5920-1 | Nuit d'Alger | Col DF-2026 |
| CL-5921-1 | Doudou | - |
| CL-5922-1 | Nuits de Miami | Col DF-2027 |

NOTE:- All these four titles were featured in the revue EN SUPER FOLIES.

Acc. by the Lecuona Cuban Boys.          Paris, November, 1936.

| CL-5973-1 | Mayari | Col BF-30 |
| CL-5974-1 | La Conga Blicoti | - |

Acc. by Wal-Berg and his Orchestra.     Paris, March, 1937.

| CL-6116-1 | Vous faites partie de moi (I've Got You Under My Skin) | Col DF-2130 |
| CL-6117-2 | C'est si facile de vous aimer (Easy To Love) | - |
| CL-6118-1 | C'est un nid charmant (There's A Small Hotel) | Col DF-2116 |
| CL-6119-1 | Toc-Toc Partout (w/Rogers) | - |

Paris, November, 1937.

| CL-6432-1 | Comme une banque (I'm Feelin' Like A Million) | Col DF-2263 |
| CL-6433-1 | I'm Feelin' Like A Million | Col DB-1743 |
| CL-6434-1 | J'ai un message pour toi (A Message From The Man In The Moon) | Col DF-2275 |
| CL-6435-1 | A Message From The Man In The Moon | Col DB-1743 |
| CL-6436-1 | J'attends votre retour | Col DF-2293 |
| CL-6445-1 | Afraid To Dream | Col DB-1742 |
| CL-6446-1 | J'ai peur de rever (Afraid To Dream) | Col DF-2263 |
| CL-6447-1 | Bonsoir, My Love (Goodnight, My Love) | Col DF-2275 |
| CL-6448-1 | The Loveliness Of You | Col DB-1742 |
| CL-6449-1 | Plus tard | Col DF-2293 |

Paris, c. January, 1939.

| CL-6995-1 | Sur deux notes | Col DF-2576 |
| CL-6996-1 | De temps en temps | - |

Miss Baker continued to record occasionally after World War II, including     several
re-makes of earlier successes.  These appear to be the versions included in a  set
of ten-inch LPs issued by Columbia in England in 1954 and 1955 under the title  of
CABARET NIGHT IN PARIS.

## KENNY  BAKER

B. Monrovia, Cal., 1912; intended to be a concert violinist, but joined a glee club.
Began working life as a labourer on the Boulder Dam, then on a farm in Mexico, and
as a mover in a Los Angeles furniture store.  Began singing commercials on a  Long
Beach radio station at $19.00 per week; won radio contest from the Cocoanut Grove,
with Eddy Duchin and his Orchestra, 1933; married, and made first films (1935-MET-
ROPOLITAN, with Lawrence Tibbett, and KING OF BURLESQUE).  Other very   successful
films :- TURN OFF THE MOON, A DAY AT THE RACES (with the Marx Brothers), THE  KING
AND THE CHORUS GIRL (1937); GOLDWYN FOLLIES (with opera star Helen Jepson and Vera
Zorina), RADIO CITY REVELS (with Jack Oakie and Bob Burns), 1938; THE MIKADO;A DAY
AT THE CIRCUS(the latter also with the Marx Brothers), 1939; HIT PARADE   OF  1941
(with Frances Langford); DOUGHBOYS IN IRELAND, 1943 (and made Broadway debut  with
Mary Martin in ONE TOUCH OF VENUS the same year); last film made 1946 (THE  HARVEY
GIRLS).

Vocal, acc. by O/Harry Sosnik.           Los Angeles, April 22, 1938.

DLA-1272-A  Lost And Found                           Dec 1795, F-6713
DLA-1273-A  Love Walked In (Film "Goldwyn Follies")    -          -
DLA-1274-A  Sing A Song Of Harvest                   Dec 1807, F-6866
DLA-1275-A  Just Let Me Look At You                    -          -

  Acc. by Eddie Dunstedter-pipe organ.   Los Angeles, November 18, 1938.

DLA-1559-   O Little Town Of Bethlehem               Dec 2189
DLA-1560-   It Came Upon The Midnight Clear          Dec 2190
DLA-1561-   Hark ! The Herald Angels Sing            Dec -
DLA-1562-   O Holy Night                             Dec 2189

  Acc. by O/Nat W. Finston.              Hollywood, April 28, 1939.

BS-036156-4  A Wandering Minstrel I (Film "The       Vic 26252, HMV BD-741
               Mikado")
BS-036157-3  The Moon And I (Film "The Mikado")        -          -
BS-036158-7  Melancholy Mood                         Vic 25268, HMV BD-732
BS-036159-7  Ain't Cha Comin' Out ?                    -          -

                                         Hollywood, June 5, 1939.

BS-036242-4  Cinderella (Stay In My Arms)            Vic 26297
BS-036243-4  Let's Make Memories Tonight
BS-036244-3  Stairway To The Stars                   Vic 26280, HMV BD-749
BS-036245-4  White Sails (Beneath A Silver Moon)       -          -

                                         Hollywood, August 15, 1939.

BS-042119-5-7  South Of The Border                   Vic 26373
BS-042120-2  Stop Kicking My Heart Around            Vic -
BS-042121-6  Two Blind Loves (Film "A Day At The     Vic 26413, HMV BD-795
               Circus")
BS-042122-3  (Why Couldn't It Last) Last Night         -          -

  Acc. by O/David Broekman.             Hollywood, December 22, 1939.

BS-042310-1  All The Things You Are                  Vic 26471, HMV BD-900
BS-042311-2  On A Little Street In Singapore         Vic 26456, HMV BD-838
BS-042312-1  Faithful Forever                          -          -
BS-042313-1  It's A Blue World                       Vic 26471

                                         Hollywood, February 9, 1940.

BS-042497-1  The Starlit Hour                        Vic 26504, HMV BD-831
BS-042498-2  Make Love With A Guitar                 Vic 26520
BS-042499-2  On The Isle Of May                        -        HMV BD-831
BS-042500-1  When You Wish Upon A Star               Vic 26504

  Acc. by orchestra.                    Los Angeles, February 26, 1940.

DLA-1958-A  Easter Parade                            Dec rejected

  Acc. by O/David Broekman.             Hollywood, March 7, 1940.

BS-042552-1  Alice Blue Gown                         Vic 26543, HMV BD-859
BS-042553-1  Down By The Old Mill Stream               -          -
BS-042554-1  A Kiss In The Dark                      Vic 26637
BS-042555-1  The Bells Of St. Mary's                 Vic 26638, HMV BD-881

                                         Hollywood, March 8, 1940.

BS-042561-1  Little Grey Home In The West            Vic 26637, HMV BD-895
BS-042562-1  Mighty Lak' A Rose                      Vic 26639    -
BS-042563-1  Kashmiri Love Song                      Vic 26638
BS-042564-1  A Little Bit Of Heaven                  Vic 26639, HMV BD-881

Hollywood, July 1, 1940.

| BS-049867-1 | Remember | Vic 26664, HMV BD-900 |
| BS-049868-1 | Cynthia | Vic 26734 |
| BS-049869-1 | A Pretty Girl Is Like A Melody | Vic 26664 |
| BS-049870-1 | One Look At You | Vic 26734 |

Acc. by O/Lou Bring.                        Hollywood, September 21, 1940.

| BS-055078-1 | Yesterthoughts | Vic 26768, HMV BD-907 |
| BS-055079-1 | Two Dreams Met | -    - |
| BS-055080-1 | Who Am I ? (Film "Hit Parade of 1941")Vic 26792 |
| BS-055081-1 | In The Cool Of The Evening (Film "Hit | - |
| |    Parade of 1941") | |

Acc. by O/Leonard Joy.                       New York, October 29, 1940.

| BS-057051-1 | Chapel In The Valley | Vic 27250 |
| BS-057052-1 | You And Your Kiss | Vic 27207 |
| BS-057053-1 | There I Go | -    HMV BD-932 |
| BS-057054-1 | You Walk By | Vic 27250    - |

Acc. by O/Harry Sosnik.                       New York, February 20, 1942.

| 70373-A | Always In My Heart | Dec 18262, Br 03366 |
| 70374-A | Blue Tahitian Moon | -    Br 03336 |
| 70375- | Two Hearts In Three-Quarter Time | Dec 24198 |
| 70376- | L'amour, toujours l'amour | |

New York, March 18, 1942.

| 70530-A | Johnny Doughboy Found A Rose In Ireland | Dec 18274, Br 03336 |
| 70531-A | There Are Rivers To Cross (Before We | -    Br 03366 |
| |    Meet Again) | |
| 70532- | Dear Old Pal Of Mine | Dec 18283 |
| 70533- | The World Is Waiting For The Sunrise | - |

New York, April 9, 1942.

| 70644- | Lover, Come Back To Me ! | Dec 18352 |
| 70645- | Softly, As In A Morning Sunrise | - |
| 70646-A | Full Moon (Noche de Luna) | Dec 18313, Br 03845 |
| 70647-A | Whisper That You Love Me | -    - |

New York, June 26, 1942.

| 70948- | Make Believe ("Show Boat") | Dec 25260 |
| 70949- | You Are Love ("Show Boat") | |
| 70950- | I Left My Heart At The Stage Door Canteen | Dec 18442, Br 03472 |
| 70951- | I'm Getting Tired So I Can Sleep | -    - |

## PHIL BAKER

Pianist, piano-accordionist, composer (e.g., STRANGE INTERLUDE, 1932), radio and revue comedian (PRIORITIES OF 1942, etc.) B. Philadelphia, August 24, 1896; d. Copenhagen, Denmark, November 30, 1963.
BAKER AND BERNIE : Phil Baker-piano accordion/Ben Bernie-violin.

New York, July 26, 1918.

| B-22071-3 | Goodbye, Alexander (Intro. My Mind's | Vic 18499 |
| |    Made Up To Marry Carolina) | |
| B-22072-2 | Waters Of Venice | - |

Piano-accordion solos.                        New York, c. September, 1919.

| 4492-1 | St. Swithin Blues | Em 1086 |
| | Just For Today | - |

PHIL BAKER AND HIS NOVELTY ORCHESTRA.     New York, August, 1923.

| 608- | Little Boy Blue | Cam 398 |

Vocal, acc. by own piano-accordion.        New York, c. September 13, 1925.

    10571     Big Butter And Egg Man                    Ed 51634

                                           New York, c. October 14, 1925.

    10636     Ann And Her Little Sedan                  Ed 51634

                                           New York, early November, 1925.

    106366    Ann In Her Little Sedan (sic)     PA 32146, Per 12225
    106367    Big Butter And Egg Man             -              -

                                           New York, November 4, 1925.

    141237-   Ann And Her Little Sedan          Col 521-D
    141238-   Big Butter And Egg Man             -

Humorous dialogue with Sid Silvers, acc. by own piano.
                                           New York, August 25, 1927.

BVE-39117-1-2  At The Theatre - Part 1          Vic rejected
BVE-39118-1  At The Theatre - Part 2             -

                                           New York, September 21, 1927.

BVE-39117-   At The Theatre - Part 1            Vic 20970, HMV B-2670
BVE-39118-   At The Theatre - Part 2             -              -

Vocal duet with Aileen Stanley, acc. by own piano-accordion and unknown violin.
                                           New York, April 8, 1929.

BVE-51612-1-2-3-4  My Melody Man                Vic rejected

Piano-accordion solos; J. H. Muldooney-v. New York, February 27, 1930.

BVE-58680-2  Humming A Song Of Love - vJHM      Vic 22350, HMV B-3438
BVE-58681-1-2-3  Like A Dream                   Rejected
BVE-58682-1  Without Your Love - vJHM            -
BVE-58683-2  Happy Days Are Here Again - vJHM   Vic 22350, HMV B-3438
See also Marion Harris.

## ERNEST R. BALL

B. Cleveland, Ohio, July 21, 1878. Studied at Cleveland Conservatory of Music; first
    job in New York as relief pianist in Keith's Union Square Theatre, then secured  a
    lifelong contract as demonstrator of popular songs for Witmarks. Wrote many  popu-
    lar songs, notably LOVE ME AND THE WORLD IS MINE (1906); MOTHER MACHREE and I LOVE
    THE NAME OF MARY (both for BARRY OF BALLYMORE, 1910, the latter with Chauncey  Ol-
    cott and George Graff, Jr.); TILL THE SANDS OF THE DESERT GROW COLD (1911)and WHEN
    IRISH EYES ARE SMILING (1912), both with Graff; A LITTLE BIT OF HEAVEN (1914,  for
    THE HEART OF PADDYWHACK); GOODBYE, GOOD LUCK, GOD BLESS YOU and TURN BACK THE UNI-
    VERSE AND GIVE ME YESTERDAY (1916); DEAR LITTLE BOY OF MINE (1918) and LET THE REST
    OF THE WORLD GO BY (1919), all with J. Keirn Brennan; ALL THE WORLD WILL BE JEALOUS
    OF ME (1917, with Al Dubin), and his last song, ROSE OF KILLARNEY (1927, with Wil-
    liam Davidson). D. May 3, 1927 in his dressing-room in a theatre in Santa Ana,Cal.

Vocal, acc. by O/? Charles A. Prince.       New York, January 25, 1916.

    46354-1-2  My Wonderful Love For Thee        Rejected
    46355-1  Goodbye, Good Luck, God Bless You - Is  Col A-1978
            All That I Can Say

## TALLULAH  BANKHEAD

B. Duntsville, Ala., January 31, 1902; d. 1968. New York debut March 15, 1918 (SQUAB
    FARM, Bijou Theatre); London debut February 15, 1923 (THE DANCERS, Wyndham's). She
    is best remembered for extravagant behaviour on stage and off, but made many films
    (e.g., TARNISHED LADY, 1931; THE DEVIL AND THE DEEP and THUNDER BELOW, 1932; LIFE-
    BOAT, 1943; CZARINA, 1945; FANATIC, 1965) and, in the fifties, LP of scenes  from
    Oscar Wilde's and other plays, and two songs on an EP.

Vocal, acc. by O/Ray Noble.              Small Queen's Hall, London, Nov. 14, 1930

Bb-20384-3  What Do I Care ?                     HMV B-3687, Par PMC-7141
Bb-20385-2  Don't Tell Him What Happened To Me           -

## JOHN BARRYMORE

B. 1882; d. May 30, 1942; r.n. John Blythe. Famed for "great profile" and the  wide
variety of parts he played, from Hamlet and Mercutio to Bulldog Drummond: also in
films such as SHERLOCK HOLMES and DR. JEKYLL AND MR. HYDE (1920);GRAND HOTEL with
Greta Garbo, and ARSENE LUPIN (1932); TRUE CONFESSION and MARIE ANTOINETTE (1938)
and PLAYMATES (1942). First film ARE YOU A MASON ? (1913); first talkie, SHOW  OF
SHOWS (1928), in which he recited from RICHARD III !  Scenes from soundtracks  of
GRAND HOTEL and MATA HARI with Greta Garbo were issued on MGM C-975, and extracts
from HAMLET, TWELFTH NIGHT, RICHARD III and MACBETH were included on Audio  Rari-
ties 2280 and 2281, all LP.

Speech, acc. by O/Nat Shilkret.          New York, April 13, 1928.

CVE-43632-1  Now I Am Alone ("Hamlet," Act 2,      Vic 6827, LCT-1112, HMV DB-1177
             Scene 2) (Music : Quartet No. 2 : Nocturne (Borodin)
CVE-43633-1  Ay, Edward Will Use Women Honorably       -                 -
             ("Henry VI," Act 3, Scene 2) (Music : Sonata Tragica: Largo)(E. Mac-
             Dowell, Op. 45)

## RICHARD  BARTHELMESS

B. New York, 1895; mother an actress. Started "walking-on" as child; graduated from
Hudson River Military Academy, Hartford, Conn., 1913; began as film extra;  first
big part in WAR BRIDES (1916). Other "silents" include D. W. Griffiths'  THE HOPE
CHEST (1919, with Dorothy Gish, then more with same team; BROKEN BLOSSOMS and WAY
DOWN EAST (1920-1922), both with Lillian Gish, made him top star. Formed partnership with Charles H. Doell (Inspiration Films, 1921-1927; big success with  TOL'-
ABLE DAVID and others); signed with First National (reputedly at $75,000 a film);
first talkie WEARY RIVER, 1929; many more including SON OF THE GODS and THE  DAWN
PATROL; after THE POSTMAN ALWAYS RINGS TWICE (1936), retired for 3 years;featured
role in ONLY ANGELS HAVE WINGS; small character part in last film (THE  SPOILERS,
1941, with Marlene Dietrich, John Wayne and Randolph Scott); joined Naval Reserve
and never acted again; d. Long Island, 1963, worth over a million dollars.

Speech.                                  New York, April, 1922.

8937    Actors' Equity - An All-Star Comedy    Voc 35010 (part side)

## ANNA  BARTHOLD

Popular vaudeville singer of the "female baritone" variety during the nineties.

Vocal, acc. by unknown pianist.          New York, date unknown.

        She Was Bred In Old Kentucky             Consol 912

        New York; issued May, 1899.      New York, issued June-end September, 1899.

Don't Be Cross                Ed 6400    Think Once Again Before We Part  Ed 7182
My Baby's Kiss                Ed 6401    Nightingale                      Ed 7183
Old Jim's Christmas Hymn      Ed 6402    Rosie Carey                      Ed 7184
Whose Pretty Girl Are You ?   Ed 6403

## NORA BAYES

B. 1880; made huge success in first decade of this century with two British numbers,
with Americanized lyrics (COME ALONG, MY MANDY and HAS ANYBODY HERE SEEN KELLY? in
THE JOLLY BACHELORS, Broadway Theatre, January 6, 1910) and Harry von Tilzer, from
a stage box in Percy Williams' Orpheum Theatre in Brooklyn in 1902 helped her plug
his DOWN WHERE THE WURZBURGER FLOWS (when she sang it in London, it flopped). Nora
Bayes and her husband, Jack Norworth composed and sang SHINE ON, HARVEST MOON with
great success in FOLLIES OF 1908, and it has never lost its popularity; she scored
again in 1917 with George M. Cohan's war song, OVER THERE, and in 1920, she introduced yet another great success to New York and London, JAPANESE SANDMAN.  She was

one of the many stars that opened Lew Fields' Music Hall (later known as the  44th
Street Theatre, and was very popular with London audiences in the twenties,   Nora
Bayes died March 19, 1928.

Vocal, acc. by studio orchestra.        New York, March 7, 1910.

B-8700-2  Has Anybody Here Seen Kelly ?       Vic 60013, Veritas 107
C-8701-1-2  Come Along, My Mandy (w/Jack Norworth) Rejected
C-8702-1-2  Shine On, Harvest Moon ("Follies of        -
            1908") (w/Jack Norworth)

                                        New York, March 14, 1910.

C-8701-5  Come Along, My Mandy ("The Jolly      Vic 70016, 55097
            Bachelors") (w/Jack Norworth)
B-8708-2  Daffydills                            Vic 60019
C-8709-2  Young America ("The Jolly Bachelors")  Vic 70015

                                        New York, April 4, 1910.

B-8791-1-2  That Lovin' Rag                     Vic rejected

                                        New York, May 20, 1910.

B-8791-3-4  That Lovin' Rag                     Rejected
C-8998-2  Rosa Rosetta (w/Jack Norworth)        Vic 70019

                                        New York, June 15, 1910.

B-8791-5  That Lovin' Rag                       Vic 60023
C-9091-2  What Good Is Water, When You're Dry ?  Vic 70020, 55101

                                        New York, November 8, 1910.

C-9633-3  How Can They Tell That Oi'm Irish ?   Vic 70030, 55101

                                        New York, January 20, 1911.

C-9830-1-2  Turn Off Your Light, Mr. Moon Man   Vic rejected
            ("Little Miss Fix-It") (w/Jack Norworth)

                                        New York, April 24, 1911.

C-9830-5  Turn Off Your Light, Mr. Moon Man    Vic 70038, 55097, LCT-1112
            ("Little Miss Fix-It") (w/Jack Norworth)

                                        New York, December 17, 1913.

B-14206-1-2  Harmony Baby                       Vic rejected
B-14209-1-2  You Can't Get Away From It            -
B-14210-1-2  The Good Ship Mary Ann               -
B-14211-1-2  I've Got A Garden In Sweden (w/Helen  -
             Clark)

                                        New York, January 22, 1914.

B-14206-4  Harmony Baby                         Vic 60115
B-14209-3  You Can't Get Away From It           Vic 60114
B-14210-4  The Good Ship Mary Ann               Vic 60113
B-14366-1  All Aboard For Dixieland             Vic 60117

                                        New York, October 21, 1914.

B-15292-1  We Take Our Hats Off To You, Mr.     Vic 60112
            Wilson !
B-15293-2  I Work Eight Hours, Sleep Eight Hours, Vic 60127
            That Leaves Eight Hours For Love
B-15294-1  Sunbeam Sal                          Vic 60130
B-15295-2  The A.O.H.'s Of The U.S.A.           Vic 60119

Acc. by O/? Charles A. Prince.        New York, December 1, 1915.

46229-1-2  When You're Down In Louisville        Col rejected
46230-1-2  I Work Eight Hours, I Sleep Eight Hours,  -
           That Leaves Eight Hours For Love

                                      New York, December 3, 1915.

46236-1-2  Hello, Hawaii, How Are You ?          Col rejected

Acc. by studio orchestra.             New York, May 4, 1916.

B-17609-2  Homesickness Blues                    Vic 45100
B-17610-2  Are You Prepared For The Summer ?     Vic 45095
B-17611-2  The Greatest Battle Song Of All       -

Acc. by O/Rosario Bourdon.            New York, June 1, 1916.

B-17761-2  For Dixie And Uncle Sam               Vic 45100
B-17762-2  Hello, Hawaii, How Are You ?          Vic 45099
B-17763-2  When Old Bill Bailey Plays The Ukulele  -
B-17764-1  Naming The Angel Child                Rejected

                                      New York, October 27, 1916.

B-18583-4  Broken Doll                           Vic 45136
B-18584-2  When John McCormack Sings A Song      Vic 45105
B-18585-1  Hicki Hoy                             -

Acc. by O/Joseph Pasternack.          New York, December 8, 1916.

B-18780-1  Cheer Up ! Eat And Grow Thin          Vic 45108
B-18781-2  Please Keep Out Of My Dreams          Vic 45136
B-18782-1  Ragging The Songs Mother Used To Sing  Vic 45108

                                      New York, April 7, 1917.

B-19559-3  Pull The Cork Out Of Erin (Let The    Vic 45123
           River Shannon Flow)
B-19560-1  Daniel In The Lion's Den              -
B-19561-1-2  I'm Out With The Boss Tonight       Rejected
B-19562-1-2  My Little Motor Car (unacc.)

                                      New York, April 10, 1917.

B-19576-1-2-3  Love America (Peace Hymn From     Vic rejected
           Civilization)
C-19577-1-2  The Lovesick Indian Squaw           -

                                      New York, July 13, 1917.

B-20335-2  Over There                            Vic 45130, AR 2290
B-20336-2  (Goodbye, And Luck Be With You) Laddie Boy  -

                                      Camden, N. J., August 13, 1917.

B-20619-1-2  Our Bungalow (w/Irving Fisher)      Vic rejected

Acc. by O/? Charles A. Prince.        New York, March, 1918.

49304-2  Someday They're Coming Home Again       Col A-6030
49305-3  I May Stay Away A Little Longer         -

                                      New York, April, 1918.

49342-1  A Little Bit Of Sunshine                Col A-6038
49343-1  Regretful Blues                         -

New York, May, 1918.

| 49385- | Mammy's Chocolate Soldier | Col A-6051 |
| 49386- | The Man Who Put The Germ In Germany | - |

New York, November 16, 1918.

| 78173-2 | Mammy's Pickaninny, Don't You Cry | Col A-2771 |
| 78174-3 | My Barney Lies Over The Ocean (The Way That He Lied To Me) | Col A-2678 |
| 78175-3 | Goodbye, France | - |

New York, December 14, 1918.

| 78202-2 | When Yankee Doodle Sails Upon The Good Ship Home Sweet Home | Col A-2687 |
| 78203-2 | Without You | Col A-2921 |

New York, December 21, 1918.

| 78218-1 | How Ya Gonna Keep 'Em Down On The Farm (After They've Seen Paree) | Col A-2687 |

New York, July 3, 1919.

| 78546-1 | Jerry | Col A-2785 |
| 78547-1 | You Can't Get Lovin' Where There Ain't Any Love | Col A-2771 |

New York, July 18, 1919.

| 78574-1 | In Miami | Col A-2785 |
| 78575-2 | Prohibition Blues | Col A-2823 |
| 78576-2 | Taxation Blues | - |
| 78578-3 | Everybody Calls Me Honey | Col A-2816 |

NOTE:- Matrix 78577 is by Billy Murray.

New York, September 11, 1919.

| 49665-2 | Just Like A Gypsy | Col A-6138 |
| 78640-3 | Freckles | Col A-2816 |

New York, September 29, 1919.

| 49670-2 | In Your Arms | Col A-6138 |
| 78698-2 | Snoops, The Lawyer | Col A-2852 |

New York, October 14, 1919.

| 78734-1 | Patches | Col A-2921 |
| 78735-2 | Oh ! How I Laugh When I Think That I Cried Over You | Col A-2852 |

New York, July 10, 1920.

| 79335-2 | Sally Green (The Village Vamp) | Col A-2980 |
| 79337-3 | The Argentines, The Portuguese And Greeks | - |

NOTE:- Matrix 79336 is by the Happy Six (jazz band).

New York, August 25, 1920.

| 79383-3 | You're Just As Beautiful At Sixty As You Were At Sweet Sixteen | Col A-2997 |

New York, August 26, 1920.

| 79386-1 | The Japanese Sandman | Col A-2997, 3008 |
| 79388-1 | Singin' The Blues | Col A-3311 |

NOTE:- Matrix 79387 is by Marion Harris, q.v.

New York, August 27, 1920.

79389-2  The Broadway Blues                    Col A-3311

Acc. by Art Hickman and his Orchestra.  New York, September 18, 1920.

79423-2  I Could Have Had You (But I Let You Get  Col A-3347
         Get By)

Acc. by O/? Charles A. Prince.          New York, November 26, 1920.

79536-3  Love Nights                           Col A-3347
79537-1-2  Home Again Blues                    Rejected

New York, December 14, 1920.

79570-1-3  Why Worry ?                          Col A-3360
79571-2  Just Snap Your Fingers At Care         -          3029
79572-1-2  Secrets                              Rejected

New York, January 25, 1921.

79655-1-2  The Little Tin Soldier (The Little Rag  Rejected
             Doll)
79656-1  Now I Lay Me Down To Sleep             Col A-3392

New York, February 14, 1921.

79723-6  Make Believe                           Col A-3392
79724-1-2  Darling                              Rejected

New York, March 8, 1921.

79779-1  Broken Moon                            Col A-3397

New York, March 12, 1921.

79784-2  In A Little Front Parlor (On An Old    Col A-3397
           Back Street)

New York, April 21, 1921.

79804-1  Cherie                                 Col A-3443
79805-1-2-3  Tea Leaves                         Rejected

New York, May 7, 1921.

79805-6  Tea Leaves                             Col A-3416
79828-1  Wyoming                                -

New York, June 14, 1921.

79887-1  When You're In, You're In, In Indiana  Col A-3443
79888-1  Saturday                               Col A-3471

New York, June 18, 1921.

79897-1-2  Tenement Rose                        Col rejected

New York, July 13, 1921.

79935-1-2  I've Got The Joys                    Col rejected

New York, July 14, 1921.

79939-2  You've Made A Chicken Of Your Mother   Col A-3471
           (But You Can't Make A Goose Of Me)

New York, November 26, 1921.

| | | |
|---|---|---|
| 80081-1-2 | The Schoolhouse Blues | Col rejected |

New York, January 9, 1922.

| | | |
|---|---|---|
| 80128-1-2 | He's A Panic | Col rejected |
| 80129-1-2 | Complainin' | - |

New York, March 6, 1922.

| | | |
|---|---|---|
| 80228- | Sing-Song Man | Col A-3592 |

New York, March 20, 1922.

| | | |
|---|---|---|
| 80249- | Oh, Sing-a-Loo | Col A-3592 |

New York, April 1, 1922.

| | | |
|---|---|---|
| 80270-3 | Kindness | Col A-3601 |
| 80271-2 | All Over Nothing At All | - |

New York, May 13, 1922.

| | | |
|---|---|---|
| 80347-1 | Cow Bells | Col A-3633 |

New York, May 19, 1922.

| | | |
|---|---|---|
| 80359-2 | Atta Baby | Col A-3633 |

New York, June 20, 1922.

| | | |
|---|---|---|
| 80389-2 | I Ain't Never Had Nobody Crazy Over Me | Col A-3652 |
| 80390-2 | You've Had Your Day | - |

New York, July 14, 1922.

| | | |
|---|---|---|
| 80455- | Good Mornin' (It's Mighty Good To Be Home) | Col A-3669 |
| 80456- | Just Like A Violin | - |

New York, August 11, 1922.

| | | |
|---|---|---|
| 80515-1-2 | Coal Black Mammy | Col rejected |
| 80516-1-2 | Whenever You're Lonesome (Just Telephone Me) | - |

New York, September 18, 1922.

| | | |
|---|---|---|
| 80549-2 | Homesick | Col A-3711 |
| 80550-3 | Tomorrow (I'll Be In My Dixie Home Again) | - |

New York, October 19, 1922.

| | | |
|---|---|---|
| 80618-2 | You Need Someone, Someone Needs You | Col A-3742 |
| 80619-1 | Mammy's Carbon Copy | - |

New York, November 11, 1922.

| | | |
|---|---|---|
| 80662-1 | Lovin' Sam (The Sheik Of Alabam') | Col A-3757 |
| 80663-1 | Daddy's Goin' Huntin' Tonight | - |

New York, November 24, 1922.

| | | |
|---|---|---|
| 80689-1 | Come On Home | Col A-3771 |
| 80690-2 | Who Did You Fool After All ? | - |

New York, January 11, 1923.

| | | |
|---|---|---|
| 80781-5 | Keep Off My Shoes | Col A-3826 |
| 80782-5 | Runnin' Wild | - |

New York, March 8, 1923.

| | | |
|---|---|---|
| 80890- | You Know You Belong To Somebody Else | Col A-3862 |
| 80891- | Dearest (You're The Nearest To My Heart) | - |

Acc. by Dudley Wilkinson-p.                Camden, N. J., November 7, 1927.

| | | |
|---|---|---|
| BVE-40445-1 | Nora/Kelly | Vic rejected |
| BVE-40446-1 | Just Like A Gypsy | - |
| BVE-40447-1 | I'm Gonna Pop My Papa | - |

## NOAH BEERY

B. Kansas City, 1884; d. 1946. Brother of Wallace Beery; usually played villainous roles on silent and talking pictures, beginning in 1918 with THE MORMON MAID; some of his greatest successes include THE MARK OF ZORRO (1920); TOL'ABLE DAVID (1921); BEAU GESTE and DON JUAN (1926); BEAU SABREUR (1927); THE FOUR FEATHERS (1929);SONG OF THE FLAME and GOLDEN DAWN (1930); THE DRIFTER (1931); SHE DONE HIM WRONG(1933); he made KING OF THE DAMNED (1935) and OUR FIGHTING NAVY (1937) in England. In 1945 he made his last film, THIS MAN'S NAVY. His son Noah Beery, Jr., b. 1913, is also a film character actor very popular on television.

Vocal, acc. by the Vitaphone Orchestra.    Los Angeles, c. May, 1930.

| | | |
|---|---|---|
| LAE-801- | The Whip (Film "Golden Dawn") | Br 4828, 1147 |
| LAE-802- | One Little Drink (Film "Song Of The Flame")- | - |

## DIGBY BELL

B. 1851; d. June 20, 1917. Vaudeville comedian of the older school who specialized in droll commentaries on everyday activities. Appeared in a film, THE EDUCATION OF MR. PIPP (1914).
Speech, unacc.                            New York, February 8, 1909.

| | |
|---|---|
| Tough Kid On The Right Field Fence | Ed 4M-156 |
| The Blind Boy In The Gallery | Ed 4M-279 |
| The Man Who Fanned Casey | Ed 4M-430 |

New York, February 27, 1909.

| | | |
|---|---|---|
| C-6837-1-3 | The Boy On The Right Field Fence | Vic 31731 |
| C-6838-1-2 | The Blind Gallery Boy | Vic 35083 |
| C-6839-1-2 | The Man Who Fanned Casey | Rejected |

New York, May 5, 1909.

| | | |
|---|---|---|
| B-7045-1-2 | Experiences Of A Commuter | Vic rejected |
| B-7046-1-2 | Day And Knight | - |
| B-7047-1-2 | A Discontented Egg | - |

New York, May 7, 1909.

| | | |
|---|---|---|
| C-6839-3 | The Man Who Fanned Casey | Vic 31733 |
| B-7045-3 | Experiences Of A Commuter | Rejected |
| B-7046-3 | Day And Knight | - |
| B-7047-3-4 | A Discontented Egg | - |

## IRVING  BERLIN

B. South Russia, May 11, 1888, youngest child of Cantor Moses Baline (his real name is Israel Baline); the family emigrated to the U.S.A. in 1893, where Cantor Baline died in 1896. Israel Baline stayed at home while his seven brothers and sisters went out to do menial jobs; at fourteen he was himself selling newspapers, singing in saloons and, later, plugging songs for his favourite composer, Harry von Tilzer in Tony Pastor's Music Hall, amongst other places. He had a short-lived job as a

singing waiter in a saloon in Chinatown run by one "Nigger Mike" Salter, who  was
also a Russian Jew, but with a swarthy complexion, and who fired young Baline for
falling asleep on the job (the hours were 8.00 p.m. to 6.00 a.m. every night). In
1907, however, he had written a lyric to a song called MARIE FROM SUNNY ITALY. It
was published, and came to the notice of Ted Snyder, the composer and  publisher,
who gave him a position in his company, collaborated with him on several numbers,
and eventually made him a partner in the firm of Waterson, Berlin & Snyder.    His
marriage to Dorothy Goetz in 1912 ended with her death five months later, and the
first sentimental song by Irving Berlin - WHEN I LOST YOU - became a hit as   his
"ragtime" and comedy songs had. (He married again in 1926).  He has  contributed
complete scores to musical productions such as WATCH YOUR STEP (1914), the   Army
show YIP YIP YAPHANK (1917) in the first World War and THIS IS THE ARMY (1942) in
the second; two editions of Ziegfeld FOLLIES and four of MUSIC BOX REVUE; the De-
pression-period revues FACE THE MUSIC (1932) and AS THOUSANDS CHEER (1933);LOUIS-
IANA PURCHASE (1939); ANNIE, GET YOUR GUN (1946); CALL ME MADAM (1951), and films
TOP HAT (1935); FOLLOW THE FLEET (1936) and ON THE AVENUE (1937), as well as BLUE
SKIES (1946) which used many earlier songs not originally included in shows.  The
huge number of these makes it impossible to list them, but there is no doubt that
GOD BLESS AMERICA, BLUE SKIES, ALWAYS, HOW DEEP IS THE OCEAN ?, AT PEACE WITH THE
WORLD and THE SONG IS ENDED must rank as some of the greatest work in the history
of twentieth-century popular culture.

Vocal, acc. by O/? Charles A. Prince.     New York, c. January, 1910.

4333-   Oh ! How That German Could Love        Col A-804, Cli K-244, Ox 4333

Acc. by Arthur Johnston-p.               New York, December 21, 1925.

        Always                           Vic test (un-numbered)

Acc. by O/Milton Rosenstock, with male chorus.
                                New York, July 28, 1942.

71228-A  Oh ! How I Hate To Get Up In The     Dec 18777, Br 03492
         Morning ("This Is The Army")

Acc. by orchestra and male chorus, with introduction by John Watt, BBC producer.*
                                London, November 22, 1943.

OEA-10096-1  This Is The Army, Mr. Jones ("This   HMV B-9355
        Is The Army")
OEA-10097-3  *My British Buddy                     -

## BARNEY BERNARD

B. 1878, d. March 21, 1924.  Well-known character comedian for his Yiddish dialect-
    sketches, and his appearance in ABE AND MAWRUSS at the Lyric Theatre, New York on
    October 21, 1915.

Speech, unacc.                           Camden, N. J., March 17, 1916.

B-17337-2  Cohen At The Tekephone          Vic 18029
B-17338-1-2  Goldstein Goes In Railroad Business  Rejected

                                Camden, N. J., April 3, 1916.

B-17338-4  Goldstein Goes In Railroad Business    Vic 18029

                                Camden, N. J., December 22, 1916.

B-18869-1-2  Cohen's Second-Handing Car      Vic rejected
B-18870-1-2  Rashkind At The Movies               -

## RHODA   BERNARD

Vocal, acc. by O/Walter B. Rogers.            Camden, N. J., March 1, 1916.

B-17241-1  Roll Your Yiddish Eyes For Me              Vic 17994
B-17242-1-2-3  My Yiddish Matinee Girl               Rejected

                                              Camden, N. J., March 8, 1916.

B-17242-4  My Yiddish Matinee Girl                   Vic 17994
B-17289-1-2-3  I Opened The Door And Closed The      Rejected
           Door

                                              Camden, N. J., April 5, 1916.

B-17451-1-2  When Isadore Sang "Il Trovatore"        Rejected
B-17452-2  Nat'an (For What Are You Waitin',         Vic 18023
           Nat'an ?)
B-17453-2  Cohen Owes Me Ninety-Seven Dollars          -

  Acc. by O/? Charles A. Prince.          New York, April 19, 1916.

  46727-   Gootmon Is A Hootmon Now                 Col rejected

                                         New York, c. April, 1916.

  43594-   Rosie Rosenblatt                          Col A-1973, E-2802
  43595-   Nathan, Nathan, What Are You Waiting For ?         -

                                         New York, c. July, 1916.

  44187-   Delegate And Shop Girl Of Cloak And       Col E-2994
           Suit Makers' Union

  Acc. by studio orchestra.              New York, c. November, 1916.

  65433    Cedro                                    Pathe 30395
  65435    Nat'an                                     -

                                         New York, c. December, 1916.

  0904     Stand Up, Sit Down, Walk Around, Do      Rex 5298
           Something

                                         New York, c. January, 1917.

           I'm Looking For Antone                   Ed 50324

                                         New York, May 25, 1918.

  77844-   Jakalie                                  Col rejected

## SARAH  BERNHARDT

"The Divine Sarah" was the greatest actress France produced in the nineteenth   century (b. 1844; d. March 26, 1923). She appeared in many tragic roles with immense
success throughout her whole career, in Europe and the U.S.A. The few records  she
made are glimpses of the parts she played; she also appeared in French films, such
as QUEEN ELIZABETH (1912), JEANNE DORE (1915) and MOTHERS OF FRANCE (1917).

Speech.                                       New York, early 1896.

           Passage dans le drame IZEYL (Eugene       Bettini cylinder
             Morand-Paul Armand Sylvestre)
           Un peu de musique (Victor Hugo)             -
           A Dramatic Phrase                           -
NOTE:- No copies of the above cylinders are known to exist; they are included   in
the Bettini catalogues of June, 1898 and April 10, 1900.

Announced by Mme. Bernhardt herself.    Paris, early 1902.

| | |
|---|---|
| La Chanson d'Eviradnus (Victor Hugo) | Pathe 2021, 4057 |
| Le Lac (Maurice Bernhardt) | Pathe 2022, 4058 |
| Passage ("Phedre" - Jean Racine) | Pathe 2023, 4059 |
| La Fiancee du Timbalier (Victor Hugo) | Pathe 2024, 4060 |
| Lucie (Alfred de Musset) | Pathe 2025, 4061 |

Paris, c. February, 1903.

| | | |
|---|---|---|
| 1501-F | Le Lac (Maurice Bernhardt) | G&T GC-31170 |
| 1502-F | Il dit encore ("La Samaritaine" - Edmond Rostand) | G&T GC-31171, HMV E-326 |
| 1503-F | Les Vieux (Mme. Edmond Rostand) | G&T GC-31172, Rococo 4002 |
| 1551-F | Un Evangile (François Coppee) | G&T GC-31102 |
| 1552-F | Oui, Prince ("Phedre" - Jean Racine) | G&T GC-31103, HMV E-326, El E-91280 (part), Rococo 4002 |
| | La Mort d'Izail (Maurice Bernhardt) | G&T GC-31104 |

Paris, c. April, 1903.

| | |
|---|---|
| Dans les profondeurs ("Theroigne de Mericourt" - Paul Hervieu) | Zon X-2129, Phonotheque Nationale PN/PR-1 (part) |
| Un peu de musique (Victor Hugo) | Zon X-2130, IRCC 3047 |
| Passage ("Izeyl" - Eugene Morand-Paul Armand Silvestre) | Rejected ? |

Not announced by Mme. Bernhardt.    Paris, c. 1908.

| | |
|---|---|
| La Brise conte ("Les Buffons" - Miguel Zamaçois) | Pathe rejected |

West Orange, N. J., c. February, 1910.

| | |
|---|---|
| Flambeau ! ("L'Aiglon" - Edmond Rostand) | Amb 35007, Varieties GS-2001, IRCC L-7028, National Vocarium 131 (part) |
| Oui, Prince ("Phedre" - Jean Racine) | Amb 35008, IRCC 5016, L-7028 |
| Le souffle ("Les Buffons" - Miguel Zamaçois) | Amb 35011      - |
| Je dormais ("La Samaritaine" - Edmond Rostand) | Amb 35013, CRS 2, AR 2465 |

London, September 28, October 2, 10, 1910.

| | |
|---|---|
| La Plaine du Wagram ("L'Aiglon" - Edmond Rostand) | Ed rejected |
| La Brise conte ("Les Buffons" - Miguel Zamaçois) | - |
| Passage ("Phedre," Act 2 - Jean Racine) | - |
| La Samaritaine rencontre Jesus au puits de Jacob ("La Samaritaine" - Edmond Rostand) | - |
| La Tirade de Nez ("Cyrano de Bergerac" - Edmond Rostand) | - |

New York, c. January, 1918.

| | |
|---|---|
| L'etoile dans la nuit (Henri Cain-E. Guerinon) | Voc 22035 |
| La Priere pour nos ennemis (Louis Payen) | -      CRS 10, Rare Records 103, History Speaks (Vol. 2), Golden Age of Opera EJS-267 |

## RALPH  BINGHAM

B. Richmond, Virginia, August 2, 1870; stage debut as child, 1876; from 1890 appeared with great success all over the U.S.A. as a character actor. D. Philadelphia, Pa., December 27, 1925.

Speech.                                  New York, April 9, 1915.

C-15871-1-2  The Boy In The Bleachers              Rejected
B-15872-2  Mrs. Rastus At The Telephone            Vic 17818
C-15873-1  My 'Possum Hunt                         Vic 35490
B-15874-1-2-3  Jests From Georgia                  Rejected


                                         New York, June 7, 1915.

C-15871-3  The Boy In The Bleachers                Vic 35490
B-15872-3-4  Mrs. Rastus At The Telephone          Rejected
C-15873-3  My 'Possum Hunt                         -
B-15874-5  Jests From Georgia                      Vic 17818


                                         New York, December 22, 1916.

B-18926-1-2-3  Mrs. Rastus Johnson At The Wedding  Vic rejected
B-18927-1-2-3  Goldstein Behind Bars               -


                                         New York, December 26, 1916.

C-18931-1  Home Run Bill's Defense                 Vic 35626
C-18932-1  The Hold-Up At Buck Run                 -


                                         New York, December 30, 1916.

B-18926-4  Mrs. Rastus Johnson At The Wedding      Vic 18231
B-18927-5  Goldstein Behind Bars                   -
B-18954-1-2  The Coster's Peep-Show                Rejected


                                         New York, September 11, 1917.

B-20657-1-2  A Few Words About Wess Jackson In     Vic rejected
             Colored Dialect


                                         New York, January 4, 1918.

B-21405-3  Brother Jones's Sermon                  Vic 18587


                                         Camden, N. J., June 9, 1919.

B-22895-4  Mrs. Rastus Johnson's Joy Ride          Vic 18587


                              JOHN BOLES

B. Greenville, Texas, October 28, 1895; intended for a doctor; served in France as an
   interpreter, 1917-1918; took up theatrical work after demobilization, New York debut as Paul Revere in LITTLE JESSIE JAMES at Longacre Theatre, August 15, 1923; in
   MERCENARY MARY (same theatre, April 13, 1925); first film SO THIS IS MARRIAGE,1925
   (silent); many successful talkies (RIO RITA, 1929; THE DESERT SONG, KING  OF JAZZ,
   both 1930; FRANKENSTEIN, ONE HEAVENLY NIGHT, both 1931; CURLY TOP, 1935;    STELLA
   DALLAS, 1937; successful return to stage in ONE TOUCH OF VENUS (Imperial   Theatre,
   New York, October 7, 1943); last film BABES IN BAGHDAD, 1952; died 1969.

Vocal, acc. by Leroy Shields-p.          New York, December 9, 1925.

            Within The Garden Of My Heart          Vic test (un-numbered)

    Acc. by O/Leroy Shields.             Culver City, Calif., November 14, 1929.

PBVE-54512-1  Love Time (Film "Song Of The West")  Vic 22231
PBVE-54513-2  Silhouette (Film "Song Of The West") -
PBVE-54514-2  West Wind (Film "Song Of The West")  Vic 22229


                                         Culver City, Calif., November 15, 1929.

PBVE-54515-4  After A Million Dreams (Film "Song    Vic 22230
              Of The West")
PBVE-54516-1  The One Girl(Film "Song Of The West")Vic 22229
PBVE-54517-1  Romance (Film "Song Of The West")     Vic 22230

Culver City, Calif., March 17, 1930.

| PBVE-54712-2 | For You (Film "Captain Of The Guard") | Vic 22373, HMV B-3467 |
| PBVE-54713-2 | It Happened In Monterey (Film "King Of Jazz") | Vic 22372, LPV-538, LSA-3074, RD-7869, HMV B-3456 |
| PBVE-54714-3 | You, You Alone (Film "Captain Of The Guard") | Vic 22373, HMV B-3467 |
| PBVE-54715-4 | Song Of The Dawn (Film "King Of Jazz") | Vic 22372, HMV B-3456 |

## EDWIN BOOTH

B. 1833; one of America's greatest actors. Debut 1849 in his father's company; 1851 played RICHARD III; 1861 debut in London. From 1863 to 1867 he was manager of the Winter Garden Theatre, New York; created a record of 100 consecutive performances of HAMLET; when the theatre was destroyed by fire, he opened his own (1869) with a performance of ROMEO AND JULIET, in which Juliet was played by Mary McVicker, his second wife (d. 1881). In 1873 he was adjudged bankrupt, but he toured U.S.A. and Europe; in England, 1880-1882, then to Germany; In 1888 he presented his house in Gramercy Park to the newly-founded Players' Club. He died June 7, 1893. Younger brother John Wilkes Booth assassinated President Abraham Lincoln in a theatre in Washington, April 14, 1865. Edwin Booth's voice is preserved very imperfectly on a wax clinder which has been transferred to three different LP issues.

Speech.                                   ? New York, c. 1891.

| Most Potent, Grave And Reverend Signiors ("Othello") | AR 2465, Delta DEL-12020, Summit LSU-3068 |

## IRENE BORDONI

B. 1894; very popular juvenile artist in Varietes, Paris, 1907-1909; New York debut in THE FIRST AFFAIR at the Winter Garden, November 2, 1912 (engaged as singer, but performed as dancer), very successful; London debut in L'IMPRESSARIO at the Palace (February 16, 1914); in various productions of HITCHY KOO in New York; big success in LITTLE MISS BLUEBEARD (Lyceum, N.Y., August 28, 1923), much less so in London production at Wyndham's (April, 1925); opened in NAUGHTY CINDERELLA, also at the Lyceum (November 9, 1925) and PARIS at the Music Box, October 8, 1928; filmed this show, 1929; other popular film PARIS IN SPRING (1935).

Vocal, acc. by vn/p.                      New York, November 5, 1923.

| B-28912-1 | I Won't Say I Will (But I Won't Say I Won't) ("Little Miss Bluebeard") | Vic 19199, HMV B-2011 |
| B-28925-1-2 | So This Is Love ("Little Miss Bluebeard") | Rejected |

New York, November 13, 1923.

| B-28925-4 | So This Is Love ("Little Miss Bluebeard") | Vic 19199, HMV B-2011 |

Acc. by Eddie Ward-p.                     New York, January 25, 1926.

| BVE-34357-1-2-3 | Do I Love You ? ("Naughty Cinderella") | Rejected |
| BVE-34358-4 | That Means Nothing To Me ("Naughty Cinderella") | Vic 19966 |
| BVE-34359-1 | Souvenir d'Argentine (in French) | Rejected |

New York, February 8, 1926.

| BVE-34357-8 | Do I Love You ? ("Naughty Cinderella") | Vic 19966 |

Acc. by Irving Aaronson and his Commanders.
                                          Camden, N. J., May 3, 1928.

| BVE-43761-1-2 | Two Little Babes In The Wood ("Paris") | Vic rejected |
| BVE-43762-1-2-3 | Let's Misbehave ("Paris") | - |
| BVE-43763-1-2 | The Land Of Going-To-Be ("Paris") | - |
| BVE-43764-1-2 | Don't Look At Me That Way ("Paris") | - |

Camden, N. J., June 24, 1928.

BVE-43761-3-4-5  Two Little Babes In The Wood        Rejected
                 ("Paris")
BVE-43762-4-5-6  Let's Misbehave ("Paris")             -
BVE-43763-4  The Land Of Going-To-Be ("Paris")     Vic 21742
BVE-43764-4  Don't Look At Me That Way ("Paris")      -          LVA-523, LSA-3078

   Acc. by studio orchestra.          New York, June 29, 1928.

BVE-45840-1-2-3  Where Is The Song Of Songs For Me  Vic rejected

New York, September 22, 1929.

149030-    Believe Me                                Col 2027-D, 5738
149031-    Just An Hour Of Love (Film "Show Of Shows")  -          -
149032-2   My Lover (Master Of My Heart) (Film      Col 1983-D, 5691
           "Paris")
149033-2   I Wonder What Is Really On His Mind (Film    -          -
           "Paris")

New York, June 13, 1935.

39631-A   Bonjour, Mam'selle (Film "Paris In        Dec S-1, F-5622
          Spring")
39632-A   Tell Me That You Love Me (Film "Paris        -          -
          In Spring")

## THE  BOSWELL SISTERS

Singing trio from New Orleans, La.: Martha (the late, who played piano), Connie, who
played 'cello and saxophone; and Helvetia ("Vet"), violin. They won a radio contest while in early teens (Connie only 12); recorded, went on tour to  California;
broadcast, filmed and recorded there (Los Angeles station KFWB, 1930); to New York
and great success on radio and in theatres; to London, July, 1933 and July,  1935;
returned to New York, disbanded in the spring of 1936.

Vocal trio, acc. by Eddie King, Vic Lubowski or Harry Pooley-p as shown.
                                New Orleans, March 22, 1925.

B-32113-1-2-3-4  You Can Call Me Baby All The Time  Vic rejected
                 - pHP
B-32132-1-2-3  Pal O' Mine - pEK                      -
   NOTE:- Matrix B-32114 is a solo by Connie Boswell; B-32115/32122 and B-32125/32131
all inclusive are by other artists on other dates.

New Orleans, March 25, 1925.

B-32123-1-2-3-4  Dad (Dedicated to the Fathers of  Rejected
                 the world) - pVL
B-32k24-4  Nights When I'm Lonely - pVL               Vic 19639

Vocalists with Jackie Taylor's Orchestra. Hollywood, July 20, 1930.

PBVE-54882-1  We're On The Highway To Heaven (Film  Vic 22500, HMV B-5921
              "Sailor Behave")
PBVE-54885-1-2-3  That's What I Like About You       Rejected

Vocal trio, acc. by Martha Boswell-p.    Los Angeles, October 3, 1930.

404407-C  My Future Just Passed                    OK 41444, Par R-787, R-1575
404408-B  Heebie Jeebies                             - Har 1428-H,Cl 5476-C,VT 2536-V,
                                                   Par R-821, R-1574, PMC-7006
404409-A-B-C  I'm Yours                            Rejected
404410-B  Gee, But I'd Like To Make You Happy      OK 41470, Par R-854, R-1575,
                                                   PMC-7006
                                Los Angeles, October 31, 1930.

404414-B  Don't Tell Her What's Happened To Me     OK 41470, Par R-850, R-1574

Acc. by the Dorsey Brothers' Orchestra, New York, March 19, 1931.

E-36491-A  Whadja Do To Me ?                    Br 6083, 80011, 01113
E-36492-A  When I Take My Sugar To Tea              -      -      -    Dec 7-3

                                    New York, April 23, 1931.

E-36654-A  Roll On, Mississippi, Roll On        Br 6109, 80012, 01136
E-36655-A  Shout, Sister, Shout                    - 6847  -   01416 -

Vocalists with Victor Young's Orchestra.  New York, May 25, 1931.

E-36825-   Sing A Little Jingle                 Br 6128, 01193
E-36826-   I Found A Million-Dollar Baby (In A     -      -
           Five-and-Ten-Cent Store)

Acc. by the Dorsey Brothers' Orchestra. New York, July 8, 1931.

E-36911-A  It's The Girl                        Br 6151, 80014, 01181
E-36912-A  It's You                                -      -      -

Acc. by the New Yorkers (studio band). New York, August 17, 1931.

E-37081-A  Makin' Faces At The Man In The Moon  Br 6170, 01221
E-37082-A  (With You On My Mind I Find) I Can't    -      -    01395
           Write The Words

Acc. by the Dorsey Brothers' Orchestra. New York, August 27, 1931.

E-37112-A  Shine On, Harvest Moon               Br 6173, 80013, 01218
E-37113-A  Heebie Jeebies                          -      -      -

                                    New York, November 5, 1931.

E-37354-A  River, Stay 'Way From My Door        Br 6218, 80014, 01251
E-37355-A  An Ev'ning In Caroline                  -      -      -

                                    New York, December 5, 1931.

E-37445-A  Nothing Is Sweeter Than You          Br 6231, 01272
E-37446-A  I Thank You, Mr. Moon                   -      -

                                    New York, February 5, 1932.

B-11240-A  (We've Got To) Put That Sun Back In The  Br rejected
           Sky
B-11241-   Was That The Human Thing To Do ?

                                    New York, February 19, 1932.

B-11320-A  Was That The Human Thing To Do ?     Br 6257, 01284
B-11321-A  (We've Got To) Put That Sun Back In The Sky -    -

                                    New York, February 24, 1932.

B-11353-B  Stop The Sun, Stop The Moon (My Man's  Br 6271, 01295
           Gone)
B-11354-A  Everybody Loves My Baby                 - 6783  -    Col 36520

                                    New York, March 21, 1932.

B-11543-A  There'll Be Some Changes Made        Br 6291, 01306, Col 36521,
                                                Epic SN-6059
B-11544-A  Between The Devil And The Deep Blue Sea Br 6291, 01306

                                    New York, April 9, 1932.

B-11684-A  If It Ain't Love                     Br 6302, 01330
B-11685-A  Got The South In My Soul                -      -

New York, June 17, 1932.

| | | |
|---|---|---|
| B-11948-A | Doggone, I've Done It ! | Br 6335, 01362, 01893 |
| B-11949-A | Hand Me Down My Walkin' Cane | -      -    Col 36520 |

Acc. by Martha Boswell-p/Dick McDonough-g/Arthur Bernstein-sb.
New York, June 29, 1932.

| | | |
|---|---|---|
| B-12000-A | Old Yazoo | Br 6360, 01379 |

Acc. by the Dorsey Brothers' Orchestra. New York, August 6, 1932.

| | | |
|---|---|---|
| B-12151-A | We Just Couldn't Say Goodbye | Br 6360, 01347 |
| B-12152-A-B | Sleep, Come On And Take Me | Rejected |
| B-12153-A | Down Among The Sheltering Palms | Br 6418, 01347, Col 36522 |

Martha Boswell-p replaces the regular Dorsey Brothers pianist (Fulton McGrath).
New York, September 13, 1932.

| | | |
|---|---|---|
| B-12290-A | Down On The Delta | Br 6395, 01403 |
| B-12291-A | Charlie Two-Step | Br 6418  - |
| B-12292-A | Sentimental Gentleman From Georgia | Br 6395, 01379, Col 36522, Rex 8910 |

New York, November 22, 1932.

| | | |
|---|---|---|
| B-12639-A | It Don't Mean A Thing (If It Ain't Got Got That Swing) | Br 6442, 01436, Voc 4546, Rex 8873, Col DB-1994 |
| B-12640-A | Louisiana Hayride | Br 6470, 01625 |
| B-12641-A | Minnie The Moocher's Wedding Day | Br 6442, 01436, Voc 4546 |

Acc. by Dick McDonough-g/Arthur Bernstein-sb.
New York, December 7, 1932.

| | | |
|---|---|---|
| B-12697-A | Crazy People | Br 6847, 01416 |

Acc. by the Dorsey Brothers' Orchestra. New York, January 9, 1933.

| | | |
|---|---|---|
| B-12860-A | Mood Indigo | Br 6470, 01543, Col 36521, DB-1960, Rex 8910 |

New York, April 11, 1933.

| | | |
|---|---|---|
| B-13222-A | Forty-Second Street | Br 6545, 01516, Epic L2N-6072 |
| B-13223-A | Shuffle Off To Buffalo | -      - |

New York, June 13, 1933.

| | | |
|---|---|---|
| B-13450-A | The Gold-Diggers' Song (We're In The Money) | Br 6596, 01556 |
| B-13451-A | It's Sunday Down In Caroline | -      - |

New York, June 15, 1933.

| | | |
|---|---|---|
| B-13466-A | Puttin' It On | Br 6625, 01576 |
| B-13467-A | Swanee Mammy | -      - |

Acc. by studio orchestra (probably dir. by Victor Young).
New York, September 11, 1933.

| | | |
|---|---|---|
| B-13990-A | Sophisticated Lady | Br 6650, 01592 |
| B-13991-A | That's How Rhythm Was Born | -      -    Col DB-1960 |

New York, November 14, 1933.

| | | |
|---|---|---|
| B-14319-A | Song Of Surrender | Br 6733, 01711 |
| B-14320-B | Coffee In The Morning (Kisses In The Night) | -      - |

New York, March 23, 1934.

B-14993-A  You Oughta Be In Pictures          Br 6798, 01751
B-14994-A  I Hate Myself (For Being So Mean To You) -      -

New York, April 27, 1934.

B-15134-A  Goin' Home                          Br 6951, 01791
B-15135-A  Lonesome Road                          -       -

New York, May 23, 1934.

B-15254-A  Alexander's Ragtime Band            Br 7412, 01893, Voc 4239,
                                               Par R-2562
B-15255-   The Darktown Strutters' Ball        Col DO-1255 (Australian only)

New York, June 21, 1934.

B-15357-A  Don't Let Your Love Go Wrong        Br 6929, 01832, Par R-2631
B-15358-A  Why Don't You Practice What You Preach ? -      -

   Acc. by Jimmy Grier and his Orchestra. Los Angeles, October 4, 1934.

LA-221-A   Rock And Roll                       Br 7302, 01957, Col 36523,
                                               Par R-2631
LA-222-A   If I Had A Million Dollars          Br 7302, 01957

   Jimmy Grier speaks.*                 Los Angeles, December 10, 1934.

LA-278-A  *The Object Of My Affection          Br 7348, 01961
LA-279-B   It's Written All Over Your Face        -       -    Col 36523

   Acc. by unknown p/Bobby Sherwood-g.   Los Angeles, December 13, 1934.

LA-294-A   Dinah                               Br 7412, 01926, Voc 4239,
                                               Rex 8873, Par R-2562

   Acc. by studio orchestra.            New York, May 21, 1935.

B-17631-1  'Way Back Home                       Br 7454, 02033
B-17632-1  Every Little Moment                    -       -

New York, May 28, 1935.

B-17645-1  Travelin' All Alone                 Br 7467, 02044, Voc 4495
B-17646-2  St. Louis Blues                        -       -    -  Col DB-1994
B-17646-3  St. Louis Blues                        -

   Acc. by Martha Boswell-p/Max Bacon-d, plus Joe Brannelly-g/Dick Ball-sb as shown.
                         London, July 19, 1935.

GB-7316-1  Fare Thee Well, Annabelle - p/d      Br 02043
GB-7317-3  Lullaby Of Broadway - p/g/sb/d         -

   Acc. by small jazz group.            New York, October 8, 1935.

60029-A    Top Hat, White Tie And Tails         Dec 574, Br 02067
60030-A    Cheek To Cheek                         -       -

New York, January 6, 1936.

60302-A    I'm Gonna Sit Right Down And Write    Dec 671, Br 02142
             Myself A Letter
60303-A    The Music Goes 'Round And Around       -       -

New York, February 12, 1936.

60463-B    Let Yourself Go                       Dec 709, Br 02165
60464-B    I'm Putting All My Eggs In One Basket   -      -
See also Bing Crosby.

B. New Orleans, 1912; worked with sisters Martha and Vet until the act broke up (see the Boswell Sisters), but had made many solo recordings before this, and continued as a solo entertainer on radio and in clubs until the fifties. A victim of polio, contracted when a child, she carried out most of her engagements in a wheel-chair, but in 1935 she married her manager, Harold Leedy, and is still happily married to him.

Vocal, acc. by Martha Boswell-p.　　　　　　New Orleans, March 22, 1925.

B-32114-1　I'm Gonna Cry (Crying Blues)　　　　Vic 19639

　Acc. by studio orchestra, probably dir. Victor Young.
　　　　　　　　　　　　　　　　　　New York, c. August 28, 1931.

E-36987-　I'm All Dressed Up With A Broken Heart　Br 6162, 01198
E-36988-　What Is It ?　　　　　　　　　　　　-　　-

　　　　　　　　　　　　　　　　　　New York, November 2, 1931.

E-37333-A　Time On My Hands (You In My Arms)　Br 6210, 01443
E-37334-A　Concentratin' (On You)　　　　　-　　01252

　　　　　　　　　　　　　　　　　　New York, c. November 18, 1931.

E-37366-　You Try Somebody Else　　　　　　Br 6223, 01257
E-37367-　Should I Be Sorry ?　　　　　　　-

　　　　　　　　　　　　　　　　　　New York, February 23, 1932.

B-11332-　I Cried For You　　　　　　　　Br 6267, 01298
B-11333-　I Can't Believe That It's You　-　　-

Vocalist with the Casa Loma Orchestra.　New York, March 16, 1932.

BX-11520-A Washboard Blues　　　　　　　Br 20108, 0110

Vocal, acc. by the Dorsey Brothers' Orchestra.
　　　　　　　　　　　　　　　　　　New York, April 9, 1932.

B-11682-A　Lullaby Of The Leaves　　　　　Br 6297, 01315
B-11683-A　My Lips Want Kisses (My Heart Wants Love) -　　-

　　　　　　　　　　　　　　　　　　New York, June 14, 1932.

B-11942-A　The Night When Love Was Born　　Br 6332, 01328
B-11943-A　(I've Got The Words, I've Got The Tune) -　　-
　　　　　　Hummin' To Myself

　　　　　　　　　　　　　　　　　　New York, September 10, 1932.

B-12278-A　Say It Isn't So　　　　　　　Br 6393, 01373
B-12279-A　Where, I Wonder Where ?　　　　-　　-

　　　　　　　　　　　　　　　　　　New York, September 27, 1932.

B-12378-A　I'll Never Have To Dream Again　Br 6405, 01382
B-12379-A　Me Minus You　　　　　　　　　-　　-

　　　　　　　　　　　　　　　　　　New York, January 9, 1933.

B-12858-A　It's All My Fault　　　　　　Br 6483, 01443, Col 38298
B-12859-A　Underneath The Arches　　　　　-　　-

　　　　　　　　　　　　　　　　　　New York, April 11, 1933.

B-13230-A　You'll Never Get Up To Heaven That Way　Br 6552, 01528
B-13231-A　In A Little Second-Hand Store　　　-　　-

Acc. by studio orchestra, probably dir. Victor Young.
                                    New York, June 10, 1933.

| | | |
|---|---|---|
| B-13445-A | I Cover The Waterfront | Br 6592, 01555 |
| B-13446-A | I Couldn't Tell Them What To Do | -      01547 |
| B-13447-A | Under A Blanket Of Blue | Br 6603, 01555 |

                                    New York, June 16, 1933.

| | | |
|---|---|---|
| B-13468-A | The River's Takin' Care Of Me | Br 6603, 01547 |

                                    New York, August 14, 1933.

| | | |
|---|---|---|
| B-13786-A | It's The Talk Of The Town | Br 6632, 01594 |
| B-13787-A | This Time It's Love | -      - |

                                    New York, August 29, 1933.

| | | |
|---|---|---|
| B-13891-A | Dinner  At Eight | Br 6640, 01595 |
| B-13892-A | Emperor Jones | -      - |

                                    New York, January 4, 1934.

| | | |
|---|---|---|
| B-14527-A | I Had To Change The Words | Br 6754, 01699 |
| B-14528-A | In Other Words - We're Through | -      - |

Acc. by the Dorsey Brothers' Orchestra.
                                    New York, March 28, 1934.

| | | |
|---|---|---|
| B-15013-A | Butterfingers | Br 6862, 01745 |

Acc. by O/Victor Young.         New York, March 30, 1934.

| | | |
|---|---|---|
| B-15024-A | I Knew You When | Br 6862, 01745 |

                                    New York, April 27, 1934.

| | | |
|---|---|---|
| B-15132- | Carioca | Br 6871, 01783 |
| B-15133- | The Boulevard Of Broken Dreams | -      - |

                                    New York, June 19, 1934.

| | | |
|---|---|---|
| B-15341-B | Little Man, You've Had A Busy Day | Br 6921, 01816 |
| B-15342-B | All I Do Is Dream Of You | -      - |

                                    New York, August 21, 1934.

| | | |
|---|---|---|
| B-15713-A | Say It | Br 6962, 01865 |
| B-15714-A | A New Moon Is Over My Shoulder | -      - |

Acc. by Jimmy Grier and his Orchestra. Los Angeles, October 4, 1934.

| | | |
|---|---|---|
| LA-219-A | Lost In A Fog | Br 7303, 01895 |
| LA-220-A | Isn't It A Shame ? | -      - |

                                    Los Angeles, December 13, 1934.

| | | |
|---|---|---|
| LA-295-A | With Every Breath I Take | Br 7354, 01982 |
| LA-296-A | I'm Growing Fonder Of You | -      - |

Acc. by studio orchestra, probably dir. Victor Young.
                                    New York, January 15, 1935.

| | | |
|---|---|---|
| B-16642-A | Blue Moon | Br 7363, 01926, Epic L2N-6072 |
| B-16643- | Clouds | -      02009 |

                                    New York, May 16, 1935.

| | | |
|---|---|---|
| B-17609-1 | Seein' Is Believin' | Br 7445, 02032 |
| B-17610-1 | Chasing Shadows | -      - |
| B-17611-2 | You're All I Need | Br 7457, 02050 |

New York, May 28, 1935.

B-17644-2  In The Middle Of A Kiss           Br 7457, 02050

   Acc. by Ambrose and his Orchestra.    London, July 19, 1935.

GB-7318-1  Things Might Have Been So Different    Br 02046
GB-7319-2  I'll Never Say "Never Again" Again         -

   Acc. by The Ramblers or Theo Uden Masman-p as shown.
                                    Casino Hamdorff, Laren, Holland,
                                    August 26, 1935.

AM-181-1  I Can't Give You Anything But Love, Baby Dec F-42108
AM-182-   Life Is A Song (Let's Sing It Together)-pTUM -

   Acc. by studio orchestra.           New York, October 4, 1935.

60025-A  You Are My Lucky Star                 Dec 575, Br 02068
60026-A  I've Got A Feelin' You're Foolin'        -        -

                                    New York, December 23, 1935.

60282-A  Moon Over Miami                       Dec 657, Br 02127
60283-A  With All My Heart                        -        -

                                    New York, March 5, 1936.

60870-A  The Panic Is On                       Dec 747, Br 02173
60873-A  Mama Don't Allow It                      -        -
   NOTE:- Matrices 60871/2 do not appear to have been allocated.

   Acc. by Bob Crosby and his Orchestra.  New York, April 13, 1936.

61034-A  You Started Me Dreaming               Dec 794
61035-A  Mommy                                    -      Br 02612

   Acc. by studio orchestra.           New York, June 9, 1936.

61148-A  On The Beach At Bali-Bali             Dec 829, Br 02235
61149-A  Swing Me A Lullaby                    Dec 840, Br 02254
61150-A  I Met My Waterloo (Down By The        Dec 829, Br 02235
            Beautiful Sea)
61151-A  You Can Call It Swing                 Dec 840, Br 02254

   Acc. by Ben Pollack and his Orchestra.  Los Angeles, February 15, 1937.

DLA-690-A  When The Poppies Bloom Again        Dec 1161
DLA-691-A  Serenade In The Night               Dec 1160
DLA-692-A  Where Are You ?                        -      Br 02401
DLA-693-A  Trust In Me                         Dec 1161    -

                                    Los Angeles, August 23, 1937.

DLA-848-A  That Old Feeling                    Dec 1420, Br 02474
DLA-849-A  The Loveliness Of You               Dec 1421, Br 02487
DLA-850-A  Afraid To Dream                        -      Br 02480
DLA-851-A  Yours And Mine                      Dec 1433, Br 02474

                                    Los Angeles, August 26, 1937.

DLA-853-A  Blossoms On Broadway                Dec 1434, Br 02487
DLA-854-A  Love Or Infatuation                    -      Br 02526
DLA-857-A  Whispers In The Dark                Dec 1420, Br 02480
   NOTE:- Matrix DLA-855 is a band side by Ben Pollack and his Orchestra; DLA-856 is a
   test of no interest.

                                    Los Angeles, August 31, 1937.

DLA-867-B  Am I In Love ?                      Dec 1433, Br 02526

Acc. by O/John Scott Trotter.              Los Angeles, September 25, 1937.

DLA-971-A  Basin Street Blues (w/Bing Crosby)      Dec 1483, 25430, DL-5390,
                                                    Br 02492, LA-8558
DLA-972-A  Bob White (Whatcha Gonna Swing Tonight ?)As above
              (w/Bing Crosby)

                                          Los Angeles, November 12, 1937.

DLA-1054-A  True Confession                  Dec 1559, Br 02544
DLA-1055-A  Ebb Tide                              -         -
DLA-1056-A  Outside Of Paradise              Dec 1568, Br 02630
DLA-1057-A  You Took The Words Right Out Of My Heart   -    Br 02612

Acc. by Bob Crosby's Bob-Cats.            Los Angeles, November 13, 1937.

DLA-1066-A  Ah ! So Pure ("Martha" - von Flotow)   Dec 1600, Br 02566, LAT-8368
DLA-1067-A  Home On The Range                         -         -
DLA-1068-A  Gypsy Love Song ("The Fortune Teller")  Dec 1678, Br 02589

                                          Los Angeles, November 16, 1937.

DLA-1086-A  Ah ! Sweet Mystery Of Life ("Naughty   Dec 1678, Br 02589
              Marietta")

Acc. by O/Victor Young.                   Los Angeles, January 26, 1938.

DLA-1152-A  Alexander's Ragtime Band (w/Bing Crosby Dec 1887, 25495, DL-5390,
              and Eddie Cantor)                      Br 02572, LA-8558
DLA-1153-A  True Confession                  Dec 1887, 25000, DL-5107,
                                                    Br 02572
NOTE:- Matrix DLA-1153-A opens with HOME ON THE RANGE sung by Bing Crosby (q.v.)

Acc. by Ben Pollack and his Orchestra.  Los Angeles, April 9, 1938.

DLA-1202-A  Fare Thee Honey, Fare Thee Well      Dec 1862, Br 02662
DLA-1203-A  Mr. Freddie Blues                         -         -

Acc. by O/Harry Sosnik.                   Los Angeles, April 16, 1938.

DLA-1223-A  All Alone                        Dec 1889, Br 02645
DLA-1224-A  (You Forgot To) Remember              -         -
DLA-1225-A  I'm Away From It All             Dec 1805
DLA-1226-A  I'm Glad For Your Sake (But I'm Sorry   -    Br 02666
              For Mine)

Acc. by studio orchestra.                 New York, June 15, 1938.

63992-A  I Hadn't Anyone Till You           Dec 1896, Br 02666
63993-A  I Let A Song Go Out Of My Heart        -    Br 02630
63994-A  If It Rains - Who Cares ?          Dec 1897, Br 02621
63995-A  You Leave Me Breathless                -         -

                                          New York, September 6, 1938.

64600-A  Simple And Sweet                   Dec 2028, Br 02689
64601-A  There's Something About An Old Love  Dec 2055, Br 02677
64602-A  Heart And Soul                     Dec 2028    -
64603-A  Summer Souvenirs                   Dec 2055, Br 02689

Acc. by Woody Herman and his Orchestra.  New York, January 10, 1939.

64877-A  Thanks For Ev'rything              Dec 2259, Br 02712
64878-A  The Umbrella Man                   Dec 2258    -
64879-A  They Say                               -    Br 02726
64880-A  Deep In A Dream                    Dec 2259    -

With the Lyn Murray Singers, acc. by p/g/sb/cel.
                                 New York, January 18, 1939.

| 64903- | When Christmas Is Gone | Dec 2264 |
| 64904-A | Memory Lane | Dec 2403, Br 02828 |
| 64905-A | Silver Threads Among The Gold | -     - |
| 64906- | You're The Only Star (In My Blue Heaven) | Dec 2264 |

Acc. by O/Ray Sinatra.           New York, April 25, 1939.

| 65456-A | Sunrise Serenade | Dec 2450, Br 02770 |
| 65457-A | You've Got Me Crying Again | Dec 2463, Br 02785 |
| 65458-A | Wishing (Will Make It So) | -     Br 02770 |
| 65459-A | You Grow Sweeter As The Years Go By | Dec 2450, Br 02785 |

Acc. by John Scott Trotter and his Orchestra.
                                 Los Angeles, June 22, 1939.

| DLA-1781-A | (Ho-dle-ay) Start The Day Right (with Bing Crosby) | Dec 2626, 25495, DL-5390, Br 02890, LA-8558 |
| DLA-1782-A | An Apple For The Teacher (w/Bing Crosby) | Dec 2640, 3602, 25496, 11022, DL-4254, DL-5390, DL-6013, Br 02839, LA-8558, LA-8742, BING-5 |
| DLA-1783-A | Soon | Dec 2879, Br 02991 |
| DLA-1784-A | They Can't Take That Away From Me | -     - |
| DLA-1785-A | At Least You Could Say "Hello" | Dec 2613, Br 02891 |
| DLA-1786-A | Stra-va-na-da (The Double-Talk Song) | Dec 2597, 3502, 25283, Br 02891 |

Acc. by O/Harry Sosnik.          Los Angeles, June 26, 1939.

| DLA-1787- | Is It Possible ? | Dec 2596 |
| DLA-1788- | Rendezvous Time In Paree | - |
| DLA-1789-A | Oh ! You Crazy Moon | Dec 2613, Br 02864 |
| DLA-1790-A | The Lamp Is Low | Dec 2597   - |

Acc. by John Scott Trotter and his Orchestra.
                                 Los Angeles, December 15, 1939.

| DLA-1910-A | Between 18th And 19th On Chestnut Street (w/Bing Crosby) | Dec 2948, 25496, DL-5390, Br 02974, LA-8558 |

                                 Los Angeles, January 19, 1940.

| DLA-1914-A | Someday You'll Find Your Bluebird | Dec 2987, Br 03051 |
| DLA-1915- | Angel | - |
| DLA-1916-A | On The Isle Of May | Dec 3004, Br 03005 |
| DLA-1917- | Gotta Get Home | - |

Acc. by O/Ray Sinatra.           New York, March 21, 1940.

| 67368-A | Lummir alla Zingen | Dec 3100 |
| 67369-A | Never Took A Lesson In My Life | Dec 3101, Br 03066 |
| 67370-A | Charming Little Fakir | Dec 3100   - |
| 67371-A | My ! My ! | Dec 3101, Br 03005 |

Acc. by O/Harry Sosnik.          New York, June 24, 1940.

| 67889-A | Blue Lovebird | Dec 3277, Br 03051 |
| 67890- | Orchids For Remembrance | - |
| 67891- | When It's Sleepy-Time Down South | Dec 3287 |
| 67892¾ | I Can't Give You Anything But Love, Baby | - |

                                 New York, August 22, 1940.

| 68000-A | Blueberry Hill | Dec 3366, Br 03072 |
| 68001-A | The Nearness Of You | -     - |
| 68002-A | Nobody's Sweetheart | Dec 3425, Br 03231 |
| 68003-A | Dinah | -     - |

New York, October 29, 1940.

| | | |
|---|---|---|
| 68301- | Remember Me | Dec 3478 |
| 68302- | The Moon Fell In The River | Dec 3481 |
| 68304- | Somewhere | - |
| 68305- | Let's Be Buddies | Dec 3478 |

NOTE:- Matrix 68303 is not by Connie Boswell.

Acc. by Bob Crosby and his Orchestra.   Los Angeles, December 13, 1940.

DLA-2271-A  Tea For Two (w/Bing Crosby)          Dec 3689, DL-5390, Br 03661,
                                                 LA-8558
DLA-2272-A  Yes Indeed (w/Bing Crosby)           As above

Acc. by O/Victor Young.          Los Angeles, January 16, 1941.

| | | |
|---|---|---|
| DLA-2365-A | The Kerry Dance | Dec 3615, Br 03194 |
| DLA-2366-A | I Hear A Rhapsody | -          - |
| DLA-2367- | You Forgot About Me | Dec 3631, Br 03156 |
| DLA-2368- | Amapola (Pretty Little Poppy) | -          - |

Los Angeles, March 27, 1941.

| | | |
|---|---|---|
| DLA-2421-A | The Clock Song | Dec 3858, Br 03299 |
| DLA-2422- | You Were Meant For Me | Dec 3837 |
| DLA-2423- | I Went Out Of My Way | - |
| DLA-2424-A | A Gay Ranchero | Dec 3858, Br 03299 |

Los Angeles, June 28, 1941.

| | | |
|---|---|---|
| DLA-2482- | Nighty-Night | Dec 3893 |
| DLA-2483-A | Sand In My Shoes | -          Br 03239 |
| DLA-2484- | Gee ! But I Hate To Go Home Alone | Dec 4046 |
| DLA-2485- | I'll Keep On Loving You | Dec 3959 |
| DLA-2486-A | Sweethearts Or Strangers | -          Br 03239 |

Acc. by studio orchestra.          Los Angeles, July 8, 1941.

| | | |
|---|---|---|
| DLA-2510-A-B | Poor Butterfly | Rejected |
| DLA-2511-A | Look For The Silver Lining | Dec 18384, 25055, Br 03388 |
| DLA-2512- | Smoke Gets In Your Eyes | -          - |
| DLA-2513- | Mighty Lak' A Rose | Dec 18423 |
| DLA-2514- | Stormy Weather | Dec 4046 |

New York, January 22, 1942.

| | | |
|---|---|---|
| 70202- | A String Of Pearls | Dec 4163, Br 03354 |
| 70203- | My Silent Love | -          - |

New York, March 4, 1942.

| | | |
|---|---|---|
| 70439-A | Music ! Music ! | Dec 4279 |
| 70440-A | When The Roses Bloom Again | -          Br 03333 |
| 70441-A | One Dozen Roses | Dec 4280, Br 03338 |
| 70442-A | On The Street Of Regret | -          Br 03333 |

New York, March 24, 1942.

| | | |
|---|---|---|
| 70574-A | Sweet Eloise | Dec 4311, Br 03338 |
| 70575-A | Johnny Doughboy Found A Rose In Ireland | - |

New York, June 12, 1942.

| | | |
|---|---|---|
| 70874- | Wonder When My Baby's Coming Home ? | Dec 18413 |
| 70875- | He Wears A Pair Of Silver Wings | Dec 18423 |
| 70876- | South Wind | Dec 18413, Br 03388 |

New York, July 29, 1942.

| | | |
|---|---|---|
| 71247-A | (As Long As You're Not In Love With | Dec 18483, Br 03392 |
| | Anyone Else) Why Don't You Fall In Love With Me ? | |
| 71248- | Moonlight Mood | Dec 18509 |
| 71249-A | Just A Letter From Home | Dec 18483, Br 03392 |
| 71250- | Savin' All I Can For Uncle Sam, Yes | Dec 18509 |
| | Ma'am (Savin' My Love For You) | |

Miss Boswell, who has for some years changed the spelling of her Christian name   to Connee, continued to record at intervals until 1956.

## FREDERICK V, BOWERS

B. Boston, Mass., June 11, 1874; in vaudeville with Charles Horwitz (1894 onwards as singing songwriters, e.g., ALWAYS (1901); later with Lew Dockstader's and Primrose and West's Minstrels; entertained troops in War of 1898 and both World Wars. D.Los Angeles, April 29, 1961.
Vocal, acc. by studio orchestra/? Charles A. Prince.
New York, c. May, 1910.

| | | |
|---|---|---|
| 4602-1 | Heigh-Ho ("The Echo") | Col A-894 |

New York, c. August, 1910.

| | | |
|---|---|---|
| 4848-3 | Here Comes A College Boy | Col A-928 |

New York, May 26, 1911.

| | | |
|---|---|---|
| 19386- | I Love The Girls From A To Z | Col A-1043 |

New York, July 17, 1911.

| | | |
|---|---|---|
| 19461- | Let's Make Love Among The Roses | Col A-1054 |
| 19462- | Love Me | - |

## AL  BOWLLY

B. Lourenco Marques, January 7, 1898.  Apprenticed as barber in uncle's shop in Johannesburg; learned to play piano, banjo, guitar and ukulele, and sang to entertain customers.  Joined Edgar Adeler's band while it was touring South Africa, 1923 and toured there and the Far East with this; left after difference of opinion and went to Calcutta to sing with Jimmy Lequime's band; left this along with the pianist, a White Russian named Monia Liter, went to Germany and sang and played in Berlin for about a year before accepting an invitation from the Spanish-American   bandleader Fred Elizalde to join his band in the Savoy Hotel, London, July, 1928.  After this band broke up in 1929, hard times followed for Al Bowlly, but in January, 1931, he was engaged by the American bandleader Roy Fox to sing and play guitar with  Fox's band at the Monseigneur Restaurant, London; after Lew Stone assumed leadership in October, 1932, Al Bowlly continued with him until going to the U.S.A. with British bandleader, songwriter and arranger Ray Noble in September, 1934.  Bowlly returned to London in 1937 after making a great impression in America, and when World  War II broke out, he entertained servicemen solo and with a partner, Jimmy Mesene.  On April 17, 1941, he was killed by a bomb in the "blitz" on London.  He had recorded and sung in public with many bands, had made a few short films and hundreds of appearances on radio on both sides of the Atlantic.

Vocalist with Arthur Briggs' Savoy Syncopators' Orchestra.
Berlin, c. July, 1927.

| | | |
|---|---|---|
| 592bd; B-41819 | Song Of The Wanderer | DG /Pol 21034 |
| 593bd; B-41821 | Muddy Water | DG /Pol 21035 |
| | | |
| 599bd; B-41820 | Hallelujah | DG /Pol 21034 |
| 600bd; B-41823 | Miss Annabelle Lee | DG /Pol 21036 |
| 601bd; B-41824 | Memphis | - |
| 603bd; B-41822 | I'm Looking For A Girl Named Mary | DG /Pol 21035 |

NOTE:- Al Bowlly's presence on matrix 601bd has not yet been confirmed, but  it is quite likely he did make it.

Vocal, acc. by Edgar Adeler-p/own u.        Berlin, September 11, 1927.

M-19372    Blue Skies                              Hom 4-2386
M-19373    Say, Mister ! Have You Met Rosie's Sister ? -

Vocalist with Fred Bird, The Salon Symphonic Jazz Band (sic).
                                            Berlin, September 12, 1927.

M-19381-2  Ain't She Sweet ?                       Hom 4-2389
M-19382    In A Little Spanish Town                 -

Vocal, acc. by Fred Bird-vn/Edgar Adeler-p/own bj or g as shown.
                                            Berlin, September 23, 1927.

M-19444    I'm Alone In Athlone - bj               Hom 4-2418
M-19445    Because I Love You - g                   -

    The following titles probably belong to this period; all other details unknown.

           A Dream Of You                           Hom 4-2411
           Muddy Water                               -
           All Day Long                             Hom 4-2414
           I'm Looking For A Bluebird (To Chase My   -
              Blues Away)

Vocalist with George Carhart's New Yorkers Jazz Orchestra.
                                            Berlin, September 28, 1927.

M-19451    Sunny Disposish                         Hom 4-2420

Vocal, acc. by Heinz Lewy-p/own g, stg or u as shown.
                                            Berlin, November 18, 1927.

M-19566    When You Played The Organ And I Sang    Hom 4-2459
             "The Rosary" - stg
M-19569    Dear Little Gadabout - u                 -
           Ev'ry Little Thing I Do                 Hom 4-2460
           Rosy Cheeks - g                          -
           My Regular Girl - g                      Hom 4-2461
           Positively - Absolutely                  -

Vocalist with Arthur Briggs' Savoy Syncopators' Orchestra.
                                            Berlin, c. December, 1927.

681bd; B-41887   Ain't She Sweet ?              DG/Pol 21124
682bd; B-41883   Do The Black Bottom With Me    DG/Pol 21122
684bd; B-41884   Souvenirs                       -

691bd; B-41889   Since I Found You              DG/Pol 21125
693bd; B-41895   Who-oo ? You-oo, That's Who !  DG/Pol 21128
694bd; B-41893   Rosy Cheeks                    DG/Pol 21127
695bd; B-41896   Roses For Remembrance          DG/Pol 21128

700bd; B-41886   Why Don't You ?                DG/Pol 21123
701bd; B-41890   I'm Coming, Virginia           DG/Pol 21125
702bd; B-41888   It All Depends On You          DG/Pol 21124
703bd; B-41892   Oole-De-Doo                    DG/Pol 21126

                                            Berlin, c. January, 1928.

717bd; B-41897   Dreamy Amazon                  DG/Pol 21129
718bd; B-41899   Me And My Shadow               DG/Pol 21130
719bd; B-41900   Are You Happy ?                 -
720bd; B-41898   You Should See My Tootsie      DG/Pol 21129
721bd ?          My Regular Girl                DG/Pol 21131
722bd; B-41903   Maybe I Will                   DG/Pol 21132
723bd ?          I'm Walking On Air             DG/Pol 21131
    NOTE:- Al Bowlly's presence on matrices 691, 700, 717, 720, 722 and 723 has not yet
    been comfirmed.

Berlin, c. January, 1928.

| | | |
|---|---|---|
| 734bd; B-41894 | Sometimes I'm Happy | DG/Pol 21127 |
| 735bd ? | Sweet Marie | DG/Pol 21134 |
| 736bd ? | The Little White House | DG/Pol 21135 |
| 739bd ? | Ain't That A Grand And Glorious Feeling ? - | |
| 740bd | Take Your Finger Out Of Your Mouth | DG/Pol 21134 |
| 741bd; B-41906 | Vo-Do-Do-De-O Blues | DG/Pol 21133 |

NOTE:- Al Bowlly's presence on matrices 735, 736 and 741 is not yet confirmed.

Vocalist with Fred Bird, The Salon Symphonic Jazz Band (sic).
Berlin, c. January, 1928.

| | | |
|---|---|---|
| | Rio Rita | Hom 4-2496 |
| | Souvenirs | - |

Vocalist with John Abriani's Six (John Abriani and his Orchestra on M-19833).
Berlin, January 17, 1928.

| | | |
|---|---|---|
| M-19826 | I Love No-One But You | Hom 4-2514 |
| M-19827 | My Blue Heaven | Hom 4-2511, 4-2611 |
| M-19828 | Just Once Again | Hom 4-2512, 4-2613 |

Berlin, January 18, 1928.

| | | |
|---|---|---|
| M-19829 | A Shady Tree | Hom 4-2613 |
| M-19830 | Are You Thinking Of Me Tonight ? | Hom 4-2612 |
| M-19831 | My Regular Girl | Hom 4-2512, 4-2611 |
| M-19833 | Shaking The Blues Away | Hom 4-2514 |

NOTE:- Matrices M-19832 and M-19834 were never issued; M-19835 has no vocal.

Berlin, January 20, 1928.

| | | |
|---|---|---|
| M-19840 | All I Want Is You | Hom 4-2532 |
| M-19841 | Can't You Hear Me Say "I Love You" ? | - |

Vocalist with Fred Elizalde and his Music.
London, c. July 25, 1928.

| | | |
|---|---|---|
| | Just Imagine | Br 189 |
| | Wherever You Are | - |
| | After My Laughter Came Tears | Rejected |

Vocalist with Van Phillips and his Band.  London, November 12, 1928.

| | | |
|---|---|---|
| WA-8089-1 | Sometimes | Col 5209 |

Vocalist with Fred Elizalde and his Music.
London, c. November 21, 1928.

| | | |
|---|---|---|
| BB-146-1 | If I Had You | Br 3948 |

London, December, 1928.

| | | |
|---|---|---|
| BB-170-3 | Misery Farm | Br 206 |
| BB-171-1 | I'm Sorry, Sally | - |

Vocalist with Percival Mackey and his Concert Orchestra ("The Ever-Bright Boys"  on
Piccadilly 264).                        London, April, 1929.

| | | |
|---|---|---|
| 1782 | When The Lilac Blooms Again | Pic 288 |
| 1783-2 | Up In The Clouds | Pic 264, Met 1141, Oct 291 |

Vocalist with Linn Milford and his Hawaiian Players and/or Singers.
London, May 15, 1929.

| | | |
|---|---|---|
| WA-9019-1 | Honeymoon Chimes | Re G-9362 |

London, November 5, 1929.

WA-9714-1  Lay My Head Beneath A Rose              Re G-9442
WA-9717-1  Last Night I Dreamed You Kissed Me         -
NOTE:- Other titles from the above two sessions have no vocal refrains.

Vocalist with the Honolulu Serenaders (same group as above).
                                London, c. November, 1929.

1577-2  The Pagan Love Song (w/Les Allen)       Dn A-219
1578-1  This Is Heaven (w/Les Allen)            Dn A-242
1579-1  S'posin' (w/Les Allen)                     -
NOTE:- Matrix 1580, the reverse of 1577, has a vocal by Les Allen only.

Vocalist with Fred Elizalde's Rhythmicians, directed by Adrian Rollini.
                                London, December 4, 1929.

3262    After The Sun Kissed The World Goodbye  Met 1241, Oct 367
3263    If Anything Happened To You                -            -

Vocalist with Linn Milford and his Hawaiian Singers.
                                London, January 24, 1930.

WA-9994-1    An Old Italian Love Song           Re MR-28
WA-9995-1-2  Love Made A Gypsy Out Of Me        Rejected
WA-9996-1-2  Waiting At The End Of The Road        -
WA-9997-1    In The Moonlight                   Re MR-28

Probable vocalist (with Cavan O'Connor) with Jay Wilbur and his Band.
                                London, c. February, 1930.

1634-2  Rio Rita                                Dn A-246

Vocalist with Linn Milford and his Hawaiian Players.
                                London, March 7, 1930.

WAR-36-1  Gypsy Dream Rose                      Rejected
WAR-37-1  Silvery Moon                          Re MR-79

Vocalist with the Brooklyn Broadcasters (Dominion C-303), the  Honolulu  Serenaders
  (Dominion C-319) or Hawaiian Octet (Celebrity 4390); apparently directed by  Linn
  Milford (pseudonym for Len Fillis, the South African guitarist and banjoist).
                                London, c. March, 1930.

1717-1  Silv'ry Moon                            Dn C-319, Cel 4390
1718-2  Happy Days Are Here Again               Dn C-303
1721-1  Gypsy Dream Rose                        Dn C-319, Cel 4390
NOTE:- Matrices 1719 and 1720 have not yet been traced.

Vocalist with Edgar Adeler's Hawaiian Players.
                                London, c. March, 1930.

S-759-1  Silv'ry Moon                           Sterno 406, Solex 6
S-760    Land Of The Might-Have-Been            Sterno 594      -
S-761    Somehow                                Sterno 429
S-763-1  Lazy Lou'siana Moon                    Sterno 406
NOTE:- Matrix S-762 has no vocal refrain.  The Solex issue is an eight-inch disc,
but it is not known whether it is dubbed from a ten-inch or simultaneously   tran-
scribed with it.

Vocal, acc. by Gideon Fagan-p.         Hayes, Middlesex, June 10, 1930.

Bb-19460-1  Ou Kaapstad is mij Hemel-land       Rejected
Bb-19461-3  Sy's in die Pad (both in Afrikaans) HMV FJ-133

   Acc. by Albert Diggenhof-p/own g.    Hayes, Middlesex, June 30, 1930.

Bb-19493-2  Alleenig (in Afrikaans)             HMV FJ-100
Bb-19494-1-2-3  Sy's mij klein Liefie (Afrikaans) Rejected ?
Bb-19495-1  Sunshine                            Rejected

Vocalist with Linn Milford and his Hawaiian Singers.
                              London, July 2, 1930.

WAR-234-1  Every Little Kindness (Makes An          Re MR-197
             Angel Smile)
WAR-235-2  My Angel Mother                          **Re MR-128**
WAR-236-2  The Golden Gates Of Paradise              -
WAR-237-1  The Hymns My Mother Used To Sing         Re MR-197

Vocal, acc. by small orchestra/Ray Noble, or Albert Diggenhof-p/own g,* all  except
    the first sung in Afrikaans.          Hayes, Middlesex, July 14, 1930.

Bb-19495-2  Sunshine                                HMV FJ-133
Bb-19552-2  Banditlied (The Prisoner's Song)         -
Bb-19553-1  The Lonesome Road                       HMV FJ-97
Bb-19554-1  Kleine Maat (Little Pal)                 -
Bb-19555-2  *Ou Kaapstad is mij Hemel-land          HMV FJ-100

Vocalist with the Aldwych Players, directed by Jay Wilbur.
                              London, August 2, 1930.

  945-1  On The Sunny Side Of The Street            Victory 253
  946-1  Sweepin' The Clouds Away                   Victory 254
  948-2  Song Of The Dawn (w/Hubert Wallace)        Victory 252
  949-1  Dancing With Tears In My Eyes              Victory 255
NOTE:- Matrix 947 has a vocal refrain by Hubert Wallace only.

Vocalist with Al Vocale and his Crooners (pseudonym for Len Fillis); all three  are
    duets with Les Allen.                 London, early September, 1930.

89867-2  Falling In Love Again                      EBR 1389
89868-2  Say A Little Prayer For Me                 EBR 1416
89869-2  One Night Alone With You                   EBR 1389

Vocalist with Harry Hudson's Melody Men (EBW 5160), as Paramount Rhythm Boys on EBW
    5161; all four are duets with Les Allen.
                              London, early September, 1930.

12964-1-2  A Bench In The Park                      EBW 5160
12965-1  Happy Feet                                  -
12966-1  Blue Is The Night                          EBW 5161
12967-1  Cheer Up And Smile                          -

Vocalist with Hawaiian Quartet (dir. Len Fillis).
                              London, September 9, 1930.

MB-1798-1-2  Aloha Oe                               Dec rejected
MB-1799-1-2  Goodbye To All That (w/Les Allen)       -

Vocalist with Linn Milford and his Hawaiian Players.
                              London, September 19, 1930.

WAR-325-2  Rose Dreams                              Re MR-216
WAR-326-2  Blue Pacific Moonlight                   Re MR-187
WAR-327-2  Here In My Heart                          -
WAR-328-2  That Little Lock Of Hair                 Re MR-216

Vocalist with Hawaiian Quartet (dir. Len Fillis); as Honolulu Quartet on Dec F-1958.
                              London, September 24, 1930.

GB-1916-2  There's A Stranger In Heaven Tonight  Dec F-1991
GB-1918-2  Aloha Oe                               Dec F-2066
GB-1919-1  Goodbye To All That (w/Les Allen)      Dec F-1958
GB-1921-2  The Golden Gates Of Paradise           Dec F-1991
  NOTE:- Matrices GB-1917 and GB-1920 are not Al Bowlly items.

Vocal, acc. by unknown h/concertina/vn/own g, all sung in Afrikaans.
                                    Hayes, Middlesex, October 10, 1930.


Bb-20441-1  Sal die Eng'le hulle Harpe speel vir   HMV FJ-103
               mij ? (Will The Angels Play Their Harps For Me ?)
Bb-20442-2  Voetslaan op oom Jacob se Leer           -
Bb-20443-2  Daar is geen ron in die Hemel           HMV FJ-120
Bb-20444-2  Die ou lelie Vallei                      -


  Acc. by ? Claude Ivy-p/own g, under the name of Jannie Viljoen, all sung in   Taal
  dialect.                           London, October 13, 1930.


GB-2049-1-2-3  Minnaarslaan (Sweetheart Lane)      Dec rejected
GB-2050-1-2  In die Droomvallei (In The Valley Of    -
               Dreams)
GB-2051-1-2  Hoe gaan dit (How Do You Do ?)          -
GB-2052-1-2  By die Vaal Rivier (By The Vaal River)  -


Vocalist with Alfredo and his Band, all titles duets with Les Allen.
                                    London, c. October 17, 1930.


13073-2  Great Day                                 EBW 5187
13074-2  Without A Song                             -
13075-2  Living In The Sunlight, Loving In The      EBW 5188
           Moonlight
13076-2  You Brought A New Kind Of Love To Me       -


Vocalist with Al Vocale and his Crooners. London, c. October 24, 1930.


13084-   Sleepy Head (w/Les Allen)                 EBW 5189
13085-   That's My Song Of Love (w/Les Allen)       -
89919-1  Waiting For That Thing Called Happiness   EBR 1416
           (w/Les Allen)


Vocalist with Jay Wilbur and his Band.   London, late October, 1930.


5516     Adeline (w/chorus)                        Imp 2355


Vocal, acc. by unknown h/concertina/? Claude Ivy-p/own g, under the name of   Jannie
  Viljoen, all sung in Afrikaans.        London, October 30, 1930.


FGB-2156-1-2-3  Sy was arm maar sy was eirlik (She Dec rejected
                  Was Poor But She Was Honest)
FGB-2157-1-2  Awend (Evening)                       -
FGB-2158-1-2  Woorhuis (Homestead)                  -
FGB-2159-1-2  Ek dink altyd aan jou (I'm Forever    -
                Thinking Of You)


Vocalist with the Phantom Players (Len Fillis and his Band).
                                    London, November 3, 1930.


GB-2177-2  Lonely Little Vagabond                  Dec F-2144
GB-2178-1  She's My Secret Passion                  -


Vocalist with Earl Melville and his Hawaiians (pseudonym for Len Fillis).
                                    London, early November, 1930.


3961-2  That's My Song Of Love (w/unknown)        Pic 673
3962    That Little Lock Of Hair (My Mother Gave    -
          To Me) (w/unknown)
3963    She's My Secret Passion                   Pic 649
3964-2  Lonely Little Vagabond                     -
3965    There's A Stranger In Heaven Tonight      Pic 685


Vocalist with Edgar Adeler's Hawaiian Players. (Matrix S-1155 is still untraced).
                                    London, early November, 1930.


S-1154-1  Sleepy Head                             Sterno 594
S-1156-1  With My Guitar And You (w/Les Allen)    Sterno 604
S-1157-1  Go Home And Tell Your Mother (w/Les Allen)   -

Vocalist with the Hawaiian Serenaders (probably identifiable with the other Len Fillis groups).                              London, November 13, 1930.

```
1040-1  Old Spanish Moon                     Victory 302
1041-2  Love Never Dies                      Victory 297
1042-1  Why Did You Turn Me Down ?           Victory 300
1043-1  Lullaby Land                         Victory 301 ?
1044-1  Love Birds Are Better Than Bluebirds Victory 298
1045-1  Headin' For Hollywood                Victory 303
```
NOTE:- We are assuming that 1043-1 was issued on Victory 301, as this is the   only
Victory record of the period which we have never seen.  Should it prove to be some
other title, it is reasonable to assume that matrix 1043-1 was rejected.

Vocalist with Ferrachini's Hawaiian Band (probably as above; Broadcast 643 and  644,
   both labelled THE WAIKIKI SERENADERS, were issued on December 12, 1930. All titles
   are duets with Les Allen.                London, November, 1930.

```
LO-797  Moonlight On The Colorado            Bcst 2605, 3018
LO-798  Cuban Love Song                        -
Z-1748  The Kiss Waltz                       Bcst 643
Z-1749  With My Guitar And You                 -
Z-1750  Bye Bye Blues                        Bcst 644
Z-1751  Old New England Moon                   -
```

Vocalist with Marius B. Winter and his Dance Orchestra.
                                            London, November, 1930.

```
LO-801  What A Perfect Night For Love        Bcst 2599
LO-802  Beware Of Love                       Bcst 2600
```

Vocalist with the New Mayfair Dance Orchestra, dir. Ray Noble. (Victor 24752 as  Ray
   Noble and his Orchestra).              Small Queen's Hall, London, Nov. 20, 1930,

```
Bb-21005-2  I'm Telling The World She's Mine  HMV B-5940, Vic 24752
Bb-21006-1  How Could I Be Lonely ?            -            -
```

Vocal, acc. by own g/Claude Ivy-p as shown,
                                            London, November 24, 1930.

```
GB-2322-2  Nigger Blues - gAB                  Dec F-2560
GB-2323-1  Frankie And Johnny - gAB (w/Ella Logan) Dec F-2206
GB-2324-2  By The Old Oak Tree - gAB/pCI (w/Ella Logan)-
```

Vocalist with The Blue Jays (EBW 5202) or the Radio Melody Boys (EBW 5203), dir.  by
   Harry Hudson, all duets with Les Allen. London, c. December 1, 1930.

```
13163-1  What A Perfect Night For Love       EBW 5202
13164-2  The "Free And Easy"                   -
13165-1  My Cradle Is The Desert             EBW 5203
13166-1  A Japanese Dream                      -
```

Vocalist with Marius B. Winter and his Dance Orchestra.
                                            London, December, 1930.

```
LO-820  Never Swat A Fly                     Bcst 2606
LO-821  Sunny Days (w/Marius B. Winter ?)    Bcst 2607
LO-822  Roamin' Thru' The Roses                -
```

Vocalist with Linn Milford and his Hawaiian Players.
                                            London, December 17, 1930.

```
WAR-450-1  There's A Stranger In Heaven Tonight  Re MR-267
WAR-451-2  Sleepy Head                          Re MR-337
WAR-452-2  In An Old Churchyard                  -
WAR-453-2  The Silver-Toned Chimes Of The Angelus  Re MR-267
```

Vocalist with the Palm Beach Hawaiians (probably a Len Fillis group).
                                            London, December 18, 1930.

```
GB-2415-2  That's What Loneliness Means To Me  Dec F-2246
```

Vocalist with Billy Hill and his Boys.    London, December 18, 1930.

GB-2416-2  The Farmyard Symphony                    Dec F-2172
GB-2417-1-2  When Bill Malone Plays The Xylophone  Rejected
GB-2418-2  The Village Jazz Band                    Dec F-2172

Vocalist with the Radio Melody Boys (EBR 1447) or the Blue Jays (EBR 1448), dir.  by
   Harry Hudson; all duets with Les Allen. London, December 30, 1930.

89986-1  My Sunshine Came On A Rainy Day      EBR 1447
89987-1  Underneath The Spanish Stars          -
89988-2  A Little Love Song                   EBR 1448
89989-2  Okay, Baby                            -

Vocalist with the New Mayfair Dance Orchestra, dir. by Ray Noble.
                                       London, December 31, 1930.

Bb-21107-1  Underneath The Spanish Stars      HMV B-5955
Bb-21108-2  Sunny Days                        HMV B-5956
Bb-21109-2  Make Yourself A Happiness Pie     HMV B-5957

Vocalist with Roy Fox and his Band at the Monseigneur Restaurant, London. (NOTE:This
   is the full designation of all Al Bowlly's records with Roy Fox and his Band).
                                       London, January 5, 1931.

GB-2498-2  Memories Of You                    Dec F-2194
GB-2499-1  You're Lucky To Me                  -
GB-2500-2  Thank Your Father                  Dec F-2312

Vocalist with the Blue Jays (EBR 1456) or Harry Hudson's Melody Men (EBR  1458),dir.
   by Harry Hudson; all duets with Les Allen.
                                       London, c. January 9, 1931.

90012-2  Old-Fashioned Girl                   EBR 1456
90013-2  Never Swat A Fly                      -
90014-2  Sweet Jennie Lee                     EBR 1458
90015-2  You're Driving Me Crazy               -

Vocalist with Roy Fox and his Band.       London, January 16, 1931.

GB-2519-3  Can't We Be Friends ?              Dec F-2220

Vocalist with Ferrachini's Hawaiian Band. London, January, 1931.

LO-845   My Bluebird Was Caught In The Rain   Bcst 3008
LO-846   Somewhere In Old Wyoming (w/Les Allen)   -
Z-1831   Oh Donna Clara ! (w/Les Allen)       Bcst 673
Z-1832   Nobody Cares If I'm Blue (w/Les Allen)   -

Vocalist with Marius B. Winter and his Dance Orchestra.
                                       London, January, 1931.

LO-848   There's Something About An Old-Fashioned Bcst 3003
            Girl
LO-849   Okay, Baby (w/? Marius B. Winter)    Bcst 3004
LO-850   A Little Love Song                    -

Vocalist with the Palm Beach Hawaiians.   London, January 23, 1931.

GB-2545-1  Somewhere In Old Wyoming (w/Les Allen) Dec F-2213
GB-2546-2  Oh ! Donna Clara (w/Les Allen)         -
GB-2548-1  Hurt                               Dec F-2317
   NOTE:- The vocalist on matrix GB-2547 is Les Allen only.

Vocalist with Roy Fox and his Band.       London, January 24, 1931.

GB-2549-3  Wedding Bells Are Ringing For Sally  Dec F-2219
GB-2550-2  Missouri Waltz                       Dec F-2233
GB-2551-3  Lady, Play Your Mandoline            Dec F-2220

London, January 28, 1931.

GB-2579-3  Hurt                                    Dec F-2239
GB-2580-3  Writing A Letter To You                Dec F-2249
GB-2581-4  A Peach Of A Pair                      Dec F-2233

London, February 9, 1931.

GB-2684-1  Between The Devil And The Deep Blue    Dec F-2240
            Sea (w/chorus)
GB-2685-2  The Peanut Vendor (w/chorus)           Dec F-2239
GB-2686-1  Maybe It's Love (w/chorus)             Dec F-2240

Vocalist with the Palm Beach Hawaiians.  London, February 9, 1931.

GB-2690-1  'Neath Hawaiian Skies                  Dec F-2255
GB-2691-   Really Mine                            Dec F-2246

Vocalist with the Radio Rhythm Boys, dir. by Harry Hudson; both duets with Les Allen
  according to some reports.        London, February, 1931.

90060-1  Tap Your Feet                            EBR 1489
90061-2  Makin' Wicki-Wacki Down In Waikiki       -

Vocalist with the New Mayfair Dance Orchestra, dir. by Ray Noble.
                                    London, February 19, 1931.

OB-368-1  Time On My Hands                   HMV B-5983, Vic 25016, Enc 140
OB-369-3  Makin' Wickey-Wackey Down In Waikiki  HMV B-5989
OB-370-3  Shout For Happiness                HMV B-5984
OB-371-2  Goodnight, Sweetheart                   -        7EG-8056, Vic 25016,
                                                     20-2950, ME MES-6816
OB-372-1  I'm Glad I Waited                  HMV B-5983  -
OB-373-2  Really Mine                        HMV B-5989
OB-374-4  Puzzle Record No. 1 - Part 2 (Al Bowlly  HMV B-3775, Vic 22745
            sings a chorus of YOU'RE DRIVING ME CRAZY; both issues as NOVELTY  ORCH-
            ESTRA)

Vocalist with Roy Fox and his Band.       London, February 26, 1931.

GB-2700-1  You're The One I Care For              Dec F-2256
GB-2701-2  Overnight                              -
GB-2702-2  Shout ! For Happiness                  Dec F-2263

Vocalist with the Blue Jays, dir. by Harry Hudson; both duets with Les Allen.
                            London, c. March 3, 1931.

13339-2  Sweet Jennie Lee                         EBW 5242
13340-2  Ti-dle-id-dle-um-pum                     -

Vocalist with Roy Fox and his Band.       London, March 5, 1931.

GB-2715-3  When Your Hair Has Turned To Silver    Dec F-2263
GB-2716-2  Bathing In The Sunshine                Dec F-2250
GB-2717-3  Reaching For The Moon                  Dec F-2279
GB-2718-1  All Through The Night                  Dec F-2249

Vocalist with Novelty Orchestra, dir. by Ray Noble.
                            London, March 9, 1931.

OB-145-1  Puzzle Record No. 2 - Part 1 (Al Bowlly  HMV B-3825
            sings a chorus of I'LL BE GOOD BECAUSE OF YOU)
OB-146-4  Puzzle Record No. 2 - Part 2 (Al Bowlly   -
            sings a chorus of GOODNIGHT, SWEETHEART)

Vocalist with Roy Fox and his Band.       London, March 10, 1931.

GB-2725-2  Them There Eyes (w/chorus)             Dec F-2252
GB-2726-2  That Lindy Hop                         Dec F-2250
GB-2727-3  Truly (w/chorus)                       Dec F-2292

London, March 13, 1931.

GB-2731-1  I'm Glad I Waited                    Dec F-2291

Vocalist with the New Mayfair Orchestra (HMV B-3836) or the New Mayfair Dance  Orchestra (HMV B-5999) (as LONDON MAYFAIR ORCHESTRA on Victor 22774 and 24499), dir.by
  Ray Noble.                              London, March 24, 1931.

OB-680-3  Pages Of Radioland - Part 1 (Al Bowlly  HMV B-3836
            sings a chorus of WITHOUT A SONG)
OB-681-2  Pages Of Radioland - Part 2 (Al Bowlly      -
            sings a chorus of FALLING IN LOVE AGAIN)
OB-682-1  We Two                              HMV B-5999
OB-683-3  Lady Of Spain                           -            Vic 22774, 24499

Vocalist with Roy Fox and his Band.       London, March 25, 1931.

GB-2751-3  One More Time                    Dec F-2294
GB-2752-2  Lady Of Spain                    Dec F-2279
GB-2753-1  Time On My Hands                 Dec F-2291

Vocalist with the New Mayfair Dance Orchestra, dir. by Ray Noble.
                                          London, March 26, 1931.

OB-694-1  Sunshine And Shadows             HMV B-6010

Vocalist with Marius B. Winter and his Dance Orchestra.
                                          London, late March, 1931.

LO-880     All Through The Night           Bcst 3034

Vocalist with the Radio Melody Boys, dir. by Harry Hudson.
                                          London, late March, 1931.

90079-2  Maybe It's Love (w/Les Allen)         EBR 1478
90080-2  Beyond The Blue Horizon                  -

Vocalist with Roy Fox and his Band.       London, April 1, 1931.

GB-2760-2  Alma Mia (w/chorus)             Dec F-2292
GB-2761-2  Koppa-Ka-Banna (w/chorus)       Dec F-2315

                                          London, April 15, 1931.

GB-2773-2  Betty Co-ed                     Dec F-2312
GB-2774-3  You Didn't Have To Tell Me      Dec F-2318
GB-2775-3  When It's Sunset On The Nile    Dec F-2315

                                          London, April 21, 1931.

GB-2784-2  Would You Like To Take A Walk ?  Dec F-2318
GB-2785-2  Laughing At The Rain            Dec F-2328
GB-2786-3  Ya Got Love                     Dec F-2329
GB-2787-2  Bubbling Over With Love         Dec F-2328

Vocalist with Percy Chandler and his Band.
                                          London, late April, 1931.

4309     Why Couldn't You ?               Pic 789
4310-1-2  Tango Lady                       Pic 764, Empire E-7, May G-2031,
                                            Oct 608
4311     Really Mine                      Pic 764, Oct 608
NOTE:- Empire as ALBERTA DANCE BAND; Mayfair as ARGENTINE TANGO ORCHESTRA.

Vocalist with the New Mayfair Dance Orchestra, dir. by Ray Noble.
                                          London, April 28, 1931.

OB-799-3  That's Somerset                 HMV B-6011
OB-800-2  Fiesta                          HMV B-6010
OB-801-2  You're Twice As Nice As The Girl In My  HMV B-6011
            My Dreams

Vocalist with Roy Fox and his Band.          London, May 5, 1931.

GB-2805-1  Fiesta                             Dec F-2341
GB-2806-3  By My Side                             -
GB-2807-1  My Temptation                      Dec F-2329

Vocalist with Len Fillis and his Novelty Orchestra; all duets with Les Allen.
                                  London, May 6, 1931.

CA-11565-1  Song Hits - Part 1 (Bowlly and Allen  Col DB-516
                sing a chorus of REACHING FOR THE MOON)
CA-11566-1  Song Hits - Part 4 (Boelly and Allen  Col DB-549
                sing a chorus of BUBBLING OVER WITH LOVE)
CA-11567-1  Song Hits - Part 3 (Bowlly and Allen     -
                sing a chorus of LADY OF SPAIN)
CA-11568-1  Song Hits - Part 2 (Bowlly and Allen  Col DB-516
                sing a chorus of HAWAIIAN STARS ARE GLEAMING)

Vocalist with the New Mayfair Orchestra (HMV B-3881) or the New Mayfair Dance  Orch-
    estra (HMV B-6023 and Victor 24004), dir. by Ray Noble.
                                  London, May 29, 1931.

OB-949-2  On With The Show - Part 1 (Al Bowlly   HMV B-3881
                sings a chorus of ON A LITTLE BALCONY IN SPAIN)
OB-950-2  Lights Of Paris                        HMV B-6023, Vic 24004
OB-951-3  June-Time Is Love Time                     -
OB-952-1  On With The Show - Part 2 (Al Bowlly   HMV B-3881
                sings a chorus of PRETTY KITTY KELLY)

Vocalist with Roy Fox and his Band.          London, June 1, 1931.

GB-2852-3  I'm So Used To You Now              Dec F-2352
GB-2853-3  I'm Gonna Get You                   Dec F-2351
GB-2854-1  It Must Be True                         -
GB-2855-2  Leave The Rest To Nature           Dec F-2352

Vocalist with the Waldorfians, dir. by Howard Godfrey.
                                  London, early June, 1931.

4360-2  My Canary Has Circles Under His Eyes   Pic 780, May Ml-2019,
                                               Simcha 10002, ACL 1204
4361-2  Miss Elizabeth Brown                   Pic 780, Empire E-12, May Ml-2019,
                                               ACL 1204
NOTE:- Empire as BASIL WINSTON AND HIS BAND; Mayfair as FIFTH AVENUE DANCE ORCHES-
TRA; Simcha as COSMOPOLITAN SYNCOPATORS.  Empire E-8 contains AT LAST I'M HAPPY by
the Waldorfians, apparently featuring Al Bowlly as vocalist, but it bears no other
means of identification of origin.  It is thought to come from this session,but it
was never issued on Piccadilly.

Vocalist with Jack Leon and his Band.          London, early June, 1931.

4362      Lights Of Paris                      Pic 782, Oct 614
4363-2  Bell-Bottom Trousers                       -            -      Simcha 10001
4364-1-2 Ya Got Love                           Pic 783
4365      Walking My Baby Back Home                 -      Empire E-12     -
NOTE:- Empire as ALBERTA DANCE BAND; Simcha as JEROME JOY AND HIS BAND.

Vocalist with the Waldorfians, dir. by Howard Godfrey.
                                  London, early June, 1931.

4366-2  Thank You Most Sincerely               Pic 781, Oct 613, Simcha 10002
4367-2  Life Is Meant For Love                     -            -
4368-2  Time On My Hands                       Pic 787, Oct 617, Empire E-9
NOTE:- Empire as BASIL WINSTON AND HIS ORCHESTRA; Simcha as THE COSMOPOLITAN  SYN-
COPATORS.

Vocalist with the Blue Jays (EBR 1507) or Radio Rhythm Boys (EBR 1508), dir. by Har-
    ry Hudson.                    London, early June, 1931.

90158-1  Walkin' My Baby Back Home             EBR 1507
90160-1  Let's Get Friendly                    EBR 1508

Vocalist with the Deauville Dance Band, dir. by Harry Hudson.
                                        London, early June, 1931.

13553-2  Time On My Hands                      EBW 5315
13554-2  I'm Glad I Waited                     -

Vocal, acc. by Claude Ivy-p.        London, June 10, 1931.

GB-2875-2  I'm So Used To You Now              Dec F-2366, ACL 1162
GB-2876-1  Leave The Rest To Nature           -

Vocalist with the New Mayfair Dance Orchestra, dir. by Ray Noble.
                                        London, June 11, 1931.

OB-976-3  Roll On, Mississippi, Roll On (w/The    HMV B-6040
             Three Ginx)
OB-977-2  Lazy Day                             HMV B-6031, Enc 160
OB-978-4  I'd Rather Be A Beggar With You      HMV B-6040

Vocalist with Roy Fox and his Band.     London, June 16, 1931.

GB-2906-1  Lazy Day                            Dec F-2396
GB-2907-2  Poor Kid                            -
GB-2908-1-2-3  By The River Sainte Marie       Rejected

Vocalist with Jack Leon and his Band.   London, mid-June, 1931.

4372-2  Leave The Rest To Nature               Pic 796
4373    I'm So Used To You Now                 -
4374-2  Goodnight, Sweetheart                  Pic 787, Oct 617

                                        London, late June, 1931.

4383-2  Shake And Let Us Be Friends            Pic 802
4384-2  I'll Keep You In My Heart Always       Pic 788
4385-2  Oh ! Rosalita                          -
4386-2  Bubbling Over With Love                Pic 802
4387    I Offer You These Roses                Pic 799

Vocalist with the New Mayfair Orchestra, dir. by Ray Noble.
                                        London, June 26, 1931.

OB-1243-3  Miracle Melodies - Part 1 (Al Bowlly     HMV B-3907
              sings a chorus of GOODNIGHT, SWEETHEART)
OB-1245-1  Holiday Hits - Part 1 (Al Bowlly sings   HMV B-3910
              a chorus of REACHING FOR THE MOON)
OB-1246-1  Holiday Hits - Part 2 (Al Bowlly sings   -
              a chorus of RIVER, STAY 'WAY FROM MY DOOR)
   NOTE:- Matrix OB-1244 has no vocal by Al Bowlly.

Vocalist with Maurice Winnick and his Orchestra.
                                        London, July 10, 1931.

CAR-740-1  Topical Tunes Medley - Part 1 (Al     Re MR-374
              Bowlly sings a chorus of WHAT A FOOL I'VE BEEN)
CAR-741-1  Springtime Reminds Me Of You         Re MR-375
CAR-742-1  The Waltz You Saved For Me           -
CAR-743-1  Topical Tunes Medley - Part 2 (Al     Re MR-374
              Bowlly sings a chorus of PARDON ME, PRETTY BABY)

Vocalist with the New Mayfair Orchestra, dir. by Ray Noble.
                                        London, July 14, 1931.

OB-1284-2  Tunes Of Not-So-Long-Ago - 1921     HMV B-3944
              (Al Bowlly sings a chorus each of COAL BLACK MAMMY and SWANEE)
OB-1285-2  Tunes Of Not-So-Long-Ago - 1923     HMV B-4012
              (Al Bowlly sings a chorus each of MY SWEETIE WENT AWAY and YES! WE HAVE
              NO BANANAS)

Vocalist with Roy Fox and his Band.          London, July 21, 1931.

GB-3026-2  When You Were The Blossom Of Buttercup  Dec F-2403
             Lane
GB-3027-1-3  Tie A Little String Around Your Finger     -
GB-3028-2  I Found You                           Dec F-2404
GB-3029-1  Love For Sale                              -

Vocalist with Rolando's Salon Orchestra.  London, c. late July, 1931.

  13708-2  Goodnight                            EBW 5361

Vocalist with Roy Fox and his Band.          London, July 31, 1931.

GB-3090-3  Roll On, Mississippi, Roll On         Dec F-2438
GB-3091-1  Out Of Nowhere                        Dec F-2439
GB-3092-1  While Hearts Are Singing                  -
GB-3093-1  I'd Rather Be A Beggar With You       Dec F-2438, F-2609

Vocalist with the Radio Melody Boys (EBR 1535) or the Blue Jays (EBR 1541), dir. by
  Harry Hudson.                          London, early August, 1931.

  90207-2  Belle Of Barcelona                    EBR 1535
  90208-1  I'm A Hundred Per Cent. In Love With You    -
  90209-1  Poor Kid                              EBR 1541
  90210-2  Mama Inez                                 -

Vocalist with the New Mayfair Dance Orchestra, dir. by Ray Noble.
                              London, August 14, 1931.

OB-1314-1  Pagan Serenade                        HMV B-6055
OB-1315-2  Belle Of Barcelona                        -
OB-1316-2  There's Something In Your Eyes        HMV B-6056
OB-1317-2  Just A Dancing Sweetheart                 -
  NOTE:- Some copies of the fourth title above show it as ONLY A DANCING SWEETHEART.

Vocalist with Roy Fox and his Band.          London, August 18, 1931.

GB-3134-1  Tell Me, Are You From Georgia ? (w/Nat  Dec F-2451
             Gonella)
GB-3135-1  You Are My Heart's Delight            Dec F-2469
GB-3137-1  Cherie, c'est vous                    Dec F-2451
  NOTE:- Matrix GB-3136 is WHISPERING, Roy Fox's signature tune, and the only  voice
  heard on it is his, introducing it.

Vocalist with the New Mayfair Dance Orchestra, dir. by Ray Noble.
                              London, August 25, 1931.

OB-1330-2  When It's Sunset On The Nile          HMV B-6057
OB-1331-2  Honeymoon Lane                        HMV B-6058
OB-1333-2  Hang Out The Stars In Indiana             -          Vic 24357,ME MES-6816
  NOTE:- The vocalist on matrix OB-1332, which is on the reverse side of HMV B-6057,
  is not Al Bowlly.

Vocalist with Sid Phillips and his Melodians.
                              London, late August, 1931.

  13772-1-2  Roll On, Mississippi, Roll On       EBW 5358, ACL 1204
  13773-1  Heartaches                               -          -
  13774-1  Time Alone Will Tell                  EBW 5356
  13775-2  Tell Me You Love Me                       -

Vocal, acc. by small orchestra.          London, September 2, 1931.

GB-3168-1  Were You Sincere ?                    Dec F-2485, ACL 1162
GB-3169-2  I'd Rather Be A Beggar With You           -          -

Vocalist with Roy Fox and his Band,        London, September 3, 1931.

GB-3170-2  You Can't Stop Me From Loving You       Dec F-2487
GB-3172-1-2  Dance Hall Doll                       Dec F-2486
GB-3173-2  What Are You Thinking About, Baby ?        -
   NOTE:- Neither of the voices on matrix GB-3171 is Al Bowlly's.

Vocalist with the Deauville Dance Band (EBR 1550) or the Radio Rhythm Boys (EBR 1551)
   dir. by Harry Hudson.                        London, September, 1931.

90225-1  Roll On, Mississippi, Roll On            EBR 1550
90226-1  Wrap Your Troubles In Dreams                -
90227-2  Honeymoon Lane                          EBR 1551
90228-2  I Can't Do Without You (w/chorus)           -

Vocalist with Roy Fox and his Band.        London, September 18, 1931.

GB-3277-1  Time Alone Will Tell                   Dec F-2513
GB-3278-2  When The Waltz Was Through                -
GB-3279-1  Sing Another Chorus, Please            Dec F-2514
GB-3280-1  Sweet And Lovely                          -

Vocalist with the Blue Jays (EBR 1556) or the Deauville Dance Band (EBR 1558),dir.by
   Harry Hudson.                             London, c. late September, 1931.

90237-1  By The River Sainte Marie               EBR 1558
90238-1  I'm Thru' With Love                         -        ACL 1204
90239-2  Hang Out The Stars In Indiana           EBR 1556
90240-3  Just One More Chance                        -

Vocalist with Roy Fox and his Band.        London, October 2, 1931.

GB-3349-2  Looking For You                        Dec F-2574
GB-3350-1  Kiss Me Goodnight                      Dec F-2581
GB-3351-3  Song Of Happiness                      Dec F-2574

                                           London, October 7, 1931.

GB-3387-2  Just One More Chance                   Dec F-2580
GB-3388-2  Smile, Darn Ya, Smile                     -
GB-3389-2  That's What I Like About You           Dec F-2581
GB-3390-2  You Forgot Your Gloves                 Dec F-2582
GB-3391-2  Take It From Me (I'm Taking To You)       -

                                           London, October 16, 1931.

GB-3456-2  Yes, Yes (My Baby Said Yes)            Dec F-2609
GB-3457-1-2-3  You Call It Madness                Rejected
GB-3458-1  I Found A Million-Dollar Baby (In A    Dec F-2610
             Five-And-Ten-Cent Store)
GB-3459-1  Look In The Looking-Glass                 -

Vocalist with the Savoy Hotel Orpheans.  London, October 19, 1931.

CA-12092-2  There's A Time And Place For Every-   Col CB-376
              thing
CA-12093-1-2  Sweet And Lovely                    Rejected

                                           London, October 29, 1931.

CA-12092-3-4  There's A Time And Place For Every- Rejected
                thing
CA-12093-4  Sweet And Lovely                      Col CB-376

                                           London, October 31, 1931.

CA-12139-1  Who Am I ?                            Col CB-377
CA-12140-2  Linda                                    -

Vocalist with the New Mayfair Dance Orchestra, dir. by Ray Noble.
                              London, October 31, 1931.

OB-1777-2  Down Sunnyside Lane                    HMV B-6091
OB-1778-1  This Is The Day Of Days                    -

Vocalist with Roy Fox and his Band.      London, November 5, 1931.

GB-3538-3  This Is The Missus                     Dec F-2682
GB-3539-3  Over The Blue                          Dec F-2683
GB-3540-2  'Neath The Spell Of Monte Carlo            -
GB-3541-2  Life Is Just A Bowl Of Cherries        Dec F-2682

Vocalist with the New Mayfair Novelty Orchestra (HMV B-4001, Victor 24090)or the New
   Mayfair Dance Orchestra (HMV B-6097, B-6098 and Victor 22953), dir. by Ray Noble.
                              London, November 14, 1931.

OB-2228-2  Got A Date With An Angel               HMV B-6098, Vic 22953
OB-2229-1-2  Guilty                               HMV B-6097
OB-2231-2  Twentieth Century Blues                HMV B-4001, Vic 24090
   NOTE:- Matrix OB-2230 has no vocal refrain at all.

Vocalist with Howard Godfrey and his Waldorfians.
                              London, November, 1931.

   4509    Looking For You                        Pic 849, Oct 133
   4510    That's What I Like About You               -
   4511-2  Got A Date With An Angel               Pic 855, Oct 133, ACL 1204
   4512    The Way With Every Sailor              Pic 856, Oct 134
   4513    Who Do You Love ?                      Pic 855    -      Ecl ECM-2048
   4514-2  Over The Blue                          Pic 856

Vocalist with the Deauville Dance Band (EBR 1584) or the Blue Jays (EBR 1585),dir.by
   Harry Hudson.                 London, November, 1931.

   90279-1  Lies                                  EBR 1584
   90280-3  Rio de Janeiro                            -
   90281-2  Linda                                 EBR 1585
   90282-2  Dear, When I Met You                      -

Vocalist with Billy Cotton and his Band.  London, December 1, 1931.

CAR-896-1  I Can't Get Mississippi Off My Mind    Re MR-463
   NOTE:- A test pressing of CAR-896-2 exists, with Al Bowlly's vocal backed by avery
   good trumpet obbligato.  It is not known if this was used for issue.

Vocalist with Ray Noble and the New Mayfair Dance Orchestra.
                              London, December 1, 1931.

OB-2031-5  Hold My Hand                           HMV B-6112, Vic 24034, Enc 160

Vocalist with Roy Fox and his Band.      London, December 2, 1931.

GB-3456-4  Yes, Yes (My Baby Said Yes)            Dec F-2720, ACL 1172
GB-3457-5  You Call It Madness (But I Call It Love)   -
GB-3664-1  Nobody's Sweetheart                    Dec F-2716, ACL 1172
GB-3665-1  Guilty                                     -

Vocalist with Ray Noble and the New Mayfair Dance Orchestra.
                              London, December 4, 1931.

OB-2484-4  Pied Piper Of Hamelin                  HMV B-6112, Vic 24034

Vocalist with the Tuff Guys, a vocal and instrumental group dir. by Harry Hudson.
                              London, December 8, 1931.

   90297-1  Eleven More Months And Ten More Days  EBR 1586
   90298-1  Foolish Facts                             -

Vocal, acc. by the Radio Rhythm Five.     London, December 9, 1931.

    14044-2  Eleven More Months And Ten More Days      EBW 5440
    14045-2  Foolish Facts                             -

Vocalist with Ray Noble and the New Mayfair Dance Orchestra.
                                          London, December 19, 1931.

    OB-2518-3  I Was True (w/chorus)                   HMV B-6118
    OB-2519-2  One Little Quarrel                      -

Vocalist with Roy Fox and his Band.       London, December 30, 1931.

    GB-3761-1  The Longer That You Linger In Virginia  Dec F-2760
    GB-3762-1-2  There's Something In Your Eyes        Rejected
    GB-3768-1  If I Didn't Have You                    Dec F-2763, ACL 1172
      NOTE:- Matrices GB-3763/6 inclusive are by other artists; GB-3767 is OH MO'NAH (on
      Decca F-2763 and many subsequent 78 and LP reissues), with vocal by Nat Gonella. A
      close examination of this side does not suggest that Al Bowlly was a member of the
      supporting chorus.

Vocalist with Jock McDermott and his Band.
                                          London, c. January 5, 1932.

    14114-1  Mona Lisa                                 EBW 5458
    14115-1  Hold My Hand                              -
    14116-2  Whispering                                EBW 5468
    14117-3  Dinah                                     -

Vocalist with Roy Fox and his Band.       London, January 7, 1932.

    GB-3762-4  There's Something In Your Eyes          Dec F-2760
    GB-3781-1-2  Prisoner Of Love                      Rejected
    GB-3782-1-2  You Didn't Know The Music             -

Vocalist with Ray Noble and the New Mayfair Dance Orchestra.
                                          London, January 8, 1932.

    OB-2102-3  Put Your Little Arms Around Me          HMV B-6131
    OB-2103-2  Meet Me Tonight In The Cowshed          HMV B-6130
               (dialogue w/Leonard Henry)
    OB-2104-1  By The Fireside                         HMV B-6131, 7EG-8186, Vic 25141,
                                                       Enc 140
    OB-2105-2  Must It End Like This ?                 HMV B-6130

Vocal, acc. by ? Harry Hudson-p.          London, c. January 13, 1932.

    14126-1  A Faded Summer Love                       EBW 5470
    14127-1  You Didn't Know The Music                 -

Vocalist with the Masqueraders (Savoy Hotel Orpheans).
                                          London, January 14, 1932.

    CA-12349-1  Actions Speak Louder Than Words        Col CB-409
    CA-12351-1  One Little Quarrel (w/Anona Winn)      Col CB-413
      NOTE:- Matrix CA-12350 has a vocal refrain by Anona Winn only.

Vocalist with Roy Fox and his Band.       London, January 21, 1932.

    GB-3781-4  Prisoner Of Love                        Dec F-2775
    GB-3782-4  You Didn't Know The Music               -
    GB-3854-2  To Be Worthy Of You                     Dec F-2793
    GB-3855-1  Jig Time                                -            ACL 1172

Vocalist with the Savoy Hotel Orpheans.   London, January 21, 1932.

    CA-12341-3  You're The Kind Of A Baby For Me       Col CB-403
      NOTE:- This is a re-make of the side made on January 7, 1932, both takes rejected.
      As Al Bowlly was not on either of the other titles made on that occasion, it seems
      likely that he did not sing on CA-12341-1 and -2.

Vocalist with the Rhythm Maniacs (on this occasion, a pseudonym for Roy Fox and his
    Band !)                                        London, January 28, 1932.

GB-3889-2  If Anything Happened To You            Dec F-3086, ACL 1204
GB-3890-2  In London On A Night Like This            -

Vocalist with the New Cumberland Dance Orchestra.
                                                London, c. January, 1932.

    1910    Falling In Love                        Film 378
    1912    You Call It Madness                    Film 379
    1915    I Idolize My Baby's Eyes               Film 378
    1916    Life Is Just A Bowl Of Cherries        Film 379
NOTE:- Matrices 1911, 1913 and 1914 are probably different takes of the above.

Vocalist with Roy Fox and his Band; he sings the word ADIOS twice near the beginning
    of this side, his sole vocal contribution to the entire session !
                                                London, February 4, 1932.

GB-3922-3  Adios                                  Dec F-2805

Vocalist with Ray Noble and the New Mayfair Dance Orchestra.
                                                London, February 12, 1932.

OB-2186-2  Sweetheart In My Dreams Tonight         HMV B-6146, Vic 24173
OB-2187-2  It's Great To Be In Love                HMV B-6147, Vic 25232
OB-2188-1  Blues In My Heart                          -         Vic 25141

Vocalist with the Savoy Hotel Orpheans.  London, February 16, 1932.

CA-12424-2  Whistling Waltz                        Col CB-425
CA-12425-2  Sweetheart In My Dreams Tonight           -
CA-12426-2  Save The Last Dance For Me             Col CB-426

    The following four sides were issued as THE MASQUERADERS.
                                                London, February 18, 1932.

CA-12443-2  Granny's Photo Album                   Col CB-434
CA-12444-2  Kiss By Kiss (w/the Carlyle Cousins)   Col CB-429
CA-12445-1  The Night You Gave Me Back The Ring       -
            (w/the Carlyle Cousins)
CA-12446-1  Only Me Knows Why                      Col CB-428

Vocalist with Roy Fox and his Band.     London, February 22, 1932.

GB-4012-2  Concentratin'                           Dec F-2839
GB-4013-3  Minnie The Moocher (w/Lew Stone and     Dec F-2834, DFE-6272, ACL 1172
           Bill Harty)
GB-4014-2  Kicking The Gong Around (Al Bowlly         -         -         -
           speaks the part of a Chinese)

Vocalist with Ray Noble and the New Mayfair Dance Orchestra.
                                                London, March 3, 1932.

OB-3008-2  There's A Ring Around The Moon          HMV B-6154, Vic 24149
OB-3009-2  With Love In My Heart                   HMV B-6157

Vocalist with the Masqueraders (Savoy Hotel Orpheans).
                                                London, March 5, 1932.

CA-12505-1  With Love In My Heart                  Col CB-442
CA-12506-2  Take Away The Moon                     Col CB-435
CA-12507-1  We'll Be Together Again                Col CB-434
CA-12508-2  Tell Tales                             Col CB-435

Vocal, acc. by studio orchestra, compered by John Watt.
                                London, March 7, 1932.

GA-4069-2  Songs From The Shows - Part 1 (Al        Dec K-645
              Bowlly sings a chorus of IT HAPPENED IN MONTEREY)
GA-4070-2  Songs From The Shows - Part 2 (Al          -
              Bowlly sings a chorus of MY BABY JUST CARES FOR ME with Elsie Carlisle)

Vocalist with Roy Fox and his Band.        London, March 7, 1932.

GB-4071-2  My Sweet Virginia                      Dec F-2866
GB-4072-1-2  If I Have To Go On Without You          -
GB-4073-3  Kiss By Kiss                           Dec F-2867
GB-4074-2  Goodnight, Moon                           -

Vocalist with the Masqueraders (Savoy Hotel Orpheans).
                                London, March 11, 1932.

CA-12527-1  The Cat And The Fiddle - Selection,    Col DB-782
              Part 1 (Al Bowlly sings a chorus of TRY TO FORGET)
CA-12528-1  The Cat And The Fiddle - Selection,      -
              Part 2 (Al Bowlly sings a chorus of SHE DIDN'T SAY YES)

Vocalist with the Durium Dance Band, dir. by Lew Stone.
                                London, March 15, 1932.

E-1003-B  All Of Me/Save The Last Dance For Me    Durium EN-8, Halcyon HAL-2
E-1004-B-C  One More Kiss/By The Fireside         Durium EN-0           -

Vocalist with Roy Fox and his Band.        London, March 22, 1932.

GB-4114-1  She Didn't Say Yes (as one of trio)    Dec F-2888, ACL 1172
GB-4115-2  Goodnight, Vienna                      Dec F-2889, Br 6375
GB-4116-2  Living In Clover                          -            -

Vocalist with the Masqueraders (Savoy Hotel Orpheans).
                                London, March 24, 1932.

CA-12544-1  The King Was In The Counting-House     Col CB-443
CA-12545-2  Goopy Geer                             Col CB-442
CA-12546-1  Sailing On The Robert E. Lee           Col CB-443

Vocalist with the Durium Dance Band, dir. by Lew Stone.
                                London, April 1, 1932.

E-1023-B  Was That The Human Thing To Do ?/Now    Durium EN-11, Halcyon HAL-2
              That You're Gone
E-1024-B-C  Goodnight, Vienna/My Sweet Virginia   Durium EN-9          -

Vocalist with Ray Noble and the New Mayfair Dance Orchestra.
                                London, April 7, 1932.

OB-3063-1  Goodnight, Vienna                      HMV B-6172, Vic 24064
OB-3064-2  Give Me A Tune                         HMV B-6182
OB-3065-2  Living In Clover                       HMV B-6172, Vic 24064

Vocalist with Roy Fox and his Band.        London, April 13, 1932.

GB-4255-2  Somebody Loves You                     Dec F-2922
GB-4256-2  I'm For You A Hundred Per Cent.        Dec F-2923
GB-4257-1-3  Can't We Talk It Over ?                -
GB-4258-2  When We're Alone                       Dec F-2922

Vocalist with the Durium Dance Band, dir. by Lew Stone.
                                London, April 20, 1932.

E-1029-A-C  Can't We Talk It Over ?/Just Humming  Durium EN-13, Halcyon HAL-2
              Along
E-1030-B  Auf Wiedersehen, My Dear/Rain On The    Durium EN-12         -
              Roof

Vocalist with Ray Noble and the New Mayfair Dance Orchestra (HMV B-6176, B-6203)  or
the New Mayfair Orchestra (HMV B-4188), dir. by Ray Noble.
London, April 21, 1932.

| | | |
|---|---|---|
| OB-2860-2 | With All My Love And Kisses | HMV B-6176,Vic 24128,ME MES-6816 |
| OB-2861-2 | We've Got The Moon And Sixpence | HMV B-6203,Vic 24212, Enc 160 |

London, May 3, 1932.

OB-2870-2  One Hour With You - Selection, Part 2   HMV B-4188
    (Al Bowlly sings a chorus of WHAT WOULD YOU DO ?)
OB-2871-1  One Hour With You - Selection, Part 1       -
    (Al Bowlly sings a chorus of ONE HOUR WITH YOU)
OB-2874-2  Sailing On The Robert E. Lee        HMV B-6176, Vic 24128, Enc 160
  NOTE:- The vocalist on matrices OB-2872 and 2873 is Cavan O'Connor.

Vocalist with Roy Fox and his Band.     London, May 4, 1932.

| | | |
|---|---|---|
| GB-4409-2 | Lovable | Dec F-2963 |
| GB-4411-2 | Love, You Funny Thing | Dec F-2964 |
| GB-4412-2 | Getting Sentimental | Dec F-2963 |

  NOTE:- The vocalist on matrix GB-4410 is Nat Gonella.

Vocalist with the Savoy Hotel Orpheans.   London, May 11, 1932.

| | | |
|---|---|---|
| CA-12691-3 | Snuggled On Your Shoulder | Col CB-458 |
| CA-12692-1-2 | Keepin' Out Of Mischief Now | Rejected |
| CA-12693-2 | When We're Alone | Col CB-459 |
| CA-12694-1 | What Makes You So Adorable ? | Col CB-469 |

Vocalist with Roy Fox and his Band.     London, May 19, 1932.

| | | | |
|---|---|---|---|
| GB-4489-2 | You've Got What Gets Me | Dec F-3014 | |
| GB-4490-3 | I Got Rhythm | - | ACL 1172 |
| GB-4491-2 | Put That Sun Back In The Sky | Dec F-3015 | |
| GB-4492-1-2 | The Echo Of A Song | Rejected | |

Vocalist with the New Mayfair Orchestra, dir. by Ray Noble.
London, May 27, 1932.

OB-2892-2  Songs Everybody Is Singing - Part 1   HMV B-4208
    (Al Bowlly sings a chorus of BY THE FIRESIDE)
OB-2893-2  Songs Everybody Is Singing - Part 2       -
    (Al Bowlly sings a chorus of WHAT MAKES YOU SO ADORABLE ?)

Vocalist with Arthur Lally and his Orchestra (Decca F-3006, F-3067), Buddy Lewis and
his Orchestra (Panachord 25240) or Jack Holmes and his Orchestra (Mayfair G-2170).
London, June 1, 1932.

GB-4537-2  A Hiking Holiday With Bert Feldman -   Dec F-3006
    Part 1 (Al Bowlly sings a chorus of WAS THAT THE HUMAN THING TO DO ?)
GB-4538-1  A Hiking Holiday With Bert Feldman -       -
    Part 2 (Al Bowlly sings a chorus of WHEN THE REST OF THE   CROWD   GOES
    HOME)
PB-1008-2  Good Evening               Dec F-3067, Pan 25240, May G-2170
PB-1009-2  My Sunny Monterey                     -           -

Vocalist with Ray Noble and the New Mayfair Dance Orchestra.
London, June 8, 1932.

| | | |
|---|---|---|
| OB-3094-3 | Good Evening | HMV B-6193 |
| OB-3095-2 | The Echo Of A Song | - |
| OB-3096-2 | Dreams That Don't Grow Old | HMV B-6192 |

Vocalist with Roy Fox and his Band.    London, June 10, 1932.

| | | |
|---|---|---|
| GB-4492-3 | The Echo Of A Song | Dec F-3015, Br 6457 |
| GB-4559-2 | It's Always Goodbye | Dec F-3028 |
| GB-4560-3 | Lullaby Of The Leaves | Dec F-3029, DFE-6271 |

  (continued on page 83)

London, June 10, 1932 (cont.)

GB-4561-2  Gone Forever                      Dec F-3029
GB-4562-2  What Makes You So Adorable ?      Dec F-3028

Vocalist with Arthur Lally and his Orchestra.
                          London, June 30, 1932.

GB-4610-2  Drums In My Heart                 Dec F-3057
GB-4611-1  Ev'ry Day's A Lucky Day              -        Ecl ECM-2048

Vocalist with the Savoy Hotel Orpheans.  London, July 18, 1932.

CA-12892-2  I Heard                          Col CB-483
CA-12893-1  What A Life !                    Col CB-482
CA-12894-2  A Great Big Bunch Of You             -

Vocalist with Roy Fox and his Band.      London, July 20, 1932.

GB-4679-3  Minnie The Moocher's Wedding Day  Dec F-3063
GB-4680-3  Roy Fox's Commentary on Minnie The   -
             Moocher's Wedding (Speech in Chinese (?) by Al Bowlly)
GB-4681-2  One More Affair                   Dec F-3093
GB-4682-1-2  Marta                           Rejected

Vocalist with Ray Noble and the New Mayfair Dance Orchestra.
                          London, July 20, 1932.

OB-2367-2  Why Be So Unkind To Me ?          HMV B-6220
OB-2368-1  Please Don't Mention It (w/Anona Winn) HMV B-6219
OB-2369-2  Where Are You (Girl Of My Dreams) HMV B-6220
             (w/Anona Winn)
OB-2370-2  Pagan Moon                        HMV B-6219

Vocalist with Arthur Lally and his Orchestra.
                          London, July 23, 1932.

GB-4689-1  We've Got The Moon And Sixpence   Dec F-3066
GB-4690-2  Is I In Love ? I Is                  -

Vocal, acc. by small instrumental group. London, July 26, 1932.

GB-4696-1  Please Don't Mention It           Dec F-3128, M-422
GB-4697-2  Wherever You Are                     -          -

Vocalist with Roy Fox and his Band.      London, August 8, 1932.

GB-4682-4  Marta                            Dec F-3093
GB-4715-1  Wherever You Are                 Dec F-3094
GB-4716-2  Just Another Dream Of You           -
GB-4717-1  Ooh ! That Kiss !                Dec F-3099
GB-4718-2  You're My Everything                -          ACL 1172

Vocalist with Ray Noble and the New Mayfair Dance Orchestra.
                          London, September 1, 1932.

OB-3182-2  Looking On The Bright Side Of Life  HMV B-6237, Vic 24212, ME MES-6816
OB-3183-2  The Younger Generation            HMV B-6238, Vic 25020
OB-3185-1  You're More Than All The World To Me  HMV B-6237
  NOTE:- Matrix OB-3184 has no vocal refrain.

Vocal, acc. by small instrumental group. London, September 7, 1932.

GB-4842-3  Happy-Go-Lucky You (And Broken-   Dec F-3145, Ecl ECM-2048
             Hearted Me)
GB-4843-1  It Was So Beautiful                  -

Vocalist with Ray Noble and the New Mayfair Dance Orchestra.
London, September 8, 1932.

| OB-3195-2 | I'll Do My Best To Make You Happy | HMV B-6245, 7EG-8056, Vic 24333, Enc 160 |
| OB-3196-2 | Love Is The Sweetest Thing | HMV B-6245, Vic 24333,ME MES-6816 |

Vocalist with Roy Fox and his Band.    London, September 9, 1932.

| GB-4866-3 | The Night When Love Was Born | Dec F-3152 |
| GB-4867-1 | Are You Prepared (To Be True ?) | - |
| GB-4868-1 | If You Were Only Mine | Dec F-3151 |
| GB-4869-2 | Call It A Day | - |

Vocal, acc. by studio orchestra.    London, September 19, 1932.

| GB-4901-1-2-3 | Love Is The Sweetest Thing | Dec rejected |
| GB-4902-1-2 | I'll Do My Best To Make You Happy | - |

Vocalist with Debroy Somers' Band.    London, September 20, 1932.

| CA-13038-1 | Listen To The German Band | Col CB-508 |

Vocalist with Arthur Lally and his Orchestra.
London, September 21, 1932.

| GB-4919-2 | Dance Of The Cuckoos | Dec F-3186 |
| GB-4921-1 | This Is My Love Song | Pan 25303, Mf G-2203 |

NOTE:- Mayfair as JACK HOLMES AND HIS ORCHESTRA. Matrix GB-4920 is by the  concert baritone Roy Henderson, apparently without connection with the Arthur Lally date.

Vocalist with Roy Fox and his Band.    London, September 23, 1932.

| GB-4936-2 | The Old Man Of The Mountain | Dec F-3181, ACL 1172 |
| GB-4937-3 | How'm I Doin' ? (Hey-Hey) (as member of chorus behind Nat Gonella) | Dec F-3198  - |
| GB-4938-2 | Moon | - |
| GB-4939-3 | All Of A Sudden | Dec F-3181 |

Vocalist with Arthur Lally and his Orchestra; Decca F-3186 as RUDY STARITA-Xylophone solo with orchestra.    London, September 29, 1932.

| GB-4957-1 | Hello Mike | Dec F-3187 | | |
| GB-4958-2 | Considerin' | - | Mf | G-2202 |
| GB-4959-3 | Looking On The Bright Side | Pan 25303, | Mf | G-2203 |
| GB-4960-2 | Wicked Mr. Punch | Dec F-3186 | | |

NOTE:- Mayfair G-2202 and G-2203 as JACK HOLMES AND HIS ORCHESTRA.

Vocal, acc. by studio orchestra.    London, October 7, 1932.

| GB-4901-6 | Love Is The Sweetest Thing | Dec F-3194, ACL 1162 |
| GB-4902-3 | I'll Do My Best To Make You Happy | -              - |
| GB-4994-1 | My Romance | Dec F-3218 |
| GB-4995-1 | Keep Your Last Goodnight For Me | - |

Vocalist with Ray Noble and the New Mayfair Dance Orchestra.
London, October 11, 1932.

| OB-4069-1 | Don't Say Goodbye | HMV B-6251 |
| OB-4070-2 | Song Of The Bells | HMV B-6249 |
| OB-4071-1 | A Bedtime Story | HMV B-6250, Vic 24226 |
| OB-4072-2 | Marching Along Together | HMV B-6249 |
| OB-4073-2 | You, Just You | HMV B-6251 |
| OB-4074-3 | Rock Your Cares Away | HMV B-6250, Vic 24302, 25262 |

Vocalist with Lew Stone and the Monseigneur Band.
                                        London, October 21, 1932.

GB-5058-1-2-3  Nightfall                        Rejected
GB-5059-1-2-3  Rain, Rain, Go Away              -
GB-5060-1-2  In The Still Of The Night          -
GB-5061-1-2 ? Why Waste Your Tears ?            -
GA-5065-2  O. K. Decca - Part 2 (Al Bowlly sings   Dec K-684
           a chorus of HAPPY-GO-LUCKY YOU AND BROKEN-HEARTED ME)
     NOTE:- Matrices GB-5062 and GB-5063 are not by the Lew Stone Band, and GA-5064  is
     Part 1 of O.K. Decca, a symposium of Decca popular artists, but not including  Al
     Bowlly.

                                        London, October 31, 1932.

GB-5058-5  Nightfall                            Dec F-3234
GB-5059-5  Rain, Rain, Go Away                  Dec F-3233
GB-5060-5  In The Still Of The Night            Dec F-3234
GB-5061-4  Why Waste Your Tears ?               Dec F-3233

                                        London, November 11, 1932.

GB-5158-1-2  I Can't Write The Words            Dec rejected
GB-5159-1-2  Let's Put Out The Lights And Go To   -
             Sleep (w/Mary Charles)

Vocal, acc. by o/George Scott-Wood (on Decca F-3275) or by George Scott-Wood-p  only
   (on Decca F-3304); matrices GB-5174 and GB-5175 are by other artists entirely.
                                        London, November 15, 1932.

GB-5172-3  So Ashamed                           Dec F-3275
GB-5173-1  Rosa Mia                             -
GB-5176-1  I'll Follow You                      Dec F-3304
GB-5177-3  A Million Dreams                     -

Vocalist with Lew Stone and the Monseigneur Band.
                                        London, November 16, 1932.

GB-5158-5  I Can't Write The Words              Dec F-3270, Mf G-277
GB-5159-4  Let's Put Out The Lights (And Go To      -          Ecl ECM-2047
           Sleep) (w/Mary Charles)

                                        London, November 29, 1932.

GB-5261-2  Junk Man Blues (w/chorus)            Dec F-3313
GB-5262-2  Balloons                             Dec F-3314
GB-5263-2  My Woman                             Dec F-3313
     NOTE:- Matrix GB-5264 was scheduled to be made at this session, but the   allotted
     time expired before it could be recorded.

                                        London, December 2, 1932.

GB-5264-2  I'll Never Be The Same               Dec F-3314
GB-5280-3  You'll Always Be The Same Sweetheart  Dec F-3345, ACL 1178
           To Me

Vocalist with Ray Noble and his Orchestra.
                                        London, December 8, 1932.

OB-4356-2  Here Lies Love                       HMV B-6283
OB-4357-1  Please                               -
OB-4358-3  Brighter Than The Sun                HMV B-6302, Vic 24314

Vocalist with Lew Stone and the Monseigneur Band.
                                        London, December 9, 1932.

GB-5314-2-3  The Girl Who Thought.....-Part 1   Dec F-3324
GB-5315-1  The Girl Who Thought.....-Part 2     -
GB-5316-1  Let's All Sing Like The Birdies Sing   Dec F-3345

Vocalist with Ray Noble and his Orchestra.

London, December 14, 1932.

OB-4365-1  What More Can I Ask ?                HMV B-6302, Vic 24314,ME MES-6816

Vocal, acc. by George Scott-Wood-p.    London, December 21, 1932.

KB-216-2  Glorious Devon                         Dec F-3369

Vocalist with Lew Stone and the Monseigneur Band.

London, December 23, 1932.

GB-5398-1  What More Can I Ask ?              Dec F-3373
GB-5399-1  Brighter Than The Sun               -
GB-5400-1  Ich Liebe Dich, My Dear             Dec F-3372
GB-5401-2  Lying In The Hay                     -           ACL 1147

London, January 10, 1933.

GB-5445-2  Little Nell (Al Bowlly speaks the part  Dec F-3394, ACL 1231
           of the villain)
GB-5446-1  A Letter To My Mother (A Brivele der   Dec F-3428, ACL 1147
           Mame) (in Yiddish)

Vocalist with Ray Noble and his Orchestra.

London, January 12, 1933.

OB-4394-2  A Little Street Where Old Friends Meet  HMV B-6305
OB-4395-2  Lying In The Hay                     HMV B-6306, Vic 24297, Enc 160
OB-4396-1  Wanderer                              -           -           -
OB-4397-1  Just An Echo In The Valley           HMV B-6305

Vocalist with Lew Stone and the Monseigneur Band.

London, January 27, 1933.

GB-5446-4  A Letter To My Mother (A Brivele der   Dec F-3428
           Mame) (in Yiddish)
GB-5521-2  What More Can I Ask ?                Dec F-3459, Br 6576
GB-5522-2  In Santa Lucia                       Dec F-3456
GB-5523-1  Please Handle With Care               -
GB-5524-1  The World Is So Small                Dec F-3455
GB-5525-1  Mediterranean Madness                 -           656

Vocalist with Ray Noble and his Orchestra; as NEW MAYFAIR DANCE ORCHESTRA on  HMV  B-
   6318.                                  London, January 31, 1933.

OB-6414-1  Butterflies In The Rain              HMV B-6316, Vic 24296
OB-6415-1  A Letter To My Mother                HMV B-6317, Vic 24308
OB-6416-1  Play, Fiddle, Play                   HMV B-6318

The next session is entered in the HMV files as by "Mr. Blunt and his Orchestra," but
   it is not known if this refers to Jack Jackson's Orchestra, or if Al Bowlly was the
   vocalist.                              London, February 1, 1933.

OB-6421-1-2  Come On, Be Happy                  HMV rejected
OB-6422-1-2  One Little Word Led To Another

Vocalist with Ray Noble and his Orchestra. Two studios were used, hence the gap  between the matrix numbers.              London, February 7, 1933.

OB-6320-1  Look What You've Done                HMV B-6321
OB-6431-2  Standing On The Corner               HMV B-6317, Vic 24308
OB-6432-2  Poor Me, Poor You                    HMV B-6318
OB-6433-1  Have You Ever Been Lonely ?          HMV B-6319, Vic 24278
OB-6434-1  Wheezy Anna                          HMV B-6316, Vic 24287
OB-6435-2  Love Tales                           HMV B-6319, Vic 24278, ME MES-6816
   NOTE:- HMV B-6318 as NEW MAYFAIR DANCE ORCHESTRA.

Vocalist with the New Mayfair Dance Orchestra, dir. by Ray Noble (a different   band
   from Ray Noble's regular group).        London, February 20, 1933.

OB-6440-1  Can't We Meet Again ?                  HMV B-6320
OB-6441-2  Sweetheart                             -

Vocalist with John (Jack) Jackson and his Orchestra.
                                       London, February 24, 1933.

OB-6421-4  Come On, Be Happy                      HMV B-6330
OB-6449-2  Let Bygones Be Bygones                 -
OB-6450-2  I'm Playing With Fire                  HMV B-6322
OB-6451-1  Sittin' In The Dark                    -

Vocalist with Ray Noble and his Orchestra.
                                       London, February 27, 1933.

OB-6452-1  The Moment I Saw You                    HMV B-6325, Vic 24610, 25313,
                                                  120859 (Canadian)
OB-6453-1  My Heart's To Let                       HMV B-6323, Vic 24341
OB-6454-1  When You've Fallen In Love              -           -

Vocalist with Lew Stone and the Monseigneur Band.
                                       London, March 2, 1933.

GB-5613-2  My Heart's To Let                       Dec F-3496
GB-5614-2  When You've Fallen In Love              -
GB-5625-1  Someone To Care For                     Dec F-3502
GB-5626-2  Won't You Stay To Tea ?                 -
   NOTE:- Matrices GB-5615/24 inclusive are by other artists on other dates.

Vocalist with Ray Noble and his Orchestra.
                                       London, March 16, 1933.

OB-6474-1  Three Wishes                            HMV B-6332, Vic 24347
OB-6476-2  Let Me Give My Happiness To You         -
OB-6478-2  Hustlin' And Bustlin' For Baby          HMV B-6331, ME MES-6816
OB-6479-1  Stay On The Right Side Of The Road      -           Vic 24375
   NOTE:- Matrices OB-6475 and OB-6477 are non-vocal versions of OB-6474 and  OB-6476
   respectively.

                                       London, March 17, 1933.

OB-6357-1-2  Brother, Can You Spare A Dime ?       HMV test
OB-6358-1-2  Sweetheart                            -

Vocalist with the Scott-Wood Accordion Quartet; Al Bowlly does not sing on CE-4951.
                                       London, c. April 3, 1933.

CE-4949-1  Sweetheart                              Par R-1476
CE-4950-1  Can't We Meet Again ?                   Par R-1506
CE-4952-1  The Goodnight Waltz                     -
CE-4953-1  Oh ! Mr. Moon                           Par R-1476

Vocalist with Lew Stone and the Monseigneur Band.
                                       London, April 5, 1933.

GB-5727-2  Oh ! Mr. Moon                           Dec F-3535
GB-5728-1  Three Wishes                            Dec F-3534
GB-5729-1  Let Me Give My Happiness To You         -           Ecl ECM-2048
GB-5730-1  And So I Married The Girl               Dec F-3535

Vocalist with the New Mayfair Orchestra, dir. by Clifford Greenwood.
                                       London, April 6, 1933.

2B-6493-1  Venetian Nights (Al Bowlly sings part   HMV C-2565
           of the BARCAROLLE from Offenbach's TALES OF HOFFMAN as a duet with Suz-
           anne Botterill)

Vocal, acc. by small instrumental group.  London, April 20, 1933.

GB-5769-2  Maria, My Own                              Dec F-3560, DFE-6245, ACL 1204
GB-5770-2  That's All That Matters To Me              -
GB-5771-1  You Must Believe Me                        Dec F-3547, Ecl ECM-2048
GB-5772-2  Goodnight But Not Goodbye                  -              -

Vocalist with Ray Noble and his Orchestra.
                                        London, April 25, 1933.

OB-6515-3  I'm One Of The Lads Of Valencia (w/Ray  HMV B-6344
              Noble and chorus)
OB-6516-1  The Village Band (w/Ray Noble and chorus)   -
OB-6517-1  Dinah                                      HMV test for Ray Noble

                                        London, May 3, 1933.

OB-6527-1  Waltzing In A Dream                        HMV B-6348
OB-6528-2  Maybe I Love You Too Much                  HMV B-6347, Enc 160
OB-6529-2  It's Within Your Power                     -

                                        London, May 10, 1933.

OB-6533-2  The Old Spinning-Wheel                     HMV B-6348, Vic 24357
OB-6534-2  When My Little Pomeranian Met Your         HMV B-6358
              Little Pekinese (w/Frances Day)
OB-6535-1  That's What Life Is Made Of                HMV B-6361, Vic 24599

                                        London, May 16, 1933.

OB-6549-1  Hiawatha's Lullaby                         HMV B-6359
OB-6550-1-2  For You Alone                            Rejected
OB-6551-4  I Shall Still Keep Smiling Along           HMV B-6359, Vic 24393

                                        London, May 24, 1933.

OB-6560-3  All Over Italy (w/chorus)                  HMV B-6364
OB-6561-1  Seven Years With The Wrong Woman           -          Vic 24388

Vocalist with Lew Stone and the Monseigneur Band. Despite the label, matrix  GB-5959
   has no vocal refrain.              London, June 7, 1933.

GB-5958-2  I Lay Me Down To Sleep                     Dec F-3603
GB-5960-1  In The Park In Paree                       Dec F-3592
GB-5961-1  The Language Of Love                       Dec F-3603

Vocalist with Ray Noble and his Orchestra (HMV B-6367, B-6370) or the New    Mayfair
   Dance Orchestra, dir. by Ray Noble (HMV B-6369).
                                        London, June 16, 1933.

OB-6593-2  You're Mine, You                           HMV B-6370, ME MES-6816
OB-6594-2  Gypsy Fiddles                              HMV B-6367
OB-6595-2  Something Came And Got Me In The Spring HMV B-6369

                                        London, June 20, 1933.

OB-6597-2  A Couple Of Fools In Love                  HMV B-6366
OB-6598-2  I Only Want One Girl                       -

                                        London, July 5, 1933.

OB-5012-2  The Shadow Waltz                           HMV B-6376
OB-5013-1  Pettin' In The Park                        HMV B-6375
OB-5015-1  I've Got To Sing A Torch-Song              -
   NOTE:- Matrices OB-5014 and OB-5016 are non-vocal versions of OB-5013 and  OB-5015
   respectively.
                                        London, July 12, 1933.

OB-4634-2  Roll Up The Carpet                         HMV B-6380,Vic 24420,25262,Enc160
OB-4635-1  It's Sunday Down In Caroline               HMV B-6381

London, July 13, 1933.

| | | |
|---|---|---|
| OB-5028-1 | Si Petite | HMV B-6381 |
| OB-5029-2 | If You'll Say "Yes," Cherie | HMV B-6379 |
| OB-5030-2 | There's A Cabin In The Pines | - |
| OB-5031-1 | On The Other Side Of Lovers' Lane | HMV B-6380, Vic 24420 |

**Vocalist** with Eddie Pola and Company, in the character of "Bang Horseby."
London, July 25, 1933.

| | | |
|---|---|---|
| CAX-6900-1 | America Calling (A Burlesque on | Col DX-499 |
| | American radio programmes) - Part 1 (Al Bowlly sings a chorus of  CUD- |
| | DLE UP CLOSE) |
| CAX-6901-1-4 | America Calling - Part 2 (Al Bowlly | - |
| | sings a chorus of YOU'LL NEVER UNDERSTAND) |

Vocal, acc. by viola/p/g.                    London, July 26, 1933.

| | | |
|---|---|---|
| GB-6056-1 | Moonstruck | Dec F-3627, ACL 1162 |
| GB-6057-1 | There's A Cabin In The Pines | Dec F-3638 |
| GB-6058-1 | Learn To Croon | Dec F-3627, ACL 1162 |
| GB-6059-2 | I'm Gettin' Sentimental Over You | Dec F-3638 |

Vocalist with Lew Stone and the Monseigneur Band.
London, August 1, 1933.

| | | |
|---|---|---|
| TB-1019-2 | Isn't It Heavenly ? | Dec F-3630, ACL 1178 |

London, September 15, 1933.

| | | |
|---|---|---|
| TB-1068-2 | Blue Prelude | Dec F-3675 |
| TB-1069-2 | Adorable | Dec F-3676 |

Vocalist with Ray Noble and his Orchestra.
London, September 18, 1933.

| | | |
|---|---|---|
| OB-5084-2 | Mademoiselle | HMV B-6394, Vic 24624 |
| OB-5085-2 | How Could We Be Wrong ? | HMV B-6396, Vic 24872, Enc 160 |

London, September 19, 1933.

| | | |
|---|---|---|
| OB-5091-2 | It's Bad For Me | HMV B-6396, Vic 24872,ME MES-6816 |
| OB-5092-2 | Trouble In Paradise | HMV B-6394 |
| OB-5093-2 | Oh ! Johanna | HMV B-6397 |
| OB-5094-1-2 | I've Got To Pass Your House To Get | Rejected |
| | To My House |

NOTE:- HMV B-6397 as NEW MAYFAIR DANCE ORCHESTRA.

London, October 12, 1933.

| | | |
|---|---|---|
| OB-4672-1 | Snow Ball | HMV B-6408 |
| OB-4673-2 | Dinner At Eight | HMV B-6409 |
| OB-4674-1 | Experiment | HMV B-6408, Vic 25006 |
| OB-5133-1 | Weep No More, My Baby | HMV B-6409 |
| OB-5134-2 | Love Locked Out | HMV B-6407, Vic 24485, Enc 140 |
| OB-5135-1 | Happy And Contented (w/Eve Becke) | - |

NOTE:- The first three titles above were made in a different studio from the  last
three, hence the large gap in matrix numbers.

Vocal, acc. by O/Carroll Gibbons.        London, October 16, 1933.

| | | |
|---|---|---|
| GB-6196-2 | Night And Day | Dec F-3695, ACL 1204 |
| GB-6197-2 | Love Locked Out | - |

Vocalist with Lew Stone and the Monseigneur Band.
London, October 18, 1933.

| | | |
|---|---|---|
| TB-1089-2 | From Me To You | Dec F-3716 |

London, October 24, 1933.

TB-1095-1  Don't Change                         Dec F-3821, 496
TB-1096-2  The Day You Came Along               Dec F-3722
TB-1097-2  Thanks                               -

Vocalist with The Bands That Matter (Ambrose, Roy Fox, Jack Hylton and Lew Stone).
London, October 25, 1933.

GB-6242-2  Al Bowlly sings a chorus of ISN'T IT    Dec F-3723
             HEAVENLY ?

Vocalist with Ray Noble and his Orchestra.
London, October 27, 1933.

OB-4680-2  Goodnight, Little Girl Of My Dreams   HMV B-6413
OB-4699-1  Thanks                               -
OB-4700-2  My Hat's On The Side Of My Head       HMV B-6421, Vic 24624

Vocalist with Lew Stone and his Band.    London, November 3, 1933.

GB-6277-1  How Could We Be Wrong ?               Dec F-3734, ACL 1178
GB-6280-1  Experiment                           -
  NOTE:- Matrices GB-6278 and GB-6279 have no vocal refrains.

Vocalist with Ray Noble and his Orchestra.
London, November 9, 1933.

OB-5181-1  Hand In Hand                          HMV B-6423
OB-5182-1  And So Goodbye                        HMV B-6422
OB-5183-1  This Is Romance                       -           ME MES-6816

Vocal, acc. by studio orchestra.    London, November 13, 1933.

GB-6317-1  Fancy Our Meeting                     Dec F-3742
GB-6318-1  Lover, Come Back To Me                -           DFE-6245, ACL 1162

Vocalist with Ray Noble and his Orchestra.
London, November 29, 1933.

OB-5200-1  Song Without Words                    HMV B-6438, Vic 24555
OB-5801-2  When You Were The Girl On The Scooter  HMV B-6432
             (w/Elsie Carlisle)

Vocalist with Lew Stone and his Band at the Cafe Anglais, London.
London, December 1, 1933.

GB-6380-2  Weep No More, My Baby                 Dec F-3783
GB-6381-3  Close Your Eyes                       -
GA-6382-1  Lew Stone Favourites ("Ten-Thirty     Dec K-715
             Tuesday Night !") - Part 1 (Al Bowlly sings a chorus of MINNIE THE MOO-
             CHER, assisted by Tiny Winters and Bill Harty)
GA-6383-1  Lew Stone Favourites ("Ten-Thirty     -           ACL 1204
             Tuesday Night !") - Part 2 (Al Bowlly sings a chorus of BROTHER,CAN YOU
             SPARE A DIME ?)

Vocalist with Ray Noble and his Orchestra.
London, December 7, 1933.

OB-5821-2  My Song Goes Round The World          HMV B-6438, Vic 24555
OB-5822-2  Oceans Of Time                        HMV B-6450, Vic 24603, Enc 160
OB-5823-1  Close Your Eyes                       HMV B-6441, 7EG-8186, Enc 140

London, December 20, 1933.

OB-5833-1  On A Steamer Coming Over              HMV B-6440, Vic 24575
OB-5834-1  Did You Ever See A Dream Walking ?    HMV B-6441
OB-5835-2  You Ought To See Sally On Sunday      HMV B-6440, Vic 24575, Enc 140

Vocalist with Lew Stone and his Band at the Cafe Anglais, London.
                              London, December 29, 1933.

GB-6441-1  Eadie Was A Lady              Dec F-3825, ACL 1147
GB-6442-2  Who'll Buy An Old Gold Ring ? Dec F-3842
GB-6443-1  Dark Clouds                   Dec F-3826, DFE-6574

Vocal, acc. by small orchestra.     London, January 4, 1934.

GB-6457-2  Everything I Have Is Yours    Dec F-3853, Ecl ECM-2048
GB-6458-2  That's My Without You            -

Vocalist with Lew Stone and his Band at the Cafe Anglais, London.
                              London, January 9, 1934.

GB-6474-2  Louisiana Hayride             Dec F-3840, Ecl ECM-2047

Vocalist with Ray Noble and his Orchestra.
                              London, February 1, 1934.

OB-4768-2  Unless                        HMV B-6453
OB-4769-2  Have A Heart                  HMV B-6459
OB-4770-1-2  Who Walks In When I Walk Out ?  HMV B-6453, Vic 24594

Vocalist with Lew Stone at the Cafe Anglais, Lobdon.
                              London, February 15, 1934.

GB-6538-1  Faint Harmony                 Dec F-3883, Ecl ECM-2048
GB-6539-1  Lullaby In Blue               Dec F-3884
GB-6540-2  Gosh ! I Must Be Falling In Love  -
GB-6574-2  Wagon Wheels                  Dec F-3905
GB-6575-1  Coffee In The Morning (Kisses In The Night) -
GB-6576-2  Vamp Till Ready               Dec F-3906, ACL 1231
  NOTE:- Matrices GB-6541/6573 inclusive are by other artists on other dates.

Vocalist with Ray Noble and his Orchestra.
                              London, February 16, 1934.

OB-5899-2  It's Time To Say Goodnight    HMV B-6459
OB-5900-2  Midnight, The Stars And You   HMV B-6461, Vic 24700,ME MES-6816
OB-5901-1  This Little Piggie Went To Market  -

                              London, February 21, 1934.

OB-4791-2  Over On The Sunny Side        HMV B-6463
OB-4792-5  Wagon Wheels                  HMV B-6469

                              London, March 12, 1934.

OB-5936-1  Not Bad                       HMV B-6471, Vic 24619
OB-5937-1  What Now ?                    HMV B-6470, Vic 24711,ME MES-6816

Vocalist with Lew Stone and his Band at the Monseigneur Restaurant, London.
                              London, March 16, 1934.

TB-1133-2  In A Shelter From A Shower    Dec F-3942

                              London, March 23, 1934.

TB-1158-2  Because It's Love             Dec F-3942
TB-1159-1  It's Psychological            Rejected
TB-1160-1  Mauna Loa                     Dec F-3952

Vocalist with Ray Noble and his Orchestra.
                              London, April 5, 1934.

OB-6858-2  You Have Taken My Heart       HMV B-6477
OB-6859-2  One Morning In May            HMV B-6478, Enc 140
OB-6860-2  You Ought To Be In Pictures   HMV B-6477

Vocal, acc. by Monia Liter-p.                    London, April 9, 1934.

GB-6684-2   True                                 Dec F-3963, DFE-6245, ACL 1162
GB-6685-2   The Very Thought Of You              -          -         -
GB-6686-2   You Oughta Be In Pictures            Dec F-3956                -
GB-6687-2   Little Dutch Mill                               -    Ecl ECM-2048

Vocalist with the Bohemians (Orchestre Raymonde), dir. by Walter Goehr.
                                                 London, April 18, 1934.

CAX-7131-1  Wonder Bar - Film Selection, Part 1    Col DX-583
            (Al Bowlly sings a chorus of WONDER BAR and GOIN' TO HEAVEN ON A MULE)
CAX-7132-1  Wonder Bar - Film Selection, Part 2    -
            (Al Bowlly sings a chorus of DON'T SAY GOODNIGHT and WONDER BAR)

Vocalist with Ray Noble and his Orchestra.
                                                 London, April 21, 1934.

OB-6872-1   The Old Covered Bridge               HMV B-6484
OB-6873-2   Little Dutch Mill                    HMV B-6482
OB-6874-1   The Very Thought Of You                        -    7EG-8186,
                                                 Vic 24657, 20-2950, Enc 140

Vocalist with Lew Stone and his Band at the Monseigneur Restaurant, London.
                                                 London, April 24, 1934.

TB-1206-1   You're My Thrill                     Dec F-3980
TB-1208-1   Melody In Spring                     Dec F-3979
  NOTE:- Matrix TB-1207 has no vocal refrain.

                                                 London, April 25, 1934.

TB-1212-2   What Is There To Take Its Place ?    Dec F-5003
TB-1214-1   Lonely Feet                          Dec F-3985
TB-1215-2   Ending With A Kiss                   Dec F-3979
  NOTE:- Matrix TB-1213 has no vocal refrain.

Vocalist with Ray Noble and his Orchestra.
                                                 London, April 27, 1934.

OB-5981-2   She Loves Me Not                     HMV B-6485
OB-5982-2   After All, You're All I'm After                -    Enc 160
OB-5983-2   My Sweet                             HMV B-6484, Vic 25232

Vocalist with Lew Stone and his Band at the Monseigneur Restaurant, London.
                                                 London, May 3, 1934.

TB-1228-2   Hand In Hand                         Dec F-3985, ACL 1178
TB-1229-2   Riding On A Hay Cart Home            Dec F-5004
TB-1230-2   I Love You Truly                     Dec F-5003, ACL 1178

Vocalist with Ray Noble and his Orchestra.
                                                 London, May 31, 1934.

OB-6956-2   The Show Is Over                     HMV B-6492
OB-6957-1   I Love You Truly                               -    Vic 24806
OB-6958-2   Little Man, You've Had A Busy Day    HMV B-6491
OB-6959-1   Beat O' My Heart                               -
OB-6960-4   Night On The Desert                  HMV B-6496

Vocalist with Lew Stone and his Band at the Monseigneur Restaurant, London.
                                                 London, June 15, 1934.

TB-1311-2   Riptide                              Dec F-5017
TB-1312-2   Night On The Desert                            -
TB-1313-1   Beat O' My Heart                     Dec F-5018, ACL 1178
TB-1314-2   Easy Come - Easy Go                            -

Vocalist with Ray Noble and his Orchestra.

London, June 28, 1934.

| | | |
|---|---|---|
| OB-7428-2 | I'll String Along With You | HMV B-6503, Enc 140 |
| OB-7429-2 | Fair And Warmer | - |
| OB-7430-1 | Hold My Hand | HMV B-6499 |

London, July 2, 1934.

| | | |
|---|---|---|
| OB-7432-3 | Over My Shoulder | HMV B-6504, Vic 24720, Enc 140 |
| OB-7433-2 | When You've Got A Little Springtime | -    -    - |
| OB-7434-1-2 | Sweetheart Darlin' | Rejected |

London, July 6, 1934.

| | | |
|---|---|---|
| OB-7435-3 | Remember Me | HMV B-6508, ME MES-6816 |
| OB-7436-1 | Moon Country | HMV B-6507 |
| OB-7437-1 | Happy | - |

London, July 11, 1934.

| | | |
|---|---|---|
| OB-7441-2 | It's All Forgotten Now | HMV B-6509, Vic 24724,ME MES-6816 |
| OB-7442-1 | All I Do Is Dream Of You | HMV B-6508 |
| OB-7443-2 | Dreamy Serenade | HMV B-6510 |

Vocal, acc. by Monia Liter-p.          London, July 16, 1934.

| | | |
|---|---|---|
| TB-1394-1 | Madonna Mine | Dec F-5121, Ecl ECM-2048 |
| TB-1395-1 | It's All Forgotten Now | -         - |

Vocalist with Ray Noble and his Orchestra.

London, July 18, 1934.

| | | |
|---|---|---|
| OB-7448-2 | I Never Had A Chance | HMV B-6509 |
| OB-7449-2 | Lady Of Madrid | HMV B-6510, Vic 24724 |
| OB-7450-2 | Little Valley In The Mountains | HMV B-6512 |
| OB-7451-1 | Driftin' Tide | HMV B-6511, Vic 25006 |

Vocalist with Lew Stone and his Band at the Monseigneur Restaurant, London.
London, July 25, 1934.

| | | |
|---|---|---|
| TB-1420-2 | I Never Had A Chance | Dec F-5131, ACL 1147 |
| TB-1421-2 | Fare Thee Well | Dec F-5130, ACL 1178 |

London, August 1, 1934.

| | | |
|---|---|---|
| TB-1440-2 | With My Eyes Wide Open I'm Dreaming | Dec F-5172, Ecl ECM-2047 |
| TB-1441-2 | Rolling Home | - |

London, August 3, 1934.

| | | |
|---|---|---|
| TB-1434-1 | As Long As I Live | Dec F-5132, Ecl ECM-2047 |
| TB-1435-1 | I've Had My Moments | Dec F-5131 |
| TB-1449-1 | Straight From The Shoulder | Dec F-5158, Ecl ECM-2048 |
| TB-1450-1 | Looking For A Little Bit Of Blue | Dec F-5270 |
| TB-1451-2 | What A Little Moonlight Can Do | -         444, ACL 1178 |
| TB-1452-1 | Love In Bloom | Dec F-5158 |

NOTE:- The vocalist on matrices TB-1448 and TB-1453, also made at this session, is Nat Gonella. Matrices TB-1438, TB-1439 and TB-1442/7 inclusive are all by various other artists on other dates. They were probably allocated prior to the recording date.

Vocal, acc. by Monia Liter-p.          London, August 21, 1934.

| | | |
|---|---|---|
| TB-1495-2 | Isle Of Capri | Dec F-5188, Ch 40032 |
| TB-1496-2 | Judy | -         -    ACL 1204 |

Vocalist with Ray Noble and his Orchestra.
                                    London, August 24, 1934.

OEA-803-2  The Prize Waltz                      HMV B-6516
OEA-805-2  Grinzing                             HMV B-6519, Vic 24771
OEA-806-2  Freckle Face, You're Beautiful       HMV B-6512
  NOTE:- Matrix OEA-804 has no vocal refrain.

                                    London, August 30, 1934.

OEA-816-2  Isle Of Capri                        HMV B-6519, Vic 24771
OEA-817-1  Love (Wonderful Love)                HMV B-6514
OEA-818-2  Dreaming A Dream                      HMV B-6520, Vic 24850, Enc 160
OEA-819-2  Sing As We Go                         HMV B-6514

Vocal, acc. by O/Victor Young.      New York, October 30, 1934.

38923-A  If I Had A Million Dollars             Dec 293, F-5326, ACL 1204
38924-A  Be Still, My Heart                        -        -        -

Vocalist with Victor Young and his Orchestra.
                                    New York, November 2, 1934.

38948-A  Say When                               Dec 278
38949-A  When Love Comes Swingin' Along            -

Vocal, acc. by O/Ray Noble.         New York, January 12, 1935.

BS-87357-1  You And The Night And The Music     Vic 24855
BS-87358-1  Blue Moon                           Vic 24849
BS-87359-1  In A Blue And Pensive Mood             -        HMV B-8302, BD-230
BS-87360-1  A Little White Gardenia             Vic 24855     -         -7EG-8186

Vocalist with Ray Noble and his Orchestra.
                                    New York, February 9, 1935.

BS-87496-1  Soon                                Vic 24879, HMV BD-140,
                                                Cam CDN-5131
BS-87497-1  Clouds                              Vic 24865, HMV BD-147
BS-87498-1  Down By The River                   Vic 24879, LPV-536, LSA-3067,
                                                RD-7881, HMV BD-140

                                    New York, March 9, 1935.

BS-89301-1-2  Flowers For Madame                Vic 24865, HMV BD-213

Vocal, acc. by O/Ray Noble.         New York, March 15, 1935.

BS-89327-1  My Melancholy Baby                  Vic 25007, HMV B-8330, BD-228
BS-89328-1  Everything's Been Done Before       Vic 25004, HMV BD-226
BS-89329-1  You Opened My Eyes                     -        HMV B-8330, BD-228
BS-89330-1-2  Basin Street Blues                Vic 25007, HMV BD-226

Vocalist with Ray Noble and his Orchestra.
                                    New York, May 10, 1935.

BS-88963-2  Paris In Spring                     Vic 25040, HMV BD-192
BS-88964-2  Bon Jour, Mam'selle                    -         -

                                    New York, June 8, 1935.

BS-92229-1  Top Hat (w/Ray Noble and The Freshmen) Vic 25094, LPV-586, LSA-3067,
                                                RD-7881, HMV BD-247

                                    New York, June 10, 1935.

BS-92231-1  Piccolino                           Vic 25094, HMV BD-247
BS-92232-1  St Louis Blues                      Vic 25082, HMV BD-5004

New York, July 20, 1935.

BS-92747-1  Why Dream ?                        Vic 25104, LPV-536, LSA-3067,
                                              RD-7881, HMV BD-210
BS-92749-1  Why Stars Come Out At Night        Vic 25105      -      Cam CDN-5131
BS-92750-1  I Wished On The Moon               Vic 25104, HMV BD-211
   NOTE:- Matrix BS-92748 has a vocal refrain by the Freshmen, with Ray Noble.

Vocal, acc. by O/Ray Noble.        New York, September 18, 1935.

BS-95042-2  Roll Along, Prairie Moon           Vic 25142, HMV BD-295
BS-95043-1  Red Sails In The Sunset             -              -

Vocalist with Ray Noble and his Orchestra.
                              New York, November 14, 1935.

BS-98064-1  I'm The Fellow Who Loves You (w/The  Vic 25190
              Freshmen)
BS-98065-1  Where Am I ?                        Vic 25187, LPV-536, LSA-3067,
                                              RD-7881, HMV BD-5072
BS-98066-1  Dinner For One, Please James        Vic 25187, LPV-536, LSA-3067,
                                              RD-7881

                              New York, December 9, 1935.

BS-98359-1  With All My Heart                  Vic 25209, LPV-536, LSA-3067,
                                              RD-7881, HMV BD-5028
BS-98360-1  I Built A Dream One Day             Vic 25200
BS-98361-1  Somebody Ought To Be Told            -
BS-98362-1  A Beautiful Lady In Blue            Vic 25209

                              New York, January 23, 1936.

BS-98670-1  Let Yourself Go (w/The Freshmen)    Vic 25241, HMV BD-5047
BS-98672-1  Let's Face The Music And Dance       -              -
BS-98673-1  If You Love Me                      Vic 25240, HMV BD-5046
   NOTE:- Matrix BS-98671 has a vocal refrain by the Freshmen.

                              New York, March 19, 1936.

BS-99900-1  Yours Truly Is Truly Yours          Vic 25277, LPV-536, LSA-3067,
                                              RD-7881
BS-99901-1  Moonlight In Hilo                   Vic 25282
BS-99902-1  The Touch Of Your Lips              Vic 25277, LPV-536, LSA-3067,
                                              RD-7881, Cam CDN-5131
BS-99903-1  Blazin' The Trail (To My Home)      Vic 25282, HMV BD-5072

                              New York, May 25, 1936.

BS-101863-1  Empty Saddles                      Vic 25346, HMV BD-5095
BS-101864-1  Big Chief De Sota (w/Sterling Bose)   -      LPV-536, LSA-3067,
                                              RD-7881, HMV BD-5095
BS-101865-1  But Definitely                    Vic 25336, HMV BD-5091
BS-101866-1  When I'm With You                   -              -

Vocalist with Ray Noble and his London Orchestra.
                              London, August 24, 1936.

2EA-3847-1  Ray Noble Medley - Part 1 (Al Bowlly   HMV C-2872, Vic 36194
              sings a chorus of THE TOUCH OF YOUR LIPS)
2EA-3848-1  Ray Noble Medley - Part 2 (Al Bowlly     -              -
              sings a chorus of GOODNIGHT, SWEETHEART)

Vocalist with Ray Noble and his Orchestra.
                              New York, September 25, 1936.

BS-0744-1  Easy To Love                         Vic 25422, HMV BD-5147,
                                              Cam CDN-5131
BS-0745-1  I've Got You Under My Skin           As above
BS-0746-1  Let's Call A Heart A Heart           Vic 25428
BS-0747-1  One, Two, Button Your Shoe            -

New York, October 16, 1936.

```
BS-02159-1  Now                                   Vic 25448, HMV BD-5287
BS-02160-1  Little Old Lady                          -            -
BS-02161-1  There's Something In The Air          Vic 25459, HMV BD-5153
BS-02162-1  Where The Lazy River Goes By              -       LPV-536, LSA-3067,
                                                  RD-7881, HMV BD-5153
```

Vocal, acc. by small orchestra/? Ronnie Munro.
                        London, June 19, 1937.

```
OEA-5035-1  Carelessly                            HMV BD-434
OEA-5036-1  On A Little Dream Ranch                   -
```

                        London, July 5, 1937.

```
OEA-5048-1  Blue Hawaii                           HMV BD-440
OEA-5049-1  Sweet Is The Word For You                 -
```

Vocalist with Ronnie Munro and his Orchestra.
                        London, July 17, 1937.

```
OEA-5060-2  Le Touquet                            HMV BD-5242
OEA-5061-1  Vieni, Vieni                              -           Vic 25668
OEA-5062-2  Smile When You Say Goodbye            HMV BD-5248
OEA-5063-2  Hometown                                  -           BB B-7334
```

Vocalist with own orchestra (studio group).
                        New York, December 3, 1937.

```
BS-017457-1  I Can Dream, Can't I ?               BB B-7332, HMV BD-5363
BS-017458-1  Half Moon On The Hudson              BB B-7317      -
BS-017459-1  Every Day's A Holiday                BB B-7319
BS-017460-1  Sweet As A Song                      BB B-7317
BS-017461-1  Outside Of Paradise                  BB B-7319
BS-017462-1  Sweet Stranger                       BB B-7332
```

Vocalist with Maurice Winnick and his Orchestra.
                        London, December 29, 1937.

```
DTB-3472-1  Bei mir bist du schoen                Dec F-6591
DTB-3473-1  There's A Gold-Mine In The Sky        Dec F-6590
DTB-3474-1  Kiss Me Goodnight                     Dec F-6591
   NOTE:- Al Bowlly is not a member of the trio singing on matrix DTB-3471.
```

Vocal, acc. by O/Ronnie Munro.          London, January 4, 1938.

```
OEA-5953-2  Bei mir bist du schoen                HMV BD-493
OEA-5954-1  Marie                                     -
```

Vocalist with Sidney Lipton and his Orchestra.
                        London, January 13, 1938.

```
DTB-3495-1  The Lonesome Trail Ain't Lonesome Any  Dec F-6608
              More
DTB-3496-2  It's A Long, Long Way To Your Heart       -
DTB-3497-1  Souvenir Of Love                      Dec F-6653
DTB-3498-1  Trusting My Luck                          -
```

Vocalist with the New Mayfair Orchestra, dir. by Ronnie Munro.
                        London, January 14, 1938.

```
OEA-5983-1  Rosalie - Selection, Part 1 (Al Bowlly HMV BD-502
              sings a chorus of ROSALIE)
OEA-5984-1  Rosalie - Selection, Part 2 (Al Bowlly    -
              sings a chorus of IN THE STILL OF THE NIGHT)
```

AL BOWLLY (cont.)

Vocalist with Maurice Winnick and his Orchestra.
                                    London, January 20, 1938.

DTB-3509-1  Rosalie                             Dec F-6605
DTB-3510-1  In The Still Of The Night            -
DTB-3511-1  Once In A While                     Dec F-6599
  NOTE:- Al Bowlly is not a member of the trio singing on matrix DTB-3512.

Vocal, acc. by O/Ronnie Munro.         London, February 2, 1938.

OEA-5998-2  You're A Sweetheart                 HMV BD-503
OEA-5999-2  The Pretty Little Patchwork Quilt    -

Vocalist with Lew Stone and his Band.   London, February 4, 1938.

DTB-3547-1  I Double Dare You                   Dec F-6606, Ecl ECM-2048
DTB-3548-2  The Girl In The Alice Blue Gown     Dec F-6607
DTB-3549-1  Little Drummer Boy                   -
DTB-3550-2  You're A Sweetheart                 Dec F-6606

Vocalist with Mantovani and his Orchestra.
                                    London, March 4, 1938.

CA-16871-2  Something To Sing About             Col FB-1925
CA-16872-1  In My Little Red Book                -

Vocalist with Lew Stone and his Band.   London, March 21, 1938.

DTB-3604-1  Sweet Genevieve                     Dec F-6642
DTB-3605-1  In My Little Red Book                -
DTB-3606-1  Moonlight On The Highway            Dec F-6641
DTB-3607-1  Have You Ever Been In Heaven ?       -

Vocal, with his Crooners Choir, acc. by ? Ronnie Munro-p.
                                    London, April 1, 1938.

OEA-6192-1  Sweet As A Song                     HMV BD-543
OEA-6193-1  Sweet Someone                        -

Vocalist with Lew Stone and his Band.   London, April 21, 1938.

DTB-3634-1  By An Old Pagoda                    Dec F-6663
DTB-3635-2  Mama, I Wanna Make Rhythm           Dec F-6664
DTB-3636-1  In Santa Margherita                 Dec F-6663
DTB-3637-1  Ti-Pi-Tin                           Dec F-6664

Vocal, acc. by George Scott-Wood-pipe organ.
                                    London, May 25, 1938.

OEA-6329-1  Goodnight, Angel                    HMV BD-565
OEA-6330-1  When The Organ Played "Oh, Promise Me"   -
OEA-6331-1-2  Maria, My Own/Marta              Rejected
OEA-6332-1-2  Stormy Weather/Brother, Can You Spare   -
            A Dime ?

Vocalist with Maurice Winnick and his Orchestra.
                                    London, June 13, 1938.

DR-2731-1  When The Organ Played "Oh, Promise Me"  Dec F-6695
DR-2732-1  Somebody's Thinking Of You Tonight
DR-2734-1  My Heaven On Earth                   Dec F-6696
  NOTE:- Al Bowlly is not a member of the trio singing on matrix DR-2733.

Vocalist with Felix Mendelssohn and his Orchestra.
                                    London, July 1, 1938.

DR-2777-1  The Blackpool Walk                   Dec F-6726
DR-2778-1  The Girl In The Upstairs Flat         -
DR-2779-1  When Granny Wore Her Crinoline       Dec F-6727
DR-2780-1  I'm Saving The Last Waltz For You     -

Vocalist with Lew Stone and his Band.     London, August 12, 1938.

```
DR-2839-1  Down And Out Blues (w/Sid Colin)     Dec F-6743
DR-2840-1  Little Lady Make-Believe             Dec F-6744
DR-2841-1  I'm Sorry I Didn't Say I'm Sorry       -
DR-2842-1  You Couldn't Be Cuter                Dec F-6745
DR-2843-1  Just Let Me Look At You                -
```

London, August 15, 1938.

```
DR-2852-1  The Red Maple Leaves                 Dec F-6777
DR-2853-2  Music, Maestro, Please                 -
DR-2854-1  I Won't Tell A Soul                  Dec F-6763
DR-2855-1  Say Goodnight To Your Old-Fashioned    -
           Mother
```

Vocalist with Don Barrigo and his Hawaiian Swing.
London, August 22, 1938.

```
CE-9278-1  Star Dust                            Par rejected
```

Vocalist with Geraldo and his Orchestra. London, September 9, 1938.

```
OEA-6553-2  My Heart Is Taking Lessons          HMV BD-5402
OEA-6554-1  On The Sentimental Side               -
  NOTE:- Neither label has any reference to the existence of a vocal refrain.
```

Vocalist with Lew Stone and his Band.     London, September 27, 1938.

```
DR-2927-1  Now It Can Be Told                   Dec F-6795
DR-2928-1  On The Sentimental Side                -
```

Vocalist with Oscar Rabin and his Romany Band (at the Hammersmith Palais de Danse).
London, September 28, 1938.

```
R-2924-1  Proud Of You                          Rex 9384
```

Vocalist with Lew Stone and his Band.     London, October 3, 1938.

```
DR-2950-2  Everyone Should Have A Sweetheart    Dec F-6811
DR-2952-2  The Frog On The Water-Lily           Dec F-6812
  NOTE:- Al Bowlly does not sing on other titles from this session, but the label of
  Decca F-6811 credits the vocal refrain to Sid Colin.
```

Vocalist with Felix Mendelssohn and his Orchestra.
London, October 10, 1938.

```
DR-2982-1  Singers On Parade - Part 2 (Al Bowlly  Dec F-6831
           sings a chorus of LITTLE LADY MAKE-BELIEVE)
```

Vocalist with Geraldo and his Orchestra. London, October 14, 1938.

```
OEA-6596-1  In A Little Toy Sail Boat           HMV BD-5421
OEA-6597-1  Small Fry                             -
```

London, November 11, 1938.

```
OEA-7071-1  Never Break A Promise               HMV BD-5428
OEA-7072-1  When Mother Nature Sings Her Lullaby HMV BD-5427
OEA-7073-1  Penny Serenade                      HMV BD-5428
OEA-7074-1  Heart And Soul                      HMV BD-5427
```

Vocal, acc. by small "novelty" group.     London, November 11, 1938.

```
DR-3053-1  When Mother Nature Sings Her Lullaby  Dec F-6877
DR-3054-1  There's Rain In My Eyes                 -           ACL 1204
DR-3055-1  Al Bowlly Remembers - Part 1 (Intro.  Dec F-6916
           Lover, Come Back To Me/Dancing In The Dark)
DR-3056-1  Al Bowlly Remembers - Part 2 (Intro.    -                        Dear)
           I'm Gonna Sit Right Down And Write Myself A Letter/Auf Wiedersehen,  My
```

Vocalist with Lew Stone and his Band.      London, November 28, 1938.

```
DR-3119-1  All Ashore                             Dec F-6890
DR-3120-1  Penny Serenade                         -
DR-3121-1  Any Broken Hearts To Mend ?            Dec F-6891
DR-3122-1  Georgia's Gotta Moon                   -
```

Vocalist with Geraldo and his Orchestra.  London, December 3, 1938.

```
OEA-6965-1  Two Sleepy People                      HMV BD-5437
OEA-6966-1  Is That The Way To Treat A Sweetheart? HMV BD-5438
OEA-6967-1  Colorado Sunset                        -
OEA-6968-2  While A Cigarette Was Burning          HMV BD-5437
```

London, December 16, 1938.

```
OEA-7264-1  Any Broken Hearts To Mend ?            HMV BD-5443
OEA-7265-1  Summer's End                           -
OEA-7266-1  My Own                                 HMV BD-5444
OEA-7267-1  You're As Pretty As A Picture          -
```

London, January 10, 1939.

```
OEA-7272-1  They Say                               HMV BD-5448
OEA-7273-1  If Ever A Heart Was In The Right Place -
OEA-7274-1  One Day When We Were Young             HMV BD-5449
OEA-7275-2  I'm In Love With Vienna                -
```

London, February 3, 1939.

```
OEA-7293-1  Grandma Said                           HMV BD-5457
OEA-7294-1  Deep In A Dream                        -
OEA-7295-1  You're A Sweet Little Headache         HMV BD-5458
```

Vocalist with Reginald Williams and his Futurists.
                                          London, February 8, 1939.

```
CA-17345-1  I'm Madly In Love With You             Col FB-2167
```

Vocal, acc. by O/Ronnie Munro.            London, February 14, 1939.

```
OEA-7298-1  Romany                                 HMV BD-666
OEA-7299-1  Lonely                                 -
OEA-7562-1  I Miss You In The Morning              HMV BD-673
OEA-7563-1  Violin In Vienna                       -
```
   NOTE:- Matrices OEA-7300/7561 inclusive are by other artists on other dates.

Vocalist with Geraldo and his Orchestra.  London, March 7, 1939.

```
OEA-7611-1  The Same Old Story                     HMV BD-5467
OEA-7612-1  Could Be                               HMV BD-5468
OEA-7613-1  Between A Kiss And A Sigh              -
```

London, April 4, 1939.

```
OEA-7628-1  To Mother, With Love                   HMV BD-5473
OEA-7629-2  Waltz Of My Heart                      Rejected
OEA-7630-1  Thanks For Everything                  HMV BD-5472
OEA-7631-1  I Miss You In The Morning              HMV BD-5473
```
   NOTE:- Matrix OEA-7629-1, issued on HMV BD-5472, has no vocal refrain.

Vocalist with Reginald Williams and his Futurists.
                                          London, May 5, 1939.

```
CA-17438-1  Small Town                             Col FB-2226
CA-17439-1  What Do You Know About Love ?          Col FB-2227
```

Vocal, acc. by O/Ronnie Munro.                London, May 11, 1939.

| OEA-7854-2 | What Do You Know About Love ? | HMV BD-706 |
| OEA-7855-1 | Hey Gypsy, Play Gypsy | HMV BD-709 |
| OEA-7856-1 | South Of The Border | HMV BD-706 |
| OEA-7857-1 | Dark Eyes | HMV BD-709 |

Vocalist with Bram Martin and his Band.   London, June 8, 1939.

| R-3678-1 | The Waves Of The Ocean Are Whisp'ring Goodnight | Rex 9590 |

Vocal, acc. by O/Ronnie Munro.                London, October 5, 1939.

| OEA-8111-1 | Moon Love | HMV BD-762 |
| OEA-8112-1 | Au Revoir But Not Goodbye | - |
| OEA-8113-1 | A Man And His Dream | HMV BD-776 |
| OEA-8114-1 | Ridin' Home | - |

The following item is entered in the HMV recording files.  It is not known if it is a genuine Al Bowlly recording.

BOWLLY-SUYMAN ORCHESTRA.                London, December 11, 1939.

OAS-217-1-2  Eken mij ou guitar              No issue number shown

Vocal, acc. by O/Ronnie Munro.                Londom, December 21, 1939.

| OEA-8334-1 | Bella Bambina | HMV BD-808 |
| OEA-8335-1 | Over The Rainbow | - |
| OEA-8336-1 | Somewhere In France With You | HMV BD-805 |
| OEA-8337-1 | Give Me My Ranch | - |

London, February 15, 1940.

| OEA-8475-1 | It's A Lovely Day Tomorrow | HMV BD-828 |
| OEA-8476-1 | Careless | - |

Vocalist with Maurice Winnick and his Orchestra.
London, March 1, 1940.

| OEA-8382-1 | Chatterbox | HMV BD-5572 |
| OEA-8383-1 | When You Wish Upon A Star | HMV BD-5573 |
| OEA-8384-1 | Turn On The Old Music Box | - |

Vocal, acc. by O/Ronnie Munro.                London, March 7, 1940.

| OEA-8500-1 | Dreaming | HMV BD-834 |
| OEA-8505-1 | A Little Rain Must Fall | HMV BD-827 |
| OEA-8506-1 | When You Wear Your Sunday Blue | - |
| OEA-8551-1 | Walkin' Thru' Mockin' Bird Lane | HMV BD-834 |

NOTE:- Matrices OEA-8501/4 and OEA-8507/50 inclusive are by other artists on  other dates.

Vocalist with Maurice Winnick and his Orchestra.
London, March 26, 1940.

| OEA-8570-1 | Who's Taking You Home Tonight ? | HMV BD-5582 |
| OEA-8571-1 | Arm In Arm | HMV BD-5583, 120944 (Canadian) |
| OEA-8572-1 | There's A Boy Coming Home On Leave | -        - |
| OEA-8573-1 | My Capri Serenade | HMV BD-5582 |

Vocalist with Ken "Snakehips" Johnson and his West Indian Orchestra and the Henderson Twins.                London, April 24, 1940.

| OEA-8582-1 | Blow, Blow, Thou Winter Wind | HMV BD-5592 |
| OEA-8583-1 | It Was A Lover And His Lass | - |

Vocalist with Macari and his Orchestra.   London, May 4, 1940.

CAR-5781-1-2  It's A Blue World                    RZ rejected
CAR-5782-1-2  This Year's Roses                    -

Vocal duets with Jimmy Mesene, acc. by their own guitars.
                                        London, July 18, 1940.

OEA-8840-1  Make Love With A Guitar/When I Dream   HMV BD-857
              Of Home
OEA-8841-2  Make-Believe Island/The Woodpecker Song

                                        London, September 12, 1940.

OEA-8741-2  Turn Your Money In Your Pocket/I'll     HMV BD-865
              Never Smile Again/We'll Go Smiling Along
OEA-8742-2  I'm Stepping Out With A Memory Tonight/  -
              I Haven't Time To Be A Millionaire

                                        London, December 6, 1940.

OEA-9058-1  Ferry Boat Serenade                     HMV BD-892
OEA-9059-1  Only Forever                            -

                                        London, April 2, 1941.

OEA-9226-1  Nicky The Greek (Has Gone)              HMV BD-922
OEA-9227-1  When That Man Is Dead And Gone          -

## LUCIENNE BOYER

French cabaret artist who made several very successful appearances in New York during
the years immediately prior to World War II; made several films in France, notably
LA BELLE SAISON (1937).

Vocal, acv. by G. van Parys-p.          Paris, c. October 27, 1926.

WL-307-2  Ca ne s'apprend pas                       Col D-6218
WL-308-1  Tu me demandes si je t'aime               -
          Je l'aimais tant                          Col D-6291
          Qui m'aurait dit                          -

  Acc. by Maurice Touhas-vn/Rex Evans-p.  Paris, January 18, 1928.

WL-861-1-2  L'Enchainee                             Col ?
WL-862-1-2  Marie Rose                              -

  Acc. by O/B. Codolban.                Paris, c. January, 1930.

WL-2175-1  Parle-moi....                            Col DF-60
WL-2176-1  Dans la fumee (Visions In The Smoke)     Col DF-61, DB-673, 205-M
WL-2177-1  Parlez-moi d'amour (Speak To Me Of Love)   -        -        -
WL-2178-1  Prenez mes roses                         Col DF-60

  Acc. by O/Costica Bagiac.             Paris, late April, 1930.

WL-2341-2  Attends                                  Col DF-173, 235-M
WL-2343-2  Le coup dur                              -         -
           Gigolette                                Col DF-388
           C'est un chagrin de femme !              -

  Acc. by L. Khotinoff-p.               Paris, c. September, 1930.

WL-2496-1  La Belle                                 Col DF-882

  Acc. by O/Iza Volpin.                 Paris, c. December, 1930.

WL-2824-1  Desir                                    Col DF-538
WL-2825-1  Ah ! pourquoi mens-tu ?                  Col DF-537
WL-2826-1  Les filles qui la nuit....               Col DF-538
WL-2827-1  Le plus joli reve !                      Col DF-537

Paris, c. October, 1931.

WL-3340-1  Le train du reve                    Col DF-882

The following titles were probably at or soon after the above session.

Je ne savais pas                    Col DFX-146
Des mots nouveaux                    -

Paris, c. March, 1932.

CL-3666-1  La Barque d'Yves                    Col DF-870
CL-3667-2  Ne dis pas toujours                 -            DB-917
CL-3668-1  Quand tu seras dans mes bras        Col DF-877   -
CL-3669-1  L'amour vient....et s'en va          -

Paris, June-July, 1932.

CL-3837-1  Fait semblant de m'aimer            Col DF-1039
CL-3838-1  Si petite                           Col DF-935, DB-1385, 228-M
CL-3840-1  Sans toi                             -         -         -

Acc. by Jean Delettre-p.              Paris, August, 1932.

CL-3936-1  C'est pas la peine                    Col DF-1039

Acc. by O/Iza Volpin.                 Paris, August, 1932.

CL-3938-1  Ballade                             Col DF-1006
CL-3939-1  Landerirette                         -

Paris, c. January, 1933.

CL-4173-4  Tourne et vire                      Col DF-1157, 229-M
CL-4174-3  J'ai laisse mon coeur (I've Lost My  Col DF-1058, DB-1386, 230-M
           Heart)
CL-4179-1  Parle-moi d'autre chose (There's No   -         -         -
           More You Can Say)
CL-4180-1  Moi, j'crache dans l'eau             Col DF-1157, 229-M

Paris, May-June, 1933.

CL-4362-1  Viens danser quand meme             Col DF-1242
CL-4363-1  Solitude                             -
CL-4364-1  L'Etoile d'Amour                    Col DF-1394, 206-M

The following titles were probably recorded about this time.

CLX-1750-1  Nuits blanches                     Col DFX-166

Acc. by Michel Emer-p.

CLX-1751-1  Dans le petit cafe du coin         Col DFX-166

Acc. by O/Iza Volpin.                 Paris, c. June, 1933.

CL-4395-3  J'ai reve de t'aimer                Col DF-1394, 206-M

Acc. by Lucien Hubert-p.              Paris, c. August, 1933.

CL-4453-3  C'est ma faute                      Col DF-1424

Acc. by O/Iza Volpin.                 Paris, September, 1933.

CL-4516-1  D'amour en amour                    Col DF-1336
CL-4517-1  La Voyageuse                         -

Paris, December, 1933.

CL-4614-1  Son regard                                    Col DF-1424
CL-4615-1  Dites-moi je vous aime                        Col DF-1529


Acc. by Lucien Hubert-p.                  Paris, May, 1934.


CL-4858-1  L'Hotel des Amours Faciles                    Col DF-1529


Acc. by O/Iza Volpin.                     Paris, September, 1934.


CL-5010-2  Comme une femme                               Col DF-1532
CL-5011-2  Beaucoup                                      Col DF-1650
CL-5012-2  Rien, rien, rien                              Col DF-1532
CL-5013-2  Un amour comme le notre                       Col DF-1650


Acc. by studio orchestra.                 New York, November 2, 1934.


16295-2  Is It The Singer Or Is It The Song ?    Col 2971-D, DC-239
16296-2  Hands Across The Table                        -           -


Acc. by O/Iza Volpin.                     Paris, c. July, 1935.


CL-5425-3  Mon ami le vent                              Col DF-1760
CL-5426-3  Ta main (Hands Across The Table)              -
CL-5427-1  Mais si tu pars                              Col DF-1804
CL-5428-1  Pourquoi rever                                -


The following session probably took place about this time, under the direction  of
Iza Volpin.


           Chez moi                                     Col DF-1815
           En se regardant                               -


Acc. by Alexandre Grunberg-p.             Paris, c. August, 1935.


CL-5459-1  Depart                                       Col DF-1816
CL-5460-1  Mon petit lit d'enfant                        -


Acc. by O/Iza Volpin.                     Paris, c. January, 1936.


CL-5735-4  Le Tango des Filles                          Col DF-1918
CL-5736-3  L'Hotel du Clair de Lune                      -
CL-5737-3  Les prenoms effaces                          Col DF-1950
CL-5738-1  Estampe Marocaine                             -


Acc. by studio orchestra.                 New York, March 2, 1936.

CO-18745-1  This Is The Kiss Of Romance                 Col 3124-D, DC-295
CO-18746-1  It's A Thrill All Over Again                Col 3123-D
CO-18747-1  I Found A Bit Of Paris In The Heart           -           -
            Of Old New York
CO-18748-1  Dancing With My Darling                     Col 3124-D

Acc. by O/Iza Volpin.                    Paris, December, 1936.

CL-5997-1  Traversee                             Col DF-2030
CL-5998-3  C'est toujours la meme chanson        Col DF-2079


                                         Paris, December, 1936-January, 1937.


CL-6003-4  Mon Rendez-vous                        Col DF-2079
CL-6004-1  Parle-moi de toi                       Col DF-2030


    Acc. by O/Wal-Berg, with chorus.     Paris, c. August, 1937.

CL-6270-1  La Chanson des Quatz' Arts ("La Belle   Col DF-2171
              Saison")
CL-6271-1  C'est a Robinson ("La Belle Saison")     -
CL-6272-1  Pour toi ("La Belle Saison")            Col DF-2172
CL-6273-1  La Vagabonde ("La Belle Saison")        -


                                         Paris, October, 1937.


CL-6374-1  La Romance du Printemps (w/Pils and    Col DF-2221
              Tabet) ("La Belle Saison")
CL-6375-1  Chez nous (w/Jacques Pils) ("La Belle   -
              Saison")


    Acc. by O/Iza Volpin.                Paris, June, 1938.

CL-6747-1  Mon ami                               Col DF-2416
CL-6748
CL-6749
CL-6750-1  Entraineuse                           Col DF-2416

    Acc. by studio orchestra.            Location unknown (? London),
                                         c. July, 1938.

CM-509-1   Je t'aime                             Col        DB-1839
CM-510-1   Embrasse-moi                                     -


                                         Paris, c. October, 1939.


CL-7146-1  Tommy et la petite Francaise          Col        DB-1914
CL-7147-1  Mon p'tit Kaki (Lettre de femme)                 -


Lucienne Boyer continued to record for Columbia after the war, and also for Decca.

Daughter of American actor-manager William A. Brady; b. 1893; studied singing at the
Boston Conservatory of Music, appeared in several operettas and Gilbert and Sullivan productions before becoming a straight actress in 1909.  First film 1915; made
many silent films as a "vamp" (BETSY ROSS, 1917; WOMAN AND WIFE, 1918; A DARK LAN-
TERN, 1919) and even a film version of LA BOHEME (1916); returned to stage career,
but made several talkies between 1933 (WHEN LADIES MEET) and 1939 (YOUNG MR. LIN-
COLN), such as THE GAY DIVORCE (1934), THREE SMART GIRLS (1937) and IN OLD CHICAGO
(1938).  She died on October 28, 1939.

Dialogues with Tom Powers.                    New York, February 8, 1931.

BVE-64675-1  Sham (made on Victor Talking Machine 7776)
BVE-64676-1  Sham (made on RCA Machine No. 1)

It is probable that neither of these recordings was intended for issue.

## BOBBY  BREEN

B. 1927; a star at 8 with Eddie Cantor on coast-to-coast radio, and later in  films,
such as RAINBOW ON THE RIVER (1936), HAWAII CALLS (1938), FISHERMAN'S WHARF,  WAY
DOWN SOUTH (1939); successful post-war tours of Great Britain, Australia, New Zealand and South Africa as cabaret entertainer.

Vocal, acc. by studio orchestra.          New York, May 11, 1936.

61100-A  It's A Sin To Tell A Lie                Dec 798, F-6086
61101-A  Let's Sing Again                         -       -

   Acc. by O/Victor Young.                 Los Angeles, September 4, 1936.

DLA-598-A  M-O-T-H-E-R (A Word That Means The    Dec 973, F-6177
              World To Me)
DLA-599-A  The Rosary                             -       -

                                          Los Angeles, November 2, 1936.

DLA-633-A  Flower Song (Film "Rainbow On The River")Dec 1053, F-6301
DLA-634-A  Rainbow On The River (Film "Rainbow On    -       -
              The River")

   Acc. by film studio orchestra, dubbed from film soundtrack.
                                          Hollywood, June 29, 1937.

PBS-09557-1  My Camp Fire Dreams (w/St. Luke's    BB B-7168, HMV BD-480
                Choristers) (Film "Make A Wish")

   Acc. by O/Hugo Reisenfeld.              Hollywood, August 20, 1937.

PBS-09649-1  Make A Wish (Film "Make A Wish")     BB B-7158, HMV BD-480
PBS-09650-1  Music In My Heart                    BB -
PBS-09651-1  Gee, But It's Great To Meet A Friend  BB B-7168
                (From Your Home Town)

   Acc. by film studio orchestra, dubbed from film soundtrack.
                                          Hollywood, October 28, 1937.

PBS-09767-1  Hawaii Calls (Film "Hawaii Calls")   Rejected
PBS-09768-1  Macushla                             BB B-7330
PBS-09769-1  Down Where The Trade Winds Blow (Film   -      HMV BD-573
                "Hawaii Calls")

                                          Hollywood, November 2, 1937.

PBS-09768-2  Macushla                             Vic rejected

                                          Hollywood, November 3, 1937.

PBS-09767-2  Hawaii Calls (Film "Hawaii Calls")   BB B-7320, HMV BD-573

Hollywood, November 4, 1937.

PBS-09789-1  Song Of The Islands (w/Max Terr's     Vic rejected
             Chorus) (Film "Hawaii Calls")

  Acc. by O/Raymond Paige.              Hollywood, November 10, 1937.

PBS-09769-2  Down Where The Trade Winds Blow       Rejected
             (Film "Hawaii Calls")
PBS-09789-2  Song Of The Islands (w/Max Terr's     BB B-7320
             Chorus) (Film "Hawaii Calls")

  Acc. by O/Harry Sosnik.              Los Angeles, April 22, 1938.

DLA-1270-A  Sleep, My Baby, Sleep                  Dec 1804, F-6747
DLA-1271-A  In A Little Dutch Kindergarten (Down      -        -
            By The Zuider Zee)

  Acc. by O/Victor Young.              Los Angeles, July 6, 1938.

DLA-1299-A  Happy As A Lark (Film "Breaking The    Dec 1950, F-6951
            Ice")
DLA-1300-A  Put Your Heart In A Song (Film "Break- Dec 1949, F-6950
            ing The Ice")
DLA-1301-A  The Sunny Side Of Things (Film "Break- Dec 1950, F-6951
            ing The Ice")
DLA-1302-A  Telling My Troubles To A Mule (Film    Dec 1949, F-6950
            "Breaking The Ice")

  Acc. by Eddie Dunstedter-pipe organ.  Los Angeles, February 18, 1939.

DLA-1709-A  Ave Maria (Schubert)                   Dec 2496, F-7303
DLA-1710-A  Largo (Ombra mai fu) ("Xerxes" - Handel)   -        -
DLA-1711-A  Blue Italian Waters (Film "Fisherman's Dec 2353, F-7113
            Wharf")
DLA-1712-A  Fisherman's Chantie (Film "Fisherman's    -        -
            Wharf")

## ELIZABETH BRICE

Stage partner of Charles King, q.v., whose only records without him are those  shown
  below. Greatest success was SLIM PRINCESS (Globe, N.Y., January 2, 1911).

Vocal, acc. by O/Walter B. Rogers.     New York, February 17, 1911.

B-9960-1  Lovie Joe                                Vic 5838

  Acc. by O/Charles A. Prince.          New York, April 20, 1917.

77000-3  Oh Johnny, Oh Johnny, Oh !                Col A-2265

## FANNY BRICE

B. New York, October 29, 1891; no relation to Elizabeth Brice, but the latter's solo
  LOVIE JOE was actually popularized by Fanny Brice.  Flo Ziegfeld discovered her as
  a teenager playing small parts, put her into FOLLIES OF 1910 (Jardin de Paris, New
  York, June 20, 1910), then a year later into FOLLIES OF 1911; in many other  Ziegfeld FOLLIES between 1920 and 1923.  In vaudeville in London, 1913; succeeded  the
  star of NOBODY HOME, Adele Rowland, Princess Theatre, November, 1915; in two Schubert FOLLIES produced after Ziegfeld's death in 1932; first film MY MAN, 1928; was
  very successful in Billy Rose's CRAZY QUILT, 1931 (m. him, her third husband); began radio career in thirties, very popular in character of Baby Snooks; d. 1951.

Vocal, acc. by O/Charles A. Prince.    New York, February 18, 1916.

46427-  I Don't Know Whether To Do It Or Not     Col A-1973
46428-  If We Could Only Take Her Word - Part 1  Col A-2122
46429-  If We Could Only Take Her Word - Part 2     -
46430-  Becky Is Back In The Ballet              Rejected

Acc. by O/Rosario Bourdon.              Camden, N. J., November 8, 1921.

B-25751-3  Second-Hand Rose                 Vic 45263, LPV-561,LSA-3076,
                                            LX-997, X LVA-1006
B-25752-6  My Man                           Vic 45263, 449-0010, LP-6804,
                                            WCT-1112, X LVA-1006, Bm 1016,
                                            Veritas 107

                                        Camden, N. J., November 15, 1921.

B-25762-3  Oh How I Hate That Fellow Nathan    Vic 45303
B-25763-1-2-3-4  Irish-Jewish Jubilee          Rejected

                                        Camden, N. J., November 18, 1921.

B-25769-3  I'm An Indian                    Vic 45303, LPV-580, LSA-3086,
                                            Veritas 107

                                        Camden, N. J., July 13, 1922.

B-26588-1-2-3  On The Shores Of The Rockaway    Rejected
B-26599-3  Becky Is Back In The Ballet          Vic 45323, LPV-561, LSA-3076

                                        Camden, N. J., July 14, 1922.

B-25763-5-6-7  Irish-Jewish Jubilee         Rejected
B-26588-4-5  On The Shores Of The Rockaway    -
B-26800-3  The Sheik Of Avenue B            Vic 45323

Acc. by O/Nat Shilkret, or by Nat Shilkret-p where shown.
                                 New York, December 20, 1927.

BVE-25752-7  My Man (Film "My Man")         Vic 21168, LPV-561, LSA-3076
BVE-41187-3  Mrs. Cohen At The Beach - Part 1   Vic 21211    -        -
             - pNS
BVE-41190-2  The Song Of The Sewing Machine    Vic 21168    -        -

                                        New York, December 21, 1927.

BVE-41194-1  Mrs. Cohen At The Beach - Part 2   Vic 21211, LPV-561, LSA-3076

                                        New York, December 22, 1927.

BVE-25752-11 My Man (Film "My Man")         Vic 21168, Cam CAL-795
BVE-41199-1-2  Is Something The Wrong With Otto    Rejected
               Kahn ?
BVE-41500-1-2  Pascha                           -

Acc. by O/Leonard Joy.                  New York, December 14, 1928.

BVE-49260-2  If You Want The Rainbow (You Must    Vic 21815, HMV B-3004, X LVA-1006
             Have The Rain) (Film "My Man")
BVE-49261-2  I'd Rather Be Blue Over You (Than    Vic LPV-561, LSA-3076
             Happy With Somebody Else ) (Film "My Man")
BVE-49261-3  I'd Rather Be Blue Over You (Than    Vic 21815, HMV B-2975, X LVA-1006
             Happy With Somebody Else) (Film "My Man")

                                        New York, December 17, 1928.

BVE-25752-12 My Man (Film "My Man")         Vic 21168, HMV B-2975
BVE-49261-4-5-6  I'd Rather Be Blue Over You    Rejected
             (Than Happy With Somebody Else) (Film "My Man")

                                        New York, January 15, 1930.

BVE-57995-1  When A Woman Loves A Man (Film "Be    X LVA-1006
             Yourself")
BVE-57995-3  When A Woman Loves A Man          Vic 22310, HMV B-3516
BVE-57996-1  Cooking Breakfast For The One I Love   X LVA-1006
BVE-57996-3  Cooking Breakfast For The One I Love   Vic 22310,LPV-538,LPV-561,LSA-3074
             (Film "Be Yourself")              LSA-3076, RD-7869, HMV B-3516

B. Copenhagen, Denmark, December 24, 1895; r.n. Carl Pederson, under which he became a famous sporting figure in Denmark (welter-weight boxer, etc.) Stage debut September, 1916 as dancer; London debut May 1921 in vaudeville; starred in THE APACHE at the London Palladium, February 14, 1927; first film THE RING (1928); great success on stage in WONDER BAR (Savoy, London, December 5, 1930); best-remembered as film actor and singer in SONG OF SOHO (1929), made in England, and ALL THE KING'S HORSES (1935), made in U.S.A. New York stage debut November, 1936 in New Amsterdam Theatre production of FORBIDDEN MELODY. Also appeared in London revival(1923) of THE MERRY WIDOW. The following are his English and American recordings; he did a number of records in Swedish in Stockholm between 1918 and 1922. D. 1958.

Vocal, acc. by unknown p.                    Hayes, Middlesex, February 28, 1927.

Yy-10224-1   When The Love-Bird Leaves The Nest        Zon 2901
Yy-10225-1-2 Let Me Hold Your Hand, Dear ("The         Rejected
             Apache")

                                             Hayes, Middlesex, March 8, 1927.

Yy-10225-3   Let Me Hold Your Hand, Dear ("The         Zon 2901
             Apache")
Yy-10257-    Since I Found You                         Zon 2902
Yy-10258-    Sweet Lady                                -

   Acc. by O/Ray Noble.             Small Queen's Hall, London, Dec. 11, 1929.

Bb-18470-2   Camille (Film "Song Of Soho")            HMV B-3295
Bb-18471-3   There's Something About You That's        -
             Different (Film "Song Of Soho")

   Acc. by t/as/p/g.                         London, August 20, 1930.

MB-1721-     It's You I Love                          Dec F-1893
MB-1722-     Why ?                                     -
MB-1723-2    Oh ! Donna Clara                         Dec F-1927
MB-1724-2    Collette                                  -

   Acc. by studio orchestra.                 London, October 13, 1930.

GB-2041-1   On The Sunny Side Of The Street           Dec F-2006
GB-2042-1-2 Dancing With Tears In My Eyes             Rejected
GB-2043-2   I Still Get A Thrill Thinking Of You      Dec F-2262
GB-2044-1   Little White Lies                         Dec F-2006

                                             London, November 30, 1930.

GB-2338-3   I've Got A Plan About You ("Wonder Bar")Dec F-2127
GB-2339-1   I'll Believe In Love ("Wonder Bar")       -
GB-2340-1   Tell Me I'm Forgiven ("Wonder Bar")      Dec F-2128
GB-2341-1   Wonder Bar ("Wonder Bar")                 -

                                             London, March 4, 1931.

GB-2710-1-2  Blame It On The Moonlight               Rejected
GB-2711-1    Reaching For The Moon                   Dec F-2251
GB-2713-2    When Your Hair Has Turned To Silver      -
GB-2714-     Leave A Little Smile                    Dec F-2262
   NOTE:- Matrix GB-2712 is not by Carl Brisson.

                                             London, June 29, 1931.

GB-2938-2   Elizabeth (in English and German)        Dec F-2397
            ("Wonder Bar")
GB-2939-3   I Surrender, Dear                          -
GB-2940-1-2-3  You're Twice As Nice As The Girl      Rejected
            In My Dreams

London, October 4, 1931.

GB-3361-    Love Is Like That (What Can You Do ?)    Dec F-2591
GB-3362-2   Whistling In The Dark                     Dec F-2579
GB-3363-2   Time Alone Will Tell                      -
GB-3364-    I'm Thru' With Love                       Dec F-2591

London, November 22, 1931.

GB-3626-    Under Your Window Tonight                 Dec F-2709
GB-3627-3   For The Sake Of The Days Gone By          Dec F-2733
GB-3628-    Nevertheless                              Dec F-2709
GB-3629-2   Was It The Moon, Or Love ?                Dec F-2733

Acc. by O/Alfredo Campoli.          London, February 9, 1932.

GB-3946-2   But Not Tonight                           Dec F-2821
GB-3947-2   An Old Spanish Tango                      -
GB-3948-2   Maxim's - Part 1 ("The Merry Widow")      Dec F-2820
GB-3949-1   Maxim's - Part 2 ("The Merry Widow")      -

Acc. by studio orchestra.          London, May 8, 1932.

GB-4461-    Was That The Human Thing To Do ?          Dec F-2982
GB-4462-    Try To Remember                           -
GB-4463-1   Let Me Hold Your Hand, Dear ("The         Dec F-3098
              Apache")
GB-4464-1   I Kiss Your Hand, Madame                  -

London, June 6, 1932.

GB-4553-    My Mom                                    Dec F-3011
GB-4554-    The Voice In The Old Village Choir        Dec F-3005
GB-4555-    Every Day Can't Be A Sunday               -
GB-4556-    I'm So Alone With The Crowd               Dec F-3011

London, October 18, 1932.

GB-5042-    We're A Couple Of Soldiers, My Baby       Dec F-3236
              And Me
GB-5043-1   A Bed-Time Story                          Dec F-3230
GB-5044-1   Silver Hair And Heart Of Gold             -
GB-5045-    While We Danced At The Mardi Gras         Dec F-3236

London, October 18, 1933.

GB-6203-2   Dinner At Eight                           Dec F-3701
GB-6204-2   Goodnight, Little Girl Of My Dreams       -
GB-6209-1-2 Thanks                                    Rejected
  NOTE:- Matrices GB-6205/8 inclusive are not by Carl Brisson.

London, November 21, 1933.

GB-6209-3   Thanks                                    Dec F-3759
GB-6354-2   A Crown Prince Of Arcadia/If I Could      -
              Only Find Her ("The Prince Of Arcadia")

London, January 1, 1934.

GB-6446-1   Give Her A Little Kiss (And Leave The     Dec F-3968
              Rest To The Girl) (Film "Two Hearts In Waltz Time")
GB-6447-2   Two Hearts That Beat In Waltz Time        -
              (Film "Two Hearts In Waltz Time")
GB-6448-1   In Old Vienna (Film "Two Hearts In        Dec F-3969
              Waltz Time")
GB-6449-2   Your Eyes So Tender (Film "Two Hearts     -
              In Waltz Time")

Acc. by Jimmie Grier and his Orchestra. Los Angeles, April 18, 1934.

LA-164-A  Live And Love Tonight                    Br 6887, Dec F-5014
LA-165-A  Cocktails For Two                           -          -        F-6997,
                                                   Epic L2N-6072

                                    Los Angeles, February 11, 1935.

LA-1003-B  Dancing The Viennese (Film "All The    Br 7398, Dec F-5495
             King's Horses")
LA-1004-A  A Little White Gardenia (Film "All The  Br 7397       -        F-6997
             King's Horses")
LA-1005-A  Be Careful, Young Lady (Film "All The   Br 7398, Dec F-5494
             King's Horses")
LA-1006-A  The King Can Do No Wrong (Film "All The Br 7397       -
             King's Horses")

   Acc. by Mahlon Merrick and his Music.  Los Angeles, July 13, 1935.

LA-1058-A-B  In A Little Gypsy Tea Room            Br rejected
LA-1059-A-B  Flowers For Madame                       -
LA-1060-A-B  Bonjour, Mam'selle                       -

   Acc. by O/? Victor Young.            Los Angeles, November 19, 1935.

DLA-268-  Fatal Fascination  (Film "Ship Cafe")   Dec F-5839
DLA-269-  Change Your Mind (Film "Ship Cafe")        -

   Acc. by studio orchestra.            London, March 4, 1939.

DR-3376-1  While A Cigarette Was Burning           Dec F-6996
DR-3377-2  The Seven-Fifteen To Dreamland             -

   Acc. by two pianos.                  London, January 4, 1940.

DR-4173-1-2  Scatterbrain                          Rejected
DR-4174-1  Where Or When                           Dec F-7352

                                    London, February 16, 1940.

DR-4173-3  Scatterbrain                            Dec F-7352

## JAMES BROCKMAN

B. December 8, 1886; vaudeville comedian and composer of many hit  songs, among  the
most memorable being I'M FOREVER BLOWING BUBBLES (1919). FEATHER YOUR NEST (1920),
and I FAW DOWN AND GO 'BOOM !' (1929). D. Santa Monica, Calif., May 22, 1967.

Vocal, acc. by studio orchestra.      New York, 1907-1909, issued as shown.

        Marianina                             Ed 9712 (December, 1907)
        Mariutch                              Ed 9730 (January, 1908)
        Garibaldi                             Ed 9750 (February, 1908)
        Moolburri                             Ed 9776 (March, 1908)
        Abie, Take An Example From Your Fa'der Ed 10165  (July, 1909)

## SHELTON BROOKS

Canadian Negro composer of such very popular and long-lived songs as SOME OF   THESE
DAYS (1910), THE DARKTOWN STRUTTERS' BALL (1915) and WALKIN' THE DOG (1917);  born
Amesburg, Ontario, May 4, 1886.    In the original PLANTATION REVUE on Broadway in
1922, with Florence Mills; also authored and produced many comedy sketches,  which
were recorded; toured Europe with Lew Leslie's BLACKBIRDS, 1923; took part in Royal
Command Performance before H.M. King George V.
Speech with supporting company and orchestra.
                                    New York, May, 1921.

7870-A  Lost Your Mind                             OK 4340

New York, May, 1921.

7874-A   Darktown Court Room                           OK 4428

7878-A   Murder In The First Degree                    OK 4340

New York, late August, 1922.

70808-B   The Chicken Thieves                          OK 4682

70813-B   Collecting Rents                             OK 4682

New York, February, 1923.

71269-   The Family Quarrel                            OK 4798
71270-   The Third Degree                              -

New York, November, 1923.

72042-B   The New Darktown Judge                       OK 4996
72043-A   Then I'll Go In That Lion's Cage             -

New York, c. November 5, 1924.

72956-   You Got To Go                                 OK 40232
72957-   That's Enough                                 -

Speech, unacc.                        New York, December 10, 1925.

73824-   The New Professor                             OK 40528
73825-   Jail Birds                                    -

New York, March, 1926.

74053-   The Fortune Teller                            OK 40605
74054-   Domestic Troubles                             -

Vocal, acc. by own (?) piano.         New York, September 23, 1926.

80135-   When You're Really Blue                       OK 40697, Par R-3259
80136-   You Sure Are One Sick Man                     -

New York, June 15, 1928.

400790-   Hard Times                                   OK rejected
400791-   Last Night                                   -

## JOE E. BROWN

B. Holgate, Ohio, July 28, 1892; in circus as child, 1901, one of the Five Ashtons,
but became a professional baseball player; m. Kathryn McGraw, 1915, and is   still
married to her (1973) !  Stage debut 1918 (LISTEN, LESTER) with Clifton Webb; made
many successes on Broadway (JIM JAM JEMS with Frank Fay, 1920; GREENWICH  VILLAGE
FOLLIES (1921-1923) with Harry Langdon and Ned Sparks; first film CROOKS CAN'T WIN
(1928); many very popular films followed, from SALLY (with Marilyn Miller,1929) to
SOME LIKE IT HOT (with Marilyn Monroe, Jack Lemmon and Tony Curtis, 1959,including
THE TENDERFOOT (1932), ELMER THE GREAT (1933), MIDSUMMER NIGHT'S DREAM (1935),WIDE
OPEN FACES (1937) and many others; son Don killed in World War II; Joe E.Brown was
awarded the Bronze Star for entertaining troops; huge stage success in HARVEY,48th
Street Theatre, November 1, 1944 for 1,680 performances: latterly in TV  -  TALENT
SCOUTS, STRIKE IT RICH, etc.; published autobiography in 1959 (LAUGHTER IS A  WON-
DERFUL THING); made 75 films in all.

Vocal, acc. by orchestra (?)          ? Hollywood, date unknown.

      Mousie                          Famous Record Co. No. 5

Three Southern-born sisters (Kathlyn, b. Winchester, Kentucky, Dagmar and Lorraine,
b. Memphis, Tenn.) who were very popular in the first MUSIC BOX REVUE at the New
York theatre of that name from 1921 to 1924; they appeared all over the U.S.A. in
similar productions and in the London version in 1923; in film KING OF JAZZ(1930).

Vocalists with Bennie Krueger and his Orchestra.
New York, c. April, 1923.

        Down Among The Sleepy Hills Of Ten-Ten- Br 2427
          Tennessee
        Little Boy Blues        -

Vocal trio, acc. by own piano (which member or members played is not stated).
New York, December 17, 1923.

        Sittin' In A Corner              Vic test (un-numbered)

Acc. by Arthur Johnston-p.       New York, March 7, 1924.

B-29588-3  Lazy                    Vic 19298
B-29589-1-2  Cover Me Up With The Sunshine Of   Rejected
           Virginia

New York, March 14, 1924.

B-29589-5  Cover Me Up With The Sunshine Of   Vic 19298
           Virginia

New York, September 5, 1924.

B-30697-1-2-3-4-5  Mandy, Make Up Your Mind    Vic rejected

Camden, N. J., September 22, 1924.

B-30697-7  Mandy, Make Up Your Mind       Vic 19510
B-30918-3  Nobody Loves You Like I Do      Vic 19478

Camden, N. J., September 23, 1924.

B-30920-3  Sweetest Little Rose In Tennessee   Vic 19478

Camden, N. J., October 4, 1924.

B-30972-2  Red Hot Mama              Vic 19510

Camden, N. J., January 16, 1925.

B-31726-3  Tokio Blues ("Music Box Revue")    Vic 19631
B-31727-4  Who ? ("Music Box Revue")       -

Chicago, December 18, 1925.

BVE-34047-1  Tie Me To Your Apron Strings Again  Vic 19921
BVE-34048-2  Kentucky's Way Of Saying "Good Morning"  -

Acc. by vn/p or g/u as shown.    New York, July 20, 1926.

BVE-35790-2  Iyone, My Own Iyone - g/u     Vic 20123, Zon 2801
BVE-35791-2  How Many Times ? - vn/p       -      -

Acc. by Arthur Johnston-p.   Camden, N. J., September 11, 1926.

BVE-35865-2  Broken-Hearted Sue        Vic 20325, Zon 2883
BVE-35866-1-2-3-4  I'm Lonely Without You   Rejected

Camden, N. J., September 18, 1926.

BVE-35866-7  I'm Lonely Without You       Vic 20232, Zon 2867

Camden, N. J., September 27, 1926.

BVE-35882-3  Lay Me Down To Sleep In Carolina       Vic 20232, Zon 2867
BVE-35883-2  Pretty Cinderella                      Vic 20325, Zon 2883

  Acc. by Arthur Johnston-p and O/Nat Shilkret.
                                    New York, September 9, 1927.

CVE-39169-1-2  Ziegfeld Follies - Selection, Part  Vic rejected
           1   (The Brox Sisters sing a chorus of OOH ! MAYBE IT'S YOU)
CVE-39170-1  Ziegfeld Follies - Selection, Part 2       -
           (The Brox Sisters sing a chorus of IT ALL BELONGS TO ME with Franklyn
           Baur, and IT'S UP TO THE BAND by themselves)

                                    New York, September 14, 1927.

CVE-39169-   Ziegfeld Follies - Selection, Part 1  Vic 35845
           (The Brox Sisters sing a chorus of OOH ! MAYBE IT'S YOU)
CVE-39170-   Ziegfeld Follies - Selection, Part 2       -
           (The Brox Sisters sing a chorus of IT ALL BELONGS TO ME with Franklyn
           Baur, and IT'S UP TO THE BAND by themselves)
See also Bing Crosby.

## CAROL BRUCE

B. Great Neck, L.I., November 15, 1919; first on stage as vocalist with Lloyd Hunt-
ley's Band in Montreal; New York debut in GEORGE WHITE'S SCANDALS OF 1939  (Alvin
Theatre, August 28, 1939), then starred in LOUISIANA PURCHASE (Imperial, May 28,
1940); made films, 1941-1944, then starred in the revival of SHOW BOAT  (Ziegfeld
Theatre, January 5, 1946).

Vocal, acc. by O/Harry Sosnik.          New York, November 29, 1940.

68421-   A Nightingale Sang In Berkeley Square   Dec 3557
68422-A  I Should Have Known You Years Ago       Dec 3566, Br 03183
68423-B  If I Feel This Way Tomorrow (Then It's Love) -          -
68424-   Wish Me Luck As You Wave Me Goodbye     Dec 3557

                                    Los Angeles, August 12, 1941.

DLA-2631-A-B  Adios                               Dec rejected
DLA-2632-A-B  Red Moon Of The Caribees               -
DLA-2633-A-B  Carioca                                -
DLA-2634-A-B  The Lamp Of Memory (Incertidumbre)     -

                                    Los Angeles, August 29, 1941.

DLA-2710-  Misirlou                             Dec 18185
DLA-2711-  Red Moon Of The Caribees                -
DLA-2712-  Adios                                Rejected ?
DLA-2713-  The Lamp Of Memory (Incertidumbre)      -

                                    Los Angeles, October 8, 1941.

DLA-2786-  A Rendezvous In Rio (Un Momento)     Dec rejected ?
DLA-2787-  My Shawl (Ombo)                         -
DLA-2788-  Rain In Spain                           -

## VIRGINIA BRUCE

B. Helen Virginia Briggs, Minneapolis, 1910; to Los Angeles as a child, toured  film
studios, noticed by William Beaudine. director; given contract for bit parts  ($25
per week) in such movies as BLUE SKIES and THE LOVE PARADE (both 1929; she had one
line to say in the latter).  She appeared as Goldwyn Girl in Eddie Cantor's   film
WHOOPEE (1930); on stage in AMERICA'S SWEETHEART (Broadhurst, N.Y., February   10,
1931), following appearance in the short-lived SMILES (November, 1930); back to Los
Angeles, 1932, to film in DOWNSTAIRS with author John Gilbert, whom she   married,
but retired when their daughter was born.  Divorced him, 1934; made JAN EYRE; John
Gilbert died 1936, leaving Virginia Bruce most of his quarter-million dollars. She
made 14 films in 16 months, including THE GREAT ZIEGFELD (she had been a  Ziegfeld
beauty), BORN TO DANCE and TURNABOUT; m. J. Walter Rubin, December 18, 1937;he was

director of BAD MAN OF BRIMSTONE, in which his wife starred; he died 1942. In 1946 she married Ali Ipar, a 23-year-old Turk, who had some difficulty over   obtaining a permanent resident's visa. Virginia Bruce made her last picture in 1960;in 1961 she was arrested in Turkey and charged with incurring heavy debts.

Vocal, acc. by Eddie Ward and his MGM Orchestra.
Los Angeles, October 5, 1936.

| | | |
|---|---|---|
| LA-1179- | I've Got You Under My Skin (Film "Easy To Love") | Br 7765, Voc 523 |
| LA-1180- | Easy To Love (Film "Easy To Love") | -       - |

## JACK  BUCHANAN

B. Helensburgh, near Glasgow, Scotland, 1891; London debut in THE GRASS WIDOWS (September 7, 1912, Apollo Theatre); enormously successful as nonchalant singer-dancer, in revues (TAILS UP, 1918; A TO Z, 1921) and musical comedies (BATTLING BUTLER,1922, TONI, 1924; SUNNY, 1926; THAT'S A GOOD GIRL, 1928; STAND UP AND SING, 1931; and MR. WHITTINGTON, 1933), all in London, and in Andre Charlot's revues in New York (Times Square, January 9, 1924, and Selwyn, November 10, 1925); made many light comedy and musical films, SHOW OF SHOWS (1929), MONTE CARLO (1930) and BAND WAGON (1953) being made in U.S.A., and MAN OF MAYFAIR (1931), GOODNIGHT, VIENNA (1932), THAT'S A  GOOD GIRL (which he directed, 1933), BIG BUSINESS and BREWSTER'S MILLIONS (1934),   COME OUT OF THE PANTRY, WHEN KNIGHTS WERE BOLD and THIS'LL MAKE YOU WHISTLE (1935-1936), all being made in England. D. October 13, 1957.

Vocal, acc. by Comedy Theatre Orchestra. London, June, 1918.

| | | |
|---|---|---|
| 76182 | Any Little Thing (w/Phyllis Monkman) ("Tails Up") | Col L-1254 |
| 76183 | Gnee-ah ! ("Tails Up") | Col L-1253 |
| 76184 | The Special Cop (w/Phyllis Monkman) ("Tails Up") | Col L-1254 |

Acc. by O/George W. Byng.                    Hayes, Middlesex, November 23, 1921.

| | | |
|---|---|---|
| Bb-703- | Keep Moving (as member of chorus behind the Trix Sisters) ("A To Z") | HMV B-1301 |
| Bb-704-2 | Dapper Dan (w/the Trix Sisters)("A To Z") And Her Mother Came Too ("A To Z") | HMV B-1302, Par PMC-7150 HMV test (un-numbered) |

Hayes, Middlesex, January 17, 1922.

| | | |
|---|---|---|
| Bb-914-1 | And Her Mother Came Too ("A To Z") | HMV B-1319 |
| Bb-915-2 | My Alco Holiday ("A To Z") | - |

Acc. by Shaftesbury Theatre Orchestra. London, June, 1924.

| | | |
|---|---|---|
| A-906 | Blotto ("Toni") | Col 3451 |
| A-907 | Take A Step ("Toni") | - |
| A-908 | Don't Love You (w/Elsie Randolph)("Toni") | Col 3453 |
| A-909 | Do It For Me (w/June) ("Toni") | Col 3452 |
| A-910 | For My Friend (w/June) ("Toni") | - |

Acc. by O/George W. Byng.          Hayes, Middlesex, April 9, 1925.

| | | |
|---|---|---|
| Bb-6021-1 | Garden Of Lies (w/June) ("Boodle") | HMV B-2005 |
| Bb-6022-2 | This Year, Next Year (w/June) ("Boodle") | - |

Acc. by studio orchestra.          New York, November 17, 1925.

| | |
|---|---|
| 141271- | A Cup Of Coffee, A Sandwich And You          Col 512-D (w/Gertrude Lawrence) ("Charlot's Revue of 1926") |

New York, November 20, 1925.

| | |
|---|---|
| 141295- | Gigolette ("Charlot's Revue of 1926")     Col 514-D |

Acc. by O/? Percival Mackey.        London, October 15, 1926.

WAX-2023-2  Let's Say Goodnight Till The Morning  Col 9147
            (w/Elsie Randolph) ("Sunny")
WAX-2024-1-2  Who ? (w/Binnie Hale) ("Sunny")    Rejected

                        London, October 19, 1926.

WA-4292-1   When We Get Our Divorce (w/Binnie    Col 4141
            Hale) ("Sunny")
WA-4293-2   I've Looked For Trouble ("Sunny")    -
WAX-2024-3  Who ? (w/Binnie Hale) ("Sunny")      Col 9147, SEG-7767

Acc. by  Debroy Somers' Band/Leonard Hornsey.
                        London, June 19, 1928.

WA-7519-1   Sweet So-And-So ("That's A Good Girl")  Col 4952
WAX-3802-2  Fancy Our Meeting (w/Elsie Randolph)    Col 9462
            ("That's A Good Girl")

                        London, June 26, 1928.

WA-7547-1   Parting Time (w/Vera Pearce-Raymond   Col 4952
            Newell) ("That's A Good Girl")
WAX-3836-2  The One I'm Looking For (w/Elsie      Col 9462
            Randolph) ("That's A Good Girl")

Acc. by the London Hippodrome Orchestra/Harry Perritt.
                        London, April 14, 1931.

WA-11451    Stand Up And Sing ("Stand Up And     Col DB-484
            Sing")
WA-11452    I Would If I Could ("Stand Up And    Col DB-486
            Sing")
WA-11453    Night Time ("Stand Up And Sing")     Col DB-484
WA-11454    It's Not You (w/Elsie Randolph)      Col DB-485
            ("Stand Up And Sing")
WA-11455    There's Always Tomorrow (W/Elsie        -          SEG-7767
            Randolph) ("Stand Up And Sing")
WA-11456    Take It Or Leave It ("Stand Up And   Col DB-486
            Sing")

Acc. by O/Ray Noble.        London, October 29, 1931.

OB-1771-    You Forgot Your Gloves               HMV B-4005
OB-1772-    Alone With My Dreams (Film "Man Of      -
            Mayfair")

                        Kingsway Hall, London, January, 1932.

OBR-100-    Living In Clover (Film "Goodnight,   HMV B-4083
            Vienna")
OBR-101-    Goodnight, Vienna (Film "Goodnight,     -
            Vienna")

                        London, March 8, 1933.

OB-6327-1   Yes, Mr. Brown (Film "Yes, Mr. Brown")  HMV B-4398
OB-6328-1   Leave A Little Love For Me (Film "Yes,  -
            Mr. Brown")

                        London, October 4, 1933.

OB-5367-2   Fancy Our Meeting (w/Elsie Randolph)  HMV B-8026
            (Film "That's A Good Girl")
OB-5368-2   Now That I've Found You (w/Elsie         -
            Randolph) (Film "That's A Good Girl")

London, October 5, 1933.

2B-5369-2  Jack Buchanan Medley - Part 1 (Intro.   HMV C-2630, 7EG-8307
           Dancing Honeymoon/And Her Mother Came Too/Fancy Our Meeting/Who ?)
2B-5370-2  Jack Buchanan Medley - Part 2 (Intro.     -           -
           Two Little Bluebirds/Goodnight, Vienna/It's Not You/There's Always  To-
           morrow)
OB-5371-2  So Green (Film "That's A Good Girl")   HMV B-8027
OB-5372-2  Oh ! La ! La ! (Film "That's A Good Girl")  -
   NOTE:- DANCING HONEYMOON was edited out of HMV 7EG-8307.

Comedy sketch with supporting cast.      London, October 6, 1933.

OB-5373-   Adapted From The French - Part 1      HMV B-8072
OB-5374-2  Adapted From The French - Part 2        -

Vocal, acc. by O/Ray Noble.          London, December 19, 1933.

OB-5524-2  Oceans Of Time (w/Elsie Randolph)      HMV B-8109
           ("Mr. Whittington")
OB-5525-2  Who Do You Think You Are ? (w/Elsie      -
           Randolph) ("Mr. Whittington")
OB-5526-2  Weep No More, My Baby ("Mr. Whitting-  HMV B-8110, 7EG-8307
           ton")

   Acc. by Carroll Gibbons and Johnny Green-2 pianos, with their Boy Friends (members
   of the Savoy Hotel Orpheans).         London, December 20, 1933.

CAX-7027-1  Mr. Whittington - Selection, Part 1    Col DX-566
            (Intro. Bow Bells Music/Oceans Of Time (w/Elsie Randolph)
CAX-7028-2  Mr. Whittington - Selection, Part 2     -
            (Intro. What A Pleasant Surprise/I'm Simply Wild About Horses/Weep  No
            More, My Baby/Who Do You Think You Are ?/Oceans Of Time (w/Elsie  Ran-
            dolph)

   Acc. by O/Ray Noble.              London, March 13, 1934.

OB-5942-1  Not Bad (Film "Big Business")          HMV B-8153
OB-5943-1  Like Monday Follows Sunday (w/Elsie      -        7EG-8307
           Randolph) (Film "Big Business")

   Acc. by Geraldo and his Orchestra with chorus.
                                       London, December 18, 1934.

CA-14809-2  I Think I Can (Film "Brewster's        Col DB-1483, FB-1130
            Millions")
CA-14810-1  One Good Tune Deserves Another (Film     -          -
            "Brewster's Millions")

                                       London, December 19, 1934.

CAX-7373-1  Brewster's Millions - Selection, Part  Col DX-662
            1 (Intro. One Good Tune Deserves Another/I Think I Can/Pull Down   The
            Blind)
CAX-7374-2  Brewster's Millions - Selection, Part    -
            2 (Intro. The Orange Seller/Caranza)

   Acc. by Harry Perritt and his Orchestra.
                                       London, May 31, 1935.

CAX-7550-1  The Flying Trapeze - Selection, Part 1 Col DX-696
            (Intro. Marie Louise/Nellie (w/Bruce Carfax)
CAX-7551-1  The Flying Trapeze - Selection, Part 2   -
            (Intro. Life In A Circus/There Won't Be Any Spring/The Flying Trapeze)

   Acc. by studio orchestra.         London, January 17, 1936.

GB-7610-1  Everything Stops For Tea (Film "Come    Br 02125
           Out Of The Pantry")
GB-7611-1  From One Minute To Another (Film "Come    -
           Out Of The Pantry") (continued on page 118)

JACK BUCHANAN (cont.)

London, January 17, 1936 (cont.)

GB-7622-1 I'm Still Dreaming (Film "When Knights   Br 02153
          Were Bold")
GB-7623-1 Let's Put Some People To Work (Film        -
          "When Knights Were Bold")

London, November 30, 1936.

TB-2668-2 I'm In A Dancing Mood (w/Elsie Ran-    Br 02348
          dolph) (Film "This'll Make You Whistle")
TB-2669-2 This'll Make You Whistle (w/Elsie Ran-      -
          dolph) (Film "This'll Make You Whistle")
TB-2670-2 Without Rhythm (Film "This'll Make You Br 02347
          Whistle")
TB-2671-2 There Isn't Any Limit To My Love (Film      -
          "This'll Make You Whistle")

## FRANK BURBECK

B. 1855, d. February 20, 1930. From the early nineties he established himself as a
Shakespearean actor par excellence, working with the dramatic productions of Rob-
son and Crane, Dion Boucicault, Maude Adams' TWELFTH NIGHT, JOAN OF ARC, etc.,and
with the Frohman company. He also made successful appearances in London in the
opening years of the century.

Speech, unacc.                        New York, July 11, 1911.

B-10702-1-2 One, Two, Three (H. C. Burner)/Love   Rejected
            Of Country (Scott)
B-10703-2  The Last Leaf (Oliver Wendell Holmes)/     -
           L'Envoi (Rudyard Kipling)
B-10704-1-2 A Life Lesson (J. Whitcomb Riley)/        -
            Three Fishers (Charles Kingsley)
B-10705-1  Abou Ben Adhem (Leigh Hunt)/Annabel    Vic 16989
           Lee (Edgar Allen Poe)

New York, July 12, 1911.

B-10703-2  The Last Leaf (Oliver Wendell Holmes)/ Vic 16989
           L'Envoi (Rudyard Kipling)
B-10705-2  Abou Ben Adhem (Leigh Hunt)/Annabel       -
           Lee (Edgar Allen Poe)
B-10715-1  An  Old Sweetheart Of Mine (J.        Vic 16913
           Whitcomb Riley)
B-10716-1  The Knight's Toast                        -
B-10717-1  What My Lover Said (Greeley)          Rejected

New York, July 13, 1911.

B-10721-1  Hamlet's Soliloquy (Shakespeare)      Vic 16912
C-10722-1  Anthony's Address Over The Body Of    Rejected
           Caesar ("Julius Caesar" - Shakespeare)
C-10723-1  Anthony's Address Over The Body Of    Vic 35216
           Caesar - Part 2 ("Julius Caesar" - Shakespeare)
C-10724-1  Brutus's Address Over The Body Of     Rejected
           Caesar ("Julius Caesar" - Shakespeare)
B-10726-1  The Fall Of Wolsey ("Henry VIII" -    Vic 16912
           Shakespeare)
B-10727-1  Speech On Discovering Treason         Rejected
           ("Henry V" - Shakespeare)
    NOTE:- Matrix B-10725 is by the baritone Reinald Werrenrath on the same date.

New York, July 26, 1911.

B-10702-3-4 One, Two, Three (H. C. Burner)/Love  Rejected
            Of Country (Scott)
C-10722-2  Anthony's Address Over The Body Of    Vic 35216
           Caesar - Part 1 ("Julius Caesar" - Shakespeare)

New York, May 2, 1912.

| | | |
|---|---|---|
| B-10721-2 | Hamlet's Soliloquy (Shakespeare) | Vic 16912 |
| C-11962-1 | Othello's Defence ("Othello" - Shake-speare) | Rejected |
| B-11963-1 | Shylock's Rebuke ("Merchant Of Venice" - Shakespaare) | Vic 17163 |
| B-11964-2 | Barbara Frietchie (J. G. Whittier) | Vic 17132 |
| B-11965-1 | The Seven Ages Of Man ("As You Like It" - Shakespeare) | Vic 17163 |
| B-11966-1 | Fool In The Forest ("As You Like It" - Shakespeare) | Rejected |
| B-11967-1 | The Water Mill (McCallum) | Vic 17132 |

New York, May 3, 1912.

| | | |
|---|---|---|
| B-11965-2 | The Seven Ages Of Man ("As You Like It" - Shakespeare) | Vic 17163 |
| B-11983-1 | Soliloquy Before Agincourt ("Henry V" - Shakespeare) | Rejected |
| C-11984-1 | The Death Of Little Nell ("Old Curio-sity Shop" - Charles Dickens) | - |

## BURNS AND ALLEN

George Burns (r.n. Nathan Birnbaum, b. 1896) and Gracie Allen (1906-1964) were among the most famous real-life husband-and-wife acts on stage, screen, radio and tele-vision between 1930 and 1964. They appeared with great success all over the U.S. and in London, making many films (THE BIG BROADCAST of 1932 and 1938, and WE'RE NOT DRESSING (1934) are among the best-remembered. Gracie Allen epitomized the scatterbrained young "flapper-wife" of the late twenties - "dizzy" was her own not inaccurate description of herself - right into the fifties.

Dialogue, unacc.                         London, October 3, 1930.

| | | |
|---|---|---|
| WA-10729-1 | Dizzy - Part 1 | Col DB-286, Par PMC-7141 |
| WA-10730-1 | Dizzy - Part 2 | - |

Acc. by studio orchestra ?         New York, June 9, 1933.

| | | |
|---|---|---|
| 152410- | George BURNS and Gracie ALLEN - Part 1 | Col 2780-D |
| 152411- | George BURNS and Gracie ALLEN - Part 2 | - |

## R. H. BURNSIDE

Dramatic author and stage director from the turn of the century into the forties; he wrote many shows, several with Anne Caldwell, such as CHIN CHIN (1914), JACK O'LAN-TERN (1917), TIP-TOP (1920), STEPPING STONES (1923), THREE CHEERS (1928); general producer at the New York Hippodrome for many years; revived ROBIN HOOD (1944), and toured with Gilbert and Sullivan companies, 1945.

Speech with effects and orchestra.         New York, June 20, 1916.

| | | |
|---|---|---|
| 46849-1-4 | A New York Hippodrome Rehearsal | Col A-2057 |

## FRANCIS X. BUSHMAN

B. 1883, d. 1966; described as "the first movie matinee idol" by Abel Green in SHOW BIZ (Permabooks); heavily-built actor whose screen career began in 1912 with a film called THE MAGIC WAND; made many other silents (ROMEO AND JULIET, 1916, was one of the more outstanding); gave up filming until 1927 when he made BEN HUR. His roles in talkies were usually small, however, and his only known record is a long-playing disc made in 1948 (Sun 147 - THE REV. DR. McARTHUR : EULOGY), but his position as a celebrity in the entertainment world is such that it merits inclusion.

## AMY BUTLER

Pioneer "coon-shouter" in the near-blues idiom also adopted by Sophie Tucker during the first decade of the twentieth century.

Vocal, acc. by studio orchestra.        New York, July 9, 1908.

    It's The Pretty Things You Say        Ed 9974

                                    New York, c. July, 1908.

    It's The Pretty Things You Say        Ind 897

                                    New York, c. May, 1909.

9195    Beautiful Eyes                    Zon 5485
9198    I Just Came Back To Say Goodbye    -

                                    New York, 1910.

    Bring Back My Lovin' Man            Zon 5827

## IRVING CAESAR

B. New York, July 4, 1895; wrote lyrics for many very popular musical comedies, such
as KISSING TIME (1919), BAMBOULA and NO, NO, NANETTE (1924), MERCENARY MARY(1925),
GEORGE WHITE'S SCANDALS OF 1929 and 1931, and WONDER BAR (1930). He also supplied
lyrics for the London production TRANSATLANTIC RHYTHM (Adelphi, October 1, 1936),
but this was not a great success. Wrote many scenarios in Hollywood during the era
of the great musicals immediately preceding World War II.

Piano duets with Ray Henderson, with vocal refrains by George Scott-Wood.
                           London, September 21, 1936.

CA-15932-1  Transatlantic Rhythm - Selection,    Col FB-1518
        Part 1 (Intro. I Heard A Song In A Taxi/Who'll Buy My Song  Of Love ?/
        Spanish Jake)
CA-15933-1  Transatlantic Rhythm - Selection,        -
        Part 2 (Intro. Breakfast In Harlem/Holiday Sweetheart/You're The Type)

## MARIE CAHILL

B. 1870; d. August 23, 1933. Prominent vaudeville impressionist, who took part in a
nearly all-girl performance at the Palace, New York, in 1925.

Vocal, acc. by O/Walter B. Rogers.       Camden, N. J., February 24, 1916.

B-17201-1-2  He's My Cousin If She's Your Niece    Vic rejected
B-17202-1-2  Drip, Drip, Drip Went The Waterfall    -
B-17203-1-2  Go Your Way And I'll Go Mine           -
B-17204-1-2  Bring Back My Barney To Me             -
B-17205-1-2-3  When I Get Back, Back To County Kerry  -
B-17206-1-2  Tell Me Some More                      -

                                Camden, N. J., March 9, 1916.

B-17201-3-4-5  He's My Cousin If She's Your Niece  Vic rejected
B-17202-3-4-5  Drip, Drip, Drip Went The Waterfall   -

    Acc. by Carl Grey-p.              Camden, N. J., November 1, 1916.

C-18653-1-2  Dallas Blues (Preceded by Mose's    Rejected
        Baptism)
B-18654-1  Faree Thee Honey, Fare Thee Well      Vic 45125
C-18655-1  An Idle Woman's Busy Day (unacc.)     Rejected

Speech, unacc.                         Camden, N. J., December 15, 1916.

C-18655-3  An Idle Woman's Busy Day              Vic 55081

Vocal, acc. by Carl Grey-p.           Camden, N. J., January 2, 1917.

C-18653-3  Dallas Blues (Preceded by Mose's      Vic 55081
        Baptism)
B-18896-1  I Never Wanted Anything So Good So Bad  Rejected

Acc. by O/Joseph Pasternack.              Camden, N. J., May 29, 1917.

B-20004-2  Under The Bamboo Tree                Vic 45125
B-20005-1-2-3  Nancy Brown (A Bucolic Wail)     Rejected

Speech, unacc.                            New York, November 4, 1921.

B-25693-1  Washing Baby                         Vic 45265
B-25694-1-2-3  Shopping                         Rejected

                                          New York, November 11, 1921.

B-25694-4  Shopping                             Vic 45265

                                          New York, October 17, 1922.

B-26965-1  In A Shoe Store                      Vic rejected
B-26966-1  Lecture On Music And Rhythm              -

                                          New York, June 12, 1923.

B-28070-1-2  The Dinner Party                   Vic rejected
B-28071-1-2-3  Mammy Vinny's Bible Lesson           -
B-28072-1-2  The Symphony Concert                   -

                                          New York, August 6, 1923.

B-26965-3  In A Shoe Store                      Vic 45370
B-28072-3  The Symphony Concert                     -
B-28347-1  Jezebel                              Rejected

                                          New York, October 8, 1923.

B-28071-4  Mammy Vinny(s Bible Lesson           Vic 45386
B-28347-3  Jezebel                                  -

                                          New York, November 6, 1924.

B-31085-1  At The Theatre                       Vic 45482
B-31086-2  Neighbors                               -

## GRACE  CAMERON

B. Storm Lake, Iowa, August 1, 1879; joined The Bostonians (debut in ROBIN HOOD, Oct-
    ober 1, 1899); also with Castle Square Opera Company, sang grand opera and Gilbert
    and Sullivan ! Appeared in THE PIED PIPER (1908).
Vocal, acc. by studio orchestra.          New York, February 19, 1909.

        Adam And Eve ("The Pied Piper")     Ed 4M-136
        If The Wind Had Only Blown The Other Ed 4M-204
          Way

                                          New York, June 15, 1909.

        Help ! Help ! Help ! I'm Falling In  Ed 10158
          Love
        If Ev'ry Girl Was A Girl Like You    Ed 10195
        Modern Love                          Ed 10235
        Oh ! Doctor                          Ed 10249
        Whose Baby Girl Are You ?            Ed 10265

                                          New York, June 26, 1909.

        I Wonder If This Funny Little Boy    Ed 4M-230
          Loves Me
        How She Gets Away With It Is More Than Ed 4M-288
          I Can See
This artist also made some titles for Edison in New York on July 14, 1910.   As none
    was ever issued, it is not known what they were.

New York, July 11, 1912.

38132-2  Since Dolly Dimple Made A Hit              Col A-1205
38133-3  I'll Bet I'd Be A Riot Down On Broadway    -

## JUDY CANOVA

B. 1916, Jacksonville, Florida; child member of family vaudeville team; New York debut 1934 in CALLING ALL STARS with Gertrude Niesen.  To Hollywood 1935,  appeared
in IN CALIENTE; then THRILL OF A LIFETIME and ARTISTS AND MODELS (1937) and  made
many "programmers" 1940-1954; very popular ha f-hour radio show, and was presented
in the first hill-billy act on television (1939); most recent film success THE AD-
VENTURES OF HUCKLEBERRY FINN (1960).  Noted for rural-type comedy and yodeling.

Vocal, acc. by unknown piano.            New York, c. October 31, 1930.

GEX-2801    I Ain't Got Nobody                     Gnt rejected
GEX-2802    Nobody Cares If I'm Blue                -

Imitations, presumably unacc.            New York, c. November 7, 1930.

GEX-2807    Whip-Poor-Will/Hog/Horse               Gnt rejected
GEX-2808    Meadow Lark/Screech Owl/Raincrow/Mocking  -
            Bird

Vocal, acc. by studio orchestra.         Hollywood, December 15, 1941.

H-602-1   I've Cried My Last Tear Over You         Rejected
H-603-1   Is It True ?                             OK 6683
H-604-1   Someone                                  -
H-605-1   I Love You Too Much                      Rejected

## EDDIE CANTOR

B. New York, January 31, 1893; stage debut in vaudeville, Clinton Music Hall, in New
York, 1907; London debut at the Alhambra, May 4, 1914 in a revue (NOT LIKELY); returned after outbreak of World War I to tour U.S.A. with Lila Lee as Cantor  & Lee
but starred alone in Ziegfeld Follies at the New Amsterdam Theatre, New York, from
1917 to 1919; long run in musical shows (KID BOOTS, Earl Carroll, December 31,1923
and WHOOPEE, New Amsterdam, December 4, 1928); began making films about this time,
including great successes based on some of the above stage hits (KID BOOTS,  1928;
WHOOPEE and GLORIFYING THE AMERICAN GIRL, 1929; PALMY DAYS, 1931;  THE  KID  FROM
SPAIN, 1932; ROMAN SCANDALS, 1933; KID MILLIONS, 1934; STRIKE ME PINK, 1935; FORTY
LITTLE MOTHERS, 1940; THANK YOUR LUCKY STARS, 1943, and IF YOU KNEW SUSIE, 1948; a
biographical film (THE EDDIE CANTOR STORY) was made in 1953, and he was awarded  a
distinction three years later "for distinguished service to the film industry." He
wrote several books between 1928 and 1962 (YOUR NEXT PRESIDENT; CAUGHT SHORT;WHO'S
HOOEY ?; BETWEEN THE ACTS; MY LIFE IS IN YOUR HANDS; TAKE MY LIFE; THE WAY I SEE IT
and AS I REMEMBER THEM).  Returned to theatre in BANJO EYES at the Shubert, N. Y.,
December 25, 1941, appeared in London several times before and after World War II.
D. October 10, 1964.  R.n. Edward Israel Isskowitz.

Vocal, acc. by O/Rosario Bourdon.        New York, July 12, 1917.

B-20216-1   The Modern Maiden's Prayer             Vic 18342
B-20217-2   That's The Kind Of A Baby For Me       -

  Acc. by studio orchestra.              New York, c. November, 1917.

            The Modern Maiden's Prayer             AV 1220
            That's The Kind Of A Baby For Me       -
            Down In Borneo Isle                    AV 1228
            Hello, Wisconsin                       -
            Dixie Volunteers                       AV 1233
            I Don't Want To Get Well               -

                                         New York, c. August, 1919.

            The Last Rose Of Summer                Pathe 22163
            We Don't Need The Wine To Have A Wonderful Time -

New York, c. September, 1919.

4467-3  You Don't Need The Wine To Have A        Em 1071
        Wonderful Time

New York, c. October, 1919.

4508-3  Don't Put A Tax On The Beautiful Girls   Em 1071
4509-1  When They're Old Enough To Know Better   Em 1094

New York, c. November, 1919.

4629-4  I Used To Call Her Baby                  Em 10102
4630-2-3  Give Me The Sultan's Harem             Em 10105

67953   When They're Old Enough To Know Better   Pathe 22201

67977   I've Got My Captain Working For Me Now   -
67979   Don't Put A Tax On The Beautiful Girls   Pathe 22260

New York, c. December, 1919.

4670-3  You'd Be Surprised                       Em 10102

New York, c. January, 1920.

4734-   The Last Rose Of Summer                  Em 10134

68091   At The High Brown Babies' Ball           Pathe 22260

New York, c. February, 1920.

4759-2  When It Comes To Lovin' The Girls I'm    Em 10105
        Away Ahead Of The Times
4760-3  Come On And Play Wiz Me, My Sweet Babee  Em 10119

68188   When It Comes To Lovin' The Girls I'm    Pathe 22318
        Away Ahead Of The Times
68189   I Never Knew I Had A Wonderful Wife
        (Until The Town Went Dry)

New York, c. March, 1920.

4779-2  All The Boys Love Mary                   Em 10119
4780-2  You Ain't Heard Nothin' Yet              Em 10134

New York, c. May, 1920.

41171-3  The Argentines, The Portuguese And      Em 10200
         Greeks
41172-1  Noah's Wife Lived A Wonderful Life      -

New York, c. June, 1920.

41207-  The Older They Get, The Younger They     Em 10212
        Want 'Em
41208-  Snoops The Lawyer                        -

New York, c. July, 1920.

41239-4  She Gives Them All The Ha ! Ha ! Ha !   Em 10292

New York, c. August, 1920.

41375-1  Dixie Made Us Jazz Band Mad             Em 10263
41376-2  When I See All The Lovin' They Waste    -
         On Babies (I Long For The Cradle Again)

# EDDIE CANTOR (cont.)

New York, October, 1920.

41453-  I Wish That I'd Been Born In Borneo    Em 10301

New York, November, 1920.

41494-  Palesteena                            Em 10292

New York, December, 1920.

41534-1  Margie                               Em 10301

41551-  You Oughta See My Baby                Em 10327

New York, late January, 1921.

41632-2  I Never Knew                         Em 10349

Timbuctoo                                     Em 10352
My Old New Jersey Home                        -

New York, June, 1921.

41852-  Anna In Indiana                       Em 10397, Re 9115
Oh, They're Such Nice People                  -

New York, April 28, 1922.

80328-  I Love Her, She Loves Me (I'm Her He -  Col A-3624
She's My She)

New York, May 10, 1922.

80342-  I'm Hungry For Beautiful Girls        Col A-3624

New York, July 5, 1922.

80439-1-2  Oh, Is She Dumb !                  Rejected
80440-  Susie                                 Col A-3682

New York, July 28, 1922.

80439-  Oh, Is She Dumb !                     Col A-3682

New York, October 30, 1922.

80636-  Sophie (I Go So Far With Sophie And   Col A-3754
Sophie Goes So Far With Me)
80637-  He Loves It                           -

New York, December 13, 1922.

80715-  Joe Is Here                           Col A-3784
80716-  How Ya Gonna Keep Your Mind On Dancing  -
(When You're Dancing With Someone You Love ?)

New York, May 4, 1923.

81004-  I Love Me (I'm Wild About Myself)     Col A-3906
81005-  Ritzi-Mitzi                           -

New York, June 12, 1923.

81073-  Oh ! Gee, Oh ! Gosh, Oh ! Golly, I'm  Col A-3934
In Love

New York, June 14, 1923.

81076-  Eddie (Steady)                        Col A-3934

New York, July 26, 1923.

81148-   No, No, Nora                           Col A-3964
81149-   (I've Got The) Yes ! We Have No Bananas        -
         Blues

Acc. by the Georgians, dir. by Frank Guarente.
                              New York, January 4, 1924.

81459-3  O, Gee, Georgie ! (sic)               Col 56-D
81460-2  If You Do - What You Do                        -

Acc. by studio orchestra.      New York, April 4, 1924.

81666-   I'll Have Vanilla                     Col 120-D
81667-   On A Windy Day 'Way Down In Waikiki            -

                              New York, May 14, 1924.

81779-   Oh Papa                               Col 140-D
81780-   Monkey Doodle                                  -

                              New York, July 18, 1924.

81878-   Charley, My Boy                       Col 182-D

                              New York, August 8, 1924.

81904-   No-One Knows What It's All About      Col 196-D

                              New York, September 12, 1924.

140037-  Doodle-Doo-Doo                        Col 213-D

                              New York, October 14, 1924.

140106-  How I Love That Girl                  Col 234-D

                              New York, November 17, 1924.

140145-  Those Panama Mamas (Are Ruinin' Me)   Col 256-D

                              New York, December 29, 1924.

140213-  Goo-Goo-Goodnight Dear !              Col 277-D

                              New York, January 6, 1925.

140223-  Laff It Off                           Col 283-D

                              New York, April 6, 1925.

140499-  If You Knew Susie ("Big Boy")         Col 364-D

                              New York, April 27, 1925.

140558-  We're Back Together Again             Col rejected

                              New York, June 1, 1925.

140558-  We're Back Together Again             Col 397-D
140641-  Row, Row, Rosie                       Col 415-D

                              New York, September 10, 1925.

140925-   Oh Boy ! What A Girl                 Col 457-D
140926-1-2  Jake, The Plumber                  Rejected
140928-1-2  Eddie's Trip Abroad                        -
   NOTE:- Matrix 140927 is by the Happiness Boys, q.v.

Acc. by George Olsen and his Music.    New York, September 6, 1928.

BVE-46989-1-2-3-4  Sonny Boy                      Vic rejected
BVE-46990-1-2  It Goes Like This (That Funny Melody)  -

Acc. by Jack Shilkret-p.          New York, September 28, 1928.

Sonny Boy                         Vic test (un-numbered)

Acc. by O/Nat Shilkret.           New York, December 18, 1928.

BVE-49001-2  Makin' Whoopee ("Whoopee")       Vic 21831, 24330, HMV B-3116
BVE-49002-4  Hungry Women ("Whoopee")           -         -          -

New York, January 28, 1929.

BVE-49688-2  Eddie Cantor's Automobile Horn Song  Vic 21862
BVE-49689-2  I Faw Down And Go 'Boom !'           -

Acc. by O/Leonard Joy.            New York, April 5, 1929.

BVE-51610-3  Hello, Sunshine, Hello           Vic 21982, HMV B-3738
BVE-51611-3  If I Give Up The Saxophone (Will You    -         -
             Come Back To Me ?)

New York, October 29, 1929.

BVE-57128-1-2-3-4  Does An Elephant Love Peanuts? Rejected
BVE-57129-3-4  My Wife Is On A Diet               Vic 22189
BVE-57130-4  Eddie Cantor's Tips On The Stock       -        LPV-580, LSA-3086
             Market

Vocalist with Gus Arnheim and his Cocoanut Grove Orchestra.
                              Hollywood, August 23, 1931.

PBVE-68306-2  There's Nothing Too Good For My      Vic 22851, HMV B-6126
              Baby (Film "Palmy Days")

Vocal, acc. by O/Philip Spitalny.    New York, c. September, 1931.

Ballyhoo ("Cheer Up")                 HoW K-6

Acc. by studio orchestra.         New York, November 2, 1932.

152316-3  What A Perfect Combination (Film "The   Col 2723-D, DB-1047
          Kid From Spain")
152317-3  Look What You've Done (Film "The Kid       -         -
          From Spain")

New York, April 16, 1934.

15075-1  Over Somebody Else's Shoulder (I Fell   Mt M-13001, Cq 8351, IB 4011
         In Love With You)
15076-1  The Man On The Flying Trapeze             -          -         -

Los Angeles, September 12, 1934.

LA-204-A  Mandy (Film "Kid Millions")            Mt M-13183, Cq 8427, Rex 8390
LA-205-A  An Earful Of Music (Film "Kid Millions")  -                    -
LA-206-A  When My Ship Comes In (Film "Kid       Rejected
          Millions")
LA-207-A  Okay, Toots (Film "Kid Millions")      Mt M-13184, Per 13063, Rex 8391

Los Angeles, October 1, 1934.

LA-206-C  When My Ship Comes In (Film "Kid       Mt M-13184, Cq 8427, Rex 8391
          Millions")

Acc. by O/Jay Wilbur.                    London, December, 1934.

F-1117-3  That's The Kind Of A Baby For Me      Rex 8389, Dec F-6748
F-1118-1  Making The Best Of Each Day            -              -

Acc. by O/Victor Young.                  Los Angeles, January 26, 1938.

DLA-1152-A  Alexander's Ragtime Band (w/Connie   Dec 1887, 25495, DL-5390,
              Boswell and Bing Crosby)           Br 02572, LA-8558

Acc. by Ambrose and his Orchestra.       London, July 23, 1938.

DR-2822-1  Says My Heart/Little Lady Make-Believe Dec F-6741
DR-2823-2  Lambeth Walk                            -

Acc. by O/Jerry Joyce.                   Los Angeles, November 26, 1939.

LA-2049-  The Only Thing I Want For Christmas    Col 35325
            (Is Just To Keep The Things That I've Got) (w/Mitchell Boychoir)
LA-2050-  If You Knew Susie (Like I Know Susie)  -

                                         Los Angeles, February 29, 1940.

LA-2171-A  Little Curly Hair In A High Chair     Col 35428, DB-1935, DC-648,
                                                 Har 11353
LA-2172-A  Margie                                As above

Acc. by studio orchestra.                New York, May 6, 1941.

69143-  Makin' Whoopee ! ("Whoopee")             Dec 3798, 11045, 23985, DL-4431,
                                                 Br 03216
69144-  Yes, Sir ! That's My Baby                Dec 24597, DL-4431, Br 03216
69145-  Oh ! Gee, Oh ! Gosh, Oh ! Golly, I'm     Dec 23986,    -       Br 04298
          In Love
69146-  They Go Wild, Simply Wild, Over Me       Dec 3873      -            -

                                         New York, March 19, 1942.

70539-  We're Having A Baby (My Baby And Me)     Dec 4314, Br 04406
          (w/June Clyde) ("Banjo Eyes")
70540-  Now's The Time To Fall In Love              - 11045, 23985 -

Eddie Cantor subsequently made a number of LPs, mostly of past successes in  modern
  recording.

## HOAGY CARMICHAEL

B. Bloomington, Indiana, November 11, 1899; studied law, but found music much  more
  to his liking; heard Bix Beiderbecke and the Wolverines at a college dance, wrote
  FREE WHEELING for them, later re-named RIVERBOAT SHUFFLE.  Organized own hot jazz
  bands, wrote several strictly jazz numbers (BONEYARD SHUFFLE, MARCH OF THE  HOOD-
  LUMS, STAR DUST, the latter as a stomp, but it was slowed down and given a  lyric
  in 1931 by Mitchell Parrish, and became one of the greatest "standards" in  popular music).  Played cornet and piano with own bands and with Jean Goldkette's Orchestra in Kansas City, 1927; to New York, 1929; turned his attention to  writing
  more sentimental ballads (GEORGIA ON MY MIND, ROCKIN' CHAIR, ONE NIGHT IN HAVANA,
  LAZY RIVER, LAZY BONES, JUDY, ONE MORNING IN MAY, TWO SLEEPY PEOPLE, many others)
  and made occasional film appearances.

HITCH'S HAPPY  HARMONISTS : Featuring Hoagy Carmichael-p and composer in place  of
  the leader, Curtis Hitch.              Richmond, Ind., May 19, 1925.

12245    Boneyard Shuffle                        Gnt 3066
12246    Washboard Blues                           -       Buddy 8005, Br 02206
  NOTE:- Buddy as MEMPHIS MELODY BOYS.  Some copies of Brunswick 02206 have  labels
  reversed; this led to a Riverside LP devoted to Bix Beiderbecke using the  above
  Hitch record instead of Bix's Rhythm Jugglers playing DAVENPORT BLUES.

CARMICHAEL'S COLLEGIANS : Hoagy Carmichael-p dir.
                                    Richmond, Ind., February 2, 1926.

12456     Watch Your Hornin'                    Gnt rejected
12457     Bridal Waltz                          -

HOAGY CARMICHAEL AND HIS PALS : Hoagy Carmichael-c-p dir.
                                    Richmond, Ind., October 28, 1927.

13183-A   One Night In Havana                   Gnt 6311, Ch 15420, Sentry 4011
13184     One Last Kiss (Waltz Supreme)         Rejected
   NOTE:- Champion as MALCOLM WEBB AND HIS BAND.

                              Richmond, Ind., October 31, 1927.

13189-A   Friday Night - cHC                    Gnt 6295, Ch 15420, Spr 310
13190     Star Dust - pHC                       Gnt 6311, Sentry 4011
13191-A   When Baby Sleeps (trio from band)     Rejected
   NOTE:- Champion as MALCOLM WEBB AND HIS BAND; Gennett 6295 as EMIL SEIDEL AND HIS
   ORCHESTRA.

Featured cornet and piano player with Emil Seidel and his Orchestra; Cliff Williams
   v.                        Richmond, Ind., November 11, 1927.

GEX-930     The Best Things In Life Are Free-vCW   Gnt 6295, Ch 15384
GEX-930-A   The Best Things In Life Are Free-vCW   Sil 5500
GEX-930-B   The Best Things In Life Are Free-vCW   Spr 309
GEX-931     Down South - vch                       Gnt 6309, Ch 15383
GEX-931-B   Down South - vch                       Bell 576, Sil 5500, Spr 307
GEX-932-A   Together, We Two - vCW                  Gnt 6324, Ch 15400
GEX-932-B   Together, We Two - vCW                  Spr 300
GEX-933-A   The Hours I Spent With You - vCW        Gnt 6309, Ch 15382
GEX-933-B   The Hours I Spent With You - vCW        Bell 573, Spr 308

Vocalist and pianist with Paul Whiteman and his Concert Orchestra.
                                    Chicago, November 18, 1927.

CVE-40901-1  Washboard Blues                    Vic 35877, 36186

Vocalist with Jean Goldkette and his Orchestra; he probably plays cornet and  piano
   in the ensemble.           Kansas City, December 12, 1927.

BVE-41367-4  My Ohio Home                       Vic 21166
BVE-41368-1  So Tired                           Vic 21150, HMV B-5479
   NOTE:- The Victor issues spell the vocalist's name "Charmichael."

CARMICHAEL'S COLLEGIANS : Hoagy Carmichael-c-p dir; v where shown.
                                    Richmond, Ind., May 5, 1928.

13722-A  March Of The Hoodlums                  Gnt 6474, Ch 16453, 40001
13723, A-B-C  Smile                             Rejected
13724-B  Walkin' The Dog - vHC                  Gnt 6474, Ch 16453, 40001,
                                                Br 02504
13725, A-B  Shimmy Shawobble (sic)              Rejected

                              Richmond, Ind., May 7, 1928.

13726, -A  One Night In Havana - cl/as/p (HC)   Gnt rejected
13727, -A  Star Dust - vn/pHC                   -

HOAGY CARMICHAEL AND HIS ORCHESTRA : Hoagy Carmichael-p-ldr; v where shown.   Frank
   Sylvano is the other vocalist.   Chicago, February 19, 1929.

BVE-48897-1-2-3  Rockin' Chair - vHC            Vic rejected
BVE-48898-1-2-3  March Of The Hoodlums          -
BVE-48899-1-2-3  One Night In Havana - vFS      -
BVE-50500-1-2-3  Walkin' The Dog - vHC          -    (Matrix BVE-50501 is  not
BVE-50502-1-2-3  Sittin' And Whittlin' - vHC    -    by Hoagy Carmichael).
BVE-50503-1-2-3  Will You, Won't You ? - vHC    -
   BVE-305-1  Sweet Lorraine                    Vic test

Vocalist with the Cotton Pickers, in duets with Harold "Scrappy" Lambert.
                              New York, March 27, 1929.

E-29523½-B  Rampart Street Blues                Br 4325, 5037
E-29524-A-B  St. Louis Gal                      Br 4440

Vocalist and percussionist with Blind Willie Dunn's Gin Bottle Four.
                              New York, April 30, 1929.

401842-B  Jet Black Blues                       OK 8689, Col DB-3440, Bm 1007,
                                                Par PMC-7106
401843-B  Blue Blood Blues                      As above

Vocalist (where shown) and pianist (doubling celeste) with Irving Mills and His Hot-
    sy-Totsy Gang.              New York, c. September 20, 1929.

E-30958/9   Harvey - vHC                        Br 4559
E-30960-    March Of The Hoodlums               -
E-30961-    Star Dust                           Br 4587

Pianist and celeste player with Eddie Lang's Orchestra; Mildred Bailey-v.
                              New York, October 5, 1929.

403031-A  What Kind O' Man Is You ? - vMB       Par R-840, PMC-7133, CBS C3L-22,
                                                BPG-62098
403032-C  Walkin' The Dog                       OK 41344, Par R-740, PMC-7133
403033-B  March Of The Hoodlums                 -        Par R-644, R-1157

Pianist and celeste player with Frankie Trumbauer and his Orchestra; Smith   Ballew-
    Joe Venuti-v; the third voice on the first side may be Hoagy Carmichael's.
                              New York, October 10, 1929.

403050-B  Turn On The Heat - vSB-JV             OK 41313, Par PNY-41313, R-499,
                                                Ar 4483
403050-C  Turn On The Heat - vSB-JV             Par PNY-41313
403051-C  Manhattan Rag                         OK 41330, Par R-1978
403052-B  Sunny Side Up - vSB                   OK 41313, Par PNY-41313, R-499,
                                                Ar 4483
   NOTE:- Parlophone PNY-41313 as JOE CURRAN'S BAND; Ariel 4483 as ARIEL DANCE  ORCH-
ESTRA.

Pianist in the orchestra acc. Seger Ellis.
                              New York, October 11, 1929.

403057-C  I'm A Dreamer - Aren't We All ?       OK 41321, Par R-502, Ar 4526
403058-B  If I Had A Talking Picture Of You     -        -        Ar 4527
403059-A-B  I Don't Want Your Kisses (If I Can't  Rejected
            Have Your Love)

Vocalist with Louis Armstrong and his Orchestra.
                              New York, December 13, 1929.

403496-C  Rockin' Chair - vLA-HC                OK 8756, Col 2688-D, Voc 3039,
                                                Par PNY-34027, R-785, PMC-7006,
   NOTE:- Parlophone PNY-34027 as TED SHAWNE'S O.  Od ONY-36027
Vocalist (where shown) and pianist (doubling celeste) with Irving Mills and his Hot-
    sy-Totsy Gang.             New York, January 6, 1930.

E-31757/8   High And Dry - vHC                  Br 4920, 01023
E-31759-    Barbaric                            -        -
E-31760-    South Breeze                        Rejected

Vocalist with own orchestra, with Irving Brodsky, Carson Robison and Joe Venuti-v(as
    shown).                    New York, May 21, 1930.

BVE-59800-2  Rockin' Chair - vHC-IB             Vic V-38139, 25494, LPT-3072,
                                                HMV B-4897, B-6288, B-8549,
                                                7EG-8037, HJCA HC-100

(continued on page 130)

New York, May 21, 1930 (cont.)

BVE-62301-1  Barnacle Bill The Sailor - vHC-CR-JV   Vic V-38139, 25371, LEJ-2,
                                                    LPM-2323, LPT-3072, RD-27225,
                                                    Cam CAL-385, CDN-112, HMV 7EG-
                                                    8037, JC1 532

New York, September 15, 1930.

BVE-63653-1  Georgia On My Mind - vHC         Vic 23013, 25494, LPT-3072,
                                              HMV B-4885, B-6133, B-8549,
                                              DLP-1106, 7EG-8037, HJCA HC-100
BVE-63654-1  One Night In Havana - vHC        Vic 23013, HMV B-4885
BVE-63655-1  Bessie Couldn't Help It - vHC    Vic 22864, LPT-3072, HMV DLP-1106
BVE-63655-2  Bessie Couldn't Help It - vHC    Vic 25371, HMV 7EG-8037, JC1 532

New York, November 20, 1930.

BVE-64365-2  Lazy River - vHC                     Vic 23034, HMV B-6500
BVE-64366-1-2  Papa's Gone Bye-Bye Blues (Jewish  Rejected
                 Boy Blues) - vHC
BVE-64367-2  Just Forget - vHC                    Vic 23034

Vocalist with the Carolina Dandies (pseudonym for Sunny Clapp and his Band  o' Sum-
   shine).                                New York, July 1, 1931.

BS-53016-3  Come Easy, Go Easy Love           Vic 22776

Vocalist with own orchestra.        New York, May 9, 1932.

BS-72557-  Dance Medley of Hoagy Carmichael    Vic L-16009
               Compositions No. 1 (Intro. Star Dust/In The Still Of The Night/  Wash-
               board Blues)
BS-72558-  Dance Medley of Hoagy Carmichael       -
               Compositions No. 2 (Intro. Rockin' Chair/Lazy River/Daybreak/  Georgia
               On My Mind)

New York, September 1, 1932.

BS-73353-2  Sing It Way Low Down               Vic 24182, HMV B-8658
   NOTE:- Three other titles made at this session, and one made the previous day, are
   credited to Hoagy Carmichael and his Orchestra, but Dick Robertson is the vocalist
   on all the products of the above date, and nowhere is there any positive  evidence
   of Hoagy Carmichael's having played.

Piano solos, with own vocal.        New York, September 13, 1933.

BS-77652-1  Snowball                           Vic 24402, HMV JO-314
BS-77653-1  Lazy Bones                              -          -

Pianist (and vocalist where shown) with his own orchestra.
                                    Chicago, October 10, 1933.

BS-77053-1  Judy - vHC                         Rejected
BS-77054-1  One Morning In May                 Vic 24505

Piano solos, with own vocal where shown.  New York, December 6, 1933.

BS-78842-1  Star Dust                          Vic 24484, Bm 1015
BS-78843-1  Cosmics                                 -

New York, December 22, 1933.

BS-78843-3-4  Cosmics                          Vic rejected
BS-78891-1-2  Washboard Blues - vHC                 -

New York, January 5, 1934.

BS-81031-1-2  Poor Old Joe - vHC               Vic rejected

New York, January 16, 1934.

BS-78891-3  Washboard Blues - vHC            Vic rejected

Vocalist and pianist with his own orchestra.
New York, March 9, 1934.

BS-81909-1  Judy                            Vic 24627
BS-81910-1  Moon Country                    -

Vocal, acc. by Perry Botkin and his Orchestra; duets with Ella Logan where shown.
Los Angeles, October 14, 1938.

LA-1730-B  Two Sleepy People (w/Ella Logan)   Br 8250, Par R-2611
LA-1731-A  Hong Kong Blues                    Br 8255, SE 5012-S, Col DB-5053

Los Angeles, October 18, 1938.

LA-1732-A  Riverboat Shuffle                  Br 8255, SE 5012-S, Col DB-5053
LA-1733-A  New Orleans (w/Ella Logan)         Br 8250, Par R-2611

Vocalist with the Casa Loma Orchestra.   New York, February 25, 1939.

65063-A  Washboard Blues                      Dec 2394, F-7157
65064-A  Little Old Lady                      -       -

Vocal, acc. by own piano.              Chicago, April 7, 1939.

91699-   Hong Kong Blues                      Dec rejected
91700-   Poor Old Joe                         -

Acc. by own p/cel/whistling, with Artie Bernstein-sb/Spike Jones-d.
Los Angeles, March 27, 1942.

DLA-2963-A  Mr. Music Master                  Dec 18396, 23942, Br 03752,
                                              Coral CP-42
DLA-2964-A  Old Man Harlem                    Dec 18397, 23933, Br 03961,
                                              Coral CP-42

Los Angeles, May 11, 1942.

DLA-2981-   Judy                              Dec 18396, 23942
DLA-2982-A  Star Dust                         Dec 18395, 23797, Br 03961,
                                              Coral CP-42
DLA-2983-B  Don't Forget To Say No, Baby      Dec 18397, 23933
DLA-2984-B  Hong Kong Blues                   Dec 18395, 23797, Br 03752,
                                              Coral CP-42

## TULLIO CARMINATI

B. Zara, Dalmatia, September 21, 1894; Italian nobleman; stage debut at the Teatro
Argentino in Rome (MIDSUMMER NIGHT'S DREAM, 1913); made films in Germany after he
had launched his own film company in Italy (1920); to Hollywood (1926) to  appear
in THE BAT; made several talkies, notably ONE NIGHT OF LOVE (1934) and THE  THREE
MAXIMS (1936).  D. 1971.

Vocal, acc. by O/Victor Schertzinger.   Los Angeles, January 3, 1935.

LA-302-   Love Passes By (Film "One Night Of     Col 3023-D
          Love")
LA-303-   I Live In My Dreams (Film "One Night Of    -
          Love")

## GEORGES  CARPENTIER

B. France, 1894; became European Heavyweight Champion in 1913 when he beat Bombardier Billy Wells; served in French Army, 1914-1918; beat Joe Beckett in an incred-
ible match lasting 74 seconds in Holborn Stadium, London, December 4, 1919;  himself beaten by Jack Dempsey in New Jersey in 1921, and the following year by  the

remarkable "Battling Siki," and in 1924 was knocked-out in the first round of contest with Gene Tunney; gave up boxing, went into light entertainment as vocalist ;
appeared in film SHOW OF SHOWS with Viola Dana and Shirley Mason (film debut 1920,
while still World Light Heavyweight Champion); five years later, in 1935, opened a
restaurant in Paris and still owns it at this writing.

Vocal, acc. by studio orchestra.              Paris, c. June, 1927.

| 200727 | La premiere fois que l'on fait ça | PA 11462 |
| 200728 | Une femme comme vous | - |

## NANCY  CARROLL

B. New York, November 19, 1906; r.n. Anna La Hiff; d. 1965. Played in straight  and
musical sound films alike; debut in ABIE'S IRISH ROSE (1928), then appeared a year
later in SHOPWORN ANGEL; PARAMOUNT ON PARADE (1930); THE KISS BEFORE THE MIRROR in
1933 and many others before retiring in 1938 (last film THAT CERTAIN AGE). Her recording career seems to have been limited to an unissued coupling with her leading
man in ABIE'S IRISH ROSE, Charles "Buddy" Rogers, q.v.

## EMMA CARUS

B. Berlin, Germany, March 18, 1879; very popular vaudeville entertainer in the opening years of the twentieth century, and is credited with introducing  Irving  Berlin's first big hit, ALEXANDER'S RAGTIME BAND (1911).  D. New York, November   18,
1927.

Vocal, acc. by studio orchestra.          New York, c. May, 1904.

| 1763- | In Zanzibar | Col 1763 |
| 1765- | Navajo | Col 1765 |

NOTE:- Prsumably matrix 1764 is a rejected title by Emma Carus.

## ENRICO  CARUSO

B. Naples, Italy, February 25, 1873; d. there, August 2, 1921.  The most  celebrated
operatic tenor of the twentieth century, who was nevertheless very much a theatrical personality, and even made two silent films ! From his Metropolitan Opera debut on November 23, 1903 until his last appearance as a singer on December 24,1920
he lived a great deal in New York, and all except two of his records made  between
those dates were recorded either there or in Camden, N. J.  Details of his career,
on stage and in the recording studio, belong properly to a book on opera, but  the
following title is the joint composition of showman Earl Carroll  and   the  singer
himself; there were also various songs about him on otherwise unimportant records,
such as MY COUSIN CARUSO; CARUSO AND TETRAZZINI, and THEY NEEDED A SONG  BIRD  IN
HEAVEN (SO GOD TOOK CARUSO AWAY (!)

Vocal, acc. by O/Walter B. Rogers.        New York, April 18, 1912.

| C-11616-3 | Dreams Of Long Ago | Vic 88376, 6015, LCT-1112, HMV 02396, DB-125 |

## CHARLEY CASE

B. Lockport, N.Y., c. 1858; negro comedian specializing in deadpan descriptions of a
variety of everyday occurrences. D. of tuberculosis at the height of his career in
New York,on November 27, 1916.

Humorous monologues.                      New York, March 18, 1909.

| B-6908-1 | Experiences In Show Business | Vic 16354 |
| B-6909-1 | How Mother Made The Soup | Vic 5693, 16547 |
| B-6910-1 | Father As A Scientist | Vic 16328 |

## WALTER CATLETT

B. San Francisco, California, February 4, 1889; d. 1960.  Stage debut 1906 at  California Theatre, S.F. (BROWNIES IN FAIRYLAND); toured U.S.A. with many "stock" companies, playing Shakespeare and minstrel shows, Irish drama and straight comedies;

New York debut in THE PRINCE OF PILSEN (Lyric, August 4, 1910); more touring,then
in SO LONG, LETTY (Shubert, October 23, 1916); ZIEGFELD FOLLIES OF 1917 (New Amsterdam, June 12, 1917); various other shows, then London debut in BABY BUNTING at
the Shaftesbury, September 27, 1919; toured England in KEYHOLE KAMEOS during the
summer of 1920; returned to New York to play in SALLY (New Amsterdam,December 21,
1920; among other notable appearances was in LADY, BE GOOD (Casino, San Francisco
April, 1926). Began film career in 1929, made countless movies as a   character
actor in supporting roles (e.g., PALMY DAYS, 1931; A TALE OF TWO CITIES, 1935; MR
DEEDS GOES TO TOWN, 1936; THE INSPECTOR GENERAL, 1949; DAVY CROCKETT AND THE RIVER
PIRATES, 1956). He was also the soundtrack voice of J. Worthington Foulfellow in
PINOCCHIO (Walt Disney, 1939).

Vocal, acc. by Shaftesbury Theatre Orchestra/Jacques Greebe.
                                        London, October, 1919.

| 76674 | At The Ball ("Baby Bunting") | Col F-1019 |
| 76675 | Listen, Baby ("Baby Bunting") | - |
| 76676 | Married Life (w/Dorothy Brunton) ("Baby | Col F-1015 |
| | Bunting") | |
| 76678 | The Green Grass Grew All Round (w/ | Col F-1016 |
| | Dorothy Brunton, Ronald Squire and Davy Burnaby) ("Baby Bunting") | |
| 76680 | Bless The Girls (w/Ronald Squire and | Col F-1020 |
| | Frank Attree) ("Baby Bunting") | |
| 76681 | Tally-Ho ! (w/Davy Burnaby) ("Baby Bunting")- | |

Acc. by studio orchestra.               Hollywood, c. October, 1939.

PBS-042396-1  Hi-Diddle-Dee-Dee (w/"Pinocchio")   Vic 26478, HMV BD-822
              (Film "Pinocchio")

## JOSEPH   CAWTHORN

B. New York, March 29, 1867, on stage at four in 1871; toured in England, 1876-1880
in minstrel shows; continued to tour on returning to U.S.A.; reappeared in London
in THE FORTUNE TELLER at the Shaftesbury in 1901; his return home brought success
in many comedies, straight and musical, among the more outstanding being THE SLIM
PRINCESS (Globe, New York, January 2, 1911); THE SUNSHINE   GIRL  (Knickerbocker,
February 3, 1913); THE GIRL FROM UTAH (Knickerbocker, August 24, 1914); SYBIL(Liberty, January 10, 1916); THE CANARY (Globe, November 4, 1918, touring with  this,
1919-1920); THE BLUE KITTEN (Selwyn, January 13, 1922); SUNNY (New Amsterdam,Sep-
tember 22, 1925). Film debut, 1927; made many before his death in 1949.

Vocal, acc. by studio orchestra.        New York, April 4, 1913.

C-13078-2  You Can't Play Every Instrument In   Vic 70098
           The Band ("The Sunshine Girl")

Acc. by O/Harold Vicars.               New York, March 9, 1916.

C-17290-1  I Can Dance With Everybody But My    Vic 55074
           Wife ("Sybil")
C-17291-3  It's A Small World                   -
C-17292-1-2  That's Why I Never Married ("The   Rejected
           Slim Princess")

Acc. by studio orchestra.              New York, May, 1922.

8937   Actors' Equity - An All-Star Comedy    Voc 35010 (part side)

## ANNA   CHANDLER

B. 1887; very popular vaudeville singer during the two decades around  World War I;
d. Hollywood, 1957.

Vocal, acc. by studio orchestra.          New York, April 26, 1911.

    In The Land Of Harmony                    Ed 4M-741

                           New York, May 20, 1911.

    I Want Everyone To Love Me (w/W. F.       Ed 4M-770
      Hooley-Steve Porter-John Bieling-Billy Murray)
    I Want Everyone To Love Me                Ed 10518

                           New York, June 9, 1911.

    When I'm Alone I'm Lonesome               Ed 4M-784
    Run Home And Tell Your Mother             Ed 4M-800

                           New York, June 30, 1911.

    When I'm Alone I'm Lonesome               Ed 10523
    Billy                                     Ed 4M-830

                           New York, July 20, 1911.

    My Lovin' Honey Man                       Ed 4M-892

                           New York, July 24, 1911.

    Maybe That Is Why I'm Lonely              Ed 4M-955

                           New York, April 17, 1912.

    Please Don't Take My Lovin' Man Away      Ed 4M-1086

                           New York, c. September, 1912.

    That Mellow Melody                        Amb 1588

                           New York, c. January, 1913.

    All Night Long                            Amb 1739

                           New York, c. February, 1913.

    Welcome Home                              Amb 1784

                           New York, c. May, 1913.

    You Made Me Love You                      Amb 1931

                           New York, c. August, 1913.

    Come Back, I'm Pining Away                Amb 2040

 Acc. by O/? Charles A. Prince.            New York, December 21, 1915.

46297-   Hello, Hawaii, How Are You ?            Col A-1939, Sil 46297
46298-1-2-3  Those Come Hither Eyes              Rejected

                           New York, January 5, 1916.

46315-   When You're Down In Louisville          Col A-1939

                           New York, January 15, 1916.

46345-   She's Good Enough To Be Your Baby's      Col A-1950
      Mother (So She's Good Enough To Vote With You)

                           New York, January 20, 1916.

46357-   You Can't Get Along With 'Em Or Without  Col A-1956
      'Em

New York, February 23, 1916.

46441-    Never Let The Same Bee Sting You Twice  Col A-1965

New York, March 18, 1916.

46650-    I'm Going 'Way Back Home And Have A      Col A-1976
          Wonderful Time

New York, May 22, 1916.

46798-    Gootmon Is A Hootmon Now                 Col A-2027
46799-    I've Got A Sweet Tooth Bothering Me      Col A-2026

New York, August 15, 1916.

46958-    The Dance Of All Nations Ragtime Ball    Col A-2086
46959-    Rolling Stones                           Rejected

New York, September 20, 1916.

47034-    Since Mary Ann McCue Came Back From      Col A-2105
          Honolulu
47035-    Sometimes You Get A Good One And               -
          Sometimes You Don't

New York, September 29, 1916.

47051-1-2-3  O'Brien Is Tryin' To Learn To Talk  Col rejected
          Hawaiian

New York, December 16, 1916.

47237-1-2-3  There Never Was A Land Like Dear     Col rejected
          Old Ireland (There Never Was A Lass Like You)
47238-1-2-3  I Love But You                             -

Acc. by Sidney Lansfield-p.          New York, May 15, 1920.

          Bold Bad Vampires                        Vic test (unnumbered)
          My Family Is Going Jazz Mad                    -

Acc. by Sidney Lansfield-p and the Rega Orchestra.
                                     New York, c. April, 1921.

7818-     Scandinavia                              OK 4297

Acc. by studio orchestra.            New York, late May, 1923.

8992-     Yes Sir ! That's Lazy Bones              Ed 51180

New York, c. July 2, 1923.

9047      My Sweetie Went Away                     Ed 51193

New York, c. September 13, 1923.

9162      He'll Always Be One Of Those Guys        Ed 51242

## CHARLIE CHAPLIN

B. London, England, April 16, 1889. Although this world-famous movie comedian  has
   never made a vocal record, he was evidently present in various recording  studios
   over the years, with the following results.  There was a spate of songs about him
   during World War I, all of them recorded, mostly in England (EVERYBODY'S    CRAZY
   OVER CHARLIE CHAPLIN; THEY ALL DO THE CHARLIE CHAPLIN WALK; CHARLIE, CHARLIE; THE
   CHARLIE CHAPLIN FOX TROT; WHEN THE MOON SHINES BRIGHT ON CHARLIE CHAPLIN (this to
   the tune of RED WING) but sung by vocalists of little importance as a rule. Debut
   at seven in music-hall sketch; appeared in GIDDY OSTEND at the London Hippodrome,
   January 15, 1900; joined Fred Karno's company, to U.S.A. on tour with this, 1910;

began in films November, 1913 (MAKING A LIVING); second film MABEL'S STRANGE PRE-
DICAMENT introduced him as the "genteel tramp" with the costume he used in dozens
of subsequent silent movies (TILLIE'S PUNCTURED ROMANCE, 1914; THE VAGABOND,1916;
THE IMMIGRANT, 1917; SHOULDER ARMS, 1918; THE KID, 1920;  THE GOLD RUSH, 1924 and
many others); steadfastly refused to make talkies (CITY LIGHTS, 1931, was silent)
but MODERN TIMES (1936) had a sequence in which he sang a number; then THE  GREAT
DICTATOR (1940) had him lampooning Adolf Hitler, in full sound, and subsequently,
MONSIEUR VERDOUX (1947), LIMELIGHT (1952), A KING IN NEW YORK (1957) and A COUNT-
ESS FROM HONG KONG (1966) gave him speaking parts, but a clown no more. He was  a
founder of United Artists Films.

METROPOLITAN MILITARY BAND : Wax autographed by Charles Chaplin, the composer of the
number.                                       New York, c. 1916.

110-1   The Peace Patrol                            Em 548 (5")

CHARLIE CHAPLIN CONDUCTING ABE LYMAN'S AMBASSADOR HOTEL ORCHESTRA playing two dance
tunes composed by him.               Los Angeles, c. July, 1925.

           Sing A Song                              Br 2912
           With You, Dear, In Bombay                  -

CHARLES CHAPLIN CONDUCTING ORCHESTRA playing his own compositions.
                                     Los Angeles, 1957.

           Mandolin Serenade (Film "A King In New  HMV POP-370
           York")
           The Spring Song (Film "A King In New York") -

## KITTY CHEATHAM

B. Nashville, Tennessee, 1864; d. January 5, 1945. Received singing lessons when  a
child; the death of her father in 1881 resulted in her going to New York with her
mother to seek an engagement.  She joined Col. McCaull's Company, her first   part
being a small one in THE BLACK HUSSAR in Toledo, Ohio.  Returned to New York, and
appeared in larger role in ERMINIE at the Casino, May 10, 1886; later sang  comic
operas; turned to comedy acting as a member of Augustin Daly's company, very successful in THE FORESTERS; also played parts established by Ada Rehan.   She also
became very interested in American negro folk-lore, and made the songs  a feature
of her concerts.

Vocal, acc. by Vess L. Ossman-bj and studio orchestra.
                                     New York, c. February 15, 1910.

30371-   Scandalize My Name/Georgia Buck            Col A-5224

30375-   When Malindy Sings                         Col A-5224

         I've Got A Pain In My Sawdust              Col A-5168
         The Visitors/The Sugar Dolly                 -
         Dixie - bj only                            Col A-5191
         The Wonderful Tar Baby Story (unacc.)        -

Acc. by Flora MacDonald-p or unacc.    Camden, N. J., January 12, 1916.

B-16998-1-2  Swing Low, Sweet Chariot/I Am          Rejected
             Seeking For A City
B-16999-1   Walk In Jerusalem Just Like John/       Vic 45086
             Sinner, Please Don't Let This Harvest Pass (unacc.)
C-17000-1   The Little Grey Lamb (unacc.)           Vic 55077

                               Camden, N. J., January 14, 1916.

B-17011-1-2-3  Nursery Rhymes No. 1 (Intro.        Vic rejected
               Little Boy Blue/Little Miss Muffet/Georgie Porgie/Pussy-Cat/Little  Bo-
               Peep)
B-17012-1-2-3  Nursery Rhymes No. 2 (Intro.             -
               Baa, Baa, Black Sheep/Baby Bunting/Pat-a-Cake/Hickory, Dickory,Dock/Mary
               Mary)

Acc. by Francis J. Lapitino-harp.        Camden, N. J., January 19, 1916.

B-17019-1-2  A Legend (Tchaikovsky, Op. 54, No. 5)Vic rejected
C-17020-1-2  Love's Lullaby                        -

Acc. by Flora MacDonald-p.               Camden, N. J., January 19, 1916.

B-17029-1-2  The Sleep Of The Child Jesus       Vic rejected
B-17030-1-2  Christmas (Voici Noël) (Weckerlin)    -
B-17031-1-2-3  Dixie                               -
B-17032-1-2  I'se Gwine Back To Dixie             -

                                         Camden, N. J., January 21, 1916.

B-17011-4  Nursery Rhymes No. 1 (Intro. Little    Vic 45082
           Boy Blue/Little Miss Muffet/Georgie Porgie/Pussy-Cat/Little Bo-Peep)
B-17012-5  Nursery Rhymes No. 2 (Intro. Baa, Baa,   -
           Black Sheep/Baby Bunting/Pat-a-Cake/Hickory, Dickory, Dock/Mary, Mary)

                                         Camden, N. J., February 11, 1916.

B-16998-3-4-5  Swing Low, Sweet Chariot/I Am      Vic rejected
           Seeking For A City
C-17000-2  The Little Grey Lamb                     -

Acc. by Harriet Johnson-p.               Camden, N. J., March 9, 1916.

B-16998-7  Swing Low, Sweet Chariot/I Am Seeking  Vic 45086
           For A City

Acc. by Francis J. Lapitino-harp or Flora MacDonald-p.
                                         Camden, N. J., April 25, 1916.

C-17020-4  Love's Lullaby - FJL                   Vic 55077
B-17031-4  Dixie - FM                             Vic 45094
B-17032-4  I'se Gwine Back To Dixie - FM            -

Acc. by Flora MacDonald-p.               Camden, N. J., September 27, 1916.

B-18472-2  Mother Goose Songs No. 2 (Intro. Three Vic 45104
           Little Kittens/Ride A Cock Horse/John Smith/Wee Willie Winkie)
B-18473-1  Once A Little Shepherd Maiden (Old French) -

Acc. by O/Joseph Pasternack.             Camden, N. J., May 18, 1917.

B-19868-1-2  Papa Haydn's Suspiro (Haydn)/Minuet  Vic rejected
           (Bach)/In The Meadow (Russian Folk Song)
B-19872-1-2-3  Butterfly (Schumann)/Children's Guard  -
           (Schumann)/Friend Husch (Herrmann)
B-19873-1-2-3  Minuet (Mozart)/Spring Song (Beethoven)-
B-19874-1-2-3  Set The Ball A-Rolling (French       -
           Canadian Folk Song)/Jasmin Flower (Chinese Folk Song)/Baby Star (adap-
           ted from Johann Strauss's THE BLUE DANUBE)

                                         Camden, N. J., September 25, 1917.

B-19872-4-5-6  Butterfly (Schumann)/Children's    Vic rejected
           Guard (Schumann)/Friend Husch (Herrmann)

                                         Camden, N. J., October 9, 1917.

B-19868-3-4  Papa Haydn's Suspiro (Haydn)/Minuet  Vic rejected
           (Bach)/In The Meadow (Russian Folk Song)
B-19873-4  Minuet (Mozart)/Spring Song (Beethoven)   -

## MAURICE CHEVALIER

B. Menilmontant, near Paris, France, September 12, 1889; d. there, January 1, 1972.
   Stage debut 1906 in Belleville as a red-nose comic; appeared in Folies-Bergere in
   1909 with Mistinguett until 1913; when World War I broke out in 1914, he   joined

the Army, was taken prisoner, and was released early in 1918.  Reappeared at  the
Folies-Bergere, thence to the Theatre Femina in LA REVUE DE FEMINA and GOBETTE DE
PARIS; London debut in HULLO, AMERICA at the Palace, February, 1919, replacing the
leading man, Owen Nares; returned to Paris, resumed work at the ˉ Folies-Bergère,
the Casino de Paris (with Mistinguett); appeared in a song-and-dance act  through
1919-1921 with Yvonne Vallee, whom he subsequently married (and divorced); played
the lead in DE-DE (1921), and appeared with his wife in London in WHITE BIRDS, at
His Majesty's Theatre, May 31, 1927; to New York, early 1929; at Ziegfeld's Amsterdam Roof Garden (July, 1929) in songs from his repertoire; film debut the same
year (INNOCENTS OF PARIS); in the London revue STOP PRESS (Adelphi, June 6,1935);
many other films (THE LOVE PARADE, PARAMOUNT ON PARADE, THE BIG POND, PLAYBOY  OF
PARIS and THE SMILING LIEUTENANT, all 1930; ONE HOUR WITH YOU and LOVE ME TONIGHT
(1932); A BEDTIME STORY (1933); THE MAN FROM THE FOLIES BERGERE (1935); following
the end of World War II, was outstandingly successful in GIGI (1958),CAN-CAN,1959
and IN SEARCH OF THE CASTAWAYS, 1962. Special Academy Award 1958 for his "contributions to the world of entertainment for more than half a century," and  decora-
ted as a Chevalier of the Legion d'Honneur (1938) "for signal services to  French
propaganda in all countries."

Vocal, acc. by O/George W. Byng.          Hayes, Middlesex, March 21, 1919.

HO-4761-AE  On The Level You're A Little Devil    HMV B-1024, Par PMC-7145
            ("Hullo America")

    Acc. by studio orchestra.          Paris, c. November, 1921.

    3410    Pour bien reussir dans la chaussure    Pathe 2030
            ("De-De")
    3411    J'ose pas ( /De-De")                   -
    3420    Si j'avais su (w/Mlle. Cocea)          Pathe 2032

                                       Paris, c. 1923-1924.

    2080    Je n'ose pas                           PA N-4372
    2085    Si les femmes etaient toutes fideles   -
    200322  Saves-vous ? (w/Yvonne Vallee)         Pathe 4266
    200325  Balance-la !                           -
            Ah ! Madam "Humpa ! Humpa ! Humpa !"   PA F-504
            Si vous saviez comme je fais ça        -

    Acc. by Jean Wiener-Clement Doucet-p duet.
                                       Paris, October 26, 1926.

WL-292-1  Quand je suis chez toi (w/Yvonne Vallee)Col 4401, DM-1303
WL-293-1  Mon coeur (w/Yvonne Vallee)             Col 4402
WL-300-   Mais ou est ma Zouzou ? (I Wonder       Col 4401, DM-1303
            Where My Baby Is Tonight ?)
WL-304-   Je ne dis pas non                        Col 4402
    NOTE:- Matrices WL-294/299 and WL-301/3 all inclusive are not by Maurice  Cheval-
    ier.

    Acc. by O/Pierre Chagnon.          Paris, November, 1927.

WL-743-   Ma Reguliere                             Col D-2023
WL-744-1  Sans avoir l'air d'y toucher             -

WL-758-1  Quand on est tout seul                   Col D-2026
WL-759-1  Dites-moi, ma mere (Tell Me, Mother)     -

    Acc. by O/Leonard Joy.             New York, March 14, 1929.

BVE-50942-2  Louise (Film "Innocents Of Paris")   Vic 21918, DPM-2033-1, LPV-538,
                                                   LPV-564, LSA-3074, RD-7869,
                                                   VPM-6055-1, HMV B-3073, JO-382
BVE-50943-2  It's A Habit Of Mine (Film "Inno-     Vic 22007, HMV B-3089
               cents Of Paris")
BVE-50944-2  On Top Of The World, Alone (Film        -      HMV B-3073
               "Innocents Of Paris")

Acc. by O/Tom Griselle.                    New York, March 15, 1929.

BVE-49783-2  Wait Till You See "Ma Cherie" (Film  Vic 21918, LPV-564, HMV B-3089
             "Innocents Of Paris")
BVE-49784-2  Les Ananas                            Vic 22093, DPM-2033-1, LPV-564,
                                                   VPM-6055-1
BVE-49785-2  Valentine (Film "Innocents Of Paris")Vic 22093, DPM-2033-1, LCT-1112,
                                                   VPM-6055-1, HMV B-3364, JO-382

Acc. by O/Leonard Joy.                     New York, January 22, 1930.

BVE-58513-2-3  Nobody's Using It Now (Film "The  Vic 22285, HMV B-3332
               Love Parade")
BVE-58514-2-3  My Love Parade (Film "The Love     **As above** plus Vic DPM-2033-1,
               Parade")                           VPM-6055-1

                                           New York, January 25, 1930.

BVE-58521-2-3  Paris, Stay The Same (Film "The   Vic 22294, HMV B-3364
               Love Parade")
BVE-58522-1-2  You've Got That Thing                -

                                           New York, March 7, 1930.

BVE-58617-    Mon Cocktail d'Amour (My Love       Vic 22368
              Parade) (Film "The Love Parade")
BVE-58618-    Personne ne s'en sert maintenant      -
              (Nobody's Using It Now) (Film "The Love Parade")

                                           New York, March 22, 1930.

BVE-59648-2  All I Want Is Just One (Girl) (Film  Vic 22378, HMV B-3480
             "Paramount On Parade")
BVE-59649-3  Sweepin' The Clouds Away (Film         - LPV-564 -
             "Paramount On Parade")

                                           New York, April 4, 1930.

BVE-59672-2  You Brought A New Kind Of Love To Me Vic 22405, DPM-2033-1, VPM-6055-1
             (Film "The Big Pond")               HMV B-3517
BVE-59673-3  Livin' In The Sunlight, Lovin' In    As above plus Vic LPM-564
             The Moonlight (Film "The Big Pond")

                                           New York, April 10, 1930.

BVE-59687-   Vous etes mon nouveau bonheur (You   Vic 22415, LPV-564
             Brought A New Kind Of Love To Me) (Film "The Big Pond")
BVE-59688-   Paris, je t'aime d'amour               -          -

                                           New York, August 15, 1930.

BVE-62387-2  My Ideal (Film "Playboy Of Paris")   Vic 22542, DPM-2033-1, VPM-6055-1
                                                  HMV B-3684
BVE-62388-3  It's A Great Life (Film "Playboy Of  Vic 22542, HMV B-3684
             Paris")
BVE-62389-2  It's A Great Life (Film "Playboy Of  Vic 22549, DPM-2033-1, VPM-6055-1
             Paris") (In French)
BVE-62390-2  My Ideal (Film "Playboy Of Paris")     -
             (In French)

Acc. by studio orchestra.              Paris, November, 1930.

BG-1152-2  Toi et moi                            HMV B-3685

BG-1166-2  Ca fait tout de meme plaisir          HMV K-6054
BG-1167-1  Oui et non                              -
BG-1168-3  Oh, Come On, Be Sociable              HMV B-3685

Acc. by Jack Hylton and his Orchestra. Paris, November 28, 1930.

BK-3064-2  Maurice Chevalier Medley - Part 1        HMV B-3686
             (Intro. Livin' In The Sunlight, Lovin' In The Moonlight/Louise/ Paris,
             Stay The Same/Valentine)
BK-3065-3  Maurice Chevalier Medley - Part 2            -
             (Intro. You Brought A New Kind Of Love To Me/Nobody's Using It Now/ Mon
             Cocktail d'Amour/Dites-moi, ma mere)
BK-3067-   Maurice Chevalier Medley - Part 3        HMV K-3065
BK-3068-   Maurice Chevalier Medley - Part 4            -
   NOTE:- Matrix BK-3066 is by Jack Hylton and his Orchestra, with a vocal trio  that
   does not include Maurice Chevalier.  The contents of Parts 3 and 4 of the  Maurice
   Chevalier Medley are not at present known.

   Acc. by O/Leonard Joy.                    New York, February 22, 1931.

BVE-67465-2  Hello, Beautiful !                    Vic 22634, DPM-2033-1, LPV-564,
                                                   VPM-6055-1, HMV B-3845
BVE-67466-2  Walkin' My Baby Back Home             As above

                                      New York, May 28, 1931.

BVE-69656-1  Moonlight-Saving Time                 Vic 22723, LPV-564, HMV B-3914
BVE-69657-2  Right Now !                              -            -            -
BVE-69661-2  Mama Inez                             Vic 22731, LPV-564, HMV B-3923
BVE-69664-2  Mama Inez (In French)                 Vic 22747
BVE-69665-2  Bon soir                              Vic 22731, DPM-2033-1, LPV-564,
                                                   VPM-6055-1, HMV B-3923
BVE-69666-1  Bon soir (In French)                  Vic 22747
   NOTE:- Matrices BVE-69658/60 and BVE-69662/3 are by other artists.

                                      New York, June 25, 1931.

BS-69976-1  Nobody Loves No Baby (Like My Baby     Vic rejected
              Loves Me)
BS-69977-1  Little Hunka Love                          -

                                      New York, February 24, 1932.

BS-71983-1  What  Would You Do ? (Film "One Hour   Vic 22941, HMV B-4173
              With You")
BS-71984-1  What  Would You Do ? (Film "One Hour   Vic 22944
              With You") (In French)
BS-71898-1  Oh ! That Mitzi (Film "One Hour With   Vic 22941, DPM-2033-1, LPV-564,
              You")                                VPM-6055-1, HMV B-4173
BS-71899-1  Oh ! That Mitzi (Film "One Hour With   Vic 22944
              You") (In French) (NOTE:- Matrices BS-71895/7 are by other artists).

   Acc. by O/Nat Finston.                    Hollywood, June 29, 1932.

PBS-68360-1  Mimi (Film "Love Me Tonight")         Vic 24063, DPM-2033-1, LPV-564,
                                                   VPM-6055-1, HMV B-4289
PBS-68361-   Mimi (Film "Love Me Tonight") (In     Vic 24066
               French),
PBS-68362-2  The Poor Ápache (Film "Love Me        Vic 24063, HMV B-4289
               Tonight")
PBS-68363-   Je suis un mechant                    Vic 24066, DPM-2033-1, LPV-564,
                                                   VPM-6055-1

                                      Hollywood, March 18, 1933.

PCS-68450-1-2  A Musical Preview of A BEDTIME       Paramount advertising record made
                 STORY                              by RCA Victor
PCS-68451-1-2  Musical Hits from A BEDTIME STORY    As above

                                      Hollywood, September 16, 1933.

PCS-68543-1-2  In A One-Room Flat/It's Oh ! It's   Paramount advertising record made
                 Wonderful (Film "The Way To Love")  by RCA Victor
PCS-68544-1-2  I'm A Lover Of Paree/It's Oh ' It's Ah ! As above

Acc. by O/Wyatt Moore.                    Hollywood, February 11, 1935.

| | | |
|---|---|---|
| PBS-79596-1 | Rhythm Of The Rain (Film "The Man From The Folies-Bergere") | Vic 24874, HMV B-8305 |
| PBS-79597-1 | Rhythm Of The Rain (Film "The Man From The Folies-Bergere") (In French) | Vic 24883 |
| PBS-79598-1 | Singing A Happy Song (Film "The Man From The Folies-Bergere") | Vic 24882, HMV B-8305 |
| PBS-79599-1 | Singing A Happy Song (Film "The Man From The Folies-Bergere") (In French) | Vic 24883 |
| PBS-90000-1 | I Was Lucky (Film "The Man From The Folies-Bergere") | Vic 24882, HMV B-8306 |
| PBS-90001-1 | I Was Lucky (Film "The Man From The Folies-Bergere") (In French) | Rejected |
| PBS-90002-1 | You Took The Words Right Out Of My Mouth (Film "The Man From The Folies-Bergere") | Vic 24874, HMV B-8306 |
| PBS-90003-1 | You Took The Words Right Out Of My Mouth (Film "The Man From The Folies-Bergere") (In French) | Rejected |

Acc. by studio orchestra.                 Paris, October, 1935.

| | | |
|---|---|---|
| OLA-668- | Donnez-moi la main (Film "Parade du Monde") | HMV K-7588 |
| OLA-669- | Prosper (Film "Parade du Monde") | — |

Paris, April 10, 1936.

| | | |
|---|---|---|
| OLA-1032-1 | You Look So Sweet, Madame (Film "The Beloved Vagabond") | HMV B-8440 |
| OLA-1033-1 | Tzinga-Doodle-Day (Film "The Beloved Vagabond") | — |

Paris, late September, 1936.

| | | |
|---|---|---|
| OLA-1267-1 | Ma Pomme | HMV B-9000 |

Paris, April, 1937.

| | | |
|---|---|---|
| OLA-1683-1 | Moi, je vous l'dir (Film "Paris en joie") | HMV K-7887 |
| OLA-1684-1 | L'amour est passe pres de vous (Film "Paris en joie") | — |

Paris, November, 1938.

| | | |
|---|---|---|
| OLA-2814-1 | Ah ! si vous connaissiez ma poule | HMV B-9000 |

Acc. by O/Marcel Cariven.                 Paris, September, 1939.

| | | |
|---|---|---|
| OLA-3187- | Mon amour | HMV JO-13 |
| OLA-3188- | Ca s'est passe un dimanche | HMV JO-11 |
| OLA-3190- | Il Pleurait | HMV JO-13 |

Paris, October 31, 1939.

| | | |
|---|---|---|
| OLA-3211- | Ca fait d'excellents Français | HMV JO-11 |
| OLA-3212- | Paris sera toujours Paris | HMV JO-14 |
| OLA-3213- | Appelez-ça comme vous voulez | HMV JOF-70 |

Paris, November 24, 1939.

| | | |
|---|---|---|
| OLA-3218-1 | Mimile | HMV JOF-44 |
| OLA-3219- | Arthur | HMV JO-14 |

Acc. by O/Marcel Pagnoul.                 Paris, October 24, 1941.

| | | |
|---|---|---|
| OLA-3627-1 | Notre espoir | HMV JOF-15 |
| OLA-3628-1 | Toi....toi....toi | — |
| OLA-3630- | La Choupetta | HMV JOF-18 |

Acc. by O/Marcel Cariven.              Paris, December, 1941.

OLA-3657-1  Ce sent si bon la France            HMV JOF-70

Maurice Chevalier made many other records in France and the U.S.A. (including one in
   French of the Beatles' success THE YELLOW SUBMARINE, which he made a green one, as
   late as 1966.

## BUDDY  CLARK

B. 1911; very popular vocalist during the thirties with the bands of Gus Arnheim,Lud
   Gluskin, Nat Brandwynne and Wayne King; successful as soloist and in duets, mainly
   with Doris Day; killed October 1, 1949 in air crash returning to Hollywood    from
   San Francisco after watching a ball-game.

Vocalist with Gus Arnheim and his Orchestra.
                                       Chicago, July 2, 1932.

BS-71765-1  Evening                             Vic 24061

Vocalist with Freddy Martin and his Orchestra.
                                       New York, September 14, 1934.

B-15917-    Stars Fell On Alabama               Br 6976
B-15918-    Isn't It A Shame ?                  Br 6982, 01881
B-15919-    In The Quiet Of An Autumn Night     -

Vocal, acc. by studio orchestra.       New York, December 6, 1934.

16453-    June In January                       Mt M-13265
16454-    With Every Breath I Take              -

Vocalist with Lud Gluskin and his Continental Orchestra.
                                       New York, September 26, 1935.

B-18108-    Here's To Romance                   Br 7536
B-18109-    Rhythm And Romance                  Br 7535
B-18110-    Red Sails In The Sunset             -
B-18111-    Midnight In Paris                   Br 7536

                                       New York, December 26, 1935.

B-18446-    I'm Shooting High                   Br 7592
B-18447-    Moon Over Miami                     Br 7590
B-18448-    I've Got My Fingers Crossed         Br 7592

Vocal, acc. by studio orchestra.       New York, March 13, 1936.

18815-    The Touch Of Your Lips                ARC 6-05-10
18816-    Lost                                  -           Cq 8652

Vocalist with Nat Brandwynne and his Stork Club Orchestra.
                                       New York, April 13, 1936.

B-19008-    Lazy Weather                        Br 7660
B-19009-    The Glory Of Love                   -
B-19010-    It's You I'm Talkin' About          Br 7655
B-19011-    There's Always A Happy Ending       -

Vocalist with Lud Gluskin and his Continental Orchestra.
                                       New York, April 23, 1936.

B-19090-    My First Thrill                     Br 7658
B-19091-    She Shall Have Music                -
B-19092-    On The Air                          Br 7664
B-19093-    Sunshine At Midnight                -

Vocalist with Nat Brandwynne and his Stork Club Orchestra.
New York, May 25, 1936.

| | | |
|---|---|---|
| B-19322-1 | Take My Heart | Br 7676, Voc 510 |
| B-19323- | These Foolish Things | - |
| B-19324- | Long Ago And Far Away | Br 7678 |
| B-19325- | Where Is My Heart ? | - |

New York, July 23, 1936.

| | | |
|---|---|---|
| B-19590- | Until Today | Br 7712 |
| B-19591- | Without A Shadow Of A Doubt | - |
| B-19592- | If We Never Meet Again | Br 7714 |
| B-19593-2 | Bye, Bye, Baby | -          Voc 510 |

Vocalist with Lud Gluskin and his Orchestra.
New York, November 13, 1936.

| | | |
|---|---|---|
| 20244- | May I Have The Next Romance With You ? | Br 7788, Voc 533 |
| 20245- | Rainbow On The River | Br 7779 |
| 20246- | Head Over Heels In Love | Br 7788, Voc 533 |
| 20247- | You're Too Good To Be True | Br 7779 |

Vocal, acc. by studio orchestra.      New York, June 14, 1938.

| | | |
|---|---|---|
| 23095- | Spring Is Here | Voc 4191 |
| 23096- | I Married An Angel | - |
| 23097- | Let Me Whisper | Voc 4207 |
| 23098- | Beside A Moonlit Stream | - |

Vocalist with Wayne King and his Orchestra.
Chicago, October 23, 1940.

| | | |
|---|---|---|
| BS-053562-1 | I Should Have Known You Years Ago | Vic 27201 |
| BS-053563-1 | He's My Uncle | - |

Vocal, acc. by studio orchestra.      Chicago, April 9, 1941.

| | | |
|---|---|---|
| C-3665-1 | A Little Old Church In England | OK 6193 |
| C-3666-1 | When That Man Is Dead And Gone | - |
| C-3667-1 | Lamplight | OK 6170 |
| C-3668-1 | G'bye Now | - |

Chicago, July 25, 1941.

| | | |
|---|---|---|
| C-3913-1 | Have You Changed ? | OK 6356 |
| C-3914-1 | Honorable Moon | OK 6368 |
| C-3915-1 | Dream Dancing | - |
| C-3916-1 | Rancho Pillow | OK 6356 |

Chicago, August 22, 1941.

| | | |
|---|---|---|
| C-3983-1 | A Sinner Kissed An Angel | OK 6403 |
| C-3984-1 | Moonlight Masquerade | OK 6392 |
| C-3985-1 | Ma-Ma-Maria (Fee-dle, ee-dle-lee, Fee-dle, ee-dle-la) | - |
| C-3986-1 | Delilah | OK 6403 |

New York, October 27, 1941.

| | | |
|---|---|---|
| 31601- | Ev'rything I Love | OK 6469 |
| 31602- | Ev'ry Time | OK 6490 |
| 31603- | I Hate You, Darling | OK 6469 |
| 31604- | It Happened In Hawaii | OK 6490 |

New York, February 25, 1942.

| | | |
|---|---|---|
| 32476- | That Old Gang Of Mine | OK 6669 |
| 32477- | My Buddy | OK 6670 |

(continued on page 139)

BUDDY CLARK (cont.)

New York, February 25, 1942 (cont.)

| | | |
|---|---|---|
| 32478- | Dear Old Pal Of Mine | OK 6668 |
| 32479- | Smiles | OK 6669 |
| 32480- | Keep The Home Fires Burning | OK 6671 |
| 32481- | Just A Baby's Prayer At Twilight | OK 6668 |
| 32482- | There's A Long, Long Trail | OK 6670 |

## ROSE COGHLAN

B. 1850; American actress who toured the world at the head of her own company after starring in both the U.S.A. and England (she appeared in Great Britain in 1869). She made a small selection of silent films, such as AS YOU LIKE IT (1912), UNDER THE RED ROBE (1923). D. April 2, 1932.

Speech.                                                   New York, January 28, 1909.

| | | |
|---|---|---|
| C-6755-1-2 | The Charge Of The Light Brigade (Tennyson) | Vic rejected |

New York, January 30, 1909.

| | | |
|---|---|---|
| C-6755-3 | The Charge Of The Light Brigade (Tennyson) | Vic 31728 |
| B-6762-1 | Penelope's Last Cry To Ulysses ("Ulysses" - Phillips) | Rejected |

## GEORGE M. COHAN

B. Providence, R.I., July 4, 1878; debut at 10 in one of his father's plays, and a member of the family vaudeville act, The Four Cohans, in his teens; began writing stage material with THE GOVERNOR'S SON, but first great success was LITTLE JOHNNY JONES (1904), followed over the next five years by FORTY-FIVE MINUTES FROM BROAD-WAY, GEORGE WASHINGTON, Jr., POPULARITY and FIFTY MILES FROM BOSTON. He composed such permanent hits as MARY'S A GRAND OLD NAME, YANKEE DOODLE DANDY, OVER THERE, the American war song of 1917, and GIVE MY REGARDS TO BROADWAY. After World War I, his biggest stage success was LITTLE NELLY KELLY at the Liberty, New York, on November 13, 1922; this also played very successfully in London (New Oxford, July 2, 1923). He appeared in several films, notably the silents SEVEN KEYS TO BALD-PATE (1917) and HIT-THE-TRAIL HOLIDAY (1918), and in talkies THE PHANTOM PRESI-DENT (1932) and GAMBLING (1934); James Cagney played him in YANKEE DOODLE DANDY, 1942, and THE SEVEN LITTLE FOYS, 1955. D. November 5, 1942.

Vocal, acc. by O/? Walter B. Rogers.      New York, May 4, 1911.

| | | |
|---|---|---|
| B-10264-1 | Life's A Funny Proposition, After All | Vic 60042, Cam CAL-745 |
| C-10265-1 | I'm Awfully Strong For You ("The Yankee Prince") | Rejected |
| B-10266-1 | I Want To Hear A Yankee Doodle Tune | Vic 60045, AR 2290 |
| B-10267-1 | Hey There ! May There | Vic 60049 |
| B-10268-1 | You Won't Do Any Business If You Haven't Got A Band | Vic 60043 |
| C-10269-1 | That Same Love ("The American Idea") | Rejected |
| C-10270-1 | I'll Go The Route For You | - |
| B-10271-1 | I'm Mighty Glad I'm Living, That's All | Vic 60044 |
| B-10272-1 | The Small Town Gal ("Fifty Miles From Boston") | Vic 60052 |
| C-10273-1 | P.S. - Mr. Johnson Sends Regards | Vic 70039 |

Speech.                                   Location unknown, probably during 30s.

         Curtain Speech                      Coral CRL-57308, AR 2465

## RONALD COLMAN

B. Richmond, Surrey, England, February 9, 1891; amateur with West Middlesex Drama-tic Society; debut on professional stage, 1914 (gave up office clerk job); wounded in action, 1916, invalided out of British Army, resumed acting career in London; made several British silent films, beginning with THE SNOW OF THE DESERT (1919). To New York, 1920; appeared in THE GREEN GODDESS (Booth, January 18, 1921), with

George Arliss; THE NIGHT CAP (39th Street, August, 1921); to Hollywood, 1922 (THE
WHITE SISTER, with Lilian Gish); many other silents (notably STELLA DALLAS, 1925;
KIKI and BEAU GESTE, 1926; THE WINNING OF BARBARA WORTH, 1928). First sound film
BULLDOG DRUMMOND (1929); other outstanding successes include RAFFLES (1931);CLIVE
OF INDIA (1935); A TALE OF TWO CITIES and UNDER TWO FLAGS (1936); LOST    HORIZON
and THE PRISONER OF ZENDA (1937); IF I WERE KING (1938); RANDOM HARVEST(1943) and
CHAMPAGNE FOR CAESAR (1950); was starred in television series HALLS OF IVY(1957).
D. 1958.

Speech, acc. by O/Victor Young, and chorus dir. Ken Darby.
                                    Los Angeles, September 17, 1941.

| | | | | | |
|---|---|---|---|---|---|
| DLA-2772-A | A Christmas Carol (as Scrooge)-Part 1 | Dec 29108, | DL-8010, | K-1078 |
| DLA-2773-A | A Christmas Carol (as Scrooge)-Part 2 | - | - | - |
| DLA-2774-A | A Christmas Carol (as Scrooge)-Part 3 | Dec 29109 | - | K-1079 |
| DLA-2775-A | A Christmas Carol (as Scrooge)-Part 4 | - | - | - |
| DLA-2776-A | A Christmas Carol (as Scrooge)-Part 5 | Dec 29110 | - | K-1080 |
| DLA-2777-A | A Christmas Carol (as Scrooge)-Part 6 | - | - | - |

## JERRY  COLONNA

B. Boston, Mass., 1904; r.n. Gerard Colonna. Originally a longshoreman, but became
a dance band musician after studying trombone and drums (played with Joe  Herlihy
and his Orchestra in mid-twenties). Played in short comedy routines on radio  in
the thirties; Pepsodent presented a show with Bob Hope and Jerry Colonna in 1938,
in which his zany humour and catch-phrases (e.g., "Who's Yehoodi ?") made a smash
hit; appeared in many films, such as ROSALIE (1937); COLLEGE SWING (1939);    THE
ROAD TO SINGAPORE (1940); SIS HOPKINS (1941); ATLANTIC CITY (1944); IT'S IN    THE
BAG (1945); THE ROAD TO RIO (1947); ANDY HARDY COMES HOME (1958). Toured   British Isles, 1956; suffered stroke, 1966, but recovered miraculously and  went with
Bob Hope to Vietnam in 1969.

Vocal, acc. by the Rhythm Wreckers.    Los Angeles, November 9, 1937.

| | | |
|---|---|---|
| LA-1522- | Hector (The Garbage Collector) | Voc 3876 |
| LA-1523- | You're My Everything | - |

Acc. by Fud (Livingston) and his Fuddy Bears.
                                    Los Angeles, April 2, 1938.

| | | |
|---|---|---|
| LA-1622-A | Sonny Boy | Voc 4056, Col FB-2084 |
| LA-1623- | On The Road To Mandalay | - |

NOTE:- Matrix LA-1623/4 are not by Jerry Colonna.

                                    Los Angeles, July 15, 1938.

| | | |
|---|---|---|
| LA-1680-A-B | Song Of The Open Road | Rejected |
| LA-1681-A | A Bird In A Gilded Cage | Voc 4382, Col FB-2084 |

                                    Los Angeles, August 6, 1938.

| | | |
|---|---|---|
| LA-1680- | Song Of The Open Road | Voc 4382 |

                                    Los Angeles, May 12, 1939.

| | | |
|---|---|---|
| LA-1885-A | Don't Send My Boy To Prison | Col 35293 |
| LA-1886-A | When You Were Sweet Sixteen | Rejected |
| LA-1887-A | Tally-Ho ! | - |
| LA-1888-A | I Came To Say Goodbye | Col 35293 |

Acc. by studio orchestra.    Los Angeles, January 13, 1940.

| | | |
|---|---|---|
| LA-2102-A | Where Is My Wandering Boy Soprano Voice Tonight ? | Col 36363 |
| LA-2103-A | The Life Of A Sailor | - |
| LA-2104-A | I Love Life | Col 35371 |
| LA-2105- | My Mother Was A Lady (If Jack Were Only Here) | - |

Los Angeles, May 13, 1940.

LA-2223-A  Who's Yehoodi ?                              Col 35512
LA-2224-A  Every Day Is Lady's Day With Me                 -

  Acc. by Orrin Tucker and his Orchestra.
                               Hollywood, November 11, 1940.

H-181-1  The Yogi Who Lost His Will Power              Col 35866

  Acc. by studio orchestra.              Hollywood, January 30, 1941.

HCO-225-1  Remember Dad (On Mother's Day)              Col 36092
HCO-226-1  Lalita                                        -

## RUSS COLUMBO

B. 1908; r.n. Ruggiero de Rudolpho Columbo.  Played violin, composed several songs,
  such as PRISONER OF LOVE, crooned in a way that appealed to the youth of the day,
  as to become a rival to Bing Crosby; led a band and appeared in several films between 1929 and 1934 (THE WOLF SONG; THE STREET GIRL; WONDER OF WOMEN;  HELLBOUND;
  DYNAMITE; BROADWAY THROUGH A KEYHOLE; MOULIN ROUGE: WAKE UP AND DREAM).  He  died
  when a photographer friend struck a match on the barrel of an ancient pistol(September 2, 1934).  Unbeknown to anyone, there was a shot and powder in the  barrel,
  which were fired, ricocheted off a table and hit Columbo in the head.

Vocalist with Gus Arnheim and his Orchestra.
                               Hollywood, June 18, 1930.

PBVE-54835-4  A Peach Of A Pair                     Vic 22546, HMV B-5953

Vocal, acc. by Con Conrad-p.          New York, July 2, 1931.

BRC-470    Out Of Nowhere                           Vic test

  Acc. by small orchestra: t/cl/vn/p/g/sb.
                          New York, **September 3, 1931.**

BS-70210-1  I Don't Know Why (I Just Do)         Vic 22801, HMV B-4042
BS-70211-1  Guilty                                          HMV B-3997
BS-70212-1  You Call It Madness (But I Call It   Vic 22802, BB B-6503, HMV B-3984
          Love)

  Acc. by O/Nat Shilkret.               New York, September 9, 1931.

BS-70224-2  Sweet And Lovely                     Vic 22802, 27635, LPM-2072,
                                      LSA-3066, HMV B-3984

                         New York, October   9, 1931.

BS-70281-1  Time On My Hands                     Vic 22826, LPM-2072, LSA-3066,
                                     BB B-6503
BS-70282-1  Goodnight, Sweetheart                Vic 22826, 27636
BS-70283-1  Prisoner Of Love                     Vic 22867, 27635, HMV B-4079

  Acc. by O/Leonard Joy.               New York, November 18, 1931.

BS-70953-1  You Try Somebody Else                Vic 22861, LPM-2072, LSA-3066
BS-70954-2  Call Me Darling (Call Me Sweetheart,   - 27634  -             -
          Call Me Dear)
BS-70955-1  Where The Blue Of The Night (Meets   Vic 22867, 27637, LPM-2072,
          The Gold Of The Day)                 LSA-3066, HMV B-4079

                       New York, December 29, 1931.

BS-71207-1  Save The Last Dance For Me           Vic 22903, 27634, LPM-2072,
                                     LSA-3066
BS-71208-1  All Of Me                            Vic 22903, LPM-2072, LSA-3066

New York, January 12, 1932.

| | | |
|---|---|---|
| BS-71218-1 | Just Friends | Vic 22909, LPM-2072, LSA-3066 |
| BS-71219-1 | You're My Everything | -        -        - |

New York, April 6, 1932.

| | | |
|---|---|---|
| BS-72243-1 | Auf Wiedersehen, My Dear | Vic 22976, 27637, LPM-2072, LSA-3066 |
| BS-72244-1 | Paradise | Vic 22976, 27636, LPM-2072, LSA-3066 |

Vocalist with his own orchestra.    New York, June 16, 1932.

| | | |
|---|---|---|
| BS-73017-1 | Just Another Dream Of You | Vic 24045 |
| BS-73018-1 | I Wanna Be Loved | Rejected |
| BS-73019-1 | Living In Dreams | Vic 24045, LPM-2072, LSA-3066 |

New York, August 3, 1932.

| | | |
|---|---|---|
| BS-73148-1 | My Love | Vic 24077 |
| BS-73149-1 | As You Desire Me | Vic 24076, HMV B-6265 |
| BS-73150-1 | Lonesome Me | Vic 24077 |
| BS-73151-1 | The Lady I Love | Vic 24076 |

New York, November 23, 1932.

| | | |
|---|---|---|
| BS-73995-1 | Street Of Dreams | Vic 24194 |
| BS-73996-1 | Make Love The Thing | Vic 24195 |
| BS-73997-1 | I Called To Say Goodnight | - |
| BS-73998-1 | Lost In A Crowd | Vic 24194 |

Vocal, acc. by Jimmie Grier and his Orchestra.
Los Angeles, August 31, 1934.

| | | |
|---|---|---|
| LA-200- | When You're In Love (Film "Wake Up And Dream") | Br 6972, Dec F-5405 |
| LA-201- | Too Beautiful For Words (Film "Wake Up And Dream") | - |
| LA-202- | Let's Pretend There's A Moon (Film "Wake Up And Dream") | Br 6972, Dec F-5596 |
| LA-203- | I See Two Lovers | Rejected |

## DOLLY CONNOLLY

The wife of composer Percy Wenrich, billed on most of her records in parentheses as such; seems to have made a few films, and appeared in GREENWICH VILLAGE FOLLIES - making a hit with her husband's then latest number, BY THE CAMP FIRE - at Greenwich Village Theatre, New York, July 15, 1919.  Many of her records are of songs written by Percy Wenrich, and are thus important as many of them again are unique examples of these numbers on record.

Vocal, acc. by studio orchestra (cond. ? Charles A. Prince).
New York, May 26, 1911.

| | | |
|---|---|---|
| 19387- | My Hula Hula Love | Col A-1028 |
| 19388- | Red Rose Rag | -        2145 |

New York, July 7, 1911.

| | | |
|---|---|---|
| 19448- | Open Your Eyes | Col A-1061 |
| 19449- | Spanish Eyes | - |

New York, September 30, 1911.

| | | |
|---|---|---|
| 19580-3 | Oh, Mr. Dream Man, Please Let Me Dream Some More | Col A-1083, 1928 |
| 19581-9 | I've Got Feathers On My Head | - |

New York, November 8, 1911.

| 19656- | Honey Man | Col A-1102 |
| 19657- | Oh, That Navajo Rag | - |

New York, December 11, 1911.

| 19686-3 | My Counterfeit Bill | Col A-1116 |

New York, December 12, 1911.

| 19687-2 | If You Talk In Your Sleep, Don't Mention My Name | Col A-1116 |

New York, January 8, 1912.

| 19720- | Moonlight Bay | Col A-1128, 1928 |
| 19721- | The Ragtime Mocking Bird | Col A-1126, 2145 |

New York, January 30, 1912.

| 19741- | Hypnotizin' Man | Col A-1140, 2041 |

New York, March 4, 1912.

| 19780- | I Want A Little Lovin' | Col rejected |

New York, March 30, 1912.

| 19835- | Ragtime Chimes | Col A-1177 |

New York, June 24, 1912.

| 19988- | Waiting For The Robert E. Lee | Col A-1197, 2026 |

New York, August 12, 1912.

| 38201- | Tennessee Moon | Col rejected |

New York, March 8, 1913.

| 38697-3 | I Miss My Mississippi Man | Col A-1312 |

New York, March 10, 1913.

| 38698-3 | My Raggyadore | Col A-1312 |

New York, May 16, 1913.

| 38857- | The Flower-Garden Ball | Col A-1346 |

New York, February 11, 1916.

| 46394-2 | Sweet Cider-Time When You Were Mine | Col A-1963 |

New York, August 16, 1916.

| 46964-3 | 'Way Out Yonder In The Golden West | Col A-2084 |

New York, c. December, 1919.

| 4652-8 | One Loving Caress | Em 10180 |

New York, c. April, 1920.

| 41077-2-3 | Daddy, You've Been A Mother To Me | Em 10159 |

NOTE:- In view of the high take number of matrix 4652-8, it is quite likely it  was
 re-made at a later date, perhaps at the same session as 41077.

B. 1914; child star at six following performance in THE KID with Charlie Chaplin in
   1920; many other silent movies (e.g., PECK'S BAD BOY and OLIVER TWIST, 1921;   MY
   BOY, 1922; DADDY, 1923; OLD CLOTHES, 1925; THE BUGLE CALL, 1927; also made a   few
   early talkies, such as TOM SAWYER (1930) and HUCKLEBERRY FINN (1931);   reappeared
   as an adult in 1938 in COLLEGE SWING, followed over the next thirty years by some
   other more or less comedy performances, ending with THE SHAKIEST GUN IN THE   WEST
   (1968) and in the TV series THE ADDAMS FAMILY (1964-1965).

Speech.                                      ? Los Angeles or Hollywood, c. 1928.

        I Want To Be A Boy Scout                    Boy Scout Record 4
        How To Spell "Boy Scout"                    -

Acc. by Carroll Gibbons-p and unknown vn where shown.
                                        Hayes, Middlesex, December 5, 1928.

Bb-15236-3  Presenting His Dad - Part 1 (w/vn)   HMV B-2893
Bb-15237-3  Presenting His Dad - Part 2           -

## OLGA   COOK


Vocal, acc. by studio orchestra.         New York, May, 1922.

   8948    Songs Of Yesterday By Stars Of Today   Voc 35010 (part side)

## JACKIE   COOPER

B. Los Angeles, September 16, 1923; both parents well-known vaudeville  performers.
   Appeared in two-reel comedies at three; member of OUR GANG and made several short
   films with this; also appeared in MOVIETONE FOLLIES (1928), SUNNY SIDE UP (1929),
   and the film that made him famous, SKIPPY (1930).  His popularity was  maintained
   in THE CHAMP (1931), THE BOWERY (1933) and TREASURE ISLAND (1934), among  others,
   but with maturity his film appearances became fewer, ending with    EVERYTHING'S
   DUCKY in 1961; appeared on TV in THE PEOPLE'S CHOICE and HENNESSEY in the sixties
   and became an executive producer in this medium.

Speech.                                      New York, May 24, 1932.

B-11884-   Talk                                  Br (Private recording)

## J.   FRED COOTS

B. Brooklyn, N.Y., May 2, 1897; wrote many hit songs,  some for theatre productions
   (SONS O' GUNS, 1929) and many as straight Tin Pan Alley numbers.  Oddly,  one  of
   the only two songs he recorded - unsuccessfully - was a hit, but J.  Fred   Coots
   was not the composer of SINGING A VAGABOND SONG.  Among his biggest successes are
   A PRECIOUS LITTLE THING CALLED LOVE (1929), I STILL GET A THRILL THINKING OF  YOU
   (1930), LOVE LETTERS IN THE SAND (1931), FOR ALL WE KNOW (1934), A BEAUTIFUL LADY
   IN BLUE (1935), YOU STARTED ME DREAMING (1936) and YOU GO TO MY HEAD (1938).

Vocal, acc. by O/Nat Shilkret.           New York, January 20, 1930.

BVE-58507-1  You Can't Stop Me From Falling In   Vic rejected
             Love With You

   Acc. by O/Leonard Joy.                New York, January 29, 1930.

BVE-58507-2-3-4  You Can't Stop Me From Falling   Vic rejected
                 In Love With You
BVE-58531-1-2-3  Singing A Vagabond Song          -

## CORRELL AND GOSDEN

Charles J. Correll and Freeman F. Gosden were a popular singing duo that   appeared
   in a revue called RED HOT in Chicago in 1925, playing piano and ukulele; in 1926,
   they introduced a blackface cross-talk act called SAM 'N' HENRY, but soon changed

their identities to AMOS 'N' ANDY, opening at McVicker's Theatre there at $250  a
week; within a year, following the signing of a radio contract, they appeared in
Balaban and Katz movie houses at $2,000 a week, rising the following year,  1928,
to $5,000.  They filmed in CHECK AND DOUBLE CHECK (1930), and were by far the most
popular radio act that year (it is said that listeners set their watches by  Amos
'n' Andy's 7.00 p.m. radio show for quarter of an hour six nights a week, and for
many years they retained this vast audience).

Vocal duets, acc. by Charles J. Correll-p, and Freeman F. Gosden-tiple where shown.
                              Chicago, December 21, 1925.

BVE-34058-1-2  Blinky Moon Bay                    Vic rejected
BVE-34059-1-2  The Kinky Kids' Parade - FFG       -


                              Chicago, March 2, 1926.

BVE-34578-2  All I Want To Do                     Vic 19986, Zon 2786
BVE-34579-5  Let's Talk About My Sweetie          -            -

SAM 'N' HENRY : Humorous dialogue.      New York, April 20, 1926.

BVE-35328-3  Sam 'Phoning His Sweetheart Liza     Vic 20032
               In Birmingham
BVE-35329-1  At The Dentist                       -
BVE-35330-1-2-3  At The Shooting Gallery          Rejected

Vocal duets, acc. by Delos Owen-p.      Chicago, May 26, 1926.

BVE-35056-3  Round-About Way To Heaven            Vic 20088, Zon 2816
BVE-35057-1  That's Why I Love You                -            -
BVE-35058-1-2-3  Where'd You Get Those Eyes ?     Rejected
BVE-35059-3  Georgianna                           Vic 20107, Zon 2866
BVE-35060-1-2  When The Red, Red Robin Comes      Rejected
               Bob, Bob, Bobbin' Along

SAM 'N' HENRY : Humorous dialogue.      Chicago, May 27, 1926.

BVE-35066-2  Sam's Speech At The Colored Lodge    Vic 20093, Zon 2831
BVE-35067-2  Sam 'n' Henry Buying Insurance       Vic 20375
BVE-35068-1  Sam 'n' Henry Rollin' The Bones      -
BVE-35073-1  Sam 'n' Henry At The Fortune Tellers Vic 20093, Zon 2831

Vocal duets, acc. by Delos Owen-p.      Chicago, September 25, 1926.

BVE-36406-4  Meadow Lark                          Vic 20286, HMV B-2412
BVE-36407-1-2  Just A Bird's-Eye View Of My Old   Rejected
               Kentucky Home


                              Chicago, September 29, 1926.

BVE-36432-3  I Never Knew What The Moonlight      Vic 20324, HMV B-2405
               Could Do
BVE-36433-2  Elsie Schultz-en-heim                Vic 20255
BVE-36434-2  I Just Wanna Be Known As Susie's Feller  -      Zon 2866
BVE-36435-2  Kiss Your Little Baby Goodnight      Vic 20286

SAM 'N' HENRY : Humorous dialogue.      Chicago, October 7, 1926.

BVE-36448-1-2  Sam 'n' Henry In Court (Violating  Vic rejected
               Traffic Regulations)
BVE-36449-1-2  Sam 'n' Henry Driving In Traffic   -

Vocal duets, acc. by Delos Owen-p.      Chicago, July 6, 1927.

BVE-39084-    Gorgeous                            Vic 20826, HMV B-2585
BVE-39085-    No Wonder I'm Happy                 Vic 20908, Zon 5055
BVE-39086-    Somebody And Me                     -            -
BVE-39087-    Who Is Your Who ?                   Vic 20826, HMV B-2585

SAM 'N' HENRY : Humorous dialogue.          Chicago, July 6, 1927.

BVE-39088-1-2-3  Sam 'n' Henry Playing Poker       Vic rejected
BVE-39089-1-2  Sam 'n' Henry Explaining Expenses    -

                                    Chicago, July 7, 1927.

BVE-39092-    Sam's Big Night                      Vic 20788
BVE-39093-    The Morning After                    -

Vocal duets, acc. by as/vn/p, vn/p or p only as shown (the latter probably by Leroy
    Shield, who was present).           Chicago, December 4, 1927.

BVE-41312-1-2-3  Changes - as/vn/p                 Rejected
BVE-41313-3  What'll You Do ? - vn/p               Vic 21143, HMV B-2738
BVE-41314-3  Oh ! Look At That Baby - p            -          -
BVE-41315-1-2-3  Liza - p                          Rejected

SAM 'N' HENRY : Humorous dialogue.          Chicago, December 8, 1927.

BVE-41347-1-2-3  The Doctor Calls On Sam           Vic rejected
BVE-41348-1-2  Henry Talks To Sam On Business      -

AMOS 'N' ANDY : Humorous dialogue.          Chicago, July 17, 1928.

BVE-46424-    Is Everybody In Your Family As Dumb  Vic 22119
                As You Is ? - Part 1
BVE-46425-    Is Everybody In Your Family As Dumb  -
                As You Is ? - Part 2
BVE-46426-2  The Presidential Election - Part 1    Vic 21608
BVE-46427-2  The Presidential Election - Part 2    -

                                    Chicago, November 22, 1929.

BVE-57444-2  At The Bullfight                      Vic 22234, HMV B-3376
BVE-57445-2  The Dairy                             - LPV-580,LSA-3086 -

                                    Chicago, April 4, 1930.

BVE-59915-2  I'se Regusted (Take Off That Shoe)    Vic 22393
BVE-59916-3  Check And Double Check (In The        -
                Gymnasium)

## SAM COSLOW

B. 1905; prolific composer of popular songs (many for films), including ONE  SUMMER
NIGHT (1927); WAS IT A DREAM ? (1928); TRUE BLUE LOU (1929); JUST ONE MORE  CHANCE
(1931); MOON SONG, LEARN TO CROON, MOONSTRUCK, THANKS and THE DAY YOU CAME  ALONG
(1933); IN THE MIDDLE OF A KISS (1935) and others.  Became a music publisher  with
Larry Spier in 1928.

Vocal, acc. unknown.                         New York,  c. April 16, 1926.

X-73    Since You Whispered "I Love You"          Gnt rejected

Vocalist with the Tracy-Brown Orchestra. Chicago, March 20, 1928.

145817-2  Chloe (Song Of The Swamp)               Col 1344-D, 5164
145818-3  Sh-h ! Here Comes My Sugar              Col 1405-D
145819-2  Beautiful (as member of trio ?)         Col 1344-D
145820-   Joline                                  Col 1541-D
145821-2  Danger  ! (Look Out For That Gal)       Col 1405-D

  Acc. by O/Leonard Joy.                    New York, August 14, 1928.

BVE-46694-4  King For A Day                        Vic 21631
BVE-46695-3  You're A Real Sweetheart             -      HMV B-2921

Vocalist with the High Hatters, dir. by Nat Shilkret.
                              New York, September 19, 1928.

BVE-47533-1  Some Sweet Someone                 Vic 21682
BVE-47534-2  I Wanna Be Loved By You            -

Vocalist with Jesse Crawford at the Wurlitzer Hall organ.
                              New York, September 20, 1928.

BVE-46461-3  Just A Night For Meditation        Vic 21713, HMV B-2949

  Acc. by O/Leonard Joy.          New York, September 25, 1928.

BVE-47561-1-2-3  Sonny Boy                       Vic rejected
BVE-47562-1-2-3  There's A Rainbow 'Round My Shoulder  -

Vocalist with the High Hatters, dir. by Nat Shilkret.
                              New York, December 20, 1928.

BVE-48499-3  The Spell Of The Blues             Vic 21835, HMV B-5626

Vocal, acc. by O/Nat Shilkret.      New York, January 21, 1929.

BVE-49668-1-2  A Love Tale Of Alsace-Lorraine   Vic rejected
BVE-49669-1-2  Glad Rag Doll                    -

Vocal, acc. by O/Nat Finston.       Hollywood, August 7, 1932.

PBS-68379-1  Announcing Bing Crosby singing PLEASE  Paramount-Publix advertisement
                                                 record (made by RCA Victor)

                              Hollywood, August 10, 1932.

PCS-68381-2  Isn't It Romantic ?               Vic 36064

                              Hollywood, September 28, 1932.

PBS-68392-1  Please                             Vic 24144, HMV B-4349
PBS-68393-3  Say It Isn't So                    Vic 24143
PBS-68394-2  Give Her A Kiss                    -
PBS-68395-2  Here Lies Love                     Vic 24144, HMV B-4349

                              Hollywood, August 9, 1933.

PBS-68526-   Lay Your Head On My Shoulder, Dear  Vic 24385, HMV B-8011
PBS-68527-   If You Ever Come Back              -        -
PBS-68528-   Learn To Croon (Film "College Humor")  Vic 24386, HMV B-8009
PBS-68529-   Moonstruck (Film "College Humor")  -        -

                              Hollywood, late August, 1933.

 B-858-   Learn To Croon (Film "College Humor")  Voc 25001, Dec F-3653
 B-859-A  Where Have I Heard That Melody ?      Voc 25002, Dec F-3710
 B-860-   Down The Old Ox Road (Film "College Humor")  -      Dec F-3653
 B-861-A  Moonstruck (Film "College Humor")     Voc 25001, Dec F-3710

  Acc. by O/Ray Noble.            London, May 9, 1934.

OB-6915-2  The Very Thought Of You             HMV B-8181
OB-6916-1  A Place In Your Heart               -

  Acc. by Geraldo and his Sweet Music.    London, November 19, 1935.

GB-7494-   The Morning After                   Dec F-5806
GB-7495-1  I've Got A Feelin' You're Foolin' (Film  Dec F-5805
            "Broadway Melody of 1936")
GB-7496-1  You Are My Lucky Star (Film "Broadway  -
            Melody of 1936")
GB-7497-   Some Other Time                     Dec F-5806

The voice of Popeye, the spinach-eating tough sailor character of Max Fleischer car-
toons between 1932 and 1950; also recorded as Red Pepper Sam in lunatic version of
DINAH, NOBODY'S SWEETHEART and other popular standards. Appeared in London 1938 -
1939.

Vocal, acc. by studio orchestra.            New York, April 27, 1935.

17393-   I'm Popeye The Sailor Man            Mt M-13402, Rex 8536, RZ MR-2897
17394-   Blow The Man Down                    -            -           -

   Acc. by O/? Jay Wilbur.                  London, August 11, 1938.

DTB-3195-1  The Man On The Flying Trapeze        Rex 9238
DTB-3196-1  The Teddy Bears' Picnic              Rex 9172
DTB-3197-1  Barnacle Bill The Sailor             Rex 9314
DTB-3198-1  Popeye Club Record - Part 1          Br SA-1345

                                           London, August 12, 1938.

DTB-3199-1  Popeye Club Record - Part 2          Br SA-1345
DTB-3200-1  Let's All Sing Like The Birdies Sing Rex 9172
DTB-3201-1  On The Good Ship Lollipop            Br SA-1346
DTB-3202-1  On The Good Ship Yacki Hicki Doo-La  Rex 9238
DTB-3203-1  The Merry-Go-Round Broke Down        Rex 9314
   NOTE:- The Brunswick issues appeared in South Africa only.

                                           London, June 1, 1939.

R-3515-1  The Three Little Fishies              Rex 9562
R-3516-2  Boogy Boogy Boo                       -

## NOËL COWARD

B. Teddington, Middlesex, England, December 16, 1899; devoted his life to  theatre,
wrote many plays, some of them musical, also films; directed and played in these,
composed a large number of songs of all kinds, from the romantic to the satirical;
first appeared on stage at the Little Theatre London, January 27, 1911 in children's play THE GOLDFISH; many other juvenile roles followed from 1911 to 1915,such
as William in WHERE THE RAINBOW ENDS and Slightly in PETER PAN, mostly directed by
Charles Hawtrey; in Army, 1918; demobbed, 1919; wrote and appeared in first of his
own plays, I'LL LEAVE IT TO YOU (New Theatre, July 21, 1920; it flopped badly) and
THE YOUNG IDEA (Savoy, February, 1923); between these (May, 1921) he was in  New
York, without much success; great success in LONDON CALLING (Duke of York's, September 4, 1923) with Gertrude Lawrence (wrote the music and lyrics); further  very
popular appearance in his own straight play THE VORTEX (Royalty, December 16,1924)
and C. B. Cochran revue ON WITH THE DANCE (London Pavilion, April 30, 1925); also
FALLEN ANGELS (Globe, April 21, 1925) and HAY FEVER (Ambassadors, June 8, 1925);to
New York to appear in THE VORTEX (Henry Miller, September 16, 1925); provided the
entire score for C. B. Cochran's revue THIS YEAR OF GRACE (London Pavilion, March
22, 1928) and appeared in New York production of this himself (Selwyn, November 7,
1928); wrote book, music and lyrics for BITTER SWEET (His Majesty's, July 18,1929)
- the hit waltz I'LL SEE YOU AGAIN was composed in 20 minutes in a taxi in a London traffic jam ! - and PRIVATE LIVES (Phoenix, September 24, 1930; Times  Square,
January 27, 1931), both immensely successful; wrote score and lyrics for COCHRAN'S
REVUE OF 1931 (London Pavilion March 19, 1931); wrote and produced CAVALCADE (His
Majesty's, October 8, 1931); wrote, composed and produced revue WORDS AND MUSIC at
the Adelphi (September 16, 1932); went into theatre management with Alfred Lunt and
his wife, Lynn Fontanne, and with them produced and appeared in his DESIGN   FOR
LIVING (Ethel Barrymore, January 24, 1933); wrote, composed and produced CONVERS-
ATION PIECE (His Majesty's, February 16, 1934), appearing in this also; after some
months touring with Gertrude Lawrence in his set of nine one-act plays originally
called TONIGHT AT 7.30, produced it as TONIGHT AT 8.30 at the Phoenix, January  9,
1936; appeared also in New York production of this (National, November 24,  1936);
did not appear on stage in London again until August, 1942 (briefly in his longest
running play, BLITHE SPIRIT, St. James'); many successful comedies followed,  such
as PRESENT LAUGHTER and THIS HAPPY BREED (1943); revue SIGH NO MORE   (Piccadilly,
August 22, 1945); subsequent musicals (PACIFIC 1860, ACE OF CLUBS)less successful;
made several films, from the silent D. W. Griffith production HEARTS OF THE WORLD,
1917 to IN WHICH WE SERVE (1942), THE ASTONISHED HEART (1950), OUR MAN IN  HAVANA
(1959), THE ITALIAN JOB (1969) and many others; elected President of the  Actors'

Orphanage, April, 1934; appeared in cabaret at London's Cafe de Paris, 1952-1953 ;
at Wilbur Clark's Desert Inn, Las Vegas, 1955-1957.  Knighted for his outstanding
contributions to the theatre, 1970; d. Jamaica, W. Indies, March 26, 1973.

Vocal, acc. by Miss April (sic)-p.      Hayes, Middlesex, August 5, 1925.

Bb-6440-1  Lady Bird ("On With The Dance")      HMV rejected
Bb-6441-1-2  He Never Did That To Me                -
Bb-6442-1  Other Girls ("London Calling")          -
Bb-6443-1  Prenez-garde, Lisette ("London Calling")  -

                                 Hayes, Middlesex, August 10, 1925.

Bb-6440-2-3  Lady Bird ("On With The Dance")      HMV rejected
Bb-6441-3-4  He Never Did That To Me                --
Bb-6472-1-2  Poor Little Rich Girl ("On With        -
             The Dance")                            -
Bb-6473-1-2  We Must All Be Very Kind To Auntie     -
             Jessie

   Acc. by O/Carroll Gibbons.         Hayes, Middlesex, April 25, 1928.

Bb-13233-1  A Room With A View ("This Year Of   HMV B-2719
            Grace")
Bb-13234-2  Dance, Little Lady ("This Year Of   HMV B-2720
            Grace")

                                 Hayes, Middlesex, April 27, 1928.

Bb-13250-3  Mary Make-Believe ("This Year Of   HMV B-2719
            Grace")
Bb-13251-3  Try To Learn To Love ("This Year Of  HMV B-2720
            Grace")

   Acc. by Carroll Gibbons-p.         Hayes, Middlesex, May 15, 1928.

Bb-13318-2  Lorelei ("This Year Of Grace")      HMV B-2737
Bb-13319-3  The Dream Is Over                       -

                       Small Queen's Hall, London, Sept. 11, 1929.

Bb-17338-1  Zigeuner ("Bitter Sweet")        HMV B-3158, CLP-1050, Vic 24772
Bb-17339-2  World Weary                          -                    -

   Acc. by O/Ray Noble.         Small Queen's Hall, London, Sept. 15, 1930.

Cc-20202-2  Private Lives : Scene from Act 2    HMV C-2043, CLP-1050, Vic 36034
            (w/Gertrude Lawrence)
Cc-20203-2  Private Lives : Love Scene from        -            -            -
            Act 1 (Intro. Someday I'll Find You) (w/Gertrude Lawrence)

                       Small Queen's Hall, London, January 2, 1931.

OB-208-1  Half-Caste Woman ("Cochran's 1931    HMV B-3794, CLP-1050, 7EG-8346,
          Revue")                              Vic 22819
OB-209-2  Any Little Fish ("Cochran's 1931      HMV B-3794, 7EG-8346, Vic 22819
          Revue")

                       Kingsway Hall, London, October 15, 1931.

2B-1162-1  Cavalcade - Vocal Medley, Part 1     HMV C-2431
OB-1163-1-2  Lover Of My Dreams (Mirabelle Waltz)Rejected
             ("Cavalcade")
OB-1164-1  Twentieth-Century Blues ("Cavalcade")     -

Kingsway Hall, London, October 20, 1931.

OB-1163-4  Lover Of My Dreams (Mirabelle Valse)   HMV B-4001, Vic 24332
               ("Cavalcade")
OB-1164-2-3  Twentieth Century Blues("Cavalcade")  Rejected
2B-1176-3  Cavalcade : Prologue                    HMV C-2289
2B-1177-3  Cavalcade : Epilogue                     -

London, c. May 25, 1932.

2B-2888-3  Cavalcade - Vocal Medley, Part 2        HMV C-2431
2B-2889-2  Noël Coward Medley - Part 1 (Intro.     HMV C-2450, Vic 39002,
               Parisian Pierrot/Poor Little Rich    Par PMC-7135
               Girl/A Room With A View/Dance, Little Lady)
2B-2890-2  Noël Coward Medley - Part 2 (Intro.     As above
               Someday I'll Find You/Any Little Fish/If You Could Only Come  With Me/
               I'll See You Again)

London, c. September 19, 1932.

OB-4207-3  Let's Say Goodbye ("Words And Music")   HMV B-4269, 7EG-8346
OB-4208-3  The Party's Over Now ("Words And        HMV B-4270
               Music")
OB-4209-2  Something To Do With Spring ("Words       -
               And Music")
OB-4210-3  Mad Dogs And Englishmen ("Words And     HMV B-4269, CLP-1050, 7EG-8300,
               Music")                               Vic 24332
OB-4211-1  Mad About The Boy ("Words And Music")   Rejected

    Acc. by Leo Reisman and his Orchestra. New York, April 11, 1933.

CS-75778-1  World Weary/Green Carnations            Vic 36239
CS-75779-1  Zigeuner/The Call Of Life ("Bitter Sweet")-
    NOTE:- The other titles on the above two sides are of Sir Noël Coward's music but
    they are not sung by him or anyone else.

    Acc. by His Majesty's Theatre Orchestra/Reginald Burston.
                                    London, February 26, 1934.

OB-5915-3  I'll Follow My Secret Heart (w/Yvonne    HMV DA-1363, CLP-1050
               Printemps) ("Conversation Piece") - Part 1
OB-5916-3  I'll Follow My Secret Heart (w/Yvonne      -              -
               Printemps) ("Conversation Piece") - Part 2

    Acc. by O/Carroll Gibbons.          London, October 26, 1934.

OEA-473-1-2  Most Of Ev'ry Day                   HMV rejected
OEA-474-1-2  I Travel Alone                         -
OEA-475-1-2  Love In Bloom                          -
OEA-476-1-2  Fare Thee Well                         -

    Acc. by Carroll Gibbons-p.          London, October 29, 1934.

OEA-657-3  I Travel Alone                        HMV B-8234
OEA-658-3  Most Of Ev'ry Day                        -
OEA-659-3  Love In Bloom                         HMV B-8237
OEA-660-3  Fare Thee Well                           -
OEA-661-1-2  Let's Fall In Love                  Rejected
OEA-662-1-2  If I Love Again                        -

    Acc. by O/Clifford Greenwood.       London, August 15, 1935.

OEA-1956-2  Mrs. Worthington                     HMV B-8369, CLP-1050, 7EG-8300,
                                                 Vic 25230
OEA-1957-1  We Were So Young                     HMV B-8369, Vic 25230
OEA-1958-1-2  Lovely To Look At                  Rejected

Acc. by the Phoenix Theatre Orchestra/Clifford Greenwood.
London, January 15, 1936.

| | | | | |
|---|---|---|---|---|
| 2EA-2666-1 | Then/Play, Orchestra, Play (w/ Gertrude Lawrence) ("Shadow Play") | HMV C-2816, CLP-1050, Vic 36191 | | |
| 2EA-2667-2 | You Were There (w/Gertrude Lawrence) ("Shadow Play") | - | - | - |
| 2EA-2668-1 | Has Anybody Seen Our Ship ? (w/ Gertrude Lawrence) ("Red Peppers") | HMV C-2815 | - | Vic 36193 |
| 2EA-2669-1 | Man About Town (w/Gertrude Lawrence) ("Red Peppers") | - | - | - |

London, January 16, 1936.

2EA-2670-2  Here's A Toast (w/Gertrude Lawrence        HMV C-2817, Vic 36192,
            and Company) ("Family Album")           Par PMC-7135
2EA-2671-2  Hearts And Flowers (The Musical Box)    As above
            (w/Gertrude Lawrence and Company) ("Family Album")
NOTE:- The above six sides are of songs and scenes in the one-act plays that   made
up the production of TONIGHT AT 8.30.

London, February 13, 1936.

OEA-2686-2  Parisian Pierrot ("London Calling")     HMV B-8414, CLP-1050, Vic 25439
OEA-2687-1  We Were Dancing ("Tonight At 8.30")     -                          -

Acc. by His Majesty's Theatre Orchestra/Francis M. Collinson.
London, February 3, 1938.

OEA-5189-   Dearest Love ("Operette")               HMV B-8721
OEA-5190-2  Where Are The Songs We Sung ?           HMV B-8722
            ("Operette")
OEA-5191-1  The Stately Homes Of England ("Operette")  -
OEA-5192-   Gipsy Melody ("Operette")               HMV B-8721

Acc. by Carroll Gibbons-p.        London, March 24, 1938.

OEA-6428-1  Dearest Love ("Operette")               HMV B-8740, Vic 27228
OEA-6429-2  I'll See You Again ("Bitter Sweet")      -  CLP-1050 -
OEA-6430-2  Just Let Me Look At You                 HMV B-8772
OEA-6431-1  Poor Little Rich Girl ("On With The      -          7EG-8300
            Dance")

London, July    , 1941.

OEA-9331-1  London Pride                            HMV B-9198, 7EG-8300
OEA-9332-1  The Last Time I Saw Paris                -          7EG-8346

Acc. by O/Carroll Gibbons, or pCG.     London, August    , 1941.

OEA-9389-1  Could You Please Oblige Us With A       HMV B-9204
            Bren Gun ?
OEA-9390-1  There Have Been Songs In England         -
OEA-9391-1  Imagine The Duchess's Feelings !-pCG    HMV B-9210
OEA-9392-1  It's Only You - pCG                      -

Sir Noël Coward made  further records, some of them on location in Las Vegas,  until
the mid-sixties.

## JANE COWL

B. Boston, Mass., December 14, 1890.  Stage debut in SWEET KITTY BELOVED   (Belasco,
New York, December 10, 1903); tremendous success in WITHIN THE LAW (Eltinge,  September 11, 1912, for 541 performances); was one of Sarah Bernhardt's three ladies-
in-waiting in a performance of PHEDRE (1917); appeared in LILAC TIME (Republic,New
York, February 6, 1917); created record run of 20 weeks in Shakespeare's ROMEO AND
JULIET (Henry Miller, January 24, 1923), and another hit was THE ROAD TO ROME   at
the Playhouse, New York, January 31, 1927; d. 1950.

Speech.                                          New York, probably early 1923.

    Romeo, Romeo, Wherefore Art Thou          AR 2465
      Romeo ? ("Romeo And Juliet" - Shakespeare)

## EUGENE  COWLES

Bass singer with the Bostonians Company in the nineties and in the opening years of
  the twentieth century; appeared in THE FORTUNE TELLER (1898) after establishing a
  huge success as Will Scarlett in Reginald de Koven's ROBIN HOOD (Chicago, June 9,
  1890). He also composed the ballad FORGOTTEN, very popular in its day. B.    Stan-
  stead, Quebec, Canada, January 17, 1860; d. Boston, Mass., September 22, 1948.
Vocal, acc. by unknown p.                        New York, October 20, 1898.

    Gypsy Love Song ("The Fortune Teller")  Ber 1909

Acc. by O/? Walter B. Rogers.              New York, May 4, 1906.

C-3114-2  Forgotten                                Vic 31533, 35474
C-3115-3  Gypsy Love Song ("The Fortune Teller")  Vic 31544    -
B-3116-2  The Armourer's Song ("Robin Hood")      Vic 4737

Acc. by studio orchestra.              New York, c. 1923.

    Forgotten                                  Ed 80686, Amb 4498

## (MISS) RAY COX

Vocal, acc. by studio orchestra.        New York, May 19, 1909.

    The Baseball Girl                          Ed 4M-196, Amb 1747

## CHARLES CRAFTS

Vocal, acc. by studio orchestra.        New York, c. March, 1923.

  341-A  The Lovelight In Your Eyes (w/Jack Haley)Cam 323

                         New York, c. May, 1923.

  425-D  Little Rover                            Cam 334

## CLIFTON CRAWFORD

B. Edinburgh, 1875; d. London, June 3, 1920;  comedian famous for writing the  song-
  hit NANCY BROWN (1901) and for appearances in stage successes MOTHER GOOSE (at the
  New Amsterdam, December 2, 1903) and THE THREE TWINS (Herald Square, June 15,1907)
  as well as his recitation, straight, of Rudyard Kipling's famous poem GUNGA DIN.

Dramatic monologue, acc. by O/? Walter B. Rogers.
                                New York, October 21, 1910.

B-9568-1-2  Two Whole Days                        Rejected
C-9569-1  Gunga Din                               Vic 70028

## JOAN  CRAWFORD

B. San Antonio, Texas, March 23, 1904; r.n. Lucille Le Sueur.  While in her    teens,
  she ran away from school and joined a vaudeville company, beginning her career  on
  stage in 1922.  Her film debut was in PRETTY LADIES (1925), followed the same year
  by the silent version of SALLY, IRENE AND MARY and OLD CLOTHES, since when she has
  appeared in dozens of others, silent and in sound, among the best-remembered being
  OUR MODERN MAIDENS and HOLLYWOOD REVUE OF 1929 (1929); GRAND HOTEL (1932); DANCING

LADY (1933); SADIE McKEE (1934); THE LAST OF MRS. CHEYNEY (1937); SUSAN  AND  GOD
and STRANGE CARGO (1940); HOLLYWOOD CANTEEN (1944); THIS WOMAN IS DANGEROUS(1952);
THE STORY OF ESTHER COSTELLO (made in England in 1957); WHATEVER HAPPENED TO BABY
JANE ? (1962); BERSERK (also in England, 1967) and TROG (1970); she was one of an
all-female cast that made THE WOMEN in 1939, and is one of the very few actresses
who have made the graceful transition from what was then termed a flapper to fine
maturity.  Her autobiography (A PORTRAIT OF JOAN) was published in 1962; she married Douglas Fairbanks, Jr. in 1929, but this broke up in 1933.

Vocalist with Gus Arnheim and his Cocoanut Grove Orchestra.
                                        Hollywood, August 23, 1931.

PBS-68307-1-2  How Long Will It Last ?              Vic rejected

Vocal, acc. by Nat Finston and the MGM Studio Orchestra.
                                        Hollywood, March 21, 1939.

PBS-036057-5  I'm In Love With The Honorable        Vic 26205, HMV B-8909
                Mr. So-and-So
PBS-036058-1-2-3-4  Tears From My Inkwell           Rejected
PBS-036059-6  It's All So New To Me                 Vic 26205, HMV B-8909
PBS-036060-1-2-3-4-5-6-7  I Never Knew Heaven       Rejected
                Could Speak

## BING  CROSBY

B. Tacoma, Wash., May 3, 1904; r.n. Harry Lillis Crosby.  Nicknamed "Bing" after an
early cartoon character in a local newspaper whose exploits he followed;  studied
law at Gonzaga University, but decided show business as vocalist with his friend,
Al Rinker, was preferable as a career.  Introduced to Paul Whiteman in  November,
1926 while working in Los Angeles; both signed to appear with Whiteman, joined by
Harry Barris to form Paul Whiteman's Rhythm Boys, stayed with him 3½ years;  made
appearance in film KING OF JAZZ (1930) with the Whiteman band, and in many  short
comedies about the same time.  When Whiteman returned to New York, the trio  sang
with Gus Arnheim at the Cocoanut Grove in Los Angeles; Bing Crosby left them during the summer of 1931 to go solo on radio and records.  To Hollywood more or less
permanently to make the following films up to 1942 : THE BIG BROADCAST(1932);COL-
LEGE HUMOR (1933); WE'RE NOT DRESSING (1934); MISSISSIPPI (1935); RHYTHM  ON  THE
RANGE (1936); PENNIES FROM HEAVEN (1936); DOCTOR RHYTHM (1937); SING, YOU SINNERS
(1938); EAST SIDE OF HEAVEN, PARIS HONEYMOON and THE ROAD TO SINGAPORE (1939); IF
I HAD MY WAY  and RHYTHM ON THE RIVER (1940); THE ROAD TO ZANZIBAR and BIRTH   OF
THE BLUES (1941); THE ROAD TO MOROCCO and HOLIDAY INN (1942); subsequent greatest
film successes include GOING MY WAY (1944); THE BELLS OF ST. MARY'S and THE  ROAD
TO UTOPIA (1945); BLUE SKIES (1946); THE ROAD TO RIO (1947); THE  EMPEROR  WALTZ
(1948); MR. MUSIC (1950); JUST FOR YOU and THE ROAD TO BALI (1952), LITTLE   BOY
LOST (1953); WHITE CHRISTMAS (1954); THE COUNTRY GIRL (which featured him in  his
first dramatic role) (1955); HIGH SOCIETY (1956); THE ROAD TO HONG KONG (made  in
England in 1962), Very popular on TV - and the golf course; autobiography,  CALL
ME LUCKY, published 1953; m. Dixie Lee Crosby, 1932 (d. 1952; four sons). Without
doubt the best-known and one of the best-liked members of the profession; the hit
song of HOLIDAY INN, Irving Berlin's WHITE CHRISTMAS, is reckoned to have sold at
least ten million copies throughout the world.

Vocalist with Don Clark and his Los Angeles Biltmore Hotel Orchestra.
                                        Los Angeles, October 18, 1926.

142785-3  I've Got The Girl (w/Al Rinker)          Col 824-D, 4310
NOTE:- Columbia 4310 as THE CHARLESTON SERENADERS.

Vocalist with Paul Whiteman and his Orchestra.
                                        Chicago, December 22, 1926.

BVE-37285-4  Wistful And Blue (w/Al Rinker)        Vic 20418
BVE-37286-1-2-3-4  Pretty Lips (w/Al Rinker)       Rejected

                                        New York, February 10, 1927.

BVE-37764-4  Shanghai Dream Man (w/Al Rinker-Jack Vic 20683, HMV B-5351
                Fulton-Charles Gaylord-Austin Young)

New York, February 25, 1927.

BVE-38118-3   That Saxophone Waltz (w/Al Rinker-     Vic 20513, HMV B-5311
              Jack Fulton-Charles Gaylord-Austin Young)

New York, February 28, 1927.

BVE-38124-1   Pretty Lips (w/Al Rinker)              Vic 20627

New York, March 3, 1927.

BVE-38135-1-2-3-4  I'm Coming, Virginia (w/Al        Vic rejected
              Rinker)

New York, March 7, 1927.

BVE-38143-3   Muddy Water                            Vic 20508

New York, April 29, 1927.

BVE-38135-7   I'm Coming, Virginia (w/Al Rinker)     Vic DPM-2027, LPM-2071, LPV-570,
                                                     RD-27075, Vik LX-995, X LVA-1000,
                                                     HMV 7EG-8251
BVE-38135-9   I'm Coming, Virginia (w/Al Rinker)     Vic 20751
BVE-38378-1   Side By Side (w/Al Rinker-Harry        Vic DPM-2027, LPV-570
              Barris)
BVE-38378-4   Side By Side (w/Al Rinker-Harry        Vic 20627, HMV B-5318,
              Barris)                                Decatur 505

Vocalist with Paul Whiteman's Rhythm Boys (Al Rinker-Harry Barris), acc. by    Harry
    Barris-p.                          New York, April 29, 1927.

              Medley (details unknown)              Vic test (un-numbered)

Vocalist with Paul Whiteman and his Orchestra.
                                      New York, May 6, 1927.

BVE-38392-1-2-3-4-5  Missouri Waltz (w/Al Rinker-  Vic rejected
              Jack Fulton-Charles Gaylord-Austin Young)

New York, May 9, 1927.

BVE-38394-3   I'm In Love Again (w/Al Rinker-Jack    Vic 20646
              Fulton-Charles Gaylord-Austin Young)

New York, May 24, 1927.

BVE-38779-1   Magnolia (Mix The Lot - What Have      Vic 20679, HMV B-5317,
              You Got ?) (w/Al Rinker-Harry         Decatur 505
              Barris)

Vocalist with Paul Whiteman's Rhythm Boys (Al Rinker-Harry Barris),  acc.  by  Harry
    Barris-p.                          New York, June 20, 1927.

BVE-39271-2   Mississippi Mud/I Left My Sugar        Vic LPV-545, LSA-3077
              Standing In The Rain
BVE-39271-3   Mississippi Mud/I Left My Sugar        Vic 20783, 24240, HMV B-2562,
              Standing In The Rain                   B-4424
BVE-39272-3   Sweet Li'l/Ain't She Sweet ?           As above

Vocalist with Paul Whiteman and his Orchestra.
                                      New York, July 6, 1927.

BVE-39627-3   My Blue Heaven (w/Al Rinker-Jack       Vic 20828, HMV B-5366
              Fulton-Charles Gaylord-Austin Young)

Camden, N. J., August 16, 1927.

BVE-39569-3   The Five-Step (w/Al Rinker-Harry       Vic 20883, HMV B-5511)
              Barris)

Camden, N. J., August 19, 1927.

BVE-39575-2  The Calinda (w/Jack Fulton-Charles    Vic 20882, HMV B-5384
                Gaylord-Austin Young)

Camden, N. J., August 20, 1927.

BVE-39577-8  It Won't Be Long Now (w/Al Rinker-    Vic 20883, HMV B-5555
                Harry Barris)

New York, September 21, 1927.

BVE-38392-7  Missouri Waltz (w/Al Rinker-Jack      Vic 20973, HMV B-5410, B-5974
                Fulton-Charles Gaylord-Austin Young)

Vocalist with Paul Whiteman's Rhythm Boys (Al Rinker-Harry Barris), acc.  by    Harry
    Barris-p.                          Chicago, November 11, 1927.

BVE-40846-3  That's Grandma                        Vic 27688, LPM-2071, RD-27075,
                                                   Vik LX-995, X LVA-1000,
                                                   HMV 7EG-8251

Chicago, November 17, 1927.

BVE-40894-2  Miss Annabelle Lee                    Vic 21104

Vocalist with Paul Whiteman and his Orchestra.
                                       Chicago, November 23, 1927.

BVE-40937-2  Changes (w/Al Rinker-Harry Barris-    Vic 25370, LPM-2323, RD-27225,
                Jack Fulton-Charles Gaylord-Austin X LVA-3040
                Young)
BVE-40937-3  Changes (w/Al Rinker-Harry Barris-    Vic 21103, LPM-2323, RD-27225,
                Jack Fulton-Charles Gaylord-Austin HMV B-5461, B-8913, DLP-1106,
                Young)                             Bm 1032

Chicago, November 25, 1927.

BVE-40945-2  Mary (What Are You Waiting For ?)     Vic 21103, HMV B-5461, Bm 1032
BVE-40945-4  Mary (What Are You Waiting For ?)     Vic 26415, LPV-584, LSA-3094,
                                                   X LVA-3040, HMV DLP-1106

New York, January 11, 1928.

BVE-41607-2  Ol' Man River                         Vic 21218, 25249, LPM-2071,
                                                   LPV-584, LSA-3094, RD-27075,
                                                   Vik LX-995, X LVA-1000,
                                                   HMV B-5471, B-8929, BD-5066,
                                                   7EG-8251, Sentry/Temple 4008

Vocalist with Paul Whiteman's Rhythm Boys (Al Rinker-Harry Barris), acc.  by    Harry
    Barris-p.                          New York, January 12, 1928.

BVE-41612-1  From Monday On                        Vic 24349
BVE-41612-3  From Monday On                        Vic 21302, HMV B-2779

Vocalist with Frankie Trumbauer and his Orchestra.
                                       New York, January 20, 1928.

400033-   From Monday On (w/Frankie Trumbauer)     Rejected
400034-A  Mississippi Mud (w/Frankie Trumbauer)    OK 40979, Par R-3526, R-2097,
                                                   DP-255, Col CL-845, GL-508,
                                                   ML-4812, 7-1644, Epic EE-22013,
                                                   EE-22014, Fon TFE-17060, Bm 1029,
                                                   Folkways FJ-2807, FP-67

Vocalist with Paul Whiteman and his Orchestra.
                              Camden, N. J., January 27, 1928.

BVE-41470-5  Make Believe                        Vic 21218, 25249, LPV-584,
                                                 LSA-3094, HMV B-5471, BD-5066,
                                                 Sentry/Temple 4008

                              New York, February 7, 1928.

BVE-41680-2  Poor Butterfly (w/Al Rinker-Jack    Vic 24078
               Fulton-Charles Gaylord-Austin Young)

                              New York, February 8, 1928.

BVE-41681-2  There Ain't No Sweet Man That's     Vic 25675, DPM-2027, LPM-2323,
               Worth The Salt Of My Tears (w/Al  LPV-570, RD-27225, HMV B-8929,
               Rinker-Harry Barris-Jack Fulton-  DLP-1106
               Charles Gaylord-Austin Young)
BVE-41681-3  There Ain't No Sweet Man That's     Vic 21464, HMV B-5515, Bm 1031
               Worth The Salt Of My Tears (w/Al
               Rinker-Harry Barris-Jack Fulton-
               Charles Gaylord-Austin Young)

                              New York, February 13, 1928.

BVE-41688-3  Sunshine (w/Al Rinker-Jack Fulton-  Vic 21240
               Charles Gaylord-Austin Young)
BVE-41689-3  From Monday On (w/Harry Barris-Jack  Vic 27688, EPAT/WPT-35, LPM-2323,
               Fulton-Charles Gaylord-Austin Young)LPT-26, RD-27225, RDM-2504,
                                                 RDS-6504, SPS-33-114, 27-0136,
                                                 HMV DLP-1106

                              New York, February 18, 1928.

BVE-41696-2  Mississippi Mud (w/Irene Taylor-Al  Vic 25366, HMV DLP-1106, Bm 1029
               Rinker-Harry Barris-Jack Fulton-
               Charles Gaylord-Austin Young)
BVE-41696-3  Mississippi Mud (w/Irene Taylor-Al  Vic 21274, DPM-2027, LPV-570
               Rinker-Harry Barris-Jack Fulton-
               Charles Gaylord-Austin Young)

                              New York, February 28, 1928.

BVE-41689-4  From Monday On (w/Harry Barris-Jack  Vic 25368
               Fulton-Charles Gaylord-Austin Young)
BVE-41689-6  From Monday On (w/Harry Barris-Jack  Vic 21274, HMV B-5492, Bm 1017
               Fulton-Charles Gaylord-Austin Young)
CVE-43117-3  High Water                          Vic 35992, 36186, HMV C-1607

Vocalist with Paul Whiteman's Rhythm Boys (Al Rinker-Harry Barris), acc.  by  Harry
  Barris-p, with ukulele.          New York, March 1, 1928.

BVE-43121-1  What Price Lyrics ?                  Vic 24349
BVE-43121-3  What Price Lyrics ?                  Vic 21302, HMV B-2779

Vocalist with Paul Whiteman and his Orchestra.
                              New York, March 12, 1928.

BVE-43140-2  I'm Wingin' Home (w/Al Rinker-Jack   Vic 21365, HMV B-5497
               Fulton-Charles Gaylord-Austin Young)

Vocalist with Paul Whiteman and his Concert Orchestra.
                              New York, March 14, 1928.

CVE-43143-4  Metropolis - Part 3 (w/Al Rinker-   Vic 35934
               Boyce Cullen-Jack Fulton-Charles Gaylord-Austin Young)

Vocalist with Paul Whiteman and his Orchestra.
New York, March 15, 1928.

BVE-43145-1  Lovable                              Vic 27685, LPV-584, LSA-3094,
                                                  HMV B-5509

New York, March 16, 1928.

BVE-43148-1  March Of The Musketeers (w/Al Rinker Vic 21315, HMV B-5807
             Boyce Cullen-Jack Fulton-Charles Gaylord-Austin Young)

New York, April 21, 1928.

BVE-43660-3  I'm Afraid Of You                    Vic 27685, LPV-584, LSA-3094
BVE-43660-4  I'm Afraid Of You                    Vic 21389, HMV B-5541

New York, April 22, 1928.

BVE-43662-1  My Pet (w/Al Rinker-Jack Fulton-     Vic 27686
             Charles Gaylord)
BVE-43662-2  My Pet (w/Al Rinker-Jack Fulton-     Vic 21389, HMV B-5504
             Charles Gaylord)
BVE-43663-2  It Was The Dawn Of Love (w/Al Rinker Vic 21453, HMV B-5522
             Jack Fulton-Charles Gaylord)
BVE-43664-1  Dancing Shadows (w/Al Rinker-Jack    Vic 21431, 27687, HMV B-5511
             Fulton-Charles Gaylord)

New York, April 23, 1928.

BVE-43667-1  Louisiana (w/Jack Fulton-Charles     Vic 21438, HMV B-5522, Bm 1030,
             Gaylord-Austin Young)                Folkways FP-59
BVE-43667-3  Louisiana (w/Jack Fulton-Charles     Vic 25369, HMV B-8913, DLP-1106
             Gaylord-Austin Young)

New York, April 24, 1928.

BVE-43669-2  Do I Hear You Saying (I Love You)    Vic 21398
             (w/Al Rinker-Charles Gaylord)

New York, April 25, 1928.

BVE-43670-1  You Took Advantage Of Me (w/Jack     Vic 21398, 25369, DPM-2027,
             Fulton-Charles Gaylord-Austin        LPM-2323, LPV-570, RD-27225,
             Young)                               HMV DLP-1106, Bm 1030

New York, May 12, 1928.

98533-1-2-3  La Paloma   (w/Al Rinker-Harry       Rejected
             Barris-Boyce Cullen-Jack Fulton-Charles Gaylord-Austin Young)
98534-3  La Golondrina (w/Al Rinker-Harry Barris Col 50070, 9459
             Boyce Cullen-Jack Fulton-Charles Gaylord-Austin Young)

New York, May 13, 1928.

146250-1-2-3  Evening Star (w/Al Rinker-Harry     Col rejected
             Barris)

New York, May 17, 1928.

146291-2  C.O.N.S.T.A.N.T.I.N.O.P.L.E. (w/Al Rin- Col 1402-D, 4951
             ker-Harry Barris-Boyce Cullen-Jack Fulton-Charles Gaylord-Austin Young)

New York, May 21, 1928.

98533-6  La Paloma (w/Al Rinker-Harry Barris-     Col 50070, 9459
             Boyce Cullen-Jack Fulton-Charles Gaylord-Austin Young)
146250-6  Evening Star (w/Al Rinker-Harry Barris) Col 1401-D, 4950
146316-1-2-3  'Tain't So, Honey, 'Tain't So      Rejected

New York, May 22, 1928.

146319-3  Get Out And Get Under The Moon (w/Al      Col 1402-D, CL-2830, 4951, 5161
          Rinker-Harry Barris-others ?)
146320-1-2-3  I'd Rather Cry Over You (w/Al          Rejected
          Rinker-Harry Barris-others ?)

New York, May 23, 1928.

146316-4-5-6  'Tain't So, Honey, 'Tain't So      Col rejected

Vocalist with Paul Whiteman's Rhythm Boys (Al Rinker-Harry Barris), acc. by Harry
    Barris-p.                          New York, May 25, 1928.

146336-1-2-3  Wa-Da-Da                             Col rejected
146344-1-2-3  That's Grandma                          -

Vocalist with Paul Whiteman and his Orchestra.
                          New York, June 10, 1928.

146316-9  'Tain't So, Honey, 'Tain't So         Col 1444-D, CL-846, CL-2830,
                                                GL-509, ML-4813, 7-1646, 4981,
                                                Epic EE-22013, EE-22014
146320-5  I'd Rather Cry Over You (w/Al Rinker-  Col 1496-D, CL-2830, 4980
          Harry Barris-others ?)

New York, June 17, 1928.

146541-3  I'm On The Crest Of A Wave (w/Al Rin-  Col 1465-D, CL-2830, 5241
          ker-Harry Barris-others ?)
146542-3  That's My Weakness Now (w/Al Rinker-   Col 1444-D, CL-846, CL-2830,
          Harry Barris)                           GL-509. ML-4813, 7-1646, 5006

146546-3  Lonesome In The Moonlight (w/Al Rinker- Col 1448-D, 5039
          Harry Barris)

New York, June 18, 1928.

146549-2  Because My Baby Don't Mean "Maybe" Now  Col 1441-D, CL-846, CL-2830,
          (w/Al Rinker-Harry Barris-others)       GL-509, ML-4813, 7-1647, 5007,
                                                  Fon TFE-17061
146550-3  Out Of Town Gal (w/Al Rinker-Harry     Col 1505-D, CL-2830, 5039
          Barris)

Vocalist with Paul Whiteman's Rhythm Boys (Al Rinker-Harry Barris), acc. by Harry
    Barris-p.                          New York, June 19, 1928.

146336-6  Wa-Da-Da                             Col 1455-D, 5006, Epic EE-22013/4
146344-6  That's Grandma                          -        5071

Vocalist with Paul Whiteman and his Orchestra.
                          New York, September 19, 1928.

 98585-3  Silent Night, Holy Night (w/Al Rinker-  Col 50098, 9561
          Harry Barris-Jack Fulton-Charles Gaylord-Austin Young-others ?)
 98586-3  Christmas Melodies (Bing Crosby sings      -        -
          NOEL)

Vocalist with Paul Whiteman's Rhythm Boys (Al Rinker-Harry Barris), acc. by Harry
    Barris-p.                          Chicago, November 10, 1928.

147500-3  My Suppressed Desire                 Col 1629-D, 5240, Epic EE-22013/4
147501-4  Rhythm King                             -        -

Vocalist with Paul Whiteman and his Orchestra.
                          New York, December 11, 1928.

147540-1-2-3-4  Makin' Whoopee (w/Al Rinker-Harry Col rejected
          Barris-Austin Young-others ?)

New York, December 22, 1928.

147540-7  Makin' Whoopee (w/Al Rinker-Harry        Col 1683-D, 5556, Epic EE-22013/4
          Barris-Austin Young-others ?)

Vocalist with the Ipana Troubadours/Sam C. Lanin.
                                New York, December 28, 1928.

147545-3  I'll Get By, As Long As I Have You      Col 1694, 5391, Epic EE-22013/4
147546-3  Rose Of Mandalay                          -      5541

Vocalist with Paul Whiteman and his Orchestra.
                                New York, January 11, 1929.

147751-1-2-3-4  My Angeline                         Col rejected

Vocalist with Paul Whiteman's Rhythm Boys (Al Rinker-Harry Barris), acc.  by   Harry
    Barris-p.                   New York, January 25, 1929.

147888-1-2-3  So The Bluebirds And The Blackbirds Col rejected
          Got Together

Vocalist with Sam Lanin and his Famous Players.
                                New York, January 25, 1929.

401555-B  I'm Crazy Over You                        OK 41228, Od ONY-41228, Par E-6148
401556-B  Susianna                                    -          - Ar 4364, Par R-339,
                                                    Epic EE-22013/4, Par PMC-7006
401557-C  If I Had You                              OK 41188, Par E-6148, PMC-7006,
                                                    Epic EE-22013/4
    NOTE:- Odeon ONY-41228 as EDDIE GORDON'S ORCHESTRA; Parlophone E-6148 as WILL PER-
    RY'S ORCHESTRA; Ariel as ARIEL DANCE ORCHESTRA.

Vocalist with the Dorsey Brothers and their Orchestra.
                                New York, January 26, 1929.

401560-B  The Spell Of The Blues                    OK 41181, Par R-385, PMC-7006,
                                                    Epic EE-22013/4
401561-B  Let's Do It (Let's Fall In Love)          OK 41181, Par R-331, PMC-7006,
                                                    Epic EE-22013/4
401562-C  My Kinda Love                             OK 41188, Par R-374, R-2475,
                                                    Har HL-7147

Vocalist with Paul Whiteman and his Orchestra.
                                New York, February 28, 1929.

147751-5-6-7-8  My Angeline                         Rejected
148013-3  Coquette                                  Col 1755-D, CL-2830, 5388

                                New York, March 7, 1929.

147751-11 My Angeline                               Col 1755-D, 5388

Vocal, acc. by Matt Malneck-vn/Roy Bargy-p/Edward "Snoozer" Quinn-g.
                                New York, March 14, 1929.

148073-3  My Kinda Love                             Col 1773-D, DB-2037,
                                                    Epic EE-22013/4
148074-3  Till We Meet                              Col 1773-D, DB-2036,
                                                    Epic EE-22013/4

Vocalist with Paul Whiteman and his Orchestra.
                                New York, March 15, 1929.

148086-3  Louise                                    Col 1771-D, 38218, 5456,
                                                    Epic EE-22013/4

New York, April 5, 1929.

148183-3  I'm In Seventh Heaven (w/Al Rinker-      Col 1877-D, 5544
          Harry Barris)
148184-1-2-3-4  Little Pal                        Rejected

Vocalist with Paul Whiteman's Rhythm Boys (Al Rinker-Harry Barris), acc. by Harry
   Barris-p.                          New York, April 10, 1929.

147888-6  So The Bluebirds And The Blackbirds Got Col 1819-D, CL-2749, 5457,
          Together                                CBS 66206
148428-2  Louise                                  Col 1819-D, 5457, Epic EE-22013/4

Vocalist with Paul Whiteman and his Orchestra.
                                    New York, April 25, 1929.

148184-8  Little Pal                              Col 1877-D, 5544

                      New York, May 3, 1929.

148408-4  Reaching For Someone And Not Finding    Col 1822-D, CL-2830, 5484
          Anyone There

                      New York, May 4, 1929.

148421-4  Oh ! Miss Hannah                        Col 1945-D, CL-846, GL-509,
                                                  ML-4813, 7-1647, DC-176,
                                                  Ph BBL-7014, Temple 529
148422-1-2-3-4  Your Mother And Mine (w/Al        Rejected
          Rinker-Harry Barris)
148423-4  Orange Blossom Time                     Col 1845-D, 5560

                      New York, May 16, 1929.

148422-8  Your Mother And Mine (w/Al Rinker-Harry Col 1845-D, 5560
          Barris)
148544-3  S'posin'                                Col 1862-D, CL-2830, 5520

Vocal, acc. by Matt Malneck-vn/Roy Bargy-p/Eddie Lang-g.
                                    New York, May 24, 1929.

148619-2  I Kiss Your Hand, Madame                Col 1851-D, DB-2036,
                                                  Epic EE-22013/4
148620-1  Baby, Oh ! Where Can You Be ?           Col 1851-D, DB-2037,
                                                  Epic EE-22013/4

Vocalist with Paul Whiteman and his Orchestra.
                                    New York, September 6, 1929.

148985-3  At Twilight (w/Al Rinker-Harry Barris-  Col 1993-D, CL-2830, 5655
          others ?)
148986-1-2-3-4  Waiting At The End Of The Road    Rejected

                      New York, September 13, 1929.

148986-8  Waiting At The End Of The Road          Col 1974-D, 5675
149005-3  When You're Counting The Stars Alone    Col 1993-D, CL-2830, 5675
          (w/Al Rinker-Harry Barris-others ?)

Vocal, acc. by small group from Paul Whiteman's Orchestra.
                                    New York, September 27, 1929.

149066-3  Can't We Be Friends ?                   Col 2001-D, DB-2035,
                                                  Epic EE-22013/4
149067-3  Gay Love                                As above, plus Cl 5476-C,
                                                  Diva 3418-G, Har 1428-H,
                                                  VT 2536-V

Vocalist with Paul Whiteman and his Orchestra.
                                        New York, c. September, 1929.

  91790-1  Moonlight And Roses (w/Al Rinker-Boyce  Col Private Recording
              Cullen-Charles Gaylord-Austin Young)
  91791-1  Southern Medley (Intro. Old Black Joe/        -
              Carry Me Back To Old Virginny - both solos by Bing Crosby - and  others
              in which he does not take part)

                                        New York, October 9, 1929.

149124-3  Great Day (w/male chorus)                Col 2023-D, CB-116, CL-2228,
                                                    CBS BPG-62545
149125-3  Without A Song                           Col 2023-D, CB-116, CBS 66210,
                                                    Epic EE-22013/4

                                        New York, October 16, 1929.

149149-4  I'm A Dreamer - Aren't We All ? (w/ch)  Col 2010-D, CL-2830, 14353
149150-4  If I Had A Talking Picture Of You             -              -
                                                    CBS 66210, Epic EE-22013/4

                                        New York, October 18, 1929.

149158-1-2-3  A Bundle Of Old Love Letters         Rejected
149159-3  After You've Gone                        Col 2098-D, 5702, CBS 66210,
                                                    Epic EE-22013/4

                                        Hollywood, October 31, 1929.

194379-3  A Bundle Of Old Love Letters             Col  2047-D, CL-2830, 5724

                                        Hollywood, February 10, 1930.

149810-1  Happy Feet (w/Al Rinker-Harry Barris)    Col 2164-D, CB-86, CL-2749,
             (Film "King Of Jazz")                  CBS 66206

                                        Hollywood, March 21, 1930.

149822-2  Song Of The Dawn (w/male chorus) (Film  Col 2163-D, CB-87
             "King Of Jazz")
                                        Hollywood, March 22, 1930.

149824-4  Livin' In The Sunlight, Lovin' In The    Col 2171-D, CB-117, DC-50,
             Moonlight                              CBS 66210, Epic EE-22013/4

                                        Hollywood, March 23, 1930.

149825-2  A Bench In The Park (w/Al Rinker-Harry  Col 2164-D, CB-86, CL-2749,
             Barris-The Brox Sisters) (Film "King Of Jazz")    CBS 66206
149826-2  I Like To Do Things For You (w/Al        Col 2170-D, CB-87, CL-2749,
             Rinker-Harry Barris) (Film "King Of Jazz")    CBS 66206
149827-4  You Brought A New Kind Of Love To Me    Col 2171-D, CB-117, CBS 66210,
                                                    Epic EE-22013/4

Vocalist with Paul Whiteman's Rhythm Boys (Al Rinker-Harry Barris), acc.  by   Harry
   Barris-p.                            Hollywood, May 23, 1930.

149840-4  A Bench In The Park (Film "King Of       Col 2223-D, CL-2749, DB-282,
             Jazz")                                 CBS 66206
149841-   Everything's Agreed Upon                 Rejected

Vocalist with Duke Ellington and his Orchestra.
                                        Hollywood, August 26, 1930.

PBVE-61013-5  Three Little Words (w/Al Rinker-     Vic 22528, 25076, 27-0031,
                Harry Barris)                       42-0031, RD-7731, VPM-6042,
                                                    HMV B-5945, BD-5755

Vocalist with Gus Arnheim and his Cocoanut Grove Orchestra.
                    Hollywood, October 29, 1930.

PBVE-61047-3  Fool Me Some More                Vic 22561, LPM-2071, LPV-584,
                                               LSA-3094, RD-27075, Vik LX-995,
                                               X LVA-1000
PBVE-61048-3  It Must Be True                  Vic 22561, 25280, LPM-2071,
                                               LPV-584, LSA-3094, RD-27075,
                                               Vik LX-995, X LVA-1000

                    Hollywood, November 20, 1930.

PBVE-61057-3  Them There Eyes (w/Al Rinker-Harry  Vic 22580, LPM-2071, RD-27075,
                Barris)                        Vik LX-995, X LVA-1000,
                                               HMV 7EG-8219

                    Hollywood, November 25, 1930.

PBVE-61058-7  The Little Things In Life        Vic 22580, LPM-2071, LPV-584,
                                               LSA-3094, RD-27075, BB B-7102,
                                               Vik LX-995, X LVA-1000,
                                               Sentry 4005

                    Hollywood, January 19, 1931.

PBVE-61068-2  I Surrender, Dear                Vic 22618, 25280, 27-0014,
                                               EPAT-5, LPT-5, LPV-584, LSA-3094,
                                               PR-119, RD-4-49-6, RDM-2356,
                                               RDS-6356, HMV 7EG-8139

                    Hollywood, March 2, 1931.

PBVE-61075-1  Thanks To You                    Vic 22700, LPM-2071, RD-27075,
                                               Vik LX-995, X LVA-1000,
                                               HMV 7EG-8251, Asterisk 951
PBVE-61075-2  Thanks To You                    Vic LPV-584, LSA-3094
PBVE-61076-2  One More Time                    Vic 22700, LPM-2071, LPV-584,
                                               LSA-3094, RD-27075, Vik LX-995,
                                               X LVA-1000, HMV B-6047, 7EG-8219,
                                               Asterisk 951

Vocal, acc. by members of Gus Arnheim's Orchestra.
                    Hollywood, March 2, 1931.

PBVE-61077-2  Wrap Your Troubles In Dreams     Vic 22701, LPM-2071, LPV-584,
                                               LSA-3094, RD-27075, PRS 400,
                                               Vik LX-995, X LVA-1000, BB B-7102,
                                               HMV B-3936, BD-470, 7EG-8219
PBVE-61078-2  Just A Gigolo                    Vic 22701, EPAT-5, LPT-5, LPV-584,
                                               LSA-3094, LOP-1509, BB B-7118,
                                               HMV BD-470, 7EG-8139, Sentry 4005

  Acc. by studio orchestra.          Los Angeles, March 30, 1931.

LA-983-A  Out Of Nowhere                       Br 6090, 80043, 9-7000, BL-54005,
                                               BL-58000, 01166, LA-8740, AH 88,
                                               Longines WL-349
LA-984-A  If You Should Ever Need Me           Br 6090, 80043, 9-7000, BL-58000,
                                               01166, LA-8740, AH-88

Vocalist with Gus Arnheim and his Cocoanut Grove Orchestra.
                    Los Angeles, May 1, 1931.

PBVE-61091-2  Ho Hum ! (w/Loyce Whiteman)      Vic 22691, LPM-2071, RD-27075,
                                               Vik LX-995, X LVA-1000,
                                               HMV 7EG-8219
PBVE-61092-2  I'm Gonna Get You                Vic 22691, LPM-2071, LPV-584,
                                               LSA-3094, RD-27075, Vik LX-995,
                                               X LVA-1000

Vocal, acc. by Victor Young and his Orchestra.
                                         Los Angeles, May 4, 1931.

LA-1036-A  Were You Sincere ?            Br 6120, 01155, AH 40
LA-1037-A  Just One More Chance          -       -      80044, 9-7000,
                                         BL-54005, BL-58000, EB-71011,
                                         02312, 04867, LA-8740, AH 88,
                                         Longines LW-349 ·


    Acc. by studio orchestra.           Los Angeles, June 12, 1931.

LA-1024-A  I'm Through With Love         Br 6140, 80045, BL-54005,
                                         BL-58000, EB-71028, 01197,
                                         LA-8740, AH 40
LA-1042-A  Many Happy Returns Of The Day Br 6145, 80058, BL-58001,
                                         EB-71029, 01182, 02695, 05934,
                                         LA-8741, AH 88
LA-1043-B  I Found A Million-Dollar Baby (In A  Br 6140, 80045, BL-54005,
           Five-and-Ten Cent Store)      BL-58000, EB-71028, 01197,
                                         LA-8740, AH 40
LA-1044-   How The Time Can Fly          Rejected

    Acc. by Harry Barris-p.             Los Angeles, June 24, 1931.

LA-1051-A  At Your Command               Br 6145
LA-1051-B  At Your Command               -       80058, BL-54005,
                                         BL-58000, EB-71029, 01182, 02534,
                                         LA-8741, AH 88
    NOTE:- Brunswick 02534 is labelled THERE'S A GOLD MINE IN THE SKY, which is matrix
DLA-1051 (q.v.), but some copies so described are pressed from the above master.

    Acc. by studio orchestra.           New York, August 19, 1931.

E-37085-A  I Apologize                   Br 6179, 80057, BL-58001,
                                         EB-71029, 01219, 05934, LA-8741,
                                         AH 88
E-37086-A  Dancing In The Dark           Br 6169, 80056, 9-7001, BL-54005,
                                         BL-58001, EB-71010, 01256, 02315,
                                         LA-8741, AH 88
E-37087-A  Star Dust                     Br 6169, 80056, 9-7001, BL-58001,
                                         EB-71010, 01252, 02101, 02312,
                                         LA-8741, AH 88


    Acc. by CBS studio orchestra, transcribed from Bing Crosby's first solo broadcast.
                                         New York, September 2, 1931.

PBS-68309-1  Just One More Chance        Vic LPV-584, LSA-3094
PBS-68311-1  I'm Through With Love       -            -
    NOTE:- Matrix PBS-68310 is not by Bing Crosby; PBS-68312 is a recording  embodying
both the above titles.

    Acc. by studio orchestra.           New York, September 14, 1931.

E-37156-A  Sweet And Lovely             Br 6179, 80057, BL-54005,
                                         BL-58001, EB-71029, 01219, 02314,
                                         LA-8741, AH-88, Longines LW-349


    Acc. by Victor Young and his Orchestra.
                                         New York, October 6, 1931.

E-37281-A  Now That You're Gone          Br 6200, 80044, 9-7000, BL-54005,
                                         BL-58000, EB-71011, 01285,
                                         LA-8740, AH 40
E-37282-A  A Faded Summer Love           Br 6200, 80055, 9-7001, BL-54005,
                                         BL-58001, EB-71010, 01240,
                                         LA-8741, AH 88

New York, October 8, 1931.

E-37284-A  Too Late                              Br 6203, 80046, BL-54005,
                                                 BL-58000, EB-71028, 01270,
                                                 LA-8740, AH 88
E-37285-A  Goodnight, Sweetheart                 Br 6203, 80046, BL-54005,
                                                 BL-58000, EB-71028, 01240, 02314,
                                                 05928, LA-8740, AH 40,
                                                 Longines LW-349

New York, October 25, 1931.

E-37320-A  Gems from GEORGE WHITE'S SCANDALS -   Br 20102, 0105, AH-40
           Part 1 (Bing Crosby sings a chorus of THE THRILL IS GONE)
E-37321-A  Gems from GEORGE WHITE'S SCANDALS -        -       -        -
           Part 2 (Bing Crosby sings a chorus of LIFE IS JUST A BOWL OF CHERRIES)

   Acc. by studio orchestra.            New York, November 23, 1931.

E-37373-A  Where The Blue Of The Night (Meets   Br 6226, 80055, 9-7001, BL-54005,
           The Gold Of The Day)                  BL-58001, EB-71010, 05928,
                                                 LA-8741, Dec DEA-7-3, AH 88,
                                                 Longines LW-349
E-37373-B  Where The Blue Of The Night (Meets   Br 6226, 01256, 01849, 02315
           The Gold Of The Day)

New York, December 3, 1931.

E-37440-A  I'm Sorry, Dear                       Br 6226, 01270, AH-40
E-37440-B  I'm Sorry, Dear                            -       -

New York, December 16, 1931.

E-37467-A  Dinah (w/The Mills Brothers)         Br 6240, 6485, 01271, 01424,
                                                 02313, 03080, Col CL-2749,
                                                 CBS 66206, AH 40

   Acc. by Helen Crawford on the organ of the Paramount Theatre.
                                        New York, December 21, 1931.

E-37474-A  Can't We Talk It Over ?              Br 6240, 01271, 02695, AH-40
E-37525-A  I Found You                          Br 6248

   Acc. by Bennie Krueger and his Orchestra.
                                        New York, January 21, 1932.

B-11163-A  Snuggled On Your Shoulder (Cuddled   Br 6248, 01285, Epic BN-26301,
           In Your Arms)                         AH 40

Vocalist with Duke Ellington and his Famous Orchestra.
                                        New York, February 11, 1932.

BX-11263-A St. Louis Blues                      Br 20105, Col 55003, CBS 66210,
                                                 Har HL-7094, Hm 520, Realm 52069,
                                                 Epic EE-22015/6, Fon TFR-6012
BX-11264-B St. Louis Blues                      Br 20105, 0116, Col 55003,
                                                 C-25006, DX-898, Epic EE-22015/6

Vocal, acc. by studio orchestra.       New York, February 16, 1932.

B-11291-A  Starlight (Help Me Find The One I    Br 6259, 01297, Col DB-2137
           Love)
B-11292-A  How Long Will It Last ?                  -       -      CBS 66210,
                                                 Epic EE-22015/6

New York, February 23, 1932.

B-11330-A  Love, You Funny Thing                Br 6268, 01304, Col DB-2009
B-11331-A  My Woman                                 -    01308, CBS 66210,
                                                 Epic EE-22015/6

New York, February 29, 1932.

B-11376-A  Shine (w/The Mills Brothers)         Br 6276, 6485, 01316, 01424,
                                                Col 4305-M, 4421-M, C-6280,
                                                CL-6027, DB-1845, 33S-1036,
                                                Philco LP-436, Ph BBE-12142

Acc. by Victor Young and his Orchestra. (Brunswick 20106 as VICTOR YOUNG AND  THE
BRUNSWICK ORCHESTRA WITH BING CROSBY). New York, March 8, 1932.

BX-11416-B  Face The Music - Medley, Part 1     Br 20106
              (Bing Crosby sings a chorus of SOFT LIGHTS AND SWEET MUSIC at the be-
              ginning and end of this side)
B-11417-B   Shadows On The Window               Br 6276, 01304

Acc. by studio orchestra.           New York, March 15, 1932.

B-11480-A  Paradise                             Br 6285, 01308, Har 1007,
                                                Col 5-1190, DB-1971, CBS 66210,
                                                Epic EE-22015/6

B-11480-B  Paradise                             Har 1007
B-11481-A  You're Still In My Heart             Br 6285, 01434, Col DB-2123

Acc. by Don Redman and his Orchestra. New York, April 13, 1932.

BX-11701-A  Lawd, You Made The Night Too Long   Br 20109, 0107, CBS 66210,
               (w/The Boswell Sisters)          Epic EE-22015/6, Bm 1013(edited)

Acc. by Isham Jones and his Orchestra. Chicago, April 23, 1932.

JC-8592-A  Sweet Georgia Brown                  Br 6320, 6635, 01316, Ban 33160,
                                                Cq 8363, 9553, Mt M-13127,
                                                Or 2962, Per 13034, Rom 2336,
                                                Voc/OK 2867, Col 4530-M, DB-1881,
                                                Epic EE-22015/6, Realm 52069
JC-8592-B  Sweet Georgia Brown                  Col 5-1166, CL-6105, Har HL-7094,
                                                HS-11313, HS-11353, Fon TFR-6012
JC-8593-A  Waltzing In A Dream                  Br 6394, 01374, Har 1008,
                                                Col DB-2074
JC-8594-A  Happy-Go-Lucky You (And Broken-      Br 6306, 01326, Col SEG-7522
              Hearted Me)

                                    Chicago, April 24, 1932.

JC-8596-B  Lazy Day                             Br 6306, 01669, Col DB-2027
JC-8597-A  Let's Try Again                      Br 6320, 01374, Col DB-2208

Acc. by Lennie Hayton and his Orchestra.
                                    Chicago, May 25, 1932.

JC-8635-1  Cabin In The Cotton                  Br 6329, 01326, CBS 66210,
                                                Epic EE-22015/6, Col DB-2030
JC-8636-1  With Summer Coming On                Br 6329, 01349

                                    Chicago, May 26, 1932.

JC-8640-1  Love Me Tonight                      Br 6351, 01349, Col SEG-7522
JC-8641-1  Some Of These Days                    -    6635, 01469, 02144,
                                                Ban 33163, Cq 8366, 9551,
                                                Mt M-13130, Or 2965, Per 13037,
                                                Rom 2339, Voc/OK 2869, Col 4305-M
                                                4421-M, CL-1927, CL-6027, DB-1845
                                                33S-1036, CBS 62144, Philco
                                                LP-436, Ph BBE-12142

Acc. by Anson Weeks and his Orchestra.  San Francisco, September 16, 1932.

SF-11-A  Please (Film "The Big Broadcast")           Br 6394, 01380, 02473,
  NOTE:- Some copies of Brunswick 6226 were      Col 4304-M, 4420-M, CL-2749,
  pressed from this master in error, instead     CL-6027, DB-1802, 33S-1036,
  of matrix E-37440, q.v.                         CBS 66206, Har HL-7094, HS-11313,
                                                Hm 520, Philco LP-436,
                                                Realm 52069, Ph BBE-12142,
                                                Fon TFE-17178, TFR-6012

  Acc. by studio orchestra.                New York, October 14, 1932.

B-12472-A  How Deep Is The Ocean ? (How High Is     Br 6406, 01421, Col 4301-M,
     The Sky ?)                            4417-M, CL-6027, DB-1985,
                                                33S-1036, SEG-7522, Har HL-7094,
                                                HS-11313, Hm 520, Realm 52069,
                                                Philco LP-435, Fon TFE-17179,
                                                TFR-6012, Z-4027
B-12473-A  Here Lies Love (Film "The Big            Br 6406, 01380, Col CL-2749,
     Broadcast")                           DB-1990, CBS 66206
B-12474-A  (I Don't Stand) A Ghost Of A Chance      Br 6454, 01423, Col DB-2030
     With You
B-12474-B  (I Don't Stand) A Ghost Of A Chance      Col 4533-M, 5-1167, CL-6027,
     With You                              CL-6105, Har 1003, HL-7094,
                                                HS-11313, Hm 520, Realm 52069,
                                                Fon TFE-17186, TFR-6012 (both
                                                edited - 17 seconds cut)

  Acc. by Lennie Hayton and his Orchestra, or Lennie Hayton-p where shown.  Matrices
  B-12503/4 are by Ruth Etting, q.v.      New York, October 25, 1932.

B-12500-A  Linger A Little Longer In The            Br 6491, 01397, Col DB-2142
     Twilight
B-12501-A  We're A Couple Of Soldiers (My Baby      Br 6696, 01397, Ban 33162,
     And Me)                               Cq 8365, Mt M-13129, Or 2964,
                                                Per 13036, Rom 2338
B-12502-A  Brother, Can You Spare A Dime ?          Br 6414, 01434, 02473,
                                                Col DB-1829
B-12505-A  Sweet Sue - Just You - pLH               CBS 66210, Epic EE-22015/6

  Acc. by studio orchestra.                New York, October 28, 1932.

B-12510-A  Let's Put Out The Lights (And Go To      Br 6414, 01404, Col 4530-M,
     Sleep)                                5-1166, CL-6105, DB-2208,
                                                Fon TFE-17179, TFR-6000, Z-4027
B-12519-A  I'll Follow You                          Br 6427, 01421, Col DB-2019
  NOTE:- Matrices B-12511/8 inclusive are by other artists on other dates.

                 New York, November 4, 1932.

B-12530-A  Just An Echo In The Valley               Br 6454, 01423, Col CL-2502,
                                                CL-2750, DB-2019, CBS 66207,
                                                Fon TFR-6000, Z-4027
B-12531-A  Some Day We'll Meet Again                Br 6427, 01404, Har 1003,
                                                Col DB-2153

                 New York, December 9, 1932.

B-12706-A  Street Of Dreams                         Br 6464, 01466, Col DB-2085
B-12707-A  It's Within Your Power                     -      -

                 New York, January 9, 1933.

B-12856-A  I'm Playing With Fire                    Br 6480, 01444, Col DB-1990
B-12857-A  Try A Little Tenderness                    -      -  Col DB-1985,
                                                SEG-7522, Bm 1013

Acc. by Guy Lombardo and his Royal Canadians.
                                    New York, January 12, 1933.

B-12887-A  You're Getting To Be A Habit With Me   Br 6472, 01480, Col DB-1901,
                                                   DC-497
B-12887-B  You're Getting To Be A Habit With Me   Col DS-290, G-31213
B-12888-A  Young And Healthy                       Br 6472
B-12888-B  Young And Healthy                       -         01456, Col DB-2027
B-12889-A  You're Beautiful Tonight, My Dear       Br 6477, 01480, Col DB-2123

Acc. by the Dorsey Brothers and their Orchestra.
                                    New York, January 26, 1933.

B-12991-A  I've Got The World On A String          Br 6491, 01531, Col 4301-M,
                                                   4417-M, CL-6027, DB-1964,
                                                   33S-1036, Har HL-7094, HS-11313,
                                                   Hm 520, Realm 52069,Philco LP-435
                                                   Fon TFR-6012
B-12992-A  My Honey's Lovin' Arms (w/The Mills     Br 6525, 01469, Col DB-1971
B-12992-B  My Honey's Lovin' Arms    Brothers)     -        Col 4304-M, 4420-M,
                                                   CL-6027, 33S-1036, Har HL-7094,
                                                   HS-11313, Hm 520, Philco LP-436,
                                                   Realm 52069, Ph BBE-12142,
                                                   Fon TFR-6012

Acc. by studio orchestra.           New York, February 9, 1933.

B-13043-A  What Do I Care ? It's Home !            Br 6515, 01503
B-13044-A  You've Got Me Crying Again              -        - Col DB-1901, DC-497

Acc. by the Dorsey Brothers and their Orchestra.
                                    New York, March 14, 1933.

B-13149-A  Someone Stole Gabriel's Horn            Br 6533, 01498, Ban 33203,
                                                   Cq 8417, Mt M-13170, Or 2998,
                                                   Per 13055, Rom 2372, Voc/OK 2879,
                                                   4522, Col DB-1894
B-13150-A  Stay On The Right Side Of The Road      Br 6533, 01498, Ban 33202,
                                                   Cq 8416, 9557, Har 1008,
                                                   Mt M-13169, Or 2997, Per 13054,
                                                   Rom 2371, Voc/OK 4522,Col DB-1964
B-13150-B  Stay On The Right Side Of The Road      IAJRC 2
B-13151-A  Here Is My Heart                        Har HL-7147

Acc. by Jimmy Grier and his Orchestra. Los Angeles, June 9, 1933.

B-779-     Learn To Croon (Film "College Humor")   Rejected
B-780-A    Moonstruck (Film "College Humor")       Br 6594, 01562, Col 4531-M,
                                                   5-1166, CL-2749, CL-6105,
                                                   CBS 66206
B-781-A    My Love                                 Br 6623, 01649
B-782-A    I've Got To Pass Your House To Get      Br 6610, 01577
             To My House
B-782-B    I've Got To Pass Your House To Get      Col 4531-M, 5-1166, CL-6105
             To My House
NOTE:- Columbia 4531-M is shown as using matrix B-782-A, but it is actually -B.

                                    Los Angeles, June 13, 1933.

B-791-A    Blue Prelude                            Br 6601, 01577, Ban 33161,
                                                   Cq 8364, Mt M-13128, Or 2963,
                                                   Per 13035, Rom 2337, Voc/OK 2868,
                                                   Rex 8957
B-791-B    Blue Prelude                            Col 5-1190, CL-2502, Fon TFR-6000
                                                   Z-4027
B-792-A    I Would If I Could But I Can't          Br 6623, 01649, AH 40
B-793-A    Learn To Croon (Film "College Humor")   Br 6594, Col CL-2502, CL-2749,
                                                   CBS 66206, Fon TFE-17178,
                                                   TFR-6000, Z-4027

(continued on page 173)

Los Angeles, June 13, 1933 (cont.)

B-793-B  Learn To Croon (Film "College Humor")    Br 6594, 01562, 02493
B-794-A  Shadow Waltz                             Br 6599, 01557, 01615, 02413,
                                                  Ban 33169, Cq 8372, Mt M-13136,
                                                  Or 2971, Per k3043, Rom 2345,
                                                  Voc/OK 2877

Los Angeles, June 16, 1933.

B-803-A  I've Got To Sing A Torch Song            Br 6599, 01563, 01615, AH 40
B-804-A  There's A Cabin In The Pines             Br 6610, 01557
B-805-A  Down The Old Ox Road  (Film "College     Br 6601, 01563, Ban 33168,
         Humor")                                  Col 4303-M, 4419-M, CL-2749,
                                                  CL-6027, DS-515, 33S-1036,
                                                  Cq 8371, Mt M-13135, Or 2970,
                                                  Per 13042, Rom 2344, CBS 66206,
                                                  Har HL-7094, HS-11313,
                                                  Philco LP-435, Realm 52069

Los Angeles, August 27, 1933.

LA-1-A  Thanks (Film "Too Much Harmony")          Br 6643, 01596, 02493,
                                                  Ban/OK 33164, Col 4303-M, 4419-M,
                                                  CL-2749, CL-6027, DB-2056,
                                                  33S-1036, Cq/Sil 8367, Mt M-13131
                                                  Or 2966, Per 13038, Rom 2340,
                                                  Voc/OK 2870, CBS 66206,
                                                  Philco LP-435

LA-2-A  The Day You Came Along (Film "Too Much    Br 6644, 01597, Ban 33165,
        Harmony")                                 Cq 8368, Mt M-13132, Or 2967,
                                                  Per 13039, Rom 2341, Voc/OK 2830,
                                                  Col CL-2749, DB-2009, CBS 66206

LA-3-A  I Guess It Had To Be That Way (Film       Br 6644, 01597, Ban 33198,
        "Too Much Harmony")                       Cq 8412, Mt M-13165, Or 2993,
                                                  Per 13050, Rom 2367, Voc/OK 2878,
                                                  Col CL-2750, DB-2137, CBS 66207

LA-4-A  Black Moonlight (Film "Too Much           Br 6643, Ban 33160, Col 4532-M,
        Harmony")                                 5-1167, CL-2750, CL-6105,
                                                  Cq 8363, 9553, Mt M-13127,
                                                  Or 2962, Per 13034, Rom 2336,
                                                  Voc/OK 2867, CBS 66207,
                                                  Fon TFR-6000, Z-4027

LA-4-B  Black Moonlight (Film "Too Much           Br 6643, 01596, Col DB-2085
        Harmony")

Acc. by Lennie Hayton and his Orchestra.
Los Angeles, September 27, 1933.

LA-19-A  Beautiful Girl (Film "Going Hollywood")  Br 6694, 01667, Ban 33165,
                                                  Cq 8368, Mt M-13132, Or 2967,
                                                  Per 13039, Rom 2341, Voc/OK 2830,
                                                  Col CL-2750, CBS 66207

LA-20-A  The Last Round-Up                        Br 6663, 01608, Ban 33203,
                                                  Col 4302-M, 4418-M, C-6063,
                                                  CL-2502, DB-1894, Cq 8417,
                                                  Mt M-13170, Or 2998, Per 13055,
                                                  Rom 2372, Voc/OK 2879, V-Disc 341
                                                  Fon TFE-17178, TFR-6000, Z-4027

LA-21-A  After Sundown (Film "Going Hollywood")   Br 6694, 01667, 02523, Ban 33168,
                                                  Cq 8371, Mt M-13135, Or 2970,
                                                  Per 13042, Rom 2344, Col DB-1881,
                                                  5-1190, CL-2750, CBS 66207

LA-22-A  Home On The Range                        Br 6663, 01608, Ban/OK 33164,
                                                  Col 4302-M, 4418-M, C-6063.
                                                  DB-1829, Cq/Sil 8367, Mt M-13131,
                                                  Or 2966, Per 13038, Rom 2340,
                                                  Voc/OK 2870, Rex 8957

Los Angeles, October 22, 1933.

LA-68-A  We'll Make Hay While The Sun Shines     Br 6695, 01668, Ban 33161,
         (Film "Going Hollywood")                Cq 8364, 9557, Mt M-13128,
                                                  Or 2963, Per 13035, Rom 2337,
                                                  Voc/OK 2868, Col CL-2750,
                                                  DB-2074, CBS 66207
LA-69-A  Temptation (Film "Going Hollywood")     Br 6695, 01668, Ban 33169,
         (20 seconds edited out of Harmony       Col 4533-M, 5-1167, CL-2502,
         HL-7094)                                 CL-2750, DB-2056, DS-670,
                                                  Cq 8372, Mt M-13136, Or 2971,
                                                  Per 13043, Rom 2345, Voc/OK 2877,
                                                  CBS 66207, Har HL-7094, HS-11313,
                                                  Hm 520, Fon TFR-6000, Z-4027,
                                                  Realm 52069
LA-69-B  Temptation (Film "Going "Hollywood")    Br 6695
LA-70-A  Our Big Love Scene (Film "Going         Br 6696, 01669, Ban 33166,
         Hollywood")                              Cq 8369, Mt M-13133, Or 2968,
                                                  Per 13040, Rom 2342, Col CL-2750,
                                                  DB-2142, CBS 66207

Los Angeles, December 11, 1933.

LA-89-A  Did You Ever See A Dream Walking ?      Br 6724, 01700, Col 4532-M,
                                                  5-1167, CL-6105, DB-2068, DS-673,
                                                  Har HL-7094, HS-11313, Hm 520,
                                                  Fon TFE-17178  TFR-6012, Z-4027,
                                                  Realm 52069
LA-90-A  Let's Spend An Evening At Home          Br 6724, 01700, Ban 33163,
                                                  Cq 8366, 9551, Mt M-13130,
                                                  Or 2965, Per 13037, Rom 2339,
                                                  Voc/OK 2869, Col DB-2153

Acc. by Nat W. Finston and his Paramount Orchestra.
                                 Los Angeles, February 25, 1934.

LA-134-A  Love Thy Neighbor  (Film "We're Not    Br 6852, 01786, Ban 33201,
          Dressing")                             Cq 8415, Mt M-13168, Or 2996,
                                                  Per 13053, Rom 2370, Voc/OK 2845,
                                                  Col CL-2750, DB-2059, CBS 66207
LA-135-A  Once In A Blue Moon (Film "We're Not   Br 6854, 01768, Ban 33162,
          Dressing")                             Cq 8365, Mt M-13129, Or 2964,
                                                  Per 13036, Rom 2338, Col CL-2750,
                                                  DB-2000, CBS 66207
LA-136-A  Goodnight, Lovely Little Lady (Film    Br 6854, 01768, Ban 33167,
          "We're Not Dressing")                  Cq 8370, Mt M-13134, Or 2969,
                                                  Per 13041, Rom 2343, Voc/OK 2834,
                                                  Col CL-2750, DB-2043, CBS 66207
LA-137-A  May I ? (Film "We're Not Dressing")    Br 6853, 01785, Ban 33200,
                                                  Cq 8414, Mt M-13167, Or 2995,
                                                  Per 13052, Rom 2369, Voc/OK 2835,
                                                  Col CL-2750, DB-2059, CBS 66207

Acc. by Jimmy Grier and his Orchestra. Los Angeles, March 10, 1934.

LA-144-A  Little Dutch Mill                       Br 6794, 01735, Ban 33166,
                                                  Cq 8369, Mt M-13133, Or 2968,
                                                  Per 13040, Rom 2342, Sentry 4010
LA-145-A  Shadows Of Love                         Br 6794, 01735, Ban 33167,
                                                  Cq 8370, Mt M-13134, Or 2969,
                                                  Per 13041, Rom 2343, Voc/OK 2834,
                                                  Sentry 4010

Los Angeles, March 13, 1934.

LA-146-A  She Reminds Me Of You (Film "We're      Br 6853, 01785, Ban 33201,
          Not Dressing")                         Cq 8415, Har 1007, Mt M-13168,
                                                  Or 2996, Per 13053, Rom 2370,
                                                  Voc/OK 2845, Col CL-2750,
(continued on page 175)             DB-2049, CBS 66207

Los Angeles, March 13, 1934 (cont.)

LA-147-A  Ridin' Around In The Rain              Br 6852, 01786, Ban 33200,Cq 8414
                                                 Mt M-13167, Or 2995, Per 13052,
                                                 Rom 2369, Voc/OK 2835,Col CL-2502
                                                 DB-2043, Fon TFR-6000, Z-4027

Acc. by Irving Aaronson and his Commanders.
                                        Los Angeles, July 5, 1934.

LA-181-A  I'm Hummin', I'm Whistlin', I'm        Br 6953, 01849, Ban 33199,
            Singin' (Film "She Loves Me Not")    Cq 8413, Mt M-13166, Or 2994,
                                                 Per 13051, Rom 2368, Col CL-2750,
                                                 DB-2068, CBS 66207
LA-182-A  Love In Bloom (Film She Loves Me Not") Br 6936, 01850, Ban 33198,
                                                 Cq 8412, Mt M-13165, Or 2993,
                                                 Per 13050, Rom 2367, Voc/OK 2878,
                                                 Col 5-1190, C-6062, DB-1802
LA-183-A  Straight From The Shoulder (Film       Br 6936, 01850, Ban 33202,
            "She Loves Me Not")                   Cq 8416, 9557, Mt M-13169,
                                                 Or 2997, Per 13054, Rom 2371,
                                                 Col C-6062, CL-2750, DB-2049,
                                                 CBS 66207
LA-184-A  Give Me A Heart To Sing To (Film "She  Br 6953, 01879, Ool DB-2000
            Loves Me Not")
LA-184-C  Give Me A Heart To Sing To (Film "She  Ban 33199, Cq 8413, Mt M-13166,
            Loves Me Not")                        Or 2994, Per 13051, Rom 2368

Acc. by Georgie Stoll and his Orchestra.
                                        Los Angeles, August 8, 1934.

DLA-6-A   I Love You Truly                       Br 01885, OE-9469
DLA-6-B   I Love You Truly                       Dec 100, Coral CPS-79
DLA-7-A   Just A-Wearyin' For You                Br 01885
DLA-7-B   Just A-Wearyin' For You                Dec 100, Coral CPS-79
DLA-8-A   Let Me Call You Sweetheart             Dec 101, Br 01925, 01992,
                                                 OE-9469, Longines LW-349,
                                                 Coral CPS-79
DLA-9-A   Someday, Sweetheart                    Dec 101, 91611, DL-8142, Br 01992,
                                                 OE-9469, AH 1

                                        Los Angeles, October 5, 1934.

DLA-64-B  The Moon Was Yellow (And The Night Was Dec 179, Br 01874, OE-9472
            Young)
DLA-65-A  The Very Thought Of You                  -      - 03079, Coral CPS-79
DLA-66-A  Two Cigarettes In The Dark             Dec 245, Br 01874
DLA-66-C  Two Cigarettes In The Dark               -
DLA-67-B  The Sweetheart Waltz                     -      - OE-9469, Coral CPS-79
DLA-67-C  The Sweetheart Waltz                     -

                                        Los Angeles, November 9, 1934.

DLA-70-A  With Every Breath I Take (Film "Here Is Dec 309, 3731, 11001, DL-4250,
            My Heart")                            DL-6008, Br 01951, BING-1,LA-8687
DLA-70-B  With Every Breath I Take (Film "Here Is Dec 309
            My Heart")
DLA-71-A  June In January (Film "Here Is My       Dec 310, Br 01951
            Heart")
DLA-71-B  June In January (Film "Here Is My         - 11000, DL-4250, DL-6008,
            Heart")                               DL-34002, Longines LW-349,
                                                 Br BING-1, LA-8687
DLA-72-A  Love Is Just Around The Corner (Film    Dec 310, 11000, DL-4250, DL-6008,
            "Here Is My Heart")                   Longines LW-349, Br 01952, BING-1,
                                                 LA-8687
DLA-72-B  Love Is Just Around The Corner (Film    Dec 310
            "Here Is My Heart")

Los Angeles, February 21, 1935.

DLA-93-A  Soon (Film "Mississippi")            Dec 392, 11002, F-49005, DL-4250,
                                               DL-6008, Br 01994, BING-1,LA-8687
DLA-94-A  Down By The River (Film "Mississippi")  Dec 11002
DLA-94-B  Down By The River (Film "Mississippi")  Dec 392, F-49005, DL-4250,DL-6008
                                               Br 01994, BING-1, LA-8687
DLA-95-B  It's Easy To Remember (w/The Rhythm-  Dec 391, 3731, 11003, DL-4250,
          ettes and Three Shades of Blue)      DL-6008, Br 01993, BING-1,
          (Film "Mississippi")                 LA-8687, Longines LW-349
DLA-96-A  Swanee River (w/The Crinoline Choir)  Dec 391, 11003, 18804, 25130,
          (Film "Mississippi")                 DL-4250, DL-5010, DL-6008,
                                               Br 01993, LA-8571, LA-8687,BING-1
DLA-97-A  Silent Night, Holy Night (w/The       Dec White Label Special (Made and
          Crinoline Choir)                     distributed for the benefit of St
                                               Columban Missionary Society)

    Acc. by unknown pipe-organist.     Los Angeles, c. February-March, 1935.

B-2078-A  Adeste Fideles (in Latin)/Lift Up Your  Decca White Label Special (as
          Hearts/Stabat Mater (in Latin)       above)

    Acc. by the Dorsey Brothers and their Orchestra.
                                       New York, August 14, 1935.

39852-A   From The Top Of Your Head (Film "Two  Dec 547, 11005, DL-4250, DL-6009,
          For Tonight")                        Br 02082, BING-1, LA-8723
39853-A   I Wish I W re Aladdin (Film "Two For  As above
          Tonight")
39854-A   Takes Two To Make A Bargain (Film "Two  Dec 548, 11004, DL-4250, DL-6009,
          For Tonight")                        Br 02070, BING-1, LA-8723
39855-A   Two For Tonight (Film "Two For Tonight")Dec 543, 11006, DL-4250, DL-6009,
                                               Br 02083, BING-1, LA-8723
39856-A   Without A Word Of Warning (Film "Two  Dec 548, 11004, DL-4250, DL-6009,
          For Tonight")                        Br 02083, BING-1, LA-8723
39857-A   I Wished On The Moon (Film "Two For   Dec 543, 11001, DL-4250, DL-6008,
          Tonight")                            Br 02070, BING-1, LA-8687

    Acc. by Victor Young and his Orchestra.
                                       Los Angeles, November 12, 1935.

DLA-253-A  Red Sails In The Sunset             Dec 616, 25380, ED-2000, Br 02101
DLA-254-A  Take Me Back To My Boots And Saddle    -    2677, 9-25003, 91120,
                                               DL-5107, DL-8210, Br 02100, 02923
                                               LAT-8152, Coral CPS-81
DLA-254-B  Take Me Back To My Boots And Saddle  Dec 616, 25003
DLA-255-A  On Treasure Island                  Dec 617, 25380
DLA-255-B  On Treasure Island                     -       -     ED-2000, Br 02100
DLA-255-C  On Treasure Island                                                 -
DLA-256-A  Adeste Fideles (O Come, All Ye      Dec 621, Br 02054
          Faithful) (in Latin and English)
          (w/the Guardsmen Quartet)
DLA-256-A  Adeste Fideles (as above)                           -
DLA-261-A  Silent Night, Holy Night (w/the        -            -
          Guardsmen Quartet)
DLA-261-B  Silent Night, Holy Night (w/the        -
          Guardsman Quartet)

    Acc. by Georgie Stoll and his Orchestra.
                                       Los Angeles, November 13, 1935.

DLA-259-A  Sailor, Beware (Film "Anything Goes")  Dec 631, 11007, DL-4251, DL-6009,
                                               Br 02143, BING-2, LA-8723
DLA-259-B  Sailor, Beware (Film "Anything Goes")    -
DLA-260-A  My Heart And I (Film "Anything Goes")  As above
DLA-260-B  My Heart And I (Film "Anything Goes")  Br 02143
DLA-262-A  Moonburn (Film "Anything Goes")      Br 02144, 02313
DLA-262-B  Moonburn (Film "Anything Goes")      Dec 617, 11006, DL-4251, DL-6009,
                                               Br 02144, 02313, BING-2, LA-8723

Acc. by Victor Young and his Orchestra. Los Angeles, March 24, 1936.

| | | |
|---|---|---|
| DLA-306-A | We'll Rest At The End Of The Trail | Dec 791, 2678, 25347, DL-5129, DL-8365, Br 02217. 02926,LAT-8253 |
| DLA-307-A | Twilight On The Trail | Dec 757, 25347, DL-5129, DL-8365, Br 02217, 02927, LAT-8253 |
| DLA-307-B | Twilight On The Trail | Dec 757, 2677 |
| DLA-308-A | The Touch Of Your Lips | -     Br 02179, 03079, Coral CPS-79 |
| DLA-308-C | The Touch Of Your Lips | Dec 757 |
| DLA-309-A | Lovely Lady | Dec 756, Br 02179, Coral CPS-79 |
| DLA-309-B | Lovely Lady | - |
| DLA-311-A | Corrine Corrina | Rejected |

NOTE:- Matrix DLA-310 is not by Bing Crosby.

Los Angeles, March 29, 1936.

| | | |
|---|---|---|
| DLA-322-A | Would You ? | Dec 756 |
| DLA-322-B | Would You ? | Dec 91611, DL-8142, Br 02223,AH 1 |
| DLA-323-A | Robins And Roses | Dec 791, Br 02223 |
| DLA-324-A | I Got Plenty O' Nuttin' | Dec 806, 25409, DL-5081, Br 02550, LA-8666 |
| DLA-324-B | I Got Plenty O' Nuttin' | Dec 25409 |
| DLA-325-A | It Ain't Necessarily So | Dec 806, Br 02550 |
| DLA-325-D | It Ain't Necessarily So | -     25409, DL-5081, Br LA-8666 |
| DLA-326- | Robins And Roses | Rejected |

NOTE:- The last title above is a parody on the lyrics of ROBINS AND ROSES,   aimed at the music publishers who controlled much of the industry in the U.S.A.

Los Angeles, probably July 8, 1936.

| | | |
|---|---|---|
| DLA-429- | Take My Heart | Dec Special (made for Jack Kapp) |

NOTE:- It is not known if matrix DLA-428 is by Bing Crosby, as the files show only a blank; DLA-427 is by Victor Young and his Orchestra, hence the assumption of the date given above.

Los Angeles, July 14, 1936.

| | | |
|---|---|---|
| DLA-436-A | Empty Saddles (Film "Rhythm On The Range") | Dec 870, 11008, 25346, DL-4251, DL-5129, DL-6010, DL-8365, Br 02270, 02924, BING-2, LA-8726, LAT-8253 |
| DLA-437-A | Round-Up Lullaby (Film "Rhythm On The Range") | Dec 870, 25346, DL-4251, DL-5129, DL-8365, Br 02272, 02928, BING-2, LAT-8253 |

Acc. by Jimmy Dorsey and his Orchestra. Los Angeles, July 17, 1936.

| | | |
|---|---|---|
| DLA-440-A | I Can't Escape From You | Dec 871, 11009, DL-4251, DL-6010, Br 02285, BING-2, LA-8726 |
| DLA-441-A | The House Jack Built For Jill | Dec 905, Br 02285 |
| DLA-441-B | The House Jack Built For Jill | Dec 11009, DL-4251, DL-6010, Br BING-2, LA-8726 |
| DLA-442-A | I'm An Old Cowhand (Film "Rhythm On The Range") | Dec 871, 2679, 11008, 25001, 91119, DL-4006, DL-4251, DL-5107, DL-6010, DL-8210, DL-34002, Br 02270, 02925, BING-2, LA-8726, LAT-8152, LAT-8368 |

Acc. by Dick McIntyre and his Harmony Hawaiians.
Los Angeles, July 23, 1936.

| | | |
|---|---|---|
| DLA-452-A | Song Of The Islands | Dec 880, 19016, 25009, 91166, DL-5122, DL-8269, Br 02320, LA-8730, Coral CPS-90 |
| DLA-453-A | Aloha Oe (Farewell To Thee) | As above, plus Dec 25425 |

Acc. by Georgie Stoll and his Orchestra.
                                Los Angeles, July 24, 1936.

DLA-462-A  So Do I (Film "Pennies From Heaven")    Dec 948, 11011, 25232, DL-4251,
                                                    DL-6010, Br 02317, BING-2,LA-8726
DLA-463-A  Pennies From Heaven (Film "Pennies       Dec 947, 11010, 25230, DEA-7-1,
           From Heaven")                            DL-4000, DL-4251, DL-6010,
                                                    Br 02316, BING-2, LA-8726

                                Los Angeles, July 29, 1936.

DLA-478-A  Let's Call A Heart A Heart (Film         Dec 947, 11010, 25230, DL-4251,
           "Pennies From Heaven")                   DL-6010, Br 02316, BING-2,LA-8726
DLA-479-A  One, Two, Button Your Shoe (Film         Dec 948, 11011, 25232, DL-4251,
           "Pennies From Heaven")                   DL-6010, Br 02317, BING-2,LA-8726

Acc. by Jimmy Dorsey and his Orchestra.
                                Los Angeles, August 4, 1936.

DLA-521-A  Shoe Shine Boy                           Dec 905, 3601, Br 02272, 03080
DLA-521-B  Shoe Shine Boy                           Dec 91612, DL-8142, AH 1

Acc. by Dick McIntyre and his Harmony Hawaiians.
                                Los Angeles, August 4, 1936.

DLA-522-A  South Sea Island Magic                   Dec 886, 19017, 25010, 91166,
                                                    DL-5122, DL-8269, Br 02263,
                                                    LA-8730, Coral CPS-90
DLA-522-B  South Sea Island Magic                   Dec 25010
DLA-523-A  Hawaiian Paradise                        Dec 886, 19017, 25010, 91166,
                                                    DL-5122, DL-8269, Br 02389,
                                                    LA-8730, Coral CPS-90
DLA-523-B  Hawaiian Paradise                        Dec 25010

Acc. by Victor Young and his Orchestra.
                                Los Angeles, August 10, 1936.

DLA-550-A  For Love Alone                           Dec 1184, Br 02281
DLA-551-A  I Never Realised                         Dec 1186,    -
DLA-551-B  I Never Realised                              -    24202, DL-5064,
                                                    Br LA-8513
DLA-552-A  Beyond Compare                           Dec 912, Br 02389, Coral CPS-79

Acc. by Ivan Ditmars-p.          Los Angeles, August 12, 1936.

DLA-554-A  Dear Old Girl (w/The Three Cheers)       Dec 1044, 91613, DL-8142,
                                                    Br 02341, AH 1
DLA-555-A  Just One Word Of Consolation (w/The      Dec 1044, 91611, Br 02341
           Three Cheers)

Acc. by Jimmy Dorsey and his Orchestra.
                                Los Angeles, August 17, 1936.

DLA-579-A  Pennies From Heaven - Medley (Bing       Dec 15027, 29226, Br 0134
           Crosby sings SO DO I as a duet with
           Frances Langford)
DLA-580-A  Pennies From Heaven (Film "Pennies            -       -       -      AH-139
           From Heaven")

Acc. by Victor Young and his Orchestra.
                                Los Angeles, August 19, 1936.

DLA-587-A  The Way You Look Tonight (w/Dixie Lee    Dec 907, 23681, 91286, DL-5001,
           Crosby)                                  Br 02291, LA-8505
DLA-588-A  A Fine Romance (w/Dixie Lee Crosby)      As above
DLA-589-A  Me And The Moon                          Dec 912, Br 02263, OE-9472

Acc. by Lani McIntyre and his Hawaiians.
                        Los Angeles, February 23, 1937.

DLA-722-A  Sweet Leilani (Film "Waikiki Wedding")  Dec 25425, Br 02412
DLA-722-B  Sweet Leilani (Film "Waikiki Wedding")  Dec 1175, 11012, 19018, 25011,
                                                   91167, DL-4000, DL-4086, DL-4252,
                                                   DL-5122, DL-6011, DL-8269,
                                                   Br 02412, 02443, BING-3, LA-8727,
                                                   LA-8730, OE-9424
DLA-723-A  Blue Hawaii (Film "Waikiki Wedding")    Dec 1175, 11012, 19018, 91167,
                                                   DL-4252, DL-5122, DL-6011,
                                                   DL-8269, Br 02444, BING-3,
                                                   LA-8727, LA-8730

Acc. by Jimmy Dorsey and his Orchestra.
                        Los Angeles, February 28, 1937.

DLA-729-A  In A Little Hula Heaven (Film           Dec 1210, Br 02443
           "Waikiki Wedding")
DLA-729-B  In A Little Hula Heaven (Film           Dec 11013, DL-4252, DL-6011,
           "Waikiki Wedding")                      Br BING-3, LA-8727
DLA-730-A  Never In A Million Years                Dec 1210, Br 02453

                        Los Angeles, March 3, 1937.

DLA-737-A  What Will I Tell My Heart ?             Dec 1185, Br 02402
DLA-738-A  Too Marvelous For Words                  -      25193, DL-5343,
                                                   Br 02452, LA-8624
DLA-738-B  Too Marvelous For Words                  -      Coral CPS-79
DLA-739-A  Peckin'                                 Dec 1301, Br 02481
    NOTE:- Decca 1301 and Brunswick 02481 as JIMMY DORSEY AND HIS ORCHESTRA    (Vocal
    Chorus by Bing Crosby).

Acc. by Victor Young and his Orchestra.
                        Los Angeles, March 5, 1937.

DLA-741-A  The One Rose (That's Left In My Heart) Dec 1201, 3541, 25367, 91169,
                                                   DL-4006, DL-5126, Br 02412,
                                                   02523, LA-8514, LAT-8368
DLA-741-C  The One Rose (That's Left In My Heart) Dec 25367
DLA-742-A  Sweet Is The Word For You (Film         Dec 1184, 11013, DL-4252, DL-6011
           "Waikiki Wedding")                      Br 02444, BING-3, LA-8727
DLA-742-B  Sweet Is The Word For You (Film          -
           "Waikiki Wedding")
DLA-743-A  Moonlight And Shadows                   Dec 1186, 25367, 91169, DL-5126,
                                                   Br 02402, LA-8514

                        Los Angeles, March 8, 1937.

DLA-745-A  Sentimental And Melancholy             Dec 1201, Br 02452
DLA-746-A  My Little Buckaroo                      Dec 1234, 2679, 25003, 91120,
                                                   DL-5107, DL-8210, Br 02413,
                                                   02925, LAT-8152
DLA-747-A  What Is Love ?                          Dec 1234, Br 02453

Acc. by John Scott Trotter and his Orchestra.
                        Los Angeles, July 12, 1937.

DLA-829-A  It's The Natural Thing To Do (Film      Dec 1376, 11015, DL-4252, DL-6011
           "Double Or Nothing")                    Br 02499, BING-3, LA-8727
DLA-830-A  All You Want To Do Is Dance (Film       As above
           "Double Or Nothing")
DLA-831-A  The Moon Got In My Eyes (Film "Double   Dec 1375, 11014, DL-4252, DL-6011
           Or Nothing")                            Br 02498, BING-3, LA-8727
DLA-832-A  Smarty (Film "Double Or Nothing")       As above

Acc. by Lani McIntyre and his Hawaiians.
                                Los Angeles, September 11, 1937.

DLA-906-A  Dancing Under The Stars              Dec 1616, 19019, 25012, 91167,
                                                DL-5122, DL-8269, Br 02485,
                                                LA-8730, Coral CPS-90
DLA-906-B  Dancing Under The Stars              Br 02485
DLA-907-A  Palace In Paradise                   -
DLA-907-B  Palace In Paradise                   As for DLA-906-A
DLA-908-A  When You Dream About Hawaii          Dec 1518
DLA-908-B  When You Dream About Hawaii          -        19021, 25021, 91291,
                                                DL-5299, Br 02646, 02826,
                                                Coral CPS-90
DLA-909-B  Sail Along, Silvery Moon             Dec 1518, 19021, 25021, 91291,
                                                DL-5299, DL-8268, Br 02604,
                                                02826, LAT-8334, OE-9472

Acc. by John Scott Trotter and his Orchestra.
                                Los Angeles, September 20, 1937.

DLA-939-A  Can I Forget You ?                   Dec 1462, Br 02484
DLA-940-A  The Folks Who Live On The Hill       -          -        Coral CPS-79
DLA-941-A  I Still Love To Kiss You Goodnight   Dec 1451, Br 02525      -
DLA-942-A  Remember Me ?                        -        18866, 91612, DL-8142,
                                                Br 02534, AH 1

                                Los Angeles, September 25, 1937.

DLA-971-A  Basin Street Blues (w/Connie Boswell) Dec 1483, 25430, DL-5390,
                                                Br 02492, LA-8558, AH 90
DLA-972-A  Bob White (Whatcha Gonna Swing       As above, except AH 90
             Tonight ?) (w/Connie Boswell)

Acc. by Eddie Dunstedter-pipe organ.  Los Angeles, November 12, 1937.

DLA-1051-A  There's A Gold Mine In The Sky      Dec 1565, 2678, 25001, 91119,
                                                DL-5107, DL-8210, Br 02534,
                                                02927, LAT-8152
DLA-1052-A  When The Organ Played "O Promise Me" Dec 1554, Br 02604

Acc. by Eddie Dunstedter-electric organ.
                                Los Angeles, November 15, 1937.

DLA-1071-B  Let's Waltz For Old Times' Sake     Dec 1554, Br 02577
DLA-1072-A  In The Mission By The Sea           Dec 1565, Br 02525

Acc. by John Scott Trotter and his Orchestra.
                                Los Angeles, January 21, 1938.

DLA-1148-A  My Heart Is Taking Lessons (Film    Dec 1648, 11020, 25233, DL-4253,
             "Doctor Rhythm")                   DL-6013, Br 02640, BING-4,LA-8742
DLA-1149-A  This Is My Night To Dream (Film     Dec 11021, DL-4253, DL-6013,
             "Doctor Rhythm")                   Br BING-4, LA-8742
DLA-1149-B  This Is My Night To Dream (Film     Dec 1649, 11021, Br 02641
             "Doctor Rhythm")
DLA-1150-A  On The Sentimental Side (Film "Doctor Dec 1648, 11020, 25233, DL-4253,
             Rhythm")                           DL-6013, DL-34002, Br 02640,
                                                BING-4, LA-8742
DLA-1151-A  The Moon Of Manakoora               Dec 1649, Br 02577
DLA-1151-B  The Moon Of Manakoora               Dec 91616, DL-8143, Br OE-9472,
                                                AH 1

Acc. by Victor Young and his Orchestra.
                                Los Angeles, January 26, 1938.

DLA-1152-A  Alexander's Ragtime Band (w/Connie  Dec 1887, 25495, DL-5390,
             Boswell and Eddie Cantor)          Br 02572, LA-8558
DLA-1153-A  Home On The Range (part side only)  Dec 1887, Br 02572
NOTE:- Eddie Cantor's introductory speech edited out of Dec DL-5390, Br LA-8558.

Acc. by Harry Owens and his Royal Hawaiian Hotel Orchestra.
Los Angeles, April 13, 1938.

DLA-1210-A  Sweet Hawaiian Chimes                  Dec 1845, 19022, 25022, 91291,
                                                   DL-5299, DL-8269, Br 02641,
                                                   Coral CPS-90
DLA-1211-A  Little Angel                           Dec 1845, 19022, 25022, 91291,
                                                   DL-5299, Br 05017

Acc. by John Scott Trotter and his Orchestra.
Los Angeles, April 22, 1938.

DLA-1276-A  Let Me Whisper I Love You (Murmullo)   Dec 1819, Br 02678, Coral CPS-79
DLA-1277-A  Don't Be That Way                      Dec 1794, 91615, DL-8143,
                                                   Br 02618, AH 1

Acc. by Eddie Dunstedter-pipe organ.    Los Angeles, April 25, 1938.

DLA-1287-A  Little Lady Make-Believe               Dec 1794, 3603, Br 02618, AH 139
DLA-1288-A  When Mother Nature Sings Her Lullaby   Dec 1874, Br 02664

Acc. by the Paul Taylor Choristers.    Los Angeles, May 3, 1938.

DLA-1289-A  Darling Nellie Gray                    Dec 1874, 3540, 24203, DL-5028,
                                                   Br 02663, LA-8585
DLA-1290-B  Swing Low, Sweet Chariot               Dec 1819, 3540, 25052, Br 02663

Acc. by John Scott Trotter and his Orchestra.
Los Angeles, May 23, 1938.

DLA-1293-A  I've Got A Pocketful Of Dreams (Film   Rejected
              "Sing, You Sinners")
DLA-1294-A  Now It Can Be Told                     Dec 1888, 25093, Br 02646
DLA-1295-A  It's The Dreamer In Me                   -     91614, DL-8143,
                                                   Br 02768, AH 1
DLA-1296-A  Don't Let That Moon Get Away (Film     Rejected
              "Sing, You Sinners")

Acc. by Victor Young's Small Fryers.    Los Angeles, July 1, 1938.

DLA-1297-A  Small Fry (w/Johnny Mercer)            Dec 1960, 3600, 11016, 24293,
                                                   91412, DL-4006, DL-4252, DL-6012,
                                                   DL-8075, DL-9064, Voc VL-3769,
                                                   Br 02653, BING-3, LA-8732,
                                                   LAT-8054, LAT-8368, LAT-8382
DLA-1298-A  Mr. Gallagher And Mr. Shean ("as       Dec 1960, 24293, AH 90
              sung by Mr. Crosby and Mr. Mercer")
DLA-1298-E  Mr. Gallagher And Mr. Shean ("as         -       -    91616, DL-8143,
              sung by Mr. Crosby and Mr. Mercer")  Br 02653, LAT-8306, AH 1

Acc. by Matty Malneck and his Orchestra.
Los Angeles, July 8, 1938.

DLA-1310-A  Summertime                             Dec 2147, 24542, DL-5081,
                                                   Br 02746, LA-8666
DLA-1310-B  Summertime                             Dec 24542
DLA-1311-A  A Blues Serenade (Film "Sing, You      Dec 1933, 3543, 25368, 91169,
              Sinners")                            DL-5126, Br 02682, LA-8514, AH 90

Acc. by John Scott Trotter and his Orchestra.
Los Angeles, July 11, 1938.

DLA-1312-A  I've Got A Pocketful Of Dreams (Film   Dec 1933, 11017, DL-4252,
              "Sing, You Sinners")                 DL-6012, DL-34002, Br 02681,
                                                   BING-3, LA-8732
DLA-1313-A  Don't Let That Moon Get Away (Film     Dec 1934, 11017, DL-4252,
              "Sing, You Sinners")                 DL-6012, Br 02682, BING-3, LA-8732
DLA-1314-A  Silver On The Sage                     Dec 2001, 25002, 91120, DL-5107,
                                                   DL-8210, 139 (Can.), Br 02664,
  (continued on page 182)                       02926, LAT-8152, Coral CPS-81

Los Angeles, July 11, 1938 (cont.)

DLA-1315-A  Laugh And Call It Love (Film "Sing,       Dec 1934, 11016, DL-4252, DL-6012,
              You Sinners")                            Br 02681, BING-3, LA-8732
DLA-1316-A  Mexicali Rose                              Dec 2001, 25002, 91120, DL-5107,
                                                       DL-8210, 139 (Can.), Br 02678,
                                                       02923, LAT-8152

    Acc. by Bob Crosby and his Orchestra.  Chicago, October 14, 1938.

C-91511-A  You Must Have Been A Beautiful Baby        Dec 2147, 91613, DL-8142,
                                                       Br 02694, AH 1
C-91511-B  You Must Have Been A Beautiful Baby        Dec 2147
C-91512-A  Old Folks                                   Dec 2123, 91615, DL-8143,
                                                       Br 02694, AH 1
C-91512-B  Old Folks                                   Dec 2123
C-91513-A  My Reverie                                  -
C-91513-B  My Reverie                                  -        91614, DL-8143, AH 1

    Acc. by John Scott Trotter and his Orchestra.
                                        Los Angeles, November 4, 1938.

DLA-1547-A  You're A Sweet Little Headache             Dec 2200, 11018, DL-4253, DL-6012,
              (Film "Paris Honeymoon")                 Br 02714, BING-4, LA-8732
DLA-1548-A  I Have Eyes (Film "Paris Honeymoon")       Dec 2201, 11019, Br 02713
DLA-1548-B  I Have Eyes (Film "Paris Honeymoon")       Dec 11019, DL-4253, DL-6012,
                                                       BING-4, LA-8732
DLA-1549-A  The Funny Old Hills (Film "Paris           Dec 2201, 11019, Br 02713
DLA-1549-B  The Funny Old Hills  Honeymoon")           Dec DL-4253, DL-6012, Br BING-4,
                                                       LA-8732
DLA-1550-A  Joobalai (Film "Paris Honeymoon")          Dec 11018, DL-4253, DL-6012,
                                                       Br BING-4, LA-8732
DLA-1550-B  Joobalai (Film "Paris Honeymoon")          Dec 2200, Br 02714

    Acc. by Victor Young and his Concert Orchestra.
                                        Los Angeles, December 2, 1938.

DLA-1605-A  When You're Away                           Dec DL-5355, Br LA-8600
DLA-1605-B  When You're Away                           Dec 2680, 23816, Br 02850
DLA-1606-A  Ah ! Sweet Mystery Of Life                 Dec 2315, 23815, DL-5355,
                                                       Br 02761, LA-8600
DLA-1607-A  Sweethearts                                Dec Y-5341 (Australian)
DLA-1607-B  Sweethearts                                Dec 2315, 23815, DL-5355,
                                                       Br 02761, LA-8600
DLA-1608-A  Thine Alone                                Dec Y-5509 (Australian)
DLA-1608-B  Thine Alone                                Dec 2680, 23816, DL-5355,
                                                       Br 02850, LA-8600

                                        Los Angeles, December 9, 1938.

DLA-1624-A  Gypsy  Love Song (w/Frances Langford) Dec 2316, 23814, DL-5355,
                                                       Br 02849, LA-8600
DLA-1625-A  I'm Falling In Love With Someone           As above, plus AH 69
              (w/Frances Langford)

    Acc. by John Scott Trotter and his Orchestra.
                                        Los Angeles, December 12, 1938.

DLA-1633-A  My Melancholy Baby                         Dec 2289, 3542, 25366, 91168,
                                                       DL-4255, DL-5126, Br 02806,
                                                       BING-6, LA-8514
DLA-1634-B  I Cried For You                            Dec 2273, 3542, 25366, 91168,
                                                       DL-5126, Br 02805, LA-8514
DLA-1634-C  I Cried For You                            Dec 25366
DLA-1635-A  The Lonesome Road                          Dec 2257, 3541, Br 02753
DLA-1636-A  When The Bloom Is On The Sage (w/          Dec 2237, 25000, 91119, 9-25000,
              The Foursome, acc. by John Scott         DL-5107, DL-8210, Br 02809,
              Trotter's Frying Pan Five)               LAT-8152

Los Angeles, December 19, 1938.

| | | |
|---|---|---|
| DLA-1689-A | Between A Kiss And A Sigh | Dec 2289, Br 02733 |
| DLA-1690-A | Just A Kid Named Joe | Dec 2257, 3601, Br 02718 |
| DLA-1691-A | It's A Lonely Trail (When You're Travelin' All Alone) | Dec 2237          -          02928 |
| DLA-1692-A | Let's Tie The Old Forget-Me-Not | Dec 2273, Br 02733 |

Los Angeles, March 10, 1939.

| | | |
|---|---|---|
| DLA-1718-A | East Side Of Heaven (Film "East Side Of Heaven") | Dec 2359, 11024, DL-4253, DL-6014, Br 02786, BING-4 |
| DLA-1719-A | Hang Your Heart On A Hickory Limb (Film "East Side Of Heaven") | Dec 2360, 11025, DL-4253, DL-6014, Br 02787, BING-4 |
| DLA-1719-B | Hang Your Heart On A Hickory Limb (Film "East Side Of Heaven") | Dec 2360 |
| DLA-1720-A | That Sly Old Gentleman (From Featherbed Lane) (Film "East Side Of Heaven") | -          88089 |
| DLA-1720-B | That Sly Old Gentleman (From Featherbed Lane) (Film "East Side Of Heaven") | Dec 2360, 3600, 11025, DL-4253, DL-6014, Br 02787, BING-4 |
| DLA-1721-A | Sing A Song Of Sunbeams (Film "East Side Of Heaven") | Dec 2359, 11024, DL-4253, DL-6014, Br 02786, BING-4, AH 139 |

Acc. by John Scott Trotter's Frying Pan Five.

Los Angeles, March 15, 1939.

| | | |
|---|---|---|
| DLA-1722-A | Ida, Sweet As Apple Cider (w/The Foursome) | Dec 2494, 25492, 9-28963, Br 02890, 05273 |
| DLA-1723-A | Poor Old Rover (w/The Foursome) | Dec 2385, Br 02873 |
| DLA-1724-A | Down By The Old Mill Stream | Dec 2447, 9-25492, Br 02807 |
| DLA-1724-B | Down By The Old Mill Stream | Dec 25492 |

Acc. by Matty Malneck and his Orchestra.

Los Angeles, March 22, 1939.

| | | |
|---|---|---|
| DLA-1733-A | Deep Purple | Dec 2374, 25285, 91168, DL-5126, Br 02746, LA-8514 |
| DLA-1734-A | Stardust | Dec 2374, 25285, 91168, DL-5126, Br 02805, LA-8514 |

Acc. by John Scott Trotter and his Orchestra.

Los Angeles, March 27, 1939.

| | | |
|---|---|---|
| DLA-1739-A | God Bless America (w/Max Terr's Mixed Chorus) | Dec 2400, 23579, Br 02810 |
| DLA-1740-A | The Star-Spangled Banner (w/Max Terr's Mixed Chorus) | -          - DL-8020 - |

Los Angeles, March 31, 1939.

| | | |
|---|---|---|
| DLA-1742-A | If I Had My Way | Dec 2448, 11030, DL-4254, DL-6015, Br 02900, BING-5 |
| DLA-1743-A | Little Sir Echo (w/The Music Maids) | Dec 2385, Voc VL-3769, Br 02753, AH 139 |
| DLA-1744-A | I Surrender, Dear | Dec 2535, 11048, 25229, 91288, DL-5105, DL-5326, DL-7019, Br 02808, LA-8595, LA-8684, LA-8728, AH 90 |
| DLA-1745-A | I'm Building A Sailboat Of Dreams | Dec 2447, Br 02768 |

Acc. by John Scott Trotter's Frying Pan Five.

Los Angeles, April 3, 1939.

| | | |
|---|---|---|
| DLA-1752-A | Alla en el Rancho Grande (w/The Foursome) | Dec 2494, 23914, 9-23914, DL-5011, DL-8846, Br 02873, LA-8529, LAT-8331 |
| DLA-1753-A | It Must Be True (w/The Music Maids) | Dec 2535, 25229, 91288, DL-5105, DL-5326, Br 03396, LA-8595, LA-8684 |

(continued on page 184)

Los Angeles, April 3, 1939.

DLA-1754-A  S'posin' (w/The Music Maids)          Dec 2413, 3543, 25368, 91169,
                                                 DL-5126, Br 02779, LA-8514, AH 90

Acc. by John Scott Trotter and his Orchestra.
                                     Los Angeles, April 5, 1939.

DLA-1757-A  Whistling In The Wildwood            Dec 2448, Br 02924, CPS 81
DLA-1758-A  And The Angels Sing                  Dec 2413, 91617, DL-8144,
                                                 Br 02779, AH 17

Los Angeles, June 9, 1939.

DLA-1767-A  Wrap Your Troubles In Dreams         Dec 2948, 25193, DL-5343,
                                                 Br 02900, LA-8624
DLA-1768-A  Girl Of My Dreams                    Dec 2671, 18866, 27551, DL-5326,
                                                 Br 03418, LA-8684, AH 90
DLA-1769-A  Missouri Waltz                       Dec 2676, 25407, Br 02809
DLA-1769-B  Missouri Waltz                       -
    NOTE:- A test of DLA-1767-C exists, and from it various illicit recordings  on  45
    rpm discs have been made and distributed.  It shows the artist inventing new words
    to describe what was happening when he sang the wrong part towards the end of  the
    side.

Los Angeles, June 12, 1939.

DLA-1770-A  Still The Bluebird Sings (Film "The  Dec 2640, 11022, DL-4254, DL-6013,
              Star Maker")                       Br 02839, BING-5, LA-8742
DLA-1771-A  Go Fly A Kite (Film "The Star Maker") Dec 2641, 11023, DL-4254, DL-6013,
                                                 Br 02840, BING-5, LA08742
DLA-1772-A  A Man And His Dream (Film "The Star  As above
              Maker")
DLA-1773-A  Just One More Chance                 Dec 2999, Br 02806

Acc. by Dick McIntyre and his Harmony Hawaiians.
                                     Los Angeles, June 13, 1939.

DLA-1774-A  To You, Sweetheart, Aloha            Dec 2775, 19023, 25023, 91292,
                                                 DL-5299, DL-8269, Br 02808
DLA-1775-A  My Isle Of Golden Dreams             Dec 2775, 19023, 25023, 91292,
                                                 91766, DL-5299, DL-8268,
                                                 Br 04342, LAT-8334

Acc. by Victor Young and his Orchestra.
                                     Los Angeles, June 14, 1939.

DLA-1776-A  Maybe                                Dec 2874, 25410, DL-5081,
                                                 Br 02986, LA-8666
DLA-1777-A  Somebody Loves Me                    As above
DLA-1778-A  Home On The Range                    Dec 2676, 25000, 91119, DL-5107,
                                                 DL-8210, Br 02807, LAT-8152,
                                                 Coral CPS-81

Acc. by John Scott Trotter and his Orchestra.
                                     Los Angeles, June 22, 1939.

DLA-1781-A  (Ho-dle-ay) Start The Day Right (w/  Dec 2626, 25495, DL-5390,
              Connie Boswell)                    Br 02890, LA-8558, AH 139
DLA-1782-A  An Apple For The Teacher (w/Connie   Dec 2640, 3602, 11022, 25496,
              Boswell) (Film "The Star Maker")   DL-4254, DL-5390, DL-6013,
                                                 Br 02839, BING-5, LA-8558, LA-8742

Los Angeles, June 30, 1939.

DLA-1793-A  Neighbors In The Sky                 Dec 2626
DLA-1794-A  What's New ?                         Dec 2671, 91618, DL-8144,
                                                 Br 04129, AH 17
DLA-1795-A  Cynthia                              Dec 3257, Br 04135
    (continued on page 185)

Los Angeles, June 30, 1939 (cont.)

DLA-1796-A  Medley of Gus Edwards' Song Hits        Dec 2700, 3602, 11021, DL-4254,
            (Bing Crosby sings a chorus of SUN-  DL-6013, Br 02841, BING-5,
            BONNET SUE, JIMMY VALENTINE and IF   LA-8742, AH 139
            I WAS A MILLIONAIRE) (w/The Music Maids)
DLA-1797-A  In My Merry Oldsmobile (w/The Music   Dec 2700, DL-4254, Br 02841,
            Maids)                                BING-5

Acc. by Joe Venuti and his Orchestra.  New York, September 20, 1939.

66632-A  Ciribiribin (w/The Andrews Sisters)     Dec 2800, ED-2037, Br 02881,
                                                  Coral CPS-91
66633-B  Yodelin' Jive (w/The Andrews Sisters)   As above

Acc. by John Scott Trotter and his Orchestra.
                                          Los Angeles, December 15, 1939.

DLA-1907-A  Too Romantic (Film "The Road To       Dec 2998, 11031, DL-4254,
            Singapore")                           DL-6015, Br 02973, BING-5
DLA-1908-A  The Moon And The Willow Tree (Film    As above, plus Br 0E-9473
            "The Road To Singapore")
DLA-1909-A  Sweet Potato Piper (w/The Foursome,   Dec 2999, Br 02974
            acc. by John Scott Trotter's Frying Pan Five) (Film "The Road To  Sin-
            gapore")
DLA-1909-B  Sweet Potato Piper (w/The Foursome,   Dec 11030, DL-4254, DL-6015,
            acc. by John Scott Trotter's Frying Br BING-5, AH 139
            Pan Five) (Film "The Road To Singapore")
DLA-1910-A  Between 18th And 19th On Chestnut     Dec 2948, 25496, DL-5390,
            Street (w/Connie Boswell)             Br 02974, LA-8558

                                          Los Angeles, February 9, 1940.

DLA-1918-A  Marcheta (A Love Song Of Old Mexico)  Dec 3133, 25407, Br 03044
DLA-1919-A  Tumbling Tumbleweeds                   Dec 3024, 4200, 25345, 9-25345,
                                                  9-30082, DL-5129, DL-8365,
                                                  Br 03010, LAT-8253, Coral CPS-81
DLA-1920-A  If I Knew Then (What I Know Now)       Dec 3024. 91618, DL-8144,
                                                  Br 03010, AH 17
DLA-1921-A  The Girl With The Pigtails In Her     Dec 3098, 3603, Br 04122
            Hair

                                          Los Angeles, February 25, 1940.

DLA-1951-A  Devil May Care                         Dec 3064, Br 02978
DLA-1952-A  The Singing Hills                      -     4200, 25345, 9-25345,
                                                  DL-5129, DL-8365, Br 02978,
                                                  LAT-8253
DLA-1953-A  I'm Waiting For Ships That Never Come Dec 3257, 26281, 91290, DL-5340,
            In                                    Br 04103, LA-8620

                                          Los Angeles, March 22, 1940.

DLA-1967-B  Beautiful Dreamer                      Dec 3118, 18802, 25128. DL-5010,
                                                  Br 03019, 05000, LA-8571
DLA-1968-A  I Dream Of Jeanie With The Light      Dec 3098, 18801, 25127, DL-5010,
            Brown Hair                            Br 04100, LA-8571
DLA-1969-A  Yours Is My Heart Alone (You Are My   Dec 3118, 23716, DL-5326,
            Heart's Delight)                      Br 03019, LA-8684
DLA-1970-A  Sierra Sue                            Dec 3133, Br 03044, Coral CPS-81

                                          Los Angeles, April 12, 1940.

DLA-1981-A  Meet The Sun Half-Way (Film "If I     Dec 3162, 11029, DL-4254, DL-6015
            Had My Way")                          DL-34002, Br 03032, BING-5
DLA-1982-A  April Played The Fiddle (Film "If I   Dec 3161, 11028, DL-4254, DL-6015
            Had My Way")                          Br 03031, BING-5
DLA-1983-A  I Haven't Time To Be A Millionaire (Film "If I Had My Way") As above
DLA-1984-A  The Pessimistic Character (With The   Dec 3162, 11029, DL-4254, DL-6015
            Crabapple Face) (Film "If I Had My Way") Br 03032, BING-5

Acc.. by Victor Young and his Orchestra.
                                    Los Angeles, April 15, 1940.

DLA-1985-A  Mister  Meadowlark (w/Johnny Mercer)   Dec 3182, 25148, 91619, DL-8144,
                                                   Br 03171, AH 17
DLA-1986-A  On  Behalf Of The Visiting Firemen     Dec 3182, 25148, 91615, DL-8143,
            (w/Johnny Mercer)                      Br 03350, AH 24

Acc.  by Dick McIntyre and his Harmony Hawaiians.
                                    Los Angeles, July 1, 1940.

DLA-2013-A  Trade Winds                            Dec 3299, 19024, 25024, 91292,
                                                   DL-5299, DL-8269, Br 03073
DLA-2014-A  A Song Of Old Hawaii                   Dec 3299, 19024, 25024, 91292,
                                                   DL-5299, DL-8269, Br 04102,
                                                   Coral CPS-90
DLA-2015-A  Aloha Kuu Ipo Aloha                    Dec 3797, 19020, 25013, 91168,
                                                   Br 04102, Coral CPS-90

Acc. by John Scott Trotter and his Orchestra.
                                    Los Angeles, July 3, 1940.

DLA-2031-A  When The Moon Comes Over Madison       Dec 3300, 11026, DL-4255,
            Square (Film "Rhythm On The River")    DL-6014, Br 03087, BING-6,
                                                   OE-9473
DLA-2032-A  That's For Me (Film "Rhythm On The     Rejected
            River")
DLA-2033-A  Only Forever (Film "Rhythm On The      Dec 3300, 11026, DL-4255,
            River")                                DL-6014, Br 03087, BING-6
DLA-2034-A  Rhythm On The River (Film "Rhythm On   Rejected
            The River")

Acc. by Victor Young and his Orchestra, with the Ken Darby Singers.
                                    Los Angeles, July 6, 1940.

DLA-2035-A  Ballad For Americans - Part 1          Dec 3297, 3554, 23580, DL-8020,
                                                   Br 03151
DLA-2036-A  Ballad For Americans - Part 2          As above, but Dec 23581
DLA-2037-A  Ballad For Americans - Part 3          Dec 3298, 3555, 23581, DL-8020,
                                                   Br 03152
DLA-2038-A  Ballad For Americans - Part 4          As above, but Dec 23580

Acc. by John Scott Trotter and his Orchestra.
                                    Los Angeles, July 10, 1940.

DLA-2042-A  Rhythm On The River (Film "Rhythm On   Dec 3309, 11027, DL-4255, DL-6014,
            The River")                            Br 03092, BING-6
DLA-2043-A  That's For Me (Film "Rhythm On The     As above
            River")
DLA-2044-A  I Found A Million-Dollar Baby (In A    Dec 3321, 25502, 91289, DL-5340,
            Five-and-Ten Cent Store)               Br 04116, LA-8620
DLA-2045-A  Can't Get Indiana Off My Mind          Dec 3321, Br 03073

Acc. by the Paradise Island Trio.     Los Angeles, July 20, 1940.

DLA-2057-A  The Waltz You Saved For Me             Dec 3354, 25186, 91765, DL-5119,
                                                   DL-8268, Br 04292, LAT-8334
DLA-2058-A  Where The Blue Of The Night (Meets     As above except Br 04292
            The Gold Of The Day)
DLA-2059-A  When You're A Long, Long Way From      Dec 3477, 25187, 91766, DL-5119,
            Home                                   DL-8268, Br 04290, LAT-8334
DLA-2060-A  When I Lost You                        Dec 3477, 25093, 25187, 91766,
                                                   DL-5119, DL-8268, Br 04103,
                                                   LAT-8334
DLA-2061-A  Paradise Isle                          Dec 3797, 19020, 25013, Br 04130,
                                                   Coral CPS-90

Acc. by Victor Young and his Orchestra. Los Angeles, July 23, 1940.

DLA-2066-A  Do You Ever Think Of Me ? (w/The Merry  Dec 3423, 25424, Br 04104
          Macs)
DLA-2067-A  You Made Me Love You (w/The Merry Macs)    -     -     -

Acc. by John Scott Trotter and his Orchestra.
                              Los Angeles, July 27, 1940.

DLA-2072-A  Legend Of Old California  Dec 3388, Br 04124, Coral CPS-81
DLA-2073-A  Please (Film "The Big Broadcast")  Dec 3450, 25502, 91289, DL-5340,
                                      Br 03220, LA-8620
DLA-2074-A  You Are The One  Dec 3450, Br 03220
DLA-2075-A  Prairieland Lullaby  Dec 3388, Br 04124, Coral CPS-81

                        Los Angeles, December 3, 1940.

DLA-2251-A  Along The Santa Fe Trail  Dec 3565, 4201, Br 03142,
                                      Coral CPS-81
DLA-2252-A  Lone Star Trail  Dec 3584, 4201, Br 03127
DLA-2253-A  It's Always You  Dec 3636, DL-4255, Br 03184,
                                      BING-6
DLA-2254-B  I'd Know You Anywhere  Dec 3565, Br 03142

Acc. by Victor Young and his Orchestra. Los Angeles, December 9, 1940.

DLA-2259-A  De Camptown Races (w/The King's Men)  Dec 3644, 18803, 25129, DL-5010,
                                      Br 03190, LA-8571
DLA-2260-A  Did Your Mother Come From Ireland ?  Dec 3609, 23787, 91165, DL-5037,
           (w/The King's Men)  DL-8207, Br 03651, LAT-8106,
                                      MCA 65002
DLA-2261-B  My Old Kentucky Home (w/The King's  Dec 3886, 18803, 25129, DL-5010,
           Men)  Br 04101, LA-8571
DLA-2262-A  Where The River Shannon Flows (w/The  Dec 3609, 23787, 91165, DL-5037,
           King's Men)  DL-8207, Br 03651, LAT-8106,
                                      MCA 65002

Acc. by Bob Crosby's Bob-Cats.       Los Angeles, December 13, 1940.

DLA-2271-A  Tea For Two (w/Connie Boswell)  Dec 3689, 25406, DL-5390,
                                      Br 03661, LA-8558
DLA-2272-A  Yes Indeed ! (w/Connie Boswell)  Dec 3689, 25406, 91414, DL-4001,
                                      DL-5390, DL-8075, DL-9064,
                                      Br 03661, LA-8558, LAT-8054,
                                      LAT-8382

Acc. by Bob Crosby and his Orchestra.  Los Angeles, December 16, 1940.

DLA-2274-A  San Antonio Rose  Dec 3590, 10299, 18766, 23968,
                                      DL-5063, Br 03171, OE-9424,
                                      Coral CPS-81
DLA-2275-B  It Makes No Difference Now  Dec 3590, 10299, 18766, 23968,
                                      DL-5063, Br 03456

Acc. by John Scott Trotter and his Orchestra.
                                Los Angeles, December 20, 1940.

DLA-2286-A  You're Dangerous  Dec 3637, DL-4255, Br 03185,
                                      BING-6
DLA-2287-A  A Nightingale Sang In Berkeley Square  Dec 3584, Br 03127
DLA-2288-A  You Lucky People, You  Dec 3636, DL-4255, Br 03184,
                                      BING-6
DLA-2289-A  Birds Of A Feather  Dec 3637, DL-4255, Br 03185,
                                      BING-6

Acc. by Bob Crosby's Bob-Cats.     Los Angeles, December 23, 1940.

DLA-2290-A  Dolores (w/The Merry Macs)  Dec 25399
DLA-2290-B  Dolores (w/The Merry Macs)  Dec 3644, 25399, Br 03190
DLA-2291-B  Pale Moon (w/The Merry Macs)  Dec 3887  -  Br 04115, OE-9473

Acc. by Victor Young and his Orchestra. Los Angeles, December 30, 1940.

| | | |
|---|---|---|
| DLA-2312-A | Chapel In The Valley | Dec 3614, Br 04739 |
| DLA-2313-A | I Only Want A Buddy - Not A Sweetheart | Dec 3736, 10302, 18769, 27554, DL-5331, Br 04739, LA-8724 |
| DLA-2314-A | When Day Is Done | Dec 3614, 25281, 91290, DL-5340, Br 03875, LA-8620 |
| DLA-2315-A | My Buddy | Dec 3736, 91619, DL-8144, Br 04740, AH 17 |

Acc. by John Scott Trotter and his Orchestra; last two as acc. by John Scott Trotter's Eight.                    Los Angeles, May 23, 1941.

| | | |
|---|---|---|
| DLA-2398-A | Who Calls ? | Dec 3887, Br 04740 |
| DLA-2399-A | Lullaby (Brahms, Op. 49, No. 6) | Dec 3840, 25052, Voc VL-3769, Br 03874, AH 139 |
| DLA-2400-A | You And I | Dec 3840, 24255, DL-5039,Br 03248 |
| DLA-2401-A | Be Honest With Me | Dec 3856, 10300, 18767, 25231, DL-8365, DL-8493, Br 03396, LAT-8228, LAT-8253, AH 31 |
| DLA-2402-A | Goodbye, Little Darlin', Goodbye | Dec 3856, 10300, 18767, DL-8365, Br LAT-8253 |
| DLA-2402-B | Goodbye, Little Darlin', Goodbye | Dec 3856, 25231, Br 04385 |

Acc. by Jack Teagarden and his Orchestra.
                    Los Angeles, May 26, 1941.

| | | |
|---|---|---|
| DLA-2411-A | The Waiter And The Porter And The Upstairs Maid (w/Mary Martin and Jack Teagarden) (Film "Birth Of The Blues") | Dec 3970, 25408, 91415, DL-4255, DL-8076, DL-9067, Br 03269, BING-6, LAT-8055, LAT-8306 |
| DLA-2412-A | The Birth Of The Blues (Film "Birth Of The Blues") | Dec 3970, 25408, DL-4255, Br 03269, BING-6 |

Acc. by John Scott Trotter and his Orchestra.
                    Los Angeles, June 14, 1941.

| | | |
|---|---|---|
| DLA-2437-A | Clementine (w/The Music Maids and Hal Hopper) | Dec 4033, 25020, DL-5129, DL-8365, V-Disc 337, Voc VL-3603, Br 04108, LAT-8253, LAT-8281 |
| DLA-2438-A | The Old Oaken Bucket (w/The Music Maids and Hal Hopper) | Dec 4343, 25020, DL-5129, DL-8365 Br 04108, LAT-8253 |
| DLA-2439-A | Lights Out 'Til Reveille | Dec 3886, Br 03248 |
| DLA-2440-A | Sweetheart Of Sigma Chi | Dec 4000, 25228, Br 04738 |

                    Los Angeles, June 16, 1941.

| | | |
|---|---|---|
| DLA-2442-A | Sweetly She Sleeps, My Alice Fair | Dec 18802, 25128, DL-5010, Br 04737, LA-8571 |
| DLA-2443-A | Dream Girl Of Pi K.A. | Dec 4000, 25228, Br 04737 |
| DLA-2444-A | I Wonder What's Become Of Sally ? | Dec 18531, 10100, 25503, 91289, DL-5340, Br 04126, LA-8620 |
| DLA-2445-A | Old Black Joe | Dec 18804, 25130, DL-5010, Br 04101, LA-8571 |
| DLA-2446-A | Mary's A Grand Old Name | Dec 18360, 10021, 25503, 91289, DL-5340, Br 03418, LA-8620 |

                    Los Angeles, July 5, 1941.

| | | |
|---|---|---|
| DLA-2500-A | Oh ! How I Miss You Tonight | Dec 4152, 25501, DL-5343, Br 04128, LA-8624 |
| DLA-2501-A | Don't Break The Spell | Br 04738 |
| DLA-2502-A | Dear Little Boy Of Mine | Dec 4152, 25415, 25501, DL-5343, Br 04282, LA-8624, MCA 65006 |
| DLA-2503-A | Nell And I | Dec 18801, 25127, DL-5010, Br 04282, LA-8571 |
| DLA-2504-A | Danny Boy | Dec 18570, 10145, 25415, Br 03782, LAT-8278, MCA 65006 |
| DLA-2505-A | Where The Turf Meets The Surf | Rejected |

Acc. by Victor Young and his Orchestra. Los Angeles, July 8, 1941.

DLA-2515-A  You Are My Sunshine

Dec 3952, 10301, 18768, 23969,
9-29634, DL-5063, DL-8076,
DL-9067, Br 03300, LAT-8055

DLA-2516-A  Ridin' Down The Canyon

Dec 3952, 10301, 18768, 23969,
DL-5063, DL-9067, Br 03528,
Coral CPS-81

DLA-2517-A  You're The Moment Of A Lifetime
            (Flores Negras) (in English and
            Spanish)

Dec 3965, 23915, DL-5011,
DL-8846, Br 04135, LA-8529,
LAT-8331

DLA-2518-B  No te importe saber (Let Me Love You
            Tonight) (In Spanish)

Dec 3965, 23915, DL-5011,
DL-8846, Br 03554, LA-8529,
LAT-8331

Los Angeles, July 14, 1941.

DLA-2538-A  Ol' Man River                              Br 04110
DLA-2539-A  Day Dreaming                               Dec 4033, Br 03300
DLA-2540-A  Darling, je vous aime beaucoup             Dec 18531, 10100, Br 04121
DLA-2541-A  The Anniversary Waltz                      Dec 4065, 23716, Br 03289

Acc. by Woody Herman and his Orchestra (first two sides) or Woody Herman and   his
Woodchoppers (last two).        Los Angeles, July 30, 1941.

DLA-2597-A  Let's All Meet At My House (w/Muriel       Dec 4162
            Lane and Woody Herman)
DLA-2598-A  Humpty-Dumpty Heart                        Dec 4064, Br 03326
DLA-2599-A  The Whistler's Mother-in-Law (w/           Dec 3971, Br 03289
            Muriel Lane)
DLA-2600-A  I Ain't Got Nobody                              -      DL-4253, DL-8144,
                                                       Br 03663, BING-4, AH 17

Acc. by Harry Sosnik and his Orchestra. New York, October 24, 1941.

69863-A  Shepherd Serenade                             Dec 4065, Br 03278
69864-A  Do You Care ?                                 Dec 4064, 28319 -

Acc. by Woody Herman and his Woodchoppers.
                                Los Angeles, January 18, 1942.

DLA-2827-A  I Want My Mama (Mama, yo quiero)           Dec 18316, 10063, DL-8143,
                                                       DL-8493, Br 03663, LAT-8228,
                                                       AH 24, AH 31
DLA-2828-A  Deep In The Heart Of Texas                 Dec 4162, 28319, DL-8076,
                                                       DL-8365, DL-9067, Br 03313,
                                                       LAT-8055, LAT-8253
DLA-2829-A  I'm Thinking Tonight Of My Blue Eyes       Dec 18316, 10003, 10302, 18769,
                                                       Br 03456

Acc. by Dick McIntyre and his Harmony Hawaiians.
                                Los Angeles, January 19, 1942.

DLA-2830-A  Sing Me A Song Of The Islands              Dec 4173, 19025, 25025,
                                                       Br 03355, Coral CPS-90
DLA-2831-A  I'm Drifting Back To Dreamland             Dec 4339, 25188, DL-5119,
                                                       DL-8268, Br 04105, LAT-8334
DLA-2832-A  The Singing Sands Of Alamosa              As above, but Br 03390
DLA-2833-A  Remember Hawaii                            Dec 4173, 19025, 25025, Br 04105

Acc. by John Scott Trotter and his Orchestra.
                                Los Angeles, January 24, 1942.

DLA-2840-A  Miss You                                   Dec 4183, 24255, DL-5039,
                                                       Br 03312
DLA-2841-A  Mandy Is Two                               Dec 4249, 25371, Br 03312
DLA-2842-A  Angels Of Mercy                            Dec Y-5771 (Australian only)
DLA-2843-B  Skylark                                    Dec 4193, Br 03326

Acc. by Victor Young and his Orchestra.
Los Angeles, January 26, 1942.

DLA-2844-A  Nobody's Darlin' But Mine              Dec 18391, 10031, 10303, 18770,
                                                   23970, 9-29634, DL-5063, Br 04123
DLA-2845-A  When The White Azaleas Start Blooming  Dec 18391, 10031, 27554, DL-5331,
                                                   Br 04130, LA-8724
DLA-2846-A  The Lamplighter's Serenade             Dec 4249, Br 03350
DLA-2847-A  Blue Shadows And White Gardenias       Dec 4193, Br 03355

Acc. by John Scott Trotter and his Orchestra.
Los Angeles, January 27, 1942.

DLA-2857-A  Blues In The Night (w/The Music Maids) Dec 4183, Br 03313
DLA-2858-A  Moonlight Cocktail                     Dec 4184, 25504, DL-5340,
                                                   Br 03321, LA-8620
DLA-2859-B  I Don't Want To Walk Without You       As above

Los Angeles, March 13, 1942.

DLA-2946-A  Lily Of Laguna (w/Mary Martin)         Dec 18278, 25091, Br 03657
DLA-2947-A  Wait Till The Sun Shines, Nellie       As above, plus Dec 91415,
            (w/Mary Martin)                        DL-4255, DL-8076, DL-9067,
                                                   DL-34002, Br BING-6, LAT-8055

Los Angeles, March 16, 1942.

DLA-2948-A  Got The Moon In My Pocket              Dec 18354, 10016, Br 04741,
                                                   OE-9473
DLA-2949-A  Just Plain Lonesome                    As above except Br OE-9473
DLA-2950-A  The Waltz Of Memory                    Dec 18360, 10021, Br 04128

Acc. by Bob Crosby and his Orchestra.  Los Angeles, May 25, 1942.

DLA-2989-B  Lazy (Film "Holiday Inn")             Dec 18427, 10063, 91620, DL-4256,
                                                   DL-8144, DL-34002, Br 03385,
                                                   BING-7, AH 17
DLA-2990-A  Let's Start The New Year Right         Dec 18429, 10065, 23823, DL-4256,
            (Film "Holiday Inn")                   DL-5092, Br 03384, BING-7,LA-8592
DLA-2991-A  I've Got Plenty To Be Thankful For     Dec 18426, 10062, 23819, DL-4256,
            (Film "Holiday Inn")                   Br 03383, BING-7, MCA 65013

Los Angeles, May 27, 1942.

DLA-2996-A  I'll Capture Your Heart (w/Fred        Dec 18427, 10063, 23823, DL-4256,
            Astaire and Margaret Leinhart)        DL-5092, Br 03385, BING-7,LA-8592
            (Film "Holiday Inn")
DLA-2998-A  When My Dream Boat Comes Home (acc.    Dec 18371, 10036, 27505, DL-5323,
            by Bob Crosby's Bob-Cats)              DL-8493, Br 04113, LA-8579,
                                                   LAT-8228, AH 31
DLA-2999-A  Walking The Floor Over You             Dec 18371, 10036, 10303, 18770,
  NOTE:- Matrix DLA-2997 is by Fred Astaire,       23970, 27505, DL-5063, DL-5323,
  q.v.                                             DL-8076, DL-8493, DL-9067,
                                                   Br 04360, LA-8579, LAT-8055,
                                                   LAT-8278, AH 31

Acc. by John Scott Trotter and his Orchestra.
Los Angeles, May 29, 1942.

DLA-3009-B  White Christmas (Film "Holiday Inn")   Dec 18429, 10065, 23778, Br 03384
DLA-3010-A  Abraham (w/the Ken Darby Singers)      Dec 18425, 10061, 23821, DL-4256,
            (Film "Holiday Inn")                   DL-5092, Br 03382, BING-7,LA-8592
DLA-3011-A  Song Of Freedom (w/the Ken Darby       Dec 18426, 10062, 23821, DL-4256,
            Singers) (Film "Holiday Inn")          DL-5092, Br 03383, BING-7,LA-8592

Los Angeles, June 1, 1942.

DLA-3012-A  The Bombardier Song (w/The Music      Dec 18432, 10042
            Maids and Hal Hopper)
DLA-3013-A  Easter Parade (Film "Holiday Inn")    Dec 18425, 10061, 23819, DL-4256,
                                                  Br 03382, BING-7, MCA 65013
DLA-3014-A  Happy Holiday (w/The Music Maids and  Dec 18424, 10060, 23820, DL-5092,
            Hal Hopper) (Film "Holiday Inn")      DL-34461, Br 03381, BING 7,
                                                  LA-8592, MCA 65013
DLA-3015-A  Be Careful, It's My Heart (Film       Dec 18424, 10060, 23820, DL-4256,
            "Holiday Inn")                         DL-5092, Br 03381,BING-7, LA-8592

Los Angeles, June 8, 1942.

L-3025-A  Adeste Fideles (O Come, All Ye Faith-   Dec 18510, 23777, DL-4258,
          ful) (w/Max Terr's Mixed Chorus) (in    DL-4283, DL-5019, DL-8128,
          English and Latin)                       Br 02054-X, 03929, BING-9,
                                                   LA-8686, LAT-8550, LAT-8556,
                                                   OE-9069, OE-9430
L-3026-A  Silent Night, Holy Night (w/Max Terr's  Dec 18510, 23777, Br 02054-X,
          Mixed Chorus)                            03929
L-3027-A  Faith Of Our Fathers (w/Max Terr's      Dec 18511, 10089, 23779, DL-5019,
          Mixed Chorus)                            DL-8128, Br 03930, LA-8686,
                                                   LAT-8556, OE-9070
L-3028-A  God Rest Ye Merry, Gentlemen (w/Max     Dec 18511, 10089, 23778, DL-5019,
          Terr's Mixed Chorus)                     DL-8128, Br 03930, LA-8686,
                                                   LAT-8556, OE-9069

  Acc. by Vic Schoen and his Orchestra.  Los Angeles, June 10, 1942.

L-3029-A  Conchita, Marquita, Lolita, Pepita,     Dec 4343, Br 03390
          Rosita, Juanita Lopez
L-3030-A  The Road To Morocco (Film "The Road     Dec 18514, 10088, Br 03410
          To Morocco")
L-3031-A  Ain't Got A Dime To My Name (Film "The    - DL-4257 -  Br 03411, BING-8
          Road To Morocco")

  Acc. by John Scott Trotter and his Orchestra.
                                    Los Angeles, June 12, 1942.

L-3032-A  My Great-Great-Grandfather (w/chorus)   Dec 18432, 10042
L-3033-A  Boy In Khaki, A Girl In Lace            Dec 4367, Br 04742
L-3034-A  Moonlight Becomes You (Film "The Road   Dec 18513, 10087, DL-4257,
          To Morocco")                             DL-8076, DL-9067, Br 03410,
                                                   BING-8, LAT-8055, Longines LW-349
L-3035-A  Constantly (Film "The Road To Morocco") Dec 18513, 10087, DL-4257,
                                                   Br 03411, BING-8

  Acc. by Capt. Eddie Dunstedter and the West Coast American Air Force Training Cen-
  ter Orchestra.                     Los Angeles, July 9, 1942.

L-3087-A  By The Light Of The Silvery Moon        Br 05000
L-3088-A  But Not For Me                          Col DB-30175 (India only)
L-3089-A  Hello, Mom                              Rejected

Los Angeles, July 27, 1942.

L-3147-B  Hello, Mom                              Dec 4367, Br 03510

Bing Crosby continued to record prolifically alone and with other artists for a number of other labels besides Decca right into the 1970s.  These are included in  a
book devoted entirely to this artist by Geoff Milne and Bob Roberts.

## DIXIE LEE CROSBY

B. Harriman, Tennessee, 1910; r.n. Wilma Winifred Wyatt.  Raised in New Orleans, but
moved to Chicago with her family, where in 1927 she won a Ruth Etting contest, de-
signed to find the girl who sang most like Ruth Etting.  To Hollywood, 1929;  made
some Fox films, met Bing Crosby  then while he was singing with Paul   Whiteman's

Rhythm Boys at the Montmartre in Los Angeles; they married in 1930, and Dixie Lee quit show business, but made a few records (see also Bing Crosby, August 19,1936) and gave her husband an incalculable amount of encouragement at the outset of his career as a soloist.  She died in 1952.

Vocal, acc. by Orville Knapp and his Orchestra.
                                          Los Angeles, March 11, 1935.

DLA-136-A  Got Me Doin' Things                    Dec 414, Br 02014
DLA-137-A  My Heart Is An Open Book                  -       -

  Acc. by Victor Young and his Orchestra. Los Angeles, July 27, 1936.

DLA-467-A  When A Lady Meets A Gentleman Down    Dec 892, Br 02302
             South
DLA-468-A  Until The Real Thing Comes Along          -       -

## FRANK CRUMIT

B. September 26, 1889; boyhood in Jackson, Ohio; attended Culver Military, Indiana.. Became known as a good sportsman, but also as singer of songs he accompanied with ukulele; featured with Paul Biese's Orchestra in Chicago and New York;   appeared in GREENWICH  VILLAGE FOLLIES at the New York theatre of that name, 1919-1920,and in TANGERINE at the Casino, August 9, 1921, which was a smash hit and for which a good deal of the material was written by Frank Crumit. M. Julia Sanderson, 1927; both on radio in Blackstone Cigar Show, 1935. President of Lamb's Club; recorded all kinds of popular songs, from Tin Pan Alley to genuine American folk-songs. D. Springfield, Mass., September 9, 1943.

Vocal, acc. by studio orchestra.     New York, December 10, 1919.

 78854-   My Gal (She Has Some Wonderful Ways)    Col A-2884

                                       New York, December 12, 1919.

 78855-   What A Day That'll Be                    Col A-2915

                                       New York, March 24, 1920.

 79065-   I've Got The Profiteering Blues          Col A-2940
 79066-   So Long ! Oo-Long (How Long You Gonna    Col A-2935
            Be Gone ?)

                                       New York, March 26, 1920.

 79078-1-2-3  The Dardanella Blues                 Col rejected

                                       New York, March 31, 1920.

 79089-   Oh ! By Jingo ! Oh ! By Gee ! (sic)      Col A-2935, 2987

                                       New York, April 14, 1920.

 79120-   I'm Coming Back To Dixie And You         Col A-3320
 79121-   Early In The Morning (Down On The Farm)  Col A-2946

                                       New York, May 12, 1920.

 79176-1-2-3  M'sieur Jimmie (Come And Shake Ze    Col rejected
            Shimmy)
 79177-1-2-3  My Dixie Rosary                         -

                                       New York, May 19, 1920.

 79185-   Marion (You'll Soon Be Marryin' Me)      Col A-2948

                                       New York, May 24, 1920.

 79199-1-2-3  Huckleberry Finn                     Col rejected
 79200-1-2-3  Goodbye Sunshine, Hello Moon            -

New York, June 1, 1920.

79210-    Sweet Inniscarra                          Rejected
79211-    Goodbye, Dixie                            Col A-2965

Vocalist with the Paul Biese Trio.        New York, June 2, 1920.

79217-    Chili Bean                                Col A-2952, 3003

Vocal, acc. by studio orchestra.          New York, June 7, 1920.

79246-1-2-3  My Wild Irish Rose                     Rejected
79247-1-2-3  They're Wearing 'Em Higher In Hawaii      -
79248-    He'd Have To Get Under, Get Out And Get  Col A-1457
              Under
NOTE:- This version of GET OUT AND GET UNDER replaces a recording made in 1913  by
Will Halley.


New York, June 14, 1920.

79275-    The Little Ford Rambled Right Along       Col A-1754
79276-1-2-3  You Don't Have To Come From Ireland  Rejected
              To Be Irish
NOTE:- This version of THE LITTLE FORD RAMBLED RIGHT ALONG replaces a    recording
made in 1915 by Arthur Fields.


New York, June 23, 1920.

79299-    Don't Take Away Those Blues               Col A-2965
79300-    Nobody To Love                            Col A-3303
79302-    And The Green Grass Grew All Around       Col A-1277
NOTE;- Matrix 79301 is by the Happy Six (no vocal); this version of AND THE  GREEN
GRASS GREW ALL AROUND replaces a recording made in 1913 by Walter van Brunt.


New York, June 26, 1920.

79311-    The Love Nest                             Col A-2973


New York, July 14, 1920.

79344-    My Little Bimbo Down On The Bamboo Isle  Col A-2981

Vocalist with Art Hickman and his Orchestra.
New York, July 21, 1920.

79354-    In Old Manila                             Col A-2982

Vocal, acc. by studio orchestra.          New York, July 23, 1920.

79357-    She Gives Them All The Ha ! Ha ! Ha !     Col A-2981
              (w/Lew Brown)


New York, August 17, 1920.

79372-    Oh You Little Bunch Of Sweetness          Col rejected

New York, August 25, 1920.

79382-    Jing-a-Bula-Jing-Jing-Jing                Col A-3303

New York, August 26, 1920.

79385-1-2-3  My Mammy                               Col rejected

New York, August 27, 1920.

79390-1-2-3  Sunny Southern Smiles (w/H. Henke)     Col rejected
79391-1-2-3  Sunny Southern Smiles (solo)              -

New York, September 1, 1920.

79397-1-2-3  Song Of The Orient                Col rejected

Vocalist with the Happy Six.          New York, September 7, 1920.

79400-   Je  ne sais pa-pa                    Col A-3304

Vocal, acc. by studio orchestra.      New York, September 22, 1920.

79429-1-2-3  Oh Girls ! What A Boy             Col rejected

New York, September 29, 1920.

79439-   Whispering (w/William Davidson)      Col A-3323

New York, October 2, 1920.

79444-   Palesteena                           Col A-3324

New York, October 7, 1920.

79453-   I Wish That I'd Been Born In Borneo   Col A-3324

New York, October 15, 1920.

79455-   There's Something About You Makes Me   Col rejected
             Love You

New York, October 20, 1920.

79460-   I'm A Lonesome Little Raindrop        Col A-3332
79461-   Margie                                   -

New York, November 17, 1920.

79523-1-2-3  Lindy (stated to be by the Crumit   Col rejected
             Quartet in the recording files)

New York, November 22, 1920.

79530-1-2-3  Caresses (w/William Davidson)     Rejected
79531-   Rosie (You Are Working Too Hard)      Col A-3346

Vocalist with the Paul Biese Trio.    New York, December 8, 1920.

79556-   Timbuctoo                            Col A-3352
79557-1-2-3  Beela Boola                      Rejected
79558-   Happy Hottentot                      Col A-3359

Vocal, acc. by studio orchestra.      New York, December 22, 1920.

79594-   No Wonder I'm Blue                   Col A-3388
79595-1-2-3  Caresses (w/Howard Marsh)        Rejected

New York, January 19, 1921.

79643-   I Used To Love You, But It's All Over   Col A-3388
             Now
79644-   Home Again Blues                     Col A-3375

Vocalist with the Paul Biese Trio.    New York, January 27, 1921.

79659-1-2-3  Ump-Pah-Pah                      Rejected
79660-   Beela Boola                          Col A-3383

Vocalist with the Happy Six.          New York, February 8, 1921.

79717-   Siam Soo                             Col A-3379

Vocal, acc. by studio orchestra.     New York, February 21, 1921.

79729-   Hortense                   Col A-3407

New York, March 5, 1921.

79755-   Nestle In Your Daddy's Arms     Col A-3406

New York, March 28, 1921.

79766-1-2-3  Vamping Rose          Col rejected

New York, April 4, 1921.

79794-   Pucker Up And Whistle (Till The Clouds  Col A-3406
          Roll By)
79795-   Oh Sweet Amelia             Col A-3407

New York, April 21, 1921.

79807-   All By Myself               Col A-3415

New York, April 22, 1921.

79808-   Moonlight                  Col A-3431
79809-   Wait Until You See My Madeline    Col A-3415

New York, May 26, 1921.

79864-   Three O'Clock In The Morning    Col A-3431

Vocalist with the Paul Biese Trio.    New York, May 28, 1921.

79870-   Mimi                     Col A-3430
79871-   Oh Me ! Oh My ! (Intro. Dolly)    -     3158

Vocal, acc. by studio orchestra.    New York, May 31, 1921.

79872-1-2-3  There's A Corner Up In Heaven    Col rejected

Vocalist with the Paul Biese Trio.    New York, June 10, 1921.

79881-   Frankie And Johnny          Col A-3459
79882-1-2-3  Ida, Sweet As Apple Cider    Rejected

New York, July 18, 1921.

79943-   I Ain't Nobody's Darling      Col A-3459, 3073
79944-   Dapper Dan               Col A-3477

Vocal, acc. by studio orchestra.    New York, July 19, 1921.

79949-   You're Just The Type For A Bungalow   Col A-3475

New York, September 7, 1921.

79972-   Sweet Lady ("Tangerine")       Col A-3475, A-3505

New York, September 12, 1921.

80021-1-2-3  Trixie              Col rejected

New York, November 14, 1921.

80061-   In My Heart, On My Mind All Day Long  Col A-3530

New York, November 16, 1921.

80070-   Da-Da-Da My Darling        Col A-3521

New York, November 26, 1921.

| | | |
|---|---|---|
| 80078- | When Frances Dances With Me | Col A-3521 |
| 80079- | Sally And Irene And Mary | Col A-3543 |

New York, December 12, 1921.

| | | |
|---|---|---|
| 80095- | Delia | Col A-3530 |
| 80096- | Boo-Hoo-Hoo (You're Gonna Cry When I'm Gone) | Col A-3543 |

New York, January 27, 1922.

80167-    She's Mine, All Mine                Col A-3573

Acc. by own ukulele.               New York, February 21, 1922.

80205-    Waikiki (I Hear You Calling Me)      Col A-3587

Acc. by studio orchestra.          New York, March 23, 1922.

80212-    Ha ! Ha ! Ha !                       Col A-3573

New York, April 5, 1922.

80276-    Down On Avenue A                     Col A-3613

New York, April 24, 1922.

80318-    Mama Loves Papa, Does Papa Love Mama ?  Col A-3613

New York, May 6, 1922.

80337-    Stumbling                            Col A-3626

New York, May 9, 1922.

80338-    The Sheik Of Avenue B                Col A-3625

New York, June 7, 1922.

80373-    Pinkie (The Flapper Song)            Col A-3651

New York, June 9, 1922.

80381-    By The Riverside                     Col A-3651

New York, July 10, 1922.

| | | |
|---|---|---|
| 80443- | The 19th Hole (Oh, How I Love The 19th Hole When The 18th Hole Is Over) | Col A-3666 |
| 80444- | In My Home Town | - |

New York, August 3, 1922.

80493-    If You Don't Think So, You're Crazy   Col A-3744

Acc. by Ray Miller's Novelty Orchestra.
                                   New York, August 4, 1922.

| | | |
|---|---|---|
| 80496- | My Honey's Lovin' Arms | Col A-3699 |
| 80497-1-2-3 | Louisian' | Rejected |

New York, August 18, 1922.

80531-    I Wish I Knew (You Really Loved Me)   Col A-3699

Acc. by studio orchestra.          New York, September 12, 1922.

80534-    True Blue Sam (The Traveling Man)     Col A-3705

New York, September 19, 1922.

| 80560- | Where The Bamboo Babies Grow | Col A-3715 |
| 80561- | I'm Through (Shedding Tears Over You) | - |

New York, October 17, 1922.

| 80614-1-2-3 | K-K-K-Kiss Me Again | Col rejected |
| 80615-1-2-3 | Do I ? | - |
| 80616-1-2-3 | He Loves It | - |

Vocalist with Phil Ohman-p/Harry Reser-bj.New York, December 9, 1922.

| 80729- | Don't Say Goodbye | Col A-3785 |
| 80730- | I Gave You Up Just Before You Threw Me Down | - |

Vocal, acc. by studio orchestra.          New York, December 16, 1922.

| 80732-1-2-3 | Honeymoon Time | Col rejected |
| 80733-1-2-3 | You Know You Belong To Somebody Else | - |
| | (So Why Don't You Leave Me Alone ?) | |

New York, January 15, 1923.

| 80793- | Jimbo Jambo | Col A-3812 |

New York, January 16, 1923.

| 80794-1-2-3 | Don't Be Silly, Sally | Col rejected |

New York, January 26, 1923.

| 80806- | Sweet One | Col A-3827 |
| 80807- | Everything Is K.O. In K.Y. | - |

New York, June 14, 1923.

| 81077- | When You Walked Out, Someone Else Walked | Col A-3933 |
| | Right In | |

New York, June 15, 1923.

| 81082- | That's My Baby | Col A-3932 |
| 81083- | Oh ! How She Lied To Me | - |

New York, August 3, 1923.

| 81160- | Stingo Stungo | Col A-3968 |
| 81161- | Maggie ! "Yes, Ma'am ?" (Come Right | Col A-3969 |
| | Upstairs) | |

New York, September 5, 1923.

| 81191- | Oh ! Min | Col A-3984 |

New York, September 6, 1923.

| 81192- | My Home Town In Kansas | Col A-3997 |
| 81193-1-2-3 | If I Can't Get The Sweetie I Want | Rejected |

New York, September 7, 1923.

| 81200- | Old-Fashioned Love | Col A-3997 |

New York, October 5, 1923.

| 81266- | Say It With A Ukulele | Col 26-D |
| 81267-1-2-3 | I'm Sitting Pretty In A Pretty | Rejected |
| | Little City | |

Acc. by O/Nat Shilkret.                    Camden, N.J., December 14, 1923.

B-29084-3  Sweet Alice                              Vic 19236
B-29089-1-2-3-4  Little Brown Road                  Rejected

   Acc. by own ukulele/Phil Ohman-p, or The Virginians.
                                    New York, December 21, 1923.

B-29154-4  Oh Baby ! (Don't Say "No," Say "Maybe")Vic 19236
           - p/u
B-29155-4  Mindin' My Business - Virginians         Vic 19259

                                    New York, February 15, 1924.

B-29515-3  You're In Kentucky Sure As You're        Vic 19275, HMV B-1861
           Born - p/u
B-29516-2  Where The Lazy Daisies Grow - p              -              -
B-29517-1-2  Iona (I Own A Bungalow) - p            Rejected

                                    New York, May 28, 1924.

B-30144-1  Ida, Sweet As Apple Cider - p            Vic 19365
B-30145-3  Roll Them Roly Boly Eyes - p                -
B-30146-3  Oh ! Didn't It Rain - p                  Vic 19469

   Acc. by Frank Banta-p/own ukulele.    New York, August 15, 1924.

B-30642-2  Knock At The Door                        Vic 19437, HMV B-2021
B-30643-1-2-3  No-One Knows What It's All About     Rejected

                                    New York, September 10, 1924.

B-30643-7  No-One Knows What It's All About         Vic 19469

   Acc. by small O/Charles A. Prince (Adam Carroll-p).
                                    Camden, N. J., September 26, 1924.

B-30939-2  The Buckeye Battle Cry (A Football       Vic 19468
           Song of Ohio State University)
B-30940-1  Hi-Hi-Ohio                                  -

   Acc. by Frank Banta-p/own ukulele.    New York, December 19, 1924.

B-31532-5  Get Yourself A Broom And Sweep Your      Vic 19549, HMV B-2021
           Troubles Away

   Sam Herman-kazoo added.                    New York, December 23, 1924.

B-31541-3  Insufficient Sweetie                     Vic 19549

   Acc. by Carson Robison-g or a Mr. Tours-p.
                                    New York, January 22, 1925.

B-31746-3  Why Couldn't It Be Poor Little Me ?-g Vic 19582
B-31747-2  Cross Word Mama (You Puzzle Me) - g         -
           Mizette - p                          Vic test (un-numbered)

   Acc. by W. McGinnes - vn/Frank Banta-p/Carson Robison-g/own ukulele, as shown.
                                    Camden, N. J., June 10, 1925.

BVE-32885-5  Ukulele Lady - WM-CR-FC                Vic 19701, HMV B-2115
BVE-32886-1-2-3-4  My Mother's Humming Lullaby      Rejected
             - WM-FB-CR
BVE-32887-2  My Sweetie Turned Me Down (What Do     Vic 19701, HMV B-2115
             I Care ?) - FB-FC
BVE-32888-2  I Married The Bootlegger's Daughter    Vic 19739, HMV B-2170
             - FB-FC

Acc. by Frank Banta-p-organ/own ukulele or g., as shown.
                              Camden, N. J., September 3, 1925.

BVE-33197-2   Old Uncle Bill - p/u                    Vic 19774
BVE-33198-4   I'se Goin' From The Cotton Field -      Vic 19777
                g/organ
BVE-33199-3   Sonya (Yup, Alay Yup) - p               Vic 19774, HMV B-2170
BVE-33402-4   The Parlor Is A Pleasant Place To       Vic 19777
                Sunday Night - g/organ

   Acc. by Joseph Pasternack-organ/W. H. Reitz-d/own g as shown.
                              Camden, N. J., December 22, 1925.

BVE-33651-1-2-3-4  Mah Lindy Lou - g                  Rejected
BVE-33652-1-2-3  My Grandfather's Clock - organ/d        -
BVE-33653-1  Billy Boy - g                            Vic 19945, HMV B-2325

   Acc. by Frank Banta-p/own ukulele.    Camden, N. J., December 31, 1925.

BVE-34073-4  I'm Sitting On Top Of The World          Vic 19928, HMV B-2293

   Acc. by Jack Shilkret-p/own ukulele.   New York, January 14, 1926.

BVE-34327-1   Show Me The Way To Go Home              Vic 19937
BVE-34328-2   I Wish't I Was In Peoria                   -

                              New York, April 13, 1926.

BVE-35310-2   Thanks For The Buggy Ride               Vic 20030, HMV B-2325
BVE-35311-1-2-3  So Is Your Old Lady                  Rejected

   Acc. by Jack Shilkret-p only.    New York, July 29, 1926.

BVE-35948-2   The Girl Friend                         Vic 20124, HMV B-2526
BVE-35949-2   Mountain Greenery                          -           -

   Acc. by Frank Banta-p.        New York, August 6, 1926.

BVE-36025-3   Get Away, Old Man, Get Away             Vic 20137, HMV B-3208
BVE-36026-2   Pretty Little Dear                         -

                              New York, January 4, 1927.

BVE-37507-2   Sunny Disposish                         Vic 20486
BVE-37508-3   High, High, High Up In The Hills        Vic 20462
BVE-37509-4   My Lady                                 Vic 20486

   Acc. by Frank Banta-p/own ukulele/Frank Garisto-lute.
                              New York, January 11, 1927.

BVE-37532-2   Crazy Words - Crazy Tune                Vic 20462
BVE-37533-3   I Miss You, Lize                        Vic 21091

   Acc. as shown.              New York, April 8, 1927.

BVE-38440-1-2-3-4  The Mermaid - pac/vn/p             Rejected
BVE-38441-2   Wake Nicodemus - organ (FB)             Vic 21098
BVE-38442-2   Abdul Abulbul Amir - gFC                Vic 20715, HMV B-3208

   Acc. by Andy Sannella-cl/Nat Shilkret-p/own g.
                              New York, May 11, 1927.

BVE-38742-   Frankie And Johnny                       Vic 20715, HMV B-3269

   Acc. by own ukulele.         New York, August 30, 1927.

BVE-39134-1-2-3  I'll Meet Her When The Sun Goes      Rejected
                Down
BVE-39135-   Bye-Bye, Pretty Baby                     Vic 20919, HMV B-2620
BVE-39136-1-2-3  They've All Got A Mate But Me        Rejected

Acc. by Andy Sannella-as/Ed Smalle-p.    New York, September 13, 1927.

BVE-39172-1-2-3  Come Along, My Mandy (w/Ed Smalle)Vic rejected
BVE-39173-1-2  I've A Garden In Sweden                -

Acc. by Andy Sannella-g.             New York, October 18, 1927.

BVE-40186-1-2-3  Who's That Knockin' At My Door ?  Rejected
BVE-40187-  Da-Da-Da My Darling                    Vic 21029

Acc. by Lou Raderman-vn/Jack Shilkret-p-organ.
                                     New York, October 25, 1927.

BVE-40506-2  That Old Wooden Rocker                Vic 21091
BVE-40507-  'S Wonderful                           Vic 21029
BVE-40508-1-2-3  Granny's Old Arm-Chair            Rejected

Acc. by own g/vn/p/bj.               New York, November 29, 1927.

BVE-41123-1  Bohunkus                              Vic 21108, HMV B-2712
BVE-41124-3  Kingdom Coming (And The Year Of Jubilo)  -          -

Acc. by as/vn/p.                     New York, January 10, 1928.

BVE-41535-1-2-3-4  Little Brown Road       Vic rejected
BVE-41536-1-2-3-4  Back In Your Own Back Yard       -

Acc. by vn/p/bj/own ukulele.        New York, January 12, 1928.

BVE-39134-4-5-6  I'll Meet Her When The Sun Goes  Vic rejected
                 Down
BVE-39136-4-5-6  They've All Got A Mate But Me      -

Acc. by vn/pac/p/g.                 New York, April 5, 1928.

BVE-43535-2  Down In De Cane Brake                 Vic 21430, HMV B-2787
BVE-43536-1  Song Of The Prune                      -          -

Acc. as shown.                      Camden, N. J., May 3, 1928.

BVE-45007-1-2-3  The Three Trees - small orch.   Rejected
BVE-45008-3  I Learned About Women From Her - S.  Vic 21735
             Pasternack-vl/own g
BVE-45009-1  The Road To Vicksburg - own bj-u/   Rejected
             W. H. Reitz-d
BVE-45010-1-2  No News, or What Killed The Dog      -
             - unacc.

                                     Camden, N. J., May 11, 1928.

BVE-45010-3-4-5  No News, or What Killed The Dog  Vic rejected
             - unacc.

                                     Camden, N. J., June 4, 1928.

BVE-45007-4  The Three Trees - small orch.        Vic 21466, HMV B-2858
BVE-45010-6  No News, or What Killed The Dog - unacc.  -          -

Vocalist with Nat Shilkret and the Victor Salon Group and Orchestra.
                                     New York, June 14, 1928.

CVE-45632-2  Foster Melodies - Part 4 (Frank      Vic 9247
             Crumit sings SOME FOLKS LIKE TO SIGH)

                                     New York, June 15, 1928.

CVE-45636-2  Foster Melodies - Part 3 (Frank      Vic 9247, HMV C-1758
             Crumit sings OH, SUSANNA)

New York, June 22, 1928.

CVE-45653-1-2-3  Foster Melodies - Part 2 (Frank   Vic rejected
          Crumit sings OH BOYS, CARRY ME 'LONG)

  Acc. by small orchestra.          New York, June 25, 1928.

BVE-45824-2  O'Hooligan's Ball                  Vic 21579, HMV B-3234
BVE-45825-3  Dolan's Poker Party                   -          -

Vocalist with Nat Shilkret and the Victor Salon Group and Orchestra.
                                    New York, June 29, 1928.

CVE-45653-7  Foster Melodies - Part 2 (Frank      Vic 9246, HMV C-1657
          Crumit sings OH BOYS, CARRY ME 'LONG)

Vocalist with Nat Shilkret and the Victor Orchestra (actually dir. by Leonard Joy).
                                    New York, July 12, 1928.

BVE-45872-3  Just A Night For Meditation         Vic 21547, HMV B-5570
BVE-45873-2  Nagasaki                            Vic 21603

Vocal, acc. by small orchestra.     New York, July 17, 1928.

BVE-46317-2  The Bride's Lament                  Vic 21668, HMV B-2921
BVE-46318-1-2-3  Jack Is Every Inch A Sailor     Rejected

                                    New York, August 31, 1928.

BVE-46318-4  Jack Is Every Inch A Sailor         Vic 21668, HMV B-3054
BVE-46972-1-2  Dearie                            Rejected

Vocal as a member of the Victor Male Chorus, acc. by Nat Shilkret and the Victor Or-
    chestra.                        New York, September 13, 1928.

CVE-47508-3  Over Here - Medley                  Vic 35937
CVE-47509-1  Over There - Medley                    -

Vocal, acc. by small O/Leonard Joy.    New York, October 2, 1928.

BVE-47583-2  A Gay Caballero                     Vic 21735, HMV B-3054

Vocalist with Jacques Renard and his Cocoanut Grove Orchestra.
                                    Boston, Mass., November 17, 1928.

BVE-47921-1-2-3-4  Ev'rybody Loves You           Vic rejected

                                    New York, December 3, 1928.

BVE-47921-6  Ev'rybody Loves You                 Vic 21811

Vocal, acc. by Carson Robison-g/d.     New York, December 4, 1928.

BVE-45009-2  The Road To Vicksburg               Vic 21899, HMV B-3065
BVE-49226-1-2  L. & W. Railroad Station In       Vic (made on approval)
          Kentucky

  Acc. by small orchestra.           New York, December 14, 1928.

BVE-48470-1-2-3  Little Boy Blue                 Vic rejected
BVE-48471-1-2  After I Fell In Love With You        -

                                    New York, January 25, 1929.

BVE-48306-3  The King Of Borneo                  Vic 21899, HMV B-3065
BVE-48307-1-2  Low Bridge (The Erie Canal Song)  Rejected

Vocal as a member of the Victor Minstrels, acc. by O/Rosario Bourdon.
New York, January 28, 1929.

CVE-49096-3  Minstrel Show of 1929 - Part 2      Vic 35961, HMV C-1739
(Frank Crumit sings ABRAHAM LINCOLN JONES)

Vocal, acc. by O/Leonard Joy.          New York, March 19, 1929.

BVE-50936-1-2-3  Let's Sit And Talk About You      Vic rejected
(w/Julia Sanderson)
BVE-50927-1-2-3  The Bee Song (You Never Saw A          -
Bee, Being Alone, Without Another Bee Being Around)

Acc. by own g/Lew Shilkret-organ.      New York, May 24, 1929.

BVE-53439-2  A High Silk Hat And A Walking Cane   Vic 22021
BVE-53440-2  The Mountains Ain't No Place For Bad Men -

Acc. by O/Leonard Joy.                 New York, September 3, 1929.

BVE-56111-1-2-3  I Done The Same Thing Over       Vic rejected
(Wasn't I The Darn Old Fool ?)
BVE-56112-1-2  She Don't See Me No More               -

New York, September 30, 1929.

BVE-56163-1  The Return Of The Gay Caballero      Vic 22154, HMV B-3269
BVE-56164-3  A Tale Of A Ticker                        -

New York, October 10, 1929.

BVE-56111-4-5-6  I Done The Same Thing Over       Vic rejected
(Wasn't I The Darn Old Fool ?)
BVE-56112-3-4-5  She Don't See Me No More               -

New York, December 2, 1929.

BVE-57184-    Granny's Old Arm-Chair            Vic 24091, HMV B-4059, B-10327
BVE-57185-    Gum Tree Canoe                           -

Acc. by O/Jack Shilkret.               New York, January 7, 1930.

BVE-57978-1-2-3  The Preacher And The Bear        Rejected
BVE-57979-1  Little Brown Jug                     Vic 24092, HMV B-4059, B-10327
BVE-57980-1-2  A Window By The Sea                Rejected

Acc. by vn/g/md.                       New York, January 21, 1930.

BVE-59106-    I Don't Work For A Living          Vic V-40214
BVE-59107-    Tramp, Tramp, Tramp, Keep On A-Trampin'  -

Acc. by O/Leonard Joy.                 New York, February 11, 1930.

BVE-58566-1-2-3  Donald The Dub                   Vic rejected
BVE-58567-1-2-3  And Then He Took Up Golf               -

New York, February 19, 1930.

BVE-58566-6  Donald The Dub                       Vic 22323, HMV B-3419
BVE-58567-5  And Then He Took Up Golf                  -           -
BVE-58585-2  Life Is Only A Merry-Go-Round        Vic 24092

New York, April 22, 1930.

BVE-62103-3  Around The Corner                    Vic 22423, HMV B-3528
BVE-62104-2  Down By The Railroad Track                -           -

New York, June 24, 1930.

BVE-62281-2  The Return Of Abdul Abulbul Amir        Vic 22482, HMV B-3569
BVE-62282-2  I'm Bettin' The Roll On Roamer            -              -

New York, July 8, 1930.

BVE-62281-4-5  The Return Of Abdul Abulbul Amir    Vic rejected
BVE-62282-4-5-6  I'm Bettin' The Roll On Roamer      -

New York, July 21, 1930.

BVE-62281-6-7-8  The Return Of Abdul Abulbul Amir  Rejected
BVE-62282-9  I'm Bettin' The Roll On Roamer          Vic 22482

  Acc. by as/vn/p/g.                    New York, August 19, 1930.

BVE-62393-1-2  The Endurance Song                    Vic rejected
BVE-62394-1-2  Miniature Golf Song (As You             -
                 Putt-Putt-Putter Along)

  Acc. by O/Leonard Joy.                New York, November 18, 1930.

BVE-64621-2  Foolish Facts                            Vic 23515, HMV B-3883
BVE-64622-2  What Kind Of A Noise Annoys An Oyster ?  -              -

New York, November 19, 1930.

BVE-64361-2  Three Little Words                       Vic 22579, HMV B-3722
BVE-64362-1  I Miss A Little Miss (Who Misses Me       -              -
               In Sunny Tennessee)

New York, February 11, 1931.

BVE-67441-2  Would You Like To Take A Walk ?          Vic 22630, HMV B-3833
               (w/Julia Sanderson)
BVE-67442-2  One Little Raindrop                       -              -

New York, October 28, 1931.

BS-70911-1  The Lady Of My Dreams Taught Me How    Vic rejected
              To Play The Second Fiddle
BS-70912-1  I'm A Specialist                           -

New York, November 11, 1931.

BS-70911-3  The Lady Of My Dreams Taught Me How    Vic 22859, HMV B-4102
              To Play The Second Fiddle
BS-70912-3  I'm A Specialist                           -              -

New York, February 17, 1932.

BS-71863-1  Plink ! Plonk ! (I Pluck My Guitar)    Vic 22943
BS-71864-1  Rhymes                                     -
 BRC-500    Sing A Song Of Contract (w/Julia       Vic test
              Sanderson)

  Acc. by O/Jack Shilkret at the piano. (Recorded for the Gramophone Co. Ltd., England).                                   New York, September 22, 1932.

BS-73561-1  I'm In Love With Susan                 HMV B-4331
BS-73562-1  They're Always Together                HMV B-4356
BS-73563-1  The Grandson Of Abdul Abulbul Amir     HMV B-4331
BS-73564-1  The Vegetable Blues                    HMV B-4356

Acc. by O/Nat Shilkret. (Recorded for the Gramophone Co. Ltd., England).
                                        New York, January 30, 1933.

| | | |
|---|---|---|
| BS-75003-1 | Minnie Skavinsky Skavar | Rejected |
| BS-75004-1 | My Girl Ran Away - Part 1 | HMV B-4441 |
| BS-75005-1 | My Girl Ran Away - Part 2 | - |
| BS-75006-1 | Brother Ezra And Sister Susan (w/ | Rejected |
| | Julia Sanderson) | |

Acc. by own g and/or Tony Colicchio-g-md as shown. (Recorded for the    Gramophone
Co. Ltd., England).                     New York, May 15, 1933.

| | | |
|---|---|---|
| BS-76123-1 | The Tarpaulin Jacket - gTC | Rejected |
| BS-76124-1 | Juanita - gTC | - |
| BS-76125-1 | The Spanish Guitar - gTC | - |
| BS-76126-1 | Riding Down From Bangor - gFC-TC | HMV B-8075 |
| BS-76127-1 | Antonio Pasquale Ramonio - gFC/mdTC | HMV B-8032 |
| BS-76128-1 | We're Trimmin' Up The Old Grey Bonnet | Rejected |
| | - gFC-TC | |

Acc. by studio orchestra. (Recorded for the Gramophone Co. Ltd., England).
                                        New York, August 15, 1933.

| | | |
|---|---|---|
| BS-77474-1 | A Rough Idea Of My Old Kentucky Home | Rejected |
| BS-77475-1 | Pale Moonlight | - |
| BS-77476-1 | The Little Mohee | - |
| BS-77478-1 | The King Of Zulu | HMV B-8075 |

NOTE:- Matrix 77477 was not allocated at all.

Acc. by small orchestra.                New York, August 17, 1934.

| | | |
|---|---|---|
| 38334 | Abdul Abulbul Amir | Dec 114, F-5385, AH 96 |
| 38335-A | A Gay Caballero | Dec 113    -       - |
| 38336-A | Harry Von Tilzer Medley - Part 1 | Dec 205, F-5257 |
| 38337-A | Harry Von Tilzer Medley - Part 2 | -       - |

                                        New York, August 23, 1934.

| | | |
|---|---|---|
| 38413-A | The Prune Song | Dec F-5210, AH 96 |
| 38414-A | Donald The Dub | -       - |
| 38415-B | Frankie And Johnnie | Dec 113       - |
| 38416-A | Gus Edwards Medley | Dec 114       - |

                                        New York, October 15, 1934.

| | | |
|---|---|---|
| 38415- | Frankie And Johnnie | Dec 113 ? |
| 38416- | Gus Edwards Medley | Dec 114 ? |

                                        New York, October 18, 1934.

| | | |
|---|---|---|
| 38856-A | The Dashing Marine | Dec 313, F-5325, AH 96 |
| 38857-A | The Pig Got Up And Slowly Walked Away | -       -       - |

                                        New York, May 20, 1935.

| | | |
|---|---|---|
| 39525-A | Whoa, Josephine | Dec 475, F-5629 |
| 39526-A | There's No-One With Endurance (Like | -       -     F-9916, AH 96 |
| | The Man Who Sells Insurance) | |

                                        New York, February 17, 1938.

| | | |
|---|---|---|
| 63290-A | The Old Apple Tree | Dec 1708, F-9916 |
| 63291-A | Connie's Got Connections In Connecticut | Dec 1697, F-6805 |
| 63292-A | Josephine | -       -     AH 96 |
| 63293-A | I Can't Stand Sitting In A Cell | Dec 1708       - |

New York, March 17, 1938.

| 63441-A | Nettie Is The Nitwit Of The Networks | Dec 1729, F-6685, AH 96 |
| 63442-A | The Girl With The Paint On Her Face | Dec 1749, F-6700 |
| 63443-A | Sissy | Dec 1729, F-6685, AH 96 |
| 63444-A | Sunday In The Park | Dec 1749, F-6700 |

Acc. by Harry Sosnik and his Orchestra. New York, April 25, 1941.

| 69050- | We'll Never Grow Old (w/Julia Sanderson) | Dec 18155 |
| 69053- | Sweet Lady (w/Julia Sanderson) ("Tangerine") | Dec 18154 |

NOTE:- Matrices 69051/2 are both by Julia Sanderson, q.v.

New York, April 28, 1941.

| 69073- | Hello ! I've Been Looking For You (w/ Julia Sanderson) | Dec 18154 |
| 69075- | Same Sort Of Girl (And The Same Sort Of Boy)(w/Julia Sanderson) | Dec 18155 |
| 69076- | You're Here And I'm Here (w/Julia Sanderson) | Dec 18156 |

NOTE:- Matrix 69074 is by Julia Sanderson only, q.v.

## BEBE DANIELS

B. Dallas, Texas, January 14, 1901; stage debut there aged four as the Duke Of York in RICHARD III; first film THE SQUAW MAN with Lewis Stone (1906); made many films with Harold Lloyd (LONESOME LUKE comedies); also in Cecil B. de Mille film in 1920 (WHY CHANGE YOUR WIFE ?) and many other silents; best-remembered are MALE AND FE-MALE (1919) and SHE'S A SHEIK (1927); great success in talkies such as **RIO RITA,in** which she played one of her own favourite parts (1929); LOVE COMES ALONG (1930); FORTY-SECOND STREET and COUNSELLOR AT LAW (1933); came to England in 1936 with her husband, Ben Lyon, appearing in HAW-HAW (Holborn Empire, London, December 22,1939), GANGWAY (London Palladium, December 17, 1941) and PANAMA HATTIE (Piccadilly,November 4, 1943); tremendously successful with Ben Lyon, Vic Oliver, and her two chil-dren, Richard and Barbara, in radio shows HI GANG (1940) and LIFE WITH THE LYONS (1950), both of which were filmed soon after becoming established on radio; worked all over the British Isles during World War II, entertaining British and American troops, and factory workers. D. London, 1971.

Vocal, acc. by studio orchestra.              New York, August 17, 1923.

| 8469 | Christmas Greetings | Gnt 5236 |

Acc. by O/Victor Baravelli.              Culver City, Calif., September 16, 1929.

| PBVE-54454-4 | You're Always In My Arms (But Only In My Dreams) (Film "Rio Rita") | Vic 22132, LPV-538, LSA-3074, RD-7869, HMV B-3211 |
| PBVE-54455- | If You're In Love, You'll Waltz (Film "Rio Rita") | Vic 22132    - |

Culver City, Calif., January 3, 1930.

| PBVE-54549-3 | Until Love Comes Along (Film "Love Comes Along") | Vic 22283 |
| PBVE-54550-2 | Night Winds (Film "Love Comes Along") | -    HMV B-3678 |

Acc. by studio orchestra.              New York, February 12, 1935.

| B-16847-A | Dream Shadows | Br 7402, Dec F-5543 |
| B-16848-A | Hollywood Holiday (w/Ben Lyon and Skeets Gallagher) | -    - |

Acc. by O/Ronnie Munro.              London, February 12, 1937.

| OEA-4815-1 | There's A Small Hotel (w/Ben Lyon) | HMV B-8543 |
| OEA-4816-1 | Sing Something In The Morning | - |

Acc. by O/Jay Wilbur.                    London, May 5, 1939.

DR-3523-1  Deep Purple                        Dec F-7046
DR-3524-1  Little Swiss Whistling Song (w/Ben Lyon)   -
DR-3525-1  Little Sir Echo (w/Ben Lyon and The   Dec F-7063
           Three Ginx)
DR-3526-2  The Masquerade Is Over                -

                                 London, June 10, 1939.

DR-3668-1  Our Love                           Dec F-7101
DR-3669-1  Three Little Fishies (Itty-Bitty-Poo)      -
           (w/Ben Lyon and The Three Ginx)

                                 London, December 11, 1939.

DR-4095-   A Mother's Prayer At Twilight (w/Rio   Dec F-7338
           Trio)
DR-4096-   Somewhere In France With You       Dec F-7329
DR-4097-   Nursie ! Nursie !                     -
DR-4098-   Ling'ring On Your Doorstep (w/Ben Lyon)Dec F-7338

                                 London, January 8, 1940.

DR-4181-1  (Ho-dle-ay) Start The Day Right (w/Ben Dec F-7349
           Lyon and the Rio Trio) ("Haw-Haw")
DR-4182-2  Your Company's Requested (w/Rio Trio)      -
           ("Haw-Haw")
DR-4183-2  Stop ! It's Wonderful (w/Ben Lyon)    Dec F-7350
           ("Haw-Haw")
DR-4184-1  As Round And Round We Go (w/Rio Trio)      -
           ("Haw-Haw")

                                 London, April 10, 1940.

DR-4510-1  There's A Boy Coming Home On Leave    Dec F-7458
           (w/Ben Lyon and The Three Ginx)
DR-4511-2  With The Wind And The Rain In Your         -
           Hair (w/The Three Sirens)
DR-4512-1  Give A Little Whistle (w/Ben Lyon and  Dec F-7474
           The Three Ginx)
DR-4513-2  In An Old Dutch Garden (By An Old          -
           Dutch Mill) (w/The Three Sirens)

                                 London, August 6, 1940.

DR-4919-1  I Can't Love You Any More (Any More   Dec F-7574
           Than I Do)
DR-4920-1  Imagination                           -
DR-4921-1-2 Rio Rita (w/Sam Browne) (Film "Rio   Rejected
           Rita")
DR-4922-1  Only A Rose (w/Sam Browne)            Dec F-7803

                                 London, October 5, 1940.

DR-5166-1  The Swiss Bell-Ringer (w/Ben Lyon)    Dec F-7679
DR-5167-1  Cheerio !                             -

                                 London, November 4, 1940.

DR-4921-3  Rio Rita (w/Sam Browne) (Film "Rio    Dec F-7803
           Rita")
DR-5073-1  Sierra Sue                           Dec F-7651
DR-5074-1  If I Only Had Wings                   -

                                 London, January 17, 1941.

DR-5256-1  I Give You My Heart                   Dec F-7710
DR-5257-2  Now I Lay Me Down To Dream            -

London, March 27, 1941.

DR-5527-1  When That Man Is Dead And Gone          Dec F-7816
DR-5528-1  Johnny Pedlar (I Got)                   -

London, May 21, 1941.

DR-5769-1  The Little Boy Who Never Told A Lie     Dec F-7878
DR-5770-1  There I Go                              -

London, November 24, 1941.

DR-6474-1  I'm Singing To A Million (But Meaning   Dec F-8012
           It Just For One) ("Hi Gang !")
DR-6475-2  It's A Small World (w/The Radio Three)  -
           ("Hi Gang !")

London, January 26, 1942.

DR-6638-   There's Something About That Town       Dec F-8084
           ("Gangway")
DR-6639-   Swing Bugler ("Gangway")                -

London, February 10, 1942.

DR-6665-2  (There'll Be Bluebirds Over) The White Dec F-8091
           Cliffs Of Dover
DR-6666-2  Elmer's Tune (w/Ben Lyon)               -

## BILLY DANIELS


Vocal, acc. by O/Leonard Joy.          New York, May 8, 1941.

BS-065095-1  Penthouse Serenade (When We're Alone)BB B-11266
BS-065096-1  Diane (I'm In Heaven When I See You   -
             Smile)

Billy Daniels subsequently made many very popular records on other labels.

## DANIELLE DARRIEUX

French film actress (b. 1917); film debut 1931; very successful in early version  of
MAYERLING (1936); as a result, to Hollywood  where she made THE RAGE OF PARIS (and
after the war, she returned there to make RICH, YOUNG AND PRETTY (1951), FIVE FIN-
GERS (1952) and ALEXANDER THE GREAT (1955).  Many films made in France before  and
after World War II, some with singing roles (LA CRISE EST FINIE (1934);  BATTEMENT
DE COEUR and RETOUR A L'AUBE (1939); among more recent films are LADY CHATTERLEY'S
LOVER (1959), MURDER AT 45 RPM (1961), THE YOUNG GIRLS OF ROCHEFORT and L'HOMME  A
LA BUICK (1967).

Vocal, acc. by O/Wal-Berg.             Paris, July, 1934.

1318½wpp  La Crise est finie (w/Pierre Mangand)   Dec PO-5106
          (Film "La Crise est Finie")
1319½wpp  On ne voit ça qu'a Paris (Film "La      Dec PO-5107
          Crise est Finie")
1320½wpp  Sans un mot (Film "La Crise est Finie") Dec PO-5106
1323wpp   Sans un mot (Film "La Crise est Finie") Dec PO-5107

  Acc. by O/Raymond Legrand.           Paris, 1939.

5254¾spp  Une charade (Film "Battement de Coeur") Pol 524606, Br 02979
5255spp   Au vent leger                           -              -
5256½spp  Dans mon coeur (Film "Retour a l'aube") Pol 524607, Br 03036
5257¾spp  Je ne sais pas si je l'aime             -              -

B. Overrysel, Holland, June 21, 1863; to U.S.A. as young actress and singer. D.  San
  Francisco, September 10, 1932.

Vocal, acc. by unknown p.                    New York, c. 1898.

          Mona                                      Ber 3674

## EDGAR L. DAVENPORT

B. Philadelphia, 1862; stage debut there as a child at the Chestnut Street Theatre ;
  appeared at the Walnut Street Theatre there, 1878-1879; toured as leading man with
  various companies; leading juvenile actor in Boston, 1887-1892.  D. 1918.

Speech.                                      New York, c. May, 1905.

          Jim Bludsoe                               Ed 9053
          Lasca                                     Ed 9087

                                             New York, April 11, 1906.

B-3266-1  Jim Bludsoe                               Vic 4701

                                             New York, April 12, 1906.

B-3273-3  In Bohemia                                Vic 4752

  Acc. by studio orchestra.                  New York, April 13, 1906.

C-3283-2  Lasca                                     Vic 31529
B-3284-2  Sheridan's Ride                           Vic 4711, 16252

  Unacc.                                     New York, June 15, 1906.

E-3475-2  Wynken, Blynken And Nod                   Vic 4809
E-3476-1-2  Sugar Plum                              Rejected
E-3477-1-2-3  I'd Like To But I Dassen't            -
E-3478-1-2  The Seven Ages Of Man                   Vic 4942
E-3479-1-2  Little Beeches                          Rejected

                                             New York, June 16, 1906.

B-3479-3-4  Little Beeches                          Rejected
B-3480-1  Barbara Freitchie                         Vic 4834
E-3481-1  Casabianca                                Rejected

                                             New York, January 28, 1909.

B-3266-5  Jim Bludsoe                               Vic 4701, 16400
C-3283-4  Lasca                                     Vic 31529, 35090
B-3479-5-6  Little Beeches                          Rejected
B-6756-1  Autobiography Of A Chicken                Vic 16260

                                             New York, August 19, 1909.

B-8157-1  The Power Of Habit                        Vic 5747
B-8158-1  The Night Before Christmas                Rejected
B-8159-1  Good Fellowship (A Toast)                 -
B-8160-1  Gunga Din                                 -
B-8161-1  The Talk Of The Postage Stamp             -

                                             New York, late May, 1910.

30505-    Sheridan's Ride                    Col A-5218, A-5970, 223
30506-    Lasca                                     -           -        -

                                             New York, c. June, 1910.

          The Talk Of A Postage Stamp               USE 267
          Chicken                                   USE 268

New York, c. June, 1910.

| | |
|---|---|
| Jim Bludsoe | Ind 1396 |
| Sheridan's Ride | Ind 3119 |
| Lasca | Ind 3143 |

New York, c. September, 1911.

| | |
|---|---|
| Lasca | USE 1381 |
| Sheridan's Ride | USE 1382 |

New York, March 13, 1913.

| | | |
|---|---|---|
| 38701- | The Charge Of The Light Brigade | Col A-1371 |

New York, 1913.

| | |
|---|---|
| Lasca | Amb 1868 |
| Sheridan's Ride | Amb 1957 |

## BENNY DAVIS

B. New York, August 21, 1895; in vaudeville at 14; toured as accompanist to Blossom Seeley and Benny Fields. Wrote many songs: MARGIE (1920): ANGEL CHILD and I'M NOBODY'S BABY (1921); YEARNING (1925); BABY FACE (1926); CAROLINA MOON (1928), etc.

Vocal, acc. by studio orchestra.          New York, September 22, 1920.

| | | |
|---|---|---|
| 79426- | Kentucky | Col A-3320 |
| 79427- | Wait'n' For Me | - |

New York, October 19, 1920.

| | | |
|---|---|---|
| 79458- | Look What You've Done With Your Doggone Dangerous Eyes | Col A-3348 |

New York, October 21, 1920.

| | | |
|---|---|---|
| 79468- | Love, Honor And O-Baby | Col A-3348 |

Vocalist with Ted Lewis's Jazz Band.     New York, November 29, 1920.

| | |
|---|---|
| 79543-1-2-3  Margie | Col rejected |

Vocal, acc. by studio orchestra.          New York, December 23, 1920.

| | |
|---|---|
| 79600-1-2-3  You Oughta See My Baby | Col rejected |

Vocalist with Lou Gold and his Orchestra. New York, May 21, 1926.

| | |
|---|---|
| 142236-    Roses Remind Me Of You | Har 188-H, Re G-8688 |

   NOTE:- Regal G-8688 as CORONA DANCE ORCHESTRA.

Vocalist with Jan Garber and his Orchestra.
                                         New York, June 29, 1926.

| | |
|---|---|
| BVE-35558-3  Baby Face | Vic 20105 |

Vocalist with Harry MacDonald's Orchestra.
                                         New York, August 27, 1926.

BVE-36136-4  Who Could Be More Wonderful Than You? Vic 20149

## JESSIE BARTLETT DAVIS

B. 1861; d. May 14, 1905. Best remembered for her performance in the original production of ROBIN HOOD (Chicago, June 9, 1890) in which she sang O PROMISE ME. She also appeared in concert and light opera, and helped to promote the songs written by Carrie Jacobs Bond (I LOVE YOU TRULY, JUST A-WEARYIN' FOR YOU, etc.)

Vocal, acc. by unknown p.                    New York, May 3, 1898.

    O Genevieve (sic)                           Ber 583

                            New York, c. May, 1898.

    Duet from the Serenade (sic) (w/W. H.    Ber 3020
    MacDonald) ("Don Jose Of Sevilla")

## EDITH DAY

B. Minneapolis, April 10, 1896; stage debut in DANCING AROUND (Shubert Theatre,  St.
Paul, Minn., September, 1915); New York debut in POM-POM (George M. Cohan Theatre,
February 28, 1916); the following November she appeared with Anna Held in   FOLLOW
ME at the Casino; big success in GOING UP (Liberty, December 25, 1917); smash  hit
in IRENE at the Vanderbilt in the title-role in IRENE (November 18, 1919);  London
debut in the same part at the Empire, April 7, 1920, with comparable success; less
so at the same theatre in the titl⌐-role of JENNY (February 10, 1922), so returned
to New York to appear in ORANGE BLOSSOMS (Fulton, September, 1922) and another big
success in WILDFLOWER (Casino, February 7, 1923); back to London to play the title
role in ROSE-MARIE at Drury Lane (March 20, 1925), which ran for two years,  to be
followed by two further enormous successes in THE DESERT SONG (April 7, 1927)  and
SHOW BOAT (May 3, 1928), also at Drury Lane.  Further success in the title role in
RIO RITA (Prince Edward, April 3, 1930), then played in revivals of these, but she
did not appear again professionally in the U.S.A.  She made several films,  starting in 1918 with THE GRAIN OF DUST, and continued to live in London, where she was
a keen patron of the theatre up to the time of her death in 1971.

Vocal, acc. by O/Rosario Bourdon.            Camden, N. J., January 26, 1920.

B-23599-1-2-3  Alice Blue Gown ("Irene")            Vic rejected
B-23700-1-2-3  Irene ("Irene")                          -

                             Camden, N. J., February 2, 1920.

B-23599-6  Alice Blue Gown ("Irene")           Vic 45173, HMV B-1115
B-23700-7  Irene ("Irene")                          -           -

  Acc. by the Empire Theatre O/Frank Tours.
                             London, c. April 10, 1920.

74053    Alice Blue Gown ("Irene")               Col F-1044
74054    To Love You (w/Robert Michaelis)        Col F-1046
       ("Irene")
74055    Irene ("Irene")                         Col F-1044

                             London, c. April 29, 1920.

74071    Sky Rocket ("Irene")                    Col F-1046
74072    Castle Of Dreams ("Irene")              Col F-1045
74073    To Be Worthy Of You ("Irene")               -

  Acc. by the Drury Lane Theatre Orchestra/Herman Finck.
                             London, April, 1925.

A-1912    Pretty Things ("Rose Marie")           Col 3638
A-1913    The Minuet Of The Minute ("Rose Marie")    -
A-1916    Door Of My Dreams ("Rose Marie")       Col 3639
AX-982    Indian Love Call (w/Derek Oldham) ("Rose Col 9038
     Marie")

                Drury Lane Theatre, London, May 6, 1927.

WA-5406-3  Romance (w/Girls' Chorus) ("The Desert  Col 4388
     Song")
WA-5407-3  The Sabre Song ("The Desert Song")         -
WAX-2685-2 The Desert Song (w/Harry Welchman)      Col 9211
     ("The Desert Song")
WAX-2686-1-2  The Desert Song ("The Desert Song")  Rejected
WAX-2687-2  French Marching Song (w/chorus) ("The Desert Song") Col 9211

Drury Lane Theatre, London, May 18, 1928.

| WAX-3659-2 | Make Believe (w/chorus) ("Show Boat") | Col 9428 |
| WAX-3660-2 | You Are Love (w/Howett Worster) ("Show Boat") | Col 9429 |
| WAX-3661-2 | Why Do I Love You ? (w/Howett Worster) ("Show Boat") | Col 9428 |
| WAX-3662-2 | Dance Away The Night (w/chorus) ("Show Boat") | Col 9429 |

Acc. by the Prince Edward Theatre Orchestra/John Heuvel.

Prince Edward Theatre, London,
April 10, 1930.

| WA-10253-1 | You're Always In My Arms ("Rio Rita") | Col DB-115 |
| WAX-5514-2 | If You're In Love, You'll Waltz (w/ Geoffrey Gwyther) ("Rio Rita") | Col DX-55 |
| WAX-5515-2 | Rio Rita (w/Geoffrey Gwyther) ("Rio Rita") | - |
| WAX-5517-1 | I'd Rather Have A Memory Of You (w/ Geoffrey Gwyther) ("Rio Rita") | Col DX-54 |

Acc. by studio orchestra.            London, early February, 1932.

| WE-4404-1 | The Desert Song (w/Robert Naylor) ("The Desert Song") | Par R-1121, F-437 |
| WE-4405-2 | Indian Love Call (w/Robert Naylor) ("Rose Marie") | -            - |

London, March, 1932.

| WE-4490-2 | One Alone (w/Robert Naylor) ("The Desert Song") | Par R-1200 |
| WE-4491-2 | Love, What Has Given You This Magic Power ? (w/Robert Naylor) ("The Land Of Smiles") | - |

London, March 2, 1934.

| GA-6608-2 | Edith Day Memories - Part 1 (Intro. Make Believe/The Desert Song/Indian Love Call) | Dec K-725 |
| GA-6609-2 | Edith Day Memories - Part 2 (Intro. Romance/Alice Blue Gown/Why Do I Love You ?) | - |

Edith Day's only other recording was of BRONXVILLE DARBY AND JOAN with Sydney Arnold, in a 1962 LP (HMV CLP-1572) of Sir Noël Coward's SAIL AWAY.

## GLORIA  DE HAVEN

B. 1925; made a considerable number of light musical films from 1940 onwards, including TWO GIRLS AND A SAILOR (1944), SUMMER HOLIDAY (1948), THREE LITTLE WORDS (1950) and TWO TICKETS TO BROADWAY (1951); sang with Jan Savitt and his Top Hatters while still a teenager, and with Bob Crosby and his Orchestra; she was the ingenue in the Charlie Chaplin film MODERN TIMES (1936), and in the 1960s made various cabaret and TV appearances.

Vocalist with Jan Savitt and his Top Hatters.

Hollywood, July 28, 1942.

| PBS-072517-1 | Romance a la Mode | BB 30-0800 |
| PBS-072519-1 | If You Ever, Ever Loved Me (Love Me Tonight) | BB B-11584 |

## VAUGHN  DE LEATH

B. Mount P  aski, Ill., September 26, 1896; concert artist as a teenager; later pioneered on early radio; appeared in LAUGH, CLOWN, LAUGH (Belasco, New York, November 23, 1923); composed many popular songs (best-known, I WASN'T LYING WHEN I SAID  "I LOVE YOU", 1936); made also early TV appearances in 1939; and in vaudeville in the twenties and thirties. D. Buffalo, N.Y., May 28, 1943.

Vocal, acc. by the Rega Orchestra.        New York, October, 1920.

  7616-A   I'm A Little Nobody That Nobody Loves    OK 4292

                                          New York, c. May, 1921.

           For Somebody Else                        OK 4303
           Vamping Rose                             -

                                          New York, c. August, 1921.

           Sweet Lady (w/Billy Jones)               OK 4454
           I Wonder Who                             OK 4455

                                          New York, November, 1921.

  70312-   I've Got The Blues But I'm Just Too     OK 4577
              Mean To Cry

  70327-A  When Frances Dances With Me (w/Billy    OK 4501
              Jones)

           Second-Hand Rose                         OK 4489
           All By My Ownsome Blues                  OK 4492
           I Ain't Gonna Be Nobody's Fool          -

                                          New York, c. April, 1922.

           Alabammy Mammy                           OK 4588, 4607
           Can't Feel Jolly Blues                  -
           Maybe You Think You're Fooling Baby     OK 4597
           Some Sunny Day                           OK 4607

  Acc. by studio orchestra.             New York, c. June 8, 1922.

  7925     I'm Just Wild About Harry                Gnt 4905
  7926     Nobody Lied                              Gnt 4907

  Acc. by Pete Lawson's Orchestra.      New York, c. March 20, 1924.

  8803     Lazy                                     Gnt rejected
  8804     Waitin' Around                          -

  Acc. by studio orchestra.             New York, December 22, 1924.

  140201-  Nobody Knows What A Red Head Mama Can    Col 271-D
              Do
  140202-  I Ain't Got Nobody To Love              -

                                          New York, February 19, 1925.

  140380-  Somebody Like You                        Col 320-D
  140381-  Polly Of Hollywood                      -

  Acc. by unknown vn/ukulele.           New York, April 6, 1925.

  140500-  Ukulele Lady                             Col 361-D, 3720

                                          New York, April 7, 1925.

  140502-  Banana Oil                               Col 361-D, 3720

  Acc. unknown.                         New York, c. June 29, 1926.

  X-199    Where'd You Get Those Eyes ?             Gnt rejected
  X-200    How Many Times ?                        -

Acc. by studio orchestra.          New York, c. July 2, 1926.

| X-206 | Where'd You Get Those Eyes ? | Gnt 3347, Ch 15135 |
| X-207 | How Many Times ? | —        Ch 15136 |

Acc. by Ed Smalle-p.               New York, July 21, 1926.

142464-  Cross Your Heart (w/Ed Smalle)        Col 711-D, 4150
142465-  Whadda You Say We Get Together ? (w/Ed      —      —
           Smalle)

                                   New York, August 16, 1926.

142533-  Looking At The World Thru' Rose-Colored  Col 717-D, 4163
           Glasses
142534-  The Good Bad Girl                            —      —

Acc. unknown.                      New York, c. September 21, 1926.

X-275, -A-B  Aloma Of The South Seas       Rejected
X-276-A  Scatter Your Smiles               Gnt 3400

Acc. by unknown p/ukulele/others ?   New York, September 27, 1926.

142693-  Give Me A Ukulele (w/Gerald Macy)     Col 799-D
142694-  Love Me (w/Gerald Macy)                   —

Acc. by unknown p.                 New York, October 6, 1926.

142739-  Susie's "Feller"                      Col 779-D, 4274
142740-  That's A Good Girl                        —      —

Acc. by the Broadway Strutters.    New York, c. October 14, 1926.

X-317-A  Here Comes Fatima          Gnt 3400, Herschel 2011
X-318    Pretty Little Thing        Gnt 3412        —
X-319, -A  Heinie Schultz-en-heim   Rejected

Acc. unknown.                      New York, October, 1926.

         Hello, Bluebird           Ed 51874
         I'm Telling The Birds, Telling The Bees    —
           (How I Love You)

Acc. by unknown p.                 New York, December 24, 1926.

143218-3 You Know - I Know - Everything's Made  Col 851-D, 4545
           For Love (w/Frank Harris)
143219-  So Will I (w/Frank Harris)                 —

                                   New York, December, 1926.

         Everything's Made For Love       Ed 51904
         Here Or There                        —

                                   New York, c. January 4, 1927.

X-428  She Said And I Said (w/Jerry Macy)  Gnt 6024, Ch 15206, Aco G-16191
X-429  I Gotta Get Myself Somebody To Love    —      Ch 15207      —
         (w/Jerry Macy)

Acc. by studio orchestra.          New York, January 10, 1927.

80292-  I'm Telling The Birds, Telling The Bees  OK 40746, Par R-3322
          How I Love You
80293-  I Gotta Get Myself Somebody To Love       —         —

                                   New York, January 11, 1927.
80296-  Blue Skies                        OK 40750, Par R-3316
80297-  There Ain't No "Maybe" In My Baby's Eyes   —         —

Acc. by unknown vn/g.                    New York, c. January 27, 1927.

GEX-483    By The Side Of The Omelette Sea        Gnt 6046, Ch 15217, Spt 9126
GEX-484-A  The Worst Rose Of Summer (w/others)       -          -       - Aco G-16210

Acc. unknown.                            New York, c. January, 1927.

E-21333    Since I Found You                        Br 3443
E-21334/5  Crazy Words - Crazy Tune                 -

           Blue Skies                              Ed 51948
           Since I Found You                        -

Acc. by studio orchestra.                New York, February 3, 1927.

80384-     Muddy Water (A Mississippi Moan)         OK 40768, Par R-3324
80385-     Some Of These Days                       -           -

Acc. by unknown p.                       New York, February 9, 1927.

143454-    That's My Hap-Hap-Happiness              Col 915-D
143455-1-2-3  I Wonder How I Look When I'm Asleep Rejected

                                         New York, February 26, 1927.

143542-    I Wonder How I Look When I'm Asleep      Col 915-D, 4443

Acc. unknown.                            New York, c. February, 1927.

           Positively - Absolutely                 Ed 51966
           It Made You Happy When You Made Me Cry    -

Acc. by unknown p.                       New York, March 17, 1927.

143663-    Down In The Old Neighborhood (w/Frank    Col 971-D
              Harris)
143673-    Oh ! Baby, Don't We Get Along ? (w/        -        4443
              Frank Harris)
   NOTE:- Matrices 143664/72 inclusive are not by Vaughn de Leath.

                                         New York, c. March, 1927.

E-22192    Just Wondering                           Br 3520
E-22196    I'm In Love Again                        -

Acc. by Murray Kellner-vn/Bill Wirges-p/Harry Reser-bj.
                                         New York, April 1, 1927.

BVE-38421-1-2-3  Kentucky Babe                      Vic rejected
BVE-38422-1-2-3  Mammy's Little Coal-Black Rose      -

Acc. by O/Nat Shilkret.                  New York, April 4, 1927.

BVE-38323-  Song Of The Wanderer                    Vic 20600

Acc. by unknown p.                       New York, April 4, 1927.

80696-     I'm On My Merry Way                      OK 40814, Par R-3341
80697-     The Whisper Song                         -           -

                                         New York, April 20, 1927.

143995-    Mister O'Toole (w/Frank Harris)          Col 994-D
143996-    Down Alongside Of The Docks (w/Frank     Col 1016-D
              Harris)

Vocalist with Don Voorhees and his Earl Carroll Vanities Orchestra.
                                         New York, c. April, 1927.
           I'll Always Remember You                 Ed 51997
           Dancing The Devil Away                   Ed 51999

Acc. unknown.                          New York, c. April, 1927.

    So Blue                              Ed 52016
    Somebody Said                        -

    I'm In Love Again                    Ed 52018
    The Whisper Song (When The Pussy Willow   -
      Whispers To The Catnip)

Acc. by 2vn/vc/p.                      New York, May 11, 1927.

BVE-38421-    Kentucky Babe                    Vic 20664, HMV B-2571
BVE-38741-    Mighty Lak' A Rose               -              -

Acc. **b**y unknown p.                 New York, May 12, 1927.

144137-2  Oh ! How I Love My Boatman           Col 1016-D, 4545

                                       New York, May 14, 1927.

144370-   I'm Gonna Dance Wit De Guy Wot Brung   Col 1091-D
          Me (The Gum-Chewer's Song) (w/Frank Harris)
144371-   Just A Little Old School House (Up On      -
          Top Of The Hill) (w/Frank Harris)

Acc. by O/Nat Shilkret.                New York, May 25, 1927.

BVE-38782-   Like An Angel You Flew Into Every-   Vic 20674
             one's Heart (Lindbergh)

Acc. by Rube Bloom-p/Eddie Lang-g.    New York, June 14, 1927.

81013-A  (What Do We Do) On A Dew-Dew-Dewy Day ? OK 40844, Par R-3386
81014-C  Vo-Do-Do-De-O Blues                    -              -
NOTE:- Parlophone as SADIE GREEN.

Acc. by 2vn/p/g.                       New York, June 24, 1927.

BVE-39291-   Sing Me A Baby Song                 Vic 20787, HMV B-2565
BVE-39292-   Who Are You Fooling Tonight ?       Vic 20825, HMV B-2590

Vocalist with Al Lynn's Music Masters.  New York, c. June, 1927.

    Sometimes I'm Happy                  Ed 52041

Acc. unknown.                          New York, c. June, 1927.

    Are You Lonesome Tonight ?           Ed 52044
    It's A Million To One You're In Love   -

                                       New York, c. July, 1927.

    Baby Feet Go Pitter-Patter ('Cross My   Ed 52073
      Floor)
    Yep ! 'Long About June               -

Acc. by studio orchestra.              New York, August 12, 1927.

BVE-39968-   Baby Your Mother (Like She Babied    Vic 20873
             You)

Acc. unknown.                          New York, August 31, 1927.

144608-   I Walked Back From The Buggy Ride (w/   Col 1110-D
          Frank Harris)

                                       New York, c. August, 1927.

E-24083   Sometimes I'm Happy                    Br 3608, 4770
E-24085   Baby Feet Go Pitter-Patter ('Cross My Floor)-

New York, c. August, 1927.

     Someday You'll Say "O.K."                    Ed 52093
     There's A Cradle In Caroline                 -

Vocalist with the OKeh Melodians (Sam Lanin's Arkansaw Travellers on Parlophone).
     New York, September 17, 1927.

81447-  My Blue Heaven                      OK 40898, Par R-3438
81448-  A Shady Tree                        OK 40905, Par R-3437
81449-B There Ain't No Land Like Dixieland  OK 40898, Par R-3438

Vocalist with Ben Bernie and his Hotel Roosevelt Orchestra.
     New York, September 20, 1927.

E-24473  There's A Cradle In Caroline       Br 3656, 3659

Vocal, acc. by ? Rube Bloom-p.        New York, September 28, 1927.

81486-  Lonely Lights Along The Shore       OK 40906, Par R-3447
81487-  Old Names Of Old Flames             -           -

Vocalist with Oreste and his Queensland Orchestra.
     New York, c. September, 1927.

     Moonlit Waters                          Ed 52103

Vocalist with Al Friedman and his Orchestra.
     New York, c. September, 1927.

     My Blue Heaven                          Ed 52128

Vocal, acc. unknown.                  New York, c. September, 1927.

     Blow, Blow, Blow                        Ed 52104
     Here Comes The Show Boat                -
     Lonely Lights Along The Shore           Ed 52120
     Make My Cot Where The Cot-Cot-Cotton    -
       Grows
     Christmas In Other Lands - Part 1       Ed 52129
     Christmas In Other Lands - Part 2       -
     The Night Before Christmas              Ed 52130

New York, October 3, 1927.

144822-  Jimmy And Mary's Christmas Eve - Part 1 Col 1153-D
144823-  Jimmy And Mary's Christmas Eve - Part 2    -

New York, October 7, 1927.

81529-C  Christmas Song                       OK 40911
81530-B  O Come, All Ye Faithful (Adeste Fideles)  -

Acc. by Ed Smalle-p.            New York, October 24, 1927.

BVE-40502-2  There's A Rickety Rackety Shack (w/  Vic 21210, HMV B-2715
     Ed Smalle)
BVE-40503-  Together, We Two (w/Ed Smalle)      Vic 21042, HMV B-2672

Vocalist with Irwin Abrams and his Orchestra.
     New York, c. October, 1927.

     Dream Kisses                            Ed 52148

Vocal, acc. by Ed Smalle-p.        New York, November 9, 1927.

144962-  When Honey Sings An Old-Time Song (w/  Col 1203-D
     The Singing Sophomores)

New York, November 10, 1927.

144965-   Playground In The Sky (w/Frank Harris)  Col 1215-D, 4779

New York, November 14, 1927.

144973-   Go Home And Tell Your Mother (That I      Col 1258-D
            Love You) (w/Frank Harris)
144974-   Just Around The Corner From An A. & P.       -
            (w/Frank Harris)

New York, November 21, 1927.

145226-   Wherever You Are (w/Franklyn Baur)      Col 1215-D, 4779
145227-   Thinking Of You (w/Franklyn Baur)          -

Acc. unknown.                    New York, c. November, 1927.

E-24690/1  Mister Aeroplane Man (Take Me Up To    Br 3683
             Heaven)
E-24693/4  Tin Pan Parade                             -

           There Must Be Somebody Else            Ed 52159
           What'll You Do ?                           -

New York, December 8, 1927.

145284-   Up In The Clouds (w/Franklyn Baur)      Col 1236-D

Vocalist with Fred Rich and his Hotel Astor Orchestra.
                                  New York, December 10, 1927.

145295-3  The Man I Love                          Col 1241-D, 4786

Vocal, acc. unknown.             New York, c. December, 1927.

           The Man I Love                         Br 3748
           Linger Longer Lane                         -

Vocalist with Don Voorhees and his Orchestra.
                                  New York, January 7, 1928.

145485-3  Can't Help Lovin' Dat Man              Col 1284-D, 4901

Vocalist with the Piccadilly Players.   New York, c. January, 1928.

           What'll You Do ?                       Ed 52198
           I Just Roll Along, Having My Ups And       -
             Downs

Vocal, acc. unknown.             New York, c. January, 1928.

           Keep Sweeping The Cobwebs Off The Moon Ed 52192
           My Blue Heaven                             -

New York, c. February, 1928.

           After My Laughter Came Tears           Br 3860
           Bluebird, Sing Me A Song                   -

           I Just Roll Along, Having My Ups And   Ed 52222
             Downs
           Sunshine                                   -

Acc. by her Buddies.             New York, c. February, 1928.

           Rambler Roses Ramble                   Ed 52212
           There Must Be A Silver Lining              -

Acc. unknown.                            New York, March 1, 1928.

145701-   I Just Roll Along (Havin' My Ups And      Col 1323-D
            Downs)
145702-   Watching For The Boogie Man              -

                                          New York, c. March, 1928.

E-27123/4  Lou'siana Lullaby                      Br 3893
E-27125/6  Little Mother                          -

                                          New York, April 24, 1928.

145871-   Giggling Gertie                          Col 1513-D

                                          New York, April, 1928.

E-27461-  Sorry For Me                            Br 3932
E-27462-  I'm Away From The World When I'm Away      -
            From You ('Cause You're All The World To Me)

                                          New York, c. April, 1928.

          Happy-Go-Lucky Lane                      Ed 52288
          After My Laughter Came Tears            -

Vocalist with Ernie Golden's Hotel McAlpine Orchestra.
                                          New York, c. April, 1928.

          I'm Away From The World When I'm Away   Ed 52289
            From You ('Cause You're All The World To Me)

Vocal, acc. unknowm.                      New York, May 26, 1928.

146350-   Dirty Hands ! Dirty Face !               Col 1556-D

                                          New York, c. May, 1928.

          Baby Your Mother (Like She Babied You)  Ed 52306
          Tin Pan Parade                          -

                                          New York, June, 1928.

E-27653-  Ginger Bread Brigade                     Br 3988
E-27654-  Mother Goose Parade                     -

                                          New York, c. June, 1928.

          Giggling Gertie                          Ed 52341
          Dusky Stevedore                         -
          Ginger Bread Brigade                     Ed 52357
          Mother Goose Parade                     -

                                          New York, July 10, 1928.

146517-   You Took Advantage Of Me (w/Frank        Col 1470-D
            Harris)
146518-   The Little Brown Shoe                    Col 1556-D
146519-   Do I Hear You Saying (I Love You) (w/    Col 1470-D
            Frank Harris)

                                          New York, c. July, 1928.

          Come Back, Chiquita                      Ed 52374
          Is It Gonna Be Long ?                   -

                                          New York, c. August, 1928.

          Nobody But Baby                          Ed 52388
          I Can't Give You Anything But Love      -

New York, September 22, 1928.

| 147030- | Pat's Night Out (w/Frank Harris) | Col 1594-D |
| 147031- | Ho-Ho-Ho-Hogan (w/Frank Harris) | - |

New York, September 27, 1928.

| 147071- | Sleep, Baby, Sleep | Col 1715-D |
| 147072- | Alice In Wonderland | - |

New York, September 28, 1928.

| 147082- | The Children's Party - Part 1 | Col 1624-D |
| 147083- | The Children's Party - Part 2 | - |

New York, c. September, 1928.

| There Ain't No Sweet Man That's Worth The Salt Of My Tears | Ed 52408 |
| I Ain't Got Nobody (And Nobody Cares For Me) | - |
| Everything We Like We Like Alike | Ed 52428 |

Acc. by her Buddies.                    New York, September-October, 1928.

| Jeannine (I Dream Of Lilac Time) | Ed 52428 |

Vocalist with the Broadway Nitelites.   New York, October 16, 1928.

| 147046- | I Wanna Be Loved By You | Col 1604-D |

Vocal, acc. unknown.                    New York, October 31, 1928.

| 147174- | Won't You Tell Me, Hon (When We're Gonna Be One ?) | Col rejected |

New York, c. November, 1928.

| Alice In Wonderland | Ed 52446 |
| Little Yaller Dog | - |
| Me And The Man In The Moon | Ed 52517 |
| Happy Days And Lonely Nights | - |

Acc. by t/as/p/g.                       New York, December 21, 1928.

| 401475-E | Me And The Man In The Moon | OK 41206 |
| 401476-B | I'll Never Ask For More | Par E-6157, Ar 4402 |

NOTE:- Parlophone as MAMIE LEE; Ariel as NANCY FOSTER.

Acc. by O/Leonard Joy.                  New York, January 4, 1929.

BVE-49618-1-2-3  I Faw Down And Go 'Boom !!    Vic rejected

New York, January 10, 1929.

BVE-49631-2  The Toymaker's Dream              Vic 21975, HMV B-3080

Acc. unknown.                           New York, February 20, 1929.

401629-  I Faw Down And Go 'Boom !!            OK rejected

Acc. by her Boys.                       New York, c. March, 1929.

| I'm Ka-razy For You | Ed 52543 |
| When I'm Walking With My Sweetness (Down Among The Sugar Cane) | - |

Acc. by O/Leonard Joy.                    New York, April 23, 1929.

BVE-51250-3  Old Fashioned Lady                    Vic 21975, HMV B-3080
BVE-51251-1-2-3  Oh Sweetheart, Where Are You      Rejected
                  Tonight ?

Acc. unknown.                             New York, c. April, 1929.

            I've Got A Feeling I'm Falling        Ed 52569
            I Got A "Code" In My "Doze"           Ed 52575
            Some Sweet Day                        -

                                          New York, c. May, 1929.

            Honey                                 Ed 52587, 52651
            Reaching For Someone (And Not Finding    -
              Anyone There)

Vocalist with B. A. Rolfe's Lucky Strike Orchestra.
                                          New York, c. May, 1929.

            Birmingham Bertha                     Ed 52604
            Am I Blue ?                           -

Vocal, acc. unknown.                      New York, c. June, 1929.

            Mah Lindy Lou                         Ed 52614
            Marianna                              -
            (If I Were You) I'd Fall In Love With  Ed 52627
              Me
            Oh Susanna                            Ed 52651

                                          New York, October, 1929.

E-30985-    Chant Of The Jungle                   Br 4533
E-30986-    He's So Unusual                       -

## DOLORES  DEL RIO

B. Durango, Mexico, August 3, 1905; r.n. Lolita Dolores Asunsolo de Martinez.  Left
   convent school at 15, m. Jaime del Rio when 16; noticed by Edwin Carewe, the film
   director, who persuaded her to leave her life in society to become a film actress
   (first film JOANNA, 1925);  star perfprmance in WHAT PRICE GLORY (1927); went  on
   to further success with RAMONA (1928), but was widowed that year.  Appeared  with
   success in  EVANGELINE (1929); THE BAD ONE (1930); m. set designer Cedric Gibbons
   (1931; div. 1941); other very popular films include BIRD OF PARADISE (1932); FLY-
   ING DOWN TO RIO (1933); WONDER BAR and MADAME DU BARRY (1934); IN CALIENTE(1935);
   INTERNATIONAL SETTLEMENT (1938); JOURNEY INTO FEAR (1942); THE FUGITIVE (1947)and
   many South American films during the 1950s; m. Lewis Riley, 1959; appeared in the
   part of Elvis Presley's mother (!) in FLAMING STAR (1960), and in CHEYENNE AUTUMN
   (1964) and MORE THAN A MIRACLE (1967).  She practices Yoga, and is as  remarkably
   beautiful today (1973) as when she first became known as an actress.

Vocal, acc. by small orchestra.           Roosevelt Hotel, Hollywood, May 6, 1928.

PBVE-42262-3  Ya va cayendo (Falling In Love)     Vic 4053, 4054, HMV E-517
                (In Spanish)
PBVE-42263-4  Ramona (in English)                 Vic 4053, LPV-538, LSA-3074,
                                                  RD-7869, HMV E-517
PBVE-42264-   Ramona (in Mexican Spanish)         Vic 4054

                                          Hollywood, February 29, 1936.

PBS-97312-1  Manon/Parlez-moi d'amour (in French) Vic rejected

## GABY  DESLYS

B. Paris, 1883; d. there, February 11, 1920,  New York debut in VERA VIOLETTA, with
   her American partner Harry Pilcer, at the Winter Garden, November 20, 1911 (they
   danced the Gaby Glide, and in Paris in 1912 were paid the highest fee ever  given

for a vaudeville entertainer.  She starred with Al Jolson in HONEYMOON EXPRESS at
the Winter Garden on February 6, 1913, and appeared in STOP ! LOOK ! LISTEN !  at
the Globe (December 25, 1915); she returned to Europe and spied for France in the
disguise of a Hungarian woman, but her experiences probably contributed to  death
at the age of 36.  She made a few films, notably INFATUATION (Pathe, 1917).

Vocal, acc. by studio orchestra.          Paris, October 17, 1910.

```
489h    Tout en rose                      HMV 2-033039
490h    Philomene                         HMV 2-033040
491h/491½h  La Parisienne                 Rejected ?
```

## MARLENE DIETRICH

B. Berlin, December 27, 1902; r.n. Maria Magdalene von Losch.   tudied music; began
film career in Germany in 1923; most successful German film THE BLUE ANGEL(1930).
To Hollywood that year; made most of her subsequent films in U.S.A., many of them
directed by Josef von Sternberg.  Best-remembered : SHANGHAI EXPRESS (1932); SONG
OF SONGS (1933); THE DEVIL IS A WOMAN (1935); GARDEN OF ALLAH (1936);DESTRY RIDES
AGAIN (1939); THE FLAME OF NEW ORLEANS (1941); FOLLOW THE BOYS (1944); GOLDEN EAR
RINGS (1947); A FOREIGN AFFAIR (1948); WITNESS FOR THE PROSECUTION (1957);  JUDG-
MENT AT NUREMBERG (1961); appeared in cabaret in Berlin in 1928, and in New York,
Las Vegas and at the Cafe de Paris in London since World War II.

Vocal, as member of the chorus "Ensemble des Nelson-Revue", acc. by O/Mischa Spoliansky.                                  Berlin, June, 1928.

```
CL-4214-2  Potpourri aus der Revue "Es liegt in  El EH-146
             der Luft" - Part 1
CL-4215-3  Potpourri aus der Revue "Es liegt in     -
             der Luft" - Part 2
```

Acc. by Mischa Spoliansky-p.              Berlin, June, 1928.

```
BL-4231-1  Wenn die beste Freunden (w/Margo Lion  El EG-892
             and Oskar Karlweis)
```

Acc. by Friedrich Holländer und sein Jazzsymphoniker.
                                          Berlin, January, 1930.

```
BLR-6034-2  Falling In Love Again (Film "The    HMV B-3524, Vic 22593, LCT-1112,
              Blue Angel") (in English)          Bm 1120
BLR-6035-2  Nimm dich in acht vor blonden        El EG-1770
              Frauen (Film "The Blue Angel") (in German)
BLR-6036-1  Blonde Women (Film "The Blue Angel")  HMV B-3524, 7EG-8257
              (in English)

BLR-6078-2  Ich bin die fesche Lola (in German)  El EG-1802, Vic 22593, HMV
                                                  7EG-8257
```

                                  Berlin, February, 1930.

```
BLR-6129-2  Ich bin von Kopf bis Fuss auf Liebe   El EG-1770
              eingestellt (Film "The Blue Angel") (in German)
BLR-6130-2  Wenn ich mir was Wünschen durfte      El EG-2265
              (in German) (acc. by Friedrich Holländer-p only)
BLR-6180-2  Kinder, heut' Abend such ich mir was  El EG-1802, HMV 7EG-8257
              aus (in German)
```

Acc. by small o/Mischa Spoliansky.        Berlin, March 12, 1931.

```
OD-250-3  Leben ohne Liebe kannst du nicht        El EG-2265
            (in German)
```

Acc. by O/Peter Kreuder.                  Berlin, late March, 1931.

```
OD-291-1  Quand l'amour meurt (in French)         El EG-2275
OD-292-1  Give Me The Man (in English)             -
```

Berlin, c. April, 1931.

| 16310 | Peter | Ul/Tel A-887, Br 7726, Dec M-447 |
| 16311 | Johnny | -    - |
| 16311-2 | Johnny | -    Epic SN-6059 - |

Acc. by l'Orchestre Wal-Berg/Peter Kreuder.

Paris, c. July, 1933.

| 6465¾bkp | Assez (in French) | Pol 524180, Br 7725, Dec M-452 |
| 6469¾bkp | Je m'ennuie (in French) | -    -    - |
| 6470 bkp | Ja, so bin ich (in German) | Pol 524182, Br 7724 |
| 6471¼bkp | Mein blondes Baby (in German) (acc. by | Pol 524181, Br 7723, Dec M-442 |
| | Peter Kreuder-p only) | |
| 6476¾bkp | Allein in einer grossen Stadt (in | Pol 524181, Br 7723, Dec M-442 |
| | German) | |
| 6477¾bkp | Wo ist der Mann ? (in German) | Pol 524182, Br 7724 |

Acc. by studio orchestra.        Los Angeles, c. November, 1934.

| B-1972-A | (If It Isn't Paris) Then It Isn't Love | Dec Special Record |
| B-1973-A | Three Sweethearts Have I | - |

Acc. by Victor Young and his Orchestra.

Los Angeles, December 11, 1939.

| DLA-1882-B | I've Been In Love Before (Film | Dec 23139, DL-5100, DL-8465, |
| | "Destry Rides Again") | Br 03014, LA-8591 |
| DLA-1883-A | You've Got That Look (That Leaves | Dec 23140, DL-5100, DL-8465, |
| | Me Weak) (Film "Destry Rides Again") | Br 03014, LA-8591 |
| DLA-1884-C | Falling In Love Again (Film "The | Dec 23141, DL-5100, DL-8465, |
| | Blue Angel") | Br 02976, LA-8591, LA-8709 |

Los Angeles, December 19, 1939.

| DLA-1911-B | The Boys In The Back Room (Film | Dec 23141, DL-5100, DL-8465, |
| | "Destry Rides Again") | Br 02976, LA-8591, LA-8709 |
| DLA-1912-A | You Go To My Head | Dec 23140, DL-5100, DL-8465. |
| | | Br 03045, LA-8591 |
| DLA-1913-A | You Do Something To Me | Dec 23139, DL-5100, DL-8465, |
| | | Br 03045, LA-8591 |

## LEW DOCKSTADER

B. 1856; r.n. George Alfred Clapp. Blackface minstrel star in Hartford, Conn., as a
teenage amateur; turned professional, 1873; joined Bloodgood's Comic Alliance, and
later, Emmett & Wilde's troupe; in 1876 organized own troupe with Charles Dockstader ("The Dockstader Brothers"); the latter retired in 1883, but Clapp kept   name
and opened his own theatre on Broadway in 1886, going into vaudeville in 1890.  He
partnered George Primrose in a minstrel act from 1898 to 1913, and travelled   the
Keith circuit from then until 1923; d. October 26, 1924. His act combined  black-
face minstrel with clown (stage "props" included a 10-yard tail-coat and shoes two
feet long and a foot wide); he is described as turning the declining minstrel show
into an instrument of social and political satire, portraying not comic Negro characters but comic whites in blackface (one of these was President Theodore  Roosevelt !)

Vocal, acc. by studio O/? Charles A. Prince.

New York, c. July, 1905.

| 3251- | Everybody Works But Father | Col/Oxford/Standard 3251, A-306, |
| | | 32927 (cylinder) |

New York, c. March, 1906.

| 3386- | Uncle Quit Work Too | Col 3386, 32937 (cyl), Marconi |
| | | 0288 |

New York, February 12, 1912.

19756-    Take A Little Tip From Father          Col rejected

New York, May 23, 1912.

19901-    Fiddle-Dee-Dee                          Col rejected

New York, July 8, 1912.

38120-    Fiddle-Dee-Dee (w/vocal quartette)      Col A-1200

New York, July 11, 1912.

38131-    If It Wasn't For My Wife And Baby       Col rejected

## LILLIAN DOREEN

British music-hall artist of the early years of the century who appeared in    vaudeville in New York in 1907.

Vocal, acc. by ? Landon Ronald-p.        London, c. June, 1903.

           Annie Laurie                        G&T GC-3451
           Rose                                G&T GC-3489

London, August 13, 1903.

4082-R    Beyond                               Rejected
4083-R    Queen Of Love                        G&T GC-3492
4084-R    Creole Cradle Song                   G&T GC-3486, Zon X-43080
4085-R    When Kate And I                      G&T GC-3512
4086-R    Mary Lee                             Rejected
4087-R    Nellie McGee                         G&T GC-3487
4088-R    My Heart Was Once                    Rejected
           Mary Lee                            G&T 3321 (7")
           Nellie McGee                        G&T 3322 (7")
           There's Nobody Just Like You        G&T 3323 (7")

Acc. unknown.                            London, 1904.

           Could You Be True To Eyes Of Blue ?    Nicole 4031 (7"), 5070
           Queen Of Love                          Nicole 5071
           Beyond                                 Nicole 5072
           Just Idle Dreams                       Nicole 5067
           Only For You, Dear Heart               Nicole 5476

London, c. 1905.

L-158    Killarney                              Od 2582
L-160    Little Mary                            Od 2595
NOTE:- The above two titles are coupled.

New York, c. July, 1907.

           Take Me Back To New York Town        Ed 9666

## EDDIE  DOWLING

B. Woonsocket, R.I., December 9, 1894; r.n. Joseph Nelson Goucher. Stage debut    in
the Opera House, Providence, in QUO VADIS ? (1909); toured England, 1911, as   member of choral party; New York debut in ZIEGFELD FOLLIES OF 1917 at the New Amsterdam, June 12, 1917; subsequently in the 1919 and 1920 editions of the same production; starred in SALLY, IRENE AND MARY (Casino, September 4, 1922), for three successive seasons, and HONEYMOON LANE (Knickerbocker, September 20, 1926), which was
a similar success, and both of which he co-authored; appeared in own management of
THUMBS UP ! (St. James, December 27, 1934); appeared in and directed many  others,
gaining Pulitzer Prize and the New York Drama Critics' Circle Award for his   production, in association with the Theatre Guild, of THE TIME OF YOUR LIFE   (Booth,
October 25, 1939); apart from writing songs for stage productions, he also   wrote

lyrics to James Hanley's music for the early musical film THE RAINBOW MAN (1929).

Vocal, acc. by O/Leonard Joy and Tom Griselle.
                              New York, March 29, 1929.

BVE-51105-1-2-3-4  Sleepy Valley (Film "The       Vic rejected
              Rainbow Man")

                              New York, April 2, 1929.

BVE-51115-1-2-3  The Rainbow Man (w/male quartet) Vic rejected
              (Film "The Rainbow Man")

                              New York, April 9, 1929.

BVE-51105-5-6-7-8  Sleepy Valley (Film "The       Vic rejected
              Rainbow Man")
BVE-51115-4-5  The Rainbow Man (w/male quartet)      -
              (Film "The Rainbow Man")

## MORTON  DOWNEY

B. of Irish parents in Wallingford, Conn., 1902; discovered singing in Sheridan by a
Paul Whiteman talent scout; sang with Whiteman's S. S. Leviathan Orchestra; made a
hit in Ziegfeld show PALM BEACH NIGHTS in Florida, 1926; appeared in London, Paris
and Berlin, 1928; opened the Delmonico Club in New York on return there; to Hollywood, 1929, made only two films (apparently unsuited to this medium), SYNCOPATION,
co-starring Barbara Bennett (m. her 1929; div. 1941; she died 1958) and LUCKY   IN
LOVE (1930).  During thirties did much radio work for Camel, Woodbury and Pall Mall
cigarettes; again appeared in London, 1933 and 1937; at the World's Fair, New York
(Aquacade); on TV, 1947, in own show, 1949; m. Margaret Schultze; she died 1964.

Vocal, acc. by studio orchestra, as MORTON JAMES.
                              New York, April 25, 1923.

        Midnight Rose                      Ed 51244

Vocalist with S. S. Leviathan Orchestra. New York, May 9, 1924.

B-29979-3  Nightingale                     Vic 19342

Vocal, a c. by studio orchestra.    New York, c. January, 1927.

        Since I Found You                  Br 3397
        The Little White House             -

  Acc. by O/Carroll Gibbons.      Small Queen's Hall, London, April 13, 1928.

Bb-12918-1  The Girl Is You And The Boy Is Me     HMV B-2749

                              Hayes, Middlesex, April 27, 1928.

Bb-13247-1-2-3  Dear, On A Night Like This   Rejected
Bb-13248-1  Paradise Isle                    HMV B-2848
Bb-13249-1  Make Believe                     HMV B-2749

                              Hayes, Middlesex, August 31, 1928.

Bb-14430-1  My Inspiration Is You            HMV B-2823
Bb-14431-1  Just A Little Fond Affection     -
Bb-14432-1-2  Left Me All Alone             Rejected
Bb-14433-1-2  For Old Times' Sake           -

                              Hayes, Middlesex, September 28, 1928.

Bb-14432-3-4  Left Me All Alone             Rejected
Bb-14434-4  For Old Times' Sake             HMV B-2848

Acc. by O/Nat Shilkret.              New York, November 14, 1928.

BVE-48162-1-2-3  How About Me ?              Vic rejected
BVE-48163-1-2-3  I'm Sorry, Sally             -

                                     New York, November 30, 1928.

BVE-48162-5  How About Me ?                  Vic 21806, HMV B-2998
BVE-48163-6  I'm Sorry Sally                 -          -

                                     New York, December 1, 1928.

BVE-48162-6-7-8  How About Me ?              Vic rejected

                                     New York, December 19, 1928.

BVE-49276-1-2-3  My Inspiration Is You       Rejected
BVE-49277-1-2  Little Irish Rose             -
BVE-49278-4  Rosemary                        Vic 21849

Acc. by O/Leonard Joy.               New York, January 11, 1929.

BVE-49276-4  My Inspiration Is You           Vic 21860
BVE-49277-3  Little Irish Rose               Vic 21849

Acc. by O/Nat Shilkret.              New York, January 21, 1929.

BVE-49670-1  I'll Always Be In Love With You  Vic 21860, HMV B-3022
             (Film "Syncopation")

Acc. by O/Leonard Joy.               New York, March 11, 1929.

BVE-50928-1-2-3  I'll Always Be Mother's Boy  Vic rejected

                                     New York, March 13, 1929.

BVE-50752-2  There'll Be You And I           Vic 21940, HMV B-3052
BVE-50753-2  The World Is Yours And Mine     Vic 21958, HMV B-3138

                                     New York, March 26, 1929.

BVE-49795-3  There's A Place In The Sun For You  Vic 21958, HMV B-3049
BVE-50928-6  I'll Always Be Mother's Boy     Vic 21940, HMV B-3052

                                     New York, April 13, 1929.

BVE-51623-1-2-3  There's The One For Me      Vic rejected
BVE-51624-1-2-3  This Is Heaven              -

                                     New York, April 29, 1929.

BVE-51623-6  There's The One For Me          Vic 21988, HMV B-3079
BVE-51624-5  This Is Heaven                  -          -

Acc. by O/Bill Wirges.               New York, May 7, 1929.

BVE-51688-3  You're Just Another Memory      Vic 22011, HMV B-3188
BVE-51689-1-2-3  That's You, Baby            Rejected

Acc. by O/Leonard Joy.               New York, June 25, 1929.

BVE-53582-3  Love Is A Dreamer               Vic 22048
BVE-53583-3  When They Sing "The Wearin' Of The  -
             Green" (In Syncopated Blues)

                                     New York, December 30, 1929.

BVE-57966-1-2-3  Shepherd's Serenade         Vic rejected
BVE-57967-1-2-3  That Wonderful Something (Is Love)  -

Acc. by O/Ray Noble.                    Small Queen's Hall, London, Sept. 8, 1930.

Bb-19981-2  Say A Little Prayer For Me        HMV B-3587, Vic 22674
Bb-19982-2  Horatio Nicholls' Gypsy Melody        -

Acc. by O/Leonard Joy.          New York, March 6, 1931.

BVE-67498-1-2  Wabash Moon                    Vic rejected

New York, March 12, 1931.

BVE-68802-1-2  If You Should Ever Need Me        Vic rejected

New York, April 9, 1931.

BVE-67498-3  Wabash Moon                    Vic 22673, HMV B-3893
BVE-68885-1  Mother's Apron Strings            -
BVE-68886-1  The Little Old Church In The Valley  Vic 22674, HMV B-3893

Acc. by unknown vn/p.           New York, October 5, 1931.

BS-70266-1-2  Carolina Moon                 Vic rejected

Acc. by studio orchestra.       New York, January 4, 1932.

11084-   Just Friends                   Mt M-12297, Cq 7932, Imp 2661
11085-   Save The Last Dance For Me        -          -        -

New York, February 15, 1932.

11284-   Auf Wiedersehen, My Dear          Mt M-12319, Cq 7933, Imp 2684
11285-   Snuggled On Your Shoulder (Cuddled In  -          -        -
         Your Arms)

Acc. by the Camel Hour Orchestra.   New York, c. March, 1932.

1200-A  Kiss Me Goodnight                HoW C-4-5
1201-C  Two Loves                        HoW C-2-3

1208-C  Dream Sweetheart/Soft Lights And Sweet  HoW E-1-2, Durium EN-24
        Music
1209-B  My Mom/I'm So Alone With The Crowd  HoW E-2-3

Acc. by studio orchestra.       New York, March 13, 1932.

11679-   Paradise                       Mt M-12353, Bcst 3198
11680-   One Hour With You                 -          -
11681-1-2  When I Was A Boy From The Mountains  Rejected
         (And You Were A Girl From The Hills)

Acc. by O/Will Osborne.         New York, September 20, 1932.

12334-   Say It Isn't So (w/Annette Hanshaw and  Mt M-12485, Cq 8044, Dec F-3272
         Singin' Sam)

Acc. by studio orchestra.       New York, November 26, 1932.

12649-   I May Never Pass Your Way Again   Mt M-12550, Bcst 3289
12650-   Street Of Dreams                 Mt M-12578, Cq 8119
12651-   A Boy And A Girl Were Dancing     Mt M-12550    -       Bcst 3289
12652-   Remember Me                      Mt M-12588, Cq 8155, Bcst 3307
12653-   Strange Interlude                Mt M-12578
12654-   That's An Irish Lullaby          Mt M-12588, Cq 8155

New York, February 7, 1933.

13033-1  Just So You'll Remember          Mt M-12627, Cq 8118, Bcst 3322
13034-1  I Bring A Song                   Mt M-12644, Cq 8117
13035-1  I Wake Up Smiling                Mt M-12627, Cq 8118, Bcst 3322
13036-   Farewell To Arms                 Mt M-12644, Cq 8117, Bcst 3307

New York, March 27, 1933.

| | | |
|---|---|---|
| BP-13181- | I'm In Love Again | ARC Special Record |
| BP-13182- | Remember Me | - |

New York, May 29, 1933.

| | | |
|---|---|---|
| 13403- | Sweetheart Darlin' | Mt M-12710 |
| 13404-1 | Isn't It Heavenly ? | -          Bcst 3341 |
| 13409- | Hold Your Man | Mt M-12734, Cq 8182 |
| 13410-1 | Love Is The Thing | -          Bcst 3352, Rex 8339 |

NOTE:- Matrices 13405/8 inclusive are of dance records made on other dates.

Acc. by O/Harry Bidgood.               London, June-July, 1933.

| | | |
|---|---|---|
| 1361-2 | Stormy Weather | Bcst 3327 |
| 1363-2 | In The Valley Of The Moon | - |
| 1364-2 | I'm P lly With Sally Again | Bcst 3351 |

NOTE:- Matrix 1362 is untraced; it is probably an unissued side by Morton Downey.

Acc. by Charles D. Smart-Wurlitzer organ.
                                       London, August, 1933.

| | | |
|---|---|---|
| 1377-2 | Night And Day | Bcst 3352, Rex 8470 |
| 1378 | A Little Bit Of Heaven | Bcst 3345, Rex 8295, Mt M-12922 |
| 1379 | Oh Promise Me | Bcst 3353 |
| 1380-2 | I Love You Truly | - |
| 1381 | Mother Machree | Bcst 3345, Rex 8295, Mt M-12922 |

NOTE:- Matrices 1378 and 1381 were dubbed for the Melotone issue, and  re-numbered 14784 and 14783 respectively.

Acc. by studio orchestra.               New York, September 12, 1934.

| | | |
|---|---|---|
| 15904- | Two Cigarettes In The Dark | Mt M-13151, Cq 8413, Rex 8307 |
| 15905- | I Saw Stars | -          -          Rex 8339 |
| 15906- | They Didn't Believe Me | Mt M-13197 |
| 15907- | If You Were The Only Girl In The World | - |

New York, January 22, 1935.

| | | |
|---|---|---|
| 16680- | A Little White Gardenia | Mt M-13317, Cq 8512, Rex 8467 |

New York, January 29, 1935.

| | | |
|---|---|---|
| 16772- | Would There Be Love ? | Mt M-13374 |
| 16773- | The Words Are In My Heart | -          Rex 8620 |
| 16774- | I Was Lucky | Mt M-13317, Cq 8512, Rex 8467 |

Acc. by Freddie Martin and his Orchestra.
                                       Chicago, May 2, 1935.

| | | |
|---|---|---|
| C-965- | In The Middle Of A Kiss | Mt M-13437, Rex 8620 |
| C-966- | You're An Angel | - |

Acc. by studio orchestra.               New York, September 5, 1935.

| | | |
|---|---|---|
| 18052- | Cheek To Cheek | ARC 5-11-08, Cq 8608, Rex 8705 |
| 18053- | Accent On Youth | -          - |
| 18054- | You Are My Lucky Star | ARC 5-12-01, Cq 8608, Rex 8675 |
| 18055- | Thanks A Million | -          - |

Acc. by O/Jay Wilbur.                   London, June, 1936.

| | | |
|---|---|---|
| F-1864-2 | The Touch Of Your Lips | Rex 8811 |
| F-1865-2 | Lovely Lady | - |

Acc. by Charles D. Smart-Wurlitzer organ.
                                       London, June, 1936.

| | | |
|---|---|---|
| F-1866 | Rose Of Tralee | Rex 8926, 9648 |
| F-1867-2 | Danny Boy | - |

Acc. by O/Jay Wilbur.                          London, July, 1936.

| F-1886 | Lost | Rex 8823 |
| F-1887 | Please Believe Me | - |

| F-1896 | Macushla | Rex 8870 |
| F-1897 | When Irish Eyes Are Smiling | - |

London, August, 1936.

| F-1927 | A Pretty Girl Is Like A Melody | Rex 8854 | |
| F-1928 | Au Revoir, But Not Goodbye | - | 9648 |
| F-1929 | Until Tomorrow | Rex 8882 | |
| F-1930 | At The Cafe Continental | - | |
| F-1931-2 | The Mountains O' Mourne | Rex 8960 | |
| F-1932 | Maire, My Girl | - | |
| F-1933 | Bonnie Mary Of Argyle | Rex 9049, ARC 6-12-01 | |
| F-1934 | Come Back To Erin | - - | |

NOTE:- Matrices F-1933 and F-1934 were dubbed for all ARC issues and re-numbered 19847 and 19848 respectively.

Acc. by ? Charles D. Smart-Wurlitzer organ.
                                            London, October 4, 1937.

| R-2425-2 | You Needn't Have Kept It A Secret | Rex 9144 |
| R-2426-2 | Goodnight To You All | - |
| R-2427-1 | Because | Rex 9170 |
| R-2428-1 | My Moonlight Madonna | - |

Acc. by studio orchestra.              New York, March 10, 1938.

| 63391-A | Home, Sweet Home | Dec 1955, Rex 9379 |
| 63392-A | Love's Old Sweet Song | - - |
| 63397-A | When Day Is Done | Dec 1738, Rex 9313 |
| 63398-A | A Perfect Day | - - |

NOTE:- Matrices 63393/6 inclusive are not by Morton Downey.

## MARIE DRESSLER

B. 1869; r.n. Leila Kerber.  Joined the first of a succession of light operatic companies, toured with these; New York stage debut in THE ROBBER OF THE RHINE(May 28, 1892, 5th Avenue Theatre), but this flopped; she went on to vaudeville success,and joined Lillian Russell's company as Flo Honeydew in THE LADY SLAVEY (Casino, February 3, 1896); appeared in vaudeville again in 1905, in London very successfully in 1907; another big hit as Tillie Blobbs in TILLIE'S NIGHTMARE (Herald Sq.,August 11, 1910), in which she sang HEAVEN WILL PROTECT THE WORKING GIRL.  This led to a film debut (TILLIE'S PUNCTURED ROMANCE, 1914, with Charles Chaplin, for Mack Sennett); many other great silent films, and such outstanding talkies as ANNA CHRISTIE (with Greta Garbo, 1930); MIN AND BILL (1931); EMMA and TUGBOAT ANNIE (1932), and DINNER AT EIGHT (with Jean Harlow, 1933).  D. July 28, 1934. Her only commercial recordings are the following cylinders, issued in the months shown after the numbers, and in excerpts from ANNA CHRISTIE (MGM C-975) and DINNER AT EIGHT (Regal Zonophone MR-1234).

Vocal, acc. by studio orchestra.              New York, 1909-1910.

| Rastus, Take Me Back | Ed 4M-401, Amb 2001 (Dec. 1909), AR 2290, IRCC 5017 |
| I'm A-Goin' To Change My Man | Ed 10318 (March, 1910) |
| He's My Soft-Shelled Crab On Toast | Ed 4M-499 (May, 1910) |
| I'm Looking For An Angel (Without Wings) | Ed 10377 (June, 1910) |
| Marie Dressler's Working Girl Song ("Tillie's Nightmare") | Ed 10416 (September, 1910) |

## THE DUNCAN SISTERS

Rosetta and Vivian Duncan were born in Los Angeles, Calif., and worked as stage partners from their debut as members of Gus Edwards' THE KIDDIES' REVUE until Rosetta was killed in a car smash in 1959.  Appeared in New York at the 5th Avenue Theatre in 1917, but scored permanent success after appearing in DOING OUR BIT at the Win-

ter Garden (October 18, 1917); two further successes at the Globe (SHE'S A GOOD
FELLOW, May 5, 1919, and TIP-TOP, October 5, 1920) before similar acclaim in London in PINS AND NEEDLES at the Gaiety (June 1, 1921); played many cabaret, revue
and vaudeville shows in London during 1922; returned to U.S.A., wrote music and
lyrics for TOPSY AND EVA (Sam. H. Harris Theatre, December 23, 1924); reappeared
in London in CLOWNS IN CLOVER (Adelphi, December 1, 1927) and TOPSY AND EVA (Gaiety, October 4, 1928; during the run of this, Rosetta was taken ill and her place
was taken by the Lancashire comedienne, Gracie Fields); the sisters resumed their
engagements in London variety theatres after Rosetta's recovery, returned to the
U.S.A., and continued to tour successfully in new productions of TOPSY AND EVA. A
tour of English music-halls took place in 1937-1938.

Vocal, acc. by O/George W. Byng or Vivian Duncan-ukulele as shown.
                                    Hayes, Middlesex, October 20, 1922.

| | | |
|---|---|---|
| Cc-1994- | The Bull Frog Patrol | HMV C-1093 |
| Cc-1995- | The Music Lesson (Do-Re-Mi) | - |
| Bb-1996-2 | Oh, Sing-a-Loo | HMV B-1419 |
| Bb-1997-2 | The Argentines, The Portuguese And Greeks - uVD | - |

Acc. by Phil Ohman-p, or Vivian Duncan-ukulele where shown.
                                    New York, March 14, 1923.

| | | |
|---|---|---|
| B-27655-2 | The Music Lesson (Do-Re-Mi) | Vic 19050 |
| B-27656-2 | Baby Sister Blues | - |

                                    New York, March 16, 1923.

| | | |
|---|---|---|
| B-27659-1-2-3-4-5 | Stick In The Mud | Vic rejected |

                                    New York, March 19, 1923.

| | | |
|---|---|---|
| B-27660-4 | The Argentines, The Portuguese And Greeks - uVD | Vic 19113 |
| B-27661-2 | Stick In The Mud | - |

Acc. by Phil Ohman or Edna Fischer, with Vivian Duncan-ukulele where shown.
                                    New York, November 19, 1923.

| | | |
|---|---|---|
| B-28966-1-2-3-4 | Um-Um-Da-Da - pPO | Rejected |
| B-28967-1 | Rememb'ring ("Topsy And Eva") - pPO | Vic 19206 |
| B-28970-3 | I Never Had A Mammy ("Topsy And Eva") - pEF/uVD | - |

                                    New York, November 20, 1923.

| | | |
|---|---|---|
| B-28972-1-2-3-4 | Aunt Susie's Picnic Day - pEF/ uVD | Vic rejected |

NOTE: Matrices B-28968/9 are by Lou Holtz, q.v., on the same day; B-28971 is by a
dance band.

Acc. by Edna Fischer-p.              Chicago, April 4, 1924.

| | | |
|---|---|---|
| B-28966-7 | Um-Um-Da-Da | Vic 19311 |
| B-28972-5 | Aunt Susie's Picnic Day | - |
| B-29834-1 | The Bull Frog Patrol | Vic 19352 |
| B-29835-1 | Vocalizing | Rejected |
| B-29836-1 | Tom Boy Blues | Vic 19352 |

Acc. by Florence Sanger-p.          Chicago, November 10, 1924.

| | | |
|---|---|---|
| C-29835-2 | Vocalizing | Vic 35751 |
| C-31157-3 | Sweet Onion Time | - |
| B-31158-1 | Mean Cicero Blues | Rejected |

                                    Chicago, November 14, 1924.

| | | |
|---|---|---|
| B-31158-4 | Mean Cicero Blues | Vic 19527 |
| B-31179-2 | Cross Word Puzzle Blues | - |

    Acc. by Mr. and Mrs. Charles Kisco-p.  New York, January 15, 1926.

BVE-33667-1-2-3-**4** The Kinky Kids' Parade     Vic rejected
BVE-33668-1-2-3-4-5 Happy-Go-Lucky Days           -

    Acc. by Mr. and Mrs. Charles Kisco-p, studio orchestra or Vivian Duncan-p.
                                         New York, January 19, 1926.

BVE-33668-6-7-8 Happy-Go-Lucky Days - 2pCK     Vic rejected

                                         New York, February 16, 1926.

BVE-33667-5  The Kinky Kids' Parade - pCK     Vic 19987, HMV B-2309
BVE-33668-10 Happy-Go-Lucky Days - pCK         -              -
BVE-34701-1-2-3-4-5  Some Day Soon - O         Rejected
BVE-34702-4  Lickens - pVD                     Vic 21226

    Acc. by Mr. and Mrs. Charles Kisco-p, with Vivian Duncan-ukulele where shown.
                                         New York, September 12, 1927.

BVE-40200-1-2  Dawning - 2pCK                  Vic rejected

                                         New York, September 13, 1927.

BVE-40201-1-2  Oh ! How I Love My Boatman - 2pCK  Rejected
BVE-40204-   Black And Blue Blues - pCK/uVD    Vic 21226

    The Duncan Sisters-2g added.          New York, September 16, 1927.

BVE-40200-   Dawning - 2p/2g                   Vic 20963
BVE-40213-   Baby Feet Go Pitter-Patter ('Cross  -
               My Floor) - 2p/2g
BVE-40214-1-2-3  Someday You'll Say "O.K."     Rejected
BVE-40215-1-2-3  Yep ! 'Long About June         -

    The next session is entered in the recording books as by "Four girls with  piano."
    It is not known if the Duncan Sisters were accompanied by two girl pianists.
                                  Small Queen's Hall, London, Dec. 13, 1927.

Bb-12127-1-2  At Sundown                       HMV rejected
Bb-12128-1  Breezin' Along With The Breeze      -

    Acc. by the Gilt-Edged Four.         London, November 13, 1928.

WA-8097-1  The Bull Frog Patrol                Col 5182
WA-8098-1  The Prune Song                       -

    Acc. by O/Carroll Gibbons.      Small Queen's Hall, London, Dec. 7, 1928.

Bb-15424-2  The Music Lesson (Do-Re-Mi)        HMV B-2715
Bb-15425-4  The Argentines, The Portuguese And  -
              Greek (sic)

    Acc. by unknown p/g, possibly their own.
                                         London, December 31, 1928.

·WA-8274-1-2-3  Just Give The Southland To Me     Col rejected

                                         London, January 1, 1929.

WA-8274-4  Just Give The Southland To Me       Col 5237
WA-8282-1  Hula-Hula Lullaby                     -

    Acc. by O/Leroy Shield.          Chicago, December 13, 1929.

BVE-57260-1-2-3  I'm Following You             Vic rejected
BVE-57261-1-2-3  House Hop                       -

Acc. by O/Leonard Joy.                    New York, January 2, 1930.

BVE-57970-1-2-3-4  Some Day Soon                    Vic rejected

                                         New York, January 3, 1930.

BVE-57279-2  I Got A "Code" In My "Doze" (RD only)  Vic 22345
BVE-57972-3  It's An Old Spanish Custom                    -

                                         New York, January 4, 1930.

BVE-57975-4  Hoosier Hop                         Vic 22269
BVE-57976-3  I'm Following You                        -       LPV-538, LSA-3074,
                                              RD-7869

Acc. unknown.                          New York, October 26, 1931.

151949-  Dusty Roads                         Col 15745-D

Acc. by 2p.                            London, May 6, 1938.

CE-9134-1  Loch Lomond In Swing Time             Par F-1191
CE-9135-1  Adam And Eve                         Par F-1156

                                         London, June 9, 1938.

CE-9209-1  Ti-Pi-Tin                            Par F-1156

                                         London, June 24, 1938.

CE-9218-1  Daniel In The Lion's Den             Par F-1215
CE-9219-1  Sweet Onion Time In Bermuda               -
CE-9220-1  In A Little Dutch Kindergarten       Par F-1191

The Duncan Sisters also recorded some sides semi-privately in San Francisco in 1947,
and Rosetta Duncan told Jim Walsh she recalled their making a side for Columbia in
1919, which was never issued.

## TODD   DUNCAN

B. Danville, Ky., February 12, 1900.  Originally an elocution teacher at Howard Uni-
versity, Washington, D.C., then musical instructor at Municipal College for Negroes
in Louisville, Ky.; stage debut in New York in 1934 in Mascagni's opera CAVALLERIA
RUSTICANA; great success as Porgy in PORGY AND BESS at the Alvin Theatre, New York
(October 10, 1935) and in many revivals of this work; London debut at Drury Lane,
June 9, 1938 in THE SUN NEVER SETS; returned to New York, appeared in CABIN IN THE
SKY (Martin Beck Theatre, October 25, 1940); later sang in opera with the New York
City Opera Company; film debut in re-make of SYNCOPATION (1942).

Vocal, acc. by Drury Lane Theatre Orchestra/Charles Prentice.
                              London, July 4, 1938.

CA-17023-2  Drums ("The Sun Never Sets")          Col DB-1778, 399-M
CA-17024-1  River God ("The Sun Never Sets")           -         -

Acc. by O/Alexander Smallens, with the Eva Jessye Choir.
                              New York, May 15, 1940.

67737-  Buzzard Song ("Porgy And Bess")          Dec 29068, Br 0153, LAT-8021
67739-  Porgy's Lament and Finale ("Porgy And    Dec 29070, Br 0155    -
        Bess")
67741-  It Ain't Necessarily So ("Porgy And Bess")Dec 29069, Br 0154, 05045 -
67742-  Bess, You Is My Woman Now (w/Anne Brown)       -         -      05046 -
        ("Porgy And Bess")
67744-  I Got Plenty O' Nuttin' ("Porgy And Bess")Dec 29068, Br 0153    -    -
NOTE:- Matrices 67738, 67740 amd 67743 are not by Todd Duncan.

New York, May 18, 1942.

70753-   What You Want Wid Bess ? (w/Anne Brown) Dec 23250, Br LAT-8021
         ("Porgy And Bess")
70754-   I Love You, Porgy (w/Anne Brown) ("Porgy      -           -
         And Bess")

Todd Duncan also recorded some of the above PORGY AND BESS songs, and other numbers
for Musicraft in New York in 1946.

## JAMES DUNN

B. New York, November 2, 1905; first was a stockbroker with his father, but decided
he preferred the stage, and eventually, films. Very popular in the 1930s, in such
movies as BAD GIRL (1931) and STAND UP AND CHEER (1934), but greatest success was
in his come-back A TREE GROWS IN BROOKLYN (1944).  D. 1967.

Speech.                              New York, February 16, 1932.

B-11293-   Talk (no other details known)      Br Private Recording

## IRENE  DUNNE

B. Louisville, Ky., July 14, 1904; trained for a musical career, and graduated from
the Chicago College of Music in 1926.  She appeared in several musical comedies -
and opera at the Metropolitan in New York - before embarking on a film career, as
a dramatic actress as well as a singing one.  Her film debut was in PRESENT  ARMS
(1930); then came CIMARRON and CONSOLATION MARRIAGE (1931); BACK STREET (1932); NO
OTHER WOMAN, BEHOLD WE LIVE, STINGAREE, THIS MAN IS MINE, AGE OF  INNOCENCE  and
ROBERTA (1933-1934); SWEET ADELINE and MAGNIFICENT OBSESSION (1935); SHOW   BOAT
and THEODORA GOES WILD (the latter gained her her first Oscar) (1936); THE   AWFUL
TRUTH and HIGH, WIDE AND HANDSOME (1937); LOVE AFFAIR (1939);  MY  FAVORITE  WIFE
(1940); PENNY SERENADE (1941); A GUY NAMED JOE (1943); THE WHITE CLIFFS OF  DOVER
(1944); ANNA AND THE KING OF SIAM (1946); LIFE WITH FATHER (1947);   I   REMEMBER
MAMA (1948); NEVER A DULL MOMENT (1950); THE MUDLARK (made in England in 1951, in
which she plated Queen Victoria); IT GROWS ON TREES (1952).  She was an Alternate
Delegate at the United Nations General Assembly in 1957; m. Dr. Griffin in  1928;
widowed 1965.

Vocal, acc. by O/Nat Shilkret.       New York, April 4, 1935.

B-17247-2  When I Grow Too Old To Dream      Br 7420, 02048, Col DB-1805
B-17248-2  Lovely To Look At (Film "Roberta")    -       -       - Epic SN-6059

    Acc. by studio orchestra.        Los Angeles, July 16, 1941.

DLA-2552-A  I've Told Ev'ry Little Star        Dec 18201, 40016, Br 03340
DLA-2553-A  Smoke Gets In Your Eyes (Film "Roberta") -        -           -
DLA-2554-A  All The Things You Are             Rejected

                                     Los Angeles, July 31, 1941.

DLA-2605-   Why Was I Born ? (Film "Roberta")   Dec 18202, 40017

                                     Los Angeles, August 4, 1941.

DLA-2626-   Babes In The Wood                   Dec 18203, 40018

                                     Los Angeles, August 24, 1941.

DLA-2679-   They Didn't Believe Me              Dec 18203, 40018
DLA-2680-   All The Things You Are              Dec 18202, 40017

## FRED  DUPREZ

B. Detroit, Mich., September 6, 1884; American vaudeville comedian  who achieved an
even greater measure of success in London from his appearances in SMILE (Garrick,
October 6, 1917); SOLDIER BOY (Apollo, June 26, 1918); THE MUSIC BOX REVUE  (Palace, May 15, 1923) and THE COCOANUTS (Garrick, March 20, 1928).  D. at sea on the
voyage to England, October 29, 1938.

Vocal and/or speech, mostly acc. by studio orchestra.  (The dates in brackets  after
the numbers of cylinder records are those of issue).

New York, c. October, 1908-April, 1909.

| | |
|---|---|
| A Vaudeville Rehearsal | Ind 930 (December, 1908) |
| Father Is A Judge | Ind 970 (January, 1909) |
| Feed The Kitty | Ind 993 (February, 1909) |
| I Looked Just Once | Ind 1008 (March, 1909) |
| Make A Noise Like A Hoop And Roll Away | Ind 1027 (April, 1909) |
| Blitz And Blatz (w/Steve Porter) | Ind 1068 (May, 1909) |
| A Little Bit Is A Whole Lot Better Than Nothing At All | Ind 1078 (June, 1909) |

New York, c. May, 1909.

3988-1  A Vaudeville Rehearsal                Col A-633

3995-1  Make A Noise Like A Hoop And Roll Away  Col A-643

New York, c. June-September, 1909.

| | |
|---|---|
| My Girl | Ind 1125 (August, 1909) |
| Blitz And Blatz At The Ball Game (w/ Bob Roberts) | Ind 1137 (August, 1909) |
| Please Don't Tell My Wife | Ind 1148 (September, 1909) |
| Blitz And Blatz At The Sea Shore (w/ Bob Roberts) | Ind 1160 (September, 1909) |
| Blitz And Blatz's Discussion (w/Bob Roberts) | Ind 1183 (October, 1909) |
| That Wasn't All | Ind 1204 (November, 1909) |
| The Actor And The Rube (w/Byron G. Harlan) | Ind 1207 (November, 1909) |

New York, c. September, 1909.

4132-   How Did The Bird Know That ?            Col A-726

New York, c. October-December, 1909.

| | |
|---|---|
| It Sounds Good To Me | Ind 1252 (January, 1910) |
| Keep Your Foot On The Soft Pedal | Ind 1296 (March, 1910) |

New York, c. November, 1909.

4190-2  Blitz And Blatz In An Aeroplane (w/Bob  Col A-758
        Roberts)

New York, c. March 26, 1910.

4390-2  I'm On My Way To Reno                   Col A-824

        When You Marry A Girl For Looks         Col A-844

New York, c. April-July, 1910.

| | |
|---|---|
| I'm On My Way To Reno | Ind 1368 (July, 1910) |
| Who Do You Suppose Went And Married My Sister ? - Thomaschefsky | Ind 1384 (August, 1910) |
| What's The Matter With Father ? | Ind 1400 (September, 1910) |
| When You Marry A Girl For Looks | Ind 1415 (October, 1910) |
| Give My Regards To Mabel | Ind 3092 (July, 1910) |
| Blitz And Blatz Among The Indians (w/ Bob Roberts) | Ind 3104 (August, 1910) |

New York, c. March, 1911.

| | |
|---|---|
| They're All Good American Names | USE 372 (2-min.) (June, 1911) |
| I Love My Wife | USE 387 (2-min.) (July, 1911) |
| You'll Do The Same Thing Over Again | USE 1271 (4-min.) (June, 1911) |

<u>FRED DUPREZ</u>  (cont.)

New York, c. April, 1911.

| | |
|---|---|
| I Love My Wife | Ind 1492 (July, 1911) |
| When Willie Took A Fancy To Miss Nancy | Ind 1499 (August, 1911) |
| First You Get The Money | Ind 1509 (September, 1911) |

New York, August 24, 1911.

19544-   The 11.69 Express                     Col A-1085, 1983, Re G-6547

New York, May 10, 1912.

19881-   Desperate Desmond - A Melodrama        Col A-1193, 2023, Climax X-712,
                                                Thomas 34190

New York, January 24, 1914.

39197-   Happy Tho' Married                     Col A-1516

New York, c. April, 1915.

3715    Happy Tho' Married                      Ed 50254, Amb 2373

3720    Desperate Desmond - Drama (Rehearsing   Ed 50254, Amb 2636
        The Orchestra)

New York, c. 1915.

You'll Do The Same Thing Over Again       Empire 1049

Acc. by the Garrick Theatre Orchestra.
                                London, October, 1917.

69066   Economise ("Smile")                    Col D-1383
69069   Telephone Scene (w/Maidie Hope)("Smile")Col D-1387
69070   Savoy Scene (w/Maidie Hope and Louis      -
        Sydney) ("Smile")

Acc. by studio O/A. W. Ketelbey.      London, c. February, 1918.

69193   Say No ! That's All                    Col 2962
69194   Wooden Clothes                           -

Acc. by the Apollo Theatre Orchestra.
                                London, c. July, 1918.

76230   Alone In A City Full Of Girls ("Soldier Col L-1263
        Boy")
76231   The Battle Front At Home ("Soldier Boy")  -

Humorous dialogue, unacc.             London, c. October, 1918.

76274   Soldier Boy (w/Maisie Gay)("Soldier     Col L-1267
        Boy")
76275   Just Chatter (w/Maisie Gay)            Col 758

London, January, 1919.

76340   Henry Comes Home Late (w/Maidie Hope)   Col 758

London, c. December, 1919.

69640   Cohen And The Company Promoter (w/Joe   Re G-7735
        Hayman)
69641   Cohen, Insurance Agent (w/Joe Hayman)     -

London, c. 1922

R-289   Do Married Men Make The Best Husbands ? World 501

Acc. by studio orchestra/? Albert W. Ketelbey.
                                    London, c. March, 1923.

73272   I Don't Want My Cigar To Go Out        Col 3282
73273   An Awfully Nice Fellow To Speak To        -


                                    London, March, 1924.

A-664   Be Satisfied                            Col 3428
A-665   Here Comes The Groom                      -

  Acc. by Madame Adami-p.         Hayes, Middlesex, October 29, 1925.

Bb-7117-1  Efficiency In Courtship              HMV rejected
Bb-7118-1  Say No ! That's All                    -


## JIMMY  DURANTE

B. New York, February 10, 1893; originally a photographic engraver, but his ability
  as a ragtime pianist secured him a position in the New Orleans Jazz Band, playing
  at the Alamo Cafe on 125th Street; he became its leader, and recorded under  this
  and his own name for Gennett and OKeh (see JAZZ RECORDS, 1897-1942), and with Sam
  Lanin's recording group Bailey's Lucky Seven (q.v. also). His sense of   showmanship and comedy led him to team up with Lou Clayton and Eddie Jackson, and    they
  first appeared in vaudeville in October, 1927 in Loew's State Theatre.  The  trio
  appeared in SHOW GIRL (Ziegfeld, July 2, 1929); Jimmy Durante (nicknamed "Schnozzle" from the size of his nose) appeared solo in THE NEW YORKERS (Broadway,Decem-
  ber 8, 1930); STRIKE ME PINK (Majestic, March 4, 1933); JUMBO (Hippodrome, November 16, 1935); RED, HOT AND BLUE (Alvin, October 29, 1936); STARS IN YOUR    EYES
  (Majestic, February 9, 1939) and others subsequently; film debut 1929, made  many
  pictures without enormous impact other than by his individual songs in such films
  as PALOOKA, STRICTLY DYNAMITE and THE GREAT SCHNOZZLE; registered better in 1940s
  in such as YOU'RE IN THE ARMY NOW and THE MAN WHO CAME TO DINNER (1941);THIS TIME
  FOR KEEPS (1946); ON AN ISLAND WITH YOU (1947) and a film version of JUMBO (1962)
  amongst others; also made many Decca and MGM records from 1944 onwards.

Vocal, acc. by studio orchestra.          New York, May 9, 1929.

148495-2  Can Broadway Do Without Me ? (w/Lou     Col 1860-D, DB-153, Har HS-11353
            Clayton and Eddie Jackson)
148496-2  So I Ups To Him (w/Lou Clayton and         -              -
            Eddie Jackson)


                                    Los Angeles, February 13, 1934.

LA-105-A  Inka Dinka Doo (Films "Palooka" and     Br 6774, 01754, Har HS-11353,
            "The Great Schnozzle")                 Col DB-1806
LA-106-A  Hot Patatta (Film "Strictly Dynamite")  Br 6774, 01754, Col DB-1806


## DEANNA  DURBIN

B. Winnipeg, Canada, December 4, 1922; r.n. Edna Mae Durbin.  Learned to sing while
  little more than a toddler; as a juvenile, appeared on Eddie Cantor's weekly radio
  shows, then was signed for THREE SMART GIRLS (1936) and success followed success:
  100 MEN AND A GIRL (1937); MAD ABOUT MUSIC, THAT CERTAIN AGE, THREE SMART   GIRLS
  GROW UP (all 1938); FIRST LOVE and IT'S A DATE (1939); SPRING PARADE,  NICE  GIRL
  (1940); many others until maturity destroyed the image of "the spirit and person-
  ification of youth" which she brought to the screen and for which she received  a
  Special Academy Award in 1938.  She married a Frenchman and lives in secluded retirement in Normandy.

Vocal, acc. by studio orchestra.          New York, December 12, 1936.

61475-A  Someone To Care For Me (Film "Three       Dec rejected
           Smart Girls")
61476-A  Il Bacio (In Italian)                       -

New York, December 15, 1936.

61481-A  Il Bacio (in Italian)                    Dec 1097, Br 02370, AH 147
61482-A  Someone To Care For Me (Film "Three        -          -          -
         Smart Girls")

Acc. by O/Charles Previn.            Los Angeles, September 23, 1937.

DLA-963-A  Libiamo ne' lieti calici (Brindisi -  Dec 1471, Br 02486, AH 93,
           "La Traviata") (Film "100 Men And A Girl") (in Italian)  Coral CP-64
DLA-964-A  It's Raining Sunbeams (Film "100 Men  Dec 1471, Br 02486, AH 60,
           And A Girl")                           Coral CP-43

Los Angeles, December 12, 1938.

DLA-1695-B  Les Filles de Cadix (Delibes) (Film  Dec 2274, DL-8785, Br 02705,
            "That Certain Age") (in French)       AH 93, Coral CP-23
DLA-1696-A  My Own (Film "That Certain Age")      Dec 2274, Br 02705, AH 93,
                                                  Coral CP-64

Los Angeles, April 5, 1939.

DLA-1755-A  Alleluja (Mozart) (Film "100 Men And  Dec 3061, Br 02975, AH 147
            A Girl")
DLA-1756-A  Ave Maria (Bach-Gounod) (Film "Mad         -     Br 02804       -
            About Music")

Los Angeles, July 7, 1939.

DLA-1810-   Because (Film "Three Smart Girls      Dec 2757, DL-8785, Br 02803,
            Grow Up")                             Coral CP-23
DLA-1811-   The Last Rose Of Summer (Film "Three  Dec 2758, Br 02803, Coral CP-43
            Smart Girls Grow Up")
DLA-1812-A  Home, Sweet Home (Film "First Love")       -     Br 02804       -
            (acc. by piano and harp only)

Los Angeles, July 21, 1939.

DLA-1828-   One Fine Day ("Madama Butterfly")-    Dec 15044, Br 0147, AH 93,
            (Film "First Love")                   Coral CP-64
DLA-1829-   Spring In My Heart (Film "First       Dec 15044, Br 0147, AH 60,
            Love")                                Coral CP-43

Los Angeles, February 28, 1940.

DLA-1960-A  Musetta's Waltz Song ("La Boheme")    Dec 3062, DL-8785, Br 03097,
            (Film "It's A Date")                  Coral CP-23
DLA-1961-A  Ave Maria (Schubert) (Film "It's A    Dec 3061, Br 02975, AH 47
            Date")
DLA-1962-A  Amapola (Film "First Love")           Dec 3063, DL-8785, Br 03007,
                                                  Coral CP-23
DLA-1963-A  Loch Lomond (Film "It's A Date")      Dec 3062, Br 03097, AH 147
DLA-1964-A  Love Is All (Film "It's A Date")      Dec 3063, Br 03007, AH 93,
                                                  Coral CP-64

Los Angeles, August 29, 1940.

DLA-2092-A  Blue Danube Dream (Film "Spring       Dec DL-8785, Coral CP-23
            Parade")
DLA-2093-A  Waltzing In The Clouds (Film "Spring  Dec 3414, Br 03125, AH 60,
            Parade")                              Coral CP-43
DLA-2094-A  It's Foolish, But It's Fun (Film      Dec 3653, Br 03163, AH 147
            "Spring Parade")
DLA-2095-A  When April Sings (Film "Spring        Dec 3414, DL-8785, Br 03125,
            Parade")                              Coral CP-23

Los Angeles, January 22, 1941.

| | | |
|---|---|---|
| DLA-2370-A | Beneath The Lights Of Home (Film "Nice Girl ?") | Dec 3653, Br 03201, AH 60, Coral CP-43 |
| DLA-2371-A | Thank You, America (Film "Nice Girl?") | Dec 3655, Br 03201, AH 147 |
| DLA-2372-A | The Old Folks At Home (Swanee River) (Film "Nice Girl ?") |    -     Br 03163, AH 93, Coral CP-64 |
| DLA-2373- | Perhaps (Film "Nice Girl ?") | Dec 3654, Br 03186, AH 93, Coral CP-64 |
| DLA-2374- | Love At Last (Film "Nice Girl ?") | Dec 3654, Br 03186, AH 147 |

Los Angeles, September 29, 1941.

| | | |
|---|---|---|
| DLA-2782- | Adeste, Fideles (O Come, All Ye Faithful) | Dec 18198, 23657, Br 03928 |
| DLA-2783- | Silent Night, Holy Night |   -     -     - |

Los Angeles, October 3, 1941.

| | | |
|---|---|---|
| DLA-2784- | Annie Laurie | Dec 18297, Br 03795, AH 147 |
| DLA-2785- | Kiss Me Again | Dec 18199, 23867, DL-8785, Br 03267, Coral CP-23 |

Acc. by O/Victor Young.                 Los Angeles, October 9, 1941.

| | | |
|---|---|---|
| DLA-2789- | My Hero | Dec 18199, 23867, Br 03267, AH 93, Coral CP-64 |
| DLA-2790- | Poor Butterfly | Dec 18297, DL-8785, Br 03795, Coral CP-23 |
| DLA-2794-A | La Estrellita (My Little Star) (in Spanish) | Dec 18216, DL-8785, Br 03375, Coral CP-23 |
| DLA-2795-A | Cielito Lindo (Beautiful Heaven) (in Spanish) | Dec 18216, Br 03375, AH 93, Coral CP-64 |

NOTE:- Matrices DLA-2791/3 inclusive are not by Deanna Durbin.

Acc. by O/Max Terr.                     Los Angeles, February 2, 1942.

| | | |
|---|---|---|
| DLA-2877-A | God Bless America | Dec 18575, Br 03500, AH 93, Coral CP-64 |
| DLA-2878- | The Star-Spangled Banner | Br 04212, AH 147 |

Los Angeles, February 4, 1942.

| | | |
|---|---|---|
| DLA-2883-A | Love's Old Sweet Song | Dec 18261, Br 03334, AH 60, Coral CP-43 |
| DLA-2884-A | When The Roses Bloom Again | Dec 18261, Br 03334, AH 93, Coral CP-64 |

## NELSON EDDY

B. Providence, R.I., June 29, 1901; studied singing under David Bispham, but career began as commercial artist and journalist; stage debut 1922; sang with the Philadelphia Civic Opera Company in New York in 1924 (I PAGLIACCI); extended repertoire to Gilbert and Sullivan and other light operas and operettas; first film BROADWAY TO HOLLYWOOD, 1933; then followed the famous series with Jeanette Macdonald as his leading lady (NAUGHTY MARIETTA and ROSE MARIE, 1935; BLOSSOM TIME and MAYTIME,1936 (later he sang and filmed with Risë Stevens). He was also the voices of the Singing Whale in Walt Disney's cartoon film MAKE MINE MUSIC (1946). D. 1967.

Vocal, acc. by O/Nat Shilkret.          New York, March 11, 1935.

| | | |
|---|---|---|
| BS-89303-1 | Tramp, Tramp, Tramp Along The Highway (Film "Naughty Marietta") | Vic 4280, LPV-526, HMV DA-1418 |
| BS-89304-1 | Ah ! Sweet Mystery Of Life (w/chorus) (Film "Naughty Marietta") | Vic 4281   -   HMV DA-1419 |
| BS-89305-1 | I'm Falling In Love With Someone (Film "Naughty Marietta") | Vic 4280   -   HMV DA-1418 |
| BS-89306-1 | 'Neath The Southern Moon (Film "Naughty Marietta") | Vic 4281   -   HMV DA-1419 |

Hollywood, June 12, 1935.

| | | |
|---|---|---|
| PBS-90262- | Auf Wiedersehen | Vic 4284, HMV DA-1435 |
| PBS-90263- | Love's Old Sweet Song | - |
| PBS-90264- | When I Grow Too Old To Dream | Vic 4285, HMV DA-1435 |
| PBS-90265- | You Are Free | - |

Hollywood, December 31, 1935.

PBS-97206-   Dusty Road                              Vic 4313, HMV DA-1502
PBS-97207-   The Mounties (w/chorus) (Film "Rose   Vic 4305, LPV-526, HMV DA-1464
             Marie")
PBS-97208-   Rose Marie (w/chorus) (Film "Rose Marie") -          -          -
PBS-97210-   Through The Years                       Vic 4313, HMV DA-1502

Hollywood, September 19, 1936.

PBS-97847-   Indian Love Call (w/Jeanette Mac-     Vic 4323, LPV-526, HMV DA-1537
             donald) (Film "Rose Marie")
PBS-97848-   Ah ! Sweet Mystery Of Life (w/                  -                -
             Jeanette Macdonald) (Film "Naughty Marietta")

Hollywood, September 21, 1936.

PBS-97855-   Farewell To Dreams (w/Jeanette Mac-   Vic 4329, LPV-526, HMV DA-1559
             donald) (Film "Maytime")
PBS-97856-   Will You Remember ? (w/Jeanette Mac-            -          -          -
             donald) (Film "Maytime")
PBS-97857-1-2  Song Of Love (w/Jeanette Macdonald) Rejected
             (Film "Blossom Time")

  Acc. unknown.                              Hollywood, May 28, 1937.

  PBS-1439-1  I Love You Truly                   Vic test
  PBS-1440-1  At Dawning                         -

  Acc. by unknown p.                         Hollywood, June 22, 1937.

PBS-09527-1-2-3  By The Waters Of Minnetonka     Vic rejected
PBS-09528-1-2  Captain Stratton's Fancy          -

  Acc. by O/Nat Shilkret.                    Hollywood, June 24, 1937.

PBS-09529-   The Rosary                              Vic 4370, HMV DA-1589
PBS-09530-   Smilin' Through                         Vic 4367, HMV DA-1579
PBS-09531-   Oh Promise Me                           Vic 4370, HMV DA-1600

Hollywood, June 29, 1937.

PBS-09558-   A Dream                                 Vic 4367, HMV DA-1703
PBS-09559-   At Dawning                              Vic 4369, HMV DA-1585
PBS-09560-2  Trees                                   Vic 4366, HMV DA-1579
PBS-09561-   Thy Beaming Eyes                        Vic 4368, HMV DA-1601
PBS-09562-   Deep River                              Vic 4371, HMV DA-1585
PBS-09563-   A Perfect Day                           Vic 4369, HMV DA-1589
PBS-09564-   The Hills Of Home                       Vic 4371, HMV DA-1600
PBS-09565-   Sylvia                                  Vic 4368, HMV DA-1601

  Acc. by Theodore Paxson-p.                 Hollywood, July 2, 1937.

PBS-09566-   By The Waters Of Minnetonka             Vic 4366, HMV DA-1579, DA-1703
PBS-09567-1  He Was Alone                            Rejected

  Acc. by O/Leonard Joy.                     New York, March 22, 1938.

BS-021613-   Sun Up To Sundown (w/male quartet)    Vic 4388, HMV DA-1632
             (Film "The Girl Of The Golden West")
BS-021614-   Soldiers Of Fortune (w/male quartet)  Vic 4389, HMV DA-1633
             (Film "The Girl Of The Golden West")
  (continued on page 239)

New York, March 22, 1938 (cont.)

BS-021615-   Who Are We To Say ? (Film "The Girl   Vic 4388, HMV DA-1633
             Of The Golden West")
BS-021616-   Señorita (Film "The Girl Of The      Vic 4389, LPV-526, HMV DA-1632
             Golden West")

   Acc. by O/Nat Finston.              New York, August 22, 1939.

WCO-26009-A  Less Than The Dust ("Four Indian     Col 17161-D, LB-57
             Love Lyrics")
WCO-26010-A  Temple Bells ("Four Indian Love Lyrics") -              -
WCO-26011-A  'Till I Wake ("Four Indian Love      Col 17162-D, LB-58
             Lyrics")
WCO-26012-A  Kashmiri Song ("Four Indian Love Lyrics")-            -

                                       Los Angeles, August 31, 1939.

LA-1979-A   None But The Lonely Heart(Tchaikovsky) Col 17171-D, LB-59
LA-1980-A   Pilgrim's Song (Tchaikovsky)              -           -

                                       New York, September 27, 1939.

WCO-26116-A  Ride, Cossack, Ride (Film            Col 17172-D, DB-1911
             "Balalaika")
WCO-26117-A  Song Of The Volga Boatmen (Film
             "Balalaika")                              -          DB-1912

                                       New York, October 9, 1939.

WCO-

WCO-26144-A  At The Balalaika  (Film "Balalaika") Col 17173-D, DB-1912

                                       New York, October 19, 1939.

WCO-26188-A  The Magic Of Your Love (Film         Col 17173-D, DB-1911
             "Balalaika")

                                       New York, August 21, 1940.

WCO-28030-C  Stout-Hearted Men (w/male chorus)    Col 4241-M, DB-1977
             (Film "The New Moon")
WCO-28031-A  Softly, As In A Morning Sunrise      Col 4240-M, DB-1976
             (Film "The New Moon")
WCO-28032-A  Wanting You (Film "The New Moon")    Col 4241-M, DB-1977
WCO-28033-B  Lover, Come Back To Me (Film "The New Col 4240-M, DB-1976
             Moon")

   Acc. by O/Robert Armbruster.        New York, August 27, 1940.

WCO-28054-A  The Star-Spangled Banner             Col 17217-D, DB-2092
WCO-28055-A  America (My Country, 'Tis Of Thee)        -          -
WXCO-28056-A Chanson du Toreador (w/chorus)       Col 70349-D, DX-990
             ("Carmen") (in French)
WXCO-28057-B Vision fugitive ("Herodiade") (in French) -          -

                                       Hollywood, October 4, 1940.

   H-31-1   Dear Little Cafe (Film "Bitter Sweet")  Col 4264-M, DB-2023
   H-32-1   Tokay (Film "Bitter Sweet")             Col 4263-M, DB-2022
   H-33-1   I'll See You Again (Film "Bitter Sweet")    -          -
   H-34-1   The Call Of Life/If You Could Only Come Col 4264-M, DB-2023
            With Me (Film "Bitter Sweet")

Hollywood, November 1, 1940.

H-120-1  Adeste Fideles (O Come, All Ye Faithful)Col 4269-M
H-121-1  Silent Night, Holy Night                        -
XH-122-  Evening Star ("Tannhäuser")            Col 71189-D

Hollywood, November 7, 1940.

XH-124-1 Jerum ! Jerum ! (Cobbler's Song) ("Die  Col 71189-D
           Meistersinger")
H-125-1  The Blind Ploughman                 Col 17292-D, DB-2114
H-126-1  Tomorrow ("Salt Water Ballads")          -          -

Hollywood, November 28, 1940.

H-149-   The Major-General's Song ("The Pirates  Col 4273-M
           Of Penzance")
H-150-   My Object All Sublime ("The Mikado")    Col 4271-M
H-151-1  I Am Monarch Of The Sea/When I Was A    Col 4273-M
           Lad ("H.M.S. Pinafore")
H-152-1  My Name Is John Wellington Wells ("The  Col 4272-M
           Sorcerer")
H-153-1  Oh ! A Private Buffoon ("The Yeomen Of  Col 4271-M
           The Guard")
H-154-1  The Lord Chancellor's Song ("The        Col 4272-M
           Mikado")

Hollywood, October 5, 1941.

HCO-534-1  Forgive (w/Risë Stevens and chorus)    Col 4283-M, DB-2071
             (Film "The Chocolate Soldier")
HCO-535-1  The Chocolate Soldier (w/Risë Stevens)    -         -
             (Film "The Chocolate Soldier")
HCO-537-1  Sympathy (w/Risë Stevens) (Film "The   Col 4281-M, DB-2069
  NOTE:- Matrix HCO-536 is a solo by Risë Stevens.

Hollywood, October 6, 1941.

HCO-541-1  My Hero (w/Risë Stevens) (Film "The    Col 4281-M, DB-2069
             Chocolate Soldier")
HCO-542-1  While My Lady Sleeps (w/male chorus)   Col 4282-M, DB-2070

Hollywood, January 18, 1942.

HCO-624-1  Gopak (Moussorgsky)                    Col 17366-D
HCO-625-1  Legend : Christ Had A Garden               -
             (Tchaikovsky, Op. 54, No. 5)
HCO-626-1  Don Juan's Serenade (Tchaikovsky)      Col 17309-D
HCO-627-1  Song Of The Flea (Moussorgsky)         Col 17312-D
HCO-628-1  Child's Evening Prayer (Moussorgsky)       -

Hollywood, January 19, 1942.

HCO-629-1  Mother Carey                           Col 17328-D
HCO-630-1  Boots                                  Col 17330-D
HCO-631-1  Route Marchin'                             -

Hollywood, January 21, 1942.

HCO-633-1  Trade Winds                            Col 17328-D
HCO-634-1  Good King Wenceslas                    Col 4296-M
HCO-635-1  The First Nowell                           -
HCO-636-1  Water Boy                              Col 17329-D, DB-2099

Hollywood, January 22, 1942.

HCO-637-1  Non piu andrai ("Le Nozze di Figaro")  Col 17331-D
HCO-638-1  Se vuol ballare ("Le Nozze di Figaro")     -
  (continued on page 241)

Hollywood, January 22, 1942 (cont.)

| | | |
|---|---|---|
| XHCO-639-1 | Rolling In Foaming Billows ("The Creation" - Haydn) | Col 71450-D |
| XHCO-640-1 | Now Heaven In Fullest Glory Shone ("The Creation" - Haydn) | - |

Hollywood, February 1, 1942.

| | | |
|---|---|---|
| HCO-647-1 | Little Work-a-Day World | Col 4294-M |
| HCO-648-1 | Spring Is Here | Col 4295-M |
| HCO-649-1 | I Married An Angel | Col 4294-M |
| HCO-650-1 | I'll Tell The Man In The Street | Col 4295-M |
| HCO-651-1 | Short'nin' Bread | Col 17329-D, DB-2099 |

## CLIFF EDWARDS

B. Hannibal, Mo., 1895; sold newspapers as a child; left school at 14, worked in   a shoe factory; to St. Louis, sang in saloons; debut at Palace Theatre. Provided the narration for silent movies, 15 shows a day, $3.50 a week.  Worked with Bob Carleton, composer of JA DA, made it a hit; the waiter in the Chicago cafe where he and Carleton worked always called him "Ike," unable to remember real name; he  adopted the nickname "Ukulele Ike" as a result.  Many films, beginning with HOLLYWOOD  RE-VUE OF 1929 (popularised SINGIN' IN THE RAIN); GEORGE WHITE'S SCANDALS (1935);GONE WITH THE WIND (1939); HIS GIRL FRIDAY (1940); SHE COULDN'T SAY NO (1945);  was the voice of Jiminy Cricket in Walt Disney's full-length cartoon PINOCCHIO (139),  and often appeared on Rudy Vallee's radio shows.  D. alone and penniless of heart  attack in Hollywood nursing-home, July 18, 1972.

Vocal, acc. by studio O/? Charles A. Prince.
                                    New York, December 4, 1919.

| | | |
|---|---|---|
| 78837-1-2-3 | There's A Lot Of Blue-Eyed Marys Down In Maryland (w/Pierce Keegan) | Col rejected |
| 78838-1-2-3 | Poor Little Butterfly Is A Fly Gal Now (w/Pierce Keegan) | - |

New York, December 26, 1919.

| | | |
|---|---|---|
| 78891-1-2-3 | Darktown Dancin' School (w/Pierce Keegan) | Col rejected |
| 78892-1-2-3 | I'm Gonna Spend My Honeymoon In Dixie (w/Pierce Keegan) | - |

New York, January 13, 1920.

| | | |
|---|---|---|
| 78923-1-2-3 | I'll Buy The Ring And Change Your Name To Mine (w/Pierce Keegan) | Col rejected |

Kazoo-player with Ladd's Black Aces.     New York, c. February 25, 1922.

| | | |
|---|---|---|
| 7782-A-B | Virginia Blues | Gnt 4843, Con 3059, Starr 9229 |

Kazoo-player with Bailey's Lucky Seven.     New York, c. June 16, 1922.

| | | |
|---|---|---|
| 7937, -C | Nobody Lied | Gnt 4909, Apex 471, Starr 9267, EBW 3796, Westport 3018 |

Vocal, acc. by own ukulele and kazoo.     New York, November, 1923.

| | | |
|---|---|---|
| 70435 | Old-Fashioned Love | PA 021097, 10654 |
| 70436 | Lovey Came Back | -          - |

New York, c. January, 1924.

| | | |
|---|---|---|
| 105052 | How My Sweetie Loves Me (She Loves Me All The Time) | PA      , Per      , Lev LV-101 |

Montreal, c. February, 1924.

| 1298 | If You'll Come Back | Apex 8162 |
| 1301 | Where The Lazy Daisies Grow | - |

New York, March, 1924.

| 105208 | Red-Hot Mama | PA        , 10858 |

New York, May, 1924.

| 105312 | You're So Cute (Mama O' Mine) | PA        , 10863, Lev LV-106 |

New York, August, 1924.

| 105518 | Little Somebody Of Mine | PA        , Per        Lev LV-101 |
| 105519 | June Night | PA 032074, 10804 |
|  | Insufficient Sweetie | - |

New York, September, 1924.

| 105552 | Charley, My Boy ! | PA        , 10862, Per        , |
|  |  | Lev LV-106 |

New York, October, 1924.

| 105615 | My Best Girl | PA 025123, 10862, Per 11557 |
| 105616 | He's The Hottest Man In Town | -         10863    - |

New York, November, 1924.

| 105668 | It's All The Same To Me | PA 025124, Per 11558 |

New York, December, 1924.

| 105713 | Fascinating Rhythm | PA 025126, 11061, Per 11560 |
| 105714 | I'll Take Her Back If She Wants To Come Back - | - |

| 105733 | All Alone | PA 025124, 10804, Per 11558 |
| 105734 | He's The Hottest Man In Town | PA 025123, 10863, Per 11557 |

NOTE:- The last title above is reported to appear on the issues shown under    both matrix numbers; probably indicating the use of two different takes.

New York, January, 1925.

| 105765 | The Only, Only One For Me | PA        , 10859, Per |
| 105787 | Nobody Knows What A Red-Head Mama Can Do | PA 025128, Per 11562 |
| 105788 | Who Takes Care Of The Caretaker's Daughter ? | -         - |
| 105799-C | Alabamy Bound | PA 025127, 10882, Per 11561 |

The following titles were probably made about this time.

|  | I Found My Sweetheart Sally | PA        , 10884, Per |
|  | Just Like A Baby | - |
|  | Heart-Breaking Creole Rose | PA        , 10885, Per |
|  | I Don't Care Any More | - |

New York, February, 1925.

| 105824 | I'll Buy The Ring And Change Your Name To Mine | PA        , 10861, Per        , |
|  |  | Lev LV-110 |

Adrian Rollini-bsx added.          New York, February, 1925.

| 105863 | That's All There Is (There Ain't No More) | PA 025132, 10855, Per 11566 |

Acc. by own ukulele and kazoo.          New York, February, 1925.

105864    Let Me Linger Longer In Your Arms      PA 025132, 10855, Per 11566
          Cheating On Me                          PA      , 10861
                                        New York, February-March, 1925.

105876    Why Couldn't It Be Poor Little Me ?    PA 025129, 10859, Per 11563
105877    Let It Rain, Let It Pour                -         10856    -
          Will You Remember Me ?                            -
                                        New York, March, 1925.

105928    If I Never See You As Long As I Live   PA      , 10860, Per
          (That'll Even Be Too Soon)
105929    Isn't She The Sweetest Thing ?                    -

                                        New York, April, 1925.

105955    I Wish It Was Me                       PA 025138, 10881, Per 11572
105956    Old Shanghai                            -         -        -

                                        New York, May, 1925.

106036    If You Knew Susie (Like I Know Susie)  PA      , 10880, 10883,
                                                 Per
          My Red Hot Gal                                    -

106039    She's My Sheba, I'm Her Sheik          PA      , 10882, Per
106040    If You Hadn't Gone Away                PA      , 10880

                                        New York, June, 1925.

106072    Every Sunday Afternoon                 PA      , 10905, Per
106073    Why Did You Let Me Get Away From You ?            -

106082    Paddlin' Madelin' Home                 PA      , 10904, Per
                                                 Lev LV-115
106086    Pretty Mary Ann                        PA      , 10903, Per
                                                 Lev LV-115
          One Smile                              PA      , 10904, Per
          When Georgia Smiles                    PA      , 10903, Per

Acc. by his Hot Combination.            New York, October, 1925.

106315-A-B  Oh ! Lovey, Be Mine                  PA 025159, 11039, Per 11593,
                                                 Starck 159
106316-A-B  Say ! Who Is That Baby Doll ?        As above

106328    How She Loves Me Is Nobody's Business  PA 025160, 11040, Per 11594
106329    The Lonesomest Girl In Town             -         -        -

                                        New York, November, 1925.

106383    Remember                               PA 025163, 11020, Per 11597,
                                                 Starck 163
106384    Someone's Stolen My Sweet, Sweet Baby  As above

106396    Dreaming Of A Castle In The Air        PA 025177, 11037, Per 11611
106397    How Can You Look So Good ?             PA 025167   -    Per 11601,
                                                 Starck 167

                                        New York, December, 1925.

106434    Dinah                                  PA 025164, 11085, Per 11598,
                                                 Starck 164
106435    Keep On Croonin' A Tune                As above

106482    Clap Hands ! Here Comes Charley        PA 025167, 11042, Per 11601,
                                                 Starck 167

New York, December, 1925.

| | | |
|---|---|---|
| 106493 | Sweet Child (I'm Wild About You) | PA 025173, 11042, Per 11607 |
| 106494 | I Want Somebody To Cheer Me Up | PA 025169, 11043, Per 11603 |
| 106495 | Sometime | PA 025173     -     Per 11607 |

Acc. by own kazoo and ukulele.        New York, c. January 5, 1926.

| | | |
|---|---|---|
| 106520 | Chip, Chip, Chippewa | PA      , 11104, Per |
| 106521 | Behind The Clouds | - |
| | In Your Green Hat | PA      , 11041, Per |
| | Don't Be Afraid To Come Home | - |

Acc. by own ukulele/Adrian Rollini-bsx.
                                      New York, April, 1926.

| | | |
|---|---|---|
| 106789 | I Don't Want Nobody But You (I Ain't<br>Got Nobody*) | PA 025192, 11290*, Per 11626 |

Acc. by own kazoo and ukulele.        New York, c. June, 1926.

| | | |
|---|---|---|
| | Who Do You Think I'm Doing It For ? | PA      , 11208, Per |
| | For No Reason At All | - |

New York, late July, 1926.

| | | |
|---|---|---|
| 107027 | Who Could Be More Wonderful Than You ? | PA 025192, 11290, Per 11626 |
| | You've Gotta Know How To Love | PA      , 11148, Per |

New York, August, 1926.

| | | |
|---|---|---|
| 107047 | I Just Wanna Be Known As "Susie's<br>Feller" | PA      , 11253, Per |
| | I'm Lonely Without You | PA      , 11148, Per |

New York, September, 1926.

| | | |
|---|---|---|
| 107098 | I Can't Get Over A Girl Like You<br>(Loving A Boy Like Me) | PA      , 11253, Per |

Acc. by his Hot Combination.        New York, October, 1926.

| | | |
|---|---|---|
| 107160-A-B | Sunday | PA 25199, Per 11633, Starck 199 |
| 107161-A-B | I Don't Mind Being All Alone | PA 25198, Per 11632, Starck 198 |

New York, November, 1926.

| | | |
|---|---|---|
| 107181 | Meadow Lark | PA 25199, 11341, Per 11633,<br>Starck 199, Ph BBL-7434 |
| 107182 | I Never Knew What The Moonlight Could<br>Do | PA 25200, 11365, Per 11634,<br>Starck 200 |
| 107194 | I'm Tellin' The Birds, Tellin' The<br>Bees (How I Love You) | PA 25200, 11341, Per 11634,<br>Starck 200 |

The following title probably belongs to one of the last sessions above.

| | | |
|---|---|---|
| | If You Can't Land 'Er On The Old<br>Verandah | PA,      , 11365, Per |

New York, December, 1926.

| | | |
|---|---|---|
| 107281 | Lonely Eyes | PA 25203, Per 11637 |
| 107282 | Since I Found You | - |
| 107283 | I Know That You Know | PA 25204, Per 11638, Spt 25201,<br>Starck 204 |

New York, March, 1927.

107418    I'm Back In Love Again                     PA 25207, Per 11641, Starck 207

          Oh, Baby ! Don't We Get Along ?           PA 25206, Per 11640
          Side By Side                                  -          -

New York, April, 1927.

          One O'Clock Baby                          PA 25208, Per 11642
          The Whisper Song                              -          -

Acc. by small instrumental groups, with own kazoo and/or ukulele on some.
                            New York, December 31, 1927.

145457-2  (I'm Cryin' 'Cause I Know I'm) Losin'     Col 1254-D, 4781
            You
145458-2  After My Laughter Came Tears                  -          -

New York, January 3, 1928.

145459-   Mary Ann                                  Col 1295-D, 4861
145460-   Together                                      -          -
145461-1-2-3  The Grass Grows Greener 'Way Down     Rejected
            Home
145462-1-2-3  When Day Is Done                          -

New York, June 5, 1928.

146396-2  Anything You Say !                         Col 1427-D, 4996
146397-4  Just Like A Melody Out Of The Sky             -          -

New York, July 3, 1928.

146621-3  Anita                                     Col 1609-D, 5221
146622-3  I Can't Give You Anything But Love        Col 1471-D, 5068
146623-5  That's My Weakness Now                        -          -

New York, July 12, 1928.

146629-2  Chiquita                                  Col 1514-D, 5153

New York, July 25, 1928.

146797-8  Stack O' Lee - Part 1                     Col 1551-D, 1820-D, Cl 5449-C,
                                                    Har 1408-H, VT 2509-V
146798-9  Stack O' Lee - Part 2                     As above

New York, August 15, 1928.

146839-3  Half-Way To Heaven                        Col 1523-D, 5113
146840-3  All Of The Time                           Col 1514-D, 5153
146841-3  It Goes Like This, That Funny Melody      Col 1523-D, 5113

New York, September 21, 1928.

147027-5  Roses Of Yesterday                        Col 1578-D, 5200
147028-3  Good Little, Bad Little You               Col 1705-D, 5185
147029-2  Just A Night For Meditation               Col 1609-D    -

New York, October 3, 1928.

147099-   I Can't Make Her Happy (That Old Girl     Col 1639-D
            Girl Of Mine)
147100-2  My Old Girl's My New Girl Now                 -          5200, Veritas 107

New York, October 5, 1928.

147106-2  Just A Sweetheart                         Col 1578-D, 5221

Acc. by Milton Charles-Pipe organ (WENR Studio).
                                    Chicago, November 24, 1928.

147527-1-2-3  Can You Blame Me ('Cause I Fell In   Col rejected
              Love With You)

Acc. by small instrumental groups, with own kazoo and/or ukulele on some.
                                    Los Angeles, May 28, 1929.

148563-    Singin' In The Rain (Film "Hollywood    Col 1869-D, 5559
              Revue of 1929")
148564-    Orange Blossom Time (Film "Hollywood        -          -
              Revue of 1929")
148565-    Sophomore Prom.                          Col 1980-D

                                    Los Angeles, May 30, 1929.

148569-3  Hang On To Me                             Col 1907-D, 5694
148570-1-2-3  Evangeline                            Rejected
148571-1-2-3  Reaching For Someone (And Not            -
              Finding Anyone There)

                                    Los Angeles, June 9, 1929.

148571-6  Reaching For Someone (And Not             Col 1980-D, 5694
              Finding Anyone There)
148581-1-2-3  My Kinda Love                         Rejected

                                    Los Angeles, June 14, 1929.

148590-    Just You - Just Me                       Col 1907-D
148591-1-2-3  When I See My Sugar (I Get A Lump     Rejected
              In My Throat)

                                    Los Angeles, February 5, 1930.

149806-    I'll See You In My Dreams                Col 2169-D
149807-    The Moon Is Low                             -

                                    Los Angeles, June 13, 1930.

149842-    Singing A Song To The Stars              Col 2235-D, DB-280
149843-    Sing (A Happy Little Thing)                 -          -
149844-1-2-3  You Never Did That Before             Rejected

                                    Los Angeles, October 24, 1930.

149861-1-2-3  My Baby Just Cares For Me            Col rejected
149862-1-2-3  Sweet Jennie Lee                        -

  Acc. by the Californians.                  New York, May 4, 1932.

B-11772-A  Dream Sweetheart                          Br 6307, 01314
B-11773-A  A Great Big Bunch Of You                  Br 6319, 01350
B-11774-A  All Of A Sudden                           Br 6307   -
B-11775-A  Crazy People                              Br 6319, 01314

  Acc. by studio orchestra.                  New York, October 13, 1933.

14143-1-2  It's Only A Paper Moon                   Voc rejected
14144-1-2  Come Up And See Me Sometime                 -
14145-1-2  You're My Past, Present And Future         -
14146-1-2  Night Owl                                  -

                                    New York, October 24, 1933.

14146-3  Night Owl                                  Voc 2587, Br 01646
14209-1  Hush My Mouth (If I Ain't Goin' South)     Voc 2578, Br 01685

New York, October 26, 1933.

| | | |
|---|---|---|
| 14143-3 | It's Only A Paper Moon | Voc 2587, Br 01646 |
| 14217-1 | I Want To Call You "Sweet Mama" | Voc 2578, Br 01685 |

London, April 9, 1934.

| | | |
|---|---|---|
| GB-6681-1 | Dancing In The Moonlight | Br 01752 |
| GB-6682-3 | I Just Couldn't Take It, Baby | - |
| GB-6683-1 | My Dog Loves Your Dog (Film "George White's Scandals") | Br 01727 |

London, April 10, 1934.

| | | |
|---|---|---|
| GB-6688-1 | Six Women (Me And Henry VIII) (Film "George White's Scandals") | Br 01727 |

New York, October 19, 1934.

| | | |
|---|---|---|
| 16211- | St. Louis Blues (w/The Eton Boys) | Mt M-13331 |
| 16212- | Old-Fashioned Love (w/The Eton Boys) | - |
| 16213- | One Little Kiss (w/The Eton Boys) | Mt M-13254 |
| 16214- | Love Is Just Around The Corner (w/The Eton Boys) | - |

Acc. by the Four Blackbirds.        Los Angeles, February 15, 1935.

| | | |
|---|---|---|
| LA-343-A | It's An Old Southern Custom (Film "George White's Scandals of 1935") | Mt M-13347, Rex 8574 |
| LA-344-B | I Got Shoes - You Got Shoesies (Film "George White's Scandals of 1935") | Mt M-13403        - |

Los Angeles, February 27, 1935.

| | | |
|---|---|---|
| LA-1010- | Hunkadola (Film "George Whie's Scandals of 1935") | Mt M-13347 |
| LA-1011- | I Was Born Too Late (Film "George White's Scandals of 1935") | Mt M-13403 |

Acc. by Andy Iona and his Islanders.   Los Angeles, December 17, 1936.

| | | |
|---|---|---|
| DLA-669-A | Somebody Loves Me (Film "George White's Scandals") | Dec 1166, Br 02408 |
| DLA-670-A | If I Had You | Dec 1106, Br 02394 |
| DLA-671-A | The Night Is Young And You're So Beautiful | -              - |
| DLA-672-A | St. Louis Blues | Dec 1166, Br 02408 |

Acc. by studio orchestra.        Hollywood, c. October, 1939.

| | | |
|---|---|---|
| PBS-042393-1 | When You Wish Upon A Star (w/chorus) (Film "Pinocchio") | Vic 26477, HMV BD-821 |
| PBS-042395-1 | Give A Little Whistle (w/"Pinocchio") (Film "Pinocchio") | -              - |
| PBS-042398-1 | Turn On The Old Music Box/When You Wish Upon A Star (w/"Pinocchio," "Geppetto" & chorus) (Film "Pinocchio") | Vic 26479, HMV BD-823 |

## JOAN EDWARDS

B. New York, February 13, 1920; niece of songwriter and producer Gus Edwards.  Very popular on radio, in clubs and hotels as singer-pianist-composer late 1930s—early 1950s.

Vocalist with Paul Whiteman and his Orchestra.
New York, May 16, 1939.

| | | |
|---|---|---|
| 65579-A | Easter Parade (w/Clark Dennis) | Dec 2692, Br 02856 |
| 65580-A | Say It Isn't So (w/Clark Dennis) | -              - |
| 65582-A | How Deep Is The Ocean ? | Dec 2693, Br 02857 |
| 65583-A | Russian Lullaby | -              - |

NOTE:- Matrix 65581 is by Paul Whiteman and his Orchestra, without Joan Edwards.

Acc. by O/Harry Sosnik.                    New York, November 26, 1940.

| | | |
|---|---|---|
| 68390-A | Lamplight | Dec 3580, F-7833 |
| 68391- | Some Of Your Sweetness (Got Into My Heart) | - |
| 68392- | There Shall Be No Night | Dec 3562 |
| 68393-A | Isola Bella (That Little Swiss Isle) | F-7833 |

Acc. by O/Mark Warnow.                     New York, February 9, 1942.

| | | |
|---|---|---|
| BS-071784-1 | Ti-Pi-Tin (w/Barry Wood and the Hit Paraders) | Vic 27865 |
| BS-071785-1 | All The Things You Are | Vic 27866 |

## PRESS ELDRIDGE

One of the true veterans in American minstrelsy; a member of Dan Bryant's troupe in the post-Civil War period, billed in the nineties and later as "Commander-in-Chief of the Army of Fun," B. Philadelphia, Pa., 1854; d. New York, December 13, 1925.

Vocal, acc. by unknown p.                  New York; all issued in May, 1899.

| | |
|---|---|
| She Was Right | Ed 5200 |
| La La Palizer | Ed 5201 |
| I Love Her Just The Same (Parody) | Ed 5202 |
| Johnnie Took The One I Wanted | Ed 5203 |
| Hannah Thompson Is My Baby's Name | Ed 5204 |
| My Coal Black Lady | Ed 5205 |
| The Patriotic Coon | Ed 5206 |
| If That's The Case, I Want To Join The Army | Ed 5207 |
| Mr. Johnson, Don't Get Gay | Ed 5208 |
| Sister Flossie's Bright Red Hair | Ed 5209 |
| Take Back Your Coal | Ed 5210 |

New York, c. February 3, 1900.

| | |
|---|---|
| Johnny Took The One I Wanted | Ber 0924 |
| My Girl's An Hawaiian Maiden | Ber 0925 |

New York, c. February 7, 1900.

| | |
|---|---|
| Let Them All Come | Ber 0931 |
| La La Palizer | Ber 0932 |

New York, January 27, 1909.

| | |
|---|---|
| Confidential Chat | Ed 10121 |

## CHICK ENDOR

Cabaret and revue artist, very popular in New York and London in the late twenties and early thirties; appeared in CLOWNS IN CLOVER at the Adelphi, London, December 1, 1927, teamed with Charles Farrell, also in London, 1932-1933.

Vocal, acc. unknown.                       New York, c. December 7, 1925.

| | | |
|---|---|---|
| E-1917 | Who's In Your Arms Tonight ? | Voc 15273 |

New York, c. December 8, 1925.

| | | |
|---|---|---|
| E-1926 | Sweet Child (I'm Wild About You) | Voc 15273 |

New York, late December, 1925.

| | | |
|---|---|---|
| E-2029 | That Certain Feeling | Voc 15270 |
| E-2031 | Sweet And Low Down | - |

New York, May-June, 1926.

| | |
|---|---|
| The Girl Friend | Voc 15352 |
| I'm In Love With You, That's Why | - |

New York, late June, 1926.

E-3297    Let's Call It A Day                         Voc 15382
E-3298/3300  Precious                                   -

New York, July, 1926.

E-3433/4  On A Quiet Evening At Home                  Voc 15404
E-3435/7  (Now That She's Off My Hands) I Can't        -
            Get Her Off My Mind

New York, September, 1926.

E-3893    Because I Love You                          Voc 15472
E-3895    That's A Good Girl                             -

New York, December, 1926.

E-4342    In A Little Spanish Town ('T Was On A       Voc 15496
            Night Like This)

E-4366    He's The Last Word                          Voc 15496

   Acc. by Fred Elizalde-p.              London, August, 1927.

          Following You Around                        Br 116
          I Got Her Off My Hands (But I Can't          -
            Get Her Off My Mind)

   Acc. by Leslie A. Hutchinson-p.       London, September, 1927.

          Maybe (w/Helen Morgan and Paul Reese)    Br 129

   Acc. by the Adelphi Theatre Orhestra/Sydney Baynes.
                                         London, January 6, 1928.

WA-6764-1  Little Boy Blues (w/June, Bobby             Col 4714
            Comber, Dennis Cowles and chorus) ("Clowns In Clover")

   Acc. by ? Eddie Ward-p/unknown g, as THE CHICK TRIO.
                                         London, February 9, 1928.

WA-6937-1  Baby's Blue                                 Col 4727
WA-6938-1  There's A Trick In Pickin' A Chick-          -
            Chick-Chicken ("Clowns In Clover")

   Acc. by Eddie Ward-p.                 London, May 1, 1928.

WA-7308-1  Ramona                                      Col 4905
WA-7309-1  I've Always Wanted To Call You My            -
            Sweetheart
WA-7310-1  Lila                                        Col 4964
WA-7311-1  She's A Great, Great Girl                    -

   Acc. by O/Nat Shilkret.              New York, December 14, 1928.

BVE-48459-1-2-3  I'll Always Be In Love With You  Rejected
BVE-48460-2  When The World Is At Rest             Vic 21848, HMV B-2993

   Acc. by O/Leonard Joy.              New York, December 15, 1928.

BVE-46394-1-2  Good Little, Bad Little You         Vic rejected

   Acc. by O/Jack Shilkret.            New York, January 11, 1929.

BVE-46394-3-4  Good Little, Bad Little You         Vic rejected
BVE-48564-1-2-3  The Monte Carlo Song                 -

    Acc. by O/Leonard Joy.                    New York, March 20, 1929.

BVE-46394-5  Good Little, Bad Little You          Vic 21922, HMV B-3115
BVE-50764-3  Love Me Or Leave Me                    -          -

                                              New York, May 6, 1929.

BVE-51287-1  Building A Nest For Mary             Vic 21978
BVE-51288-1  What A Day !                          -

                                              New York, August 20, 1929.

BVE-55185-1-2-3  Let Me Sing In My Bathtub        Vic rejected
BVE-55186-1-2-3  For One Another (w/Belle Mann)    -

                                              New York, August 21, 1929.

BVE-55186-4-5  For One Another (w/Belle Mann)     Vic rejected
BVE-55187-1-2-3  She Goes For Everybody Else But Me   -
BVE-55188-1-2-3  Everybody Knew It But Me         -

                                              New York, September 16, 1929.

BVE-56131-2  That's Where You Come In             Vic 22151
BVE-56132-3  It's Unanimous Now                    -

                                              New York, November 29, 1929.

BVE-57182-2  Singin' In The Bathtub               Vic 22245, HMV B-3359
BVE-57183-3  Lady Luck                             -          -

                                              New York, December 24, 1929.

BVE-57948-1  Sunny Side Up                        Vic 22274, HMV B-3373
BVE-57949-1-2-3  You Do Something To Me           Rejected

                                              New York, January 13, 1930.

BVE-57949-6  You Do Something To Me               Vic 22274

The remaining records are all duets with Charlie Farrell,

    Acc. by unknown p.                        London, May 31, 1932.

CA-12757-1  It's The Woman Who Pays              Col DB-866
CA-12758-1  My Wife's First Husband, John         -

    Acc. by unknown p/g.                      London, June 3, 1932.

CA-12775-2  She's Lazy, She's Lousy And She Loves  Col DB-852
              It
CA-12776-1  One Of Us Is Crazy                    -

    Acc. by O/Carroll Gibbons ?               London, June 9, 1932.

CA-12795-1  My Mom                               Col DB-867
CA-12798-1  If We Never Meet Again                -
  NOTE:- Matrices CA-12796/7 are organ solos by Sidney Torch, on the following day.

                                              London, June 16, 1932.

CA-12814-2  I Don't Blame You                    Col DB-887

    Acc. by unknown p/g.                      London, July 6, 1932.

CA-12865-1  I'm The Guy Whose Wife Is The Life Of  Col DB-888
              The Party
CA-12866-1  Where's The Girl ?                    -

Acc. by O/? Carroll Gibbons.                    London, July 7, 1932.

| CA-12870-1 | My Extraordinary Gal | Col DB-887 |
| CA-12871-1 | I Got Her Off My Hands (But I Can't Get Her Off My Mind) | Col DB-901 |

London, July 16, 1932.

| CA-12889-1 | I Got The Potatoes, I Got The Tomatoes (But Someone Else Has Got My Girl) | Col DB-918 |
| CA-12890-1 | My Consolation | - |
| CA-12891-2 | 'Leven Pounds Of Heaven | Col DB-901 |

Acc. by unknown p/g.                            London, September 12, 1932.

| CA-13012-1 | All Of A Sudden | Col DB-922 |
| CA-13013-2 | We Just Couldn't Say Goodbye | - |
| CA-13014-1-2 | I Told You Lies | Rejected |
| CAX-6513-1 | Endor and Farrell Medley - Part 1 | Col DX-384 |

(Intro. My Extraordinary Gal/My Mom/I Don't Blame You/I Got Her Off My Hands)

| CAX-6514-1 | Endor and Farrell Medley - Part 2 | - |

(Intro. One Of Us Is Crazy/My Wife's First Husband, John/I'm  The Guy Whose Wife Is The Life Of The Party/It's The Woman Who Pays/She's Lazy She's Lousy And She Loves It)

New York, December 9, 1932.

| 265008-1-2 | Happy Times | Rejected |
| 265009-2 | Try A Little Tenderness | Col DB-1049 |
| 265010-1-2 | I Got A Date With Kate | Rejected |

New York, December 14, 1932.

| 265011-2 | I've Got A Roof Over My Head | Col DB-1080 |
| 265012-1-2 | Then You Went And Changed Your Mind | Rejected |
| 265013-2 | Let's Sit This One Out | Col DB-1049 |
| 265014-1-2 | Isn't It The Truth ? | Rejected |

New York, December 29, 1932.

| 265023-2 | Just An Echo In The Valley | Col DB-1073 |
| 265024-2 | Well ! Well ! Well ! | Col DB-1080 |

Comedy sketch with Eddie Pola, unacc.          London, October 6, 1933.

| CA-13993-1 | Three Loose Screws - Part 1 | Col DB-1217 |
| CA-13994-1 | Three Loose Screws - Part 2 | - |

Vocal duets with Charlie Farrell, acc. by studio orchestra.
New York, May 2, 1935.

| P-17442- | Cheer Up, Everything's Going To Be Lousy | LMS L- |
| P-17443- | We've Always Wanted To Meet The Man (The Women Go To See About A Dog) | - |

## RUTH ETTING

B. David City, Neb., November 23, 1907; educated there and at the Chicago Academy of Fine Arts; originally intended to be a fashion designer; stage debut in chorus  of revue at the Marigold Gardens Theatre. Chicago, 1925; New York stage debut in  the 1927 edition of ZIEGFELD FOLLIES (New Amsterdam, August 16, 1927); appeared in the same theatre, December 4, 1928, in WHOOPEE with Eddie Cantor; several other revues including the ZIEGFELD FOLLIES OF 1931 (Ziegfeld Theatre, July 1, 1931); debut  in London in TRANSATLANTIC RHYTHM (Adelphi, October 1, 1936); made several films,  the best-remembered being ROMAN SCANDALS (1933); composed several popular songs, WIST-FUL AND BLUE (1926) and WHEN YOU'RE WITH SOMEBODY ELSE (1928) being among them.

Vocal, acc. by own piano.                    Chicago, April 4, 1924.

        You're In Kentucky Sure As You're Born  Vic test (un-numbered)
        My Sweetie's Sweeter Than That          -

                                    Chicago, February, 1926.

141670-   Nothing Else To Do                    Col 580-D
141671-   Let's Talk About My Sweetie           -

                                    New York, April 14, 1926.

141961-   There's Nothing Sweeter Than A Sweet, Col 764-D
            Sweet Sweetie
141962-   What A Man !                          Col 675-D
141963-   You've Got Those Wanna-Go-Back-Again Blues  -
141964-   So Is Your Old Lady                   Col 633-D, 4126
141968-   Lonesome And Sorry                    Col 644-D, 4127
141969-   Could I ? I Certainly Could           Col 633-D, 4126
   NOTE:- Matrices 141965/7 inclusive are not by Ruth Etting.

                                    New York, April 15, 1926.

141970-   But I Do, You Know I Do               Col 644-D, 4127
141971-   Stars                                 Rejected

                                    Chicago, July 7, 1926.

142400-   That's Why I Love You                 Col 692-D
142401-   I Ain't Got Nobody                    -
142402-   Stars                                 Rejected

                                    Chicago, July 12, 1926.

142418-1-2-3  Precious                          Col rejected
142419-1-2-3  Her Beaus Are Only Rainbows       -

                                    Chicago, July 26, 1926.

142402-   Stars                                 Col 764-D
142418-   Precious                              Col 722-D
142419-   Her Beaus Are Only Rainbows           -

Vocalist with Art Kahn and his Orchestra.
                                    Chicago, July 27, 1926.

142449-2  Hello, Baby                           Col 716-D, Re G-8745
   NOTE:- Regal as RAYMOND DANCE BAND (With Vocal Chorus).

Vocal, acc. by own piano.                    Chicago, July 28, 1926.

142504-1-2-3  Looking At The World Through Rose- Col rejected
              Colored Glasses
142505-1-2-3  The Good Bad Girl                 -

                                    Chicago, November 24, 1926.

142958-   Wistful And Blue                      Col 924-D
142959-   Just A Bird's-Eye View Of My Old      Col 827-D
            Kentucky Home
142960-   Thinking Of You                       -
142961-1-2-3  My Man                            Rejected

                                    Chicago, November 29, 1926.

142966-1-2-3  Counting The Days (Till I Get     Col rejected
              Back To Georgia)
142967-1-2-3  After You've Gone                 -

Chicago, December 1, 1926.

| 142974- | 'Deed I Do | Col 865-D |
| 142975- | There Ain't No Maybe In My Baby's Eyes | - |

New York, February 28, 1927.

| 143548- | (What Do We Do) On A Dew-Dew-Dewy Day ? | Col 979-D |
| 143549- | Wherever You Go - Whatever You Do (I Want You To Know I Love You) | - |
| 143550- | Hoosier Sweetheart (Say Who) | Col 924-D |
| 143551- | It All Depends On You | Col 908-D |

New York, March 1, 1927.

| 143561- | My Man (Mon Homme) | Col 995-D |
| 143562- | I'm Nobody's Baby | Col 1104-D |
| 143563- | After You've Gone | Col 995-D |
| 143564- | Sam, The Old Accordion Man | Col 908-D |

Chicago, June 27, 1927.

| 144402- | At Sundown | Col 1052-D |
| 144403- | Sing Me A Baby Song | - |

Chicago, July 1, 1927.

| 144418- | You Don't Like It - Not Much ! | Col 1104-D |

New York, July 13, 1927.

| 144366- | Swanee Shore | Col 1075-D |
| 144367- | Just Once Again | - |

New York, August 30, 1927.

| 144592- | Shaking The Blues Away ("Ziegfeld Follies of 1927") | Col 1113-D |
| 144593- | It All Belongs To Me ("Ziegfeld Follies of 1927") | - |

New York, November 3, 1927.

| 144952-1-2-3 | I Ain't Got Nobody | Col rejected |
| 144953-1-2-3 | Blue River | - |

Acc. by unknown vn/p.                    New York, November 11, 1927.

| 144968- | Together, We Two | Col 1196-D |
| 144969-2 | The Song Is Ended (But The Melody Lingers On) | - |
| 144970- | Love Is Just A Little Bit Of Heaven | Col 1208-D |

Acc. by unknown p.                       New York, November 15, 1927.

| 144952- | I Ain't Got Nobody | Col 1312-D |
| 144953-6 | Blue River | Col 1208-D, 4778 |
| 144981- | Don't Leave Me, Daddy | Col 1312-D |

New York, December 15, 1927.

| 145413- | The Varsity Drag | Col 1237-D |

Vocalist with Ted Lewis and his Band.     New York, December 23, 1927.

| 145395-2 | Keep Sweeping The Cobwebs Off The Moon | Col 1242-D, 4747 |

Vocal, acc. by Phil Schwartz-p.           New York, January 3, 1928.

| 145465-2 | Back In Your Own Back Yard | Col 1288-D, 4903 |
| 145466-2 | When You're With Somebody Else | - - |

Chicago, March 28, 1928.

| | | |
|---|---|---|
| 145848- | Ramona | Col 1352-D |
| 145849-2 | Bluebird, Sing Me A Song | Col 1393-D, 4974 |
| 145850-3 | I Must Be Dreaming | -           - |
| 145851- | Say "Yes" Today | Col 1352-D |

Acc. by small instrumental group.    New York, May 24, 1928.

| | | |
|---|---|---|
| 146340-3 | Happy Days And Lonely Nights | Col 1454-D, 5110 |
| 146341-1-2-3 | Lonely Little Bluebird | Rejected |

New York, May 25, 1928.

| | | |
|---|---|---|
| 146346- | Because My Baby Don't Mean "Maybe" Now | Col 1420-D |
| 146347-4 | Beloved | -           5110 |

New York, June 1, 1928.

| | | |
|---|---|---|
| 146341- | Lonely Little Bluebird | Col 1454-D |

Acc. by unknown vn/vc/p.    New York, September 18, 1928.

| | | |
|---|---|---|
| 147017-3 | I Still Keep Dreaming Of You | Col 1563-D, 5180 |
| 147018-1 | Sonny Boy | -        - |
| 147019-1-2-3 | Sleepy Baby | Rejected |

Acc. by unknown c/p.    New York, October 2, 1928.

| | | |
|---|---|---|
| 147092- | My Blackbirds Are Bluebirds Now | Col 1595-D |
| 147093-2 | You're In Love And I'm In Love | -        DB-19 |

Acc. by unknown vn/vc/p/Eddie Lang-g.    New York, December 17, 1928.

| | | |
|---|---|---|
| 147710-1 | I'm Bringing A Red, Red Rose ("Whoopee") | Col 1680-D, 5553 |
| 147711-2 | Love Me Or Leave Me ("Whoopee") | -        - |

Acc. by unknown vn/vc/p.    New York, January 14, 1929.

| | | |
|---|---|---|
| 147779-3 | You're The Cream In My Coffee | Col 1707-D, 5422 |
| 147780-3 | To Know You Is To Love You | -        - |
| 147781- | Glad Rag Doll | Col 1733-D |

Acc. by t/vn/p/g.    New York, February 11, 1929.

| | | |
|---|---|---|
| 147955-3 | I'll Get By As Long As I Have You | Col 1733-D, 5446 |

Acc. by small orchestra.    New York, March 11, 1929.

| | | |
|---|---|---|
| 148029-3 | Button Up Your Overcoat | Col 1762-D, 5600 |
| 148030- | Mean To Me | -        5446 |

New York, April 8, 1929.

| | | |
|---|---|---|
| 148193- | Deep Night | Col 1801-D |
| 148194- | Maybe - Who Knows ? | - |

New York, May 2, 1929.

| | | |
|---|---|---|
| 148404-2 | The One In The World | Col 1830-D, 5506 |
| 148405-1 | I'm Walkin' Around In A Dream | -        - |

New York, June 14, 1929.

| | | |
|---|---|---|
| 148701-1-2-3 | I Want To Meander In The Meadow | Col rejected |
| 148702-1-2-3 | Now I'm In Love | - |

New York, June 25, 1929.

| | | |
|---|---|---|
| 148701- | I Want To Meander In The Meadow | Col 1883-D |
| 148702-6 | Now I'm In Love | -        5615 |

New York, August 20, 1929.

148905-1-2-3  Ain't Misbehavin'                     Col rejected
148906-1-2-3  At Twilight                               -

New York, September 3, 1929.

148905-6  Ain't Misbehavin'                        Col 1958-D, 5615
148906-7  At Twilight                                 -        DB-42

New York, October 4, 1929.

149098-1  What Wouldn't I Do For That Man ?       Col 1998-D, DB-19
149099-1  The Right Kind Of Man                       -        DB-42

   Acc. by unknown vn/p/g.           New York, November 12, 1929.

149412-   More Than You Know                       Col 2038-D, DB-217
149413-   A Place To Call Home                        -        -

   Acc. by small instrumental group.  New York, December 10, 1929.

149705-2  If He Cared                              Col 2073-D, DB-83
149706-2  Crying For The Carolines                    -        -

   Acc. by small orchestra.          New York, March 4, 1930.

150062-3  Ten Cents A Dance                        Col 2146-D, DB-440
150063-2  Funny, Dear, What Love Can Do               -        DB-147

                                     New York, March 25, 1930.

150118-   Let Me Sing And I'm Happy                Col 2172-D
150119-   A Cottage For Sale                          -

                                     New York, April 30, 1930.

150512-   It Happened In Monterey                  Col 2199-D
150513-   Exactly Like You                            -        Epic SN-6059

Vocalist with Ben Selvin and his Orchestra.
                                     New York, May 16, 1930.

150437-   I Remember You From Somewhere            Col 2207-D, CB-128
150438-   Dancing With Tears In My Eyes            Col 2206-D, CB-119

Vocal, acc. unknown.                 New York, May 27, 1930.

150547-   I Never Dreamt (You'd Fall In Love       Rejected
             With Me)

   Acc. by small orchestra.          New York, June 2, 1930.

150560-   I Never Dreamt (You'd Fall In Love       Col 2216-D
             With Me)
150561-3  Dancing With Tears In My Eyes               -        DB-218

                                     New York, July 11, 1930.

150647-1-2-3  Grieving For You                     Col rejected
150648-1-2-3  Shine On, Harvest Moon                  -

                                     New York, August 27, 1930.

150740-3  Don't Tell Her What's Happened To Me     Col 2280-D, DB-311
150741-3  The Kiss Waltz                              -        -
150742-3  I'm Yours                                Col 2318-D, DB-409

New York, August 28, 1930.

150743-1-2-3  Just A Little Closer              Col rejected
150744-1-2-3  I'll Be Blue, Just Thinking Of You      -

New York, September 18, 1930.

150743-7  Just A Little Closer              Col 2307-D, DB-341
150744-6  I'll Be Blue, Just Thinking Of You        -         DB-355
150826-3  If I Could Be With You            Col 2300-D, DB-341

New York, September 29, 1930.

150844-   Body And Soul                     Col 2300-D
150845-3  Laughing At Life                  Col 2318-D, DB-409

New York, January 13, 1931.

151202-   Reaching For The Moon             Col 2377-D
151203-   Overnight                             -
151204-3  Love Is Like That (What Can You Do ?)  Col 2398-D, DB-440

New York, January 16, 1931.

151227-   You're The One I Care For         Col 2398-D

  Acc. by unknown p.                  New York, April 13, 1931.

151515-   Falling In Love Again             Col 2445-D, Epic L2N-6072
151516-   Were You Sincere ?                    -         DB-546

New York, April 16, 1931.

151519-   Out Of Nowhere                    Col 2454-D, DB-546
151520-   Say A Little Prayer For Me            -

New York, May 26, 1931.

151569-   Faithfully Yours                  Col 2470-D, DB-571
151570-2  (There Ought To Be A) Moonlight-Saving Time -        -

New York, June 9, 1931.

10692-2   Without That Gal !                Per 12732, Dec F-2483, EBW 5373,
                                            Imp 2625
10693-2   Nevertheless                      Per 12732, Dec F-2483, EBW 5373,
                                            Imp 2625

New York, July 8, 1931.

10724-1-2-3  Cigarettes, Cigars !           ARC rejected
10725-1-2-3  Shine On, Harvest Moon             -

New York, July 16, 1931.

151688-   I'm Good For Nothing But Love     Col 2505-D
151689-   I'm Falling In Love                   -

New York, July 24, 1931.

10738-3   Just One More Chance              Ban 32231, Or 2311, Per 12739,
                                            Rom 1681, Imp 2579, Pic 846
10739-3   Have You Forgotten ?              As above, but Imp 2601

New York, July 28, 1931.

10724-    Cigarettes, Cigars !              Ban 32229, Or 2308, Per 12737
10725-    Shine On, Harvest Moon                -         -          -

New York, September 1, 1931.

| 151761- | Guilty | Col 2529-D, Re MR-458 |
| 151762- | Now That You're Gone | - |

New York, September 9, 1931.

| 10798-3 | Love Letters In The Sand | Cq 7828, Per 12754, Imp 2625 |
| 10799-1 | Me ! | -         -        Imp 2601 |

New York, October 6, 1931.

| 10827-1 | If I Didn't Have You | Ban 32289, Per 12757, Imp 2645 |
| 10828-1 | Let Me Call You Sweetheart | -         - |

New York, October 21, 1931.

| 151858- | A Faded Summer Love | Col 2557-D, Re MR-458 |
| 151859- | Goodnight, Sweetheart | - |

New York, December 9, 1931.

| 152037-2 | Too Late | Col 2580-D, Re MR-507 |
| 152038-3 | Cuban Love Song | -         - |

New York, December 11, 1931.

| 11064-3 | All Of Me | Cq 7918, Per 12771, Imp 2652 |
| 11065-2 | Home | -         -         - |

New York, March 7, 1932.

| 152123- | When We're Alone | Col 2630-D |
| 152124- | Kiss Me Goodnight | - |

New York, March 8, 1932.

| 11419- | Love, You Funny Thing ! | Mt M-12352, Per 12791 |
| 11420- | Can't We Talk It Over ? | -         - |

New York, May 9, 1932.

| 11791-1 | Happy-Go-Lucky You (And Broken-Hearted Me) | Mt M-12375, Per 12809, Imp 2769 |
| 11792- | That's What Heaven Means To Me | -         - |

New York, May 10, 1932.

| 152190- | That's Something To Be Thankful For | Col 2660-D |
| 152191- | The Voice In The Old Village Choir | - |

New York, June 2, 1932.

| 11889-2 | Lazy Day | Mt M-12394, Cq 8042, Per 12810, Re 233 |
| 11890-1 | (I'm Still Without A Sweetheart) With Summer Coming On | As above |

New York, June 30, 1932.

| 152229-2 | Holding My Honey's Hand | Col 2681-D, DB-945 |
| 152230-2 | The Night When Love Was Born | -         - |

New York, July 26, 1932.

| 12115-1 | It Was So Beautiful | Mt M-12450, Bwy 4021, Cq 7997, Per 12828, Imp 2769 |
| 12116- | I'll Never Be The Same | As above, except Imp 2769 |

New York, October 25, 1932.

| 12503-1 | I'll Follow You | Ban 32595, Cq 8075, Mt M-12528, Per 12855 |
| 12504-1 | I'll Never Have To Dream Again | As above |

New York, December 5, 1932.

| 12688- | Take Me In Your Arms | Ban 32634, Mt M-12563, Per 12869 |
| 12689- | Some Day We'll Meet Again | -        -        - |

New York, February 8, 1933.

| 13039-1 | Hey ! Young Fella | Mt M-12625, Cq 8122, Per 12887, Imp 2840 |
| 13040-1 | Try A Little Tenderness | As above |

New York, March 1, 1933.

| 13105- | How Can I Go On Without You ? | Ban 32714, Cq 8123, Mt M-12643, Or 2663, Per 12896, Rom 2036 |
| 13106- | Linger A Little Longer In The Twilight | As above |

New York, March 29, 1933.

| 13185- | You've Got Me Crying Again | Ban 32739, Cq 8154, Mt M-12668, Or 2679, Per 12904, Rom 2052 |
| 13186- | Hold Me | As above |

Los Angeles, September 19, 1933.

| LA-5-A | No More Love (Film "Roman Scandals") | Br 6697, 01674 |
| LA-6-A | Build A Little Home (Film "Roman Scandals") | - |
| LA-7-A | You're My Past, Present And Future | Br 6671, 01634 |
| LA-8-A | Dancing In The Moonlight | Br 6719, 01684 |

Los Angeles, September 21, 1933.

| LA-10-A | What Is Sweeter (Than The Sweetness Of "I Love You" ?) | Br 6671, 01684 |
| LA-11-A | Summer Is Over (So Is My Dream Of Love) | Br 6657, 01614 |
| LA-12-A | Everything I Have Is Yours | Br 6719, 01634 |
| LA-13-A | Close Your Eyes | Br 6657, 01614 |

New York, January 23, 1934.

| B-14667-A | Tired Of It All | Br 6761, 01740 |
| B-14668-A | Keep Romance Alive | -        - |

New York, February 9, 1934.

| B-14817-A | This Little Piggie Went To Market | Br 6769 |
| B-14818-A | Smoke Gets In Your Eyes | -        01879 |

New York, May 10, 1934.

| B-15188-A | Riptide | Br 6892, 01794 |
| B-15189-A | Easy Come, Easy Go | -        - |
| B-15190-A | With My Eyes Wide Open, I'm Dreaming | Br 6914, 01829 |
| B-15191-A | Were Your Ears Burning ? | -        - |

Acc. by Jimmie Grier and his Orchestra. Los Angeles, August 29, 1934.

| LA-196- | Talkin' To Myself | Col 2954-D |
| LA-197- | Tomorrow Who Cares ? | - |
| LA-198-A | What About Me ? | Col 2955-D, DB-1499 |
| LA-199- | Out In The Cold Again | - |

Acc. by studio orchestra.                    New York, November 21, 1934.

CO-16349-1  Stay As Sweet As You Are              Col 2979-D, DB-1499
CO-16350-1  A Needle In A Haystack                   -        DB-1512
CO-16351-1  Am I To Blame ?                       Col 2985-D
CO-16352-1  I've Got An Invitation To A Dance        -        DB-1512

                                             New York, February 11, 1935.

CO-16841-3  Things Might Have Been So Diff'rent   Col 3014-D, DB-1539
CO-16842-1  March Winds And April Showers            -         -

                                             New York, April 5, 1935.

CO-17249-   It's Easy To Remember                 Col 3031-D, FB-1140
CO-17250-   Life Is A Song (Let's Sing It Together)   -        -

                                             New York, July 1, 1935.

CO-17751-   Ten Cents A Dance                     Col 3085-D
CO-17752-   Shine On, Harvest Moon                   -

                                             New York, July 3, 1935.

CO-17774-   I Wished On The Moon                   Col 3070-D
CO-17775-   Why Dream ?                              -

                                             New York, July 19, 1935.

CO-17752-   Shine On, Harvest Moon                Col 3085-D

                                             New York, March 30, 1936.

B-18895-1  Lost                                  Br 7646, 02218
B-18896-1  It's Been So Long                        -         -

Acc. by O/Jay Wilbur.                        London, August, 1936.

F-1940-1  You                                    Rex 8852
F-1941-1  It's Love Again                           -
F-1942-1-2  It's A Sin To Tell A Lie             Rex 8853
F-1943-2  Take My Heart                             -

                                             London, September, 1936.

F-1990-2  Holiday Sweethearts                    Rex 8881
F-1991-2  Who'll Buy My Song Of Love ?              -

Acc. by studio orchestra.                    New York, December 12, 1936.

61477-A  Goodnight, My Love                      Dec 1107, F-6294
61478-   In The Chapel In The Moonlight          Dec 1084, F-6257
61479-A  There's Something In The Air               -      F-6294
61480-   May I Have The Next Romance With You ?  Dec 1107, F-6257

                                             New York, April 1, 1937.

62090-A  It's Swell Of You                       Dec 1212, Br 02446
62091-A  On A Little Dream Ranch                  Dec 1259, Br 02420
62092-A  There's A Lull In My Life (acc. p only) Dec 1212, Br 02446

Acc. by Frank Signorelli-Harold Solomon-p.
                                             New York, April 5, 1937.

62103-A  A Message From The Man In The Moon      Dec 1259, Br 02420

B. 1890; baritone with the Chicago Civic Opera, then to New York to star in  EILEEN;
also in BLOSSOM TIME (Ambassador, September 29, 1921) and THE STUDENT PRINCE (Jolson, September 2, 1924); d. Norwalk, Conn., January 28, 1967.
Vocal, acc. by chorus of 8 and O/Victor Herbert.
                                                    Camden, N. J., April 5, 1917.

B-19445-1  Free Trade And A Misty Moon ("Eileen")  Vic 18285

   Acc. by O/? Charles A. Prince.         New York, October 4, 1917.

   77402-   Homeward Bound                    Col A-2423
   77403-1-2-3  Wasn't It Yesterday ?         Rejected

                                        New York, November 2, 1917.

   77483-   That's A Mother's Liberty Loan    Col A-2471

                                        New York, November 19, 1917.

   77517-1-2-3  There's A Green Hill Out In         Col rejected
               Flanders (There's A Green Hill Up In Maine)

                                        New York, December 20, 1917.

   77593-1-2-3  It's A Mighty Good World After All  Col rejected

                             MAURICE  EVANS

B. Dorchester, Dorset, England, June 3, 1901; first public appearances as a boy soprano, then as an amateur actor, in his father's productions of Thomas Hardy novels
in Dorchester; first stage appearance as professional at the Festival Theatre,Cam-
bridge, in THE ORESTIA (Aeschylus), November 26, 1926; London debut at  Wyndham's
in THE ONE-EYED HERRING (August 25, 1927); greatest success in London was  at  the
Savoy in JOURNEY'S END (January 21, 1929); many other varied but successful  shows
in London (including the musical comedy BALL AT THE SAVOY at Drury Lane, September
8, 1933); joined the Old Vic.-Sadler's Wells Company a year later; to U.S.A.a year
later still, toured with Katherine Cornell; New York debut with her in the  title
roles of ROMEO AND JULIET (Martin Block, December 23, 1935); particularly successful in RICHARD II (St. James, February, 1937); toured in this and many other parts
of Shakespeare plays; became a citizen of U.S.A. in August, 1941; commissioned  as
Captain, Army Entertainments Section, August, 1942; in charge of this in the Central Pacific from December, 1942 to June, 1945; made several films, beginning 1929;
most memorable are WHITE CARGO (1930); SCROOGE (1935); ANDROCLES AND THE LION  and
THE STORY OF GILBERT AND SULLIVAN (1953), playing Julius Caesar and Sir Arthur Sullivan respectively; PLANET OF THE APES (1967) and ROSEMARY'S BABY (1968).

Speech, unacc.                           New York, April 16, 1937.

XCO-20987-   Richard II, Act 3, Scene 2 (The      Col 11044-D, 11219-D
             Coast Of Wales) - Part 1 (Shakespeare)
XCO-20988-   Richard II, Act 3, Scene 2 (The         -        11220-D
             Coast Of Wales) - Part 2 (Shakespeare)
XCO-20989-   Richard II, Act 3, Scene 2 (The      Col 11045-D, 11221-D
             Coast Of Wales) - Part 3 (Shakespeare)
XCO-20990-   Richard II, Act 3, Scene 3 (Before      -        11222-D
             Flint Castle) - Part 1 (Shakespeare)
XCO-20991-   Richard II, Act 3, Scene 3 (Before   Col 11046-D, 11223-D
             Flint Castle) - Part 2 (Shakespeare)

                                        New York, April 30, 1937.

XCO-21076-   Richard II, Act 4, Scene 1 (West-    Col 11046-D, 11223-D
             minster Hall, Deposition Scene) - Part 1 (Shakespeare)
XCO-21077-   Richard II, Act 4, Scene 1 (West-    Col 11047-D, 11222-D
             minster Hall, Deposition Scene) - Part 2 (Shakespeare)
XCO-21078-   Richard II, Act 4, Scene 1 (West-       -        11221-D
             minster Hall, Deposition Scene) - Part 3 (Shakespeare)
XCO-21079-   Richard II, Act 5, Scene 5 (Pomfret  Col 11048-D, 11220-D
             Castle, Prison Scene) - Part 1 (Shakespeare)
XCO-21080-   Richard II, Act 5, Scene 5 (Pomfret     -        11219-D
             Castle, Prison Scene) - Part 2 (Shakespeare)

New York, November 22, 1938.

| XCO-23743- | Hamlet : **To Be Or** Not To Be (Shakespeare) | Col 11135-D |
| XCO-23744- | Hamlet : How All Occasions (Shakespeare) | - |
| XCO-23745- | Hamlet : O, That This Too, Too Solid Flesh (Shakespeare) | Col 11136-D |

New York, December 1, 1938.

| XCO-23746- | Hamlet : O What A Rogue And Peasant Slave (Shakespeare) | Col 11136-D |

## SAMMY FAIN

B. 1902; wrote first song 1925; soon began producing big hits, many in collaboration with Irving Kahal; outstanding and well-remembered numbers for which he   composed the music are THERE'S SOMETHING ABOUT A ROSE (1929); WEDDING BELLS (1929);   YOU BROUGHT A NEW KIND OF LOVE TO ME (1930); WHEN I TAKE MY SUGAR TO TEA (1931);   WAS THAT THE HUMAN THING TO DO ? (1932); BY A WATERFALL (1933); I WENT MERRILY MERRILY ON MY WAY (1935) and THAT OLD FEELING (1937).  He recorded quite extensively, using the sub-title "The Crooning Composer."

Vocal, acc. by small instrumental group. New York, c. February, 1928.

| | And Then You Came Along (w/Artie Dunn) | PA 32344, Per 12423 |
| | There's Something About A Rose (That Reminds Me Of You) (w/Artie Dunn) | - - |

New York, December 4, 1928.

| 147688-1-2-3 | You Took Advantage Of Me | Col rejected |
| 147689-1-2-3 | Baby | - |

New York, February 6, 1929.

| 147933- | Wedding Bells (Are Breaking Up That Gang Of Mine) | Har 843-H |
| 147934- | Love Me Or Leave Me | - |

New York, March 26, 1929.

| 148139-2 | What Didja Wanna Make Me Love You For ? | Har 904-H |
| 148140-3 | (You Can't Take Away) The Things That Were Made For Love | - |

New York, May 10, 1929.

| 148508-2 | To Be In Love (Espesh'lly With You) | Har 943-H |
| 148509-1 | What A Day ! | - |
| 148510-2 | Why Can't You ? | Har 961-H, SR 1043-P |

New York, July 16, 1929.

| 148816-1 | Liza (All The Clouds'll Roll Away) | Har 993-H |
| 148817-3 | Ain't Misbehavin' | - SR 1044-P |

New York, September 20, 1929.

| 149028-3 | Painting The Clouds With Sunshine | Har 1014-H |
| 149029-3 | Lovable And Sweet | - |

New York, March 3, 1930.

| 150051- | The One I Love (Just Can't Be Bothered With Me) | Har 1114-H |
| 150052- | Watching My Dreams Go By | - |

New York, May 14, 1930.

| | | |
|---|---|---|
| 150420-3 | You Brought A New Kind Of Love To Me | Har 1179-H |
| 150421- | I'm In The Market For You | Har 1103-H, Cl 5016-C |
| 150422- | Mia Cara | - |

New York, June 16, 1930.

| | | |
|---|---|---|
| 150589- | Ro-Ro-Rollin' Along | Har 1179-H |

New York, July 25, 1930.

| | | |
|---|---|---|
| 150680-1-2-3 | Confessin' (That I Love You) | Col rejected |

New York, August 19, 1930.

| | | | |
|---|---|---|---|
| 150680- | Confessin' (That I Love You) | Har 1203-H, | Cl 5053-C |
| 150717- | Don't Tell Her (What's Happened To Me) | - | Cl 5055-C |
| 150718- | I'd Rather Mean A Little To You | | - |
| 150719- | I'm In Love With All The World | | Cl 5053-C |

New York, December 8, 1930.

| | | | |
|---|---|---|---|
| 151150- | You're Driving Me Crazy (What Did I Do) | Har 1250-H, | Cl 5183-C |
| 151151- | I'm Alone Because I Love You | - | Cl 5184-C |

New York, July 14, 1931.

| | | |
|---|---|---|
| 365027- | Begging For Love | Har 1355-H, VT 2431-V |
| 365028- | Just One More Chance | -       - |

New York, March 19, 1932.

| | | |
|---|---|---|
| B-11540- | Walking Home With Your Goodnight Kiss | Br Private Recording |

Acc. by unknown vn/p.                    New York, February 8, 1933.

| | | |
|---|---|---|
| 265036- | If You Don't Want To Be Sweethearts (I Don't Want To Be Friends) | Col DB-1095 |
| 265037- | The Handwriting's On The Wall | Col DB-1117 |
| 265038- | A Kiss In The Moonlight (And The World Began) | - |
| 265039- | In Every Nook And Corner You Are Missing | Col DB-1095 |

New York, April 7, 1933.

| | | |
|---|---|---|
| 265096- | I'll Pin Another Petal On The Daisy | Col rejected |
| 265097- | In The Valley Of The Moon | - |
| 265098- | There's A New Moon Over My Shoulder | - |
| 265099- | My Picture Puzzle Of You | - |

## DOUGLAS FAIRBANKS, Jr.

B. New York, December 9, 1909; began studying art and sculpture in London and Paris; film debut in STEPHEN STEPS OUT (1923); many others, silent and talking, since; he is best remembered for his appearances in CATHERINE THE GREAT (1934, made in Great Britain, where he has lived since 1945); THE AMATEUR GENTLEMAN (1936, also British made), THE PRISONER OF ZENDA (1937); THE SUN NEVER SETS (1939); GREEN HELL (1940); MR. DRAKE'S DUCK (1953). Debut on stage in England in Manchester in May, 1934, in THE WINDING JOURNEY; London debut in MOONLIGHT IS SILVER (Queen's, September 19, 1934); formed own film company, 1935; served in U.S. Navy during World War II; is author of many short stories, articles and TV plays, some of which he produced and in which he sometimes played. M. Joan Crawford (1929), divorced; m. Mary Lee Epling Hartford.

Vocal and speech, acc. by O/Carroll Gibbons.
London, November 20, 1934.

2EA-693-2  Scene and Song (w/Gertrude Lawrence)   HMV C-2710
            ("Moonlight Is Silver") - Part 1
2EA-694-2  Scene and Song (w/Gertrude Lawrence)      -
            ("Moonlight Is Silver") - Part 2

Also appeared as D'Artagnan in THE THREE MUSKETEERS on Decca LK-4050 (LP) and reading poetry on HMV CLP-1435 (LP) in 1951 and 1958 respectively.

## THE FARBER SISTERS

Vocal duets, acc. by studio orchestra.   New York, March 8, 1918.

77715-   How'd You Like To Be My Daddy ?        Col A-2525, LW 884

New York, March 29, 1918.

77743-   I Want A Daddy Like You                Col A-2544

New York, April 4, 1918.

77754-   Won't You Be A Dear, Dear Daddy (To    Col A-2544
          A Itta Bitta Doll Like Me ?)

New York, April 23, 1918.

77777-   If He Can Fight Like He Can Love,      Col A-2556
          Goodnight Germany

New York, May 4, 1918.

77809-   I'm So Glad My Mama Don't Know Where    Col A-2573
          I'm At

New York, May 17, 1918.

77829-   I Can't Let 'Em Suffer                 Col A-2573

New York, c. May-June, 1918.

66778    They Were All Out Of Step But Jim      Pathe 20338
          (Constance Farber only)
66779    Won't You Be A Dear, Dear Daddy (To       -
          A Itta Bitta Doll Like Me ?)

         How'd You Like To Be My Daddy ?        Pathe 20355
         There's A Lump Of Sugar Down In Dixie     -

New York, c. October, 1918.

67168    I'm Crazy About My Daddy In A Uniform  Pathe 22017
         Everything Is Peaches Down In Georgia  Pathe 20435

## MAURICE FARKOA

B. Smyrna, Syria, 1864; d. March 21, 1916.  Became famous throught Europe as perhaps
the greatest interpreter of French chansonettes of his time; appeared with success
in AN ARTIST'S MODEL at Daly's, London, February 2, 1895; toured with this in  the
U.S.A. in 1896; returned to London, appeared in  KITTY GREY (Apollo, September  7,
1901) and LADY MADCAP (Prince of Wales, December 17, 1904).

Vocal, acc. by  Frank Lambert-p.        washington, May 8, 1896.

        Laughing Song ("An Artist's Model")     Ber 1302

London, October 19, 1898.

|  | Mrs. 'Enery 'Awkins (in French !) | Ber 2124 |
|  | Le Fou Rire ("An Artist's Model") (in French) | Ber 2125 |
|  | I Want Yer, Ma Honey (in French) | Ber 2127 |
|  | Laughing Song ("An Artist's Model") (in English) | Ber 2128 |
|  | Les Blondes (in French) | Ber 2129 |

London, October, 1899.

|  | Laughing Song (Le Fou Rire) ("An Artist's Model) (in French) | Ber 32111 |
|  | The Honeysuckle And The Bee (in French) | Ber 32112 |
|  | Laughing Song (in English)(?) | Ber 32651 |
| 4094 | Nini, Ninette, Ninon (in French) | Ber 32653 |
| 4095 | Laughing Song (Le Fou Rire) ("An Artist's Model") (in French) | Ber 32654 |
|  | I Was Born In Turkey (in English) | Ber 2701 |
|  | I Love You All (in English) | Ber 2702 |

London, c. November, 1901.

| 1108 | Nini, Ninette, Ninon (in French) | G&T GC2-2527 |
| 1109 | Kitty Grey ("Kitty Grey") (in English) | G&T GC2-2528 |

Acc. by studio orchestra.                   London, March 10, 1905.

| 1911e | Do I Like Love ? ("Lady Madcap") (in English) | Rejected |
| 1914e | I Like You In Velvet ("Lady Madcap") (in English) | G&T GC3-2254 |
| 1916e | My Portuguese Princess(w/Delia Mason) ("Lady Madcap") (in English) | G&T GC-4374 |
| 1917e | Do I Like Love ? ("Lady Madcap") (in English) | G&T GC3-2255 |

London, March 16, 1905.

| 1958e | Laughing Song (Le Fou Rire) ("An Artist's Model") (in French) | G&T GC3-2261, HMV E-325 |

Unacc.                                      London, August 15, 1906.

| 8659e | Laughs I Have Met (w/Amy Augarde-Will Evans-Burt Shepard-Fred Monk) | G&T GC3-2468, Vic 17232 |

Acc. by unknown p.                          London, December 15, 1908.

| 2746f | I Like You In Velvet ("Lady Madcap") (in English) | G&T rejected |
| 2747f | Tes Baisers (in French) | - |

London, December 16, 1908.

| 9306e | I Like You In Velvet ("Lady Madcap") | HMV 4-2016, B-453 |
| 9307e | Two Dirty Little Hands (in English) | HMV 4-2012, B-343 |
| 9308e | I Beg Your Pardon (in English) | Rejected |
| 9309e | Who'll Marry Me ? (in English) | HMV 4-2029, E-324 |

Acc. by studio orchestra.                   London, c. October, 1910.

| 77162 | I Like You In Velvet ("Lady Madcap") (in English) | Pathe 694 |
| 77163 | I Beg Your Pardon (in English) | - |
|  | I Beg Your Pardon (in English) | Amb 12251 |

Irish-American musical comedy and revue star of the second and third decades of the
twentieth century; decided on theatrical career while in her teens; appeared in a
small part in THE ROGERS BROTHERS IN IRELAND (Liberty, New York, September 4,1905
- it is uncertain that she actually appeared in the original staging), then had a
season in vaudeville with The Four College Girls.  Six months' voice training led
to acceptance by Oscar Hammerstein, and she appeared in twenty-eight grand operas
in one season; she turned to comic opera and appeared in MISS PRINCESS and AMERI-
CAN MAID; then worked with Lillian Russell, eventually appearing in STEP THIS WAY
(Lew Fields' version of the 1907 musical, THE GIRL BEHIND THE COUNTER); b. Providence, R.I., September 16, 1888; d. Buffalo, N.Y., January 26, 1951.

Vocal, acc. by studio orchestra/? Charles A. Prince.
                                        New York, October 27, 1915.

46158-1   Out Of A City Of Six Million People      Col A-1870
            (Why Did You Pick On Me ?)
46161-1-2-3  Some Beautiful Morning (You'll        Rejected
            Find Me Gone)
  NOTE:- Matrices 46159/60 are by George O'Connor, q.v.

                                        New York, December 8, 1915.

46250-    Along The Rocky Road To Dublin           Col A-1920

                                        New York, December 10, 1915.

46256-1-2-3  I'm Just A Little Naughty But I'm     Rejected
            Nice
46257-1   At The Fountain Of Youth                 Col A-1962
46260-    He's The Son Of An Irishman              Col A-1920
  NOTE:- Matrices 46258/9 are by other artists.

                                        New York, December 20, 1915.

46292-1   Oh, Oh, Oh, He's Breaking My Heart       Col A-1925

                                        New York, February 17, 1916.

46424-2   When Priscilla Tries To Reach High C     Col A-1962
46425-    Pretty Please                            Col A-2006

                                        New York, March 14, 1916.

46636-    Arrah Go On, I'm Gonna Go Back To        Col A-1981
            Oregon

                                        New York, March 15, 1916.

46638-    Now's The Time (The Great Leap Year      Col A-1981
            Song)

                                        New York, May 20, 1916.

46797-    (Sweet Babette) She Always Did The       Col A-2020
            Minuet

                                        New York, June 16, 1916.

46847-3   If I Knock The 'L' Out Of Kelly (It      Col A-2040, Sil 46847
            Would Still Be Kelly To Me) ("Step This Way")

Acc. by O/Eddie King, w/male chorus.    New York, June 26, 1916.

B-17930-1-2  If I Knock The 'L' Out Of Kelly (It   Vic rejected
            Would Still Be Kelly To Me) ("Step This Way")
B-17931-1-2-3  By The Sad Luana Shore ("Step This Way")_

New York, July 10, 1916.

B-17930-3  If I Knock The 'L' Out Of Kelly (It      Vic 18105
           Would Still Be Kelly To Me) ("Step This Way")
B-17931-4  By The Sad Luana Shore ("Step This Way")   -

Acc. by studio O/? Charles A. Prince.  New York, July 18, 1916.

46923-     This Great Big World Owes Me A Living    Col A-2063
           (w/M. J. O'Connell)
46924-1-2-3  You've Got Me Going With Your           Rejected
           Irish Eyes

Acc. by O/Rosario Bourdon.            New York, August 7, 1916.

B-18183-2  You've Got Me Going With Your Irish      Vic 18135
           Eyes
B-18184-1  Since Maggie Dooley Learned The          Vic 18131
           Hooley-Hooley
B-18185-1-2-3  Bring Her Back To Me                 Rejected
B-18186-2  Come On And Baby Me                      Vic 18131
B-18187-1  Sweet Babette, She Always Did The        Vic 18135
           Minuet

Acc. by studio O/? Charles A. Prince.  New York, August 12, 1916.

46952-     You Were Just Made To Order For Me       Col A-2088
           (w/M. J. O'Connell)
46953-3    Come On And Baby Me                      Col A-2082

Acc. by O/Eddie King.          Camden, N. J., December 11, 1916.

B-18830-3  Naughty, Naughty, Naughty                Vic 18213

                                New York, July 18, 1917.

B-20228-2  Says I To Myself, Says I                 Vic 18346
B-20229-3  Wonderful Girl, Goodnight                  -

Acc. by studio orchestra.       New York, January 14, 1921.

7739       To The Strains Of That Wedding March     Ed 50769, Amb 4280

                                New York, c. October, 1921.

8025       Yo-Lay-Ee-Oo                             Ed 50819, Amb 4408
           I've Got The Traveling Choo Choo Blues   Ed 50808
           Arrah, Go 'Long With You                   -        Amb 4338

                                New York, c. July, 1922.

8475       I Certainly Must Be In Love              Ed 51006

                                New York, March, 1923.

8876       If You Go, You'll Come Back, By And By   Ed 51139

## FRANK FAY

B. San Francisco, November 17, 1897; stage debut in Chicago at four (QUO VADIS);   in
1903 appeared there in BABES IN TOYLAND; New York debut as an extra in Sir   Henry
Irving's production of THE MERCHANT OF VENICE (Broadway, October 26, 1903); toured
in many shows in juvenile parts, then into vaudeville with a partner as Dyer & Fay
(1914-1917); appeared in THE PASSING SHOW OF 1918 (Winter Garden, July 25. 1918;in
JIM JAM JEMS (Cort, October 4, 1920); wrote, produced and acted in   FRANK FAY'S
FABLES (Park, February, 1922, short-running); great success in ARTISTS AND  MODELS
(Shubert, August 20, 1923); made successful return to vaudeville, began filming in
1929; huge success as Elwood P. Dowd in HARVEY (48th Street, November 1, 1944), as
this ran for over two years; well-known as raconteur and master of ceremonies;  m.
Frances White (div.), then Barbara Stanwyck (also div.)

Vocal, acc. by own piano.              New York, November 12, 1926.

  Take In The Sun, Hang Out The Moon  Vic test (un-numbered)

Also took part in a 1958 LP recording (BE FRANK WITH FAY) on Bally BAL-12015.

## ALICE FAYE

B. New York, May 5, 1912 (r.n. Alice Jeane Leppert; of Scottish, Irish, German and French ancestry). in Ziegfeld Follies chorus in 1930; toured with Chester Hale, 1930-1933; changed name to Faye; in chorus of GEORGE WHITE'S SCANDALS; at a party with the cast, she made a record for fun of MIMI, with Rudy Vallee at the piano; he booked her for his radio show (Fleischmann Hour) and paid her salary, but the sponsors were unimpressed. She sang with Vallee's band, however, and was becoming popular in this work when she was involved in a car smash, was badly injured; plastic surgery restored her attractive features, enabling her to appear in films starting with GEORGE WHITE'S SCANDALS (1934), in which she sang NASTY MAN, taking Lillian Harvey's part; three-year contract with Fox; second film was straight(NOW I'LL TALK, with Spencer Tracy and Helen Twelvetrees); outstanding films: GEORGE WHITE'S SCANDALS OF 1935; SHE LEARNED ABOUT SAILORS; 365 NIGHTS IN HOLLYWOOD and EVERY NIGHT AT EIGHT (1935); KING OF BURLESQUE; POOR LITTLE RICH GIRL; SING, BABY SING (1936); STOWAWAY and ON THE AVENUE (1937); WAKE UP AND LIVE; YOU CAN'T HAVE EVERYTHING and YOU'RE A SWEETHEART (1938); to Universal Films; SALLY, IRENE AND MARY; IN OLD CHICAGO; ALEXANDER'S RAGTIME BAND (1938); TAILSPIN; HOLLYWOOD CAVALCADE and ROSE OF WASHINGTON SQUARE (1939); LILIAN RUSSELL (1940); she was to have appeared in DOWN ARGENTINA WAY (1940), but appendicitis prevented this, and Betty Grable replaced her (in TIN PAN ALLEY, 1940, Betty Grable played her sister);THAT NIGHT IN RIO and WEEKEND IN HAVANA (1941); m. Tony Martin, 1937; div. 1940;m.Phil Harris, bandleader, May 12, 1941; retired from show business in 1942 to have his child; made HELLO, FRISCO, HELLO (1943); again retired, to have second daughter; guested in FOUR JILLS IN A JEEP and THE GANG'S ALL HERE (1944); last film FALLEN ANGEL (1945) until STATE FAIR (1961); between these dates she worked with husband on radio and TV, refusing many offers to resume film career.

Vocalist with Rudy Vallee and his Connecticut Yankees.
          New York, September 6, 1933.

| | | |
|---|---|---|
| BS-77619-1 | Shame On You | BB B-5175, Eld 2069, Sr S-3256 |
| BS-77620-1 | Happy Boy - Happy Girl (w/Rudy Vallee) | BB B-5182, Eld 2075, Sr S-3262 |
| BS-77621-1 | Honeymoon Hotel | BB B-5171, Eld 2065, Sr S-3252 |

 Acc. by O/Freddie Martin.   New York, July 13, 1934.

| | | |
|---|---|---|
| 15421- | Nasty Man (Film "George White's Scandals") | Col CL-3068 |
| 15422- | Here's The Key To My Heart (Film "She Learned About Sailors") | - |

 Acc. by studio orchestra.   New York, September 26, 1934.

| | | | |
|---|---|---|---|
| 16065-1 | My Future Star (Film "365 Nights In Hollywood") | Mt M-13220, Rex 8450 | |
| 16066-1 | Yes To You | - - | Col CL-3068 |

       New York, February 26, 1935.

| | | | |
|---|---|---|---|
| 16921- | According To The Moonlight (Film "George White's Scandals of 1935") | Mt M-13346, Rex 8573 | |
| 16922- | Oh, I Didn't Know (Film "George White's Scandals of 1935") | - - | Col CL-3068 |

       Los Angeles, July 6, 1935.

| | | |
|---|---|---|
| LA-379- | Speaking Confidentially (Film "Every Night At Eight") | Col CL-3068 |
| LA-380- | I Feel A Song Coming On (Film "Every Night At Eight") | - |

Acc. by O/Cy Feuer.                        Los Angeles, January 4, 1936.

| LA-449- | I've Got My Fingers Crossed (Film "King Of Burlesque") | ARC 6-03-09, Rex 8779, Col CL-3068 |
| LA-450-A | I Love To Ride The Horses (On A Merry-Go-Round) (Film "King Of Burlesque") | ARC 6-03-09, Rex 8778 |
| LA-451-A | I'm Shootin' High (Film "King Of Burlesque") | ARC 6-03-08, Rex 8778, Col CL-3068 |
| LA-452- | Spreadin' Rhythm Around (Film "King Of Burlesque") | ARC 6-03-08, Rex 8779, Col CL-3068 |

Los Angeles, December 6, 1936.

| LA-1202-B | Goodnight, My Love (Film "Stowaway") | Br 7821, 02406, Col DB-1831, CL-3068 |

Los Angeles, January 24, 1937.

| LA-1240-A | This Year's Kisses (Film "On The Avenue") | Br 7825, 02454, Col CL-3068 |
| LA-1241-B | Slumming On Park Avenue (Film "On The Avenue") | - | - | - |
| LA-1242- | I've Got My Love To Keep Me Warm (Film "On The Avenue") | Br 7821, 02516 | - |

Los Angeles, March 18, 1937.

| LA-1304-A | Never In A Million Years (Film "Wake Up And Live") | Br 7860, 02436, Col DB-1831, CL-3068 |
| LA-1305-A | It's Swell Of You (Film "Wake Up And Live") | Br 7860, 02436, Col CL-3068 |
| LA-1306-A | There's A Lull In My Life (Film "Wake Up And Live") | Br 7876, 02435, - -Epic SN-6059 |
| LA-1307-A | Wake Up And Live (Film "Wake Up And Live") | - | - | - |

## BENNY FIELDS

Showman-vocalist (husband of Blossom Seeley, q.v.) B. Milwaukee, Wis., June 14, 1894; d. New York, August 16, 1959.

Vocal, acc. by studio orchestra.          New York, March 26, 1936.

| 60944-A | Welcome Stranger | Dec 752, Br 02193 |
| 60945-A | Lost | - | - |

New York, June 26, 1936.

| 61199- | These Foolish Things (Remind Me Of You) | Dec 849 |
| 61200- | Heaven In My Heart | - |

## DOROTHY FIELDS

Daughter of actor-producer Lew Fields, b. New York; supplied lyrics to many popular songs in shows and films, some to music by Jimmy McHugh, some by her brother Herbert, and others :- Songs (GO HOME AND TELL YOUR MOTHER and BLUE AGAIN, 1930; DINNER AT EIGHT (1933); LOVELY TO LOOK AT (with Jerome Kern, 1934); THE WAY YOU LOOK TONIGHT and A FINE ROMANCE, also with Jerome Kern, 1936); and shows :- HELLO DADDY and BLACKBIRDS OF 1928 (1928); LET'S FACE IT (1941); SOMETHING FOR THE BOYS (1942), MEXICAN HAYRIDE and UP IN CENTRAL PARK (1944). The numbers I CAN'T GIVE YOU ANYTHING BUT LOVE and DIGA DIGA DOO, both from BLACKBIRDS OF 1928, have become standards.

Speech, with Jimmy McHugh and Jack Kapp.  New York, February 21, 1933.

B-13099-A  Exploitation Record for "Blackbirds"    Br Promotional Record

## GRACIE FIELDS

B. Rochdale, Lancashire, England, January 9, 1898 (r.n. Grace Stansfield); began her career as vocalist in a cinema in 1906; appeared with various juvenile troupes; as

soloist in 1913; only appearance in pantomime in DICK WHITTINGTON (Grand,  Oldham,
December 24, 1914); London debut in a revue, YES, I THINK SO (Middlesex Music Hall
July 5, 1915); huge success in Archie Pitt's touring revue MR. TOWER OF LONDON, in
which she appeared from 1918 to 1925 (over 4,000 performances); played in this  at
the Alhambra, London, July 30, 1923; m. Archie Pitt (later div.;)made success with
Sir Gerald Du Maurier's production of S.O.S. (St. James, February 11, 1928); later
that year she deputised for Rosetta Duncan in TOPSY AND EVA (Gaiety); appeared  in
revue THE SHOW'S THE THING (Victoria Palace, June 4, 1929, later to Lyceum and the
Winter Garden, London); to New York, October, 1930 to sing at the Palace; returned
to London, appeared in WALK THIS WAY (Winter Garden, December 17, 1931); began her
film career with SALLY IN OUR ALLEY (1931); several appearances at the London Palladium (1931-1935); to U.S.A., 1940; gave many shows for troops and munition workers during World War II in U.S.A., England, Africa, etc.; granted Freedom of Rochdale, May, 1937; Officer Sister of the Order of St. John of Jerusalem, April,1938;
(first actress to receive this honour); two months later was created Commander  of
the British Empire in the King's Birthday Honours; founded the Orphanage in Sussex
bearing her name in April, 1935.  Other films :- LOOKING ON THE BRIGHT SIDE(1932);
SING AS WE GO (1934); QUEEN OF HEARTS (1936); THE SHOW GOES ON (1937);    SHIPYARD
SALLY (1939); and in U.S.A., HOLY MATRIMONY (1943); MOLLY AND ME (1944);    MADAME
PIMPERNEL (1945).  Autobiography, SING AS WE GO (1960).


Vocal, acc. by Madame Adami-p.                Hayes, Middlesex, November 15, 1923.

Bb-3851-1-2  Deedle-Deedle-Dum                       HMV rejected
Bb-3852-1-2  Romany Love                             -

  Acc. by O/? Carroll Gibbons.                Hayes, Middlesex, April 3, 1928.

Bb-13151-1-2  Because I Love You                     HMV rejected
Bb-13152-1-2  As Long As He Loves Me                 -


                                              Hayes, Middlesex, May 3, 1928.

Bb-13151-4  Because I Love You                       HMV B-2733, RZ MR-1815
Bb-13261-1  My Blue Heaven                           -          RZ MR-1846
Bb-13262-2  We're Living At "The Cloisters"          HMV B-2739, RZ MR-2115

  Acc. by O/"own conductor" (sic).            Hayes, Middlesex, May 24, 1928.

Bb-13398-3  Our Avenue                               HMV B-2758, RZ MR-2086
Bb-13399-2  So Tired                                 HMV B-2739
Bb-13400-3  Under The Moon                           HMV B-2758


                                              Hayes, Middlesex, June 26, 1928.

Bb-13580-1  Serenade (Toselli)                       HMV B-3104, RZ MR-1845
Bb-13581-1  Oh ! You Have No Idea                    HMV B-2795


                                              Hayes, Middlesex, July 6, 1928.

Bb-14038-2  In The Woodshed She Said She Would       HMV B-2782
Bb-14039-2  How About Me ?                           HMV B-2795
Bb-14040-3  Laugh, Clown, Laugh                      HMV B-2782, RZ MR-1845

  Acc. by O/William Pether.                   Hayes, Middlesex, September 20, 1928.

Bb-14521-2  Why Does The Hyena Laugh ?               HMV B-2839, RZ MR-1814
Bb-14522-1  Ramona                                   -
Bb-14523-1-2  My Ohio Home                           Rejected

                                              Hayes, Middlesex, November 13, 1928.

Bb-14523-3  My Ohio Home                             HMV B-2880
Bb-14929-1  Ee, By Gum !                             -
Bb-14930-2  If I Didn't Miss You                     HMV B-2914

Acc. by O/Carroll Gibbons.                    Hayes, Middlesex, December 11, 1928.

Bb-15243-2  I've Always Wanted To Call You My        HMV B-2914
              Sweetheart
Bb-15244-1-2  I Can't Give You Anything But Love     Rejected
Bb-15246-2  Like The Big Pots Do                     HMV B-2923
Bb-15247-1  I Think Of What You Used To Think Of Me    -
  NOTE:- Matrix Bb-15245 is a rejected by Betty Fields.

                                              Small Queen's Hall, London, Jan. 13, 1929.

Bb-15547-3  Take A Look At Mine                      HMV B-2965
Bb-15548-4  Reviens (in French, announced in English)  -

   Acc. by unknown orchestra.                 Liverpool, March 12, 1929.

BR-2293-1  Hot Pot                                   HMV B-3008
BR-2294-2  Would A Manx Cat Wag Its Tail ?           HMV B-3032
BR-2295-1  I Lift Up My Finger And I Say "Tweet      HMV B-2999
              Tweet"

                                              Liverpool, March 14, 1929.

BR-2300-1  Sonny Boy                                 HMV B-3008
BR-2301-1-2  I Kiss Your Hand, Madame                Rejected
BR-2302-3  She's Funny That Way                      HMV B-2999

   Acc. by O/Carroll Gibbons.                 Hayes, Middlesex, April 19, 1929.

Bb-16445-3  That's What Puts The "Sweet" In          HMV B-3032
              "Home, Sweet Home"
Bb-16446-2  Scented Soap                             HMV B-3061
Bb-16447-1-2-3-4  She's Funny That Way               Rejected
Bb-16448-2  Nagasaki                                 HMV B-3061, RZ MR-1950

                                              Hayes, Middlesex, July 5, 1929.

Bb-17435-1-2  Unlucky Number Thirteen                Rejected
Bb-17436-2  I Got A "Code" In My "Doze"              HMV B-3092
Bb-17437-3  When Summer Is Gone                       -

                                              Hayes, Middlesex, August 26, 1929.

Bb-17535-1  Little Pal                               HMV B-3147
Bb-17536-2  That's How I Feel About You,             HMV B-3176
              Sweetheart
Bb-17537-2  Cute Little Flat (w/Archie Pitt)         HMV B-3134
Bb-17538-2  When You're Gone                          -

                                              Hayes, Middlesex, September 2, 1929.

Bb-17561-2  Why Can't You ?                          HMV B-3147
Bb-17562-1  Thoughts Of You                          HMV B-3176
Bb-17563-1  Oh Maggie, What Have You Been Up To ?  HMV B-3202

                                              Hayes, Middlesex, September 13, 1929.

Bb-17629-2  I Got A "Code" In My "Doze"              HMV B-3092
Bb-17630-2  Unlucky Number Thirteen                  HMV B-3104
Bb-17631-1-2-3  I've Got A Feeling I'm Falling       Rejected
Bb-17632-1-2  Peace Of Mind                           -

   Acc. by O/Ray Noble.                       Hayes, Middlesex, October 18, 1929.

Bb-17723-2  Nowt About Owt                           HMV B-3291
Bb-17724-3  I've Got A Man                           HMV B-3202
Bb-17725-1-2-3  Sentimental Fool                     Rejected

Acc. by O/Carroll Gibbons.                    Hayes, Middlesex, November 29, 1929.

Bb-18216-3  Moscow                            HMV B-3244
Bb-18217-3  This Is Heaven                    -
Bb-18218-2  If I Had A Talking Picture Of You  HMV B-3259, RZ MR-2134
Bb-18219-2  I'm A Dreamer (Aren't We All ?)   -              -

Acc. by O/Ray Noble.                          Hayes, Middlesex, January 9, 1930.

Bb-18272-2  Coople O' Dooks                   HMV B-3305
Bb-18273-3  Stop And Shop At The Co-op Shop   -              7EG-8299
Bb-18274-3  Painting The Clouds With Sunshine  HMV B-3291

Acc. by O/Miss Lipman.                        Hayes, Middlesex, February 14, 1930.

Bb-18357-2  The Punch And Judy Show           HMV B-3326
Bb-18358-3  Singing In The Bathtub            -              7EG-8299, RZ MR-2087
Bb-18359-1-2  Just You - Just Me             Rejected

                                              Hayes, Middlesex, March 21, 1930.

Bb-19060-1  Body And Soul                     HMV B-3383, RZ MR-1900
Bb-19061-1  You Can't Kill Flies By Scratching  -
Bb-19062-2  The Clatter Of The Clogs          HMV B-3415, RZ MR-2068

Organ acc. by Herbert Dawson.         Kingsway Hall, London, March 25, 1930.

Bb-18715-2  Three Green Bonnets               HMV B-3595, 7EG-8071, RZ MR-1917
Bb-18716-1  A Little Love, A Little Kiss      HMV B-3415, RZ MR-2068
Cc-18717-1  Private record for Douglas Gordon  HMV Private Recording

Acc. by O/Ray Noble.                          Hayes, Middlesex, May 22, 1930.

Bb-19198-3  Little Pudden Basin               HMV B-3494
Bb-19199-2  Around The Corner                 -
Bb-19200-2  A Cottage For Sale                HMV B-3463, RZ MR-2195
Bb-19401-2  Cryin' For The Carolines          -              -

                                              Hayes, Middlesex, June 6, 1930.

Bb-19451-1-2-3  'Fonso (My Hot Spanish Knight)  Rejected
Bb-19452-2  It's Nothing To Do With You       HMV B-3505
Bb-19453-2  Dream Lover                       -              RZ MR-1815

                                              Hayes, Middlesex, August 14, 1930.

Bb-19451-5  'Fonso (My Hot Spanish Knight)    HMV B-3565
Bb-19583-1-2-3  Dancing With The Devil        Rejected
Bb-19584-2  I Just Can't Figure It Out At All  HMV B-3565

                                              Hayes, Middlesex, August 22, 1930.

Bb-19593-2  Falling In Love Again             HMV B-3592
Bb-19594-2  The Barmaid's Song                HMV B-3573, RZ MR-2012
Bb-19595-1  Over The Garden Wall              HMV B-3600

                                              Hayes, Middlesex, August 29, 1930.

Bb-20002-2  What Archibald Says, Goes         HMV B-3592
Bb-20003-1  I'm In The Market For You         HMV B-3573
Bb-20004-1  I'll Be Good Because Of You       HMV B-3600

                                              Hayes, Middlesex, November 19, 1930.

Bb-20507-1  The Lovely Aspidistra In The Old  HMV B-3688
              Art Pot
Bb-20508-1  Dancing With Tears In My Eyes     -              RZ MR-2012

Hayes, Middlesex, November 27, 1930.

Bb-20528-2  Fred Fannakapan                    HMV B-3595, RZ MR-2067
Bb-20529-2  Lancashire Blues                   HMV B-3708, RZ MR-2086
Bb-20530-2  What Good Am I Without You ?             -

Hayes, Middlesex, January 8, 1931.

OB-13-2  Sitting On A Five-Barred Gate         HMV B-3724
OB-14-2  Go Home And Tell Your Mother               -
OB-15-2  The Kiss Waltz                        HMV B-3780, RZ MR-2133

Hayes, Middlesex, February 24, 1931.

OB-127-2  Pass, Shoot, Goal !                  HMV B-3795
OB-128-2  The Bargain Hunter                   HMV B-3912
OB-129-3  You're Driving Me Crazy              HMV B-3780, RZ MR-2133

Hayes, Middlesex, March 20, 1931.

OB-170-2  That Must Have Been Our Walter       HMV B-3824, RZ MR-2011
OB-171-2  River, Stay 'Way From My Door            -          -
OB-172-3  The Clockwork Courtship              HMV B-3795

Small Queen's Hall, London, April 24,1931.

OB-791-5  Fall In And Follow The Band (w/      HMV B-3879, RZ MR-1791
            children's chorus) (Film "Sally In Our Alley")
OB-792-4  Sally (Film "Sally In Our Alley")        - 7EG-8071 -

Small Queen's Hall, London, June 29, 1931.

OB-1247-2  Oh, Sailor Behave                   HMV B-3912
OB-1248-2  The Party's Getting Rough           HMV B-3908
OB-1249-2  I'll Always Be True                      -
OB-1250-1  A Little Bit Of Chinese Music       Rejected

Small Queen's Hall, London, July 13, 1931.

OB-1277-2  Granny's Little Old Skin Rug        HMV B-3920
OB-1278-2  Only A Dancing Sweetheart               -
OB-1279-1-2  I'm One Of God's Children (Who    Rejected
              Hasn't Got Wings)
OB-1280-1-2  When The Circus Comes To Town         -

Kingsway Hall, London, October 2, 1931.

OB-1126-3  The Mocking Bird Went "Cuckoo"      HMV B-3968
OB-1127-   Obadiah's Mother                    HMV B-3998
OB-1128-1-2  Just One More Chance              Rejected
OB-1129-   Oh ! Glory                          HMV B-3998

Small Queen's Hall, London, Nov. 3, 1931.

OB-1128-3  Just One More Chance                HMV B-3968
OB-2214-2  Down At Our Charity Bazaar          HMV B-4051
OB-2215-2  They All Fall In Love But Me        HMV B-4000
OB-2216-2  Life's Desire                           -
OB-2217-2  Song Of The Highway                 HMV B-4051

London, February 8, 1932.

2B-2683-1  Gracie Fields Medley - Part 1 (Intro.   HMV C-2378
              Charmaine/Because I Love You/My Blue Heaven)
2B-2684-3  Gracie Fields Medley - Part 2 (Intro.        -
              Ramona/Ee, By Gum/Laugh, Clown, Laugh)

London, February 29, 1932.

| | | |
|---|---|---|
| OB-2754-2 | He Forgot To Come Back | HMV B-4101 |
| OB-2755-2 | When The Rest Of The Crowd Goes Home | HMV B-4109 |
| OB-2756-2 | Home | HMV B-4101 |

London, March 15, 1932.

| | | |
|---|---|---|
| OB-3037-1-2-3 | When We All Went To The Zoo | Rejected |
| OB-3038-2 | Rochdale Hounds | HMV B-4109, 7EG-8299, RZ .MR-2237 |
| OB-3039-1-2 | Now That You're Gone | Rejected |

London, March 29, 1932.

| | | |
|---|---|---|
| OB-3037-6 | When We All Went To The Zoo | HMV B-4168 |
| OB-3039-4 | Now That You're Gone | - |

London, May 12, 1932.

| | | |
|---|---|---|
| OB-3387-2 | Antonio | HMV B-4198 |
| OB-3388-1 | Can't We Talk It Over ? | - |

London, May 27, 1932.

| | | |
|---|---|---|
| OB-2267-1-2 | 'Appy 'Ampstead | Rejected |
| OB-2268-2 | Waltzing Time In Old Vienna | HMV B-4214 |
| OB-2269-2 | A Fly's Day Out | - |

London, July 27, 1932.

| | | |
|---|---|---|
| OB-2267-4 | 'Appy 'Ampstead | HMV B-4259 |
| OB-2386-2 | After Tonight We Say Goodbye (Film "Looking On The Bright Side") | HMV B-4260 |
| OB-2387-2 | I Hate You (Film "Looking On The Bright Side") | - |
| OB-2388-2 | You're More Than All The World To Me (Film "Looking On The Bright Side") | HMV B-4259 |
| OB-2389-3 | He's Dead But He Won't Lie Down (Film "Looking On The Bright Side") | HMV B-4258, RZ MR-1814 |
| OB-2390-2 | Looking On The Bright Side Of Life (Film "Looking On The Bright Side") | - |

London, September 22, 1932.

| | | |
|---|---|---|
| OB-4212-2 | Round The Bend Of The Road | HMV B-4281 |
| OB-4213-2 | Underneath The Arches | HMV B-4277, RZ MR-2115 |
| OB-4214-1-2 | Free | Rejected |
| OB-4215-1-2 | Grandfather's Bagpipes | - |
| OB-4216-2 | Why Waste Your Tears ? | HMV B-4281 |
| OB-4217-2 | John Willie's Farm | HMV B-4277 |

London, October 24, 1932.

| | | |
|---|---|---|
| 2B-4421-2 | Gracie's Christmas Party - Part 1 (w/ her Mother) | HMV C-2487, RZ MR-1881 (10-inch edition of 12-inch |
| 2B-4422-3 | Gracie's Christmas Party - Part 2 (w/ her Mother) | -            -            original) |

London, October 25, 1932.

| | | |
|---|---|---|
| OB-4279-2 | Let's All Go Posh | HMV B-4316 |
| OB-4280-2 | Mary Ellen's Hot Pot Party | HMV B-4317, RZ MR-2067 |
| OB-4281-3 | Song Of The Bells | HMV B-4316 |
| OB-4282-2 | Say It Isn't So | HMV B-4317 |

London; November 22, 1932.

| | | |
|---|---|---|
| OB-4336-2 | One Little Hair On His Head | HMV B-4343 |
| OB-4337-1-2-3 | In Old Siberia | Rejected |
| OB-4338-2 | How Deep Is The Ocean ? | HMV B-4343, RZ MR-2114 |

London, January 3, 1933.

OB-4337-5  In Old Siberia                         HMV B-4362
OB-4600-2  Balloons                               -
OB-6201-2  Play, Fiddle, Play                     HMV B-4368

London, January 13, 1933.

OB-6216-1-2  Pu-leeze ! Mr. Hemingway            Rejected
OB-6217-2  Heaven Will Protect An Honest Girl    HMV B-4470, RZ MR-2040
OB-6218-1-2  Invitation to the Press Lunch       HMV Private Recording
             (speaking, with Messrs. Dodgson and Streeton)

London, January 23, 1933.

OB-6218-3-4  Invitation to the Press Lunch       HMV Private Recording
             (speaking, with Messrs. Dodgson and Streeton)

London, February 6, 1933.

OB-6429-1-2  Musical Menu Lancashire Lunch       Rejected
OB-6430-1-2  So Long, Lads, We're Off            HMV B-4368

London, February 21, 1933.

OB-6443-2  Fiddler Joe                            HMV B-4383
OB-6444-2  Poor Me, Poor You                      -

London, March 24, 1933.

OB-6367-2  The Photograph Of Mother's Wedding     HMV B-4407
             Group
OB-6368-1  I'm Playing With Fire                  -
OB-6369-2  Poor Little Willie                     HMV B-4469

London, June 9, 1933.

OB-6745-1  My Lucky Day (Film "This Week Of Grace")HMV B-4471, RZ MR-2041
OB-6746-2  I Can't Remember                       HMV B-4464
OB-6747-2  Whiskers And All                       -
OB-6748-1  Mary Rose (Film "This Week Of Grace")  HMV B-4471, RZ MR-2041

London, June 13, 1933.

OB-6756-2  Happy Ending (Film "This Week Of Grace")HMV B-4469, RZ MR-2040
OB-6757-2  Stormy Weather                         HMV B-4470
OB-6758-2  A Melody At Dawn                       HMV B-4472, RZ MR-2042
OB-6759-2  When Cupid Calls                       -          -

London, July 25, 1933.

OB-5037-2  I Had To Go And Find Another Job       HMV B-4493
OB-5038-1-2  In A Little Second-Hand Store        Rejected
OB-5039-1  There's A Cabin In The Pines           HMV B-4493, RZ MR-2156

Acc. by the Holborn Empire Orchestra.   Holborn Empire, October 11, 1933.

            Gracie In The Theatre - Part 1 (Intro.  HMV C-2625, RZ MR-1878
             There's A Cabin In The Pines/Whiskers And All)
            Gracie In The Theatre - Part 2 (Intro.    -            -
             The Punch And Judy Show/Rochdale Hounds)
            Gracie In The Theatre - Part 3 (Intro.  HMV C-2626, RZ MR-1879
             Rochdale Hounds (w/patter)/A May Morning (Burlesque)
            Gracie In The Theatre - Part 4 (Intro.    -            -
             Out In The Cold, Cold Snow/I Can't Remember)
            Gracie In The Theatre - Part 5 (Intro.  HMV C-2627, RZ MR-1880
             Applause and calls for encores/Sally/Speech/Sally (by the audience)
            Gracie In The Theatre - Part 6 (Intro.    -            -
             Applause/Stormy Weather/Further calls, Final Speech and Curtain)

Acc. by O/Ray Noble.                    London, October 30, 1933.

OB-5150-2  Christmas Bells At Eventide        HMV B-8065
OB-5152-1  It Isn't Fair                      HMV B-8064
OB-5153-1  I Took My Harp To A Party          HMV B-8065, RZ MR-2237
  NOTE:- Matrix OB-5151 was never allocated.

                                        London, October 31, 1933.

2B-5158-2  Gracie At Home (w/her Parents, Sister  HMV C-2622, RZ MR-1881
             and Brother) - Part 1
2B-5159-2  Gracie At Home (w/her Parents, Sister        -            -
             and Brother) - Part 2
OB-5160-2  Laugh At Life                      HMV B-8064

                                        London, January 12, 1934.

OB-5854-2  Cherie (Film "Love, Life And       HMV B-8140
             Laughter")
OB-5855-2  Riding On The Clouds (Film "Love,  HMV B-8141
             Life And Laughter")

                                        London, February 12, 1934.

OB-5891-2  Love, Life And Laughter (Film "Love,  HMV B-8140
             Life And Laughter")
OB-5892-1  Out In The Cold, Cold Snow         HMV B-8185
OB-5893-1  Play To Me, Gypsy                  HMV B-8130, RZ MR-2069

                                        London, February 13, 1934.

OB-5894-1-2  How Happy The Lover              Rejected
OB-5895-2  I'm A Failure (Film "Love, Life And  HMV B-8141
             Laughter")
OB-5896-1  Keep It In The Family Circle       HMV B-8130

                                        London, May 17, 1934.

OB-7221-2  Love's Last Word Is Spoken         HMV B-8185, 7EG-8071, RZ MR-1949
OB-7222-2  Will You Love Me When I'm Mutton ?  HMV B-8192, RZ MR-2156
OB-7223-2  At The Court Of Old King Cole           -

                                        London, July 1, 1934.

OB-7293-2  Love (Wonderful Love) (Film "Sing As  HMV B-8208
             We Go")
OB-7294-2  Just A Catchy Little Tune (Film "Sing      -
             As We Go")
OB-7295-2  In My Little Bottom Drawer (Film   HMV B-8209, RZ MR-1846
             "Sing As We Go")

                                        London, July 8, 1934.

OB-7438-6  Little Man, You've Had A Busy Day   HMV B-8210
OB-7439-2  Sing As We Go (w/chorus) (Film "Sing  HMV B-8209, RZ MR-2114
             As We Go")
OB-7440-2  There's Millions And Millions Of   HMV B-8210
             Women

Acc. by O/Percival Mackey.              London, October 9, 1934.

OEA-634-2  What Can You Give A Nudist On His   HMV B-8232
             Birthday ?
OEA-635-2  How Changed Is The Old Place Now   HMV B-8233
OEA-636-3  The House Is Haunted                    -         RZ MR-1949
OEA-637-2  Isle Of Capri                      HMV B-8232, RZ MR-2069

Organ acc. by Herbert Dawson.              Kingsway Hall, London, October 25, 1934.

2EA-1011-3  Ave Maria (Bach-Gounod) (in Latin)     HMV C-2705, 7EG-8071, RZ MR-1917
2EA-1012-2  Medley of Film Waltz Songs (Intro.        -                  RZ MR-1983
            Sally/You're More Than All The World To Me/Cherie)

    Acc. by O/Percival Mackey.                 London, October 26, 1934.

OEA-865-2  I Taught Her How To Play Br-oop, Br-oop HMV B-8243
OEA-866-3  Love In Bloom                             -        RZ MR-2087

    Acc. by Jack Jackson and his Orchestra. London, December 15, 1934.

OEA-711-2  Gracie In The Children's Ward           HMV B-8261

    Acc. by O/Clifford Greenwood.              London, February 1, 1935.

OEA-754-2  Born To Be A Clown                      HMV B-8298
OEA-755-2  If All The World Were Mine              HMV B-8286
OEA-756-2  Your Dog's Come Home Again              -
OEA-757-2  You Haven't Altered A Bit               HMV B-8298, RZ MR-1847

                                London, March 5, 1935.

OEA-1809-   One Night Of Love                      RZ MR-1792
OEA-1810-1-2  When The Robin Sings His Song Again  Rejected
OEA-1811-1-2  Egbert 'Enery 'Epplethwaite          -
OEA-1812-   You And The Night And The Music        RZ MR-1792

                                London, May 19, 1935.

OEA-1873-   Anna From Anacapresi (w/Tommy Fields-  RZ MR-1793
            Douglas Wakefield-Billy Nelson) (Film "Look Up And Laugh")
OEA-1374-   Love Is Everywhere (w/Tommy Fields)    -
            (Film "Look Up And Laugh")
OEA-1875-2  Things Might Have Been So Diff'rent     HMV B-8331
OEA-1876-   Look Up And Laugh (w/chorus) (Film     RZ MR-1794
            "Look Up And Laugh")
OEA-1877-   Shall I Be An Old Man's Darling ?      -
OEA-1878-2  I Haven't Been The Same Girl Since     HMV B-8331, RZ MR-1847

    Acc. by O/Jay Wilbur.                      London, July-August, 1935.

F-1417-3  When I Grow Too Old To Dream            Rex 8557, 9690, Dec F-9700
F-1418-3  Turn 'Erbert's Face To The Wall, Mother   -        9515
F-1419-1-2  Life Is A Song/The Words Are In My    Rex 8558
            Heart/Lullaby Of Broadway
F-1420-4  I'm Ninety-Nine Today                   -

    Acc. by O/Fred Hartley.                    London, August, 1935.

F-1449-2  Trees                                   Rex 8636
F-1450-2  Smilin' Through                         -
F-1451-1  Roll Along, Prairie Moon                Rex 8633
F-1452-3  Red Sails In The Sunset                 Rex 8585

F-1461-2  South American Joe                      Rex 8585
F-1462-2  There's A Lovely Lake In London         Rex 8592
F-1463-1  We've Got To Keep Up With The Joneses     -        9431
F-1464-1  Love Me Forever                         Rex 8599

                                London, September, 1935.

F-1481-1-2  When You Grow Up, Little Lady         Rex 8599
F-1482-1-2  Danny Boy                            Rex 8687, 9603
F-1483-1  I Give My Heart                         Rex 8749, 9515
F-1484-1  The General's Fast Asleep               Rex 8617

London, September, 1935.

F-1499-2  Look To The Left And Look To The          Rex 8718
          Right  (w/The Corona Babes)
F-1500-1  One Of The Little Orphans Of The          Rex 8818, 9478
          Storm (Film "Queen Of Hearts")
F-1501-2  Grandfather's Bagpipes                    Rex 8617, 9603

F-1503-1  Why Did I Have To Meet You ? (Film        Rex 8819
          "Queen Of Hearts")

F-1512-   Old Soldiers Never Die - Part 1 (Intro. Rex 8618
          Fall In And Follow Me/Let The Great Big World Keep Turning/Hello,Hello,
          Who's Your Lady Friend ?/Mademoiselle From Armentieres)
F-1513-   Old Soldiers Never Die - Part 2 (Intro.      -
          There's A Long, Long Trail/Take Me Back To Dear Old Blighty/If You Were
          The Only Girl In The World/It's A Long Way To Tipperary)

F-1515-2  Do You Remember My First Love Song ?      Rex 8819
          (Film "Queen Of Hearts")

London, October, 1935.

F-1561-2  I'm Only Her Mother                       Rex 8687
F-1562-2  Queen Of Hearts (Film "Queen Of           Rex 8818
          Hearts")
F-1563-2  She Fought Like A Tiger For 'Er Honour  Rex 8749, 9478

F-1565-2  Clogs And Shawl                           Rex 8718
F-1566-2  Winter Draws On                           Rex 8633, 9431

   Acc. by O/Jay Wilbur.              London, April, 1936.

F-1792-1-2  Alone                                   Rex 8768
F-1793-1  Why Did She Fall For The Leader Of The      -
          Band ?

London, May, 1936.

F-1837-2  The Glory Of Love                         Rex 8786
F-1838-2  Poor Little Angeline                        -

London, June, 1936.

F-1860-2  Sweetheart, Let's Grow Old Together       Rex 8806
F-1861-1  She Came From Alsace-Lorraine               -

London, July, 1936.

F-1900-2  Would You ?                               Rex 8840
F-1901-2  Laughing Irish Eyes                         -

London, August, 1936.

F-1952-1  Gracie's Request Record - Part 1          Rex 8868
          (Intro. Sally/My Blue Heaven/Looking On The Bright Side)
F-1953-2  Gracie's Request Record - Part 2            -
          (Intro. Sing As We Go/Because I Love You/The Rochdale Hounds)

London, September, 1936.

F-1970-2  Indian Love Call (w/male chorus)          Rex 8893
F-1971-2  Rose Marie (w/male chorus)                  -

London, late September, 1936.

F-2001-2  Gracie And Sandy's Party (w/Sandy         Rex 8905
          Powell-Larry Adler-Joe Peterson etc.) - Part 1
F-2002-2  Gracie And Sandy's Party - Part 2           -

London, October, 1936.

```
F-2048-1  Serenade In The Night                  Rex 8921
F-2049-1  In A Little Lancashire Town (Film "The      -      9097
            Show Goes On")
```

London, November, 1936.

```
F-2088-1  Did Your Mother Come From Ireland ?    Rex 8936
F-2089-1  A Feather In Her Tyrolean Hat             -
```

London, early January, 1937.

```
F-2136-1  Show Boat - Vocal Gems from the Film    Rex 8967
            - Part 1 (Intro. Can't Help Lovin' Dat Man/Why Do I Love You ?/Bill)(w/
            Lyle Evans and chorus)
F-2137-1  Show Boat - Vocal Gems from the Film      -
            - Part 2 (Intro. Ol' Man River/You Are Love/Make Believe)(w/Lyle  Evans
            and chorus)
F-2138-2  In The Chapel In The Moonlight          Rex 8968
F-2139-2  Have You Forgotten So Soon ?              -
```

London, February, 1937.

```
F-2202-1  Smile When You Say Goodbye (Film "The   Rex 9095, 9649
            Show Goes On")
F-2203-1  We're All Good Pals Together (Film      Rex 9096
            "The Show Goes On")
F-2204-1  Gracie And Sandy At The Coronation -    Rex 9022
            Part 1 (w/Sandy Powell and supporting cast)
F-2205-1  Gracie And Sandy At The Coronation -      -
            Part 2 (w/Sandy Powell and supporting cast)
```

Acc. by Fred Hartley and his Quintet.  London, February-March, 1937.

```
F-2210-1  There's A Small Hotel                   Rex 9114, Dec F-6331
F-2211-1  A Nice Cup Of Tea                         -           -
F-2212-1  The Song In Your Heart (Film "The       Rex 9096
            Show Goes On")
F-2213-1  My Love For You (Film "The Show Goes    Rex 9097
            On")
F-2214-1  I Never Cried So Much In All My Life    Rex 9095
            (Film "The Show Goes On")
F-2215-1  The Desert Song                         Rex 9115, Dec F-6388
F-2216-1  Ah ! Sweet Mystery Of Life                -           -
```

London, May 21, 1937.

```
TB-3071-3  Goodnight, My Love                     Rex 9116, Dec F-6403
TB-3072-1  Coronation Waltz                         -           -
```

London, June  18 , 1937.

```
R-2337-1  Will You Remember ?                     Rex 9117
R-2338-1  On A Little Dream Ranch                   -
```

London, August  11, 1937.

```
R-2378-1  Medley - Part 1 (Intro. When My Dream   Rex 9101
            Boat Comes Home/September In The Rain)
R-2379-1  Medley - Part 2 (Intro. Where Is The      -
            Sun ?/When The Harvest Moon Is Shining)
R-2380-1  Our Song                                Rex 9133
R-2381-1  Where Are You ?                           -
```

London, October  11, 1937.

```
R-2433-1  It Looks Like Rain In Cherry Blossom    Rex 9140
            Lane
R-2434-1  The Greatest Mistake Of My Life           -    (continued on page 280)
```
(continued on page 280)

London, October 11, 1937 (cont.)

R-2435-1  The Organ, The Monkey And Me          Rex 9161
R-2436-1  Gypsy Lullaby                         -

London, November 8, 1937.

R-2495-1  Little Old Lady              Rex 9166, 9690, Dec F-9700
R-2496-1  The First Time I Saw You              -
R-2497-1  Giannina Mia                          Rex 9195
R-2498-1  Sympathy                              -

London, January 5, 1938.

R-2563-1  A Foggy Day                           Rex 9237
R-2564-1  Remember Me ?                         Rex 9221
R-2565-1  Sailing Home                          -
R-2566-1  The Family Tree                       Rex 9237

London, January 18, 1938.

R-2567-1  Walter, Walter                        Rex 9307
R-2568-1-2  The Sweetest Song In The World      Rejected
R-2569-2  The Trek Song                         Rex 9307

London, January 25, 1938.

R-2570-1-2  My Only Dream                       Rejected
R-2585-1  Rosalie                               Rex 9255
R-2586-1  London Is Saying Goodnight            -

London, February 22, 1938.

R-2623-1  In Me 'Oroscope                       Rex 9278
R-2624-1  Someday My Prince Will Come           Rex 9258
R-2625-1  Whistle While You Work                -
R-2626-1  The Girl In The Alice Blue Gown       Rex 9278
R-2627-1  Outside An Old Stage Door             Rex 9302
R-2628-1  Old Father Thames                     -

  Acc. by O/? Jay Wilbur.        London, May 11, 1938.

R-2697-1  Lambeth Walk (w/The Corona Babes)     Rex 9308
R-2698-2  Little Drummer Boy                    -        9649

London, May 20, 1938.

R-2718-1  There Is A Tavern In The Town         Rex 9325
R-2719-1  The Sweetest Song In The World        -
R-2720-1  When The Organ Played "O Promise Me"  Rex 9328
R-2721-1  I Love To Whistle                     -

London, August 2, 1938.

R-2828-1  Little Lady Make-Believe              Rex 9354
R-2829-1  My Heaven In The Pines                -
R-2830-1  Somebody's Thinking Of You Tonight    Rex 9350
R-2831-1  Oh Ma-Ma (The Butcher Boy)            -

London, August 17, 1938.

R-2856-1  Goodnight, Angel                      Rex 9361
R-2857-1  Please Be Kind/I Won't Tell A Soul    -
R-2858-1  Music, Maestro, Please               Rex 9377
R-2859-1  Love Walked In                        -

  Acc. by organ and orchestra.   London, November 10, 1938.

OGF-5-1  The Holy City (w/choir)               RZ MR-2892
OGF-6-1  Land Of Hope And Glory (w/choir)      -

Acc. by O/? George Scott Wood.        London, November 12, 1938.

OGF-7-1   The Donkey's Serenade                RZ MR-2893
OGF-8-1   Christopher Robin Is Saying His Prayers    -
OGF-9-1   Christopher Robin Is Saying His Prayers  Rejected
            ("cod" version)
OGF-10-1  O Come, All Ye Faithful              RZ MR-2924
OGF-11-1  You've Got To Be Smart In The Army   RZ MR-3001
            Nowadays (Film "Keep Smiling")
OGF-12-1  Giddy-Up (Film "Keep Smiling")       RZ MR-2950
OGF-13-1  Swing Your Way To Happiness (Film       -
            "Keep Smiling")

                              London, November 18, 1938.

OGF-14-1  One Of Those Old-Fashioned Ladies    RZ MR-2929
OGF-15-1  Snow White And The Seven Dwarfs -    RZ MR-2917
            Medley. (Intro. With A Smile And A Song/I'm Wishing/Heigh Ho)
OGF-16-1  Gracie's Hit Medley (1938) (Intro.      -
            Any Broken Hearts To Mend ?/When Mother Nature Sings Her Lullaby/A-Tis-
            ket A-Tasket)
OGF-17-1  Alexander's Ragtime Band             RZ MR-2929
OGF-18-1  The Biggest Aspidistra In The World  RZ MR-3001, HMV 7EG-8299
            (Film "Keep Smiling")

                              London, February 17, 1939.

OGF-19-1  Mrs. Binns' Twins (Film "Keep Smiling") RZ MR-3000
OGF-20-1  Two Sleepy People (w/Tommy Fields)   RZ MR-2996
OGF-21-1  Peace Of Mind (Film "Keep Smiling")  RZ MR-3000
OGF-22-1  The Umbrella Man (w/Tommy Fields)    RZ MR-2996

                              London, May 12, 1939.

OGF-23-1  Gracie's Hit Medley (No. 2), Part 1     RZ MR-3054
            (Intro. Little Swiss Whistling Song/They Say/Jeepers Creepers)
OGF-24-1  Gracie's Hit Medley (No. 2), Part 2
            (Intro. Little Sir Echo/I Promise You/Sweethearts)
OGF-25-1  Romany                               RZ MR-3055
OGF-26-1  One Day When We Were Young              -

Acc. by film studio orchestra.        Recorded July 26, 1939 from soundtrack of
                                        film.

OGF-27-1  Danny Boy (Film "Shipyard Sally")    RZ MR-3118
OGF-28-1  Wish Me Luck As You Wave Me Goodbye     -
            (Film "Shipyard Sally")
OGF-29-1  I've Got The Jitterbugs (Film "Ship- RZ MR-3119
            yard Sally")
OGF-30-1  Grandfather's Bagpipes (Intro. Annie    -
            Laurie) (w/choir) (Film "Shipyard Sally")

Acc. by unknown p.                    London, July 30, 1939.

OGF-31-1-2  Speech (Broadcast)                 Rejected
OGF-32-1  I Love The Moon                      RZ MR-3189

Acc. by film studio orchestra.        Recorded August 1, 1939 from soundtrack  of
                                        film.

OGF-33-1  In Pernambuco (Film "Shipyard Sally")  RZ rejected

Acc. by O/George Scott Wood.          Chelsea Barracks, London, October 26, 1939.

OGF-34-1  Gracie With The Troops - Part 1 (Intro. RZ MR-3156
            Run, Rabbit, Run/If You Were The Only Girl In The World/There'll  Always
            Be An England)
OGF-35-1  Gracie With The Troops - Part 2 (Intro.    -
            The Old Lady From Armentieres/The Biggest Aspidistra In The World/  Wish
            Me Luck As You Wave Me Goodbye)

Acc. by O/Phil Cardew.                    London, November 7, 1939.

OGF-36-1  The Last Rose Of Summer              Col FB-2496
OGF-37-1  The Fairy On The Christmas Tree      RZ MR-3180
OGF-38-1  Crash ! Bang ! I Want To Go Home     RZ MR-3189
OGF-39-1  I'm Sending A Letter To Santa Claus  RZ MR-3180

Acc. by unknown orchestra, introduced by Sir Seymour Hicks, with BEF chorus.
                          "Somewhere in France," November 17, 1939.

OGF-40-1  Our Gracie With The Boys In France   RZ MR-3181
          - Part 1 (Intro. Sing As We Go/I Never Cried So Much In All My Life)
OGF-41-1  Our Gracie With The Boys In France   -
          - Part 2 (Intro. An Old Violin)
OGF-42-1  Our Gracie With The Boys In France   RZ MR-3182
          - Part 3 (Intro. When I Grow Too Old To Dream/Walter, Walter/I'm Sending
          A Letter To Santa Claus)
OGF-43-1  Our Gracie With The Boys In France   -
          - Part 4 (Intro. Wish Me Luck As You Wave Me Goodbye)

Acc. by unknown p, and RAF chorus.    "Somewhere in France," December 25, 1939.

OGF-48-1  Our Gracie With The Air Force - Part 1 RZ MR-3228
          (Intro. F.D.R. Jones/Please Leave My Butter Alone)
OGF-49-1  Our Gracie With The Air Force - Part 2
          (Intro. Romany/The Bells Of St. Mary's/O Come, All Ye Faithful)

Acc. by unknown p, and Navy chorus.    Location unknown, January 8, 1940.

OGF-50-1  Our Gracie With The Navy - Part 1     RZ MR-3229
          (Intro. They Can't Ration Love/Christopher Robin Is Saying His Prayers)
OGF-51-1  Our Gracie With The Navy - Part 2     -
          (Intro. I Hear A Dream/Out In The Cold, Cold Snow/Red Sails In The  Sun-
          set)

Acc. by O/George Scott Wood.              London, January 10, 1940.

OGF-44-1  Over The Rainbow (w/chorus)          RZ MR-3227
OGF-45-1  Goodnight, Children, Everywhere (w/ch.) RZ MR-3226
OGF-46-1  Gulliver's Travels - Film Selection  -
          (w/chorus) (Intro. It's A Hap-Hap-Happy Day/I Hear A Dream/We're All To-
          gether)
OGF-47-1  Bella Bambina                        RZ MR-3227

Acc. by O/Lou Bring.                      Hollywood, March 7, 1940.

PBS-042556-1  Pinocchio - Vocal Film Selection,   RZ MR-3287
          **Part 1 (Intro. When You Wish Upon A Star/Give A Little Whistle/Hi-Diddle**
          Dee Dee)
PBS-042557-1  Pinocchio - Vocal Film Selection,   -
          Part 2 (Intro. Turn On The Old Music Box/Little Wooden Head/I've Got  No
          Strings)
PBS-042558-1  The Woodpecker Song              RZ MR-3288
PBS-042559-1  Little Curly Hair In A High Chair  Col FB-2448

Acc. by unknown p.                        London, April 25, 1940.

OGF-52-1  What's The Good Of A Birthday ?      Col FB-2448
OGF-53-1  Medley (Intro. When Irish Eyes Are   Rejected
          Smiling/My Blue Heaven/Land Of Hope And Glory)
OGF-62-2  I Never Cried So Much In All My Life  Col FB-2463

                          Theatre Royal, Drury Lane, London,
                          May 6, 1940.

OGF-54-1  The Grandest Song Of All             RZ MR-3288
OGF-55-1  Stop And Shop At The Co-op. Shop     Col FB-2449
OGF-56-1  Indian Summer                        Col FB-2463

Acc. by O/Ben Frankel.                     London, May 15, 1940.

OGF-57-1  When Our Dreams Grow Old                RZ MR-3308
OGF-58-1  If I Should Fall In Love Again          -
OGF-59-1  Angels Guard Thee                       Rejected
OGF-60-1  Begin The Beguine                       Col FB-2449
OGF-61-1  Roses Of Picardy (acc. by piano only)   Col FB-2496

Acc. by O/Victor Young.                    Los Angeles, June 24, 1941.

DLA-2455-A  He's Dead - But He Won't Lie Down     Dec 18183, 23897, F-7981
DLA-2456-A  The Biggest Aspidistra In The World     -        -
DLA-2457-A  The Biggest Aspidistra In The World   Dec F-7981, DFE-6246
            (Special English version)
DLA-2458-A  Ave Maria (Schubert)                  Dec 23896, F-8015
DLA-2459-A  An Old Violin                           -        -

                                           Los Angeles, February 2, 1942.

DLA-2879-A  Rose O'Day (The Filla-Ga-Dusha Song)  Dec 18218, F-8132
DLA-2880-A  O'Brien Has Gone Hawaiian               -        -
DLA-2881-A  The Bleeding Heart                    Dec 18263, 23893, F-8173
DLA-2882-A  All For One And One For All             -        -        -

Acc. by studio orchestra.                  New York, June 25, 1942.

70932-A  Nighty-Night, Little Sailor Boy          Dec 23894
70933-A  That Lovely Week-End                     Dec 23895
70934-A  The Thingummy-bob (That's Going To       Dec 23894
         Win The War)
70935-A  Walter, Walter (Lead Me To The Altar)    Dec 23895, DFE-6246

## W. C. FIELDS

B. Philadelphia, Pa., January 29, 1879; r.n. William Claude Dukinfield. Stage debut
as juggler at open-air theatre, Plymouth Park, Pa., July, 1897; New York debut at
the London Theatre in the Bowery the following year, also as a juggler; as such -
in February, 1900 - appeared in London at the Palace Theatre, then in many European countries; took part in WATCH YOUR STEP (New Amsterdam, December 8, 1914,and
later in the ZIEGFELD FOLLIES series, 1915-1921; great success in POPPY (Apollo,
September 3, 1923); began film career in 1915 (POOL SHARKS); made many more films
(JANICE MEREDITH (1924); SALLY OF THE SAWDUST (1925); SO'S YOUR OLD MAN (1926); a
re-make of TILLIE'S PUNCTURED ROMANCE (1928), all silent; talkies included ALICE
IN WONDERLAND (1933); TILLIE AND GUS and MRS. WIGGS OF THE CABBAGE PATCH (1934);
outstanding as Mr. Micawber in DAVID COPPERFIELD (1934); MISSISSIPPI (1935);POPPY
(1936); MY LITTLE CHICKADEE (1940); many others. D. 1946. The only records issued
commercially containing lengthy examples of his voice are the following,    transferred from public broadcasts and film soundtracks made on unknown dates; the records are LPs.

           The Temperance Lecture (w/cast and p)   Proscenium PR-22
           The Day I Drank A Glass Of Water           -
           Talk                                     Har HS-11353

## JAY C. FLIPPEN

B. 1898; d. 1971. Vaudeville singer and light comedian whose screen debut was  not
until 1949 (A WOMAN'S SECRET); also made THUNDER BAY (1953), THE WILD ONE (1954),
CAT BALLOU (1965), HELLFIGHTERS (1968) and many more.  Also took part in the 1950
Capitol LP recording of OKLAHOMA ! (T-595, LCT-6100).  Although his singing style
was in the idiom of its time - the later twenties - his films usually showed  him
as a rather tough Western sheriff or police officer.

Vocal, acc. by studio orchestra.           New York, June 11, 1924.

81819-  Something Tells Me You Are Going (Far   Col 159-D
        Away From Here)
81820-  Often                                     -

New York, August 8, 1924.

| | | |
|---|---|---|
| 81902- | Darktown Broadcasting - **Part 1** | Col 198-D |
| 81903- | Darktown Broadcasting - Part 2 | - |

Acc. by small jazz band.                    New York, July, 1926.

| | | |
|---|---|---|
| 106970 | How Many Times ? | PA        , 11255, Per |
| 106972 | Hard-To-Get Gertie | - |

New York, September, 1926.

| | | |
|---|---|---|
| 107060 | Baby Face | PA        , 11286, Per |
| 107061 | Sadie Green, The Vamp Of New Orleans | - |
| 107062 | She Knows Her "Onions" (sic) | PA 32218, Per 12297 |

New York, November, 1926.

| | | |
|---|---|---|
| 107207 | How Could Red Riding Hood ? | PA 32218, Per 12297 |
| 107217 | For My Sweetheart | PA 32223, Per 12302 |
| 107218 | Short And Sweet | -        - |

New York, December, 1926.

| | | |
|---|---|---|
| 107284 | Hello Bluebird | PA 32229, 11364, Per 12308 |
| 107286 | If I Didn't Know Your Husband (And You Didn't Know My Wife) | -        -        - |

Acc. by his Hot Combination.          New York, May, 1927.

| | |
|---|---|
| Sixty Seconds Every Minute | PA 32260, 11436, Per 12339 |
| South Wind | -        -        - |

Acc. by his Gang (small contingent from the California Ramblers).
New York, August 4, 1927.

| | | |
|---|---|---|
| 107697 | Clementine (From New Orleans) | PA 32288, 11531, Per 12367 |
| 107698 | An' Furthermore | PA 32294    -    Per 12373 |
| 107699 | You Don't Like It - Not Much | PA 32288, 11522, Per 12367 |
| 107700 | I Ain't Got Nobody | PA 32294    -    Per 12373 |

New York, November, 1927.

| | | |
|---|---|---|
| 107892 | Is She My Girl Friend ? | PA 32321, 11541, Per 12400 |
| 107893 | Did You Mean It ? | PA 32313    -    Per 12392 |
| | Oh ! My Operation | -        - |
| | I Told Them All About You | PA 32321, Per 12400 |

Acc. unknown.                    New York, c. February, 1928.

| | |
|---|---|
| Away Down South In Heaven | PA 32329, Per 12406 |
| Let A Smile Be Your Umbrella | -        - |

New York, August, 1928.

| | | |
|---|---|---|
| E-28005- | Ace In The Hole | Br 4051 |
| E-28006- | I Love That Girl | Br 4113 |
| E-28007- | I'm A Ding-Dong Daddy From Dumas | Br 4051 |

New York, c. March 5, 1929.

| | | |
|---|---|---|
| E-29391- | Out Where The Blues Begin | Br 4289 |
| E-29392- | You're Just A Little Bit Of Everything I Love | - |

Three unidentified girls, known to have been members of the cast of the original New
York production of FLORODORA (opened at the Casino, November 10, 1900), with Joe
Belmont, Byron G. Harlan and Frank C. Stanley, made one record that can claim to
be the first ever made in the U.S.A. by members of the cast of a musical comedy.

Vocal sextette, acc. by unknown p.       New York, c.February, 1902.

647-    Tell Me, Pretty Maiden ("Florodora")      Col 647, 31604 (cyl.),
                                                   Marconi 0376

## LYNN FONTANNE

B. Woodford, Essex, England, December 6, 1887; studied with Ellen Terry; London debut in pantomime (CINDERELLA, Drury Lane, December 26, 1905); many small parts in
Lobdon productions with such as Lewis Waller and Sir Herbert Beerbohm Tree; debut
in New York in MR. PREEDY AND THE COUNTESS (Nazimova's 39th Street Theatre,  November 7, 1910); many London appearances between 1911 and the end of 1915, notably
in MY LADY'S DRESS (two parts) at the Royalty (April 23, 1914); to U.S.A., worked
outside New York for a time, then appeared in THE HARP OF LIFE (Globe,November 23,
1916); many further performances there, then in Chicago in June, 1919,appeared in
A YOUNG MAN'S FANCY; played in CHRIS at the Broad Street Theatre, Philadelphia in
March, 1920; returned to London to appear in ONE NIGHT IN ROME (Garrick,  May  3,
1920); very successful in DULCY (Cort, Chicago, February, 1921, and Frazee, N.Y.,
August 23, 1921); other successes include IN LOVE WITH LOVE (Ritz, August 6,1923);
THE GUARDSMAN (Garrick, October 13, 1924); ARMS AND THE MAN (Guild, September 14,
1925); AT MRS. BEAM'S (Guild, April 26, 1926); PYGMALION (as Eliza Doolittle,  at
the Guild, November 15, 1926); THE SECOND MAN (Guild, April 11, 1927); THE   DOC-
TOR'S DILEMMA (Guild, November 21, 1927); STRANGE INTERLUDE (John Golden, January
30, 1928); CAPRICE (Guild, December 31, 1928); to London to appear in the    last-
named play (St. James's, June, 1929); returned to New York, notably successful in
ELIZABETH THE QUEEN (Guild, November 3, 1930); REUNION IN VIENNA (Martin Beck,Nov-
ember 16, 1931, touring in this from September, 1932 to January, 1933);  produced
and appeared in Noel Coward's DESIGN FOR LIVING, at the Ethel Barrymore, January
24, 1933, in conjunction with the author and Alfred Lunt, her husband; to London,
again very successful in REUNION IN VIENNA (Lyric, January 3, 1934); to New York,
long run in IDIOT'S DELIGHT (Shubert, March 24, 1936); AMPHITRYON 38 (also   Shubert, November 1, 1937); appeared in London six months later in this, at the Lyric, but less successfully than in New York; toured the U.S.A. in the last two and
THE SEAGULL; next big success in New York in THERE SHALL BE NO NIGHT (Alvin,April
29, 1940); played the same show in London (Aldwych, December 15, 1943);  remained
in London to appear in LOVE IN IDLENESS (Lyric, December 20, 1944); toured Europe
for the troops, returning to U.S.A. to play in LOVE IN IDLENESS (under the  title
O MISTRESS MINE) in Toledo, Ohio, December, 1945; also in New York (Empire, January 23, 1946); awarded the American Academy of Arts and Letters Medal for diction
in November, 1935; made only very few films (SECOND YOUTH, 1926; THE   GUARDSMAN,
1932, and STAGE DOOR CANTEEN (1943).

Poetry reading, acc. by O/Arthur Lang.     Hollywood, March 3, 1941.

PCS-055463-2  The White Cliffs - A Poem by Alice  Vic 13610, HMV C-3240
               Duer Miller - Part 1
PCS-055464-1  The White Cliffs - Part 2              -           -
PCS-055465-1  The White Cliffs - Part 3           Vic 13611, HMV C-3241
PCS-055466-1  The White Cliffs - Part 4              -           -
PCS-055467-1  The White Cliffs - Part 5           Vic 13612, HMV C-3242
PCS-055468-1  The White Cliffs - Part 6              -           -

## DICK FORAN

B. 1910; light comedian star of many Westerns (STAND UP AND CHEER, 1934;  TRAVELIN'
WEST, 1936; THE PERFECT SPECIMEN, 1938; HORROR ISLAND, 1941; GUEST  WIFE,  1944;
ATOMIC SUBMARINE, 1960; TAGGART, 1965).

Vocal, acc. by O/Victor Young.         Los Angeles, October 14, 1936.

DLA-627-A-B  The Prairie Is My Home           Rejected ?
DLA-628-A  Moonlight Valley (Film "Travelin'  Dec 1039, F-6296
             West")
DLA-629-A  Mexicali Rose                         -
DLA-630-A-B  Whisper While You're Waltzing    Rejected ?

Cabaret entertainer during the second decade of the century; appeared in silent film
  BEATRICE FAIRFAX (1916). B. Pomona, Calif., 1882; d. Woodland Hills, Calif.,  July
  20, 1959.
Vocal, acc. by studio O/? Charles A. Prince.

New York, April 16, 1918.

77772-5  I'm Always Chasing Rainbows              Col A-2557

New York, June 20, 1918.

77905-   Oh ! You La ! La !                       Col A-2600

New York, July 11, 1918.

77949-   Oui, Oui, Marie                          Col rejected

New York, April 1, 1919.

78375-3  Anything Is Nice If It Comes From        Col A-2732
         Dixieland

New York, May 23, 1919.

78446-5  I'm Goin' To Break That Mason-Dixon Line Col A-2769

New York, July 19, 1919.

78579-2  Alexander's Band Is Back In Dixieland    Col A-2787

New York, September 13, 1919.

78649-3  I Lost My Heart In Dixieland             Col A-2828

New York, September 30, 1919.

78716-   Bless My Swanee River Home               Col A-2828

New York, March 10, 1920.

79035-   I'd Love To Fall Asleep And Wake Up In   Col A-2964
         My Mammy's Arms

New York, March 14, 1920.

79045-5  'Way Down Barcelona Way                  Col A-2942

New York, June 17, 1920.

79284-2  Rock-a-Bye Lullaby Mammy                 Col A-2964

## ADELINE   FRANCIS

Versatile American vaudeville singer, b. 1876, d. New York, August 11, 1956.

Vocal, acc. by studio orchestra.        New York, c. November, 1909.

         He Falls For The Ladies Every Time       Ind 1259
         Man, Man, Man                            Ind 1299

New York, May 29, 1911.

19389-2  Take A Look At Me Now                    Col A-1039
19390-2  When I'm Alone, I'm Lonesome              -           Lakeside 70414

New York, April 22, 1913.

38805-1-2-3  Finnegan                    Col rejected

New York, June 6, 1917.

77111-  Says I To Myself, Says I          Col A-2345

## IRENE FRANKLIN

B. 1876; vivacious red-haired comedienne-mimic on the Keith-Albee circuit in   1909.
M. pianist Burton Green; d. June 16, 1941.

Vocal, acc. by Burton Green-p.          New York, November 7, 1911.

I've Got The Mumps                Ed 4M-950, Amb 1813
The Talkative Waitress            Ed 4M-951, Amb 1814
I Want To Be A Janitor's Child    Ed 4M-952, Amb 1815
The Chambermaid                   Ed 4M-1016

New York, November 11, 1911.

19658-  I Want To Be A Janitor's Child    Col A-1105
19659-  Don't Never Trust A Traveling Man    -

New York, February 8, 1912.

I'm A-Bringing Up The Family      Ed 4M-1041, Amb 1816

New York, September 1, 1915.

45978-  Red-Head                   Col A-1873, AR 2290
45979-1-2-3  Dimples               Rejected

New York, September 8, 1915.

45990-  All Wrong (The Wail Of A Chorus Lady)  Col A-1873
45991-1-2-3  You Can't Fool A New York Kid     Rejected

New York, c. April, 1917.

2481-2  Red-Head                   Em 7165
2482-   Dirty Face                 Em 7209

New York, c. July, 1917.

2565-   I'm A-Bringin' Up The Family    Em 7228
2566-   The Awkward Age            Em 7209

## CLIFF FRIEND

Song-writer who has contributed the following to the literature of popular music   in
the twentieth century :- WANA (WHEN I WANNA, YOU NO WANNA) (1921); I LOVE MY CHILI
BOM-BOM (with Walter Donaldson, 1923); MAMA LOVES PAPA, PAPA LOVES MAMA (with Abel
Baer, 1923); WHERE THE LAZY DAISIES GROW (1924); THERE'S YES ! YES ! IN YOUR  EYES
(1924); I'M TELLIN' THE BIRDS, TELLIN' THE BEES (with Lew Brown, 1926);   TAMIAMI
TRAIL (with Joseph Santly, 1926); GIVE ME A NIGHT IN JUNE (1927); I TOLD THEM   ALL
ABOUT YOU (1928); SWEETHEARTS FOREVER (with Irving Caesar, 1932); WAH HOO ! (1936)
and the following with Dave Franklin :- WHEN MY DREAM BOAT COMES HOME (1936);   THE
MERRY-GO-ROUND BROKE DOWN and YOU CAN'T STOP ME FROM DREAMING (1937); I  MUST  SEE
ANNIE TONIGHT (1938); CONCERT IN THE PARK (1939); and the following with  Charles
Tobias :- TRADE WINDS (1940); DON'T SWEETHEART ME (1943); TIME WAITS FOR  NO  ONE
(1944).

Vocal, acc. by own piano.          New York, February 29, 1928.

BVE-43300-1  Bob White                   Vic rejected
BVE-43301-1  Disappointed                -
BVE-43302-1  I Told Them All About You   -

New York, March 29, 1928.

| BVE-43516-2 | Daffy Ditties - Part 1 | Vic 21460, Zon 5214 |
|---|---|---|
| BVE-43517-2 | Daffy Ditties - Part 2 | -          - |

## RUDOLF FRIML

B. Prague, Czechoslovakia, December 7, 1881; d. 1973. Pianist and composer; first
   appearance in U.S.A. as accompanist to the violinist Jan Kubelik in 1903; worked
   with him for five years. Wrote the music to the following musical plays, operettas and films :- THE FIREFLY (1912, filmed 1937); HIGH JINKS  and  THE  BALLET
   GIRL (1914); KATINKA (1915); THE PEA ANT GIRL (1916); YOU'RE IN LOVE and    KITTY
   DARLIN' (1917); GLORIANNA and SOMETIME (1918); THE LITTLE WHOPPER and  TUMBLE INN
   (1919); JUNE LOVE (1920); ZIEGFELD FOLLIES OF 1921 and  THE  BLUE  KITTEN (1921);
   BIBI OF THE BOULEVARDS (1922); CINDERS (1923); ROSE-MARIE (with Herbert Stothart,
   1924); THE VAGABOND KING (1925); THE WILD ROSE (1926); WHITE EAGLES (1927);   THE
   THREE MUSKETEERS (1928); LUANA (1930); AMINA and MUSIC HATH CHARMS (1934).

Piano solos.                              New York, December 15, 1925.

| 141391- | Song Of The Vagabonds ("The Vagabond  King") | Col 533-D, 4377 |
|---|---|---|
| 141392- | Chansonette | -        3980 |

New York, November 29, 1929.

| CVE-57179-2 | Amour Coquet/Improvisation | Vic 9649 |
|---|---|---|
| CVE-57180-1 | Chansonette/Improvisation | Rejected |
| CVE-57181-1 | Improvisation | - |

New York, December 10, 1929.

| BVE-57901-1-2 | Chansonette | Rejected |
|---|---|---|
| BVE-57902-3 | Huguette ("The Vagabond King") | Vic 22540 |
| BVE-57903-1-2 | Valse Lucille | Rejected |
| BVE-57904-2 | Indian Love Call ("Rose Marie") | Vic 22540 |

RUDOLF FRIML AND HIS ORCHESTRA.       New York, December 12, 1929.

| CVE-58101-1 | Arabian Suite - Part 1 | Vic rejected |
|---|---|---|
| CVE-58102-1 | Arabian Suite - Part 2 | - |
| CVE-58103-1-2 | Arabian Suite - Part 3 | - |
| CVE-58104-1 | Arabian Suite - Part 4 | - |

Piano solos.                              New York, September 24, 1930.

| BVE-57903-3-4 | Valse Lucille | Vic rejected |
|---|---|---|
| BVE-63668-1-2 | Luana ("Luana") | - |
| BVE-63669-1-2 | L'amour, toujours l'amour | - |

Rudolf Friml also made an LP for Decca in 1950 of some of his best-known numbers, as
   piano solos. All the above are his own compositions.

## JANE   FROMAN

Vocalist with Henry Thies and his Orchestra.
                              Hotel Sinton, Cincinnati, June 10, 1930.

| BVE-62647- | Sharing | Vic 22461 |
|---|---|---|
| BVE-62649-2 | June Kisses | Vic 22460 |
| BVE-327 | St. Louis Blues (acc. by small  group from the band) | Vic test |

Vocal, acc. by studio orchestra.        New York, September 14, 1934.

| 38658-A | My Melancholy Baby | Br 01927 |
| 38659-A | I Only Have Eyes For You | - |
| 38660-A | Lost In A Fog | Br 01902 |
| 38661-A | A New Moon Is Over My Shoulder | - |

New York, February 13, 1936.

| 60466-A | But Where Are You ? | Dec 710, Br 02166 |
| 60467-A | If You Love Me | Dec 725 - |
| 60468-A | It's Great To Be In Love Again | - Br 02174 |
| 60469-A | Please Believe Me | Dec 710 - |

Jane Froman also made a number of sides for Capitol after 1945.

## GEORGE  B.  FROTHINGHAM

B. Boston, Mass., April 12, 1844; began professional career with minstrel  companies
   in the late 1860's; created role of Friar Tuck in ROBIN HOOD(Chicago,June 9,1890);
   played the part over 3,000 times.  D. c. 1920.
Vocal, acc. by unknown p.               New York, c. July, 1898.

Rolling To The Sea                      Ber 1833

## WILL FYFFE

B. Dundee, Scotland, 1884 (despite his most famous song asserting I BELONG TO  GLAS-
   GOW); toured Scotland in his father's stock company, playing every role from  Pol-
   onius in HAMLET to Little Willie in EAST LYNNE; appeared in revue in his own Scottish character sketches after Sir Harry Lauder and Neil Kenyon had refused   them.
   He was a fine character actor who made a great success both on British music-halls
   and in American vaudeville theatres (appeared in New York in the spring of  1927),
   and was awarded the honour of Commander of the British Empire during World War II.
   He made many films, such as HAPPY (1934); ANNIE LAURIE (1936); COTTON QUEEN(1937);
   OWD BOB (1938); THE MIND OF MR. READER (1939); FOR FREEDOM and NEUTRAL PORT(1940);
   HEAVEN IS ROUND THE CORNER (1944); THE BROTHERS (1947).  D. 1947.

Vocal, acc. by O/Albert W. Ketelbey.    London, September, 1921.

| 71404 | I'm 94 Today | Re G-7693, Col 183-D |
| 71405 | I Belong To Glasgow | - - |
| 71406 | The Engineer | Re G-7703 |
| 71407 | Sandy's Holiday | - |

London, April, 1922.

| 71694 | Maggie | Re G-7800 |

| 71705 | New Year's Day | Re G-7800 |
| 71706 | The First Wee Drappie In The Morning | Re G-7794 |
| 71707 | Goodbye, Jenny | - |

London, October, 1922.

| 71974 | The Hieland Jazz | Re G-7873 |
| 71975 | I'm Going To Sea | - |

London, c. May, 1923.

| 73401 | I'm Tight, Too | Re G-7987 |
| 73402 | Up Among The Heather | - |

London, November 21, 1923.

| AX-237 | I'm 94 Today | Col 961 |
| AX-238 | I Belong To Glasgow | - |

                                    London, November 25, 1923.

A-470   I Love My Mary                          Re G-8129
A-471   I'm Verra Glad I'm Marrit Tae The Wife    -

                                    London, March, 1924.

A-801   Ah'm A Very Happy Fellow When Ah'm       Re G-8218
          Working
A-802   Ma Maggie Mackay                          -
        Jessie MacDonald                         Re G-8208
        The Elder                                 -

                                    London, c. December, 1924.

A-1555  Tobermory Treasure                       Re G-8312
A-1556  Come And Hae A Walk Wi' Me                -
        Give My Regards To Uncle Sandy           Re G-8311
        Let's Sing "Auld Lang Syne"               -
        When McKay Started Learning To Play      Re G-8313
          The Bagpipes
        The Inverary Inn                          -

                                    London, June 2, 1926.

WA-3332-1  Down In The Quarry Where The          Re G-8681
             Bluebells Grow
WA-3333-1  Dr. McGregor                           -
WAX-1554-2 Dr. McGregor                          Col 9108
WAX-1555-1 The Engineer                           -

   Acc. by studio orchestra.        New York, April 28, 1927.

144059-  I'm 94 Today                 Col 976-D, Re G-7693
144060-  I Belong To Glasgow            -           -
144061-  The Engineer                 Col 993-D, Re G-7703
144062-  Sandy's Holiday                -           -

                                    New York, May 24, 1927.

144208-  The Centenarian             Col 1272-D, Re G-9171
144209-  The Gamekeeper                 -           -

   Acc. by O/Albert W. Ketelbey.     London, June 13, 1928.

WA-7496-1  Sailing Up The Clyde                Re MR-258, Col 1746-D
WA-7497-1  Ye Can Come And See The Baby Any Time   -          -
WAX-3764-1 Sailing Up The Clyde                Col 9468
WAX-3765-1 Ye Can Come And See The Baby Any Time   -

                                    London, August 29, 1929.

WA-9403-2  She Was The Belle Of The Ball       Re G-9390
WA-9404-1  Sheila McKay                        Re G-9462
WA-9405-1  Twelve And A Tanner A Bottle        Re G-9390
WA-9406-2  The Train That's Taking You Home    Re G-9462

                                    London, October 17, 1929.

WAX-5220-1  I'm 94 Today                       Col 9928
WAX-5221-1  I Belong To Glasgow                 -
WAX-5222-1  The Train That's Taking You Home   Col 9775
WAX-5223-2  Sheila McKay                        -

                                    London, July 2, 1930.

WAR-233-1  McPherson's Wedding Breakfast       Re MR-206
WAX-5640-1 Daft Sandy - Part 1                 Col DX-107
WAX-5641-2 Daft Sandy - Part 2                  -

London, July 4, 1930.

```
WAR-244-1  The Railway Guard                      Re MR-206
WAR-245-1  Daft Sandy - Part 1                    Re MR-176
WAR-246-1  Daft Sandy - Part 2                        -
WAX-5642-1 MacPherson's Wedding Breakfast         Col DX-138
WAX-5643-1 The Railway Guard                          -
```

London, July 8, 1931.

```
CAR-704-1  The Spirit Of A Man From Aberdeen      Re MR-413
CAR-705-1  The Waddin' O' Mary Maclean                -
CAX-6165-1 The Spirit Of A Man From Aberdeen      Col DX-275
CAX-6166-1 The Waddin' O' Mary Maclean                -
```

London, July 15, 1931.

```
CAR-748-1  Ah'm Feared For Mrs. McKie             Re MR-456
CAR-749-1  Uncle Mac                                  -
CAX-6181-1 Ah'm Feared For Mrs. McKie             Col DX-354
CAX-6182-1 Uncle Mac                                  -
```

London, April 8, 1932.

```
CAX-6369-2 It Isn't The Hen                       Col DX-437
CAX-6370-1 If  Scotland Turns Republic                -
CAX-6371-1 He's Been On The Bottle Since A Baby   Col DX-381
CAX-6372-1 I'm The Landlord Of The Inn In Aberfoyle   -
```

London, April 10, 1932.

```
CAX-6375-1 A Trip Round Scotland With Will Fyffe  Col DX-369
              - Part 1
CAX-6376-1 A Trip Round Scotland With Will Fyffe      -
```

## ED GALLAGHER-AL  SHEAN

Ed Gallagher and Al Shean (the latter b. Dornum, Germany, in May, 1868; d. 1949) met in partnership in vaudeville in 1910.  They were very popular as a team until they split up in 1925, but they had a brief reunion in the thirties.  As creators of an unforgettable comedy song bearing their own names as a title, they have made  sure of immortality, but they only made one published recording.  They introduced  this number in ZIEGFELD FOLLIES OF 1922 (New Amsterdam, June 5, 1922), which ran longer than any other of the long series (541 performances).  Al Shean, uncle of the Marx Brothers, also appeared solo in THE ROSE MAID (Globe, April 22, 1912);THE PRINCESS PAT (Cort, September 29, 1915); CINDERELLA ON BROADWAY (Winter Garden,  June   24, 1920); MUSIC IN THE AIR (Alvin, November 8, 1932); in the title role of FATHER MAL-ACHY'S MIRACLE (St. James, November 17, 1937); many other shows and several films.

Vocal duets, acc. by studio orchestra.   New York, July 20, 1922.

```
B-26703-4  Mr. Gallagher And Mr. Shean - Part 1   Vic 18941
              ("Positively, Mr. Gallagher ?")
B-26704-1-2-3-4  Quietly                          Rejected
```

Acc. by O/Eddie King.                 New York, August 3, 1922.

```
B-26709-1-2-3-4-5  Boola-Boola                    Vic rejected
```

Acc  by O/Nat Shilkret.               New York, August 18, 1922.

```
B-26728-2  Mr. Gallagher And Mr. Shean - Part 2   Vic 18941
              ("Absolutely, Mr. Shean !")
```

Acc. by Jeff Clarkson-p.              New York, July 12, 1933.

```
LBS-1054-1-2  Absolutely - Positively             Vic test
```

NOTE:- A track entitled BY, ABOUT AND FOR THEMSELVES, origin unknown, by these  art-ists appeared on an LP (Veritas 107), and Al Shean re-made their signature tune on Coral 60033 with a different partner in the mid-forties.

B. Wimbledon, London, England, February 27, 1903; began career in an architect's office; studied for the stage at the Royal Academy of Dramatic Art; London debut  in
walking-on part in THE PRISONER OF ZENDA (Haymarket, August 23, 1923); this led to
tours outside London, and to many successful appearances in "silly-ass" roles,such
as THE MIDDLE WATCH (Shaftesbury, August 12, 1929); LEAVE IT TO PSMITH (also Shaftesbury, September 29, 1930); MAKE UP YOUR MIND (Criterion, December 1, 1931); introduced his famous TRAINS monologue at this time; PLEASURE CRUISE (Apollo, April
26, 1932); MOTHER OF PEARL (Gaiety, January 27, 1933); New York debut in AT  HOME
ABROAD (Winter Garden, September 19, 1935); at the same theatre, THE  SHOW  IS  ON
(December 25, 1936); to Hollywood, continuing film career begun in 1932 with LOVE-
LORN LADY; U.S. films include BORN TO DANCE (1936); EVERYBODY SING (1937);   MARIE
ANTOINETTE (1938); SWEETHEARTS (1939); THE GREAT DICTATOR (1940); THE MAN WHO CAME
TO DINNER (1941); CAPTAINS OF THE CLOUDS (1942); THE IMMORTAL SERGEANT (1943);MOL-
LY AND ME (1944); CLUNY BROWN (1946); HALLS OF MONTEZUMA (1951); THE BIRDS AND THE
BEES (1956); MR. HOBBS TAKES A VACATION (1962); DO NOT DISTURB (1965), and others,
all in supporting roles.  Also appeared in TV series THE PRUITTS OF SOUTHAMPTON.

Speech, unacc.                              London, c. December 30, 1931.

OY-2542-1  Impressions Of A Train Journey - Part 1 Zon rejected
OY-2543-1  Impressions Of A Train Journey - Part 2      -

                                            London, September 13, 1934.

TB-1540-2  Trains - Part 1                       Dec F-5278, 23212
TB-1541-1  Trains - Part 2                        -          -

                                            Los Angeles, January 23, 1941.

DLA-2375-  Trains - Part 1                       Dec 23022
DLA-2376-  Trains - Part 2                        -
DLA-2377-  Trains - Part 3                       Rejected ?
DLA-2378-  Trains - Part 4                        -

### JUDY GARLAND

B. 1922 (r.n. Frances Gumm), d. 1969.  Daughter of stage performers, own debut at 5,
screen debut in 1936 in EVERY SUNDAY and PIGSKIN PARADE; huge success in the  fol-
lowing :- BROADWAY MELODY OF 1938; THOROUGHBREDS DON'T CRY; LISTEN DARLING; EVERY-
BODY SING and LOVE FINDS ANDY HARDY (1938); THE WIZARD OF OZ, BABES IN ARMS,  ANDY
HARDY MEETS A DEBUTANTE (1939); STRIKE UP THE BAND and LITTLE NELLIE KELLY (1940);
ZIEGFELD GIRL, LIFE BEGINS FOR ANDY HARDY and BABES ON BROADWAY (1941); FOR ME AND
MY GAL, PRESENTING LILY MARS and GIRL CRAZY (1942); MEET ME IN ST. LOUIS and ZIEG-
FELD FOLLIES (1944); UNDER THE CLOCK (1945); THE HARVEY GIRLS (1946); EASTER PAR-
ADE (1948); IN THE GOOD OLD SUMMERTIME (1949); A STAR IS BORN (1954); JUDGMENT  AT
NUREMBERG (1960); and her British film I COULD GO ON SINGING (1963); also appeared
as guest star in AS THOUSANDS CHEER (1943); TILL THE CLOUDS ROLL BY (1946),  WORDS
AND MUSIC (1948); Special Academy Award (1939) "for her outstanding performance as
a screen juvenile."  Frequently appeared in cabaret in London in the 1960s;  final
performance there in TALK OF THE TOWN a few months before her death there.

Vocal, acc. by O/Victor Young.              Los Angeles, November 27, 1935.

DLA-280-A  No Other One                          Dec rejected
DLA-283-A  All's Well                             -
  NOTE:- Matrices DLA-281/2 are by Ginger Rogers, q.v.

  Acc. by Bob Crosby and his Orchestra.     New York, June 12, 1936.

61165-A  Stompin' At The Savoy                   Dec 848, Br 02267, 03352,
                                                 Coral CP-53
61166-A  Swing, Mr. Charlie                      As above, except Br 03352

  Acc. by O/Victor Young.                    Los Angeles, August 30, 1937.

DLA-860-  Everybody Sing (Film "Broadway Melody  Dec 1432, Br 02478, Coral CP-53
            of 1938")
DLA-861-  All God's Chillun Got Rhythm            -          -           -

Acc. by Harry Sosnik and his Orchestra.

Los Angeles, September 24, 1937.

| | | |
|---|---|---|
| DLA-967-A | (Dear Mr. Gable) You Made Me Love You (Film "Broadway Melody of 1938") | Dec 1463, 25393, 75150, Br 02488, AH 11 |
| DLA-968-A | You Can't Have Everything | Dec 1463, Br 02488, Coral CP-53 |

Los Angeles, April 25, 1938.

| | | |
|---|---|---|
| DLA-1284-A | Sleep, My Baby, Sleep | Dec 1796, 25393, Br 02611, Coral CP-53 |
| DLA-1285-A | Cry, Baby, Cry | As above except Dec 25393 |

Los Angeles, August 21, 1938.

| | | |
|---|---|---|
| DLA-1436-C | Ten Pins In The Sky (Film "Listen, Darling") | Br 02656, Coral CP-53 |
| DLA-1437-A | It Never Rains But It Pours (Film "Love Finds Andy Hardy") | —          — |

Acc. by O/Victor Young.          Los Angeles, July 28, 1939.

| | | |
|---|---|---|
| DLA-1840-A | Over The Rainbow (Film "The Wizard Of Oz") | Dec 2672, 23961, 75150, Br 02886, LA-8725, AH 11 |
| DLA-1841-A | The Jitterbug (Film "The Wizard Of Oz") | Dec 2672, 23961, Br 02886 |
| DLA-1842-A | In Between (Film "Love Finds Andy Hardy") | Dec 15045, 29233, Br 0148, LA-8725, AH 11 |
| DLA-1843-A | Sweet Sixteen | As above |

Los Angeles, July 29, 1939.

| | | |
|---|---|---|
| DLA-1850-A | Zing ! Went The Strings Of My Heart | Dec 18543, Br 02969 |
| DLA-1851-A | I'm Just Wild About Harry (Film "Babes In Arms") | — |
| DLA-1852-A | Swanee | Rejected |
| DLA-1853-A | Fascinating Rhythm | Dec 18543, AH 48 |

Los Angeles, October 16, 1939.

| | | |
|---|---|---|
| DLA-1868-B | Oceans Apart | Dec 2873, Br 02943, Coral CP-53 |
| DLA-1869-A | Embraceable You (Film "Girl Crazy") | Dec 2881, Br 02993, Coral CP-54 |
| DLA-1870-A | Swanee | —          — |
| DLA-1871-A | Figaro (Film "Babes In Arms") | Dec 2873, Br 02943 |

Acc. by O/Bobby Sherwood.          Los Angeles, April 10, 1940.

| | | |
|---|---|---|
| DLA-1971-A | (Can This Be) The End Of The Rainbow | Dec 3231, 4081, Br 03172, Coral CP-53 |
| DLA-1972-A | I'm Nobody's Baby (Film "Andy Hardy Meets A Debutante") | Dec 3174, 75150, Br 03038 |
| DLA-1973-A | Buds Won't Bud (Film "Andy Hardy Meets A Debutantante") | —          — Coral CP-53 |
| DLA-1974-A | The Wearing Of The Green | Dec 3165, Br 03172, Coral CP-54 |

Acc. by O/Victor Young.          Los Angeles, April 15, 1940.

| | | |
|---|---|---|
| DLA-1987-A | Friendship (w/Johnny Mercer) | Dec 3165, Br 03393, AH 48 |

Acc. by O/David Rose.          Los Angeles, December 18, 1940.

| | | |
|---|---|---|
| DLA-2282- | I'm Always Chasing Rainbows | Dec 3593, 75150, Br 03128 |
| DLA-2283- | Our Love Affair | —          — |
| DLA-2284-A | A Pretty Girl Milking Her Cow (Film "Little Nellie Kelly") | Dec 3604, 25043, 75150, Br 03211 |
| DLA-2285-A | It's A Great Day For The Irish (Film "Little Nellie Kelly") | —          — Coral CP-54 — |

Los Angeles, July 20, 1941.

| | | |
|---|---|---|
| DLA-2578-A | The Birthday Of A King | Dec 4050, 23568, Br 03924 |
| DLA-2579-A | The Star Of The East | -        -        - |

Los Angeles, October 24, 1941.

| | | |
|---|---|---|
| DLA-2798-A | How About You ? (Film "Babes On Broadway") | Dec 4072, Br 03305, AH 11, Coral CP-54 |
| DLA-2799-A | Blues In The Night | Dec 4081, Br 03352, Coral CP-54 |
| DLA-2800-A | F. D. R. Jones (Film "Babes On Broadway") | Dec 4072, Br 03305 |

Los Angeles, April 3, 1942.

| | | |
|---|---|---|
| DLA-2968-A | The Last Call For Love | Dec 18320, Br 03358 |
| DLA-2969-A | Poor You | -        - |
| DLA-2970-A | On The Sunny Side Of The Street | Dec 18524 |
| DLA-2971-A | Poor Little Rich Girl | Dec 18540, Br 03446, AH 48 |

Los Angeles, July 26, 1942.

| | | |
|---|---|---|
| DLA-3140-A | For Me And My Gal (w/Gene Kelly) (Film "For Me And My Gal") | Dec 18480, 25115, 10013, 75150, Br 03432, LA-8725, AH 11 |
| DLA-3141-A | When You Wore A Tulip (And I Wore A Big Red Rose) (w/Gene Kelly) (Film "For Me And My Gal") | As above |
| DLA-3142-A | That Old Black Magic | Dec 18540, Br 03446 |
| DLA-3143-A | I Never Knew | Dec 18524 |

## GEORGE GERSHWIN

B. New York, September 26, 1898; studied piano with famous teachers, including Joseph Schillinger; composed first song (WHEN YOU WANT 'EM, YOU CAN'T GET 'EM), 1916; sold it to Harry von Tilzer, was given a weekly drawing-account and a room with a piano so he could produce more numbers.   Worked as pianist with saxophonist   Bert Ralton and banjoist Fred van Eps; wrote SWANEE (1919) and a complete musical score for LA, LA, LUCILLE; wrote for five GEORGE WHITE'S SCANDALS (1920-1924), many fine popular songs (LIMEHOUSE NIGHTS, 1920; DRIFTING ALONG WITH THE TIDE, SHE'S JUST  A BABY and SOUTH SEA ISLES (1921); DO IT AGAIN (in THE FRENCH DOLL) and THE   YANKEE DOODLE BLUES (1922); THAT AMERICAN BOY OF MINE (in THE DANCING GIRL, 1923);   while in London in 1923 began work on the famous RHAPSODY IN BLUE, first played by  Paul Whiteman and his Orchestra at an Aeolian Hall concert, February 12, 1924;   commissioned by conductor Walter Damrosch to write a CONCERTO FOR PIANO AND ORCHESTRA, in 1928; also wrote set of PRELUDES and AN AMERICAN IN PARIS (1928); SECOND  RHAPSODY (1931); CUBAN OVERTURE (1932); folk-opera PORGY AND BESS (1935); music for a great many more musical comedies (LADY, BE GOOD, 1924; TIP-TOES; OH, KAY ! (1926);STRIKE UP THE BAND and FUNNY FACE (1927); GIRL CRAZY (1930); also films (SHALL WE DANCE ? and A DAMSEL IN DISTRESS (1937), both for Fred Astaire and Ginger Rogers, q.v.  D. in Hollywood, July 11, 1937.

THE GERSHWIN TRIO : Bert Ralton-cl-o/George Gershwin-p/Eddie King-bj.
New York, July 28, 1920.

| | |
|---|---|
| Kismet | Vic test (un-numbered) |
| Chica | - |

Piano soloist with Paul Whiteman and his Concert Orchestra.
New York, June 10, 1924.

| | | |
|---|---|---|
| C-30173-2 | Rhapsody In Blue - Part 2 | Vic 55225, HMV C-1171 |
| C-30174-1 | Rhapsody In Blue - Part 1 | -        - |

Piano solos.                            London, July 6, 1926.

| | | |
|---|---|---|
| WA-3553-1 | Sweet And Low-Down ("Tip-Toes") | Col 4065, ME MES-7037 |
| WA-3554-1 | That Certain Feeling ("Tip-Toes") | Col 4066     - |
| WA-3555-2 | Looking For A Boy ("Tip-Toes") | Col 4065     - |
| WA-3556-1 | When Do We Dance ? ("Tip-Toes") | Col 4066     - |

New York, November 8, 1926.

142924-1  Do-Do-Do ("Oh, Kay !")                Col 809-D, 4538
142925-   Someone To Watch Over Me ("Oh, Kay !")  Col 812-D, 4539

New York, November 12, 1926.

142931-4  Clap Yo' Hands ("Oh, Kay !")          Col 809-D, 4538
142932-   Maybe ("Oh, Kay !")                   Col 812-D, 4539

Piano soloist with Paul Whiteman and his Concert Orchestra.
                              Camden, N. J., April 21, 1927.

CVE-30173-8  Rhapsody In Blue - Part 2          Vic 35822, HMV C-1395
CVE-30174-6  Rhapsody In Blue - Part 1            -           -

Piano solos.
                              London, June 8, 1928.

WA-7465-1   My One And Only ("Funny Face")      Col 5109, ME MES-7037
WAX-3758-   Preludes, Nos. 1 and 2              Col 50107-D
WAX-3759-   Prelude No. 3/Andante from Rhapsody In Blue-

                              London, June 12, 1928.

WA-7483-2  'S Wonderful/Funny Face ("Funny Face")  Col 5109, ME MES-7037

Piano and celeste soloist with the Victor Symphony Orchestra (New Light Symphony Orchestra on HMV)/Nat Shilkret.    New York, February 4, 1929.

CVE-49710-2  An American In Paris - Part 1      Vic 35963, HMV C-1698
CVE-49711-2  An American In Paris - Part 2        -           -
CVE-49712-2  An American In Paris - Part 3      Vic 35964, HMV C-1699
CVE-49713-3  An American In Paris - Part 4        -           -

See also Fred Astaire (accompaniments to Columbia recordings of LADY, BE GOOD, 1926).

## L. WOLFE GILBERT

Composer of a great number of popular songs ranging from the ragtime-flavoured to the
  Latin-American styled, e.g., HITCHY KOO, WAITING FOR THE ROBERT E. LEE and  RAGGING
  THE BABY TO SLEEP (all with music by Lewis F. Muir, 1912); I'VE GOT THE ARMY  BLUES
  (with Carey Morgan) and LILY OF THE VALLEY (with Anatole Friedland), 1917;   GRANNY
  (with Alex Belledna), 1919; O KATHARINA ! (with Richard Fall, in CHAUVE SOURIS)1924
  and I MISS MY SWISS (with Abel Baer, in the following year's edition of the  show);
  DON'T WAKE ME UP, LET ME DREAM (with Mabel Wayne and Abel Baer), 1925; HELLO,ALOHA,
  HOW ARE YOU ? (with Abel Baer), 1926; RAMONA (with Mabel Wayne), 1927;  JEANNINE, I
  DREAM OF LILAC TIME (with Nat Shilkret), 1928; TNE PEANUT VENDOR (with  additional
  words by Marion Sunshine to music by Moises Simons), 1930; MARTA (with Moises  Simons), 1931; MAMA INEZ (with Eliseo Grenet), 1931; and A GRAND VACATION WITH PAY,  a
  World War II recruiting song (with Jimmy McHugh).  He recorded one of his own songs
  as shown below; it is one of his least-known.

Vocalist with the Broadway Dance Orchestra (alleged by some to have been a  pseudonym
  for Vincent Lopez and his Hotel Pennsylvania Orchestra).
                              New York, February, 1923.

8835    The Natchez And The Robert E. Lee        Ed 51133

## ART  GILLHAM

"The Whispering Pianist" was born in St. Louis, January 1, 1895; d. June 6, 1961.  He
  left school at 19 to study orchestration; served in the Army in World War I, worked
  in a Chicago music store and on the road as a music salesman; pioneer  broadcasting
  artist, sang as well as played one night for a dare, and was a hit; gave up  broadcasting in 1937, moved to Atlanta, Ga., and became Principal of Crichton's Business
  College for 15 years; composed many numbers, and is said to have recorded   several
  more sides than are shown below (for Gennett and OKeh, but these have never come to
  light).

Vocal, acc. by own piano.                    Richmond, Ind., May 2, 1924.

```
11848    The Deacon Told Me I Was Good        Gnt (rejected ?)
11849    Mean Blues                                 -
11850    You May Be Lonesome                        -
11851    Hesitation Blues                           -
```

New York, c. October, 1924.

```
105600-A-B  The Deacon Told Me I Was Good    PA 032096, Per 12175
105602      How Do You Do ?                  PA 032087, 10799, Per 12166
```

New York, October 22, 1924.

```
140113-1  Way Out West In Kansas             Col 238-D
140114-3  How Do You Do ?                        -
```

New York, November 6, 1924.

```
140123-   The Deacon Told Me I Was Good      Col 297-D
140125-1-2-3  You May Be Lonesome            Rejected
  NOTE:- Matrix 140124 is not by Art Gillham.
```

New York, January 20, 1925.

```
140125-7  You May Be Lonesome (But You'll Be  Col 328-D
            Lonesome Alone)
140270-   Carolina Blues                      Col 297-D
```

New York, January 21, 1925.

```
140274-3  Second-Hand Love                    Col 343-D
140275-   Doo Wacka Doo                       Rejected
```

New York, February 25, 1925.

```
140390-2  Hesitation Blues                    Col 343-D
140391-   Heart Broken Strain                 Rejected
140394-2  I Had Someone Else Before I Had You  Col 328-D, 3748
  NOTE:- Matrix 140392/3 are not by Art Gillham.
```

New York, February 26, 1925.

```
140395-1  How's Your Folks And My Folks ?     Col 387-D, 3855
140399-3  Can't Your Friend Get A Friend For Me ?  Col 326-D
  NOTE:- Matrices 140396/8 inclusive are by other artists on the same day.
```

New York, February 27, 1925.

```
140404-3  Hot Tamale Molly                    Col 326-D
```

New York, June 26, 1925.

```
140725-1  Smile All The While                 Col 411-D, 3748
140726-1  Are You Sorry ?                     Col 458-D
140727-1  Angry                               Col 411-D, 3855
140728-   Page Mr. Handy                      Rejected
```

New York, June 27, 1925.

```
140731-3  So That's The Kind Of A Girl You Are  Col 442-D
140732-1  Cecilia                             Col 425-D
140733-3  Feelin' Kind O' Blue                Col 442-D
```

New York, June 29, 1925.

```
140734-   Words Of Love                       Rejected
140735-3  Loving Just You                     Col 458-D
140736-1  If You Leave Me I'll Never Cry      Col 425-D
```

Vocalist with Lanin's Red Heads.            New York, October 19, 1925.

141156-3  Five Foot Two, Eyes Of Blue              Col 483-D

Vocal, acc. by own piano.                   New York, October 19, 1925.

141157-   Let Me Call You Sweetheart              Rejected
141158-   Let Us Waltz As We Say Goodbye            -
141159-4  Hello, Little Girl Of My Dreams         Col 737-D

                                            New York, October 20, 1925.

141165-3  Mean Blues                              Col 550-D
141166-7  Just Waiting For You                    Col 771-D
141167-1  Don't Let Me Stand In Your Way          Col 529-D
141168-   Where Can I Find You ?                  Rejected

                                            New York, October 21, 1925.

141172-2  She's My Gal                            Col 550-D
141173-1  You're More Than A Pal To Me            Col 505-D
141174-3  Bam Bam Bammy Shore                     Col 529-D

                                            New York, October 24, 1925.

141190-2  I'm Sitting On Top Of The World         Col 505-D
141191-   Little Southern Pal Of Mine             Rejected
141192-   Memphis Blues (Piano solo)               -

  Acc. by own p/Horace Seavey-bb, and Lew Pollack-p where shown.
                                            New York, March 16, 1926.

141802-2  In Your Green Hat - pLP                 Col 614-D
141803-3  Let's Make Up                           Col 892-D
141804-   You're The One I'm Looking For          Rejected
141805-1  I Can't Keep You Out Of My Dreams       Col 737-D

  Acc. by Frances Spur-p/Horace Seavey-bb.
                                            New York, March 17, 1926.

141814-2  I'd Climb The Highest Mountain If I     Col 626-D
            Knew I'd Find You
141815-2  He Ain't Done Right By Nell             Col 657-D
141816-1  (I Don't Believe It, But) Say It Again  Col 626-D
141817-1  It's Too Late To Be Sorry Now (no bb)   Col 614-D

  Acc. by own p/Horace Seavey-bb, and Louis Hooper-p where shown.
                                            New York, March 18, 1926.

141823-4  It Don't Do Nothing But Rain - pLH      Col 657-D
141824-2  I'm Leaving You - pLH                   Col 685-D
141825-   If You're Old-Fashioned Your Long       Rejected
            Underwear - pLH
141826-5  Crying Again                            Col 771-D

  Acc. by own piano.                        New York, March 19, 1926.

141827-   The Waltz We Love                       Col rejected

                                            New York, March 22, 1926.

141835-   Gone                                    Rejected
141836-5  I Don't Want To Forget                  Col 842-D
141837-2  I Wish I Had My Old Gal Back Again      Col 685-D

                                            New York, July 8, 1926.

142376-1  Tenderly                                Col 710-D
142377-2  Thinking                                 -

Acc. by own p/Horace Seavey-bb, with Bob Bagar-p where shown.
                                    New York, October 18, 1926.

| | | |
|---|---|---|
| 142831-4 | Just A Little Longer | Col 806-D |
| 142832- | Red Hot Flo (From Kokomo) - pBB | Rejected |
| 142833-3 | Broken-Hearted - pBB | Col 972-D |
| 142834-3 | If I Get A Sweetie Now - pBB | - |

Acc. by own piano, with Peter DeRose-p or Sid Wolff-p/Horace Seavey-bb where shown.
                                    New York, October 19, 1926.

| | | |
|---|---|---|
| 142839-1 | Broken-Hearted Sue - pPD | Col 842-D |
| 142840-3 | Pretty Little Thing - pSW/bbHS | Col 1051-D |
| 142841-3 | Things That Remind Me Of You | Col 892-D |
| 142842-3 | I'm Missing The Kissing Of Someone | Col 1472-D |
| 142843-3 | I'm Only Another To You | Col 955-D |
| 142844-5 | I'm Drifting Back To Dreamland (p solo) | - |

Acc. by own p/Abner Silver-p.        New York, November 3, 1926.

| | | |
|---|---|---|
| 142904-3 | Rags | Col 806-D |

Acc. by own p/Andy Sannella-as-g.    New York, April 25, 1927.

| | | |
|---|---|---|
| 144044-5 | Tonight You Belong To Me - gAS | Col 1007-D |
| 144045-5 | I'm Waiting For Ships That Never Come In - gAS | Col 1051-D |

                                    New York, April 26, 1927.

| | | |
|---|---|---|
| 144048-6 | That Saxophone Waltz - asAS | Col 1081-D |

Acc. by his Southland Syncopators.    New York, April 26, 1927.

| | | |
|---|---|---|
| 144049-3 | I Crave You | Col 1007-D |
| 144050-3 | Twiddlin' My Thumbs (Fiddlin' My Time Away) | Col 1194-D |
| 144051-3 | Flutter By, Butterfly | Col 1116-D |

                                    New York, April 27, 1927.

| | | |
|---|---|---|
| 144056-1 | Now I Won't Be Blue | Col 1253-D |
| 144057-3 | I'd Walk A Million Miles To Be A Little Bit Nearer To You | Col 1116-D |
| 144058-2 | I Love You But I Don't Know Why | Col 1152-D |

Acc. by own piano or Eddie King-p where shown.
                                    New York, May 4, 1927.

| | | |
|---|---|---|
| 144087-2 | (Don't Forget) The Pal You Left At Home | Col 1194-D |
| 144088-2 | I Could Waltz On Forever With You, Sweetheart | Col 1081-D |
| 144089-4 | What A Wonderful Night This Would Be | Col 1253-D |
| 144090-3 | Just Before You Broke My Heart - pEK | Col 1152-D |

Acc. by Rube Bloom-p.               New York, May 16, 1927.

| | | |
|---|---|---|
| 144152-3 | I'm Looking For My Old Gal Sal | Col 1392-D |
| 144153- | I Told You I'd Never Forget You | Rejected |

Acc. by cl-as-g/vn/p/cel.           New York, January 9, 1928.

| | | |
|---|---|---|
| 145491-3 | Gee ! But I'm Blue | Col 1392-D |
| 145492-3 | Nobody's Lonesome But Me | Col 1492-D |
| 145493-3 | Just For Tonight | Col 1619-D |

Acc. by Murray Kellner-vn/Rube Bloom-p. New York, January 10, 1928.

| | | |
|---|---|---|
| 145499-3 | So Tired | Col 1282-D |
| 145500-3 | You'd Rather Forget Than Forgive | -    (continued on page 299) |

Acc. by Murray Kellner-vn/Rube Bloom-p.
                              New York, January 10, 1928 (cont.)

145501-1  In My Sweetheart's Arms                  Col 1492-D
145502-3  Silver-Haired Sweetheart                 Col 1319-D

   Acc. by Andy Sannella-cl-as-f-g-effects/Murray Kellner-vn/Rube Bloom-p, or own  p
   where shown.                   New York, January 11, 1928.

145505-3  Chinatown, My Chinatown                  Col 1619-D
145506-2  My Heart's Aching For My Old Gal         Col 1472-D
145507-3  Who Gives You All Your Kisses ?          Col 1319-D
145508-   I'm Just A Rollin' Stone - own p         Rejected

                              New York, January 17, 1928.

145539-1  The Hours I Spent With You               Col 1353-D

   Acc. by own p/Dale Wimbrow-harmonola (composer of the number).
                              New York, January 19, 1928.

145553-   Think Of Me, Thinking Of You             Col rejected

BARREL-HOUSE PETE : Piano solos by Art Gillham.
                              New York, January 23, 1928.

145562-2  I'm Just A Rollin' Stone                 Col 14308-D
145563-2  Pussy                                        -

Vocal, acc. by own piano.        New York, February 23, 1928.

145676-1  I Found You Out When I Found You In      Col 1353-D
             Somebody Else's Arms

BARREL-HOUSE PETE : Piano solos by Art Gillham.
                              New Orleans, April 24, 1928.

146181-1-2  St. Louis Blues                        Col rejected
146182-1-2  Memphis Blues                              -
146182-1-2  Some Of These Days                         -
146183-1-2  Hesitation Blues                           -

Vocal, acc. by own piano.        New York, August 15, 1928.

146845-3  It's Never Too Late To Be Sorry          Col 1540-D
146846-3  My Heart Cries Out For You               Col 1572-D
146847-2  You Can't Take My Mem'ries From Me       Col 1663-D

   Acc. by unknown c/Arthur Schutt-p.    New York, August 16, 1928.

146848-3  The Lamp Of Aladdin                      Col 1663-D
146849-3  Right Or Wrong                           Col 1540-D
146850-2  Somebody Else May Be Telling Her         Col 1572-D
             Something She'd Love To Hear From You

   Acc. by small orchestra/Ben Selvin.   New York, February 28, 1929.

148008-2  Some Sweet Day                           Col 1726-D
148009-2  I Love You-I Love You-I Love You,
             Sweetheart Of All My Dreams

                              New York, March 5, 1929.

148019-1  Two Little Rooms                         Col 1919-D
148020-3  Somewhere There's Someone                Col 1802-D
148025-5  You've Made My Dreams Come True           Col 1873-D
   NOTE:- Matrices 148022/4 inclusive are not by Art Gillham.

New York, March 6, 1929.

| | | |
|---|---|---|
| 148034- | My Swanee River Home | Rejected |
| 148035-3 | Tell Me There's Hope For Me | Col 1944-D |
| 148036-1 | What Wouldn't I Do ? | Col 1802-D |

New York, March 7, 1929.

| | | |
|---|---|---|
| 148041- | I'm Nobody's Baby | Rejected |
| 148042-3 | True Blue | Col 1919-D |
| 148043-2 | On The Alamo | Col 1944-D |

New York, March 8, 1929.

| | | |
|---|---|---|
| 148047-5 | Blue Little You And Blue Little Me | Col 2016-D |

Acc. by unknown vn/p.          New York, March 18, 1929.

| | | |
|---|---|---|
| 148101-5 | I'm Still Caring | Col 1873-D |

New York, March 29, 1929.

| | | |
|---|---|---|
| 148148-2 | If You Know What I Know | Col 2016-D |

New York, November 25, 1929.

| | | |
|---|---|---|
| 149485-1 | Absence Makes The Heart Grow Fonder (For | Col 2119-D |
| | Somebody Else) | |
| 149486-2 | If You Were The Only Girl In The World | Col 2051-D |
| 149487-2 | Hollywood | - |
| 149492-2 | Have A Little Faith In Me | Col 2119-D |

NOTE:- Matrices 149488/91 inclusive are not by Art Gillham.

New York, November 26, 1929.

| | | |
|---|---|---|
| 149640-6 | If I Had To Do Without You | Col 2189-D |
| 149641- | (You'll Always Be) Welcome | Rejected |
| 149642- | Would You Care ? | - |

Acc. by vn/p (his own ?)/train effects and bells, or own piano only where shown.
                              New York, November 27, 1929.

| | | |
|---|---|---|
| 149648-3 | Just Forget | Col 2245-D, Voc 3028 |
| 149649-5 | Tonight | -              - |
| 149650-8 | You Don't Care - pAG | Col 2189-D |

Acc. by quintet/Ben Selvin.     New York, July 24, 1930.

| | | |
|---|---|---|
| 150661-2 | Good Evenin' | Col 2291-D |
| 150662-1 | Confessin' (That I Love You) | Col 2265-D |
| 150665-2 | My Heart Belongs To The Girl Who Belongs | - |
| | To Somebody Else | |
| 150666-3 | I'm Drifting Back To Dreamland | Col 2291-D |

NOTE:- Matrices 150663/4 are not by Art Gillham.

Acc. by Alex Hill-p.           New York, October 7, 1930.

| | | |
|---|---|---|
| 150865-1 | Passing Time With Me | Col 2331-D |
| 150866-1 | When They Changed My Name To A Number | - |

Acc. by own piano.             New York, November 6, 1930.

| | | |
|---|---|---|
| 150939-3 | Gazing At The Stars | Col 2349-D |
| 150940-3 | To Whom It May Concern | - |

Acc. by unknown cl-as/p.        New York, January 5, 1931.

| | | |
|---|---|---|
| 151144-3 | Shine On, Harvest Moon (w/The Rondoliers) | Col 2374-D, Voc 3027 |
| 151145-2 | If You're Happy, I'll Be Glad | -              - |

Acc. by own piano.                     New York, February 4, 1931.

151272-2  Something Reminds Me Of You        Col 2451-D
151273-3  If You Haven't Got A Girl          -

                                       New York, March 12, 1931.

151415-   Another Broken Heart               Col rejected
151416-   As Long As We Have Each Other      -

                                       New York, May 12, 1931.

151551-4  You Are The Rose Of My Heart       Col 2506-D
151552-   You Treat Me Like A Baby           Rejected

                                       New York, May 26, 1931.

151571-2  Just A Minute More To Say Goodbye  Col 2506-D

Acc. by Billy Smythe—p.                Texas Hotel, San Antonio, March 31, 1934.

BS-82740-1  Somebody Painted My Dream Castle Blue  BB B-5454
BS-82741-1  Alone (I'd Rather Be Alone)            -

## CHARLES S. GILPIN

B. 1878; many years in vaudeville as minstrel; manager of first all-negro stock com-
pany (Lafayette Theatre, New York, 1916); played negro clergyman in ABRAHAM LINCOLN
(Cort, December 15, 1919); very successful in emotional part of Brutus Jones in THE
EMPEROR JONES (Neighborhood, November 1, 1920); played the part for three years in
New York and on tour.  D. May 6, 1930.

Speech, unacc.                         New York, c. July, 1921.

        A Humorous Address To The Musicians     Arto 9102

## LOTTIE GILSON

"The Little Magnet" was a famous vaudeville singer during the nineties and the opening years of the twentieth century.  She made famous songs such as SIDEWALKS OF NEW
YORK (which she sang at the London Theatre in the Bowery, New York, in 1894);YOU'RE
NOT THE ONLY PEBBLE ON THE BEACH (1896); COAX ME, in which she reflected the spot-
light on the audience in the front rows with mirrors.  She encouraged Harry von Tilzer to come to New York before he had ever written any big hits, and helped to plug
his MY OLD NEW HAMPSHIRE HOME (1898).  She allegedly made brown-wax cylinders for
various small companies in the nineties, but no details are known: she is known to
have recorded cylinders for Edison on August 19, September 14 and November 10, 1911
(in addition to the titles mentioned below), but nothing more is known;  it is of
some interest to note that her recording fee on September 14, 1911, was $400, in-
stead of the usual $200 !

Vocal, acc. by studio orchestra.       New York, July 8, 1911.

        Can't You Take It Back And Change It     Ed 4M-890
          For A Boy ?

                                       New York, September 15, 1911.

        Don't Be Ashamed You're Irish (w/John    Ed 4M-934
          Bieling-William F. Hooley-Steve Porter)
        I Want Someone To Care For Me            Ed 4M-990
        Just A Plain Little Irish Girl           Ed 4M-1101

## GEORGE GOBEL (GOEBEL)

B. 1920; child star on radio, became a TV comedian with adulthood, and appeared only
twice in films : THE BIRDS AND THE BEES (1956) and I MARRIED A WOMAN (1957).

Vocal, acc. unknown (g ?)                 Chicago, April 12, 1933.

C-544-   Berry Picking Time                    Rejected ?
C-545-   Billy Richardson's Last Ride          -
C-546-   A Cowboy's Best Friend Is His Horse   Cq 8157
C-547-   Night Herding Song                    -

## ARTHUR GODFREY

B. New York City, August 31, 1903; joined U.S. Navy after attending the Naval Radio
   School, Great Lakes, Ill.; began radio career, 1929 as "The Warbling Banjoist,"and
   was a radio announcer and compere for many years; also popular on TV.

Vocal, acc. by Johnny Salb-elo.           New York, September 14, 1938.

BS-027107-1  (Be It Ever So Thrilling) There's No  BB B-7829
               Place Like Your Arms
BS-027108-1  Old Folks                               -
BS-027109-1  Indiana Moonlight                        BB B-7842, HMV BD-651
BS-027110-1  A Song Of Old Hawaii                     -           -

   Acc. by studio orchestra.              New York, December 2, 1939.

66915-   Back Home On Sunday Night             Dec 2958
66916-   I'd Give A Million Tomorrows          Dec 3014
66917-   Lay My Head Beneath A Rose            -
66918-   I'd Love To Live In Loveland With A   Dec 2958
           Girl Like You

## RUBE   GOLDBERG

Newspaper cartoonist of the Taft-Wilson era who wrote a hit comedy number called I'M
   THE GUY in 1912, and became a popular vaudeville comedian.

Vocal, acc. by studio orchestra.          New York, c. January, 1918.

66518    Father Was Right                     Pathe 20279

## GLORIA GRAFTON

Vocal, acc. by Carroll Gibbons and his Boy Friends.
                                          London, February 28, 1934.

CA-14363-2  I'll Follow My Secret Heart       Col DB-1350
CA-14364-2  Nevermore                          -

   Acc. by studio orchestra.              New York, August 30, 1934.
BS-84070-1  Two Cigarettes In The Dark ("Kill      Vic 24717
              That Story")
BS-84071-2  Lost In A Fog                          -

Vocalist with Paul Whiteman and his Orchestra.
                                          New York, March 10, 1936.

BS-99444-1  My Romance (w/Donald Novis) ("Jumbo")  Vic 25269
BS-99445-1  Little Girl Blue ("Jumbo")             -

## ALEXANDER GRAY

Vocal, acc. by studio orchestra.          New York, April 23, 1925.

140549-  Three Times A Day ("Tell Me More")   Col 368-D
140550-  Tell Me More ! ("Tell Me More")      -

New York, July 15, 1925.

| | | |
|---|---|---|
| 140767- | What A World This Would Be | Col 427-D |
| 140768- | Remembering You | - |

## EDDIE GREEN

Negro composer and comedian, best-remembered for his having written A GOOD MAN IS HARD TO FIND (1918) and other blues-flavoured popular songs, and for his appearance in HOT CHOCOLATES, an all-negro revue, at the Hudson, New York, June 20, 1929.

Speech, unacc.                          New York, August 17, 1929.

| | | |
|---|---|---|
| 402863- | Sending A Wire - Part 1 | OK 8721 |
| 402864- | Sending A Wire - Part 2 | - |

Acc. by Fats Waller-p.            New York, October 14, 1929.

| | | |
|---|---|---|
| BVE-56782-3 | Big Business - Part 1 (w/Billy Higgins & Co.) ("Hot Chocolates") | Vic V-38552 |
| BVE-56783-2 | Big Business - Part 2 (w/Billy Higgins & Co.) ("Hot Chocolates") | - |

## JANE GREEN

American vaudeville singer popular during the 1920s; although she does not seem to have appeared in England, her records were very well-received there.

Vocal, acc. by studio orchestra.        New York, c. December, 1920.

| | |
|---|---|
| Lonely Blues | PA 020480 |
| Wild Romantic Blues | - |

Acc. by Jack Shilkret-p.          New York, November 13, 1923.

| | | |
|---|---|---|
| B-28942-1-2-3 | Mama Goes Where Papa Goes | Vic rejected |
| B-28943-1-2-3-4 | Mama Loves Papa (Papa Loves Mama) | - |

Acc. by the Virginians/Ross Gorman.    New York, December 4, 1923.

| | | |
|---|---|---|
| B-29103-2 | Mama Loves Papa (Papa Loves Mama) | Vic 19215 |
| B-29104-2 | Mama Goes Where Papa Goes (Or Papa Don't Go Out Tonight) | - |

Acc. by O/Nat Shilkret.           New York, November 11, 1924.

| | | |
|---|---|---|
| B-31401-1-2-3 | Old Maid Jim | Rejected |
| B-31402-5 | Me And The Boy Friend | Vic 19502 |

New York, November 26, 1924.

| | | |
|---|---|---|
| B-31451-1-2-3 | Somebody Like You | Rejected |
| B-31455-2 | The Blues Have Got Me | Vic 19609 |

NOTE:- Matrices B-31452/4 inclusive are not by Jane Green.

New York, January 30, 1925.

| | | |
|---|---|---|
| B-31451-6 | Somebody Like You | Vic 19604 |
| B-31793-2 | A Mama Like You And A Papa Like Me | - |

Camden, N. J., May 28, 1925.

| | | |
|---|---|---|
| BVE-32829-1 | If You Hadn't Gone Away | Vic 19707 |
| BVE-32830-1 | We're Back Together Again (My Baby And Me) | Vic 19687 |
| BVE-32831-1-2-3 | Sweet Georgia Brown | Rejected |
| BVE-32832-1 | Can't Your Friend Get A Friend For Me ? | - |
| BVE-32833-4 | Got No Time | Vic 19687 |

Camden, N. J., June 11, 1925.

| | | |
|---|---|---|
| BVE-32731-4  Ida - I Do | Vic 19707 | |
| BVE-32732-1-2-3  Headin' For Home | Rejected | |
| BVE-32831-4-5-6  Sweet Georgia Brown | - | |

Acc. by Frank Banta-p.                  New York, February 9, 1926.

BVE-34604-1-2-3-4  Poor Papa (He's Got Nothin'     Vic rejected
               At All)                                -
BVE-34605-1-2-3-4  Go South                          -

Acc. by O/Nat Shilkret.                 New York, March 4, 1926.

BVE-34680-4  My Castle In Spain                Vic 19995, Zon 2784
BVE-34681-4  Honey Bunch                          -        -

Acc. by O/Leroy Shield.                 New York, November 1, 1926.

BVE-36891-3  Won't Be Long Before He Belongs To Me Vic 20323
BVE-36892-2  Hard-To-Get Gertie                         -
BVE-36893-1-2  If I'd Only Believed In You       Vic 20391, HMV B-2521

Acc. by O/Nat Shilkret.                 New York, February 18, 1927.

BVE-37795-3  You Went Away Too Far (And Stayed   Vic 20509, HMV B-2482
               Away Too Long)
BVE-37796-2  I'm Gonna Meet My Sweetie Now            -           -

New York, December 8, 1927.

BVE-41153-3  Mine, All Mine                      Vic 21114, HMV B-2702
BVE-41154-3  My One And Only                         -           -

## GENE   GREENE

B. Aurora, Ill., June 9, 1877; known as "The Ragtime King," he developed a style   of
singing that was more sophisticated than the "coon-shouting" of the vaudeville artists of the turn of the century; wrote much of his material, including his greatest
hit, KING OF THE BUNGALOOS; appeared in London with great success, 1912-1914,   at a
time when commercial "ragtime" was all the rage. D. New York, April 5, 1930.

Vocal, acc. by Charley Straight-p.      New York, February 17, 1911.

19242-   Cancel That Wedding March          Col A-994
19243-   King Of The Bungaloos                 -        2064

London, c. September, 1912.

92133   Waiting For The Robert E. Lee       Pathe 5347
92134   Ragtime Violin                         -
        Blarney Barney Finn                 Pathe 5348
        King Of The Bungaloos                  -
        Rum Tum Tiddle                      Pathe 5349
        All Night Long                         -
        When You're Married                 Pathe 5350
        Ragtime Melodies                       -
        Dublin Daisies                      Pathe 5351
        That Was Me                            -
        Moonlight Bay                       Pathe 5296
        In Dear Old Tennessee                  -

London, c. November, 1912.

92159   Hitchy Koo                          Pathe 5369
92160   Mocking Bird Rag                       -

92179   Ragtime Soldier Man                 Pathe 100
92183   Drinking                               -

London, c. December, 1912.

| | |
|---|---|
| My Lady Angeline | Pathe 90 |
| My Ever-Loving Two-Step Man | - |
| Go Back | Pathe 5370 |
| Frankie And Johnny | - |

London, c. January, 1913.

| | |
|---|---|
| Raggin' The Baby To Sleep | Pathe 305 |
| That London Rag | - |
| Stop That Bear Cat, Sadie | Pathe 142 |
| Hello, Go On, Goodbye ! | - |

London, c. February, 1913.

| | |
|---|---|
| Whistling Rag | Pathe 167 |
| Heinze | - |
| My Rose Of Old Kildare | Pathe 148 |
| Long Lost Chord | - |

London, c. March, 1913.

| | |
|---|---|
| Beautiful Doll, Goodbye | Pathe 11 |
| Oh, You Beautiful Doll | - |
| Maybe You Think I'm Happy | Pathe 447 |
| That Coontown Quartet | - |

London, c. April, 1913.

| | |
|---|---|
| On The Mississippi | Pathe 544 |
| Rag, Rag, Rag | - |
| Ghost Of The Violin | Pathe 555 |
| Mammy's Shufflin' Dance | - |

London, c. May, 1913.

| | |
|---|---|
| Ragtime Goblin Man | Pathe 538 |
| That Organ **Rag** | - |
| Everybody Two-Step | Pathe 151 |
| You're My Baby | - |

London, c. June, 1913.

| | |
|---|---|
| Oh, You Circus Day | Pathe 5222 |
| Be My Little Baby Bumble Bee | - |
| Ragtime Cowboy Joe | Pathe 529 |
| That Haunting Melody | - |

London, c. July, 1913.

| | |
|---|---|
| Row, Row, Row | Pathe 644 |
| 'Way Down South | - |
| Keep Away From The Fellow Who Owns An Automobile | Pathe 446 |
| One O'Clock In The Morning I Get Lonesome | - |

London, c. August, 1913.

| | |
|---|---|
| I Want To Be In Dixie | Pathe 536 |
| When The Midnight Choo Choo Leaves For Alabam' | - |
| Casey Jones | Pathe 563 |
| Parisienne | - |

London, c. October, 1913.

| | |
|---|---|
| Jimmy Valentine | Pathe 551 |
| That Baboon Baby Dance | - |

London, c. November, 1913.

| They All Kept Time With Their Feet | Pathe 5185 |
| You'll Never Know The Good Fellow I've Been | - |
| Down In Dear Old New Orleans | Pathe 558 |
| Kentucky Days | - |

The dates of recording of the above have been based on the date of issue; the following cannot be determined so nearly at present, but they obviously date from about
the same period.

| 92247 | Piano Fingers | Pathe 150 |
| 92249 | Billy Green | - |

| | No Man Can Do It Like My Father | Pathe 106 |
| | I'm Going To Stay In Solid Ground | - |
| | There's A Big Cry-Baby In The Moon | Pathe 99 |
| | My Little Hong Kong Baby | - |

New York, c. December, 1916.

| 1219-1 | Chinese Blues | Em 5175 (5") |

| 2400- | King Of The Bungaloos | Em 7228 (7") |
| 2401- | Chinese Blues | Em 7140 (7") |

Acc. by O/Rosario Bourdon.          New York, January 30, 1917.

| B-19143-4 | From Here To Shanghai | Vic 18242 |
| B-19144-1-2-3 | Ruff Johnson's Harmony Band | Rejected |
| B-19145-1 | Dance And Grow Thin | - |

New York, March 9, 1917.

| B-19144-6 | Ruff Johnson's Harmony Band | Vic 18266 |
| B-19356-1-2 | Frankie And Johnnie | Rejected ("made on approval") |

Acc. by O/? Charles A. Prince.          New York, April 6, 1917.

| 47465- | Buzzin' The Bee | Col A-2276 |

New York, November 3, 1917.

| 77485-1-2-3-4 | Chin Chin Chinaman | Col rejected |

New York, November 9, 1917.

| 77500- | Alexander's Got A Jazz Band Now | Col A-2472 |

## CHARLOTTE GREENWOOD

B. Philadelphia, Pa., June 25, 1893; stage debut in chorus of THE WHITE CAT (New Amsterdam, November 2, 1905); various other small parts in New York, Chicago and touring; first big success in THE PASSING SHOW OF 1912 (Winter Garden, July 22, 1912);
further successes included THE PASSING SHOW OF 1913 (Winter Garden, July 24, 1913);
SO LONG, LETTY (Shubert, October 23, 1916); various sequels on the "Letty" character between November, 1919 and the spring of 1922; MUSIC BOX REVUE (Music Box, October 23, 1922); HASSARD SHORT'S RITZ REVUE (Ritz, September 17, 1924); on tour from
Chicago to San Francisco between 1930 and 1932; London debut in WILD VIOLETS (Drury
Lane, October 31, 1932); returned to U.S.A. and played in THE LATE CHRISTOPHER BEAN
(El Capitan, Hollywood, October, 1933); again appeared in London at Drury Lane, in
THREE SISTERS (April 9, 1934), and in THE GAY DECEIVERS (Gaiety, May 23, 1935); returned to U.S.A., began long series of appearances in LEANING ON LETTY in San Francisco (December, 1935); toured in U.S.A. and Australia in this, 1936-1943; made her
first film in 1918 (JANE); others include PALMY DAYS (1932); DOWN ARGENTINE WAY
(1940); SPRINGTIME IN THE ROCKIES (1943); UP IN MABEL'S ROOM (1944); OKLAHOMA ! and
THE OPPOSITE SEX (1956); also an appearance in LITTLE MISS WONDERFUL with Jack Oakie and Shirley Temple, with whom she sang TRA-LA-LA-LA, included on Music For Pleasure (LP) MFP-1141. She was noted for her extraordinary ability in high-kicking in
eccentric dance routines.

Vocal, acc. unknown.                    New York, July 30, 1928.

BVE-123   Too Tall                            Vic test

  Acc. by studio orchestra.             London, May 3, 1935.

OEA-2051-2  It Happened In The Moonlight ("The    HMV B-8324
               Gay Deceivers")
OEA-2052-2  Serenade ("The Gay Deceivers")        -

## BEN  GREET

B. in England, 1857 (r.n. Philip Barling; knighted as Sir Philip Greet, 1929,   for
   services to the theatre); first open-air production of Shakespeare, 1886;   formed
   touring company, toured U.S.A. for many years; back to London, 1914, where he was
   one of the founders of the Old Vic Company; many Shakespearean productions   there
   up to the time of his death on May 17, 1936.

Speech, all scenes from Shakespeare.    New York, April 30, 1912.

B-11944-1  The Seven Ages Of Man ("As You Like    Rejected
              It," Act 2, Scene 7)
C-11945-1  The Duke's Opening Speech ("As You      Vic 35235
              Like It," Act 2, Scene 1)
B-11948-1  Marc Antony's Oration ("Julius         Rejected
              Caesar," Act 3, Scene 2)
   NOTE:- Matrices B-11946/7 are not by Ben Greet.

                                        New York, May 1, 1912.

B-11956-1  Prospero's Speech ("The Tempest")      Vic rejected
B-11957-1  Queen Mab Speech ("Romeo and Juliet,"  -
              Act 1, Scene 4)
B-11958-1  The Plea For Mercy ("The Merchant Of    -
              Venice," Act 4, Scene 1)
B-11959-1  Hamlet's Advice To The Players ("Hamlet," -
              Act 3, Scene 2)
B-11960-1  The Charm Of Music ("Twelfth Night,"   -
              Act 1, Scene 1)
B-11961-1  The Power Of Music ("The Merchant Of    -
              Venice," Act 5, Scene 1)

                                        New York, May 3, 1912.

B-11944-2  The Seven Ages Of Man ("As You Like    Rejected
              It," Act 2, Scene 7)
B-11985-1  Henry V Before Harfleur ("Henry V,"    -
              Act 3, Scene 3)
B-11986-1  Othello's Story Before The Senate       -
              ("Othello," Act 1, Scene 3)
C-11987-1  Strike Upon The Bell ("Macbeth,"       Vic 35235
              Act 2, Scene 1)
B-11988-1  Hamlet On Friendship ("Hamlet," Act 2, Vic 17115
              Scene 2)
B-11989-1  Benedick's Ideal Of A Wife ("Much Ado   -
              About Nothing," Act 2, Scene 3)
B-11990-1  St. Crispin's Day ("Henry V," Act 4,   Rejected
              Scene 3)

## LOUISE  GROODY

B. Waco, Texas, March 26, 1897; appeared in several musicals, but star role was  in
   HIT THE DECK (Belasco, N.Y., April 25, 1927). D. September 16, 1961.

Vocal, acc. by studio orchestra.        New York, May, 1922.

 8948   Songs Of Yesterday By Stars Of Today   Voc 35010 (part side)

Acc. by Frank Banta-p.                New York, April 12, 1927.

BVE-38601-4  Sometimes I'm Happy (w/Charles King) Vic 20609, HMV B-2520
             ("Hit The Deck")

## EDGAR A. GUEST

B. Birmingham, England, 1881; to U.S.A. at ten; office boy in Detroit; began contributing witty verse and articles to syndicated press; author of many humorous books
   and short stories. D. Detroit, Mich., August 5, 1959.
Speech.                               Camden, N. J., October 22, 1921.

B-25735-1  Ma And The Auto                      Vic 45258
B-25736-1  It Couldn't Be Done/Wait Until Your Pa    -
           Comes Home
B-25737-1  A Heap O' Livin'                      Vic 45341
B-25738-1  The Boy And The Flag/Selling The House Rejected

                                      Camden, N. J., June 8, 1922.

B-26521-1  The Old Wooden Tub                    Vic 45320
B-26522-2  The Lost Pocket Book                  -
B-26523-2  The Boy And The Flag/At The Door      Vic 45341

                                      Camden, N. J., June 5, 1923.

B-27945-1  Bread And Gravy/Pretending Not To See  Vic 45419
B-27946-1  Proud Father/Dirty Hands               Vic 45454
B-27947-1  Ten Little Mice/When Father Shakes     Vic 45368
           The Stove
B-27948-2  She Powders Her Nose/The Good Little Boy   -
B-27949-2  The Man To Be/Compensation            Vic 45454
B-27999-1  Out Fishin'/The Junk Box              Vic 45419
   NOTE:- Matrices B-27950/27998 inclusive are by other artists on other dates.

## YVETTE  GUILBERT

B. Paris, 1865; well-loved French diseuse who made her debut at the Theatre des Varietes in 1889, singing songs specially written for her; appeared in London at Empire
   and Coliseum variety theatres many times, also in New York. All her songs were recorded in French with the exception of the first two below. She made one film  (for
   UFA in Germany) of FAUST, in 1926.  D. February 3, 1944.

Vocal, acc. by studio orchestra.      Paris, c. November, 1907.

   5275h    I Want Yer, Ma Honey             G&T GC-3735
   5276h    The Keys Of Heaven               G&T GC-3736, HMV E-181

                                      Paris, c. 1908.

        Le Fiacre                           Pathe 1481

                                      New York, October 16, 1918.

   78110-   La Glu                           Col A-2735
   78111-   Ah ! que l'amour cause de peine   -
   78112-   Le Cycle du Vin                  Col A-2736, 18-M
   78113-   Ma Grandmere                     -

                                      New York, October 17, 1918.

   78123-   St. Nicholas                     Col A-2737
   78124-   Le Voyage a Bethlehem            -

                                      New York, October 23, 1918.

   78129-   Le Roy a fait battre tambour     Col A-2738
   78130-   Est-il donc bien ?               -
   (continued on page 309; matrices 78131/3 are not by Yvette Guilbert).

New York, October 23, 1918 (cont.)

| | | |
|---|---|---|
| 78134- | A l'Hotel du Numero 3 | Col A-2739 |
| 78135- | La Defense inutile | -    18-M |
| 78136- | Une mouvement de curiosite | Col A-2740 |
| 78137- | La Femme | - |

Acc. by unknown p.                    Small Queen's Hall, London, June 11, 1928.

| | | |
|---|---|---|
| Bb-13809-1 | Pourquoi me bat mon mari ? | HMV E-527 |
| Bb-13810-2 | Dites-moi si je suis belle | - |
| Cc-13811-2 | Elle etait tres bien | Rejected ? |
| Cc-13812-1 | Je m'embrouille | - |

Small Queen's Hall, London, June 14, 1928.

| | | |
|---|---|---|
| Cc-13825-1-2 | C'est le mai | HMV rejected ? |
| Cc-13826-1-2 | La Delaisee | - |

## MIZZI HAJOS

B. Budapest, Hungary, April 27, 1891; r.n. Magdalena Hajos, and for some time during the twenties, she was known simply as "Mitzi." Stage debut in Budapest as a child and later in Vienna as a teenager; New York debut (and first English-speaking part also) in THE BARNYARD ROMEO, American Roof Garden, June 6, 1910; appeared in vaudeville, then in LA BELLE PAREE (Winter Garden, March 20, 1911); toured U.S.A.,1912, in THE SPRING MAID; her next big success was in the title-role of SARI in New York (Liberty, January 13, 1914); further outstanding successes in POM-POM (George   M. Cohan, February 28, 1916); HEAD OVER HEELS (Cohan, August 29, 1918); LADY   BILLY (Liberty, December 14, 1920); YOU CAN'T TAKE IT WITH YOU (Booth, December 14,1936) and CAFE CROWN (Cort, January 23, 1942); during twenties and early thirties toured U.S.A. and also appeared in New York.

Vocal, acc. by O/Walter B. Rogers.           Camden, N. J., March 28, 1916.

| | |
|---|---|
| B-17386-1-2  In The Dark ("Pom-Pom") | Rejected |
| B-17387-3  Evelyn ("Pom-Pom") | Vic 45091 |

Camden, N. J., April 14, 1916.

| | |
|---|---|
| B-17386-3-4-5-6  In The Dark ("Pom-Pom") | Vic rejected |

Camden, N. J., June 26, 1916.

| | |
|---|---|
| B-17386-7-8-9-10  In The Dark ("Pom-Pom") | Vic rejected |
| B-17387-4-5  Evelyn ("Pom-Pom") | - |

Camden, N. J., July 10, 1916.

| | |
|---|---|
| B-17386-12  In The Dark ("Pom-Pom") | Vic 45091 |
| B-17387-6-7  Evelyn ("Pom-Pom") | Rejected |

The following titles are listed in the Gennett files and catalogues as by Mitzi, but it is not certain that Mizzi Hajos made them.

Vocal, acc. unknown.                    New York, c. August 21, 1923.

| | | |
|---|---|---|
| 8475 | My Christmas Wish | Gnt 5242 |

Acc. by small instrumental group.        New York, c. April 2, 1928.

| | | |
|---|---|---|
| GEX-1163 | Lila | Gnt rejected |
| GEX-1164 | Without You, Sweetheart | - |

New York, c. May 17, 1928.

| | | |
|---|---|---|
| GEX-1299 | After My Laughter Came Tears | Gnt rejected |
| GEX-1300 | Sweet Sue - Just You | - |

New York, c. June 18, 1928.

GEX-1455    After My Laughter Came Tears          Spt 8028
GEX-1456    Sweet Sue - Just You                  -

## JACK HALEY

B. Boston, Mass., 1902; stage debut in vaudeville; New York debut in ROUND THE  TOWN
(Century Roof, May 21, 1924); subsequent stage successes include GAY PAREE  (Shubert, August 18, 1925); revival of this (Winter Garden, November 9, 1926);  FOLLOW
THRU' (46th Street, January 9, 1929); TAKE A CHANCE (Apollo, November 26, 1932);in
films since 1930, many very popular performances (SITTING PRETTY, with Jack Oakie,
1933; CORONADO (1935); WAKE UP AND LIVE, with Alice Faye, 1937; REBECCA OF  SUNNY-
BROOK FARM, with Shirley Temple, 1938; ALEXANDER'S RAGTIME BAND, with Alice  Faye,
1938;THE WIZARD OF OZ (as the Tin Man and Hickory, with Judy Garland), 1939; HIGH-
ER AND HIGHER (film version of 1940 stage hit), 1942; GEORGE WHITE'S SCANDALS,1945
and many others); m. Florence McFadden, 1923; son Jack Haley, Jr. produced NORWOOD
(1970) for which his father came out of retirement for a part; other more  recent
stage appearances include SHOW TIME (1942, with Ella Logan) and INSIDE U.S.A.,with
Beatrice Lillie (1948).

Vocal, acc. by studio orchestra.          New York, c. May, 1923.

  426-B  I Love Me (I'm Wild About Myself)          Cam 327

Jack Haley also appears on MGM C-757 (LP), in extracts from the soundtrack  of  THE
WIZARD OF OZ.

## ADELAIDE  HALL

B. Brooklyn, N.Y., 1895; spotted by Lew Leslie, producer of BLACKBIRDS when she sang
at a school Christmas concert (one of her childhood friends was a sister of  Florence Mills, the star of BLACKBIRDS); appeared in SHUFFLE ALONG (63rd Street,  May
23, 1921), which ran for 504 performances; took Florence Mills's place when  "the
little blackbird" died in 1927; London debut in cabaret, 1931; returned to New York
and starred at the Cotton Club in Harlem, having sung with Duke Ellington and  his
Orchestra that had played there for over three years; opened own night-club, known
as The Big Apple, in Paris, and ran it with her husband and manager, Bert Hicks;he
was a Trinidadian, thus British, and after a tour of Europe, they decided to  settle in London, where Adelaide Hall lives yet (at this writing).  She made a number
of films in England (THE THIEF OF BAGDAD, 1940, and NIGHT AND THE CITY), and  took
part in stage productions such as THE SUN NEVER SETS (Drury Lane, June 9,1938)KISS
ME KATE (Coliseum, March 8, 1951) and LOVE FROM JUDY (Saville, September 25, 1952).
Widowed in 1963, but still accepts engagements all over England, and appeared in a
Broadway production of JAMAICA, with Lena Horne, in 1957.

Vocalist with Duke Ellington and his Orchestra.
                                     New York, October 26, 1927.

BVE-39370-1  Creole Love Call                    Vic 21137, 24861, LPM-1715,
                                                 RD-27133, X LVA-3037, HMV B-4895,
                                                 B-6252, BD-5758, DLP-1094
BVE-39370-2  Creole Love Call                    Vic 21137
BVE-39371-1  The Blues I Love To Sing            Vic 21490, 22985, 68-0837,
                                                 BB B-6531, HMV B-4966, B-6343,
                                                 BD-5760
BVE-39371-2  The Blues I Love To Sing            X LVA-3037

Vocal, acc. by George Rickson-p.          New York, June 21, 1928.

             Baby ("Blackbirds of 1928")          Vic test (un-numbered)
             I Must Have That Man ("Blackbirds of    -
             1928")

  Acc. by Lew Leslie's Blackbirds Orchestra.
                                     New York, August, 1928.

E-28059-   I Must Have That Man ("Blackbirds of   Br 4031
           1928")
E-28060-   Baby ("Blackbirds of 1928")                -

Acc. by Francis J. Carter-Bennie Paine-p.
                                    London, October, 1931.

| R-218 | Rhapsody In Love | Br 01217 |
| R-221 | Minnie The Moocher | - |
| R-225 | Too Darn Fickle | Or P-108, Br 01307 |
| R-229 | I Got Rhythm | Or P-109    - |
| R-230 | Baby Mine | - |
| R-232 | I'm Red-Hot From Harlem | Or P-108 |

NOTE:- Matrix R-231 is a twelve-inch piano solo of a Chopin waltz by an  unidentified pianist; the other missing numbers have not been traced.

Acc. by small studio group.        New York, August 5, 1932.

| B-12148-A | Strange As It Seems | Br 6376, 01348 |
| B-12149-A | I'll Never Be The Same | Br 6362    - |

Acc. by Art Tatum-Francis J. Carter-p, with unknown vib*.
                                    New York, August 10, 1932.

| B-12166-A | *You Gave Me Everything But Love | Br 6376, 01442, Par F-1425 |
| B-12167-A | This Time It's Love | Br 6362    -      - |

Vocalist with Duke Ellington and his Famous Orchestra.
                                    New York, December 21, 1932.

| B-12773-B | I Must Have That Man ("Blackbirds of 1928") | CBS OL-6770 |
| B-12774-B | Baby ("Blackbirds of 1928") | - |

                                    New York, January 7, 1933.

| B-12773-C | I Must Have That Man ("Blackbirds of 1928") | Br 6518, 01519 |
| B-12774-C | Baby ("Blackbirds of 1928") | -      - |

Vocalist with Mills Blue Rhythm Band.    New York, December 4, 1933.

| BS-78827-1-2 | Drop Me Off In Harlem | Vic rejected |
| BS-78828-1-2-3 | Reaching For The Cotton Moon | - |

Vocal, acc. by Francis J. Carter-p.    Paris, January, 1936.

| P-77612 | I'm In The Mood For Love | Ul AP-1574 |
| P-77613 | Truckin' | - |

Acc. by John Ellsworth and his Orchestra.
                                    Paris, January, 1936.

| P-77616 | East Of The Sun (And West Of The Moon) | Ul AP-1575 |
| P-77618 | Solitude | - |

Vocalist with Willie Lewis and his Orchestra.
                                    Paris, May 5, 1936.

| CPT-2649-1 | I'm Shooting High | PA PA-914 |
| CPT-2652-1 | Say You're Mine | PA PA-915 |

NOTE:- Adelaide Hall does not sing on matrices CPT-2650 and 2651.

Vocal, acc. by Kai Ewans' Orkester.    Copenhagen, November, 1937.

| C-596- | There's A Lull In My Life | Tono K-6001, T-1213, Ekko 135 |
| C-597- | Stormy Weather | Tono K-6002    - |
| C-598- | Where Or When | -    T-1214 |
| C-599- | Medley (Intro. Dinah/Margie/After You've Gone/I Ain't Got Nobody) | Tono K-6001    -    Ekko 135 |

Acc. by Fats Waller-pipe organ-v.          London, August 28, 1938.

OEA-6391-1  That Old Feeling                        HMV B-8849
OEA-6392-2  I Can't Give You Anything But Love       -

Acc. by Fela Sowande-elo/unknown d.      London, April 27, 1939.

DR-3517-1  I Have Eyes                               Dec F-7049
DR-3518-1  I Promise You                             -

                                          London, May 15, 1939.

DR-3580-1  Deep Purple                               Dec F-7083
DR-3581-1  Solitude                                  -

                                          London, June  8, 1939.

DR-3660-1  A New Moon And An Old Serenade            Dec F-7095
DR-3661-1  Our Love                                  -

                                          London, June 23, 1939.

DR-3691-2  Don't Worry 'Bout Me                      Dec F-7121
DR-3692-2  'Tain't What You Do (It's The Way          -
               That You Do It)

                                          London, July 26, 1939.

DR-3765-1  Transatlantic Lullaby                     Dec F-7132
DR-3766-1  I Get Along Without You Very Well          -

                                          London, October 17, 1939.

DR-3921-1  Moon Love                                 Dec F-7272
DR-3922-1  Yours For A Song                          -

                                          London, November 8, 1939.

DR-4013-1  Day In - Day Out                          Dec F-7304
DR-4014-1  I Poured My Heart Into A Song             -
DR-4015-2  My Heart Belongs To Daddy                 Dec F-7305
DR-4016-1  Have You Met Miss Jones ?                 -

                                          London, December 27, 1939.

DR-4119-1  Serenade In Blue                          Dec F-7340
DR-4120-1  Fare Thee Well                            -

                                          London, January 19, 1940.

DR-4229-1  Where Or When                             Dec F-7345
DR-4230-1  The Lady Is A Tramp                        -

Acc. by Robin Richmond-pipe organ/Gerry Moore-p/Al Craig-d.
                                          London, March 11, 1940.

DR-4409-1  Careless                                  Dec F-7430
DR-4410-1  Don't Make Me Laugh                       -

Acc. by studio orchestra/? Jay Wilbur.  London, April 15, 1940.

DR-4526-1  Chloe (Song Of The Swamp)                 Dec F-7460
DR-4527-1  Begin The Beguine                         -

Acc. by small instrumental group,       London, May  3, 1940.

DR-4632-1  This Can't Be Love                        Dec F-7501
DR-4633-1  No Souvenirs                              -  ·

London, May 31, 1940.

DR-4762-1  Who Told You I Cared ?              Dec F-7522
DR-4763-1  Shake Down The Stars                    -

London, August 15, 1940.

DR-4962-1  Mist On The River                   Dec F-7583
DR-4963-2  Fools Rush In                           -

London, October 9, 1940.

DR-5045-1  All The Things You Are              Dec F-7636
DR-5046-1  I Wanna Be Loved                        -

London, December 12, 1940.

DR-5160-1  Goodnight Again                     Dec F-7678
DR-5161-1  Trade Winds                             -
DR-5162-1  Our Love Affair                     Dec F-7681
DR-5163-1  And So Do I

London, February 7, 1941.

DR-5325-1  Moon For Sale                       Dec F-7708
DR-5326-1  Yesterday's Dreams                      -
DR-5327-1  Ain't It A Shame About Mame ?       Dec F-7709
DR-5328-1  Room Five Hundred And Four

London, May 23, 1941.

DR-5783-1  It's Always You                     Dec F-7879
DR-5784-1  How Did He Look ?                       -
DR-5785-1  Yes, My Darling Daughter            Dec F-7891
DR-5786-1  The Things I Love

London, July 3, 1941.

DR-5957-1  I Hear A Rhapsody                   Dec F-7918
DR-5958-1  Mississippi Mama                        -

Acc. by studio orchestra/? Jay Wilbur.  London, August 7, 1941.

DR-6103-1  I, Yi, Yi, Yi, Yi (I Like You Very   Dec F-7942
             Much)
DR-6104-1  Moonlight In Mexico                     -

London, November 5, 1941.

DR-6401-1  As If You Didn't Know               Dec F-8030
DR-6402-1  I Take To You                           -
DR-6403-1  Minnie From Trinidad                Dec F-8031
DR-6404-1  Sand In My Shoes

Acc. by Roland Peachey and his Royal Hawaiians.
                                     London, November 7, 1941.

DR-6433-1  Song Of The Islands                 Dec F-8058
DR-6434-1  Pagan Love Song                         -

Acc. by Gerry Moore-p.               London, November 18, 1941.

DR-6468-1  I Don't Want To Set The World On Fire  Dec F-8043
DR-6469-1  My Sister And I                         -

Acc. by studio orchestra.            London, February 2, 1942.

DR-6648-1  A Sinner Kissed An Angel            Dec F-8092
DR-6649-1  Tropical Magic                      Dec F-8118
DR-6650-1  Why Don't We Do This More Often ?   Dec F-8092
DR-6651-1  Intermezzo                          Dec F-8118

"The Red-Headed Music Maker" was a folk-singer whose nonsense song IT  AIN'T  GONNA RAIN NO MO' propelled him and his ukulele into the limelight of vaudeville appearances (and later, radio shows) throughout the latter half of the twenties and  the early thirties.

Vocal, acc. by own ukulele.          New York, c. October 1, 1923.

    8541    Red-Headed Music Maker              $^G$nt 5271
    8542    It Ain't Gonna Rain No Mo'              -     EBW 4027
    NOTE:- Some copies of Edison Bell Winner 4027 as WILL HALL, others as REGENT ORCHESTRA.

                                     New York, October 12, 1923.

B-28740-1  Red Headed Music Maker (Intro. Red    Vic 19171
             Hot Blues)
B-28741-2  It Ain't Gonna Rain No Mo'              -

    Acc. by the Virginians.          New York, October 23, 1923.

B-28760-3  Blue Island Blues                     Vic 19226
B-28761-4  Bluebird Blues                          -

    Acc. by own ukulele.           New York, c. October, 1923.

           It Ain't Gonna Rain No Mo'           Ed 51261

                                     New York, January 15, 1924.

B-29312-3  It Looks Like Rain                    Vic 19270
B-29313-3  Comfortin' Gal                          -

    Acc. by the Virginians.          New York, January 18, 1924.

B-29330-1-2-3-4  Brother, You've Got Me Wrong    Vic rejected
B-29331-1-2-3-4  31st Street Blues                 -

    Acc. by O/Rosario Bourdon.       Camden, N. J., January 22, 1924.

B-29407-1-2-3  Land Of My Sunset Dreams          Vic rejected

    Acc. by Rosario Bourdon-p/Lawrence Rizzolli-bj.
                                     Camden, N. J., January 24, 1924.

B-29416-1-2-3-4  Gwine To Run All Night (w/The   Vic rejected
             Shannon Four)
B-29417-1  Oh Susanna                              -

    Acc. by Phil Ohman-p.
                                     New York, February 4, 1924.

B-29377-1-2-3-4  Land Of My Sunset Dreams        Vic rejected

    Acc. by Lou Raderman-vn/Leroy Shield-p, or O/Eddie King, with Frank Reino-bj.
                                     New York, February 8, 1924.

B-29377-7  Land Of My Sunset Dreams - vn/p       Vic 19282
B-29416-6  Gwine To Run All Night (w/The Shannon Vic 19290
             Four and O/EK-bjFR)
B-29417-3  Oh Susanna (w/The Shannon Four and bjFR)  -

Vocal duets with Carson Robison, acc. by their own g/u respectively.
                                     New York, May 1, 1924.

B-29954-2  Song Birds In Georgia                 Vic 19338
B-29955-1  Whistling The Blues Away                -

Unknown p added.                        New York, May 5, 1924.

B-29963-1-2-3-4  Swanee River Dreams              Rejected
B-29964-3  Old Plantation Melody (CR does not     Vic 19392
           sing)

Vocal, acc. by own u/Carson Robison-g.  New York, May 7, 1924.

B-29971-1-2-3-4  Lilac (Don't Lie Like That)      Vic rejected
B-29972-1-2-3-4  Pretty Pettin' Man               -

   Lou Raderman-vn added.               New York, June 10, 1924.

B-29963-8  Swanee River Dreams (w/Carson Robison) Vic 19479
B-29964-4-5-6  Old Plantation Lullaby             Rejected

   Acc. by Lou Raderman-vn/Nat Shilkret-p/own u/Carson Robison-g-whistling.
                                        New York, June 11, 1924.

B-30178-3  Lonely Lane                            Vic 19479
B-30179-2  Pickaninny Lullaby                     Vic 19392

   No p used.                           New York, November 5, 1924.

B-31077-1-2-3-4  Little Lindy Lou                 Rejected
B-31078-4  We're Gonna Have Weather (Whether Or   Vic 19501
           Not)

   Acc. by own u/Carson Robison-g-stg; unknown f/Leroy Shields-p added where shown.
                                        New York, November 7, 1924.

B-31092-2  I Couldn't Get To It In Time - u/g     Vic 19565
B-31093-4  Don't Say "Aloha" - f/p/stg/u          Vic 19653
B-31094-2  Rose Of Hawaii - f/p/stg/u             -

   Acc. by own ukulele.                 Camden, N. J., June 15, 1925.

BVE-32898-1-2-3-4-5  Sunshine (Ain't The          Vic rejected
               Sunshine Grand ?)
BVE-32899-1-2-3-4  It Struck My Funny Bone         -

                                        Camden, N. J., June 29, 1925.

BVE-32898-7  Sunshine (Ain't The Sunshine Grand ?)Vic 19725, HMV B-2176
BVE-32899-5  It Struck My Funny Bone              -         HMV B-2152

Vocal duets with Marjorie Lamkin, acc. by her bj.
                                        Camden, N. J., June 29, 1925.

BVE-33041-1-2-3-4  Gwine Lay Down Mah Life Fo'     Vic rejected
               Mah Lord)
BVE-33042-1-2-3-4  I'm On De Right Side (Brother,  -
               What's You ?)

Vocal, acc. by own ukulele.             Camden, N. J., July 15, 1925.

BVE-32777-2  Hokey Pokey Diddle Dee Rum           Vic 19792
BVE-32778-2  I Don't Think So                     -

   Acc. by Lou Raderman-vn/Leroy Shield-p/Carson Robison-g/own u, as shown.
                                        Camden, N. J., July 24, 1925.

BVE-31077-8  Little Lindy Lou - vn/g/u            Vic 19744, HMV B-2176
BVE-33098-2  Over The Rainbow Trail - vn/p        Vic 19762
BVE-33099-1-2-3  Your Eyes (Your Shining Eyes)    Rejected

Acc. by own ukulele.                        Camden, N. J., July 29, 1925.

BVE-28740-6  Red Headed Music Maker (Intro. Red   Vic 19886
                Hot Blues)
BVE-28741-5  It Ain't Gonna Rain No Mo'            -
BVE-33203-3  It Ain't Gonna Rain No Mo' - Part 2  Vic 19890
BVE-33204-1-2-3-4  Fuzzy Wuzzy Bird                Rejected

Acc. by own ukulele and tiple, with Lou Raderman-vn/Nat Shilkret-p/Carson Robison-
g, as shown.                                Camden, N. J., August 7, 1925.

BVE-29377-9-10  Land Of My Sunset Dreams - vn/p   Rejected
BVE-31078-6  We're Gonna Have Weather (Whether    Vic 19890, HMV B-2152
                Or Not) - t/g
BVE-33099-4  Your Eyes (Your Shining Eyes)-vn/p   Vic 19762
BVE-33150-3  Whisp'ring Trees (Memories And You)  Vic 19819
                - vn/p

Acc. by Lou Raderman-vn/Nat Shilkret-p.
                                   Camden, N. J., October 6, 1925.

BVE-29377-12  Land Of My Sunset Dreams -          Vic 20170
BVE-33451-4  Angry                                Vic 19819

Acc. by own tarapatch (kind of ukulele).
                                   New York, c. December, 1925.

E-17191    Honkey Pokey Diddle Dee Rum            Br 3006
E-17194    Kentucky's Way Of Saying "Good Morning"  -

                                   New York, c. March, 1926.

E-17814    Say, Mister ! Have You Met Rosie's     Br 3086
              Sister ?
           Spanish Shawl                          -

                                   New York, c. June, 1926.

E-19653    That's Why I Love You                  Br 3236
E-19655    My Dream Sweetheart                    -

                                   New York, c. July, 1926.

E-19770/1  Mandy                                  Br 3265
E-19772/3  Precious                               -

Acc. by vn/vc/p/g.                 New York, c. September, 1926.

E-20215/6  She's Still My Baby                    Br 3330

Acc. by vn/vc/p.                   New York, c. September, 1926.

E-20391/2  No-One But You Knows How To Love       Br 3330
E-20393/5  Just A Bird's-Eye View (Of My Old      Br 3331
              Kentucky Home)
E-20396/7  Meadow Lark                            -

Acc. by own ukulele/Carson Robison-g.  New York, c. November, 1926.

           I'm Tellin' The Birds, Tellin' The     Br 3387
              Bees (How I Love You)
           Take In The Sun, Hang Out The Moon     -

                                   New York, February 24, 1927.

143521-    Down Kentucky Way                      Col 942-D
143522-    Hot Feet                               -

Acc. by studio orchestra.                    New York, c. March, 1927.

E-22003/4  Down Kentucky Way                        Br 3507
E-22005/7  Yesterday                                  -

  Acc. unknown.                            New York, c. April 1, 1927.

GEX-560   Down Kentucky Way                     Gnt 6084, Ch 15256
GEX-561   Hot Feet                                  -      Ch 15259

                                           New York, May 21, 1927.

144188-   Headin' Home (Bound For Birmingham)   Col 1028-D
144189-   There's A Trick In Pickin' A Chick-Chick-   -
          Chicken

                                           New York, June 17, 1927.

 7151-   Ain't She Sweet ?                     Ban ? Dom ? Or ?

  Acc. by studio orchestra.              New York, c. April, 1928.

E-        Will You Remember (What I Can't Forget)  Br 3903
          I Told You I'd Never Forget You           -

                                           New York, June, 1928.

E-27793-  Oh ! Lucindy                          Br 3983, 3925
E-27794-  Headin' Home (Bound For Birmingham)   Br 3984    -
E-27795-  My Dream Sweetheart                   Br 4004, 3880

                                           New York, July, 1928.

E-27802-  Polly Wolly Doodle                    Br 4024, 3880
E-27803-  Hot Feet                              Br 3983

E-27815-  Easy Goin'                            Br 4004
E-27816-  If I Only Knew                        Br 4024
E-27817-  Old-Fashioned Locket                  Br 3984

                                           Chicago, December 16, 1928.

C-2680-   In The Big Rock Candy Mountains       Br 4174
C-2681-   Who Said I Was A Bum ?                  -

                                           New York, February, 1929.

E-29322-  Ploddin' Along                        Br 4271
E-29323-  Dear Heart Of Mine                    Br 4270
E-29324-  There's A Four-Leaf Clover In My      Br 4271
          Pocket
E-29326-  My Angeline                           Br 4270
E-29327-  (Underneath The) Mellow Moon          Br 4879
E-29328-  Land Of My Sunset Dreams                -

E-29369-  Eleven Cent Cotton And Forty Cent Meat  Br 4279
E-29370-  Seven Times Seven Is Forty-Nine         -
  NOTE:- Matrix E-29325 is untraced.

  Acc. by own tiple/2vn/vc/sb.        Chicago, December 13, 1933.

BS-77335-1  Where's Elmer ?                   BB B-5291, Eld 2162, Sr S-3372
BS-77336-1  Jimmy Had A Nickel                   -          -         -
BS-77337-1  Where The Dear Old Rockies Tip-Toe  BB B-5410
            To The Sea
BS-77338-1  My Carolina Home                     -
BS-77339-1  New It Ain't Gonna Rain No Mo' (no vn) BB B-5332, Sr S-3413
            - Part 3
BS-77340-1  You So-And-So (no vn)                 -          -

B. New York, October 18, 1910; liked to sing as a child, but never learned to read
music; heard by Pathe executive Herman Rose while singing at a party when she was
fifteen; he signed her to make records (and eventually married her). Although she
could play piano and ukulele, she never liked show business, and despite fame and
success in short films and regular radio appearances, she retired to become house-
wife in 1934, and even after her husband died in 1954, she never tried to make any
sort of come-back. Billed as "The Personality Girl," she has a great gift of mim-
icry, and her impressions of Helen Kane drew applause from Miss Kane herself.

Vocal, acc. by own piano.                    New York, July 28, 1926.

E-2476    Medley                                  PA test
E-2477    Medley                                  -

   Acc. by small jazz band.               New York, September 12, 1926.

E-2518-C *Black Bottom                       PA 32207, 11248, Per 12286, Hal 5
E-2519-D *Six Feet Of Papa                   PA 32211, Per 12290, Apex 774   -

   Acc. by own piano.                      New York, September 13, 1926.

E-2522    That's Why I Love You             Apex 774
E-2523-A-C *Lay Me Down To Sleep In Carolina PA 32207, 11248, Per 12286,
                                             Apex 780
E-2524-A *Falling In Love With You           PA 32211, Per 12290

   Acc. by the Red Heads (small jazz band).
                                          New York, October, 1926.

107133-A-B *Don't Take That Black Bottom Away   PA 32213, Per 12292 (-A on Hal 5)
107133-D  Don't Take That Black Bottom Away     -

   Acc. by Murray Kellner-vn/Own p, with unknown as where shown.
                                          New York, October 20, 1926.

E-2565-B *Cherie, I Love You - as            PA 32213, 11361, Per 12292,
                                             Apex 791
E-2566-A *Calling Me Home                    PA 32222, 11361, Per 12301,
                                             Apex 791

   Acc. by Irving Brodsky-p.              New York, October 22, 1926.

E-2567-B *If I'd Only Believed In You        PA 32226, Per 12305, Apex 26023
E-2568-C *My Baby Knows How                  PA 32222, Per 12301, Apex 26006

                                          New York, November 26, 1926.

E-2608    *Do-Do-Do                          PA 32226, 11492, Per 12305,
                                             Apex 26006
E-2609-B *Everything's Made For Love         PA 32230, 11338, Per 12309
E-2610-B *Kiss Your Little Baby Goodnight    -          -          -
E-2611-B *One Sweet Letter From You (W/own u also) PA 32259, Per 12338

   Acc. by the Red Heads (Murray Kellner-vn/Irving Brodsky-p).
                                          New York, November, 1926.

107189-A *If You Can't Tell The World She's A    PA 32217, Per 12296
         Good Little Girl Just Say Nothing At All
107190-A *I'm All Alone In A Palace Of Stone     -          -
         (The "Peaches" and Browning Song)
   (All above titles marked * issued on Fountain FV-201).
   Acc. by Irving Brodsky-p.             New York, January 28, 1927.

E-2666    He's The Last Word                 PA 32240, 11463, Per 12319,
                                             Apex 26023
E-2667    I'm Gonna Meet My Sweetie Now      As above, except Apex 26023
E-2668    Ain't He Sweet ?                   PA 32244, 11388, Per 12323
E-2669    It All Depends On You              -          -          - Apex 26026

Acc. by Jimmy Lytell-cl/Irving Brodsky-p.
                              New York, c. February 2, 1927.

107340    Here Or There                       PA 32235, 11433, Per 12314
107341    I Gotta Get Myself Somebody To Love   -        -        -

     Acc. by Irving Brodsky-p.          New York, February 26, 1927.

107398    Song Of The Wanderer              PA 32250, 11409, Per 12329, Hal 5
107399, -A  If You See Sally                  -    Apex 26026   -         -

     Acc. by J. Russel Robinson-p, with unknown vn where shown.
                              New York, April 1, 1927.

107458    So Blue - vn                      PA 32255, 11409, Per 12334
107459    My Idea Of Heaven                     -    11472   -
107460    Aw Gee ! Don't Be That Way Now    PA 32267, 11517, Per 12346

Vocalist with the Original Memphis Five. New York, c. April 14, 1927.

107487    Wistful And Blue                  PA 36623, 11421, Per 14804
107488    What Do I Care What Somebody Said ?   -        -        -
107489    Nothin'                           PA 11471

Vocal, acc. by Irving Brodsky-p.        New York, April 29, 1927.

107513    Just Like A Butterfly             PA 32267, 11472, Per 12346
107514    Rosy Cheeks                       PA 32259, 11517, Per 12338
107515    It's Just Because I'm Falling In Love  Rejected
             With You

     Acc. by the Four Instrumental Stars, under which name the first two sides were is-
     sued.                    New York, June, 1927.

107645    I'm Somebody's Somebody Now       PA 36664, 11485, Per 14845, Hal 5
107646    I Like What You Like                  -        -    - VJM VEP-31 -
107647    Ain't That A Grand And Glorious Feeling PA 32275, 11495, Per 12354  -    -
107648    Who-oo·? You-oo, That's Who !     PA 11540                          -
107650    Under The Moon                    PA 32275, 11495, Per 12354,
                                            VJM VEP-31

     Acc. by Phil Wall-p.               New York, August, 1927.

107720    Miss Annabelle Lee (w/own u also)   PA 32283, 11523, Per 12362
107721    From Now On (You're Gonna Be Mine)      -    11535    -

     Acc. by her Sizzlin' Syncopators.    New York, September 8, 1927.

107765    It Was Only A Sunshower           PA 32293, 11546, Per 12372, Hal 5
107766    Who's That Knockin' At My Door ?      -        -    - VJM VEP-31 -

     Acc. by self or    Willard Robison-p.  New York, October, 1927.

107833    Just Another Day Wasted Away - pWR  PA 32309, 11523, Per 12388
107834    Are You Happy ? - pAH                 -    11540    -

     Acc. by small string orchestra.    New York, c. November 23, 1927.

107921    The Song Is Ended                 PA 32314, 11535, Per 12393
          Thinking Of You                       -        -
          Mine - All Mine                   PA 32320, Per 12399
          There Must Be Somebody Else           -

Vocalist (sometimes described as "Miss Annette") with Lou Gold and his Orchestra.
                              New York, November, 1927.

107941    Mary (What Are You Waiting For ?)   PA 36725, Per 14906, P-416
          What'll You Do ?                  PA 36726, Per 14907

New York, December, 1927.

      Plenty Of Sunshine                           PA 36733, 11547, Per 14914
      Who Gives You All Your Kisses ?              -                  -

New York, January, 1928.

108011-1  After My Laughter Came Tears         PA 36759, Per 14940, P-379
      You Gotta Be Good To Me              PA 36751, Per 14932
      In The Sing-Song Sycamore Tree       PA 36752, Per 14933
      (I'm Cryin' 'Cause I Know) I'm Losin'    PA 36761, Per 14942
        You
  NOTE:- All Pathe Actuelles as THE VIRGINIA CREEPERS; Perfect P-379 as MEYER'S   DANCE
ORCHESTRA.

Vocal, acc. by small orchestra.          New York, January, 1928.

108018    The Man I Love                      PA 32332, 11554, Per 12411
108019    When You're With Somebody Else       -          -          -

  Acc. by Peter de Rose-p/Harry Reser-bj-g, with Jimmy Lytell-cl-as where shown.
                New York, February, 1928.

108054    There Must Be A Silver Lining       PA 32340, 11559, Per 12419
108055    I Just Roll Along (Having My Ups And  -          -          -
      Downs) - clJL

Vocalist with Frank Ferera's Hawaiian Trio.
                New York, March, 1928.

108084-1  I'm Longing To Belong To Someone    PA      , Per      , P-411
  NOTE:- Perfect P-411 as THE HAWAIIAN SERENADERS.

Vocal, acc. by Jimmy Lytell-cl/Peter de Rose-p/Harry Reser-bj-g.
                New York, March, 1928.

108087    Lila                                PA 32348, 11565, Per 12427
108088    'Cause I Feel Low Down               -          -          -

Vocalist with Willard Robison and his Orchestra.
                New York, c. March, 1928.

      I Love My Old-Fashioned Man           PA 36782, Per 14963
      Speedy Boy                            PA 36785, Per 14966
  NOTE:- Pathe Actuelle 36785 and Perfect 14966 as LEVEE LOUNGERS.

New York, April, 1928.

108116    There Ain't No Sweet Man That's Worth  PA 36782, 11563, Per 14963
      The Salt Of My Tears
      Japanese Sandman                    PA 36796, Per 14977
      Smiles                               -          -
  NOTE:- Pathe Actuelle 11563 as DEEP RIVER ORCHESTRA.

Vocal, acc. by Jimmy Lytell-cl-as/Rube Bloom-p/Harry Reser-bj-g.
                New York, April, 1928.

108150    'Tain't No-One But You - clJL       PA 32358, 11577, Per 12437
108151    Ready For The River - asJL           -          -          -

  Reser omitted.                         New York, May, 1928.

108196    Get Out And Get Under The Moon      PA 32365, 11568, Per 12444, Hal 5
108197    We Love It                           -          -          -          -

At this point, Annette Hanshaw began recording for Columbia, OKeh, Harmony,  Clarion,
  Diva and Velvet Tone.  Although she was given her own name on most of these,  some
  were issued as by Gay Ellis (for sentimental numbers), Dot Dare or Patsy Young  for
  her Helen Kane impersonations.  It is possible to find the identical recording  as
  by Annette Hanshaw on one label and Gay Ellis on another !

Vocalist with Frank Ferera's Hawaiian Trio.
                              New York, June 12, 1928.

146432-3  Was It A Dream ?                    Har 666-H
146433-1  For Old Times' Sake                    -

Vocal, acc. unknown.              New York, June 14, 1928.

146450-1-2-3  Get Out And Get Under The Moon      Col rejected

   Acc. by her Sizzlin' Syncopators.    New York, July 24, 1928.

146791-3  I Can't Give You Anything But Love  Har 706-H, SR 1005-P, 1023-S
146792-2  I Must Have That Man                 -          -         -

Vocalist with Frank Ferera's Hawaiian Trio.
                              New York, August 10, 1928.

146833-   Get Out And Get Under The Moon       Har 713-H
146834-   Lonely Nights In Hawaii                 -

Vocal, acc. by the University Six.    New York, September 13, 1928.

146993-3  That's Just My Way Of Forgetting You  Har 734-H
146994-3  High Upon A Hill-Top                     -

   Acc. by her Novelty Orchestra.     New York, October 19, 1928.

147153-2  If You Want The Rainbow (You Must Have  Har 766-H
             The Rain)
147154-2  My Blackbirds Are Bluebirds Now          -

                              New York, November 8, 1928.

147451-1  You're The Cream In My Coffee        Har 785-H
147452-3  My Inspiration Is You                    -

Vocalist with Frank Ferera's Hawaiian Trio.
                              New York, November 9, 1928.

147453-   Sonny Boy                            Har 782-H
147454-   Sweet Lei Lehua                          -

Vocal, acc. by small orchestra.    New York, November 22, 1928.

147482-3  I Wanna Be Loved By You              Har 792-H
147483-3  Is There Anything Wrong In That ?        -
   NOTE:- Harmony as DOT DARE, Velvet Tone 1792-V as PATSY YOUNG.

Vocalist with Frank Ferera's Hawaiian Trio.
                              New York, January 11, 1929.

147774-2  Carolina Moon                        Har 826-H,
147775-3  Maui Chimes                              -        Cl 5057-C

Vocal, acc. by unknown as/ts/p/bb.    New York, January 15, 1929.

147787-3  I Faw Down And Go 'Boom' !           Har 829-H
147788-2  Don't Be Like That                       -
   NOTE:- This issue as DOT DARE.

   Acc. by the Connecticut Yankees.    New York, January 17, 1929.

147855-2  In A Great Big Way                   Har 832-H
147856-1  When The World Is At Rest                -

   Acc. by the New England Yankees.    New York, February 20, 1929.

147974-2  A Precious Little Thing Called Love  Har 859-H
147976-3  Mean To Me                               -
   NOTE:- Matrix 147975 is not by Annette Hanshaw.

                                      New York, March 14, 1929.

148076-4  Button Up Your Overcoat            Har 878-H
148077-2  I Want To Be Bad                    -

    Acc. by small orchestra.          New York, March 15, 1929.

148082-3  Lover, Come Back To Me !            Col 1769-D
148083-1  You Wouldn't Fool Me, Would You ?    -        5600

                                      New York, April 5, 1929.

148181-2  That's You, Baby                    Col 1812-D, 5425
148182-2  Big City Blues                       -        -

    Acc. by the New Englanders.       New York, April 30, 1929.

148393-2  My Sin                              Har 910-H, SR 1018-P
148394-2  I Get The Blues When It Rains        -        SR 1023-P

                                      New York, May 9, 1929.

148489-3  I've Got A Feeling I'm Falling      Har 915-H, SR 1021-P
148490-1  The One In The World                 -

                                      New York, May 31, 1929.

148647-1  Am I Blue ?                         Har 940-H, SR 1022-P, 1038-P
148648-4  Daddy, Won't You Please Come Home ?  -        SR 1021-P

Vocalist with Frank Ferera's Hawaiian Trio.
                                      New York, June 4, 1929.

148655-3  Pagan Love Song                     Har 945-H, SR 1026-P, 1037-P
148656-1  Ua Like No A Like (Sweet Constancy)  -

Vocal, acc. by the New Englanders.   New York, July 24, 1929.

148848-2-3  Here We Are                       Har 981-H, SR 1040-P
148849-2-3  True Blue Lou                      -        SR 1071-P

    Acc. by small jazz band.          New York, August 29, 1929.

402887-A  Moanin' Low                         OK 41292, Par R-850
402888-D  Lovable And Sweet                   -        Par R-477

    Acc. by unknown cl-as/p/g.        New York, September 16, 1929.

149008-1-2-3-4-5  Tip-Toe Thru' The Tulips With Me Rejected
149009-4  What Wouldn't I Do For That Man ?   Har 1012-H, SR 1050-P

    Acc. by unknown t/vn/p/g.         New York, September 20, 1929.

149008-7  Tip-Toe Thru' The Tulips With Me    Har 1012-H

    Acc. by small jazz band.          New York, October 19, 1929.

403080-A  The Right Kind Of Man               OK 41327, Par R-546
403081-A  If I Can't Have You                 Rejected

                                      New York, October 28, 1929.

149195-3  He's So Unusual                     Har 1047-H, SR 1057-P
149196-3  I Think You'll Like It               -        -
    NOTE:- This issue as PATSY YOUNG.

                                      New York, October 31, 1929.

403081-B  If I Can't Have You                 Od 193450 (Arg.), A-221203 (Fr.)
403081-D  If I Can't Have You                 OK 41327, Par R-546, Ar 4499
    NOTE:- Ariel as LEILA SANDFORD.

Vocalist with Ben Selvin and his Orchestra, as FRANK AUBURN AND HIS ORCHESTRA.
New York, November 27, 1929.

| | | |
|---|---|---|
| 149645- | When I'm Housekeeping For You | SR 1070-P |
| 149646-1 | I Have To Have You | Har 1075-H, SR 1069-P, 2008-P |
| 149647- | Ain'tcha ? | - |

Vocal, acc. by the Three Blue Streaks.   New York, December 4, 1929.

| | | |
|---|---|---|
| 149676-2 | I'm A Dreamer - Aren't We All ? | Har 1066-H, SR 2000-P, 2007-P |
| 149677-4 | If I Had A Talking Picture Of You | -          -          - |

Acc. by unknown t/bar/vn/p.          New York, December 13, 1929.

| | | |
|---|---|---|
| 403499-B | When I Am Housekeeping For You | OK 41351, Od ONY-36033, Par R-642 |

Acc. by small jazz band.          New York, December 16, 1929.

| | | |
|---|---|---|
| 403521-B | I Have To Have You | OK 41351, Od ONY-36033, Par R-642 |
| | | PMC-7006 |

New York, January 27, 1930.

| | | |
|---|---|---|
| 403692-A | Cooking Breakfast For The One I Love | OK 41370, Par PNY-34037, R-654 |
| 403693-B | When A Woman Loves A Man | -          -          - |

NOTE:- Parlophone PNY-34037 as JANET SHAW.

New York, February 11, 1930.

| | | |
|---|---|---|
| 149973-3 | I'm Following You ! | Har 1106-H |
| 149974-1-2-3 | What Do I Care ? | Rejected |
| 149975-3 | Happy Days Are Here Again (w/male chorus) | Har 1106-H |

Vocalist with Sam Lanin and his Famous Players.
New York, February 25, 1930.

| | | |
|---|---|---|
| 403771-B | Cooking Breakfast For The One I Love | OK 41383, Par R-674 |

Vocalist with Frank Ferera's Hawaiian Trio.
New York, March 10, 1930.

| | | |
|---|---|---|
| 150076-2 | Lazy Lou'siana Moon | Har 1121-H |
| 150077-4 | Pale Blue Waters | -          Cl 5029-C |

Vocal, acc. by small orchestra.          New York, March 11, 1930.

| | | |
|---|---|---|
| 403847-C | The One I Love Just Can't Be Bothered With Me | OK 41397, Par PNY-34060, R-697 |
| 403848-B | With You | -          -          - |

NOTE:- Parlophone PNY-34060 as JANET SHAW.
Vocalist with Frank Ferera's Hawaiian Trio.
New York, April 17, 1930.

| | | |
|---|---|---|
| 150480- | I Love A Ukulele | Har 1144-H, Cl 5029-C |
| 150481- | It Happened In Monterey | - |

Vocal, acc. by small jazz band.          New York, May 5, 1930.

| | | |
|---|---|---|
| 150387-2 | Telling It To The Daisies (But It Never Gets Back To You) | Har 1155-H, Col DB-252 |
| 150388-3 | I've Got "It" (But It Don't Do Me No Good) | -          Col DB-313, SR 2022-P |

Acc. by small orchestra.          New York, June 16, 1930.

| | | |
|---|---|---|
| 150587-1-3 | If I Had A Girl Like You | Har 1178-H, Cl 5017-C |
| 150588-2-3 | My Future Just Passed | - |

New York, July 21, 1930.

| | | |
|---|---|---|
| 150651-2 | Little White Lies | Har 1196-H, Cl 5037-C |
| 150652-2 | Nobody Cares If I'm Blue | -          Col DB-313, Par PMC-7006 |
| 150653-1 | I Want A Good Man (And I Want Him Bad) | Cl 5017-C |
| 150654-2 | The Way I Feel Today | Cl 5037-C |

New York, October 7, 1930.

```
150863-5  Body And Soul                           Har 1224-H, Cl 5093-C
150864-3  Wasting My Love On You                       -      Cl 5081-C, VT 2289-V
```

New York, October 21, 1930.

```
150898-3  Yes Indeedy (He Do)                     Cl 5093-C
150899-2  Now I Know (I Love You)                 Cl 5101-C, VT 2289-V
```

New York, January 16, 1931.

```
151223-1-2  I'll Lock You In My Arms              Cl 5217-C, VT 2273-V
151224-3  Crying To The Moon                      Cl 5216-C, VT 2274-V
```

New York, January 20, 1931.

```
151234-1  I Hate Myself (For Falling In Love With  Har 1273-H, Cl 5217-C, VT 2274-V,
          You)                                     Col DB-470
151235-2  You're The One I Care For                As above, but CL 5216-C
151236-2  Would You Like To Take A Walk ?          Har 1288-H, Cl 5249-C, VT 2315-V
          (Sump'n Good'll Come From That)
151237-1-2-3  Walkin' My Baby Back Home           Rejected
```

New York, February 20, 1931.

```
151331-1  Ever Since Time Began                   Cl 5248-C, VT 2314-V
151332-2  Walkin' My Baby Back Home                   -          -         Har 1288-H
151333-2  You're Just To Sweet For Words, Honey   Cl 5249-C, VT 2315-V
          O' Mine
```

Acc. by Jimmy Dorsey-cl/Sammy Prager-p/Eddie Lang-g.
                              New York, May 9, 1931.

```
365007-1-2  There Ought To Be A Moonlight-Saving  Har 1324-H, Cl 5327-C, VT 2393-V,
          Time                                     Par R-967
365008-2-3  Ho Hum !                               As above
```

Acc. by small instrumental group.    New York, September 22, 1931.

```
365033-1-2  Sweet And Lovely                      Rejected
365034-2  Guilty                                  Har 1376-H, Cl 5390-C, VT 2454-V
365035-2  I Don't Know Why (I Just Do)                -          -         -
```

Acc. by studio orchestra.            New York, August 16, 1932.

```
12198-A  It Was So Beautiful                      Rejected
12199-A  We Just Couldn't Say "Goodbye"           Ban 32541, Cq 8046, Mt M-12471,
                                                  Or 2546, Per 12835, Pan 25270
```

New York, August 18, 1932.

```
12209-1  Love Me Tonight                          Ban 32541,Cq 8046, Mt M-12471,
                                                  Or 2546, Per 12835, Pan 25270
```

New York, September 12, 1932.

```
12283-2  Say It Isn't So                          Ban 32565, Bwy 4022, Mt M-12486,
                                                  Or 2561, Per 12842, Ro 1935,
                                                  Pan 25324
12284-1  You'll Always Be The Same Sweetheart     As above, plus Cq 8044
          To Me
```

Acc. by O/Will Osborne.              New York, September 20, 1932.

```
12334-  Say It Isn't So (w/Morton Downey and      Mt M-12485, Cq 8044, Dec F-3272
          Singin' Sam)
```

New York, December 2, 1932.

12670-1  I'm Sure Of Everything But You          Ban 32616, Cq 8125, Mt M-12551,
                                                 Or 2598, Per 12866, Ro 1972,
                                                 Pan 25413, Mf G-265
12671-1  Fit As A Fiddle                         As above
 NOTE:- Mayfair G-265 as MARION LEE.

New York, January 25, 1933.

12983-1  Moon Song (That Wasn't Meant For Me)    Ban 32671, Cq 8124, Mt M-12604,
                                                 Or 2638, Per 12882, Ro 2011,
                                                 Pan 25469, Key K-604, Mf G-318
12984-1  Twenty Million People                   As above, but Key K-611
 NOTE:- Key K-604 and K-611 as ETHEL BINGHAM; Mayfair G-318 as MARION LEE.

New York, June 3, 1933.

13422-1  I Cover The Waterfront                  Ban 32788, Cq 8185, Mt M-12721,
                                                 Or 2713, Per 12921, Ro 2083,
                                                 Pan 25551
13423-1  Sweetheart Darlin'                      As above

New York, September 1, 1933.

13905-1  Don't Blame Me                          Ban 32846, Cq 8256, Mt M-12775,
                                                 Or 2747, Per 12937, Ro 2120,
                                                 EBW W-20
13906-1  It's The Talk Of The Town               As above

New York, November 22, 1933.

14367-1  Give Me Liberty Or Give Me Love         Ban 32908, Mt M-12851, Or 2799,
                                                 Per 12959, Ro 2172, EBW W-71
14368-1  Sing A Little Low-Down Tune             As above

New York, February 3, 1934.

14705-1  This Little Piggie Went To Market       Voc 2735, EBW W-94
14706-1  Let's Fall In Love                        -         -

## THE HAPPINESS BOYS

Billy Jones (William Reese Jones) (b. New York, March 15, 1889) and Ernest Hare (b.
 Norfolk, Va., March 16, 1883) met in a recording studio and were given a test  as
 a recording team, both having made many solo records; it was successful, and they
 became one of the most popular acts on radio, as well as records, during the next
 decade; Ernest Hare had understudied Al Jolson in several shows, and was able  to
 sing all kinds of music, secular and sacred. He died in Jamaica, N.Y.,  March  9,
 1939; Billy Jones died on November 23, 1940.

Vocal duets, acc. by studio O/? Milo Rega.
                                                 New York, c. May, 1921.

   I Like It                                     OK 4325

   Down Yonder                                   OK 4347

                                                 New York, c. July, 1921.

   Down By The Old Swimming Hole                 OK 4375

Acc. by studio orchestra.                        New York, c. August, 1921.

   Down At The Old Swimming Hole                 Ed 50841

                                                 New York, c. September, 1921.

   Ten Little Fingers And Ten Little Toes        Ed 50855

New York, c. September, 1921.

Ten Little Fingers And Ten Little Toes    OK 4456

New York, c. November, 1921.

Operatic Syncopation                      Ed 50917
Dapper Dan                                Ed 50918

New York, April 20, 1922.

70638-   Mr. Gallagher And Mr. Shean          OK 4608, Par E-5109

New York, c. April, 1922.

Atta Baby !                               Ed 50956
In The Little Red School House            Ed 50962

New York, c. July, 1922.

Oh ! Is She Dumb ?                        OK 4676
For The Sake Of Auld Lang Syne            OK 4690

New York, October-November, 1922.

70982-   Toot, Toot, Tootsie (Goo'bye)        OK 4726, Par E-5088
         Hello ! Hello ! Hello !                -

New York, c. November 16, 1922.

8113    You Tell Her - I Stutter             Gnt 5007

New York, c. November, 1922.

You Tell Her - I Stutter                  Ed 51079

New York, c. January, 1923.

Down By The Old Apple Tree                Ed 51106
Open Your Arms, My Alabammy               Ed 51131

Down By The Old Apple Tree                OK 4756
You Tell Her - I Stutter                    -

New York, c. February 7, 1923.

8204    Down By The Old Apple Tree           Gnt 5055

Acc. by unknown p.              New York, March, 1923.

71336-   Barney Google                        OK 4828, Par E-5088
71337-   No-One Loves You Better Than Your      -
         M-A-double-M-Y

Acc. by studio orchestra.       New York, c. March 27, 1923.

8295    No-One Loves You Better Than Your    Gnt 5121
        M-A-double-M-Y

New York, April, 1923.

Barney Google                             Ed 51155
Old King Tut                                -

New York, c. July 12, 1923.

8459    Hi-Lee Hi-Lo                         Gnt 5208

New York, c. August 23, 1923.

71794-   Last Night On The Back Porch            OK 4948, Par E-5120

New York, c. October, 1923.

Maggie ! "Yes Ma'am !" - Come Right       Ed 51180
  Upstairs
Oh ! Gee, Oh ! Gosh, Oh ! Golly, I'm      Ed 51193
  In Love
From De Ol' Home Town (The Meeting of     Ed 51199
  Lincoln and Glascoe)
Cut Yourself A Piece Of Cake (And Make    Ed 51206
  Yourself At Home)

New York, c. November 30, 1923.

72125-   Say It With A Ukulele                   OK 40040, Par E-5188

New York, c. December, 1923.

That Old Gang Of Mine                     Ed 51235
That's A Lot Of Bunk                      -

New York, c. February 11, 1924.

837-A   Does The Spearmint Lose Its Flavor On    Cam 504
  The Bedpost Overnight ?

New York, c. March, 1924.

Me No Speak-a Good English                Ed 51322
What Does The Pussy-Cat Mean When She     -
  Says "Me-ow" ?
Down Where The South Begins               Ed 51333

New York, c. April 5, 1924.

72423-   What Does The Pussy-Cat Mean When She   OK 40093, Par E-5240
  Says "Me-ow" ?

New York, c. May, 1924.

Hard-Boiled Rose                          Ed 51357
He Looks At Her And Then He Goes          -
  "Ha-Ha-Ha-Ha-Ha !"
I'm Gonna Bring A Water Melon To My       Ed 51365
  Girl Tonight

New York, October 24, 1924.

140119-   Everything Has Got My Goat             Col 234-D

New York, c. October, 1924.

Oh, You Can't Fool An Old Hoss Fly        Ed 51415
It Ain't Gonna Rain No Mo' (2nd edn.)     Ed 51430

New York, November 26, 1924.

73002-   Gotta Getta Girl                        OK 40243, Par E-5333

New York, c. November, 1924.

No-One Knows What It's All About          Ed 51454
Laff It Off                               Ed 51470
On My Ukulele                             -
How Do You Do ?                           Ed 51500

New York, January 7, 1925.

| | | |
|---|---|---|
| 140228- | Oh, Mabel ! | Col 283-D |
| 140229- | Sweet Onion Time | Col 332-D |

New York, April 2, 1925.

| | | |
|---|---|---|
| 73287- | As A Porcupine Pines For Its Pork (That's How I Pine For You) | OK 40421, Par E-5427 |
| 73288-B | Don't Bring Lulu | OK 40354, Par E-5387 |

New York, April 6, 1925.

| | | |
|---|---|---|
| 140498- | As A Porcupine Pines For Its Pork (That's How I Pine For You) | Col 378-D |

New York, April, 1925.

| | |
|---|---|
| As A Porcupine Pines For Its Pork (That's How I Pine For You) | Ed 51535 |
| Don't Bring Lulu | Ed 51555 |

Acc. by Dave Kaplan-p.            New York, June 11, 1925.

| | | |
|---|---|---|
| 73427- | We're Gonna Have Weather (Whether Or Not) | OK 40397, Par E-5427 |

New York, June 25, 1925.

| | | |
|---|---|---|
| 140722- | The Farmer Took Another Load Away | Col 415-D |
| 140723- | Collegiate | Col 410-D |
| 140724- | I Miss My Swiss | -            3811 |

New York, c. June, 1925.

| | |
|---|---|
| The Farmer Took Another Load Away (Hay ! Hay !) | Ed 51577 |

Camden, N. J., July 1, 1925.

| | | |
|---|---|---|
| BVE-33045-2 | How's Your Folks And My Folks (Down In Norfolk Town) | Vic 19739, HMV B-2128 |
| BVE-33046-1 | As A Porcupine Pines For Its Pork (That's How I Pine For You) | Vic 19718 |
| BVE-33047-4 | I Miss My Swiss (My Swiss Miss Misses Me) | -            HMV B-2128 |

New York, August 10, 1925.

| | | |
|---|---|---|
| 140833- | I Miss My Swiss | Har 9-H |
| 140834- | Oh Say ! Can I See You Tonight ? | - |

Camden, N. J., August 21, 1925.

| | | |
|---|---|---|
| BVE-33243-2 | Pardon Me (Ha-Ha, Ha-Ha !) | Vic 19760 |
| BVE-33244-2 | I Would Rather Be Alone In The South | Vic 19826 |
| BVE-33245-3 | There Ain't No Flies On Auntie | Vic 19848, HMV B-2276 |
| BVE-33246-3 | Pretty Puppy | Vic 19760 |

New York, c. August, 1925.

| | |
|---|---|
| How's Your Folks And My Folks (Down In Norfolk Town) | Ed 51618 |
| Old Grey Mare | - |

New York, September 10, 1925.

| | |
|---|---|
| 140927- | Pardon Me (Ha-Ha, Ha-Ha, While I Laugh) Col 457-D |

New York, September 14, 1925.

73613-   Hurray ! Hurray ! My Wife's So Good To   OK 40520
       Me

It is believed that the following titles may have been recorded at the above session
or near to it, but no copies of any issue could be found to uphold this.

        There Ain't No Flies On Auntie      OK     , Par E-5444
        There's One Born Every Minute           -

                            New York, c. September, 1925.

        Pardon Me While I Laugh (Ha-Ha, Ha-Ha !) Ed 51624

Acc. by the Bow-Wows.            New York, c. November 20, 1925.

73768-   I Would Rather Be Alone In The South    OK 40520
73769-   Hokey Pokey (Diddle-Dee-Rum)        OK 40519

Acc. by Dave Kaplan-p.          New York, c. November, 1925.

        Show Me The Way To Go Home       Ed 51660
        I Would Rather Be Alone In The South   -

                   Camden, N. J., November 25, 1925.

BVE-33626-1-2-3  Frank And Ernest          Rejected
BVE-33627-1-2-3  That Certain Party          -
BVE-33628-1-2-3  Whispering Leaves           -
BVE-33629-1  Why Aren't Yez Eatin' More Oranges ?  Vic 19865, HMV B-2283
         (From Cal-I-For-Ny-A)
BVE-33630-1-2-3  An Operatic Syncopation      Rejected

                  Camden, N. J., December 4, 1925.

BVE-33627-5  That Certain Party         Vic 19865, HMV B-2283

                 New York, December 22, 1925.

141425-   I Wish't I Was In Peoria        Col 534-D
141426-   Hot Coffee                   -

                 New York, c. December, 1925.

        Hokey-Pokey Diddle-Dee-Rum      Ed 51677
        I Wish't I Was In Peoria          -

                 New York, January 13, 1926.

141485-   What ? No Women !           Col 553-D
141486-   The Village Blacksmith Owns The Village Now  -

                 Camden, N. J., January 26, 1926.

BVE-33682-1-2-3  In My Gondola          Rejected
BVE-33683-2  What ! No Women ?         Vic 19973, HMV B-2301
BVE-33684-3  The Village Blacksmith Owns The    -       -
         Village Now

                 New York, c. January, 1926.

        What ! No Women ?         Ed 51695
        Nobody's Business           -

        Hooray For The Irish !       Voc 15285
        I'm Gonna Let The Bumble Bee Be   -

New York, c. February, 1926.

|          | In My Gondola          | Ed 51704 |
|          | Wimmin - Aaah !        | -        |

New York, April 15, 1926.

| 141972- | Spring Is Here             | Col 645-D |
| 141973- | Show That Fellow The Door  | Rejected  |

New York, c. April, 1926.

|          | Spring Is Here                | Ed 51741 |
|          | It Don't Do Nothing But Rain  | -        |

New York, April 30, 1926.

| 142116- | That's Where I Meet My Girl | Col 645-D |

New York, c. May, 1926.

|          | Lunatic's Lullaby | Ed 51755 |
|          | The Pump Song     | -        |

New York, June 7, 1926.

| 142281- | What ! No Spinach ? | Col 674-D |
| 142282- | Lo-Do-De-O          | -         |

The following four titles were probably made about this time, but here again, it  has
not been possible to locate copies for inspection.

|          | The Pump Song               | OK    | , Par E-5646 |
|          | Hi-Ho-The Merrio            |       | -            |
|          | Oh ! Boy, How It Was Raining | OK   | , Par E-5679 |
|          | Lo-Do-De-O                  |       | -            |

New York, c. June, 1926.

|          | Hi-Diddle-Diddle | Ed 51767 |

New York, July 13, 1926.

| 142391- | My Cutey's Due At Two-To-Two Today | Col 700-D |
| 142392- | How Many Times ?                   | -         |

New York, c. July, 1926.

|          | Gentlemen Prefer Blondes                 | Ed 51802 |
|          | Sing, Katie (But Leave The Piano Alone)  | -        |

|          | My Cutey's Due At Two-To-Two Today | PA | , 11232, Per |
|          | It Don't Do Nothin' But Rain       | PA | , 11256, Per |

New York, August 11, 1926.

| 74254- | How Many Times ?            | OK 40669, Par E-5691 |
| 74255- | Where'd You Get Those Eyes ? | -        -           |

Camden, N. J., August 25, 1926.

| BVE-36131-1-2-3 | Sing, Katie (But Leave The Piano Alone) | Rejected |
| BVE-36132-1     | She Knows Her Onions        | Vic 20208, LPV-557, LSA-3075 |
| BVE-36133-1     | It Won't Be Long Now        | -        |
| BVE-36134-1-2-3 | I Haven't Mentioned Mammy   | Rejected |
| BVE-36135-1-2-3 | And Then I Forget !         | -        |

New York, January 27, 1927.

| | | |
|---|---|---|
| 143363- | Where Do You Work-a, John ? | Col 875-D |
| 143364- | Bridget O'Flynn (Where've Ya Been ?) | - |

New York, February 23, 1927.

| | | |
|---|---|---|
| BVE-38106-2 | That's My Hap-Hap-Happiness | Vic 20500, LPV-545, LSA-3077, RD-7903 |
| BVE-38107-2 | Cock-a-Doodle, I'm Off My Noodle | Vic 20500 |

New York, c. February, 1927.

| | |
|---|---|
| I've Never Seen A Straight Banana | Ed 51973 |
| That's My Hap-Hap-Happiness | - |

New York, May 4, 1927.

| | | |
|---|---|---|
| 144083- | Ask Me Another | Col 1010-D |
| 144084- | You Never Get Nowhere Holding Hands | - |

New York, June 14, 1927.

| | | |
|---|---|---|
| BVE-39249- | Oh, Ja Ja | Vic 20756 |
| BVE-39250- | You Don't Like It - Not Much | - |
| BVE-39251- | When Lindy Comes Home | Vic 20741 |

New York, c. June, 1927.

| | |
|---|---|
| Just A Little Old School House | Ed 52050 |
| Oh ! Ya ! Ya ! | - |

New York, July 6, 1927.

| | | |
|---|---|---|
| 144432- | Gid-ap, Garibaldi | Col 1074-D |
| 144433- | Oh ! Ya ! Ya ! | - |

New York, September 8, 1927.

| | | |
|---|---|---|
| BVE-39165- | Pastafazoola | Vic 20925 |
| BVE-39166-1-2 | From Saturday Night Till Monday Morning | Rejected |
| BVE-39167- | Since Henry Ford Apologized To Me | Vic 20925 |

New York, September, 1927.

| | | |
|---|---|---|
| 107778 | She Don't Wanna | PA     , 11509, Per |
| 107779 | Oh, Ya ! Ya ! | - |

New York, c. October, 1927.

| | |
|---|---|
| Who's That Pretty Baby ? | Ed 52137 |
| Get 'Em In A Rumble Seat | Ed 52149 |
| Go Home And Tell Your Mother | - |

New York, December 21, 1927.

| | | |
|---|---|---|
| BVE-41191-1-2 | Go Home And Tell Your Mother | Rejected |
| BVE-41192-1-2 | Poor Lizzie | - |
| BVE-41193- | It's In The Bag | Vic 21174 |

New York, December 22, 1927.

| | | |
|---|---|---|
| 145383- | I Love To Catch Brass Rings On A Merry-Go-Round | Col 1245-D |
| 145384- | Poor Lizzie | - |

New York, January 4, 1928.

| | | |
|---|---|---|
| BVE-41514- | Henry's Made A Lady Out Of Lizzie | Vic 21174, HMV B-2704 |

New York, c. January, 1928.

Henry's Made A Lady Out Of Lizzie          Ed 52200
Poor Lizzie                                -

New York, c. February, 1928.

It's In The Bag                            Ed 52236
Stay Out Of The South                      -

New York, March 26, 1928.

BVE-43399-3  He Ain't Never Been To College      Vic 21332
BVE-43500-1  She's The Sweetheart Of Six Other Guys    -
BVE-43501-1-2-3  Hello, Montreal !               Rejected

New York, April 19, 1928.

146266-    She'll Never Find A Fellow Like Me     Col 1373-D
146267-    She's The Sweetheart Of Six Other Guys    -

New York, June 19, 1928.

BVE-45800-3  Must You Wear A Moustache ?        Vic 21529
BVE-45801-2  Giggling Gertie                    -

New York, c. June, 1928.

Must You Wear A Moustache ?                 Ed 52333
Shout Hallelujah ! 'Cause I'm Home          -

New York, July 24, 1928.

BVE-46603-1-2-3  I Love To Dunk A Hunk Of Sponge   Rejected
                 Cake
BVE-46604-2  Mr. Hoover - Mr. Smith             Vic 21607
BVE-46605-3  Sing, Sister, Sing                 -

New York, August 3, 1928.

BVE-46661-1  Etiquette Blues                    Vic 21797

New York, c. August, 1928.

Mr. Hoover And Mr. Smith                    Ed 52367
I Love To Dunk A Hunk Of Sponge Cake        -

New York, October 31, 1928.

BVE-48106-2  Where Did You Get That Name ?      Vic 21797
CVE-48107-2  Twisting The Dials - Part 1        Vic 35953, Zon A-362

New York, November 12, 1928.

CVE-48149-2  Twisting The Dials - Part 2        Vic 35953, Zon A-362

New York, December 26, 1928.

147727-    A Gay Caballero                      Col 1692-D
147728-    All By Yourself In The Moonlight      -

Acc. by Dave Kaplan-p and O/Bill Wirges. New York, May 16, 1929.

BVE-53418-  She Has A Little Dimple On Her Chin   Vic 22087
BVE-53419-1-2-3  Misery Farm                     Rejected
BVE-53420-  Who Cares Anyhow ?                   Vic 22087

Acc. by Dave Kaplan-p.              New York, c. May, 1929.
She Has A Little Dimple On Her Chin    Ed 52598
It Ain't No Fault Of Mine              -

New York, September 25, 1929.

BVE-56149-1-2-3  Billy And Ernie Thank You For      Vic rejected
                Your Information - Part 1
BVE-56150-1-2-3  Billy And Ernie Thank You For        -
                Your Information - Part 2

Acc. by O/Leonard Joy.              New York, October 8, 1929.

BVE-56759-2  Sergeant Flagg And Sergeant Quirt    Vic 22150
             (w/Baroness Erzi)
BVE-56760-2  I Can't Sleep In The Movies Any More     -

                        New York, July 16, 1930.

BVE-62350-2  The Happiness Boys Going Abroad       Vic 22491
BVE-62351-2  The Happiness Boys In London             -

## MARION  HARRIS

B. 1896; became very popular vaudeville singer and night-club entertainer in  U.S.A.
   and England (appeared with great success at the Cafe de Paris, London, in 1931 and
   made several subsequent appearances in London during the 1930s); she died  tragic-
   ally when the hotel where she was staying in New York caught fire on April 23,1944.

Vocal, acc. by O/Rosario Bourdon.     New York, August 9, 1916.

B-18192-1  I Ain't Got Nobody Much            Vic 18133
B-18193-1-2-3  My Syncopated Melody Man       Rejected

                        New York, August 31, 1916.

B-18318-1-2-3  I'm Gonna Make Hay While The Sun   Vic rejected
               Shines In Virginia
B-18319-1-2-3  Paradise Blues                     -

Acc. by O/Eddie King.               New York, October 5, 1916.

B-18604-1  Don't Leave Me, Daddy              Vic 18185

                        New York, November 17, 1916.

B-18193-7  My Syncopated Melody Man          Vic 18152
B-18319-5  Paradise Blues                        -

Acc. by O/Joseph Pasternack.        New York, February 28, 1917.

B-19317-3  I Wonder Why (w/Billy Murray)      Vic 18270
B-19318-1-2-3  Some Sweet Day (w/American Quartet)Rejected

                        New York, March 16, 1917.

B-19380-1-2-3  The Maiden's Prayer (w/American    Vic rejected
               Quartet)

Acc. by O/Rosario Bourdon.          New York, July 12, 1917.

B-20213-2  They Go Wild, Simply Wild Over Me    Vic 18343
B-20214-1-2  Plant Plenty Of Potatoes           Rejected
B-20215-1  Some Sweet Day                        Vic 18343

Acc. by O/Eddie King.               New York, July 18, 1917.

B-20230-2  When I Hear That Jazz Band Play      Vic 18398

Acc. by O/Joseph Pasternack.        New York, November 5, 1917.
B-21052-1-2-3  Cleopatra Had A Jazz Band          Vic rejected
B-21053-1-2-3  My Sweetie                           -

## MARION HARRIS (cont.)

New York, November 26, 1917.

B-21208-1-2-3  Quaker Girl           Vic rejected
B-21209-1-2-3  I Want Someone To Kiss The Blues Away  -

New York, December 6, 1917.

B-21243-2  Everybody's Crazy 'Bout The Doggone   Vic 18443
           Blues
B-21244-1-2-3  I Should Worry           Rejected

Camden, N. J., June 12, 1918.

B-21208-4-5-6  Quaker Girl           Vic rejected
B-21983-1-2-3  When Alexander Takes His Ragtime    -
           Band To France

Camden, N. J., June 18, 1918.

B-21983-5  When Alexander Takes His Ragtime Band  Vic 18486
           To France
B-21994-4  There's A Lump Of Sugar Down In Dixie  Vic 18482
B-21995-1  Mammy's Chocolate Soldier         Vic 18493

Camden, N. J., July 15, 1918.

B-22159-1-2-3  Goodbye, Alexander        Vic rejected
B-22160-1-2-3  After You've Gone          -

Camden, N. J., July 22, 1918.

B-22159-4  Goodbye, Alexander          Vic 18495
B-22160-4  After You've Gone           Vic 18509

   Acc. by O/Rosario Bourdon.     Camden, N. J., August 12, 1918.

B-22208-1-2-3  I Always Think I'm Up In Heaven   Vic rejected

Camden, N. J., August 14, 1918.

B-22213-1-2-3-4  Navy Blues           Vic rejected

Camden, N. J., August 15, 1918.

B-22214-1-2-3  Everything Is Hunky Dory Down In   Vic rejected
           Honky-Tonk Town

Camden, N. J., October 18, 1918.

B-22160-7  After You've Gone           Vic 18509
B-22287-1-2-3  At The Dixie Military Ball     Rejected

   Acc. by O/Joseph Pasternack.     Camden, N. J., October 30, 1918.

B-22400-1-2-3  Those Draftin' Blues        Vic rejected

Camden, N. J., November 29, 1918.

B-22440-1-2-3  When You Get Back (O/Pasternack)   Vic rejected
B-22441-1-2-3  I'm Crazy 'Bout My Daddy (O/Bourdon)   -

Camden, N. J., February 18, 1919.

B-22590-1  For Johnny And Me           Vic 18535
B-22591-1-2-3  I Don't Want To Love No One But   Rejected
           You

Camden, N. J., February 19, 1919.

B-22592-1-2-3  Oh ! Lawdy           Rejected
B-22593-3  A Good Man Is Hard To Find     Vic 18535

Acc. by O/Rosario Bourdon.              Camden, N. J., April 18, 1919.

B-22695-1  Jazz Baby                        Vic 18555

Acc. by O/Joseph Pasternack.            Camden, N. J., May 9, 1919.

B-22592-4-5-6  Oh ! Lawdy                    Vic rejected
B-22841-1-2-3  You Can Have It, I Don't Want It        -

Acc. by O/Rosario Bourdon.              Camden, N. J., June 11, 1919.

B-22899-3  Take Me To The Land Of Jazz      Vic 18593

Acc. by O/Joseph Pasternack.            Camden, N. J., July 18, 1919.

B-23081-1-2-3  You Can't Get Lovin' Where There    Vic rejected
                Ain't Any Love
B-23082-1-2-3  Sweet Kisses                     -

Acc. by O/Rosario Bourdon.              Camden, N. J., August 6, 1919.

B-23110-1-2-3  Tia-Da-Tia-Da-Dee             Vic rejected
B-23111-1-2-3  Regretful Blues                  -
B-23112-1-2-3  Southern Girl Medley             -
B-23113-1-2-3  Musical Comedy Blues             -

                                        Camden, N. J., October 30, 1919.

B-23110-4-5  Tia-Da-Tia-Da-Dee               Vic rejected
B-23111-4-5-6  Regretful Blues                  -
B-23113-4-5-6  Musical Comedy Blues             -

                                        Camden, N. J., November 18, 1919.

B-23110-6-7-9  Tia-Da-Tia-Da-Dee             Vic rejected
B-23113-7-8-9-10  Musical Comedy Blues         -

Acc. by O/? Charles A. Prince.          New York, March 25, 1920.

79067-1-2-3  Stop That Band                  Col rejected

                                        New York, March 26, 1920.

79072-    Left All Alone Again Blues           Col A-2939

                                        New York, April 7, 1920.

79104-    Oh ! Judge (He Treats Me Mean)       Col A-2968
79105-    Everybody But Me                     Col A-2939

                                        New York, April 15, 1920.

79123-1-2-3  That Thing Called Love           Col rejected

                                        New York, April 16, 1920.

79124-    The St. Louis Blues                  Col A-2944
79125-    Homesickness Blues                   -

                                        New York, April 20, 1920.

79131-    He Done Me Wrong (The Death Of Bill   Col A-2968
            Bailey)

                                        New York, April 21, 1920.

79134-    I Ain't Got Nobody                   Col A-3371

New York, August 26, 1920.

79387-    I Told You So                          Col A-3300

New York, August 31, 1920.

79394-    Sweet Mama (Papa's Getting Mad)        Col A-3300
79395-    Long Gone                              Rejected

New York, September 17, 1920.

79422-1-2-3  I've Got The A-B-C-D Blues          Col rejected

New York, October 1, 1920.

79443-    I'm A Jazz Vampire                     Col A-3328

New York, October 6, 1920.

79451-    Where Is My Daddy Now Blues            Col A-3371
79452-    Never Let No One Man Worry Your Mind   Col A-3328

New York, November 29, 1920.

79539-    Yankee                                 Col A-3353
79540-    Grieving For You                       -

New York, December 29, 1920.

79612-    Look For The Silver Lining             Col A-3367

New York, December 30, 1920.

79617-    I'm Gonna Do It If I Like It           Col A-3367

New York, March 2, 1921.

79747-    The Memphis Blues                      Col A-3474
79748-    Beale Street Blues                     -

New York, March 24, 1921.

79790-1-2-3  I'm Nobody's Baby                   Col rejected
79793-1-2-3  I Wonder Where My Sweet Daddy's Gone   -
NOTE:- Matrices 79791/2 are not by Marion Harris.

New York, May 27, 1921.

79866-    I'm Nobody's Baby                      Col A-3433

New York, June 22, 1921.

79904-    I'm Looking For A Bluebird             Col A-3457

New York, July 25, 1921.

79961-    Sweet Cookie                           Col A-3457

New York, September 7, 1921.

79973-1-2-3  No-One's Fool                       Col rejected
79974-1-2-3  Cry Baby Blues                      -

New York, January 16, 1922.

80135-    Cuddle Up Blues                        Col A-3555

New York, January 20, 1922.

80147-    I've Got The Wonder Where He Went      Col A-3555
          And When He's Coming Back Blues

New York, January 21, 1922.

80155-    Poor Little Me                          Col A-3593

New York, March 15, 1922.

80241-    Some Sunny Day                          Col A-3593

New York, April 5, 1922.

80277-    Malinda Brown                           Col A-3604
80278-    Maybe You Think You're Fooling, Baby        -

New York, May 11, 1922.

80343-    Who'll Take My Place ?                  Col A-3630

New York, May 16, 1922.

80350-    Fickle Flo (From Kokomo)                Col A-3630

New York, June 8, 1922.

80376-    Nobody Lied (When They Said That I      Col A-3646
              Cried Over You)
80377-    Haunting Blues                              -

New York, June 21, 1922.

80411-    Away Down South                         Col A-3659
80412-    Send Back My Honeyman                       -

Acc. by O/? Carl Fenton.        New York, c. August, 1922.

          I'm Just Wild About Harry              Br 2309
          My Cradle Melody                           -
          Sweet Indiana Home                     Br 2310
          Blue                                       -

New York, c. September, 1922.

          Dixie Highway                          Br 2318
          Brother-in-Law Dan                         -
          Carolina In The Morning                Br 2329
          Homesick                                   -

New York, c. October, 1922.

          Aggravatin' Papa                       Br 2345
          Hot Lips                                   -
          Mississippi Choo Choo                  Br 2461
          Who Cares ?                                -

New York, c. November, 1922.

          Rose Of The Rio Grande                 Br 2370
          I Gave You Up Just Before You Threw Me     -
              Down

New York, c. December, 1922.

          I Ain't Got Nobody                     Br 2395
          St. Louis Blues                            -

New York, c. February, 1923.

          Runnin' Wild                           Br 2410
          You've Got To See Mama Every Night         -

New York, c. March, 1923.

| | |
|---|---|
| Beside A Babbling Brook | Br 2421 |
| Dearest (You're The Nearest To My Heart) | - |

New York, c. April, 1923.

| | |
|---|---|
| That Red-Head Gal | Br 2434 |
| Two-Time Dan | - |

New York, c. May, 1923.

| | |
|---|---|
| Waitin' For The Evenin' Mail | Br 2443 |
| Who's Sorry Now ? | - |

New York, c. June, 1923.

| | |
|---|---|
| Dirty Hands, Dirty Face | Br 2458 |
| When You Walked Out, Someone Else Walked | - |
|   Right In | |

New York, c. July, 1923.

| | |
|---|---|
| 'Tain't Nuthin' Else | Br 2470 |
| I've Been Saving For A Rainy Day | - |

New York, c. September, 1923.

| | |
|---|---|
| Lovey Came Back | Br 2494 |
| I've Got A Cross-Eyed Papa, But He | - |
|   Looks Straight To Me | |

New York, c. October, 1923.

| | |
|---|---|
| Stealing To Virginia | Br 2513 |
| Your Mama's Gonna Slow You Down | - |

New York, c. December, 1923.

| | |
|---|---|
| Before You Go | Br 2539 |
| Nashville Nightingale | - |

New York, c. January, 1924.

| | |
|---|---|
| I Don't Want You To Cry Over Me | Br 2552 |
| St. Louis Gal | - |

New York, c. March, 1924.

| | |
|---|---|
| It Had To Be You | Br 2610 |
| How Come You Do Me Like You Do ? | - |

New York, c. April, 1924.

| | |
|---|---|
| Jealous | Br 2622 |
| Hey Hey And Hee Hee (I'm Charleston Crazy) | - |

New York, c. June, 1924.

| | |
|---|---|
| There'll Be Some Changes Made | Br 2651 |
| I Can't Get The One I Want | - |

New York, c. August, 1924.

| | |
|---|---|
| Go, Emmaline | Br 2672 |
| Wanted - Someone To Love | - |

New York, c. October, 1924.

| | |
|---|---|
| Somebody Loves Me | Br 2735 |
| Charleston Charlie | - |

New York, c. November, 1924.

Tea For Two                                 Br 2747
The Blues Have Got Me                       -

New York, c. January, 1925.

I'll See You In My Dreams                   Br 2784
Why Couldn't It Be Poor Little Me ?         -

New York, c. March, 1925.

Does My Sweetie Do - And How !              Br 2807
I Can't Realize                             -

New York, c. April, 1925.

When You And I Were Seventeen               Br 2836
No One                                      -

Acc. by unknown vn/p, with Phil Baker-piano accordion (and part-composer) or   unknown g as shown, dir. Leroy Shield.   Chicago, December 8, 1927.

BVE-41345-1  Did You Mean It ? - PB              Vic 21116
BVE-41346-4  The Man I Love - g                  -

Acc. by various studio orchestras.     Chicago, early December, 1929.

C-4774-    Nobody's Sweetheart                   Br 4681, Dec F-3436
C-4776-    Funny, Dear, What Love Can Do         Br 4663

C-4779-    My Fate Is In Your Hands              Br 4681
C-4780-    Nobody's Using It Now                 Br 4663

New York, May, 1930.

E-32773-   You Do Something To Me                Br 4806
E-32774-   Wasn't It Nice ?                      -

New York, June, 1930.

E-32835-   I Remember You From Somewhere         Br 4812, 01015
E-32836-   Nobody Cares If I'm Blue              -       -

New York, c. August, 1930.

E-34202-   If I Could Be With You                Br 4873
E-34203-   Little White Lies                     -

New York, November, 1930.

E-35061-   He's Not Worth Your Tears             Br 4972
E-35062-   My Man From Caroline                  -

New York, c. December 14, 1930.

E-35742-   Blue Again                            Br 6016, 01086, Dec F-3436
E-35743-   He's My Secret Passion                -

Acc. by Billy Mason and his Cafe de Paris Band.
                                       London, March 17, 1931.

WA-11364-1  My Canary Has Circles Under His Eyes  Col DB-453
WA-11365-1  Would You Like To Take A Walk ?       -

Acc. by studio orchestra.              London, April 25, 1932.

CA-12664-1  Gettin' Sentimental                   Col DB-851

London, May 3, 1932.

CA-12662-2  Is I In Love ? I Is                Col DB-822
CA-12663-1  An Ev'ning In Caroline              -
  NOTE:- The matrix number CA-12664 was allocated at the time of the above  session,
  although the artist made it on the date shown on page 339.

London, June 2, 1932.

CA-12774-1  Spring Is Here Again               Col DB-851

London, March 29, 1934.

GB-6677-1  One Morning In May                   Dec F-3954
GB-6678-2  Oo-Oo-Ooh ! Honey (What You Do To Me)  -
           (Intro. Ooh ! That Kiss)

London, August 2, 1934.

TB-1447-2  Mobday, Tuesday, Wednesday           Dec F-5160
TB-1461-2  Singing The Blues                    -
  NOTE:- Matrix TB-1461 was originally numbered TB-1448, but this had already  been
  allocated to a side by Lew Stone and his Band, so the Marion Harris record was re-
  numbered as shown.

## PHIL  HARRIS

B. 1906; originally drummer with Henry Halstead's Orchestra in Los Angeles, 1924-27;
led his own band at the St. Francis Hotel in San Francisco, 1931-1932, then at the
Cocoanut Grove in Los Angeles; began film career in 1933 and appeared in such pictures as MELODY CRUISE (1936); TURN OFF THE MOON (1937); BUCK BENNY RIDES    AGAIN
(1938); THUNDER ACROSS THE PACIFIC (1950, in which he sang his hit-song THE THING);
and he was the voice of Baloo the Bear in Walt Disney's adaptation of THE    JUNGLE
BOOK; made many post-1942 hit records, mainly of numbers originally introduced  by
Bert Williams, q.v., thirty or more years earlier. M. Alice Faye, 1941.

Vocalist with the Lofner-Harris St. Francis Hotel Orchestra.
                                  San Francisco, October 13, 1931.

PBS-68313-2  I Got The Ritz (From The One I Love)  Vic 22830

San Francisco, October 14, 1931.

PBS-68319-2  River, Stay 'Way From My Door      Vic 22831
 PBS-1306-1  When It's Sleepy Time Down South    Vic 22855
 PBS-1307-1  Constantly                          -
  NOTE:- The last two titles were made as tests, and were never allocated numbers in
  the regular series.

Vocalist with his Cocoanut Grove Orchestra.
                          ? New York, March 3, 1933.

152382-  You've Got Me Crying Again            Col 2761-D
152383-  What Have We Got To Lose ? (Hi-Ho-Lack-a-Day)-
152384-  How's About It ?                       Col 2766-D
152385-  Was My Face Red ?                      -

Vocalist with his own Orchestra.      New York, September 16, 1935.

39979-A  I'd Love To Take Orders From You      Dec 564, Br 02130
39980-   Just As Long As The World Goes 'Round  Dec 565, Br RL-311
         And Around
39981-   Now You've Got Me Doing It             -        -
39982-A  I'd Rather Listen To Your Eyes         Dec 564, Br 02130
                          Los Angeles, December 17, 1936.

LA-1219-  Jelly Bean (He's A Curbstone Cutie)   Voc 3430
LA-1220-  Nobody                                -
LA-1221-  Where The Lazy River Goes By          Voc 3419
LA-1222-  You Can Tell She Comes From Dixie     -

Los Angeles, January 18, 1937.

| | | |
|---|---|---|
| LA-1236- | Swingin' For The King | Voc 3466 |
| LA-1237- | Goodnight, My Love | Voc 3447 |
| LA-1238- | Woodman, Spare That Tree | Voc 3466 |
| LA-1239- | Swing High, Swing Low | Voc 3447 |

Los Angeles, February 27, 1937.

| | | | |
|---|---|---|---|
| LA-1259- | The Darktown Strutters' Ball | Voc 3565 | |
| LA-1260- | Between The Devil And The Deep Blue Sea | - | 555 |
| LA-1261- | Too Marvelous For Words | Voc 3488 | |
| LA-1262- | Sentimental And Melancholy | - | |
| LA-1263- | Rhythm Record (sic) | Rejected | |

Los Angeles, March 31, 1937.

| | | |
|---|---|---|
| LA-1324- | Jammin' (Film "Turn Off The Moon") | Voc 3533, 567 |
| LA-1325- | That's Southern Hospitality (Film "Turn Off The Moon") | -          - |
| LA-1326- | That's What I Like About The South | Voc 3583 |
| LA-1327- | Constantly | - |

## WILLIAM  S.  HART

B. Newburgh, New York, 1869; literally moved west as a young man and witnessed  Cus-
ter's last battle (and took part in many battles with Indians; stage debut  in New
York, 1888 (Bowery Theatre); began film career in 1914 in TWO-GUN HICKS; then fol-
lowed many very popular Western movies, all silent, such as HELL'S HINGES  and THE
ARYAN (1916); THE NARROW TRAIL and THE GUN FIGHTER (1917); THE TOLL GATE and a war
propaganda film called WAR RELIEF (1918); WAGON TRACKS (1919); TRAVELIN' ON(1921);
WHITE OAK (1922); WILD BILL HICKOK (1923); TUMBLEWEEDS (1925); also wrote MY  LIFE
EAST AND WEST, his autobiography (1929) and many poems, including PINTO BEN.  Died
June 24, 1946.

Speech.                                            Camden, N. J., October 18, 1928.

| | |
|---|---|
| BVE-47847-1-2  Annabelle Lee | Rejected |
| BVE-47848-1-2-3  Just Plain Dog | - |
| CVE-47849-2  Lasca | Vic 9297 |
| CVE-47850-1  Pinto Ben | - |

## GRACE  HAYES

Vocal, acc. by O/Leonard Joy.                      New York, December 19, 1927.

| | |
|---|---|
| BVE-41185-    The Man I Love | HMV B-2688 |
| BVE-41186-    Did You Mean It ? | - |

NOTE:- These two sides were made specially for the Gramophone Co. Ltd., England.

New York, July 19, 1928.

| | |
|---|---|
| BVE-45893-1-2-3  I Can't Give You Anything But Love | Vic rejected |
| BVE-45894-1-2-3  What D'Ya Say ? | - |

Acc. by O/Nat Shilkret.                            New York, August 6, 1928.

| | |
|---|---|
| BVE-45893-4  I Can't Give You Anything But Love | Vic 21571, HMV B-2900 |
| BVE-46662-2  I Must Have That Man | -              - |

Acc. by O/Leonard Joy.                             New York, July 3, 1929.

| | |
|---|---|
| BVE-53902-1-2-3-4  Am I Blue ? | Vic rejected |

Acc. by O/Nat Shilkret.                     New York, July 10, 1929.

BVE-53902-5-6-7  Am I Blue ?                      Vic rejected
BVE-53911-1  Big City Blues                            -

Acc. by O/Leroy Shield.                    Culver City, Calif., March 21, 1930.

PBVE-54738-2  My Lover                        Vic 22388, HMV B-3585
PBVE-54739-1  I Like To Do Things For You          -       HMV B-3632

                                           Culver City, Calif., May 1, 1930.

PBVE-54774-3  Exactly Like You                Vic 22428, HMV B-3534
PBVE-54775-2  On The Sunny Side Of The Street      -       HMV B-3585

                                             Hollywood, June 19, 1930.

PBVE-54844-1-2-3  Say It In A Nutshell        Vic 22479 (never issued)
PBVE-54845-1-2-3-4  What's The Use Of Living Without   -
                  Love ?

                                             Hollywood, July 16, 1930.

PBVE-54868-    My Future Just Passed          HMV B-3678
PBVE-54869-1-2-3-4  Ten Cents A Dance         Rejected

## HELEN HAYES

B. Washington, D.C., October 10, 1900 (r.n. Helen Brown); stage debut at five in  THE
   ROYAL FAMILY (National Theatre, Washington); during the next four years appeared in
   many other roles as a child; New York debut in OLD DUTCH (Herald Square,   November
   22, 1909); subsequent outstanding successes in DEAR BRUTUS (Empire,  December   23,
   1918); CLARENCE (Hudson, September 20, 1919); TO THE LADIES (Liberty,  February 20,
   1922, in which she played for two years); DANCING MOTHERS (Booth, August 11, 1924);
   Cleopatra in CAESAR AND CLEOPATRA (Guild, April 13, 1925); WHAT EVERY WOMAN   KNOWS
   (Bijou, April 13, 1926); COQUETTE (Maxine Elliott, November 8, 1927, touring   with
   this during 1928-1929); THE GOOD FAIRY (Henry Miller, November 24, 1931); MARY   OF
   SCOTLAND (title role, Alvin, for Theatre Guild, November 27, 1933); toured in  this
   in 1934-1935; title role in VICTORIA REGINA (Broadhurst, December 26, 1935;   great
   success throughout season and coast-to-coast tour, 1937-1938, earning Drama  League
   of New York medal for the most distinguished performance of 1936); LADIES AND GENT-
   LEMEN (Martin Beck, October 17, 1939); title role (Harriet Beecher Stowe) in   HAR-
   RIET (Henry Miller, March 3, 1943, and on tour for two years); began film career in
   1917 (THE WEAVERS OF LIFE) and appeared in BABS (1920, film of stage play in  which
   she also played that year); A FAREWELL TO ARMS (1932); THE WHITE SISTER (1933);WHAT
   EVERY WOMAN KNOWS (1934); VANESSA (1935); MY SON JOHN (1951); ANASTASIA (1956), and
   AIRPORT (1969) among others.

Speech, acc. by O/Leroy Shield.             Chicago, March 30, 1942.

CS-074178-2  America                             Vic 11-8222
CS-074179-2  The Star-Spangled Banner            Vic 11-8221

                                            Chicago, March 31, 1942.

CS-074186-1  Battle Hymn Of The Republic         Vic 11-8221
CS-074187-2  Beat, Beat, Drums                   Vic 11-8222

## JOE HAYMAN

Vaudeville comedian well-known on both sides of the Atlantic for his Jewish  sketches
   on topics of the day (1912-1930).

Speech.                                     London, July, 1913.

28563    Abe Levi's Wedding Day               Col 2190, Re G-6450
28564    Cohen On The Telephone                  -       -

                                        London, c. May, 1915.

          Cohen At The Call Office                Re G-7066
          Cohen Is Arrested For Exceeding The        -
            Speed Limit

                                        London, c. July, 1915.

          Cohen's Recruiting Speech              Re G-7134
          Cohen 'Phones His Tailor                  -

                                        London, October, 1922.

71978     Cohen And Wireless : Cohen Listens In   Re G-7871
71979     Cohen And Wireless : Cohen Buys A Wireless  -

                                        New York, April 14, 1923.

80956-    Cohen 'Phones For A 'Phone             Col 3-D
80957-    Cohen 'Phones His Son At College       Col 123-D

                                        New York, April 16, 1923.

80958-    Cohen 'Phones The Plumber              Col A-3904
80959-    Cohen 'Phones Mrs. Levi (Regarding A   Col 3-D
            Matter Of Money)

                                        New York, April 19, 1923.

80972-    Cohen On Telephone Etiquette           Col A-3904
80974-    Cohen At The Fight                     Col 123-D
          NOTE:- Matrix 80973 is not by Joe Hayman.

                                        London, June 14, 1926.

WA-3416-1  Cohen On The Telephone                Col 4036, 792-D
WA-3417-1  Abe Levi's Wedding Day                   -       -

                                        Hayes, Middlesex, November 27, 1928.

Yy-14994-1-2  Cohen Broadcasts                      Rejected
Yy-14995-1  Abe Levi's Anniversary                  Zon 5831
Yy-14996-2  Cohen At A Prize Fight                  Zon 5239
Yy-14997-1-2  Cohen's Troubles                      Rejected
Yy-14998-2  Cohen Forms A New Company               Zon 5239

                                        Hayes, Middlesex, December 3, 1928.

Yy-14998-3-4  Cohen Forms A New Company             Rejected
Yy-15222-1  Cohen On Telephone Deportment           Zon 5831

## MARY HEALY

B. 1917; singing star of many typical films of the late thirties and early thirties,
  such as SECOND FIDDLE (1939); STAR DUST, SIS BOOM BAH, STRICTLY IN THE GROOVE  and
  FIVE THOUSAND FINGERS OF DR. T. (1940-1944).

Vocal, acc. by O/Cy Feuer.                Los Angeles, June 14, 1939.

LA-1905-A  The Song Of The Metronome (Film    Br 8436, Col DB-1879
             "Second Fiddle")
LA-1906-A  I Poured My Heart Into A Song (Film    -       -
             "Second Fiddle")
LA-1907-A  I'm Sorry For Myself (Film "Second  Br 8437, Col DB-1880
             Fiddle")
LA-1908-A  When Winter Comes (Film "Second Fiddle")  -       -

Los Angeles, January 5, 1940.

| | | | |
|---|---|---|---|
| LA-2098-A | Between You And Me (Film "Broadway Melody of 1940") | Col | , DB-1927 |
| LA-2099- | I Happen To Be In Love (Film "Broadway Melody of 1940") | Col | |
| LA-2100-B | I Concentrate On You (Film "Broadway Melody of 1940") | Col | , DB-1927 |
| LA-2101- | I've Got My Eyes On You (Film "Broadway Melody of 1940") | Col | |

Hollywood, October 8, 1940.

| | | |
|---|---|---|
| H-35-1 | I Hear A Rhapsody | OK 5864 |
| H-36-1 | Down Argentina Way | - |
| H-37-1 | What Is There To Say ? | OK 6002 |
| H-38-1 | I'll See You Again | - |

## RAY  HENDERSON

B. 1896; d. 1969.  Composer of hundreds of extremely popular tunes during the    years between the wars, most of them in collaboration with B. G. ("Bud") de Sylva and Lew Brown (e.g., BLACK BOTTOM and THE BIRTH OF THE BLUES,(1926); IT ALL DEPENDS  ON YOU and SO BLUE (1927); JUST IMAGINE; TOGETHER; FORGETTING YOU; JUST A MEMORY and SONNY BOY (1927-1928); LITTLE PAL; I'M A DREAMER - AREN'T WE ALL ? and IF I HAD A TALKING PICTURE OF YOU (1929); THIS IS THE MISSUS and LIFE IS JUST A BOWL OF CHERRIES(1931) and many others); also wrote I HEARD A SONG IN A TAXI for the London production  of TRANSATLANTIC RHYTHM (1936) and recorded it and other numbers from the show in Lon-don with co-author Irving Caesar, q.v.

## EVELYN HERBERT

B. Philadelphia, 1898; trained to sing in opera, and among her teachers was    Enrico Caruso; stage debut in Chicago in LA BOHEME (Auditorium Theatre, February, 1920, as member of Chicago Opera Company); New York debut in the Lexington Opera House later that year in the same part (Mimi); other New York stage successes include  STEPPING STONES (Globe, November 6, 1923); THE LOVE SONG (Century, January 13, 1925);  PRIN-CESS FLAVIA (Century, November 2, 1925); MY MARYLAND (Jolson, September 12,  1927); THE NEW MOON (Imperial, September 19, 1928); London debut in WALTZES FROM VIENNA at the Alhambra, August 17, 1931.

Vocal, acc. by O/Leroy Shield.        New York, October 5, 1927.

| | | |
|---|---|---|
| BVE-39877- | Silver Moon ("My Maryland") | Vic 20995, HMV B-3938 |
| BVE-39878- | Mother (w/Franklyn Baur) ("My Maryland")  - | - |

Acc. by O/Leonard Joy.          New York, December 28, 1928.

| | |
|---|---|
| BVE-49605-1-2-3  Lover, Come Back To Me ("New Moon") | Rejected |
| BVE-49606-5  One Kiss ("New Moon") | Vic 21883 |

New York, January 8, 1929.

| | |
|---|---|
| BVE-49605-5  Lover, Come Back To Me ("New Moon") | Vic 21883 |

New York, February 5, 1929.

| | |
|---|---|
| BVE-49605-8  Lover, Come Back To Me ("New Moon") | Vic 21883 |
| BVE-49924-1-2-3-4  Wanting You ("New Moon") | Rejected |

New York, February 20, 1929.

| | |
|---|---|
| BVE-49924-5-6-7  Wanting You ("New Moon") | Vic rejected |

New York, May 27, 1930.

| | |
|---|---|
| BVE-62171-2  Prince Charming | Vic 22454 |
| BVE-62172-1  Love Comes Only Once In A Lifetime | - |

B. Dublin, February 1, 1959; educated and trained as musician in Germany; made great
study ·of the 'cello, played in orchestras conducted by Franz Liszt,Johannes Brahms
and others; became engaged in 1886 to Therese Foerster, a soprano in the Stuttgart
Opera House, who was offered a contract by Walter Damrosch for the   Metropolitan,
New York, which she accepted on condition that her fiance became first 'cellist in
the orchestra.  He made many public appearances as soloist, writing a concerto for
'cello and orchestra, also SERENADE FOR STRINGS and AMERICAN FANTASY; in 1893,  he
was appointed leader of Patrick S. Gilmore's 22nd Regiment Band of New York; later
became conductor of the Pittsburgh Symphony Orchestra for six years.  Began   work
on operettas and musical comedies, subsequently recording selections and  individual numbers from these.  Founded the American Society of Composers, Authors    and
Publishers (ASCAP) in 1914; also composed two grand operas (NATOMA, 1911 and MADE-
LEINE, 1914), neither very successful; d. New York, March 27, 1924. All the under-
mentioned titles are Victor Herbert compositions, recorded under his personal direction; the dates in brackets after the titles are those of first performances.

VICTOR HERBERT'S ORCHESTRA.                  New York, c. 1903.

        Battle Of Manila  (1899)                Zon A-9128

                              New York, c. March, 1909.

        Mademoiselle Modiste - Selection (1905)  Ed 4M-195
        The Red Mill - Selection (1906)          Ed 4M-215, Amb 1872
        It Happened In Nordland - Selection      Ed 4M-229
          (1906)

                              New York, July 6, 1909.

        Oriental March ("The Tattooed Man" -     Ed 10280
          1907)
        Little Nemo - Selection (1908)           Ed 4M-287
        Mademoiselle Modiste - Selection (1905)  Ed 4M-330, Amb 5376
        Rose Of The World (?)                    Ed 4M-345, Amb 5270
        Badinage (1897)                          Ed 4M-369, Amb 5288

                              New York, c. October, 1909.

        Babes In Toyland - Selection (1903)      Ed 4M-396, Amb 5244

                              New York, November 17, 1909.

        Entr'acte ("The Prima Donna" - 1908)     Ed 4M-420
        The Tattooed Man - Selection (1907)      Ed 4M-440, Amb 5350
        Old Dutch - Selection (1909)             Ed 4M-453, Amb 5319

                              New York, May 9 to May 13, 1910.

        If You Love But Me (?)                   Ed 10406
        L'Encore (Duet for Flute & Clarinet)(?)  Ed 10413
        Spanish Dance ("The Nations" - ?)        Ed 10470
        Berceuse (?)                             Ed 10480
        The Fortune Teller - Fantasy (1898)      Ed 4M-547, Amb 5456
        The Wizard Of The Nile - Selection(1895) Ed 4M-569
        Dream Melody ("Naughty Marietta"-1910)   Ed 4M-683, Amb 1775
        Wild Rose (?)                            Ed 4M-704
        Naughty Marietta - Selection (1910)      Ed 4M-729, Amb 5487
        The Singing Girl - Selection (1899)      Ed 4M-918, Amb 1950
        The Ameer - Selection (1899)             Ed 4M-1037
        The Idol's Eye - Selection (1897)        Amb 1731

                              New York, June 19, 1911.

C-10546-5  Intermezzo ("Naughty Marietta" - 1910)  Vic 70075
C-10547-4  Badinage (1897)                          Vic 70053
C-10567-1-2  When Sweet Sixteen - Selection (1910) Rejected
B-10568-1  Mademoiselle Rosita (?)                  Vic 60087

New York, June 21, 1911.

C-10571-1-2-3  The Red Mill - Selection (1906)      Rejected
B-10572-3  Al Fresco ("It Happened In Nordland" -  Vic 60086
           1906)

New York, June 22, 1911.

B-10568-3-4  Mademoiselle Rosita                    Rejected
C-10582-2  Dagger Dance ("Natoma" - 1911)           Vic 70049
C-10583-3  March Of The Toys ("Babes In Toyland" - Vic 70048, 55054
           1903)

New York, June 23, 1911.

B-10587-1  Yesterthoughts (Op. 37)                  Vic 60054
B-10588-1-2  Punchinello (Op. 37)                   Rejected

New York, June 24, 1911.

B-10588-3-4-5  Punchinello (Op. 37)                 Vic rejected
C-10591-1-2-3  Mademoiselle Modiste - Selection        -
           (1905)

New York, October 9, 1911.

C-10591-4-5-6  Mademoiselle Modiste - Selection  Rejected
           (1905)
C-11070-2  The Sultan's Entrance ("Rose Of          Vic 70056
           Algeria" - 1909)

New York, October 10, 1911.

C-11072-1-2  The Birth Of The Butterfly ("Babes    Vic rejected
           In Toyland" - 1903)

New York, October 13, 1911.

C-11097-1  Entr'acte ("The Prima Donna" - 1908)     Vic 70092

New York, October 14, 1911.

C-11101-1  The Military Ball ("Babes In Toyland" - Vic 70091, 55104
           1903)
B-11103-1  They Were Irish ("Little Nemo" - 1908)  Vic 60089
B-11104-2  Sextette ("Babette" - 1903)             Vic 60088

Violoncello solos, acc. by Rosario Bourdon-p.
                              New York, January 25, 1912.

B-11516-1  Petite Valse a Pablo Casals (1911)       Vic 64297, 677

New York, January 26, 1912.

C-11519-2  Pensee Amoureuse (1911)                  Vic 74286

VICTOR HERBERT'S ORCHESTRA, acc. artists named in brackets after each title, or  per-
    forming without soloists.          New York, April 3, 1912.

C-11820-1-2-3  Spring Song ("Natoma") (Agnes       Rejected
           Kimball) (1911)
B-11821-3  Serenade (When The Sunlight Dies)        Vic 60072
           ("Natoma"- 1911) (Reinald Werrenrath)
C-11822-1  Paul's Address (No Country Can My Own  Vic 74295
           Outvie) ("Natoma" - 1911) (John McCormack)

NOTE:- John McCormack made four other records on this date, all accompanied by Victor
    Herbert's Orchestra, but all of Irish and other popular ballads by other composers.

New York, June 10, 1912.

C-12103-1  Spring Song ("Natoma" - 1911) (Alma       Vic 74274, 6147, HMV 03348,DB-281
           Gluck)
C-12105-1-2  The Enchantress - Selection (1911)      Rejected
B-12106-1-2  Habañera ("Natoma" - 1911)                -

New York, June 11, 1912.

C-12108-1-2  Spring Song ("Natoma" - 1911) (Lucy    Vic rejected
             Isabelle Marsh)

New York, June 25, 1912.

C-12105-3-4  The Enchantress - Selection (1911)      Vic rejected
B-12106-3-4  Habañera ("Natoma" - 1911)                -

New York, June 26, 1912.

C-12105-5  The Enchantress - Selection               Vic 70090

New York, July 27, 1912.

C-12251-2  Pan-Americana (1901)                      Vic 70089
B-12252-1-2  Saxtette (There Once Was An Owl)        Vic 60088
             ("Babette" - 1903)
B-12255-1  Kiss Me Again ("Mademoiselle Modiste" -  Vic 45165
           1905)

New York, July 28, 1912.

B-12257-4  The Toymaker's Shop ("Babes In Toyland"  Vic 60080
           - 1903)

New York, May 20, 1913.

C-13336-4  Sweethearts - Selection (1913)            Vic 55039
C-13337-1-2  The Lady Of The Slipper - Selection     Rejected
             (1912)

New York, May 23, 1913.

C-13336-5  Sweethearts - Selection (1913)            Vic rejected
C-13348-1-2  Natoma - Selection (1911)                 -

New York, May 24, 1913.

C-13337-3  The Lady Of The Slipper - Selection       Vic 55039
           (1912)

New York, May 27, 1913.

B-10587-4  Yesterthoughts (Op. 37)                   Vic 60054 (not used ?)
C-13348-3-4-5-6  Natoma - Selection (1911)           Rejected

New York, May 29, 1913.

B-13368-1-2-3  Forget-Me-Not (?)                     Vic rejected

Camden, N. J., April 5,1917.

B-19445-1  Free Trade And A Misty Moon ("Eileen" -  Vic 18285
           1917) (Greek Evans and chorus)
B-19446-2  The Irish Have A Great Day Tonight          -
           ("Eileen" - 1917) (Scott Welsh and chorus)

New York, May 7, 1917.

C-19812-1-2-3  American Fantasy - Part 1 (1888)      Vic rejected
C-19813-1-2  American Fantasy - Part 2 (1888)          -

New York, May 8, 1917.

C-19813-3-4  American Fantasy - Part 2 (1888)      Vic rejected
C-19814-1-2  Eileen - Selection (1917)             -

New York, May 10, 1917.

C-19819-1-2  The American Rose - Waltz (1917)      Vic rejected

New York, May 11, 1917.

C-19812-4-5  American Fantasy - Part 1 (1888)      Vic rejected
C-19813-5-6  American Fantasy - Part 2 (1888)      -

New York, May 20, 1917.

C-19812-6  American Fantasy - Part 1 (1888)        Vic 55093

Camden, N. J., May 20, 1918.

C-19813-8  American Fantasy - Part 2 (1888)        Vic 55093
B-21926-1  Kiss Me Again ("Mademoiselle Modiste" - Vic 45165
           1905)

Camden, N. J., May 23, 1918.

C-13336-7  Sweethearts - Selection (1913)          Vic 55039

Camden, N. J., November 18, 1921.

C-25767-1-2-3  Devotion (?)                         Vic rejected
C-25768-1-2-3-4  Indian Summer (1919)              -

Camden, N. J., May 3, 1923.

C-10582-4  Dagger Dance ("Natoma" - 1911)          Vic 55200
C-13336-9  Sweethearts - Selection (1913)          Vic 55223

Camden, N. J., May 22, 1923.

C-25767-4  Devotion (?)                             Vic 55223
C-25768-5-6-7  Indian Summer (1919)                Rejected

Camden, N. J., June 7, 1923.

C-25768-10  Indian Summer (1919)                    Vic 55200

## AL  HERMAN

Vocal, acc. by studio orchestra.        New York, c. November, 1916.

  2358-1  Ida, Sweet As Apple Cider               Em 7129 (7")

New York, October 14, 1921.

80024-3  I Hold Her Hand And She Holds Mine        Col A-3507

New York, October 29, 1921.

80045-3  They Call It Dancing                      Col A-3507

New York, November 30, 1921.

80085-1-2-3  Ta-Ta                                 Rejected
80086-5  Which Hazel                               Col A-3536

                               New York, December 23, 1921.

80121-4  You're Out O' Luck                   Col A-3536

     Piano acc. by Leonard Joy.         New York, July 12, 1927.

          Ain't She Sweet ?                    Vic rejected

     Acc. unknown.                 New York, October 24, 1927.

144894-   I Thought I'd Die - Part 1          Col 1230-D
144895-   I Thought I'd Die - Part 2               -


                               New York, November 8, 1930.

150942-   Letter From Heliotrope To Eclipse     Col rejected
150943-   Letter From Eclipse To Heliotrope          -

## HARRY HERSHFIELD

Jewish character comedian very popular in vaudeville during the years around  World
  War I.

Humorous monologues.                    New York, 1917-1918.

          Abe Kabibble "Does His Bit"             LW 684

                               New York, January 29, 1920.

 78952-3  Abe Kabibble Dictates A Letter      Col A-2907
 78953-3  Abe Kabibble At The Ball Game            -
 NOTE:- According to the original files, the above two sides were recorded by  Jaek
 Kaufman, but they were issued under Harry Hershfield's name.  The latter also took
 part in an LP (Jubilee JGM-2041) in the mid-fifties, entitled THE PRESIDENT'S JES-
 TER.

## RALPH   C. HERZ

B. Paris, March 25,  1878.  Actor and light comedian best-remembered for his appear-
  ance in THE SOUL KISS (New York Theatre, January 28, 1908).  D. Atlantic City,N.J.,
  July 12, 1921.
Vocal, acc. by the Victor Orchestra.    New York, November 27, 1908.

B-6618-1  An Educated Fool                    Vic rejected
C-6619-1  I'd Sooner Be A Has-Been                -
B-6620-1  Very Well, Then ("The Soul Kiss")       -
B-6621-1  That Wasn't All ("The Soul Kiss")       -


                               New York, December 1, 1908.

B-6618-2  An Educated Fool                    Vic rejected
B-6620-2  Very Well, Then ("The Soul Kiss")       -
B-6621-2-3  That Wasn't All ("The Soul Kiss")     -


                               New York, December 4, 1908.

B-6620-3-4  Very Well, Then ("The Soul Kiss")   Rejected
B-6621-5  That Wasn't All ("The Soul Kiss")     Vic 5654
C-6648-1  The Perils Of Invisibility ("The Baba  Rejected
            Ballads") (unacc.)
B-6649-1  Mephisto's Soliloquy ("The Soul Kiss")    -
            (unacc.)
                               New York, December 8, 1908.

B-6620-5  Very Well, Then ("The Soul Kiss")     Vic 5661
C-6648-2  The Perils Of Invisibility (unacc.)   Rejected
B-6649-2  Mephisto's Soliloquy ("The Soul Kiss")    -
B-6656-1  Other Things                             -

New York, December 11, 1908.

B-6663-1-2-3  The Rake's Progress (unacc.)          Rejected
B-6664-2  Non, merci ("Cyrano de Bergerac") (in     Vic 5681
          French, unacc.)
B-6665-1-2  One-a-Strike                            Rejected

## HILDEGARDE

French cabaret star who made her London debut in 1933; New York 1936; resident U.S.A.
  from early in 1939; popularized THE LAST TIME I SAW PARIS (1941) and LILI  MARLENE
  (1943); originally discovered by Gus Edwards as a child singer and dancer.

Vocal, acc. by O/? George Scott Wood.     London, October 17, 1933.

CAR-2301-1  Why Don't They Leave Us Alone ?       Col DB-1247, FB-1523
CAR-2302-1  I Was In The Mood

   Acc. by O/? Carroll Gibbons.          London, May 10, 1935.

CA-15051-1  I Believe In Miracles                 Col DB-1552
CA-15052-2  Listen To The German Band                -

   Acc. by Carroll Gibbons and his Boy Friends.
                                    London, May 20, 1935.

CA-15064-2  For Me, For You                       Col DB-1556
CA-15065-1  Darling, je vous aime beaucoup           -

   Acc. by Henry Hall and the BBC Dance Orchestra.
                                    London, September 21, 1935.

CA-15272-1  Honey-Coloured Moon                   Col FB-1123

   Acc. by O/? Carroll Gibbons.          London, October 5, 1935.

CA-15317-1  I'm In The Mood For Love              Col FB-1170
CA-15318-1  You Are My Lucky Star                    -

   Acc. by Carroll Gibbons and his Boy Friends.
                                    London, October 15, 1935.

CA-15360-1  Cheek To Cheek                        Col FB-1190
CA-15361-2  Isn't This A Lovely Day ?                -

   Acc. by Mantovani and his Tipica Orchestra.
                                    London, December 19, 1935.

CA-15504-1  Thanks A Million                      Col FB-1266
CA-15505-1  Love Is A Dancing Thing                  -

                                    London, February 7, 1936.

CA-15600-1  I Dream Too Much                      Col FB-1308

                                    London, February 8, 1936.

CA-15605-1  Eeny Meeny Miney Mo                   Col FB-1308

                                    London, February 14, 1936.

CM-149-1  Comme une boite a musique (in French)   Col DF-1897, MC-3085
CM-150-1  Cheek To Cheek (in French)                 -        -
CM-151-1  C'etait ecrit (in French)              Col DF-1892, MC-3084
CM-152-1  Quand un Vicomte (in French)               -        -

                                    London, March 25, 1936.
CA-15674-1  But Where Are You ? (Intro. Let's     Col FB-1354
            Face The Music And Dance)
CA-15675-1  Life Begins When You're In Love          -
            (Intro. Rolling Along)

Acc. by the Albert Sandler Trio.          London, April 3, 1936.

CA-15708-2  Gloomy Sunday                          Col FB-1366

Acc. by Carroll Gibbons and his Boy Friends (third title as HILDIE AND HER   SWING-
London, May 1, 1936.

CA-15739-1  The Glory Of Love                      Col FB-1401
CA-15740-1  The Touch Of Your Lips/The Very Thought   -
            Of You
CA-15741-1  Swing, Mister Charlie                  Col FB-1415

Acc. by O/? Carroll Gibbons.          London, May 29, 1936.

CA-15776-1  Practising The Piano                   Col FB-1468
CA-15777-1  Fritz (Intro. The Village Band)        Col FB-1466

London, July 3, 1936.

CA-15835-1  A Pretty Girl Is Like A Melody         Col FB-1468
CA-15836-1  The Scene Changes                      Col FB-1466
CA-15847-1  Hildegarde Looks Back - Part 1 (Intro. Col FB-1541
            Why Do I Love You ?/Sometimes I'm Happy/Look For The Silver Lining)
CA-15848-1  Hildegarde Looks Back - Part 2 (Intro.    -
            Always/'S Wonderful/I Got Rhythm)
  NOTE:- Matrices CA-15837/15846 inclusive are not by Hildegarde.

London, July 14, 1936.

CA-15863-1  When I'm With You                      Col FB-1523
CA-15864-1  There's A Small Hotel                  Col FB-1598

Acc. by studio orchestra.          New York, November 19, 1936.

CO-20286-1  Pennies From Heaven                    Col FB-1598
CO-20287-2  Goodnight, My Love                     Col FB-1641
CO-20288-1  For Sentimental Reasons                   -
CO-20289-1-2  I Wanna Go To The Zoo                Rejected

Acc. by O/? Carroll Gibbons.          London, May 11, 1937.

CA-16388-1-2  Will You Remember ?                  Col rejected
CA-16389-1-2  Trying To Say That I Love You           -

London, May 20, 1937.

CA-16393-1  Let's Call The Whole Thing Off         Col FB-1712
CA-16394-1  They Can't Take That Away From Me         -

London, June 8, 1937.

CA-16388-4  Will You Remember ?                    Col FB-1700
CA-16389-3  Trying To Say That I Love You             -

Acc. by Carroll Gibbons and his Orchestra.
London, July 20, 1937.

CA-16395-1  This Year's Kisses                     Col FB-1726
CA-16396-1  I've Got My Love To Keep Me Warm          -
CAX-8045-1  Gershwin - King Of Rhythm - Part 1     Col DX-786
            (Hildegarde sings a chorus of THE MAN I LOVE)
CAX-8046-1  Gershwin - King Of Rhythm - Part 2        -
            (Hildegarde sings a chorus of THE MAN I LOVE)

London, August 30, 1937.

CA-16526-1  Yours And Mine                         Col FB-1768
CA-16527-1  So Rare                                Col FB-1758
CA-16528-1  I'm Feeling Like A Million             Col FB-1768
CA-16529-1  Ten Pretty Girls                       Col FB-1758

London, September 4, 1937.

| | | |
|---|---|---|
| CA-16540-1 | Can I Forget You ? | Col FB-1841 |
| CA-16541-1 | It's The Natural Thing To Do | Col FB-1799 |
| CA-16542-1 | Bon soir | Col FB-1841 |
| CA-16543-1 | The Moon Got In My Eyes (Intro. All You Want To Do Is Dance) | Col FB-1799 |

London, July 1, 1938.

| | | |
|---|---|---|
| CA-17021-1 | Love Walked In | Col FB-1992 |
| CA-17022-1 | Goodnight, Angel | - |

London, July 11, 1938.

| | | |
|---|---|---|
| CA-17059-1 | Let's Try Again | Col FB-2004 |
| CA-17060-1 | Say Goodnight To Your Old Fashioned Mother | - |

Acc. by Clive Richardson-Rene Pougnet-p/unknown g/sb.
London, July 13, 1938.

| | | |
|---|---|---|
| CA-17C67-1 | Now It Can Be Told | Col FB-2043 |
| CA-17068-1 | Alexander's Ragtime Band - Selection (Intro. Blue Skies/Alexander's Ragtime Band/What'll I Do ?) | - |

Acc. by 0/Ray Sinatra.                    New York, May 22, 1939.

| | | |
|---|---|---|
| 65622-A | Dance, Little Lady | Dec 23099, F-7310 |
| 65623-A | Someday I'll Find You | -    -    - |
| 65624-A | I'll Follow My Secret Heart | Dec 23100, F-7542 |

New York, May 29, 1939.

| | | |
|---|---|---|
| 65672-A | I'll See You Again | Dec 23101, F-7608 |
| 65673-A | A Room With A View | -    - |
| 65674-A | Zigeuner | Dec 23100, F-7542 |

New York, June 12, 1939.

| | | |
|---|---|---|
| 65754-A | The Blue Room | Dec 23134, F-7754 |
| 65755-A | My Heart Stood Still | Dec 23133, F-7652 |
| 65761-A | With A Song In My Heart | Dec 23135, F-7853 |

NOTE:- Matrices 65756/60 inclusive are not by Hildegarde.

New York, June 19, 1939.

| | | |
|---|---|---|
| 65845-A | Thou Swell | Dec 23133, F-7652 |
| 65846-A | Isn't It Romantic ? | Dec 23135, F-7853 |
| 65847-A | Lover | Dec 23134, F-7754 |

New York, January 9, 1940.

| | | |
|---|---|---|
| 67032- | I Didn't Know What Time It Was | Dec 23115 |
| 67033- | All The Things You Are | - |

New York, May 23, 1940.

| | | |
|---|---|---|
| 67809- | Now | Dec 23161 |
| 67810- | April In Paris | - |
| 67811- | I Can't Get Started | Dec 23162 |

New York, July 2, 1940.

| | | |
|---|---|---|
| 67907- | What Is There To Say ? | Dec 23163 |
| 67908- | Suddenly | Dec 23162 |

New York, July 9, 1940.

| | | |
|---|---|---|
| 67927- | I Cling To You | Dec 23163 |

New York, October 16, 1940.

| 68256- | The Last Time I Saw Paris | Dec 23183, DL-8656 |
| 68257- | Why Do I Love You ? | - |

Acc. by O/Harry Sosnik, with Hildegarde at the piano.
New York, February 2, 1941.

| 68644- | The Saga Of Jenny - Part 1 (w/chorus) | Dec 23206, Br 03512 |
| 68645- | The Saga Of Jenny - Part 2 (w/chorus) | - - |
| 68647- | This Is New | Dec 23207 |
| 68648- | My Ship (w/chorus) | Dec 23208, Br 03513 |
| 68649- | One Life To Live | - |

NOTE:- Matrix 68646 is not by Hildegarde.

New York, April 14, 1941.

| 68987- | Darling, je vous aime beaucoup | Dec 23218, DL-8656, 7-2, F-7976 |
| 68988- | I Worship You | - |
| 68989- | A Little Cafe Down The Street | Dec 23219 |
| 68990- | You Will Remember Vienna | - F-7976 |

New York, October 13, 1941.

| 69809- | A Little Rumba Numba | Dec 23243 |
| 69810- | You Irritate Me So | - |
| 69811-A | Ev'rything I Love | Dec 23242, F-8178 |
| 69814-A | I Hate You, Darling | Dec 23244 - |
| 69815- | Ace In The Hole | Dec 23242 |
| 69816- | Farming | Dec 23244 |

NOTE:- Matrices 69812/3 are not by Hildegarde.

Acc. by Bob Grant and the Savoy-Plaza Orchestra.
New York, November 22, 1941.

| 69965-A | A Pink Cocktail For A Blue Lady | Dec 23245, F-8133 |
| 69966-A | I Said No | - - |

New York, January 7, 1942.

| 70131- | You Made Me Love You | Dec 23246 |
| 70132- | My Cousin In Milwaukee | - |

Acc. by O/Harry Sosnik, with Hildegarde at the piano.
New York, June 9, 1942.

| 70840- | Careless Rhapsody | Dec 23253 |
| 70841- | Ev'rything I've Got | Dec 23254 |
| 70842- | Nobody's Heart | - |
| 70843- | Jupiter Forbid | Dec 23253 |

NOTE:- Hildegarde continued to record for Decca until 1949, and sang LILI MARLENE on the RCA Victor SHOW BIZ LP in 1953.

## MURRY K. HILL

B. New York, April 15, 1865; prominent vaudeville comedian during the 1890s and early years of the twentieth century; vocalist and raconteur; d, Chicago, October 23,1942.

Vocal, acc. by studio orchestra.          New York, c. June, 1907.

In The Good Old Steamboat Days          Ed 9619

New York, c. July, 1908.

Oh, Glory !          Ed 9940

New York, c. August, 1908.

| The Stranded Minstrel Man | Ed 4M-16 (October, 1908) |
| A Bunch Of Nonsense | Ed 4M-41 (November, 1908) |
| A Comedy Dream | Ed 4M-66 (December, 1908) |
| A String Of Laughs | Ed 4M-101 (January, 1909), |
| | Amb 2112 |
| There's A Woman In The Case | Ed 4M-185 (April, 1909) |
| Grandma's Mustard Plaster | Ed 4M-291 (August, 1909),Amb 1969 |
| A Monolog On Married Life | Ed 4M-370 (November, 1909) |

NOTE:- The dates after the catalogue numbers of the above are those of issue.

New York, November 9, 1909.

| B-8354-1-2 | A Bunch Of Nonsense | Vic 5760, 16446 |
| B-8355-1-2 | Four Hundred Nursery Rhymes | - |

New York, November 10, 1909.

| C-8356-3 | The Tale Of The Cheese | Vic 35093 |
| B-8360-2 | Father Was Out | Vic 16436 |
| B-8361-3 | The Alphabet Song | Vic 16458 |
| B-8362-2 | A Talk On Married Life | Vic 16463 |

New York, March 14, 1910.

| Don't Go Up In That Big Balloon, Dad | Ed 10375 |
| Noah's Ark | Ed 10388 |

New York, c. October, 1910.

| A Bunch Of Nonsense | USE 1172 |
| Married Life | USE 1178 |

New York, January 30, 1911.

| B-9865-1 | A Bit Of Grand Opera | Vic 16837, 16954 |
| B-9866-1 | A Bit Of Drama | Vic 16846, 16944 |
| B-9867-1-2 | The Old Jokes | Rejected |
| B-9868-1 | How Columbus Discovered America | Vic 16890 |
| B-9869-2 | Adventures In A Department Store | Vic 16861, 16944 |

New York, January 31, 1911.

| B-9880-1-2 | Jack Faust (w/Billy Murray) | Rejected |
| C-9881-1 | Seated Around An Oil Stove (w/Billy Murray) | Vic 35186 |
| B-9882-1-2 | Kling Wing King And Sing (w/Billy Murray) | Rejected |
| B-9883-2 | Through A Hole In The Fence | Vic 16844, 16954 |
| B-9884-1-2 | A Talk On Trusts (unacc.) | Rejected |

New York, c. January, 1911.

| A Bunch Of Nonsense | Ind 3230 |

New York, February 15, 1911.

| B-9867-4 | The Old Jokes | Vic 16867 |
| B-9884-3 | A Talk On Trusts | Vic 16903 |
| B-9955-1 | Burbank The Wizard | Vic 16849 |
| B-9956-1-2 | Four Hundred Nursery Rhymes | Rejected |

New York, March 3, 1911.

| 19247-1 | The Old Jokes | Col A-995 |
| 19248-1 | Some Talk and Songs | - |

New York, c. March, 1911.

| | |
|---|---|
| Fireman's Song | USE 235 |
| Oh Fiddle ! | USE 374 |
| The Trusts | USE 1242 |
| Father Was Out | USE 1491 |
| Oh Fiddle ! | USE 1501 |
| Oh Glory ! | USE 1493 |
| A Talk On Married Life | USE 3240 |
| The Tale Of The Cheese | USE 3249 |

New York, April 11, 1911.

| | | |
|---|---|---|
| 19274- | Father Was Out | Col A-1011 |
| 19275- | A Discourse On The Trusts | - |
| 19276-1-2-3 | Connubial Bliss | Rejected |

New York, c. April, 1912.

| | |
|---|---|
| Seated Around An Oil Stove | Ed 4M-1019 (June, 1912), Amb 1909 |
| Father's Eccentricities | Amb B (Special) |
| The Honest Hold-Up Man /Billy Beans | Amb 2166 |

## FRED  HILLEBRAND

B. Brooklyn, N.Y., December 25, 1893; comedian, songwriter (e.g., PLEASE RETURN  MY
HEART and SHAKE HANDS WITH THE MAN); wrote for and appeared in various shows  for
twenty-five years; d. New York, September 15, 1963.

Vocal, acc. by studio orchestra.          New York, c. March, 1910.

| | |
|---|---|
| Mandy, How Do You Do ? (w/Walter van Brunt) | Ind 1326 |
| 'Way Down In Cotton Town (w/Walter van Brunt) | Ind 1370 |

New York, c. September, 1919.

| | |
|---|---|
| I've Got My Captain Working For Me Now | Ed 50603, Amb 3882 |

New York, c. March, 1920.

| | |
|---|---|
| 'Way Down Barcelona Way | Ed 50663, Amb 4260 |
| I'll See You In C-U-B-A | Amb 4072 |

New York, c. June, 1920.

| | | |
|---|---|---|
| 41246- | 'Way Down Barcelona Way | Em 10234 |

New York, c. August, 1920.

| | | |
|---|---|---|
| 41345- | Ding-a-Ring | Em 10255 |

New York, c. December, 1920.

| | | |
|---|---|---|
| 41549- | He Always Goes Farther Than Father | Em 10320 |

New York, c. March 1, 1921.

| | | |
|---|---|---|
| 41667- | Vamping Rose | Em 10354 |

New York, March, 1921.

| | | |
|---|---|---|
| 41686- | Hortense | Em 10364 |

New York, April, 1921.

| | | |
|---|---|---|
| 41739- | Ain't We Got Fun ? | Em 10386, Re 993 |

New York, c. July 21, 1921.

| 41915- | Ma ! | Em | , Re 9116 |
| | Kill 'Em With Kindness | | Re 9115 |

New York, October, 1921.

| 42005- | When Frances Dances With Me | Em 10475 |
| | Molly On A Trolley | Em | , Re 9119 |

New York, early September, 1923.

| 71818-B | Oh ! Min | OK 4941 |
| 71819-E | Three Thousand Years Ago | - |

New York, September 28, 1934.

38748-A　Home, James, And Don't Spare The　　　　Dec 215, F-5723, Pan 25668
　　　　　Horses - Part 1 (w/The Cavaliers)
38749-A　Home, James, And Don't Spare The　　　　-　　-　　-
　　　　　Horses - Part 2 (w/The Cavaliers)
38750-A　The Drunkard Song - Part 1 (Intro.　　　Dec 216, Pan 25689
　　　　　There Is A Tavern In The Town) (w/The Cavaliers)
38751-A　The Drunkard Song - Part 2 (Intro.　　　-　　-
　　　　　Fare-Thee-Well, For I Must Leave Thee) (w/The Cavaliers)
38752-A　The Man On The Flying Trapeze - Part 1　Dec 217, Pan 25667
　　　　　(w/The Cavaliers)
38753-A　The Man On The Flying Trapeze - Part 2　-　　-
　　　　　(w/The Cavaliers)

## ROBERT HILLIARD

Speech.　　　　　　　　　　　　　　New York, April 24, 1911.

B-10220-1　The Vampire (Rudyard Kipling)　　　Vic rejected
C-10221-1　A Fool There Was - Scene　　　　　-

New York, April 27, 1911.

C-10239-1　The Littlest Girl (A dramatization of　Vic rejected
　　　　　　Richard Harding Davis's story "Her First Appearance") - Part 1
C-10240-1　The Littlest Girl - Part 2　　　　-
C-10241-1　Como (Miller)　　　　　　　　　-

New York, October 5, 1911.

C-10222-2　A Fool There Was - Scene　　　　　Vic 70057, 55100

New York, October 6, 1911.

C-10239-2　The Littlest Girl - Part 1　　　　Vic 70058, 55099
C-10240-2　The Littlest Girl - Part 2　　　　-　　-

New York, November 8, 1912.

C-10241-2　Como (Miller)　　　　　　　　　Rejected
C-12602-1　Christmas Day In The Workhouse (Sims)　Vic 70093, 55100

New York, April 7, 1913.

C-13090-1　The Night Before Christmas　　　　Vic rejected

B. Auburn, N.Y., 1865; first stage success in title-role of KING DODO in 1901; later
hits include THE YANKEE CONSUL (Broadway, February 22, 1904); THE YANKEE    TOURIST
(Astor, August 12, 1907); THE MAN WHO OWNS BROADWAY (New York, October  11, 1909);
THE RED WIDOW (Astor, November 6, 1911); THE BEAUTY SHOP (a short run only, summer
1914); MY VALET (Knickerbocker, September 23, 1915); London debut and only appearance there, in MR. MANHATTAN (Prince of Wales, March 30, 1916); returned to U.S.A.
and appeared in BETTY (another short run,  September,   1916); greatest   success
in HITCHY KOO (Cohan and Harris, June 7, 1917, and new editions through 1921);most
famous straight part in THE OLD SOAK (Plymouth, August 22, 1922). D. November  25,
1929. (Also filmed in MY VALET (1915) and THE BEAUTY SHOP (1922).

Vocal, acc. by studio orchestra.          New York, January 25, 1910.

30342-2  Wal I Swan                            Col A-5162
30343-1  So What's The Use ?                   Col A-5165, 605

                                          New York, late May, 1910.

30503-2  Ain't It Funny What A Difference Just A  Col A-5231, 605
           Few Hours Make ?
30504-1  And The World Goes On                    -   606

                                          New York, c. mid-August, 1910.

30555-2  In The Days Of Old                    Col A-5257
30556-2  Recollections                         -

Humorous monologues, unacc.               New York, June 26, 1914.

C-15018-1-2  Mr. Hitchcock's Curtain Speech ("The  Vic rejected
           Beauty Shop")

                                          New York, July 21, 1914.

C-15018-3  Mr. Hitchcock's Curtain Speech ("The   Vic 55046, HMV 01114
           Beauty Shop")
C-15075-1-2  Burglar Story and The High Cost Of    Rejected
           Living
   NOTE:- HMV 01114 is entitled MR. HITCHCOCK - CANDIDATE FOR THE U.S. PRESIDENCY.

                                          New York, July 30, 1914.

C-15075-4  Burglar Story and The High Cost Of      Vic 55046, HMV 01115
           Living

Vocal, acc. by studio orchestra/G. W. Byng.
                                  Hayes, Middlesex, April 14, 1916.

HO-1766-AC  When You're All Dressed Up And No       HMV 02660, D-413
           Place To Go ("Mr. Manhattan")
HO-1767-AC  When You're All Dressed Up And No       Rejected
           Place To Go ("Mr. Manhattan")
HO-1768-AC/HO-1769-AC  My First Call On The Nobility  -

  Acc. by O/Eddie King.             New York, November 23, 1916.

C-18693-1-2-3  Sometime (w/Peerless Quartet)        Vic rejected
           ("Betty")
C-18694-1-2  Here Comes The Groom ("Betty")         -

                                          New York, December 11, 1916.

C-18693-4  Sometime (w/Peerless Quartet) ("Betty") Vic 55080
C-18694-3  Here Comes The Groom ("Betty")           -

Humorous monologue.                       New York, May, 1922.

  8937    Actors' Equity - An All-Star Comedy       Voc 35010 (part side)

B. Cincinnati, May 23, 1906; amateur actress who turned professional in 1924, touring in THE FOOL; New York debut in GARRICK GAIETIES (Garrick, June 8, 1925); other
Broadway successes included appearance in GREENWICH VILLAGE FOLLIES (46th Street,
May, 1926); MERRY-GO-ROUND (Klaw, May 31, 1927); outstanding in THE LITTLE SHOW at
the Music Box (April 30, 1929), with Fred Allen and Clifton Webb, and in   THREE'S
A CROWD (Selwyn, October 15, 1930); and REVENGE WITH MUSIC (New Amsterdam,   November 28, 1934); afflicted by personal tragedy (murder of husband Zachary Reynolds,
on July 5, 1932, after only a few months of marriage; their son killed, mountain-
climbing, aged 17; second husband Ralph Holmes took overdose of sleeping pills after they had separated); tried to make come-back with modest success in the 1960s;
d. Stamford, Conn., June 18, 1971.

Vocal, acc. by studio orchestra.          New York, c. September, 1927.

E-24576/7   Who's That Knockin' At My Door ?       Br 3667
E-24581     Carefree                               -

                                          New York, c. February, 1928.

            There Ain't No Sweet Man That's Worth   Br 3798
              The Salt Of My Tears
            The Way He Loves Is Just Too Bad         -

Acc. by Ralph Rainger-p.                  New York, June 5, 1929.

BVE-417     Can't We Be Friends ? ("The Little Show")Vic test
BVE-418     Moanin' Low ("The Little Show")        -

Acc. by studio orchestra.                 New York, July, 1929.

E-30296-    Am I Blue ?                            Br 4445
E-30297-    Moanin' Low ("The Little Show")        -       01058, Dec 7-2

                                          New York, September, 1929.

E-30829-    Can't We Be Friends ? ("The Little    Br 4506
              Show")
E-30830-    I May Be Wrong (But I Think You're     -
              Wonderful)

                                          New York, November, 1929.

E-31148-    Here Am I                              Br 4570
E-31149-    Why Was I Born ?                       -

                                          New York, December, 1929.

E-31526-    Happy Because I'm In Love              Br 4613
E-31527-    More Than You Know                     -

                                          New York, late January, 1930.

E-31973-    A Ship Without A Sail                  Br 4700
E-31974-    What Is This Thing Called Love ?       -

                                          New York, October, 1930.

E-34705/6   Body And Soul ("Three's A Crowd")      Br 4910
E-34708-    Something To Remember You By ("Three's  -      01058
              A Crowd")

                                          New York, late January, 1931.

E-35972-    I'm One Of God's Children (Who Hasn't  Br 6045, 01183
              Got Wings)
E-35973-    Love For Sale                          -

Vocalist with Richard Himber and his Ritz-Carlton Orchestra.
New York, December 19, 1934.

| | | |
|---|---|---|
| BS-86484-1 | You And The Night And The Music | Vic 24839 |
| BS-86485-1 | When You Love Only One | - |
| BS-86486-1 | Wand'ring Heart | Rejected |

Vocal, acc. by Josh White-g.                    New York, March 23, 1942.

| | | |
|---|---|---|
| 70561- | Baby, Baby | Dec 18304 |
| 70562- | Hansom' Winsome Johnny/Old Smoky | Dec 18306 |
| 70563- | The House Of The Risin' Sun | - |
| 70564- | When The Sun Goes Down | Dec 18305 |
| 70565- | Good Morning Blues | - |
| 70566- | Fare Thee Well | Dec 18304 |

Libby Holman also made two LPs in the 1960s of the songs she made famous (as above).

## TAYLOR  HOLMES

B. Newark, N.J., May 16, 1878; originally a concert entertainer; first professional appearance at Keith's, Boston, in vaudeville, May, 1899; debut in London later in the same year; many very successful appearances in New York and on tour : A GRAND ARMY MAN (Stuyvesant, October 16, 1907); THE MIDNIGHT SONS (Broadway, May 22,1909); THE COMMUTERS (Criterion, August 15, 1910); THE MILLION (39th Street, October 23, 1911); THE THIRD PARTY (Shubert, August 3, 1914); NOT SO FAST (Morosco, May 22, 1923); THAT'S GRATITUDE (Waldorf, June 16, 1932); I'D RATHER BE RIGHT(Alvin, November 2, 1937); MARINKA (Winter Garden, July 18, 1945) and many others; appeared in many films, beginning with EFFICIENCY EDGAR'S COURTSHIP (1917), followed during the next 40 years by RUGGLES OF RED GAP (title role) (1918); ONE HOUR OF LOVE (1928); THE FIRST BABY (1936); BOOMERANG (1947); FATHER OF THE BRIDE (1950); FIRST LEGION (1951); BEWARE MY LOVELY (1952); THE MAVERICK QUEEN (1956). D. 1959.

Speech, unacc., or acc. by Eddie King-p where shown.
New York, July 8, 1915.

| | | |
|---|---|---|
| B-16179-1-2 | I Couldn't Distinguish The Words - pEK | Rejected |
| B-16180-1-2 | If I Could Be By Her | - |
| B-16181-1-2 | Mrs. Dugan's Discovery | - |
| C-16182-1 | Gunga Din | Vic 55057 |
| C-16183-1 | Boots | - |

Acc. by O/Walter B. Rogers where shown. New York, July 29, 1915.

| | | |
|---|---|---|
| B-16180-3 | If I Could Be By Her | Vic 45073 |
| B-16181-3 | Mrs. Dugan's Discovery | Rejected |
| B-16277-2 | I Couldn't Distinguish The Words - O/WBR | Vic 45073 |
| C-16278-1-2 | The Green Eye Of The Little Yellow God - O/WBR | Rejected |
| B-16279-1-2 | The Spell Of The Yukon | - |

Acc. by Nat Shilkret-p.                     New York, October 27, 1923.

| | | |
|---|---|---|
| C-28784-1-2 | The Shooting Of Dan McGrew | Rejected |
| C-28785-1 | The Face On The Barroom Floor | Vic 55218 |

New York, December 11, 1923.

| | | |
|---|---|---|
| C-28784-3 | The Shooting Of Dan McGrew | Vic 55218 |

New York, December 13, 1923.

| | | |
|---|---|---|
| C-28784-4-5 | The Shooting Of Dan McGrew | Vic rejected |

Acc. by unknown p.                     New York, May 3, 1940.

| | | |
|---|---|---|
| 67670- | Casey At The Bat | Dec 15048 |

B. San Francisco, April 11, 1898; stage debut in vaudeville, Proctor's Theatre, New Jersey, 1914; New York debut also in vaudeville at the Palace, March, 1914; made a success in SCANDALS OF 1919 (Liberty, June 2, 1919); SCANDALS OF 1920 (Globe, June 7, 1920); MANHATTAN MARY (Apollo, September 26, 1927) and many other revues at the Liberty and Winter Garden theatres in New York from 1921 to 1926; YOU SAID IT(46th Street, January, 1931); London debut in TRANSATLANTIC RHYTHM (Adelphi, October 1, 1936), also appeared there in LAUGHTER OVER LONDON (Victoria Palace, December 7, 1936); made several films, beginning with FOLLOW THE LEADER in 1928.

Vocal, acc. by O/Rosario Bourdon.           Camden, N. J., April 30, 1923.

B-27787-1-2-3-4  Oh Sole, Oh Me !                   Vic rejected
B-27788-1-2-3-4  That's My Baby                        -

                                            Camden, N. J., May 10, 1923.

B-27787-6  Oh Sole, Oh Me !                  Vic 19079
B-27788-7  That's My Baby                       -

  Acc. by O/Eddie King.                     New York, November 19, 1923.

B-28968-4  Lovey Came Back                   Vic 19205
B-28969-4  When It's Night Time In Italy (It's    -
           Wednesday Over Here)

                                            New York, June 25, 1924.

B-30324-1  Oh Sole, Oh Me ! - 2nd Instalment    Vic 19403
B-30325-1  I Can't Get The One I Want              -

## BOB HOPE

B. Eltham, Kent, England; r.n. Leslie Townes Hope. To U.S.A. as a child, educated in Cleveland, Ohio; first a commercial clerk, then went into vaudeville; New York debut in SIDEWALKS OF NEW YORK (Knickerbocker, October 3, 1927); subsequently appeared in SMILES (Ziegfeld, November, 1930); ROBERTA (Ambassadors, November 18, 1933); SAY WHEN (Imperial, November, 1934); ZIEGFELD FOLLIES (Winter Garden, January 30, 1936); RED HOT AND BLUE (Alvin, October 29, 1936); to Hollywood, 1937, to begin film career with THE BIG BROADCAST OF 1938; many hilarious subsequent films, such as THANKS FOR THE MEMORY (1938); THE GHOST BREAKERS (1941); MY FAVORITE BLONDE (1942); STAR SPANGLED RHYTHM (1943); MY FAVORITE BRUNETTE (1946); THE PALEFACE (1947); THE SEVEN LITTLE FOYS (1955); THE FACTS OF LIFE (1960); CALL ME BWANA and CRITIC'S CHOICE (1963); and all the "Road" series of films with Bing Crosby, q.v., and Dorothy Lamour; tirelessly toured the war zones in World War II, Korea, Vietnam; Special Academy Awards, 1940, 1944, 1952; many very successful appearances in London in 1950s and 1960s. For records made in the period covered by this volume, see Shirley Ross.

## DE WOLF HOPPER

B. 1858, d. September 23, 1935; began law career, but deserted studies in 1879 to go on tour with own company (bass singer in light opera); most famous for his humorous monologue CASEY AT THE BAT, first performed at Wallack's Theater, New York, May 13, 1888, and subsequently some 10,000 times; produced and acted in various musicals from 1891; Sousa's EL CAPITAN (New York and on tour, 1896-1898, and in London, 1899); patter-songs in Gilbert and Sullivan were his specialty. He was married 6 times; published memoirs (ONCE A CLOWN, ALWAYS A CLOWN) in 1927; filmed in silent version of DON QUIXOTE, 1915; r.n. William D'Wolf.

Humorous monologues, unacc.              New York, July 17, 1907.

C-3537-1  Casey At The Bat                  Vic 31559

                                           New York, June 16, 1909.

C-3537-4  Casey At The Bat                  Vic 31559, 35290

                                           New York, May, 1922.

  8937  Actors' Equity - An All-Star Comedy    Voc 35010  (part side)

Vocal, acc. by O/Joseph Pasternack.          Camden, N. J., May 29, 1925.

       Tit Willow                                 Vic test
       The Man With An Elephant On His Hands           -

Humorous monologues, unacc.                  New York, August 25, 1926.

CVE-3537-5-6  Casey At The Bat                    Vic rejected
CVE-36130-1-2-3  O'Toole's Touchdown                   -

                     New York, September 1, 1926.

CVE-3537-9  Casey At The Bat                      Vic 35783, LCT-1112
CVE-36130-6  O'Toole's Touchdown                       -

## LENA HORNE

B. 1918; began professional career singing in night-clubs with dance bands,  notably
  Noble Sissle's; took part in NBC CHAMBER MUSIC SOCIETY OF LOWER BASIN STREET radio
  shows, 1940-1942; to Hollywood to begin film career with well-remembered  pictures
  as CABIN IN THE SKY and STORMY WEATHER (1943); TWO GIRLS AND A SAILOR (1944); TILL
  THE CLOUDS ROLL BY (1945); continued cabaret work, appearing in London very  successfully.

Vocalist with Noble Sissle and his Orchestra.
                     New York, March 11, 1936.

60888-A  That's What Love Did To Me               Dec 778
60892-A  I Take To You                            Dec 847, Col DB-5032
  NOTE:- Other titles from this session do not feature Lena Horne.

Vocalist with Henry Levine and the Dixieland Jazz Group of NBC's Chamber Music Society of Lower Basin Street.          New York, June 23, 1941.

BS-066127-1  St. Louis Blues                      Vic 27542, HMV BD-5819
BS-066128-1  Careless Love                        Vic 27545, HMV BD-5827

                     New York, June 25, 1941.

BS-066144-1  Aunt Hagar's Blues                   Vic 27544
BS-066145-1  Beale Street Blues                   Vic 27543, HMV BD-5819

Vocalist with Artie Shaw and his Orchestra.
                     New York, June 26, 1941.

BS-066147-1  Love Me A Little Little               Vic 27509, 20-2994, HMV B-9322
BS-066149-1  Don't Take Your Love From Me            - 20-1593, 20-2865     -
  NOTE:- Other titles from this session do not feature Lena Horne.

Vocalist with Teddy Wilson and his Orchestra.
                     New York, September 16, 1941.

31320-1  Out Of Nowhere                           Col 36737
31321-1  Prisoner Of Love                         V-Disc 317

Vocal, acc. by O/Lou Bring.             Hollywood, December 15, 1941.

PBS-061977-1  Stormy Weather                       Vic 27819
PBS-061978-1  What Is This Thing Called Love ?     Vic 27820
PBS-061979-1  Ill Wind (You're Blowin' Me No Good) Vic 27819
PBS-061980-1  The Man I Love                       Vic 27818

                 Hollywood, December 17, 1941.

PBS-061985-1  Where Or When                        Vic 27818
PBS-061986-1  I Gotta Right To Sing The Blues      Vic 27817
PBS-061987-1  Mad About The Boy                    Vic 27820
PBS-061988-1  Moanin' Low                          Vic 27817

Lena Horne made many records, mostly for MGM, after 1942.

B. New York, February 12, 1878; boy soprano in vaudeville at eleven; toured in stock
   company production of LITTLE EVA; produced, directed and wrote music for  Broadway
   shows; many other individual hits (HELLO, MY BABY (1899); GOODBYE, MY LADY  LOVE
   (1900); I WONDER WHO'S KISSING HER NOW (1909), the latter being the title of a 1947
   film of the composer's life; appeared at the St. Louis Fair, 1904; night clubs,  on
   radio (notably GAY NINETIES REVUE), TV; d. on stage in Chicago, May 19, 1961.


Vocal, acc. by studio orchestra.            New York, March, 1920.

  68375    Whistle A Song                         Pathe 22361

                                            New York, c. April, 1929.

E-29457-   Honeymoon                        Br 4340
E-29460-   Blow The Smoke Away               -
  NOTE:- Matrices E-29458/9 are not by Joe Howard.

                                            New York, October 15, 1936.

  20077-   I Wonder Who's Kissing Her Now/Honeymoon Voc 3357
  20078-   Hello, My Baby/Goodbye, My Lady Love        -

Acc. by Gene Kardos and his Orchestra.  New York, February 17, 1938.

P-22442-   What's The Use Of Dreaming ?      Br Private Recording
P-22443-   If You Should Stop Caring          -
P-22444-   I Wonder Who's Kissing Her Now ?   -
P-22445-   Meet Me At The New York Fair       -
P-22446-   Goodbye, My Lady Love              -
P-22447-   Medley (no details known)          -

Joe Howard also recorded eight sides for De Luxe records in Cincinnati in 1947,  com-
prising eight of his own songs used in the film.

## LESLIE  HOWARD

B. London, April 24, 1893; originally a bank clerk, but on being invalided out of the
   Army in 1917, took up stage work.  Made several small-part films, then went to U.S.
   to play prominent role in OUTWARD BOUND (1930); subsequently played important parts
   in SMILING THROUGH (1932); BERKELEY SQUARE (1933); OF HUMAN BONDAGE; BRITISH AGENT;
   THE SCARLET PIMPERNEL (all 1934); THE PETRIFIED FOREST and ROMEO AND JULIET (1936);
   PYGMALION (which he co-directed, 1938); GONE WITH THE WIND and INTERMEZZO or ESCAPE
   TO HAPPINESS (1939); 49TH PARALLEL (1941); THE FIRST OF THE FEW (1942), the  latter
   two being made in England.  The plane in which he was travelling from Portugal back
   to London on June 1, 1943 was shot down by Nazi fighters, and Leslie Howard died.

Speech.                                     Location unknown, c. 1925.

        A Serious Obstacle                      Spoken Word 203

## WILLIE  HOWARD

B. Neustadt, Germany, April 13, 1886; debut in Proctor's 125th St. Theatre, N.Y.; appeared in THE LITTLE DUCHESS with Anna Held (Casino, October 14, 1901); on tour all
   over U.S.A. in vaudeville with brother (Eugene), 1902-1912; took part in nine PASS-
   ING SHOWS at the Winter Garden (July 22, 1912; July 24, 1913; June 10, 1914;May 29,
   1915; June 22, 1916; April 26, 1917; July 25, 1918; October 23, 1919;  December 29,
   1920), also at the same theatre in THE WHIRL OF THE WORLD (January 10, 1914)and THE
   SHOW OF WONDERS (October 26, 1916); toured in vaudeville again, 1922-1925;  starred
   in SKY HIGH (Shubert, March 2, 1925); in four editions of GEORGE WHITE'S  SCANDALS,
   at the Apollo (June 14, 1926; July 2, 1928; September 23, 1929; September 14,1931);
   two further editions of the same production (New Amsterdam, December 25, 1935,  and
   Alvin, August 28, 1939); also two further Winter Garden shows (ZIEGFELD FOLLIES  OF
   1934, January 4, 1934, and THE SHOW IS ON, which he joined in June, 1937);  various
   other shows in New York and Chicago, toured with THE PASSING SHOW, 1945-1946; r. n.
   William Levkowitz; d. New York, January 12, 1949.

Vocal, acc. by studio orchestra.          New York, April 22, 1925.

140547-   The Barber Of Seville ("Sky High")      Col 370-D
140548-   Let It Rain ("Sky High")                 -

New York, September 3, 1925.

140897-   My Yiddishe Momme                        Col 473-D
140898-   When Nathan Was Married To Rose Of       Col 455-D
          Washington Square ("Ziegfeld Follies of 1925")

New York, September 4, 1925.

140903-   Valeska (My Russian Rose)                Col 455-D
140904-   After The Opera (w/Eugene Howard)        Col 473-D

New York, c. early 1936.

B-2416   Got A Gal In Calif-orn-ia               Dec Private Recording

Willie Howard also made a Gala LP and appeared on Jubilee 3507 in two numbers, SALTY
PAUL PETER and (with Al "Doubletalk" Kelly), PROFESSOR PIERRE MARQUETTE.

## WALTER HUSTON

B. Toronto, Canada, April 6, 1884; stage debut there in 1902; New York debut in 1905
followed by minor roles; left stage, but returned in vaudeville, 1909, and toured
in this medium with his first wife (Bayonne Whipple) in sketches; returned to New
York and appeared in many successful shows, e.g., DESIRE UNDER THE ELMS (Greenwich
Village, November 11, 1924); KONGO (Biltmore, March 30, 1926); THE BARKER(Biltmore
January 18, 1927); DODSWORTH (in title role) (Shubert, February 24, 1934, touring
in this, 1935-1936, also in OTHELLO); KNICKERBOCKER HOLIDAY (Ethel Barrymore, Oct-
ober 19, 1938); APPLE OF HIS EYE (Biltmore, February 5, 1946); made many very pop-
ular films, beginning with GENTLEMEN OF THE PRESS (1928); then in such as ABRAHAM
LINCOLN (1930); LAW AND ORDER (as Wyatt Earp, 1932); KONGO and RAIN (1932); RHODES
OF AFRICA (made in England in 1936); THE LIGHT THAT FAILED (1940); ALWAYS IN MY
HEART; YANKEE DOODLE DANDY and MISSION TO MOSCOW (all 1942); DRAGON SEED (1944);
DUEL IN THE SUN (1946); THE TREASURE OF SIERRA MADRE (1947). D. 1950.

Vocal, acc. by O/Maurice Abravanel.       New York, November 24, 1938.

B-23732-   September Song ("Knickerbocker Holiday")Br 8272, Fon TFE-17186
B-23733-   The Scars ("Knickerbocker Holiday")     -

Walter Huston re-made his famous SEPTEMBER SONG for Decca in 1947.

## BETTY HUTTON

B. 1921; first professional work as vivacious singer with Vincent Lopez and his Suave
Swing Orchestra, 1939; stage debut in New York in PANAMA HATTIE (46th Street, Oct-
ober 30, 1940); to Hollywood, 1942, to begin film career in THE FLEET'S IN; other
outstanding pictures include THE MIRACLE OF MORGAN'S CREEK and LET'S FACE IT(1943);
HERE COME THE WAVES and AND THE ANGELS SING (1944); INCENDIARY BLONDE (1945); THE
PERILS OF PAULINE (1947); ANNIE, GET YOUR GUN (1950); SOMEBODY LOVES ME '1952);THE
GREATEST SHOW ON EARTH (1953). She has made a number of records as soloist in the
years since 1942, mostly for Victor and Capitol.

Vocalist with Vincent Lopez and his Suave Swing Orchestra.
                                          Chicago, May 8, 1939.

BS-036457-1-2 Igloo                       BB rejected

Chicago, May 25, 1939.

BS-036457-3 Igloo                         BB B-10300
BS-034904-1 Concert In The Park (w/Sonny Schuyler)  -

Chicago, July 5, 1939.

BS-040247-1  The Jitterbug                BB B-10367

Negro vocal quartet consisting of Charles Fuqua-tenor voice-g-u/Bill Kenny-tenor-cym-
bal/Ivory Watson-baritone-g/Orville Jones-baritone-sb, formed in 1934, and imported
into England by impresario-bandleader Jack Hylton. Fame followed on their   return,
and for two decades they were among the most consistently popular artists on radio,
theatre and records; they visited and entertained at service camps all over America
during the war, and afterwards made very successful visits to Great Britain.

Vocal, self-acc.                                    New York, January 4, 1935.

BS-87269-1   Swingin' On The Strings               Vic 24851, BB B-6530,  HMV BD-146
BS-87270-1   Your Feet's Too Big                       -            -              -
BS-87271-1   Don't 'Low No Swingin' In Here        Vic 24876, HMV B-8418
BS-87272-1   Swing, Gate, Swing                        -            -

                                                    New York, May 12, 1936.

61104-A   Your Feet's Too Big                       Dec 817, Col DB-5031
61105-A   'Tain't Nobody's Biz-ness If I Do             -            -

                                                    New York, June 18, 1936.

61188-A   Stompin' At The Savoy                     Dec 1036, Br 02280, Col FB-1513
61189-A   Old Joe's Hittin' The Jug                 Dec 883
61190-A   Keep Away From My Doorstep                Dec 1036, Br 02280, Col FB-1513
61191-A   Christopher Columbus                      Dec 883

                                                    New York, February 5, 1937.

61581-A   Alabama Barbecue                          Dec 1154, Br 02422
61582-A   Don't Let Old Age Creep Up On You         Dec 1731, Br 02407
61583-A   With Plenty Of Money And You              Dec 1154, Br 02422
61584-A   Yes Suh !                                 Dec 1731, Br 02407

                                                    New York, April 9, 1937.

62120-A   Whoa Babe !                               Dec 1236, Br 02431
62121-A   Let's Call The Whole Thing Off            Dec 1251, Br 02440
62122-A   Swing High, Swing Low                     Dec 1236, Br 02431
62123-A   Slap That Bass                            Dec 1251, Br 02440

                                                    New York, March 25, 1938.

63494-A   Oh ! Red                                  Dec 1789, Br 02606
63495-B   That Cat Is High                              -            -

                                                    New York, May 19, 1938.

63813-A   I Wish You The Best Of Everything         Dec 1870, Br 02637
63814-B   When The Sun Goes Down                        -            -

                                                    New York, August 31, 1938.

64485-A   Pork Chops And Gravy                      Dec 2044, Br 02673
64486-A   Brown Gal                                     -            -

                                                    New York, January 12, 1939.

64891-A   If I Didn't Care                          Dec 2286, 23632, DL-4297,
                                                    DX-182, Br 02734, Coral CP-46
64892-A   Just For A Thrill                         Dec 2507, Br 02812       -
64893-A   Knock-Kneed Sal (On The Mourner's Bench)  Dec 2286, Br 02734

                                                    New York, May 17, 1939.

65584-A   It's Funny To Everyone But Me             Dec 2507, 29750, DL-4297,
                                                    Br 02812

New York, August 17, 1939.

| 66118-A | You Bring Me Down | Dec 2707, Br 02902 |
| 66119-A | I Don't Want Sympathy, I Want Love | Dec 2841, Br 03433 |
| 66120-A | Address Unknown | Dec 2707, DL-4297, DX-182, Br 02902 |
| 66121-A | Coquette | Dec 3077, Br 03017, Coral CP-46 |

New York, September 18, 1939.

| 66608-A | My Prayer | Dec 2790, DL-4297, DX-182, Br 02935 |
| 66609-A | Give Her My Love | As above |

New York, October 3, 1939.

| 66463-B | Memories Of You | Dec 2966, 29750, Br 02981 |
| 66464-A-B | Puttin' And Takin' | Rejected |

New York, October 6, 1939.

| 66737-A | Thoughtless | Dec 18711, Br 03040 |
| 66738-A | I'm Through | Dec 2966, Br 02981 |
| 66739-A | What Can I Do ? | Dec 3195, Br 03054 |

New York, October 11, 1939.

| 66752-B | I'm Gettin' Sentimental Over You | Dec 3077, 25239, Br 03017, Coral CP-46 |
| 66753-A | Bless You | Dec 2841, 23757, Br 03040 |

New York, May 13, 1940.

| 67718-A | When The Swallows Come Back To Capistrano | Dec 3195, 25240, DX-182, Br 03054 |

New York, June 11, 1940.

| 67862-A | Whispering Grass (Don't Tell The Trees) | Dec 3258, 23632, DL-4297, DX-182, Br 03075, Coral CP-46 |
| 67863-A | Maybe | Dec 3258, 23634, DX-182, Br 03075 Coral CP-46 |

New York, June 18, 1940.

| 67876-A-B | You're Breaking My Heart All Over Again | Dec rejected |

New York, June 26, 1940.

| 67898-A | Stop Pretending (So Hep You See) | Dec 3288, Br 03095 |
| 67899-A | I'm Only Human | Dec 3468, Br 04189 |
| 67900-A | You're Breaking My Heart All Over Again | Dec 3288, Br 03095 |

New York, July 16, 1940.

| 67928-A | We Three (My Echo, My Shadow And Me) | Dec 3379, 23634, DL-4297, DX-182, Br 03109, Coral CP-46 |
| 67929-A-B | So Sorry | Rejected |
| 67930-A | Puttin' And Takin' | Dec 3468 |
| 67931-A | Java Jive | Dec 3432, 23633, DX-182, Br 03197, Coral CP-46 |

New York, August 8, 1940.

| 67968-A | I'll Never Smile Again (Until I Smile At You) | Dec 3346, 23635, DX-182, Br 03081, Coral CP-46 |
| 67969-A-B | I Could Make You Care | Rejected |
| 67970-A | Do I Worry ? | Dec 3432, 23633, DL-4297, DX-182, Br 03197, Coral CP-46 |

New York, August 20, 1940.

| | | |
|---|---|---|
| 67969-D | I Could Make You Care | Dec 3346, Br 03109 |
| 67990-A | My Greatest Mistake | Dec 3379, 25237, Br 03081 |
| 67991-A | Don't Ever Break A Promise | Br 04183 |
| 67992-A-B | Ring, Telephone, Ring | Rejected |

New York, August 21, 1940.

| | | |
|---|---|---|
| 67999-A-B | In The Doorway (Where We Used To Kiss<br>Goodnight) | Dec rejected |

New York, December 23, 1940.

| | | |
|---|---|---|
| 68532-A | So Sorry | Dec 3806, Br 03173 |
| 68533-A | Ring, Telephone, Ring | Dec 3626, 25378 - |
| 68534-B | You're Looking For Romance (And I'm<br>Looking For Love) | Dec 3656, Br 04183 |
| 68535- | I Can't Stand Losing You | Br 04184 |
| 68536- | That's When Your Heartaches Begin | Dec 3720, Br 03674 |
| 68537- | I'm Still Without A Sweetheart ('Cause<br>I'm Still In Love With You) | Dec 3806, Br 04184 |
| 68538- | Why Didn't You Tell Me ? | Br 03673 |
| 68539- | I Wish I Could Say The Same | - |
| 68540- | I'd Climb The Highest Mountain (If I<br>Knew I'd Find You) | Dec 18711, 25239, 10262 |
| 68541- | What Good Would It Do ? | Dec 3720, Br 03674 |

New York, January 23, 1941.

| | | |
|---|---|---|
| TNY-911 | Please Take A Letter, Miss Brown | Dec 3626 |

New York, February 4, 1941.

| | | |
|---|---|---|
| 68655- | Driftwood | Dec 29957, Br 04188 |
| 68656- | We'll Meet Again | Dec 3656, DX-182, Br 04187,<br>Coral CP-46 |

New York, July 25, 1941.

| | | |
|---|---|---|
| 69565- | Keep Cool, Fool | Dec 3958, 25237, Br 04188 |
| 69566- | (It Will Have To Do) Until The Real<br>Thing Comes Along | -          23635, DX-182,<br>Br 04187, Coral CP-46 |
| 69567- | Hey Doc ! | Dec 3987, Br 03260 |

New York, August 12, 1941.

| | | |
|---|---|---|
| 69633-A | It Isn't A Dream Any More | Dec 4194, Br 03377 |
| 69634-A | Nothin' | Dec 4045, Br 03314 |

New York, August 27, 1941.

| | | |
|---|---|---|
| 69660- | I Don't Want To Set The World On Fire | Dec 3987, DL-4297, DX-182,<br>Br 03260 |
| 69671-A | Don't Leave Now | Dec 4303, 25378, Br 03360 |

NOTE:- Matrices 69661/70 inclusive are not by the Ink Spots.

New York, October 6, 1941.

| | | |
|---|---|---|
| 69786-A | Foo-Gee | Dec 4303, Br 03360 |
| 69787- | Mine, All Mine, My My | Dec 18528, Br 04189 |
| 69788-A | I'm Not The Same Old Me | Dec 18461, Br 03460 |

New York, October 13, 1941.

| | | |
|---|---|---|
| 69807-A | Someone's Rocking My Dreamboat | Dec 4045, DL-4297, DX-182,<br>Br 03314 |
| 69808-A | Shout, Brother, Shout | Dec 4194, ·Br 03377 |

New York, November 17, 1941.

| 69949-A | It's A Sin To Tell A Lie | Dec 4112, Br 03653 |
| 69950-A | Is It A Sin (My Loving You) | -        - |

New York, May 19, 1942.

| 70762-A | Don't Tell A Lie About Me, Dear (And I Won't Tell The Truth About You) | Dec 18383, Br 04014 |
| 70763-A | Who Wouldn't Love You ? | -       Br 03404 |

New York, June 23, 1942.

| 70917-A | Ev'ry Night About This Time | Dec 18461, 29957, Br 03433 |
| 70918-A-B | Knock Me A Kiss | Rejected |

New York, July 28, 1942.

| 71233-A | Street Of Dreams | Dec 18503, DL-4297, DX-182, Br 03524 |
| 71234- | I'll Never Make The Same Mistake Again | Dec 18542, Br 04190 |
| 71235-B | Just As Though You Were Here | Dec 18466, Br 04014 |
| 71236- | If I Cared A Little Bit Less | Dec 18528, Br 04190 |
| 71237-A | Don't Get Around Much Any More | Dec 18503, DL-4297, DX-182, Br 03460 |
| 71238-A | This Is Worth Fighting For | Dec 18466, Br 03404 |

## MAY IRWIN

B. Whitby, Ontario, Canada, June 27, 1862; r.n. Ada Campbell; made stage debut with her sister Flora (February 8, 1875), and worked at Tony Pastor's in New York; in 1893 she composed MAMIE and sang it in A COUNTRY SPORT (Bijou, December 25, 1893) - most of her other hits were adaptations of genuine negro ragtime songs - and later, she introduced her biggest success, THE BULLY SONG (I'M LOOKIN' FOR THE BULLY OF THE TOWN) by sports writer Charles E. Trevathan, in THE WIDOW JONES (Bijou, February 16, 1896); he also composed her FROG SONG. She also appeared in COURTED IN COURT (Bijou, December 29, 1896), in which she sang the white ragtime composer Ben Harney's MISTER JOHNSON, TURN ME LOOSE, and introduced the teenage George M. Cohan as a songwriter by featuring his HOT TAMALE ALLEY the previous year. An early song by Gus Edwards, I COULDN'T STAND TO SEE MY BABY LOSE, became part of her repertoire in 1899. Filmed THE KISS SCENE from THE WIDOW JONES in 1896 and MRS. BLACK IS BACK for the Famous Players in 1914. D. October 22, 1938.

Vocal, acc. by studio orchestra.              New York, May 20, 1907.

| C-4510-1 | Moses Andrew Jackson, Goodbye | Vic 31641 |
| C-4511-1 | The Bully ("The Widow Jones") | Vic 31642, 35050 |
| B-4512-1-2 | Mat-ri-money | Rejected |

New York, May 21, 1907.

| B-4512-4 | Mat-ri-money | Vic 5151 |
| C-4513-2 | When You Ain't Got No Money, You Needn't Come Around | Vic 31648, 35050 |
| B-4514-1 | May Irwin's Frog Song | Vic 5156, 17253 |

New York, May 22, 1907.

| C-4510-3 | Moses Andrew Jackson, Goodbye | Rejected |
| B-4520-2 | Don't Argify | Vic 5157, 16058 |

## HARRY JAMES

The namesake of the famous "swing" trumpet player, and of the man who discovered the Original Dixieland Jazz Band, was an Englishman who made a great hit on radio during its earliest days in the U.S.A., having entertained American soldiers in World War I, and having supervised the entertainment work in 42 reconstruction hospitals, for 75,000 wounded American and Allied soldiers. Needless to say, he is not in any way identifiable with either of the other show-business personalities of this name!

Humorous monologues.                            Richmond, Ind., February 27, 1923.

| 11331 | An Englishman At A Ball Game | Gnt 5092 |
| 11332 | An Englishman's Idea Of American Wit | - |

                                                Richmond, Ind., February 28, 1923.

| 11334 | When Knighthood Blooms | Gnt 5093 |
| 11335 | Jokes Too Deep For An Englishman - Part 1 | |
| 11336 | Jokes Too Deep For An Englishman - Part 2 | |
| 11337 | American Wit - Part 1 | |
| 11338 | American Wit - Part 2 | |

Speech.                                         Richmond, Ind., March 3, 1923.

| 11339 | A Republican's Creed | Gnt rejected |
| 11340 | Lincoln's Gettysburg Address | - |
| 11341 | American Wit - Part 3 | - |

NOTE:- The reverse of Gennett 5093 is labelled IS MARRIAGE A FAILURE ?  This is presumably a re-titling of one of the other four sides made on February 28, 1923,  but
at the time of writing, no copy has been found by which this can be identified.

## ELSIE  JANIS

B. Columbus, Ohio, March 16, 1889; stage debut there as Cain (a boy) in THE   CHARITY
BALL (December 24, 1897); New York debut in vaudeville at the Casino Theatre   Roof
Garden, June, 1900; toured for three years all over the U.S.A.; appeared in WHEN WE
WERE FORTY-ONE IN July, 1905 at the New York Roof Garden, imitating famous artists;
as a result was engaged to take part in THE VANDERBILT CUP (Broadway, January   16,
1906); very successful run, followed by long tour; returned to New York to play   in
THE HOYDEN (Knickerbocker, October 14, 1907); toured in THE FAIR CO-ED, opening   in
this at the Knickerbocker, February 1, 1909; toured in THE SLIM PRINCESS, appearing
in this at the Globe, N.Y., January 2, 1911; followed this on March 30, 1911 in her
own play A STAR FOR A NIGHT; toured again in THE SLIM PRINCESS; returned to   Globe
in THE LADY OF THE SLIPPER (October 28, 1912); London debut in THE PASSING SHOW, at
the Palace, April 20, 1914 (huge success); returned to U.S.A., but was re-engaged a
year later for THE PASSING SHOW OF 1915 (Palace, March 9, 1915); returned to U.S.A.
to appear in various productions, notably THE CENTURY GIRL (Century, Nov. 6, 1916);
returned to Europe to entertain front-line troops in France, 1918; starred again at
the Palace in HULLO, AMERICA (September 25, 1918); devised her own show  under  the
name ELSIE JANIS AND HER GANG (Academy of Music, Baltimore, November, 1919; Gaiety,
New York, January, 1922; Queen's, London, November, 1924); entered on management of
the Queen's Theatre, London, opening December 13, 1920 with her own revue IT'S   ALL
WRONG; also wrote and appeared in PUZZLES OF 1925 (Fulton, N.Y., February 2, 1925);
toured U.S.A. in 1927 in title-role of OH ! KAY; last appearance in London in  September, 1928 in CLOWNS IN CLOVER (Adelphi); wrote dozens of songs and three  books:
LOVE LETTERS OF AN ACTRESS; IF I KNOW WHAT I MEAN and her autobiography, SO FAR, SO
GOOD.  Film career began 1917 with PRETTY MRS. SMITH; then made BETTY IN SEARCH  OF
A THRILL; A REGULAR GIRL; A MERRY MADCAP; NEARLY A LADY; 'TWAS EVER THUS, and other
silents; only one talkie, WOMEN IN WAR (1942).  D. Hollywood, February 27, 1956.

Vocal, acc. by the Victor Orchestra/? Walter B. Rogers.
                                      New York, October 22, 1912.

| B-12527-1 | That Fascinating Baseball Slide | Vic 60090 |
| B-12528-1 | When Antelo Plays The 'Cello ("The Slim | Vic 60093 |
| | Princess") | |
| B-12529-1 | Fo' De Lawd's Sake, Play A Waltz | Vic 60091, AR 2290 |

   Acc. by studio orchestra/? George W. Byng.
                                      London, June 4, 1914.

| AK-17912e | Florrie Was A Flapper ("The Passing | HMV 2-3029, B-488 |
| | Show") | |
| AK-17914e | You're Here And I'm Here (w/Basil | HMV 2-4201     - |
| | Hallam) ("The Passing Show") | |
| AL-8002f | I've Got Everything I Want But You (w/ | HMV 04116, C-597 |
| | Basil Hallam) ("The Passing Show") | |

   NOTE:- Matrices AK-17913e and AL-8001f are rejected takes of the titles following.

Hayes, Middlesex, June 30, 1914.

| AK-18015e | When We Tango To "The Wearing Of The Green" | HMV 2-3053, B-489 |
| AK-18017e | The Anti-Ragtime Girl | Rejected |
| AK-18018e | I Want A Dancing Man | HMV 2-3040, B-489 |

NOTE:- Matrix AK-18016e is a rejected take of the preceding title.

Acc. by the Palace Theatre Orchestra/Herman Finck.

Hayes, Middlesex, April 15, 1915.

| HO-1381-AE | Ballin' The Jack (w/Basil Hallam) ("The Passing Show of 1915") | HMV 2-4251, B-485 |
| HO-755-AF | Prudence ("The Passing Show of 1915") | HMV 03403, C-566 |
| HO-757-AF | The Fortune Teller ("The Passing Show of 1915") | HMV 03402, C-569 |
| HO-758-AF | The Same Old Song (w/Basil Hallam) ("The Passing Show of 1915") | HMV 04126, C-566 |

NOTE:- Matrix HO-756-AF is by Basil Hallam, Elsie Janis's fiance (killed in action August 20, 1916; note the last title of the next session).

Hayes, Middlesex, August 22, 1916.

| HO-2094-AF | Yaaka Hula Hickey Dula | HMV 03511, D-388 |
| HO-2095-AF | I'm Not Prepared | HMV 03526 |
| HO-2096-AF | Along The Rocky Road To Dublin | HMV 03512 |
| HO-2097-AF | When You're Down In Louisville (Call On Me) | HMV 03516 |
| HO-2098-AF | A Little Love (But Not For Me) | Rejected |

Hayes, Middlesex, November 22, 1918.

| HO-4513-AE | I Love Them All A Little Bit (w/ chorus) ("Hullo, America") | HMV 2-3315, E-174 |
| HO-4515-AE | The Jazz Band ("Hullo, America") | HMV 2-3314    - |
| HO-3518-AF | Apres la Guerre (w/Owen Nares-Stanley Lupino-Will West) ("Hullo, America") | HMV 04248, D-434 |
| HO-3520-AF | The Picture I Want To See (w/Owen Nares) ("Hullo, America") | HMV 04247    - |
| HO-3522-AF | Give Me The Moonlight, Give Me The Girl - Part 2 ("Hullo, America") | HMV 03630, D-435 |
| HO-3523-AF | Give Me The Moonlight, Give Me The Girl - Part 1 ("Hullo, America") | HMV 03629    - |

NOTE:- Matrices HO-4512-AE, HO-4514-AE, HO-3517-AF and HO-3519-AF are rejected recordings of the titles following them; HO-3521-AF is a speech by the Rt. Hon. Winston Churchill, M.P., all recorded on the same day !

Acc. by studio orchestra/George W. Byng.

Hayes, Middlesex, March 21, 1919.

| HO-4764-AE | The Darktown Strutters' Ball (A Jazz Melody) | HMV 2-3329, E-167 |
| HO-3652/3-AF | Homesickness Blues | Rejected |
| HO-3654/5-AF | Mr. Jazz Himself | - |
| HO-3656-AF | Smiles | HMV 03645, D-388 |

NOTE· Matrices HO-4763-AE and HO-3657-AF are rejected takes of the succeeding and preceding titles respectively.

## HARRY JANS-HAROLD WHALEN

Cross-talk comedians very popular briefly in radio and cabaret during the 1920s.

Humorous dialogue, unacc.                New York, August 25, 1927.

| BVE-39116-1-2 | Just A Couple Of Good Guys Gone Wrong | Vic rejected |

New York, September 12, 1927.

| BVE-39116- | Just A Couple Of Good Guys Gone Wrong | Vic 21022, HMV B-2675 |
| BVE-39174- | Well ! Well ! Well ! | -        - |

Vocal, acc. by O/Nat Shilkret.            New York, April 16, 1928.

BVE-43566-3-4  Well, The Irish And The Germans     Vic 21367
               Got Together

## GLORIA  JEAN

B. 1928; signed by Universal Pictures as rival to Deanna Durbin; appeared in various
   singing roles in such films as THE UNDERPUP (1939); IF I HAD MY WAY; A LITTLE  BIT
   OF HEAVEN and PARDON MY RHYTHM (1940); MOONLIGHT IN VERMONT (1941); SHE'S MY LOVE-
   LY (1942); OLD-FASHIONED GIRL (1943); I'LL REMEMBER APRIL (1944); COPACABANA(1947);
   THERE'S A GIRL IN MY HEART (1949) and others; retired, but emerged to appear in THE
   LADIES' MAN (1961); r.n. Gloria Jean Schoonover.

Vocal, acc. by O/Victor Young.            Los Angeles, December 12, 1939.

DLA-1885-A  Annie Laurie (Film "The Underpup")      Dec 3116, Br 03113
DLA-1886-A  Love's Old Sweet Song                   Dec 3117      -
DLA-1887-A  If I Only Were A Swallow (La Vilanelle)     -      Br 02970

                                          Los Angeles, December 14, 1939.

DLA-1904-A  Penguin Song (To the music of "High    Dec 3116, Br 02970
              School Cadets March" - Sousa) (Film "The Underpup")
DLA-1905-A  Lo ! Hear (sic) The Gentle Lark        Dec 15047, Br 0149
DLA-1906-A  I'm Like A Bird (Film "The Underpup")       -        -

Acc. by O/Charles Previn.                 Los Angeles, October 1, 1940.

DLA-2163-   After Ev'ry Rainstorm (Film "A Little  Dec 3449
              Bit Of Heaven")
DLA-2164-   A Little Bit Of Heaven (Film "A Little     -
              Bit Of Heaven")

## JOSEPH JEFFERSON

B. 1829; debut with Jim Crow 1833 (tumbled out of a sack !); toured with family, but
   his father died in 1842 and there followed a long period of unrewarding hard work.
   Began to be famous as actor by 1849; to Europe, 1856; joined Laura Keene's  company
   on return to U.S.A., success at the theatre in New York bearing her name  in    OUR
   AMERICAN COUSIN (October 18, 1858); first wife died 1861, but he went on a tour  of
   Australia until 1865, then to London to play his most famous part for the first  of
   many times: the title role in RIP VAN WINKLE under Boucicault's direction (Adelphi,
   September 4, 1865); played it in New York first time 1866, and little else     until
   1880; succeded Edwin Booth as President of the Players' Club, 1893; last appearance
   on stage May 7, 1904 (in DOT, first played by him at the Winter Garden in 1860); d.
   April 23, 1905.  Only daughter m. B. L. Farjeon; their children included revue com-
   pilers and writers Herbert and Eleanor Farjeon.  Filmed scenes from RIP VAN WINKLE,
   1903, for Biograph.
Dramatic monologues.                      New York, December 27, 1897.

          The Toast ("Rip Van Winkle")          Ber 698-Z

                                New York, c. April, 1903.

1468-   Scene in the Mountains ("Rip Van Winkle")Col 1468, A-385, 32229 (cyl.)
1469-   Rip Meets Meenie After Twenty Years       Col 1469, A-390, 32230 (cyl.),
          ("Rip Van Winkle")                      Folkways 3886
NOTE:- The cylinders are different takes from the discs.

## GEORGE  JESSEL

B. New York, April 3, 1898; stage debut in vaudeville in 1907 with Gus Edwards'  BOYS
   AND GIRLS; London debut, 1914 at the Victoria Palace; produced HELEN OF TROY, N.Y.,
   with Rufus Lemaire (Selwyn, June 19, 1923); played his most successful role in  THE
   JAZZ SINGER (Fulton, September 14, 1925); other subsequent successes include  SWEET
   AND LOW (46th Street, November 17, 1930) and HIGH KICKERS (Broadhurst, October  31,
   1941), which he presented and which he part-authored; retired 1943 to produce films
   (own film career began 1927 with silent SAILOR IZZY MURPHY; also sang in LUCKY  BOY
   (1929) and appeared as Death in HIERONYMUS MERKIN (1969); composer of many  popular

songs, one of the best-known being AND HE'D SAY "OO-LA-LA ! WEE-WEE !" (1919).  He
also recorded Hebrew songs for Banner in the late 1940s, and compered the SHOW BIZ
album for RCA Victor (LOC-1011) in 1953. Autobiography SO HELP ME published 1943.

Vocal, acc. by studio orchestra.              New York, October 11, 1919.

  78730-1-2-3  You Know What I Mean                    Col rejected

                                              New York, October 28, 1919.

  78764-1-2-3  Give Me The Sultan's Harem (Won't   Col rejected
               You Give Me That Harem ?)
  78765-1-2-3  When They're Old Enough To Know Better    -
               (It's Better To Leave Them Alone)

                                              New York, c. July, 1920.

  68587     Marcelle                          Pathe 22418, Operaphone 31186
  68588     Dolls                                -                  -

                                              New York, c. September, 1920.

  41371-   Jing-A-Bula-Jing-Jing-Jing            Em 10264

   Acc. by Harry Selinger's Ensemble/Leroy Shield.
                                              Chicago, January 18, 1929.

BVE-48804-2  My Mother's Eyes (Film "Lucky Boy")   Vic 21852, LPV-538, LSA-3074,
                                                   RD-7869, HMV B-3049
BVE-48805-2  When The Curtain Comes Down            Vic 21852

Humorous monologue.                           Los Angeles, September 10, 1937.

DLA-894-A  Hello, Momma - Part 1                  Dec 1484, 7-2, 9-11075, Br 02524
DLA-895-A  Hello, Momma - Part 2                     -        -      -         -

## AL   JOLSON

B. New York, May 26, 1886 (r.n. Asa Yoelson); stage debut at Harald Square   Theatre,
in "mob" chorus in THE CHILDREN OF THE GHETTO (October 16, 1899); toured with  circus companies, Lew Dockstader's Minstrels and in vaudeville; first New York success
in LA BELLE PAREE (Winter Garden, March 20, 1911); subsequently starred there in a
long run of hit shows (VERA VIOLETTA, November 20, 1911; THE WHIRL OF SOCIETY, Mar.
5, 1912; THE HONEYMOON EXPRESS, February 6, 1913; DANCING AROUND, October 10, 1914;
ROBINSON CRUSOE, Jr., February 17, 1916; SINBAD, February 14, 1918); toured for two
years in the last-named; resumed in New York at Jolson's 59th Street Theatre   with
BOMBO (October 6, 1921); toured in this until 1924; returned to the Winter  Garden,
January, 1925 to play in BIG BOY; began film career with the first talkie, THE JAZZ
SINGER (1927); other great hit talkies include THE SINGING FOOL (1928);MAMMY(1930);
WONDER BAR (1933); HALLELUJAH, I'M A BUM (1934); GO INTO YOUR DANCE (1936); ROSE OF
WASHINGTON SQUARE (1939); SWANEE RIVER (1940); guested in RHAPSODY IN BLUE in 1945,
and provided the voice to which Larry Parks mimed in THE JOLSON STORY (1946),  fol-
lowed in 1949 by JOLSON SINGS AGAIN; entertained troops fighting in Korea up to the
time of his death on October 24, 1950; only other important stage appearance was in
HOLD ON TO YOUR HATS (Shubert, September 11, 1940).

Vocal, acc. by studio orchestra.              New York, December 22, 1911.

B-11409-2  That Haunting Melody                    Vic 17037
B-11410-3  Rum-Tum-Tiddle                             -
B-11411-2  Asleep In The Deep (Parody)              Vic 17915

                                              New York, March 15, 1912.

B-11730-1  The Villain Song                        Rejected
B-11731-1  My Sunshine Girl                           -
B-11732-3  Snap Your Fingers                        Vic 17075
B-11733-1  Brass Band Ephraham Jones                Vic 17068

New York, April 17, 1912.

B-11883-1  Ragging The Baby To Sleep                Vic 17081
B-11884-1  That Lovin' Träumerei                    Vic 17119
B-11885-1  Movin' Man, Don't Take My Baby Grand     Vic 17081
  NOTE:- Matrix B-11886-1 is a whistling solo (UNCLE SAMMY MARCH AND TWO-STEP) by  an
  unidentified performer, on the same date as the above.  It was never issued, but it
  could have been made by Al Jolson.

New York, March 7, 1913.

B-12971-1  My Yellow Jacket Girl                     Vic 17318, Cam CAL-745
B-12972-1  The Spaniard That Blighted My Life             -             -

New York, June 4, 1913.

38901-     Pullman Porters' Parade                   Col A-1374
38902-     You Made Me Love You                           -            2301
38903-     That Little German Band (Al Jolson's      Col A-1356
             La-La Song)
38904-     Everybody Snap Your Fingers With Me            -

New York, September 19, 1914.

39567-     Back To The Carolina You Love             Col A-1621
39568-     Revival Day                                    -
           Back To The Carolina You Love             LW 20 (anonymous)

New York, December 3, 1914.

39664-     Sister Susie's Sewing Shirts For Soldiers Col A-1671
39665-     When The Grown-Up Ladies Act Like Babies       -

New York, January 12, 1916.

46335-     There's A Broken Heart For Every Light On Rejected
             Broadway
46336-     Eeny Meany Miney Moe                           -
46337-     Yaaka Hula Hickey Doola                   Col A-1956, 2711

New York, February 28, 1916.

46459-     Where Did Robinson Crusoe Go With Friday  Col A-1976
             On Saturday Night ?
46460-     Down Where The Swanee River Flows         Col A-2007, 2760
46463-     Now He's Got A Beautiful Girl             Col A-2080, 2794
  NOTE:- Matrices 46461/2 are not by Al Jolson.

New York, May 17, 1916.

46786-     I Sent My Wife To The Thousand Isles      Col A-2021, 2817
46787-     You're A Dangerous Girl                   Col A-2041, 2752

New York, June 9, 1916.

46820-     I'm Saving Up The Means To Get To New     Col A-2064
             Orleans

New York, September 19, 1916.

47029-1    Someone Else May Be There While I'm Gone  Col A-2124
47030-     I'm Down In Honolulu Looking Them Over    Rejected
47031-     Don't Write Me Letters                    Col A-2106

New York, November 27, 1916.

47191-     A Broken Doll                             Col A-2154
47192-     Ev'ry Little While                        Col A-2181

New York, December 11, 1916.

47217-  Pray For Sunshine                        Col A-2169
47218-  From Here To Shanghai                    Col A-2224, 2817

New York, May 29, 1917.

77079-  Tillie Titwillow ("Robinson Crusoe, Jr.")Col A-2296

New York, December 13, 1917.

77571-  Wedding Bells (Will You Ever Ring For    Col A-2512
        Me ?)
77572-  I'm All Bound 'Round With The Mason-     Col A-2478
        Dixon Line

New York, Decemer 27, 1917.

77602-  'N' Everything                           Col A-2519
77603-  There's A Lump Of Sugar Down In Dixie    Col A-2491

New York, March 13, 1918.

77720-  Rock-a-Bye Your Baby With A Dixie Melody Col A-2560

New York, April 3, 1918.

77753-1 Hello Central, Give Me No-Man's-Land     Col A-2542

New York, September 11, 1918.

78046-1 Tell That To The Marines                 Col A-2657
78047-  I Wonder Why She Kept On Saying "Si-Si-  Col A-2671
        Si Señor" ?

New York, October 24, 1918.

78153-3 I'll Say She Does ("Sinbad")             Col A-2746

New York, December 9, 1918.

78193-  On The Road To Calais                    Col A-2690

New York, December 14, 1918.

78201-  Don't Forget The Boys                    Col rejected

New York, July 24, 1919.

78593-4 Some Beautiful Morning                   Col A-2940
78594-  Who Played Poker With Pocahontas (When   Col A-2787
        John Smith Went Away)

New York, July 25, 1919.

78600-  Her Danny                                Col rejected

New York, September 15, 1919.

78652-2 I've Got My Captain Working For Me Now   Col A-2794

New York, September 22, 1919.

78684-  You Ain't Heard Nothin' Yet              Col A-2836, 2974
78685-  I Gave Her That                          Col A-2835

New York, October 4, 1919.

78722-  Tell Me                                  Col A-2821, 2957

New York, October 20, 1919.

78743-   Chloe                                    Col A-2861

New York, January 9, 1920.

78916-   That Wonderful Kid From Madrid           Col A-2898
78917-   Swanee                                   Col A-2884, 2974

New York, May 10, 1920.

79152-3  In Sweet September                       Col A-2946, 3011

New York, August 16, 1920.

79371-   Avalon                                   Col A-2995, 3011

New York, December 13, 1920.

79568-   O-H-I-O (O-My ! O !)                     Col A-3361, 3029

New York, January 4, 1921.

79624-   Ding-A-Ring-A-Ring                       Col A-3375

New York, February 14, 1921.

79726-2  Scandinavia                              Col A-3382

New York, July 20, 1921.

79953-   She Knows It                             Col rejected

New York, October 22, 1921.

80041-   April Showers ("Bombo")                  Col A-3500
80042-   Give Me My Mammy                         Col A-3540

New York, November 7, 1921.

80052-   Yoo Hoo                                  Col A-3513

New York, January 17, 1922.

80140-   Angel Child                              Col A-3568

New York, March 10, 1922.

80232-   Oogie-Oogie-Wa-Wa                        Col A-3588

New York, April 24, 1922.

80317-   Coo Coo                                  Col A-3626

New York, August 5, 1922.

80500-   I'll Stand Beneath Your Window Tonight   Col A-3694
           And Whistle

New York, September 11, 1922.

80532-   Toot, Toot, Tootsie (Goo'bye)            Col A-3705
80533-   Do I ? (Do I Love You ?)                 Rejected

New York, October 13, 1922.

80609-   Some Of These Days                       Col rejected

Chicago, October 23, 1922.

80593-   Lost (A Wonderful Girl)                  Col A-3744

Chicago, December 8, 1922.

| 80631- | Who Cares ? | Col A-3779 |

New York, January 4, 1923.

| 80761- | Coal Black Mammy | Col A-3854 |
| 80762- | Wanita (Wanna Eat - Wanna Eat) | Col A-3812 |

New York, March 30, 1923.

| 80929- | Morning Will Come | Col A-3880 |

New York, May 15, 1923.

| 81016- | Stella | Col A-3913 |

New York, June 12, 1923.

| 81072- | Waitin' For The Evening Mail | Col A-3933 |

New York, July 27, 1923.

| 81152- | That Big Blonde Mama | Col A-3968 |

New York, September 7, 1923.

| 81201- | You've Simply Got Me Cuckoo | Col A-3984 |

New York, October 13, 1923.

| 81281- | Mama Loves Papa | Col rejected |

New York, November 23, 1923.

| 81368- | Arcady | Col 43-D |

New York, December 18, 1923.

| 81423- | I'm Goin' South | Col 61-D |

New York, December 20, 1923.

| 81429- | Twelve O'Clock At Night | Col 79-D |

Acc. by Isham Jones and his Orchestra, with Bud de Sylva-u where shown.
Chicago, March, 1924.

| 142-CH | Steppin' Out | Br 2567 |
| 144-CH | The One I Love Belongs To Somebody Else | - |
| | California, Here I Come - uBdeS | Br 2569 |
| | I'm Goin' South | - |
| | Home In Pasadena | Br 2582 |
| | Mr. Radio Man | - |
| | Lazy | Br 2595 |
| | My Papa Doesn't Two-Time No Time | - |
| | Feeling The Way I Do | Br 2611 |
| | Never Again | - |

New York, c. June, 1924.

| | Mandalay | Br 2650 |
| | Who Wants A Bad Little Boy ? | - |
| | Follow The Swallow | Br 2671 |
| | I Wonder What's Become Of Sally ? | - |

Acc. by Ray Miller and his Orchestra.    New York, c. November, 1924.

    All Alone                                          Br 2743
    I'm Gonna Tramp, Tramp, Tramp                      -
    Hello, 'Tucky                                      Br 2763
    Trouble's A Bubble                                 -

Acc. by Carl Fenton and his Orchestra.   New York, c. December, 1925.

    Miami                                              Br 3013
    You Forgot To Remember                             -
    I'm Sitting On Top Of The World                    Br 3014
    You Flew Away From The Nest                        -

                                  New York, c. May, 1926.

    I Wish I Had My Old Gal Back Again         Br 3183
    I'd Climb The Highest Mountain (If I Knew  -
       I'd Find You)
    At Peace With The World                    Br 3196
    Tonight's My Night With Baby               -

                                New York, c. June, 1926.

    Here I Am                                          Br 3222
    When The Red, Red Robin Comes Bob, Bob,            -
       Bobbin' Along

Acc. by Bill Wirges and his Orchestra.   New York, c. October, 1927.

E-25184/5  Mother Of Mine, I Still Have You (Film   Br 3719, 3696
       "The Jazz Singer")
E-25188/9  Blue River                                 -        -

                            New York, c. December, 1927.

    Four Walls                                         Br 3775
    Golden Gate                                        -

                            New York, c. January, 1928.

    Ol' Man River                                     Br 3867, 3771
    Back In Your Own Back Yard                        -      -

Acc. by Abe Lyman and his California Orchestra.
                           Chicago, c. March 31, 1928.

C-1832    My Mammy                                     Br 3912, 3790
C-1833    Dirty Hands ! Dirty Face !                   -      -

Acc. by studio orchestra.                Los Angeles, August 20, 1928.

LAE-249-  There's A Rainbow 'Round My Shoulder   Br 4033, 3879, 01364
        (Film "The Jazz Singer")
LAE-250-  Sonny Boy (Film "The Singing Fool")    -      -      -

                           Los Angeles, April 7, 1929.

LAE-446-  I'm In Seventh Heaven (Film "Say It With  Br 4400, 10286
        Songs")
LAE-447-  Little Pal (Film "Say It With Songs")      -      -
LAE-448-  Used To You (Film "Say It With Songs")    Br 4401, 10287
LAE-449-  Why Can't You ? (Film "Say It With Songs")  -      -
LAE-450-  One Sweet Kiss                             Br 4402

                              New York, July, 1929.

E-30576-  Liza (All The Clouds'll Roll Away)         Br 4402

Los Angeles, c. February, 1930.

| | | |
|---|---|---|
| LAE-685- | Let Me Sing, And I'm Happy (Film "Mammy") | Br 4721, 01059, Dec 7-3 |
| LAE-686- | To My Mammy (Film "Mammy") | Br 4722, 01060 |
| LAE-687- | Looking At You Across The Breakfast Table (Film "Mammy") | Br 4721, 01059, Dec 7-1 |
| LAE-688- | When The Little Red Roses Get The Blues For You | Br 4722, 01060 |

New York, December 20, 1932.

| | | |
|---|---|---|
| B-12760-A | The Cantor (In Hebrew) | Br 6501, 01459, Col DB-2637 |
| B-12761-A | Hallelujah ! I'm A Bum (Film "Hallelujah ! I'm A Bum") (Br 01507 as | Br 6500, 01507, Har 1005 HALLELUJAH ! I'M A TRAMP) |
| B-12762-A | You Are Too Beautiful (Film "Hallelujah ! I'm A Bum") | Br 6500, 01507, Har 1004, Col DB-2637, Epic L2N-6072 |
| B-12763-A | April Showers | Br 6502, 01440, Har 1005, Col DB-2613 |
| B-12764-A | Rock-a-Bye Your Baby With A Dixie Melody | Br 6502, 01440, Har 1004, HS-11353, Col DB-2613 |

Al Jolson resumed recording in the mid-forties coincident with the making of the film of his life.  These are Decca (English Brunswick) records.

## ALLAN  JONES

B. Scranton, Pa., October 14, 1908, son of Welsh coal-miner; worked in mines    during school vacations to earn money for singing lessons, and also drove coal trucks   and steam shovels.  Continued studying in Europe, finally won film contract (1935);made film debut in A DAY AT THE RACES (1937) with Marx Brothers; then starred in EVERY-BODY SING   and   THE FIREFLY (1937); THE BOYS FROM SYRACUSE (1939); THE GREAT VIC-TOR HERBERT (1940);  SHOW  BOAT  (1941); WHEN JOHNNY COMES MARCHING HOME (1943) and others; visited England and gave many successful concerts there during later 1940s; son Jack also a very popular singer during 1960s and 1970s.

Vocal, acc. by unknown p.                    New York, December 12, 1930.

| | | |
|---|---|---|
| BVE-67706-1-2 | Dweller In Dreams | Vic rejected |

Acc. by O/Nat Shilkret.                    Hollywood, January 13, 1938.

| | | |
|---|---|---|
| PBS-09934-1 | The One I Love (Film "Everybody Sing") | Vic 4381, HMV B-8724 |
| PBS-09935-1 | The Donkey Serenade (Film "The Firefly") | Vic 4380, Cam CAL-2256,HMV B-8714 |
| PBS-09936-1 | Giannina Mia (Film "The Firefly") | -        -        - |
| PBS-09937-1 | Cosi Cosa (Film "Everybody Sing") | Vic 4381, HMV B-8724 |

Acc. by O/Nat W. Finston.                    Hollywood, August 27, 1939.

| | | |
|---|---|---|
| PBS-036456-4 | Sweethearts (Film "The Great Victor Herbert") | Vic 4447, HMV B-8999 |
| PBS-036457-2-4 | Some Day (Film "The Great Victor Herbert") (w/chorus) | -       HMV B-9032 |
| PBS-036458-4 | Thine Alone (Film "The Great Victor Herbert") | Vic 4446       - |
| PBS-036459-3 | I'm Falling In Love With Someone (Film "The Great Victor Herbert") | -       HMV B-8999 |

Acc. by O/Charles Previn.                    Hollywood, June 14, 1940.

| | | |
|---|---|---|
| PBS-049851-1 | Sylvia | Vic 4539, HMV B-9234 |
| PBS-049852-1 | The Sleigh | Cam CAL-2256 |
| PBS-049853-1 | Falling In Love With Love (Film "The Boys From Syracuse") | Vic 4525, Cam CAL-2256, HMV B-9106 |
| PBS-049854-1 | Who Are You ? (Film "The Boys From Syracuse") | Vic 4525, HMV B-9106 |

Acc. by O/Lou Bring.                    Hollywood, May 13, 1941.

| | | |
|---|---|---|
| PBS-061247-1 | Intermezzo (Escape To Happiness) | Vic 4552, HMV B-9234 |
| PBS-061248-1 | Why Do I Love You ? (Film "Show Boat") | Vic 4555, HMV B-9242 |
| PBS-061249-1 | Amapola | Vic 4552 |
| PBS-061250-1 | Make Believe (Film "Show Boat") | Vic 4555,Cam CAL-2256,HMV B-9242 |

Member of the cast of the smash hit POTASH AND PERLMUTTER (Cohan, August 16, 1913 for
457 continuous performances).

Humorous monologue.                       New York, c. February, 1917.

2436-2  Four Minutes With Jules Jordan - Part 1   Em 7152 (7")
2437-2  Four Minutes With Jules Jordan - Part 2        -

## RICHARD JOSE

B. England, June 5, 1869; to U.S.A. as a boy, became blacksmith in Reno, Nevada;  took
singing lessons and joined Charlie Reed's Minstrels in San Francisco, later in  Lew
Dockstader's company in the East; provided incidental singing in THE OLD HOMESTEAD,
for its 8-year run (including revivals) from January 10, 1887 (14th Street Theatre,
New York, and others); his best-known number was SILVER THREADS AMONG THE GOLD; retired from stage, 1920, but continued to sing on radio; d. San Francisco,   October
20, 1941.
Vocal, acc. by studio orchestra.          New York, October 27, 1903.

B-598-1  Silver Threads Among The Gold        Vic 2556
B-599-1  Belle Brandon                        Vic 2554

                                           New York, October 31, 1904.

C-616-1  Dear Old Girl                         Rejected
C-617-1  When I'm Away From You, Dear          Vic 31154
C-618-1  With All Her Faults, I Love Her Still Vic 31171

Acc. by C. H. H. Booth-p or organ.        New York, January 12, 1904.

C-616-2  Dear Old Girl                         Vic 31172
C-617-3  When I'm Away From You, Dear          Rejected ?
C-618-3  With All Her Faults, I Love Her Still     -
B-897-1  Dear Old Songs                        Vic 2629
B-898-1-2 Your Mother Wants You Home, Boy, And Vic 2632
          She Wants You Mighty Bad
B-899-1  The Brotherhood Of Man                Vic 2631
A-900-1/B-900-1  May, Sweet May                Vic 2630 (7"/10")

                                           New York, January 14, 1904.

C-616-3  Dear Old Girl                         Rejected ?
C-897-2  Dear Old Songs                        Vic 31170
B-899-2  The Brotherhood Of Man                Vic 2631
B-914-1  Abide With Me (w/organ)               Vic 2633
B-915-1  Softly Now The Light Of Day (w/organ) Vic 2686

                                           New York, January 18, 1904.

B-915-2  Softly Now The Light Of Day (w/organ) Vic 2686
C-930-1  Glory To God (w/organ)                Vic 31192
B-931-1  Sun Of My Soul (w/organ)              Vic 2669
B-932-1  Oh Come All Ye Faithful (Adeste Fideles) Rejected
B-933-1  Oh Paradise                           Vic 2724
B-934-1  The Palms                             Rejected

                                           New York, January 20, 1904.

B-915-3  Softly Now The Light Of Day (w/organ) Vic 2686 ?
B-942-2  Oh Come, All Ye Faithful (Adeste Fideles) Vic 2725

Acc. by studio orchestra.                 New York, December 8, 1904.

B-2023-2  Silver Threads Among The Gold        Vic 2556
C-2023-1  Silver Threads Among The Gold        Rejected
C-2024-1  When I'm Away From You, Dear          Vic 31154
B-2025-1  Bonnie Eloise                        Vic 4288
C-2026-1  She Fought On By His Side             Vic 31345
C-2027-1  The Day That You Grew Colder          Vic 31348
C-2028-1  Too Late !                            Vic 31344

New York, December 9, 1904.

| | | |
|---|---|---|
| B-2024-1 | When I'm Away From You, Dear | Vic 4208 |
| B-2026-1 | She Fought On By His Side | Vic 4261 |
| B-2028-1 | Too Late ! | Vic 4227 |
| C-2040-1 | Killarney | Vic 31343 |
| B-2041-1 | Dear Old Girl | Rejected |
| C-2041-1-2 | Dear Old Girl | - |
| C-2042-1 | With All Her Faults, I Love Her Still | - |
| B-2043-1 | Belle Brandon | Vic 2554, 16666 |
| B-2044-1 | Rose Of My Life | Vic 4219 |
| C-2045-1 | Time And Tide | Vic 31355 |

New York, December 10, 1904.

| | | |
|---|---|---|
| C-2023-2 | Silver Threads Among The Gold | Vic 31342 |
| B-2041-2 | Dear Old Girl | Vic 4226 |
| C-2041-3 | Dear Old Girl | Vic 31172 |
| C-2042-2 | With All Her Faults, I Love Her Still | Vic 31171 |
| B-2044-2 | Rose Of My Life | Rejected |

New York, December 19, 1905.

| | | |
|---|---|---|
| C-2963-2 | Since Nellie Went Away | Vic 31489 |

New York, December 20, 1905.

| | | |
|---|---|---|
| C-2964-1 | When You And I Were Young, Maggie | Vic 31485 |
| C-2965-1 | Katie Dear | Vic 31484 |

New York, December 21, 1905.

| | | |
|---|---|---|
| C-2966-1 | I Cannot Sing The Old Songs | Vic 31496 |
| C-2967-1-2 | The Ninety And Nine (w/cornet, organ and tubes (? chimes) added) | Rejected |

New York, December 22, 1905.

| | | |
|---|---|---|
| B/C-2023-3 | Silver Threads Among The Gold | Both rejected ? |
| C-2968-1 | Ben Bolt | Vic 31497 |
| C-2969-1 | The Angel At The Window | Vic 31490 |
| B-2970-1 | Rock Of Ages (w/cornet, organ and tubes) | Vic 4782 |

New York, February 22, 1906.

| | | |
|---|---|---|
| C-3137-1 | The Blind Boy | Vic 31513 |

New York, February 23, 1906.

| | | |
|---|---|---|
| B-3138-1 | Darling Nellie Gray | Rejected |
| C-3139-1 | We've Been Chums For Fifty Years | Vic 31516 |
| C-3140-1 | A Flower From My Angel Mother's Grave | Rejected |
| C-3141-1 | Home, Sweet Home | Vic 31515 |
| B-3142-1 | The Ninety And Nine | Vic 4755 |
| B-3143-1 | Sun Of My Soul (w/String Quartet) | Vic 2669 |
| B-3144-1 | Abide With Me (w/String Quartet) | Vic 2633, 16660 |
| B-3145-1 | Nearer, My God, To Thee | Vic 4818 |
| B-3146-1 | Softly Now The Light Of Day | Rejected ? |

New York, March 15, 1909.

| | | |
|---|---|---|
| B/C-2023-4 | Silver Threads Among The Gold | Vic rejected |
| C-3141-2 | Home, Sweet Home | - |

New York, September 16, 1909.

| | | |
|---|---|---|
| B-2043-2-3 | Belle Brandon | Vic rejected |
| B-2044-3 | Rose Of My Life | - |
| C-2968-2-3 | Ben Bolt | - |
| B-3145-2 | Nearer, My God, To Thee | - |

B. 1904; r.n. Helen Schroder. Stage debut in a Marx Brothers' revue; made hit  with
her "boop-boop-a-doop" style of "scat" singing; starred in GOOD BOY (Hammerstein,
New York, September 5, 1928); signed with Paramount Pictures in 1929 and  appeared
in SWEETIE; NOTHING BUT THE TRUTH; POINTED HEELS; DANGEROUS NAN McGREW;  PARAMOUNT
ON PARADE; HEADS UP; FLYING HIGH; YOUNG MEN OF MANHATTAN, all in the following two
years. Her essentially "flapper" style lost its appeal during the Depression, but
she provided the voice for I WANNA BE LOVED BY YOU, one of her biggest hits,  when
the film THREE LITTLE WORDS was made by MGM with Debbie Reynolds miming, in  1950.
Helen Kane died in 1966.

Vocal, acc. by Mike Cleary-p.          New York, June 7, 1928.

BVE-106    That's My Weakness Now            Vic test

Acc. by O/Nat Shilkret.          New York, July 16, 1928.

BVE-45880-3  Get Out And Get Under The Moon    Vic 21557, Zon 5227
BVE-45881-2  That's My Weakness Now            -              -

Acc. by O/Leonard Joy.           New York, September 20, 1928.

BVE-47539-3  I Wanna Be Loved By You ("Good Boy")  Vic 21684, LVA-523, LSA-3078,
                                                    HMV B-4042
BVE-47540-3  Is There Anything Wrong In That ?     Vic 21684, HMV B-2953

                                 New York, December 20, 1928.

BVE-48501-2  Don't Be Like That               Vic 21830, HMV B-2977
BVE-48502-3  Me And The Man In The Moon        -              -

                                 New York, January 30, 1929.

BVE-49698-3  Button Up Your Overcoat          Vic 21863, HMV B-3133
BVE-49699-3  I Want To Be Bad                 -              -

                                 New York, March 15, 1929.

BVE-50945-3  Do Something (Film "Nothing But The  Vic 21917, HMV B-3050
               Truth")
BVE-50946-4  That's Why I'm Happy             -              -

                                 New York, June 13, 1929.

BVE-53560-1-2  I'd Do Anything For You        Vic rejected

                                 New York, June 14, 1929.

BVE-53560-   I'd Do Anything For You          Vic 22080, HMV B-3195
BVE-53563-   He's So Unusual (Film "Sweetie")    -     LPV-538, LSA-3074,
                                                 RD-7869, HMV B-3195

                                 New York, October 29, 1929.

BVE-57126-4  Ain'tcha ? (Film "Pointed Heels")    Vic 22192, HMV B-3296
BVE-57127-2  I Have To Have You (Film "Pointed Heels") - LCT-1112 -

                                 New York, March 18, 1930.

BVE-59639-3  I'd Go Barefoot All Winter Long (If  Vic 22397
               You'd Fall For Me In The Spring)

                                 New York, April 12, 1930.

BVE-59695-3  Dangerous Nan McGrew (Film "Dangerous Vic 22407
               Nan McGrew")
BVE-59696-2  Thank Your Father (Film "Flying High")Vic 22397
BVE-59697-3  I Owe You (Film "Dangerous Nan        Vic 22407
               McGrew")

New York, July 1, 1930.

BVE-63102-3  Readin' Ritin' Rhythm (Film "Heads     Vic 22520
                Up")
BVE-63103-3  I've Got "It" (But It Don't Do Me      Vic 22475
                No Good) (Film "Young Men Of Manhattan")

New York, July 2, 1930.

BVE-63106-3  My Man Is On The Make (Film "Heads     Vic 22475
                Up")
BVE-63107-3  If I Knew You Better (Film "Heads      Vic 22520
                Up")

## DOLLY KAY

Vocal, acc. by studio orchestra.       New York, June 28, 1921.

79917-1-2  I Ain't Gonna Be Nobody's Fool          Col rejected

New York, October 20, 1921.

80034-2  Cry Baby Blues                           Col A-3502
80035-1  No-One's Fool                                 -
80036-1-2  The Schoolhouse Blues                  Rejected

New York, December 22, 1921.

80117-  Wabash Blues                              Col A-3534
80118-  Got To Have My Daddy Blues                     -

New York, June 7, 1922.

80374-3  It's The Last Time You'll Ever Do Me     Col A-3644
            Wrong
80375-2  Buzz Mirandy                                  -

New York, June 29, 1922.

80430-  If I Can't Have You, I Don't Want         Col A-3664
            Nobody At All
80431-  Lonesome Longin' Blues                         -

New York, August 15, 1922.

80526-2  I'm Nobody's Gal                         Col A-3692
80527-3  Sweet Man O' Mine                             -

New York, October 27, 1922.

80626-2  Hot Lips                                 Col A-3758
80627-2  Blue                                          -

Acc. by Frank Westphal and his Orchestra.
                                    Chicago, January 9, 1923.

80759-2  You've Got To See Mama Ev'ry Night       Col A-3808
            (Or You Can't See Mama At All)
80760-3  I Loved You Once But You Stayed Away          -
            Too Long

Acc. by studio orchestra.        New York, January 30, 1923.

80813-3  Aggravatin' Papa (Don't You Try To       Col A-3828.
            Two-Time Me)
80814-3  Seven Or Eleven (My Dixie Pair O' Dice)       -

New York, March 9, 1923.

80892-1  Wet Yo' Thumb                              Col A-3882
80893-6  Don't Think You'll Be Missed              —

Acc. by Phil Phillips-p.          New York, July 16, 1923.

81138-3  My Sweetie Went Away                      Col A-3955
81139-3  Oh ! Sister, Ain't That Hot !             —

New York, August 11, 1923.

81173-3  The Gold-Digger                           Col A-3980
81174-3  Sweet Henry (The Pride Of Tennessee)      —

Acc. by the Georgians/Frank Guarente.  New York, January 9, 1924.

81467-1-2-3  Ain't You Ashamed ?                   Rejected
81468-1  Hula Lou                                  Col 70-D

New York, January 11, 1924.

81474-2  Maybe                                     Col 70-D
81475-1-2-3-4  Take A Look At This                 Rejected

New York, March 27, 1924.

81654-1  Big Boy                                   Col 117-D
81655-2  Someday, Sweetheart                       —

Acc. by studio orchestra.         New York, May 28, 1924.

81796-3  I Can't Get The One I Want                Col 151-D
81797-4  Hard Hearted Hannah                       —

New York, October 7, 1924.

140088-  Red-Hot Mama                              Col 226-D
140089-  Big Bad Bill (Is Sweet William Now)       —

New York, November 11, 1924.

140132-1  Any Way The Wind Blows                   Col 246-D
140133-3  I Want To See My Tennessee               —

Acc. by Phil Phillips-p.          New York, October 5, 1926.

142732-1  How Could Red Riding Hood ?              Har 268-H
142733-3  It Takes A Good Woman (To Keep A Good    —
            Man At Home)

New York, October 27, 1926.

142879-2  Pretty Little Thing                      Har 294-H
142880-2  Rags                                     —

New York, May 4, 1927.

144085-  I Haven't Told Her - She Hasn't Told Me  Har 411-H
            (But We Know It Just The Same)
144086-  Fifty Million Frenchmen Can't Be Wrong    —

New York, July 1, 1927.

144420-3  Magnolia                                 Har 449-H
144421-1  I Ain't That Kind Of A Baby              —

Acc. by the University Six.              New York, January 24, 1928.

145569-2  The Grass Grows Greener ('Way Down Home) Har 581-H
145570-3  Let A Smile Be Your Umbrella (On A Rainy Day)-

## GRETA KELLER

B. Vienna, Austria, 1913; trained as a dancer and hoped to be an opera singer; stage
debut at twelve in a boy's part, took elocution and drama lessons; appeared at age
of 16 in non-singing part in Berlin in EINBRECHER; returned to Vienna, and was offered a major part in SHOW BOAT - singing in English ! Invited to broadcast  from
London, 1930; instant success with her "perfect microphone voice"; engaged to sing
and dance with Fred Astaire in New York in THE FOURTH LITTLE SHOW, but the Depression killed this; she accepted radio contracts instead.  Returned to Europe, 1936;
appeared in Berlin at Die Scala as part of the entertainment for visitors to Olym-
pic Games; anschluss with Austria forced her to tour Holland, France and England -
all very successfully - before returning to New York and eventually Hollywood. Her
husband's murder brought on ill-health, but she recovered and made propaganda recordings that were smuggled into Germany; made a very successful come-back and now
divides her working time between Vienna and New York.

Vocal, acc. by studio orchestra.         London, November 21, 1930.

WAR-427-2  It's For You                           Re MR-244
WAR-428-1  What Good Am I Without You ?


                                         London, February 19, 1931.

WAR-543-2  He's My Secret Passion                 Re MR-297
WAR-544-1  Moanin' Low                            -


                                         London, March 14, 1931.

WAR-561-2  Ten Cents A Dance                      Re MR-319
WAR-562-1-2  Three Little Words                   Rejected
WAR-563-1  Would You Like To Take A Walk ?        Re MR-369
WAR-564-1-2  Writing A Letter To You              Rejected


                                         London, October 5, 1931.

GB-3372-1  Kiss Me "Goodnight"                    Dec F-2578
GB-3373-2  Looking For You                        -
GB-3392-  Blues In My Heart                       Dec F-2592
GB-3393-  Come To Me                              -
   NOTE:- Matrices GB-3374/3391 inclusive are not by Greta Keller.


                                         London, October 13, 1931.

GB-3439-1  Just One More Chance                   Dec F-2669
GB-3440-1  I Apologise                            -


                                         London, November 4, 1931.

GB-3532-  Guilty                                  Dec F-2689

  Acc. by instrumental quintet.          London, November 13, 1931.

GB-3586-1-2  Just Because I Lost My Heart To You  Dec rejected


                                         London, January 12, 1932.

GB-3586-3-4  Just Because I Lost My Heart To You  Dec rejected
GB-3812-1-2  One Of Us Was Wrong                  -


                                         London, January 20, 1932.

GB-3842-2  Tu ne sais pas aimer                   Dec F-40171
GB-3843-2  Ne dis pas toujours                    -
GB-3844-  Keiner weiss wie ich (acc. 2 pianos)    Dec ?
GB-3845-  Wer weint heut' ans (acc. 2 pianos)     -

London, January 22, 1932.

| | | |
|---|---|---|
| GB-3586- | Just Because I Lost My Heart To You | Dec F-2689 |
| GB-3812- | One Of Us Was Wrong | Dec F-2887 |
| GB-3856- | A Faded Summer Love | Dec F-2843 |
| GB-3857-1 | Speak To Me Of Love | Dec F-2813 |

London, January 27, 1932.

| | | |
|---|---|---|
| GB-3884-2 | Just Friends | Dec F-2813 |
| GB-3885- | All Of Me | Dec F-2843 |
| GB-3886- | What A Life ! (Trying To Live Without You) | Dec F-3159, Ecl ECM-2049 |
| GB-3887- | Dancing In The Dark | Dec F-2799 |
| GB-3888- | Hold My Hand | - |

London, March 24, 1932.

| | | |
|---|---|---|
| GB-4117- | You Try Somebody Else | Dec F-2887 |

London, April 5, 1932.

| | | |
|---|---|---|
| GB-4197-2 | Can't We Talk It Over ? | Dec F-3157, M-403 |
| GB-4198-1 | Too Late | -          - |
| GB-4199-2 | Auf Wiedersehen, My Dear | Dec F-3158, M-404, Ecl ECM-2049 |
| GB-4200-2 | With All My Love And Kisses | -          -          - |

London, April 29, 1932.

| | | |
|---|---|---|
| GB-4368- | Paradise | Dec F-3159 |
| GB-4369- | Oui, j'aime | Dec F-40227 |
| GB-4370- | Dis-moi "Je t'aime" | -          Ecl ECM-2049 |

London, June 22, 1932.

| | | |
|---|---|---|
| GB-4585-4 | A Great Big Bunch Of You | Dec M-418 |
| GB-4586-4 | Thank You For The Flowers | - |
| GB-4587-1-2-3 | Take Me In Your Arms | Rejected |
| GB-4588-1-2-3 | The Echo Of A Song | - |

Acc. by studio orchestra.                    New York, August 24, 1932.

| | | |
|---|---|---|
| 12226-B | Love Me Tonight | Dec F-3184 |
| 12227-B | I'll Never Be The Same | - |

New York, November 10, 1932.

| | | |
|---|---|---|
| 12554-A | (I Don't Stand) A Ghost Of A Chance | Dec F-3295 |
| 12555-A | Say It Isn't So | - |

Acc. by O/Nat Shilkret.                    New York, January 23, 1933.

| | | |
|---|---|---|
| BS-74967-1-2 | One More Night | Rejected |
| BS-74968-1-2 | Mary Make-Believe | - |
| BS-74969-1 | Was hat eine Frau von der Treue ? | El EG- ? |
| BS-74970-1 | Wonderful You | - |

Acc. by studio orchestra.                    New York, January 24, 1933.

| | | |
|---|---|---|
| 12977-A | I'll Never Have To Dream Again | Br 6506, Dec F-3470 |
| 12978-A | Willow, Weep For Me | -          Dec F-3483 |
| 12979-A | I'm Playing With Fire | - |
| 12980-A | I'm Sure Of Everything But You | Dec F-3470 |

Acc. by O/Nat Shilkret.                    New York, February 13, 1933.

| | | |
|---|---|---|
| BS-74967- | One More Night | Vic 24228 |
| BS-74968- | Mary Make-Believe | - |

Acc. by studio orchestra.                     New York, March 22, 1933.

| | | |
|---|---|---|
| 13168-A | Maybe I Love You Too Much | Br 6544, Dec F-3562 |
| 13169-A | I Wake Up Smiling | Dec F-3586 |
| 13170-A | Lover | Br 6544, Dec F-3601 |

New York, May 11, 1933.

| | | |
|---|---|---|
| 13324-A | Stormy Weather (Keeps Rainin' All The Time) | Dec F-3562 |
| 13325-A | I Can't Remember | Dec F-3586 |
| 13326-A | Hold Me | Dec F-3601 |

Acc. by O/Victor Young.                       New York, June 2, 1934.

| | | |
|---|---|---|
| B-15282-A | Don't Let It Happen Again | Dec F-5078, Ecl ECM-2049 |
| B-15283-A | Give Me A Heart To Sing To | Dec F-5281 |
| B-15284-A | Easy Come, Easy Go | Dec F-5078 |
| B-15285-A | With My Eyes Wide Open, I'm Dreaming | Dec F-5203 |

Acc. by Fred Hartley and his Quintet.     London, September 7, 1934.

| | | |
|---|---|---|
| TB-1513-1 | For All We Know | Dec F-5217, Ecl ECM-2049 |
| TB-1514-1 | Trust In Me | Dec F-5203, F-6319 - |
| TB-1515-2 | Lamplights | Dec F-5193, F-6783 |
| TB-1516- | I Never Had A Chance | - |

London, September 20, 1934.

| | | |
|---|---|---|
| TB-1567- | I Love You Very Much, Madame | Dec F-5217 |
| TB-1568-1 | A Little Ramble In Springtime With You (Eine Kleinereise) | Dec F-5281, F-6319 |

Acc. by studio orchestra/? Victor Young. New York, October 20, 1934.

| | | |
|---|---|---|
| 38858-A | Am I To Blame ? | Dec 292, F-5327 |
| 38859-A | One Night Of Love | - - |

New York, January 29, 1935.

| | | |
|---|---|---|
| 39292- | I Believe In Miracles | Dec F-5460 |
| 39293- | Blue Moon | - |

Acc. by Fred Hartley and his Quintet.     London, June 24, 1935.

| | | |
|---|---|---|
| GB-7253-1 | Call Me Sweetheart | Dec F-5595 |
| GB-7254-2 | Chasing Shadows | Dec F-5587 |
| GB-7255-1 | Let Me Sing You To Sleep With A Love Song | - |
| GB-7256-1 | In A Little Gypsy Tea Room | Dec F-5595 |

Acc. by O/Peter Kreuder.                   Berlin, August, 1935.

| | | |
|---|---|---|
| 20841 | Schlaf, mein Engel, schlaf ein | Tel A-1846 |
| 20842 | Zwischen heute und Morgen | Tel A-1845 |
| 20843 | Du sollst der Kaiser meine Seele sein | Tel A-1833 |
| 20844 | Mein blondes Baby | Tel A-1846 |
| 20845 | Drunt' in der Lobau | Tel A-1833 |
| 20847 | Ich spür in mir | Tel A-1837 |
| 20848 | Nur eine Stunde | - |
| 20849 | Aus gerechnet du ! | Tel A-1845 |
| 20850 | Bei zärtlicher Musik du kann man herrlich träumen | Tel A-1835 |
| 20851 | Geh' schlafen, mein Junge | - |

NOTE:- Matrix 20846 is untraced.

Acc. by Fred Hartley and his Quintet.     London, November 27, 1935.

| | | |
|---|---|---|
| GB-7523-1 | In The Dark | Dec F-5813 |
| GB-7524-1 | I Wished On The Moon | Dec F-5814 |
| GB-7525-1 | On Treasure Island | Dec F-5813 |
| GB-7526-1 | When Budapest Was Young | Dec F-5814 |

London, January 16, 1936.

GB-7620-2  Bird On The Wing                       Dec F-5863
GB-7621-1  If I Should Lose You                       -        Ecl ECM-2049

   Acc. by O/Peter Kreuder.            Berlin, February, 1936.

21040   In Wien gibt's man in winziger Gasserl   Tel A-1922
21041   Liebe                                     Tel A-1911
21042   Du wachen in der Wachau                   Tel A-1922
21043   Ich will nicht auf den Frühling warten    Tel A-1913
21044   Wenn die Sonne hinter den Dächern versinkt    -
21045   Lied vom Schwachen Stündchen              Tel A-1911

   Acc. by Fred Hartley and his Quintet.   London, April 25, 1936.

TB-2154-   Gloomy Sunday                          Dec F-5966
TB-2155-   Let It Be Me                               -
TB-2156-2  The Touch Of Your Lips                 Dec F-5965
TB-2157-1  Alone                                      -

   Acc. by studio orchestra.           Paris, May 23, 1936.

6587gr   Lights Out                               Dec F-5987
6588gr   These Foolish Things                         -

Amsterdam, August 14, 1936.

AM-286-3  Take My Heart                           Dec F-6054
AM-287-2  Would You ?                                 -

   Acc. by O/Peter Kreuder.            Berlin, October 23, 1936.

21513   Sag' beim Abschied leise "Servus"         Tel A-2081
21514   Das is a Wein !                               -
21515   Wann muss man denn immer verliebt sein    Tel A-2082
21516   Lied der Adrinne                              -

   Acc. by studio orchestra.           Paris, October 26, 1936.

6728gr   Foolish Heart                            Rejected ?
6729gr   When I Learn French                      Dec F-6390
6730gr   Me And The Moon                          Dec F-6189
6731gr   Drop In Next Time You're Passing             -

   Acc. by Fred Hartley and his Quintet.   London, December 29, 1936.

TB-2733-1  Have You Forgotten So Soon ?           Dec F-6246
TB-2734-   Saving Up My Time To Spend On You      Dec F-6256
TB-2735-1  Did You Mean It ?                      Dec F-6246, Ecl ECM-2049
TB-2736-   There's A Small Hotel                  Dec F-6256

London, February 4, 1937.

TB-2813-1  At The Balalaika (Intro. If The World  Dec F-6263
              Were Mine)
TB-2814-   The Laugh Was On Me (w/Archie Campbell) Dec F-6390
TB-2815-1  I've Got You Under My Skin             Dec F-6263

   Acc. by O/Fred Hartley.             London, June 24, 1937.

TB-3116-1  Carelessly                             Dec F-6439
TB-3117-1  The Mood That I'm In                       -        Ecl ECM-2049
TB-3118-1  Let's Call The Whole Thing Off (w/     Dec F-6461
              Brian Lawrence)
TB-3119-1  They Can't Take That Away From Me          -

Acc. by O/Peter Kreuder.                    Berlin, September 6, 1937.

| | | |
|---|---|---|
| 22300 | Ich hab' eine tiefe Sehnsucht in mir | Tel A-2276 |
| 22301 | Ich steh' im Regen | - |
| 22302 | Yes Sir ! | Tel A-2277 |
| 22303 | In einem kleinen Nachtlokal | |

Berlin, September 13, 1937.

| | | |
|---|---|---|
| 22322 | Mei' Muatterl war a Wienerin | Tel A-2325 |
| 22323 | A Klane Drahrerei | - |
| 22324 | In Sankt Anton am Arlberg | Tel A-2292 |
| 22325 | Liebesgeschwichten sind meistens nicht war ! | - |

Acc. by unknown p/g.                    London, October 19, 1937.

| | | |
|---|---|---|
| DTB-3285-1 | You're Here, You're There, You're Everywhere | Dec F-6513 |
| DTB-3286-1 | In The Mountains Of The Moon | - |

Acc. by Rae Jenkins' Quartet.          London, January 12, 1938.

| | | |
|---|---|---|
| DTB-3489-1 | Bei mir bist du schoen (Means That You're Grand) | Dec F-6603 |
| DTB-3490-1 | Roses In December | - |

Acc. by unknown p/g.                    London, March 8, 1938.

| | | |
|---|---|---|
| DTB-3602-1 | Thanks For The Memory | Dec F-6640 |
| DTB-3603-1 | Once In A While | -          Ecl ECM-2049 |

Acc. by studio orchestra.              Amsterdam, March 24, 1938.

| | | |
|---|---|---|
| AM-478-3 | You're A Sweetheart | Dec F-6683, Ecl ECM-2049 |
| AM-479-2 | My Fine Feathered Friend | - |

New York, July 12, 1938.

| | | |
|---|---|---|
| 64301-A | So Little Time | Dec F-6750 |
| 64302-A | You Leave Me Breathless | - |
| 64303-A | Music, Maestro, Please ! | Dec F-6783 |

Acc. by jazz quintet.                  Paris, September 27, 1938.

| | | |
|---|---|---|
| 4453hpp | Goodbye To Summer | Dec F-6821 |
| 4454½hpp | I'm Gonna Lock My Heart And Throw Away The Key | - |

Acc. by O/Ray Sinatra.                 New York, March 6, 1939.

| | | |
|---|---|---|
| 65201-A | They Say | Dec F-7025 |
| 65202-A | Deep In A Dream | - |

New York, July 13, 1939.

| | | |
|---|---|---|
| 65976- | Don't Worry 'Bout Me | Dec F-7194 |
| 65977- | Stairway To The Stars | - |

Acc. by unknown p/g; others ?          New York, c. July, 1939.

| | | |
|---|---|---|
| R-159-1 | Danger In The Dark | LMS L-262 |
| R-161-1 | Once Upon A Dream | - |

NOTE:- Matrix R-160, and perhaos others from this session, are untraced.

Acc. by unknown p/g.                    New York, October 17, 1939.

| | | |
|---|---|---|
| 66778- | Moon Love | Dec F-7331, Ecl ECM-2049 |
| 66779-A | The Lamp Is Low | Dec F-7433          - |
| 66780- | Day In - Day Out | Dec F-7331 |
| 66781-A | Melancholy Mood | Dec F-7433 |

B. Mineville, N.Y., October 29, 1873; as a young man he operated a cafe in  Virginia,
   where he was able to observe the many different characters he afterwards  portrayed
   in his vaudeville act "The Virginian Judge," for he was a master of dialects.  Died
   in Philadelphia, Pa., January 6, 1939.

Humorous monologues.                              Camden, N. J., July 6, 1920.

B-24197-2  Virginian Judge (Southern Court Scene)  Vic 45180
              (First session) - Part 1
B-24198-1  Virginian Judge (First session) - Part 2    -
B-24199-1  Virginian Judge (Second session) -        Rejected
              Part 1
B-24300-1  Virginian Judge (Second session) - Part 2    -

                                                  Camden, N. J., July 19, 1920.

B-24199-2  Virginian Judge (Second session) -        Vic 45202
              Part 1
B-24300-3  Virginian Judge (Second session) - Part 2    -

                                                  New York, May 4, 1921.

B-25074-1-2-3  Darky Stories                      Vic rejected
B-25075-1-2  Irish Stories                         -
B-25076-1-2  Virginian Judge (Third session) - Part 1  -
B-25077-1-2  Virginian Judge (Third session) - Part 2  -

                                                  New York, May 19, 1921.

B-25074-5  Darky Stories                          Vic 45255
B-25075-4  Irish Stories                           -
B-25076-4  Virginian Judge (Third session)-Part 1  Vic 45250
B-25077-4  Virginian Judge (Third session)-Part 2  -

                                                  New York, April 8, 1926.

BVE-35297-1  Virginian Judge (Fourth session)      Vic 20136
                - Part 1
BVE-35298-3  Virginian Judge (Fourth session)-Part 2  -

                                                  New York, May 12, 1926.

BVE-35396-1-2-3  Virginian Judge (Fifth session)   Rejected
                - Part 1
BVE-35397-4  Virginian Judge (Fifth session) -     Vic 20388
                - Part 2

                                                  New York, May 21, 1926.

BVE-35396-6  Virginian Judge (Fifth session)-Pt. 1 Vic 20388

### CHARLES KING

B. 1891; dancer and singer, stage partner for some years of Elizabeth Brice;  starred
   with her in THE SLIM PRINCESS (Globe, New York, January 2, 1911); appeared in  many
   ZIEGFELD FOLLIES productions in the ensuing decade, and in HIT THE DECK   (Belasco,
   April 25, 1927); to Hollywood, 1929, to star in BROADWAY MELODY (1929),   HOLLYWOOD
   REVUE OF 1929; CHASING RAINBOWS; OH SAILOR, BEHAVE (1930); but a few years   before
   his death on January 11, 1944, he was a member of a trio entertaining at the tables
   in the Victoria Hotel, New York, and in a nostalgic revue, BILL'S GAY NINETIES.

Vocal, acc. by studio orchestra.               New York, January 26, 1911.

B-9853-1-2  Let Me Stay And Live In Dixieland       Vic rejected
              (w/Elizabeth Brice) ("The Slim Princess")
B-9854-1-2  That's Ever-Loving Love (w/Elizabeth Brice)-
              ("The Slim Princess")

New York, February 17, 1911.

B-9853-3-4 Let Me Stay And Live In Dixieland      Rejected
    (W/Elizabeth Brice) ("The Slim Princess")
B-9854-3-4-5 That's Ever-Loving Love (w/Elizabeth      -
    Brice) ("The Slim Princess")
B-9959-2 Virginia Lou                             Vic 5842

New York, March 24, 1911.

B-9853-6 Let Me Stay And Live In Dixieland      Vic 5843
    (w/Elizabeth Brice) ("The Slim Princess")
B-9854-6 That's Ever-Loving Love (w/Elizabeth      Vic 5847
    Brice) ("The Slim Princess")

Acc. by O/? Charles A. Prince.      New York, January 6, 1916.

46317-1  I've Gotta Go Back To Texas (w/Elizabeth Col A-1944
    Brice)

New York, January 11, 1916.

46329-1-2-3  If I Were A Bee And You Were A Red,  Col rejected
    Red Rose (w/Elizabeth Brice)
46330-1-2-3  Medley (Intro. I Love To Have The      -
    Boys Around/They Always Follow Me Around/When It's Night-Time  In  Dixie-
    land/When I Discovered You/Settle Down In A One-Horse Town) (w/ Elizabeth
    Brice)

New York, January 13, 1916.

46338-2  That Hula-Hula (w/Elizabeth Brice)      Col A-1944
46339-1-2-3  Siam (w/Elizabeth Brice)            Rejected
46340-1-2-3  An Old-Fashioned Garden In Virginia      -
    (w/Elizabeth Brice)

New York, June 13, 1916.

46827-1  When The Sun Goes Down In Romany (My      Col A-2059
    Heart Goes Roaming Back To You) (w/Elizabeth Brice)

New York, June 14, 1916.

46830-  My Own Iona (Moi-One-Iona) (w/Elizabeth  Col A-2059
    Brice)

New York, March 13, 1917.

47414-1  Hawaiian Butterfly (w/Elizabeth Brice)  Col A-2226
47415-2  If You Ever Get Lonely (w/Elizabeth     Col A-2229
    Brice)

New York, March 16, 1917.

47426-  Hong Kong (w/Elizabeth Brice)            Col A-2232

New York, April 17, 1917.

47495-2  The Ghost Of The Ukulele (w/Elizabeth   Col A-2257
    Brice)

New York, June 11, 1917.

77131-2  In Lilac Time (When You Stole This      Col A-2339
    Heart Of Mine) (w/Elizabeth Brice)

New York, November 8, 1917.

77495-1-3  I'll Take You Back To Italy (w/       Col A-2459
    Elizabeth Brice)

New York, December 13, 1917.

77569-    Sweet Patootie (w/Elizabeth Brice)        Col rejected

New York, December 19, 1918.

78212-    I've A Million Girls Around Me        Col rejected

New York, March 26, 1921.

79765-    Oh ! Sweet Amelia                     Col rejected

Acc. by Frank Banta-p.              New York, April 12, 1927.

BVE-38601-4  Sometimes I'm Happy (w/Louise Groody) Vic 20609, HMV B-2520
            ("Hit The Deck")

Acc. by O/Leroy Shield.              Hollywood, April 3, 1929.

PBVE-50578-2  Broadway Melody (Film "Broadway       Vic 21964, LPV-538, LSA-3074,
              Melody")                              RD-7869, HMV B-3087
PBVE-50579-1-2-3-4  The Wedding Of The Painted      Rejected
              Doll (Film "Broadway Melody")

Hollywood, April 5, 1929.

PBVE-50579-5  The Wedding Of The Painted Doll       Vic rejected
              (Film "Broadway Melody")
PBVE-50588-1-2-3-4  You Were Meant For Me (Film         -
              "Broadway Melody")
PBVE-50589-1-2-3-4  Love Boat (Film "Broadway Melody") -

Hollywood, April 11, 1929.

PBVE-50579-7  The Wedding Of The Painted Doll       Vic 21964, HMV B-3070
              (Film "Broadway Melody")
PBVE-50588-5  You Were Meant For Me (Film "Broad-   Vic 21965        -
              way Melody")
PBVE-50589-7  Love Boat (Film "Broadway Melody")        -        HMV B-3087

Acc. by Earl Burtnett's Biltmore Trio.  Los Angeles, November, 1929.

LAE-628-    Love Ain't Nothin' But The Blues (Film  Br 4615
              "Chasing Rainbows")
LAE-629/630  Happy Days Are Here Again (Film            -
              "Chasing Rainbows")
LAE-631-    Everybody Tap (Film "Road Show")        Br 4616
LAE-632-    Lucky Me, Lovable You (Film "Road Show")  -

Acc. by Earl Burtnett and his Los Angeles Biltmore Hotel Orchestra.
                                    Los Angeles, April, 1930.

LAE-772-    Love Comes In The Moonlight (Film "Oh   Br 4840
              Sailor, Behave")
LAE-773-    Highway To Heaven (Film "Oh Sailor, Behave")-
LAE-774-    Here Comes The Sun                      Br 4849, 01020
LAE-775-    Leave A Little Smile                        -        -

## DENNIS KING

B. Coventry, Warwickshire, England, November 2, 1897; stage debut at Birmingham Repertory Theatre, 1916, where he had been call-boy and afterwards assistant stage-man-
ager; London debut in MONSIEUR BEAUCAIRE (Palace, September, 1919); to New York, in
many straight plays, then took star part in ROSE-MARIE (Imperial, September 2,1924);
greatest success was in THE VAGABOND KING (Casino, September 21, 1925), which   ran
for over two years; this was followed by THE THREE MUSKETEERS, musical version   of
Alexandre Dumas's novel (Lyric, March 13, 1928); starred in the same production   in
London (Drury Lane, March 28, 1930); returned to New York a year later, appeared in
many shows; also in London; PETTICOAT FEVER (Ritz, March 4, 1935) and the same show
in London at Daly's a year later; two more successful musicals in New York   before

retiring from the theatre (I MARRIED AN ANGEL, Shubert, May 11, 1938, and a revival of THREE SISTERS (Ethel Barrymore, December 21, 1942); also made two films: THE
VAGABOND KING (1929) and FRA DIAVOLO (1933).

Vocal, acc. by O/Rosario Bourdon.　　　　Camden, N. J., December 10, 1925.

BVE-33980-5　Song Of The Vagabonds (w/chorus)　　Vic 19897, HMV B-2426
　　　　　　　("The Vagabond King")

　Acc. by O/Nat Shilkret.　　　　　　New York, June 6, 1929.

BVE-53547-1-2-3　Love Me Tonight (w/Josefa Chekova)Vic rejected
　　　　　　　(Film "The Vagabond King")
BVE-53548-1-2　Drinking Song (w/male chorus) (Film　　-
　　　　　　　"The Vagabond King")

　　　　　　　　　　　　New York, December 13, 1929.

BVE-58106-3　If I Were King　　　　　　Vic 22263, HMV B-3363

　　　　　　　　　　　　New York, December 31, 1929.

BVE-53547-4-5-6-7　Love Me Tonight (w/Josefa　　Vic rejected
　　　　　　　Chekova) (Film "The Vagabond King")

　　　　　　　　　　　　New York, January 17, 1930.

BVE-58604-1　Nichavo ! (Nothing Matters)　　　Vic 22263, LPV-538, LSA-3074,
　　　　　　　　　　　　　　　　　　　RD-7869, HMV B-3363
BVE-58605-1-2　Because　　　　　　　　Rejected
BVE-58606-1-2　Vale　　　　　　　　　-
BVE-58607-1-2　Love Me Tonight (Film "The　　-
　　　　　　　Vagabond King")

　Acc. by Drury Lane Theatre Orchestra/Herman Finck.
　　　　　　　　　　Drury Lane Theatre, London, May 12, 1930.

WA-10381-1-2　One Kiss (w/Adrienne Brune) ("The　　Col rejected
　　　　　　　Three Musketeers")

　　　　　　　　　Drury Lane Theatre, London, May 13, 1930.

WA-10382-3　Gascony (w/chorus) ("The Three　　　Col DB-127
　　　　　　　Musketeers")
WA-10383-2　Your Eyes (w/Adrienne Brune) ("The　　Col DB-128
　　　　　　　Three Musketeers")
WAX-5575-1　March Of The Musketeers (w/Raymond　　Col DX-58
　　　　　　　Newell-Jack Livesey-Robert Woollard  & chorus)("The Three Musketeers")

　　　　　　　　　Drury Lane Theatre, London, May 16, 1930.

WA-10381-3　One Kiss (w/Adrienne Brune) ("The　　Col DB-128
　　　　　　　Three Musketeers")
WA-10392-2　My Sword And I (w/chorus) ("The Three　Col DB-127
　　　　　　　Musketeers")

　Acc. by O/Ray Noble.　　　　　Small Queen's Hall, London, June 23, 1930.

Bb-19848-1　Blue Is The Night　　　　　　HMV B-3523
Bb-19849-2　Without A Song　　　　　　　-

## DOROTHY LAMOUR

B. New Orleans, 1914; r.n. Dorothy Kaumeyer.  Titled "Miss New Orleans of 1931";  her
first film was THE JUNGLE PRINCESS (1936); famed for appearances in the Bing Crosby
and Bob Hope ROAD series of comedies (see Bing Crosby), she also appeared as  leading lady in SWING HIGH, SWING LOW; HIGH, WIDE AND HANDSOME; THE THRILL OF A  LIFE-
TIME and THE HURRICANE (1937); THE BIG BROADCAST OF 1938; HER JUNGLE LOVE;  TROPIC
HOLIDAY and SPAWN OF THE NORTH (1938); MAN ABOUT TOWN; ST. LOUIS BLUES; TYPHOON and
DISPUTED PASSAGE, also THE ROAD TO SINGAPORE, the first of the series (1939); JOHNNY

APOLLO; MOON OVER BURMA and CHAD HANNA (1940); ALOMA OF THE SOUTH SEAS;THE FLEET'S
IN (1941); BEYOND THE BLUE HORIZON (1942); DIXIE and AND THE ANGELS SING (1943); MY
FAVOURITE BRUNETTE (with Bob Hope but not Bing Crosby - officially, anyway !)(1947)
and many others; retired in 1953, but made guest appearances in THE  ROAD  TO HONG
KONG (1961), DONOVAN'S REEF (1963) and PAJAMA PARTY (1965).

Vocal, acc. by O/Cy Feuer.                    Los Angeles, February 4, 1937.

LA-1243-C  Moonlight And Shadows (Film "The Jungle   Br 7829, 02416, Col DB-1803
              Princess")
LA-1244-A  Panamania (Film "Swing High, Swing Low")    -         -     Col DB-1811,
                                                     Epic SN-6059
LA-1245-   Swing High, Swing Low (Film "Swing     Br 7838, 02421
              High, Swing Low")
LA-1246-   I Hear A Call To Arms (Film "Swing        -         -     Col DC-416
              High, Swing Low")

                                      Los Angeles, November 5, 1937.

LA-1515-B  You Took The Words Right Out Of My     Br 8017, 02562, Col DC-416
              Heart (Film "The Big Broadcast of 1938")
LA-1516-B  Thanks For The Memory (Film "The Big      -         -     Col DB-1803
              Broadcast of 1938")

  Acc. by O/Herbie Kay.                      Los Angeles, April 30, 1938.

LA-1633-A  Lovelight In The Starlight (Film "Her   Br 8132, Col DB-1777
              Jungle Love")
LA-1634-A  Little Lady Make-Believe                  -        Col DB-1783
LA-1635-A  Tonight Will Live (Film "Tropic          Br 8154     -
              Holiday")
LA-1636-A  On A Tropic Night (Film "Tropic Holiday")  -     Col DB-1811

  Acc. by O/Jerry Joyce.                     Los Angeles, December 15, 1938.

LA-1777-A  I Go For That (Film "St. Louis Blues")   Br 8291, Col DB-1851
LA-1778-A  Junior (Film "St. Louis Blues")          Br 8304, Col DB-1852
LA-1779-A  Kinda Lonesome (Film "St. Louis Blues")    -         -
LA-1780-A  Let's Dream In The Moonlight (Film      Br 8291, Col DB-1851
              "St. Louis Blues")

  Acc. by O/Lou Bring.                       Hollywood, April 26, 1939.

PBS-036149-3  Strange Enchantment (Film "Man      BB B-10265, HMV B-8940
                 About Town")
PBS-036150-3  That Sentimental Sandwich (Film        -           -
                 "Man About Town")
PBS-036151-3  The Lamp Is Low                     BB B-10302
PBS-036152-2  The Man I Love                         -         HMV B-8963

                                      Hollywood, July 28, 1939.

PBS-036374-4  You Took Me Out Of This World      BB B-10382, HMV B-8963
PBS-036375-5  Comes Love                             -         HMV B-8992
PBS-036376-2  My Heart Keeps Cryin'                            -
PBS-036377-2  I'll Take An Option On You         BB B-10494
PBS-036378-3  I'm All A-Tremble Over You                       HMV B-9016
PBS-036379-2  Paradise                           BB B-10494     -

                                      Hollywood, November 21, 1939.

PBS-042263-2  Sweet Potato Piper (Film "The Road  BB B-10651, HMV B-9055
                 To Singapore")
PBS-042264-2  Palms Of Paradise (Film "Typhoon")     -           -
PBS-042265-1  The Moon And The Willow Tree (Film  BB B-10608, HMV B-9049
                 "The Road To Singapore")
PBS-042266-2  Too Romantic (Film "The Road To        -           -
                 Singapore")

Hollywood, January 19, 1940.

| | | |
|---|---|---|
| PBS-042384-1 | I Gotta Right To Sing The Blues | BB B-10758, HMV B-9098 |
| PBS-042385-2 | It Had To Be You | —            — |
| PBS-042386-2 | Your Kiss | BB B-10630 |
| PBS-042387-1 | This Is The Beginning Of The End (Film "Johnny Apollo") | — |

Hollywood, August 5, 1940.

| | | |
|---|---|---|
| PBS-049976-2 | Moon Over Burma (Film "Moon Over Burma") | BB B-10891, HMV B-9203 |
| PBS-049977-2 | There's Danger In Your Eyes, Cherie | BB B-10864 |
| PBS-049978-2 | I'm Gettin' Sentimental Over You | — |
| PBS-049979-1 | Mexican Magic (Film "Moon Over Burma") | BB B-10891, HMV B-9203 |

## FRANCES LANGFORD

B. Lakeland, Fla., 1914; majored in music at Southern College, wanted to sing opera professionally, but tonsillectomy changed her vocal capacity from soprano to contralto; Rudy Vallee heard her in New Orleans, guested her on his radio show (1932); she appeared in New York in a bad flop (HERE GOES THE BRIDE, November 7, 1933),but she sang NIGHT AND DAY for composer Cole Porter, who arranged with Walter Wanger - powerful film producer at the time - for her to be signed for film work without an audition or test. Her best-known films are :- EVERY NIGHT AT EIGHT (with George Raft) and COLLEGIATE (1935); BROADWAY MELODY OF 1936; HOLLYWOOD HOTEL (1937); TOO MANY GIRLS (1940); HIT PARADE OF 1941; many others, with guest appearance in 1953 in THE GLENN MILLER STORY; chosen as All-American Girl in 1939; began long working association with Bob Hope, 1941; toured with him throughout the war and received a citation from General Eisenhower as a result; subsequently entertained troops in Korea and Vietnam.

Vocal, acc. by Frank Leithner-p.          New York, June 15, 1931.

    Wabash Moon                              Vic test (un-numbered)

New York, July 1, 1931.

BRC-1118  I'm Thru' With Love/Makin' Faces At The  Vic test
    Man In The Moon

Acc. by the Four New Yorkers.          New York, August 1, 1932.

| | | |
|---|---|---|
| 152247- | I Can't Believe It's True | Col 2696-D |
| 152248- | Having A Good Time, Wish You Were Here | — |

Acc. by Jesse Crawford at the Paramount Theatre Organ.
New York, October 25, 1932.

BS-71773-1  When Mother Played The Organ (And     Vic 24191
    Daddy Sang A Hymn)

Acc. by small instrumental group.          New York, February 16, 1933.

| | | |
|---|---|---|
| 265053-1 | Stormy Weather | Col DB-1124 |
| 265054-1 | You Hi-De-Hi-ing Me | — |

Acc. by studio orchestra.          New York, March 17, 1933.

| | | |
|---|---|---|
| BS-75535-1 | Moon Song (That Wasn't Meant For Me) | BB B-5016, 1840, Eld 1954 |
| BS-75536-1 | Meet Me In The Gloaming | —        —        — |

New York, March 22, 1934.

| | | |
|---|---|---|
| 14983-1 | Hold My Hand | Ban 33027, Mt M-12986, Or 2872, Per 12994, Ro 2252, Rex 8231 |
| 14984-1 | Nasty Man | As above |

Acc. by Mahlon Merrick and his Music.   Los Angeles, July 31, 1935.

LA-1066-B  Speaking Confidentially (Film "Every    Br 7513, 02085
           Night At Eight")
LA-1067-A  I Feel A Song Coming On (Film "Every     Br 7512, 02084
           Night At Eight")
LA-1068-A  Then You've Never Been Blue (Film              -        -
           "Every Night At Eight")
LA-1069-A  I'm In The Mood For Love (Film "Every    Br 7513, 02085, 02961,
           Night At Eight")                         Epic SN-6059

Acc. by O/Victor Young.                   Los Angeles, November 19, 1935.

DLA-265-A  You Hit The Spot (Film "Collegiate")    Dec 663, Br 02156
DLA-266-A  Will I Ever Know ? (Film "Palm Springs")   -    Br 02252
DLA-267-A  Dream Girl Of Pi K.A.                   Dec Special Record for the artist

                                          Los Angeles, April 4, 1936.

DLA-343-A  The Hills Of Old Wyomin' (w/The         Dec 783, Br 02242
           Uptowners Quartet) (Film "Palm Springs")
DLA-344-A  I Don't Want To Make History (I Just          -        -
           Want To Make Love) (Film "Palm Springs")
DLA-345-A  Melody From The Sky                     Dec 775, Br 02216
DLA-346-A  Is It True What They Say About Dixie ?        -        -

                                          Los Angeles, July 30, 1936.

DLA-489-A-B  When Did You Leave Heaven ?           Rejected
DLA-490-   Long Ago And Far Away                   Dec 893, Br 02378
DLA-491-   It's Like Reaching For The Moon              -        -
DLA-492-A  Deep Shadows                            Dec 902, Br 02287

                                          Los Angeles, August 3, 1936.

DLA-508-A  Easy To Love (Film "Born To Dance")     Dec 940, Br 02359
DLA-509-A  Rap Tap On Wood (Film "Born To Dance")  Dec 939, Br 02358

                                          Los Angeles, August 5, 1936.

DLA-537-A  I've Got You Under My Skin (Film "Born  Dec 939, Br 02358
           To Dance")

                                          Los Angeles, August 12, 1936.

DLA-556-A  Swingin' The Jinx Away (Film "Born To   Dec 940, Br 02359
           Dance")

                                          Los Angeles, August 13, 1936.

DLA-573-A  When Did You Leave Heaven ?             Dec 902, Br 02287

Acc. by Jimmy Dorsey and his Orchestra. Los Angeles, August 17, 1936.

DLA-579-A  Pennies From Heaven  - Medley          Dec 15027, 29226, Br 0134
           (Frances Langford sings LET'S CALL A HEART A HEART, and SO DO I as duet
           with Bing Crosby)
DLA-580-A  Pennies From Heaven (w/Bing Crosby and       -        -        -        AH-139
           Louis Armstrong)

Acc. by O/Victor Young.                   Los Angeles, March 14, 1937.

DLA-755-   Sweet Heartache                         Dec 1202, Br 02430
DLA-756-   Was It Rain ?                                -        -
                                          Los Angeles, September 14, 1937.

DLA-916-   Harbor Lights                           Dec 1441
DLA-917-   Stardust On The Moon                    Dec 1440, Br 02479
DLA-918-   My Cabin Of Dreams                      Dec 1441    -
DLA-919-   So Many Memories                        Dec 1440, Br 02537

Los Angeles, September 16, 1937.

| | | |
|---|---|---|
| DLA-926- | Dream Girl Of Pi K.A. | Dec 1454 |
| DLA-927-A | Little Fraternity Pin | -        Br 02563 |
| DLA-928- | If It's The Last Thing I Do | Dec 1464, Br 02494 |
| DLA-929- | Everything You Said Came True | -        - |

Acc. by O/Harry Sosnik.                    Los Angeles, November 7, 1937.

| | | |
|---|---|---|
| DLA-1025-A | I'm Gettin' Sentimental Over You | Dec 1577, Br 02537 |
| DLA-1026-A | Sweet Someone | -        Br 02583 |
| DLA-1027-A | Once In A While | Dec 1542, Br 02563 |
| DLA-1028-A | Farewell My Love | |

Los Angeles, April 6, 1938.

| | | |
|---|---|---|
| DLA-1192-A | Please Be Kind | Dec 1760, Br 02599 |
| DLA-1193-A | At Your Beck And Call | -        Br 02647 |
| DLA-1194-A | Night And Day | Dec 1831     - |

Los Angeles, April 11, 1938.

| | | |
|---|---|---|
| DLA-1205- | Carry Me Back To Old Virginny (w/male  Dec 15040, Br 0139 | |
| | octet) | |
| DLA-1206- | Little Grey Home In The West (w/male octet)- | - |

Los Angeles, April 25, 1938.

| | | |
|---|---|---|
| DLA-1286-A | Then You've Never Been Blue (Film        Dec 1831, Br 02730 | |
| | "Every Night At Eight") | |

Los Angeles, May 3, 1938.

| | | |
|---|---|---|
| DLA-1291-A | Serenade (Schubert)(w/Paul Taylor Ch.) Dec 2124, Br 02655 | |
| DLA-1292-A | The Last Rose Of Summer (w/Paul Taylor Ch.)- | - |

Acc. by Eddie Dunstedter-pipe organ.    Los Angeles, November 10, 1938.

| | | |
|---|---|---|
| DLA-1556-A | Silent Night, Holy Night | Dec 2188, Br 02876 |
| DLA-1557-A | O Come All Ye Faithful | -        - |

Acc. by O/Victor Young.                    Los Angeles, November 19, 1938.

| | | |
|---|---|---|
| DLA-1563- | At Long Last Love | Dec 2197 |
| DLA-1564-A | Hurry Home | -        Br 02730 |
| DLA-1565-A | I Won't Tell A Soul | Dec 2218, Br 02872, 02965 |

Los Angeles, November 23, 1938.

| | | |
|---|---|---|
| DLA-1581- | Everybody's Laughing | Dec 2218 |

Los Angeles, December 9, 1938.

| | | |
|---|---|---|
| DLA-1624-A | Gypsy Love Song (w/Bing Crosby) | Dec 2316, Br 02849 |
| DLA-1625-A | I'm Falling In Love With Someone | -        - |
| | (w/Bing Crosby) | |
| DLA-1626-A | 'Neath The Southern Moon | Dec 2681, Br 02853 |
| DLA-1627-A | A Kiss In The Dark | -        - |

Los Angeles, December 14, 1938.

| | | |
|---|---|---|
| DLA-1653- | From Now On | Dec 2229 |
| DLA-1654-A | Get Out Of Town | -        Br 02872 |
| DLA-1655-A | Falling In Love With Love | Dec 2247, Br 02946 |
| DLA-1656- | You Have Cast Your Shadow On The Sea | - |

Los Angeles, December 18, 1938.

| | | |
|---|---|---|
| DLA-1685-A | This Can't Be Love (w/Rudy Vallee) | Dec 2248, Br 02883 |
| DLA-1686-A | The Shortest Day Of The Year (w/Rudy | -        - |
| | Vallee) | |

                                        Los Angeles, March 17, 1939.

DLA-1729-   This Is It                              Dec 2376
DLA-1730-   It's All Yours                          -
DLA-1731-   Tears From My Inkwell                   Dec 2386, Br 02813
DLA-1732-   A Fool For Love                         -          -

    Acc. by O/Harry Sosnik.             Los Angeles, March 24, 1939.

DLA-1738-A  Blue Evening                            Dec 2438, Br 02965

                                        Los Angeles, March 30, 1939.

DLA-1741-A  (I'm In Love With) The Honorable Mr.    Dec 2438, Br 02946
                So-and-So

                                        Los Angeles, June 30, 1939.

DLA-1791-A  Someone To Watch Over Me               Dec 2882, Br 02994
DLA-1792-A  The Man I Love                          -          -

                                        Los Angeles, July 1, 1939.

DLA-1798-A  Moonglow                                Dec 2861, Br 02962
DLA-1799-A  I'm In The Mood For Love (Film "Every   Dec 2860
                Night At Eight")
DLA-1800-A  Blue Moon                               Dec 2860, Br 02961
DLA-1801-A  Paradise                                Dec 2862, Br 02963

                                        Los Angeles, July 3, 1939.

DLA-1802-A  Body And Soul                           Dec 2862, Br 02963
DLA-1803-A  The Boulevard Of Broken Dreams          Dec 2861, Br 02962
DLA-1804-A  Am I Blue ?                             Dec 2747, Br 02964
DLA-1805-A  Echoes Of Hawaii                        Dec 2595, Br 02829
DLA-1806-A  The Man With The Mandolin               -          -
DLA-1807-A  Between The Devil And The Deep Blue Sea Dec 2747, Br 02964

                                        Los Angeles, February 19, 1940.

DLA-1930-   Kuu Ipo (My Sweetheart)                 Dec 3046, 25164
DLA-1931-   Moonlight Over Molokai                  Dec 3047, 25166
DLA-1932-   When Hilo Hattie Does The Hilo Hop      Dec 3046, 25164
DLA-1933-   Manuela Boy                             Dec 3047, 25166

                                        Los Angeles, February 24, 1940.

DLA-1947-A  With The Wind And The Rain In Your Hair Dec 3050, Br 02977
DLA-1948-A  Say It                                  Dec 3076, Br 03022
DLA-1949-A  Palms Of Paradise                       -          -
DLA-1950-A  When You Wish Upon A Star               Dec 3050, Br 02977

    Acc. by O/Victor Young.             Los Angeles, July 30, 1940.

DLA-2078-A  Love Lies                               Dec 3345, Br 03096
DLA-2079-A  Dreaming Out Loud                       Dec 3400, Br 03204
DLA-2080-A  You're Nearer                           -          -
DLA-2081-A  And So Do I                             Dec 3345, Br 03096

                                        Los Angeles, September 6, 1940.

DLA-2128-A  Two Dreams Met (w/Tony Martin)          Dec 3415, F-7725
DLA-2129-A  Our Love Affair (w/Tony Martin)         -          -

                                        Los Angeles, September 10, 1940.

DLA-2143-A  Who Am I ? (Film "Hit Parade of 1941")  Dec 3433, Br 03134
DLA-2144-A  In The Cool Of The Evening (Film "Hit   -          -
                Parade of 1941")

Acc. by Dick McIntyre and his Harmony Hawaiians.
                                         Los Angeles, August 20, 1941.

DLA-2660-    Lovely Hula Hands                        Dec 25165
DLA-2661-    South Sea Sadie                             -
DLA-2662-    In Waikiki                               Dec 3990
DLA-2663-    White Ginger Blossoms                       -

    Acc. by O/Victor Young.             Los Angeles, September 9, 1941.

DLA-2742-    White Blossoms Of Tah-Ni                 Dec 4035, Br 03322
DLA-2743-    Tropical Magic                              -        -
DLA-2744-A   Smilin' Through                          Dec 4020, Br 03277
DLA-2745-B   A Little Love, A Little Kiss                -        -


                                         Los Angeles, January 28, 1942.

DLA-2863-    April In My Heart                        Dec 4195
DLA-2864-    Baltimore Oriole (w/whistling by the     Dec 29216
                composer, Hoagy Carmichael)


                                         Los Angeles, February 6, 1942.

DLA-2889-    Blue Tahitian Moon                       Dec 4195
DLA-2890-    I'll Be Seeing You                       Dec 18505
DLA-2891-    In The Blue Hills Of Maine               Rejected ?

    Acc. by O/Harry Sosnik.             New York, June 14, 1942.

70881-       Can't Help Lovin' Dat Man                Dec 18765
70882-       Bill                                        -
70883-       Serenade In Blue                         Dec 18434, Br 03415
70884-       At Last                                     -        -

    Acc. by O/Victor Young.             Los Angeles, July 19, 1942.

DLA-3108-    Why Do I Love You ? (w/Tony Martin)      Dec 18763, 25262

## GRACE LA RUE

B. Kansas City, Mo., 1882; stage debut at 11 as member of Julia Marlowe's company; a
few years later appeared in vaudeville with a partner as Burke and La Rue; New York
debut in THE BLUE MOON (Casino, November 3, 1906); appeared in FOLLIES OF 1908(New
York Roof, June 15, 1908) and other musical productions before coming to London to
appear in vaudeville at the Palace, August 4, 1913, where she created a  sensation
with her singing of YOU MADE ME LOVE YOU; appeared at the Lyric there in  THE GIRL
WHO DIDN'T (December 18, 1913); returned to U.S.A., continued vaudeville   career:
then took part in HITCHY-KOO (Cohan and Harris, June 7, 1917); DEAR ME  (Republic,
January 17, 1921); THE MUSIC BOX REVUE at the Music Box, New York (October 23,1922
for a year); more vaudeville appearances, notably in Chicago (October, 1923)and in
London (Coliseum, July, 1924, in a sketch with her husband Hale Hamilton,  DANGER-
OUS ADVICE; they appeared also in the only film she ever made, THAT'S GOOD  (1919)
under the pseudonym Stella Gray; last major success in GREENWICH VILLAGE  FOLLIES,
Winter Garden, April 9, 1928.  D. 1956.

Vocal, acc. by studio orchestra/? Charles A. Prince.
                                         New York, May, 1910.

4475-2   Clap Hands                               Col A-904
4476-2   Does Anybody Here Know Nancy ?              -

                                         New York, December  16; 1910.

19167-1-2  What's Your Hurry, Birdie ?            Col rejected

    Acc. by studio orchestra/? Herman Finck. London, August 22, 1913.

AL-7482f  You Made Me Love You                    HMV 03343, C-576
AL-7483f  Highland Mary                           HMV 03344.

Acc. by unknown p.                           London, November 27, 1913.

AL-7667f  Not Your Money, Just Your Heart        HMV 03358, C-576

                                             London, February 6, 1914.

AL-7796f  A Tango Dream ("The Girl Who Didn't")  HMV 03373, C-575

## GEORGE LASHWOOD

B. London (?), 1862; British music-hall comedian with impeccable diction who special-
ised in the rousing chorus number; active in British and American vaudeville during
the "golden years"; d. Worcestershire, England, January 20, 1942.

Vocal, acc. by Fred Gaisberg-p.          London, c. September, 1898.

          Parody on "I Want Yer, Ma Honey"      Ber 2059
          It's A Thing I Never Interfere With   Ber 2076

Acc. by unknown p.                           London, April 29, 1903.

  99-R   I'm Coming Home To You              G&T 02017
 100-R   W-O-M-A-N                           G&T 02018
3547-R   There's A Girl Wanted There         G&T GC2-2856
3548-R   Fol-The-Rol-Lol                     Rejected
3549-R   Woman All Over                      G&T GC2-2852

                                             London, June, 1904.

25627-   W-O-M-A-N                           Col 25627, 201032 (cyl.)
25628-   There's A Girl Wanted There         Col 25628, 201033 (cyl.)
25629-   The Latch Key                       Col 25629, 201034 (cyl.)
25630-   Why Doesn't She Do That To Me ?     Col 25630, 201035 (cyl.)
25631-   Twenty Girls, Thirty Girls          Col 25631, 201037 (cyl.)

Acc. by studio orchestra.                    London, July 13, 1905.

2256/7b   The Statues In Trafalgar Square    Rejected
2258/9b   The Best World                     G&T GC3-2286
  2260b   Riding On Top Of A Car             G&T GC3-2284
  2261b   My Latch Key                       G&T GC3-2285
  2264b   The Ladies I've Met                Rejected
          The Best World                     G&T 3-2603 (7")
          The Ladies I've Met                G&T 3-2604 (7")
          My Latch Key                       G&T 3-2605 (7")
NOTE:- Matrices 2262/3b are not by George Lashwood.

                                             London, May, 1907.

  6194e   Twilight                           Zon X-42616, 543
          Feathers                           Zon X-42624
          The Serpentine                     Zon X-42670

                                             London, early September, 1908.

  8886e   Hang Out The Front Door Key        Zon 39
  8887e   Saturday-aturday                   -
  8889e   Dear Mr. Admiral                   Zon 58
  8891e   Shall I Meet You On The Bois de    Zon X-42816
            Boulogne ?
  8892e   The Baby's Parade                  Zon 58

                                             London, June 23, 1909.

 10328e   One Of The Girls                   Zon 214
 10329e   I've Been Out With Charlie Brown   Zon 170
 10330e   Sea, Sea, Sea                      -
 10331e   Send For A Policeman               Zon 162, 195
 10332e   There's Another Fellow Looks Like Me        -

London, c. August, 1909.

| 26644- | What A Don | Col 26644, 1175 |
|--------|-----------|-----------------|
| 26645- | One Of The Girls | Col 26645    - |

| | I've Been Out With Charlie Brown | Col 1163 |
|---|-------------------------------|----------|
| | Sea, Sea, Sea | - |

New York, mid-January, 1910.

| 30328-2 | There's Another Fellow Looks Like Me | Col A-5164 |
|---------|--------------------------------------|-----------|
| 30329-1 | My Latch Key | - |
| 30330-2 | Send For A P'liceman (sic) | Col A-5167 |

| 30335-1 | Sea, Sea, Sea | Col A-5157 |
|---------|---------------|-----------|
| 30336-1 | In The Twi-Twi-Twilight | - |

London, September 2, 1910.

| 12199e | Just For A Girl | Zon 415 |
|--------|-----------------|---------|
| 12200e | The Moonlight Promenade | Zon X2-42031 |
| 12202e | Mr. Pat O'Hare | Zon 378 |
| 12203e | Oh, Blow The Scenery On The Railway ! | Zon X2-42030, 544 |
| 12204e | Rainy Afternoon | Zon X2-42039, 543 |

London, c. October, 1912.

| 92144 | A Long, Long Walk | Pathe 5352 |
|-------|-------------------|-----------|
| 92146 | The Number On The Door | - |
| 92148 | Alexander's Bagpipe Band | Pathe 112 |
| | The Ragtime Sea | Pathe 5353 |
| | Take A Tip From Father | - |

London, c. December, 1912.

| | I Forgot The Number On The Door | Col 2065 |
|---|-------------------------------|----------|
| | It's A Long, Long Walk | - |
| | Take A Tip From Father | Col 2092 |
| | Alexander's Bagpipe Band | - |

London, c. February, 1913.

| 92189 | My Latch Key | Pathe 112 |
|-------|--------------|-----------|
| | Rainy Afternoon | Pathe 124 |
| | There's A Good Time Coming For Charlie | - |

## HARRY LAUDER

B. Portobello, Scotland, August 4, 1870; as a boy worked in flax mill, and in a coal-
mine for ten years; stage debut in travelling show competition in Arbroath, August
24, 1882; London debut at Gatti's Music Hall, Westminster, March 19, 1900, making a
huge hit with TOBERMORY; CALLAGHAN, and THE LASS O' KILLIECRANKIE; repeated success
at the Royal, Holborn, London, December 24, 1900; established his reputation at the
Oxford and London Pavilion; became the highest-paid music-hall artist, touring the
country, the U.S.A. (twenty-five times there between 1909 and 1932), Canada, Australia, New Zealand and Africa; appeared before H.M. King Edward VII in 1908; during World War I he organized many concerts and entertainments for troops (his only
son was killed in action on December 28, 1916); knighted for these services in 1919.
One appearance in revue (THREE CHEERS, Shaftesbury, London, December 22, 1916); made
several short films based on his best-known songs.  Retired to Lauder Ha', Strath-
aven, Lanarkshire, Scotland, and died there in February, 1950.

Vocal, acc. by ? Landon Ronald-p.          London, February, 1902.

| 1571 | To Jericho | G&T GC2-2657 |
|------|-----------|--------------|
| 1572 | Killiecrankie | G&T GC2-2636 |
| 1573 | Early In The Morning | G&T GC2-2644 |
| 1574 | I Took Him Up To Take Him Down | G&T GC2-2658 |
| 1575 | Tobermory | G&T GC2-2671 |
| 1576 | The Referee | G&T GC2-2645 |

London, February, 1902.

| 4257 | Rob Roy Tam O'Shanter O'Brian | G&T 2-2075 (7") |
|------|------------------------------|-----------------|
|      | Mrs. Macfarlane              | G&T 2-2074 (7") |
|      | To Jericho                   | G&T 2-2162 (7") |

London, December 15, 1903.

| 4692 | The Saftest Of The Family               | G&T GC3-2031    |
|------|------------------------------------------|-----------------|
| 4693 | I Took The Prize                        | G&T GC3-2032    |
| 4694 | Callaghan ("Calligan" on the label)     | G&T GC3-2033    |
|      | The Saftest Of The Family               | G&T 2-2414 (7") |
|      | Hielan' Mary                            | G&T 2-2417 (7") |
|      | Callaghan ("Calligan" on the label)     | G&T 2-2418 (7") |

London, December 17, 1903.

| 4718 | The Magistrate          | G&T GC3-2003                 |
|------|-------------------------|------------------------------|
| 4719 | The Last Of The Sandies | G&T GC3-2034, Zon X-42328    |
| 4720 | If I Were In            | Rejected                     |
| 4721 | Title unknown           | G&T GC3-2035                 |
| 4722 | I Am The Man            | Rejected                     |
| 5787 | Hey Donal'              | G&T 2-2442 (7")              |
|      | Tattie Soup             | G&T 2-2430 (7")              |
|      | To Jericho              | G&T 2-2423 (7")              |

London, December 22, 1903.

| 4735 | Stop Your Ticklin', Jock | G&T GC3-2004, Zon X-42355       |
|------|--------------------------|---------------------------------|
| 4736 | Mr. John Mackay          | G&T GC3-2005                    |
| 4737 | Mr. John Mackay          | Rejected                        |
| 4738 | Jean McNeil              | G&T GC3-2006                    |
| 5803 | Stop Your Ticklin', Jock | G&T 2-2420, Zon 42230 (7")      |
| 5806 | Mrs. Macfarlane          | G&T 2-2422 (7")                 |
|      | Killiecrankie            | G&T 2-2421 (7")                 |

London, January 6, 1904.

| 4800/1 | The Saftest Of The Family    | G&T rejected |
|--------|-------------------------------|--------------|
| 4802   | The Councillor Magistrate     | –            |
| 4803   | Killiecrankie                 | –            |

London, February 12, 1904.

| 5032/3 | Killiecrankie | G&T rejected |
|--------|---------------|--------------|

London, c. October, 1904.

| 60453 | A Trip To Tobermory | Pathe 60453, 276, 1161, 4030 |
|-------|---------------------|------------------------------|
| 60454 | Calligam, Call Again | Pathe 60454, 281, 1166, 8029 |
| 60457 | Mrs. Jean Macfarlane | Pathe 60457, 280, 1165 |
| 60458 | Rising Early In The Morning | Pathe 60458, 284, 1169, 8029 |
| 60459 | Hey, Donal' | Pathe 60459, 283, 1168, 8693 |
| 60460 | Jericho | Pathe 60460   –     –     – 4046 |
| 60462 | Inverary | Pathe 60462 |
| 60463 | Stop Your Ticklin', Jock | Pathe 60463, 276, 1161, 8685 |
| 60464 | The Waddin' O' Lauchie MacGraw (sic) | Pathe 60464, 282, 1167 |
| 60465 | Harry Lauder in a snatch from his | Pathe 60465, 281, 1166 |
|       | famous TOBERMORY (Intro. Rocked In The Cradle Of The Deep) | |
| 60466 | The Saftest O' The Family | Pathe 60466, 274, 1159 |
| 60467 | Tattie Soup | Pathe 60467, 280, 1165, 8686 |
| 60468 | She's Ma Daisy | Pathe 60468, 279, 1164, 4030 |
| 60469 | Fu' The Noo | Pathe 60469   –     – 8685 |

London, November 9, 1904.

| 6225b | The Wedding Of Lauchie McGraw    | G&T GC3-2174 |
|-------|-----------------------------------|--------------|
| 6226b | A Trip To Inverary                | G&T GC3-2175 |
| 6227b | Rocked In The Cradle Of The Deep  | Rejected     |

Acc. by studio orchestra.                    London, November 29, 1904.

| | | |
|---|---|---|
| 6592½a | Rising Early In The Morning | G&T 3-2542 (7") |
| 6593½a | Mr. John Mackay | G&T 3-2544 (7") |
| 6594½a | Stop Your Tickling, Jock | G&T 3-2543, Zon 42350 (7") |
| 6278½b | Killiecrankie | G&T GC3-2184 |
| 6279½b | Rising Early In The Morning | G&T GC3-2179, Zon X-42202 |
| 6280½b | The Saftest Of The Family | Rejected |
| 6281b | The Saftest Of The Family | G&T GC3-2185, Zon X-42203 |
| 6282½b | Stop Your Tickling, Jock | G&T GC3-2180 |
| 6283½b | **Mr. John Mackay** | G&T GC3-2186, Zon X-42305 |

London, May 18, 1905.

| | | |
|---|---|---|
| 970d | She Is Ma Daisy | G&T 3-2602, Zon 42351 (7") |
| 971d | I've Something In The Bottle For The Morning | G&T 3-2615 (7") |
| | Tobermory | G&T 3-2600 (7") |
| 2100e | She Is Ma Daisy | G&T GC3-2267 |
| 2101e | She Is Ma Daisy | Rejected |
| | I've Something In The Bottle For The Morning | G&T GC3-2271 |

London, August 26, 1905.

| | | |
|---|---|---|
| | I Love A **Lassie** | G&T 3-2633, Zon 42352 (7") |
| | Ticklie Geordie | Zon 42277 |
| 2521/2e | Sound Advice | G&T GC3-2362, Zon X-42581, 545 |
| 2523e | I Love A Lassie | G&T GC3-2322, Zon 547 |
| 2524e | Ticklie Geordie | G&T GC3-2321 |
| 2525e | Sandy MacPherson's Cauld (w/Russell Hunting as "Casey") | Zon X-41012 |

London, c. June, 1906.

| | | |
|---|---|---|
| 60286 | We Parted On The Shore - Part 1 | Pathe 60286, 277, 1162 |
| 60287 | We Parted On The Shore - Part 2 | Pathe 60287  -   - |
| 60288 | I Love A Lassie, Ma Scotch Bluebell | Pathe 60288, 278, 1163, 8021 |
| 60289 | Sound Advice | Pathe 60289  -   -  4046 |
| 60290 | Rob Roy McIntosh | Pathe 60290, 275, 1160, 8021 |
| 60291 | The Bonnie Wee Man | Pathe 60291, 273, 1158 |
| 60292 | A Cough Lozenge | Pathe 60292  -   - |
| 60293 | Fu' The Noo (2nd edition) | Pathe 60293, 275, 1160 |
| 60294 | Tobermory (2nd edition) | Pathe 60294, 274, 1159 |
| 60295 | She Is Ma Daisy (2nd edition) | Pathe 60295, 284, 1169 |
| | | |
| 60300 | Piper Macfarlane | Pathe 60300, 285, 1170 |
| 60301 | I Wish I Had Someone To Love Me | Pathe 60301, 286, 1171 |
| 60302 | The Reason Noo I Wear A Kilt | Pathe 60302, 282, 1167, 8686 |
| 60303 | Aye Waken O ! | Pathe 60303, 286, 1171 |
| 60304 | Jean M'Neill (sic) | Pathe 60304, 285, 1170 |

London, August 16, 1906.

| | | |
|---|---|---|
| 8671b | We Parted On The Shore | G&T GC3-2470, Zon X-42582, 548 |
| 8672b | We Parted On The Shore | As above or rejected ? |
| 8673b | Aye Waken O ! | G&T GC3-2469, Zon X-42572 |
| 8674b | Aye Waken O ! | As above or rejected ? |
| 8675b | I Wish I Had Someone To Love Me | G&T GC3-2473, HMV E-170 |
| 8676b | Tobermory | Rejected |
| 8677b | Tobermory | G&T GC3-2860 |
| 8678b | Calligan | Rejected |
| 8691b | Wearing Kilts | G&T GC3-2474 |
| 8692b | Jean McNeill | G&T GC3-2764 |
| 8693b | The Lass O' Killiecrankie | Zon X-42891, 604 |
| 8694b | A Trip To Inverary | G&T GC3-2765, Zon X-42859, 604 |
| 8695b | Stop Your Tickling, Jock | G&T GC3-2475, Zon X-42573, 545 |
| 8696b | The Wedding Of Lauchie McGraw | G&T GC3-2861 |
| 8697b | The Meeting Of Marry Lauder And Will Evans | Zon X-41016 |

NOTE:- Matrices 8679/8690 inclusive are not by Harry Lauder.

London, March, 1907.

| | | |
|---|---|---|
| 10246b | Gilt-Edged Bertie | G&T GC3-2851, Zon X2-42056 |
| 10248b | The Saftest Of The Family | G&T GC3-2864 |
| 1880f | Stop Your Tickling, Jock | G&T 02089, HMV D-402 |
| 1883f | Rob Roy McIntosh | G&T 02093 |
| 1888f | A Nicht Wi' Burns | G&T 01002 |

London, c. August, 1907.

| | | |
|---|---|---|
| 2022f | I've Something In The Bottle For The Morning | G&T 01003, HMV D-396 |
| 2026f | She Is My Daisy | G&T 01004, HMV D-399 |
| 2028f | I Love A Lassie | G&T 02116, HMV D-393 |

London, c. November, 1907 (all issued 2-08)

| | | |
|---|---|---|
| | Rob Roy Mackintosh | Ed 19173 |
| | She's My Daisy | Ed 19174 |
| | Tobermory | Ed 19175 |
| | We Parted On The Shore | Ed 19176 |
| | The Saftest O' The Family | Ed 19177, Sc 877 (LP) |
| | I Love A Lassie | Ed 19178 |
| | Stop Yer Ticklin', Jock (sic) | Ed 19179 |

London, March, 1908.

| | | |
|---|---|---|
| 2349f | The Wedding Of Lauchie McGraw | HMV 02138, D-441 |
| 2351f | A Trip To Inverary | HMV 02155 |
| 2352f | The Wedding Of Sandy McNab | HMV 02132, D-406 |
| 2355f | When I Get Back To Bonnie Scotland | HMV 02135, D-409 |

London, June, 1908.

| | | |
|---|---|---|
| 8487e | When I Get Back To Bonnie Scotland | Zon X-42801, 549 |
| 8490e | The Wedding Of Sandy McNab | Zon X-42793  - |
| 2481f | That's The Reason Noo I Wear A Kilt | HMV 02142, D-403 |
| 2482f | Tobermory | HMV 02146, D-408 |
| 2483f | McGregor's Toast (spoken, unacc.) | HMV 01013 |

London, September 22, 1908.

| | | |
|---|---|---|
| 8950e | Rocked In The Cradle Of The Deep | Zon 941 |
| 8951e | He Was Very, Very Kind To Me | Zon 550 |
| 2593f | Mr. John McKay | HMV 02170, D-396 |
| 2594f | He Was Very, Very Kind To Me | HMV 02161 |
| 2595f | The Lass O' Killiecrankie | HMV 02165, D-402 |

London, April 29, 1909.

| | | |
|---|---|---|
| 10052e | Bonnie Leezie Lindsay | Zon 689 |
| 10053e | The Referee | - |
| 10054e | I've Loved Her Ever Since She Was A Baby | Zon 547 |
| 3015f | The Saftest O' The Family | Rejected |
| 3016f | The Saftest O' The Family | HMV 02227, D-398 |
| 3017f | Bonnie Leezie Lindsay | Rejected |
| 3018f | Bonnie Leezie Lindsay | HMV 02186, D-391 |
| 3019f | Aye Waken O ! | HMV 02202 |
| 3020f | The Referee | HMV 02210 |
| 3021f | I've Loved Her Ever Since She Was A Baby | HMV 02189, D-395 |
| 3022f | Jean McNeil | Rejected |
| 3023f | Jean McNeil | HMV 02190 |

London, September 30, 1909.

| | | |
|---|---|---|
| 10780e | Rising Early In The Morning | Zon X-42992, 546 |
| 10781e | The Bounding Bounder | Zon X-42940, 550 |
| 3666f | Rising Early In The Morning | Rejected |
| 3667f | We Parted On The Shore | HMV 02224, D-407 |
| 3668f | Ticklie Geordie | Rejected |
| 3669f | Ticklie Geordie | HMV 02217, D-408 |
| 3670f | The Bounding Bounder | HMV 02212 |

London, c. October, 1909.

| | |
|---|---|
| The Bounding Sea | Amb 12119, 5455 |
| When I Get Back Again To Bonnie Scotland | Amb 12132, 5318, Sc 877 (LP) |

Acc. by O/? Walter B. Rogers.          New York, December 12, 1909.

| | | |
|---|---|---|
| B-8446-1 | Stop Your Ticklin', Jock | Vic 60002, 45197 |
| B-8447-1 | Tobermory | Vic 60003, 45206 |
| C-8448-1 | The Bounding Bounder (or, On The Bounding Sea) | Vic 70010, 55121 |
| B-8449-1 | I've Something In The Bottle For The Morning | Vic 60000 |
| C-8449-1 | Fu' Th' Noo' (I've Something In The Bottle) | Vic 70000 |
| B-8458-1 | Wee Jean McGregor | Vic 60028, 45211 |
| C-8459-2 | The Wedding Of Sandy McNab | Vic 70008, 55117 |
| C-8460-2 | The Saftest Of The Family | Vic 70005, 55127 |
| C-8461-1 | When I Get Back Again To Bonnie Scotland | Vic 70009, 55131 |
| B-8462-1 | I Love A Lassie (My Scotch Bluebell) | Vic 60001 |
| C-8462-1 | I Love A Lassie (My Scotch Bluebell) | Vic 70002 |
| B-8463-1 | Wearing Kilts (That's The Reason Noo I Wear A Kilt) | Vic 60004, 45206, Zon X-42810, GO-56 |
| B-8464-1 | Hey ! Donal' | Vic 60005, 45207 |
| B-8465-1 | A Trip To Inverary | Vic 60006  - |
| C-8466-1 | The Wedding O' Lauchie McGraw | Vic 70007, 55128 |
| B-8467-1 | She Is My Daisy | Rejected |
| C-8467-1 | She Is My Daisy | Vic 70006, 55123 |
| B-8468-1 | Rising Early In The Morning | Vic 60007 (never issued) |
| B-8469-1 | Mr. John McKay | Vic 60008, 45195 |
| B-8470-1 | I've Loved Her Ever Since She Was A Baby | Vic 60009, 45212 |
| C-8471-1 | He Was Very Kind To Me | Vic 70001, 55127 |
| C-8472-1 | Rob Roy MacIntosh | Vic 70004, 55128 |
| C-8473-1 | MacGregor's Toast (spoken, unacc.) | Vic 70003, 55131 |
| B-8474-1 | Queen Among The Heather | Vic 60010, 45208 |
| B-8475-1 | Bonnie Leezie Lindsay | Vic 60011  - |

Acc. by O/Fred Quintrell.          New York, February 25, 1910.

| | | |
|---|---|---|
| C-8660-1 | We Parted On The Shore | Vic 70013, 55118 |
| B-8661-1 | Jean MacNiell (sic) | Vic 60021, 45213 |
| C-8661-1 | Jean MacNiell (sic) | Rejected |
| C-8662-1 | The Blarney Stone | Vic 70018 |
| B-8663-2 | Killiecrankie | Vic 60018, 45211 |

Acc. by studio orchestra.          London, September 22, 1910.

| | | |
|---|---|---|
| 12309e | Hey Donal' | HMV 4-2104, E-169 |
| 12310e | Every Lassie Loves A Laddie (The Picnic) | HMV 4-2097 |
| 12311e | Queen Among The Heather | HMV 4-2105, E-168 |
| 12312e | Breakfast In Bed On Sunday Morning | Zon 664 |
| 12313/4e | The Weddin' O' Lauchie McGraw | Rejected |
| 12315e | Foo The Noo (sic) | Zon 618 |
| 12316e | John Mackay (sic) | Zon X2-42051 |
| 12317e | Tobermory | Zon X2-42045, 618 |

London, September 23, 1910.

| | | |
|---|---|---|
| 4455f | Hey, Donal' | Rejected |
| 4456f | Every Lassie Loves A Laddie (The Picnic) | HMV 02287, D-392 |
| 4457f | Queen Among The Heather | Rejected |
| 4458f | Breakfast In Bed | HMV 02282, D-392 |

London, December 18, 1910.

| | | |
|---|---|---|
| 12971e | The Message Boy | Zon 664 |
| 12972e | Goodbye Till We Meet Again | HMV 4-2124, E-168 |
| 12973e | It's Just Like Being At Hame | Zon 634 |
| 4703f | The Message Boy | HMV 02300, D-403 |

(continued on page 404)

4704/5f  Goodbye Till We Meet Again                Rejected
4706f  It's Just Like Being At Hame                HMV 02303

London, c. January, 1911.

The Picnic                                 Amb 12288, 5218
Roamin' In The Gloamin'                    Amb 12320, Sc 877 (LP)

London, March 28, 1911.

13457e  Roamin' In The Gloamin'            Zon 634
13458e  Wee Jean McGregor                  HMV 4-2146, E-169
4941f  Roamin' In The Gloamin'             Rejected
4942f  Roamin' In The Gloamin'             HMV 02320, D-397
4943f  Wee Jean McGregor                   Rejected

London, c. July, 1911.

Just Like Being At Hame                    Amb 12342, 23163
Mr. John McKie (sic)                       Amb 12359, 5392
Jean M'Neil (sic)                          Amb 12360, 5364
The Blarney Stone                          Amb 12361, 5303, Sc 877 (LP)
That's The Reason Noo I Wear A Kilt        Amb 12362, 13757, 5472
Killiecrankie                              Amb 12363, 5351
The Wedding Of Sandy McNab                 Amb 12372, 13742, 5243

Hey, Donal' !                              Amb 13741
Fou The Noo (sic)                          Amb 13743
When I Get Back Again Tae Bonnie Scotland  Amb 13744, 5318

Inverary                                   Amb 13758
Callaghan                                  Amb 13759

He Was Very Kind To Me                     Amb 13783
Rising Early In The Morning                Amb 13784
The Weddin' O' Lauchie McGraw              Amb 13785

Bonnie Leezy (sic) Lindsay                 Amb 5380
Goodbye Until We Meet Again                Amb 1818
I Wish I Had Someone To Love Me            Amb 5443
I've Loved Her Ever Since She Was A Baby   Amb 5271
McGregor's Toast (spoken, unacc.)          Amb 5258, Sc 877 (LP)
Queen Amang The Heather                    Amb 5506
The Referee                                Amb 5425
The Scotch Errand Boy                      Amb 5335
She's My Daisy                             Amb 1817

Acc. by O/Fred Quintrell.        New York, October 18, 1911.

C-11121-1  The Picnic (Every Lassie Loves A Laddie)Vic 70060, 55122
B-11122-1  Roamin' In The Gloamin'         Vic 60105, 45209
C-11122-1-2  Roamin' In The Gloamin'       Vic 70061, 55129
C-11123-1  Just Like Being At Home         Rejected
C-11124-1  Breakfast In Bed On Sunday Morning  Vic 70063, 55119
C-11125-1  A Wee Deoch-an-Doris            Vic 70062, 55120

Acc. by studio orchestra.        London, April 23, 1912.

15165e  The Same As His Father Did Before Him    Zon 899
15166e  It's Nice When You Love A Wee Lassie     Zon 941
15167e  The Blarney Stone                        Zon 899
6247f  It's Nice When You Love A Wee Lassie      HMV 02390, D-394
6248f  The Same As His Father Did Before Him     HMV 02395, D-405
6249f  The Blarney Stone                         Rejected
6250f  A Wee Deoch an' Doris (sic)               HMV 02371, D-389
6251f  A Wee Deoch an' Doris (sic)               Rejected

London, c. June, 1912.

| | | |
|---|---|---|
| Just A Wee Deoch-an-Doris | Amb 12469, 1819 | |
| Same As His Father Did Before Him | Amb 12484, 5287 | |
| It's Nice When You Love A Wee Lassie | Amb 12489, 1820 | |
| I Love A Lassie | Amb 12501, 1821, Sc 877 (LP) | |

London, November 8, 1912.

| | | |
|---|---|---|
| 15946e | She's The Lass For Me | Zon 1117 |
| 15947e | The Kilty Lads | Zon 1189 |
| 15948e | A Wee Hoose 'Mang The Heather | Zon 1117 |
| 6776f | She's The Lass For Me | HMV 02435, D-400 |
| 6777f | The Kilty Lads | HMV 02428, D-404 |
| 6778f | A Wee Hoose 'Mang The Heather | HMV 02446, D-390 |

Acc. by O/ —— Schwartz and Walter B. Rogers.

New York, January 18, 1913.

| | | |
|---|---|---|
| B-8462-2 | I Love A Lassie (My Scotch Bluebell) | Vic 60001, 45212 |
| B-12809-1 | Trixie From Dixie | Vic 60110, 45210, HMV 4-2642, E-170 |
| C-12809-1 | Trixie From Dixie | Vic 70095, 55130 |
| B-12810-1 | She's The Lass For Me | Vic 60107, 45210 |
| C-12810-1 | She's The Lass For Me | Vic 70096, 55130 |
| B-12811-1 | The Same As His Father Was Before Him | Vic 60094, 45205 |
| C-12811-1 | The Same As His Father Was Before Him | Vic 70104, 55126 |
| C-12812-1 | The Kiltie Lads | Vic 70097, 55132 |
| B-12813-1 | The Wee Hoose 'Mang The Heather | Vic 60106, 45209 |
| C-12813-1 | The Wee Hoose 'Mang The Heather | Vic 70096, 55129, Cam CAL-479 |

Acc. by O/George W. Byng.                    Hayes, Middlesex, May 20, 1913.

| | | |
|---|---|---|
| HO-500/1-AK | Portobello Lass | Zon 1166 |
| HO-502-AK | It's Nicer To Be In Bed | Zon 1189 |
| HO-503-AK | Ta-Ta, My Bonnie Maggie Darling | Zon 1166 |
| HO-487-AL | The Portobello Lass | HMV 02488, D-405 |
| HO-488-AL | It's Nicer To Be In Bed | HMV 02484, D-395 |
| HO-489-AL | Ta-Ta, My Bonnie Maggie Darling | HMV 02478, D-401 |
| HO-490-AL | Just A Wee Deoch-an-Doris | Rejected |
| HO-491-AL | Test (unidentified song) | - |

Acc. by studio orchestra.                    London, c. October, 1913.

| | | |
|---|---|---|
| Roamin' In The Gloamin' | Amb 23003 | |
| Breakfast In Bed | Amb 23017, Sc 877 (LP) | |
| Wee Hoose 'Mang The Heather | Amb 23022, 1822 | |
| The Kilty Lads | Amb 23059 | |
| She's The Lass For Me | Amb 23073 | |

Acc. by O/Horace Sheldon.                    New York, January 15, 1914.

| | | |
|---|---|---|
| B-14327-1 | It's Nice To Get Up In The Morning (But It's Nicer To Stay In Bed) | Vic 60143, 45146 |
| C-14327-1 | It's Nice To Get Up In The Morning (But It's Nicer To Stay In Bed) | Vic 70107, 55115 |
| B-14328-1 | Ta-Ta, My Bonnie Maggie Darling | Rejected |
| C-14328-1 | Ta-Ta, My Bonnie Maggie Darling | Vic 70108, 55124 |
| C-14329-1 | Rocked In The Cradle Of The Deep | Rejected |
| B-14330-1 | The Portobello Lass | - |
| C-14330-1 | The Portobello Lass | Vic 70106 |
| C-14331-1 | The Message Boy | Vic 70110, 55132 |

Acc. by O/? George W. Byng.                    Hayes, Middlesex, April 1, 1915.

| | | |
|---|---|---|
| HO-1334-AB | Doughie The Baker | Zon GO-18 |
| HO-1335-AB | Bonnie Maggie Tamson | - |
| HO-1336-AB | Jean | Zon 1473 |
| HO-1337-AB | The British Bulldog's Watching At The Door | - |

(continued on page 406)

Hayes, Middlesex, April 1, 1915 (cont.)

| | | |
|---|---|---|
| HO-735-AC | Doughie The Baker | HMV 02601, D-393 |
| HO-736-AC | Bonnie Maggie Tamson | Rejected |
| HO-737-AC | Bonnie Maggie Tamson | HMV 02588, D-389 |
| HO-738-AC | Jean | Rejected |
| HO-739-AC | Jean | HMV 02572, D-440 |
| HO-740-AC | The British Bulldog's Watching At The Door | HMV 02571, D-404 |
| HO-741-AC | The British Bulldog's Watching At The Door | Rejected |

Acc. by O/Walter B. Rogers.                    New York, November 20, 1915.

| | | |
|---|---|---|
| B-16789-2 | Rosie (She's My Rosie) | Vic 60142, 45197 |
| C-16789-1 | Rosie (She's My Rosie) | Vic 70113, 55116 |
| B-16798-2 | Doughie The Baker | Vic 60141, 45196 |
| C-16798-1 | Doughie The Baker | Vic 70112, 55115 |

NOTE:- Matrices B/C-16790/7 inclusive are not by Harry Lauder.

Camden, N. J., February 18, 1916.

| | | |
|---|---|---|
| C-17188-1 | Jean (My Bonnie Jean) | Vic 70115, 55119 |
| B-17189-1 | The British Bulldog's Watching At The Door | Vic 60138 |
| B-17190-1 | In The R-O-T-A-R-Y | Vic 60139, 45195 |
| B-17191-1 | Mary Of Argyle | Vic 45126 |

Acc. by O/? George W. Byng.                    Hayes, Middlesex, August 28, 1916.

| | | |
|---|---|---|
| HO-3101/2-AE | I Love To Be A Sailor | Zon GO-22 |
| HO-3103-AE | I'm Going To Marry-arry | - |
| HO-3104-AE | Nanny, or I Never Loved Another Lass But You | Zon GO-27 |
| HO-3105/6-AE | She Is My Rosie | Zon GO-23 |
| HO-3107-AE | The Lads Who Fought And Won | - |
| HO-3108-AE | Loch Lomond | Rejected |
| HO-3109-AE | Loch Lomond | HMV 4-2821, E-67 |
| HO-2108-AF | I Love To Be A Sailor | HMV 02685, D-440 |
| HO-2109-AF | I'm Going To Marry-arry | HMV 02681, D-394 |
| HO-2110-AF | Nanny (I Never Loved Another Lass But You) | HMV 02704, D-397 |
| HO-2111-AF | Nanny (I Never Loved Another Lass But You) | Rejected |
| HO-2112-AF | She Is My Rosie | HMV 02689, D-400 |
| HO-2113-AF | The Lads Who Fought And Won | Rejected |
| HO-2114-AF | The Lads Who Fought And Won | HMV 02688, D-441 |

Hayes, Middlesex, July 2, 1917.

| | | |
|---|---|---|
| HO-3636-AE | The Waggle O' The Kilt | Zon GO-27 |
| HO-3637-AE | I Think I'll Get Wed In The Summer | Zon GO-28 |
| HO-3638-AE | O, Sing To Me The Auld Scotch Sangs | Zon GO-33 |
| HO-3639-AE | Back, Back To Where The Heather Grows | Zon GO-28 |
| HO-2710-AF | The Waggle O' The Kilt | HMV 02740, D-406 |
| HO-2711-AF | I Think I'll Get Wed In The Summer | HNV 02765, D-391 |
| HO-2712-AF | O, Sing To Me The Auld Scotch Sangs | HMV 02763, D-399 |
| HO-2713-AF | O, Sing To Me The Auld Scotch Sangs | Rejected |
| HO-2714-AF | Back, Back To Where The Heather Grows | HMV 02756, D-390 |

Hayes, Middlesex, August 20, 1917.

| | | |
|---|---|---|
| 20878e | We All Go Home The Same Way | Zon GO-33 |
| 20879e | Shouther To Shouther | Zon GO-29 |
| 20880e | Appeal for £1,000,000 for Maimed Scottish Soldiers and Sailors | Rejected |
| HO-2837/8-AF | We All Go Home The Same Way | HMV 02781, D-407 |
| HO-2839/40-AF | Shouther To Shouther | HMV D-1 |
| HO-2841-AF | Appeal for £1,000,000 for Maimed Scottish Soldiers and Sailors | - |

Hayes, Middlesex, September 27, 1917.

| | | |
|---|---|---|
| 20911e | Appeal for £1,000,000 for Maimed Scottish Soldiers and Sailors | Zon GO-29 |
| 20912e | Somebody's Waiting For Me | Zon GO-38 |

Acc. by O/Joseph Pasternack.                    New York, November 2, 1917.

| | | |
|---|---|---|
| C-21042-1 | I Love To Be A Sailor | Vic 70118 |
| C-21043-1 | I'm Going To Marry 'Arry On The 5th Of January (sic) | Vic 55138 |
| C-21044-2 | The Waggle O' The Kilt | Vic 55153 |
| C-21045-1 | The Laddies Who Fought And Won | Vic 70117, 55172 |
| C-21046-2 | There Is Somebody Waiting For Me | Vic 70119 |

Camden, N. J., April 11, 1918.

| | | |
|---|---|---|
| C-21669-1 | From The North, South, East And West (Marching With The President) | Vic 70120 |
| B-21671-1 | Old Scotch Song (acc. by JP-p only) | Vic 45256 |
| C-21672-1 | Granny's Laddie | Vic 70121 |
| NOTE:- Matrix B-21670 is not by Harry Lauder. | | |

Acc. by O/George W. Byng.                Hayes, Middlesex, October 1, 1918.

| | | |
|---|---|---|
| 21313/4e | Somebody's Waiting For Me | Zon GO-38 |
| 21315e | When I Was Twenty-One | Zon GO-36 |
| 21316e | North, South, East And West | - |
| 21317e | Bonnie Wee Annie | Zon GO-38 |
| HO-3469-AF | Somebody's Waiting For Me | HMV 02820, D-401 |
| HO-3470-AF | When I Was Twenty-One | HMV 02806, D-409 |
| HO-3471-AF | North, South, East And West | HMV D2808, D-398 |
| HO-3472-AF | North, South, East And West | Rejected |
| HO-3473-AF | Bonnie Wee Annie | - |

Acc. by O/Joseph Pasternack.              Camden, N. J., December 10, 1918.

| | | |
|---|---|---|
| C-22456-2 | Back, Back To Where The Heather Grows | Vic 55153 |
| C-22457-2 | When I Was Twenty-One | Vic 70123 |
| C-22458-2 | Don't Let Us Sing Any More About War; Just Let Us Sing Of Love | Vic 70122 |

Camden, N. J., February 20, 1920.

| | | |
|---|---|---|
| C-23743-1 | O'er The Hill To Ardenteny | Vic 55138 |
| C-23744-1 | O-Hi-O | Rejected |
| C-23745-1 | I Wish You Were Here Again | Vic 55173 |
| C-23746-1 | I Think I'll Get Wed In The Summer | Vic 70125 |

Acc. by O/George W. Byng.              Hayes, Middlesex, December 13, 1920.

| | | |
|---|---|---|
| Y-22244e | O-Hi-O | Zon GO-51 |
| Y-22245e | I Wish You Were Here Again | Zon GO-52 |
| Y-22246e | The Sunshine O' A Bonnie Lassie's Smile | - |
| Y-22247e | O'er The Hills To Ardentenny (sic) | Zon GO-51 |
| HO-4663-AF | O-Hi-O | HMV D-535 |
| HO-4664-AF | I Wish You Were Here Again | HMV D-544 |
| HO-4665-AF | The Sunshine O' A Bonnie Lassie's Smile | HMV D-535 |
| HO-4666-AF | O'er The Hills To Ardentenny (sic) | HMV D-544 |

Hayes, Middlesex, May 30, 1921.

| | | |
|---|---|---|
| Cc-197-1 | The Harry Lauder Toronto Notary Record | HMV Private Recording |

Hayes, Middlesex, June 8, 1922.

| | | |
|---|---|---|
| Yy-1444- | Saturday Night | Zon GO-57 |
| Cc-1445-1 | Saturday Night | HMV D-642 |

(continued on page 408)

Hayes, Middlesex, June 8, 1922.

| | | |
|---|---|---|
| Yy-1446- | Bella, The Belle O' Dunoon | Zon GO-57 |
| Cc-1447-1 | Bella, The Belle O' Dunoon | HMV D-642 |
| Yy-1448- | Hame O' Mine | Zon GO-58 |
| Cc-1449- | Hame O' Mine | HMV D-647 |
| Yy-1450- | It's A Fine Thing To Sing | Zon GO-58 |
| Cc-1451- | It's A Fine Thing To Sing | HMV D-647 |

Acc. by O/Joseph Pasternack or Charles Frank.

Camden, N. J., October 19, 1922.

| | | |
|---|---|---|
| C-27039-2 | Saturday Night (O/JP) | Vic 55180 |
| C-27040-2 | The Sunshine Of A Bonnie Lassie's Smile (O/CF) | Vic 55179 |
| C-27041-2 | It's A Fine Thing To Sing (O/CF) | Vic 55180 |
| C-27042-2 | Bella, The Belle O' Dunoon (O/CF) | Vic 55179 |

Acc. by O/Fred Quintrell.          Camden, N. J., February 12, 1924.

| | | |
|---|---|---|
| C-29462-2 | Love Makes The World A Merry-Go-Round | Vic 55222 |
| C-29463-1-2 | I Like My Old Home Town | Rejected |
| C-29464-1 | Australian Girls Are Good Enough For Me | - |
| C-29465-1 | Canadian Girls Are Good Enough For Me | - |
| C-29466-1 | Dixie Girls Are Good Enough For Me | Vic 55221 |

New York, March 31, 1924.

| | | |
|---|---|---|
| C-8459-4 | The Wedding Of Sandy McNab | Vic 55117 |
| C-8461-5 | When I Get Back Again To Bonnie Scotland | Vic 55131 |
| C-8467-3 | She Is My Daisy | Vic 55123 |
| C-8473-1 | McGregor's Toast (spoken unacc.) | Vic 55131 |
| C-8600-2-3 | We Parted On The Shore | Rejected |

Acc. by O/George W. Byng.          Hayes, Middlesex, April 29, 1924.

| | | |
|---|---|---|
| Cc-4522- | The Boss Of The Hoose | HMV D-869 |
| Cc-4523- | I'm Looking For A Bonny Lass To Love Me | HMV D-918 |
| Cc-4524- | Love Makes The World A Merry-Go-Round | - |
| Cc-4525- | I Like My Old Home Town | HMV D-869 |
| Yy-4526-1 | Music And Song (unacc.) | Zon GO-64 |
| Cc-4527-1-2 | The End Of The Road | Rejected |

Hayes, Middlesex, September 29, 1924.

| | | |
|---|---|---|
| Yy-5141- | The Boss Of The Hoose | Zon GO-63 |
| Yy-5142- | I'm Looking For A Bonny Lass To Love Me | Zon GO-62 |
| Yy-5143- | Love Makes The World A Merry-Go-Round | - |
| Yy-5144- | I Like My Old Home Town | Zon GO-63 |
| Yy-5145-1 | The End Of The Road | Zon GO-64 |

Hayes, Middlesex, October 26, 1925.

| | | |
|---|---|---|
| Cc-7061-1 | I Like My Old Home Town | HMV D-1043 |
| Cc-7062-1 | I'm Looking For A Bonny Lass To Love Me | HMV D-1064 |
| Cc-7072-2 | Love Makes The World A Merry-Go-Round | - |
| Cc-7073-1 | Keep Right On To The End Of The Road | HMV D-1085, DLP-1089 |
| Cc-7074-2 | I'm The Boss Of The Hoose | HMV D-1043 |

NOTE:- Matrices Bb/Cc-7063/7071 inclusive are not by Harry Lauder.

Hayes, Middlesex, March 3, 1926.

| | | |
|---|---|---|
| Cc-7997-1 | It's Nicer To Be In Bed | HMV D-1100 |
| Cc-7998-1 | Just A Wee Deoch-an-Doris | HMV D-1134, C-4089, DLP-1089 |
| Cc-7999-1 | Doughie The Baker | HMV D-1197 |
| Cc-8000-1 | The Waggle O' The Kilt | HMV D-1112, DLP-1089 |
| Cc-8001-2 | The Wedding Of Sandy McNab | -          - |
| Cc-8002-1 | I Love A Lassie | HMV D-1197, C-4090, DLP-1089,Vic |
| Cc-8003-1 | Bonnie Maggie Tamson | HMV D-1134                  )9012 |

(continued on page 409)

Hayes, Middlesex, March 3, 1926 (cont.)

| | | |
|---|---|---|
| Cc-8004-1 | Nanny | HMV D-1277 |
| Yy-8005-1 | It's Nicer To Be In Bed | Zon GO-86 |
| Yy-8006-1 | Just A Wee Deoch-an-Doris | Zon GO-68 |
| Yy-8007-1 | Doughie The Baker | Zon GO-77 |
| Yy-8008-1 | The Waggle O' The Kilt | Zon GO-78 |
| Yy-8009-1 | The Wedding Of Sandy McNab | Zon GO-68 |
| Yy-8010-1 | I Love A Lassie | Zon GO-81 |
| Yy-8011-1 | Bonnie Maggie Tamson | Zon GO-77 |
| Yy-8012-1 | Nanny (I Never Loved Another Lass But You | Zon GO-78 |
| Cc-8016-1 | Roamin' In The Gloamin' | HMV D-1277, C-4091, DLP-1089, Vic |
| Yy-8017-1 | Roamin' In The Gloamin' | Zon GO-80                              )9012 |

NOTE:- Matrices Bb/Cc-8013/5 inclusive are not by Harry Lauder.

Hayes, Middlesex, March 4, 1926.

| | | |
|---|---|---|
| Cc-8023-1 | I've Loved Her Ever Since She Was A Baby | HMV D-1100 |
| Yy-8024-1 | I've Loved Her Ever Since She Was A Baby | Zon GO-69 |
| Cc-8025-1 | Soosie Maclean | HMV D-1078 |
| Yy-8026-1 | Soosie Maclean | Zon GO-69 |
| Cc-8027-1 | The Lass O' Killiecrankie | HMV D-1106 |
| Yy-8028-1 | The Lass O' Killiecrankie | Zon GO-83 |
| Cc-8029-1 | Loch Lomond | Rejected |
| Yy-8030-1 | Loch Lomond | - |
| Cc-8031-1 | Bonnie Mary Of Argyle | - |
| Cc-8032-1 | The Road To The Isles | HMV D-1085 |
| Cc-8033-1 | Stop Your Tickling, Jock | HMV D-1106, C-4091, DLP-1089 |

Hayes, Middlesex, March 5, 1926.

| | | |
|---|---|---|
| Cc-8031-2 | Bonnie Mary Of Argyle | HMV D-1229 |
| Cc-8035-1 | I Like My Old Home Town | Rejected |
| Cc-8036-1 | Tobermory | HMV D-1229 |
| Yy-8037-1 | Tobermory | Zon GO-85 |
| Yy-8038-1 | The End Of The Road | Zon GO-82 |
| Cc-8039-2 | When I Meet Mackay | HMV D-1078, Vic 9024 |
| Yy-8055-1 | Love Makes The World A Merry-Go-Round | Zon GO-84 |

NOTE:- Matrices Bb/Cc-8040/8054 inclusive are not by Harry Lauder.

Acc. by O/Rosario Bourdon.          Camden, N. J., November 1, 1926.

| | | |
|---|---|---|
| BVE-17191-2 | Mary Of Argyle | Rejected |
| CVE-21046-3 | There Is Somebody Waiting For Me | Vic 9022, Cam CAL-479 |
| CVE-22457-3 | When I Was Twenty-One | Vic 9020 |
| CVE-36748-1 | Soosie Maclean | Vic 9000, Cam CAL-479 |
| CVE-36749-2 | The End Of The Road | Vic 9024     - |

Camden, N. J., November 2, 1926.

| | | |
|---|---|---|
| CVE-8467-4 | She Is My Daisy | Vic 9020 |
| CVE-11124-2 | Breakfast In Bed On Sunday Morning | Vic 9021, Cam CAL-479 |
| CVE-11125-2 | A Wee Deoch-an-Doris | - LOP-1509    - |
| CVE-12813-2 | The Wee Hoose 'Mang The Heather | Vic 9022 |
| BVE-16789-3 | She Is My Rosie | Vic 4021 |
| CVE-17188-3 | Jean (My Bonnie Jean) | Rejected |

Camden, N. J., December 7, 1926.

| | | |
|---|---|---|
| BVE-8446-2 | Stop Your Ticklin', Jock | Vic 4021 |
| BVE-37300-1 | Auld Scotch Sangs | Vic 4002, Zon GO-74 |
| BVE-37301-2 | Mary Of Argyle (unacc.) | -        - |
| BVE-37302-1 | Scottish Mixture | Rejected |

Acc. by O/George W. Byng.      Small Queen's Hall, London, May 20, 1927.

| | | |
|---|---|---|
| Cc-10886-1 | The Pirate | HMV D-1434 |
| Yy-10887-1 | The Pirate | Zon GO-75 |
| Cc-10888-1 | Oh, How I Weary, Dearie | HMV D-1493 |
| Yy-10889-1 | Oh, How I Weary, Dearie | Zon GO-75 |
| Cc-10890-1 | Just Got Off The Chain | HMV D-1434 |

Acc. by O/Charles Frank.                    Camden, N. J., April 18, 1928.

BVE-37302-2-3  Scottish Mixture             Rejected
CVE-43731-1  I've Just Got Off The Chain    Vic 9205, Cam CAL-479
CVE-43732-1  Oh, How I Weary, Dearie           -              -

Acc. by O/George W. Byng.                   Hayes, Middlesex, May 17, 1928.

Cc-13335-1  Music And Song (unacc.)         HMV D-1665
Yy-13336-1  Music And Song (unacc.)         Zon GO-82
Yy-13337-1  When I Get Back Again To Bonnie Zon GO-81
              Scotland
Cc-13338-2  That's The Reason Noo I Wear A Kilt  HMV D-1493
Yy-13339-   That's The Reason Noo I Wear A Kilt  Zon GO-83
Cc-13340-1  Flower O' The Heather           HMV D-1665
Yy-13341-   Flower O' The Heather           Zon GO-80
Cc-13342-   I'm Looking For A Bonnie Lass To Love  HMV D-1064
              Me
Yy-13343-   I'm Looking For A Bonnie Lass To Love  Zon GO-84
              Me

                                            Hayes, Middlesex, October 22, 1928.

Cc-14820-1  Rising Early In The Morning     HMV D-1622
Cc-14821-1  Ta-Ta, My Bonnie Maggie Darlin'    -
Cc-14822-2  Portobello Lass                 HMV D-1623
Yy-14823-1  Ta-Ta, My Bonnie Maggie Darlin' Zon GO-90
Yy-14824-1  Portobello Lass                    -
Yy-14825-1  She Is My Daisy                 Zon GO-89
Yy-14826-1  Rising Early In The Morning        -
Yy-14827-1  The Kilty Lads                  Zon GO-86
Yy-14828-1  It's Just Like Being At Hame    Zon GO-85
Cc-14829-1  Wee Hoose 'Mang The Heather     HMV D-1623

                                            Hayes, Middlesex, May 27, 1930.

Yy-19406-   I Love To Be A Sailor           Zon GO-98
Cc-19407-1  I'd Love To Be A Sailor (sic)   HMV D-1968
Yy-19408-   She's The Lass For Me           Zon GO-92
Cc-19409-1  She's The Lass For Me           HMV D-1968
Yy-19410-   Sound Advice                    Zon GO-91
Cc-19411-1-2  Sound Advice                  Rejected
Yy-19412-   Back, Back To Where The Heather Grows  Zon GO-95
Cc-19413-1  Back, Back To Where The Heather Grows  HMV D-1884
Yy-19414-   I Think I'll Get Wed In The Summer  Zon GO-95
Cc-19415-1  I Think I'll Get Wed In The Summer  HMV D-1884
Yy-19416-   Saturday Night                  Zon GO-96
Cc-19417-   Saturday Night                  HMV D-1883
Yy-19418-   O'er The Hills To Ardentenny (sic)  Zon GO-97
Cc-19419-1  O'er The Hills To Ardentenny (sic)  HMV D-1901
Yy-19420-   Stop Your Tickling, Jock        Zon GO-91
Yy-19421-   O-Hi-O                          Zon GO-97
Cc-19422-1-2  O-Hi-O                        Rejected
Yy-19423-   Bella, The Belle O' Dunoon      Zon GO-96
Cc-19424-1  Bella, The Belle O' Dunoon      HMV D-1883
Yy-19425-   Somebody's Waiting For Me       Zon GO-100
Cc-19426-1  Somebody's Waiting For Me       HMV D-1901, C-4092
Yy-19427-   I'm Going To Marry-arry         Zon GO-98

                                            Small Queen's Hall, London, May 28, 1930.

Cc-19344-1  Dear Old Cronies                HMV DB-4003
Cc-19347-1  We All Go Home The Same Way        -            C-4093
Yy-19349-1  Hame O' Mine                    Zon GO-99
Cc-19350-1  It's A Fine Thing To Sing       Rejected
Yy-19351-1  Bonnie Leezie Lindsay           Zon GO-102
Yy-19352-1  It's A Fine Thing To Sing       Zon GO-99

Hayes, Middlesex, February 3, 1931.

| OY-72-1 | Jean | Rejected |
| OY-73-1 | Pin Your Faith On The Motherland | Zon GO-101 |
| OY-74-1 | I Wish You Were Here Again | - |
| OY-75-1 | The Referee | Zon GO-102 |

London, March 13, 1932.

| 2B-3040-1-2 | It's A' Roon Th' Toon | Rejected |
| 2B-3041-2 | I Wonder If You're Missing Me | HMV DB-4014 |
| OY-3042-1-2 | I Wonder If You're Missing Me | Rejected |
| OY-3043-1-2 | It's A.' Roon Th' Toon | - |

London, July 22, 1932.

2B-3155-2 Harry Lauder's Songs - Part 1 (Intro.   HMV DB-4015
          I Love A Lassie/Saftest O' The Family/Stop Your Tickling, Jock/Waggle O'
          The Kilt/It's Nicer To Be In Bed/Keep Right On To The End Of The Road)
2B-3156-1 Harry Lauder's Songs - Part 2 (Intro.   -
          She Is Ma Daisy/We Parted On The Shore/Roaming In The Gloaming/I've Some-
          thing In The Bottle For The Morning/The Wedding Of Sandy McNab/The Lass
          O' Killiecrankie/Just A Wee Deoch and Doris (sic)

| 2B-3157-2 | Breakfast In Bed | HMV DB-4014 |
| 2B-3158-1 | Mr. John McKay | HMV DB-4027 |
| 2B-3159-1 | I've Something In The Bottle For The Morning | -   C-4090 |
| 2B-3160-1 | We Parted On The Shore | HMV DB-4028, C-4092, DLP-1089 |
| 2B-3161- | It's A Fine Thing To Sing | - |
| 2B-3162-1-2 | It's A.' Roon Th' Toon | Rejected |

Acc. by O/John Firman.                London, May 31, 1933.

| 2B-6575-3 | Always Take Care Of Your Pennies | HMV DB-4026 |
| 2B-6576-1 | It's A' Roon Th' Toon | - |
| 2B-6577-1-2 | She Says She Can Never | Rejected |
| 2B-6578-1 | Bonnie Sweet Annie | - |

Acc. by O/George Scott Wood.          London, December 11, 1935.

| 2EA-2848-1-2 | Jubilee | HMV rejected |
| 2EA-2849-1-2 | When I Go Down The Town | - |
| 2EA-2850-1 | Kettle | - |
| 2EA-2851-1 | O-Hi-O | - |

## CHARLES LAUGHTON

B. Scarborough, Yorks., England, July 1, 1899; Gold Medallist at Royal Academy of Dramatic Art; debut in THE GOVERNMENT INSPECTOR (Barnes Theatre, April 28, 1926); made
many very successful stage appearances in London up to 1931 (particularly in   THE
HAPPY HUSBAND, Criterion, June 15, 1927, and as Hercule Poirot, Agatha Christie's
famous French detective character, in ALIBI, Prince of Wales's, May 15, 1928);   to
New York, appearing in PAYMENT DEFERRED (Lyceum, September 24, 1931); many   subsequent successes in straight drama in New York and London, and on May 9, 1936,   became the first English actor to appear at the Comedie Française, Paris (in   second
act of Moliere's LE MEDECIN MALGRE LUI, in French); began film career in 1927;   to
Hollywood where he made many well-remembered films (THE SIGN OF THE CROSS;   ISLAND
OF LOST SOULS and PAYMENT DEFERRED (1932); WHITE WOMAN (1933); THE BARRETTS OF WIM-
POLE STREET (1934); RUGGIES OF RED GAP and MUTINY ON THE BOUNTY (1935), the latter
being made in England; as was his best-remembered of all films, THE PRIVATE   LIVES
OF HENRY VIII (1932), and MUTINY ON THE BOUNTY (1935); REMBRANDT (1936); VESSEL OF
WRATH (1937); ST. MARTIN'S LANE (1938) and JAMAICA INN (1939); other memorable per-
formances in such American films as THE HUNCHBACK OF NOTRE DAME (1939);   TALES   OF
MANHATTAN (1942); CAPTAIN KIDD (1945); m. Elsa Lanchester, who wrote his biography
CHARLES LAUGHTON AND I.   Became U.S. citizen, 1939; d. 1962.

Speech.                               Los Angeles, c. January 6, 1937.

CP-253   Lincoln's Gettysburg Address          Col S-271-M

Stanley Laurel (r.n. Arthur Stanley Jefferson) b. Ulverston, Lancs., England,   1890;
son of actor-theatre manager; joined Juvenile Parts Company, 1903; to U.S.A., 1910,
with Fred Karno's Company (understudied Charlie Chaplin); stayed in vaudeville as a
mimic, especially of Chaplin, until film debut in NUTS IN MAY (1918); several other
films in character part of Hickory Hiram, then signed with Hal Roach, 1926,   making
many short comedies before teaming with Oliver Hardy in 1927; first film  as a team
SLIPPING WIVES; first co-starred in PUTTING PANTS ON PHILIP, then many more   silent
shorts; first talkie ANGORA LOVE (1928); took part in HOLLYWOOD REVUE OF 1929,;sup-
ported Lawrence Tibbett in THE ROGUE SONG (1930); first full-length starring    film
together was PARDON US (1931); Oscar award 1932 for best short-subject comedy; made
FRA DIAVOLO (1933); BABES IN TOYLAND (1934); BONNIE SCOTLAND (1935); BLOCKHEADS and
SWISS MISS (1938); THE FLYING DEUCES (1939); A CHUMP AT OXFORD and SAPS AT SEA,both
1940, and many others.  Oliver Hardy was born in Atlanta, Ga., 1892; d. 1957;   Stan
Laurel died in 1965.  He received a Special Oscar, 1960, for "creative pioneering in
the field of cinema comedy."

Humorous dialogue.                          London, August 18, 1932.

CAX-6486-1  Hal Roach-MGM Present Laurel and Hardy  Col DX-370
            - Part 1
CAX-6488-1  Hal Roach-MGM Present Laurel and Hardy       -
            - Part 2 (with signature-tune, DANCE OF THE CUCKOOS, played by a studio
            orchestra/Van Phillips)
    NOTE:- Matrix CAX-6487 is not by Laurel and Hardy.  Extracts from their films  were
    issued on an LP (Douglas 10) in the 1950s.

## JOE LAURIE, Jr.

B. New York, 1892; vaudeville comedian who became a favourite radio star; author of a
book (SHOW BIZ) with Abel Green; d. New York, April 29, 1954.

Humorous monologue, acc. by unknown p.     New York, May 3, 1940.

67671-   Casey's Revenge                           Dec 15048

## GERTRUDE  LAWRENCE

B. London, July 4, 1898; studied dancing under Mme. Espinosa and elocution and    acting under Italia Conti; stage debut at the Brixton Theatre, London, as a child dancer in the pantomime THE BABES IN THE WOOD (December 26, 1910); toured in  sketches
in vaudeville until 1916; while appearing in MONEY FOR NOTHING at the    Hippodrome,
Dover, was seen by Lee White and Clay Smith who engaged her as principal dancer and
understudy to Billie Carleton in their revue SOME (Vaudeville, June 29, 1916);   she
toured in this, then returned to the Vaudeville to be general understudy in CHEEP !
(played all leading parts at times during the run, which began on April  26, 1917);
appeared in TABS (Vaudeville, May 15, 1918, subsequently played Beatrice   Lillie's
part in this for two months); made great impression in BUZZ-BUZZ (Vaudeville,   December 20, 1918), and during the run was engaged as leading lady in Murray's    Club,
in London's first cabaret; toured in THE MIDNIGHT FROLICS; starred in A TO Z revue,
Prince of Wales', October 11, 1921; and in DEDE (Garrick, October 17, 1922);   leading lady in THE MIDNIGHT FOLLIES at the Metropole Hotel, December, 1922; and in the
revue RATS ! (Vaudeville, February 4, 1923) and LONDON CALLING (Duke of York's,Sep-
tember 4, 1923); to U.S.A.; New York debut in ANDRE CHARLOT'S REVUE OF 1924,   sharing leading part with Beatrice Lillie (Times Square, January 9, 1924); a year later
she returned to London to star in CHARLOT'S REVUE (Prince of Wales', March 30,1925)
then back to New York to star with Beatrice Lillie and Jack Buchanan in THE CHARLOT
REVUE, 1926 (Selwyn, November 10, 1925); remained in New York to lead in OH,KAY! at
the Imperial, November 8, 1926; played the same show in London (His Majesty's, September 21, 1927); various other straight roles in England and U.S.A., notably  PRI-
VATE LIVES (Phoenix, London, September 24, 1930; Times Square, N.Y.,     January 27,
1931); CAN THE LEOPARD....? (Haymarket, London, December 15, 1931); BEHOLD WE  LIVE
(St. James's, London, August 16, 1932); returned to musical comedy in NYMPH  ERRANT
(Adelphi, London, October 6, 1933); MOONLIGHT IS SILVER (Queen's, London, September
19, 1934); toured with Noel Coward in TONIGHT AT 7.30, his series of nine   one-act
plays, re-named TONIGHT AT 8.30 for opening at the Phoenix, London, January 9,1936;
played in these at the National, New York, November 24, 1936; SUSAN AND GOD   (Plymouth, N.Y., October 7, 1937); toured in this and SKYLARK, appearing in the latter,
Morosco, N.Y., October 11, 1939; great success in musical LADY IN THE DARK   (Alvin,
N.Y., January 23, 1941); toured in England, 1944, entertaining troops; also   France

and Belgium, and in 1945 toured Pacific Ocean area for U.S.O. with her own company
(including playing BLITHE SPIRIT in Hawaii in July that year); returned to U.S.A.,
played Eliza Doolittle in revival of PYGMALION (Ethel Barrymore, December 26,1945);
last major stage appearance in THE KING AND I in 1951; d. September 6, 1952. Began
film career with THE BATTLE OF PARIS and INNOCENT (1929); others include AREN'T WE
ALL ? (1931); NO FUNNY BUSINESS (1932); MIMI (1935); REMBRANDT (1936); MEN ARE NOT
GODS (1937); THE GLASS MENAGERIE (1950). She was President of the American branch
of ENSA, and director of British Actors' Orphanage.

Vocal, acc. by Vaudeville Theatre Orchestra.
                                          London, February, 1919.

| 76349 | I've Been Waiting For Someone Like You | Col L-1296, Par PMC-7145 |
|  | (w/Walter Williams) ("Buzz-Buzz") | |
| 76350 | Winnie The Window-Cleaner (w/chorus) | - |
|  | ("Buzz-Buzz") | |
| 76351 | I've Lost My Heart In Maoriland | Col L-1293 |
|  | (w/chorus) ("Buzz-Buzz") | |

Acc. by O/George W. Byng.          Hayes, Middlesex, March 31, 1922.

Bb-1172-1-2  When I'm Dressed In Blue ("A To Z")    HMV rejected
Bb-1173-1-2  Come On And Kiss Your Angel Child,     -
              Sweetie Dear ("A To Z")

Acc. by unknown as/vn/p/bj.          Hayes, Middlesex, May 6, 1925.

Cc-6097-  Broadway Medley - Part 1 (Intro.        HMV C-1206, Par PMC-7135
            Sweet And Low/Lazy/So This Is Venice/My Honey Lou/Doo Wacka Doo/Big Boy)
            (w/Beatrice Lillie)
Cc-6098-  Broadway Medley - Part 2 (Intro. Chloe/    -            -
            Cover Me Up With The Sunshine Of Virginia/I Wonder What's Become Of Sal-
            ly ?/I'm So Unlucky/My Best Girl) (w/Beatrice Lillie)

Acc. by studio orchestra.          New York, November 17, 1925.

141271-  A Cup Of Coffee, A Sandwich And You    Col 512-D
            (w/Jack Buchanan) ("The Charlot Revue, 1926")
141272-  Poor Little Rich Girl ("The Charlot    Col 513-D
            Revue, 1926")
141273-  Russian Blues ("The Charlot Revue, 1926")Col 514-D
141274-  Carrie ("The Charlot Revue, 1926")       Col 512-D

Acc. by Tom Waring-p.          Camden, N. J., October 29, 1926.

BVE-36653-3  Do-Do-Do ("Oh, Kay !")              Vic 20331, LPV-545, SLA-3077,
                                                  RD-7903, HMV B-2563
BVE-36654-3  Someone To Watch Over Me ("Oh, Kay !")Vic 20331    -

Acc. by Milton Rettenberg-p.          Camden, N. J., November 15, 1926.

BVE-36653-5-6-7  Do-Do-Do ("Oh, Kay !")          Vic rejected
BVE-36654-4  Someone To Watch Over Me (w/Nat      -
              Shilkret-p also) ("Oh, Kay !")

Acc. by His Majesty's Theatre Orchestra/Arthur Wood.
                              His Majesty's Theatre, London, Oct.4,1927.

WA-6325-1-2  Do-Do-Do (w/Harold French) ("Oh,    Col rejected
              Kay !")
WA-6326-1-2  Someone To Watch Over Me ("Oh, Kay !")  -
WA-6327-1-2  Maybe (w/Harold French) ("Oh, Kay !")   -

                              His Majesty's Theatre,London,Oct. 17,1927.

WA-6327-3  Maybe (w/Harold French) ("Oh, Kay !")  Col rejected
                              His Majesty's Theatre,London,Oct. 25, 1927.
WA-6325-4  Do-Do-Do (w/Harold French) ("Oh, Kay !")Col 4617, MFP 1245
WA-6326-4  Someone To Watch Over Me ("Oh, Kay !")  Col 4618    -
WA-6327-5  Maybe (w/Harold French) ("Oh, Kay !")   -          -

Acc. by O/Ray Noble.                    Small Queen's Hall, London, Sept.15, 1930.

Cc-20202-2  Private Lives : Scene from Act 2      HMV C-2043, CLP-1050, Vic 36034
            (w/Noël Coward)
Cc-20203-2  Private Lives : Love Scene from Act 1      -          -          -
            (Intro. Someday I'll Find You) (w/Noël Coward)

Acc. by Ord Hamilton-p.                  London, October 2, 1931.

GB-3352-1-2  At Your Command                      Dec rejected

                                         London, October 5, 1931.

GB-3370-1-2  You're My Decline And Fall           Dec rejected

                                         London, October 13, 1931.

GB-3352-3-4  At Your Command                      Dec rejected

                                         London, October 15, 1931.

GB-3352-5-6  At Your Command                      Dec rejected
GB-3370-3-4-5  You're My Decline And Fall             -

                                         London, October 20, 1931.

GB-3352-7    At Your Command                      Dec F-2577, ACL-1171
GB-3370-6    You're My Decline And Fall               -          -
GB-3464-2    Now You Are Here                     Dec F-2755        -
GB-3465-     Impossible You                           -

Acc. by studio orchestra.               London, November 3, 1931.

GB-3520-1  Limehouse Blues ("A To Z")             Dec F-3578, ACL 1171
GB-3521-1-2-3  Parisian Pierrot ("London Calling") Rejected

                                         London, December 21, 1931.

GB-3464-5  Now You Are Here                       Dec F-3578
GB-3744-1-2-3  Stealing For You                   Rejected
GB-3745-2  You're Blase                           Dec F-2755

                                         London, March 11, 1932.

GB-4079-1  My Sweet (Film "Aren't We All ?")      Dec F-3140, M-400, ACL 1171
GB-4080-1  Someday I'll Find You ("Private Lives")    -          -          -

Acc. by unknown vc/Claude Ivy-p.        London, May 13, 1932.

GB-4483-1  Tired                                  Dec F-3141, M-412
GB-4484-1-3  Shadows On The Window                    -          -      ACL 1171

                                         London, July 27, 1932.

GB-4944-3  Nothing But A Lie                      Dec F-3192, ACL 1171
GB-4945-2  Why Waste Your Tears ?                     -          -

Acc. by O/Claude Ivy-p.                 London, October 11, 1932.

GB-5004-3  Let's Say Goodbye                      Dec F-3214, ACL 1182
GB-5005-2  Mad About The Boy                          -          -

                                         London, November 24, 1932.

GA-5247-   Songs She Made Famous - Part 1 (Intro.  Dec K-689, ACL 1171
           I Said Goodbye/You Were Meant For Me)
GA-5248-   Songs She Made Famous - Part 2 (Intro.      -          -
           A Cup Of Coffee, A Sandwich And You/Someone To Watch Over Me)

Acc. by O/Ray Noble.                          London, October 11, 1933.

OEA-5381-1-2  How Could We Be Wrong ? ("Nymph       HMV B-8030, DLP-1099, MFP 1245
              Errant")
OEA-5382-2  It's Bad For Me ("Nymph Errant")             -            -           -

                                              London, October 18, 1933.

OEA-5137-2  The Physician ("Nymph Errant")          HMV B-8029, DLP-1099, MFP 1245
OEA-5138-2  Experiment ("Nymph Errant")                  -            -           -
OEA-5139-1-2  Nymph Errant ("Nymph Errant")         HMV B-8031       -           -

                                              London, February 7, 1934.

OEA-5880-2  An Hour Ago This Minute                  HMV B-8137, Par PMC-7135
OEA-5881-2  What Now ?                                    -            -

    Acc. by O/Carroll Gibbons.                London, November 20, 1934.

2EA-693-2  Scene and Song (w/Douglas Fairbanks, Jr.)HMV C-2710, MFP 1245
           ("Moonlight Is Silver") - Part 1
2EA-694-2  Scene and Song (w/Douglas Fairbanks, Jr.)    -            -
           ("Moonlight Is Silver") - Part 2

    Acc. by the Phoenix Theatre Orchestra/Clifford Greenwood.
                                              London, January 15, 1936.

2EA-2666-1  Then/Play, Orchestra, Play (w/Noël       HMV C-2816, CLP-1050, Vic 36191
            Coward) ("Shadow Play")
2EA-2667-2  You Were There (w/Noël Coward) ("Shadow Play")-      -           -
2EA-2668-1  Has Anybody Seen Our Ship ? (w/Noël       HMV C-2815       -       Vic 36193
            Coward) ("Red Peppers")
2EA-2669-1  Man About Town (w/Noël Coward) ("Red         -            -           -
            Peppers")

                                              London, January 16, 1936.

2EA-2670-2  Here's A Toast (w/Noël Coward and        HMV C-2817, Vic 36192, MFP 1245,
            Company) ("Family Album")              Par PMC-7135
2EA-2671-2  Hearts And Flowers (The Musical Box)     As above
            (w/Noël Coward and Company) ("Family Album")

    Acc. by O/Carroll Gibbons.                London, March 4, 1936.

2EA-2708-1  Gertrude Lawrence Medley (Medley of       HMV C-2835, C-4198, Par PMC-7135
            Song Successes) - Part 1 (Intro. Limehouse Blues/You Were Meant For Me/
            Do-Do-Do)
2EA-2709-2  Gertrude Lawrence Medley (Medley of           -            -           -
            Song Successes) - Part 2 (Intro. Someone To Watch Over Me/A Cup Of Cof-
            fee, A Sandwich And You/Wild Thyme/Experiment)

    Acc. by O/Leonard Joy.                    New York, February 23, 1941.

BS-060679-1  This Is New ("Lady In The Dark")         Vic 27331, HMV DLP-1099
BS-060680-1  One Life To Live ("Lady In The Dark")         -            -
BS-060681-1  The Princess Of Pure Delight ("Lady      Vic 27332         -
             In The Dark")
BS-060682-1-2  My Ship ("Lady In The Dark")           Vic 27330         -
BS-060683-1  Jenny ("Lady In The Dark")                    -            -
BS-060684-1  Glamor Music (Gertrude Lawrence          Vic 27332         -
             sings HUXLEY; the other two songs on the side are by a male quartet)

Shortly before her death, Gertrude Lawrence recorded her numbers from THE KING AND I,
    for Decca.

## BUDDY LEE

American vaudeville comedian who replaced Cliff Edwards in the cast of LADY, BE GOOD,
    when this was presented in London (Empire, April 14, 1926).

Vocal, acc. by studio orchestra.           New York, c. June 29, 1925.

| 9627 | Oh, Say ! Can I See You Tonight ? | Gnt 3090, Voc X-9771 |
| 9628 | If I Had My Way 'Bout My Sweetie |    -      Voc X-9791 |

New York, c. August 13, 1925.

| 9685 | Want A Little Lovin' | Gnt 3132, Voc X-9771 |
| 9686 | Some Other Bird Whistled A Tune |    -      Voc X-9791 |

Acc. by the Gilt-Edged Four.               London, May 17, 1926.

| WA-3256-2 | Lady, Be Good ("Lady, Be Good") | Col 3981 |
| WA-3257-1 | Fascinating Rhythm ("Lady, Be Good") |   -      |

## DAVEY  LEE

American child-actor whose chief claim to fame is that he was the original Sonny  Boy
in Al Jolson's famous film THE SINGING FOOL (1928), and on the strength of this, he
made one record. B. Hollywood, January 5, 1925.

Vocal, unacc.                              New York, c. September, 1929.

| E-30693- | Sonny Boy's Bear Story - Part 2 | Br 4491 |
| E-30698- | Sonny Boy's Bear Story - Part 1 |   -      |

## EDDIE  LEONARD

B. Richmond, Va., October 18, 1875; r.n. Lemuel Gordon Toney. Professional  baseball
player who joined minstrel shows; served in the Spanish-American War, 1898; sang at
Tony Pastor's and other variety theatres, and with Primrose and West Minstrel show,
1902; appeared in ROLY-BOLY EYES (Knickerbocker, N.Y., September 25, 1919) and in a
few films, notably IF I HAD MY WAY (1940); last professional engagement was in 1940
at Billy Rose's Diamond Horseshoe.  Best-remembered as composer of IDA,  SWEET  AS
APPLE CIDER (1903) and ROLL DEM ROLY-BOLY EYES (1912). D. New York, July 29, 1941.

Vocal, acc. unknown.                       New York, June 20, 1932.

| CS-73020-1 | Don't You Never Tell A Lie - Part 1 (w/vocal trio) | Vic rejected |
| CS-73021-1 | Don't You Never Tell A Lie - Part 2 (w/vocal trio) |    -      |

Acc. by N. Gluck-p.                        New York, July 5, 1932.

| CS-73058-1 | Sugar Round My Door (w/vocal trio) | Vic rejected |

Acc. unknown.                              New York, July 28, 1932.

| 152243-1-2 | Marching Into Minstrelsy - Part 1 | Col rejected |
| 152244-1-2 | Marching Into Minstrelsy - Part 2 |    -      |

## HENRI  LEONI

French musical comedy and cabaret entertainer who made a hit in New York in  PARISIAN
MODEL (Broadway, November 27, 1906), and was a great favourite in London throughout
World War I and afterwards (BUSINESS AS USUAL, Hippodrome, November 16, 1914;   TO-
NIGHT'S THE NIGHT, Gaiety, April 18, 1915; THEODORE & CO., Gaiety, September  19,
1916; YES, UNCLE, Prince of Wales's, December 29, 1917; THE CAT AND THE FIDDLE,Pal-
ace, March 4, 1932); introduced the smash-hit VALENCIA in 1925.

Vocal, acc. by studio orchestra.           New York, June 17, 1907.

| B-4593-2 | I Love You, Ma Cherie ("Parisian Model") | Vic 5201, 16173 |

Paris, c. May, 1914.

| 694 | Je sais que vous etes jolie | Pathe 3268 |
| 729 | En passant devant ta maison |   -      |

London, late November, 1914.

| | | |
|---|---|---|
| 29219 | When The Angelus Is Ringing ("Business As Usual") | Col 2485 |
| 29220 | The Red, White And Blue ("Business As Usual")- | |

London, May, 1915.

| | | |
|---|---|---|
| 29568 | Couldn't You ? | Col 2679 |
| 29572 | Summertime | - |

Acc. by the Gaiety Theatre Orchestra/Manuel Klein.
Hayes, Middlesex, February 8, 1916.

| | | |
|---|---|---|
| HO-2464-AE | Pink And White ("Tonight's The Night") | Rejected |
| HO-2465-AE | Please Don't Flirt With Me ("Tonight's The Night") | - |
| HO-1524-AF | March along, mon ami | HMV C-685 |
| HO-1525-AF | March along, mon ami | Rejected |
| HO-1526-AF | Au revoir, Paree | HMV C-685 |
| HO-1527-AF | Pink And White ("Tonight's The Night") | HMV C-657 |
| HO-1528-AF | Please Don't Flirt With Me ("Tonight's The Night") | - |
| HO-1529-AF | Please Don't Flirt With Me ("Tonight's The Night") | Rejected |

Acc. by the Gaiety Theatre Orchestra/Willy Redstone.
Hayes, Middlesex, October 27, 1916.

| | | |
|---|---|---|
| HO-3251-AE | Oh ! How I Want To Marry All The Little Candy Girls (w/chorus) ("Theodore & Co.") | Rejected |
| HO-3252-AE | Oh ! How I Want To Marry All The Little Candy Girls (w/chorus) ("Theodore & Co.") | HMV B-753 |
| HO-2269-AF | Any Old Where (w/chorus) ("Theodore & Co.") | Rejected |
| HO-2270-AF | Any Old Where (w/chorus) ("Theodore & Co.") | HMV C-749 |

Acc. by the Prince of Wales's Theatre Orchestra/Willy Redstone.
Hayes, Middlesex, April 26, 1918.

| | | |
|---|---|---|
| HO-4096-AE | Think Of Me (w/Mimi Crawford) ("Yes, Uncle") | Rejected |
| HO-4097-AE | Think Of Me (w/Mimi Crawford) ("Yes, Uncle") | HMV B-908 |
| HO-4098-AE | Play Me That Marching Melody ("Yes, Uncle") | Rejected |
| HO-4099-AE | Play Me That Marching Melody ("Yes, Uncle") | HMV B-909 |
| HO-4100-AE | You May Take Me Around Paree (w/Mimi Crawford) ("Yes, Uncle") | HMV B-908 |
| HO-4101-AE | You May Take Me Around Paree (w/Mimi Crawford) ("Yes, Uncle") | Rejected |

Acc. by unknown p.                    London, c. October, 1920.

| | | |
|---|---|---|
| 02023 | Hindustan | Voc X-9023 |
| 02026 | I Love You, Ma Cherie ("Parisian Model") | - |
| | Some Day Waiting Will End | Voc X-9035 |
| | Underneath The Stars | - |

Acc. by studio orchestra.            London, March 18, 1926.

| | | |
|---|---|---|
| WA-3067-2 | Have You Forgotten Yvonne ? | Col 3935 |
| WA-3068-3 | Valencia | - |

Acc. by Napoleon Lambelet (composer)-p. Small Queen's Hall, London, Feb. 24, 1927.

| | | |
|---|---|---|
| Bb-9960-1 | Epistepsa (In Greek) | HMV rejected |

Acc. by studio orchestra.                          London, May 5, 1933.

CAX-6834-1  Henri Leoni Memories - Part 1 (Intro.   Col DX-471
            I Like You In Velvet/Please Don't Flirt With Me/Nini,Ninette,Ninon/Come
            To The Ball)
CAX-6835-1  Henri Leoni Memories - Part 2 (Intro.          -
            Au revoir, Paree/Three Cheers For The Red, White And Blue/Think  Of  Me
            When The Band Is Playing/When The Angelus Is Ringing)

## ETHEL  LEVEY

B. San Francisco, November 22, 1881; stage debut there at 16  in  A MILK WHITE FLAG,
Columbia Theatre, December 31, 1897; New York debut at Weber and Fields' Music Hall
(1898); appeared with Weber and Fields for some time, and with Koster and Bial; she
became associated with George M. Cohan in 1901, and appeared in all his productions
from then until 1907 (q.v.); London debut - for one night only - on  Mafeking Night
(May 18, 1900), at the Tivoli Music Hall; toured U.S.A. on her return, m. George M.
Cohan (div.); reappeared in London at the Alhambra, September 20, 1909; toured Europe in revue; returned to London to star in HULLO, RAGTIME ! (Hippodrome,  December
23, 1912); HULLO, TANGO ! (Hippodrome, December 23, 1913); WATCH YOUR STEP (Empire,
May 4, 1915); FOLLOW THE CROWD (Empire, February 19, 1916); LOOK WHO'S HERE (London
Opera House, July 17, 1916); THREE CHEERS (Shaftesbury, December 22, 1916);HERE AND
THERE (Empire, November 29, 1917); title-role in OH ! JULIE (Shaftesbury,  June 22,
1920); YES (Vaudeville, November 29, 1923); THE BLUE KITTEN (Gaiety,  December  23,
1925); vaudeville   in England, toured there before returning to U.S.A.; made film
(CALL ME MAME) and appeared in MARINKA (Winter Garden, N.Y., July 18, 1945).


Vocal, acc. by studio orchestra.                   London, October 7, 1911.

    5555f    Sweet Italian Love                        HMV rejected

                                                   London, March 8, 1914.

    17587e   Melinda's Wedding Day                     Rejected
    17588e   Bye And Bye You Will Miss Me              HMV 2-3012, HMV B-490
    7830f    How Do You Do, Miss Ragtime ? ("Hullo,    HMV 03377, C-572
             Ragtime !")
    7831f    My Tango Girl ("Hullo, Tango !")          HMV 03376, C-573
    7832f    Goodbye, Summer, So Long Fall, Hello,     HMV 03385, C-572
             Wintertime
    7833f    That Haunting Melody                      HMV 03375, C-573

                                                   London, November 22, 1914.

    8169f    Carry On                                  Rejected
    8170f    Carry On                                  HMV 03394, C-575

Acc. by the Empire Theatre Orchestra/Jacques Heuvel.
                                    Hayes, Middlesex, October 26, 1915.

HO-2005-AE  Discoveries (w/Joe Coyne) ("Watch Your  HMV B-536
            Step")
HO-1157/8-AE  The Minstrel Parade (w/Joe Coyne-d)    HMV C-611
            ("Watch Your Step")
HO-1159/60-AE That Simple Melody (w/Blanche Tomlin)       -
            ("Watch Your Step")
HO-1161-AE  The Syncopated Walk (w/Blanche Tomlin-   HMV C-610
            Joe Coyne)
HO-1162-AE  Settle Down In A One-Horse Town          HMV C-612
            ("Watch Your Step")
HO-1163-AE  My Bird Of Paradise ("Watch Your Step")      -

                                    Hayes, Middlesex, April 13, 1916.

HO-1757-AF  I Love A Piano ("Follow The Crowd")       HMV 03476
HO-1758-AF  That Hula Hula ("Follow The Crowd")       Rejected
HO-1759-AF  That Hula Hula ("Follow The Crowd")       HMV 03477
HO-1760-AF  Where Did Robinson Crusoe Go With         HMV 03478
            Friday On Saturday Night ? ("Follow The Crowd")

Acc. by the Shaftesbury Theatre Orchestra/Maurice Jacobi. (Matrices HO-2469/2470-
AF are not by Ethel Levey).                    Hayes, Middlesex, January 26, 1917.

| | | |
|---|---|---|
| HO-2467-AF | Hold Me In Your Loving Arms (w/Walter Williams) ("Three Cheers") | Rejected |
| HO-2468-AF | Hold Me In Your Loving Arms (w/Walter Williams) ("Three Cheers") | HMV 04194 |
| HO-2471-AF | The Ragtime Bagpipe Band (w/chorus) ("Three Cheers") | HMV 03544 |
| HO-2472-AF | The Ragtime Bagpipe Band (w/chorus) ("Three Cheers") | Rejected |

Acc. by Gaiety Theatre O/Howard Carr.  Hayes, Middlesex, January 7, 1926.

| | | |
|---|---|---|
| Cc-7639- | Cutie (w/Roy Royston)("The Blue Kitten")| HMV C-1239 |
| Cc-7640- | Blue Kitten Blues (w/girls' chorus) ("The Blue Kitten") | HMV C-1242 |
| Cc-7641- | I'm Head Over Heels In Love (w/Roy Royston) ("The Blue Kitten") | - |

Acc. by small jazz band.                    London, August 27, 1929.

| | | |
|---|---|---|
| WA-9399-1 | Kansas City Kitty | Col rejected |
| WA-9400-1 | That's How I Feel About You, Sweetheart | - |

Acc. by O/Ray Noble.                    London, February 16, 1933.

| | | |
|---|---|---|
| OB-6301-1-2 | I May Never Pass Your Way Again | Rejected |
| OB-6302-1-2 | Brother, Can You Spare A Dime ? | - |
| OB-6303-2 | What A Perfect Combination | HMV B-4384 |
| OB-6304-1 | Look What You've Done | - |

London, March 10, 1933.

| | | |
|---|---|---|
| OB-6301-4 | I May Never Pass Your Way Again | HMV B-4401 |
| OB-6471-2 | I Want To Go Home | - |

## J.  ALDRICH LIBBEY

B. 1872; appeared in several musical productions in the 1880s and 1890s, notably a
revival of A TRIP TO CHINATOWN (Hoyt's, New York, November 9, 1891; ran 657 performances), in which he introduced AFTER THE BALL. D. San Francisco, April 29, 1925.

Vocal, acc. by unknown piano.          New York, issued as shown in brackets.

| | |
|---|---|
| On A Sunday Afternoon | Ed 8018 (June, 1902) |
| The Song The Soldiers Sang | Ed 8019 (June, 1902) |
| Where The Silvery Colorado Wends Its Way | Ed 8020 (June, 1902) |
| Only A Summer Girl | Ed 8171 (October, 1902) |
| Marie-Louise | Ed 8204 (October, 1902) |
| In The Sweet Bye-and-Bye | Ed 8300 (January-February, 1903) |

## BEATRICE  LILLIE

B. Toronto, Canada, May 29, 1898; stage debut in Chatham Music Hall (England),early
1914; London debut in THE DARING OF DIANE (Pavilion, April, 1914); later appeared
in three Alhambra revues (NOT LIKELY !, October, 1914; 5064 GERRARD    (March 19,
1915); NOW'S THE TIME (October 13, 1915); to the Vaudeville in SAMPLES(succeeding
Mabel Russell, March, 1916); SOME (June 29, 1916); CHEEP ! (April 26, 1917); TABS
(May 15, 1918); further hits in OH, JOY ! (Kingsway, January 27, 1919); BRAN  PIE
(Prince of Wales', August 28, 1919); NOW AND THEN (Vaudeville, October, 1921);  A
TO Z (Prince of Wales', September, 1922); THE NINE O'CLOCK REVUE (Little, October
25, 1922; ran 385 performances); New York debut in ANDRE CHARLOT'S REVUE OF  1924
(Times Square, January 9, 1924, 285 performances); to London for CHARLOT'S  REVUE
(Prince of Wales', March 30, 1925); returned to New York to star with Jack Buchanan and Gertrude Lawrence in a new edition of this (Selwyn, November 10, 1925);it
was followed by OH PLEASE ! (Fulton, December, 1926) and THIS YEAR OF GRACE (Selwyn, November 7, 1928); she returned to London to star in CHARLOT'S MASQUERADE at
the Cambridge, September 4, 1930; this had a much shorter run; she then  returned

to New York to appear in THE THIRD LITTLE SHOW (Music Box, June 1, 1931); and  WALK
A LITTLE FASTER (St. James, December 7, 1932); to London for PLEASE (Savoy,November
16, 1933); further success at the Winter Garden, N.Y. in AT HOME ABROAD  (September
19, 1935) and THE SHOW IS ON (December 25, 1936); appeared in HAPPY RETURNS  (Adelphi, London, May 19, 1938); then in New York in SET TO MUSIC (Music Box,January 18,
1939); in cabaret at the Cafe de Paris, London, June, 1939; ALL CLEAR (Queen's,Dec-
ember 20, 1939); toured England in TONIGHT AT 8.30 and other shows in aid of   Actors' Orphanage; BIG TOP (His Majesty's May 8, 1942); long tour covering   Gibraltar
and North Africa, entertaining troops; back to New York for SEVEN LIVELY ARTS(Ziegfeld, December 7, 1944); first post-war London appearance, BETTER LATE(Garrick, April 24, 1946); began film career in 1927 (EXIT SMILING); other films include DOCTOR
RHYTHM (1938); AROUND THE WORLD IN 80 DAYS (1956); THOROUGHLY MODERN MILLIE (1967).

Vocal, acc. by studio orchestra.              London, November, 1915.

35855     Now's The Time (w/chorus) ("Now's The      Col 2632
            Time")
35856     We'll Have A Jubilee In My Old Kentucky      -
            Home (w/Lee White) ("Now's The Time")

Acc. by O/Albert W. Ketelbey.              London, May, 1917.

75922     Julia ("Cheep !")                        Col L-1194, Par PMC-7135
75923     Shoot The Rabbit ("Cheep !")               -              -
75924     When I Am With Her Again ("Cheep !")     Col L-1192
75925     Where The Black-Eyed Susans Grow ("Cheep !") -
75928     Take Me Back To The Land Of Promise      Col L-1193
            ("Cheep !") NOTE:- Matrices 75926/7 are not by Beatrice Lillie.

Acc. by Vaudeville Theatre Orchestra.   London, June, 1918.

76164     I Hate To Give Trouble (w/Margaret       Col L-1257
            Campbell) ("Tabs")
76165     My River Girl (w/Alfred Austin) ("Tabs") Col L-1258
76166     Maryland (w/Trio) ("Tabs")               Col L-1257
76167     I Said Goodbye (w/Trio) ("Tabs")         Col L-1256
76169     Sammy (w/Trio) ("Tabs")                    -
NOTE:- Matrix 76168 is not by Beatrice Lillie.

Acc. by Kingsway Theatre Orchestra/Leonard Hornsey.
                                       London, February, 1919.

76375     Till The Clouds Roll By (w/Tom Powers)   Col L-1285
            ("Oh Joy")
76376     March Quarter Day (w/Tom Powers-Billy    Col L-1289
            Leonard) ("Oh Joy")
76378     Rolled Into One ("Oh Joy")               Col L-1285, Par PMC-7135
76379     A Pal Like You(w/Billy Leonard)("Oh Joy")Col L-1286
76380     Nestling Time ("Oh Joy")                   -
NOTE:- Matrix 76377 is not by Beatrice Lillie.

Acc. by Prince of Wales's Theatre Orchestra/Philip Braham.
                                       London, September, 1919.

76630     Hullo ! (w/Jack Hulbert) ("Bran Pie")    Col F-1008
76631     By The Camp Fire (w/Jose de Moraes)      Col F-1009
            ("Bran Pie")
76632     Won't You Come Along, Mary ?("Bran Pie") Col F-1008
76633     A Striking Dip (Bolshevik Quartette)     Col F-1009
            (w/Jack Barker-Jack Tully-Rebla) ("Bran Pie")

76658     That Wonderful Lamp ("Bran Pie")         Col F-1010
76659     I'm Going 'Way Back Home ("Bran Pie")      -
76660     Someone Else May Be There When I'm Gone  Col F-1011
            ("Bran Pie")

Acc. by Muriel Lillie (composer)-p.    Hayes, Middlesex, May 2, 1923.

Bb-2926-1-2  Susannah's Squeakin' Shoes              HMV rejected

Acc. by unknown as/vn/p/bj.              Hayes, Middlesex, May 6, 1925.

Cc-6097-   Broadway Medley - Part 1 (Intro.      HMV C-1206, Par PMC-7135
           Sweet And Low/Lazy/So This Is Venice/My Honey Lou/Doo Wacka Doo/Big Boy)
           (w/Gertrude Lawrence)
Cc-6098-   Broadway Medley - Part 2 (Intro.          -            -
           Cover Me Up With The Sunshine Of Virginia/I Wonder What's Become Of Sal-
           ly ?/I'm So Unlucky/My Best Girl) (w/Gertrude Lawrence)

Acc. by studio orchestra.                New York, November 23, 1925.

141300-    Susannah's Squeaking Shoes ("The       Col 513-D
           Charlot Revue, 1926")

Acc. by Vincent Youmans (composer)-p.    Camden, N. J., November 27, 1926.

BVE-37051-1-2  Like He Loves Me ("Oh, Please !")   Rejected
BVE-37052-2    Nicodemus ("Oh, Please !")          Vic 20361
BVE-37053-1    Like He Loves Me (w/male chorus)    Vic LPV-557, LSA-3075
               ("Oh, Please !")
BVE-37053-2    Like He Loves Me (w/male chorus)    Vic 20361
               ("Oh, Please !")

Acc. by Sam Walsh-p.                      New York, July 3, 1934.

170752-2   He Was A Gentleman                     GSV 1003
170753-1   There Are Fairies At The Bottom Of Our  GSV 1002
           Garden
170754-1   Snoops, The Lawyer                     -
170755-1   I'm A Camp Fire Girl                   GSV 1003

Acc. by Edward Cooper-p.                  London, October 24, 1934.

OEA-471-1  Baby Didn't Know                       HMV B-8362,Vic 25165,Par PMC-7135
OEA-472-1  A Baby's Best Friend                      -          -           -

Acc. by studio orchestra.                New York, October 31, 1935.

60120-B    Mother Told Me So ("Flying Colors")    LMS L-189, 1002 (LP)
60121-A    Paree ("At Home Abroad")                  -         -

                                         New York, February 13-14, 1939.

P-24114-   Mad About The Boy-Pt.1 ("Set To Music")  LMS L-    , 1002 (LP), JJC M-3003
P-24115-   Mad About The Boy-Pt.2 ("Set To Music")    -         -          -
P-24116-   Weary Of It All ("Set To Music")       LMS L-    -         -
P-24117-   Three White Feathers ("Set To Music")            -         --
P-24118-   Get Yourself A Geisha ("At Home Abroad")         -         -
P-24119-   I Hate Spring                                    -         -
P-24120-   The Gutter Song ("New Faces of 1934")            -         -
P-24121-   Marvelous Party ("Set To Music")                 -         -

## ALICE  LLOYD

Cockney music-hall and pantomime star; debut at Forresters' Music Hall, London, with
Grace Lloyd as The Lloyd Sisters, February 20, 1888; very successful tour of U.S.A.
in 1907; continued stage career long after her return. D. 1949.

Vocal, acc. by unknown p.                London, c. November, 1902.

           Mary Green                             Zon X-2362
           That's A Man                           Zon X-2364
           Father And Mother's Out                Zon X-2365
           Who You Getting At, Eh ?               Zon X-2366
           Young Men Lodgers                      Zon X-2367

                                         London, November 5, 1903.

4208       Mary Green                             G&T rejected
4209       Tottie                                 -

London, c. June, 1904.

Nancy Brown                                    Zon 43015 (7")
Father And Mother's Out                        Zon 43016 (7")

Acc. by studio orchestra.             New York, May 23, 1907.

B-4526-1-2  May, May, May                      Vic rejected
C-4527-1-2  The Tale Of The Clothes Line          -
B-4528-1-2  You Splash Me And I'll Splash You     -
B-4529-1-2  Who Are You Getting At ?              -

New York, May 24, 1907.

B-4526-3-4  May, May, May                      Vic 5158
B-4530-2  Young Men Lodgers                    Vic 5159, G&T GC-3727
C-4531-1-2  Never Introduce Your Bloke To Your   Vic 31646
            Lady Friend

New York, June 1, 1907.

C-4527-4  The Tale Of The Clothes Line         Vic 31662
B-4528-4  You Splash Me And I'll Splash You    Vic 5225, 16058
B-4529-4-4  Who Are You Getting At ?           Rejected

London, December, 1933.

EB-1100-2  Marie Lloyd Memoirs - Part 1 (Alice       EBW 5623
           Lloyd sings a verse and chorus of WHO ARE YOU GETTING AT ?)
EB-1101-2  Marie Lloyd Memoirs - Part 2 (Alice       -
           Lloyd sings a verse and chorus of THE NEARER THE BONE, THE SWEETER     THE
           MEAT)

## CISSIE  LOFTUS

B. London, 1876; daughter of Marie Loftus, variety artist; debut with great success at
the Oxford Music Hall, London, 1893; great mimic and straight actress in widely dif-
fering productions such as FAUST, A DOLL'S HOUSE and PETER PAN (Duke of York's. Dee-
ember 27. 1904); very successful in U.S.A. (vaudeville at the Palace, New York, many
times); films include EAST LYNNE (1931); THE BLUEBIRD (1940). D. July 12, 1943.

Vocal, acc. by Fred Gaisberg-p.        London, November 22, 1898.

231     Imitation of Mr. Hayden Coffin in THE     Ber E-3048
        GEISHA
235     Imitation of Miss Edna May in THE BELLE   Ber E-3050
        OF NEW YORK
        Imitation of Miss Phyllis Rankin in THE   Ber E-3049
        BELLE OF NEW YORK
        Imitation of Mlle. Yvette Guilbert        Ber E-3052
        Imitation of Mr. Eugene Stratton in THE   Ber E-3053
        CHRISTENING

London, December 5, 1898.

304     Imitation of Miss Marie Tempest in THE    Ber E-3055
        GEISHA

## ELLA LOGAN

B. Glasgow, 1913; became famous first as a teenage dance-band vocalist in London, then
as soloist in variety and cabaret; to U.S.A. in 1933, where she remained, a popular
radio and cabaret artist, until her death in 1969, apart from occasional engagements
in London (e.g., with Louis Armstrong and his All-Stars in 1956).

Vocalist with Jack Hylton and his Orchestra.
                            Small Queen's Hall, London, Feb. 26, 1930.

Bb-18886-3  Moanin' Low                         HMV B-5952
Bb-18887-1  Can't We Be Friends ?                -

Vocalist with Ambrose and his Orchestra from the May Fair Hotel, London.
                                Small Queen's Hall, London, July 4, 1930.

Bb-19884-2  Shoo The Hoodoo Away                    HMV B-5877

Vocalist with Jack Hylton and his Orchestra.
                                Small Queen's Hall, London, Aug. 27, 1930.

Bb-19951-1  If Your Kisses Can't Hold The Man You   HMV B-5891
            Love

Vocalist with the Rhythm Maniacs.          London, September 5, 1930.

MB-1785-    I'm Still At Your Beck And Call         Dec F-2015
MB-1786-    He's My Secret Passion                  -

Vocal, acc. by Arthur Young-p/Len Fillis-g.
                                London, October 20, 1930.

GB-2095-2  Whispering Out Of The South              Dec F-2025
GB-2096-1-2  I Need A Good Kind Man                 Rejected
GB-2097-1  Waiting For That Thing Called Happiness  -
GB-2098-1  Dinah                                    Dec F-2025

Vocalist with the Phantom Players.         London, November 3, 1930.

GB-2176-   Dancing With The Devil                   Dec F-2078

Vocal, acc. by Al Bowlly-g, and Claude Ivy-p where shown.
                                London, November 24, 1930.

GB-2321-2  She Walked Right Up And Took My Man      Dec F-2560
           Away
GB-2323-1  Frankie And Johnny (w/Al Bowlly)         Dec F-2206
GB-2324-2  By The Old Oak Tree (w/Al Bowlly)-pCI    -
  NOTE:- Matrix GB-2322 is by Al Bowlly alone, q.v., but Ella Logan makes comments.

Vocalist with Jack Payne and the BBC Dance Orchestra.
                                London, March 24, 1931.

CA-11275-3-4  Ten Cents A Dance                     Col rejected
  NOTE:- Takes 1 and 2 of this title were made a little earlier with Elsie   Carlisle
  as the vocalist, one of them being used for issue.

Vocalist with Abe Lyman and his California Orchestra.
                                New York, October 12, 1933.

B-14140-   Doin' The Uptown Low Down                Br 6674, 01633

Vocalist with Adrian (Rollini)'s Ramblers. New York, May 4, 1934.

B-15168-A  I Wish I Were Twins                      Br 6889, 01775

Vocalist with Adrian Rollini and his Orchestra.
                                New York, October 23, 1934.

38874    It Had To Be You                           Dec rejected

Vocal, acc. by Victor Young and his Orchestra.
                                New York, May 20, 1935.

39529-A  'Way Back Home - Part 1 (w/Bob Crosby-     Dec 473, M-464
         Johnny Davis-The Tune Twisters)
39530-A  'Way Back Home - Part 2 (w/Cleo Brown-     -     -
         Johnny Davis-The Tune Twisters)

Acc. by O/Bill Harty.                    Los Angeles, December 30, 1937.

LA-1556-C  Oh, Dear ! What Can The Matter Be ?   Br 8057, Col 35318, Voc 578
LA-1557-A  I Was Doing All Right                 Br 8064
LA-1558-A  Love Is Here To Stay                  -
LA-1559-A  Jingle (Bingle) Bells                 Br 8057, Col 35318, Voc 578

Acc. unknown.                            New York, April 15, 1938.

B-22739-   My Bonnie Lies Over The Ocean         Br  rejected
B-22740-   I'm Off To Philadelphia               -
B-22741-   Comin' Thru' The Rye                  -
B-22742-   Phil The Fluter's Ball                -

Acc. by O/Perry Botkin.                  Los Angeles, July 17, 1938.

LA-1684-A  Phil The Fluter's Ball                Br 8300, Col FB-2631
LA-1685-A  My Bonnie Lies Over The Ocean         Br 8196, Col 36313, C-454,
                                                 Par R-2583
LA-1686-A  The Bluebells Of Scotland             Br 8196 -
LA-1687-A  Come To The Fair                      Br 8232, Col 36313, C-454

                                         Los Angeles, September 13, 1938.

LA-1714-A  Adios, Muchachos (Farewell, Boys)     Br 8277, Col 36309, Par R-2635
LA-1715-A  Cielito Lindo (Beautiful Heaven)      Br 8300
LA-1716-A  I'm Forever Blowing Bubbles           Br 8277, Col 36309, Par R-2635
LA-1717-A  Ragtime Cowboy Joe                    Br 8232

                                         Los Angeles, October 14, 1938.

LA-1730-A  Two Sleepy People (w/Hoagy Carmichael)  Br 8250, Par R-2611

                                         Los Angeles, October 18, 1938.

LA-1733-A  New Orleans (w/Hoagy Carmichael)      Br 8250, Par R-2611

Acc. by O/Bill Harty.                    Los Angeles, April 8, 1939.

LA-1843-   The Old Kent Road                     Br 8376
LA-1844-   Bonnie Mary Of Argyle                 -
LA-1845-A  There's Nae Luck Aboot The Hoose      Br 8364, Col FB-2631
LA-1846-   It's The Same The Whole World Over    -

Acc. by studio orchestra.                New York, September 26, 1939.

WCO-26112- Are You Havin' Any Fun ?             Col 35251
WCO-26113- Waikiki                              Col 35243
WCO-26114- Goodnight, My Beautiful              -
WCO-26115- Something I Dreamed Last Night       Col 35251, Epic SN-6059

Acc. by O/Perry Botkin.                  Los Angeles, April 2, 1940.

LA-2184-   The Curse Of An Aching Heart          Col 35874
LA-2185-   The Whiffenpoof Song (Baa ! Baa ! Baa !)  Col 35701
LA-2186-   I Wonder Where My Baby Is Tonight     Col 35874
LA-2187-   Oh By Jingo ! (Oh By Gee, You're The   Col 35701
              Only Girl For Me)

                                         Hollywood, May 18, 1941.

H-303-1  Take Me Out To The Ball Game            Col 36257

                                         New York, May 22, 1941.

30524-   The Mountains O' Mourne                 Col 36257
30525-   Bill                                    Col 36173
30526-   My Yiddishe Momme                       Col 36373
30528-   The Spaniard That Blighted My Life      -
30529-   The Hut-Sut Song                        Col 36173

Acc. by the Spirits of Rhythm,                    Hollywood, September 4, 1941.

H-498-2  It's A Long, Long Way To Tipperary         Epic LN-24047, SN-6042, EP-335,
                                                    Col 33SX-1499
H-499-1  I Woke Up With A Teardrop In My Eye        Rejected
H-500-1  From Monday On                                 -
H-501-1  Exactly Like You                               -

## LILLIAN LORRAINE

B. San Francisco, January 1, 1892; r.n. Ealallean de Jacques; stage debut there as  a
  small child in UNCLE TOM'S CABIN (1896); continued to play children's parts as member of various stock companies until her New York debut in THE GAY WHITE WAY,  with
  Blanche Ring, Casino, October 9, 1907; then followed other New York successes, such
  as MISS INNOCENCE (New York, November 30, 1908); regular appearances in  FOLLIES OF
  1909, 1910 and 1911 (Jardin de Paris); OVER THE RIVER (Globe, January 8, 1912); THE
  WHIRL OF THE WORLD (Winter Garden, January 10, 1914); ODDS AND ENDS (Bijou,  Novem-
  19, 1917); ZIEGFELD FOLLIES OF 1918 (New Amsterdam, June 18, 1918); THE BLUE KITTEN
  (Selwyn, January 13, 1922).  D. 1955.

Vocal, acc. by studio orchestra.          New York, May, 1922.

   8948    Songs of Yesterday by Stars of Today     Voc 35010 (part side)

## NICK LUCAS

B. 1900; played guitar and banjo with various dance bands (Sam Lanin's, Russo-Fiorito
  Oriole Orchestra, etc.), sometimes contributing vocal refrains; began career  as  a
  soloist, self-accompanied, in 1924, and at this writing continues to entertain   in
  clubs and on TV; may lay fair claim to having originated the "intimate" style.

Guitar solos.                             New York, c. July, 1922.

         Pickin' The Guitar                     PA 020794, 10392, Sil 1207
         Teasin' The Frets                         -           -        -

Vocal, acc. by own guitar.                New York, c. November, 1924.

         My Best Girl                           Br 2768
         Dreamer Of Dreams                         -

                                          New York, c. February 7, 1925.

E-14845  Because They All Love You               Br 2803
         Somebody Like You                          -

                                          New York, March, 1925.

E-14989  I've Named My Pillow After You          Br 2827
         If I Can't Have You                        -

                                          New York, July, 1925.

E-15921  Isn't She The Sweetest Thing ?          Br 2906
E-15932  By The Light Of The Stars                  -
E-15997  I Might Have Known                      Br 2940
         I'm Tired Of Everything But You            -

   Acc. by unknown p/own g.                New York, September, 1925.

E-16347  I Found Somebody To Love               Br 2990
E-16374  If You Hadn't Gone Away                 Br 2961
E-16456  Brown Eyes, Why Are You Blue ?            -

                                          New York, c. November, 1925.

E-17082  Sleepy-Time Gal                         Br 2990
         Forever And Ever With You               Br 3021
         Smile A Little Bit                         -

Acc. by unknown p.                          New York, c. December, 1925.

E-17138    Whose Who Are You ?                       Br 3052

Acc. by own guitar.                         New York, c. January, 1926.

E-17746    A Cup Of Coffee, A Sandwich And You      Br 3052

Acc. by unknown vn/vc/own g.                New York, February, 1926.

E-17937    I Don't Believe It - But Say It Again    Br 3088
E-17978    Always                                   -

Acc. by unknown vn/own g.                   New York, c. May, 1926.

E-18876    Adorable                                 Br 3184
E-18878    Bye-Bye, Blackbird                       -

Acc. by own g, and Sammy Stept-p-cel where shown.
                                            New York, c. July, 1926.

E-19430/2  Looking At The World Thru' Rose-Colored  Br 3283
             Glasses
           Sleepy Head                              Br 3229
E-19596    Let Me Live And Love You Just For        Br 3283
             Tonight - pSS
E-19597    How Many Times ? - pSS                   Br 3229

                                            New York, October, 1926.

           Because I Love You - celSS              Br 3367
E-20524/5  When You're Lonely - pSS                 -
E-20527    Precious                                 Br 3369

E-20562/3  Hello, Bluebird - pSS                    Br 3370
E-20564    I'd Love To Call You My Sweetheart       Br 3369
E-20568/70 I've Got The Girl - pSS                  Br 3370

                                            New York, January, 1927.

E-21274/5  Put Your Arms Where They Belong          Br 3433
E-21277    In A Little Spanish Town - 2g used       -

E-21304/5  I'm Looking Over A Four-Leaf Clover-2g   Br 3439
E-21307/8  High, High, High Up In The Hills         -

                                            New York, February, 1927.

E-21480/1  I'm Looking For A Girl Named Mary        Br 3466
E-21483    Underneath The Weeping Willow            -

                                            New York, March, 1927.

E-21825    Moonbeam ! Kiss Her For Me               Br 3492
E-21829    So Blue (w/David Rubinoff-vn)            -

                                            New York, April, 1927.

E-22106/8  Side By Side                             Br 3512
E-22109    Why Should I Say That I'm Sorry ?        -
             (When Nobody's Sorry For Me) - pSS

E-22146    Rosy Cheeks - pSS                        Br 3518
E-22148    Underneath The Stars With You            -

Acc. by Bill Wirges-p.                      New York, July, 1927.

E-23859    Sing Me A Baby Song                      Br 3602
E-23860    Broken Hearted                           -

New York, August, 1927.

E-24118/20 Sweet Someone                                          Br 3614
E-24121/2  I Can't Believe That You're In Love With Me -

                                          Chicago, October, 1927.

C-1270/1   I Can't Believe That You're In Love        Br 3614
               With Me

                                          Chicago, November, 1927.

C-1364/5   The Song Is Ended                          Br 3736
C-1368/9   Kiss And Make Up                                -

                                          New York, November, 1927.

E-25514    Keep Sweeping The Cobwebs Off The Moon     Br 3749
E-25516    Together                                       -
           Without You, Sweetheart                    Br 3773
           My Ohio Home                                    -

                                          New York, February, 1928.

E-26669    I'm Waiting For Ships That Never Come In Br 3853, 3968
           Marcheta                                        -
           Sunshine                                   Br 3850
           I Still Love You                                -

                                          New York, May, 1928.

E-27721-   When You Said "Goodnight" (Did You         Br 3966
               Really Mean "Goodbye" ?)
E-27722-   You're A Real Sweetheart                        -

                                          New York, June, 1928.

E-27690-   Marcheta                                   Br 3968
E-27691-   Just Like A Melody Out Of The Sky          Br 3965

                                          New York, August, 1928.

E-27837-   For Old Times' Sake                        Br 3965

                                          New York, September, 1928.

E-27955-   Someday, Somewhere (We'll Meet Again)      Br 4026
E-27956-   Chiquita                                        -

                                          New York, December, 1928.

E-28882-   My Tonia                                   Br 4141
E-28883-   The Song I Love                                 -    3926

                                          New York, January, 1929.

E-29000-   I'll Get By (As Long As I Have You)        Br 4156
E-29001-   How About Me ?                                  -

                                          Chicago, January 17, 1929.

C-2817-    I'll Get By (as Long As I Have You)        Br 4156
C-2818-    (You're Not Asking Me) I'm Telling You     Br 4214
C-2819-    Some Rainy Day                                  -    3949

                                          Chicago, January 18, 1929.

C-2831-    Old Timer                                  Br 4215, 3949
C-2832-    Heart O' Mine                                   -    5007
C-2833-    How About Me ?                             Br 4156

New York, January, 1929.

| | | |
|---|---|---|
| E-29012- | When The World Is At Rest | Br 4171 |
| E-29013- | I'll Never Ask For More | - |

Los Angeles, late March, 1929.

| | | |
|---|---|---|
| LAE-434- | I've Got A Feeling I'm Falling | Br 4302 |
| LAE-438- | Coquette | - |

Los Angeles, May, 1929.

| | | | |
|---|---|---|---|
| LAE-496- | Just Another Kiss | Br 4390 | |
| LAE-497- | Painting The Clouds With Sunshine | Br 4418 | |
| LAE-498- | Tip-Toe Thru' The Tulips With Me | - | Dec 7-1 |
| | | | |
| LAE-505- | When My Dreams Come True | Br 4390 | |

Los Angeles, June, 1929.

| | | |
|---|---|---|
| LAE-584- | I Don't Want Your Kisses (If I Can't Have Your Love) | Br 4547 |

New York, July, 1929.

| | | |
|---|---|---|
| E-30535- | Where Are You, Dream Girl ? | Br 4468 |

New York, August, 1929.

| | | |
|---|---|---|
| E-30365- | Ich liebe dich (I Love You) | Br 4464 |
| E-30366- | Until The End | Br 4547 |
| E-30368- | Sweethearts' Holiday | Br 4468 |
| | | |
| E-30394- | My Song Of The Nile | Br 4464 |

New York, May, 1930.

| | | |
|---|---|---|
| E-33039- | Dancing With Tears In My Eyes | Br 4834, 01012 |
| E-33040- | Telling It To The Daisies (But It Never Gets Back To You) | -       - |

New York, late June, 1930.

| | | |
|---|---|---|
| E-33292- | My Heart Belongs To The Girl Who Belongs To Somebody Else | Br 4847 |
| E-33293- | Singing A Song To The Stars | - |

New York, July, 1930.

| | | |
|---|---|---|
| E-33430- | Singing A Song To The Stars | Br 4860 |
| E-33431- | My Heart Belongs To The Girl Who Belongs To Somebody Else | - |

New York, August, 1930.

| | | |
|---|---|---|
| E-34075- | Just A Little Closer | Br 4896, 01057 |

New York, c. August 25, 1930.

| | | |
|---|---|---|
| E-34106- | Don't Tell Her What's Happened To Me | Br 4896, 01030 |

New York, September, 1930.

| | | |
|---|---|---|
| E-34197- | The Kiss Waltz | Br 4900, 01026 |
| E-34198- | Go Home And Tell Your Mother | -       - |
| | | |
| E-33989- | Wasting My Love On You | Br 4959 |
| E-33990- | Maybe It's Love | Br 4960, 01057 |

New York, October, 1930.

| | | |
|---|---|---|
| E-34017- | Three Little Words | Br 4959 |
| E-34018- | I'm Yours | - |

   Acc. by his Crooning Troubadours.    New York, November, 1930.

| | | |
|---|---|---|
| E-35404- | You're Driving Me Crazy | Br 4987, 01055 |
| E-35405- | I Miss A Little Miss (Who Misses Me In Sunny Tennessee) | -    - |

New York, late December, 1930.

| | | |
|---|---|---|
| E-35771- | Lady, Play Your Mandolin | Br 6013, 01081 |
| E-35772- | Say "Hello" To The Folks Back Home | -    - |

New York, late January, 1931.

| | | |
|---|---|---|
| E-35967- | You Didn't Have To Tell Me (I Knew It All The Time) | Br 6045, 01100 |
| E-35968- | Hello ! Beautiful | Br 6049, 01102 |
| E-35969- | When You Were The Blossom Of Buttercup Lane And I Was Your Little Boy Blue | Br 6045, 01100 |

New York, early February, 1931.

| | | |
|---|---|---|
| E-36029- | Walkin' My Baby Back Home | Br 6048, 01119 |
| E-36030- | Falling In Love Again | - |
| E-36031- | Running Between The Raindrops | Br 6049, 01102 |

New York, March, 1931.

| | | |
|---|---|---|
| E-36425- | Wabash Moon | Br 6089, 01138 |
| E-36449- | Can't You Read Between The Lines ? | Br 6104 |
| E-36450- | Boy ! Oh ! Boy ! Oh ! Boy ! I've Got It Bad | Br 6098, 01141 |
| E-36451- | Now You're In My Arms | Br 6104 |
| E-36452- | Let's Get Friendly | Br 6098, 01141 |
| E-36453- | I Surrender, Dear | Br 6089, 01138 |

New York, c. June 30, 1931.

| | | |
|---|---|---|
| E-36894- | That's My Desire | Br 6147, 01190 |
| E-36895- | When The Moon Comes Over The Mountain | -    01214 |

   Acc. by O/Victor Young.    New York, c. October 5, 1931.

| | | |
|---|---|---|
| E-37237- | Goodnight, Sweetheart | Br 6195 |

   Acc. by his Troubadours.    New York, January, 1932.

| | | |
|---|---|---|
| 1193-A | An Evening In Caroline | HoW B-3-4 |
| 1194-A | All Of Me/Goodnight, Ladies (no vocal) | HoW A-4-B-1 |

Guitar solos.    New York, December 6, 1932.

| | | |
|---|---|---|
| B-12690- | Picking The Guitar | Br 6508, 01433 |
| B-12691- | Teasing The Frets | -    - |

Vocal, acc. by own guitar.    New York, December 21, 1932.

| | | |
|---|---|---|
| B-12767- | I'm Sure Of Everything But You | Br 6459, 01437 |
| B-12768- | More Beautiful Than Ever | - |
| B-12769- | Till Tomorrow | Br 6462, 01437 |
| B-12770- | I Called To Say Goodnight | -    01465 |

Acc. by O/Victor Young.                    New York, May 8, 1934.

15177-   Love Thy Neighbour                  Mt M-13026
15178-   A Thousand Goodnights               -
15179-   Carry Me Back To The Lone Prairie   Mt M-13027
15180-   Goin' Home                          -

                                        New York, August 3, 1934.

15535-   Moon Glow                           Mt M-13091
15536-   For All We Know                     -

## BEN LYON

B. Atlanta, Ga., February 6, 1901; stage debut in Providence, R.I., 1919; played    in
various stock companies there and in Buffalo, N.Y.; toured with Jeanne Eagels,1920,
in THE WONDERFUL THING; first N.Y. success in MARY THE THIRD (39th Street, February
5, 1923, playing three parts); began film career that year; best-known films HELL'S
ANGELS (1930); I COVER THE WATERFRONT (1935); I KILLED THE COUNT (1938); HI GANG (a
film of his famous wartime British radio show with his wife Bebe Daniels, q.v.   for
details of his recordings) (1940); LIFE WITH THE LYONS (1954). Film executive, but
resident in London, 1939-1972.

## CHRISTIE MACDONALD

B. Picton, Nova Scotia, Canada, February 28, 1875; stage debut as member of    Pauline
Hall's Company in PURITANIA; with Francis Wilson's Company in 1893 appeared in    THE
DEVIL'S DEPUTY; ERMINIE; THE CHIEFTAIN and other productions; 1897-1899 played    in
another Sousa operetta, THE BRIDE ELECT; various other shows on tour, then rejoined
Francis Wilson to play in THE TOREADOR (1901); New York debut in THE SHO-GUN (Wallack's, October 10, 1904); subsequent successes in THE BELLE OF MAYFAIR(Daly's,Dec-
ember 3, 1906); MISS HOOK OF HOLLAND (Criterion, December 31, 1907); THE PRINCE OF
BOHEMIA (Hackett, January, 1910); THE SPRING MAID (Liberty, December 26, 1910); she
played the latter role throughout 1911 and 1912; SWEETHEARTS (first in Baltimore in
March, 1913, then at the New Amsterdam, September 8, 1913); toured in this  show in
1915, then retired temporarily until she appeared at the Palace in CUPID'S   MIRROR,
June, 1918, and a revival of FLORODORA (Century, April 5, 1920). Retired    permanently; d. 1962.

Vocal, acc. by O/ ── Magee.            New York, October 23, 1911.

B-11128-1-2  Day Dreams (w/Lyric Quartet) ("The      Rejected
                Spring Maid")
B-11129-2   Two Little Love Bees (w/Reinald Werren-  Vic 60060
                rath) ("The Spring Maid")

                                        New York, October 27, 1911.

B-11128-4   Day Dreams (w/Lyric Quartet) ("The       Vic 60061
                Spring Maid")

                                        New York, April 22, 1913.

B-13177-3   The Cricket On The Hearth (w/Reinald      Vic 60102
                Werrenrath) ("Sweethearts")
B-13178-2   Sweethearts ("Sweethearts")              Vic 60101

                                        New York, April 25, 1913.

B-13200-1   Sweethearts (w/chorus) ("Sweethearts")   Rejected
C-13201-1   Angelus (w/Reinald Werrenrath) ("Sweet-  Vic 70099
                hearts")
B-13202-1   Mother Goose (w/chorus) ("Sweethearts")  Rejected

## JEANETTE MacDONALD

B. Philadelphia, Pa., June 18, 1907; stage debut in chorus of THE DEMI-TASSE   REVUE,
Capitol N.Y., January, 1920; appeared in THE NIGHT BOAT (Liberty, April, 1920) and
IRENE (presented in Chicago while Edith Day was playing in it in London); appeared
in TANGERINE in October, 1921 (two months after it opened at the Casino, New York);

A FANTASTIC FRICASSEE (Greenwich Village, September 11, 1922); TIP-TOES (Liberty, December 28, 1925); SUNNY DAYS (Imperial, February 8, 1928); many other musicals in New York during the 1920s; began film career 1929, and starred in THE LOVE PARADE, her first (1929); ONE HOUR WITH YOU and LOVE ME TONIGHT (1932); all these with Maurice Chevalier; THE MERRY WIDOW (1934); then she teamed with Nelson Eddy in several famous operettas on film : NAUGHTY MARIETTA (1935); ROSE-MARIE (1936);MAYTIME(1937); THE GIRL OF THE GOLDEN WEST (1938); SWEETHEARTS (1939); NEW MOON (1940); I MARRIED AN ANGEL (1942); also starred in SAN FRANCISCO (1936); THE FIREFLY (1937); BITTER SWEET (1940); SMILIN' THROUGH (1941), and others. Visited Europe in 1931 and sang at the Empire, Paris (September 4) and the Dominion, London, September 21; appeared successfully on concert platform during the 1940s and 1950s. D. 1965. Her husband Gene Raymond wrote LET ME ALWAYS SING for her.

Vocal, acc. by O/Nat Shilkret.                    New York, December 11, 1929.

BVE-57596-1  March Of The Grenadiers (w/The        Vic 22247, HMV B-3289
             Revelers) (Film "The Love Parade")
BVE-57597-3  Dream Lover (Film "The Love Parade")  As above plus Vic LPV-538,
                                                   LSA-3074, RD-7869

    Acc. by O/Leroy Shield.                    Culver City, Calif., January 19, 1930.

PBVE-54560-1-2-3-4  Dream Lover (Film "The Love    Vic rejected
             Parade")

                                         Hollywood, August 4, 1930.

PBVE-61007-2  Always In All Ways (Film "Monte      Vic 22514, HMV B-3633
              Carlo")

                                         Hollywood, August 5, 1930.

PBVE-61008-3  Beyond The Blue Horizon (w/The       Vic 22514, HMV B-3633
              Rounders) (Film "Monte Carlo")

    Acc. by O/Ray Noble.              Small Queen's Hall, London, Sept. 25, 1931.

OB-1486-2  Dear, When I Met You                     HMV B-3953
OB-1487-2  Pardon, Madame                           HMV B-3952
OB-1488-3  Goodnight                                -
OB-1489-3  Reviens (In French)                      HMV B-3953

    Acc. by Nat W. Finston and the Paramount Studio Orchestra.
                                    Hollywood, April 24, 1932.

PBS-68350-1-2-3  One Hour With You (Film "One
             Hour With You")                        Vic rejected
PBS-68351-1-2  One Hour With You (Film "One Hour    -
             With You") (In French)
PBS-68352-  We Will Always Be Sweethearts (Film     Vic 24019
             "One Hour With You") (in French)
PBS-68353-1-2-3  We Will Always Be Sweethearts      Rejected
             (Film "One Hour With You")

                                         Hollywood, April 27, 1932.

PBS-68350-  One Hour With You (Film "One Hour       Vic 24013, HMV B-4210
            With You")
PBS-68351-  One Hour With You (Film "One Hour       Vic 24019
            With You") (In French)
PBS-68353-  We Will Always Be Sweethearts (Film     Vic 24013, HMV B-4210
            "One Hour With You")

                                         Hollywood, July 5, 1932.

PBS-68366-3  Love Me Tonight (Film "Love Me         Vic 24067, HMV B-4288
             Tonight")
PBS-68367-  Love Me Tonight (Film "Love Me          Vic 24068
             Tonight") (In French)
(continued on page 432)

Hollywood, July 5, 1932 (cont.)

PBS-68368-2   Isn't It Romantic ? (Film "Love Me      Vic 24067, HMV B-4288
              Tonight")
PBS-68369-    Isn't It Romantic ? (Film "Love Me      Vic 24068
              Tonight") (in French)

Acc. by the MGM Studio Orchestra/Herbert Stothart.
                                    Hollywood, August 14, 1934.

PBS-79313-    I Love You So (Film "The Merry Widow")Vic 24729, HMV B-8247
PBS-79314-1-2 I Love You So (Film "The Merry Widow")Rejected
              (In French)
PBS-79315-    Vilia (Film "The Merry Widow")          Vic 24729, HMV B-8247, B-8972
PBS-79316-1-2-3 Vilia (Film "The Merry Widow")        Rejected
              (In French)

                                    Hollywood, August 30, 1934.

PBS-79326-1-2-3 Tonight Will Teach Me To Forget       Rejected
              (Film "The Cat And The Fiddle") (In French)
PBS-79327-    Tonight Will Teach Me To Forget         Vic 24754, HMV B-8251
              (Film "The Cat And The Fiddle")

                                    Hollywood, September 20, 1934.

PBS-79371-1-2-3 Try To Forget (Film "The Cat And      Rejected
              The Fiddle") (In French)
PBS-79372-    Try To Forget (Film "The Cat And The    Vic 24754, HMV B-8251
              Fiddle")

                                    Hollywood, March 20, 1935.

PBS-90072-    Italian Street Song (Film "Naughty      Vic 24896, LPV-526, HMV B-8320
              Marietta")
PBS-90073-1-2 Italian Street Song (Film "Naughty      Rejected
              Marietta") (In French)
PBS-90074-    Ah ! Sweet Mystery Of Life (Film        Vic 24896, LPV-526, HMV B-8320,
              "Naughty Marietta")                     B-8972
PBS-90075-1-2 Ah ! Sweet Mystery Of Life (Film        Rejected
              "Naughty Marietta")

Acc. by O/Nat Shilkret.              Hollywood, September 19, 1936.

PBS-97847-    Indian Love Call (w/Nelson Eddy)        Vic 4323, LPV-526, HMV DA-1537
              (Film "Rose Marie")
PBS-97848-    Ah ! Sweet Mystery Of Life (w/Nelson        -                    -
              Eddy) (Film "Naughty Marietta")

                                    Hollywood, September 21, 1936.

PBS-97855-    Farewell To Dreams (w/Nelson Eddy)      Vic 4329, LPV-526, HMV DA-1559
              (Film "Maytime")
PBS-97856-    Will You Remember ? (w/Nelson Eddy)         -            -         -
              (Film "Maytime")
PBS-97857-1-2 Song Of Love (w/Nelson Eddy) (Film      Rejected
              "Blossom Time")

Acc. by Giuseppe Bamboschek-p.       Hollywood, September 11, 1939.

PBS-036488-5  When I Have Sung My Songs               Vic 2047
PBS-036489-6  Do Not Go, My Love                          -
PBS-036490-5  Annie Laurie/Comin' Thro' The Rye       Vic 2055, HMV DA-1735
PBS-036491-2  From The Land Of The Sky-Blue Water/    Rejected
              Let Me Always Sing

Acc. by O/Giuseppe Bamboschek.          Hollywood, September 13, 1939.

PBS-042102-5   Ave Maria (Bach-Gounod)          Vic 2049, HMV DA-1739
PBS-042103-6   Les Filles de Cadix (Delibes)      - HMV DA-1735 -
PCS-042104-1-2-3  Depuis le jour ou je me suis    Rejected
               donnee ("Louise" - Charpentier)

                                        Hollywood, September 15, 1939.

PBS-042116-1-2-3-4  Air de Bijoux ("Faust"-Gounod) Rejected
               - Part 1
PBS-042117-1-2  Air de Bijoux ("Faust" - Gounod)      -
               - Part 2
PBS-042118-    Je veux vivre dans cette reve     Vic 15850, HMV DB-3940
               ("Romeo et Juliette" - Gounod)

                                        Hollywood, September 16, 1939.

PBS-036491-10  From The Land Of The Sky-Blue Water/Rejected
               Let Me Always Sing (Acc. by Gene Raymond-p)
PCS-042104-    Depuis le jour ou je me suis    Vic 15850, HMV DB-3940
               donnee ("Louise" - Charpentier)
PBS-042123-5   Lover, Come Back To Me (Film "New  Vic 2048, LPV-526, HMV DA-1721
               Moon")
PBS-042124-5   One Kiss (Film "New Moon")            -                      -

                                        Hollywood, October 5, 1939.

PBS-036491-    From The Land Of The Sky-Blue Water/Vic 2055
               Let Me Always Sing (Acc. by Gene Raymond-p)

Acc. by the Victor Concert Orchestra/Herbert Stothart.
                                        Hollywood, September 22, 1941.

PCS-061675-1   Drink To Me Only With Thine Eyes   Vic 18317, HMV C-3285
               (Film "Smilin' Through")
PCS-061676-1   Smilin' Through (Film "Smilin'    Vic 18315, HMV C-3284
               Through")
PCS-061677-3   The Kerry Dance (Film "Smilin'    Vic 18316, HMV C-3285
               Through")
PCS-061678-2   Ouvre ton coeur - Bolero (Bizet)      -
               (Film "Smilin' Through")
PCS-061679-2   A Little Love, A Little Kiss (Film  Vic 18315, HMV C-3284
               "Smilin' Through")
PCS-061680-1   Land Of Hope And Glory (Film      Vic 18317
               "Smilin' Through")

## GEORGE  MacFARLANE

B. Kingston, Ontario, Canada, 1877.  Very popular baritone singer and actor who made
great successes out of his appearances in THE MIDNIGHT GIRL (44th Street, New York,
February 23, 1914) and MISS SPRINGTIME (New Amsterdam, September 25, 1916), and in
other short-lived productions (MISS CAPRICE, 1913; SHAMEEN DHU; THE HEART OF PADDY
WHACK (1914); TRILBY; LADY LUXURY (1915); HEART O' TH' HEATHER (1916); he also sang
in Gilbert and Sullivan operas.  D. Hollywood, February 22, 1932.

Vocal, acc. by studio orchestra.        New York, October 17, 1913.

C-13966-1-2   Somewhere A Voice Is Calling     Vic rejected
B-13967-1-2   Look In Her Eyes ("Miss Caprice")      -
B-13968-1-2   Take Your Time ("Miss Caprice")        -
B-13969-1-2   The Garden By The Sea                  -

                                        New York, May  5,  1914.

B-13967-3   Look In Her Eyes ("Miss Caprice")    Vic 60120
B-14799-2   Oh ! Gustave (w/Margaret Romaine)    Vic 60118
            ("The Midnight Girl")
B-14801-2   That's An Irish Lullaby ("Shameen Dhu") Vic 60125

New York, June 17, 1914.

C-13969-1-2  The Garden By The Sea              Vic rejected
B-14964-1-2  When It's Night-Time Down In Burgundy    -

New York, July 6, 1914.

C-13969-3  The Garden By The Sea                Vic 70109
B-14964-3  When It's Night-Time Down In Burgundy  Vic 60121
B-15045-2  Can't You Hear Me Calling, Caroline ?  Vic 60123

New York, August 26, 1914.

C-15148-2  Your Eyes                            Vic 70111
B-15149-1  Roll On, Beautiful World, Roll On    Rejected

    Acc. by O/Walter B. Rogers.        New York, December 21, 1914.

B-15535-1-2  California (The Girl I Adore)       Vic rejected
B-15537-1-2  A Little Bit Of Heaven ("The Heart    -
               Of Paddy Whack")
    NOTE:- Matrix B-15536 is not by George MacFarlane.

New York, January 29, 1915.

B-15537-3  A Little Bit Of Heaven ("The Heart Of  Vic 60132
             Paddy Whack")
B-15646-1  Fair Moon ("H.M.S. Pinafore")        Vic 60136

New York, February 2, 1915.

B-15658-1  Dreamy Eyes                          Vic 60134
B-15659-1-2  Mother Machree                     Rejected

New York, May 14, 1915.

B-16024-2  Irish Eyes Of Love ("The Heart Of    Vic 60137
             Paddy Whack")
B-16025-2  A Breath O' Blooming Heather From My  Vic 45068
             Little Highland Hame ("Trilby")
B-16026-2  To The Lass We Love, A Toast ("Trilby")   -

New York, August 3, 1915.

B-16306-2  You're The Best Little Mother That God  Vic 45079
             Ever Made
B-16307-1-2  I Would Find You, Dear             Rejected
B-16308-1  Goodnight, Goodnight                  -
B-16309-2  Ireland                              Vic 45074

New York, August 4, 1915.

B-16306-3-4  You're The Best Little Mother That  Rejected
               God Ever Made
B-16307-3-4  I Would Find You, Dear               -
B-16308-2  Goodnight, Goodnight                 Vic 45079
B-16316-1-2  The Heart                          Rejected
B-16317-1  My Home Town In Ireland              Vic 45074
B-16318-1  I Will Always Love You (As I Do Today)  Rejected

New York, August 5, 1915.

B-16307-5-6  I Would Find You, Dear             Vic rejected
B-16316-3-4  The Heart                            -
B-16318-2-3  I Will Always Love You (As I Do Today)  -
B-16319-1-2  Longing Just For You ("Lady Luxury")   -

Acc. by O/Walter B. Rogers or Eddie King.
                              New York, December 10, 1915.

B-16318-4-5  I Will Always Love You (As I Do Today)Vic rejected
                 - O/WBR
B-16879-1-2  Kitty MacFadden - O/WBR                  -
B-16891-1-2-3  What An Irishman Means By Machree      -
                 - O/EK

Acc. by O/Walter B. Rogers.         New York, April 26, 1916.

B-17543-1-2-3  The Heart Of The Heather ("The       Rejected
                 Heart Of The Heather")
B-17544-2  Don't Believe All You Hear In The        Vic 45097
                 Moonlight ("The Heart Of The Heather")
B-17545-1  In Scotland ("The Heart Of The Heather")   -
B-17546-1-2  Lass O' My Dreams ("The Heart Of The  Rejected
                 Heather")

                              New York, January 12, 1917.

B-19039-3  My Castle In The Air ("Miss Springtime")Vic 45110
B-19040-2  My Old Rose
B-19041-2  Won't Yez Kape Me Company ?              Vic 45112
B-19042-1-2  My Old Briar Pipe                      Rejected

Acc. by O/? Charles A. Prince.      New York, August 1, 1918.

77982-   When You Come Back, And You Will Come   Col A-2624
             Back, There's The Whole World Waiting For You
77983-   What A Wonderful Message From Home          -

                              New York, August 23, 1918.

78024-1-2-3  Mother Machree                     Col rejected

## FRED MACMURRAY

B. 1908; began professional career as tenor saxophonist and vocalist with dance bands led by George Olsen (1929) and Gus Arnheim (1930); turned to acting bit parts in an enormous number of films, then established himself as a versatile actor.  Among his best-remembered films are :- HANDS ACROSS THE TABLE and THE TRAIL OF THE   LONESOME PINE (1936); CHAMPAGNE WALTZ and SWING HIGH, SWING LOW (1937); TRUE CONFESSION and SING, YOU SINNERS (1938); CAFE SOCIETY (1939); LITTLE OLD NEW YORK (1940); NEW YORK TOWN and DIVE BOMBER (1941); THE LADY IS WILLING; TAKE A LETTER, DARLING and FOREST RANGERS (1942); AND THE ANGELS SING (1943); WHERE DO WE GO FROM HERE ? (1945); SUD-DENLY IT'S SPRING (1946); THE EGG AND I (1947); THE MIRACLE OF THE BELLS and ON OUR MERRY WAY (1948); NEVER A DULL MOMENT (1951); CALLAWAY WENT THATAWAY (1952);WOMAN'S WORLD and THE CAINE MUTINY (1954); THE SHAGGY DOG (1959); THE APARTMENT (1960); SON OF FLUBBER (1963); THE HAPPIEST MILLIONAIRE (1967). Also appeared in long TV series MY THREE SONS (1960-1969).

Vocalist with George Olsen and his Music. Culver City, Calif., November 10, 1929.

PBVE-54498-2  After A Million Dreams              Vic 22248

Vocalist with Gus Arnheim and his Orchestra.
                              Culver City, Calif., March 20, 1930.

PBVE-54730-3  All I Want Is Just One (Girl)       Vic 22384

## FRANCES MADDUX

B. Hollywood, Calif., 1908; studied piano as a child, and as a teenager appeared as a soloist with the Los Angeles Philharmonic Orchestra; became attracted to    popular music in 1928, learned to sing it, very successfully, in New York cabarets,   clubs, theatres and on radio; made unheralded entrance in London's Cafe de Paris in  July, 1929 and created a sensation; went on to Deauville and Biarritz, then back to   New York to sing with Leo Reisman and his Orchestra at the Central Park Casino;   reap-peared briefly in London in 1933.

Vocalist with Leo Reisman and his Orchestra.
                                        New York, October 10, 1930.

BVE-62370-17  Body And Soul                     Vic 22537
BVE-64315-1-2-3  Trees                          Rejected

                                        New York, December 28, 1931.

BS-71205-2  Paradise                            Vic 22904
BS-71206-1  Someday I'll Find You                  -        HMV B-6156

Vocal, acc. by own (?) p/unknown g.     London, February 2, 1933.

CA-13386-1  Ev'ry Little While                  Col DB-1089
CA-13387-1  Try Gettin' A Good Night's Sleep       -

   Acc. by own p or her Play Boys.      New York, September 13, 1934.

P-15892-  It's All Forgotten Now - PB            LMS L-
P-15893-  It Happens To The Best Of Friends - PB
P-15894-  Sin-Tax (The Movie Star Song) - PB
P-15895-  I'm A Divorcee - p
P-15896-  I'm On The Brink Of Disaster - p
P-15897-  Ho Hum ! - p

   Acc. by own piano.                   New York, November 2, 1934.

P-16294-  April Woman                           LMS L-

                                        New York, October 19, 1935.

P-18181-  I'd Like To Learn A Lot (From A Nice   LMS L-
            Young Man)
P-18182-  The Country Maiden

                                        New York, May 19, 1936.

P-19285-  These Foolish Things Remind Me Of You  LMS L-
P-19286-  There's Not A Real New Yorker In New York

## MADGE MAITLAND


Vocal, acc. by studio orchestra.        New York, c. November, 1905.

   3328-1  My Lovin' Henry                       Col 3328, Standard 3328
   NOTE:- The Standard issue is anonymous : "Contralto Solo."

                                        New York, c. December, 1905.

      Is Everybody Happy ?                      Ed 9210 (February, 1906)

## LOUIS MANN

B. New York, April 20, 1865; became well-known straight actor in the 1880s,  appearing
   in many plays, notably DR. JEKYLL AND MR. HYDE.  Later he extended his scope to comedy routines.  D. New York, February 15, 1931.

Humorous monologue, unacc.              New York, c. 1917.

      Cohen Stories                             Em 783

## EVERETT MARSHALL

B. Lawrence, Mass., December 31, 1901; educated in Cincinnati, London and Milan; began
   his career in an office, but turned to the theatre and had his debut in October,1926
   in Palermo, Italy, as the Conte di Luna in Verdi's IL TROVATORE; New York debut   at
   the Metropolitan Opera House, November 12, 1927, as the Herald in Wagner's LOHENGRIN

(remaining a member of that company until 1931); turned to the lighter musical pro-
ductions and appeared in GEORGE WHITE'S SCANDALS (Apollo, September 14, 1931); also
ZIEGFELD FOLLIES (Winter Garden, January 4, 1934) and many other musicals;    played
Schubert in BLOSSOM TIME (46th Street, December, 1938), sang at the New York World's
Fair, 1939; made a few films, beginning with DIXIANA (1930); I LIVE FOR YOU (1935).

Vocal, acc. by O/Leroy Shield.                  Hollywood, May 23, 1930.

PBVE-54828-1-2-3  My Guiding Star                  Vic rejected
PBVE-54829-1-2-3  Carl's Entrance                  -

   Acc. by O/Nat Shilkret.              New York, June 10, 1930.

BVE-62707-1-2  My Shining Silver Star            Rejected
BVE-62708-2  Goodbye, Old Pals (Film "Dixiana")  Vic 22471, HMV B-3570
BVE-62709-2  Mr. And Mrs. Sippi (Film "Dixiana") As above plus Vic LPV-538,
                                                 LSA-3074, RD-7869

   Acc. by the Brunswick Hour Orchestra/Victor Young.
                           New York, late October, 1931.

E-37322-   That's Why Darkies Were Born ("George  Br 6215, 01250
             White's Scandals")

                           New York, late November, 1931.

E-37388-   The Thrill Is Gone ("George White's    Br 6215, 01250
             Scandals")

   Acc. by studio orchestra, featuring Jack Jenney-tb.
                           New York, August 16, 1934.

38331-C  Lonely Heart - tbJJ                    Dec 15002, K-746
38332-C  Let Me Be Born Again (w/The Cavaliers)  -        -
38333-A-B  Song Of Love ("Blossom Time")        Rejected

                           New York, September 20, 1934.

38333-C-D  Song Of Love ("Blossom Time")        Dec 225
38697    Yours Is My Heart Alone                -

                           New York, October 10, 1935.

BS-95372-1-2  Mine Alone (Film "I Live For You")  Vic rejected
BS-95373-1  Silver Wings (Film "I Live For You")  -

                           New York, October 31, 1935.

BS-95372-3  Mine Alone (Film "I Live For You")   Vic 25164, HMV B-8399
BS-95373-2  Silver Wings (Film "I Live For You")  -        -

## HENRY I. MARSHALL

B. Boston, Mass., February 22, 1883; actor, director, song-writer and radio producer;
acted in and directed THE RUNAWAYS (Casino, N.Y., May 11, 1903); appeared in vaudeville as pianist and arranger; wrote song hits such as BE MY LITTLE BABY BUMBLE BEE
(1912); MARY, YOU'RE A LITTLE BIT OLD-FASHIONED and ON THE 5.15 (1914); LOADING  UP
THE MANDY LEE (1916); produced first amateur radio show (1929) and the award-winner
CAVALCADE OF YOUTH.  D. Plainfield, N.J., April 4, 1958.  Neither of the two  songs
he recorded  is his own.

Vocal, acc. by studio orchestra/? Charles A. Prince.
                           New York, September 22, 1916.

47042-1-2-3  Take Me To My Alabam'               Col rejected

                           New York, November 14, 1916.

47154-   Whose Pretty Baby Are You Now ?         Col A-2153

B. London, May 23, 1890; began career as an articled clerk to a firm of chartered ac-
countants, but took up acting in 1911; London debut in BREWSTER'S MILLIONS (Prince's
Theatre, May 12, 1913); accompanied Cyril Maude on tour in U.S.A. and Canada (q.v.),
1915; served in British Army in France, lost a leg and was demobilized in 1918; despite this handicap, resumed acting career with the company at the Lyric,   Hammersmith, London; played in many productions there (including Shakespeare); in    BROWN
SUGAR (Duke of York's, July 7, 1920); A SAFETY MATCH (Strand, January 13, 1921); in
August, 1921 accompanied Marie Löhr on her tour of the U.S.A. and Canada, appearing
in several shows; resumed in London in April, 1922, with success in AREN'T WE ALL ?
(Globe, April 10, 1923); THE PELICAN (Ambassadors, October 20, 1924); THE  LAVENDER
LADIES (Comedy, July 29, 1925); to New York for THESE CHARMING PEOPLE (Gaiety, Oct-
ober 6, 1925); in London, THE QUEEN WAS IN THE PARLOUR(St.Martin's, August 24,1926);
INTERFÉRENCE (St. James's, January 29, 1927); S.O.S. (St. James's, February 11,1928);
again to New York, for THE HIGH ROAD (Fulton, September 10, 1928); in London,at St.
James's for two successful shows (MICHAEL AND MARY, February 1, 1930, and THE SWAN,
June 30, 1930); played in TOMORROW AND TOMORROW in New York (January 13, 1931), and
in THERE'S ALWAYS JULIET in London (Apollo, October 12, 1931) and New York (Empire,
February 15, 1932); returned briefly to London before resuming his film career that
had begun in 1927 with MUMSIE and which had included MICHAEL AND MARY (1931); films
of the next six years include I WAS A SPY (1933); FOUR FRIGHTENED PEOPLE (1934);THE
DARK ANGEL (1936) and IF YOU COULD ONLY COOK (1937);  others of the 1940s and later
include THE MOON AND SIXPENCE (1942); DUEL IN THE SUN and THE RAZOR'S EDGE  (1946);
THE VIRGIN QUEEN (1955); THE THIRD DAY (1965), and many others.  D. 1966.

Speech in title-role, with supporting cast and acc. by O/Victor Young, dir. by   Nat
Wolff.                                    Los Angeles, June 30, 1942.

| L-3079- | The Count Of Monte Cristo - Part 1 | Dec 29122, Br LAT-8534 |
| L-3080- | The Count Of Monte Cristo - Part 2 | - | - |
| L-3081- | The Count Of Monte Cristo - Part 3 | Dec 29123 | - |
| L-3082- | The Count Of Monte Cristo - Part 4 | - | - |
| L-3083- | The Count Of Monte Cristo - Part 5 | Dec 29124 | - |
| L-3084- | The Count Of Monte Cristo - Part 6 | - | - |
| L-3085- | The Count Of Monte Cristo - Part 7 | Dec 29125 | - |
| L-3086- | The Count Of Monte Cristo - Part 8 | - | - |

                                          Los Angeles, July 13, 1942.

| L-3094- | The Count Of Monte Cristo - Part 3 | Dec 29123 ? |
| L-3095- | The Count Of Monte Cristo - Part 5 | Dec 29124 ? |

## MARY  MARTIN

B. Weatherford, Texas, December 1, 1913; studied and taught dancing; first public appearance as vocalist at the Trocadero night club, Hollywood; stage debut in New York
in LEAVE IT TO ME (Imperial, November 9, 1938); back to Hollywood to make many musical films (THE GREAT VICTOR HERBERT (1939); RHYTHM ON THE RIVER (1940);  NEW  YORK
TOWN; KISS THE BOYS GOODBYE and THE BIRTH OF THE BLUES (1941); STAR-SPANGLED RHYTHM
(1943); HAPPY-GO-LUCKY (1943) and many others); reappeared in New York in the great
hit ONE TOUCH OF VENUS (Imperial, October 7, 1943); toured in this until June,1945;
LUTE SONG (Plymouth, February 6, 1946); in London to appear in PACIFIC 1860 (Drury
Lane, December 19, 1946); this flopped, and Mary Martin vowed she would return   to
London in a hit show.  She did so on November 1, 1951 in SOUTH PACIFIC (also  Drury
Lane), after making a huge hit with it in New York (1,694 performances from April7,
1949).

Vocal, acc. by Eddy Duchin and his Orchestra.
                                          New York, November 30, 1938.

| B-23778- | My Heart Belongs To Daddy ("Leave It To Me") | Br 8282, Par F-1619 | | |
| B-23779- | Most Gentlemen Don't Like Love ("Leave It To Me") | - | - | Epic SN-6059 |

Acc. by Woody Herman and his Orchestra.  New York, December 22, 1938.

| 64833-A | Who'll Buy My Violets ? | Dec 2362, Br 02760 |
| 64834-A | Listen To The Mocking Bird | Dec 2265, Br 02749 |

New York, January 24, 1939.

```
64940-A  The Maids Of Cadiz                 Dec 2265, Br 02937
64941-A  Il Bacio                           Dec 2377
64941-B  Il Bacio                               -      Br 02749
```

  Acc. by O/Ray Sinatra.            New York, March 20, 1939.

```
65194-A  Our Love                           Dec 2377, Br 02937
65195-A  Deep Purple                        Dec 2362, Br 02760
```

New York, January 25, 1940.

```
67127-   Why Shouldn't I ?                  Dec 23148
67128-A  Let's Do It                            -      Br 03229
67129-   My Heart Belongs To Daddy ("Leave It To  Dec 23149, 7-2, AH 67
           Me")
```

Los Angeles, April 16, 1940.

```
DLA-1992-   You're Lonely And I'm Lonely     Dec 23151
```

New York, May 2, 1940.

```
67164-A  I Get A Kick Out Of You            Dec 23149, Br 03229
67165-   What Is This Thing Called Love ?   Dec 23150
67166-A  Katie Went To Haiti                    -      Br 03393
67167-   Just A-Whistlin', Just A-Whittlin'  Dec 23151
```

  Acc. by O/Victor Young.          Los Angeles, August 26, 1940.

```
DLA-2090-A  I Don't Want To Cry Any More (Film   Dec 23164, Br 03103
              (Film "Rhythm On The River")
DLA-2091-A  Ain't It A Shame About Mame ? (Film      -        -
              "Rhythm On The River")
```

Acc. by Jack Teagarden and his Orchestra. (From the soundtrack of the film   BIRTH
OF THE BLUES).                          Hollywood, May, 1941.

```
         Wait Till The Sun Shines, Nellie (w/    V-Disc 542
           Bing Crosby)
         The Waiter And The Porter And The Upstairs     -
         Maid (w/Bing Crosby and Jack Teagarden)
```

Los Angeles, May 26, 1941.

```
DLA-2411-A  The Waiter And The Porter And The   Dec 3970, 25408, 9-25408, 91415,
              Upstairs Maid (Film "Birth Of The  DL-8076, DL-9067, Br 03269,BING-6
                                                 LAT-8055, LAT-8306
```

  Acc. by O/Richard Himber.        Los Angeles, July 17, 1941.

```
DLA-2565-   Kiss The Boys Goodbye (Film "Kiss The  Dec 18184, Br 03253, AH 67
              Boys Goodbye")
DLA-2566-   Do It Again                           -        -
```

  Acc. by John Scott Trotter and his Orchestra.
                                        Los Angeles, March 13, 1942.

```
DLA-2946-A  Lily Of Laguna (w/Bing Crosby)     Dec 18278, 25091, Br 03657
DLA-2947-A  Wait Till The Sun Shines, Nellie   As above, plus Dec 91415,
              (w/Bing Crosby)                  DL-4255, DL-8076, DL-9067,
                                               DL-34002, Br BING-6, LAT-8055
```

Vocalist with Horace Heidt and his Musical Knights.
                                        Hollywood, April 8, 1942.

```
HCO-792-1  Pound Your Table Polka             Col 36595
```

B. 1913; began as dance-band vocalist with Tom Gerun and others; film debut in SING,
BABY, SING (1936); then followed FOLLOW THE FLEET (1936); BANJO ON MY KNEE (1937);
ALI BABA GOES TO TOWN (1938); KENTUCKY MOONSHINE and THANKS FOR EVERYTHING (1939);
SALLY, IRENE AND MARY and MUSIC IN MY HEART (1940); ZIEGFELD GIRL and THE BIG STORE
(1941); TILL THE CLOUDS ROLL BY (1946); CASBAH (1948); TWO TICKETS TO BROADWAY and
EASY TO LOVE (1952); HERE COME THE GIRLS (1953); DEEP IN MY HEART (1954);  HIT  THE
DECK (1955); and his British-made film LET'S BE HAPPY (1957); appeared in London in
vaudeville and cabaret, 1948.  M. first Alice Faye (q.v.), then Cyd Charisse; r. n.
Alvin Norris.

Vocal, acc. by O/Victor Young.                Los Angeles, July 18, 1936.

DLA-445-A  A Star Fell Out Of Heaven                   Dec 884, F-6102
DLA-446-A  When Did You Leave Heaven ? (Film "Sing,    - 7-1 -
           Baby, Sing")

                                              Los Angeles, September 17, 1936.

DLA-615-   It's Love I'm After                         Dec 957, F-6292
DLA-616-   You're Slightly Terrific                     -       -
DLA-617-A  Sweetheart, Let's Grow Old Together         Dec 970, F-6234
DLA-618-A  The World Is Mine (Tonight)                  -       -        F-7084

   Acc. by O/Cy Feuer.                        Los Angeles, November 5, 1936.

LA-1185-   There's Something In The Air (Film    Br 7782, Voc 528
              "Banjo On My Knee")
LA-1186-   Rainbow On The River                  Br 7791
LA-1187-   So Do I                               -
LA-1188-   Where The Lazy River Goes By ("Banjo On  Br 7782, Voc 528
              My Knee")

Vocalist with Ray Noble and his Orchestra. Los Angeles, January 29, 1938.

LA-1568-   Just Let Me Look At You               Br 8076, Col FB-2010
LA-1569-   The Moon Of Manakoora                 Br 8079, Col FB-2002
LA-1570-A-B  I Hadn't Anyone Till You            Rejected
LA-1571-   You Couldn't Be Cuter                 Br 8076, Col FB-2010

                                              Los Angeles, February 3, 1938.

LA-1570-C  I Hadn't Anyone Till You             Br 8079, Col FB-2024

                                              Los Angeles, March 20, 1938.

LA-1598-A  My Walking Stick                     Br 8153, Col FB-2045
LA-1599-A  Now It Can Be Told                   -        -
LA-1600-A  Marching Along With Time             Br 8180, Col FB-2044

Vocal, acc. by Manny Klein and his Swing-a-Hulas.
                                  Los Angeles, June 5, 1938.

LA-1652-   A Song Of Old Hawaii                 Voc 4254, Col FB-2049
LA-1653-A  The Island Of Maui Hula (Aloha Ia No  Voc 4508, Col FB-2131
              O Maui)
LA-1654-   My Sweetheart (Kuu Ipo)              Voc 4254, Col FB-2049
LA-1655-A  Rhythm Of The Waves                  Voc 4508, Col FB-2131

   Acc. by O/Jerry Joyce.                      Los Angeles, July 20, 1938.

LA-1688-A  A Mist Is Over The Moon              Voc 4320, Col FB-2212
LA-1689-A  This May Be The Night                Voc 4255, Col FB-2066
LA-1690-A  That Week In Paris                   Voc 4320, Col FB-2212
LA-1691-B  By A Wishing Well                    Voc 4255, Col FB-2066

   Acc. by O/Ray Sinatra.                      New York, March 14, 1939.

65177-B  Begin The Beguine                     Dec 2375, 25018, DL-8366, F-7084,
                                               F-7552, Br LA-8713
65178-A  September Song                         Dec 2375, 25018, DL-8366,
                                               Br 04655, LA-8713

Acc. by Abe Lyman and his Orchestra.    New York, March 15, 1939.

| 65184- | Avalon | Dec 2434 |
| 65185- | Rose Room | Dec 2433 |
| 65186- | Home In Pasadena | - |
| 65187- | California, Here I Come | Dec 2434 |

Acc. by O/Victor Young.    Los Angeles, July 12, 1939.

| DLA-1815-A | White Sails (Beneath A Yellow Moon) | Dec 2651, F-7226 |
| DLA-1816- | Cinderella, Stay In My Arms | Dec 2627 |
| DLA-1817-A | All I Remember Is You | -   F-7226 |

Los Angeles, July 14, 1939.

| DLA-1819-A | Don't Forget Me, Don't Forget Me | Dec 2883, Br 02995 |
| DLA-1820-A | Song Of The Flame | - |
| DLA-1821-A | To You | Dec 2651, F-7494 |

Acc. by Abe Lyman and his Orchestra.    New York, September 26, 1939.

| 66668-A | Does Your Heart Beat For Me ? | Dec 2788, F-7391 |
| 66669- | South Of The Border | - |
| 66670-A | Lilacs In The Rain | Dec 2791, F-7391 |
| 66671- | Day In - Day Out | -   25379, DL-8366, Br LA-8713 |

Acc. by O/Ray Sinatra.    New York, December 19, 1939.

| 66988-A | Indian Summer | Dec 2936, 4235, F-7449, F-7552 |
| 66989-A | It's A Blue World | Dec 2932, F-7494 |
| 66990-A | Careless | Dec 2936, F-7449 |
| 66991-B | All The Things You Are | Dec 2932, 4236, 25042, 25262, F-7645 |

New York, March 20, 1940.

| 67351- | Love Song Of Renaldo | Dec 3087, F-7621 |
| 67352- | A Young Man Sings | -   4236 |
| 67353- | The Creaking Old Mill On The Creek | Dec 3099, F-7557 |
| 67354-A | Hear My Song, Violetta | -   F-7565 |

New York, March 31, 1940.

| 67437-A | Havana For A Night | Dec 3120, 4234, F-7645 |
| 67438-A | Tonight (Perfidia) | Dec 3119  -  F-7656 |
| 67439- | The Sky Fell Down | Dec 3120 |
| 67440- | Fools Rush In (Where Angels Fear To Tread) | Dec 3119, 25297, F-7557 |

Acc. by O/Victor Young.    Los Angeles, April 16, 1940.

| DLA-1988-A | The Donkey Serenade | Dec 3183, F-7565, DL-8366, Br LA-8713 |
| DLA-1989- | You're Lonely And I'm Lonely | Dec 3175 |
| DLA-1990- | Fools Fall In Love | - |
| DLA-1991-A | Help Me (Cuatro Vidas) | Dec 3183, F-8016 |

Acc. by O/Ray Sinatra.    New York, May 28, 1940.

| 67843-A | Where Was I ? | Dec 3246, F-7656 |
| 67844- | When The Swallows Come Back To Capistrano | -   F-7621 |
| 67845- | I'll Never Smile Again (Until I Smile At You) | Dec 3247, F-7610 |
| 67846- | I'm Stepping Out With A Memory Tonight | - 25054 - |

Acc. by O/Victor Young.                    Los Angeles, September 6, 1940.

DLA-2128-A  Two Dreams Met (w/Frances Langford)   Dec 3415, F-7725
DLA-2129-A  Our Love Affair (w/Frances Langford)    -          -
DLA-2130-A  Yesterthoughts                         Dec 3424, 4235
DLA-2131-A  My Next Romance                        Dec 3403, F-8921

                                           Los Angeles, September 10, 1940.

DLA-2145-A  A Handful Of Stars                     Dec 3424
DLA-2146-A  The Call Of The Canyon                 Dec 3403, F-7799

                                           Los Angeles, December 24, 1940.

DLA-2294-   Now I Lay Me Down To Dream             Dec 3592, F-7799
DLA-2295-   Dream Valley                             -      F-7795
DLA-2296-   The Last Time I Saw Paris              Dec 3591, 25042, F-7795
DLA-2297-   Till The Lights Of London Shine Again    -

                                           Los Angeles, January 15, 1941.

DLA-2361-A  They Met In Rio (A Midnight Serenade)  Dec 3624, F-7913
DLA-2362-A  Boa Noite                                -          -
DLA-2363-A  You Stepped Out Of A Dream (Film       Dec 3645, F-7954
              "Ziegfeld Girl")
DLA-2364-A  Too Beautiful To Last (Film "Ziegfeld Girl")-      -

Acc. by O/David Rose.                      Los Angeles, May 29, 1941.

DLA-2429-A  Intermezzo (w/chorus)                  Dec 3842, 25273, DL-8366, F-8024,
                                                   Br LA-8713
DLA-2430-A  Taboo                                  Dec 3842                -
DLA-2431-A  Flamingo                               Dec 3857, DL-8366, F-8007
DLA-2432-A  Where In The World                       -          -

Acc. by O/Dick Winslow.                    Los Angeles, June 24, 1941.

DLA-2451-A  Beautiful Ohio                         Dec F-8901
DLA-2452-A  By The River Sainte Marie              Dec F-8921
DLA-2453-   On Miami Shore                         Rejected
DLA-2454-   Old Pal, Why Don't You Answer Me ?       -

Acc. by O/David Rose.                      Los Angeles, June 27, 1941.

DLA-2472-   Don't Take Your Love From Me           Dec 3879, 25054
DLA-2473-A  The Angelus Rings Again                Dec 4250, F-8152
DLA-2474-   Below The Equator                      Dec 3967
DLA-2475-A  If It's You (Film "The Big Store")     Dec 3879, F-8016

Acc. by O/Dick Winslow.                    Los Angeles, July 1, 1941.

DLA-2451-   Beautiful Ohio                         Rejected ?
DLA-2452-   By The River Sainte Marie              Dec 4185
DLA-2453-   On Miami Shore                           -
DLA-2454-   Old Pal, Why Don't You Answer Me ?     Rejected ?

Acc. by O/David Rose.                      Los Angeles, July 11, 1941.

DLA-2525-A  Cuban Love Song                        Dec F-8900
DLA-2526-A  Just A Gigolo                            -
DLA-2527-A  Jealous                                Dec 3967, F-8071
DLA-2528-   Under Your Window                      Dec 4413
DLA-2529-A  Don't Ask Me Why                       Dec 4394, DL-8366, F-8286

                                           Los Angeles, July 20, 1941.

DLA-2576-   Nazareth (A Sacred Song)               Dec 4051, 25235
DLA-2577-   Christmas Candle                         -          -

Los Angeles, August 18, 1941.

| | | |
|---|---|---|
| DLA-2651-A | I Guess I'll Have To Dream The Rest | Dec 3988 |
| DLA-2652- | The Cowboy Serenade (While I'm Rolling | Dec 3989 |
| | My Last Cigarette) | |
| DLA-2653-A | Tonight We Love | Dec 3988, 25273, DL-8366, F-8205, |
| | | Br LA-8713 |
| DLA-2654-A | A Pretty Girl Is Like A Melody | Dec 18763, F-8901 |
| DLA-2655- | The Hills Of Home | Dec 3989, DL-8366, Br LA-8713 |

Acc. by O/Harry Sosnik.              New York, November 18, 1941.

| | | |
|---|---|---|
| 69961-A | 'Tis Autumn | Dec 4101, DL-8366, F-8119 |
| 69962-A | Cancel The Flowers | -              - |
| 69963- | Abe Lincoln Had Just One Country | Dec 4111 |
| 69964-A | Somebody Else Is Taking My Place | -      F-8152 |

Acc. by O/Victor Young.            Los Angeles, February 1, 1942.

| | | |
|---|---|---|
| DLA-2871- | Junior Miss | Dec 4310 |
| DLA-2872-A | Sleepy Lagoon | Dec 4250, DL-8366, F-8205 |
| DLA-2873- | After Taps | Dec 18321 |
| DLA-2874-A | Here You Are | Dec 4310, F-8230 |
| DLA-2875-A | Anywhere On Earth Is Heaven | Dec 18321  - |
| DLA-2876-A | (I Don't Stand) A Ghost Of A Chance | Dec 4413, 25379, DL-8366, |
| | (With You) | Br 04655, LA-8713 |

Los Angeles, July 19, 1942.

| | | |
|---|---|---|
| L-3105-A | I Had The Craziest Dream | Dec 4394, F-8286 |
| L-3106- | Yesterday's Gardenias | Dec 4378 |
| L-3107- | Lullaby Of The Rain | - |
| L-3108- | Why Do I Love You ? (w/Frances Langford) | Dec 18763, 25262 |

## NINO MARTINI

B. Italy, 1904; concert tenor who made some films in the U.S.A. and England   between
1935 and 1948 (HERE'S TO ROMANCE, 1935; THE GAY DESPERADO (1936); ONE NIGHT   WITH
YOU (in England in 1948); in the early and middle thirties he was a popular   member
of the Metropolitan Opera Company, New York.

Vocal, acc. by studio orchestra.        New York, September 21, 1933.

| | | |
|---|---|---|
| BS-77656-1 | El Trust de los Tenorios (in Spanish) | Vic 4231 |
| BS-77696-1 | La Dolorosa (in Spanish) | - |

New York, September 30, 1935.

| | | |
|---|---|---|
| BS-95302-1 | Mattinata (Film "Here's To Romance") | Vic 4295, HMV B-8411 |
| BS-95303-1 | Here's To Romance (Film "Here's To | Vic 4296, HMV B-8401 |
| | Romance") | |
| BS-95304-1 | I Carry You In My Pocket (Film "Here's | -      HMV B-8411 |
| | To Romance") | |
| BS-95305-1 | Midnight In Paris (Film "Here's To | Vic 4295, HMV B-8401 |
| | Romance") | |

## JOHNNY  MARVIN

B. Butler, Okla., July 11, 1897; stage debut in HONEYMOON LANE (Knickerbocker,   September 20, 1926); better known as cabaret entertainer, radio compere, and as singer
of popular songs accompanying himself on ukulele or guitar; had own radio show  for
five years in New York, then went to California during the 1930s, wrote music   for
Gene Autry films.  Appeared in London in the early summer of 1928, greatly  admired
by the then Prince of Wales.  D. Hollywood, Calif., December 20, 1944.

Vocal, acc. by own ukulele.          New York, c. May 6, 1924.

| | | |
|---|---|---|
| 72505- | Somebody Stole My Gal (w/Jack Kaufman) | OK 40127, Par E-5346 |

New York, October 30, 1925.

141226-  'Way Down South In Chicago By The Old      Rejected
             Pacific Shore
141227-  Down By The Winegar Woiks                  Col 511-D

New York, c. November 4, 1925.

73747-  Show Me The Way To Go Home                  OK 40508
73748-  Wait 'Til Tomorrow Night                    -

New York, November 20, 1925.

141292-  I Love My Baby (My Baby Loves Me)          Col 511-D

New York, December 30, 1925.

141447-  I Ain't In Love No More                    Col 547-D
141448-  In My Gondola                              -

New York, January 6, 1926.

141459-  Hot Coffee                                 Har 94-H
141460-  That Certain Party                         -
     NOTE:- This, and all the Harmony records listed in this chapter, are labelled HONEY
DUKE AND HIS UKE.

New York, January 22, 1926.

141545-  12th Street Rag (no vocal)                 Har 115-H, Re G-8591
141546-  Memphis Blues (no vocal)                   -          -

New York, February 10, 1926.

141619-  So Does Your Old Mandarin                  Rejected
141620-  I'm Gonna Let The Bumble Bee Be            Har 145-H

New York, February 24, 1926.

141720-  Sleepy Town                                Har 152-H
141721-  I'd Rather Be Alone                        -
141722-  Hooray For The Irish !                     Har 145-H

New York, c. February, 1926.

         I Ain't In Love No More                    Ed 51707
         Hooray For The Irish !                     -
         The Memphis Blues (no vocal)               Ed 51709
         12th Street Rag (no vocal)                 -

New York, March 10, 1926.

141788-  Thanks For The Buggy Ride                  Col 606-D
141789-  Under The Ukulele Tree                     -

New York, April 15, 1926.

141974-  So Is Your Old Lady                        Har 169-H
141975-  Hello, Aloha ! How Are You ?               -

New York, May 12, 1926.

142198-  Somebody's Lonely                          Col 648-D
142199-  (There's A Blue Ridge In My Heart) Virginia  -

New York, May 27, 1926.

142261-  I'm Full Of Love For Her                   Har 199-H
142262-  Oh Boy ! How It Was Raining                -

New York, June 29, 1926.

| | | |
|---|---|---|
| 142355- | Breezin' Along With The Breeze | Col 699-D |
| 142356- | Hello, Baby | - |

New York, July 16, 1926.

| | | |
|---|---|---|
| 142456- | Calling Me Home | Har 221-H |
| 142457- | Precious | - |

New York, c. July, 1926.

| | |
|---|---|
| Breezin' Along With The Breeze | Ed 51793 |
| Who Wouldn't ? | - |

New York, August 11, 1926.

80074-A-B  Calling Me Home                    OK rejected

New York, August 23, 1926.

| | | |
|---|---|---|
| 142558- | Half A Moon ("Honeymoon Lane") | Col 750-D |
| 142559- | Jersey Walk ("Honeymoon Lane") | - |

New York, August 26, 1926.

| | | |
|---|---|---|
| 142574- | I Can't Keep You Out Of My Dreams | Rejected |
| 142575- | Pretty Cinderella | Har 259-H |

New York, September 24, 1926.

142687-  Mary Lou                            Har 259-H

Vocalist and ukulele player with Nat Shilkret and the Victor Orchestra.

New York, September 24, 1926.

| | | |
|---|---|---|
| BVE-36352-2 | Half A Moon ("Honeymoon Lane") | Vic 20231, HMV B-5225 |
| BVE-36352-3 | Half A Moon ("Honeymoon Lane") | Vic LPV-557, LSA-3075 |

Vocal, acc. by own ukulele.

New York, c. September, 1926.

| | |
|---|---|
| Half A Moon ("Honeymoon Lane") | Ed 51841 |
| Jersey Walk ("Honeymoon Lane") | - |

Vocalist and ukulele player with Nat Shilkret and the Victor Orchestra.

New York, October 8, 1926.

BVE-36802-  All Alone Monday                 Vic 20259

Vocal, acc. by own ukulele.

New York, c. October 12, 1926.

| | | |
|---|---|---|
| 80163- | I'm On My Way Home | OK 40704 |
| 80164- | The Little White House ("Honeymoon Lane") | - |

New York, c. October 20, 1926.

| | | |
|---|---|---|
| X-325 | Jersey Walk ("Honeymoon Lane") | Gnt rejected |
| X-326 | Hum A Little Tune | - |

New York, October 21, 1926.

| | | |
|---|---|---|
| 142850- | Baby Face | Har 284-H |
| 142851- | Just A Little Longer | - |

New York, October 26, 1926.

| | | |
|---|---|---|
| BVE-36872-4 | I'd Love To Call You My Sweetheart (w/Lou Raderman-vn) | Vic 20288, HMV B-2402 |
| BVE-36873-3 | Hum Your Troubles Away | -           - |

Vocalist and ukulele player with Roger Wolfe Kahn and his Orchestra.
New York, November 4, 1926.

BVE-36903-1  We'll Have A Kingdom                Vic 20338

Vocal, acc. by own ukulele.          New York, c. November 10, 1926.

X-343    Jersey Walk ("Honeymoon Lane")          Gnt rejected
X-344    I Can't Get Over A Girl Like You Loving    -
         A Boy Like Me
X-345    I've Seen My Baby (And It Won't Be Long Now) -
X-346    I Can't Believe That You're In Love With Me  -


Vocalist and ukulele player with Nat Shilkret and the Victor Orchestra.
New York, November 16, 1926.

BVE-36932-  Sweet Thing                          Vic 20352, HMV B-5269

Vocalist and ukulele player with the Knickerbockers.
New York, November 17, 1926.

142940-   Someone                         Col 832-D
142941-4  Half A Moon ("Honeymoon Lane")        -      4418

Vocal, acc. by own ukulele.          New York, November 18, 1926.

142949-   It Made You Happy When You Made Me Cry  Har 306-H
143120-   I've Grown So Lonesome Thinking Of You    -
   NOTE:- Matrices 142950/143119 inclusive were recorded in Chicago or Atlanta.

New York, November 19, 1926.

143130-   A Little Music In The Moonlight        Col 831-D
143131-   My Lady                                  -

New York, c. November, 1926.

          I'd Love To Call You My Sweetheart    Ed 51881
          I Can't Get Over A Girl Like You Loving    -
            A Boy Like Me

Guitar duet with William Carola.     New York, December 2, 1926.

BVE-36991-3  12th Street Rag                     Vic 20386

New York, December 6, 1926.

BVE-37103-4  Memphis Blues                       Vic 20386
BVE-37104-1-2-3  Aloha Oe                        Rejected

Vocal, acc. by own ukulele.          New York, c. December 13, 1926.

GEX-390   Jersey Walk ("Honeymoon Lane")        Gnt 6011, Ch 15196, Gmn 2019
GEX-391   I Can't Get Over A Girl Like You Loving   -     Ch 15195, Chg 223,
            A Boy Like Me                        Sil 5045
GEX-392   Hello, Swanee, Hello                   Gnt 6023, Ch 15196, Sil 5045,
                                                 Gmn 2019
   NOTE:- The above Gennett issues, and all others on this label listed in this  chap-
   ter, are labelled DUKE AND HIS UKE.  The other subsidiary labels probably use their
   own pseudonyms.

New York, December 17, 1926.

BVE-37146-1-2-3  Oh ! How She Could Play A Ukulele Rejected
BVE-37150-2  'Deed I Do (w/3cl/p/own u)         Vic 20397, HMV B-2422

New York, December 21, 1926.

143207-   Angel Eyes                            Har 326-H
143208-   Since I Found You                         -

New York, December 29, 1926.

BVE-37146-7  Oh ! How She Could Play A Ukulele (w/  Vic 20478, HMV B-2455
             Lou Raderman-vn)

New York, c. December, 1926.

'Deed I Do                              Ed 51928
Strumming                                  —

Acc. by Andy Sannella-as-stg/Ed Smalle-p/own g.
                                      New York, January 17, 1927.

BVE-37541-2  Blue Skies (w/Ed Smalle)          Vic 20457, HMV B-2441

Vocalist with Roger Wolfe Kahn and his Orchestra.
                                      New York, January 25, 1927.

BVE-37569-2  A Little Birdie Told Me So        Vic 20493, HMV B-5292

Vocal, acc. by Andy Sannella-cl-stg/own ukulele, as shown.
                                      New York, February 8, 1927.

80405-    Since I Found You - stg             OK 40769, Par R-3340
80406-    Ain't She Sweet ? - cl/u               —          —

Vocalist with the Columbians.          New York, February 9, 1927.

143453-   Proud (Of A Baby Like You)           Col 891-D

Vocal, acc. by own ukulele.            New York, February 11, 1927.

143467-   If You See Sally                     Rejected
143468-   At Sundown (When Love Is Calling Me Home) Har 368-H

Vocalist and ukulele player with Jacques Renard and his Orchestra.
                                      New York, February 14, 1927.

BVE-37772-1  You Went Away Too Far And Stayed Away  Vic 20487
             Too Long

Vocal, acc. by Andy Sannella-cl-stg/Frank Banta-p/own g or u.
                                      New York, February 17, 1927.

BVE-37792-   I Can't Believe That You're In Love    Vic 20997, HMV B-2643
             With Me - p/g/stg
BVE-37793-1-2-3-4  Strumming My Blues Away - cl/p/u Rejected

Acc. by own ukulele.                   New York, February 25, 1927.

143540-   At Sundown (When Love Is Calling Me Home) Rejected
143541-   If You See Sally                     Har 368-H

Vocalist with Nat Shilkret and the Victor Orchestra.
                                      New York, March 24, 1927.

BVE-38405-1-2-3  You Can't Cry Over My Shoulder      Vic rejected

Vocal, acc. by own ukulele and perhaps others.
                                      New York, March 28, 1927.

80676-    At Sundown (When Love Is Calling Me Home) OK 40802
80677-    Wherever You Go - Whatever You Do        —

Vocalist with Nat Shilkret and the Victor Orchestra.
                                      New York, March 31, 1927.

BVE-38312-1-2-3-4  Judy - Medley Fox Trot (Johnny    Vic rejected
             Marvin sings a chorus of WEAR YOUR SUNDAY SMILE)

Vocalist with the Columbians.              New York, April 1, 1927.

143738-   A Lane In Spain                   Col 961-D, 4558

Vocalist with the Hilo Hawaiian Orchestra/Nat Shilkret.
                                           New York, April 1, 1927.

BVE-38134-7 Honolulu Moon                  Vic 20596, HMV B-2497
   NOTE:- Takes 1, 2, 3 and 4 of this title, made on March 18, have no vocalist.

Vocal duets with Andy Sannella, acc. by own ukulele and steel guitar respectively.
                                           New York, c. April 2, 1927.

GEX-562    You'll Never Be Missed A Hundred Years  Gnt 6085, Ch 15257
           From Now
GEX-563    I'll Just Go Along                    -      Ch 15256

Vocalist and ukulele player with Nat Shilkret and the Victor Orchestra.
                                           New York, April 14, 1927.

BVE-38312-5  Judy - Medley Fox Trot (Johnny Marvin Vic 20601, HMV B-5531
           sings a chorus of WEAR YOUR SUNDAY SMILE, the title shown on the HMV)

Vocal, acc. by own ukulele.               New York, April 18, 1927.

144039-   Just The Same                    Har 409-H
144040-   Red Lips - Kiss My Blues Away !        -

Vocalist and ukulele player with Nat Shilkret and the Victor Orchestra.
                                           New York, April 19, 1927.

BVE-38357-3  There's Everything Nice About You (w/ Vic 20603, HMV B-5319
           Ed Smalle)

Vocal, acc. by Andy Sannella-cl-g-stg/? Frank Banta-p/own u, as shown.
                                           New York, April 22, 1927.

BVE-38486-1-2-3-4  Side By Side - stg       Rejected
BVE-38487-3  There's Everything Nice About You -   Vic 20612, HMV B-2517
           cl-stg/p/u
BVE-38488-2  In A Shady Nook By A Babbling Brook - Vic 20741, HMV B-2541
           g/u

   Acc. by own ukulele.                    New York, c. April, 1927.

           Ain't She Sweet ?                 Ed 51992
           I Can't Believe That You're In Love With Me -

Vocalist and ukulele player with Nat Shilkret and the Victor Orchestra.
                                           New York, May 12, 1927.

BVE-38399-4  Me And My Shadow               Vic 20675

                                           New York, May 19, 1927.

BVE-38814-1  Who-oo ? You-oo, That's Who !   Vic 20727, HMV B-5327

                                           New York, May 20, 1927.

BVE-38767-   I Could Waltz On Forever       Vic 20729

Vocalist with Charlie Fry and his Million-Dollar Pier Orchestra.
                                           Camden, N. J., May 21, 1927.

BVE-38265-1-2-3  My Wife's In Europe Today   Vic rejected

Vocal, acc. by own ukulele.               New York, May 23, 1927.
144200-   Roamin' Into The Sunset (Thinking Of   Rejected
           You, Just You)
144201-   Me And My Shadow                   Col 1020-D

Vocal, acc. by cl/p/g/own u.                    New York, May 25, 1927.

BVE-38780-3  Side By Side (w/Aileen Stanley)      Vic 20714, HMV B-2519
BVE-38781-3  Red Lips, Kiss My Blues Away (w/Aileen       -           -
             Stanley)

Vocalist and ukulele player with Nat Shilkret and the Victor Orchestra.
                                    New York, May 26, 1927.

BVE-38842-   Stop Go                              Vic 20682
BVE-38843-   Something To Tell

Vocal, acc. by Andy Sannella-cl-as-stg/Milt Rette berg-p-cel/Ed Smalle-p-v/Nat   Shil-
    kret-cel/own g-u.                 New York, May 27, 1927.

BVE-38845-1-2-3-4  Vo-Do-Do-De-O Blues - cl-stg/    Rejected
             pMR/celNS/u)
BVE-38846-   Just Another Day Wasted Away (as-stg/  Vic 20758, HMV B-2554
             p-vES/celMR/g)

Vocalist and ukulele player with Nat Shilkret and the Victor Orchestra.
                                    New York, June 2, 1927.

BVE-39205-   Just Like A Butterfly (That's Caught   Vic 20732
             In The Rain)

Vocalist with Charlie Fry and his Million-Dollar Pier Orchestra.
                          **Camden**, N. J., June 4, 1927.

BVE-38265-   My Wife's In Europe Today             Vic 20726

Vocal, acc. by cl/p/g/own u/Leonard Joy, or cl/vn/p/g/own stg/Nat Shilkret, or own stg
    only, as shown.                   New York, June 7, 1927.

BVE-39224-3  Magnolia (Mix The Lot - What Have You  Vic 20731, HMV B-2554
             Got ?) - LJ
BVE-39225-1  Ain't That A Grand And Glorious        Rejected
             Feeling ? - stg
BVE-39225-3  Ain't That A Grand And Glorious        Vic 20731, HMV B-2529
             Feeling ? - NS

Vocalist and ukulele player with Nat Shilkret and the Victor Orchestra.
                                    New York, June 9, 1927.

BVE-38892-3  There's A Trick In Pickin' A Chick-    Vic 20759, HMV B-5352
             Chick-Chicken

Vocal, acc. by vn/p/g.                          New York, June 22, 1927.

BVE-39284-3  Under The Moon (w/Aileen Stanley)      Vic 20787, HMV B-2565
BVE-39285-   I Walked Back From The Buggy Ride      Vic 20822, HMV B-2578
             (w/Aileen Stanley, plus Joe Green-d)

Vocalist and ukulele player with Nat Shilkret and the Victor Orchestra.
                                    New York, July 1, 1927.

BVE-39618-2  What Do We Do On A Dew-Dew-Dewy Day ?  Vic 20819

Vocalist and ukulele player with Jan Garber and his Orchestra.
                                    New York, July 21, 1927.

BVE-38759-9  Sixty Seconds Every Minute            Vic 20848
BVE-39403-7  Sweet Marie                           Vic 20833, HMV B-5367
BVE-39449-2  Bye-Bye, Pretty Baby                         -

Vocal, acc. by cl/p/pac/own u.                  New York, July 27, 1927.

BVE-39909-2  It's A Million To One You're In Love   Vic 20832, HMV B-2591
BVE-39910-2  I'm Afraid You Sing That Song To Some-       -           -
             body Else

Vocalist and ukulele player with Nat Shilkret and the Victor Orchestra, as The Troubadours on Victor 20848, HMV B-5367.    New York, August 11, 1927.

BVE-39957-2  Tired Hands                        Vic 20848, HMV B-5367
BVE-39958-2  Where Have You Been All My Life ?

Vocalist with Roger Wolfe Kahn and his Orchestra.
                                        New York, August 12, 1927.

BVE-39969-1-2-3  Say It With A Red, Red Rose       Vic rejected

Vocalist with Nat Shilkret and the Victor Orchestra.
                                        New York, August 18, 1927.

BVE-39989-2  Baby's Blue                         Vic 20882, HMV B-5384
BVE-39990-3  Are You Thinking Of Me Tonight ? (w/  Vic 20899
               Elliott Shaw-Franklyn Baur)

                                  ·     New York, August 22, 1927.

BVE-39101-2  Pull Yourself Together             Vic 20902

Vocal, acc. by c/cl/p/own u.          New York, August 24, 1927.

BVE-39109-1  Marvelous                          Vic 20893, HMV B-2636
BVE-39110-3  It All Belongs To Me                 -        HMV B-2643

Vocalist with Jacques Renard and his Cocoanut Grove Orchestra.
                                        New York, September 26, 1927.

BVE-40118-1-2-3  Underneath The Wabash Moon        Rejected
BVE-40120-1  When The Morning Glories Wake Up In   Vic 20981
               The Morning (Then I'll Kiss Your Two Lips Goodnight)

Vocal, acc. by O/Nat Shilkret.        New York, September 28, 1927.

BVE-40131-   After I've Called You Sweetheart    Vic 20984
BVE-40132-   Give Me A Night In June               -        HMV B-2636

Vocal, acc. by O/Jack Shilkret.       New York, November 1, 1927.

BVE-40679-   Old Fashioned Locket               Vic 21299
BVE-40680-   Kiss And Make Up (w/Ed Smalle)     Vic 21042, HMV B-2704

Vocalist with Nat Shilkret and the Victor Orchestra.
                                        New York, November 3, 1927.

BVE-40539-2  There's A Cradle In Caroline (w/Ed   Vic 21040
               Smalle)

Vocalist with Edwin J. McEnelly's Orchestra.
                                        New York, December 5, 1927.

BVE-41098-3  What Are You Waiting For ?           Vic 21154, HMV B-5445

Vocal, acc. by c/cl/p/own u.          New York, December 6, 1927.

BVE-41099-1  Is She My Girl Friend ? (How-De-Ow-  Vic 21153, HMV B-2736
               Dow)
BVE-41200-1-2  From Midnight Till Dawn           Vic 21230

Vocalist with Victor Arden-Phil Ohman and their Orchestra.
                                        New York, December 8, 1927.

BVE-41151-   Funny Face                          Vic 21114, HMV B-5527
BVE-41152-   'S Wonderful                          -            -

Vocal, acc. by O/Leonard Joy.         New York, December 9, 1927.

BVE-41155-2  Keep Sweeping The Cobwebs Off The Moon Vic 21153

Vocal, acc. by Andy Sannella-as/Ed Smalle-p/own u.
                                      New York, December 27, 1927.

BVE-41509-3  Rain (w/Ed Smalle)                      Vic 21172, HMV B-2705
BVE-41510-3  After My Laughter Came Tears (w/Ed Smalle)-          -

   Acc. by c/cl/vn/p/own u.           New York, January 27, 1928.

BVE-41586-1-2-3  Mary Ann (w/Ed Smalle)              Vic rejected
BVE-41587-1-2-3  There Must Be A Silver Lining (w/Ed Smalle) -

Vocal and guitarist with Nat Shilkret and the Victor Orchestra.
                                      New York, February 23, 1928.

BVE-43107-2  Without You, Sweetheart                 Vic 21259

Vocal, acc. by cl/vn/p.               New York, February 28, 1928.

BVE-41586-4  Mary Ann (w/Ed Smalle)                  Vic 21299
BVE-41587-4-5-6  There Must Be A Silver Lining (w/ Rejected
                Ed Smalle)

   Acc. by Andy Sannella-cl-g/vn/p/own u.  New York, March 6, 1928.

BVE-43319-1-2-3  Sunshine                            Rejected
BVE-43320-1  Old Fashioned Locket                    Vic 21299

   Acc. by O/Nat Shilkret.            New York, April 18, 1928.

BVE-43578-1  Angel                                   Vic 21376, HMV B-2789
BVE-43579-3  My Pet                                  Vic 21435, HMV B-2812

                                      New York, April 19, 1928.

BVE-43654-2  I Still Love You                        Vic 21435, HMV B-2812
BVE-43655-3  Sweetheart O' Mine                      Vic 21376

                                      New York, May 2, 1928.

BVE-43695-4  Think Of Me Thinking Of You             Vic 21427, HMV B-2786
BVE-43696-3  Oh ! You Have No Idea                   Vic 21509
BVE-43697-2  Golden Gate                             Vic 21427, HMV B-2786

Vocalist with Nat Shilkret and the Victor Orchestra.
                                      New York, May 3, 1928.

BVE-43698-3  I'd Rather Cry Over You                 Vic 21463, HMV B-5523
BVE-43699-3  Get Out And Get Under The Moon          Vic 21432, HMV B-5504

Vocal, acc. by O/Leonard Joy.         New York, August 8, 1928.

BVE-46672-2  Old Man Sunshine, Little Boy Bluebird Vic 21609, HMV B-2872
BVE-46673-3  If You Don't Love Me                      -            -

Vocalist with Johnny Hamp and his Kentucky Serenaders.
                                      New York, August 14, 1928.

BVE-46364-2  What D'Ya Say ?                         Vic 21632

Vocalist with Roger Wolfe Kahn and his Orchestra.
                                      New York, August 21, 1928.

BVE-46922-1-2-3  Anything You Say !                  Vic rejected

Vocal, acc. by O/? Roger Wolfe Kahn.      New York, August 21, 1928.
BVE-46923-   Water Melon Smilin' On The Vine         Vic 21653
BVE-46924-1-2  Don't Send My Boy To Prison           Rejected
BVE-46925-1  Crazy Rhythm                            Vic 21650 .
BVE-46926-3  Heartbroken And Lonely                    -

Vocal, acc. by c/as/vn/p.                    New York, October 19, 1928.

BVE-47768-1-2  Ev'rybody Loves You                Rejected
BVE-47769-2  Happy Days And Lonely Nights         Vic 21780, HMV B-2926

  Acc. by O/Leonard Joy.                     New York, November 7, 1928.

BVE-48130-3  There's A Rainbow 'Round My Shoulder  Vic 21780, HMV B-2926
BVE-48131-1-2-3  You Lied - I Cried               Rejected

                                             New York, December 12, 1928.

BVE-49253-3  The Sun Is At My Window (w/Ed Smalle)  Vic 21866, HMV B-3024
BVE-49254-3  Why Did You Leave Me ? (w/Ed Smalle)   Vic 21990, HMV B-3091

Vocalist with Nat Shilkret and the Victor Orchestra.
                                             New York, December 13, 1928.

BVE-49257-  I'd Rather Be Blue                     Vic 21814, HMV B-5609

Vocal, acc. by O/Leonard Joy.                New York, December 15, 1928.

BVE-46392-2  Sweethearts On Parade                 Vic 21820, HMV B-2983
BVE-46393-2  Where The Shy Little Violets Grow      -          -

                                             New York, December 31, 1928.

BVE-49029-1-2-3  All By Yourself In The Moonlight  Rejected
BVE-49030-3  You Wanted Someone To Play With        Vic 21839, HMV B-2993

Vocalist with Nat Shilkret and the Victor Orchestra.
                                             New York, January 3, 1929.

BVE-49617-1-2  That's Why I'm Happy                Vic rejected

Vocal, acc. by studio orchestra.             New York, January 11, 1929.

BVE-49057-1-2-3  Won't You Tell Me, Hon (When      Rejected
        We're Gonna Be One ?) (w/Aileen Stanley)
BVE-49058-2  Ev'rybody Loves You (w/Aileen Stanley) Vic 21848, HMV B-2991

Vocal, acc. by O/Nat Shilkret.               New York, January 18, 1929.

BVE-48589-2  Sweetheart Of All My Dreams           Vic 21851, HMV B-3004
BVE-49029-6  All By Yourself In The Moonlight       -

Vocalist with Nat Shilkret and the Victor Orchestra.
                                             New York, January 22, 1929.

BVE-49671-2  You Wouldn't Fool Me, Would You ?      Vic 21859

Vocal, acc. by O/Thomas Griselle.            New York, February 20, 1929.

BVE-49976-1-2-3  A Precious Little Thing Called     Vic rejected
        Love (w/Ed Smalle)
BVE-49977-1-2-3  Caressing You (w/Ed Smalle)        -

  Acc. by c/as/vn/Ed Smalle-p.               New York, February 27, 1929.

BVE-49976-6  A Precious Little Thing Called Love    Vic 21892
        (w/Ed Smalle)
BVE-49977-5  Caressing You (w/Ed Smalle)            -          HMV B-3024

Vocalist with Bennie Krueger and his Orchestra.
                                             New York, February 28, 1929.

BVE-49999-  That's The Good Old Sunny South         Vic 21903, HMV B-5643
BVE-50900-  Down Among The Sugar Cane               -

Vocal, acc. by O/Leonard Joy.                    New York, April 5, 1929.

BVE-51608-1  I'm In Seventh Heaven                    Vic 21955, HMV B-3119
BVE-51609-3  Used To You                              —            —

New York, April 11, 1929.

BVE-51615-3  Down Among The Sugar Cane               Vic 21959, HMV B-3077
BVE-51616-2  I Get The Blues When It Rains (with     —
             Ed Smalle)

  Acc. by O/Nat Shilkret.                        New York, April 18, 1929.

BVE-51641-2  Some Sweet Day                          Vic 21990, HMV B-3091
BVE-51642-1-2-3  Underneath The Russian Moon         Rejected

New York, May 22, 1929.

BVE-53428-1-2-3  Singin' In The Rain                 Rejected
BVE-53429-2  Your Mother And Mine                    Vic 22022, HMV B-3129
BVE-53430-3  Finding The Long Way Home               —        HMV B-3130

Vocalist with Nat Shilkret and the Victor Orchestra.
                                                New York, May 27, 1929.

BVE-53442-1-2-3  Kiddies' Kabaret                    Vic rejected

Vocal, acc. by O/Leonard Joy.                    New York, June 14, 1929.

BVE-53575-2  (If I Were You) I'd Fall In Love        Vic 22039
             With Me
BVE-53576-2  Baby, Oh ! Where Can You Be ?           —

Vocalist with Nat Shilkret and the Victor Orchestra.
                                                New York, June 28, 1929.

BVE-53475-1  I'm The Medicine Man For The Blues      Vic rejected

Vocal duets with Frank Marvin, acc. by own stgs.
                                                New York, July 8, 1929.

BVE-53909-1-2  Sweetheart, You're In My Dreams       Vic rejected
BVE-53910-1-2  She's Old And Bent (But She Just      —
               Keeps Hoofin' Along)

Vocal, acc. by O/Leonard Joy.                    New York, July 12, 1929.

BVE-53916-1-2-3  Singin' In The Rain (w/The Frohne Rejected
                 Sisters)
BVE-53917-3  Orange Blossom Time                     Vic 22057, HMV B-3129

Vocalist with Nat Shilkret and the Victor Orchestra.
                                                New York, July 15, 1929.

BVE-53475-2  I'm The Medicine Man For The Blues      Vic 22055, HMV B-5750
BVE-55608-1  Wouldn't It Be Wonderful ?              —            —

Vocal, acc. by O/Leonard Joy.                    New York, July 19, 1929.

BVE-53916-5  Singin' In The Rain (w/The Frohne       Vic 22057, HMV B-3130
             Sisters)

New York, August 2, 1929.

BVE-55184-   Ev'ry Day Away From You                 Vic 22076

New York, August 3, 1929.

BVE-55644-   Little By Little                        Vic 22070, HMV B-3185

New York, September 5, 1929.

BVE-56119-    Tip-Toe Thru' The Tulips With Me    Vic 22113, HMV B-3204
BVE-56120-    I'm Painting The Clouds With Sunshine     -          -

New York, September 17, 1929.

BVE-56133-1-2-3  True Blue Lou                   Rejected
BVE-56134-    Same Old Moon (Same Old June, But Not  Vic 22125
                 The Same Old You)

New York, September 23, 1929.

BVE-56133-    True Blue Lou                       Vic 22125, HMV B-3220

    Acc. by O/Nat Shilkret.          New York, September 30, 1929.

BVE-56729-1-2  If I Had A Talking Picture Of You    Vic rejected
BVE-56730-1-2-3  I'm A Dreamer - Aren't We All ?       -
BVE-56731-1-2-3  Have A Little Faith In Me           -

New York, October 8, 1929.

BVE-56729-5  If I Had A Talking Picture Of You    Vic 22148, HMV B-3373
BVE-56730-7  I'm A Dreamer - Aren't We All ?         -

    Acc. by O/Leonard Joy.            New York, October 16, 1929.

BVE-56186-3  Melancholy                          Vic 22180, HMV B-3452
BVE-56187-4  Satisfied                              -

Vocalist with Nat Shilkret and the Victor Orchestra.
                                     New York, October 17, 1929.

BVE-56787-1  Georgia Pines                       Vic 22195

Vocal, acc. by O/Leonard Joy.        New York, October 23, 1929.

BVE-57112-1  Lucky Me - Lovable You              Vic 22186, HMV B-3331
BVE-57113-3  Happy Days Are Here Again              -

New York, January 6, 1930.

BVE-56731-6  Have A Little Faith In Me           Vic 22273
BVE-57977-3  With You                               -        HMV B-3417

Vocalist with the High Hatters/Leonard Joy.
                                     New York, January 17, 1930.

BVE-58504-3  Red Hot And Blue Rhythm             Vic 22314

Vocal, acc. by O/Leonard Joy.        New York, January 27, 1930.

BVE-58525-3  Cryin' For The Carolines            Vic 22302, HMV B-3417
BVE-58526-1  Blue Eyes (Get Red-Red-Ready For Love)

    Acc. by O/Nat Shilkret.          New York, February 24, 1930.

BVE-58600-1-2  Lazy Lou'siana Moon               Vic rejected

    Acc. by O/Leonard Joy.           New York, March 11, 1930.

BVE-58600-4  Lazy Lou'siana Moon                 Vic 22348, HMV B-3452
BVE-59624-3  The One I Love Just Can't Be Bothered    -
                 With Me

Vocal, acc. by O/Nat Shilkret.              New York, April 29, 1930.

BVE-59768-1  Ro-Ro-Rollin' Along                      Vic 22418, HMV B-3497
BVE-59769-2  Down The River Of Golden Dreams          -
BVE-59770-1  Dancing With Tears In My Eyes            Vic 22440, HMV B-3572

Vocalist with Don Azpiazu and his Havana Casino Orchestra.
                                            New York, May 15, 1930.

BVE-62156-2  Be Careful With Those Eyes              Vic 22441, HMV B-5934

Vocal, acc. by O/Leonard Joy.               New York, May 28, 1930.

BVE-62251-1  I'm In The Market For You               Vic 22440

                                            New York, July 28, 1930.

BVE-62374-1  Go Home And Tell Your Mother            Vic 22502
BVE-62375-2  Little White Lies                       -

                                            New York, September 17, 1930.

BVE-63659-1  I Still Get A Thrill (Thinking Of You)Vic 22534
BVE-63660-3  Bye Bye Blues                           -

  Acc. by Jack Erby-cl/own u (as HONEY DUKE AND HIS UKE).
                                            New York, October 6, 1930.

BVE-63695-1  Underneath Those Weeping Willow Trees Vic 23531
BVE-63696-1  I'm Looking For A Gal                   -

  Acc. by O/Leonard Joy.                    New York, October 16, 1930.

BVE-63157-2  You Darlin'                             Vic 22555
BVE-63158-1  I'm Yours                               -

Vocalist with the High Hatters/Leonard Joy.
                                            New York, October 28, 1930.

BVE-63177-3  Overnight                               Vic 22566
BVE-63178-2  Cheerful Little Earful                  -

Vocal, acc. by O/Leonard Joy.               New York, December 12, 1930.

BVE-64829-1-2-3  To Whom It May Concern (w/Aileen  Vic rejected
                 Stanley)

                                            New York, December 19, 1930.

BVE-64830-1-2  (I Am The Words) You Are The Melody Vic rejected
               (w/Aileen Stanley)
BVE-64831-1-2  Yours And Mine                         -

                                            New York, December 20, 1930.

BVE-64829-4-5  To Whom It May Concern (w/Aileen    Vic rejected
               Stanley)

                                            New York, January 2, 1931.

BVE-64631-1  To Whom It May Concern                  Vic 22604
BVE-64632-2  Yours And Mine                          -

                                            New York, February 25, 1931.

BVE-67470-1  Little Sweetheart Of The Prairie       Vic 22649, HMV B-3903
BVE-67471-2  Little Sweetheart Of The Mountains       -        HMV B-3904

New York, March 31, 1931.

BVE-53003-1  Would You Take Me Back Again ?        Vic 22666, HMV B-3904
BVE-53004-1  Rocky Mountain Rose                    -

  Acc. by O/Nat Shilkret, with own u.     New York, June 11, 1931.

BVE-69926-1  Dr. Cheer - Part 1 (Intro. Runnin'    Vic 22741
                Wild/Lonesome Road)
BVE-69927-1  Dr. Cheer - Part 2 (Intro. Slow And        -
                Easy/When Your Hair Has Turned To Silver/I Walked Back From The    Buggy
                Ride)

  Acc. by studio orchestra.               New York, October 8, 1931.

  10833-   Guilty                               ARC ?
  10834-   Now That You're Gone                  -

  Acc. by own guitar.                     New York, March 2, 1932.

  152112-  Seven Come Eleven                     Col 15750-D
  152114-  Yodelin' My Way To Heaven             -
  152115-  Medley - Part 1 (Intro. Bend Down,    Col 2655-D
              Sister/Take Your Girlie To The Movies/Take It Slow And Easy/Old Grey Mare)
              (w/Norman Brokenshire)
  152116-  Medley - Part 2 (Intro. They're Wearing 'Em    -
              Higher In Hawaii/So's Your Old Lady/Etiquette/Seven Come Eleven) (w/Norman
              Brokenshire)
     NOTE:- Matrix 152113 is not by Johnny Marvin.

                                         New York, May 31, 1932.

BS-72825-1  When You Hear Me Call                 Vic 23691
BS-72826-1  Jack And Jill                         Vic 23728
BS-72827-1  The Man With The Big Black Mustache   Vic 23708
BS-72828-1  Go Along Bum And Keep On Bumming Along Vic 23728
BS-72829-1  Seven Come Eleven                     Vic 23708
BS-72830-1  I'm Gonna Yodel My Way To Heaven      Vic 23691

                                         New York, July 28, 1932.

  12130-   I'm The Man That's Been Forgotten-Part 1  Mt M-12460
  12131-   I'm The Man That's Been Forgotten-Part 2      -

  Acc. by studio orchestra.               New York, January 25, 1933

  12981-   Rock-a-Bye Moon                       Mt M-12610, Pan 25471
  12982-   I'm Playing With Fire                   -          -

  Acc. by own guitar.                     New York, November 12, 1934.

  38997-A  I Want My Boots On When I Die         Dec 5056, Pan 25682
  39005-A  Lazy Texas Longhorns (w/Frankie Marvin)    -          -
     NOTE:- Matrices 38998/39004 inclusive are not by Johnny Marvin.

                                         New York, February 18, 1935.

  39368-A  The Last Mile                         Pan 25973
  39369-A  Beneath A Bed Of Daisies              -
  39370-   Grandma's Rockin' Chair               Rejected ?
  39371-   By Big Swiss Cheese                   -

  Acc. by small instrumental group.       Los Angeles, September 11, 1940.

DLA-2151-  We Like It                            Dec 5891
DLA-2152-  Me And My Shadow                      -
DLA-2153-  No-One To Kiss Me Goodnight           Dec 5904
DLA-2154   As Long As I Live                     -

Originally the five Marks brothers (as spelt) consisted of Leonard (Chico, the crazy Italian-type pianist) (1891-1961); Arthur (Harpo, the mute harpist) (1893-1964)who published his autobiography HARPO SPEAKS ! in 1961; Gummo, who left the act  early on; Zeppo, who provided the romantic characterization in the first five films, and Julius (Groucho, b. 1895, and sole survivor). They were well-known in  vaudeville long before their first film (THE COCONUTS, 1929), but it was this and classics of lunatic comedy such as ANIMAL CRACKERS (1930), MONKEY BUSINESS (1931), HORSE FEAT-HERS (1932), DUCK SOUP (1933) and A NIGHT AT THE OPERA (1935) that established the brothers as unsurpassed exponents of lively, clean offbeat humour.  Their only re-cording is an LP (MCA MUP-395) which gives excerpts from the soundtracks of  their greatest films, narrated by Gary Owens.

## SHIRLEY MASON

B. 1900; r.n. Leona Flugrath.  Prominent star of silents from 1915 onwards (debut in VANITY FAIR); others include GOODBYE BILL and SEVEN DEADLY SINS (1917-1918); MERE-LY MARY ANN and TREASURE ISLAND (1920); LIGHTS OF THE DESERT (1922); WHAT    FOOLS MEN (1925); DON JUAN'S THREE NIGHTS (1926); SALLY IN OUR ALLEY (1927);   SHOW   OF STARS (1929), and others.

Speech, unacc. (?)                          New York, c. August 13, 1923.

8464    Christmas In Hollywood                     Gnt 5237

## RAYMOND MASSEY

B. Toronto, Ontario, Canada, August 30, 1896; stage debut at the Everyman Theatre in IN THE ZONE (July, 1922) after war service in France and Siberia; many successes in London (AT MRS. BEAM'S, Royalty, April 2, 1923; SAINT JOAN , New, March 26,   1924; THE TRANSIT OF VENUS, Ambassadors, April, 1927; THE SECOND MAN, Playhouse,April 24, 1928; LATE NIGHT FINAL, Phoenix, June 25, 1931; THE RATS OF NORWAY, Playhouse, Ap-ril 6, 1933, which he also produced; THE SHINING HOUR, St. James's, September    4, 1934; IDIOT'S DELIGHT, Apollo, March 22, 1938; and many more) and New York  (debut in HAMLET, Broadhurst, November 5, 1931; THE SHINING HOUR, Booth, Feb. 13,    1934; ETHAN FROME, National, January 21, 1936; ABE LINCOLN IN ILLINOIS, Plymouth,October 15, 1938; THE DOCTOR'S DILEMMA, Shubert, March 11, 1941; LOVERS AND FRIENDS,  Ply-mouth, November 29, 1943; PYGMALION, Ethel Barrymore, December 26, 1945); produced dozens of plays; began film career in 1931 in THE SPECKLED BAND; other outstanding films include THE SCARLET PIMPERNEL (1934); THINGS TO COME (1936); THE PRISONER OF ZENDA (1937); ABE LINCOLN IN ILLINOIS (1939); ARSENIC AND OLD LACE (1944); A  MAT-TER OF LIFE AND DEATH (1946); DAVID AND BATHSHEBA (1951); EAST OF EDEN (1955);OMAR KHAYYAM (1957); THE NAKED AND THE DEAD (1958); HOW THE WEST WAS WON (1962); played part of Dr. Gillespie in very popular TV series DR. KILDARE (1961-1965).

Dramatic speech with supporting cast in excerpts from ABE LINCOLN IN ILLINOIS.
                                        New York, July 14, 1939.

| CS-038265-1 | The Proposal To Ann Rutledge | Vic 36230 |
| CS-038266-1 | Lincoln's Law Office | - |
| CS-038267-1 | Lincoln's Prayer | Vic 36231 |
| CS-038268-1 | Lincoln's Reply To Stephen A. Douglas - Part 1 | - |
| CS-038269-1 | Lincoln's Reply To Stephen A. Douglas - Part 2 | Vic 36232 |
| CS-038270-1 | Lincoln's Farewell To Springfield | - |

## JESSIE MATTHEWS

B. London, March 11, 1907; stage debut in BLUEBELL IN FAIRYLAND (Alhambra, December, 1917); appeared in THE MUSIC BOX REVUE (Palace, May 15, 1923); in chorus of  CHAR-LOT'S REVUE (Prince of Wales's, September 23, 1924); went to U.S.A. in this as un-derstudy for Gertrude Lawrence, and made first hit in this capacity; appeared   in THE CHARLOT SHOW OF 1926 (Prince of Wales's, October 5, 1926); engaged by C.B.Coch-ran to take part in ONE DAM THING AFTER ANOTHER (Pavilion, May 20, 1927);    great success, so re-engaged to star in THIS YEAR OF GRACE (March 22, 1928) and WAKE  UP AND DREAM (March 27, 1929), both at London Pavilion; to New York to play in   WAKE UP AND DREAM (Selwyn, December 30, 1929); returned to London to star in EVER GREEN (Adelphi, December 3, 1930); HOLD MY HAND (Gaiety, December 23, 1931); began a six year film career with OUT OF THE BLUE (1931); then THERE GOES THE BRIDE;   THE GOOD COMPANIONS; THE MAN FROM TORONTO; THE MIDSHIPMAID (1932); FRIDAY THE    THIRTEENTH

and WALTZES FROM VIENNA (1933); EVER GREEN (1934); FIRST A GIRL (1935); IT'S   LOVE
AGAIN (1936); HEAD OVER HEELS and GANGWAY (1937); SAILING ALONG  (1938) ;  CLIMBING
HIGH (1939); returned to theatre in I CAN TAKE IT, touring in this during 1939, and
appearing in COME OUT TO PLAY (Phoenix, March 19, 1940); to U.S.A. in December,1941
to play in THE LADY COMES ACROSS (Shubert, New Heaven); returned to London to  star
in WILD ROSE (new version of SALLY, in which she played the title role, at Prince's
August 6, 1942); three further films (FOREVER AND A DAY and CANDLES AT NINE,  1943;
TOM THUMB, 1958); for long played the title role in British radio soap-opera,  MRS.
DALE'S DIARY.

Vocal, acc. by the Prince of Wales's Theatre Orchestra.
                                            London, November 16, 1926.

WA-4457-1-2  The Good Little Girl And The Bad     Rejected
             Little Girl ("The Charlot Show of 1926")
WA-4458-1    Silly Little Hill (w/Henry Lytton, Jr.) Col 4189, Par PMC-7150
             ("The Charlot Show of 1926")
WA-4460-1    Friendly Ghosts ("The Charlot Show of   Col 4192
             1926")
WA-4461-1    Journey's End (w/the Company) ("The       -
             Charlot Show of 1926")

                                            London, November 24, 1926.

WA-4457-3  The Good Little Girl And The Bad     Col 4189
           Little Girl ("The Charlot Show of 1926")

  Acc. by Leslie A. Hutchinson ("Hutch")-p.
                                            London, c. October, 1927.

           My Heart Stood Still ("One Dam Thing     Br 135
             After Another")
           Just A Memory                             -

  Acc. by studio orchestra/Carroll Gibbons.
                                            London, January 27, 1932.

CA-12383-1  Hold My Hand (w/Sonnie Hale and      Col DB-760
            Gaiety Theatre chorus)
CA-12384-1  Turn On The Music (w/Sonnie Hale and     -
            Gaiety Theatre chorus)

                                            London, March 22, 1932.

CA-12542-1  By The Fireside                      Col DB-803, MFP 1127
CA-12543-1  One More Kiss                             -       -

                                            London, February 1, 1933.

CA-13384-1  I'll Stay With You (Film "There Goes  Col DB-1048, MFP 1127
            The Bride")
CA-13385-1  One Little Kiss (Film "The Midshipmaid")  -        -

                                            London, April 2, 1933.

CA-13551-1  Three Wishes (Film "The Good         Col DB-1102, MFP 1127
            Companions")
CA-13552-1  Let Me Give My Happiness To You (Film    -        -
            "The Good Companions")

                                            London, May 4, 1934.

CA-14472-1  Just By Your Example (Film "Evergreen")Col DB-1403, MFP 1127
CA-14473-1  Dancing On The Ceiling (Film "Evergreen")  -       -    WRC SH-183
CA-14474-1  When You've Got A Little Springtime   Col DB-1404      -
            In Your Heart (Film "Evergreen")
CA-14475-1  Tinkle, Tinkle, Tinkle/Over My Shoulder   -          -
            (Film "Evergreen")

Acc. by studio orchestra.                    London, August 22, 1935.

GB-7357-1-2  Say The Word And It's Yours (Film       Dec rejected
             "First A Girl")
GB-7358-1-2  Everything's In Rhythm With My Heart        -
             (Film "First A Girl")


                                             London, September 18, 1935.

GB-7357-3    Say The Word And It's Yours (Film       Dec F-5728
             "First A Girl")
GB-7358-3    Everything's In Rhythm With My Heart     Dec F-5729, ACL 1140
             (Film "First A Girl")
GB-7398-1    I Can Wiggle My Ears (Film "First A      Dec F-5728
             Girl")
GB-7399-1    The Little Silk Worm (Film "First A      Dec F-5729
             Girl")


Acc. by O/Louis Levy.                         London, April 17, 1936.

TB-2122-2    It's Love Again (Film "It's Love Again")  Dec F-5982
TB-2123-1    Tony's In Town (w/The Three Ginx) (Film      -        ACL 1140
             "It's Love Again")
TB-2124-2    I Nearly Let Love Go Slipping Through     Dec F-5983
             My Fingers (Film "It's Love Again")
TB-2125-1    Got To Dance My Way To Heaven (w/tap-        -
             dancing) (Film "It's Love Again")


Acc. by studio orchestra.                    London, January 13, 1937.

TB-2748-     There's That Look In Your Eyes Again     Dec F-6287
             (Film "Head Over Heels")
TB-2749-1    Head Over Heels In Love (Film "Head      Dec F-6286, ACL 1140
             Over Heels")
TB-2750-2    Looking Around Corners For You (Film        -
             "Head Over Heels")
TB-2751-     May I Have The Next Romance With You ?   Dec F-6287, ACL 1140
             (Film "Head Over Heels")


Acc. by O/Jay Wilbur.                         London, August 7, 1937.

DTA-3189-3   Jessie Matthews Memories - Part 1        Dec K-871
             (Intro. One Little Kiss/Let Me Give My Happiness To You/When You've Got
             A Little Springtime In Your Heart/Over My Shoulder)
DTA-3190-1   Jessie Matthews Memories - Part 2
             (Intro. I Nearly Let Love Go Slipping Through My Fingers/Got To   Dance
             My Way To Heaven/Everything's In Rhythm With My Heart/I Can  Wiggle  My
             Ears)
DTB-3191-1   Lord And Lady Whozis (Film "Gangway")    Dec F-6471
DTB-3192-1   Gangway (Film "Gangway")                    -        ACL 1140
DTB-3193-1   Moon Or No Moon (Film "Gangway")         Dec F-6470
DTB-3194-1   When You Gotta Sing, You Gotta Sing         -        ACL 1140
             (Film "Gangway")


Acc. by O/Peter Yorke.                        London, December 23, 1937.

DTB-3467-1   Trusting My Luck (Film "Sailing Along")  Dec F-6672
DTB-3468-2   My River (Film "Sailing Along")             -
DTB-3469-1   Your Heart Skips A Beat (Film "Sailing   Dec F-6673
             Along")
DTB-3470-1   Souvenir Of Love (Film "Sailing Along")     -


Acc. by O/Debroy Somers.                      London, September 15, 1942.

CA-19057-1   Look For The Silver Lining ("Wild Rose")Col DB-2094, MFP 1127,WRC SH-174
CA-19058-1   Whip-Poor-Will ("Wild Rose")                -           -           -


Jessie Matthews made other records, mostly LPs and for children, after 1942.

B. London, April 24, 1862; studied for the stage as young man, but ill health forced
   him to leave England for Canada, eventually the U.S.A.; stage debut in Denver,Col.,
   as a member of Daniel Bandmann's Company (as servant in EAST LYNNE, April, 1884);
   New York debut in THE COLONEL (Stetson's Fifth Avenue Theatre, October 27, 1884);
   returned to England, 1885; London debut in THE GREAT DIVORCE CASE (Criterion, February 18, 1886); during the next sixty years he appeared in and/or produced dozens
   of plays in London and New York; most memorable in London are WOODCOCK'S    LITTLE
   GAME, Gaiety, October 8, 1887; HANDFAST, Prince of Wales's, December 13, 1887; was
   engaged for the Vaudeville, beginning with JOSEPH'S SWEETHEART, March 8, 1888;  he
   appeared there for three years, then joined Charles Wyndham at the Criterion (LON-
   DON ASSURANCE, November 27, 1890) and other shows there for three years, including
   a production of SCHOOL FOR SCANDAL in 1891; THE SECOND MRS. TANQUERAY (St.James's,
   May 27, 1893); joined Comyns Carr at the Comedy for three years; in partnership at
   the Haymarket with Frederick Harrison, October, 1896-July, 1905; during this  time
   his principal successes were UNDER THE RED ROBE (October 17, 1896); A MARRIAGE  OF
   CONVENIENCE (June 5, 1897); THE LITTLE MINISTER (November 6, 1897); THE SECOND  IN
   COMMAND (November 27, 1900); FROCKS AND FRILLS (January 2, 1902); THE    UNFORESEEN
   (December 2, 1902); BEAUTY AND THE BARGE (staged at the New Theatre while the Haymarket was undergoing alterations, August 30, 1904); after leaving the Haymarket he
   acquired the Avenue Theatre, which was wrecked by the roof of adjoining     Charing
   Cross Station collapsing on December 5, 1905; rebuilt and re-named the  Playhouse,
   it opened on January 28, 1907; played many roles there before sailing for U. S. A.
   and Canada; appeared in THE SECOND IN COMMAND (Wallack's, N.Y., November 3, 1913);
   very successful in GRUMPY (same theatre, November 19, 1913); toured U.S.A.,  ended
   lease of Playhouse, London, September, 1915; made a film of PEER GYNT about   then;
   also other silents (GRUMPY; THESE CHARMING PEOPLE; COUNSEL'S OPINION and ORDERS IS
   ORDERS, etc.); toured in Australia, 1917-1918; returned to London for a great  hit
   (LORD RICHARD IN THE PANTRY, Criterion, November 11, 1919, which ran for 576  performances); returned to New York early in 1923 and remained there for three years;
   reappeared in London in 1927, and again in 1932 and 1933; made many appearances in
   aid of charity, culminating in one his 80th birthday in 1942 at the Haymarket, for
   the RAF Benevolent Fund and the Actors' Orphanage; m. Winifred Emery, who died  in
   1924, then Mrs. P. H. Trew.

Dramatic speech, unacc.                    London, February 3, 1899.

  1161      Scene from "The Little Minister" (w/      Ber 1065
          Winifred Emery)

                             London, February 16, 1909.

  2825f     Quarrel Scene (w/Winifred Emery) ("The    Rejected
          School For Scandal")
  2828f     Speech on behalf of the Actors'           HMV 01023, D-372
          Benevolent Fund

                             London, January 11, 1913.

  6976f     Theatre Shouts                            HMV Private Recording
  6977f     Theatre Shouts                            -

                             New York, October 24, 1915.

37440-    Dinky                                     Col A-5746, 593
37441-    A Telephone Reconciliation (Conversation   -        -
          overheard in London during the Great War)

## JOE  MAXWELL

Vocal, acc. by studio orchestra.          New York, issued as shown in brackets.

      I'd Like To Be The Fellow             Ed 4M-427 (February, 1910)
      The Garden Of Roses (w/chorus)        Ed 4M-434 (March, 1910)
      You Taught Me How To Love You         Ed 4M-456 (April, 1910)
      Come To The Land Of Bohemia           Ed 10358 (May, 1910)
      Dreamy Town                           Ed 10373 (June, 1910)
(continued on page 461)

New York, issued as shown in brackets.

| | |
|---|---|
| Dear Mayme, I Love You | Ed 4M-491 (June, 1910) |
| I'll Make A Ring Around Rosie | Ed 10381 (July, 1910) |
| Mary, You're A Big Girl Now | Ed 10403 (August, 1910) |
| Nobody Seems To Love Me Now | Ed 10443 (November, 1910) |
| My Heart Has Learned To Love You | Ed 4M-554 (December, 1910) |
| Planning | Ed 4M-571 (January, 1911) |
| You're Just A Little Bit O' Sugar | Ed D-18 (?) |

## EDNA MAY

B. Syracuse, N.Y., September 2, 1878; r.n. Edna Pettie; stage debut there as a child in 1883; professional stage debut(after studying music and taking part in local Gilbert and Sullivan productions) in SI STEBBINGS (Syracuse, February 21, 1895); debut in New York in SANTA MARIA (Hammerstein's, September 14, 1896); engaged by George W. Lederer to play in THE BELLE OF NEW YORK (Casino, September 28, 1897); made London debut in this at Shaftesbury, April 12, 1898; this great success was followed by AN AMERICAN BEAUTY (same theatre, April 25, 1900; returned briefly to New York, appearing in THE GIRL FROM UP THERE (Herald Square, January 7, 1901); played in the same show in London (Duke of York's, April 23, 1901); joined George Edwardes at the Apollo, appearing in KITTY GREY (September 7, 1901) and THREE LITTLE MAIDS (March 10, 1902); then appeared in THE SCHOOL GIRL (Prince of Wales's, May 9, 1903); then revival of LA POUPEE there (April 9, 1904); returned to New York to play THE SCHOOL GIRL (Daly's, September 1, 1904) and THE CATCH OF THE SEASON (also Daly's,August28, 1905); reappeared in London in THE BELLE OF MAYFAIR (Vaudeville, April 11, 1906);in September she suddenly resigned from this company, but appeared in title role of NELLY NEIL (Aldwych, January 10, 1907); after this ended, she married and left the profession, but appeared for one week at the Savoy, London, in February, 1911 in a series of performances including THE BELLE OF NEW YORK in aid of charity.

Vocal, acc. by Landon Ronald-p.          London, May 8, 1900.

| | | |
|---|---|---|
| J-588 | They All Follow Me ("The Belle Of New York") | Ber 3192 |
| J-589 | Dear Little Baby ("An American Beauty") | Ber 3191 |
| J-590 | The Purity Brigade ("The Belle Of New York") | Ber 3193 |

## STELLA MAYHEW

B. Waynesburg, Ohio, c. 1874; d. New York, May 2, 1934. Very popular vaudeville artist at the beginning of the century, starring with Al Jolson in THE WHIRL OF SOCIETY (Winter Garden, March 5, 1912).

Vocal, acc. by studio orchestra.          New York, c. December, 1909.

I'm Looking For Something To Eat          Ed 10298

New York, March 8, 1910.

I'm A Woman Of Importance          Ed 4M-374

New York, April 7, 1910.

You'll Come Back          Ed 10396
Savannah          Ed 4M-467

New York, April 19, 1910.

The Grizzly Bear          Ed 4M-479

New York, July 15, 1910.

That Beautiful Rag (w/Billie Taylor)          Ed 10438

New York, April 24, 1911.

De Devilin' Tune          Ed 4M-744

New York, January 8, 1912.

A Songologue ("The Whirl Of Society")        Ed 4M-987
My Lou (w/Billie Taylor) ("The Whirl Of      Ed 4M-995
  Society")

New York, April 25, 1912.

Lead Me To That Beautiful Band               Ed 4M-1082, Amb 2173
Oh ! You Circus Day                          Ed 4M-1122

New York, date unknown.

There Are Fifty-Seven Ways To Catch A Man Ed D-23

## MABEL McKINLEY

Vocal, acc. by studio orchestra.        New York, February 3 and 8, 1909.

Golden Rod                                   Ed 4M-122
Anona                                        Ed 4M-150
My Rancho Maid                               Ed 4M-157

New York, August 31, 1909.

Ma Li'l Sweet Sunbeam                        Ed 10289

NOTE:- There is evidence in the Edison files that this artist made further cylinders
in New York on December 23, 1909 and July 18, 1910, but it is not known what titles
were made.

## TOM McNAUGHTON

B. England, July 1, 1867; better known in U.S.A., where his appearance in THE SPRING
  MAID (Liberty, December 26, 1910) was outstanding, making his only recording a best-
  seller for many years. D. London, November 28, 1923.

Humorous monologue, acc. by O/ —— Magee.
                                        New York, October 23, 1911.

B-11130-1 The Three Trees ("The Spring Maid")      Vic 5866, 17222

## RAQUEL  MELLER

B. Madrid, Spain, 1888; r.n. Francisca Marquez Lopez. One of the few native  Spanish
  artists to achieve fame outside their own country; appeared very successfully in New
  York in 1926 in vaudeville. D. Barcelona, July 26, 1962. The following listing  of
  records is not necessarily complete; she seems to have recorded only in Barcelona.

Vocal in Spanish, with orchestra.        Barcelona, 1927-1933.

SO-1156     Vaya una palabra                     Od A-138176
SO-1183     La Bella Sol                         -
            Lagarteranas                         Par R-554
            Rafaelito                            -
            El Relicario                         Par R-1334
            La Violetera                         -
            Flor del Mal                         Par R-2294
            Clavelito del Genil                  -

## JAMES MELTON

B. 1904; began singing career with the Revelers (alias the Merrymakers or the Singing
  Sophomores, all q.v.) after leaving his position as saxophonist-vocalist with Fran-
  cis Craig's Orchestra in Atlanta in 1926; eventually reached the Metropolitan Opera
  Company in New York as tenor, and as romantic singing-actor in films such as  STARS
  OVER BROADWAY (1935); SING ME A LOVE SONG; COME UP SMILING (1936); MELODY FOR   TWO

(1937); ZIEGFELD FOLLIES (1945). D. 1961.

Vocal, acc. by small studio orchestra.   New York, November 10, 1927.

| 144966- | I'm In Heaven When I See You Smile, Diane | Col 1206-D |
| 144967- | An Old Guitar And An Old Refrain (A Song Of Spain) | - |

New York, December 14, 1927.

| 145407- | Among My Souvenirs | Col 1238-D |
| 145408- | Dear, On A Night Like This | - |

New York, January 16, 1928.

| 145532- | My Heart Stood Still | Col 1294-D |

New York, March 1, 1928.

| 145706- | When Love Comes Stealing | Col rejected |

New York, March 9, 1928.

| 145745- | I Can't Do Without You | Col 1329-D |
| 145746- | La Rosita | Col 1400-D |
| 145747- | My Heart Is In The Roses | Col 1329-D |

New York, April 11, 1928.

| 145994- | Fleur-de-Lis | Re G-9247 |

New York, June 6, 1928.

| 146410- | The Call Of Love | Col rejected |
| 146411- | Dear Little Mother Of Mine | - |

Acc. by Nat Shilkret and the Victor Salon Group and Orchestra.
New York, June 15, 1928.

CVE-45636-2  Foster Melodies - Part 3 (James      Vic 9247, HMV C-1758
   Melton sings I DREAM OF JEANIE WITH THE LIGHT BROWN HAIR)

Acc. by small studio orchestra.   New York, June 20, 1928.

| 146563- | Angela Mia (My Angel) | Col 1493-D |

New York, June 27, 1928.

| 145706- | When Love Comes Stealing | Col 1400-D, Re G-9302 |
| 146588- | Neapolitan Nights | Col 1493-D, Re G-9247 |

New York, October 17, 1928.

| 147132- | I Loved You Then As I Love You Now | Col 1614-D, Re G-9302 |
| 147133- | Sally Of My Dreams | -     Re G-9328 |

New York, November 23, 1928.

| 147486- | Ceasing To Care | Col 1640-D |
| 147487- | Where Is The Song Of Songs For Me ? | -     Re G-9402 |

New York, December 10, 1928.

| 147404- | Marcheta (A Love Song Of Old Mexico) | Col 1760-D |
| 147405- | Roses Of Picardy | - |

New York, December 18, 1928.

| 147716- | Macushla | Col 1932-D |
| 147717- | Because | - |

New York, December 28, 1928.

| | | |
|---|---|---|
| 147736- | Sleepy Valley | Col 1797-D, Re G-9449 |
| 147737- | Dawn | - |

New York, January 16, 1929.

| | | |
|---|---|---|
| 147795- | The Song I Love | Col 1711-D, Re G-9328 |
| 147796- | My Tonia | - |

New York, April 3, 1929.

| | | |
|---|---|---|
| 148168- | Little Pal | Col 1879-D |
| 148169- | Why Can't You ? | - |

New York, May 27, 1929.

| | | |
|---|---|---|
| 148634- | With A Song In My Heart | Col 1853-D, Re MR-41 |
| 148635- | Pagan Love Song | -          Re G-9402 |

New York, July 19, 1929.

| | | |
|---|---|---|
| 148829- | At Close Of Day | Col 1917-D |
| 148830- | Love Is A Dreamer | Col 1986-D, Re G-9442 |
| 148831- | Ich liebe dich (I Love You) | Col 1917-D |

New York, September 24, 1929.

| | | |
|---|---|---|
| 149040- | I'm Only Making Believe | Col 2015-D, Re G-9465 |
| 149041- | Dance Away The Night | Col 1986-D    - |
| 149042- | I'll Still Go On Wanting You | Col 2015-D, Re MR-12 |

New York, November 11, 1929.

| | | |
|---|---|---|
| 149406- | Chant Of The Jungle | Col 2050-D |
| 149407- | A Bundle Of Old Love Letters | Col 2065-D, Re MR-100 |

New York, November 19, 1929.

| | | |
|---|---|---|
| 149445-3 | Love (Your Spell Is Everywhere) | Col 2050-D, Re MR-12 |
| 149446-6 | The Shepherd's Serenade (Do You Hear Me | Col 2084-D |
| | Calling You ?) | |

New York, December 6, 1929.

| | | |
|---|---|---|
| 149695-3 | There Will Never Be Another Mary | Col 2065-D, Re MR-59 |
| 149696-3 | The Sacred Flame | Col 2084-D, Re MR-41 |

Vocalist with Nat Shilkret and the Victor Orchestra.

New York, January 20, 1930.

| | | |
|---|---|---|
| BVE-58506-1 | Blue Is The Night | Vic 22290 |

Vocal, acc. by O/Rosario Bourdon.     New York, January 24, 1930.

| | | |
|---|---|---|
| BVE-58622-1-2-3 | There's Danger In Your Eyes, | Rejected |
| | Cherie | |
| BVE-58623-4 | A Year From Today | Vic 22335 |

New York, February 7, 1930.

| | | |
|---|---|---|
| BVE-58622-4 | There's Danger In Your Eyes, Cherie | Vic 22335, HMV B-3469 |
| BVE-58651-2 | The Hills Of Home | Vic 22336 (not issued) |
| BVE-58652-3 | The Old Refrain | -          - |

New York, February 25, 1930.

| | | |
|---|---|---|
| BVE-58651-5 | The Hills Of Home | Vic 22336 |
| BVE-58652-6 | The Old Refrain | - |

Acc. by O/Nat Shilkret.                    New York, May 26, 1930.

BVE-62310-1  Blue Is The Night                   Vic 22439
BVE-62311-1  I Remember You From Somewhere          -

Acc. by O/? Ben Selvin.                    New York, May 15, 1931.

151553-   Now You're In My Arms                  Col 2465-D
151554-   Beautiful Love                            -

Acc. by O/Victor Young.                    New York, July 20, 1932.

BX-12094-A  You Are Love                         Br 20115, 0112
BX-12095-   Make-Believe                         Rejected

                                           New York, August 9, 1932.

BX-12160-A  Make-Believe                         Br 20115, 0112

                                           New York, November 7, 1932.

B-12540-A  Deep In Your Eyes                     Br 6428, 01418
B-12541-A  I May Never Pass Your Way Again          -        -

Acc. by Charles O'Connell-pipe organ.   Camden, N. J., June 28, 1933.

BS-76299-1  A Broken Rosary                       Vic 24356
BS-76300-1  In The Little White Church On The Hill   -

Acc. by unknown p, or g, as shown.   New York, March 19, 1934.

B-14969-   She Rested By The Broken Brook - p      Br rejected
B-14970-   Come, Love With Me - p                     -
B-14971-   Carry Me Back To The Lone Prairie - g      -
B-14972-   Short'nin' Bread  - g                      -

                                           New York, April 3, 1934.

B-14972-   Short'nin' Bread - g                     Br rejected

                                           New York, April 5, 1934.

B-14969-   She Rested By The Broken Brook - p      Br rejected
B-14970-   Come, Love With Me - p                     -

Acc. by unknown p.                         New York, July 23, 1934.

B-15441-   Your Eyes Have Told Me So              Br rejected
B-15442-   A Little Love, A Little Kiss (Un peu       -
             d'amour)

                                           New York, November 2, 1934.

B-15442-   A Little Love, A Little Kiss (Un peu   Br rejected
             d'amour)
B-16239-   My Little Nest Of Heavenly Blue            -

Acc. by O/Rosario Bourdon.        New York, November 27, 1934.

B-16371-   Adeste Fideles (O Come, All Ye Faithful)Br 7341
B-16372-   Silent Night, Holy Night                   -
B-16373-   The Palms                             Br 7396
B-16374-   Agnus Dei (Lamb Of God)                    -

Acc. by O/Frank Black.                     New York, March 4, 1935.

B-16961-   I Hear You Calling Me                  Col rejected
B-16962-   Mah Lindy Lou                              -
B-16963-   A Dream                                    -
B-16964-   Then You'll Remember Me                    -

New York, March 20, 1935.

| | | |
|---|---|---|
| B-16964- | Then You'll Remember Me | Br rejected |
| B-17157- | Serenade | - |
| B-17158- | Mavis | - |

New York, June 6, 1935.

| | | |
|---|---|---|
| B-17158- | Mavis | Br rejected |
| B-17668- | Ah ! Sweet Mystery Of Life | - |
| B-17669- | I'm Falling In Love With Someone | - |
| B-17670- | The Song Of Songs | - |

Acc. by O/Nat Shilkret.         New York, October 31, 1935.

BS-95684-1  Where Am I ? (Am I In Heaven ?)         Vic 25185, HMV B-8444
                (Film "Stars Over Broadway")
BS-95685-1  Carry Me Back To The Lone Prairie         -              -


The following two sides are entered in the Victor recording files "Dubs from    records
   supplied by Ed Kirkeby." Nothing is known of the location or   recording date.

CS-98357-1  M'appari tutt' amor ("Martha" - von Flotow)
CS-98358-1  Celeste Aida, forma divina ("Aida" - Verdi)

Acc. by studio orchestra.         New York, December 16, 1936.

61485-A  A Little House That Love Built (Film         Dec 1093, F-6366
              "Come Up Smiling")
61486-A  Summer Night (Film "Come Up Smiling")         -              -
61487-A  Your Eyes Have Told Me So         Dec         , F-6822

New York, January 27, 1937.

61554-  Love, Here Is My Heart         Dec rejected

Acc. by O/Bobby Dolan.         New York, April 20, 1937.

62137-A  September In The Rain (Film "Melody         Dec 1247, F-6404
              For Two")
62138-A  Melody For Two (Film "Melody For Two")         -              -

Acc. by Philip Evans-p.         New York, June 11, 1940.

BS-051267-1  The Green Hills Of Ireland         Vic 4533
BS-051268-1  The Little Irish Girl (Kitty Me Love, Rejected
                Will You Marry Me ?)
BS-051269-1  Sunrise And You         Vic 4533
BS-051270-1  Tommy Lad         Rejected

Acc. by Jacques Zayde-vn/Karl Kritz-p. New York, June 26, 1940.

CS-051371-1  Elegie (Song Of Mourning) (Massenet)  Vic 13431
CS-051372-1  Angel's Serenade (Braga)         -
CS-051373-1  Pleasing Pain (Haydn)         Rejected
CS-051374-1-2  The Sailor's Song (Haydn)         -

Acc. by John Gart-elo, with Jacques Zayde-vn where shown.
                                New York, January 28, 1941.

CS-060386-1  The Holy City         Vic 13592
CS-060387-1  Ave Maria (Kahn) - vnJZ         Vic 13593
CS-060388-1  Ave Maria (Mascagni) - vnJZ         -
CS-060389-2  The Palms (Faure)         Vic 13592

Acc. by O/Wilfred Pelletier.            Lotus Club, New York, May 28, 1941.

| | | |
|---|---|---|
| CS-065367-1 | I'll Take You Home Again, Kathleen | Vic 18219 |
| CS-065368-1 | Harlequin's Serenade ("I Pagliacci" - Vic 18365 |
| | Leoncavallo) | |
| CS-065369-2 | Siciliana ("Cavalleria Rusticana" - | — |
| | Mascagni) | |
| CS-065370-2 | O Dry Those Tears | Vic 18219 |
| CS-065371-1 | Rose Of The World | Vic 18466 |
| CS-065372-1 | Then You'll Remember Me ("The | Rejected |
| | Bohemian Girl" - Balfe) | |

Lotus Club, New York, September 3, 1941.

| | | |
|---|---|---|
| CS-065372-2-3-4 | Then You'll Remember Me ("The | Rejected |
| | Bohemian Girl" - Balfe) | |
| CS-066747-1 | You Haunt My Heart | Vic 18466 |

## ADOLPHE MENJOU

B. 1890; some stage experience before beginning impressive film career in Hollywood in 1919; appeared in THE SHEIK (1921); THE THREE MUSKETEERS (1922); A WOMAN IN PARIS and THE MARRIAGE CIRCLE (1923); various other silents, some made in France; made an enormous number of talkies, gaining reputation of being the best-dressed film actor. These include MORNING GLORY and TWO WHITE ARMS (1932); THE MIGHTY BARNUM (1934); THE MILKY WAY and GOLD DIGGERS OF 1935 (1935); SING, BABY, SING (1936); ONE HUNDRED MEN AND A GIRL (1937); THE GOLDWYN FOLLIES (1938); A BILL OF DIVORCEMENT (1940); FATHER TAKES A WIFE (1941); ROXIE HART; SYNCOPATION and YOU WERE NEVER LOVELIER (1942); MAN ALIVE (1945); ACROSS THE WIDE MISSOURI (1951); POLLYANNA (1960), many others. Although many of his films were musicals, he had no singing parts; the one record made by him may explain why. D. 1963.

Vocal, acc. by O/? Carroll Gibbons.        London, March 6, 1932.

CA-12509-1  Two White Arms (Film "Two White Arms") Col DB-798

## JOHNNY MERCER

B. 1909; composer of many popular songs (lyrics and scores); wrote LAZY BONES in 1933 to Hoagy Carmichael's music; since then hits such as BLUES IN THE NIGHT (1941); THAT OLD BLACK MAGIC (1942); AC-CEN-CHUATE THE POSITIVE (1945); composed scores to films such as THE HARVEY GIRLS (1946); SEVEN BRIDES FOR SEVEN BROTHERS (1954); LI'L ABNER (1959).

Vocalist with Frankie Trumbauer and his Orchestra.
New York, April 5, 1932.

255004-1  Sizzling One-Step Medley (Johnny Mercer
sings DINAH (with The Nitecaps) and MY HONEY'S LOVIN' ARMS)

Vocalist with the Dorsey Brothers' Orchestra.
New York, October 17, 1933.

B-14158-A  Dr. Heckle And Mr. Jibe            Br 01834

Vocalist with Paul Whiteman and his Orchestra.
New York, February 16, 1934.

BS-81715-1  Fare-Thee-Well To Harlem (w/Jack      Vic 24571, BB B-10969
Teagarden)

New York, April 17, 1934.

BS-82320-1-2  Christmas Night In Harlem (w/Jack   Vic 24615, BB B-10969, HMV B-6549
Teagarden)

Vocal, acc. by O/Victor Young.      New York, August 24, 1934.

| | | |
|---|---|---|
| 38417-A | Lord, I Give You My Children | Dec 142 |
| 38418-A-B | If I Could Only Read Your Mind | Rejected |
| 38419-A | The Bathtub Ran Over Again | Dec 142 |

. Vocal, acc. by studio orchestra.          Los Angeles, June 14, 1935.

LA-1043-   I Never Saw A Better Night              Br rejected
LA-1044-   Comes The Revolution, Baby                -
LA-1045-   Old Man Rhythm                            -
LA-1046-   I Never Had A College Education           -

Vocalist with Wingy Manone and his Orchestra.
                                            New York, October 8, 1935.

 18136-1-2  I've Got A Note (w/Wingy Manone-Jack   Voc 3071
              Teagarden)

Vocal, acc. by O/Victor Young.              Los Angeles, November 27, 1935.

DLA-282-A  Eeny Meeny Miney Mo (w/Ginger Rogers)    Dec 638, F-5838

   Acc. by studio orchestra, with Six Hits and a Miss.
                                            Los Angeles, October 14, 1937.

LA-1458-A  The Murder Of J. B. Markham            Br 8011, Har 1010, Voc 578
LA-1459-B  Last Night On The Back Porch             -       Har 1009      -
LA-1460-   Bob White (What You Gonna Swing Tonight) Br 7988      -
LA-1461-   Jamboree Jones                           --      Har 1010

   Acc. by Victor Young's Small Fryers.     Los Angeles, July 1, 1938.

DLA-1297-A  Small Fry (w/Bing Crosby)             Dec 1960, 3600, 11016, 24293,
                                                  91412, DL-4006, DL-4252, DL-6012,
                                                  DL-8075, DL-9064, Voc VL-3769,
                                                  Br 02653, BING-3, LA-8732,
                                                  LAT-8054, LAT-8368, LAT-8382
DLA-1298-A  Mr. Gallagher And Mr. Shean ("as      Dec 1960, 24293, AH 90
              sung by Mr. Crosby and Mr. Mercer")
DLA-1298-E  Mr. Gallagher And Mr. Shean ("as         -       -    91616, DL-8143,
              sung by Mr. Crosby and Mr. Mercer")  Br 02653, LAT-8306, AH 1

Vocalist with Benny Goodman and his Orchestra.
                                            New York, February 1, 1939.

BS-031874-1  Cuckoo In The Clock                   Vic 26175, Cam CAL-624, CAL-872,
                                                   CDN-148
BS-031876-1  Sent For You Yesterday And Here You   Vic 26170, LPT-6703        -
               Come Today

                                            New York, April 7, 1939.

BS-035713-1-2  Show Your Linen, Miss Richardson    Vic 26211

Vocal, acc. by O/Victor Young.              Los Angeles, April 15, 1940.

DLA-1985-A  Mister Meadowlark (w/Bing Crosby)      Dec 3182, 25148, 91619, DL-8144,
                                                   Br 03171, AH 17
DLA-1986-A  On Behalf Of The Visiting Fireman      Dec 3182, 25148, 91615, DL-8143,
              (w/Bing Crosby)                      Br 03350, AH 24

Vocalist with Paul Whiteman and his Orchestra.
                                            Los Angeles, June 12, 1942.

CAP-31-A  The Old Music Master (w/Jack Teagarden)   Cap 137, CL-13845

                              ETHEL MERMAN

B. Astoria, Long Island City, N.Y., January 16, 1909; trained as typist and secretary
   to a company President; stage debut (in cabaret), 1928; appeared in vaudeville with
   Clayton, Jackson and Durante (Palace, July, 1929); made several short films  before
   making regular stage debut in GIRL CRAZY (Alvin, October 14, 1930); all  subsequent
   appearances were great successes (GEORGE WHITE'S SCANDALS, Apollo, Sept. 14, 1931);
   TAKE A CHANCE (Apollo, November 26, 1932); ANYTHING GOES (Alvin, November 21,1934);
   RED HOT AND BLUE (Alvin, October 29, 1936); STARS IN YOUR EYES (Majestic, Feb.  9,

1939); DU BARRY WAS A LADY (December 6, 1939) and PANAMA HATTIE (October 30, 1940),
both at 46th Street Theatre; SOMETHING FOR THE BOYS (Alvin, January 7,1943); ANNIE,
GET YOUR GUN (Imperial, May 16, 1946); CALL ME MADAM
Appeared in several films : WE'RE NOT DRESSING (1934); THE BIG BROADCAST Of   1936;
ANYTHING GOES (1936); ALEXANDER'S RAGTIME BAND (1938); CALL ME MADAM (1953);THERE'S
NO BUSINESS LIKE SHOW BUSINESS (1954); IT'S A MAD, MAD, MAD, MAD WORLD (1963);   THE
ART OF LOVE (1965).  R.n. Ethel Agnes Zimmerman.

Vocal, acc. by Frank Leithner-p.          New York, October 1, 1931.

BRC-475   Life Is Just A Bowl Of Cherries/My Song  Vic test
             ("George White's Scandals")
BRC-476   Ladies And Gentlemen, That's Love              -
             ("George White's Scandals")

   Acc. by O/Nat Shilkret.                  New York, September 29, 1932.

BS-73708-1  How-Deep-Is-The-Ocean ? (How-High-Is-  Vic 24146, Cam CAL-745
               The-Sky ?)
BS-73709-1  I'll Follow You                          -      HMV B-4348
BS-73710-1  Satan's Li'l Lamb                    Vic 24145
BS-73711-1  I Gotta Right To Sing The Blues          -      HMV B-4348

   Acc. by O/? Victor Young.                New York, December 16, 1932.

B-12735-B  Eadie Was A Lady - Part 1 ("Take A     Br 6456, Col CL-2751
              Chance")
B-12736-B  Eadie Was A Lady - Part 2 ("Take A Chance") -          -

   Acc. by O/Johnny Green.                  New York, October 8, 1934.

B-16117-A  An Earful Of Music (Film "Kid Millions") Br 6995, 01945, Col CL-2751
B-16118-A  You're A Builder-Upper                     -             -

                                           New York, December 4, 1934.

B-16397-A  I Get A Kick Out Of You ("Anything Goes")Br 7342, 02028, Col CL-2751,
                                                     Epic SN-6059
B-16398-A  You're The Top ("Anything Goes")        As above except Epic SN-6059

   Acc. by O/Al Goodman.                    New York, July 17, 1935.

B-17824-1  The Lady In Red                        Br 7491, Col CL-2751
B-17825-1  It's The Animal In Me (Film "The Big      -             -
              Broadcast of 1936")

   Acc. by Fairchild-Carroll and their Orchestra.
                                           New York, November 6, 1936.

P-20201-   Down In The Depths On The 90th Floor    LMS L-206
              ("Red Hot And Blue")
P-20202-   It's De-Lovely ("Red Hot And Blue")        -
P-20203-   Ridin' High ("Red Hot And Blue")        LMS L-207
P-20204-   Red Hot And Blue ("Red Hot And Blue")      -

   Acc. by O/Al Goodman.                    New York, February 22, 1939.

P-24163-1  A Lady Needs A Change ("Stars In Your   LMS L-256, JJC M-3004
              Eyes")
P-24165-1  I'll Pay The Check ("Stars In Your Eyes")   -            -
           This Is It ("Stars In Your Eyes")       LMS L-          -
           Just A Little Bit More ("Stars In Your Eyes")-           -
   Acc. by O/Harry Sosnik.                  New York, December 2, 1940.

68425-    My Mother Would Love You ("Panama Hattie")Dec 23200, Br 03270
68426-    I've Still Got My Health ("Panama Hattie")  -
68427-    Let's Be Buddies (w/Joan Carroll)        Dec 23199, Br 03270
             ("Panama Hattie")
68428-    Make It Another Old-Fashioned, Please       -
             ("Panama Hattie")

American singing quartette consisting of three men and a girl, whose personnel   did
not remain constant for any length of time, but whose popularity was very   great,
on both sides of the Atlantic, particularly during the latter part of World War II
and after (they appeared in London at the Palladium in 1948).

Vocal, acc. by unknown p.                    Chicago, January 27, 1933.

BS-75487-1  In The Little White Church On The Hill Vic 23806
BS-75488-1  We're Together Again                 Vic 24313, HMV B-4473
BS-75489-1  Hiawatha's Lullaby                   Vic 23806
BS-75490-1  Love Songs Of The Nile               Vic 24313, HMV B-4473

Vocalists with Jack Hylton's Orchestra.   Chicago, January 2, 1936.

BS-96540-1  A Little Bit Independent                 Vic rejected

Vocal, acc. by studio orchestra.             New York, August 4, 1938.

64412-    There's Honey On The Moon Tonight      Dec 1969
64413-A   Pop Goes The Weasel                    Dec 1968, F-6879
64414-    On The Bumpy Road To Love              Dec 1969
64415-A   Stop Beatin' 'Round The Mulberry Bush  Dec 1968, F-6879

                                        New York, December29, 1938.

64837-    Chopsticks                             Rejected
64838-A   I Got Rings On My Fingers (And Bells On Dec 2238, F-6973
            My Toes)
64839-A   Ferdinand The Bull                        -        -
64840-    Put On Your Old Grey Bonnet            Rejected

                                        New York, February 24, 1939.

65059-A   Cuckoo In The Clock                    Dec 2334, F-7035
65060-B   Patty-Cake, Patty-Cake (Baker Man)        -        -
65061-A   Chopsticks                             Dec 2333, F-7050
65062-A   Ta-Hu-Wa Hu-Wai (Hawaiian War Chant)      -        -

                                        New York, March 31, 1939.

65322-A   A-Ruble A-Rhumba                       Dec 2404, F-7098
65323-A   Hello 'Frisco                          Dec 2471, F-7179
65324-A   Chinatown, My Chinatown                   -        -
65325-B   La Paloma                              Dec 2404, F-7098

                                        New York, May 9, 1939.

65560-A   Rumpel-Stilts-Kin (Oh, Could He Sew,   Dec 2495, F-7227
            Could He Sew)
65561-A   Igloo                                  Dec 2506, F-7208
65562-A   Too Tired                              Dec 2495, F-7227
65563-A   I'm Forever Blowing Bubbles            Dec 2506, F-7208

                                        New York, September 5, 1939.

66270-A   Vol Vistu Gaily Star                   Dec 2759, F-7434
66271-A   Clap Yo' Hands                         Dec 2877    -    Br 02989
66272-A   I Got Rhythm                              -             -
66273-A   My Cat Fell In The Well                Dec 2759

                                        New York, November 9, 1939.

66496-A   Shoot The Sherbet To Me, Herbert !     Dec 2842, F-7392
66497-A   In The Mood                               -        -

                                        New York, February 20, 1940.

67216-    Breezin' Along With The Breeze         Dec 3025, F-7589
67217-    Ma ! (He's Making Eyes At Me)             -        -

New York, March 8, 1940.

| | | |
|---|---|---|
| 67276-A | Johnson Rag | Dec 3088, F-7643 |
| 67277-B | Ho ! Sa Bonnie | -          - |

Acc. by O/Victor Young.                  Los Angeles, July 23, 1940.

| | | |
|---|---|---|
| DLA-2064- | Dry Bones | Dec 3390 |
| DLA-2065- | Red Wing | - |
| DLA-2066-A | Do You Ever Think Of Me ? (w/Bing Crosby) | Dec 3423, 25424, Br 04104 |
| DLA-2067-A | You Made Me Love You (w/Bing Crosby) | -          -          - |

Los Angeles, July 27, 1940.

| | | |
|---|---|---|
| DLA-2076-A | I Get The Blues When It Rains | Dec 3347, Br 03871 |
| DLA-2077-A | The Way You Look Tonight | -          - |

Acc. by studio orchestra.               New York, October 30, 1940.

| | | |
|---|---|---|
| 68305-A | Isn't That Just Like Love ? | Dec 3483, F-7887 |
| 68306-A | Do You Know Why ? | -          - |

Acc. by O/Victor Young.                  Los Angeles, January 23, 1941.

| | | |
|---|---|---|
| DLA-2379- | It Just Isn't True | Dec rejected |
| DLA-2380- | You'll Never Get Rich | - |

Los Angeles, May 14, 1941.

| | | |
|---|---|---|
| DLA-2393-A | The Hut-Sut Song (A Swedish Serenade) | Dec 3810, F-7960 |
| DLA-2394-A | Mary Lou | -          - |

Los Angeles, July 5, 1941.

| | | |
|---|---|---|
| DLA-2497- | Kiss The Boys Goodbye | Dec 3930, F-8017 |
| DLA-2498- | Sunday | Dec 18527 |
| DLA-2499- | Honk, Honk (The Rumble Seat Song) | Dec 3930, F-8017 |

Los Angeles, September 12, 1941.

| | | |
|---|---|---|
| DLA-2759- | Annabella | Dec 4074 |
| DLA-2760- | By-U-By-O (The Lou'siana Lullaby) | Dec 4023, F-8064 |
| DLA-2761-A | Rose O'Day (The Filla-Ga-Dusha Song) | -          - |
| DLA-2762- | The Little Guppy | Dec 4074 |

Los Angeles, December 23, 1941.

| | | |
|---|---|---|
| DLA-2817- | Deep In The Heart Of Texas | Dec 4136, F-8131 |
| DLA-2818- | Down On Ami Ami Oni Oni Isle | Rejected |
| DLA-2819- | Kimaneero Down To Cairo (A Frog Went A-Courting) | Dec 4136, F-8131 |
| DLA-2820- | Tee-Oli-Ee-Go | Rejected |

Los Angeles, February 14, 1942.

| | | |
|---|---|---|
| DLA-2904-A | Hey Mabel | Dec 4265, F-8211 |
| DLA-2905- | Olivia | Dec 4313 |
| DLA-2906- | Breathless | Dec 4265, F-8206 |

Los Angeles, February 21, 1942.

| | | |
|---|---|---|
| DLA-2911-A | Idaho | Dec 4313, F-8249 |
| DLA-2912- | Cheatin' On The Sandman | Dec 18361 |
| DLA-2913- | Jingle Jangle Jingle | -          F-8206 |

Los Angeles, June 19, 1942.

| | | |
|---|---|---|
| DLA-3050-A | Pass The Biscuits, Mirandy | Dec 18478, F-8278 |
| DLA-3051- | Put On Your Old Grey Bonnet | Dec 18436 |
| DLA-3052- | Rolleo-Rolling Along (The Bicycle Song) | -          F-8211 |

Los Angeles, July 29, 1942.

| | | |
|---|---|---|
| L-3152- | Praise The Lord And Pass The Ammunition | Dec 18498, F-8249 |
| L-3153- | I Wanna Go Back To West Virginia | Dec 18527 |
| L-3154- | Tweedle O'Twill | Dec 18498 |
| L-3155-A | Under A Strawberry Moon | Dec 18478, F-8278 |

## THE  MERRYMAKERS

The name used by Brunswick for the very popular cabaret act usually presented under the identity of The Revelers (q.v.; see also The Singing Sophomores).

Vocal, acc. by Ed Smalle-p.                    New York, November, 1925.

| | |
|---|---|
| I Never Knew How Wonderful You Were | Br 3004 |
| Keep On Croonin' A Tune | - |

New York, December, 1925.

| | |
|---|---|
| Clap Hands, Here Comes Charlie ! | Br 3049 |
| That Certain Party | - |

New York, January, 1926.

| | |
|---|---|
| My Castle In Spain | Br 3059 |
| Sweet Child (I'm Wild About You) | - |

New York, April, 1926.

| | | |
|---|---|---|
| E-19248 | How D' Y' Do, Miss Springtime ? | Br 3154 |
| | Mah Lindy Lou | - |

New York, May, 1926.

| | | |
|---|---|---|
| EX-19836 | The Merrymakers In Spain | Br 20049 |
| EX-19852 | The Merrymakers In Hawaii | - |
| | The Merrymakers' Carnival - Part 1 | Br 20044 |
| | The Merrymakers' Carnival - Part 2 | - |

NOTE:- Brunswick 20044 features other Brunswick artists of the time.

New York, July, 1926.

| | |
|---|---|
| Barcelona | Br 3289 |
| Baby Face | - |

New York, September, 1926.

| | | |
|---|---|---|
| E-20116 | Sunny Disposish | Br 3312 |
| E-20122 | Down On The Banks Of The Old Yazoo | - |

New York, December, 1926.

| | | |
|---|---|---|
| E-21311/2 | Mine | Br 3441 |
| E-21522 | Blue Skies | - |

## MILLER AND LYLES

Negro vaudeville act responsible for the book of the first all-negro revue  SHUFFLE ALONG (63rd Street Theatre, New York, May 23, 1921; ran for 504 performances).

Humorous dialogue.                          New York, c. August 29, 1921.

| | | |
|---|---|---|
| 70123- | You Can't Come In | OK 4428 |

New York, May 12, 1924.

| | | |
|---|---|---|
| 72516- | The Raid | OK 40118 |

New York, c. May 14, 1924.

72523-  Traveling                          OK 40118

New York, early July, 1924.

72648-  The Fight                          OK 40186

New York, early August, 1924.

72732-  Sam And Steve                      OK 40186

New York, October 18, 1927.

7575-1  Evolution                          Re 8435
7576-1  The Lost Aviators                  -

New York, October 31, 1927.

7575-   Evolution                          ARC rejected ?
7576-   The Lost Aviators                  -

New York, November 3, 1927.

7599-   Gwine To Africa                    Rejected
7600-   Moneyless Debts                    Ban 2173

New York, November 18, 1927.

7599-   Gwine To Africa                    Ban 2173

## MARILYN MILLER

B. 1898; r.n. Marilyn Reynolds.  Star of colossal stage hit SALLY (New   Amsterdam,
December 21, 1920; ran for 570 performances) and AS THOUSANDS CHEER (Music   Box,
September 30, 1933, 400 performances); also made films (SALLY, 1930; SUNNY, 1931;
HER MAJESTY LOVE, 1932).  D. April 7, 1936.

Vocal, acc. by own p.                    New York, June 12, 1928.

        Rosalie                           Vic test (un-numbered)
        How Long Has This Been Going On ?     -

## THE MILLS BROTHERS

The best-known of the negro singing groups of the 1930s; originally four  brothers,
born a year apart in Piqua, Ohio (John, Herbert, Harry and Donald); they   started
in small-time vaudeville as a singing quartet using kazoos for effect, until   one
night they forgot them and had to improvise the instrumental sound by using their
voices and cupped hands.  This was a sensation; they were auditioned successfully
for a radio station in Cincinnati, worked on this for ten months, toured  in Ohio
and neighbouring states until they came to the attention of Tommy Rockwell, whose
enthusiasm for their act secured them work on CBS.  Records, appearances throughout the country, films (THE BIG BROADCAST (1932); OPERATOR 13 (1933); and  TWENTY
MILLION SWEETHEARTS (1934), amongst others) led to world fame (appeared in London
in 1934, at the Palladium and at a Royal Command performance; in 1935, 1937    and
1939).  John Mills died in January, 1936, but his father, also John, took  on the
part his son had played, and continued to sing and "play" with his three  remaining sons up to the time of his own death after the war.  The only musical instrument used on the records included here is one guitar; the original labels take  a
good deal of space in drawing attention to this, and the sub-title of the act was
"Four Boys and a Guitar."

Vocal, acc. by John Mills-g.             New York, c. October 12, 1931.

E-37288-  Nobody's Sweetheart             Br 6197, 01229
E-37289-A Tiger Rag                       -        -    01415, 02020

Acc. by Victor Young and his Orchestra. New York, October 25, 1931.

E-37321-A  Gems from GEORGE WHITE'S SCANDALS -     Br 20102, 0105, AH 40
           Part 2 (The Mills Brothers sing half a chorus of LIFE IS JUST  A  BOWL
           OF CHERRIES)

Acc. by John Mills-g.                      New York, late November, 1931.

E-37391-   You Rascal, You                      Br 6225, 01255
E-37392-A  Baby, Won't You Please Come Home ?        -          -

                                         New York, December 16, 1931.

E-37467-A  Dinah (w/Bing Crosby)                 Br 6240, 6485, 01271, 01424,
                                                 02313, 03080, Col CL-2749,
                                                 CBS 66206, AH 40

                                         New York, February 16, 1932.

B-11376-A  Shine (w/Bing Crosby)                 Br 6276, 6485, 01316, 01424,
                                                 Col 4305-M, 4421-M, C-6280,
                                                 DB-1845, CL-6027, 33S-1036,
                                                 Philco LP-436, Ph BBE-12142
B-11377-   I Heard                               Br 6269, 01283
B-11378-A  How'm I Doin', Hey-Hey                    -          -    Mt M-13179,
                                                 Col DB-1959, Rex 8896

                                         New York, March 8, 1932.

B-11421-   Rockin' Chair                         Br 6278, 01296
B-11422-A  Goodbye Blues                             -          -    01415, Ro 2381,
                                                 Col DB-1947

                                         New York, April 14, 1932.

BX-11704-  O. K. America - Part 2 (The Mills     Br 20112
           Brothers sing THE OLD MAN OF THE MOUNTAINS)
B-11708-A  Chinatown, My Chinatown               Br 6305, 01331, Mt M-13182
B-11709-A  Sweet Sue - Just You                  Br 6330, 01305, Mt M-13181
B-11710-A  Loveless Love                         Br 6305   -
B-11711-A  St. Louis Blues                       Br 6330, 01331, Ban 33211,
           NOTE:- Matrices 11705/7 are not by the Brothers. Har 1001, Per 13057, Col DB-1947

                                         Chicago, late May, 1932.

C-8651-1   Bugle Call Rag                        Br 6357, 01346, Mt M-13182,
                                                 Rex 8896

                                         Chicago, early June, 1932.

C-8663-1   The Old Man Of The Mountains          Br 6357, 01346
C-8664-1   It Don't Mean A Thing (If It Ain't Got  Br 01363
           That Swing)
C-8665-1   Coney Island Washboard                Ban 33211, Per 13057, Br 01363

                                         New York, November 21, 1932.

B-12626-B  Dirt-Dishin' Daisy                    Br 6430, 01419, Per 13082
B-12627-A  Git Along                                 -          -

                                         New York, December 22, 1932.

B-12781-A  Diga Diga Doo (w/Duke Ellington and his  Br 6519, 01520
           Famous Orchestra)
B-12782-A  I Can't Give You Anything But Love         -          -

                                         New York, December 29, 1932.

B-12811-A  Doin' The New Low-Down (w/Cab Calloway  Br 6517, 01518
           and Don Redman and his Orchestra)

New York, January 25, 1933.

| | | |
|---|---|---|
| B-12985-A | Smoke Rings | Br 6525, 01497, Har 1002, Col DB-1959 |
| B-12986-A | Fiddlin' Joe | Per 13082, Br 01497, Col DB-2010 |

New York, January 26, 1933.

| | | |
|---|---|---|
| B-12992-A | My Honey's Lovin' Arms (w/Bing Crosby) | Br 6525, 01469, Col DB-1971 |
| B-12992-B | My Honey's Lovin' Arms (w/Bing Crosby) |     -     Col 4304-M, 4420-M, CL-6027, 33S-1036, Har HL-7094, HS-11313, Hm 520, Philco LP-436 Realm 52069, Ph BBE-12142, Fon TFR-6012 |
| B-12993-A | Anytime, Any Day, Anywhere | Har 1001, Col DB-2001 |

New York, February 2, 1933.

| | | |
|---|---|---|
| B-13014-A | That's Georgia | Br 01531 |

Los Angeles, February 24, 1934.

| | | |
|---|---|---|
| LA-129-A | Swing It, Sister | Br 6894, 01756 |
| LA-130-A | Money In My Pockets |   -     - |
| LA-131-A | Jungle Fever | Br 6785, 01766, Col DB-2010 |
| LA-132-A | I've Found A New Baby |   -   01761, Col DB-2001, Epic L2N-6072 |
| LA-133-A | My Little Grass Shack In Keal kekua, Hawaii | Rejected |

San Francisco, March 29, 1934.

| | | |
|---|---|---|
| SF-104-A | Put On Your Old Grey Bonnet | Br 6913, 01761, Har 1002 |
| SF-105-A | Sleepy Head (Film "Operation 13") |   -   01766 |

London, June 13, 1934.

| | | |
|---|---|---|
| TB-1298-2 | Lazybones | Br 01800, Dec 176 |
| TB-1299-2 | Nagasaki |   -     - |

New York, September 12, 1934.

| | | |
|---|---|---|
| 38606-A | Sweet Georgia Brown | Dec 380, Br 01987, Coral CP-68 |
| 38607-A | Old-Fashioned Love | Dec 166, Br 01943 |
| 38612-A | Miss Otis Regrets (She's Unable To Lunch Today)- | Nr 01887, Coral CP-68 |
| 38613-A | Sweeter Than Sugar | Dec 267, Br 01987   - |

NOTE:- Matrices 38608/11 inclusive are not by the Mills Brothers.

New York, September 13, 1934.

| | | |
|---|---|---|
| 38615-A | Ida, Sweet As Apple Cider | Dec 165, Br 01863 |
| 38616-A | My Gal Sal |   -     -   Coral CP-68 |

New York, September 14, 1934.

| | | |
|---|---|---|
| 38637-A | Some Of These Days | Dec 228, Br 02020, Coral CP-68 |
| 38638 | I've Found A New Baby |   -     - |
| 38639 | Limehouse Blues | Dec 267, Br 01943 |
| 38640 | Rockin' Chair | Dec 167, Br 02062, Coral CP-68 |
| 38641-A | Tiger Rag |   - 7-3, Br 02020 |
| 38642-A | There Goes My Headache | Dec 380 |

Los Angeles, February 20, 1935.

| | | |
|---|---|---|
| DLA-88-A | Sweet Lucy Brown | Dec 497, Br 02035 |
| DLA-89-B | Don't Be Afraid To Tell Your Mother | Dec 402   - |
| DLA-90-A | Since We Fell Out Of Love | Dec 1495, Br 01999 |
| DLA-91-B | Moanin' For You | Dec 497, Br 02062 |
| DLA-92-B | What's The Reason (I'm Not Pleasin' You?) | Dec 402, Br 01999, Coral CP-68 |

Chicago, October 28, 1935.

| | | |
|---|---|---|
| C-90402-A | Lulu's Back In Town | Br 02093, Coral CP-68 |
| C-90403-A | Sweet And Slow | -          - |

Bernard Addison-g replaces John Mills.  London, June 23, 1936.

| | | |
|---|---|---|
| TB-2250-2 | Rhythm Saved The World | Br 02245, Dec 961 |
| TB-2251-2 | Shoe Shine Boy | -          - |

London, September 10, 1936.

| | | |
|---|---|---|
| TB-2442-1 | London Rhythm | Br 02284, Dec 1082 |
| TB-2443-1 | Solitude | -          - |
| TB-2444- | Swing Is The Thing | Br 02298 |
| TB-2445- | 'Long About Midnight | -       Dec 1360 |

New York, December 17, 1936.

| | | |
|---|---|---|
| 61492- | Pennies From Heaven | Dec rejected |
| 61493- | Swing For Sale | - |

New York, January 14, 1937.

| | | |
|---|---|---|
| 61529-A | Big Boy Blue (w/Ella Fitzgerald) | Dec 1148, Br 02399 |

New York, February 3, 1937.

| | | |
|---|---|---|
| 61574-A | Swing For Sale | Dec 1147, Br 02367 |
| 61575-A | Pennies From Heaven | -          -- |
| 61576-A | Dedicated To You (w/Ella Fitzgerald) | Dec 1148, Br 02399 |

New York, April 5, 1937.

| | | |
|---|---|---|
| 62106-A | The Love Bug Will Bite You | Dec 1227, Br 02415, Coral CP-68 |

New York, April 7, 1937.

| | | |
|---|---|---|
| 62115-A | Rockin' Chair Swing | Dec 1227, Br 02415, Coral CP-68 |
| 62116-A | Carry Me Back To Old Virginny (w/Louis Armstrong) | Dec 1245, Br 02445 |
| 62117-A | Darling Nellie Gray (w/Louis Armstrong) | -          - |
| 62117-B | Darling Nellie Gray (w/Louis Armstrong) | - |

New York, June 29, 1937.

| | | |
|---|---|---|
| 62322-A | In The Shade Of The Old Apple Tree (w/ Louis Armstrong) | Dec 1495, Br 02461 |
| 62322-B | In The Shade Of The Old Apple Tree (w/ Louis Armstrong) | Dec Y-5182 (Australian issue) |
| 62323-A | The Old Folks At Home | Dec 1360, Br 02461 |

London, July 23, 1937.

| | | |
|---|---|---|
| TB-3174-1 | Organ Grinder's Swing | Br 02460 |
| TB-3175-1 | Let Me Dream | - |

London, December 17, 1937.

| | | |
|---|---|---|
| TB-3456-1 | Caravan | Br 02542 |
| TB-3457-2 | Little Old Lady | - |
| TB-3458-1 | The Song Is Ended | Br 02648 |

   NOTE:- Brunswick 02648 bears the matrix number 63831 on the label, but as far as
   can be ascertained, the American recording was not used for this issue.

New York, May 20, 1938.

| | | |
|---|---|---|
| 63829- | Asleep In The Deep | Rejected |
| 63830-A | Caravan | Dec 1816  Br 02622 |
| 63831- | The Song Is Ended | Rejected |

New York, June 10, 1938.

63950-A  The Flat Foot Floogie (w/Louis Armstrong) Dec 1876, Br 02622

New York, June 13, 1938.

63967-A  The Song Is Ended (w/Louis Armstrong)      Dec 1892
63968-A  My Walking Stick (w/Louis Armstrong)          -

New York, June 20, 1938.

64223-A  Funiculi, Funicula                          Dec 2029, Br 02709
64224-A  Asleep In The Deep                          Dec 2804      -

New York, June 29, 1938.

64249-A  Side-Kick Joe                               Dec 2599, Br 03002

New York, July 19, 1938.

64323-A  Julius Caesar                               Dec 1964, Br 02642
64324-A  Sixty Seconds Got Together                      -         -

New York, August 19, 1938.

64466-A  Just A Kid Named Joe                        Dec 2029, Br 02679

New York, August 23, 1938.

64475-A  The Yam                                     Dec 2008, Br 02679
64480-A  The Lambeth Walk                                -     Br 02648
  NOTE:- Matrices 64476/9 inclusive are not by the Mills Brothers.
                                        New York, January 24, 1939.

64934-A  Sweet Adeline                               Dec 2285, 23623, Br 02932
64935-A  Meet Me Tonight In Dreamland                Dec 2804, Br 03704

New York, January 25, 1939.

64948-A  You Tell Me Your Dream, I'll Tell You       Dec 2285, 23623, Br 02932
           Mine
64949-   'Way Down Home                              Dec 2599, Br 04450
64959-A  Sweet Sue - Just You                        Dec 2441, Br 02764
64960-B  Goodbye Blues                                   -     Br 03002
  NOTE:- Matrices 64950/8 inclusive are not by the Mills Brothers.

London, February 17, 1939.

DR-3330-1  Jeepers Creepers                          Br 02725
DR-3331-1  Stop Beatin' 'Round The Mulberry Bush       -
DR-3332-1  Put On Your Old Grey Bonnet               Br 02832, Dec 2982
DR-3333-1  F. D. R. Jones                              -

London, February 18, 1939.

DR-3334-1  It Don't Mean A Thing (If It Ain't Got    Br 02782, Dec 2982
             That Swing)
DR-3335-1  Smoke Rings                                 -
DR-3336-1  (Mr. Paganini) You'll Have To Swing It    Br 02741
DR-3337-1  Stardust                                    -

London, July 5, 1939.

DR-3739-1  Shine                                     Br 02844, Dec 3688
DR-3740-1  Basin Street Blues                          -
DR-3741-1  Strawberry Fair                           Br 02800

London, July 7, 1939.

DR-3746-1  Three Little Fishies (Itty Bitty Poo)     Br 02800
DR-3747-1  Georgia On My Mind                        Br 02892, Dec 3688

London, August 17, 1939.

DR-3824-1  And The Angels Sing                          Br 02823
DR-3825-1  South Of The Border (Down Mexico Way)        -

London, August 23, 1939.

DR-3860-1  Ain't Misbehavin'                            Br 02892

New York, March 18, 1940.

67339-A  Sleepy-Time Gal                 Dec 3291, Br 03042
67340-A  Moonlight Bay                   Dec 3331, 23626, Br 04150
67341-A  My Gal Sal                      Dec 3225, 23624, Br 03042

New York, March 19, 1940.

67350-  Break The News To Mother         Dec 3705, Br 03659
67355-  Darling Nellie Gray              -         -
67356-  Old Black Joe                    Dec 3132, Br 04148
67357-  Swanee River                     -         -
NOTE:- Matrices 67351/4 inclusive are not by the Mills Brothers.

New York, March 21, 1940.

67366-  Can't Yo' Heah Me Callin', Caroline ?   Dec 3455, 23625, Br 03687
67367-B  On The Banks Of The Wabash             Dec 3331, 23626, Br 03436

New York, March 22, 1940.

67380-  Just A Dream Of You, Dear        Dec 3225, 23624
67381-  Love's Old Sweet Song            Dec 3455, Br 03687
67382-A  When You Were Sweet Sixteen     Dec 3381, 23627, Br 03139

New York, April 10, 1940.

67519-A  W. P. A. (w/Louis Armstrong)    Dec 3151
67520-A  Boog It (w/Louis Armstrong)     Dec 3180, Br 03150

New York, April 11, 1940.

67529-A  Once Upon A Dream               Dec 3381, Br 03139
67530-A  Cherry (w/Louis Armstrong)      Dec 3180, Br 03065
67531-A  Marie (w/Louis Armstrong)       Dec 3151, 3291 -

New York, October 24, 1940.

68284-A  By The Watermelon Vine, Lindy Lou   Dec 3545, Br 03232
             (w/Benny Carter and his Orchestra)
68288-  When You Said "Goodbye"             Dec 3486
68289-  A Bird In The Hand                  -
NOTE:- Matrices 68285/7 inclusive are not by the Mills Brothers.

New York, November 27, 1940.

68406-  How Did She Look ?               Dec 3567, Br 03150
68407-  Did Anyone Call ?                -

Acc. by unknown g/sb/d.           New York, April 10, 1941.

68972-  Down, Down, Down (What A Song)   Dec 3763, Br 03362
68973-A  I Yi Yi Yi (Cielito Lindo)      Dec 25046, Br 04155

Acc. by studio orchestra.         New York, April 15, 1941.

68995-  If It's True                     Rejected
68996-  Brazilian Nuts                   Dec 3789, Br 04151
69001-  Love Is Fun                      -
NOTE:- Matrices 68997/69000 inclusive are not by the Mills Brothers.

New York, April 17, 1941.

| | | |
|---|---|---|
| 9016-A | If It's True | Dec 3901, 25284 |
| 9017-A | The Very Thought Of You | - - Br 04150 |
| 9018- | Rig-a-Jig-Jig | Dec 3763, Br 03362 |

New York, October 15, 1941.

| | | |
|---|---|---|
| 9825- | The Bells Of San Raquel | Dec 4070, Br 03296 |
| 9826- | I Guess I'll Be On My Way | - - |

New York, October 22, 1941.

| | | |
|---|---|---|
| 9854-A | Lazy River | Dec 4187, Br 04155, 05058 |

New York, November 13, 1941.

| | | |
|---|---|---|
| 9943- | Delilah | Dec 4108, Br 03304 |
| 9944- | 627 Stomp | Dec 4187 |
| 9945-A | The Window Washer Man | Dec 4108, Br 03304 |

New York, January 30, 1942.

| | | |
|---|---|---|
| 0268- | When I See An Elephant Fly | Rejected |
| 0269- | Beyond The Stars | Dec 4251, Br 04156 |
| 0270- | In Old Champlain | Rejected |

New York, February 12, 1942.

| | | |
|---|---|---|
| 0314-A | Dreamsville, Ohio | Dec 4251, Br 04152 |

New York, February 18, 1942.

| | | |
|---|---|---|
| 0348- | Paper Doll | Dec 18318, DL-4084, DX-193, Br 03464 |
| 0349- | I'll Be Around | As above |
| 0350- | In Old Champlain | Dec 18473, Br 04156 |

New York, July 9, 1942.

| | | |
|---|---|---|
| 71019-B | I Met Her On Monday | Dec 18473, Br 03436 |

## FLORENCE MILLS

Washington, D.C., January 25, 1895; best-loved negro actress for superb appearances in vaudeville (Lincoln Theatre, in Harlem, New York) and in the PLANTATION
REVUE (Lafayette, February 18, 1924); she also captivated London in two Pavilion
revues (DOVER STREET TO DIXIE, May 31, 1923, and BLACKBIRDS (September 11, 1926).
She overworked herself during the phenomenal success of the latter, however, and
on November 1, 1927, a few weeks after returning to New York, she died.

ocal, acc. by Arthur Johnston (composer)-p.
New York, December 12, 1924.

| | |
|---|---|
| Dixie Dreams ("Dixie To Broadway") | Vic test (un-numbered) |
| I'm A Little Blackbird Looking For A Bluebird ("Dixie To Broadway") | - |

## CARMEN MIRANDA

Rio de Janeiro, Brazil, 1909; very popular as cabaret entertainer there before
going to Hollywood in 1939 for her film debut in DOWN ARGENTINE WAY (though she
had made four films in Rio between 1934 and 1938); also appeared with success in
THAT NIGHT IN RIO and WEEK-END IN HAVANA (1941); THE GANG'S ALL HERE (1942); THE
GIRLS HE LEFT BEHIND (1943); FOUR JILLS IN A JEEP and GREENWICH VILLAGE (1944);
COPACABANA (1947); A DATE WITH JUDY (1948); NANCY GOES TO RIO (1950) and SCARED
STIFF (1953), amongst others. R.n. Maria de Carmo Miranda da Cunha. D. 1955.

Vocal, acc. by Bando da Lua.          New York, December 26, 1939.

| 67000-B | Mama, eu quero (I Want My Mama) | Dec 23132, Br 03111 |
| 67001-A | Bambu-Bambu | - - |
| 67002-A | Que e que a Bahiana tem ? | Dec 23131, Br 03149 |
| 67003- | South American Way (Film "Down Argen-tina Way") (in Portuguese) | Dec 23130 |
| 67004-A | South American Way (Film "Down Argen-tina Way") | Br 03178 |
| 67005-A | Co, Co, Co, Co, Co, Co, Ro | Dec 23131, Br 03149 |
| 67006- | Touradas em Madrid | Dec 23130, Br 03178 |

Los Angeles, January 5, 1941.

| DLA-2341- | I, Yi, Yi, Yi, Yi (I Like You Very Much) (Film "That Night In Rio") | Dec 23209, Br 03207 |
| DLA-2342- | Chica Chica Boom Chic (Film "That Night In Rio") | Dec 23210     - |
| DLA-2343- | Cae Cae | Dec 23211, Br 03237 |
| DLA-2344- | Alo Alo | Dec 23209 |
| DLA-2345-A | Bambale | Dec 23210, Br 03954 |
| DLA-2346-A | Arca de Noe | Dec 23211    - |

New York, October 9, 1941.

| 69803-A | A Week-End In Havana (Film "Week-End In Havana") | Dec 23239, Br 03271 |
| 69804-A | The Man With The Lollipop Song (Film "Week-End In Havana") | Dec 23241, Br 03273 |
| 69805-A | Rebola a Bola (Film "Week-End In Havana") | Dec 23240, Br 03272 |
| 69806-A | When I Love, I Love (Film "Week-End In Havana") | - - |

New York, October 13, 1941.

| 69812-A | Ella diz que tem | Dec 23239, Br 03271 |
| 69813-A | Não te dou a chupeta | Dec 23241, Br 03273 |

New York, December 23, 1941.

| 70097- | Thank You, North America | Dec 23226 |
| 70098- | Manuelo | - |
| 70099- | When I Love, I Love (Film "Week-End In Havana") | Dec 23240 |

Los Angeles, July 25, 1942.

| L-3133-A | Chattanooga Choo-Choo (In Portuguese) | Dec 23265, Br 03437 |
| L-3134-A | Tic-Tac do meu Coraçao | Dec 23266, Br 03243 |
| L-3135-A | O Passo do Kanguru (Brazilly Willy) | - - |
| L-3136-A | Boneca de Pixe | Dec 23265, Br 03437 |

NOTE:- Where a title is given in Portuguese, it is sung in that language.

## MITZI

See Mizzi Hajos.

## MONTGOMERY AND STONE

David Craig Montgomery (b. St. Joseph, Mo., April 21, 1870) and Fred Andrew  Stone (b. Longmont, Colorado, August 19, 1873) formed one of the best-known vaudeville and musical comedy partnerships of the last eighty years in Kansas City in 1895. They refused a film offer of $104,000 in 1913, to remain in "live" theatre  until Montgomery died on April 20, 1917.  (His partner survived him until March 6, 1959 without going into partnership with anyone else).  Their biggest successes  were in two shows at the Globe, New York: THE OLD TOWN (January 10, 1910) and THE LADY OF THE SLIPPER (October 28, 1912).  Despite their great popularity, they made an inexplicably small number of records.

Humorous dialogue.                    New York, January 24, 1911.

C-9845-1  Travel, Travel, Little Star ("The Old      Vic 70033
           Town")
C-9846-2  Moriah (A Scotch Medley) ("The Old Town")  Vic 70044, AR 2290

                              New York, February 4, 1911.

C-9906-1  Gay Paree                         Vic rejected
C-9907-1  The Lobster Song                  -

                              New York, May 18, 1911.

B-10409-1  Hurrah For Baffin Bay            Vic rejected
C-10410-1  At The Seashore                  -

                              New York, May 19, 1911.

C-9846-3  Moriah (A Scotch Medley) ("The Old Town")  Vic 70044
C-9906-2  Gay Paree                                  Vic 70042

## FLORENCE MOORE

B. Philadelphia, Pa., 1886; best-remembered for her appearance in the first    Irving
  Berlin MUSIC BOX REVUE at the newly-opened Music Box Theatre (September 22, 1921);
  it ran for 407 performances.  She was also the first Mistress of Ceremonies at the
  Palace (1927).  She died in Darby, Pa., March 23, 1935.

Humorous speech.                      New York, April, 1922.

  8937    Actors' Equity - An All-Star Comedy    Voc 35010 (part side)

## GRACE  MOORE

B. Del Rio, Cocke County, Tenn., December 5, 1901; studied singing under Dr.  P.  M.
  Marafioti, a great friend of Enrico Caruso; stage debut in HITCHY-KOO in Boston at
  the Colonial Theatre,(September 7, 1920; New York debut in the same show at theNew
  Amsterdam (October 19, 1920); appeared in two MUSIC BOX REVUES (Music Box, September 22, 1923 and December 1, 1924); adopted concert stage and made her debut as an
  operatic soprano in LA BOHEME (as Mimi) at the Metropolitan, New York, February 7,
  1928; during the next three seasons there she sang in ROMEO ET JULIETTE;   CARMEN;
  FAUST, and MANON; sang LOUISE at L'Opera-Comique, Paris, 1929; London debut, Royal
  Opera House, Covent Garden, in LA BOHEME (again as Mimi), June 6, 1935: made  some
  musical films such as NEW MOON (1932); ONE NIGHT OF LOVE (1934); LOVE  ME  FOREVER
  (1935); THE KING STEPS OUT (1936); FOR YOU ALONE and I'LL TAKE ROMANCE (1937); was
  created Chevalier du Legion d'Honneur, and twelve other countries awarded her honours in recognition of her art.  She died in an air crash in 1947.

Vocal, acc. by O/Rosario Bourdon.      New York, January 19, 1925.

B-31661-1-2-3  Tell Her In The Springtime ("Music   Vic rejected
                Box Revue")
B-31662-1-2-3  Listening ("Music Box Revue")         -
B-31663-1-2-3  Rock-a-Bye Baby ("Music Box Revue")   -

                              New York, January 30, 1925.

B-31661-4-5-6  Tell Her In The Springtime ("Music   Rejected
                Box Revue")
B-31662-4-5-6  Listening ("Music Box Revue")         -
B-31663-4  Rock-a-Bye Baby ("Music Box Revue")       Vic 19668

                              New York, February 26, 1925.

B-31661-10 Tell Her In The Springtime ("Music Box   Vic 19613
              Revue")
B-31662-8  Listening ("Music Box Revue")             -

                              New York, March 2, 1925.

B-31663-7-8  Rock-a-Bye Baby ("Music Box Revue")     Vic rejected

Acc. by studio orchestra.                 New York, c. October, 1927.

<pre>
        They Call Me Mimi ("La Boheme" - Puccini) Br 50140, 0129
        Farewell ("La Boheme" - Puccini)              -        -
        By The Bend Of The River                  Br 15186, 02031
        For You (Pour toi)                            - 10277 -
        Musetta's Waltz Song ("La Boheme" -       Br     , 02102
          Puccini)
        Funiculi, Funicula                            -
        Habanera ("Carmen" - Bizet)               Br ?
        Butterfly's Entrance ("Madame Butterfly"  Br ?
          - Puccini)
        One Fine Day ("Madame Butterfly" -        Br ?
          - Puccini)
</pre>

Acc. by O/Nat Shilkret.                    New York, December 19, 1932.

BS-74707-2  Without Your Love (w/Richard Crooks)  Vic 1615, HMV DA-1306
              ("The Dubarry")
BS-74708-2  I Give My Heart ("The Dubarry")       Vic 1614, HMV DA-1309
BS-74709-2  The Dubarry ("The Dubarry")                -          -

Acc. by O/Wilfred Pelletier, with Metropolitan Opera Chorus.
                                           New York, October 4, 1934.

B-16101-A  Ciribiribin (Film "One Night Of Love")  Br 6994, 01922, Rex 8871,
                                                      Col DB-1801
B-16102-A  One Night Of Love (Film "One Night Of   As above, plus Epic SN-6059
             Love")

Acc. by O/Joseph Pasternack.               Los Angeles, November 27, 1935.

DLA-284-C  Un bel di vedremo (One Fine Day)        Dec 29000, Br 0130
             ("Madame Butterfly" - Puccini)
DLA-285-C  Love Me Forever (Film "Love Me Forever")    -    7-1    -

                                           New York, March 23, 1936.

60920-A  What Shall Remain ? (The Old Refrain)     Dec 23000, Br 02233
           (Film "The King Steps Out")
60921-A  Stars In My Eyes (Film "The King Steps     Dec 23001, Br 02234
           Out")

                                           New York, March 25, 1936.

60932-A  Learn How To Lose (Film "The King Steps   Dec 23001, Br 02234
           Out")
60933-A  The End Begins (Film "The King Steps       Dec 23000, Br 02233
           Out")

Acc. by O/Victor Young.                    Los Angeles, February 10, 1937.

DLA-686-A  Our Song (Film "For You Alone")         Dec 23023, Br 02400
DLA-687-B  The Whistling Boy (Film "For You Alone")    -       -

Acc. by O/Alexander Smallens.              New York, April 8, 1937.

62118-A  Vissi d'arte, vissi d'amore (Love And     Dec 29010, Br 0136
           Music) ("La Tosca" - Puccini)
62119-A  Serenade (Schubert)                           -       -

Acc. by the Victor Symphony Orchestra/Wilfred Pelletier.
                                           New York, February 12, 1940.

CS-047051-  Mi chiamano Mimi (They Call Me Mimi)  Vic 17189
              ("La Boheme" - Puccini)
CS-047052-  Depuis le jour ou je me suis donnee        -
              ("Louise" - Charpentier)
CS-047053-1  Toi seule                             Rejected

New York, October 7, 1940.

| | | |
|---|---|---|
| CS-056449-1-2-3  Adieu, notre petite table | Vic rejected | ? |
|   ("Manon" - Massenet) | | |
| CS-056450-1-2  Gavotte ("Manon" - Massenet) | - | |
| CS-056451-1  L'Absence ("Nuits d'Hiver" - Berlioz) | - | |
| CS-056452-1-2  Que deviennent les roses | - | |
| CS-056453-1-2  Toi seule | - | |
| CS-056454-1  Valse (Arensky, Op. 49, No. 5) | - | |

Acc. by Isaac van Grove-p.            New York, May 20, 1942.

| | |
|---|---|
| CS-075211-1  Red Rosy Bush | Vic rejected ? |
| CS-075212-1  Forgotten | - |
| CS-075213-1  Danny Boy | - |
| CS-075214-1-2  Ma Curly-Headed Babby | - |
| CS-075215-1  The Old Refrain (Film "The King Steps Out")- | |
| CS-075216-1  Stars In My Eyes (Film "The King Steps | - |
|   Out") | |
| CS-075217-1  Valse (Arensky, Op. 49, No. 5) | - |
| CS-075218-1  Canto Andaluz | - |
| CS-075219-1  The Last Rose Of Summer | - |

## MORAN AND MACK

George Moran (b. Elwood, Kansas, 1881) and Charles E. Mack (**b.** White Cloud, Kansas, 1888) formed their famous vaudeville act "The Two Black Crows" in 1926, becoming stars of stage and radio before Amos 'n' Andy; they made one film (WHY BRING THAT UP ? in 1930) but soon afterwards they split up owing to the ill-health of Mack, whose real name was Sellers. He died in Mesa, Arizona, January 11, 1934; George Moran outlived him until August 1, 1949, when he died in Oakland, California.

Humorous dialogue, acc. by —— Richards. New York, January 11, 1927.

| | |
|---|---|
| The Darktown Poker Club | Vic test (un-numbered) |
| Two Black Crows | - |

New York, March 14, 1927.

| | | | |
|---|---|---|---|
| 143602-3  Two Black Crows - Part 1 (The Early Bird | Col 935-D, 38481, 4441 | | |
|   Catches The Worm) | | | |
| 143603-2  Two Black Crows - Part 2 (The Early Bird | - | - | - |
|   Catches The Worm) | | | |

New York, May 23, 1927.

| | |
|---|---|
| 144198-1-2-3  Two Black Crows - Part 3 (All About | Col rejected |
|   Lions) | |
| 144199-1-2-3  Two Black Crows - Part 4 (All About | - |
|   Lions) | |

New York, July 19, 1927.

| | | |
|---|---|---|
| 144198-6  Two Black Crows - Part 3 (All About | Col 1094-D, 4616 | |
|   Lions) | | |
| 144467-3  Two Black Crows - Part 4 (All About Lions) | - | - |

New York, November 14, 1927.

| | | |
|---|---|---|
| 144975-3  Two Black Crows - Part 5 (Curiosities | Col 1198-D, 4686 | |
|   On The Farm) | | |
| 144976-1  Two Black Crows - Part 6 (Curiosities | - | - |
|   On The Farm) | | |

New York, November 25, 1927.

| | |
|---|---|
| 145235-3  Two Black Crows - Part 8 (No Matter How | Col 1350-D, 4927 |
|   Hungry A Horse Is, He Cannot Eat A Bit) | |

Acc. by C. Luckeyth Roberts—p.          New York, December 22, 1927.

98411-3  Our Child (Charles E. Mack only)          Col 50061-D

Acc. by unknown p (organ where shown).  New York, December 23, 1927.

98413-2  Elder Eatmore's Sermon On Throwing      Col 50061-D
         Stones (Charles E. Mack only, w/organ)
145396-2  Two Black Crows - Part 7 (No Matter How  Col 1350-D, 4927
         Hungry A Horse Is, He Cannot Eat A Bit)

Acc. by Guy Lombardo and his Royal Canadians.
                                        Chicago, March 22, 1928.

145828-1-2-3  Two Black Crows (no other details)  Col rejected

Unacc. ?                                New York, c. May, 1928.

170330-4  Two Black Crows In The AEF (Dialogue    Col Personal Recording
         from the novel by Charles E. Mack)

Acc. by unknown p.                      New York, September 6, 1928.

146958-6  Two Black Crows In Jail - Part 1        Col 1560-D, 5148

                                        New York, September 7, 1928.

146970-5  Two Black Crows In Jail - Part 2        Col 1560-D, 5148

                                        New York, November 14, 1928.

147458-2  Two Black Crows In Hades - Part 1       Col 1652-D, 5259
147459-2  Two Black Crows In Hades - Part 2           -           -

                                        Los Angeles, January 23, 1929.

147825-  Two Black Crows a la Carte - Part 1      Col rejected
147826-  Two Black Crows a la Carte - Part 2          -
147827-  Esau Buck And The Buck Saw                   -

                                        Los Angeles, May 31, 1929.

148572-  Untitled selection                      Col rejected

                                        Los Angeles, June 4, 1929.

148573-1  Two Black Crows - Part 13 (Foolishments) Col 1929-D, 5604
148574-  The Two Black Crows At The Party         Rejected
148575-  Two Black Crows - Part 14 (Esau Buck And Col 1929-D, 5604
         The Buck Saw)

## HELEN MORGAN

B. 1900;  cabaret entertainer (renowned for sitting on the grand piano) who made a
    successful debut in London (summer-autumn, 1927) and New York (SHOW BOAT, Zieg-
    feld, December 27, 1927); SWEET ADELINE (Hammerstein, September 3, 1929);  ZIEG-
    FELD FOLLIES OF 1931 (Ziegfeld, July 1, 1931); made  films (GLORIFYING THE AMER-
    ICAN GIRL and APPLAUSE (1929); ROADHOUSE NIGHTS (1930); YOU BELONG TO ME;  MARIE
    GALANTE, and FRANKIE AND JOHNNY (1934); GO INTO YOUR DANCE; SWEET MUSIC and SHOW
    BOAT (1936), and others); d. October 8, 1941.  A film of her life, BOTH  ENDS OF
    THE CANDLE, was made in 1957.

Vocal, acc. by Leslie A. Hutchinson ("Hutch")—p, who sings where shown.
                                        London, c. June, 1927.

                 Me And My Shadow (w/Leslie Hutchinson)   Br 104
                 When I Discover My Man                       -
                 Just Like A Butterfly                     Br 110
                 You Remind Me Of A Naughty Springtime        -
                    Cuckoo

London, July-August, 1927.

A Tree In The Park                    Br 111
Where's That Rainbow ?                  -

Acc. by small studio orchestra.    London, July-August, 1927.

R-181  Lazy Weather                   Br 113
                                        -
       Nothing But                    Br 122
       Wanting You                      -

Acc. by Leslie A. Hutchinson ("Hutch")-p.
                         London, September, 1927.

       Do-Do-Do (w/Chick Endor-Paul Reese)    Br 129
       Maybe (w/Chick Endor-Paul Reese)         -

Acc. by O/Victor Baravalli.       New York, February 14, 1928.

BVE-42442-1  Can't Help Lovin' Dat Man ("Show    Vic 21238, 25248, 27681, LPV-561,
             Boat")                              LSA-3076, X LVA-1006, HMV B-2735,
                                                 BD-343
BVE-42443-2  Bill ("Show Boat")                  Vic 21238, 25248, 27681,LCT-1112,
                                                 LPV-523, LPV-561, LSA-3076,
                                                 LSA-3078, HMV BD-343, Bm 1016

Acc. by O/Leonard Joy.            New York, March 6, 1929.

BVE-50917-3  Who Cares What You Have Been ?    Vic 21930, HMV B-3050
BVE-50918-2  Mean To Me                          -         -        X LVA-1006

                         New York, September 24, 1929.

BVE-56711-1-2-3  What Wouldn't I Do For That    Vic rejected
             Man ? (Films "Glorifying The American Girl" and "Applause")
BVE-56712-1-2-3  More Than You Know               -

                         New York, October 8, 1929.

BVE-56711-5  What Wouldn't I Do For That Man ?    Vic 22149, LPV-538, LPV-561,
             (Films "Glorifying The American      LSA-3074, LSA-3076, RD-7869,
             Girl" and "Applause")                HMV B-3258
BVE-56712-4  More Than You Know                   Vic 22149, 27684, LPV-561,
                                                  LSA-3076, HMV B-3534

                         New York, October 16, 1929.

BVE-56191-2  Why Was I Born ? ("Sweet Adeline")   Vic 22199, 27682, X LVA-1006

                         New York, November 12, 1929.

BVE-57142-4  Don't Ever Leave Me ("Sweet Adeline")Vic 22199, 27682, LPV 561,
                                                  LSA-3076

                         New York, September 5, 1930.

BVE-63625-1-2-3  Body And Soul                    Vic rejected
BVE-63626-1-2-3  Something To Remember You By       -

                         New York, September 12, 1930.

BVE-63625-5  Body And Soul                        Vic 22532, 27683, LPV-561,
                                                  LSA-3076, X LVA-1006
BVE-63626-4  Something To Remember You By         Vic 22532, 27683  -

Acc. by Victor Young and the Brunswick Orchestra.
                                     New York, August 9, 1932.

BX-12161-A  Bill ("Show Boat")                  Br 20115, 0113, Col 55005
BX-12162-A  Can't Help Lovin' Dat Man ("Show Boat")    -        -      - Epic SN-6059

Vocalist with George Hall and his Hotel Taft Orchestra.
                                     New York, March 12, 1934.

BS-81880-1  A Fool There Was                    Vic rejected

Vocal, acc. by O/Nat Shilkret.      New York, March 21, 1934.

BS-81968-1  Give Me A Heart To Sing To (Film    Vic 24650, 27684, LPV-561,
              "Frankie And Johnny")              LSA-3076
BS-81969-1  Frankie And Johnny (Film "Frankie   Vic 24650, LPV-561, LSA-3076,
              And Johnny")                        X LVA-1006

    Acc. by studio orchestra.       Los Angeles, September, 1934.

CPB-1126-A  It's Home (Film "Marie Galante")    Br 7329, 01968
CPB-1127-A  When He Comes Home To Me (Film "You  Br 6984, 01917
              Belong To Me")
CPB-1128-A  Song Of A Dreamer (Film "Marie      Br 7329, 01968
              Galante")
CPB-1129-A  (I've Got) Sand In My Shoes (Film   Br 6984, 01917
              "Convention Girl")

    Acc. by Jimmie Grier and his Orchestra. Los Angeles, December 5, 1934.

LA-274-     Winter Overnight                    Br 7391, 02036, Epic L2N-6072
LA-275-     I See Two Lovers                    Rejected

    Acc. by O/Bakaleinikoff.         Los Angeles, January 9, 1935.

LA-275-     I See Two Lovers                    Br 7391, 02036
LA-309-A    The Little Things You Used To Do (Film   Br 7424, 02086
              "Casino de Paree")
LA-310-A    I Was Taken By Storm (Film "Casino de Paree")-    -

                              ELIDA MORRIS

B. Philadelphia, Pa., November 12, 1886; one of the great "coon-shouters" and exponents of syncopated popular music, who performed in the idiom while touring in
the British Isles, France, South Africa and the U.S.A. in the years between 1910
and 1922.  Later she appeared in opera and in her church choir, and at the  time
of writing still does so.

Vocal, acc. by O/? Walter B. Rogers.      New York, January 21, 1910.

B-8570-1-2  The Sting Of The Bumble Bee         Vic rejected
B-8571-1-2  Has Anybody Here Seen Kelly ?          -
B-8572-1-2  You'll Come Back (w/Billy Murray)      -

    Acc. by O/? Charles A. Prince.       New York, c. March 28, 1910.

    4394-1  You'll Come Back                    Col/Utd A-826, Aretino D-678

                                   New York, c. May, 1910.

    4593-3  Kiss Me, My Honey, Kiss Me         Col A-906

    Acc. by O/? Walter B. Rogers.       New York, May 16, 1910.

B-8572-4   You'll Come Back (w/Billy Murray)    Vic 16653
B-8958-2   Angel Eyes (w/Billy Murray)         Vic 5782

Acc. by studio orchestra.                    New York, c. August, 1910.

      You'll Come Back                          Ind 1414
      Kiss Me, My Honey, Kiss Me                 Ind 1439

Acc. by O/? Walter B. Rogers.                New York, September 13, 1910.

B-9145-3  Kiss Me                                    Vic 16807
B-9146-2  Stop ! Stop ! Stop ! (Come Over And        Vic 16687
      Love Me Some More)

Acc. by O/? Charles A. Prince.               New York, late September, 1910.

4941-5  Stop ! Stop ! Stop ! (Come Over And          Col/Utd A-253, Climax K-253
      Love Me Some More)

Acc. by studio orchestra.                    New York, c. October, 1910.

      Stop ! Stop ! Stop ! (Come Over And       Ind 1457
      Love Me Some More)
      I've Got Your Number (w/Walter van Brunt)Ind 3191

Acc. by O/? Walter B. Rogers.                New York, January 23, 1912.

B-11479-1  If Every Star Was A Little Pickaninny    Vic 17061
B-11490-2  Play Me A Good Old-Fashioned Melody      Vic 17048
B-11491-4  The Trolley Car Swing                    -

Acc. by O/? Charles A. Prince.               New York, March 4, 1912.

19782-1-2-3  Movin' Man, Don't Take My Baby Grand  Col rejected

Acc. by O/? Walter B. Rogers.                New York, June 5, 1913.

B-13385-1-2  They've Got Me Doin' It Now            Vic rejected
B-13386-1-2  I Was Waiting Around                   -
B-13387-1-2  Happy Little Country Girl             -

                                   New York, July 31, 1913.

B-13386-3-4  I Was Waiting Around                   Rejected
B-13387-4  Happy Little Country Girl               Vic 17430

Acc. by studio orchestra.                    New York, c. January, 1914.

      You're Here And I'm Here                  Pathe B-5030
      All He Does Is Follow Them Around         -

Acc. by O/? Charles A. Prince.               New York, March 9, 1914.

39269-  If I Had Someone At Home Like You            Col A-1523

                                   New York, May 28, 1914.

39421-  The Little Things That Count                 Col A-1581
39422-  Some Day You'll Know Who Loves You           Col A-1564

                                   New York, July 17, 1914.

39496-  I Want To Go Back To The Farm                Col A-1592
39497-  The High Cost Of Loving                      -

Acc. by studio orchestra.                    New York, c. July, 1914.

      The High Cost Of Loving                   Ind 1520
      I Want To Go Back To Michigan             Ind 3339

Acc. by O/? Charles A. Prince.               New York, June 30, 1915.

45831-  Hello ! 'Frisco (w/Sam Ash)                  Col A-1801

New York, August 24, 1915.

45963-1-2-3  We're Going To Celebrate The End Of  Col rejected
             The War In Ragtime

  Acc. by studio orchestra.              New York, c. October, 1916.

          Flora Bella                           Pathe 20081
          Bachelor Girl And Boy (w/Henry Burr)  Pathe 20088

  Acc. by Madame Adami-p.                Hayes, Middlesex, June 1, 1921.

Bb-208-1-2  My Mammy                            HMV rejected
Bb-209-1-2  I'd Love To But I'm Afraid          -

## JOE MORRISON

Popular singing film star of the mid-thirties appearing in ONE HOUR LATE (debut, in
  1934); LOVE IN BLOOM (1935); HOLLYWOOD REVELS OF 1936 and IT'S A GREAT LIFE (both
  1936).


Vocal, acc. by Jimmie Grier and his Orchestra.
                                    Los Angeles, November 14, 1934.

LA-267-A  Me Without You (Film "One Hour Late")  Br 7347, Dec F-5501
LA-268-A  A Little Angel Told Me So (Film "One   -            -
          Hour Late")

                                    Los Angeles, December 8, 1934.

LA-276-   Old Faithful                           Br 7359
LA-277-   Home On The Range                      -

  Acc. by Harry Jackson and his Orchestra.
                                    Los Angeles, November 21, 1935.

LA-1074-  Lazy Bones Gotta Job Now (w/The Four   Br 7574
          Esquires)
LA-1075-B  I Lost My Heart (Film "It's A Great Life") -     02252

  Acc. by Jack Shilkret and his Orchestra.
                                    New York, December 16, 1935.

18393-   Moonburn                                Br 7588
18394-   A Little Bit Independent                Br 7583
18395-1  When April Comes Again (Film "Hollywood  -     02156
         Revels of 1936")
18396-   I Dream Too Much                        Br 7588

## LEE   MORSE

B. Tennessee, c. 1900; father a minister; stage debut in vaudeville in Los Angeles,
  1920; played on Pantages circuit throughout the West for two years, then was Raymond Hitchcock's leading lady in a later edition of HITCHY-KOO, and was  the star
  of ARTISTS AND MODELS (Shubert, August 20, 1923). She appeared in London at  the
  Piccadilly Theatre in 1926, but personal problems forced her retirement from  the
  profession during the 1930s. She made an unsuccessful attempt at a come-back  in
  1951, and died in 1954.

Vocal, acc. by own ukulele, guitar and kazoo.
                                    New York, c. December, 1924.

          Everybody Loves My Baby              PA        , 10816, Per
          Better Shoot Straight With Your Mama          -

                                    New York, c. February, 1925.

          Me Neenyah                           PA        , 10878, Per
          Golden Dream Girl                             -

New York, c. April, 1925.

|  | Those D<sub>a</sub>isy Days | PA 025140, Per 11574 |
|  | Yearning (Just For You) | -       - |

Acc. by small jazz band, own u-kazoo.   New York, May,   1925.

| 106009 | Ukulele Lady | PA        , 10949, Per |
| 106010 ? | My Sweetie Turned Me Down | PA        , 11004, Per |
| 106011 | Blue Soldier Blues | PA 025152, 10950, **Per** 11586 |
| 106012 | Yes, **Sir**, That's My Baby | PA        , 10949, Per |

New York, June, 1925.

| 106098 | Are You Sorry ? | PA        , 11052, Per |
|  | Cecilia | PA 025152, 10950, Per 11586 |

New York, August, 1925.

| 106192 | Sweet Man | PA 025157, Per 11591 |
|  | Only This Time I'll Be True | PA 025156, Per 11590 |
|  | What-Cha-Call-'Em Blues | -       - |
|  | I'se Gwan Back To Dixie (sic) | PA        , 11003, Per |

New York, August-September, 1925.

| 106224 | Oh, Boy ! What A Girl | PA 025158, 11004, Per 11592 |
| 106225 | Want A Little Lovin' | PA 025161, Per 11595 |
| 106226 | I Love You So | PA 025158, 11003, Per 11592 |

New York, early November, 1925.

| 106390 | I Wonder Where My Baby Is Tonight ? | PA        , 11052, Per |

New York, November-December, 1925.

| 106459-B | I Love My Baby (My Baby Loves Me) | PA 025168, 11105, Per 11602 |

| 106466-A | Deep Wide Ocean Blues | PA 025168, 11313, Per 11602 |

New York, c. February 16, 1926.

| 106646 | Tentin' Down In Tennessee | PA 025174, Per 11608 |
| 106647 | Poor Papa (He's Got Nothin' At All) | -  11105   - |

New York, c. March, 1926.

|  | Thanks For The Buggy Ride | PA        , 11124, Per |
|  | A Garland Of Old-Fashioned Roses | - |
|  | Lonesome And Sorry | PA        , 11147 |

New York, c. April 20, 1926.

| 106813 | Could I - I Certainly Could | PA 025182, 11176, Per 11616 |
|  | In The Middle Of The Night | PA        , 11313, Per |

New York, May,   1926.

| 106874 | Hoodle-Dee-Doo-Dee-Doo-Doo | PA 025187, 11176, Per 11621 |

New York, c. June, 1926.

| 106960 | Daddy's Girl | PA        , 11207, Per |
|  | Where'd You Get Those Eyes ? | - |

Acc. by her Blue Grass Boys.            New York, August, 1926.

107033    He's Still My Baby                    PA         , 11247, Per
          Someone Is Losin' Susan                           -

                                        New York, November, 1926.

107199    The Little White House (In Honeymoon   PA 25201, 11410, Per 11635
          Lane)
107200    Ain't That Too Bad ?                   PA 25205, 11434, Per 11639
107201    With All My Heart                      PA 25202,   -      Per 11636
107202    The Jersey Walk                            -       11410    -

Acc. by own guitar, ukulele and kazoo, sometimes with piano acc. also.
                                        New York, March 16, 1927.

143659-   I'd Love To Be In Love                 Col 1011-D
143660-   Where The Wild, Wild Flowers Grow        -
143661-   My Idea Of Heaven (Is To Be In Love With  Col 974-D
          You)
143662-   Side By Side                             -

Acc. by her Southern Serenaders.        New York, March 17, 1927.

143678-   I Hate To Say Goodbye                  Col 1063-D
143679-   What Do I Care What Somebody Said ?      -
143680-   Ain't She Sweet ?                      Col 939-D
143681-   Mollie, Make Up Your Mind                -

Acc. by own (?) g/unknown p.            New York, June 30, 1927.

144414-   Rosita                                 Col 1082-D
144415-   I'm A Red-Hot Hot-House Flower (But My  Rejected
          Daddy Is An Ice-Cream Cone)
144416-   We (My Honey And Me)                   Col 1082-D
144417-   I've Looked All Over (For A Girl Like  Rejected
          You)

                                        New York, August 27, 1927.

144579-   Dawning                                Col 1149-D
144580-   I've Looked All Over (For A Boy Like You)  -

                                        New York, October 10, 1927.

144845-   Old-Fashioned Romance                  Col 1199-D
144846-   Did You Mean It ?                        -
144847-   Someday You'll Say "O.K."              Rejected

Acc. by her Southern Serenaders or (more usually) her Blue Grass Boys.
                                        New York, December 9, 1927.

145292-   Keep Sweeping The Cobwebs Off The Moon  Col 1276-D
145293-   I'm Lonely                             Col 1381-D, Re G-9215
145294-   Give Me A Goodnight Kiss               Col 1276-D

                                        New York, January 23, 1928.

145564-   Let A Smile Be Your Umbrella (On A Rainy  Col 1303-D
          Day)
145565-   There Must Be A Silver Lining (That's    -
          Shining For Me)
145566-   In The Sing-Song Sycamore Tree         Col 1381-D

                                        New York, January 25, 1928.

145584-   After We Kiss                          Col 1328-D
145585-   Poor Butterfly Waits For Me              -

New York, June 6, 1928.

| 146407- | Mother And Dad | Col 1497-D |
| 146408- | When I Lost You | Col 1434-D |
| 146409- | Lonesome For You | - |

New York, June 25, 1928.

| 146578- | Be Sweet To Me | Col 1466-D |
| 146579- | Don't Keep Me In The Dark, Bright Eyes | - |
| 146580- | Shadows On The Wall | Col 1497-D |

New York, September 13, 1928.

| 146989- | Main Street | Col 1752-D |
| 146990- | I Must Have That Man ! | Col 1584-D |
| 146991- | Mississippi Mud | - |

New York, September 28, 1928.

| 147087- | You Are My Own | Col 1716-D |

New York, October 23, 1928.

| 147136- | Old Man Sunshine, Little Boy Bluebird | Col 1621-D | |
| 147137-3 | Don't Be Like That | - | 5359 |
| 147138- | Where The Shy Little Violets Grow | Col 1716-D | |

New York, November 3, 1928.

| 147442- | If You Want The Rainbow (You Must Have The Rain) | Col 1659-D |

New York, December 7, 1928.

| 147396-3 | Let's Do It (Let's Fall In Love) | Col 1659-D, 5359 |
| 147397- | Susianna | Col 1752-D |
| 147398- | Adelleria (sic) | Rejected |

New York, December 10, 1928.

| 147403- | Just You And I | Col 2270-D |

New York, May 27, 1929.

| 148632-6 | He's A Good Man To Have Around | Col 1866-D, 5588 |
| 148633-6 | I'm Doing What I'm Doing For Love | -        - |

New York, July 3, 1929.

| 148784- | Miss You | Col 1896-D |
| 148785- | In The Hush Of The Night | - |

New York, July 24, 1929.

| 148846-1 | Moanin' Low | Col 1922-D, DB-370 |
| 148847-1 | Sweetness | -        DB-161 |

New York, September 11, 1929.

| 148992-2 | Sweethearts' Holiday | Col 1972-D, DB-8 |
| 148993-3 | Love Me | -        DB-34 |

New York, October 18, 1929.

| 149156-2 | Look What You've Done To Me | Col 2012-D, DB-34 |
| 149160- | If I Can't Have You | - |

NOTE:- Matrices 149157/9 inclusive are not by Lee Morse.

New York, November 4, 1929.

149469-3  My Fate Is In Your Hands              Col 2037-D, DB-8
149470-   To Be Forgotten                           -

New York, December 5, 1929.

149684-   A Little Kiss Each Morning (A Little   Col 2063-D
          Kiss Each Night)
149685-   I Love You, Believe Me, I Love You        -

New York, January 16, 1930.

149773-   Until Love Comes Along                 Col 2101-D
149774-1  Blue, Turning Grey Over You                -        DB-140

New York, February 27, 1930.

150032-3  'Tain't No Sin (To Dance Around In Your  Col 2136-D, DB-140
          Bones)
150033-   I'm Following You                         -

New York, March 27, 1930.

150138-2  Cooking Breakfast For The One I Love   Col 2165-D, DB-147
150139-2  Sing, You Sinners                         -        DB-161

New York, June 5, 1930.

150570-   Swingin' In A Hammock                  Col 2225-D, DB-252
150571-   Seems To Me                               -

New York, July 7, 1930.

150623-   Little White Lies                      Col 2248-D
150624-   Nobody Cares If I'm Blue                  -

New York, July 25, 1930.

150675-   I Still Get A Thrill (Thinking Of You)  Col 2270-D
150676-   So Beats My Heart For You                 -

New York, September 26, 1930.

150842-2  Just A Little While                    Col 2308-D, DB-355
150843-   When The Organ Played At Twilight         -

New York, October 31, 1930.

150924-1  Wasting My Love On You                 Col 2333-D, DB-370
150925-3  Loving You The Way I Do                   -        DB-413

New York, November 26, 1930.

150986-   You're Driving Me Crazy ! (What Did I Do)Col 2348-D
150987-3  He's My Secret Passion                    -

New York, December 23, 1930.

151173-   The Little Things In Life              Col 2365-D
151174-   Tears                                     -

New York, January 16, 1931.

151225-   I'm One Of God's Children (Who Hasn't  Col 2388-D, DB-579
          Got Wings)
151226-   Blue Again                                -

                                          New York, February 20, 1931.

151334-3  Walkin' My Baby Back Home                 Col 2417-D
151335-3  I've Got Five Dollars                          -

                                          New York, March 27, 1931.

151470-   The Tune That Never Grows Old               Col 2436-D
151471-   By My Side                                     -

                                          New York, June 3, 1931.

151585-   Let's Get Friendly                          Col 2474-D
151586-   I'm Thru' With Love                            -

                                          New York, July 8, 1931.

151670-1  It's The Girl !                             Col 2497-D
151671-3  I'm An Unemployed Sweetheart (Waiting For      -
              Somebody To Love)

                                          New York, April 28, 1932.

152173-   When The Lights Are Soft And Low            Col 2650-D
152174-   Lawd, You Made The Night Too Long              -

                                          New York, August 26, 1932.

152290-   Moonlight On The River                      Col 2705-D
152291-   Something In The Night                         -

   Acc. by B. Downey-p/John Cali-g.     New York, April 11, 1933.

BS-75786-1  I've Got To Sing A Torch Song        BB B-5052, Eld 1978
BS-75787-1  Pettin' In The Park                     -              -
BS-75788-1  In The Little White Church On The Hill BB B-5044, Eld 1970, Sr S-3122
BS-75789-1  While The Rest Of The World Is Sleeping  -            -            -

   Acc. by small instrumental group.    New York, March 2, 1938.

63361-    When I Lost You                             Dec 1919
63362-    Shadows On The Wall                            -
63363-    I See Your Face Before Me                   Rejected
63364-    Careless Love                               Dec 1737
63365-    Sing Me A Song Of Texas                        -
63366-    I Need Lovin'                               Rejected

## EDDIE MORTON

B. Philadelphia, Pa., May 15, 1870; famous vaudeville comedian during the first two
  decades of the twentieth century.  D. Wildwood, N.J., April 11, 1938.

Vocal, acc. by O/? Walter B. Rogers.    New York, July 25, 1907.

C-4709-2  That's Gratitude                            Vic 31661, 35051
B-4710-2  Just A Friend Of The Family                 Vic 5281, 16284

                                          New York, August 1, 1907.

B-4735-1-2  Ain't Goin' To Be No River               Rejected
B-4736-1    Mariuccia Dance Da-Hotch-a-ma-Kooch       Vic 5220, 16530
B-4737-1-2  Brother Noah Gave Out Checks For Rain     Rejected

                                          New York, February 20, 1908.

B-5088-1-2-3  Just Because He Couldn't Sing "Love  Vic rejected
                Me And The World Is Mine"
B-5089-1-2  Nothing Ever Troubles Me                    -

New York, February 21, 1908.

B-5090-1-2  Here's Where Friendship Ends          Rejected
B-5091-1-2  I'd Like To See You Get Along (On Crutches)-
B-5092-2   The Peach That Tastes The Sweetest     Vic 5403, 16150
           Hangs The Highest On The Tree
E-5092-1   The Peach That Tastes The Sweetest     Rejected (8")
           Hangs The Highest On The Tree

New York, June 11, 1908.

B-6263-3  The Right Church But The Wrong Pew     Vic 5501, 16555
B-6264-1-2-3  Fluff-a-da-Ruff                    Rejected
B-6265-1  The Party That Wrote "Home, Sweet Home"  Vic 5513, 16758
          Never Was A Married Man

   Acc. by studio orchestra.               New York, July 2, 1908.

          Don't Take Me Home                      Ed 9949

   Acc. by 0/? Walter B. Rogers.          New York, July 13, 1908.

B-6298-1  Don't Take Me Home                     Vic 5545
B-6299-2  Somebody Lied                          Vic 5546, 16784
B-6300-1  A Singer Sang A Song                   Rejected
B-6312-1-2  Music Makes Me Sentimental           Vic 16011
   NOTE:- Matrices B-6301/11 inclusive are not by Eddie Morton.

New York, July 17, 1908.

B-6300-4  A Singer Sang A Song                   Vic 16012

   Acc. by studio orchestra.              New York, c. July, 1908.

          In The Right Church But In The Wrong Pew  Ind 854
          A Singer Sang A Song                   Ind 880

          Don't Take Me Home                     Zon 1176
          A Singer Sang A Song                   Zon 5151

New York, August 19, 1908.

          A Singer Sang A Song                   Ed 4M-29

   Acc. by 0/? Walter B. Rogers.          New York, April 23, 1909.

B-7007-2-3  I'm A Member Of The Midnight Crew    Vic 16324

New York, April 28, 1909.

B-7018-2  In Ireland                             Vic 16333

New York, May 28, 1909.

B-8015-1  I'd Rather Be A Minstrel Man Than A    Vic 16697
          Multi-Millionaire
C-8016-1  That's The Doctor, Bill                Vic 35079

New York, July 6, 1909.

B-8091-1-2  The Girl I Left Before I Left The    Rejected
            Girl I Left Behind Me
B-8092-1-2-3  Abraham Lincoln Jones              -
B-8093-2  Please Don't Tell My Wife              Vic 16445

   Acc. by 0/? Charles A. Prince.      New York, c. September, 1909.

   4151-2  Wild Cherry Rag (sic)                 Col A-737, D & R 3645

New York, c. October, 1909.

4175-1  Then We'll All Go Home                    Col A-758, Climax X-712
4177-1  Don't Take Me Home                        Col A-742, D & R 3643

New York, c. December, 1909.

4271-4  You Ain't Talking To Me                   Col A-777, Climax X-786

Acc. by O/? Walter B. Rogers.        New York, July 25, 1910.

B-9322-2  If He Comes In, I'm Going Out           Vic 16650, 16938
B-9323-1-2  I Won't Be Back 'Til August           Rejected

New York, July 27, 1910.

B-9323-4  I Won't Be Back 'Til August             Vic 16706, 16926
B-9326-2  Wild Cherries Rag                       Vic 16792
B-9327-3  Let George Do It                        Vic 16648

Acc. by O/? Charles A. Prince.       New York, c. August, 1910.

4862-3  Oh, You Dream                             Col A-928
4863-1  That's The Fellow I Want To Get           Col A-956

New York, late September, 1910.

4944-2  Don't Make Me Laugh, Bill                 Col A-956
4945-1-2  If I Could See As Far Ahead As I Can    Col A-977
         See Behind

Acc. by studio orchestra.            New York, c. January, 1911.

        What's The Matter With Father ?           USE 328
        Nothing To Do Until Tomorrow              USE 439
        If I Could See As Far Ahead As I Can      USE 1113
          See Behind
        Play That Barber Shop Chord               USE 1114

Acc. by O/? Charles A. Prince.       New York, July 11, 1911.

19455-  That Peculiar Rag                         Col A-1058

Acc. by O/? Walter B. Rogers.        New York, July 12, 1911.

B-10712-1  The Oceana Roll                        Vic 16908
B-10713-1  You Can Lead A Mule To Water, But You  Vic 16911
           Can't Make Him Drink
B-10714-3  They're All Good American Names        Vic 16938

Acc. by O/? Charles A. Prince.       New York, October 21, 1911.

19614-  Bill From Louisville                      Col A-1106

New York, February 12, 1912.

19757-  The Trolley Car Swing                     Col A-1147

Acc. by O/? Walter B. Rogers.        New York, February 14, 1912.

B-11594-1-2  The Last Shot Got Him                Vic rejected

New York, March 21, 1912.

B-11594-4  The Last Shot Got Him                  Vic 17071
B-11751-1  Beans, Beans, Beans                    Vic 17108
B-11752-2  There's A Lot Of Stations On My        Vic 17128
           Railroad Track
B-11753-2  I've Got You, Steve !                  Vic 17094

Acc. by O/? Charles A. Prince.          New York, June 19, 1912.

| | | |
|---|---|---|
| 19972- | Somebody Else Is Gettin' It | Col rejected |
| 19973- | The Villain Still Pursued Her | - |
| 19974- | Ragtime Cowboy Joe | - |

Acc. by O/? Walter B. Rogers.          New York, June 24, 1912.

| | | |
|---|---|---|
| B-12141-2 | Somebody Else Is Gettin' it | Vic 17151 |
| B-12142-2 | Waiting For Me | Vic 17214 |
| B-12143-1-2 | The Ragtime Sailor's Rag | Rejected |
| B-12144-1-2 | Be Sure He's Irish | - |

Acc. by O/? Charles A. Prince.          New York, June 20, 1913.

38916-    They've Got Me Doin' It Now          Col A-1381

Acc. by O/? Walter B. Rogers.          New York, August 13, 1913.

| | | |
|---|---|---|
| B-13696-2 | Noodle Soup Rag | Vic 17451 |
| B-13697-2 | Ever Since You Told Me That You Loved Me | Vic 17425 |
| B-13698-1-2 | The Kellys Are At It Again | Rejected |
| B-13699-1-2 | What D'Ya Mean, You Lost Your Dog ? (Where's That Dog-Gone, Dog-Gone Dog Of Mine ?) | - |

New York, September 19, 1913.

| | | |
|---|---|---|
| B-13830-1-2-3 | Your Mother's Gone Away To Join The Army | Rejected |
| B-13831-1-2-3 | She's Waiting For You To Love Her All The Time | - |
| B-13832-1 | Isch-Ga-Bibble (I Should Worry) | Vic 17451 |

Acc. by O/? Charles A. Prince.          New York, December 1, 1913.

39127-    I'm Crying Just For You          Col A-1456

New York, December 18, 1913.

39156-    While They Were Dancing Around          Col A-1484

New York, March 18, 1914.

39288-    He's A Devil In His Own Home Town          Col A-1525

New York, May 19, 1914.

39387-    Goodbye, Broadway (w/The Peerless          Col A-1552
          Quartet)

New York, May 20, 1914.

39391-    They're On Their Way To Mexico          Col rejected

New York, May 28, 1914.

39423-    You're Here And I'm Here          Col A-1557

New York, c. July, 1917.

| | | |
|---|---|---|
| 1205-2 | Just A Little Bit Of Monkey Left In You And Me | Em 5164 (6") |
| | Come Out Of The Kitchen, Mary Ann | Em 7128 (7") |

## ARTHUR MOSS-ED. FRYE

Arthur Moss (b. Iowa) and Ed. Frye (b. Kansas) were popular vaudeville comedians of
the 1920s, specializing in contrasting dialogue between the cheerful and the dour
respectively.

Humorous dialogue.                          New York, April 6, 1923.

B-27805-1-2  How High Is Up ? - Part 1              Vic rejected
B-27806-1-2  Be Like The Early Bird                      -
B-27807-1-2  How High Is Up ? - Part 2                   -

                                            New York, April 13, 1923.

B-27805-3-4-5  How High Is Up ? - Part 1            Vic rejected
B-27807-3-4-5-6  How High Is Up ? - Part 2                -

                                            New York, May 4, 1923.

B-27805-10  How High Is Up ? - Part 1               Vic 19081
B-27807-10  How High Is Up ? - Part 2                    -

                                            New York, August 30, 1923.

B-28518-1-2-3-4  Why Adam Sinned (w/Nat Shilkret-p)Vic rejected
B-28519-1-2-3-4  Story No. 4                             -

                                            New York, September 7, 1923.

B-27806-3-4-5-6  Be Like The Early Bird               Vic rejected

                                            New York, September 14, 1923.

B-27806-9   Be Like The Early Bird                  Vic 19190
B-28518-7   Why Adam Sinned (w/Nat Shilkret-p)            -

## PAUL MUNI

B. Vienna, September 22, 1897; r.n. Muni Weisenfreund; family emigrated to New York
  when he was a child; began career as character-actor at eleven; trained for stage
  work in the Yiddish Art Theatre and with the Theatre Guild; to Hollywood, 1929,to
  begin film career with THE VALIANT and SEVEN FACES; subsequent great success with
  SCARFACE and I AM A FUGITIVE FROM A CHAIN GANG (1932); DOCTOR SOCRATES (1935);THE
  STORY OF LOUIS PASTEUR (1936); THE GOOD EARTH and THE LIFE OF EMILE ZOLA (1937);
  THE WOMAN I LOVE (1938); THE COMMANDOS STRIKE AT DAWN (1942); A SONG TO REMEMBER
  (1944); STRANGER ON THE PROWL (1951); THE LAST ANGRY MAN (1959).  D. 1967.

Dramatic monologue.                         New York, January 22, 1942.

BS-071713-1  The Crisis (Thomas Payn) - Part 1     Vic 10-1005
BS-071714-1  The Crisis (Thomas Payn) - Part 2          -

## ELIZABETH MURRAY

B. 1870; one of the foremost exponents of the art of "coon-shouting" in the   years
  preceding World War I.  D. Philadelphia, Pa., March 27, 1946.

Vocal, acc. by studio orchestra.            New York, c. November, 1919.

  4636-3-5  (Down Around The River) At The Dixie   Em 10235
            Jubilee

## J. HAROLD MURRAY

B. South Berwick, Maine, February 17, 1891; popular singer of romantic ballads, and
  notable for his part in RIO RITA (Ziegfeld, New York, February 2, 1927).  D. Kil-
  lingsworth, Conn., December 11, 1940.

Vocal, acc. by studio orchestra.            New York, c. June, 1921.

            Stand Up And Sing For Your Father (w/    Amb 4375
               Gladys Rice)
            Just Keep A Thought For Me               Ed 50790

New York, c. June, 1922.

Just Keep On Smiling (w/mixed chorus)     Ed 51005, Amb 4625
When Knighthood Was In Flower (w/Eliza-   Ed 51087
    beth Spencer)

New York, c. November, 1922.

Will She Come From The East ?            Ed 51099, Amb 4727
Faded Love Letters (w/The Homestead Trio) Ed 51110

Acc. by  O/Rosario Bourdon.        Camden, N. J., February 21, 1927.

CVE-37833-4  Rio Rita - Vocal Gems (w/Victor Light  Vic 35816, HMV C-1780
               Opera Company)

## KEN MURRAY

B. 1907 (?); r.n. Don Court; famous as comedy actor, on stage, screen, radio and of
    more recent date, TV; presented the first TV commercial (1930) for Libby's; BLACK-
    OUTS (his stage show) lasted seven years in Hollywood up to 1945, but flopped  in
    as many weeks in New York; awarded special Oscar for his bird fantasy film  (1947)
    BILL AND COO; appeared in HALF MARRIAGE (1929); A NIGHT AT EARL CARROLL'S  (1941);
    FOLLOW ME BOYS (1966).

KEN MURRAY AND OSWALD : Ken Murray and Tony Labriola, with Marlyn Stuart -  humorous
    dialogue.                        New York, September 18, 1936.

BS-0416-1  Mama, That Man's Here Again (O-oh      Vic 25418
               Ye-a-h) - Part 1
BS-0459-1  Mama, That Man's Here Again (O-oh        -
               Ye-a-h) - Part 2
    NOTE:- Matrices BS-0417/0458 inclusive are not by Ken Murray.

## PETE  MURRAY

B. New York, March 28, 1875; famous vaudeville comedian between the nineties and the
    twenties; d, December, 1940.

Vocal, acc. by studio orchestra.        New York, c. April, 1915.

On The 5.15                        Ed 50234, Amb 2561

Pete Murray also recorded 4-minute Edison cylinders in New York on May 14, 1909, and
2-minute ones on June 11 and July 20, 1909, but nothing is known of their titles.

## MAY  NAUDAIN

B. Burlington, Iowa, October 12, 1880; well-known singing actress remembered for her
    work in KATINKA (44th Street, New York, December 23, 1915), and THE GIRL BEHIND THE
    COUNTER, in which she sang THE GLOW WORM. D. Jacksonville, Fla., February 8,1923.

Vocal, acc. by studio orchestra.        New York, c. January, 1916.

Rackety-Coo ("Katinka")                Operaphone 1076

## CLIFF  NAZARRO

Vocal, acc. by unknown piano.          New York, October 29, 1925.

141210-  Headin' For Louisville              Har 59-H
141213-    I Wonder Where My Baby Is Tonight ?     -
    NOTE:- Matrices 141211/2 are not by Cliff Nazarro.

New York, January 16, 1926.

141504-  You Ought To See What's Waiting For Me  Har 108-H
141505-  Why Don't You Marry The Girl ?           -

New York, September 21, 1926.

142661-   I Want To Be Known As "Susie's Feller"  Har 263-H
142662-   Gone Again Gal                          -

Acc. by Helen Myers-p-organ.          New York, September 13, 1939.

BS-042675-1  I'll Remember                         Vic rejected
BS-042676-1  How To Learn How To Tap-Dance         -

Acc. by Maurine Ward-pipe-organ.      New York, September 18, 1939.

BS-042675-2  I'll Remember                         BB B-10433
BS-042676-2  How To Learn How To Tap-Dance         -

Acc. by O/Leonard Joy, or unacc.      New York, March 25, 1942.

BS-073478-1  News Of The World (unacc.)            BB B-11545
BS-073479-1  You Go Your Way (And I'll Go Crazy)   -

## POLA NEGRI

B. Poland, 1897; r.n. Appolonia Chalupek. Stage debut in Germany before World War I (and made films there also); to Hollywood in 1922 and became world-famous for her work in BELLA DONNA (1923);,FORBIDDEN PARADISE (1924); HOTEL IMPERIAL (1926); THE SECRET HOUR (1927); other silents in which she appeared include THE SPANISH DAN-CER (1923, with Adolphe Menjou) and LILY OF THE DUST (1924, with Ben Lyon); also made a few talkies :- A WOMAN COMMANDS (1931); MADAME BOVARY (1935); HI - DIDDLE-DIDDLE (1943); THE MOONSPINNERS (1964) amongst others.

Vocal, acc. by Boris Golovka and two others-g.
                          Small Queen's Hall, London, March 12,1931.

OB-641-   Ve Chastasni (The Hour Of Longing)     HMV EK-114
OB-642-   Sto nam gore ? (Why Are You Sorry ?)   -
OB-643-   Os sho tass                            Rejected ?

                          Small Queen's Hall, London, March 13,1931.

OB-647-   Dark Eyes (Ochye Tchornia)             HMV B-3820
OB-648-   Why Fall In Love ?                     HMV EK-115
OB-649-   Farewell, My Gypsy Camp                HMV B-3820
OB-650-   Gypsy, Sing ! (Dedicated to Pola Negri HMV EK-115
            by Boris Golovka)

Acc. by studio orchestra.             Berlin, c. early 1936.

128337-   Stay Close To Me (Film "Mazurka")      Par R-2271
128338-   For That One Hour Of Passion (Film     -
            "Mazurka")

                          Berlin, December 30, 1938.

Be-12171  Siehst du die Sterne ? (Film "Night Of  Par R-2640
            Fate")
Be-12172  Zeig der Welt nicht dein Herz (Film     -
            "Night Of Fate")

## ALICE  NIELSEN

B. Nashville, Tenn., June 7, 1876; star of several Victor Herbert operettas  (THE SINGING GIRL; THE SERENADE; THE FORTUNE TELLER) in the nineties before taking up concert and operatic work.  D. New York, March 8, 1943.  She made many records of concert and operatic music for Columbia from 1912 onwards, but they are  outside the scope of this book in view of the nature of the music on them.

Vocal, acc. by unknown piano.         New York, 1898.

          Always Do As People Say You Should    Ber 3180
            (w/chorus)

B. at sea, July 8, 1910; professional debut in cabaret in New York, at the 300 Club;
then in St. Louis with the Municipal Opera Company in various operettas and musical comedies (THE VAGABOND KING; SUNNY; GOOD NEWS, etc.); regular stage debut December 13, 1934 in CALLING ALL STARS (Hollywood, New York); then starred in   ZIEG-
FELD FOLLIES (Winter Garden, January 30, 1936); London debut in NO SKY SO BLUE, at
the Savoy, June 8, 1938; stayed in London to appear in BOBBY, GET YOUR GUN  (Adelphi, October 7, 1938); returned to U.S.A.; great success in FOLLOW THE GIRLS (Century, New York, April 8, 1944; film debut in TOP OF THE TOWN (1937).

Vocal, acc. by O/? Ben Selvin.              New York, February 9, 1933.

152376-2  You're Mine, You !                     Col 2759-D, DB-1135
152377-2  Tony's Wife                                 -         -

                                            New York, June 23, 1933.

152424-   My ! Oh, My !                          Rejected
152425-   Hold Your Man                          Col 2787-D

                                            New York, July 5, 1933.

152434-   I've Got To Pass Your House To Get To   Col 2787-D
            My House

   **Acc.**  by     Isham Jones and his Orchestra.
                                            New York, October 13, 1933.

BS-78182-2  Supper Time                          Vic 24435
BS-78201-1  Jealousy                             Vic 24454
BS-78202-1  Harlem On My Mind                    Vic 24435
   NOTE:- Matrices BS-78183/78200 inclusive are not by Gertrude Niesen.

   Acc. by O/Ray Sinatra.            New York, November 1, 1933.

BS-78377-1  Smoke Gets In Your Eyes              Vic 24454

   Acc. by O/Lud Gluskin.            New York, October 26, 1934.

CO-16148-   Be Still, My Heart !                 Col rejected

   Acc. by Joe Reichman and his Orchestra. New York, November 8, 1934.

CO-16148-   Be Still, My Heart !             Col 2972-D
CO-16247-   The Continental (You Kiss While You're   -
              Dancing)

                                            New York, November 10, 1934.

CO-16311-   Just Mention Joe                     Col rejected
CO-16312-   Stepping Out Of The Picture          -

                                            New York, February 1, 1935.

CO-16788-   Devil In The Moon                    Col 3021-D
CO-16789-   Would There Be Love ?                -

                                            New York, May 15, 1935.

CO-17605-   She's A Latin From Manhattan         Col 3047-D
CO-17606-   In The Middle Of A Kiss              -

   Acc. by O/Cy Feuer.             Los Angeles, January 7, 1937.

LA-1223-   Top Of The Town (Film "Top Of The Town")Br 7818, 02428
LA-1224-   .Blame It On The Rhumba (Film "Top Of The    -        -
             Town")
LA-1225-B  Where Are You ? (Film "Top Of The Town")Br 7837, 02429, Epic SN-6059
                                            Los Angeles, January 14, 1937.

LA-1234-A  Jamboree (Film "Top Of The Town")        Br 7837, 02429

Acc. by the Savoy Theatre Orchestra/Fred Hartley.
London, July 4, 1938.

| | | |
|---|---|---|
| CA-17025-1 | My Heaven On Earth | Col DB-1780 |
| CA-17026-1 | In Paree It's Love ("No Sky So Blue") | - |
| CA-17027-1 | What Is Romance ? ("No Sky So Blue") | Col DB-1779 |
| CA-17028-1 | Rhythm Is My Romeo ("No Sky So Blue") | - |

Acc. by the Lecuona Cuban Boys.          London, October 26, 1938.

| | | |
|---|---|---|
| CA-17154-1 | La Cucaracha | Col DB-1824 |
| CA-17155-1 | La Conga (Havane a Paris) ("Bobby, Get Your Gun") | - |

Vocalist with Leo Reisman and his Orchestra.
New York, November 17, 1939.

BS-043387-1  Katie From Haiti                  Vic rejected

New York, November 25, 1939.

| | | |
|---|---|---|
| BS-043387-2 | Katie From Haiti | Vic 26421 |
| BS-043918-1 | When Love Beckoned | Vic 26434 |

Vocal, acc. by studio orchestra.     New York, March 19, 1942.

| | | |
|---|---|---|
| 70547-A | Temptation | Dec 18351 |
| 70548-A | Body And Soul | - |
| 70549-A | The Lamplighter's Serenade | Dec 18284, Br 03347 |
| 70550-A | Skylark | - - |

## OLIVE NORTH

B. Indianapolis, c. 1885; stage debut in a fantasy called WOODLAND (as The Dove);in
New York she appeared in THE PRINCE OF PILSEN (Broadway, March 17, 1903);A KNIGHT
FOR A DAY (Wallack's, December 16, 1907), and was a member of the New York Hippo-
drome Company for three years, turning to vaudeville in 1915.

Vocal, acc. by O/Walter B. Rogers.        Camden, N. J., January 12, 1916.

| | | |
|---|---|---|
| B-17005-3 | I'm Neutral | Vic 17956 |
| B-17006-3 | I'm A Lonesome Melody | - |

## RUBY NORTON

American character-actress whose great success in vaudeville at the Palace Theatre,
New York, during the twenties was carried beyond the U.S.A. to Great Britain, New
Zealand and Australia. She was also a pioneer radio artist.

Humorous monologue.                       New York, c. February 11, 1924.

835-D  Listenin' In On Ruby Norton              Cam 504

## JACK NORWORTH

B. Philadelphia, Pa., January 5, 1879; stage debut as black-face comedian in vaudeville, 1898; continued in this style for seven years; then New York debut in regular theatre in ABOUT TOWN (Herald Square, August 30, 1906); many successes there
(e.g., THE JOLLY BACHELORS, Broadway, January 6, 1910; LITTLE MISS FIX-IT, Globe,
April, 1911); to London to appear in HULLO ! TANGO (Hippodrome, June 2, 1914); he
later appeared at the Pavilion and other variety theatres; ROSY RAPTURE (Duke of
York's, March 30, 1915); toured in A SYNCOPATED ROMANCE; returned to London, and
appeared in LOOKING AROUND (Garrick, November 6, 1915) and OH ! LA-LA (Queen's,
December 27, 1915); returned to New York in 1917, and appeared in ODDS AND ENDS
OF 1917 (Bijou, November 19, 1917); reverted to vaudeville, but toured in MY LADY
FRIENDS (July, 1920-late 1921); worked again in vaudeville until 1937, when  he
played some relatively small parts before retiring.  M. Nora Bayes (q.v.) and was
her stage partner and co-author of songs with her, notably SHINE ON, HARVEST MOON
(1908).  D. 1962.

Vocal, acc. by studio orchestra.          New York, March 7, 1910.

C-8701-1-2  Come Along, My Mandy (w/Nora Bayes)    Vic rejected
C-8702-1-2  Shine On, Harvest Moon (w/Nora Bayes)     -
            ("Follies of 1908")                       -
B-8703-1  Jack Norworth's College Medley             -

                                          New York, March 14, 1910.

C-8701-5  Come Along, My Mandy (w/Nora Bayes)    Vic 70016, 55097
          ("The Jolly Bachelors")
B-8707-2  Back To My Old Home Town                Vic 60020

                                          New York, April 4, 1910.

B-8703-2-3  Jack Norworth's College Medley         Vic rejected

                                          New York, April 25, 1910.

B-8703-4-5  Jack Norworth's College Medley         Rejected
B-8888-3  Sadie Brady, Listen Good To Me           Vic 60022

                                          New York, May 20, 1910.

C-8998-2  Rosa Rosetta (w/Nora Bayes)              Vic 70019

                                          New York, November 8, 1910.

B-9632-2  For Months And Months And Months         Vic 60030

                                          New York, January 20, 1911.

B-9829-1-2-3  Everyone In Favor Say "Aye"          Vic rejected
C-9830-1-2  Turn Off Your Light, Mr. Moon Man       -
            (w/Nora Bayes) ("Little Miss Fix-It")

                                          New York, April 24, 1911.

C-9830-5  Turn Off Your Light, Mr. Moon Man     Vic 70038, 55097, LCT-1112
          (w/Nora Bayes) ("Little Miss Fix-It")

Acc. by O/? Albert W. Ketelbey.          London, c. December, 1914.

29299     Molly McCarthy                         Col 2526
29300     Kitty, The Telephone Girl              Col 2539
29302     Sister Susie's Sewing Shirts For       Col 2526
            Soldiers

                                          London, c. January, 1915.

29323     Mother's Sitting Knitting Little Mittens Col 2539
          Oh ! How He Could Sing An Irish Song     Col 2548
          My Boy                                    -

                                          London, late March, 1915.

6462      Which Switch Is The Switch, Miss, For    Col 524
            Ipswich ? ("Rosy Rapture")
6463      Sally From Calais ("Rosy Rapture")       Col 525
6464      Safe In Our Wardrobe For Two (w/
            Gertrude Lang) ("Rosy Rapture")         -
6465      When I'm With You (w/Gertrude Lang)       Col 524
            ("Rosy Rapture")

                                          London, early April, 1915.

6475      The Same Sort Of Mother And Same Sort    Col 526
            Of Child ("Rosy Rapture")
          Give Me A Tinkle On The Telephone        Col 555
          Sister Susie Is Marrying Tommy Atkins     -

London, c. July, 1915.

| 29927 | You Can't Get Away From It ("A Syncopated Romance") | Col 2608 |
| 29928 | When We Are M-A-R-R-I-E-D (w/Gertrude Lang) ("A Syncopated Romance") | - |
| 29948 | Go Away, Mr. Moon (w/Gertrude Lang) ("A Syncopated Romance") | Col 2609 |
| 29949 | Private Michael Cassidy ("A Syncopated Romance") | - |
| | She Wants To Marry Me ("A Syncopated Romance") | Col 2607 |
| | Waiting 'Neath Your Window (w/Gertrude Lang) ("A Syncopated Romance") | - |

London, c. November, 1915.

| 35886 | Private Michael Cassidy ("A Syncopated Romance") - Part 1 | Re G-7217 |
| 35887 | Private Michael Cassidy ("A Syncopated Romance") - Part 2 | - |
| | On His First Day Home On Leave | Re G-7355 |
| | Keep Your Head Down, Fritzie Boy | - |

Acc. by studio orchestra.                    New York, c. August, 1918.

| 66826 | I Stopped, I Looked And I Listened | Pathe 29208 |
| 66833 | Ten Little Bridesmaids | Pathe 29208 |
| 66834 | His Wonderful Irish Brogue | Pathe 29211 |
| 66835 | I Want To Go Back There Again | Pathe 29220 |
| 66836 | Do You Want Us To Lose The War ? | Pathe 29211 |
| 66837 | Fancy You Fancying Me | Pathe 29210 |
| 66838 | The Further It Is From Tipperary | - |

New York, December, 1918.

| 67214 | A Good Man Is Hard To Find | Pathe 29235 |
| 67215 | Can You Tame Wild Wimmen ? | Pathe 29231 |
| 67216 | Oh ! Tomorrow Night | - |
| 67217 | My Boy | Pathe 29235 |

New York, January, 1919.

| 67319 | That Ain't All | Pathe 29242 |
| 67320 | Salvation Nell | - |
| 67321 | Mickey Slater | Pathe 29245 |
| 67322 | I'm Goin' To Settle Down Outside Of London Town | - |
| 67323 | In These Hard Times | Pathe 29246 |

New York, late March, 1919.

| 67544 | On The First Day He Came Home | Pathe 29246 |

New York, c. August, 1919.

| | You'd Be Surprised | Pathe 22235 |
| | Honeymoon Bells | - |

New York, December, 1919.

| 68223 | Me And My Wife | Pathe 22290 |
| 68224 | It's Hard To Settle Down To Civilian Life Once More | Pathe 22335 |
| 68225 | Never Let No One Gal Worry Your Mind | Pathe 22290 |
| 68226 | The Argentines, Portuguese And Greeks | Pathe 22335 |

New York, c. August, 1920.

| | | |
|---|---|---|
| 68534 | Ten Little Bottles | Pathe 20458 |
| 68535 | Lonesome Alimony Blues | Pathe 20466 |
| 68536 | The Body's Upstairs | - |
| 68537 | I'm On Strike | Pathe 20458 |
| 68538 | You'n Me | Pathe 20473 |
| 68539 | The Broadway Blues | - |

New York, c. October, 1920.

| | | |
|---|---|---|
| 68679 | I Want To Spread A Little Sunshine | Pathe 20462 |
| | ("My Lady Friends") | |
| 68680 | Orange Blossom Time | - |

New York, March, 1921.

| | | |
|---|---|---|
| 69137 | Singin' The Blues ('Till My Daddy Comes | PA 020553, 10138 |
| | Home) | |
| 69138 | Vamping Rose | PA 020535 |
| 69139 | Ain't We Got Fun ? | PA 020553, 10138 |
| 69140 | My Old New Jersey Home | PA 020535 |

New York, c. March 31, 1922.

| | | |
|---|---|---|
| 42243-1 | People Like Us | Re 9216 |
| 42244-1 | A Sleepy Little Village (Where The | - |
| | Dixie Cotton Grows) | |

## RAMON  NOVARRO

B. Durango, Mexico, February 6, 1899; r.n. Ramon Gil Samaniegos; a revolution   in 1913 wiped out his family fortunes, and he and one of his many brothers went  to Los Angeles, where he experienced hard times until he secured a part in THE PRI- SONER OF ZENDA (1922), establishing him as a film actor.  The same year he  made SCARAMOUCHE; then followed THE MIDSHIPMAN (1925); BEN HUR (1926); THE    STUDENT PRINCE (1927), among many other silents; talkies include THE PAGAN (1929); DEVIL MAY CARE and CALL OF THE FLESH (1930); MATA HARI (with Greta Garbo) (1932);  THE BARBARIAN and A NIGHT IN CAIRO (1933); LAUGHING BOY and THE CAT AND THE   FIDDLE (1934); THE NIGHT IS YOUNG (1935); to London to appear in A ROYAL EXCHANGE  (His Majesty's, December 6, 1935); returned to Hollywood and resumed film career with THE SHEIK STEPS OUT (1937); DESPERATE ADVENTURE (1938); WE WERE STRANGERS (1949), with Jennifer Jones and John Garfield; CRISIS (1950) with Cary Grant; HELLER  IN PINK TIGHTS (1960); never married; found murdered in his Hollywood home at   the end of December, 1969.

Vocal, acc. by O/Clifford Greenwood.    London, September 16, 1935.

| | | |
|---|---|---|
| 2EA-2200-1 | Ramon Novarro Medley - Part 1 | HMV C-2778 |
| | (Intro. Love Songs Of The Nile (Film "A Night In Cairo")/Lonely(Film | |
| | "Call Of The Flesh")/Pagan Love Song (Film "The Pagan") | |
| 2EA-2401-1 | Ramon Novarro Medley - Part 2 | - |
| | (Intro. Charming/Shepherd's Serenade (both film "Devil May Care")/The | |
| | Night Is Young (Film "The Night Is Young") | |

London, March 23, 1936.

| | | |
|---|---|---|
| OEA-2724-2 | Long Ago In Alcala | HMV B-8426 |
| OEA-2725-2 | El Relicario | - |

## DONALD NOVIS

B. 1906; very popular tenor on radio, in a few musicals such as JUMBO, his biggest hit, at the New York Hippodrome (November 16, 1935); began professional   career as vocalist with various dance orchestras (see below), then appeared in   films; retired in 1963 after a run of 11,000 performances at the Golden Horseshoe, Dis- neyland.  D. Norwalk, Calif., July 23, 1966.

Vocal, acc. by O/Marie Golden.          Culver City, Calif., November 11, 1929.

PBVE-54501-3  Alone In The Rain              Vic 22286, HMV B-3362
PBVE-54502-3  Molly                                     -

Vocalist with George Olsen and his Music. Culver City, Calif., March 19, 1930.

PBVE-54718-2  Song Of The Dawn                Vic 22370

Vocalist with Gus Arnheim and his Cocoanut Grove Orchestra.
                                    Hollywood, May 15, 1931.

PBVE-61093-   To Whisper, Dear, I Love You     Vic 22702

                                    Hollywood, July 6, 1931.

PBVE-61095-2  Just One More Chance            Vic 22758
PBVE-61096-1  At Your Command                          -

                                    Hollywood, July 19, 1931.

PBVE-61099-   Sweet And Lovely                Vic 22770

Vocalist with Jimmie Grier and his Cocoanut Grove Orchestra.
                                    Hollywood, March 28, 1932.

PBS-68346-1   One Hour With You               Vic 22971
PBS-68348-2   Music In The Moonlight                 -        HMV B-6201
PBS-68349-1   Bon Voyage To Your Ship Of Dreams   Vic 22970, HMV B-6206

Vocal, acc. by O/Ray Heindorff-p.       Hollywood, May 11, 1932.

PBS-68356-2   (In The Gloaming) By The Fireside   Vic 24020
PBS-68357-2   Deep In Your Eyes               Vic 24021, HMV B-4226
PBS-68358-2   The Voice In The Old Village Choir     -           -
PBS-68359-2   Goodnight, My Love              Vic 24020

Acc. by O/Leonard Joy.                  New York, July 14, 1932.

BS-73114-1    Somewhere In The West           Vic 24071
BS-73115-1    As You Desire Me

Acc. by O/Victor Young.                 New York, January 26, 1933.

B-12987-A     Rock-a-Bye Moon
B-12988-A     The Whisper Waltz               Br 6489, 01514
B-12989-A     Trees                                  -        -
B-12990-A     The Rosary                      Br 6538, 01453
                                                     -        -

                                    New York, April 20, 1933.

B-13268-      When The Sun Bids The Moon Goodnight   Br 6557
B-13271-      I Lay Me Down To Sleep                    -
NOTE:- Matrices B-13269/70 are not by Donald Novis.

Vocalist with Paul Whiteman and his Orchestra.
                                    New York, March 10, 1936.

BS-99444-1    My Romance (w/Gloria Grafton) ("Jumbo")Vic 25269
                                                     -
Vocal, acc. by Eddie Dunstedter-Pipe organ.
                                    Los Angeles, April 20, 1938.

DLA-1260-A    Diane
DLA-1261-A    Alice Blue Gown                 Dec 2047, F-6842
DLA-1262-A    Angela Mia (My Angel)                  -        -
DLA-1263-A    Charmaine                       Dec 1833, F-6722
                                                     -        -

DONALD NOVIS (cont.)

Los Angeles, August 12, 1938.

| | | |
|---|---|---|
| DLA-1396-A | At Dawning | Dec 2101, F-6921 |
| DLA-1397-A | Oh, Promise Me | - - |
| DLA-1398-A | Trees | Dec 2186, F-6953 |
| DLA-1399-A | The Song Of Songs | - - |

## JACK OAKIE

B. Sedalia, Mo., November 14, 1903; r.n. Lewis D. Offield; began career as clerk in Wall Street brokers' office, but found amateur theatricals more interesting; took up partnership in vaudeville act, eventually obtained a small part in 1927 silent (FINDERS KEEPERS, with Laura La Plante); subsequent films include SWEETIE (1929, with Helen Kane); PARAMOUNT ON PARADE (1930); MILLION DOLLAR LEGS and IF I HAD A MILLION (1932); TOO MUCH HARMONY and COLLEGE HUMOUR (1933, both with Bing Crosby); MURDER AT THE VANITIES; SHOOT THE WORKS; LOOKING FOR TROUBLE (with Spencer Tracy) and COLLEGE RHYTHM (1934); THE BIG BROADCAST OF 1936; FLORIDA SPECIAL; THE TEXAS RANGERS (1936); THE TOAST OF NEW YORK (1937); THANKS FOR EVERYTHING (1938); RISE AND SHINE (1939); THE GREAT DICTATOR (1940, with Charles Chaplin); FOOTLIGHT SERENADE and SONG OF THE ISLANDS (1942); ON STAGE EVERYBODY (1945); WHEN MY BABY SMILES AT ME (1948, with Betty Grable); AROUND THE WORLD IN 80 DAYS (1956); THE WONDERFUL COUNTRY (1959); THE RAT RACE (1960); LOVER COME BACK (1962).

Humorous monologue.                         Camden, N. J., July 10, 1930.

BVE-62676-1-2 Let's Go Native            Vic rejected

Vocal, acc. by studio orchestra.        Los Angeles, October 24, 1934.

| | | |
|---|---|---|
| LA-253- | Take A Number From One To Ten (Film "College Rhythm") | Mt M-13236 |
| LA-254- | College Rhythm (Film "College Rhythm") | - |

Los Angeles, July 12, 1935.

| | | |
|---|---|---|
| LA-1057- | Miss Brown To You (Film "The Big Broadcast of 1936") | ARC 35-10-01 |

Los Angeles, July 16, 1935.

| | | |
|---|---|---|
| LA-1061- | Why Dream ? (Film "The Big Broadcast of 1936") | ARC 35-10-01 |

## WILL OAKLAND

B. Jersey City, N. J., January 15, 1880; r.n. Herman Hinrichs; counter-tenor, with the highest male voice ever heard on the stage. Began professionally in 1904, in vaudeville, minstrel troupes, radio, night-clubs, TV; sang on TV until shortly before his death (in a bus en route to Newark, N. J., May 15, 1956).

Vocal, acc. by studio orchestra.       New York, c. May, 1908.

When The Autumn Moon Is Creeping Thru'    Ed 9902
    The Woodlands

New York, c. August, 1908.

When You And I Were Young, Maggie      Ed 9980
Silver Threads Among The Gold         Ed 4M-47, Amb 1547

New York, c. October, 1908.

There Is No Love Like Mine         Ed 4M-107.

New York, c. November, 1908.

The Longest Way Round Is The Sweetest    Ed 4M-145
    Way Home

New York, c. December, 1908.

Only A Pansy Blossom                          Ed 51536, 4M-170, Amb 1778

Acc. by O/? Walter B. Rogers.          New York, February 19, 1909.

B-6822-1  When You And I Were Young, Maggie      Vic 5682, 16666
B-6823-1-2  Silver Threads Among The Gold        Rejected

Acc. by studio orchestra.          New York, c. February, 1909.

      While The Kids Play Ring-a-Rosie          Ed 4M-190
      Dearie                                    Ed 4M-201

Acc. by O/? Walter B. Rogers.          New York, March 10, 1909.

B-6823-3  Silver Threads Among The Gold         Vic 5691, 16786
B-6870-2  When The Autumn Moon Is Creeping Thro'  Vic 16376
      The Woodlands
B-6871-1-2  When The Winter Days Are Over        Rejected
B-6872-1  The Longest Way Round Is The Sweetest  Vic 16310
      Way Home

Acc. by studio orchestra.          New York, c. March, 1909.

      If I Only Had A Home, Sweet Home          Ed 4M-227

                              New York, c. April, 1909.
      Nobody Knows, Nobody Cares               Ed 10163
      Won't You Come Over To My House ?        Ed 4M-239

                              New York, c. June, 1909.
      Dear Old Dear                            Ed 10187
      I'm Tired Of Living Without You          Ed 10203
      Just Before The Battle, Mother           Ed 4M-297, Amb 1516

                              New York, c. July, 1909.

      In The Gloaming                          Ed 4M-320

Acc. by O/? Walter B. Rogers.          New York, August 13, 1909.

B-6870-3  When The Autumn Moon Is Creeping Thro'  Vic 16376
      The Woodlands
B-6871-3-4  When The Winter Days Are Over        Rejected
B-8146-2-3  I'm Tired Of Living Without You      Vic 16439
B-8147-1  White Wings                          Vic 16355

Acc. by studio orchestra.          New York, c. August, 1909.

      We've Been Chums For Fifty Years          Ed 10245

                              New York, c. September, 1909.

      Ring Me Up Heaven, Please Central         Ed 10263

                              New York, c. December, 1909.

      When You And I Were Young, Maggie         Ed 4M-454, Amb 1873

                              New York, c. January, 1910.

      Who Will Care For Mother Now ?            Ed 4M-475, Amb 3128

                              New York, c. February, 1910.

      If This Rose Told You All That It Knows   Ed 4M-503
        (w/William Thompson)
      If Dreams Are True                        Ed 4M-511

New York, c. March, 1910.

When The Robins Nest Again                    Ed 4M-537

Acc. by O/? Walter B. Rogers.        New York, May 6, 1910.

B-8920-1  Only A Pansy Blossom              Vic 16496
B-8921-1-2  My Wild Irish Rose              Rejected
B-8922-1-2  The Story Of The Rose           -

Acc. by studio orchestra.            New York, c. May, 1910.

Mack's Lullaby                               Ed 10401

Acc. by O/? Walter B. Rogers.        New York, July 12, 1910.

B-9161-2  In The Gloaming (w/American Quartet)   Vic 16646, 16928
B-9162-1-2  Who Will Care For Mother Now ?       Rejected
B-9163-2  Wait 'Till The Clouds Roll By          Vic 16608, 16928
B-9164-1-2  Mack's Lullaby                       Rejected
C-9165-2  When The Robins Nest Again             Vic 35126

Acc. by studio orchestra.            New York, c. July, 1910.

You Can't Make Me Stop Loving You        Ed 10418
I'll Await My Love                       Ed 10431

Bonnie Sweet Bessie                      USE 1094

New York, c. August, 1910.

I Wonder How The Old Folks Are At Home  Ed 10439

My Wild Irish Rose                       USE 1109

New York, c. September, 1910.

There's A Clock Upon The Mantel          Ed 10447
   Striking One-Two-Three
My Old Lady                              Ed 4M-557

Mother Machree                           USE 1132
I Love The Name Of Mary                  USE 1133

Gee, But It's Great To Meet A Friend     USE 346
   From Your Home Town (w/W. H. Thompson)
Somebody Loves You, Dear                 USE 1139

New York, c. October, 1910.

Dear Old Ma                                       Ed 10461
My Wild Irish Rose (w/William Thompson)  Ed 4M-567
Mother Machree                                    Ed 4M-583

Only A Pansy Blossom                     USE 1149
When The Autumn Moon Is Creeping         USE 1151
   Through The Woodland
Who Will Care For Mother Now ?           USE 1152
Won't You Come Over To My House ?        USE 1156
You've Changed The Winter Of My Heart    USE 1159
   To Glad Springtime

Acc. by O/? Walter B. Rogers.        New York, November 15, 1910.

B-9650-1-2  Mother Machree                        Rejected
B-9651-2  Eileen Alannah                          Vic 16701
B-9652-1-2  The Star, The Rose And The Dream      Rejected

Acc. by studio orchestra.                    New York, c. November, 1910.

    There's A Light In The Window          Ed 10473

    Poverty's Tears Ebb And Flow            USE 1169

Acc. by O/? Charles A. Prince.                New York, November 29, 1910.

19133-  I Love The Name Of Mary                 Col A-969, 1792
19134-  The Longest Way Round Is The Sweetest      -      1708, Re G-7366
    Way Home


                    New York, December 30, 1910.

19178-  Goodnight, Beloved, Goodnight           Col A-980, 1723
19179-  I'll Change The Thorns To Roses            -      1708, Re G-7366

Acc. by studio orchestra.                    New York, c. December, 1910.

    Old Popular Songs Medley                USE 1184


                    New York, c. January, 1911.

    Where The River Shannon Flows            Ed 4M-623

    You Can't Make Me Stop Loving You        USE 1232

Acc. by O/? Walter B. Rogers.                 New York, February 10, 1911.

19234-  When The Swallows Homeward Fly           Col A-993, 1723
19235-  Poverty's Tears Ebb And Flow               -      1792

Acc. by studio orchestra.                    New York, c. February, 1911.

    On Mobile Bay (w/John Bieling-William F. Ed 10495
      Hooley-Steve Porter)
    Peek-a-Boo                              Ed 4M-651

    It's A Long Way Back To Dear Old        USE 1248
      Mother's Knee
    Think It Over, Mary                     USE 1253
    Emmett's Lullaby                        USE 1255

Acc. by O/? Charles A. Prince.                New York, March 9, 1911.

19255-  The Lass From County Mayo               Col A-1002, 2431, Re G-7377
19256-  You Can't Make Me Stop Loving You          -       -        -

Acc. by studio orchestra.                    New York, c. March, 1911.

    Rock Me To Sleep, Mother                Ed 4M-681

    Wait Till The Clouds Roll By            Ind 1467
    Only A Pansy Blossom                    Ind 3209
    Belle Brandon                           Ind 3211
    The Longest Way Round Is The Sweetest   Ind 3217
      Way Home
    Silver Threads Among The Gold           Ind 3223

    Just One Word Of Consolation            USE 1267

Acc. by O/? Charles A. Prince.                New York, April 7, 1911.

19269-  Only A Pansy Blossom                    Col A-1007, 2058, Re G-7371
19270-  It's A Long Way Back To Dear Old           -       1927, Re G-7369
    Mother's Knee


                    New York, April 25, 1911.

19308-  I'll Await My Love                      Col A-1017, 2171, Re G-7373
19309-  We're Growing Old Together                 -       -        -

Acc. by studio orchestra.                    New York, c. April, 1911.

    Wait Till The Clouds Roll By              Ed 4M-711

    Wanted, A Harp Like The Angels Play       USE 1283

                               New York, c. May, 1911.

    Pretty Pond Lilies                        Ed 4M-749
    In All My Dreams, I Dream Of You          Ed 4M-752

Acc. by O/? Charles A. Prince.                New York, June 15, 1911.

19408-  White Wings                           Col A-1093, 1889, Re G-7368
19409-  Just One Word Of Consolation          Col A-1077, 1927, Re G-7369

Acc. by studio orchestra.                    New York, c. June, 1911.

    Wanted, A Harp Like The Angels Play       Ed 4M-773
    Stick To Your Mother, Tom                 Ed 4M-783, Amb 2380

    Take This Letter To My Mother             USE 1318
    When The Kids Played Ring-a-Rosie         USE 1319

Acc. by O/Charles A. Prince.                  New York, July 12, 1911.

19456-  Peek-a-Boo                            Col A-1145, 1821, Re G-7367
19457-  Baby Mine                             -       -          -
19459-  Take This Letter To My Mother         Col A-1077, 2058, Re G-7371

                               New York, July 17, 1911.

19460-  Only To See Her Face Again            Col A-1093, 1889, Re G-7368
NOTE:- Matrix 19458 is by Prince's Orchestra on the same date as 19456/7/9.

Acc. by studio orchestra.                    New York, c. July, 1911.

    Wanted, A Harp Like The Angels Play       Ed 10517
    I'll Remember You, Love, In My Prayers    Ed 4M-808

    Nora Acushla                              USE 1326

                               New York, c. August, 1911.

    Only To See Her Face Again                Ed 4M-819, Amb 1947

                               New York, c. October, 1911.

    Eileen Alannah                            Ed 10532

                               New York, c. January, 1912.

    With All Her Faults, I Love Her Still      USE 1446

                               New York, c. February, 1912.

    Molly Darling                             Ed 4M-963

    Sweet Genevieve (w/W. H. Thompson)        USE 1484
    My Sweetheart's The Man In The Moon       USE 1485
      (w/W. H. Thompson)
    Say "Au Revoir" (w/W. H. Thompson)        USE 1493
    Where The River Shannon Flows (w/W. H.    USE 1495
      Thompson)

Acc. by O/? Charles A. Prince.                New York, March 16, 1912.

19817-  When The Robins Nest Again            Col A-1183, 2161, Re G-7372
19818-  Mother Machree                        Col A-1204   -        -
(continued on page 511)

New York, March 16, 1912 (cont.)

| | | |
|---|---|---|
| 19819- | Wait Till The Clouds Roll By, Jennie | Col A-1183, 1995. Re G-7370 |
| 19820- | We've Been Chums For Fifty Years | Col A-1204 - - |

Acc. by studio orchestra.      New York, c. March, 1912.

Say "Au Revoir" But Not "Goodbye"      Ed 4M-1022, Amb 1911

New York, c. April, 1912.

As I Sat Upon My Dear Old Mother's Knee   Ind 3314

The Girl I'll Call My Sweetheart Must    USE 1519
   Look Like You

New York, c. May, 1912.

Goodbye Rose                           USE 1531
The Lass From County Mayo          USE 1532

Acc. by O/? Walter B. Rogers.      New York, June 7, 1912.

| | | |
|---|---|---|
| B-12085-1 | 'Way Down South (w/American Quartet) | Vic 17146 |
| B-12086-1 | Emmett's Lullaby (w/American Quartet) | Vic 17217 |

New York, July 11, 1912.

| | | |
|---|---|---|
| B-12179-1-2 | When The Rainbow Shines Bright At Morn (w/American Quartet) | Rejected |
| B-12180-1 | On A Beautiful Night With A Beautiful Girl (w/American Quartet) | Vic 17152 |
| B-12181-2 | Waiting For The Robert E. Lee (w/ American Quartet) | Vic 17141 |

NOTE:- Victor 17141 and 17152 as HEIDELBERG QUINTET; no reference to Will    Oakland on the labels.

New York, July 26, 1912.

| | | |
|---|---|---|
| B-12085-4 | 'Way Down South (w/American Quartet) | Vic 17146 |
| B-12241-2 | My Little Lovin' Sugar Baby (w/American Quartet) | Vic 17236 |
| B-12242-2 | Tennessee Moon (w/American Quartet) | Vic 17207 |

NOTE:- Victor 17146, 17207 and 17236 as HEIDELBERG QUINTET; again, no   reference to Will Oakland.

Acc. by studio orchestra.      New York, c. July, 1912.

With All Her Faults, I Love Her Still   Ed 4M-1124

Where The Silvery Colorado Wends Its    USE 1561
   Way

Acc. by O/Charles A. Prince.      New York, August 2, 1912.

| | | |
|---|---|---|
| 38172- | With All Her Faults, I Love Her Still | Col A-1306, 2212, Re G-7374 |
| 38173- | As I Sat Upon My Dear Old Mother's Knee | - - - |

Acc. by studio orchestra.      New York, c. August, 1912.

Under The Love Tree (as by Heidelberg    Ed 4M-1131
   Quintet)
'Way Down South (as by Heidelberg Qt.)   Amb 1531
I Want To Love You While The Music's    Amb 1565
   Playing (as by Heidelberg Quintet)

New York, c. September, 1912.

Nora Acushla                        Ed 4M-1157, Amb 1569
I'll Wait At The Golden Gate For You    Ed D-2

New York, c. October, 1912.

Dear Robin, I'll Be True                     Amb 1580

New York, c. January, 1913.

You're Just As Sweet At Sixty As You        Amb 1746
    Were At Sweet Sixteen

Acc. by O/Charles A. Prince.          New York, April 21, 1913.

38800-  Emmett's Lullaby                Col A-1468, 2383, Re G-7376

New York, April 22, 1913.

38801-  A Garland Of Old-Fashioned Roses    Col A-1370, 2296, Re G-7375
38802-  You're Just As Sweet At Sixty As You Col A-1468    -        -
        Were At Sweet Sixteen
38803-  Pretty Pond Lilies                   Col A-1370, 2383, Re G-7376

Acc. by O/? Walter B. Rogers.         New York, May 29, 1913.

B-13369-1-2-3  That Tinkling Tango (w/American    Vic rejected
               Quartet)
B-13371-1-2  Boom-Tum-Ta-Ra-Zing-Boom (w/American       -
             Quartet)
    NOTE:- Matrix B-13370 is by the American Quartet, without Will Oakland.

Acc. by studio orchestra.             New York, c. May, 1913.

        Emmett's Lullaby                     Amb 1923

Acc. by O/? Walter B. Rogers.         New York, June 13, 1913.

B-13369-4-5-6  That Tinkling Tango (w/American    Rejected
               Quartet)
B-13424-2  The Curse Of An Aching Heart           Vic 17372,
B-13426-1  In The Heart Of The Kentucky Hills     Vic 17378
           (w/American Quartet)
    NOTE:- Will Oakland does not sing on matrix B-13425; Victor 17378 as   HEIDELBERG
QUINTET.

Acc. by studio orchestra.             New York, c. June, 1913.

        The Curse Of An Aching Heart          Amb 2022
        There's A Mother Always Waiting For You  Amb 2030
            At Home, Sweet Home

New York, c. July, 1913.

        Dear Old Girl                         Amb 2075

New York, c. August, 1913.

        I'll Take You Home Again, Kathleen    Amb 2103

New York, c. September, 1913.

        My Mother's Old Red Shawl            Amb 2126

Acc. by O/? Walter B. Rogers.         New York, November 13, 1913.

B-14064-3  Dream Days                         Vic 17503
B-14065-3  Sing Rock-a-Bye Baby To Me        Vic 17518

New York, November 18, 1913.

B-14091-1  I'm On My Way To Mandalay (w/Henry    Vic 17503
           Burr-Albert Campbell)

New York, November 19, 1913.

B-14095-1-2-3  You Tell Me Your Dream, I'll Tell      Rejected
        You Mine (w/Billy Murray)
B-14096-1  Evalyne (w/Billy Murray)                   Vic 17518

   Acc. by studio orchestra.            New York, c. February, 1914.

       Sing Rock-a-Bye Baby To Me            Amb 2331

   Acc. by O/? Walter B. Rogers.        New York, June 24, 1914.

B-14996-1  Meet Me In Blossom Time (w/Henry Burr-  Vic 17629
        Albert Campbell)
B-14997-2  Dear Love Days (w/Henry Burr-Albert       Vic 17789
        Campbell)
B-14998-3  Everything Reminds Me Of That Old         Vic 17697
        Sweetheart Of Mine

   Acc. by O/Charles A. Prince, as THE LYRIC TRIO (w/Henry Burr-Albert Campbell).
                 New York, June 29, 1914.

39467-     Dear Love Days                             Col A-1577
39468-     Everything  Reminds Me Of That Old         Col A-1684
        Sweetheart Of Mine

   Acc. by studio orchestra.            New York, c. June, 1914.

       Ma Pickaninny Babe                    Amb 2416

   Acc. by O/? Walter B. Rogers.        New York, July 6, 1914.

B-15042-1-2-3  In The Town Where I Was Born          Rejected
        (w/Billy Murray)
B-15043-2  Ma Pickaninny Babe (w/Billy Murray)       Vic 17819
B-15044-2  Just For Tonight (w/Billy Murray)         Vic 17622

                 New York, July 7, 1914.

B-8143-3  White Wings                                Vic 16355
B-15046-1-2  Belle Brandon                           Rejected
B-15047-1-2-3  When You're Away From Home            -

   Acc. by studio orchestra.            New York, c. 1914-1915.

       Take This Letter To My Mother         Amb 3097

   Acc. by O/Theodore Levy.             New York, June 4, 1915.

B-16071-1  Old-Time Song Medley (Intro. When The   Vic 17823
        Robins Nest Again/My Mother's Old Red Shawl/White Wings/Stick To  Your
        Mother, Tom/Wait Till The Clouds Roll By)
B-16075-1  When It's Moonlight In Mayo (Two Irish  Vic 17819
        Eyes Are Shining)

   Acc. by O/Walter B. Rogers.          Camden, N. J., February 11, 1916.

B-17144-1-2-3  Mother's Old Sweet Lullaby            Rejected
B-17145-1  Norah Acushla                             Vic 18011
B-17146-3  Sighing                                   Vic 17984
B-17147-2  Good Luck, God Bless You (Is All I Can Say) -

               Camden, N. J., March 1, 1916.

B-17239-1-2-3  Oh Promise Me That You'll Come        Vic rejected
        Back To Alabama (w/Billy Murray)

              Camden, N. J., March 13, 1916.

B-17144-4-5-6-7  Mother's Old Sweet Lullaby          Vic rejected
B-17239-4-5-6  Oh Promise Me That You'll Come Back   -
        To Alabama (w/Billy Murray)

Camden, N. J., June 8, 1916.

B-17144-8-9-10  Mother's Old Sweet Lullaby        Vic rejected

  Acc. by O/Rosario Bourdon.        New York, December 8, 1916.

B-18779-1-2-3  Ireland, My Ireland               Vic rejected

  Acc. by studio orchestra.        New York, c. November, 1917.

| | | |
|---|---|---|
| Mother's Old Sweet Lullaby (w/chorus) | Ed 50481, Amb 3472 | |
| My Irish Song Of Songs | Ed 51536, Amb 3484 | |

New York, c. December, 1918.

6583    Dear Little Boy Of Mine             Ed 50526, Amb 3781
      Bring Back The Rose                 Ed 50506, Amb 3678

New York, c. March, 1919.

6682    That Wonderful Mother Of Mine       Ed 50526, 51210, Amb 3758
      That Tumbledown Shack In Athlone    Ed 50586, Amb 3876

New York, c. April, 1919.

622-B   When Ireland Comes Into Her Own     OK 1220
623-B   Peg Aroon                           -

New York, c. May, 1920.

7403-   Norah Acushla                       OK 4176

New York, March 29, 1926.

141881-   Let's Grow Old Together           Har 162-H
141882-   Gone                              -

## GEORGE O'CONNOR

B. Washington, D.C., August 20, 1874; trained as lawyer, but became comedian in minstrel shows in the 1890s.  He was a favourite entertainer of successive Presidents
of the U.S.A.  D. Washington, D.C., September 28, 1946.

Vocal, acc. unknown.        New York, February 21, 1914.

B-14504-1  'Tain't No Disgrace To Run When You're  Vic Personal Recording
        Skeered
B-14505-1  Oh Lord, These Feet Of Mine             -

  Acc. by O/Charles A. Prince.        New York, November 27, 1914.

39649-    The Mississippi Barbecue          Col A-1669

New York, November 30, 1914.

39650-    Alabama Jamboree                  Col A-1669

New York, January 22, 1915.

39790-    At The Mississippi Cabaret        Col rejected
39791-    Roaming Around                    -

New York, February 10, 1915.

39842-    Everybody Rag With Me             Col A-1706
39843-    On My Way To New Orleans          -

New York, May 22, 1915.

45677-    Hop A Jitney With Me              Col A-1768
45678-    Circus Day In Dixie               -

New York, July 26, 1915.

45881-  Gasoline Gus And His Jitney Bus             Col A-1806
45882-  I Guess I'll Soon Be Back In Dixieland      Col A-1901
45885-  Scaddle-De-Mooch                            Col A-1806
NOTE:- Matrices 45883/4 are not by George O'Connor.

New York, October 27, 1915.

46159-  I'm Homesick                                Col A-1870
46160-  These Feet Of Mine                          Col A-1901

New York, December 3, 1915.

46233-  Loading Up The Mandy Lee                    Col A-1911
46234-  I'm Gone                                    Col A-1980
46235-  P. S. - Mr. Johnson Sends Regards           Col A-1911

New York, March 20, 1916.

46654-  Oh, Joe, With Your Fiddle And Bow You       Col A-1980
          Stole My Heart Away
46655-  Come On To Nashville, Tennessee             Col A-2008

New York, July 18, 1916.

46920-  Nigger Blues                                Col A-2064
46921-  You Ain't No Relation Of Mine               Col A-2080
46922-2  I Ain't Prepared For That                  Col A-2124

New York, October 18, 1916.

47079-  Oh ! Southern City (Send Us Some            Col A-2127
          Beautiful Girls)
47080-  Pray For The Lights To Go Out               Col A-2143
47081-  Misery                                      Col A-2184

New York, February 10, 1917.

47362-  She's Dixie All The Time                    Col A-2210
47363-  Ephraham's Jazbo Band                       Col A-2211

New York, April 16, 1917.

47492-  They May Call You Hawaiian On Broadway      Col A-2441
          (But You're Just Plain Nigger To Me)
47493-  Ever Since That Town Of Mine Went Dry       Rejected
47494-  I Ain't Got Nobody (And Nobody Cares        Col A-2481
          For Me)

New York, June 8, 1917.

77123-  Sons Of America                             Col A-2294
77124-  Ain't You Coming Back To Dixieland ?        Col A-2293

New York, October 4, 1917.

77404-  Down Where The Sweet Potatoes Grow          Col A-2411
          (w/Columbia Quartet)
77405-  Down South Everybody's Happy                   -
77406-  There's Always Something Doin' Down In      Col A-2507
          Dixie

New York, November 9, 1917.

77503-  Everybody's Crazy 'Bout The Doggone         Col A-2481
          Blues, But I'm Happy

New York, January 12, 1918.

77629-    It Makes No Diff'rence Whose Sweetie      Rejected
          You Were
77630-    Jazzin' The Cotton Town Blues            Col A-2507

## GEOFFREY O'HARA

An early collector of native American Indian songs, appointed in 1914 by the  U. S.
    Government as Instructor in the subject, who lived among the Navajo for some time
    and served as an organizer of entertainments for service personnel in World War I.
    He was also composer of such very different styles of songs as the absurd but ex-
    tremely popular K-K-K-KATY (1918) and THERE IS NO DEATH (1919); began his  career
    as a musician with various concert groups singing sacred music (some of which was
    recorded - for Zonophone in 1905 as the Criterion Quartet - but which is  outside
    the scope of this book).  D. 1955.

Vocal, as member of the Knickerbocker Quartet.
                                    New York, issued August, 1905.

        The Rosary                              Ed 9052

Vocal, acc. by tom-tom.              New York, July 14, 1914.

B-15063-3  Navajo Indian Song                   Vic 17635

                                    New York, c. August, 1914.

        Navajo Indian Songs                     Amb 2451

    Acc. by O/Walter B. Rogers.      Camden, N. J., March 29, 1916.

B-17397-2  Dixieland, My Home                   Vic 18024
B-17398-3  All I Want Is A Cottage, Some Roses  Vic 18022
          And You

    Acc. by O/Charles A. Prince.     New York, April 20, 1916.

46728-    There's Someone More Lonesome Than You  Col rejected

    Acc. by O/Rosario Bourdon.       New York, May 2, 1916.

B-17590-1  Where The Shamrock Grows             Vic 18053
B-17591-1  They Made It Twice As Nice As Paradise  Vic 18051
          (And They Called It Dixieland)

                                    New York, September 29, 1916.

B-18518-1  Ma Li'l Starlight (w/Marguerite Dunlap, Vic 18166
          as Lillian Davis)
B-18519-2  I'll Make You Want Me (w/Marguerite           -
          Dunlap, as Lillian Davis)

                                    New York, September 10, 1917.

B-20653-1-2-3  Send Me A Curl                   Rejected
B-20654-2  The South Will Do Her Part           Vic 18391

    Acc. by O/Joseph Pasternack.     New York, February 5, 1918.

B-20653-6  Send Me A Curl                       Vic 18441

    Acc. by O/Rosario Bourdon.       New York, February 20, 1918.

B-21461-1-2-3  Parodies Of The Camp             Vic rejected
B-21462-1-2-3  A Soldier's Day                          -

                                    New York, April 18, 1918.

B-21461-5  Parodies Of The Camp                 Vic 18451
B-21462-5  A Soldier's Day                              -

Camden, N. J., September 3, 1918.

B-22218-1-2-3  When It's Peach Jam Makin' Time    Vic rejected
B-22219-1-2-3  Over Yonder Where The Lilies Grow      -

Camden, N. J., October 3, 1918.

B-22219-4-5-6-7  Over Yonder Where The Lilies Grow Vic rejected

Camden, N. J., May 5, 1919.

B-22829-1-2-3  You're Making A Miser Of Me          Vic rejected

Acc. by O/Theodore Levy.          Camden, N. J., December 4, 1923.

B-29059-1-2-3-4-5  Leetle Bateese                   Vic rejected

Acc. by own piano.             New York, May 22, 1929.

BVE-643   Give A Man A Horse He Can Ride          Vic test

## WALTER O'KEEFE

B. Hartford, Conn., August 18, 1900; served in U.S. Marine Corps in World War I, and turned to entertaining in night clubs and vaudeville during the 1920s; own show on radio for many years; composed THE MAN ON THE FLYING TRAPEZE and THE TATTOOED LADY amongst others.

Vocal, acc. by Wayne R. Euchner-p/Perry Botkin-g.
                              New York, March 14, 1928.

BVE-43361-1-2-3  Was Last Night The Last Night    Vic rejected
                   With You ?
BVE-43362-1-2-3  You've Got A Lot To Learn            -

New York, April 3, 1928.

BVE-43528-1-2  Henry's Made A Lady Out Of Lizzie  Vic rejected

New York, April 16, 1928.

BVE-43568-1-2  Maybe It's All For The Best         Rejected
BVE-43569-1-2  Sorry For Me                          -
BVE-43570-5  I'm Lookin' For A Girl                Vic 21436
BVE-43571-1-2-3  Gee ! I'm Marvelous In The        Rejected
                   Bathroom

New York, May 2, 1928.

BVE-43569-4-5-6  Sorry For Me                       Rejected
BVE-43571-6  Gee ! I'm Marvelous In The Bathroom  Vic 21436

Acc. by p/g (same as above ?)      New York, November 12, 1928.

BVE-48150-1-2-3  Ever Since The Movies Learned    Vic rejected
                   To Talk

Acc. by O/? Leonard Joy.          New York, December 3, 1928.

BVE-48422-1-2-3  Me And The Man In The Moon       Vic rejected
BVE-48423-1-2-3  My Inspiration Is You                -

Acc. by O/Jack Shilkret.          New York, October 13, 1932.

BS-73809-1  The Man On The Flying Trapeze - Part 1 Vic 24172, HMV B-8050
BS-73810-1  The Man On The Flying Trapeze - Part 2     -            -

Acc. by vm/pac/p/g.                    New York, September 27, 1933.

BS-77988-1  The Tattooed Lady - Part 1           Vic 24416
BS-77989-1  The Tattooed Lady - Part 2              -

Acc. by studio orchestra.              New York, October 26, 1934.

16238-A  The Gambler's Wife                  Br 7408, Dec F-5541
16276-   Father Put The Cow Away               -
16277-   The Bearded Lady                    Br 7336
16278-A  Always A Bridesmaid                   -        Dec F-5541
NOTE:- Matrices 16239/16275 inclusive are not by Walter O'Keefe.

## CHAUNCEY  OLCOTT

B. Providence, R.I., July 21, 1857; began professional career as a minstrel with the
Alabama Serenaders on February 21, 1876; he remained in various minstrel companies
(London debut with Haverley's Mastodons at Drury Lane, July 31, 1880) for a little
over ten years, becoming a solo performer, composer and actor; appeared in musical
shows to which he contributed some songs (BARRY OF BALLYMORE, 1910; THE HEART   OF
PADDY WHACK, 1914, and others); d. Monte Carlo, March 18, 1932.

Vocal, acc. by studio orchestra.       New York, January 5, 1906.

B-2985-1  My Wild Irish Rose                   Vic rejected
B-2986-1  My Beautiful Irish Maid                -

Acc. by O/Charles A. Prince.           New York, February 25, 1913.

38656-2  When Irish Eyes Are Smiling ("Isle Of   Col A-1310
            Dreams")
38657-1  My Wild Irish Rose                  Col A-1308, Re G-6267
38658-1-2  Sweet Inniscarra                  Col A-1309

                                       New York, February 26, 1913.

38659-1  Molly-O                            Col A-1309
38660-1  Mother Machree ("Barry Of Mallymore")   Col A-1337

                                       New York, February 27, 1913.

38662-2  My Beautiful Irish Maid             Col A-1337
38663-1  I Used To Believe In Fairies        Col A-1308
38664-1  I Love The Name Of Mary             Col A-1310

                                       New York, June 20, 1913.

38913-   Where The River Shannon Flows       Col rejected
38914-   Isle Of Dreams ("Isle Of Dreams")     -
38915-   In The Garden Of My Heart             -

                                       New York, July 30, 1913.

38968-1  Too-Ra-Loo-Ra-Loo-Ral (That's An Irish  Col A-1410
            Lullaby)
38969-1  Peggy Darlin'                      Col A-1411
38970-1  Me Little Dudeen                      -
38974-   I Never Met Before A Girl Like You      Rejected
NOTE:- Matrices 38971/3 inclusive are not by Chauncey Olcott.

                                       New York, August 2, 1913.

38983-1  Dream Girl Of Mine                 Col A-1410

                                       New York, June 29, 1920.

79320-2  That's How The Shannon Flows ("Macushla")Col A-3525
79321-2  'Tis An Irish Girl I Love And She's   Col A-2988
            Just Like You

New York, June 30, 1920.

79323-1   Macushla Asthore (Pulse Of My Heart)    Col A-2988
79324-2   I'll Miss You, Old Ireland, God Bless   Col A-3525
          You, Goodbye ("Macushla")

## OLSEN AND JOHNSON

John Siguard Olsen (b. Peru, Ind., November 6, 1892) and Chic Johnson (b. 1891) made
    one of the craziest comedy teams in the history of the American stage and   screen;
    formed partnership in 1915 after some years of vaudeville experience; they   toured
    the U.S.A., Australia and Great Britain through the 1920s, began making films    in
    1930 with OH, SAILOR, BEHAVE; then FIFTY MILLION FRENCHMEN (1931); biggest success
    on stage and screen was HELLZAPOPPIN (New York, 46th Street Theatre, September 22,
    1938, and filmed in 1942); also SONS O' FUN (Winter Garden, December 1, 1941); and
    LAFFIN' ROOM ONLY (Winter Garden, December 23, 1944).  Olsen died in 1965, Johnson
    in 1962.

Vocal, acc. by O/Spud Murphy, with the Four Belles.
                                   New York, c. May, 1940.

US-1716-1   Oh ! Gee, Oh ! Gosh, Oh ! Golly, I'm   Var 8308
              In Love
US-1718-1   My Heartzapoppin' ("Hellzapoppin'")       -

## ZELMA O'NEAL

B. Rock Falls, Ind., May 29, 1907; educated in Chicago, where she first appeared  on
    stage (as singer and dancer); in vaudeville on Orpheum circuit; New York debut  in
    GOOD NEWS (46th Street, September 6, 1927); London debut in the same show, opening
    the Carlton Theatre, August 15, 1928; returned to New York and starred in   FOLLOW
    THROUGH (46th Street, January 9, 1929); after some other New York and    Hollywood
    appearances, returned to London to play in NICE GOINGS ON (Strand, September    13,
    1933); JACK O'DIAMONDS (Gaiety, February 25, 1935); SWING ALONG (Gaiety, September
    2, 1936); subsequently retired to U.S.A.  Made several films, such as FREEDOM   OF
    THE SEAS; FOLLOW THROUGH; GIVE HER A RING (in Britain, 1934); MR. CINDERS, etc.

Vocal, acc. unknown.                    Camden, N. J., August 19, 1927.

          The 'Varsity Drag ("Good News")      Vic test (un-numbered)

Acc. by unknown piano.                  New York, c. March, 1928.

          The 'Varsity Drag ("Good News")        Br 3864, 3832
          Can't Help Lovin' Dat Man               -      -

Acc. by Al Goodman and his "Follow Through" Orchestra.
                                   New York, c. January 21, 1929.

E-29078-   Button Up Your Overcoat ("Follow       Br 4207
             Through")
E-29079-   I Want To Be Bad ("Follow Through")       -

Vocalist with Ben Bernie and his Hotel Roosevelt Orchestra.
                                   New York, February, 1929.

E-29130-   I Want To Be Bad ("Follow Through")     Br 4204, 5045

Vocal, acc. by Al Goodman and his Orchestra.
                                   New York, April, 1929.

E-29488-   What Didja Wanna Make Me Love You For ? Br 4330, 3999
E-29489-   Do Something                             -      -

E-29567-   I Got A "Code" In My "Doze"             Br 4322
E-29568-   I'm "Ka-Razy" For You                     -

                                   New York, August, 1929.
E-30592-   Do What You Do                          Br 4476
E-30594-   I've Made A Habit Of You                  -

B. Walkerville, Iowa, 1890; educated in Germany; stage debut at the Deutsche Opera-
House in Charlottenberg in OBERON; stayed in Germany two years; to New York, took
part in first performance of DER ROSENKAVALIER there; abandoned grand opera,  and
appeared in THE LILAC DOMINO (44th Street, October 28, 1914); then PRINCESS   PAT
(Cort, September 29, 1915); the successful revival of FLORADORA (Century, April 5,
1920); THE LAST WALTZ (Century, May 10, 1921); THE CHIFFON GIRL (Lyric, February
19, 1924); other shows also, including the part of Jenny Lind in THE  NIGHTINGALE
(Jolson, January, 1927).

Vocal, acc. by O/? Charles A. Prince.     New York, November 20, 1915.

46213-   Love Is Best Of All ("Princess Pat")     Col A-1937

                                          New York, November 26, 1915.

46226-   The Lilac Domino ("The Lilac Domino")     Col A-1937

## BEE PALMER

B. Chicago, c. 1898; introduced the Shimmy dance to New York in 1918 and was sensational; toured the Mid-West during the 1920s in vaudeville, singing popular songs
in a sensuous manner that shocked - or attracted; noted also for her accompanying
band being out-and-out jazz, and her pianist and husband the bandleader Al Siegel
(who appeared in London as a cabaret act in 1926 without his wife; her  accompanist on the first session below looks interesting !)

Vocal, acc. by C. Coolidge-p.            New York, May 15, 1918.

        When Alexander Takes His Ragtime Band    Vic test (un-numbered)
           To France

Acc. unknown.                            New York, June 3, 1918.

77869-   At Half-Past Nine                       Col rejected

Acc. by unknown vn/own p.          Camden, N. J., July 14, 1925.

        I'll See You In My Dreams                Vic test (un-numbered)
        Sweet Georgia Brown                         -
        The Bee Palmer Strut (g added; no vocal)    -

Acc. unknown.                            New York, May 10, 1928.

        I'm Coming, Virginia                      Vic test (un-numbered)

Acc. by Frankie Trumbauer and his Orchestra, presented by Paul Whiteman.
                                   New York, January 10, 1929.

147770-1-2-3  Don't Leave Me, Daddy              Col rejected
147771-1-2-3  Singin' The Blues                     -

## ISABELLA PATRICOLA

Vocal, acc. by studio orchestra.         New York, c. May, 1919.

        Ballyhoo Bay                             Pathe 22144
        Take Your Girlie To The Movies (If You      -
           Can't Make Love At Home)

                                         New York, c. September, 1919.

        Alexander's Band Is Back In Dixieland    Pathe 22218
        When Mariutch Shake-a Da Shimmie-Sha-Wob    -

New York, c. November, 1919.

All The Quakers Are Shoulder-Shakers     Pathe 22241
    Down In Quaker Town
The Vamp                                   -

New York, c. September, 1920.

68640    Pretty Kitty Kelly                Pathe 22405
68641    Since Mariella Learned The Dardanella    -

New York, c. November, 1920.

68784    Laughing Vamp                     Pathe 22448
68785 ?  Sweetie O' Mine                   -

New York, c. December, 1920.

68826    I Want To Go To The Land Where The    Pathe 22462
            Sweet Daddies Grow
68827    Nobody To Love                    -

New York, September, 1921.

69390    When Frances Dances With Me       PA 020639
69391    I Ain't Gonna Be Nobody's Fool    -

New York, c. September, 1921.

         I Ain't Gonna Be Nobody's Fool    Ed      , Amb 4444
         Little Min-Nee-Ha ! Ha !                  Amb 4468

Acc. by O/Joseph Pasternack.            Camden, N. J., November 22, 1921.

B-25772-1  Happy Hottentot               Vic 18838
B-25773-1-2-3-4  He's The Cat's Meow     Rejected
B-25776-1-2-3  You're A Good Old Car (But You    -
            Can't Climb Hills)
B-25777-4  I've Got My Habits On         Vic 18838
    NOTE:- Matrices B-25774/5 are not by Isabella Patricola.

Camden, N. J., November 25, 1921.

B-25778-1-2-3  Thrills                   Vic rejected
B-25779-1-2-3-4  Sally And Irene And Mary    -

Camden, N. J., October 3, 1922.

B-27000-2  All For The Love Of Mike      Vic 18967
B-27001-1-2-3  Hot Lips                  Rejected

Camden, N. J., October 6, 1922.

B-27001-7  Hot Lips                      Vic 18967

Acc. by the Virginians.                 New York, October 24, 1922.

B-26994-1-2-3  Lovin' Sam (The Sheik Of Alabam')  Vic rejected

New York, October 31, 1922.

B-26994-6  Lovin' Sam (The Sheik Of Alabam')    Vic 18976
B-27107-4  Away Down East In Maine       -

New York, December 20, 1922.

B-27246-3  When You And I Were Young Maggie    Vic 19010
            Blues (w/Billy Murray)

New York, December 27, 1922.

B-27262-1   Come On Home                        Vic 19010
B-27263-1   Runnin' Wild                        Vic 19027

New York, January 5, 1923.

B-27283-1-2-3-4-5  Aggravatin' Papa             Vic rejected

Acc. by studio orchestra.         New York, June, 1923.

11642      Oh, Sister ! Ain't That Hot ?        Voc 14623, Aco G-15289
11645      Stingo Stungo                             -          -
NOTE:- Aco as SADIE PETERS.

New York, July, 1923.

           Abie's Irish Rose                     Voc 14645
           I've Got The Yes ! We Have No Banana Blues   -

Acc. by O/Rosario Bourdon.        Camden, N. J., August 29, 1923.

B-28451-1-2-3-4-5  Dirty Hands ! Dirty Face !    Vic rejected

Acc. by the Virginians.          New York, September 11, 1923.

B-28549-4  Struttin' Jim                         Vic 19160

Acc. by studio orchestra.        New York, September, 1923.

           Mama's Gonna Slow You Down            Voc 14669
           Walk, Jennie, Walk                        -

11956      If I Can't Get The Sweetie I Want (I  Voc 14676
              Pity The Sweetie I Get)
11959      Mama Goes Where Papa Goes (Or Papa         -
              Don't Go Out Tonight)

New York, c. October, 1923.

           Lovey Came Back                       Vic 14701
           Somebody's Wrong                           -

New York, November, 1923.

12345      Mama Loves Papa (Papa Loves Mama)     Voc 14722
12347      Dancin' Dan                                -

New York, December, 1923.

           Who Is The Meanest Gal In Town ?      Voc 14743
              Josephine
           Hula Lou                                   -

New York, January, 1924.

12580      Whose Izzy Is He ? (Is He Yours Or Is  Voc 14755
              He Mine ?)
12583      Me No Speak-a Good English                 -

New York, August, 1924.

13513-     Somebody Loves Me (w/Tom Patricola-as)  Voc 14866, X-9506

Acc. by the Ambassadors.         New York, August, 1924.

13532      Doodle-Doo-Doo                        Voc 14866, X-9506
13538      No-One Knows What It's All About           -       X-9518

Acc. unknown.                         New York, c. February, 1929.

    Olaf (You Oughta Hear Olaf Laugh)        Ed 52563
    Nothing To Do But Think Of You            -

## BERTRAM PEACOCK

B. Philadelphia, Pa., 1883; well-known vaudeville artist in the first quarter of the
  twentieth century.  D. Bloomfield, N. J., April 28, 1963.

Vocal, acc. by studio orchestra.          New York, April, 1922.

    Songs of Yesterday by Stars of Today     Voc 35010 (part side)

## JAN PEERCE

B. New York, 1913; began singing at eleven in a synagogue; hired as young tenor  by
  Radio City Music Hall for regular Sunday afternoon broadcasts; auditioned by con-
  ductor Arturo Toscanini, and thus set his future in grand opera; debut in this in
  San Francisco, then became a member of the Metropolitan Opera Company (debut   as
  Alfredo in LA TRAVIATA); first American singer to appear at the Bolshoi Opera  in
  Moscow (1946); appeared in films (CARNEGIE HALL; TONIGHT WE SING; HYMN   OF  ALL
  NATIONS and GOODBYE, COLUMBUS).  Made many operatic and popular records after the
  end of World War II.

Vocal, acc. by O/Jack Shilkret.           New York, March 13, 1936.

B-18813-   My Romance                     Br 7635
B-18814-   A Beautiful Lady In Blue        -

## THE  PICKENS SISTERS

Helen, Georgia and Patti Pickens were born in Atlanta, Ga., between 1910 and  1914;
  very popular on radio, in cabarets and theatres from 1932 until their act   broke
  up in the mid-thirties on Helen and Patti getting married (they appeared in films
  such as SITTING PRETTY, 1933); Georgia, then known as Jane Pickens, returned solo
  to show business in 1948.

Vocal trio, acc. unknown.                 New York, September 21, 1931.

151800-    Blue Kentucky Moon             Col rejected
151801-    The Kiss That You've Forgotten  -

    Acc. by cl-as/p/g/sb.                 New York, February 16, 1932.

BS-71860-1  Was That The Human Thing To Do ?     Vic 22929, HMV B-4176
BS-71861-1  Goodnight, Moon                       -        -

                                    New York, March 21, 1932.

BS-71977-1  Too Many Tears                 Vic 22965, HMV B-4191
BS-71978-1  Somebody Loves You              -        -

    Acc. by cl/p/g.                       New York, April 6, 1932.

BS-72241-1  Dream Sweetheart               Vic 22975, HMV B-4212
BS-72242-1  Lawd, You Made The Night Too Long    -        -

    Acc. by cl/p/g/sb.                    New York, May 17, 1932.

BS-72593-1  San                           Vic 24025, HMV B-4250
BS-72594-1  Sweet Georgia Brown            -        -

    Acc. by t/cl/p/g.                     New York, July 26, 1932.

BS-73122-1  The Darktown Strutters' Ball (w/sb)  Vic 24355
BS-73123-1  China Boy                      -

Acc. by cl/p/g/sb.                     New York, November 2, 1932.

BS-73905-1  Back In The Old Sunday School          Vic 24180
BS-73906-1  Sentimental Gentleman From Georgia     Vic 24190
BS-73907-1  When Mother Played The Organ (And      Vic 24180
              Daddy Sang A Hymn)

Vocalists with Paul Whiteman and his Concert Orchestra.
                                       New York, February 2, 1933.

CS-75028-1  Night And Day (w/Phil Dewey)       Vic 36085, HMV C-2606
CS-75030-1  Cole Porter Medley (The Pickens Sisters    -          -
              sing a chorus of WHAT IS THIS THING CALLED LOVE ?)
   NOTE:- The Pickens Sisters do not sing on matrix BS-75029.

Vocal trio, acc. by small orchestra/Nat W. Finston.
                                       Hollywood, October 25, 1933.

PBS-68591-1  Many Moons Ago (Film "Sitting Pretty")Vic 24471
PBS-68592-1  You're Such A Comfort To Me (Film      Rejected
               "Sitting Pretty")
PBS-68593-2  May I ?                                 Vic 24625
PBS-68594-1  Good Morning, Glory (Film "Sitting     Rejected
               Pretty")

Acc. by p/g.                           Hollywood, November 1, 1933.

PBS-68604-3  Did You Ever See A Dream Walking ?   Vic 24468
               (Film "Sitting Pretty")

Acc. by small orchestra/Nat W. Finston. Hollywood, November 8, 1933.

PBS-68592-2  You're Such A Comfort To Me (Film    Vic 24471, HMV B-8108
               "Sitting Pretty")                           -
PBS-68594-2  Good Morning, Glory (Film "Sitting   Vic 24468     -
               Pretty")

Acc. by c/cl/as/p/g/sb.                New York, May 4, 1934.

BS-82373-1  The Beat O' My Heart                  Vic 24625
BS-82374-1  Riptide                               Vic 24630
BS-82375-1  Little Man, You've Had A Busy Day        -

THE PICKENS SISTERS AND THEIR ORCHESTRA.  New York, October 11, 1934.

BS-84466-1  Be Still, My Heart                    Vic 24751
BS-84467-1  Happiness Ahead                          -       HMV BD-116
BS-84468-1  The Thief Of Bagdad                   Vic 24753
BS-84469-1  Love Is Just Around The Corner        Vic 24815

## MOLLY PICON

B. New York, June 1, 1898; educated in Philadelphia (stage debut there im 1904);she
   toured for some time as Topsy in UNCLE TOM'S CABIN; engaged at Chestnut St.  Theatre, Philadelphia, 1915-1919 in English stock company; toured in Europe,    1920-
   1923; appeared in many Yiddish productions in Kessler's, New York, 1923-1927; returned to Europe with her husband and toured there, and in the Near East,    South
   Africa and the Argentine, 1927-1935; appeared in London before returning to   New
   York, 1936; resumed career in Yiddish theatre, recording many numbers from  these
   productions.

Vocal, acc. by O/Abraham Ellstein.     London, May 16, 1936.

OEA-3633-1  Busy, Busy                            HMV B-8453
OEA-3634-1  The Song Of The Tenement                 -

                                       London, June 19, 1936.

OEA-2993-1  A New York Symphony                   HMV B-8460
OEA-2994-1  What People Make A Living From           -

London, September 2, 1936.

| OEA-4048-1 | It's Love | HMV B-8486 |
| OEA-4049-1 | Nervous | - |

## WALTER PIDGEON

B. Canada, 1897; sang in London, 1924 before coming to New York to appear in  PUZZ-
LES OF 1925 (Fulton, February 2, 1925); to Hollywood, made film debut (MANNEQUIN,
1926) and appeared or starred in many more during the next forty years  (notably:
A MOST IMMORAL LADY (1930); FATAL LADY (1936); SARATOGA (1937); THE GIRL  OF  THE
GOLDEN WEST (1938); NICK CARTER, MASTER DETECTIVE (1939); HOW GREEN WAS MY VALLEY
(1941); MRS. MINIVER (1942); MADAME CURIE (1943); IF WINTER COMES (1947);THE FOR-
SYTE SAGA (1949); CALLING BULLDOG DRUMMOND (1951); THE BAD AND THE BEAUTIFUL(1952)
and FUNNY GIRL (1968).

Vocal, acc. by Lester Hodges-p.          Hayes, Middlesex, July 15, 1924.

| Bb-4896-2 | What'll I Do ? | HMV B-1882, Par PMC-7141 |
| Bb-4897-1-2 | Invictus | Rejected |
| Bb-4898-2 | Duna | HMV B-1882 |
| Bb-4899-1-2 | Trade Winds | Rejected |

Acc. by Joseph Pasternack-p.          New York, June 13, 1925.

Duna                          Vic test (un-numbered)

## FRANK  POLLOCK

Tenor star of the revival of Reginald de Koven's ROB ROY in New York, October, 1913,
with Henrietta Wakefield.

Vocal, acc. by O/? Walter B. Rogers.      New York, July 17, 1913.

| C-13605-3 | Who Can Tell Me Where She Dwells ? | Vic 70101 |
| | (w/Henrietta Wakefield) ("Rob Roy") | |

## THE  PONCE SISTERS

Ethel and Dorothea Ponce were born in New York, the daughters of Phil Ponce, composer, author, publisher and radio executive (1886-1945); Ethel, b. August 4, 1910,
is also a pianist, and at this writing teaches music in a small school.  The  act
was very popular in vaudeville, on records and radio between 1925 and 1933.

Vocal duets, acc. unknown (? Ethel Ponce-p).
                          New York, October 15, 1925.

| 141137- | What Could Be Sweeter Than You ? | Col rejected |
| 141138- | I Care For Her, She Cares For Me | - |

New York, November 2, 1925.

| 141232- | What Could Be Sweeter Than You ? | Col 501-D |
| 141233- | I Care For Her, She Cares For Me | Rejected |
| 141236- | That Certain Party | Col 501-D |

NOTE:- Matrices 141234/5 are not by the Ponce Sisters.

New York, c. November 14, 1925.

| 9833 | Forever | Gnt rejected |
| 9834 | That Certain Party | - |

Acc. by as/p/bj.          New York, c. December 4, 1925.

| 9885 | That Certain Party | Gnt 3207 |
| 9886 | Forever | - |

Acc. by ? Ethel Ponce-p.          New York, c. December, 1925.

| | That Certain Party | PA      , 11086, Per |
| | There's Nothing On My Mind | - |

New York, c. March, 1926.

Everything's Gonna Be All Right          PA          , 11150, Per
I Found A Round-about Way To Heaven                  -

New York, April 28, 1926.

142108-   Hi-Diddle-Diddle                    Col 651-D
142109-   I'd Climb The Highest Mountain (If I   Rejected
            Knew I'd Find You)

New York, May 12, 1926.

142189-   Happy-Go-Lucky Days                  Col 651-D

New York, July 28, 1926.

142474-   Who Wouldn't ?                       Col 736-D
142475-   I'd Leave Ten Men Like Yours (To Love  Rejected
            One Man Like Mine)

New York, c. August, 1926.

Someone Is Losin' Susan              Ed 51816
Put Your Arms Where They Belong          -

New York, October 14, 1926.

142814-   For My Sweetheart                    Col 791-D
142815-   Tonight You Belong To Me                 -

New York, late October, 1926.

2155-B  Mary Lou                             Cam 1029

New York, February 21, 1927.

143505-   Moonbeam ! Kiss Her For Me           Col 983-D
143506-   Honolulu Moon                            -

New York, March 21, 1927.

143699-   Nesting Time                         Col rejected

New York, April 5, 1927.

143745-   That's What I Call A Pal             Col rejected

Chicago, June 8, 1927.

144304-   Sailin' On                           Col 1228-D
144305-   Under The Moon                       Col 1039-D
144306-   Nesting Time                             -

Chicago, June 9, 1927.

144307-   Then You'll Come Back To Me          Col rejected
144308-   Let's Be The Same Old Pals               -

New York, March 3, 1928.

145723-   Happy-Go-Lucky Lane                  Col 1347-D
145724-   Hush-a-Bye Baby                          -

New York, c. June, 1928.

Tomorrow                             Ed 52318
I'd Rather Cry Over You                  -

New York, November 7, 1928.

| | | |
|---|---|---|
| 147443- | Down Where The Lolly-Pops Grow | Col 1698-D |
| 147444- | Motherhood | Rejected |

New York, January 2, 1929.

| | | |
|---|---|---|
| 147746- | In A Little Town Called Home, Sweet Home | Rejected |
| 147747- | I Faw Down An' Go 'Boom !' | Col 1698-D |

Acc. by small jazz band.                  New York, December 16, 1932.

| | | |
|---|---|---|
| 265015-3 | Fit As A Fiddle | Col DB-1051 |
| 265016- | Contented | Rejected |
| 265017-2 | So At Last It's Come To This | Col DB-1051 |
| 265018-1 | A Million Dreams | Col DB-1073 |

## COLE PORTER

B. Peru, Ind., June 9, 1892; attended Yale and Harvard Universities; studied   music
under Vincent d'Indy; composed score of SEE AMERICA FIRST (1916); served in France
in AEF in World War I, and for a time was in the French Foreign Legion;    resumed
musical career on returning home, and wrote the scores for HITCHY-KOO 1919; GREEN-
WICH VILLAGE FOLLIES, 1924; PARIS, 1928; WAKE UP AND DREAM; FIFTY MILLION FRENCH-
MEN, both 1929; THE NEW YORKERS, 1930; GAY DIVORCE, 1932; NYMPH ERRANT, 1933; ANY-
THING GOES, 1934; JUBILEE, 1935; RED HOT AND BLUE, 1936; part lyrics and music for
YOU NEVER KNOW and LEAVE IT TO ME, 1938; DU BARRY WAS A LADY, 1939; PANAMA HATTIE,
1940; LET'S FACE IT, 1941; SOMETHING FOR THE BOYS, 1943; SEVEN LIVELY ARTS, 1944;
AROUND THE WORLD, 1946; the film HIGH SOCIETY (1956); and contributed to   MAYFAIR
AND MONTMARTRE and PHI-PHI, 1922, and THE SUN NEVER SETS, 1938.  D.   October  15,
1964.

Vocal, acc. by own piano.                  New York, October 26, 1934.

| | | |
|---|---|---|
| BS-84900-1 | Thank You So Much, Mrs. Lowsborough-Goodby | Vic 24766, HMV B-8284 |
| BS-84901-1 | You're The Top ("Anything Goes") | —   HMV B-8332 |

New York, November 27, 1934.

| | | |
|---|---|---|
| BS-86065-1 | Anything Goes ("Anything Goes") | Vic 24825, HMV B-8332 |
| BS-86066-1 | Two Little Babes In The Wood ("Paris") | —   HMV B-8284 |

New York, January 3, 1935.

| | | |
|---|---|---|
| BS-86374-1 | Be Like The Bluebird ("Anything Goes") | Vic 24843 |
| BS-86375-1 | The Physician ("Nymph Errant") | Vic 24859 |
| BS-86376-1 | The Cocotte | - |
| BS-86377-1 | I'm A Gigolo | Vic 24843 |

## DICK  POWELL

B. Mountain View, Ark., November 14, 1904; family moved to Little Rock while he  was
a child; he sang in a church there; studied singing while working for a  telephone
company, and in 1927 he joined Charlie Davis's Orchestra as vocalist; his  records
and broadcasting led to a screen test, and he began his film career with   BLESSED
EVENT in 1932.  A number of star-roles followed in FORTY-SECOND STREET (1933);WON-
DER BAR, DAMES and FLIRTATION WALK (1934); GOLD DIGGERS OF 1935;   BROADWAY GONDO-
LIER  and SHIPMATES FOREVER (1935); ON THE AVENUE and HOLLYWOOD HOTEL (1937); COW-
BOY FROM BROOKLYN and ROMANCE AND RHYTHM (1938); CHRISTMAS IN JULY (1940);   MODEL
WIFE (1941); HAPPY GO LUCKY (1942); TRUE TO LIFE (1943); IT HAPPENED TOMORROW  and
FAREWELL MY LOVELY (1944); CORNERED (1945); JOHNNY O'CLOCK (1946); TO THE ENDS  OF
THE EARTH (1948); THE REFORMER AND THE REDHEAD (1950); THE TALL TARGET (1951); THE
BAD AND THE BEAUTIFUL (1952); SUSAN SLEPT HERE (1954); produced and/or directed  a
large number of other films in the 1950s; founded Four-Star Television; began with
romantic crooning roles, changed in 1940s to tough character parts. D. 1963.

Vocal, acc. by Emil Seidel-p.              Richmond, Ind., November 30, 1927.

| | | |
|---|---|---|
| GEX-980 | Time Will Tell | Gnt rejected |
| GEX-981 | Beautiful | - |

Acc. unknown.                                      ? Chicago, c. December, 1927.

      Is She My Girl Friend ? (How-De-Ow-Dow)  Voc 15647
      Beautiful                                 -
      There's No End To My Love For You          Voc 15648

                                 ? Chicago, c. March, 1928.

      Beloved                                   Voc 15674
      Mary Ann                                  -
      Coquette                                  Voc 15675
      Together                                  -

                            Chicago, c. March 28, 1928.

C-1814; E-7246   There Must Be A Silver Lining    Voc 15686
         (That's Shining For Me)
C-1817; E-7249   Suppose Nobody Cared             -

                          Indianapolis, June, 1928.

IND-633; E-7406  Last Night I Dreamed You         Voc 15699
         Kissed Me
IND-634; E-7407  Was It A Dream ?                 -
IND-635; E-7408  If You Don't Love Me             Voc 15700
IND-636; E-7409  Rosette                          -

Vocalist with Charlie Davis and his Orchestra.
                          Indianapolis, June, 1928.

IND-649   Suppose Nobody Cared                    Br 4037

Vocal, acc. by studio orchestra.        New York, c. July 5, 1930.

E-33337-   June Kisses                            Br 4884
E-33338-   With My Guitar And You                 -

                         New York, May 25, 1933.

13386-1  The Gold Diggers' Song (Film "Gold      Cq 8184, Ro 2084, Bcst 3339,
      Diggers of 1933")                        Col C2L-44
13387-1  Pettin' In The Park (Film "Gold          Cq 8183, Bcst 3339, Col C2L-44
      Diggers of 1933")
13388-1  Shadow Waltz (Film "Gold Diggers of         -       Bcst 3340       -
      1933")
13389-1  I've Got To Sing A Torch Song (Film      Cq 8184, Ro 2084, Bcst 3340,
      "Gold Diggers of 1933")                  Col C2L-44

                        Los Angeles, September 27, 1933.

LA-14-   By A Waterfall (Film "Footlight Parade")  Br 6667, Dec F-3773, Col C2L-44
LA-15-   The Road Is Open Again (Film "Footlight   Br 6685, Dec F-3824       -
      Parade")
LA-16-   Lonely Lane (Film "Footlight Parade")        -       Dec F-3773       -
LA-17-   Ah ! The Moon Is Here (Film "Footlight Parade")   Dec F-3772       -
LA-18-   Honeymoon Hotel (Film "Footlight Parade")Br 6667       -             -

Vocalist with Ted Fio Rito and his Orchestra.
                        San Francisco, March 1, 1934.

SF-95-   Why Do I Dream Those Dreams ? (Film      Br 6792, Dec F-5106, Col C2L-44
      "Wonder Bar")
SF-96-   Wonder Bar (Film "Wonder Bar")              -       Dec F-3944
SF-97-   I'll String Along With You (Film         Br 6793, Dec F-5106       -
      "Twenty Million Sweethearts")
SF-98-   Don't Say Goodnight (Film "Twenty           -       Dec F-3944
      Million Sweethearts")

Acc. by studio orchestra.                  New York, September 16, 1934.

B-15920-  Pop ! Goes Your Heart (Film "Happiness  Br 6979, Dec F-5404, Col C2L-44
          Ahead")
B-15921-  I See Two Lovers (Film "Flirtation Walk")          Dec F-5596          -
B-15922-A Mr. And Mrs. Is The Name (Film        Br 7328, Dec F-5650,
          "Flirtation Walk")                     Epic L2N-6072
B-15923-  Happiness Ahead (Film "Happiness Ahead")Br 6979, Dec F-5404
B-15924-A Beauty Must Be Loved (Film "Happiness Ahead")   Dec F-5503, Col C2L-44
B-15925-A Flirtation Walk (Film "Flirtation Walk")Br 7328, Dec F-5650

                                           New York, October 2, 1934.

P-16080-  Happiness Ahead (Film "Happiness Ahead")Warner Bros. Exploitation Record
P-16081-  Beauty Must Be Loved (Film "Happiness Ahead")  -

Acc. by Jimmie Grier and his Orchestra. Los Angeles, January 13, 1935.

LA-321-   Lullaby Of Broadway (Film "Gold Diggers  Br 7374, Dec F-5548, Col C2L-44
          of 1935")
LA-322-   I'm Goin' Shoppin' With You (Film "Gold  Br 7407          -               -
          Diggers of 1935")
LA-323-   The Words Are In My Heart (Film "Gold         -      Dec F-5549           -
          Diggers of 1935")
LA-324-A  I Believe In Miracles                    Br 7374, Dec F-5503             -
LA-325-   Down Sunshine Lane                               Dec F-5549             -

Acc. by O/Victor Arden.                    New York, June 21, 1935.

B-17722-1 Outside Of You (Film "Broadway          -Br 7468, Dec F-5693, Col C2L-44
          Gondolier")
B-17723-  Lulu's Back In Town (Film "Broadway      Br 7469, Dec F-5694            -
          Gondolier")
B-17724-  The Rose In Her Hair (Film "Broadway          -          -             -
          Gondolier")
B-17725-1 Lonely Gondolier (Film "Broadway         Br 7468, Dec F-5693           -
          Gondolier")

Acc. by O/Victor Young.                    Los Angeles, November 3, 1935.

DLA-249-A-B  Don't Give Up The Ship (w/male octet) Dec 613, 3266, F-5823
             (Film "Shipmates Forever")
DLA-250-A  I've Got A Pocketful Of Sunshine         Dec 612, F-5822
DLA-251-A  Thanks A Million                              -          -     DL-8837
DLA-252-A-B  I'm Sitting High On A Hill-Top         Dec 613, F-5823

                                           Los Angeles, July 18, 1936.

DLA-443-A  When The Moon Hangs High (And The        Dec 889, F-6044
           Prairie Stars Hang Low)
DLA-444-A  Did I Remember ?                              -          -     DL-8837

                                           Los Angeles, August 4, 1936.

DLA-524-A  Fancy Meeting You                        Dec 924, F-6293, DL-8837
DLA-525-A  Two Hearts Divided                       Dec 900, F-6126
DLA-526-A  My Kingdom For A Kiss                         -          -     DL-8837

                                           Los Angeles, August 13, 1936.

DLA-571-A  I Want The Whole World To Love You       Dec F-6194
DLA-572-A  There's Two Sides To Every Story         Dec 924 -
DLA-575-A  In Your Own Quiet Way                    Dec F-6293
  NOTE:- Matrices DLA-573/4 are not by Dick Powell.

                                           Los Angeles, November 11, 1936.

DLA-635-A  With Plenty Of Money And You (Film       Dec 1067, F-6394, DL-8837, 7-1
DLA-636-A  Let's Put Our Heads Together ("Gold      Dec 1068, F-6395
DLA-637-A  All's Fair In Love And War  (Diggers          -          -
DLA-638-A  Speaking Of The Weather     (of 1937") Dec 1067, F-6394

Los Angeles, February 6, 1937.

DLA-682-A  I've Got My Love To Keep Me Warm (Film   Dec 1149, F-6453, DL-8837
           "On The Avenue")
DLA-683-A  The Girl On The Police Gazette (Film      Dec 1150, F-6454      -
           "On The Avenue")
DLA-684-A  This Year's Kisses (Film "On The          Dec 1149, F-6453      -
           Avenue")
DLA-685-A  You're Laughing At Me (Film "On The       Dec 1150, F-6454
           Avenue")

   Acc. by the Music of Lou Forbes.        Los Angeles, May 31, 1937.

DLA-815-A  You Can't Run Away From Love Tonight      Dec 1311, F-6479
           (Film "The Singing Marine")
DLA-816-A-B 'Cause My Baby Says It's So (Film         Dec 1310, F-6478, DL-8837
           "The Singing Marine")
DLA-817-A  I Know Now (Film "The Singing Marine")       -        -
DLA-818-A  Song Of The Marines (Film "The Singing    Dec 1311, 3266, F-6479
           Marine")

                                    Los Angeles, August 30, 1937.

DLA-862-A  You've Got Something There (Film          Dec 1431, F-6638
           "Varsity Show")
DLA-863-A  Love Is On The Air Tonight (Film            -        -
           "Varsity Show")
DLA-864-A  Have You Got Any Castles, Baby ? (Film  Dec 1430, F-6637, DL-8837
           "Varsity Show")
DLA-865-A  Moonlight On The Campus (Film "Varsity      -        -
           Show")

   Acc. by O/Harry Sosnik.              Los Angeles, November 5, 1937.

DLA-1021-A  I've Hitched My Wagon To A Star          Dec 1557, F-6652
            (Film "Hollywood Hotel")
DLA-1022-A  I'm Like A Fish Out Of Water (Film        -        -
            "Hollywood Hotel")
DLA-1023-A  You Can't Stop Me From Dreamin'         Dec 1543, F-6569
DLA-1024-A  Roses In December                         -        -

                                    Los Angeles, April 16, 1938.

DLA-1227-A  The Girl In The Bonnet Of Blue           Dec 1782, F-6694
DLA-1228-A  Ride, Tenderfoot, Ride (Film "Cowboy    Dec 1820, F-6784, DL-8837
            From Brooklyn")
DLA-1229-A  Daddy's Boy                                -        -
DLA-1230-A  In My Little Red Book (w/male quartet) Dec 1782, F-6694, DL-8837

                                    Los Angeles, August 12, 1938.

DLA-1400-A  On, Wisconsin ! (w/The Foursome)         Dec 2013
DLA-1401-A  Stein Song (w/The Foursome)              Dec 2024, F-7097
DLA-1402-A  The Eyes Of Texas Are Upon You (w/       Dec 2013
            The Foursome)
DLA-1403-A  Victory March (w/The Foursome)           Dec 2025, Br 03994

                                    Los Angeles, August 21, 1938.

DLA-1438-A  Rambling Wreck From Georgia Tech.        Dec 2025, Br 03994
            (w/The Foursome)
DLA-1439-A  The Illinois Loyalty Song (We're         Dec 2024
            Loyal To You, Illinois) (w/The Foursome)

                                    Los Angeles, March 24, 1939.

DLA-1736-A  Mr. And Mrs. America                     Dec 2387
DLA-1737-A  In A Moment Of Weakness                    -        F-7097

Los Angeles, July 19, 1939.

DLA-1824-A  They Would Wind Him Up And He Would    Dec 2655, F-7413
                Whistle (w/The Foursome)
DLA-1825-A  I Like Mountain Music (w/The Goursome)       -      F-7307
DLA-1826-A  Jingle Bells (w/The Foursome)       Dec 2760       -
DLA-1827-A  Good Fellows Medley (Intro. Hail !         -
                Hail ! The Gang's All Here/The More We Are Together/For He's A    Jolly
                Good Fellow/Hail ! Hail ! The Gang's All Here) (w/The Foursome)

New York, November 10, 1939.

66855-A  The Army Air Corps (w/The Norsemen)       Dec 2975
66856-A  Semper Paratus (U. S. Coast Guard)        Dec 3267, F-7413
            (w/The Norsemen)
66857-A  The Marines' Hymn (w/The Norsemen)        Dec 2975
66858-A  On, Brave Old Army Team (West Point)      Dec 3267
            (w/The Norsemen)

Los Angeles, August 26, 1940.

DLA-2088-A  Old Shep                             Dec 3389
DLA-2089-A  Tumbledown Ranch In Arizona              -

  Acc. by O/Victor Young.              Los Angeles, October 9, 1940.

DLA-2201-A  He's My Uncle                        Dec 3458, F-7846
DLA-2202-A  America, I Love You                      -       -

Los Angeles, December 27, 1940.

DLA-2303-A  Life's Railway To Heaven (w/Sleepy    Dec 3784
                Hollow Quartet)
DLA-2304-A  When They Ring The Golden Bells           -
                (w/Sleepy Hollow Quartet)
DLA-2305-A  Where The Morning Glories Twine       Dec 3662
                Around The Door (w/Sleepy Hollow Quartet)
DLA-2306-A  I Wonder How The Old Folks Are At  Home   -
                (w/Sleepy Hollow Quartet)

New York, January 28, 1942.

70231-A  Over There (w/The American Four)        Dec 4174
70237-A  Captains Of The Clouds (w/The American       -
            Four)
  NOTE:- Matrices 70232/6 inclusive are not by Dick Powell.

## ELEANOR POWELL

B. Springfield, Mass., November 21, 1912; studied dancing and appeared with the  Gus
Edwards children's company; stage debut as an adult in New York in THE  OPTIMISTS,
Casino de Paris, January 29, 1928; afterwards in FOLLOW THROUGH (46th Street, January 9, 1929); FINE AND DANDY (Erlanger's, September 23, 1930); HOT-CHA (Ziegfeld,
March 8, 1932); AT HOME ABROAD (Winter Garden, September 19, 1935); began her film
career with GEORGE WHITE'S SCANDALS OF 1935, then starred in BROADWAY MELODY   OF
1936; ROSALIE (1937); HONOLULU (1938); BROADWAY MELODY OF 1940 and I DOOD IT(1940);
LADY BE GOOD (1941); BORN TO DANCE (1942), and many others, mostly demonstrating a
skill at acrobatic dancing that has never been surpassed.

Vocal, acc. by Tommy Dorsey and his Orchestra.
                              New York, October 11, 1935.

BS-95379-1  You Are My Lucky Star (Film "Broadway Vic 25158, HMV B-8396
                Melody of 1936")
BS-95380-1  I've Got A Feelin' You're Foolin'         -             -
                (Film "Broadway Melody of 1936")
BS-95381-1  Got A Bran' New Suit                  Vic 25173, HMV B-8406

New York, October 14, 1935.

BS-95505-1  That's Not Cricket                    Vic 25173
BS-95506-1-2  What A Wonderful World              Rejected

## TYRONE POWER, Sr.

B. Dublin (?), 1869; worked mostly in U.S.A. as leading man for Julia Marlowe, etc.
in Shakespearean parts. Began film career with A TEXAS STEER (1915); then in JOHN
NEEDHAM'S DOUBLE and WHERE ARE MY CHILDREN ? (1916); FOOTFALLS (1921); BRIDE   OF
THE STORM (1926). D. December 30, 1931.

Speech, unacc.                                    London, c. May, 1902.

        Signor Antonio, Many A Time And Oft      G&T GC-1229
        ("The Merchant of Venice" - Act 1, Scene 3) (Shakespeare)
        Street Scene ("The Merchant of Venice")  G&T GC-1230
        (Shakespeare)

                                    New York, June 16, 1927.

        The Breeches And The Petticoats          Vic test (un-numbered)
        The Twenty-Third Psalm                      -

## TYRONE POWER, Jr.

B. Cincinnati, Ohio, May 5, 1914; worked in various rather menial jobs while studying under his father's teaching for the stage; professional debut in Chicago in a
small part in THE MERCHANT OF VENICE (1931); New York debut in HAMLET (as a page)
on November 19, 1931 (Royale); various other stage performances of Shakespeare and
others (George Bernard Shaw); began film career in 1932 in TOM BROWN OF   CULVER
and followed this with many successful films, some with music (LLOYDS OF  LONDON,
1937; IN OLD CHICAGO and ALEXANDER'S RAGTIME BAND (1938); JESSE JAMES;   THE RAINS
CAME; SECOND FIDDLE and ROSE OF WASHINGTON SQUARE (1939); JOHNNY APOLLO;  BRIGHAM
YOUNG and THE MARK OF ZORRO (1940); A YANK IN THE RAF and BLOOD AND SAND (1941) ;
after war service resumed film work and made many very different pictures,e.g.THE
RAZOR'S EDGE (1946); THE EDDY DUCHIN STORY (1956); THE SUN ALSO RISES and WITNESS
FOR THE PROSECUTION (1957); was filming SOLOMON AND SHEBA at the time of his sud-
den death; Yul Brynner took over his role.

Vocal, acc. by Al Goodman and his Orchestra and Ray Block's Choir.
                                    New York, August 28, 1941.

CS-067663-1-2  Ballad Of The Leatherneck Corps    Vic 36404

## TOM POWERS

B. Owensboro', Ky., July 7, 1890; studied for the stage at the American Academy  of
Dramatic Art; stage debut in Lancaster, Pa., in IN MIZZOURA (February, 1911);   in
New York in SIX WHO PASS WHILE THE LENTILS BOIL (Portmanteau, July 21, 1915); appeared in MR. LAZARUS (Shubert, September 5, 1916); many others; OH, BOY ! (Princess, February 20, 1917); same show, re-named OH, JOY ! for London debut  (Kings-
way, January 27, 1919); returned to New York for a lifetime of widely    different
parts there and on tour (New York outstanding successes include WHY NOT ?   (48th
Street, December 25, 1922); TARNISH (Belmont, October 2, 1923);  THE  WILD   DUCK
(48th Street, February 24, 1925); LOVE IN A MIST (Gaiety, April 12, 1926);STRANGE
INTERLUDE (John Golden, January 30, 1928, 426 performances); THE  END  OF  SUMMER
(Guild, February 17, 1936); succeeded Orson Welles as Brutus in modern-dress JUL-
IUS CAESAR (Mercury, May, 1938); WHEN WE ARE MARRIED (Lyceum, December 25, 1939);
and the revival of THE THREE SISTERS (Ethel Barrymore, December 21, 1942). Began
film career for Vitagraph as far back as 1911 (SAVING AN AUDIENCE); also made THE
AUCTION BLOCK (1917); JULIUS CAESAR (as Metellus Cimber) (1953).

Vocal, acc. by the Kingsway Theatre Orchestra/Leonard Hornsey.
                                    London, February, 1919.

    76371      Words Are Not Needed (w/Dot Temple)    Col L-1287
               ("Oh, Joy !")
    76372      You Never Knew About Me (w/Dot Temple)  Col L-1288
               ("Oh, Joy !")  (continued on page 533)

London, February, 1919 (cont.)

| 76373 | Loving By Proxy (w/Dot Temple-Tom Payne) Col L-1290 ("Oh, Joy !") |
| 76374 | Wedding Bells (w/Billy Leonard-Tom Payne)Col L-1288 ("Oh, Joy !") |
| 76375 | Till The Clouds Roll By (w/Beatrice      Col L-1285 Lillie) ("Oh, Joy !") |
| 76376 | March Quarter Day (w/Beatrice Lillie-    Col L-1289 Billy Leonard) ("Oh, Joy !") |

Dialogues with Alice Brady.               New York, February 8, 1931.

BVE-64675-1  Sham (made on Victor Talking Machine 7776)
BVE-64676-1  Sham (made on RCA Machine No. 1)
  NOTE:- These two recordings were probably not intended for issue.  Tom Powers  can
  also be heard in the MGM LP recording of the Soundtrack of JULIUS CAESAR (C-751).

## GEORGIE  PRICE

B. New York, January 5, 1900; member of Gus Edwards' vaudeville act SCHOOLBOYS  AND
   SCHOOLGIRLS as a teenager; became comedian in vaudeville and night-clubs; appeared
   in ARTISTS AND MODELS (Shubert, August 20, 1923); A NIGHT IN PARIS (Casino de Paris
   January 5, 1926); founded American Guild of Variety Artists.  D. New York, May 10,
   1964.

Vocal, acc. by O/Eddie King.             New York, March 26, 1923.

B-27673-4  Dearest (You're The Nearest To My Heart)Vic 19047
B-27674-4  Morning Will Come                             -

   Acc. by O/Rosario Bourdon.            Camden, N. J., April 24, 1923.

B-27775-1-2-3  Barney Google                     Vic rejected
B-27776-1-2-3  Beside A Babbling Brook                -

                                         Camden, N. J., April 26, 1923.

B-27775-6  Barney Google                         Vic 19066
B-27776-7  Beside A Babbling Brook               Vic 19065

                                         Camden, N. J., December 18, 1923.

B-29097-1-2-3  Ellis Island Blues                Vic rejected

   Acc. by the Manhattan Merrymakers, the Troubadours or the Virginians, as shown.
                                         New York, December 28, 1923.

B-29162-1-2-3-4  Yes Dear - MM                   Rejected
B-29164-4  I'm Goin' South - V                   Vic 19261

                                         New York, January 28, 1924.

B-29162-5-6-7  Yes Dear - MM                     Rejected
B-29355-1-2-3-4  Nita (I Need You) - MM              -
B-29356-3  California, Here I Come - MM          Vic 19261

                                         New York, May 23, 1924.

B-30132-3  Nobody's Child - T                    Vic 19355
B-30133-5  You Know Me, Alabam' - T                  -

   Acc. by the International Novelty Orchestra.
                                         New York, September 12, 1924.

B-30814-2  Bring Back Those Rock-a-Bye Baby Days  Vic 19465

   Acc. by O/Nat Shilkret.               New York, September 19, 1924.

B-30834-3  My Best Girl                          Vic 19465

Acc. by O/Nat Shilkret.                    New York, April 10, 1925.

BVE-32415-3  Isn't She The Sweetest Thing ?      Vic 19654
BVE-32416-1  Swanee Butterfly                    -
BVE-32417-1  All Aboard For Heaven               Vic 19680

                                           New York, October 30, 1925.

BVE-33827-2  Mother Me, Tennessee               Vic 19826
BVE-33828-1-2-3  Clap Hands ! Here Comes Charley  Rejected

                                           New York, December 9, 1925.

BVE-34131-1-2-3-4  Where The Huckleberries Grow   Vic rejected

Acc. by O/Leroy Shield.                    New York, December 14, 1925.

BVE-34140-1-2-3-4  Miami - You Owe A Lot To Me    Vic rejected

Acc. by own piano.                         New York, August 20, 1928.

          Song Of The South                    Vic test (un-numbered)

Acc. by studio orchestra.                  New York, January, 1931.

E-35124-    The Song Of The Fool                Br 4997

E-35469-    The Mender Of Broken Dreams          Br 4997

                                           New York, June 19, 1934.

15339-1  I Never Had A Chance              Mt M-13062, Per 13015, Rex 8267
15340-   I Only Have Eyes For You          -                   -

                                           New York, August 9, 1934.

15583-  Love In Bloom                      Mt M-13104, Per 13030, Rex 8281
15584-  A New Moon Is Over My Shoulder     -                   -

Georgie Price made a few sides for Stinson in 1947.

## MAE QUESTAL

Known as "The Betty Boop" girl, Mae Questal was an accurate impersonator of Shirley
  Temple (in her heyday as a child-star) and Helen Kane, and by this means    became
  famous by her broadcasts and cabaret and theatre appearances in the 1930s.

Vocal, acc. by O/Nat Shilkret.             New York, February 13, 1933.

BS-75211-1  Sweet Betty (Don't Take My Boop-Oop-a- Vic 24261
              Doop Away) (w/Dick Robertson)
BS-75212-1  The Girl In The Little Green Hat      -

Acc. by O/Victor Young.                    New York, January 16, 1935.

39250-B  I've Got A Pain In My Sawdust     Dec 346, F-5452, F-6042
39251-A  On The Good Ship Lollipop         -       F-5565

                                           New York, April 19, 1935.

39484-A  The Choc'late Soldier Man         Dec 447, F-5899
39485-A  Practising The Piano              -       F-5565

                                           New York, August 13, 1935.

39850-A  When I Grow Up                    Dec 540, F-5849
39851-A  Animal Crackers In My Soup        -       -

New York, December 23, 1935.

60280-B  The Wedding Of Jack And Jill              Dec 653, F-5871
60281-A  Polly-Wolly-Doodle                          -    F-6042

New York, January 8, 1936.

60316-A  The Music Goes 'Round And Around          Dec 680, F-5871
60317-A  The Broken Record                           -    F-5899

New York, April 3, 1936.

60975-A  At The Codfish Ball                       Dec 769, F-6084
60976-A  The Right Somebody To Love                  -      -

New York, June 15, 1936.

61169-   Medley of Songs from Shirley Temple       Dec 876
            Pictures - Part 1
61170-   Medley of Songs from Shirley Temple         -
            Pictures - Part 2
61171-   Oh ! My Goodness                          Dec 832, F-6015
61172-   You've Gotta Eat Your Spinach, Baby         -      -

New York, November 10, 1937.

62757-A  In Our Little Wooden Shoes                Dec 1544, F-6843
62758-A  I Want You For Christmas                    -      -

New York, January 11, 1940.

67036-   Oh ! Gee, Oh ! Gosh, Oh ! Golly, I'm In   Dec 2974
            Love
67037-   You'd Be Surprised                          -

## RALPH RAINGER

B. New York, 1901; pianist who accompanied Clifton Webb in vaudeville, and was    his
   rehearsal pianist in THE FIRST LITTLE SHOW (1929) in which Webb sang Ralph    Rain-
   ger's MOANIN' LOW; composed many songs for films with Leo Robin (PLEASE, from  THE
   BIG BROADCAST (1932); I LIKE A GUY WHAT TAKES HIS TIME (from SHE DONE HIM    WRONG
   (1933); LOVE IN BLOOM (from SHE LOVES ME NOT (1934); JUNE IN JANUARY (from HERE IS
   MY HEART (1934); I DON'T WANT TO MAKE HISTORY (from PALM SPRINGS (1936); BLUE HAW-
   AII (from WAIKIKI WEDDING (1937); THANKS FOR THE MEMORY (from THE BIG BROADCAST OF
   1938); the songs from GULLIVER'S TRAVELS (1939); YOU STARTED SOMETHING (from  MOON
   OVER MIAMI), OH, THE PITY OF IT ALL (from MY GAL SAL) and TAKE IT FROM THERE (from
   CONEY ISLAND), all 1940-1941; also composed WHEN A WOMAN LOVES A MAN with   showman
   Billy Rose (from BE YOURSELF, 1930) and I WISHED ON THE MOON with Dorothy    Parker
   (from THE BIG BROADCAST OF 1936).  D. in air crash, 1942; his real name was  Ralph
   Reichenthal.  He and Edgar Fairchild played their duets in both shows recorded.

Piano duets with Edgar Fairchild.        New York, December 13, 1926.

BVE-37124-  Oh Kay ! - Selection                   Vic 20435, HMV B-2552

New York, December 27, 1926.

BVE-37180-2  Queen High - Selection (Intro.        Vic 20435, HMV B-2431
            Everything Will Happen For The Best/Cross Your Heart/Don't Forget)

Piano solo, acc. by Nat W. Finston and the Paramount Studio Orchestra.
                         Hollywood, January 14, 1934.

PBS-68699-1  Raftero (Film "Bolero")               Vic 24515

## BASIL RATHBONE

B. Johannesburg, Transvaal, June 13, 1892; originally an insurance clerk, but worked
   to become an actor, and made stage debut at the Theatre Royal, Ipswich,   April 22,
   1911, in Sir Frank Benson's No. 2 Company's production of THE TAMING OF THE SHREW;

to U.S.A., October, 1912 with this company, touring in Shakespeare productions; to London for debut there in THE SIN OF DAVID (Savoy, July 9, 1914); toured U.K. with the Benson company, then joined London Scottish Regt. as private, took a commission and gained the Military Cross (September, 1918); returned to civilian life in 1919 and had a great success in the title-role of PETER IBBETSON (Savoy, Feb. 4, 1920); also in THE EDGE O' BEYOND (Garrick, August 9, 1921); to New York to play in THE CZARINA (Empire, January 31, 1922); returned to London, more big successes in EAST OF SUEZ (His Majesty's, September 2, 1922) and R.U.R. (St. Martin's, April 24,1923); to New York to appear in THE SWAN (Cort, October 23, 1923); remained in U.S.A. for nine years, with outstanding success in THE CAPTIVE (Empire, New York, September 29, 1926); THE COMMAND TO LOVE (Longacre, September 20, 1927); began film career in 1921 with THE FRUITFUL VINE; made many films establishing himself as a great Sherlock Holmes (1939, followed by several other "Holmes" films in modern settings)and as a superb villain, amongst other parts; best-remembered films include THE LAST OF MRS. CHEYNEY (1930); DAVID COPPERFIELD (1934); ANNA KARENINA; THE LAST DAYS OF POMPEII and CAPTAIN BLOOD (1935); A TALE OF TWO CITIES (1936); THE GARDEN OF ALLAH and THE ADVENTURES OF MARCO POLO (1937); DAWN PATROL and THE ADVENTURES OF ROBIN HOOD (1938); SON OF FRANKENSTEIN (1939); THE MARK OF ZORRO (1940); CROSSROADS and FINGERS AT THE WINDOW (1942); FRENCHMAN'S CREEK (1944); and many others, mainly in "terror" vein, ending with PREHISTORIC PLANET WOMEN and THE GHOST IN THE INVISIBLE BIKINI (1966). D. 1967.

Speech, acc. by the All-American Orchestra/Leopold Stokowski.
                                    New York, July 11, 1941.

| | | | |
|---|---|---|---|
| XCO-31172-1 | Peter And The Wolf - Part 1(Prokofiev)Col 11647-D, | 11650-D |
| XCO-31173-1 | Peter And The Wolf - Part 2 | - | - | 11651-D |
| XCO-31174-1 | Peter And The Wolf - Part 3 | - | Col 11648-D, 11652-D |
| XCO-31175-1 | Peter And The Wolf - Part 4 | - | - | - |
| XCO-31176-1 | Peter And The Wolf - Part 5 | - | Col 11649-D, 11651-D |
| XCO-31177-1 | Peter And The Wolf - Part 6 | - | - | 11650-D |

Unacc. readings for MASTERPIECES OF LITERATURE, Vol. III (GREAT THEMES IN POETRY, ALBUM II).                            Hollywood, October 29, 1941.

HCO-553-1  God's World (Millay)/Loveliest Of Trees Col 36481
           (Housman)/The Vagabond (Stevenson)
HCO-554-1  Ode On A Grecian Urn (Keats)               -
HCO-555-1  Abou Ben Adhem (Hunt)/Hate (Stephens)   Col 36482
HCO-556-1  Sonnet XXIX (Shakespeare)/The Arrow And    -
           The Song (Longfellow)/Sonnet XLIII (Browning)
HCO-557-1  The Passionate Shepherd To His Love (   Col 36483
           (Marlowe)/Go, Lovely Rose (Waller)/To The Virgins To Make Much Of  Time
           (Herrick)
HCO-558-1  The World Is Too Much With Us (Wordsworth)/ -
           Travel (Millay)/On First Looking Into Chapman's Homer (Keats)
HCO-559-1  Ode To The West Wind (Shelley)          Col 36484
HCO-560-1  From In Memoriam (Section LV) (Tennyson)/  -
           To A Waterfowl (Bryant)
HCO-561-1  On The Late Massacre In Piedmont(Milton)Col 36485
           /Stupidity Street (Hodgson)/In Memoriam F.A.S. (Stevenson)
HCO-562-1  Sonnet (Brooks)/Prospice (Browning)        -
HCO-563-1  The Waste Places (Stephens)/Say Not The Col 36486
           Struggle Naught Availeth (Clough)/Invictus (Henley)
HCO-564-1  The Old Woman Of The Roads (Colum)/My Own,  -
           My Native Land (scott)/America (Lanier)

Speech, with supporting cast and music/Leith Stevens, in the part of Scrooge.
                                    Hollywood, July 26, 1942.

| | | | |
|---|---|---|---|
| XHCO-921-1 | Dickens' A CHRISTMAS CAROL - Part 1 | Col 11880-D, 11883-D |
| XHCO-922-1 | Dickens' A CHRISTMAS CAROL - Part 2 | - | 11884-D |
| XHCO-923-1 | Dickens' A CHRISTMAS CAROL - Part 3 | Col 11881-D, 11885-D |
| XHCO-924-1 | Dickens' A CHRISTMAS CAROL - Part 4 | - | - |
| XHCO-925-1 | Dickens' A CHRISTMAS CAROL - Part 5 | Col 11882-D, 11884-D |
| XHCO-926-1 | Dickens' A CHRISTMAS CAROL - Part 6 | - | 11883-D |

Narration with Blanche Yurka and chorus.  Hollywood, December 7, 1942.

XHCO-947-1 through XHCO-952-1  The Murder Of          Col MM-536 (6 sides, all -1)
            Lidice (Parts 1-6) (Edna St. Vincent Millay)

## MARTHA  RAYE

B. 1916; popular American comedienne on radio, TV and in films, her first being  in
   1936 (RHYTHM ON THE RANGE), followed by WAIKIKI WEDDING (1937);ARTISTS AND MODELS
   (1938); THE BOYS FROM SYRACUSE (1940); KEEP 'EM FLYING (1941); HELLZAPOPPIN(1942);
   PIN-UP GIRL (1943); FOUR JILLS IN A JEEP (1944); MONSIEUR VERDOUX (1947);   JUMBO
   (1962), and many others; r.n. Margie Yvonne Reed.

Vocal, acc. by Bobby Henderson-p/Lonnie Johnson-g.
                                         New York, October 6, 1932.

BS-73783-1-2  I Heard                            Vic rejected
BS-73784-1-2  How'm I Doin' (Hey-Hey)            -

  Acc. by O/Dave  Rose.              Los Angeles, May 27, 1939.

LA-1893-   Stairway To The Stars                 Br 8394, Col DB-1873
LA-1894-   Ol' Man River                         Br 8433, Col 36322
LA-1895-   (If You Can't Sing It) You'll Have To    -          -
             Swing It
LA-1896-   Melancholy Mood                       Br 8394, Col DB-1873

                                     Los Angeles, September 17, 1939.

LA-1988-A  Jeanie With The Light Brown Hair      Col 35305
LA-1989-A  Body And Soul                         Col 35522
LA-1990-A  It Ain't Necessarily So               Col 35394
LA-1991-A  I Walk Alone                          Col 35260

                                     Los Angeles, October 8, 1939.

LA-2020-   Once In A While                       Col 35260, Epic SN-6059
LA-2021-   Yesterdays                            Col 35305
LA-2022-   Gone With The Wind                    Col 35394
LA-2023-   Peter, Peter, Pumpkin Eater           Col 35522

                                     New York, March 20, 1942.

70551-A  Pig Foot Pete (Film "Keep 'Em Flying")  Dec 18298, Br 03363
70552-A  My Little Cousin                        Dec 18279, Br 03424
70553-A  Three Little Sisters                    Dec 18298, Br 03363
70554-A  Oh ! The Pity Of It All                 Dec 18279, Br 03424

## GENE RAYMOND

B. New York, August 13, 1908; r.n. Raymond Guion (changed on taking up film  career
   in 1931; debut in PERSONAL MAID); stage debut as a small child in 1913; first big
   success in WHY NOT ? (48th Street, December 25, 1922); then in THE POTTERS  (Plymouth, December 8, 1923); CRADLE SNATCHERS (Music Box, September 7, 1925);  YOUNG
   SINNERS (Morosco, November 28, 1929); other films include FLYING DOWN TO RIO(with
   Fred Astaire and Ginger Rogers, 1933); SEVEN KEYS TO BALDPATE (1934); HATS    OFF
   (1936); THAT GIRL FROM PARIS (1937); SMILIN' THROUGH (with his wife,Jeanette Mac-
   Donald, 1941); HIT THE DECK (1955); THE BEST MAN (1964).

Vocal, acc. by O/Cy Feuer.          Los Angeles, November 19, 1936.

LA-1189-A  Will You ? (Film "Hats Off")          Br 7796
LA-1190-A  Twinkle, Twinkle, Little Star (Film      -       02516
            "Hats Off")

## MAUDE  RAYMOND

B. 1871; became a famous exponent of "coon-shouting" in the opening years of   this
   century; d. Rockville Centre, New York, May 10, 1961.

Vocal, acc. by O/? Walter B. Rogers.        New York, January 29, 1909.

B-6760-1-2  Goodbye, Molly  Brown                    Vic rejected
B-6761-1-2  The Dusky Salome                         -

                                            New York, February 8, 1909.

B-6760-4  Goodbye, Molly  Brown                      Vic 5715
B-6761-4  The Dusky Salome                           Vic 5671
B-6780-2  Bye-Bye, My Caroline                       Vic 5678, 16780

                                            New York, June 4, 1909.

B-8023-1-2  Acting Song No. 1                        Vic rejected
B-8024-1-2  Acting Song No. 2                        -

                                            New York, June 5, 1909.

B-8023-3  Acting Song No. 1                          Vic rejected
B-8024-3  Acting Song No. 2                          -
B-8025-1-2  Coony Spoony Rag                         -
B-8026-1-2  It Sounds Good To Me                     -

                                            New York, April 29, 1910.

B-8025-3  Coony Spoony Rag                           Vic rejected
B-8901-1-2  Grizzly Bear Rag                         -
B-8902-1-2  Rag Baby                                 -
B-8903-1-2  Phoebe Brown                             -
B-8904-1-2  Under The Harvest Moon                   -
B-8905-1-2  That Dreamy Barcarolle Tune              -
B-8906-1  The Stage-Struck Girl - Medley             -

   Acc. by studio orchestra.                New York, c. July, 1910.

        Rag Baby's Gwine To Be Mine                  Ed 10463
        Phoebe Brown                                 Ed 4M-505

   Acc. by O/? Walter B. Rogers.            New York, December 2, 1910.

B-8901-3  Grizzly Bear Rag                           Vic rejected
B-8902-3  Rag Baby                                   -
B-8903-3  Phoebe Brown                               -
B-8904-3  Under The Harvest Moon                     -
B-8905-3-4  That Dreamy Barcarolle Tune              -
B-9683-1-2  The Masquerade                           -

## ANDY RAZAF

B. Washington, D. C., December 16, 1895; grandson of John I. Waller, the first negro
   member of the U.S. Diplomatic Corps; related to the Royal House of Madagascar(r.n.
   Andrea Paul Razafinkeriefo).  Composer of many permanently popular songs(S'POSIN',
   with Paul Denniker, 1929; LOUISIANA and DUSKY STEVEDORE with J. C. Johnson, 1928;
   MEMORIES OF YOU with Eubie Blake, 1930; AIN'T MISBEHAVIN' and HONEYSUCKLE ROSE with
   "Fats" Waller, 1929, and many others) and of scores for shows such as HOT  CHOCO-
   LATES and KEEP SHUFFLIN' (1929) and BLACKBIRDS OF 1930.  D. North Hollywood,Calif-
   ornia, February 3, 1973.

Vocal, acc. by own piano.                   New York, March 7, 1925.

   9396    Don't Forget, You'll Regret Day By Day   Gnt 3082
   9397    He Rambled (Till The Butcher Cut Him     Rejected
           Down)

                                            New York, c. April 24, 1925.

   9490    Who Takes Care Of The Caretaker's         Gnt 3052
           Daughter ?
   9491    Yes, Sir ! That's My Baby                 -

New York, c. May 25, 1925.

| | | |
|---|---|---|
| 9561 | On Rainy Days | Gnt 3119 |
| 9562 | Someday We'll Meet Again | Rejected |

Acc. by unknown ukulele.            New York, c. June 17, 1925.

| | | |
|---|---|---|
| 9592 | Because Of You (The World Is Mine) | Gnt rejected |
| 9593 | Her Have Went, Her Have Gone (Her Have Left I All Alone) | - |

Acc. by unknown bj/u.               New York, c. July 1, 1925.

| | | |
|---|---|---|
| 9632 | Cecilia | Gnt 3102 |
| 9633 | I'm Gonna Charleston Back To Charleston | - |

Acc. unknown.                       New York, August 6, 1925.

| | | |
|---|---|---|
| 6121- | Because Of You (The World Is Mine) | ARC rejected |

New York, c. September 15, 1925.

| | | |
|---|---|---|
| 9728 | When A Blonde Makes Up Her Mind To Do You Good | Gnt rejected |
| 9729 | My Sweetie Turned Me Down | - |
| 9730 | Her Have Went, Her Have Gone (Her Have Left I All Alone) | - |

CROONING ANDY RAZAF : Vocal, acc. by "Fats" Waller-p.
New York, November 4, 1927.

| | | |
|---|---|---|
| 144956- | Empty Arms | Col 14265-D |
| 144957- | All The World Is Lonely (For A Little Blackbird) | - |

## PHIL REGAN

B. 1906; popular radio and TV singer before entering politics in the 1960s; he made many films, e.g., DAMES; STUDENT TOUR and SWEET ADELINE (1934); BROADWAY HOSTESS; WE'RE IN THE MONEY and IN CALIENTE (1935); LAUGHING IRISH EYES; HAPPY GO LUCKY and HIT PARADE (1936); MANHATTAN MUSIC BOX and OUTSIDE OF PARADISE (1937).

Vocal, acc. by O/? Ben Selvin.      New York, February 9, 1933.

| | | |
|---|---|---|
| 152374- | Close To My Heart | Col 2755-D |
| 152375- | You're Beautiful Tonight, My Dear | - |

Vocalist with Fred Rich and his Orchestra.
New York, December 20, 1933.

| | | |
|---|---|---|
| 152655-1 | Let's Fall In Love | Col 2868-D, CB-728 |
| 152656-2 | You Have Taken My Heart | Col 2866-D  - |

Vocal, acc. by studio orchestra.    New York, August 7, 1934.

| | | |
|---|---|---|
| CO-15541- | By The Taj Mahal | Col 2948-D |
| CO-15542- | A New Moon Is Over My Shoulder | - |
| CO-15543- | I Only Have Eyes For You (Film "Dames") | Col 2942-D |
| CO-15544- | My Journey's End | - |

Acc. by Jimmie Grier and his Orchestra. Los Angeles, November 14, 1934.

| | | |
|---|---|---|
| LA-269- | We Were So Young (Film "Sweet Adeline") | Col 2990-D, RZ MR-1757 |
| LA-270- | Molly O'Donahue (Film "Sweet Adeline") | -        - |

Acc. by Mahlon Merrick and his Music.   Los Angeles, April 11, 1935.

| | | |
|---|---|---|
| LA-1012- | To Call You My Own (Film "In Caliente") | Col 3035-D, RZ MR-1894 |
| LA-1013- | Muchacha (Film "In Caliente") | -        - |

Acc. by studio orchestra.                    New York, July 24, 1935.

CO-17869-   So Nice Seeing You Again              Col 3075-D
CO-17870-   A Sunbonnet Blue (And A Yellow Straw Hat)

Acc. by O/Harry Jackson.                     Los Angeles, November 21, 1935.

LA-1076-    Let It Be Me (Film "Broadway Hostess")  Col 3106-D, RZ MR-2063
LA-1077-    Weary (Film "Broadway Hostess")         -              -
                                                                   .

Acc. by studio orchestra.                    New York, February 20, 1936.

B-18702-2   Laughing Irish Eyes (Film "Laughing     Br 7623, 02227
              Irish Eyes")
B-18703-1   All My Life (Film "Laughing Irish Eyes")  -        -

Acc. by O/Cy Feuer.                          Los Angeles, March 17, 1937.

LA-1300-    Sweet Heartache (Film "Hit Parade")     Br 7869
LA-1301-    Last Night I Dreamed Of You             Br 7864, Dec F-6486
LA-1302-    Was It Rain ? (Film "Hit Parade")       Br 7864
LA-1303-    Seventh Heaven                          Br 7869, Dec F-6486

                                             Los Angeles, October 8, 1937.

LA-1448-    I Owe You (Film "Manhattan Music Box")  Br 7984, Dec F-6643
LA-1449-    Have You Ever Been In Heaven ? (Film    -           -
              "Manhattan Music Box")
LA-1450-    When Irish Eyes Are Smiling             Br 8086

                                             Los Angeles, December 17, 1937.

LA-1553-A   A Sweet Irish Sweetheart Of Mine (Film  Br 8051, Col FB-1993
              "Outside Of Paradise")
LA-1554-A   Outside Of Paradise (Film "Outside Of   -           -
              Paradise")
LA-1555-    Come Back To Erin                       Br 8086

## THE REVELERS

The most popular singing group in the U.S.A. during the latter half of the 1920s, in
vaudeville and cabaret, on the air and on records, the sales of which in England
were enough to warrant the quintet appearing there at the New Prince's Restaurant
in London in October, 1926. Originally known as the Shannon Quartet, consisting
of Lewis James and Franklyn Baur (tenors), Elliott Shaw (baritone) and    Wilfred
Glenn (bass), they were augmented by Ed Smalle (baritone, piano accompanist    and
arranger) in 1924, and secured radio work which made them more than just    another
recording unit. The name The Revelers is the one by which they are best    remembered, and under which they made Victor (HMV) records; on Brunswick they recorded
as The Merrymakers, and on Columbia as The Singing Sophomores (q.v.) Duos, trios
and quartets from within their ranks recorded vocal refrains on hundreds of sides
by dance bands of all kinds, frequently anonymously; but as the unique sound that
brought them fame for nearly a decade is that associated with all five    singers,
only the recordings they made as a group are listed here.

Vocal quintet, acc. by Ed Smalle-p/Carson Robison-g-w.
                                  Camden, N. J., July 13, 1925.

BVE-33072-1-2-3-4  Just A Bundle Of Sunshine       Vic rejected
BVE-33076-1-2-3-4-5  Every Sunday Afternoon          -

                                  Camden, N. J., July 20, 1925.

BVE-33072-7  Just A Bundle Of Sunshine             Vic 19731, HMV B-2304
BVE-33076-7  Every Sunday Afternoon                  -              -
   NOTE:- Matrices BVE-33073/5 inclusive are not by The Revelers.

Robison omitted.                        Camden, N..J., September 4, 1925.

BVE-33251-2  I'm Gonna Charleston Back To        Vic 19778, HMV B-2182
             Charleston
BVE-33252-5  Dinah                               Vic 19796        -

                                        Camden, N. J., September 12, 1925.

BVE-33273-1-2-3-4-5  Collegiate                  Vic rejected

                                        Camden, N. J., September 15, 1925.

BVE-33273-8  Collegiate                          Vic 19778, HMV B-2236
BVE-33281-6  Oh, Miss Hannah                     Vic 19796        -

                                        New York, November 5, 1925.

BVE-33850-4  Bam Bam Bammy Shore                 Vic 19848, HMV B-2276

                                        New York, January 6, 1926.

BVE-34300-2  Where Is My Rose Of Waikiki ? (w/   Vic 19949, HMV B-2303
             May Singhi Brden-u)

                                        New York, January 13, 1926.

BVE-33252-9  Dinah                               Vic 19796

                                        New York, January 26, 1926.

BVE-34360-1  Don't Wait Too Long                 Vic 19949, HMV B-2303

                                        New York, February 12, 1926.

CVE-34614-2  Tip-Toes - Vocal Gems (Intro. These   Vic 35772, HMV C-1293
             Charming People/That Certain Feeling/When Do We Dance ?/Looking For A
             Boy/Sweet And Low Down) (w/Gladys Rice)
BVE-34615-4  Just Around The Corner              Vic 19968, HMV B-2340

                                        New York, February 25, 1926.

BVE-34650-1-2-3-4-5  Swinging On The Gate        Vic rejected

                                        New York, March 17, 1926.

BVE-34699-1-2-3-4-5  Tentin' Down In Tennessee   Vic rejected

                                        New York, May 10, 1926.

BVE-35386-5  No Foolin'                          Vic 20064, HMV B-2334

                                        New York, May 17, 1926.

BVE-35609-1  Talking To The Moon                 Vic 20064, HMV B-2334

                                        New York, June 2, 1926.

BVE-35653-1  Valencia (A Song Of Spain)          Vic 20082, HMV B-2340

                                        New York, June 8, 1926.

BVE-35666-2  The Blue Room                       Vic 20082, HMV B-2541

                                        New York, July 14, 1926.

BVE-35769-2  Lucky Day                           Vic 20111, LPV-557, LSA-3075,
                                                 HMV B-2504
BVE-35770-4  The Birth Of The Blues              Vic 20111, HMV B-2468

New York, August 13, 1926.

BVE-36045-1  Moonlight On The Ganges              Vic 20140, HMV B-2360

New York, August 16, 1926.

BVE-36046-1  Breezin' Along With The Breeze      Vic 20140, HMV B-2360

  Smalle leaves the group; Frank Black-p except on dance band vocals by the quartet.


Vocalists with Nat Shilkret and the Victor Orchestra.
                                New York, November 29, 1926.

BVE-36981-3  The Riff Song                        Vic 20373, HMV B-5233

Vocal quartet, acc. by Frank Black-p.    New York, December 2, 1926.

BVE-36993-3  Mary Lou                             Vic 20380, HMV B-2443

                                New York, December 8, 1926.

BVE-37113-1  I Know That You Know                 Vic 20380

                                New York, December 24, 1926.

BVE-37179-1  All Alone Monday                     Vic 20417

                                New York, December 29, 1926.

BVE-37187-1-2-3  You Remind Me Of A Naughty       Vic rejected
                 Springtime Cuckoo


                                New York, January 14, 1927.

CVE-37723-1  Oh, Kay ! - Vocal Gems (Intro. Clap    Vic 35811, HMV C-1396
             Yo' Hands/Someone To Watch Over Me/Maybe/Do-Do-Do) (w/Gladys Rice and
             extra pianist-Adam Carroll)

                                New York, January 20, 1927.

BVE-37556-1  In A Little Spanish Town             Vic 20457, LPV-523, LSA-3078,
                                                  HMV B-2443

Vocalists with the International Novelty Orchestra.
                                New York, February 17, 1927.

BVE-37790-1-2-3-4  Muddy Water                    Vic rejected

Vocal quartet (Lewis James-Franklyn Baur-Elliott Shaw-Wilfred Glenn), acc. by  Frank
   Black-p.                      New York, March 16, 1927.

BVE-38173-1-2-3  Yankee Rose                      Vic rejected

                                New York, March 25, 1927.

BVE-38409-3  So Blue                              Vic 20564, HMV B-2468

  Charles Harrison-tenor replaces Baur.   New York, March 28, 1927.

BVE-38173-4  Yankee Rose                          Vic 20564, HMV B-2518

Vocalists with Nat Shilkret and the Victor Orchestra.
                                New York, April 7, 1927.

BVE-38438-2  The More We Are Together             Vic 20603
BVE-38439-2  Yesterday                            Vic 20597, HMV B-5324

Vocal quartet (Lewis James-Franklyn Baur-Elliott Shaw-Wilfred Glenn), acc. by Frank
   Black-p.                                    New York, April 25, 1927.

BVE-38489-2  Hallelujah !                              Vic 20609, LPV-545, LSA-3077,
                                                       RD-7903, HMV B-2520

                             New York, May 13, 1927.

BVE-38751-   I'm Looking Over A Four-Leaf Clover   Vic 20678, HMV B-2504

                             New York, May 23, 1927.

BVE-38776-   I'm In Love Again                      Vic 20678, HMV B-2518

  Charles Harrison-tenor replaces James.  New York, May 27, 1927.

BVE-38794-   Honolulu Moon                          Vic 20719

  Lewis James-tenor replaces Harrison; vocalists with The Troubadours/Nat Shilkret.
                             New York, September 8, 1927.

BVE-39164-1  Baby Feet Go Pitter-Patter (¶Cross    Vic 20967, HMV B-5416
           My Floor)

  Acc. by Frank Black-p.                    New York, September 8, 1927.

BVE-39168-   Roam On, My Little Gypsy Sweetheart   Vic 20920, HMV B-2611

                             New York, September 12, 1927.

BVE-39171-   Blue River                             Vic 20920, HMV B-2611

  Frank Luther-tenor replaces Baur; as VICTOR SALON GROUP, acc. by Milt Rettenberg-p
  and Nat Shilkret and the Victor Orchestra.
                             New York, September 23, 1927.

BVE-40112-   C'est vous (It's You)                  Vic 20985, HMV B-2639
BVE-40113-   Dawn Of Tomorrow                          -           -

Vocal quartet (Lewis James-Ed Smalle-Elliott Shaw-Wilfred Glenn),acc. by Frank Black
p.                                              New York, October 26, 1927.

BVE-40514-   The 'Varsity Drag                      Vic 21039, HMV B-2766

  James Melton-tenor replaces Smalle.    New York, November 18, 1927.

BVE-40597-1  Nola                                   Vic 21100, HMV B-2680

Vocal trio (James-Shaw-Glenn only, but labelled THE REVELERS (!), acc. by 3vn/vc/p/d
  - Frank Black probably the pianist).    New York, November 23, 1927.

BVE-41106-2  Among My Souvenirs (Souvenirs*)       Vic 21100, HMV B-2680*

  James Melton-tenor returns; vocalists with The Troubadours/Nat Shilkret.
                             New York, December 2, 1927.

BVE-41093-1-2-3  The Song Is Ended (But The Melody Vic rejected
           Lingers On)

                             New York, December 15, 1927.

BVE-41178-2  Tin Pan Parade                         Vic 21149, HMV B-5462

Vocal quartet, acc. by Frank Black-p.    New York, December 15, 1927.

BVE-41179-2  Oh ! Lucindy                           Vic 21241, HMV B-2816

Vocalists with Nat Shilkret and the Victor Orchestra.
                             New York, December 22, 1927.

BVE-41197-2  The Whip                               Vic 21170

Vocal quartet (Lewis James-James Melton-Elliott Shaw-Wilfred Glenn), acc. by    Frank
    Black-p.                          New York, January 11, 1928.

BVE-41539-2   Ol' Man River                      Vic 21241, HMV B-2735

Vocalists with Nat Shilkret and the Victor Orchestra.
                                      New York, March 15, 1928.

CVE-43365-   Mask And Wig Medley ("Tarantella")   Vic 35915

Vocal quartet as for January 11, 1928,   New York, March 27, 1928.

BVE-43505-1   Dream River (w/Roy Smeck-octochorda)  Vic 21448, HMV B-2816

Vocalists with Victor Arden-Phil Ohman and their Orchestra.
                                      New York, April 5, 1928.

CVE-43533-2   Good News-Selection(The Revelers sing Vic 35918, HMV C-1547
              a chorus of LUCKY IN LOVE and half a chorus of GOOD NEWS)
CVE-43534-    Funny Face - Selection (Intro.          -        HMV C-1586
              'S Wonderful/My One And Only/He Loves And She Loves/Funny Face)

Vocal quartet as last, acc. by Frank Black-p.
                                      New York, April 27, 1928.

BVE-43927-    Narcissus                          HMV B-2804

                                      New York, May 4, 1928.

BVE-43949-1-2-3-4  Canzone amoroso               Vic rejected

                                      New York, May 11, 1928.

BVE-43972-3  Mammy Is Gone                       Vic 21448, HMV B-2804

                                      New York, May 16, 1928.

BVE-43989-1-2-3  Was It A Dream ?                Vic rejected

Vocalists with the International Novelty Orchestra.
                                      Camden, N. J., May 17, 1928.

CVE-41991-1-2-3  The Blue Danube                 Vic rejected

Vocal quartet as last, acc. by Frank Black-p.
                                      New York, June 8, 1928.

BVE-43989-4  Was It A Dream ?                     Vic 21516, HMV B-2834

At this point, The Revelers supplied some of the vocal part of an album of    Stephen
    Foster songs, mostly as a background to other soloists (Frank Crumit, Olive Kline,
    Vaughn de Leath, Gladys Rice and others).

                                      New York, September 20, 1928.

BVE-47537-1-2  Blue Shadows                       Vic rejected
BVE-47538-1-2-3  Dusky Stevedore                      -

                                      New York, October 23, 1928.

BVE-47537-3  Blue Shadows                         Vic 21765, HMV B-2912
BVE-47538-4  Dusky Stevedore                          -          -

Vocalists with Victor Arden-Phil Ohman and their Orchestra.
                                      New York, October 25, 1928.

BVE-47782-3  Lover, Come Back To Me !             Vic 21776, HMV B-5634
BVE-47783-4  Marianne                                 -          -

Vocal quartet as before, acc. by Frank Black-p.
                              New York, November 6, 1928.

BVE-47537-6-7-8  Blue Shadows                    Vic rejected
BVE-47538-9-10   Dusky Stevedore                     -

Vocalists with the High Hatters/Leonard Joy.
                              New York, November 8, 1928.

BVE-48137-1  Wipin' The Pan                      Vic 21835, HMV B-5626

Vocal quartet as before, acc. by Frank Black-p.
                              New York, November 14, 1928.

BVE-46381-3  Comin' Home                         Vic 21807, HMV B-2972
BVE-46382-1  Evenin'                                 -           -

Vocalists with Victor Arden-Phil Ohman and their Orchestra.
                              New York, November 22, 1928.

BVE-48194-3  Got A Rainbow                       Vic 21795

Vocal quartet as before, acc. by Frank Black-p.
                              New York, January 8, 1929.

BVE-49048-1-2-3  Raquel                          Vic rejected

                              New York, January 23, 1929.

BVE-49048-6  Raquel                              Vic 21911, HMV B-3059

   Jack Parker-tenor replaces Melton.    New York, May 2, 1929.

BVE-51680-1-2-3-4  Wake Up, Chillun, Wake Up     Vic rejected

   James Melton-tenor replaces Parker.    New York, May 21, 1929.

BVE-53423-2  Ploddin' Along                      Vic 22036, HMV B-3156

                              New York, June 11, 1929.

BVE-51680-7  Wake Up, Chillun, Wake Up           Vic 22036, HMV B-3156

                              New York, November 22, 1929.

BVE-57552-1-2-3  Waiting At The End Of The Road  Rejected
BVE-57553-1  Kentucky Babe                       Vic 22249, HMV B-3416

                              New York, December 2, 1929.

BVE-57552-4-5  Waiting At The End Of The Road    Rejected
BVE-57569-1-2-3  Love, Your Spell Is Everywhere      -
BVE-57570-1  Little Cotton Dolly                 Vic 22249, HMV B-3416

                              New York, January 2, 1930.

BVE-57552-8  Waiting At The End Of The Road      Vic 22270
BVE-57971-1  Chant Of The Jungle                     -

                              New York, January 30, 1930.

BVE-58536-2  A Cottage For Sale                  Vic 22382

Vocalists with Victor Arden-Phil Ohman and their Orchestra.
                              New York, January 31, 1930.

BVE-58640-3  Strike Up The Band                  Vic 22308

Vocal quartet (Lewis James-James Melton-Elliott Shaw-Wilfred Glenn), acc. by   Frank
    Black-p.                            New York, March 21, 1930.

BVE-59647-2  The Woman In The Shoe              Vic 22382, HMV B-3531

                                         New York, March 31, 193D.

BVE-59659-1-2-3  The Snowball Men               Rejected
BVE-59660-3  Strike Up The Band                 Vic 22401

                                         New York, April 10, 1930.

BVE-59689-3  Singin' A Vagabond Song            Vic 22401, HMV B-3497

                                         New York, May 7, 1930.

BVE-62217-2  Sing, You Sinners                  Vic 22422, HMV B-3531

                                         New York, October 2, 1930.

BVE-63691-3  Sing Something Simple              Vic 22547, HMV B-3704

                                         New York, October 7, 1930.

BVE-64302-1-2-3  So Beats My Heart For You      Rejected
BVE-64303-1  Happy Feet                         Vic 22547, HMV B-3704

                                         New York, January 19, 1931.

BVE-64856-1-2-3  Lady, Play Your Mandolin (w/John  Vic rejected
            Cali-bj-g)

                                         New York, January 26, 1931.

BVE-64856-4  Lady, Play Your Mandolin (w/Dick   Vic 22612, HMV B-3840
            Maffei-md)
BVE-67419-2  Blue Again                         Vic 22622      -

                                         New York, April 28, 1931.

BVE-53064-1-2  Hosanna !                        Vic rejected
BVE-53065-1-2  The King's Horses (And The King's Men)  -

                                         New York, July 24, 1931.

BS-70203-1  When Yuba Plays The Rumba On The Tuba  Vic 22772, HMV B-4164
BS-70204-1  Dancing In The Dark                 -        24707, HMV B-4077

   Jack Parker-tenor replaces Melton.    New York, January 2, 1934.

BS-81017-1-2  The Ginger Bread Parade           Vic rejected
BS-81018-1  Grandfather's Clock                 -
BS-81019-1  The Last Round-Up                   -

                                         New York, January 25, 1934.

BS-81019-2  The Last Round-Up                   Vic rejected

See also Jeanette MacDonald.

## HARRY RICHMAN

B. Cincinnati, Ohio, August 10, 1895; became pianist in a cafe there at eleven;  one
year later he was singing in vaudeville with the Jewel City Trio, and later, Those
Three Boys; then after some experience on the Keith theatre circuit, he became the
accompanist in a New York 7th Avenue honky-tonk to Mae West, also the Dolly   Sis-
ters; caught the attention of radio promoter Nils Granlund of WHN, on which  Harry
Richman first broadcast (1924); appeared in many Broadway shows (e.g.,   QUEEN O'
HEARTS (1922); GEORGE WHITE'S SCANDALS (Apollo, June 14, 1926 and July 2,  1928);
SONS O' GUNS (Imperial, November 26, 1929); appeared in some films (PUTTIN' ON THE

RITZ (1930); THE MUSIC GOES ROUND (1936); STARS OVER ARIZONA (1937); KICKING  THE
MOON AROUND (with Bob Hope, in England, 1938); NEWCOMERS OF 1926 (1959); appeared
in London in the spring and summer of 1937 and 1938; very popular at the   Desert
Inn, Las Vegas, and the Latin Quarter, New York, 1963; composed several very successful songs (THERE'S DANGER IN YOUR EYES, CHERIE (1929); SINGIN' A VAGABOND SONG
(1930); WALKIN' MY BABY BACK HOME (1931) and others).  D. Hollywood,  November 3,
1972.

Vocal, acc. by unknown g (and studio orchestra where shown).
                                        New York, c. January 30, 1925.

    5833-3  Will You Remember Me ? (w/orchestra)     Ban 1493
    5834-2  California Poppy                           -

    Acc. by studio orchestra.                   New York, July, 1926.

E-3621; E-23058  The Birth Of The Blues           Voc 15412
E-3625/6; E-23062/3  Lucky Day                      -         Br 3523

                                        New York, September, 1926.

E-3826     Here I Am                              Voc 15457
E-3828/9   I Want To Be Known As "Susie's Feller"   -

                                        New York, c. January, 1927.

E-4410/2  Mine                                    Voc 15511, Br 5-15511

E-4449    Blue Skies                              Voc 15511, Br 5-15511

E-21259/61  Muddy Water                           Br 3435
E-21262/3/4  Ain't She Sweet ?                      -

                                        New York, February, 1927.

E-21881½  What Does It Matter ?                   Br 3501
E-21882   It All Depends On You                     -         Br 4626

                                        New York, March, 1927.

E-4691    Moonbeam, Kiss Her For Me               Voc 15540

E-4705    So Blue                                 Voc 15540, Br 3523

                                        New York, April, 1927.

E-5047    Rosy Cheeks                             Voc 15560
E-5050    Dixie Vagabond                            -

E-22877   My Idea Of Heaven                       Br 3538

                                        New York, May, 1927.

E-23298   Hallelujah !                            Br 3569, 4770

                                        New York, June, 1927.

E-23539   Ain't That A Grand And Glorious Feeling? Br 3583

E-23614   Magnolia                               Br 3583
E-23616   Just Like A Butterfly                  Br 3569
E-23617   C'est vous (It's You)                  Br 3538

    Acc. by O/Nat Shilkret.             New York, March 1, 1928.

BVE-43305-1-2  Back In Your Own Back Yard          Vic rejected
BVE-43306-1-2  Laugh, Clown, Laugh !                -

Acc. by studio orchestra.                    New York, March, 1928.

E-27101/2   I Just Roll Along (Having My Ups And        Br 3889
               Downs)
E-27103     I'm Riding To Glory (With A Glorious        Br 3890
               Girl)

E-27181/2   Laugh, Clown, Laugh !                       Br 3889
E-27184     That's My Mammy                             Br 3890

                                              New York, c. July 31, 1928.

E-27904-    I'm On The Crest Of A Wave                  Br 4008
E-27905-    What D'Ya Say ?                             -

                                              New York, August, 1928.

E-28106-    King For A Day                              Br 4035, 3873
E-28107-    I Can't Give You Anything But Love, Baby    -       -

E-28148-    Moonlight Madness (Then You Were Gone)  Voc 15725
E-28149-    Out Of The Dawn                             -

                                              New York, November, 1928.

E-29010-    You're The Cream In My Coffee               Br 4173
E-29011-    She's Funny That Way                        -

                                              New York, December, 1928.

E-29043-    Makin' Whoopee                              Br 4197, 4626
E-29044-    Don't Be Like That                          -

                                              New York, c. May 31, 1929.

E-29980-    My Dear                                     Br 4420
E-29981-    Now I'm In Love                             -

Acc. by Earl Burtnett and his Los Angeles Biltmore Hotel Orchestra.
                                        Los Angeles, c. February, 1930.

LAE-671-    Singing A Vagabond Song (Film "Puttin'   Br 4678, 01014
               On The Ritz")
LAE-672-    Puttin' On The Ritz (Film "Puttin' On    Br 4677, 01010
               The Ritz")
LAE-673-    There's Danger In Your Eyes, Cherie         -       -
               (Film "Puttin' On The Ritz")
LAE-674-    With You (Film "Puttin' On The Ritz")    Br 4678, 01014

Acc. by studio orchestra.              New York, c. April, 1930.

E-32425-    Exactly Like You ("International Revue")  Br 4747
E-32426-    On The Sunny Side Of The Street             -
               ("International Revue")

                                              New York, May, 1930.

E-32767-    Thank Your Father                           Br 4799, 01107
E-32768-    Without Love                                -       -

                                              New York, June, 1930.

E-32851-    Dream Avenue                                Br 4817
E-32852-    Ro-Ro-Rollin' Along                         -

                                              New York, February, 1931.

E-36057-    Just A Gigolo                               Br 6052
E-36058-    When Your Lover Has Gone                    -

New York, August 15, 1932.

152265-2  I Love A Parade                    Col 2701-D, DB-981,Epic L2N-6072
152266-2  It Was So Beautiful                    -          -

New York, October 17, 1934.

P-16192-   Song Of The Evening ("Say When")    Col Personal Recording
CO-16193-  Song Of The Evening ("Say When")    Rejected
CO-16194-  Say When ("Say When")               Col 2965-D
CO-16195-  When Love Comes Swinging Along ("Say    -
           When")

New York, December 21, 1934.

CO-16527-  June In January                     Col 2995-D
CO-16528-  With Every Breath I Take               -

New York, January 22, 1935.

CO-16678-  I'm Facing The Music                Col 3017-D
CO-16679-  According To The Moonlight             -

Acc. by small jazz band.              New York, January 26, 1936.

60391-A  Life Begins When You're In Love (Film    Dec 700, Br 02161
         "The Music Goes Round")
60392-A  Let's Go (Film "The Music Goes Round")     -        -
60393-A  Suzannah (Film "The Music Goes Round")   Dec 701, Br 02162
60394-A  There'll Be No South (Film "The Music      -        -
         Goes Round")

Acc. by studio orchestra.             New York, February 5, 1936.

60440-A  Alone                                 Dec 702, Br 02154
60441-A  If I Should Lose You                     -        -

Acc. by O/Carroll Gibbons.            London, May 10, 1937.

CA-16375-1  The Night Is Young And You're So    Col DB-1698
            Beautiful
CA-16376-1  Pennies From Heaven                    -

London, July 20,,1937.

CA-16480-1  Broken-Hearted Clown                Col DB-1711
CA-16481-1  They All Laughed                       -
CA-16488-1  The Music Goes 'Round And Around    Rejected
   NOTE:- Matrices CA-16482/7 inclusive are not by Harry Richman.

London, September 25, 1937.

CA-16578-1  Shake Hands With A Millionaire      Col DB-1728
CA-16579-1  Your Broadway And My Broadway          -

Acc. by O/Jack Golden.                London, June 10, 1938.

OEA-6357-1  Weep And You Dance Alone            HMV B-8760
OEA-6358-1  The Sweetest Sweetheart Of All         -

London, June 29, 1938.

OEA-6507-1  Daddy's Boy                         HMV B-8770
OEA-6508-1  Down And Out Blues                     -
OEA-6509-2  Say Goodnight To Your Old-Fashioned  HMV B-8774
            Mother
OEA-6510-2  You're What's The Matter With Me       -

B. Greenfield, Ind., October 7, 1849; author of many well-known poems, which he began writing while contributing to various Indiana newspapers in 1873 (he was with
the Indianapolis Journal, 1877-1885). D. Indianapolis, July 22, 1916.

Speech, unacc.                                    New York, April 29, 1912.

C-11972-1-2  An Old Sweetheart Of Mine ("After-    Rejected
                whiles")
B-11973-1  When The Frost Is On The Punkin           -
                ("Afterwhiles")
B-11974-1  On The Banks Of Deer Crick ("Farm Rhymes")  -
C-11975-1-2  Out To Old Aunt Mary's                  -
B-11976-1  Thoughts For The Discouraged Farmer       -
                ("Neighborly Poems") (in Hoosier dialect)
B-11977-1  Little Orphant Annie ("Afterwhiles")   Vic 60075, 45190
B-11978-1  The Raggedy Man ("Poems From Here At    Vic 60076    -
                Home")
B-11979-1  The Old Band ("Poems From Here At Home")Rejected
C-11980-1  The Happy Little Cripple ("Rhymes Of    Vic 70079, 55095
                Childhood")

                                    New York, June 4, 1912.

C-12087-1  The Old Man And Jim ("Here At Home")    Vic rejected
C-12088-1  Dot Leedle Boy ("Green Fields And        -
                Running Brooks")
B-12089-1  Her Beautiful Hands ("Lockerbie Book")   -

                                    New York, June 5, 1912.

C-11972-2  An Old Sweetheart Of Mine ("After-       Rejected
                whiles")
C-11975-3  Out To Old Aunt Mary's                  Vic 70078, 55095
C-12090-1  The Name Of Old Glory, 1898             Rejected
C-12091-1  The Soldier's Story                      -
C-12092-1  The Boy's Bear Story                     -
C-12093-1  The Object Lesson Of A Peanut            -
C-12094-1  Tradin' Jim ("Poems Of Here At Home")    -
B-12095-1  A Life's Lesson/In The Dark              -
B-12096-1  Kissing The Rod/The Prayer Perfect       -
B-12097-1  The Harper/The Rain                      -

## BLANCHE RING

B. Boston, Mass., April 24, 1877; played small parts in and around Boston until her
New York debut in TOMMY ROT (Mrs. Osborn's Playhouse, 1902); then followed more
sophisticated roles (THE BLONDE IN BLACK,(Knickerbocker, June 8, 1903);THE JERSEY
LILY (Victoria, September 14, 1903); London debut in a programme of songs in variety (vaudeville) at the Palace, November 16, 1903, and in THE LOVE BIRDS (Savoy,
February 10, 1904); returned to America and after a tour in VIVIAN'S PAPAS,played
in SERGEANT BRUE (Knickerbocker, April 24, 1905); IT HAPPENED IN NORDLAND (revival, Lew Fields' Theatre, August 31, 1905); ABOUT TOWN (Lew Fields, November 15,
1906); toured in this and other shows, returned to New York to play in THE GREAT
WHITE WAY (Casino, October 7, 1907); THE MIDNIGHT SONS (Broadway, May 22, 1909);
toured through the mid-West to California for ten years, returning to New York to
appear in THE PASSING SHOW OF 1919 (Winter Garden, October 23, 1919); THE BROAD-
WAY WHIRL (Times Square, June 8, 1921); THE HOUSE BOAT ON THE STYX (Liberty, December 25, 1928, playing Queen Elizabeth I); STRIKE UP THE BAND (Times Square,Jan-
uary 14, 1930); in the mid-twenties on tour in Chicago and elsewhere, and in New
York, she played every kind of part from the title-role of NO, NO, NANETTE to Mrs.
Quickly in Shakespeare's KING HENRY IV, Part 1; she made two silent pictures,both
in 1915 (PRETTY MRS. SMITH, with Elsie Janis and Fritzi Scheff) and THE YANKEE
GIRL); her two most famous songs are IN THE GOOD OLD SUMMER TIME and YIP-I-ADDY-I
AY. D. Santa Monica, Calif., January 13, 1961.

Vocal, acc. by O/? Walter B. Rogers.    New York, March 20, 1909.

B-6914-3  Yip ! I Adee ! I Aye ! (sic)            Vic 5692, 60017, 45188,
                                                  HMV 3817, AR 2290

New York, June 24, 1909.

B-8073-2  The Billiken Man                     Vic 5731, 60015
B-8074-2  I've Got Rings On My Fingers         Vic 5737, 60016 , 45188

New York, July 11, 1910.

B-9308-1-2  The Top O' The Morning             Vic rejected
B-9309-1-2-3  Louisiana Lizabeth               -
B-9310-3  Nora Malone                          Vic 60024

New York, July 21, 1910.

B-9308-3  The Top O' The Morning               Vic 60025
B-9309-4-5  Louisiana Lizabeth                 Rejected

New York, December 22, 1910.

B-9735-1  Come, Josephine, In My Flying Machine  Vic 60032
B-9736-1-2  Let's Make Love Among The Roses      Rejected

Acc. by studio orchestra.          New York, c. September, 1920.

68607    Barney, Come Over Here          Pathe 22419, Cleartone 819

## LYDA ROBERTI

B. Warsaw (?), 1910; was a child cafe-singer before obtaining work in many Holly-
wood films (MILLION DOLLAR LEGS and THE KID FROM SPAIN (1932); THREE-CORNERED MOON
(1933); COLLEGE RHYTHM (1934); GEORGE WHITE'S SCANDALS (1935); PICK A STAR and WIDE
OPEN FACES (1937), and others); d. March 12, 1938. Also appeared in New York with
Lou Holtz in YOU SAID IT (46th Street, January 19, 1931).
Vocal, acc. by Jimmie Grier and his Orchestra.
                              Los Angeles, October 5, 1934.

LA-227-  Take A Number From One To Ten (Film   Col 2967-D, CL-2751
           "College Rhythm")
LA-228-  College Rhythm (Film "College Rhythm")    -        -

## PAUL ROBESON

B. Princeton, N.J., April 9, 1898; educated at Rutger's University (B.A.,  Honorary
M.A., 1932); Columbia University (LL.B., admitted to the Bar in New York); took up
acting as profession and made his debut in SIMON THE CYRENIAN (Lafayette, 1921); in
TABOO (Sam H. Harris Theatre, April, 1922); English debut in the same play(but re-
named THE VOODOO for its presentation in the Opera House, Blackpool, July 20,1922,
with Mrs. Patrick Campbell playing the female lead); returned to New York and made
a great impression in ALL GOD'S CHILLUN GOT WINGS (Provincetown, May, 1924); later
in THE EMPEROR JONES (52nd Street, February, 1925); London debut in this  (Ambassadors, September 10, 1925); played various other parts in New York before  coming
back to London for his greatest triumph in SHOW BOAT (Drury Lane, May 3, 1928); he
also gave song recitals during the run of this, and afterwards toured England as a
concert artist; in 1929 he toured Europe in this capacity, also playing THE  EMPE-
ROR JONES in Berlin in April, 1930; to New York for revival of SHOW BOAT  (Casino,
May 19, 1932); returned to London in October and remained there until after  World
War II had broken out; his starring as OTHELLO (Shubert, October 19, 1943) set  up
a record for the longest run of any Shakespearean production (295); starred in   a
number of British films (THE EMPEROR JONES (1933); SANDERS OF THE RIVER (1935);the
second filming of SHOW BOAT (1936); SONG OF FREEDOM and KING SOLOMON'S MINES(1937);
JERICHO (1938); THE PROUD VALLEY (1939); and an excellent American production with
an all-star cast, TALES OF MANHATTAN (1942).

Vocal, acc. by Lawrence Brown-p (and voice where shown).
                              Camden, N. J., July 16, 1925.

BVE-33084-1-2  Water Boy                       Rejected
BVE-33085-2  Bye And Bye                       Vic 19743, HMV B-2126
BVE-33086-1-2  Were You There ?                Rejected
BVE-33087-1-2  Steal Away                      -
BVE-33088-1  Joshua Fit De Battle Ob Jericho (w/LB)   -

Camden, N. J., July 27, 1925.

```
BVE-32798-1-2  Li'l Gal                          Rejected
BVE-32799-1-2  I'll Hear The Trumpet Sound         -
BVE-33084-3-4  Water Boy                           -
BVE-33086-4  Were You There ?               Vic 19742, HMV B-2126
BVE-33087-4  Steal Away                         -        HMV B-2187
BVE-33088-2-3  Joshua Fit De Battle Ob Jericho   Rejected
               (w/Lawrence Brown)
```

Camden, N. J., July 30, 1925.

```
BVE-33085-3-4  Bye And Bye (w/Lawrence Brown)    Rejected
BVE-33088-5  Joshua Fit De Battle Ob Jericho (w/LB)  Vic 19743, HMV B-2339
BVE-33119-1-2  Swing Low, Sweet Chariot          Rejected
```

Camden, N. J., January 7, 1926.

```
BVE-32798-3-4  Li'l Gal                          Rejected
BVE-33084-6  Water Boy                        Vic 19824, HMV B-2187
BVE-33119-3  Swing Low, Sweet Chariot         Vic 20068, HMV B-2339
BVE-34077-2  Sometimes I Feel Like A Motherless  Vic 20013, HMV B-2326
             Child
```

Camden, N. J., January 25, 1926.

```
BVE-32798-5  Li'l Gal                          Vic 19824
BVE-32799-3-4-5  I'll Hear The Trumpet Sound   Rejected
BVE-34438-1  Nobody Knows De Trouble I've Seen  Vic 20068
BVE-34439-3  On Ma Journey                     Vic 20013, HMV B-2326
```

New York, March 30, 1927.

```
BVE-38414-1-2-3  Down De Lovers' Lane          Rejected
BVE-38415-1-2-3  Since You Went Away             -
BVE-38416-1-2  I'm Goin' To Tell God All O' My Troubles -
BVE-38417-1-2-3  I Got A Home In Dat Rock        -
BVE-38418-1-2  Deep River                        -
BVE-38419-  Hear De Lam's A-Cryin' (w/L. Brown)   Vic 20604, HMV B-2838
BVE-38420-  Ezekiel Saw De Wheel (w/Lawrence Brown)    -        -
```

New York, May 10, 1927.

```
BVE-38414-4-5  Down De Lovers' Lane          Rejected
BVE-38416-  I'm Goin' To Tell God All O' My   Vic 20793, HMV B-2619
            Troubles
BVE-38417-  I Got A Home In Dat Rock       Vic 21109, HMV B-2727
BVE-38418-5  Deep River                    Vic 20793, HMV B-2619, B-9021
BVE-38740-  Witness (w/Lawrence Brown)     Vic 21109, HMV B-2727
```

Vocalist with Paul Whiteman and his Concert Orchestra.
New York, March 1, 1928.

CVE-43122-3  Ol' Man River (w/chorus) ("Show Boat") Vic 35912, HMV C-1505

Vocal, acc. by the Drury Lane Theatre Orchestra/Herman Finck.
Drury Lane Theatre, London, May 15, 1928.

WAX-3624-1-2  Ol' Man River (w/chorus)("Show Boat") Col rejected

Acc. by O/Carroll Gibbons.          Small Queen's Hall, London, June 15, 1928.

```
Bb-13827-2  Seem Lak' To Me               HMV B-2777
Bb-13828-2  Down De Lovers' Lane            -
```

Acc. by Lawrence Brown-p.          Hayes, Middlesex, June 19, 1928.

```
Bb-13544-1-2  Go Down, Moses               Rejected
Bb-13545-2  Scandalize My Name             HMV B-2771
Bb-13546-1-2  Weepin' Mary                 Rejected
Bb-13547-2  Sinner, Please Doan' Let Dis Harves'  HMV B-2771
            Pass
```

Small Queen's Hall, London, Sept.13,1928.

Bb-14349-4  Weepin' Mary/I Want To Be Ready      HMV B-2897, Vic 22225
Bb-14350-2  My Lord, What A Mornin'              -
Bb-14351-1-2  De Li'l Pickaninny's Gone To Sleep  HMV B-2948
Bb-14352-2  Git On Board, Li'l Children/Dere's No  HMV B-3033, Vic 22225
            Hidin' Place

Acc. by O/Carroll Gibbons.          Small Queen's Hall, London, Oct. 2, 1928.

Cc-14611-3  Plantation Songs - Part 1 (Intro. So   HMV C-1585
            Early In The Morning/Carry Me Back To Old Virginny/Old Folks At Home/
            Goodnight, Ladies) (w/chorus)
Cc-14612-1-2  Plantation Songs - Part 2 (Intro. Away   -
            Down South In Dixie/Poor Old Joe/Oh, Susanna/My Old Kentucky Home)(w/
            chorus)

Acc. by Lawrence Brown-p.            Small Queen's Hall, London, Oct. 4, 1928.

Bb-14622-1  Oh ! Rock Me, Julie/Oh, Didn't It      HMV B-3033
            Rain

Acc. by O/Carroll Gibbons.          Kingsway Hall, London, November 5, 1928.

Cc-13750-1-2-3  Mammy                             HMV rejected
Cc-13751-1-2-3  Roll Away, Clouds                 -

                                    Kingsway Hall, London, November 15, 1928.

Cc-13750-6  Mammy                                 HMV C-1591
Cc-13751-6  Roll Away, Clouds                     -

                                    Small Queen's Hall, London, Jan. 28,1929.

Bb-15802-1  Sonny Boy                             HMV B-2948
.Bb-15803-1-2  Mountain Top Blues                 Rejected

Acc. by O/Ray Noble.                 Hayes, Middlesex, August 30, 1929.

Bb-17550-2  Little Pal                            HMV B-3146
Bb-17551-2  Lonesome Road                         -
Bb-17552-3  Just Keepin' On                       HMV B-3199

                                    Hayes, Middlesex, October 2, 1929.

Bb-17698-2  Mighty Lak' A Rose                    HMV B-3199, B-9110
Bb-17699-1-2  High Water                          Rejected
Bb-17700-2  Mammy Is Gone                         HMV B-3663

Acc. by Lawrence Brown-p.            Small Queen's Hall, London, Feb.27, 1930.

Bb-18893-2  Hail De Crown                         HMV B-3409
Bb-18894-2  Exhortation                           -
Bb-18895-2  I Stood On De Ribber/Peter, Go Ring   HMV B-3381
            Dem Bells

Acc. by O/Ray Noble.                 Hayes, Middlesex, September 11, 1930.

Bb-17699-4  High Water                            HMV B-3663
Bb-20072-1  Swanee River (The Old Folks At Home)  HMV B-3664
Bb-20073-2  Poor Old Joe                          -

                                    Hayes, Middlesex, September 12, 1930.

Bb-20083-1  My Old Kentucky Home                  HMV B-3653
Bb-20084-3  Ol' Man River ("Show Boat")          -

                                    Small Queen's Hall, London, Aug.25, 1931.

OB-1334-1  River, Stay 'Way From My Door          HMV B-3956, Vic 22889
OB-1335-1-2  Without A Song                       Rejected

London, September 17, 1931.

```
OB-1664-1-2  My Heart Is Where The Mohawk Flows    Rejected
             Tonight
OB-1665-1-2  Without A Song                         -
OB-1666-1-2  The Folks I Used To Know               -
OB-1667-1    Rockin' Chair                          HMV B-3956, Vic 22889
```

Acc. by Jack Hylton and his Orchestra.  Small Queen's Hall, London, Sept.24,1931.

```
2B-1094-2  Negro Spiritual Medley - Part 1 (Intro. HMV C-2287
           I'm A Rolling And Sing-a-Ho !/Hail De Crown/Joshua Fit De Battle Ob Je-
           richo/I Got A Robe/ Oh Lord I Done/De Gospel Train) (w/chorus)
2B-1095-1  Negro Spiritual Medley - Part 2 (Intro.    -
           Black Sheep/Heav'n Bells Are Ringin'/I'll Hear De Trumpet Sound/ Swing
           Low/Walk Together, Children) (w/chorus)
```

Small Queen's Hall, London, Nov.26, 1931.

```
OB-1664-4    My Heart Is Where The Mohawk Flows    HMV B-4052
             Tonight
OB-1666-4    The Folks I Used To Know               -
OB-2249-1-2  Travellin' All Alone                   Rejected
OB-2250-1-2  'Tain't No Use Tellin' The World       -
```

London, December 16, 1931.

```
OB-2503-1  Mary Had A Baby (Yes, Lord)             HMV B-4336
OB-2504-1  Li'l Gal                                HMV B-4093
OB-2505-2  Bear De Burden/All God's Chillun Got    HMV B-4336
           Wings
```

London, December 18, 1931.

```
OB-2515-1  That's Why Darkies Were Born            HMV B-4058, B-8973
OB-2516-1  When It's Sleepy-Time Down South        -
OB-2517-2  Seekin'                                 HMV B-4093
```

Acc. by Victor Young and the Brunswick Orchestra.
New York, July 21, 1932.

```
BX-12096-A  Ol' Man River ("Show Boat")      Br 20114, 0111, 0133, Col 55004
```

Acc. by Herbert Dawson-Pipe organ.      Kingsway Hall, October 19, 1932.

```
2B-3465-2  Nearer, My God, To Thee                 HMV C-2517
2B-3466-2  There Is A Green Hill
```

Acc. by O/Ray Noble.                    London, October 20, 1932.

```
OB-4404-2  Mah Lindy Lou                           HMV B-4309
OB-4405-1  Ma Curly-Headed Baby                    -
```

Acc. by Ruthland Clapham-p.             London, December 13, 1932.

```
OB-4582-2  Pilgrim's Song                          HMV B-4421
OB-4583-2  Roll The Chariot Along                  -
OB-4584-2  Since You Went Away                     HMV B-4396
OB-4585-1  Wid De Moon, Moon, Moon                 -
```

Acc. by O/Ray Noble.                    London, December 15, 1932.

```
OB-4368-2    Got The South In My Soul              HMV B-4354
OB-4369-2    Hush-a-Bye Lullaby                    -
OB-4370-1-2  Round The Bend Of The Road            Rejected
```

London, February 3, 1933.

```
OB-4370-3    Round The Bend Of The Road            HMV B-4352, Vic 24318
OB-6427-2    Take Me Away From The River           -
OB-6428-1-2  Beware, Beware (You'll Be Swept Away) Rejected
```

Acc. by Ruthland Clapham-p.              London, February 15, 1933.

OB-6295-1  Swing Low, Sweet Chariot              HMV B-8372, B-8973, Vic 25547
OB-6296-1  On Mah Journey                             -                    -
OB-6297-1  Bye And Bye                          HMV B-4480
OB-6298-1  Were You There ?                         -

Acc. by O/Ray Noble.                     London, May 2, 1933.

OB-6523-1  Swing Along                          HMV B-8018
OB-6524-1  Piccaninny Shoes                     HMV B-4499
OB-6525-2  In A Narrow Street                       -
OB-6526-1-2  Baa, Baa, Black Sheep              Rejected

                                         London, September 8, 1933.

OB-5311-2  Carry Me Back To Green Pastures      HMV B-8010
OB-5312-2  Lazy Bones                               -
OB-5313-2  Blue Prelude                         HMV B-8018

                                         London, September 20, 1933.

2B-5095-2  Paul Robeson Medley - Part 1 (Intro.    HMV C-2621
              Roll De Ole Chariot/Mary Had A Baby/Swing Low/Heav'n, Heav'n)
2B-5096-2  Paul Robeson Medley - Part 2 (Intro.
              Carry Me Back/Mighty Lak' A Rose/Round The Bend Of The Road/River, Stay
              'Way From My Door/Ol' Man River)

                                         London, October 20, 1933.

OB-5146-2  Fat Li'l Feller Wid His Mammy's Eyes/   HMV B-8060
              Short'nin' Bread
OB-5147-2  Snowball                                 -

Acc. by Ruthland Clapham (?)-p.          London, December 14, 1933.

OB-5827-3  Water Boy                            HMV B-8103
OB-5828-1  Doan You Cry, Ma Honey               HMV B-8156
OB-5829-2  Steal Away                           HMV B-8103

Acc. by O/Ray Noble.                     London, February 16, 1934.

OB-5902-2  Scarecrow                            HMV B-8132
OB-5903-1  Wagon Wheels                         HMV B-8135, Vic 24635
OB-5904-2  So Shy                               HMV B-8132

                                         London, February 20, 1934.

OB-5905-2  Piccaninny Slumber Song              HMV B-8156
OB-5906-2  St. Louis Blues                      HMV B-8219, Vic 24635
OB-5907-2  Mammy's Little Kinky-Headed Boy      HMV B-8135

                                         London, June 21, 1934.

OB-7423-2  Little Man, You've Had A Busy Day    HMV B-8202
OB-7424-2  I Ain't Lazy, I'm Just Dreamin'          -
OB-7425-1  The Banjo Song                       HMV B-8219

Acc. by O/Percival Mackey.               London, November 13, 1934.

2EA-532-1  Paul Robeson Medley (No. 2) - Part 1   HMV C-2708
              (Intro. Lazy Bones/Scarecrow/Fat Li'l Feller/Wagon Wheels)
2EA-533-2  Paul Robeson Medley (No. 2) - Part 2      -
              (Intro. Deep River/Ma Curly-Headed Baby/Carry Me Back To Green Pastures
              /Old Folks At Home)

Acc. by O/Muir Matheson.                 London, April 15, 1935.

OEA-1850-1  Love Song (Film "Sanders Of The River")HMV B-8316, Vic 25107
OEA-1851-2  Congo Lullaby (Film "Sanders Of The   HMV B-8315, Vic 25106
              River")

London, April 16, 1935.

OEA-1481-1-2-3  Canoe Song (Film "Sanders Of The      HMV rejected
                River")
OEA-1482-1-2-3  Killing Song (Film "Sanders Of        -
                The River")

London, May 14, 1935.

OEA-1481-6  Canoe Song (Film "Sanders Of The      HMV B-8315, Vic 25106
            River")
OEA-1482-4  Killing Song (Film "Sanders Of The    HMV B-8316, Vic 25107
            River")

Acc. by Lawrence Brown-p (and voice where shown).
                                London, May 24, 1936.

OEA-2726-1  Shenandoah                             HMV B-8438, Vic 27430
OEA-2727-1  Jes' Mah Song                          -           Vic 26289
OEA-2728-1  De Ole Ark's A-Movering/Ezekiel Saw    HMV B-8478
            De Wheel (w/Lawrence Brown)
OEA-2729-2  Joshua Fit De Battle Ob Jericho (w/    -
            Lawrence Brown)

Acc. by O/? Clifford Greenwood.     London, March 26, 1936.

OEA-2736-2  Honey (Dat's All)                      HMV B-8423, Vic 25362
OEA-2737-2  Gloomy Sunday                          -           -

London, May 18, 1936.

OEA-2935-1  Ol' Man River (Film "Show Boat")       HMV B-8497, Vic 25376
            (w/chorus)
OEA-2936-1  I Still Suits Me (w/Elisabeth Welch)   -           -
            (Film "Show Boat")

London, May 20, 1936.

OEA-2937-1  Sleepy River (w/Elisabeth Welch and    HMV B-8482
            chorus) (Film "Song Of Freedom")
OEA-2938-1  Lonely Road (Film "Song Of Freedom")   HMV B-8483

London, May 21, 1936.

OEA-2939-1  Song Of Freedom (w/chorus) (Film       HMV B-8482
            "Song Of Freedom")
OEA-2940-1  The Black Emperor (w/chorus) (Film     HMV B-8483
            "Song Of Freedom")

Acc. by Lawrence Brown-p.           London, January 27, 1937.

OEA-4560-1  Mam'selle Marie/Dere's No Hidin' Place HMV B-8550
OEA-4561-1  Oh ! No John                           HMV B-8541
OEA-4562-1  Passing By                             -
OEA-4563-1  Hammer Song/Li'l David (w/Lawrence     HMV B-8550
            Brown)

Acc. by O/? Clifford Greenwood.     London, April 29, 1937.

OEA-4775-1  My Way (Film "Jericho")                HMV B-8572, B-8621, Vic 25743
OEA-4776-1  Golden River (Film "Jericho")          -

London, May 1, 1937.

OEA-4905-1  Ho ! Ho ! (Wagon Song) (w/chorus)      HMV B-8586
            (Film "King Solomon's Mines")
OEA-4906-1  Climbing Up (Mountain Song) (w/chorus) -
            (Film "King Solomon's Mines")

London, May 3, 1937.

| | | |
|---|---|---|
| OEA-5006-2 | Lazin' (Film "Big Fella") | HMV B-8607 |
| OEA-5007-1 | I Don't Know What's Wrong | HMV B-8591 |
| OEA-5008-1 | Roll Up, Sailorman (Film "Big Fella") | – |
| OEA-5009-1 | You Didn't Oughta Do Such Things (Film "Big Fella") | HMV B-8607 |

London, July 2, 1937.

| | | |
|---|---|---|
| OEA-5296-1 | Deep Desert (Film "Jericho") | HMV B-8621, Vic 25743 |

Acc. by Lawrence Brown-p.          London, July 5, 1937.

| | | |
|---|---|---|
| OEA-4996-1 | Sometimes I Feel Like A Motherless Child/Minstrel Man (spoken, unacc.) | HMV B-8604 |
| OEA-4997-1 | Speech/How Long, Brethren ? (spoken, unacc.) | Rejected |
| OEA-4998-1 | The Wanderer | HMV B-8604 |
| OEA-4999-1 | Lay Down Late | Rejected |

London, October 8, 1937.

| | | |
|---|---|---|
| OEA-5477-1 | Dere's A Man Goin' Roun' Takin' Names | HMV B-8637, Vic 25809 |
| OEA-5478-1 | No More | HMV B-8781, Vic 26289 |
| OEA-5479-1 | Work All De Summer/Didn't My Lord Deliver Daniel ? | HMV B-8637, Vic 25809 |

Acc. by O/? Clifford Greenwood.          London, October 18, 1937.

| | | |
|---|---|---|
| OEA-5814-1 | Still Night, Holy Night | HMV B-8668 |
| OEA-5815-2 | All Through The Night | –            B-9021 |
| OEA-5816-1 | Solitude | HMV B-8664 |
| OEA-5817-1 | Mood Indigo | – |

London, January 14, 1938.

| | | |
|---|---|---|
| OEA-5171-1 | Summertime (Lullaby) | HMV B-8698, Vic 26359 |
| OEA-5172-1 | It Take A Long Pull To Get There | –            – |

London, January 21, 1938.

| | | |
|---|---|---|
| OEA-5991-1 | It Ain't Necessarily So | HMV B-8711, Vic 26358 |
| OEA-5992-1 | A Woman Is A Sometime Thing | –            – |

London, March 15, 1938.

| | | |
|---|---|---|
| OEA-6271-1-2-3 | Just A-Wearyin' For You | HMV rejected |
| OEA-6272-1-2-3 | At Dawning | – |

London, March 24, 1938.

| | | |
|---|---|---|
| OEA-6271-4 | Just A-Wearyin' For You | HMV B-8731, Vic 25873 |
| OEA-6272-5 | At Dawning | –            – |

London, March 28, 1938.

| | | |
|---|---|---|
| OEA-6162-1 | Song Of The Volga Boatmen | HMV B-8750 |
| OEA-6163-1-2 | Kishmul's Galley | Rejected |

London, April 13, 1938.

| | | |
|---|---|---|
| OEA-6163-3-4 | Kishmul's Galley | Rejected |
| OEA-6601-1 | An Eriskay Love Lilt | HMV B-8750 |
| OEA-6602-1 | Encantadora Maria | HMV B-8781 |

    Acc. by Lawrence Brown-p.              London, September 15, 1938.

OEA-6570-1-2  After The Battle                    Rejected
OEA-6571-1    David Of The White Rock             —
OEA-6572-1    Goin' To Ride Up In De Chariot/Every
              Time I Feel De Spirit        HMV B-8813, Vic 26251
OEA-6573-1    Lay Down Late                        —            —

                                         London, October 25, 1938.

OEA-6570-3    After The Battle             HMV B-9149
OEA-6571-2    David Of The White Rock              —

    Acc. by O/? Clifford Greenwood.       London, November 20, 1938.

OEA-7087-1    Trees                        HMV B-8830, Vic 26168
OEA-7088-1    Songs My Mother Taught Me            —
OEA-7089-1    Loch Lomond                  HMV B-8831, Vic 27227
OEA-7090-1    Drink To Me Only With Thine Eyes     —       Vic 26168

    Acc. by Lawrence Brown-p.             London, May 9, 1939.

OEA-7694-1    Down De Lovers' Lane         HMV B-8915, Vic 27430
OEA-7695-1    Lullaby ("The Moor Of Peter The Great"   —      Vic 26409
              - Gambs) (in English and Russian)
OEA-7696-1    Night (Russian Folk Song)    HMV B-8918      —
OEA-7697-1    The Little Black Boy ("Songs Of      —
              Innocence" - William Blake) (spoken, unacc.)

    Acc. by O/? Clifford Greenwood.       London, September 26, 1939.

OEA-8283-1    Dear Old Southland           HMV B-9001, Vic 26741
OEA-8284-1    Jerusalem                    HMV B-9010, Vic 27348
OEA-8285-1    The Blind Ploughman          HMV B-8977      —
OEA-8286-1    The Cobbler's Song                   —
OEA-8287-1    Oh, Could I But Express In Song  HMV B-8989, Vic 26651

                                         London, September 27, 1939.

OEA-8291-1    Love At My Heart             HMV B-9281
OEA-8292-1    Nothin'                      HMV B-9001, Vic 26741
OEA-8293-1    The Rosary                   HMV B-8988, Vic 26498
OEA-8294-1    A Perfect Day                        —            —
OEA-8295-1    Absent                       HMV B-9257, Vic 27366
OEA-8296-1    Black Eyes                   HMV B-8989, Vic 26651

                                         London, September 28, 1939.

OEA-8102-1    Oh, Promise Me               HMV B-9059
OEA-8103-1    Plaisir d'amour                      —
OEA-8104-1    Sylvia                       HMV B-9037, Vic 27366
OEA-8105-1    She Is Far From The Land     HMV B-9010
OEA-8106-1    Thora                        HMV B-9037

    Acc. by unknown piano.                London, September 29, 1939.

OEA-8099-2    Now Sleeps The Crimson Petal  HMV B-9281
OEA-8100-1    Sea Fever                     HMV B-9257
OEA-8301-2    Ebenezer (Film "The Proud Valley")  HMV B-9020
OEA-8302-1    Land Of My Fathers (Film "The Proud     —      Vic 27227
              Valley")

The following two sides were transcribed from the soundtrack of THE PROUD VALLEY,
on February 26 and March 6, 1940 respectively.

OEA-8504-1    Deep River                   HMV B-9024
OEA-8243-1    Rehearsal Scene, including Baal Chorus    —
              and Lord God Of Abraham ("Elijah" - Mendelssohn)

Acc. by the Victor Symphony Orchestra and American People's Chorus/Nat Shilkret.
New York, February 9, 1940.

| | | |
|---|---|---|
| BS-047035-1 | Ballad For Americans - Part 1 | Vic 26516, HMV B-9160 |
| BS-047036-1 | Ballad For Americans - Part 2 | -           - |
| BS-047037-1 | Ballad For Americans - Part 3 | Vic 26517, HMV B-9161 |
| BS-047038-1 | Ballad For Americans - Part 4 | -           - |

Acc. by Count Basie and his Orchestra.  New York, October 1, 1941.

| | | |
|---|---|---|
| 31373-1 | King Joe - Part 1 | OK 6475, Col C-516, Par R-2966 |
| 31374-1 | King Joe - Part 2 | -          -          - |

Paul Robeson made some records for Keynote of Chinese, Russian and other songs, and
some re-makes of his most popular spirituals, for Columbia, after 1942.

## BILL  ROBINSON

B. Richmond, Va., May 25, 1878; gained a reputation as a dancer in vaudeville, then
made a sensational appearance in BLACKBIRDS OF 1928 (Liberty, New York, May   9,
1928); then appeared there in BROWN BUDDIES (October 7, 1930); several other successes on Broadway, but reached world audiences and international acclaim as   the
finest tap-dancer in the history of the theatre by means of films (THE LITTLE COL-
ONEL (1935); IN OLD KENTUCKY (1936); REBECCA OF SUNNYBROOK FARM (1938);   STORMY
WEATHER (1943).  D. 1949.

Tap-dancing and vocal acc. by Irving Mills' Hotsy-Totsy Gang.
New York, September 11, 1929.

| | | |
|---|---|---|
| E-30526- | Ain't Misbehavin' | Br 4535, 7706, 01112 |
| E-30527- | Doin' The New Low-Down  ("Blackbirds of 1928") | -          -          - |

Acc. by studio orchestra.            New York, May 27, 1931.

| | | |
|---|---|---|
| E-36833- | Keep A Song In Your Soul | Br 6134, 7705, 01168 |
| E-36834- | Just A Crazy Song (Hi-Hi-Hi) | -          -          -          Dec 7-2 |

Acc. by Don Redman and his Orchestra.   New York, December 29, 1932.

B-12810-A  Doin' The New Low-Down ("Blackbirds of  Br 6520, 01521
1928")

## J. RUSSEL ROBINSON

B. Indianapolis, July 8, 1892; formed piano-and-drums act with his brother;   toured
South and mid-West on vaudeville circuits with this while composing genuine rags;
best-known of these are ECCENTRIC and DYNAMITE RAG; played solo piano before moving to Chicago to play in a New Orleans jazz band there; to New York, joined   the
Original Dixieland Jazz Band as replacement for their late pianist and   appeared
with them in London; left England on account of wife's health and began composing
popular songs (MARGIE (1920); TOMORROW and AGGRAVATIN' PAPA (1922); LET ME BE THE
FIRST TO KISS YOU GOOD MORNING and BLUE EYED SALLY (1924); MARY LOU (1926); IS  I
IN LOVE ? I IS (1932); A PORTRAIT OF JENNIE (1949) and dozens of others; rejoined
the ODJB on their return from London, July, 1920; left them in April, 1921; later
teamed with Al Bernard, "The Boy From Dixie," as The Dixie Stars; toured in shows
(vaudeville theatres) for three years; rejoined the Original Dixieland Jazz  Band
in 1936 when they were re-formed; after they broke up in January, 1938, he  moved
to California and resumed composing, including incidental film music.  D.   Palm-
dale, Calif., September 30, 1963.  Only his vocal records are listed here; he was
a member of the Wiedoeft-Wadsworth Quartet (with composer Harry Akst, q.v.),  and
may have been one of the Dixie Trio on Pathe and Perfect records, but if so,it is
not certain that he sings on these.

Vocal, acc. by own piano.            Hayes, Middlesex, August 21, 1919.

HO-5135-AE  Oh Death, Where Is Thy Sting ?        HMV rejected
HO-5136-AE  A Good Man Is Hard To Find             -

Acc. by studio orchestra (or possibly the Prince of Wales' Theatre Orchestra/Philip Braham.                              London, September, 1919.

76655-   Pip-Pip, Toot-Toot, Goodbye-ee ("Bran    Col F-1039
            Pie")

BERNARD AND ROBINSON : Al Bernard-J. Russel  Robinson-vocal duets, acc. by J. Russel
   Robinson-p.                              New York, July, 1924.

1060-    Let My Home Be Your Home                  Cam 596

THE DIXIE STARS : As last above.        New York, December 30, 1924.

140214-  Let Me Be The First To Kiss You Good    Col 275-D
            Morning
140215-  Blue-Eyed Sally                          -

                                   New York, January 16, 1925.

140257-  Birmingham Papa, Your Memphis Mama's    Col 309-D
            Comin' To Town
140258-  Never Gettin' No Place Blues             -

                                   New York, May 21, 1925.

140618-  New York Ain't New York Any More         Col 389-D
140619-  What Do I Care - What Do I Care, My      -
            Sweetie Turned Me Down

Vocal duets with Martin Hurt, acc. by own piano.
                                   New York, March 8, 1929.

BVE-49774-1-2  Rhythm King                        Vic rejected
BVE-49775-1-2  You Ain't Quittin' Me Without Two   -
            Weeks' Notice

Vocalist with Nick LaRocca and his Original Dixieland Band.
                                   New York, September 25, 1936.

BS-0492-1  Old Joe Blade                          Vic 26039

## THE  ROGERS BROTHERS

Gus and Max Rogers (r.n. Solomon) were very popular vaudeville and musical     comedy
artists in the nineties and the opening years of the century; Gus was born in  New
York in 1869 and died there on October 19, 1908, and Max, born in 1873 in New York
died in Far Rockaway, N.Y., December 26, 1932.  Their biggest successes  on Broad-
were THE ROGERS BROTHERS IN WALL STREET (Victoria, September 18, 1899); THE ROGERS
BROTHERS IN IRELAND (Liberty, September 4, 1905).

Humorous dialogues.                     New York, c. June, 1901.

296-   How To Play Golf In Central Park         Col/Climax 296

                                   New York, February 6, 1902.

A-1207-1-2  An Original Parody on MAMIE          Vic 1207 (7" and 10")

## BUDDY ROGERS

B. Olathe, Kansas, 1904; played in small band (trombone, saxophone and drums)  as  a
schoolboy; learned to act at Paramount's acting school, under contract, in Astoria
(L.I.); graduated; film debut in FASCINATING YOUTH (1926), and SO'S YOUR OLD   MAN
(with W. C. Fields); then came WINGS (with Richard Arlen and Clara Bow); MY   BEST
GIRL (with Mary Pickford, whom he married in 1936 after her divorce from   Douglas
Fairbanks, Sr.), both 1927; ABIE'S IRISH ROSE (with Nancy Carroll); SAFETY IN NUM-
BERS (with Virginia Bruce, 1930); most of his records were made as a bandleader,in
which capacity he visited London in 1935 to appear in cabaret, and they will  thus
be listed in THE AMERICAN DANCE BANDS DISCOGRAPHY.  His vocal records with  studio
groups accompanying are shown on page 561.

CHARLES (BUDDY) ROGERS (America's Boy Friend) : Vocal, acc. by small jazz band.
                                New York, February 27, 1930.

150027-3  (It'd  Like To Be) A Bee In Your Boudoir   Col 2183-D, DB-242
              (Film  "Safety In Numbers")
150028-1-2-3  My Future Just Passed (Film "Safety Rejected
              In  Numbers")

                                New York, March 4, 1930.

150028-5   My Future Just Passed (Film "Safety In   Col 2183-D, DB-242
              Numbers")
150056-3   Any Time's The Time To Fall In Love       Col 2143-D, DB-162
150057-3   (Up On Top Of A Rainbow) Sweepin' The         -        -
              Clouds Away (both from film "Paramount On Parade")

Humorous dialogue with Nancy Carroll.     Camden, N. J., July 10, 1930.

BVE-62675-1-2  Follow Through                      Vic rejected

## DUKE  ROGERS

Alleged by some to be a pseudonym for Bert Williams, q.v., on the strength of a sole
  Edison Diamond Disc (50976) and Blue Amberol cylinder (4565) of SAVE A LITTLE DRAM
  FOR ME.  It is likely that this was made soon after Williams' death, but even  if
  it were found to have been made in his lifetime, we remain unconvinced that it  is
  the great comedian himself.

## GINGER  ROGERS

B. Independence, Mo., July 16, 1911; r.n. Virginia Katherine McMath; won many awards
  as a teenage dancer, and made a hit in two Broadway shows : TOP SPEED (46th Street
  Theatre, December 25, 1929) and GIRL CRAZY (Alvin, October 14, 1930); began career
  in films with YOUNG MAN OF MANHATTAN (1930), and appeared in FORTY-SECOND   STREET
  (1932); then came the series of musicals with Fred Astaire, q.v., with others such
  as IN PERSON between making these; THE STORY OF VERNON AND IRENE CASTLE (1939) was
  the last film with Fred Astaire for ten years, after which she made BACHELOR MOTHER
  (1939); KITTY FOYLE (1940); ROXIE HART (1942); THE MAJOR AND THE MINOR and LADY IN
  THE DARK (1943); I'LL BE SEEING YOU (1944); WEEKEND AT THE WALDORF (1945); IT   HAD
  TO BE YOU (1948), and many others. She appeared in London as the star of MAME   in
  1970.

Vocal, acc. by O/Victor Young.          Los Angeles, June 14, 1935.

DLA-182-   The Piccolino (Film "Top Hat")           Dec rejected
DLA-183-   Isn't This A Lovely Day ? (Film "Top Hat")  -
DLA-184-   Cheek To Cheek (Film "Top Hat")             -
DLA-185-   No Strings (Film "Top Hat")                 -

                                Los Angeles, August 25, 1935.

DLA-228-A  No Strings (Film "Top Hat")              Dec F-5746
DLA-229-A  Isn't This A Lovely Day ? (Film "Top Hat")  -
DLA-230-A  The Piccolino (Film "Top Hat")           Dec F-5747
DLA-231-A  Cheek To Cheek                              -

                                Los Angeles, November 22, 1935.

DLA-274-A-B  Got A New Lease On Love (Film "In      Rejected
              Person")
DLA-275-B  Don't Mention Love To Me (Film "In       Dec 638, Dec F-5838
              Person")

                                Los Angeles, November 27, 1935.

DLA-281-C  Out Of Sight, Out Of Mind                Dec F-6822
DLA-282-A  Eeny, Meeny, Miney Mo (w/Johnny Mercer)  Dec 638, F-5838

Acc. by Jimmy Dorsey and his Orchestra. Los Angeles, April 3, 1936.

DLA-335-A  I'm Putting All My Eggs In One Basket     Dec F-5963
           (Film "Follow The Fleet")
DLA-336-A  Let Yourself Go (Film "Follow The Fleet")    -

Acc. by O/Hal Boone.                        Hollywood, October 6, 1938.

PBS-026169-1  I Used To Be Color Blind (Film       BB B-7981, HMV B-8822
              "Carefree")
PBS-026170-1  The Yam (Film "Carefree")               -              -

## WILL  ROGERS

B. Claremore, Oklahoma, November 4, 1879; r.n. William Penn Adair Rogers; very eager
   for adventure as a young man (became cattle-puncher at 17, tried to serve in  Boer
   War by working his way from Argentina to Cape Town to join up, but the war    ended
   before he arrived); joined travelling Wild West show and eventually became a  star
   of vaudeville; appeared in the ZIEGFELD FOLLIES shows of 1912-1918; began his film
   career with LAUGHING BILL HYDE (1918), then was in many silents, but his first appearance in talkies (THEY HAD TO SEE PARIS, 1930) proved his value as a   comedian;
   others include A CONNECTICUT YANKEE AT THE COURT OF KING ARTHUR (1930); STATE FAIR
   (1933); DAVID HARUM; HANDY ANDY and JUDGE PRIEST (1934); IN OLD KENTUCKY (1935).He
   was killed in August, 1935 in a 'plane crash. He had appeared in London in 1926 at
   the Pavilion with enormous success.

Humorous monologues.                        New York, February 6, 1923.

B-27457-2  A New Slant On War                   Vic 45347, 25126
B-27458-2  Timely Topics                          -           -         LCT-1112
B-27459-1-2  The United States Senate And The    Rejected
             Government
B-27460-1-2  Prohibition                          -

                                            New York, May 31, 1923.

B-28043-1  Will Rogers Talks To The Bankers     Vic 45374, 25127
B-28044-2  Will Rogers' First Political Speech     -            -
B-28045-3  Will Rogers Nominates Henry Ford For  Vic 45369
           President

                                            New York, June 2, 1923.

B-28049-2  Will Rogers Tells Traffic Chiefs How  Vic 45369
           To Direct Traffic

The following examples of Will Rogers' style of humour, sources unknown, have   been
   issued on LP :-

            Yankee Philosophy               Veritas 107
            Talk                            Har HS-11353

## MANUEL  ROMAIN

B. Cambridge, Mass., October 1, 1872; sang in churches and concerts until 1893, when
   he joined Primrose and West's Minstrels and appeared in New York with them;   later
   worked with Lew Dockstader; began vaudeville career in 1906-1907 with DOWN IN MUSIC
   ROW, followed by BEFORE AND AFTER THE BALL (1908), which he produced. He was very
   active as a tenor singer until shortly before his death in Quincy, Mass., December
   22, 1926.

Vocal, acc. by studio orchestra. (Manuel Romain began his recording career on Edison
   2-minute, and later 4-minute cylinders, the exact recording dates of which are not
   known; we have therefore listed them en bloc, showing the dates of issue after the
   catalogue numbers, in brackets).        New York, c. June, 1907-c. July, 1912.

            When The Blue Birds Nest Again, Sweet    Ed 9628 (September, 1907)
               Nellie Gray
            Meet Me, Sweet Kathleen, In Honeysuckle  Ed 9664 (October, 1907)
            Time                          (continued on page

New York, c. June, 1907-c. July, 1912.

| | |
|---|---|
| When Summer Tells Autumn Goodbye | Ed 9675 (November, 1907) |
| When The Sheep Are In The Fold, Jennie Dear | Ed 9718 (December, 1907) |
| When It's Moonlight, Mary Darling, 'Neath The Old Grape Arbor Shade | Ed 9728 (January, 1908) |
| When The Springtime Brings The Roses, Jessie Dear | Ed 9771 (March, 1908) |
| When We Listened To The Chiming Of The Old Church Bell | Ed 9802 (April, 1908) |
| Somebody That I Know And You Know Too | Ed 9822 (May, 1908) |
| Just Someone | Ed 9847 (June, 1908) |
| You Have Changed The Winter In My Heart To Glad Spring-Time | Ed 9878 (July, 1908) |
| Only An Old-Fashioned Cottage | Ed 9891 (August, 1908) |
| Let Me Crown You Queen Of May With Orange Blossoms | Ed 9925 (September, 1908) |
| I Lost My Heart When I Saw Your Eyes | Ed 9954 (October, 1908) |
| Roses Bring Dreams Of You | Ed 4M-2 (October, 1908) |
| I'm Starving For One Sight Of You | Ed 9977 (November, 1908) |
| Belle Brandon | Ed 4M-27 (November, 1908) |
| When Darling Bess First Whispered "Yes" | Ed 10012 (December, 1908) |
| Ask Mammy | Ed 4M-52 (December, 1908) |
| Somebody Just Like You | Ed 10042 (January, 1909) |
| To The End Of The World With You | Ed 4M-118 (January, 1909) |
| I Wish I Had A Girl | Ed 10068 (February, 1909) |
| As The Years Roll On | Ed 4M-138 (February, 1909) |
| Just One Sweet Girl | Ed 10083 (March, 1909) |
| What Might Have Been | Ed 10098 (April, 1909) |
| Won't You Even Say "Hello" ? | Ed 10118 (May, 1909) |
| No-One Knows | Ed 10138 (June, 1909) |
| Just Someone | Ed 4M-278 (August, 1909), Amb 1945 |
| Pansies Mean Thoughts, Dear | Ed 4M-294 (September, 1909) |
| When The Evening Bells Are Chiming Songs Of Auld Lang Syne | Ed 4M-306 (October, 1909), Amb 1869 |
| Pennyland | Ed 10238 (November, 1909) |
| When You Were Sweet Sixteen | Ed 4M-331 (November, 1909) |
| You Can't Stop Me From Loving You | Ed 10258 (December, 1909) |
| When The Bloom Is On The Cotton, Dixie Lee | Ed 4M-353 (December, 1909), Amb 2238 |
| White Wings | Ed 4M-372 (December, 1909) |
| Sweetheart's A Pretty Name When It's Y-O-U | Ed 10279 (January, 1910) |
| I Wonder Who's Kissing Her Now ? | Ed 10287 (January, 1910) |
| I'm Longing For The Old Days, Marguerite | Ed 4M-394 (January, 1910) |
| When I Dream In The Gloaming Of You | Ed 10306 (February, 1910) |
| I Wish You Was My Gal, Molly | Ed 4M-414 (February, 1910) |
| When I Am Away From You | Ed 10321 (March, 1910) |
| Molly Lee | Ed 4M-441 (March, 1910) |
| I'd Rather Say "Hello" Than Say "Goodbye" | Ed 10336 (April, 1910) |
| There's No Girl Like Your Old Girl | Ed 4M-459 (April, 1910) |
| Christmas Time Seems Years And Years Away | Ed 10351 (May, 1910) |
| I'm Afraid Of You | Ed 4M-482 (May, 1910) |
| I've Set My Heart On You | Ed 10371 (June, 1910) |
| You'll Never Find Another Love Like Mine | Ed 4M-497 (June, 1910) |
| Think Of The Girl Down Home | Ed 10386 (July, 1910) |
| Daisies Won't Tell | Ed 10399 (August, 1910) |
| Gee, But There's Class To A Girl Like You | Ed 4M-528 (August, 1910) |
| Pal Of Mine | Ed 10414 (September, 1910) |
| Does The Girl You Left Behind....? | Ed 4M-661 (May, 1911) |
| Gee, But The Moon Makes Me Lonesome | Ed 4M-694 (July, 1911) |
| Sweet Old Rose ( | Ed 4M-717 (August, 1911) |
| Wishing | Ed 4M-750 (August, 1911) |
| Down In Sunshine Valley | Ed 4M-780 (September, 1911) |

(continued on page 564)

New York, c. June, 1907-c. July, 1912.

| | |
|---|---|
| Your Eyes Have Told Me So | Ed 4M-781 (September, 1911) |
| Down In Sunshine Valley | Ed 10519 (October, 1911) |
| Under Southern Skies | Ed 4M-810 (Oct. 1911), Amb 1894 |
| I'll Love You When The Silver Threads | Ed 4M-821 (November, 1911), |
| Are Shining Among The Gold | Amb 1538 |
| Peggy Gray | Ed 4M-999 (June, 1912) |
| I Long To See The Girl I Left Behind | Ed 4M-1029 (July,1912), Amb 2053 |
| Come Back To Playland With Me | Ed 4M-1099 (September, 1912) |
| When The Old Folks Were Young Folks | Ed 4M-1136 (Oct. 1912), Amb 2007 |
| Where The Ivy's Clinging, Dearie | Ed D-14 (?) |
| If I Must Say Farewell, Kate | Ed C (?) |

Acc. by O/? Walter B. Rogers.        New York, August 20, 1909.

| | | |
|---|---|---|
| B-8164-1-2 | When The Sheep Are In The Fold, Jennie Dear | Vic 16478 |
| B-8165-2 | When We Listened To The Chiming Of The Old Church Bell | Vic 16363 |
| B-8166-1-2 | No-One Knows | Rejected |
| C-8167-2 | I Long To See The Girl I Left Behind | Vic 35083 |

Acc. by studio orchestra.        New York, c. January, 1912.

| | |
|---|---|
| I Will Love You When The Silver Threads | Ind 3305 |
| Are Shining Among The Gold | |
| When It Rains, Sweetheart | Ind 3309 |
| My Rosary Of Dreams | Ind 3315 |

Acc. by O/? Charles A. Prince.        New York, May 23 (? 24), 1912.

| | | |
|---|---|---|
| 19903- | Let's Grow Old Together, Honey | Col A-1192 |
| 19904- | I Love The Girl My Father Loved | -        2353 |

Acc. by studio orchestra.        New York, c. June, 1912.

| | |
|---|---|
| Gee, But The Moon Makes Me Lonesome | USE 1548 |
| When It Rains, Sweetheart | USE 1549 |
| Meet Me, Sweet Kathleen, In Honeysuckle Time | USE 1550 |
| I Will Love You When The Silver Threads | USE 1557 |
| Are Shining Among The Gold | |
| When I Dream Of Old Erin | USE 1622 |

Acc. by O/Charles A. Prince.        New York, July 12, 1912.

| | | |
|---|---|---|
| 38135- | When It Rains, Sweetheart, When It Rains | Col A-1217, 2162 |
| 38136- | Gee, But The Moon Makes Me Lonesome | - |

New York, August 12, 1912.

| | | |
|---|---|---|
| 38198- | Always Think Of Mother | Col A-1231, 2107 |
| 38199- | That's How I Need You | -        - |

New York, December 3, 1912.

| | | |
|---|---|---|
| 38469- | When I Lost You | Col A-1288, 2162 |
| 38470- | When Sally In Our Alley Sings Those Old-Time Songs To Me | -        2213 |

New York, March 22, 1913.

| | | |
|---|---|---|
| 38721- | Daddy Has A Sweetheart | Col A-1320, 2213 |
| 38722- | Why Did You Make Me Care ? | -        2353 |

Acc. by studio orchestra.        New York, c. March, 1913.

| | |
|---|---|
| The Trail Of The Lonesome Pine | Amb 1743 |

Acc. by O/? Charles A. Prince.          New York, May 24, 1913.

38881-   There's One In A Million Like You (w/    Col A-1336
            Peerless Quartet)

                                        New York, July 15, 1913.

38947-   The Curse Of An Aching Heart             Col A-1380, 2301

                                        New York, October 10, 1913.

39039-   Love Has Done Wonders For Me             Col A-1444, 2371

                                        New York, December 2, 1913.

39129-   I Miss You Most Of All                   Col A-1454

                                        New York, December 3, 1913.

39130-   Would You Take Me Back Again ?           Col A-1454, 2371

                                        New York, February 24, 1914.

39262-   She's Dancing Her Heart Away             Col A-1514, Re G-7384

  Acc. by studio orchestra.             New York, c. February, 1914.

         That's An Irish Lullaby                  Ed 50230
         When I Dream Of Old Erin                     -
         She's Dancing Her Heart Away             Amb 2310

  Acc. by O/? Charles A. Prince.        New York, March 21, 1914.

39295-   That's A Real Moving Picture From Life   Col A-1524, Re G-7384

                                        New York, April 24, 1914.

39338-   My Love Would Fill A Thousand Hearts     Col A-1553

                                        New York, May 26, 1914.

39419-   Rose Of The Glen                         Col A-1561

                                        New York, June 29, 1914.

39469-   You're More Than All The World To Me     Col A-1577

                                        New York, June 28, 1915.

45826-   You're Plenty Up-To-Date For Me          Col rejected

                                        New York, July 19, 1915.

45865-   That's The Song Of Songs For Me          Col rejected

                                        New York, December 16, 1915.

46280-   When It's Orange Blossom Time In         Col A-1922
            Loveland

                                        New York, January 17, 1916.

46347-   She's The Daughter Of Mother Machree    Col A-1951
46348-3  No-One But Your Dear Old Dad            Col A-1950

                                        New York, February 16, 1916.

46420-   There's A Broken Heart For Every Light   Col A-1964
            On Broadway
46421-   Where The Shamrock Grows                 Rejected

New York, March 15, 1916.

46639-    The Ashes Of My Heart                    Col A-1983

New York, May 3, 1916.

46746-    Goodbye, Mother Dear                     Col rejected

Acc. by studio orchestra.              New York, c. June, 1916.

2266-5    Hippodrome Minstrel Medley              Em 7117 (7")
2267-3    Where The Sunset Turns The Ocean's Blue        -
          To Gold

New York, c. November, 1916.

          A Broken Doll                          Amb 3189

New York, c. June, 1917.

          If You Had All The World And Its Gold   Ed 50465
          Mammy's Little Coal Black Rose                -
          My Sunshine Jane                        Ed 50481

New York, c. August, 1923.

          I Will Love You When The Silver Threads Ed 51231
            Are Shining Among The Gold
          Why Don't You Come Back Home Again ?         -

New York, April, 1926.

10902     I Wish I Had My Old Gal Back Again      Ed 51728
10908     Am I Wasting My Time On You ?                 -

New York, September, 1926.

11202     She May Have Seen Better Days           Ed 51837

11217     My Sweetheart's The Man In The Moon     Ed 51837

## MARGARET ROMAINE

American-born, European-trained operatic soprano who made a considerable impression
  by her appearances in THE MIDNIGHT GIRL (44th Street, New York, February 23,1914)
  and CHIN-CHIN (Globe, October 20, 1914). Her Columbias of 1919-1921 are of concert
  music and opera, and somewhat outside the scope of this book.
Vocal, acc. by O/? Walter B. Rogers.      New York, May 5, 1914.

B-14799-2  Oh ! Gustave (w/George MacFarlane)       Vic 60118
             ("The Midnight Girl")
B-14800-2  The Castillian Maid                       Vic 60119
B-14802-1-2  Knowest Thou The Land ? ("Mignon" -   Rejected
             Thomas)

New York, June 24, 1914.

B-15004-1  Goodnight (Bonne nuit) (Massenet)       Rejected
B-15005-1-2  The Star-Spangled Banner                   -
B-15006-1  The Sun Whose Rays ("The Mikado")       Vic 60112
B-15007-1-2  Serenade (Smile, Sing, Slumber)       Rejected
             (Gounod)

New York, July 6, 1914.

B-15005-3-4  The Star-Spangled Banner             Vic rejected
B-15006-2  The Sun Whose Rays ("The Mikado")           -

Acc. by O/Theodore Levy.              New York, August 26, 1914.

B-15005-5-6  The Star-Spangled Banner         Rejected
B-15150-2   Absent                            Vic 60124

Acc. by O/Walter B. Rogers.           New York, December 21, 1914.

B-15534-1-2  My Skylark Love                   Vic rejected
B-15536-1-2  The Grey Dove ("Chin-Chin")        -

                                      New York, January 29, 1915.

B-15534-3-4  My Skylark Love                   Vic rejected
B-15536-3-4  The Grey Dove ("Chin-Chin")        -

                                      New York, February 2, 1915.

B-15534-6  My Skylark Love                     Vic 60135
B-15536-5  The Grey Dove ("Chin-Chin")         Vic 60133
C-15660-1-2  Resignation                       Rejected
   NOTE:- Matrix B-15535 is by George MacFarlane, q.v.

## HAROLD ROME

B. Hartford, Conn., May 27, 1908; educated at Yale; pianist in the college band, and
   wrote musical revues (PINS AND NEEDLES, Labor Stage, November 27, 1937, for 1,108
   performances); SING OUT THE NEWS (Music Box, September 24, 1938); CALL ME MISTER
   (National, April 18, 1946); served in U.S. Army during World War II, and wrote the
   material for STARS AND GRIPES; also wrote many very popular songs (SUNDAY IN THE
   PARK (1938); SOITH AMERICA, TAKE IT AWAY (1947); HAVE I TOLD YOU LATELY THAT I LOVE
   YOU ? (1949); ALL OF A SUDDEN MY HEART SINGS (1945).

Vocal, acc. by unknown piano.         New York, November 25, 1938.

64771-   Plaza 6-9423 ("Sing Out The News")    Dec 23078
64772-   Yip-Ahoy ("Sing Out The News")          -

## ANN RONELL

B. Omaha, Neb., December 25, 1910 (?) Educated at Radcliffe College; interviewed the
   late George Gershwin for the college magazine, decided on music as a career;  pro-
   tege of Gershwin; taught music and coached singers for theatre and radio; was  rehearsal pianist for several Broadway musicals; first woman to compose and  conduct
   for films (wrote many film scores, the English libretti for the operas MARTHA  and
   THE GYPSY BARON; also wrote two very popular perennial favourites : WILLOW,  WEEP
   FOR ME (1932) and WHO'S AFRAID OF THE BIG BAD WOLF ? (1933).

Vocal, acc. by own piano.             New York, October 4, 1933.

BS-1176   Who's Afraid Of The Big Bad Wolf ?       Vic test
          (Walt Disney Silly Symphony "Three Little Pigs")

## JULIAN ROSE

Jewish-American comedian with a long career in vaudeville in U.S.A. and music-hall in
London.

Vocal, acc. by studio orchestra.      New York, issued on the dates shown.

          Rip Van Winkle Was A Lucky Man (Parody)   Ed 8383 (April, 1903)
          In The Good Old Summer Time (Parody)      Ed 8403 (May, 1903)
          When The Boys Go Marching By (Parody)     Ed 8417 (June, 1903)
          Go 'Way Back And Sit Down (Parody)        Ed 8423 (June, 1903)
          On A Sunday Afternoon (Parody)            Ed 8448 (July, 1903)
          Ain't Dat A Shame ? (Parody)              Ed 8498 (September, 1903)

          In The Shade Of The Old Apple Tree        Ed 9176 (January, 1906)
            (Parody)
          Then I'd Be Satisfied With Life (Parody) Ed 9223 (March, 1906)

Humorous monologues.                         New York, March 16, 1917.

47429-   Levinsky At The Wedding - Part 1        Col A-2310, 2892
47430-   Levinsky At The Wedding - Part 2           -       -
47431-   Levinsky At The Wedding - Part 3        Col A-2366, 2893
47432-   Levinsky At The Wedding - Part 4           -       -

Vocal, acc. by studio orchestra.             New York, c. March, 1922.

         Sadie's Birthday Party               Ed 50952, Amb 4435
         Becky, The Spanish Dancer               -     Amb 4603
         Levinsky's Jubilee                   Ed 51024, Amb 4561
         Yiddisher Jazz                          -     Amb 4579

Humorous monologues.                         London, November 28, 1928.

WA-8152-1  Levinsky At The Wedding - Part 1     Col 5216
WA-8153-1  Levinsky At The Wedding - Part 2       -
WA-8154-1  Levinsky At The Wedding - Part 3     Col 5217
WA-8155-1  Levinsky At The Wedding - Part 4       -

   Acc. by O/? Harry Bidgood.                London, c. March, 1932.

J-105    Mrs. Blumberg's Jewish Boarding House    Bcst 829 (9")
            - Part 1
J-106    Mrs. Blumberg's Jewish Boarding House      -
            - Part 2

J-119    Mrs. Blumberg's Jewish Boarding House    Bcst 854 (9")
            - Part 3
J-120    Mrs. Blumberg's Villa By The Sea           -

## LANNY ROSS

B. Seattle, Wash., January 19, 1906; educated Yale, Columbia and Juilliard School of
   Music; was soloist with Yale Glee Club; radio debut 1928; took part in SHOW    BOAT
   radio series with Annette Hanshaw for five years; also in vaudeville, night clubs,
   theatres, films; gave Town Hall recitals and concert tours; own radio shows; wrote
   several songs; served in U.S. Army in World War II (rank of Major).

Vocal, acc. by own piano.                    New York, July 17, 1929.

BVE-657    I Kiss Your Hand, Madame/Finding The    Vic test
              Long Way Home

   Acc. by O/Billy Burton.                   New York, October 23, 1933.

BS-78268-1  Many Moons Ago                          Vic rejected
BS-78269-1  One Morning In May                        -

   Acc. by O/Ray Sinatra.                    New York, November 27, 1933.

BS-78702-1  One Morning In May                   Vic 24493, HMV B-8176
BS-78703-1  The Harbor Of Home, Sweet Home         -        -

   Acc. by Nat W. Finston and his Paramount Recording Orchestra.
                                 Los Angeles, October 21, 1934.

LA-247-A   Stay As Sweet As You Are             Br 7318, 01936, Col DB-1830,
                                                Epic L2N-6072
LA-248-    Let's Give Three Cheers For Love     Br 7318, 01936
LA-249-    Water Under The Bridge               Br 7314, 01977
LA-250-    The World Is Mine                      -       -

   Acc. by studio orchestra.                 New York, February 8, 1935.

B-16828-   I'm Misunderstood                    Br 7403
B-16829-   The Rose Of Tralee                   Br 02012
B-16830-A  Moonlight And Roses                    -      Col DB-1830
B-16831-   Two Heads Against The Moon           Br 7403

Acc. by O/Russ Morgan.                    New York, July 23, 1935.

| B-17855- | I'm In The Mood For Love | Br 7496, 02057 |
| B-17856-1 | Nothing Lives Longer Than Love | Br 7508, 02094 |
| B-17857- | I Wished On The Moon | Br 7496, 02057 |
| B-17858-1 | Whenever I Think Of You | Br 7508, 02094 |

New York, October 4, 1935.

| B-18127- | Thanks A Million | Br 7540 |
| B-18128- | Day Dreams | - |

New York, November 5, 1935.

| B-18237- | If You Were Mine | Br 7557 |
| B-18238- | Red Sails In The Sunset | - |

Acc. by O/Roy Bargy-p.                    New York, October 10, 1940.

| BS-056473- | Moonlight And Roses | Vic 26784 |
| BS-056474-1 | Crosstown | Vic 27202 |
| BS-056475-1 | Marianna Annabella (The Little Girl With The Big Name) | - |
| BS-056476- | Whispering | Vic 26784 |

New York, November 28, 1940.

| BS-057683-1 | High On A Windy Hill | Vic 27254, HMV BD-985 |
| BS-057684-1 | The Last Time I Saw Paris | - |
| BS-057685- | Till The Lights Of London Shine Again | Vic 27269 |
| BS-057686- | Music In The Evening (Romance In The Night) | - |

New York, February 14, 1941.

| BS-060646-1 | There's Nothing Like The Smile Of The Irish | Vic 27346 |
| BS-060647-1 | Bendemeer's Stream | - |
| BS-060648-1 | The Night We Met In Honomu | Vic 27379, HMV BD-988 |
| BS-060649-1 | Somewhere In England | - |

New York, April 8, 1941.

| BS-063722-1 | The Mother's Day Song | Vic 27390, HMV BD-988 |
| BS-063723-1 | Ave Maria (Bach-Gounod) | - |
| BS-063724-1 | Come Back To Sorrento | Vic 27413 |

New York, May 6, 1941.

| BS-063854- | Estrellita (Little Star) | Vic 27413 |
| BS-063855-1 | Tulip Time | Rejected |
| BS-063856-1 | 'Neath The South Sea Moon | - |

New York, June 4, 1941.

| BS-065678-1 | The Bard Of Armagh | Vic 27674 |
| BS-065679-1 | Norah O'Neale | Vic 27672 |
| BS-065680-1 | The Light Of The Moon | Vic 27673 |
| BS-065681-1 | Lady Be Tranquil/The Leprechaun | Vic 27672 |
| BS-065682-1 | The Boreen Of Derry | Vic 27671 |
| BS-065683-1 | The Rose Of Kildare | - |
| BS-065684-1 | She Moved Thro' The Fair | Vic 27673 |
| BS-065685-1 | The Star Of The County Down | Vic 27674 |

Acc. by O/Leonard Joy.                    New York, July 18, 1941.

| BS-066871-1 | Shepherd Serenade | Vic 27572, HMV BD-985 |
| BS-066872-1 | 'Til Reveille | Vic 27538, HMV BD-974 |
| BS-066873-1 | Lament To Love | Vic 27572 |
| BS-066874-2 | I Guess I'll Have To Dream The Rest | Vic 27538, HMV BD-974 |

New York, October 22, 1941.

BS-068100-1  Sleigh-Bell Serenade                        Vic 27669
BS-068101-   As We Walk Into The Sunset                    -
BS-068102-1  Your Love To Hold                           Vic 27723
BS-068103-1  You Haunt My Heart                            -

New York, January 21, 1942.

BS-071705-1  Blue Shadows And White Gardenias            Vic 27799
BS-071706-1  All Through The Night                       Vic 27807
BS-071707-1  The Lamp Of Memory                          Vic 27799
BS-071708-1  I'll Pray For You                           Vic 27807

## SHIRLEY ROSS

B. Omaha, Neb., 1909; family moved to Hollywood when she was very small, and she was
   educated there, excelling at piano, singing and acting; in her second year at University of California, she was auditioned by Gus Arnheim to sing with his band; in
   1935 she began her film career with THE AGE OF INDISCRETION, followed by SAN FRAN-
   CISCO (1936); BLOSSOMS ON BROADWAY and WAIKIKI WEDDING (1937); THE BIG BROADCAST OF
   1938 and THANKS FOR THE MEMORY (1938); PARIS HONEYMOON and SOME LIKE IT HOT (1939)
   and A SONG FOR MISS JULIE (1945), among many others.

Vocalist with Gus Arnheim and his Orchestra.
                                              Los Angeles, October 20, 1933.

LA-65-A  I'm No Angel                                Br 6683, 01637

Vocal, acc. by O/Harry Sosnik.        Los Angeles, November 23, 1938.

DLA-1582-A  Two **Sleepy People** (w/Bob Hope) (Film   Dec 2219, Br 02697
              "Thanks For The Memory")
DLA-1583-A  Thanks For The Memory (w/Bob Hope)            - 7-1   -
              (Film "The Big Broadcast of 1938")

                                              Los Angeles, June 16, 1939.

DLA-1779-A  The Lady's In Love With You (w/Bob    Dec 2568, Br 02822
              Hope) (Film "Some Like It Hot")
DLA-1780-A  Penthouse Serenade (When We're Alone)       -        -
              (w/Bob Hope)

Acc. by O/Victor Young.              Los Angeles, July 5, 1939.

DLA-1808-  Mine (w/The Foursome)                   Dec 2878, Br 02990
DLA-1809-  That Certain Feeling (w/The Foursome)         -

Acc. by O/Ray Sinatra.              New York, March 2, 1940.

67259-A  It Never Entered My Mind                    Dec 3066
67260-A  From Another World                          Dec 3067
67261-A  Nothing But You                             Dec 3066
67262-A  Ev'ry Sunday Afternoon                      Dec 3067

## LILLIAN ROTH

B. Boston, Mass., December 13, 1910; stage debut as child in THE INNER MEN (Lyric,
   New York, August 13, 1917); played in THE BETROTHAL (Shubert, November 18, 1918);
   SHAVINGS (Knickerbocker, February 16, 1920); ARTISTS AND MODELS (Shubert, August
   20, 1923); DELMAR'S REVEL (Shubert, November 28, 1927); EARL CARROLL VANITIES at
   Earl Carroll Theatre (August 6, 1928 - as VANITIES - and August 27, 1931); debut
   in films as child in 1915; made several talkies (ILLUSION (1929); THE LOVE PARADE;
   THE VAGABOND KING; PARAMOUNT ON PARADE and MADAM SATAN (1930); ANIMAL CRACKERS and
   SEA LEGS (1931); LADIES THEY TALK ABOUT (1933); TAKE A CHANCE (1934); her career
   was interrupted by personal problems, which she overcame and appeared with Barbra
   Streisand in I CAN GET IT FOR YOU WHOLESALE (Broadway, 1962); her autobiography -
   I'LL CRY TOMORROW - was filmed with Susan Hayward playing her part (1955).

Vocal, acc. by own piano.                    New York, July 15, 1927.

      Hannah Lee/Oh Boy ! How It Was Raining/ Vic test (un-numbered)
        Somebody, Somebody

Lillian Roth also made an LP in the 1950s of some of the songs from her films.

## ADELE  ROWLAND

Began career in vaudeville in 1911; reached stardom with UP IN MABEL'S ROOM at  the
   Eltinge Theatre, New York, January 15, 1919; also made a silent movie in 1923 for
   Goldwyn (VANITY FAIR).

Vocal, acc. by studio orchestra.            New York, early February, 1919.

| 67421 | When I Get In Indiana In The Morning | Pathe 22095 |
| 67422 | When You See Another Sweetie Hanging Around | - |

  Acc. by O/Charles A. Prince.              New York, March 5, 1919.

| 78334- | The Hesitating Blues | Col A-2769 |
| 78335- | Rainy Day Blues | Rejected |

  Acc. by O/Joseph Pasternack.            Camden, N. J., April 23, 1919.

| B-22801-2 | Mammy O' Mine | Vic 18560 |
| B-22802-3 | When You See Another Sweetie Hanging Around | - |

  Acc. by O/Charles A. Prince.              New York, June 19, 1919.

| 78512- | Granny | Col A-2820 |

  Acc. by O/Joseph Pasternack.            Camden, N. J., July 3, 1919.

| B-23045-1-2-3 | Granny | Vic rejected |
| B-23046-1-2-3 | When The Preacher Makes You Mine | - |

                            Camden, N. J., July 29, 1919.

| B-23045-4 | Granny | Vic 18621 |
| B-23046-5 | When The Preacher Makes You Mine | - |

## RUTH  ROYE

Vaudeville top-liner who introduced the song ABA DABA HONEYMOON in the summer 1914,
   and had the logest run ever at the Palace, New York, that year.

Vocal, acc. by studio orchestra.            New York, c. September, 1916.

| Mammy's Little Coal-Black Rose (w/ —— | Pathe 20103 |
|   Winsch) | |
| When They Go Through A Tunnel | Pathe 20104 |
| Since Maggie Dooley Learned The Hooley | Pathe 20105 |
|   Hooley | |

                            New York, c. November, 1916.

| Honolulu, America Loves You | Pathe 20128 |
| Put On Your Slippers And Fill Up Your | Pathe 20135 |
|   Pipe | |
| Keep Your Eye On The Girlie You Love | Pathe 20136 |

                            New York, September 19, 1922.

| 80558- | Georgette | Col A-3714 |
| 80559- | I'm Askin' Ye Ain't It The Truth ? | - |

RUTH ROYE (cont.)

                                    New York, April 14, 1923.

80962-   Louisville Lou (The Vampin' Lady)      Col A-3881
80963-   Hotsy Totsy Town                       -

                                    New York, January 2, 1924.

81446-   Dancin' Dan                            Col 63-D
81447-   Big-Hearted Bennie                     -

## RUTH RUBENSTEIN

American comedienne noted for her appearance in PINS AND NEEDLES (Labor Stage Theatre
in New York, November 27, 1937).

Vocal, acc. by Harold Rome (composer)-Baldwin Bergesen-p.
                                    New York, February 1, 1938.

63235-A  Chain Store Daisy ("Pins And Needles")    Dec 23061, Br 02616

## YVETTE RUGEL

B. Philadelphia, Pa., c. 1899; became a vaudeville star during the 1920s.

Vocal, acc. by Rosario Bourdon.        Camden, N. J., December 16, 1921.

B-25903-3  Granny (You're My Mammy's Mammy)       Vic 18854, HMV B-1398
B-25904-1-2-3  In Blue Bird Land                  Rejected

                                    Camden, N. J., January 16, 1922.

B-25954-1-2-3  April Showers                      Vic rejected
B-25955-1-2-3  Leave Me With A Smile              -

  Acc. by studio orchestra.            New York, February, 1925.

  5845-   Listening                             Apex 8321

                                    New York, c. February 19, 1925.

  5863-   Honest And Truly                       Do 3464
  5864-2  Indian Love Call                       Do 3467, Imp 1426

## LILLIAN RUSSELL

B. 1861; became an outstanding vaudeville and musical comedy artist after some years
as an operetta star (she sang in Gilbert and Sullivan's THE SORCERER in the 1880s)
and her burlesquing of light opera (debut at Tony Pastor's Theatre, New York,1881),
her biggest success was in TWIRLY WHIRLY (Weber and Fields, September 18, 1902) in
which she sang COME DOWN, MA EVENING STAR. She formed the Gamut Club for  members
of the profession in 1910, ran her own opera company, and appeared in one   silent
film, WILDFIRE (1915).  D. June 6, 1922.

Vocal, acc. by O/Charles A. Prince.     New York, March 22, 1912.

19831-   When You're Away                       Col rejected
19832-   The Island Of Roses And Love           -

                                    New York, c. 1912.

       Come Down, Ma Evening Star ("Twirly     Collectors Record Shop 8, AR 2290
          Whirly")                             (dubbed from privately made original)

One of the most famous of all French popular singers of the 1930s and 1940s; he made
his debut as the vocalist with Don Marino Barreto and his Orchestra at Melody's Bar
in Paris in 1932; New York debut in the summer of 1937, returning there in spring,
1939 and staying until after World War II.

Vocal (in French where the titles are given first in that language; if shown in English, they are sung thus), acc. by Don Barreto et son Orchestre du Melody's Bar.
Paris, c. March, 1932.

      Beguin-Biguine                             Col DF-878

Acc. by Mireille-p.                          Paris, c. July, 1932.

      Quand on est au volant                     Col DF-917
      Vingt et vingt                             Col DF-947
      Ma grand'mere etait garde-barriere         -

                                 Paris, c. December, 1932.

      C'est un jardinier qui boite (w/Pils       Col DF-1074
        and Tabet and Mireille) ("Un mois de vacances")
      Les pieds dans l'eau (w/Mireille) ("Un     Col DF-1075
        mois de vacances")

Acc. by Clement Doucet or G. Tabet-p.   Paris, c. December, 1932.

      Presque oui (w/Mireille) ("Un mois de      Col DF-1076
        vacances") - pCD
      La partie de bridge (w/Pils and Tabet      Col DF-1077
        and Mireille) ("Un mois de vacances") - pGT
      Plus rien - pCD                            Col DF-1177
      Mimi - pCD                                 -
      Eteignons tout et couchons-nous (Let's     Col DF-1274
        Put Out The Lights And Go To Sleep) - pCD
      Mon chant d'amour est une valse ("L'Auberge
        du Cheval Blanc" ("The White Horse Inn")-pCD

Acc. by vn/p/cel/g/d.                     Paris, March, 1933.

CL-4257-1  Le meme coup                       Col DF-1191
CL-4258-1  Je suis Sex-Appeal                 -

Acc. by Mireille-p.                        Paris, c. November, 1933.

      Ce petit chemin                            Col DF-1353

Acc. by Andre Ekyan and his Orchestra.  Paris, January 15, 1934.

CL-4661-1  Le jour ou je te vis (The Day You Came  Col DF-1406
        Along)
CL-4662-1-2  Un sou dans la poche              Rejected
CL-4663-1  Prenez garde au mechant loup (Who's    Col DF-1406
        Afraid Of The Big Bad Wolf ?)
CL-4664-1  Pas sur la bouche                  Rejected

Acc. by Andre Ekyan-cl/Alec Siniavine-p/Django Reinhardt-g.
                        Paris, April 16, 1934.

CL-4807-1  Je sais que vous etes jolie !     Col DF-1506, BF-404, 4191-M
CL-4808-1  Par Correspondance                 -          -        -

Acc. by Garland Wilson or Alec Siniavine-p/Django Reinhardt-g as shown.
                        Paris, January 7, 1935.

CL-5176-2  The Continental - pGW/gDR         Col DF-1672
CL-5177-1  Miss Otis Regrets - pGW            -
CL-5178-3  Un Baiser - pGW/gDR               Col DF-1714, 4178-M
CL-5179-1  La Derniere Bergere - pAS/gDR      -          -
      Je m'en fous car je l'aime - pAS          Col DF-1715
      La Baignoire - pAS                         -

Paris, c. August, 1935.

Ferme jusqu'a lundi (w/Mireille) - pAS    Col DF-1846
Puisque vous partez en voyage (w/Mireille)    -
    - pAS

Acc. by Stephane Grappelly-p/Django Reinhardt-g.
                                     Paris, August, 1935.

CL-5487-1-2  Cette chanson est pour vous         Col rejected
CL-5488-1-2  Darling, je vous aime beaucoup          -
CL-5489-1    Dermiere chanson                         -

Acc. by Stephane Grappelly-vn/Django Reinhardt-Joseph Reinhardt-g/Louis Vola-sb.
                                     Paris, September, 1935.

CL-5487-3  Cette chanson est pour vous         Col DF-1847
CL-5518-1  Rendez-vous sous la pluie               -        4222-M

    Acc. by O/Wal-Berg.              Paris, c. October, 1935.

Ça vient tout doucement (w/Loulou        Col DF-1868
    Hegoburu) (Film "Mademoiselle Mozart")
Le bonheur c'est un rien (w/Loulou           -
    Hegoburu) (Film "Mademoiseele Mozart")
Deux sur un trapeze (w/Loulou Hegoburu) Col DF-1881
Le moulin qui jase (w/Loulou Hegoburu)       -

Acc. by Garland Wilson-p.           Paris, c. January, 1936.

CL-5651-1  Un seul couvert, please James      Col DF-1903, 4174-M
CL-5652-1  Si tu m'aimes                          - DB-1709, 4175-M

    Acc. by O/Wal-Berg, with Alec Siniavine-p, where shown.
                                     Paris, c. March, 1936.

CL-5796-1  Un  poisson dans l'eau - pAS     Col DF-1951, DB-1709
CL-5797-1  Vous  qui passez sans me voir - pAS   Col DF-1977, DB-1670
           Ces  petites choses (These Foolish Things)-pAS -
           Alobe  (Seul) - pAS               Col DF-1951

                          Paris, c. October, 1936.

CL-5905-1  La Chanson des Rues           Col DF-2029, DF-2147, DB-1670
           Duo des aveux (w/Germaine Sablon) ("Le    -
             Chant des Tropiques")
           Quand je te parle d'amour (Tormented)   Col DF-2010
           Il ne faut pas briser un reve              -

                          Paris, c. February, 1937.

CL-6034-1  Melancolie - pAS             Col DF-2084, DB-1691
CL-6035-1  Pour vous j'avais fait cette chanson - pAS -         -
           Plus rien n'existe - pAS     Col DF-2147

    Acc. by O/Norman Cloutier.       New York, August 5, 1937.

BS-011654-1  Can I Forget You ?               Vic 25643, HMV B-8635
BS-011655-1  Comment t'oublier (Can I Forget You ?)Vic 25654
BS-011656-1  Afraid To Dream                  Vic 25643, HMV B-8635
BS-011657-   J'ai peur de rever (Afraid To Dream)  Vic 25654
BS-011658-1  Le Doux Caboulet                 Vic 25655
BS-011659-   Si mon coeur pouvait te dire           -

    Acc. by O/Lou Bring.            Hollywood, October 12, 1938.

BS-026186-   J'ai ta main                     Vic 26078
BS-026187-1  Two Sleepy People                Vic 26092, HMV B-8848
BS-026188-1  Two Sleepy People (in French)    Rejected ?
BS-026189-   Stardust (in English and French)
BS-026190-1  Stardust (in English only)       Vic 26078, HMV B-8848
BS-026191-1  Blue Nightfall                   Vic 26092

Acc. by O/Wal-Berg.                          Paris, c. April, 1939.

OLA-3002-2  Sur le Pont d'Avignon              HMV B-9054

OLA-3009-2  Le Fiacre (The Cab)                HMV B-8986
OLA-3010-2  Je tire ma reverence               HMV B-9054

OLA-3015-2  Paris, tu n'as pas change (Paris, You  HMV B-8986
              Have Not Changed)

Acc. by O/Leonard Joy.                       New York, May 24, 1939.

BS-037148-1  Rendezvous Time In Paree          Vic 26269
BS-037149-1  Is It Possible ?                  Vic 26286
BS-037150-1  We Can Live On Love (We Haven't Got A  Vic 26269
              Pot To Cook In)
BS-037151-1  South American Way                Vic 26286

                                             New York, June 2, 1941.

BS-065670-1  Sur les quais du vieux Paris      Vic 27500
BS-065671-1  J'attendrai                       Vic 27475
BS-065672-1  Le Fiacre (The Cab)               -
BS-065673-1  I'm Misunderstood                 Vic 27500

Acc. by O/Paul Baron.                        New York, May 28, 1942.

70788-A  Ma Mie                               Dec 23255, Br 03873
70789-A  Serenade (Charles Trenet)            -             -
70790-   Dis-lui que je l'aime                Dec 23256

                                             New York, June 8, 1942.

70829-   Jean, Jean                           Dec 23255
70830-   Je n'en connais pas la fin           Dec 23257
70831-   Elle n'est pas si mal que ça         Dec 23256

## SABU

B. Mysore, India, 1924; r.n. Sabu Dastagir; originally a stable lad who was  noticed
by film director Robert Flaherty on location in India; film debut ELEPHANT BOY (in
1937); came to England and later U.S.A.; starred in THE DRUM (1938); THE THIEF  OF
BAGDAD (1940); THE JUNGLE BOOK (1942); WHITE SAVAGE (1943); COBRA WOMAN(1944);TAN-
GIER (1946); THE END OF THE RIVER (1947); MANEATER OF KUMAON (1948); SONG OF INDIA
(1949); HELLO, ELEPHANT (1952); JAGUAR (1956); A TIGER WALKS (1963), and others.D.
1963.

Narration, acc. by O/Miklos Rosza.          Lotus Club, New York, March 24, 1942.

CS-073223-1  Kipling's "Jungle Book" - Part 1   Vic 11-8206
CS-073224-2  Kipling's "Jungle Book" - Part 2   -
CS-073225-1  Kipling's "Jungle Book" - Part 3   Vic 11-8207
CS-073226-1  Kipling's "Jungle Book" - Part 4   -
CS-073227-1  Kipling's "Jungle Book" - Part 5   Vic 11-8208
CS-073228-1  Kipling's "Jungle Book" - Part 6   -

## JOSIE SADLER

Very popular vaudeville artiste in New York during the opening years of the century.

Vocal, acc. by studio orchestra.            New York, October, 1907.

3815-   I'd Like To Make A Smash Mit You       Col 3815, A-581, Climax 3815

                                             New York, c. January, 1908.

3901-   Come And Hear The Orchestra            Col 3901, A-582, 33291 (cyl.)

New York, c. February, 1908.

3931-    A Little German Trouble                Col 3931, A-596, 33303 (cyl.),
                                                Diamond A-596

3934-    One Good Turn Deserves Another         Col A-604

Acc. by O/? Walter B. Rogers.        New York, December 31, 1908.

B-6695-1-2-3  If I Could Only Get Some Sleep    Rejected
B-6696-3  What's The Use Of Working ?           Vic 5669

Acc. by studio orchestra.          New York, March 31, 1909.

         He Falls For The Ladies Every Time     Ed 10179

Acc. by O/? Walter B. Rogers.        New York, April 23, 1909.

B-7008-2  He Falls For The Ladies Every Time    Vic 5702, 16784
B-7009-1-3  Come And Hear The Orchestra         Vic 5719
B-7010-1-2  One Good Turn Deserves Another      Rejected

Acc. by studio orchestra.          New York, April 28, 1909.

         Come And Hear The Orchestra            Ed 4M-184

                                     New York, May 17, 1909.

         Lena From Germany                      Ed 10198
         One Good Turn Deserves Another         Ed 10229

Acc. by O/? Walter B. Rogers.        New York, June 11, 1909.

B-8043-1-2  Hilda Loses Her Job                 Vic 5749, 16783
B-8044-1  I'd Like To Make A Smash Mit You      Vic 5762
B-8045-1-2  Heinie Waltzed Round On His Hickory Vic 5729
            Limb
B-8046-1  Beer Land                             Vic 16486

Acc. by studio orchestra.          New York, June 23, 1909.

         Bl-nd And P-g (sic)                    Ed 10267

Acc. by O/? Walter B. Rogers.        New York, November 19, 1909.

B-8388-1-2  I Love My Husband, But Oh, You Henry  Vic rejected

Acc. by studio orchestra.          New York, March 1, 1910.

         The German Fifth                       Ed 4M-438

## CHARLES "CHIC" SALE

B. **Huron**, South Dakota, August 25, 1885; famous during the 1910s and 1920s as mono-
    loguist and character comedian, especially for his book THE SPECIALIST; d. Los An-
    geles, November 7, 1936.

Humorous monologues, unacc.          New York, May 10, 1917.

77042-   Lem Underdunk's New Cap                Rejected
77043-   Lem Underdunk's Sleigh Riding Party    Col A-2404

                                     New York, July 12, 1917.

77205-   Mr. Lem Underdunk, "Leading Horner Of  Col A-2404
            The Silver Cornet Band"

Acc. by Frank Black-Pipe organ/Nat Shilkret-chimes, with choir.
New York, December 24, 1927.

BVE-41266-    The Substitute Parson - Part 1       Vic 22103
BVE-41267-    The Substitute Parson - Part 2         -

## JULIA  SANDERSON

B. Springfield, Mass., August 20, 1887; popular star of light opera and musical comedy for many years, notably TANGERINE (Casino, New York, August 9, 1921), in which
   she appeared with her husband, the late Frank Crumit, and with whom she had a very
   successful radio spot for some time during the 1930s (she continued to appear   on
   the air with her own show after his death in 1943).  She only made one film,   THE
   RUNAWAY (silent, 1917); also starred in THE GIRL FROM UTAH (Knickerbocker, August
   24, 1914).
Vocal, acc. by O/Leonard Joy.             New York, February 11, 1931.

BVE-67441-2  Would You Like To Take A Walk ?       Vic 22630, HMV B-3833
             (w/Frank Crumit)

                                          New York, February 17, 1932.

BRC-500       Sing A Song Of Contract (w/Frank      Vic test
              Crumit)

Acc. by Jack Shilkret-p.                  New York, March 16, 1932.

BS-71959-1  Lamb's Gambol Dialogue and Singing     Vic rejected

Acc. by O/Harry Sosnik.                   New York, April 25, 1941.

69050-    We'll Never Grow Old (w/Frank Crumit)    Dec 18155
69051-    They Didn't Believe Me ("The Girl From Utah")Dec 18157, DL-6019
69052-    The Girl With The Brogue                    -
69053-    Sweet Lady (w/Frank Crumit) ("Tangerine")Dec 18154

                                          New York, April 28, 1941.

69073-    Hello ! I've Been Looking For You (w/    Dec 18154
          Frank Crumit)
69074-    Bring Me A Rose                          Dec 18156
69075-    Same Sort Of Girl (And The Same Sort Of  Dec 18155
          Boy) (w/Frank Crumit) ("The Girl From Utah")
69076-    You're Here And I'm Here (w/Frank Crumit)Dec 18156

## JERE SANFORD

Popular vaudeville personality of the opening years of the century.

Vocal, whistling and yodling, acc. by studio orchestra.
New York, c. June, 1910.

              Jere Sanford's Yodling and Whistling    Ed 4M-523, Amb 1988
              Specialty

## JOSEPH SANTLEY

B. Salt Lake City, Utah, January 10, 1889; stage debut at three, under mother's tui-
   tion; played many juvenile parts; first New York success in THE QUEEN OF THE  MOU-
   LIN ROUGE (Circle, December 7, 1908); extended his scope to vaudeville and  revue,
   after many other Broadway shows; in STOP ! LOOK ! LISTEN ! (Globe, December   25,
   1915); OH, MY DEAR ! (Princess, November 27, 1918); SHE'S A GOOD FELLOW(Globe, May
   5, 1919); MUSIC BOX REVUE (Music Box, September 22, 1921 and September 22, 1923) ;
   between these shows, he appeared in a revue of the same name as his London  debut,
   Palace, May 15, 1923; made many films, beginning with THE SMARTEST GIRL  IN  TOWN,
   1932; among others, SWING, SISTER, SWING (1941); HITTING  THE   HEADLINES  (1942);
   BRAZIL (1944); SHADOW OF A WOMAN (1947); MAKE-BELIEVE BALLROOM (1949); m. Ivy Sawyer, q.v.

JOSEPH SANTLEY (cont.)

Vocal, acc. by studio orchestra.           New York, May, 1922.

  8948    Songs of Yesterday by Stars of Today      Voc 35010 (part side)

## IVY SAWYER

B. London, 1896; pupil of Stedman's Academy; stage debut in ALICE IN WONDERLAND    (as
the Dormouse) at the Prince of Wales's, December, 1906; appeared in MY DARLING    at
the Hicks Theatre, March 2, 1907; toured with Seymour Hicks in this, 1908; made    a
number of other appearances in different performances of ALICE IN WONDERLAND; in the
Russian Ballet at Covent Garden in May, 1912; toured England and appeared in Paris,
1913; to U.S.A., 1916; New York debut in title role of BETTY (Globe, October 3,1916
- met Joseph Santley and married him, thereafter appearing in the same productions,
q.v.)

Vocal, acc. by studio orchestra.           New York, May, 1922.

  8948    Songs of Yesterday by Stars of Today      Voc 35010 (part side)

## JOE  SCHENCK

See Van and Schenck.

## VICTOR  SCHERTZINGER

B. 1889; film director, formerly concert violinist and pianist, also wrote   hundreds
of popular songs, mostly for films; best-known probably MARCHETA (A LOVE-SONG    OF
OLD MEXICO), 1922; first film music was for CIVILIZATION (1915); subsequently HEADS
UP (1929); PARAMOUNT ON PARADE and SAFETY IN NUMBERS (1930); ONE NIGHT OF LOVE (and
directed this, 1934); LOVE ME FOREVER (1935); THE MUSIC GOES ROUND (1936);SOMETHING
TO SING ABOUT (1937); THE ROAD TO SINGAPORE (1940); THE ROAD TO ZANZIBAR; RHYTHM ON
THE RIVER; KISS THE BOYS GOODBYE; BIRTH OF THE BLUES and THE FLEET'S IN (1941);   d.
October 26, 1941.

Piano solo, dubbed from film soundtrack.  Hollywood, December 16, 1935.

PBS-97164-1  Let's Go                          Vic rejected

## SONNY SCHUYLER

Vocalist with George Hall's Hotel Taft Orchestra in New York (1934-1935) who   became
a member of the cast of the long-running PINS AND NEEDLES (Labor Stage,November 27,
1937).

Vocalist with George Hall and his Hotel Taft Orchestra.
                              New York, November 13, 1934.

| | | |
|---|---|---|
| BS-84971- | Santa Claus Is Coming To Town | BB B-5711 |
| BS-84974-1 | Flirtation Walk | BB B-5709, RZ MR-1681 |
| BS-84976-1 | Mr. And Mrs. Is The Name (w/Loretta Lee) | - |
| BS-84980-1 | Imagine Me Without You (w/Loretta Lee) | Rejected |
| BS-84981-1 | No ! No ! A Thousand Times No ! (w/ | BB B-5711 |
| | Loretta Lee) | |

  NOTE:- Sonny Schuyler does not sing on the missing numbers above.

                              New York, December 19, 1934.

| | | |
|---|---|---|
| BS-86477-1 | You're The Top (w/Loretta Lee) | BB B-5765 |
| BS-86478-1 | Au revoir l'amour | BB B-5802 |
| BS-86479-1 | Maria | BB B-5768 |
| BS-86483-1 | When I Grow Too Old To Dream | BB B-5787, RZ MR-1640 |

  NOTE:- Sonny Schuyler does not sing on matrices BS-86480/2 inclusive.

                              New York, March 5, 1935.

| | | |
|---|---|---|
| BS-88771-1 | According To The Moonlight | BB B-5865, RZ MR-1787 |
| BS-88772-1 | Everything's Been Done Before | RZ MR-1875 |
| BS-88773-1 | I Won't Dance (w/Loretta Lee) | BB B-5863 |
| BS-88775-1 | Oh Susannah (Dust Off That Old Pianna) | BB B-5864 |
| | (w/Loretta Lee) | |

New York, July 12, 1935.

| | | |
|---|---|---|
| BS-92597-1 | Why Dream ? | BB B-6014 |
| BS-92598-1 | Through The Doorway Of Dreams | - |
| BS-92599-1 | My Very Good Friend The Milkman (w/ Dolly Dawn) | BB B-6015 |
| BS-92700-1 | Roll Along, Prairie Moon | BB B-6017, RZ MR-1865 |
| BS-92701-1 | I Never Saw A Better Night | BB B-6018 |

New York, September 14, 1935.

| | | |
|---|---|---|
| BS-95028-1 | Every Now And Then | BB B-6099, RZ MR-1916 |
| BS-95029-1 | You're A Vision To Behold | BB B-6115 |
| BS-95030-1 | It Never Dawned On Me | BB B-6101 |

New York, September 27, 1935.

BS-95082-1  A Picture Of Me Without You (w/Dolly  BB B-6127
           Dawn)

Vocal, acc. by Harold Rome (composer)-Baldwin Bergeson-p.
                         New York, February 9, 1938.

63260-A  One Big Union For Two (w/Kay Weber)    Dec 23060, Br 02617
        ("Pins And Needles")

New York, February 10, 1938.

63267-A  Sing Me A Song With Social Significance  Dec 23061, Br 02616
        (w/Kay Weber) ("Pins And Needles")

## ARTHUR SCHWARTZ

B. Newark, N. J., November 25, 1900; composer of music for many Broadway shows from 1929 onwards (e.g., THE LITTLE SHOW (1929); THE SECOND LITTLE SHOW; HERE COMES THE BRIDE; THE CO-OPTIMISTS OF 1930; THREE'S A CROWD and PRINCESS CHARMING (1930); THE BAND WAGON (1931); FLYING COLORS (1932); NICE GOINGS ON (1933); REVENGE WITH MUSIC (1934); AT HOME ABROAD and FOLLOW THE SUN (1935); BETWEEN THE DEVIL (1937); STARS IN YOUR EYES (1939), and others); visited London in the 1930s to supervise musical arrangements of shows for which he wrote scores.

Vocalist with Leo Reisman and his Orchestra.
                       New York, October 5, 1932.

BS-73766-1  Louisiana Hayride (w/Eva Jessye Choir) Vic 24157, HMV B-6419
          ("Flying Colors")

Piano solos, with own vocal where shown.  London, December 6, 1935.

CA-15479-1  Follow The Sun - Selection, Part 1    Col FB-1269
          (Intro. Love Is A Dancing Thing/How High Can A Little Bird Fly ?-vAS / Nicotina)
CA-15480-1  Follow The Sun - Selection, Part 2      -
          (Intro. Got A Bran' New Suit-vAS/Dangerous You/Follow The Sun)

## BLOSSOM SEELEY

Pioneer "coon-shouter" who achieved fame, and a certain amount of notoriety, in 1908 in San Francisco by singing PUT YOUR ARMS AROUND ME, HONEY and TODDLIN' THE TODALO (with demonstration of the dance); made a similar sensation in cabaret in New York in 1912, and continued to be a top-liner in this and vaudeville for many years; m. Benny Fields, q.v.

Vocal, acc. by O/? Charles A. Prince.    New York, May 22, 1911.

19379-2  He's Coming Back
                          Col A-1042
                      New York, February 5, 1921.

| | | |
|---|---|---|
| 79713- | Hawaiian Blues | **Col** rejected |
| 79714- | Spanish Lou | - |

New York, February 14, 1921.

79725-3  Funeral Blues (Eat Custard And You'll     Col A-3382
           Never Break A Tooth)

New York, September 29, 1922.

80571-3  'Way Down Yonder In New Orleans          Col A-3731
80572-3  Mississippi Choo Choo                       -

New York, March 28, 1923.

80914-1  Down Among The Sleepy Hills Of Ten-Ten-  Col A-3868
           Tennessee

New York, April 4, 1923.

80922-2  You Said Something When You Said "Dixie"  Col A-3868

  Acc. by The Georgians/Frank Guarente.    New York, March 27, 1924.

81652-1  Don't Mind The Rain                      Col 114-D
81653-2  Lazy                                        -

New York, May 10, 1924.

81771-2  Bringin' Home The Bacon                  Col 136-D
81772-1  A New Kind Of Man With A New Kind Of Love    -
           For Me

  Acc. by studio orchestra.                 New York, January 29, 1925.

140372-  Everybody Loves My Baby                  Col 304-D
140373-  Alabamy Bound                               -

New York, March 12, 1925.

140427-  All Aboard For Heaven                    Col rejected
140428-  It's Just That Feeling For Home             -

New York, May 15, 1925.

140608-  Yes Sir, That's My Baby                  Col 386-D
140609-  It's Just That Feeling For Home             -

New York, March 25, 1926.

141862-3  Spanish Shawl                           Col 613-D
141863-3  I Found A Round-About Way To Heaven        -

New York, February 20, 1933.

265055-  What Have We Got To Lose ? (w/Al Fields)  Col rejected

## ALICE J.  SHAW

Mrs. Alice Shaw was a headliner at Keith-Albee's Union Square Theatre, New York, when
  it opened in 1893; she was also well-known in London, where she had appeared  as a
  "high-class" music-hall act in the 1880s.

Whistling, acc. by O/Walter B. Rogers.     New York, May 29, 1907.

B-4541-2  In Venice                               Vic 5175, 16052
B-4542-2  La Gazelle                              Vic 5306
B-4543-2  Manzanilla                              Vic 5174

B. Philadelphia, Pa., 1889; r.n. Oscar Schwartz; stage debut in chorus of THE MIMIC
WORLD (Casino, New York, July 9, 1908); several other shows there, then to Winter
Garden, July 22, 1912, to appear in THE PASSING SHOW OF 1912; to London; appeared
in KILL THAT FLY (Alhambra, October 14, 1912); COME OVER HERE (Hammerstein's Lon-
don Opera House, April 19, 1913); THE HONEYMOON EXPRESS (Oxford, April 13, 1914);
DORA'S DOZE (Palladium, July 6, 1914); 5064 GERRARD (Alhambra, March 19, 1915); to
New York and starred in VERY GOOD, EDDIE (Princess, December 23, 1915); LEAVE IT
TO JANE (Longacre, August 28, 1917); TWO LITTLE GIRLS IN BLUE (Cohan, May 3,1921);
GOOD MORNING, DEARIE (Globe, November 1, 1921); MUSIC BOX REVUE (Music Box, Decem-
ber 1, 1924); OH, KAY ! (Imperial, November 8, 1926); THE FIVE O'CLOCK GIRL (44th
Street, October 10, 1927); FLYING HIGH (Apollo, March 3, 1930); EVERYBODY'S WEL-
COME (Shubert, October 13, 1931), and many others. He made one film (THE GREAT
WHITE WAY, 1924).

Vocal, acc. by O/Charles A. Prince.      New York, April 21, 1916.

46732-2  I've Got The Blues For Home, Sweet Home  Col A-2003

                                         New York, May 16, 1916.

46781-1  The Stormy Sea Of Love              Col A-2026
46782-1  Michael And His Motor-Cycle         Col A-2027

                                         New York, June 20, 1916.

46860-1  Some Girls Do And Some Girls Don't   Col A-2043

Acc. by studio orchestra.                New York, May, 1922.

8948     Songs of Yesterday by Stars of Today   Voc 35010 (part side)

## WINIFRED SHAW

B. 1910; child performer in parents' vaudeville act for some time before film debut
in 1934; supplied the voice of non-singing stars in many musicals produced by the
Warner Brothers studios; appeared in person in such as THE GIFT OF GAB;WAKE UP AND
DREAM (1934); SWEET ADELINE; GOLD DIGGERS OF 1935; IN CALIENTE and BROADWAY HOST-
ESS (1935); READY, WILLING AND ABLE and MELODY FOR TWO (1937); r.n. Winifred Lei
Momi (she is of Hawaiian descent).

Vocal, acc. by Dick Jurgens and his Orchestra.
                                     Los Angeles, February 28, 1935.

DLA-110-A  Lullaby Of Broadway (Film "Gold        Dec 408, 7-1, Br 02026
             Diggers of 1935")
DLA-111-A  I'm Goin' Shoppin' With You (Film "Gold     -           -
             Diggers of 1935")

## AL SHEAN

See Ed. Gallagher.

## NORMA SHEARER

B. Montreal, Canada, August 10, 1904, of Anglo-Scottish parents; now naturalised American. Widow of MGM executive producer Irving Thalberg (1899-1936); after years of
hard work in small parts on stage, secured Hollywood contract and began film work;
debut in silents, THE STEALERS (1920); in talkies, THE TRIAL OF MARY DUGAN (1929);
star of many great films since (e.g., THE LAST OF MRS. CHEYNEY (1929); STRANGE IN-
TERLUDE and PRIVATE LIVES (1931); SMILIN' THROUGH (1932); RIPTIDE and THE BARRETTS
OF WIMPOLE STREET (1934); ROMEO AND JULIET (1936); MARIE ANTOINETTE (1938);IDIOT'S
DELIGHT (1939); HER CARDBOARD LOVER (1942).

Speech.                          ? Hollywood, March 31, 1931.

      A Sunkist Radio Interview from "The       Flexo (un-numbered)
      Sunkist Musical Cocktail" (Parts 1-2) (w/Louella Parsons)
                             Hollywood, September 1, 1931.

BVE-68308-1  Test (no other details known)      Dub from MGM 13130 (LP)

B. Nashville (?), Tenn., 1917; debut in radio 1938; sang with Xavier Cugat's Orchestra at the Waldorf-Astoria Hotel, New York, 1939-1940; made great impression  with
her singing in the radio programme NBC CHAMBER MUSIC SOCIETY OF LOWER BASIN STREET
(1940-1942); began film work then, appearing in THANK YOUR LUCKY STARS (1943);   UP
IN ARMS (1944); BELLE OF THE YUKON (1945); TILL THE CLOUDS ROLL BY (1946);    AARON
SLICK FROM PUNKIN CRICK (1952); now a well-established TV star. Sang in  England,
1944, with Major Glenn Miller and the AEF Dance Orchestra, and has appeared  since
in London as a civilian; m. film star George Montgomery.

Vocalist with Xavier Cugat and his Waldorf-Astoria Orchestra.
                                        New York, June 12, 1939.

BS-037625-1  The Thrill Of A New Romance        Vic 26299
BS-037627-1  Quiereme mucho (Yours)             Vic 26384
  NOTE:- Dinah Shore does not sing on matrix BS-037626.

                                        New York, September 27, 1939.

BS-042740-1  La Cumparsita                       Vic 26426, HMV B-9072

Vocal, acc. by O/Leonard Joy.        New York, October 3, 1939.

BS-042776-1  Who Told You I Cared ?             BB B-10454, RZ MR-3317
BS-042777-1  I Like To Recognize The Tune        -
BS-042778-1  I Thought About You                BB B-10473
BS-042779-1  (Why Couldn't It Last) Last Night   -

Vocalist with Xavier Cugat and his Waldorf-Astoria Orchestra.
                                        New York, October 5, 1939.

BS-042789-1  San Domingo                         Rejected
BS-042790-1  Jungle Drums                        Vic 26426

Vocal, acc. by O/Leonard Joy.        New York, December 28, 1939.

BS-046037-   Careless                            BB B-10564
BS-046038-1  Watching The Clock                  BB B-10592
BS-046039-   Darn That Dream                     BB B-10564
BS-046040-1  I've Got My Eyes On You             BB B-10592, RZ MR-3317

                                        New York, March 28, 1940.

BS-048470-1  Just A-Whistlin' And A-Whittlin'    BB B-10714
               (And A-Watchin' The World Go By)
BS-048471-   Imagination                         BB B-10668
BS-048472-1  Say It                              BB B-10714
BS-048473-1  Shake Down The Stars                BB B-10668

                                        New York, April 15, 1940.

BS-048907-1  You Can't Brush Me Off (w/Dick Todd)  BB B-10720
BS-048908-1  Outside Of That I Love You (w/Dick Todd) -

  Acc. by O/Paul Wetstein (Weston).      New York, June 25, 1940.

BS-051561-1  How Come You Do Me Like You Do ?    BB B-10824
BS-051562-1  Smoke Gets In Your Eyes              -           HMV BD-1084
BS-051563-1  The Nearness Of You                 BB B-10793, RZ MR-3382
BS-051564-1  Maybe                                -           -

Vocalist with Xavier Cugat and his Waldorf-Astoria Orchestra.
                                        New York, June 26, 1940.

BS-051569-1  The Rhumba-Cardi (The Rhumba Of The   Vic 26665
               Heart)
BS-051570-   Whatever Happened To You ?                    -

Vocal, acc. by O/Leonard Joy.                    New York, October 4, 1940.

BS-056437-1  My Man                               BB B-10978, HMV BD-1092
BS-056438-1  Yes, My Darling Daughter             BB B-10920
BS-056439-1  Down Argentina Way                   -
BS-056440-1  Somewhere                            BB B-10991

Vocalist with Maestro Paul Laval and his Woodwindy Ten.
                                                 New York, November 11, 1940.

BS-057616-1  Mood Indigo                          Vic 27302
BS-057619-   Dinah's Blues                        Vic 27303
   NOTE:- "Mlle. Dinah Shore" (so-described) does not sing on matrices BS-057617/8.

Vocal, acc. by O/Leonard Joy.                    New York, December 10, 1940.

BS-058246-1  Somebody Loves Me                    BB B-10978, HMV BD-1092
BS-058247-1  I Hear A Rhapsody                    BB B-11003
BS-058248-1  Memphis Blues                        BB B-10991, HMV BD-1043
BS-058249-   I Do, Do You ? (Do You Believe In    BB B-11003
             Love ?)

   Acc. by O/Lou Bring (Paul Weston-a).    Hollywood, February 20, 1941.

PBS-055296-1  Number Ten, Lullaby Lane            BB B-11084
PBS-055297-2  I'm Thru' With Love                 BB B-11204
PBS-055298-1  Honeysuckle Rose                    BB B-11191, RZ MR-3569
PBS-055299-1  For All Time                        BB B-11084

   Acc. by O/? Leonard Joy.              New York, May 9, 1941.

BS-063875-1  Do You Care ?                        BB B-11191, RZ MR-3605
BS-063876-1  Jim                                  BB B-11204       -
BS-063877-1  Where You Are                        BB B-11164
BS-063878-1  Mocking Bird Lament                     -            RZ MR-3592

   Acc. by O/Paul Weston.               New York, July 2, 1941.

BS-066176-1  You And I                            BB B-11233, HMV BD-1048
BS-066177-2  All Alone                            BB B-11278
BS-066178-1  If It's You                          BB B-11301
BS-066179-1  On A Bicycle Built For Two (Daisy    BB B-11233
             Bell)

   Acc. by Dr. Henry Levine's Barefoot Dixieland Philharmonic.
                                                 New York, August 11, 1941.

BS-067550-1  Love Me Or Leave Me                  BB B-11278
BS-067551-1  Sophisticated Lady                   Vic 27624, HMV BD-1035

   Acc. by Maestro Paul Laval and his Woodwindy Ten.
                                                 New York, August 18, 1941.

BS-067595-1  Star Dust                            Vic 27622, HMV BD-1035
BS-067596-1  Chloe (Song Of The Swamp)            Vic 27625, HMV BD-1026

   Acc. by Dr. Henry Levine's Barefoot Dixieland Philharmonic (first side);  remainder
   dir. by Leonard Joy.                  New York, September 9, 1941.

BS-067761-1  Body And Soul                        Vic 27623, HMV BD-1026
BS-067762-1  Somebody Nobody Loves                BB B-11301
BS-067763-1  Is It Taboo ? (To Fall In Love With  BB B-11322
             You)
BS-067764-1  I Got It Bad And That Ain't Good     BB B-11357
BS-067765-1  Miss You                             BB B-11322

                                    New York, October 28, 1941.

BS-068124-1  This Is No Laughing Matter           BB B-11357
BS-068125-1  Don't Leave Me, Daddy                BB B-11370
BS-068126-1  As We Walk Into The Sunset              -            HMV BD-1020

New York, January 12, 1942.

BS-068852-1  Sometimes                              BB B-11436, HMV BD-1017
BS-068853-1  Blues In The Night                        -          RZ MR-3642

     Acc. by O/Rosario Bourdon.        New York, February 10, 1942.

BS-071795-1  Not Mine                               BB B-11500
BS-071796-1  Goodnight, Captain Curly Head          BB B-11473
BS-071797-1  Skylark                                   -          RZ MR-3642
BS-071798-1-2  She'll Always Remember               Rejected

                                       New York, February 19, 1942.

BS-071798-3  She'll Always Remember                 BB B-11500

     Acc. by Freddy Martin and his Orchestra. New York, March 6, 1942.

BS-073509-1  I Look At Heaven (When I Look At You)   BB B-11487
BS-073510-1  I Can't Give You Anything But Love         -

     Acc. by O/Leonard Joy.            New York, April 9, 1942.

BS-073824-1  Three Little Sisters                   Vic 27875, HMV BD-1020
BS-073825-1  One Dozen Roses                        Vic 27881
BS-073826-1  Sleepy Lagoon                          Vic 27875
BS-073827-1  All I Need Is You                      Vic 27881

     Acc. by O/Gordon Jenkins.         Hollywood, June 12, 1942.

PBS-072423-1  Mad About Him, Sad Without Him, How   Vic 27940
                Can I Be Glad Without Him Blues
PBS-072424-1  Be Careful, It's My Heart                -
PBS-072425-1  He Wears A Pair Of Silver Wings       Vic 27931
PBS-072426-1  Conchita, Marcheta, Lolita, Pepita,      -
                Rosita, Juanita Lopez

                                       Hollywood, July 21, 1942.

PBS-072483-1  A Boy In Khaki, A Girl In Lace        Rejected
PBS-072484-1  Murder, He Says                       Vic      , HMV BD-1058
PBS-072485-1  Manhattan Serenade                    Rejected
PBS-072486-1  Something To Remember You By          Vic      , HMV BD-1058

     Acc. by O/Paul Weston.            Hollywood, July 30, 1942.

PBS-072483-2  A Boy In Khaki, A Girl In Lace        Vic 27963, HMV BD-1031
PBS-072485-2  Manhattan Serenade                    Vic 20-1519, HMV BD-1043
PBS-072558-1  (As Long As You're Not In Love With   Vic 27970
                Anyone Else) Why Don't You Fall In Love With Me ?
PBS-072559-1  Dearly Beloved                           -
PBS-072560-1  (Nobody Knows Better Than I) He's My  Vic 27963, HMV BD-1031
                Guy
PBS-072561-1  You'd Be So Nice To Come Home To      Vic 20-1519, HMV BD-1048

## ETHEL SHUTTA

B. 1897; long career on musical stage (she appeared in one of the FOLLIES revues  in
  a number called I'M IN LOVE WITH EDDIE CANTOR) during the 1920s, and in 1971  took
  part in a FOLLIES revival on Broadway; m. bandleader George Olsen and sang on many
  records made by his Music (see below).

Vocalist with George Olsen and his Music.  Camden, N. J., October 3, 1928.

BVE-47801-1  A Precious Little Thing Called Love    Vic 21832

                                       New York, May 29, 1929.

BVE-53530-1  Or What Have You ? (w/Fran Frey)       Vic rejected

Culver City, Calif., November 3, 1929.

PBVE-54482-6  South Sea Rose                     Vic 22213

Culver City, Calif., November 10, 1929.

PBVE-54499-3  Sweet Nothings Of Love              Vic 22251, HMV B-5796

Culver City, Calif., December 22, 1929.

PBVE-54544-2  I'm On A Diet Of Love               Vic 22259, HMV B-5805

New York, February 24, 1932.

BS-71895-1  There I Go Dreaming Again             Vic 22937, HMV B-6202

New York, March 4, 1932.

BS-71915-1  By The Fireside (w/Bob Borger)        Vic 22947

New York, March 23, 1932.

BS-71988-1  There's Nothing The Matter With Me    Vic 22968

New York, April 14, 1932.

BS-72288-1  Gosh Darn ! (w/Fran Frey)             Vic 22994, HMV B-6197
BS-72289-1  I'm So Alone With The Crowd             -              -

New York, July 13, 1932.

BS-73107-1  Listen To The German Band             Vic 24090, LPV-549

New York, September 2, 1932.

BS-73358-1  And So To Bed (w/Paul Small)          Vic 24125

New York, September 24, 1932.

BS-73576-1  Rock-a-Bye Moon                       Vic rejected

New York, October 20, 1932.

BS-73576-2  Rock-a-Bye Moon                       Vic 24165, HMV B-6333
BS-73845-1  Ah, But I've Learned                  Vic 24166        -

New York, January 11, 1933.

BS-74796-1  Underneath The Arches                 Vic 24229

New York, July 11, 1933.

152435-  Lou'siana Lullaby                        Col 2790-D, CB-656
152438-  Let's Make Up                              -              -

Vocal, acc. by studio orchestra.    New York, September 15, 1933.

152499-  Who's Afraid Of The Big Bad Wolf ?       Col 2849-D
152500-  Snowball                                   -

Vocalist with George Olsen and his Music.  New York, October 30, 1933.

152546-  Sing A Little Low-Down Tune              Col 2843-D, CB-714

There may be other Columbia records by George Olsen and his Music made in 1933-1934,
  with Ethel Shutta as vocalist, but owing to their great rarity - as most    popular
  records of the Depression years tend to be - it has not been possible to check all
  of them.

B. Brooklyn, New York, January 1, 1907; on the staff of a music publishing    company
   for two years, partner in vaudeville of accordionist Phil Baker, q.v. also,     for
   eight; wrote much of the material for films such as BABES IN ARMS; FOR ME AND    MY
   GAL and THE WIZARD OF OZ; appeared in BROADWAY MELODY OF 1936 (and 1938) and   BORN
   TO DANCE (1936).

Vocal, acc. by studio orchestra.              New York, April, 1929.

E-29761-   Little Pal                              Voc 15811
E-29762-   Why Can't You ?                             -

## FRANK  SINATRA

B. Hoboken, N. J., December 12, 1915; on radio in 1936, but became more widely known
   through his singing with first, Harry James and then Tommy Dorsey (1939-1942); began film career in LAS VEGAS NIGHTS (1941); acting career in HIGHER AND HIGHER   in
   1943; since then has appeared in dozens of films of all kinds, from light musicals
   to tense drama (e.g., ANCHORS AWEIGH (1945); TILL THE CLOUDS ROLL BY and IT    HAP-
   PENED IN BROOKLYN (1946); ON THE TOWN (1949); FROM HERE TO ETERNITY (1953);   YOUNG
   AT HEART (1954); THE TENDER TRAP (1955); THE MAN WITH THE GOLDEN ARM; HIGH SOCIETY
   and GUYS AND DOLLS (1956); PAL JOEY (1957); CAN CAN (1959); SERGEANTS THREE(1962);
   ROBIN AND THE SEVEN HOODS (1964); THE NAKED RUNNER (1967, in England).

Vocalist with Harry James and his Orchestra.
                                        New York, July 13, 1939.

B-25057-1  From The Bottom Of My Heart            Br 8443, Col DB-2150, BRS 995
B-25059-1  Melancholy Mood                            -                    -
NOTE:- Frank Sinatra does not sing on the other titles made at this session.

                                        New York, August 17, 1939.

25212-2  My Buddy                                 Col 35242, 37520
25215-1  It's Funny To Everyone But Me            Col 35209, 36738

                                        New York, September 17, 1939.

25285-1  Here Comes The Night                     Col 35227, DB-2150
25288-1  All Or Nothing At All                    Col 35587, C-707, DB-2145

                                        Chicago, October 13, 1939.

WC-2798-A  On A Little Street In Singapore        Col 35261, 36700
WC-2799-A  Who Told You I Cared ?                     -

                                        Los Angeles, November 8, 1939.

LA-2046-A  Ciribiribin                            Col 35316, 37141, C-6045,
                                                  DB-2145, V-Disc 138
LA-2047-A  Every Day Of My Life                   Col 35531, 36700, C-47

Vocalist with Tommy Dorsey and his Orchestra. All these have been issued in a box of
   six LPs (RCA SD-1000) unless marked *.  Chicago, February 1, 1940.

BS-044680-1  The Sky Fell Down                    Vic 26518
BS-044682-1  Too Romantic                         Vic 26500

                                        New York, February 26, 1940.

BS-047706-1  Shake Down The Stars                 Vic 26525, HMV BD-5601
BS-047707-1  Moments In The Moonlight                 -
BS-047708-1  I'll Be Seeing You                   Vic 26539, 20-1574

                                        New York, March 4, 1940.

BS-047746-1  Say It                               Vic 26535
BS-047747-1  Polka Dots And Moonbeams             Vic 26539

New York, March 13, 1940.

| | | |
|---|---|---|
| BS-048129-1 | The Fable Of The Rose | Vic 26555 |
| BS-048130-1 | This Is The Beginning Of The End | - |

New York, March 25, 1940.

| | | |
|---|---|---|
| BS-048430-1-2 | Imagination | Vic rejected |
| BS-048431-1-2 | Yours Is My Heart Alone | - |

New York, March 29, 1940.

| | | |
|---|---|---|
| BS-048479-1 | Hear My Song, Violetta | Vic 26616, HMV BD-1166 |
| BS-048480-1 | Fools Rush In | Vic 26593 |
| BS-048481-1 | Devil May Care | - |

New York, April 10, 1940.

| | | |
|---|---|---|
| BS-048430-3 | Imagination | Vic 26581 |
| BS-048431-3 | Yours Is My Heart Alone | Vic 26616 |
| BS-048758-1 | April Played The Fiddle | Vic 26606, HMV BD-5611 |
| BS-048762-1 | I Haven't Time To Be A Millionaire | -          - |

New York, April 23, 1940.

| | | |
|---|---|---|
| BS-048938-1 | You're Lonely And I'm Lonely | Vic 26596 |
| BS-048939-1 | East Of The Sun (And West Of The Moon) | BB B-10726, HMV BD-5665 |
| BS-048940-1 | Head On My Pillow | - |
| BS-048941-1 | It's A Lovely Day Tomorrow | Vic 26596 |
| BS-048942-1-2-3 | I'll Never Smile Again (w/The Pied Pipers) | Rejected |

New York, May 23, 1940.

| | | |
|---|---|---|
| BS-048942-4 | I'll Never Smile Again (w/The Pied Pipers) | Vic 26628, 27521, HMV B-9102, V-Disc 582 |
| BS-050852-1 | All This And Heaven Too | Vic 26653, HMV BD-5656 |
| BS-050853-1 | Where Do You Keep Your Heart ? | - |

New York, June 13, 1940.

| | | |
|---|---|---|
| BS-051279-1 | Whispering (w/The Pied Pipers) | BB B-10771, Vic 20-1579, HMV B-9102 |

New York, June 27, 1940.

| | | |
|---|---|---|
| BS-051579-1 | Trade Winds | Vic 26666, HMV BD-5645 |
| BS-051581- | The One I Love Belongs To Somebody Else (w/The Pied Pipers) | Vic 26660, 20-2446, HMV BD-5665 |

New York, July 17, 1940.

| | | |
|---|---|---|
| BS-051874-1 | The Call Of The Canyon | Vic 26678 |
| BS-051875-1 | Love Lies | - |
| BS-051876-1 | I Could Make You Care | Vic 26717 |
| BS-051877-1 | The World Is In My Arms | - |

New York, August 29, 1940.

| | | |
|---|---|---|
| BS-055543-1 | Our Love Affair | Vic 26736, HMV BD-5650 |
| BS-055563-1 | Looking For Yesterday | Vic 26738 |
| BS-055564-1 | Tell Me At Midnight | Vic 26747 |
| BS-055565-1 | We Three | -          HMV BD-5655 |

New York, September 9, 1940.

| | | |
|---|---|---|
| BS-055960-1 | When You Awake | Vic 26764 |
| BS-055960-2 | When You Awake | HMV EA-2806 (Australian only) |
| BS-055961-1 | Anything | Vic 27208 |

New York, September 17, 1940.

| BS-056131-1 | Shadows On The Sand | Vic 26761 |
| BS-056133-2 | You're Breaking My Heart All Over Again | - |
| BS-056135-1 | I'd Know You Anywhere | Vic 26770 |

Hollywood, October 16, 1940.

| BS-055110-1 | Do You Know Why ? | Vic 26798 |

Hollywood, October 17, 1940.

| | *Marie (w/chorus) | Vic LPM-6003 |

Hollywood, November 7, 1940.

| | *Yearning (Just For You) | Vic LPM-6003 |

Hollywood, November 11, 1940.

| PBS-055157-1 | Not So Long Ago | Vic 27219 |
| PBS-055158-1 | Star Dust (w/The Pied Pipers) | Vic 27233, 27520, HMV BD-5679 |

Hollywood, November 28, 1940.

| | *How Am I To Know ? (w/The Pied Pipers) | Vic LPM-6003 |

New York, January 6, 1941.

| BS-058760-1 | Oh ! Look At Me Know (w/connie Haines- | Vic 27274, 20-1578 |
| | The Pied Pipers) | |
| BS-058571-1 | You Might Have Belonged To Another (w/ | - |
| | Connie Haines-The Pied Pipers) | |

New York, January 15, 1941.

| BS-058877-1 | You Lucky People | Vic 27350 |
| BS-058879-1 | It's Always You | Vic 27345, 20-1530 |

New York, January 20, 1941.

| BS-060346-1 | I Tried | Vic 27317 |
| BS-060347-1 | Dolores | - HMV BD-5688 |
| CS-060349-2 | Without A Song | Vic 36396, HMV C-3262, |
| | | V-Disc 33, 582 |

New York, February 7, 1941.

| BS-060626-1 | Do I Worry ? (w/The Pied Pipers) | Vic 27338, HMV BD-5719 |
| BS-060628-1 | Everything Happens To Me | Vic 27359, 20-1577 |

New York, February 17, 1941.

| BS-060903-1 | Let's Get Away From It All - Part 2 | Vic 27377 |
| | (w/Connie Haines-The Pied Pipers) | |

New York, May 28, 1941.

| BS-065913-1 | I'll Never Let A Day Pass By | Vic 27461, HMV BD-5712 |
| BS-065915-1 | Love Me As I Am | Vic 27483 |
| BS-065916-1 | Free For All (w/The Pied Pipers) | Rejected |
| BS-065917-1 | This Love Of Mine | Vic 27508, 20-2848 |

New York, June 27, 1941.

| BS-065916-2 | Free For All (w/The Pied Pipers) | Vic 27532 |
| BS-066430-1 | I Guess I'll Have To Dream The Rest | Vic 27526, HMV BD-5719 |
| | (w/The Pied Pipers) | |
| BS-066431-1 | You And I | Vic 27532 |
| BS-066432- | Neiani (w/The Pied Pipers) | Vic 27508 |

New York, July 15, 1941.

BS-066923-1  Blue Skies (w/chorus)                    Vic 27566, HMV BD-564, V-Disc 1

New York, August 19, 1941.

BS-067651-1  Two In Love                              Vic 27611, 20-1597, HMV BD-5739
BS-067652-1-2  Violets For Your Furs                  Rejected
BS-067653-1  The Sunshine Of Your Smile              -
BS-067654-1  Pale Moon                                Vic 27591

New York, September 18, 1941.

BS-067913-1  I Think Of You                           Vic 27701
BS-067914-1  How Do You Do Without Me ?               Vic 27710
BS-067915-1  A Sinner Kissed An Angel                 Vic 27611, HMV BD-5739

New York, September 26, 1941.

BS-067652-3  Violets For Your Furs                    Vic 27690, 20-1597
BS-067653-2  The Sunshine Of Your Smile               Vic 27638, HMV BD-1230

Hollywood, December 22, 1941.

PBS-061991-1  How About You ?                         Vic 27749

Vocal, acc. by O/Axel Stordahl.          Hollywood, January 19, 1942.

PBS-072042-1  The Night We Called It A Day            BB B-11463
PBS-072043-1  The Lamplighter's Serenade              BB B-11515
PBS-072044-1  The Song Is You                         -
PBS-072045-1  Night And Day                           BB B-11463, Vic LOP-1509

Vocalist with Tommy Dorsey and his Orchestra.
                                         Hollywood, February 19, 1942.

PBS-072107-1  Snootie Little Cutie (w/Connie          Vic 27876, 20-2116
                Haines-The Pied Pipers)
PBS-072108-1  Poor You                                Vic 27849
PBS-072109-1  I'll Take Tallulah (w/Tommy Dorsey-     Vic 27869
                The Pied Pipers)
PBS-072111-1  The Last Call For Love                  Vic 27849

Hollywood, March 9, 1942.

PBS-072171-1  Somewhere A Voice Is Calling            Vic  27887, 20-2006

New York, May 3, 1942.

        *My Melancholy Baby                           Vic LPM-6003

New York, May 18, 1942.

BS-075204-1  Just As Though You Were Here (w/The      Vic 27903
                Pied Pipers)
BS-075205-1  Street Of Dreams (w/The Pied Pipers)     -

New York, June 9, 1942.

BS-075264-1  Take Me                                  Vic 27923
BS-075265-1  Be Careful, It's My Heart                -

New York, June 17, 1942.

BS-075282-1  In The Blue Of The Evening               Vic 27947, 20-1530, V-Disc 18
BS-075285-1  Dig Down Deep (w/The Pied Pipers)        Vic 20-1539

New York, July 1, 1942.

BS-075400-1  There Are Such Things (w/The Pied          Vic 27974
                Pipers)
BS-075402-1  Daybreak                                        -
BS-075403-1  It Started All Over Again (w/The Pied   Vic 20-1522
                Pipers)

New York, July 2, 1942.

BS-075407-1  Light A Candle In The Chapel              Vic 27941

New York, July 30, 1942.

        *I'll Take Tallulah (w/Jo Stafford-The   Vic LPM-6003
           Pied Pipers)

New York, September 3, 1942.

        *The Song Is You                          Vic LPM-6003

## THE SINGING SOPHOMORES

The name used by Columbia for the quintet/quartet of male singers known more usually
as The Revelers (q.v.), consisting originally of Lewis James-Franklyn Baur-tenors;
Elliott Shaw-baritone; Ed Smalle-baritone-p-a and Wilfred Glenn-bass. Other alterations in the personnel are noted by the appropriate session.

Vocal quintet, acc. by Ed Smalle-p.      New York, October 13, 1925.

141102-8  Show Me The Way To Go Home              Col 485-D, 3957

New York, October 20, 1925.

141162-    I'd Rather Be Alone In The South        Col 485-D, 3956

New York, December 14, 1925.

141388-    Then I'll Be Happy                      Col 530-D, 3956
141389-3  Collegiate Blues                           -      3957

New York, January 27, 1926.

141567-4  Who ?                                   Col 568-D, 4102

New York, February 1, 1926.

141585-    Sweet And Low-Down                      Col 568-D, 4081

New York, March 18, 1926.

141818-5  Georgianna                              Col 625-D, 4001

Vocalists with the Ipana Troubadours/Sam C. Lanin.
                                         New York, March 22, 1926.

141831-    Goodnight (I'll See You In The Morning)  Col 609-D, 3962

Vocal quintet as before.                 New York, March 29, 1926.

141880-7  Honey Mine                              Col 625-D, 4001

New York, April 29, 1926.

142113-    Hello, Aloha ! How Are You ?            Col 646-D, 4025

New York, May 6, 1926.

142164-    Honey Bunch                             Col 646-D, 4025

New York, June 11, 1926.

142293-4  All I Want To Do Is To Be With You        Col 682-D, 4102

New York, June 15, 1926.

142296-   When The Red, Red Robin Comes Bob, Bob,  Col 682-D, 4081
             Bobbin' Along

New York, August 5, 1926.

142510-   Barcelona                                 Col 732-D
142511-8  I'd Love To Meet That Old Sweetheart Of Mine -      4193

New York, September 13, 1926.

142605-3  Why Do You Roll Those Eyes ?              Col 756-D, 4272

New York, September 16, 1926.

142628-3  Lay Me Down To Sleep In Carolina         Col 756-D, 4272

London, October 27, 1926.

WA-4342-1  Ya Gotta Know How To Love               Col 4168
WA-4343-1  In My Gondola                           Col 4235
WA-4344-1  Breezin' Along With The Breeze            -

London, October 28, 1926.

WA-4347-2  The Girl Friend                         Col 4564
WA-4348-2  Here In My Arms                         Col 4193

   Ed Smalle leaves; Frank Black replaces him as piano accompanist.
                                   New York, November 30, 1926.

143160-5  Clap Yo' Hands                           Col 838-D, 4619
143161-   Take In The Sun, Hang Out The Moon         -      4346

New York, January 19, 1927.

143320-   Sing                                     Col 927-D, 4346

New York, February 2, 1927.

143380-   Somebody Else                            Col 985-D

New York, February 10, 1927.

143457-   Mother                                   Col 897-D

New York, February 23, 1927.

143515-   Where's That Rainbow ?                   Col 927-D, 4620

New York, April 22, 1927.

143999-   Russian Lullaby                          Col 985-D

New York, May 14, 1927.

144148-   Just Like A Butterfly (That's Caught In  Col 1032-D, 4690
             The Rain)

   Charles Harrison-tenor replaces James.  New York, May 26, 1927.

144207-   Sweet Marie                              Col 1057-D, 4690

New York, May 27, 1927.
144237-2  Slow River                               Col 1032-D, 4619

                                        London, June 27, 1927.

WA-5779-1-2-3  Hallelujah !                  Col rejected

                                        London, July 4, 1927.

WA-5816-2  Peggy Ann - Medley                Col 4541

                                        London, July 6, 1927.

WA-5779-6  Hallelujah !                      Col 4620

                                        London, July 7, 1927.

WA-5839-2  One Dam Thing After Another - Medley    Col 4541
           (Intro. The Birth Of The Blues/My Heart Stood Still)

                                        London, July 15, 1927.

WA-5906-2  The Girl Friend - Medley (Intro.       Col 4564
           The Blue Room/Mountain Greenery)

Lewis James-tenor/Ed Smalle-baritone-p-a/Elliott Shaw-baritone/Wilfred Glenn-bass.
                                   New York, October 3, 1927.

144821-    I'm Coming, Virginia                Col 1178-D

                                   New York, October 11, 1927.

144851-    Just A Memory                       Col 1178-D

                                   New York, October 25, 1927.

144908-    My Blue Heaven                      Col 1203-D

                                   New York, November 9, 1927.

144962-    When Honey Sings An Old-Time Song (w/    Col 1203-D
           Vaughn de Leath)

  James Melton-tenor replaces Smalle; Frank Black-p acc.
                                   New York, November 29, 1927.

146256-1  Chloe (Song Of The Swamp) (w/guitar)    Col 1257-D, 4866

                                   New York, December 16, 1927.

145419-    Good News                          Col 1237-D

                                   New York, December 22, 1927.

145387-    Cornfield Medley                    Col rejected

                                   New York, January 9, 1928.

145487-3  My Ohio Home                         Col 1257-D, 4866

## CORNELIA  OTIS  SKINNER

B. Chicago, May 30, 1902; studied for the stage in Paris; debut in Buffalo, N.Y., in
   BLOOD AND SAND (August, 1921),  as member of her father's company; New York  debut
   in the same play (Empire, September 20, 1921); several other New York appearances,
   ending with WHITE COLLARS (Cort, February 23, 1925); then devoted herself to performances of character sketches, touring the U.S.A.; London debut at St.  James's,
   June, 1929 in these; on returning to New York, continued with this form of  entertainment, touring also with various plays; wrote the play CAPTAIN FURY, and  books
   (TINY GARMENTS, EXCUSE IT PLEASE, DITHERS AND JITTERS, SOAP BEHIND THE EARS;   co-
   authoress of OUR HEARTS WERE YOUNG AND GAY (with Emily Kimbrough); awarded degrees
   of D.Litt. (U. of Pennsylvania); L.H.D. (St. Laurence, New York, Rochester, Temple
   Universities; also Doctor of Fine Arts at Clark University. Films : KISMET and THE
   UNINVITED (1944).

Dramatic speech, with Otis Skinner (father).
                                 New York, January 13, 1941.

CS-060320-1  The Wooing Scene ("The Taming Of The  Vic 17763
                Shrew", Act 2, Scene 2) (Shakespeare)
CS-060321-1  The Wooing Scene (concluded) and         -
                Katherine's Advice ("The Taming Of The Shrew," Act 2, Scene 2)(Shake-
                speare)
CS-060322-1  The Murder Scene ("Macbeth," Act 1,  Vic 17762
                Scene 7, and Act 2, Scene 1) (Shakespeare)
CS-060323-1  The Murder Scene ("Macbeth," Act 2,       -
                Scenes 1 and 2) (Shakespeare)


                                 New York, January 17, 1941.

CS-060341-1  Marc Antony's Oration ("Julius         Vic 17764
                Caesar," Act 3, Scene 2) (Shakespeare) (Otis Skinner only)
CS-060342-1  Potion Speech ("Romeo And Juliet")/     -
                Portia's Mercy Speech ("The Merchant Of Venice")/The Seven Ages Of Man
                ("As You Like It") (Shakespeare)

Poetry reading, acc. by Frederick Fradkin-vn/Emil Stark-vc/Ted Dale-p.
                                 New York, January 22, 1941.

CS-060355-1  Elizabethan Period : The Parting      Vic 18111
                (Michael Drayton)/Cards And Kisses (John Lyly)/Two Sonnets and   Full
                Fathom Five (William Shakespeare)
CS-060356-1  Romantic Poets of the 17th and 18th      -
                Centuries : On His Blindness (John Milton)/Why So Pale And Wan ? (Sir
                John Suckling)/The Spacious Firmament On High (Joseph Addison)/  The
                Piper; The Tiger (William Blake)
CS-060357-1  Romantic Poets of the 17th and 18th  Vic 18112
                Centuries : The Solitary Reaper; The World - Sonnet (William   Words-
                worth)/Night (Percy Bysshe Shelley)/We'll Go No More A-Roving   (Lord
                Byron)
CS-060358-1  Romantic and Victorian Poets : Ode       -
                On A Grecian Urn (William Keats)/Meeting At Night (Robert  Browning)/
                Crossing The Bar (Alfred Lord Tennyson)
CS-060359-1  Victorian Poets : A Musical Instru-   Vic 18113
                ment (Elizabeth Barrett Browning)/The Tugs (Coventry Patmore)/ Uphill
                (Christina G. Rosetti)
CS-060360-1  Modern Poets : Sea Fever (John Masefield)/-
                The Soldier (Rupert Brooke)/The Runaway(Robert Frost)/Recuerdo  (Edna
                St. Vincent Millay)/Grass (Carl Sandburg)

## JACK SMITH

B. New York, 1899; served in World War I in France, where a gas-shell reduced   his
   singing ability to a "confidential" murmur, earning him the sobriquet "The   Whispering Baritone," with which he introduced the style in 1925; much in demand  as a
   night-club entertainer and on stage both in U.S.A. amd England (debut in London at
   the Hotel Metropole "Midnight Follies," 1926; returned there, 1927; starred in the
   revue BLUE SKIES (Vaudeville, June 27, 1927); short time in New York, then back to
   London to star in WILL-O'-THE-WHISPERS (Shaftesbury, April 4, 1928); appeared very
   successfully in Berlin, August, 1928; returned to New York briefly; one more  season in London, then to Hollywood to take part in the Fox musical CHEER UP AND SMILE
   (1930); the coming of "crooning" supplanted his unique style in the 1930s, but  he
   made a short-lived come-back in 1940; d. May, 1951.

Vocal, acc. by own piano.                 New York, August 28, 1925.

            Alone At Last                     Vic test (un-numbered)
            My Sweetie Turned Me Down           -

                                 New York, September 15, 1925.

BVE-33383-1-2-3  Cecilia                      Vic rejected
BVE-33384-1-2-3  I Care For Her, She Cares For Me    -

Acc. by Lew Pollack or Leroy Shield-p as shown, or own piano.
New York, September 21, 1925.

BVE-33383-4  Cecilia - pJS                              Vic 19787, HMV B-2226
BVE-33384-6  I Care For Her, She Cares For Me-pJS       Vic 19800      -
BVE-33397-3  I'm Knee Deep In Daisies (And Head         Vic 19787, HMV B-2192
               Over Heels In Love) - pLS
BVE-33398-3  Feelin' Kind 0' Blue - pLS                 Vic 19800      -
BVE-33399-3  Loud Speakin' Papa (You'd Better           HMV B-2333
               Speak Easy To Me) - pLP

New York, November 4, 1925.

BVE-33848-1-2-3  Some Other Bird Whistled A Tune        Rejected
               - pJS (w/Carson Robison-w)
BVE-33849-2  What Did I Tell Ya ? - pLS                 Vic 19914, HMV B-2260

New York, November 24, 1925.

BVE-33848-4  Some Other Bird Whistled A Tune -          Vic 19914, HMV B-2270
               pJS/with Carson Robison-w)
BVE-33895-2  Are You Sorry ? - pLP                      Vic 19856      -
BVE-33896-1  I Wanna Go Where You Go - Do What You         -       HMV B-2260
               Do - Then I'll Be Happy

Acc. by Abner Silver or self-p.        New York, February 5, 1926.

BVE-34398-2  When Autumn Leaves Are Falling - pAS  Vic 19959, HMV B-2333
BVE-34399-4  I Don't Believe It, But Say It Again  Vic 20038, HMV B-2319
               - pAS
BVE-34600-1  Don't Be A Fool, You Fool - pJS            Vic 19998, HMV B-2310
  NOTE:- Abner Silver is the composer of both the numbers he accompanies above.

Acc. by own piano.                    New York, February 19, 1926.

BVE-34638-4  Pretty Little Baby                         Vic 19978, HMV B-2312
BVE-34639-1  Poor Papa (He's Got Nothin' At All)        Vic 19998, HMV B-2310

New York, March 5, 1926.

BVE-34683-3  Gimme A Li'l Kiss, Will Ya, Huh ?          Vic 19978, HMV B-2312
BVE-34683-4  Gimme A Li'l Kiss, Will Ya, Huh ?          Vic LPV-557, LSA-3075
BVE-34684-1  I'd Climb The Highest Mountain If I        Vic 20038, HMV B-2319
               Knew I'd Find You

New York, April 28, 1926.

BVE-35350-3  When The Red, Red Robin Comes Bob,         Vic 20069, HMV B-2337
               Bob, Bobbin' Along
BVE-35351-3  Tonight's My Night With Baby                  -          -
BVE-35352-1-2-3-4  Talking To The Moon                  Rejected

Acc. by Arthur Johnston-p.             New York, September 22, 1926.

BVE-36342-2  I'm On My Way Home                         Vic 20229, HMV B-2383
BVE-36343-3  Baby Face                                     -          -

New York, October 1, 1926.

BVE-36377-3  That's A Good Girl                         Vic 20254, HMV B-2659
BVE-36378-1  Precious                                      -

New York, October 30, 1926.

BVE-36886-3  No-One But You Knows How To Love           Vic 20312
               (plus own piano)
BVE-3688701-2  I'm Tellin' The Birds - Tellin'          Rejected
               The Bees (How I Love You)
BVE-36888-1  There Ain't No Maybe In My Baby's          Vic 20312, HMV B-2414
               Eyes

New York, December 1, 1926.

BVE-36887-5  I'm Tellin' The Birds, Tellin' The     Vic 20372, HMV B-2414
             Bees (How I Love You)
BVE-36992-1  Clap Yo' Hands                             -        HMV B-2564
BVE-36992-3  Clap Yo' Hands                             -

  Acc. by own piano.                         New York, December 23, 1926.

BVE-37177-1  So Will I                             Vic 20413, HMV B-2435
BVE-37178-3  If I Didn't Know Your Husband And You    -            -
             Didn't Know My Wife

                                        Camden, N. J., March 18, 1927.

BVE-38222-1-2-3  It's Just Because I'm Falling In  Rejected
                 Love With You
BVE-38223-3  My Sunday Girl                         Vic 20572
BVE-38224-2  I've Never Seen A Straight Banana         -
BVE-38225-1-2-3  My Idea Of Heaven                  Rejected

  Acc. by Dave Dreyer-p where shown.      New York, April 28, 1927.

BVE-38702-1-2-3  Where The Wild, Wild Flowers Grow Rejected
                 - pDD
BVE-38703-2  Rosy Cheeks - pDD                      Vic 20845, HMV B-2555
BVE-38704-3  Me And My Shadow - pDD (composer)      Vic 20626, LPV-523, LSA-3076,
                                                    HMV B-2496
BVE-38705-3  Oo ! Golly Ain't She Cute ? - pJS      Vic 20845, HMV B-2496
BVE-38706-2  You Won't See Me If I See You (With    Vic 20626, HMV B-2555
             Anyone Else At All) - pJS

  Acc. by the Metropole Hotel Orchestra/Jay Whidden.
                                        Metropole Hotel, London, May 17, 1927.

BR-1052-1-2-3  Blue Skies                           HMV rejected
BR-1053-1  Some Other Bird Whistled A Tune            -

  Acc. by own piano.                 Small Queen's Hall, London, May 23, 1927.

Bb-10899-1-2-3  It All Depends On You               HMV rejected

                                        Hayes, Middlesex, June 17, 1927.

Bb-10899-   It All Depends On You                   HMV B-2494
Bb-11038-   Blue Skies ("Blue Skies")                 -

                                        Hayes, Middlesex, July 7, 1927.

Bb-11099-4  Possibly                                HMV B-2516
Bb-11100-2  The Birth Of The Blues                    -

                                        Hayes, Middlesex, October 3, 1927.

Bb-11563-2  There's Always A Way Into Trouble       HMV B-2607
Bb-11564-2  Half A Moon                               -

                                        New York, October 25, 1927.

BVE-40509-   The Song Is Ended                      Vic 21028
BVE-40510-3  There Must Be Somebody Else            Vic 21041, HMV B-2659
BVE-40511-2  I'll Be Lonely                         Vic 21028, HMV B-2676

                                        Camden, N. J., October 28, 1927.

BVE-39378-1-2  Where Have You Been All My Life ?    Rejected
BVE-39379-2  The Best Things In Life Are Free       Vic 21039, HMV B-2766
BVE-39380-1-2-3  Playground In The Sky              Rejected
BVE-39381-3  For My Baby                            Vic 21210, HMV B-2715

Camden, N. J., November 1, 1927.

BVE-39380-6  Playground In The Sky                Vic 21041, HMV B-2676

  Acc. by the Whispering Orchestra/Bert Ambrose.

Hayes, Middlesex, January 10, 1928.

Bb-12338-3  My Blue Heaven ("Will-O'-The-Whispers")HMV B-2665
Bb-12339-3  The Song Is Ended ("Will-O'-The-Whispers")  -

Hayes, Middlesex, January 12, 1928.

Bb-12352-3  Miss Annabelle Lee("Will-O'-The-      HMV B-2666, Par PMC-7150
        Whispers")
Bb-12353-3  When Day Is Done ("Will-O'-The-Whispers")  -

Hayes, Middlesex, March 2, 1928.

Bb-13007-3  Sunshine ("Will-O'-The-Whispers")     HMV B-2706
Bb-13008-3  Whispering ("Will-O'-The-Whispers")      -

Hayes, Middlesex, April 2, 1928.

Bb-13145-3  I Never Dreamt (You'd Fall In Love    HMV B-2718
        With Me) ("Will-O'-The-Whispers")
Bb-13146-2  Afraid Of You                            -

  Acc. by two unknown pianists.           Berlin, August 27, 1928.

BL-4446-2  Ich küsse ihre Hand, Madame (in        El EG-962
       English and German)
BL-4447-2  Ramona                                    -

  Acc. by O/Carroll Gibbons.              Hayes, Middlesex, September 18, 1928.

Bb-14509-3  'S Wonderful                          HMV B-2863
Bb-14510-3  My One And Only                          -

Hayes, Middlesex, September 19, 1928.

Bb-14514-3  Crazy Rhythm                          HMV B-2864       ＊
Bb-14515-3  Funny Face                               -

Hayes, Middlesex, October 11, 1928.

Bb-14587-1-2-3-4  I Can't Give You Anything But   Rejected
        Love
Bb-14588-3  If I Had You                          HMV B-2925
Bb-14589-2  That's My Weakness Now                HMV B-2871
Bb-14590-3  The Song I Love                          -

Hayes, Middlesex, December 28, 1928.

Bb-15296-2  All By Yourself In The Moonlight      HMV B-2925
Bb-15297-2  I'm Crazy Over You                    HMV B-2962
Bb-15298-1-2-3  Peace Of Mind                     Rejected

Hayes, Middlesex, January 29, 1929.

Bb-15298-6  Peace Of Mind                         HMV B-2968
Bb-15684-3  I Faw Down And Go 'Boom !'               -
Bb-15685-3  Sally Of My Dreams                    HMV B-2962

  Acc. by O/Leonard Joy.                  New York, February 13, 1929.

BVE-49946-1  Glad Rag Doll                        Vic 21882
BVE-49947-1  Sweet Forget-Me-Not                     -        HMV B-3022

New York, April 24, 1929.

BVE-51658-2  I Kiss Your Hand, Madame              Vic 21973
BVE-51659-1  She's A New Kind Of Old-Fashioned Girl    -       HMV B-3191

New York, April 30, 1929.

BVE-51667-2  From Sunrise To Sunset (From Sunset   Vic 21987, HMV B-3090
                'Til Dawn)

New York, May 8, 1929.

BVE-51690-2  To Be In Love (Espesh'lly With You)   Vic 21987, HMV B-3090

  Acc. by Clarence Gaskill-p.        New York, July 30, 1929.

BVE-187   Who Conquers The Mighty Benkei ?/All    Vic test
             Hail To The Bantam Prince

  Acc. by O/Leonard Joy.           New York, August 20, 1929.

BVE-53999-1-2-3-4  I'm Just A Vagabond Lover      Vic rejected
BVE-56100-1-2-3-4  Mistakes                         -

New York, August 26, 1929.

BVE-53999-5-6-7  I'm Just A Vagabond Lover      Vic rejected
BVE-56100-5-6-7  Mistakes                         -

New York, August 28, 1929.

BVE-55812-1-2-3  Then You've Never Been Blue    Vic rejected
BVE-55813-1-2-3  You Wanted Me, I Wanted You      -

  Acc. by O/Carroll Gibbons.       Hayes, Middlesex, October 10, 1929.

Bb-17708-2  Encore                             HMV B-3193
Bb-17709-3  I'll Be Getting Along               -
Bb-17710-3  Lily Of Laguna                     HMV B-3191

  Acc. by Ruby Ward-Henry Santley-p.    New York, October 25, 1929.

BVE-57122-1-2-3  On The Road To Rainbow Bay     Vic rejected
BVE-57123-1-2-3  Congratulations                  -

  Acc. by O/? Leroy Shield.        Culver City, Calif., April 24, 1930.

▸PBVE-54769-1-2-3  When You Look In My Eyes      Vic rejected
PBVE-54770-1-2-3  You May Not Like It (But It's A    -
                Great Idea) (Film "Cheer Up And Smile")

Hollywood, May 20, 1930.

PBVE-54770-6  You May Not Like It (But It's A    Vic 22443, HMV B-3540
                Great Idea) (Film "Cheer Up And Smile")
PBVE-54820-2  'Leven-Thirty Saturday Night       Vic 22452
PBVE-54821-3  Where Can You Be ? (Film "Cheer Up  Vic 22443, HMV B-3540
                And Smile")

Hollywood, May 23, 1930.

PBVE-54831-2  A Slave To Love                    Vic 22452

  Acc. by own piano.             New York, July 29, 1931.

10754-1-2-3-4  Pardon Me, Pretty Baby          Rejected
10755-2  Little Girl                           Imp 2600, Pic 847

New York, August 7, 1931.

10754-8   Pardon Me, Pretty Baby                 Imp 2600, Pic 847

Acc. by p/g/sb.                          New York, April 16, 1940.

67557-B   Cecilia                                Dec 3156, 25077, F-7647
67558-A   I'm Knee Deep In Daisies (And Head Over      -        -        -
          Heels In Love)

New York, September 13, 1940.

68095-A   I Wish You Were Jealous Of Me          Dec 3437, F-7783
68096-A   A Faded Photograph                           -        -

## KATE SMITH

B. Greenville, Va., May 1, 1909; sang in church chour at four; stage debut in HONEY-
MOON LANE (Knickerbocker, New York, September 20, 1926); by 1931 she was   popular
enough to appear for ten consecutive weeks at the Palace, and she made her   first
film (HELLO, EVERYBODY) in 1932. She was one of the first radio personalities   to
use a signature tune (WHEN THE MOON COMES OVER THE MOUNTAIN), and her singing of a
patriotic song by Irving Berlin, GOD BLESS AMERICA, almost brought about its being
installed as the official national anthem.

Vocal, acc. by own piano.                Camden, N. J., September 16, 1926.

          Mary Dear ("Honeymoon Lane")         Vic test (un-numbered)
          The Little White House ("Honeymoon Lane")    -
          Jersey Walk ("Honeymoon Lane")             -

Acc. by James F. Hanley (composer)-p.   New York, October 7, 1926.

BVE-36396-1-2-3  The Little White House ("Honey-   Vic rejected
          moon Lane")
BVE-36397-1-2  Mary Dear ("Honeymoon Lane")           -
BVE-36398-1-2-3  Jersey Walk ("Honeymoon Lane")       -

New York, October 28, 1926.

142884-   The Little White House ("Honeymoon Lane")Col 810-D
142885-   Mary Dear ("Honeymoon Lane")                 -
142886-   Jersey Walk ("Honeymoon Lane")        Rejected

Acc. by the Charleston Chasers/Red Nichols.
                                         New York, February 14, 1927.

143476-3  One Sweet Letter From You              Col 911-D
143477-3  I'm Gonna Meet My Sweetie Now                -

Acc. by studio orchestra.                New York, May 26, 1927.

144233-   In The Evening                         Col 1348-D
144234-   Just Another Day Wasted Away           Col 1132-D

New York, July 28, 1927.

144522-   Worryin'                               Rejected
144523-   A Little Smile, A Little Kiss          Col 1348-D
144524-   Clementine (From New Orleans)          Col 1132-D

Acc. by the Harmonians/Ben Selvin.      New York, July 12, 1929.

148806-   He's A Good Man To Have Around         Har 970-H
148807-   Maybe - Who Knows ?                          -        SR 1043-P

New York, August 27, 1929.

148937-   Moanin' Low                            Har 999-H, SR 1050-P, 1073-P
148938-   Waiting At The End Of The Road           - SR-1052-P - 1087-P - 1093-P

New York, November 1, 1929.

149457-   I May Be Wrong, But I Think You're      Har 1050-H, SR 1087-P
          Wonderful
149458-   Love (Your Spell Is Everywhere)          -

New York, November 29, 1929.

149651-   Chant Of The Jungle                      Har 1069-H, SR 2014-P
149652-   That Wonderful Something (Is Love)       -        SR 2011-P

Acc. unknown.                      New York, December 13, 1929.

149722-   St. Louis Blues                          Col rejected
149723-   Frankie And Johnny                       -

Acc. by O/Ben Selvin.              New York, May 20, 1930.

150447-   Sharing                                  Har 1170-H
150448-   Dancing With Tears In My Eyes            -        Cl 5015-C

New York, July 8, 1930.

150631-   Don't Let Me Hold You, Baby Mine         Cl 5015-C
150632-   I Don't Mind Walkin' In The Rain (When   Har 1191-H, Cl 5074-C
          I'm Walkin' In The Rain With You)
150633-   Swingin' In A Hammock                    -        Cl 5038-C
150634-   You'll Be Coming Back To Me              -

New York, September 23, 1930.

150835-   Maybe It's Love                          Har 1216-H
150836-   You'll Never Know, Sweetheart            -        Cl 5074-C

New York, November 6, 1930.

150937-   Here Comes The Sun                       Har 1235-H, Cl 5124-C
150938-   I Got Rhythm                             -        Cl 5123-C

New York, November 17, 1930.

150958-   Morning, Noon And Night                  Cl 5124-C
150959-   Held By The Spell Of The Moon            Cl 5123-C

New York, January 29, 1931.

151247-   Overnight                                Har 1280-H, Cl 5228-C, VT 2293-V
151248-   Reaching For The Moon                    -        Cl 5227-C, VT 2292-V
151251-   Grievin'                                 Cl 5228-C, VT 2293-V
151252-   You Don't Want Me Any More               Cl 5227-C, VT 2292-V
     NOTE:- Matrices 151249/50 are not by Kate Smith.

New York, March 13, 1931.

151419-   You Didn't Have To Tell Me (I Knew It    Rejected
          All The Time)
151420-   Wabash Moon                              Har 1303-H, Cl 5278-C, VT 2334-V
151421-   Now's The Time                           Cl 5279-C, VT 2345-V
151422-   At Dusk                                  Rejected

New York, March 20, 1931.

151449-   Dinah Lee From Tennessee                 Cl 5278-C, VT 2344-V
151450-   You Didn't Have To Tell Me (I Knew It    Har 1303-H, Cl 5279-C, VT 2345-V
          All The Time)

Acc. by her Swanee Music.          New York, July 7, 1931.

365025-   Makin' Faces At The Man In The Moon      Har 1347-H, VT 2423-V
365026-3  When The Moon Comes Over The Mountain    - HS-11353  -        Col DB-683

Acc. by O/Ben Selvin.                    New York, August 17, 1931.

151735-3  If I Have To Go On Without You          Col 2516-D, DB-683
151736-   When The Moon Comes Over The Mountain   -

                                         New York, September 15, 1931.

151786-   You Call It Madness, But I Call It Love  Col 2539-D, DB-709
151787-   I Don't Know Why (I Just Do)            -              -
365031-   Shine On, Harvest Moon                  Har 1371-H, VT 2448-V
365032-   I Apologize                             -              -        Col DB-734
   NOTE:- The accompaniment on the last two sides is described as "Her Swanee Music."

                                         New York, October 28, 1931.

151866-   That's Why Darkies Were Born            Col 2563-D
151867-   Tell Me With A Love Song                -
365038-   You Try Somebody Else (We'll Be Back    VT 2465-V, Col DB-734
             Together Again)
365039-   Goodnight, Sweetheart                   -

Vocalist with Guy Lombardo and his Royal Canadians.
                                         New York, December 8, 1931.

152031-   Too Late                                Col 2579-D
152032-   River, Stay 'Way From My Door           -

Vocal, acc. by her Swanee Music.         New York, December 10, 1931.

365048-   River, Stay 'Way From My Door           VT 2483-V
365049-   All Of Me                               -

Acc. by O/Ben Selvin.                    New York, January 28, 1932.

152096-   In The Baggage Coach Ahead              Col 2605-D
365059-   Just Friends                            VT 2512-V
365060-   Between The Devil And The Deep Blue Sea  -

                                         New York, January 29, 1932.

152099-   Twenty-One Years                        Col 2605-D

                                         New York, March 1, 1932.

152111; 365069-   My Mom                          Rejected
152121-2  Snuggled On Your Shoulder (Cuddled In   Col 2624-D, DB-871, Epic L2N-6072
             Your Arms)
152122-2  Love, You Funny Thing !                 -              -
   NOTE:- Matrices 152112/152120 inclusive are not by Kate Smith.

                                         New York, March 4, 1932.

365073-   By The Fireside                         Col rejected

Acc. by O/? Victor Young.                New York, February 9, 1933.

B-13045-A  Pickaninnies' Heaven (Film "Hello      Br 6497, 01479
             Everybody")
B-13046-A  Twenty Million People (Film "Hello     Br 6496, 01481
             Everybody")
B-13047-A  My Queen Of Lullaby Land (Film "Hello  -              -
             Everybody")
B-13048-A  Moon Song (That Wasn't Meant For Me)   Br 6497, 01479, Epic SN-6059
             (Film "Hello Everybody")

Acc. by her Swanee Music.                New York, ? October 31, 1934.

38928-A  The Continental (w/The Ambassadors Trio)  Dec 288, Br 01937

New York, November 1, 1934.

| | | |
|---|---|---|
| 38937-A | College Rhythm (w/Ambassadors Trio) | Dec 277, Br 01937 |
| 38938-A | Let's Give Three Cheers To Love (w/ | - - |
| | Ambassadors Trio) | |
| 38939-A | When My Ship Comes In | Dec 288, Br 01970 |
| 38940-A | I'm Growing Fonder Of You | Dec 276, Br 01991 |
| 38941-A | Stay As Sweet As You Are | - 7-3, Br 01970 |

Acc. by O/Jack Miller.                New York, December 28, 1937.

| | | |
|---|---|---|
| BS-017776-1 | When The Moon Comes Over The | Vic 25760, HMV BD-522 |
| | Mountain (w/The Ambassadors) | |
| BS-017777-1 | There's A Gold Mine In The Sky (w/ | Vic 25752 - |
| | The Girls) | |
| BS-017778-1 | You're A Sweetheart | Vic 25760. HMV BD-507 |
| BS-017779-1 | Bei mir bist du schoen (Means That | Vic 25752 - |
| | You're Grand) | |

New York, March 21, 1939.

| | | |
|---|---|---|
| BS-035319-1 | God Bless America (w/mixed chorus) | Vic 26198 |
| BS-035320-2 | The Star-Spangled Banner (w/mixed chorus) | - |
| BS-035321-1 | It's Never Too Late | Vic 26214, HMV BD-715 |
| BS-035322-1 | I Cried For You | - - |

New York, April 17, 1939.

| | | |
|---|---|---|
| BS-035753-1 | Don't Worry 'Bout Me | Vic 26235, HMV BD-718 |
| BS-035754-1 | If I Had My Way | Vic 26245 |
| BS-035755-1 | And The Angels Sing | Vic 26235, HMV BD-718 |
| BS-035756-1 | If I Didn't Care | Vic 26245 |

New York, February, 1940.

| | |
|---|---|
| The Woodpecker Song | Col 35398 |
| I'm Stepping Out With A Memory Tonight | - |
| So Long | Col 35413 |
| When You Wish Upon A Star | - |

New York, March, 1940.

| | |
|---|---|
| Imagination | Col 35486 |
| Make-Believe Island | - |

New York, April, 1940.

| | |
|---|---|
| You're Lonely And I'm Lonely | Col 35501 |
| The Lord Done Fixed Up My Soul | - |
| It's A Lovely Day Tomorrow | Col 35502 |
| You Can't Brush Me Off | - |

New York, June 27, 1940.

| | | |
|---|---|---|
| WCO-26960-2 | Trade Winds | Col 35638, FB-2536 |
| WCO-26961-2 | Goodnight Again | - - |
| | Maybe | Col 35564 |
| | Can't Get Indiana Off My Mind | - |

New York, September, 1940.

| | |
|---|---|
| Two Dreams Met | Col 35778 |
| A Nightingale Sang In Berkeley Square | - |
| Adeste Fideles (O Come, All Ye | Col 35791 |
| Faithful) | |
| Silent Night, Holy Night | - |

New York, c. November, 1940.

| Along The Santa Fe Trail | Col 35802 |
| The Last Time I Saw Paris | - |
| My Buddy | Col 35822 |
| Sometime | - |

New York, c. January, 1941.

| It's Sad But True | Col 35965 |
| Love Is | - |

New York, February, 1941.

| Lamplight | Col 35996 |
| We're All Americans (All True Blue) | - |
| It All Comes Back To Me Now | Col 36015 |
| A Little Old Church In England | - |

New York, March, 1941.

| I Do, Do You ? (Do You Believe In Love ?) | Col 36043 |
| Two Hearts That Pass In The Night | - |
| When Day Is Done | Col 36045 |
| When The Moon Comes Over The Mountain | - |
| Macushla | Col 36046 |
| Your Eyes Have Told Me So | - |
| The Sunshine Of Your Smile | Col 36047 |
| Thine Alone | - |
| Kiss Me Again | Col 36048 |
| The Rosary | - |

New York, May, 1941.

| Until Tomorrow | Col 36210 |
| You And I | - |
| Don't Cry, Cherie | Col 36220 |
| Will You Still Be Mine ? | - |

New York, June, 1941.

| Dancing In A Dream With You | Col 36247 |
| Wasn't It You ? | - |
| Along 'Bout Sundown | Col 36272 |
| Time Was | - |

## E. H. SOTHERN-JULIA MARLOWE

B. 1859; educated in England, intended to be an artist, but decided on stage career; (toured in U.S.A.); became leading man in Daniel Frohman's Lyceum Company, 1884-1898; his performance in THE PRISONER OF ZENDA was very popular; opened New Lyceum (New York), November 2, 1903 in THE PROUD PRINCE; m. Julia Marlowe(second wife) in 1911; together they headed a Shakespeare repertory company until she retired,1924, he continued acting until 1927; d. October 28, 1933. Julia Marlowe b. Caldbeck, 8 miles from Keswick, Cumberland, England, August 17, 1866; taken to U.S.A. at four; educated in Cincinnati and Kansas City; debut in Vincennes, Ind., 1878 in juvenile production of H.M.S. PINAFORE; studied for the stage for ten years, appearing as a star for the first time in in INGOMAR in New London, Conn., April 25, 1887; debut in New York in the same play (Bijou, October 20, 1887); she had a long and distinguished career principally in Shakespearean productions in New York and on tour;d. 1950. Their records are all of Shakespearean scenes unless otherwise noted.

Dramatic speech, unacc.                     Camden, N. J., April 14, 1920.

| C-23936-1 | Balcony Scene ("Romeo And Juliet") | Vic rejected |
| C-23937-1 | To Be Or Not To Be ("Hamlet") (EHS only) | - |
| C-23938-1 | The Speech To The Players ("Hamlet") (EHS) | - |
| C-23939-1 | The Seven Ages Of Man ("As You Like It") | - |

Camden, N. J., April 15, 1920.

C-23937-2  To Be Or Not To Be ("Hamlet") (EHS only)Vic rejected
C-23938-2  The Speech To The Players ("Hamlet") (EHS)  -
C-23940-1-2-3  The Fool's Speech ("As You Like It")    -
           (EHS only)

Camden, N. J., May 24, 1920.

B-23937-1-2  To Be Or Not To Be ("Hamlet") (EHS)   Vic rejected
C-23938-3-4  The Speech To The Players ("Hamlet")(EHS) -

Camden, N. J., October 25, 1920.

C-24661-1-2  Good Morrow, Kate ("The Taming Of The Vic rejected
             Shrew")
C-24662-1-2  What Is Your Will ? ("The Taming Of      -
             The Shrew")

Camden, N. J., October 26, 1920.

C-24663-1-2  Balcony Scene, Part 1 ("Romeo And      Vic rejected
             Juliet")
C-24664-1-2  Balcony Scene, Part 2 ("Romeo And        -
             Juliet")

Camden, N. J., October 27, 1920.

B-23937-3-4  To Be Or Not To Be ("Hamlet") (EHS)   Vic rejected
C-23938-5-6  The Speech To The Players ("Hamlet")(EHS) -
C-23939-2-3  The Seven Ages Of Man ("As You Like It")  -

Camden, N. J., October 28, 1920.

C-23939-4  The Seven Ages Of Man ("As You Like It")Vic 74701
C-24666-1  Antony's Oration, Part 1 ("Julius      Vic 74699, 6295
           Caesar") (EHS only)
C-24667-1  Antony's Oration, Part 2 ("Julius      Vic 74700    -
           Caesar") (EHS only)

Camden, N. J., October 29, 1920.

C-24671-1-2  Shylock's Speech (EHS)/Portia's      Vic rejected
             Mercy Speech ("The Merchant Of Venice") (JM)

Camden, N. J., November 1, 1920.

C-23937-4  To Be Or Not To Be ("Hamlet") (EHS)    Vic 74702, 6294
C-24663-4  Balcony Scene, Part 1 ("Romeo and      Vic 74662, 6298
           Juliet")
C-24664-4  Balcony Scene, Part 2 ("Romeo and      Vic 74663    -
           Juliet")
C-24674-1  The Casket Scene ("The Merchant Of     Vic 74708, 6297
           Venice")

Camden, N. J., November 3, 1920.

B-24678-1-2-3  Love Scene In The Forest Of Arden   Vic rejected
               - Part 2 ("As You Like It")
B-24679-1  Love Scene In The Forest Of Arden -        -
           Part 3 ("As You Like It")
B-24680-1  Love Scene In The Forest Of Arden -        -
           Part 4 ("As You Like It")
B-24681-1-2  Love Scene In The Forest Of Arden -      -
             Part 1 ("As You Like It")

Camden, N. J., January 13, 1921.

| | | |
|---|---|---|
| C-24661-3 | Good Morrow, Kate ("The Taming Of The Shrew") | Vic 74704, 6299 |
| C-24662-3 | What Is Your Will ? ("The Taming Of The Shrew") | Rejected |
| C-24671-3 | Shylock's Speech (EHS)/Portia's Mercy Speech (JM) ("The Merchant Of Venice") | Vic 74673, 6297 |
| C-24789-1 | Brutus and Portia Scene ("Julius Caesar") | Vic 74706, 6296 |

Camden, N. J., January 14, 1921.

| | | |
|---|---|---|
| C-23938-8 | The Speech To The Players ("Hamlet") (EHS) | Vic 74703, 6294 |
| C-24662-4 | What Is Your Will ? ("The Taming Of The Shrew") | Vic 74705, 6299 |
| C-24793-1 | Crossing The Bar (Tennyson)/The Sleep (Browning) (JM) | Rejected |
| C-24794-1 | If Villon Were King Of France (Villon)/ The Sorrows Of Yesterday (McCarthy) (EHS) | - |
| C-24795-1 | Battle Hymn Of The Republic (Ward Howe)(JM) | - |

Camden, N. J., February 15, 1921.

| | | |
|---|---|---|
| C-24940-1-2 | Love Scene In The Forest Of Arden - Part 1 ("As You Like It") | Rejected |
| C-24941-1 | Love Scene In The Forest Of Arden - Part 2 ("As You Like It") | - |
| C-24942-2 | Duke and Viola Scene ("Twelfth Night") | Vic 74707 |
| C-24943-1 | Murder Scene ("Macbeth") | Rejected |

## PAUL SOUTHE

B. 1888; prominent vaudevillian in the years preceding World War I; d. New York,August 25, 1946.

Vocal, acc. by O/? Charles A. Prince.    New York, early January, 1910.

| | | |
|---|---|---|
| 4276-5 | He's A College Boy | Col A-790 |
| 4277-1 | Take Me Out For A Joy Ride | Col A-791 |

New York, late January, 1910.

| | | |
|---|---|---|
| 4324-1 | Cubanola Glide | Col A-800 |

NOTE:- This record was issued in April, 1910, and withdrawn a month later, to be replaced by Arthur Collins and Byron G. Harlan singing the same number, also Columbia A-800.

New York, late February, 1910.

| | | |
|---|---|---|
| 4352-2 | Whoop-la, Willie, Don't Let Me Go | Col A-810 |

## AILEEN STANLEY

B. 1897; stage debut at six, followed by many years as an increasingly    successful vaudeville and cabaret artist, very popular on both sides of the Atlantic (she appeared in London in 1925, 1927, 1934 and 1937); at this writing she lives in California.

Vocal, acc. by O/Rosario Bourdon.        Camden, N. J., August 10, 1920.

| | | |
|---|---|---|
| B-24371-2 | Broadway Blues | Vic 18691 |
| B-24372-3 | My Little Bimbo Down On The Bamboo Isle | - |
| B-24373-1-2-3-4 | Early To Bed And Early To Rise (Never Made Anyone Wise) | Rejected |

Acc. by studio orchestra.                New York, c. August, 1920.

My Little Bimbo Down On The Bamboo Isle Amb 4147

Acc. by O/Rosario Bourdon.              Camden, N. J., October 22, 1920.

B-24655-3  I've Got The Blues For My Old Kentucky  Vic 18703
            Home
B-24656-1-2-3  I'm A Little Nobody           Rejected
B-24657-1-2-3  Singin' The Blues                -

                                        Camden, N. J., October 27, 1920.

B-24656-4-5-6  I'm A Little Nobody           Rejected
B-24657-6  Singin' The Blues                 Vic 18703
B-24665-1-2-3  I Told You So                 Rejected

  Acc. by studio orchestra.             New York, c. October, 1920.

        Look What You've Done With Your     Voc 14124
          Doggone Dangerous Eyes
        Whatcha Gonna Do When There Ain't No Jazz ? -

                                        New York, c. November, 1920.

  6484    Sweet Mama, Your Papa's Getting Mad  Voc 14134
  6485    It's All Over Now                    -

        Where Is My Daddy Now Blues          Amb 4204
        She Walks In Her Husband's Sleep     Ed 50729, Amb 4233

                                        New York, c. January, 1921.

        O-HI-O                               Voc 14151
        Timbuctoo                            Voc 14161

        I'm Missin' Mammy's Kissin'          Gnt 4689

        Gone Are The Days                    OK 4275
        My Mammy                             -

                                        New York, c. February, 1921.

        There's A Little Bit Of Irish In All  Amb 4256
          Of Us
        Scandinavia                          Ed 50761, Amb 4268

                                        New York, c. March, 1921.

        I Was Born In Michigan               Gnt 4719
        Scandinavia                          -
        Emaline                              Gnt 4728

        I Was Born In Michigan               Voc 14172
        I'm Nobody's Baby                    -

  Acc. by O/Rosario Bourdon.            Camden, N. J., April 21, 1921.

B-25174-1-2-3  All By Myself                 Rejected
B-25175-1-2-3  I'm Looking For A Bluebird (To   -
            Chase The Blues Away)
B-25176-3  Home Again Blues                  Vic 18760

  Acc. by studio orchestra.             New York, c. April, 1921.

        Honey Rose                           Voc 14188
        Hortense                             -
        You Made Me Forget How To Cry        Voc 14202
        It Takes A Good Man To Do That       Voc 14216

  Acc. by the Rega Orchestra.           New York, May, 1921.

  7875-A  My Man                             OK 4326
  7876-C  I've Got The Traveling Choo Choo Blues    -

Acc. by O/Rosario Bourdon.                    Camden, N. J., May 3, 1921.

B-25174-4-5-6  All By Myself                   Rejected
B-25251-2  I Wonder Where My Sweet Daddy's Gone ?   Vic 18784

                                              Camden, N. J., May 16, 1921.

B-25174-9  All By Myself                       Vic 18774

Acc. by studio orchestra.                     New York, c. May-June, 1921.

          Just A Week From Today               Amb 4293
          I'm Nobody's Baby                    Amb 4327

Acc. by the Rega Orchestra.                   New York, June, 1921.

7964-C  It Takes A Good Man To Do That        OK 4358
7965-A  Mimi (Mee-Mee)                        -

Acc. by studio orchestra.                     New York, c. July, 1921.

          Anna In Indiana                      **Ed** 50804, Amb 4349

          Stand Up And Sing For Your Father An   Voc 14230
            Old-Time Song
          Cry Baby Blues                       Voc 14237

Acc. by the Rega Orchestra.                   New York, c. July-August, 1921.

          I Want My Mammy                      OK 4409
          Mandy 'n' Me                         OK 4415
          'Tain't Nothin' Else But Jazz        -

Acc. by O/Rosario Bourdon.                    Camden, N. J., August 16, 1921.

B-25515-1-2-3-4  Saturday                     Rejected
B-25516-3  I've Got The Joys                  Vic 18799
B-25517-1-2-3-4  I'm Nobody's Gal             Rejected
B-25518-1-2-3-4  Bimini Bay                   -

Acc. by studio orchestra.                     New York, c. October, 1921.

          Weep No More, My Mammy               OK 4513
          Write And Tell Your Mammy (I'm Coming)   -

                                              New York, c. November, 1921.

          I'm Looking For A Bluebird (To Chase   Amb 4413
            The Blues Away)

                                              New York, early December, 1921.

70355-A  Bow Wow Blues (My Mama Treats Me Like A   OK 4524
           Dog)

70366-A  Granny (You're My Mammy's Mammy)     OK 4524
70367-A  On The 'Gin 'Gin 'Ginny Shore        OK 4543

                                              New York, January, 1922.

7721  I've Got The Red, White And Blues       Gnt 4819
7722  Boo Hoo Hoo                             -

          My Home Town                         Gnt 4836

          Boo Hoo Hoo                          Ed 50919, Amb 4487

                                              New York, August, 1922.

70767-B  True Blue Sam                        OK 4698
          Coal Black Mammy                     OK 4677

New York, c. September, 1922.

Homesick                                     Voc 14451

New York, c. November 18, 1922.

8112    Don't Bring Me Posies (It's Shoes I Need)Gnt 5007

New York, January, 1923.

71256-A  Chicago                                OK 4792
71258-B  Lovin' Sam (The Sheik Of Alabam')      -
71259-B  Lost (A Wonderful Girl)                OK 4794

New York, c. February 8, 1923.

8208    Seven Or Eleven                         Gnt 5071

Acc. by The Virginians/Ross Gorman.    New York, March 2, 1923.

B-27635-4  Don't Think You'll Be Missed         Vic 19039

Acc. by studio orchestra.              New York, c. May, 1923.

        Louisiana                               Voc 14614
        I'll Hop, Skip And Jump Into My Mammy's  -
        Arms

        On The Isle Of Wicki Wacki Woo          Ed 51207

Acc. by O/Rosario Bourdon.             Camden, N. J., June 26, 1923.

B-28145-4  I'm A Lonesome Cry Baby              Vic 19144
B-28146-1-2-3  Under The 'Sip 'Sip 'Sippi Moon   Rejected

Acc. by studio orchestra.              New York, November, 1923.

72098-   Sittin' In A Corner                    OK 40003

Acc. by O/? Nat Shilkret.              New York, December 10, 1923.

B-29119-1-2  Lonesome Cry Baby                  Vic Personal Recording

Acc. by O/Rosario Bourdon.             Camden, N. J., December 12, 1923.

B-29076-3  Big-Hearted Bennie (w/Billy Murray)  Vic 19221

Acc. by Ed Smalle-p or The Virginians/Ross Gorman, as shown.
                                       New York, December 13, 1923.

B-29125-1-2-3-4-5  It's A Man Ev'ry Time, It's A  Rejected
            Man - pES
B-29126-2  You May Be Fast, But Mama's Gonna Slow  Vic 19231
            You Down (w/Billy Murray) - V
B-29127-4  Promise Me Everything, Never Get Anything  -
            Blues (w/Billy Murray) - V

Acc. by O/Charles A. Prince.           New York, June 5, 1924.

B-30247-3  It Had To Be You (w/Billy Murray)    Vic 19373
B-30248-4  Nobody's Sweetheart                   -

                                       Camden, N. J., August 19, 1924.

B-30586-7  You'll Never Get To Heaven With Those  Vic 19431
            Eyes (w/Billy Murray)
B-30587-1-2-3-4  The Last Sweetheart Of Mine (w/  Rejected
            Billy Murray)                        -
B-30593-1-2-3-4  When I Was The Dandy And You Were  -
            The Belle (w/Billy Murray)
B-30594-1-2-3-4  In A Little Rendezvous (w/Billy Murray)-

Acc. by studio orchestra.                  New York, c. August 20, 1924.

9047     Too Tired                         Gnt rejected ?
9048     Charley, My Boy                        —

Acc. by O/Nat Shilkret (as "The Southwinders" on the first side).
                                           New York, August 22, 1924.

B-30666-3  When I Was The Dandy And You Were The   Vic 19443
              Belle (w/Billy Murray)
B-30667-3  All Alone With You (in A Little           Vic 19454
              Rendezvous)(w/Billy Murray)

                                           New York, September 9, 1924.

B-30807-3  Somebody Loves Me                Vic 19454
B-30808-1  Put Away A Little Ray Of Golden  Vic 19443, HMV B-1975
              Sunshine For A Rainy Day

                                           New York, September 12, 1924.

B-30815-1-2-3  Everybody Loves My Baby          Vic rejected

                                           New York, September 19, 1924.

B-30815-6  Everybody Loves My Baby              Vic 19486, HMV B-1976

                                           New York, September 25, 1924.

B-30857-1-2-3-4  Back Where The Daffodils Grow   Vic rejected
              (Carson Robison-w)
B-30858-1-2-3  If You Don't Want Me              —

  Acc. by studio orchestra.                New York, c. September 26, 1924.

9098     I'm In Love With The Prince of Wales   Gnt rejected ?
9099     Me And The Boy Friend                  —

                                           New York, October 2, 1924.

B-30857-5-6-7-8  Back Where The Daffodils Grow   Vic rejected
              (Carson Robison-w)

  Acc. by studio orchestra.                New York, c. October 6, 1924.

9113     Cradle Of The Blues                  Gnt rejected ?
9114     My Best Girl                           —

  Acc. by O/Nat Shilkret.                  New York, October 29, 1924.

B-30857-12  Back Where The Daffodils Grow (Carson  Vic 19502
              Robison-w)

                                           New York, January 20, 1925.

B-31738-1-2-3  I Ain't Got Nobody To Love       Vic rejected
B-31739-1-2-3  It's All The Same To Me          —

                                           New York, January 22, 1925.

B-31757-1-2-3-4-5  Everybody Loves My Baby      Vic Personal Record for Miss
                                               Stanley (take chosen not known)

                                           New York, January 30, 1925.

B-31738-7  I Ain't Got Nobody To Love        Vic 19585, HMV B-2006
B-31739-4-5-6  It's All The Same To Me        Rejected
B-31792-1  When My Sugar Walks Down The Street  Vic 19585, HMV B-2006
              (w/Gene Austin)

Acc. by Robert Buttenuth-p.                    Hayes, Middlesex, March 26, 1925.

Bb-5940-1-2-3  Everybody Loves My Baby (w/chorus)  Private talking record
Bb-5941-1  My Best Girl                            HMV rejected
Bb-5942-1  You're In Wrong With The Right Baby      -

                                               Hayes, Middlesex, April 21, 1925.

Bb-5941-3  My Best Girl                            HMV B-2015
Bb-5942-3  You're In Wrong With The Right Baby      -
Bb-6046-1  It Was Only A Dream                     HMV B-2022
Bb-6047-2  Alabamy Bound                            -
Dd-6048-1  Special test for Aileen Stanley "Kit-Cat" (sic)

                                               Hayes, Middlesex, July 15, 1925.

Bb-6358-1-2  How Do You Do ?                       Rejected
Bb-6359-2  Can't Your Friend Find A Friend For Me  HMV B-2087
Bb-6360-2  Make Hay, Hay                           HMV B-2106
Bb-6361-1  If You Hadn't Gone Away                  -
Bb-6362-1  Give Me Just A Little Bit Of Your Love  HMV B-2087
Bb-6363-1  We're Back Together Again               Rejected

   Acc. by O/Rosario Bourdon,or Frank Banta-p where shown.
                                        Camden, N. J., August 20, 1925.

BVE-33179-1-2-3-4  If I Had A Girl Like You (w/   Rejected
          Billy Murray)
BVE-33180-1-2-3  Give Me Just A Little Bit Of Your   -
          Love - pFB
BVE-33181-3  You're In Wrong With The Right Baby   Vic 19767
          - pFB
BVE-33239-1-2-3-4  Mighty Blue - pFB              Rejected
BVE-33240-1-2-3-4  I Know Someone Loves Me - pFB    -

   Acc. by Frank Banta-p.              Camden, N. J., August 25, 1925.

BVE-33179-5-6-7-8  If I had A Girl Like You (w/    Rejected
          Billy Murray)
BVE-33182-3  Keep Your Skirts Down, Mary Ann       Vic 19795
          (w/Billy Murray)
BVE-33183-1  Want A Little Lovin'                  Vic 19767
BVE-33239-5-6-7-8  Mighty Blue                     Rejected

                                        New York, September 21, 1925.

BVE-33239-9-10-11-12  Mighty Blue                 Vic rejected

                                        New York, September 22, 1925.

BVE-33239-13-14  Mighty Blue                      Rejected
BVE-33503-5  If I Had A Girl Like You (w/Billy     Vic 19795
          Murray)

   Acc. by Jack Shilkret-p/Billy Carpenter-u.
                                        New York, October 5, 1925.

BVE-33540-1-2-3  Better Call The Preacher Now      Rejected
          (w/Billy Murray)
BVE-33541-1  Flaming Mamie                         Vic 19828

                                        New York, October 12, 1925.

BVE-33558-1-2-3  Sweet Man                         Vic rejected

                                        New York, October 23, 1925.

BVE-33558-4-5-6-7  Sweet Man                       Vic rejected

New York, October 28, 1925.

BVE-33822-1-2-3-4  No Man's Mama - pJS only       Vic rejected
BVE-33823-3  I Love My Baby (My Baby Loves Me)    Vic 19950, HMV B-2278

   Acc. by O/Rosario Bourdon or Frank Banta-p as shown.
                                        Camden, N. J., November 4, 1925.

BVE-33239-18  Mighty Blue - pFB                   Vic 19863
BVE-33753-4   Down By The Winegar Woiks (w/Billy  Vic 19838
                Murray) - O/RB
BVE-33822-6   No Man's Mama - pFB                 Vic 19863, HMV B-2278

                                        Camden, N. J., November 6, 1925.

BVE-33758-1-2-3  D'Ye Love Me ? (w/Billy Murray)  Vic rejected
                - O/RB

   Acc. by O/Nat Shilkret.              New York, April 1, 1926.

BVE-35265-1-2-3  I'd Give A Lot Of Love           Vic rejected
BVE-35266-1-2-3-4  What A Man !                       -

                                        New York, April 16, 1926.

BVE-35265-4-5-6-7  I'd Give A Lot Of Love         Vic rejected
BVE-35266-5-6-7  What A Man !                         -

   Acc. by Frank Banta-p.               New York, May 12, 1926.

BVE-35393-3  What A Man !                          Vic 20056
BVE-35394-1-2-3-4  I'd Give A Lot Of Love          Rejected
BVE-35395-1  I Wonder What's Become Of Joe ?       Vic 20056

   Acc. by O/Rosario Bourdon.          Camden, N. J., May 19, 1926.

BVE-35468-3  Whaddya Say We Get Together ? (w/    Vic 20065, HMV B-2338
               Billy Murray)

                                        Camden, N. J., May 21, 1926.

BVE-35394-5-6-7  I'd Give A Lot Of Love - pFB     Rejected
BVE-35472-1-2-3  Hi-Diddle-Diddle (w/Billy Murray)    -
BVE-35473-3  Any Ice Today, Lady ? (w/Billy Murray)Vic 20065, HMV B-2338

   Acc. by Frank Banta-Rosario Bourdon-p.  Camden, N. J., May 26, 1926.

BVE-35164-3  Down By The Gas House               Vic 20096

   Acc. by Frank Banta-p.               New York, August 20, 1926.

BVE-36056-2  I Can't Get Over A Girl Like You     Vic 20148, HMV B-2381
               (Loving A Boy Like Me) (w/Billy Murray)

                                        New York, August 24, 1926.

BVE-36062-1  Who Wouldn't ? (w/Billy Murray)      Vic 20148, HMV B-2381
BVE-36063-1  Bridget O'Flynn (Where've Ya Been ?)  Vic 20240, HMV B-2392
               (w/Billy Murray)

                                        New York, August 26, 1926.

BVE-36068-2  Who Could Be More Wonderful Than You? Vic 20240, HMV B-2392
               (w/Billy Murray)

   Acc. by vn/vc/p.                     New York, August 27, 1926.

BVE-36072-2  Don't Be Angry With Me               Vic 20391, HMV B-2521
BVE-36073-1  Looking At The World Thru' Rose-      Vic 20198
               Colored Glasses
BVE-36074-2  Six Feet Of Papa                         -

New York, September 1, 1926.

BVE-36088-1-2-3-4  I Ain't Got Nobody To Love Me    Vic rejected
BVE-36089-1-2-3-4  Precious                         -

   Acc. by O/Nat Shilkret, or Robert Buttenuth-p where shown.
                                     New York, March 4, 1927.

BVE-38138-1-2-3  Song Of The Wanderer              Rejected
BVE-38139-    Nay ! Nay ! Neighbor                 Vic 20511
BVE-38140-    Gonna Get A Girl - pRB               -

                                     New York, March 17, 1927.

BVE-38179-1-2  I'm Back In Love Again (w/Billy     Vic rejected
                 Murray)                             -
BVE-38180-1-2-3  Does She Love Me ? (Positively -    -
                 Absolutely) (w/Billy Murray)
BVE-38181-1-2  Mama Wants To Go To Bye-Bye (w/       -
                 Billy Murray)

                                     New York, March 18, 1927.

BVE-38138-4-5  Song Of The Wanderer               Vic rejected

   Acc. by O/Leonard Joy.            New York, April 15, 1927.

BVE-38179-3  I'm Back In Love Again (w/Billy      Vic 20643, HMV B-2502
               Murray)
BVE-38180-7  Does She Love Me ? (Positively -        -            -
               Absolutely) (w/Billy Murray)

   Acc. by cl/p/g/Johnny Marvin-u-v.   New York, May 25, 1927.

BVE-38780-3  Side By Side - u-vJM                 Vic 20714, HMV B-2519
BVE-38781-3  Red Lips, Kiss My Blues Away  - u-vJM    -            -

   Acc. by c/p/g, with Johnny Marvin-stg.* New York, May 26, 1927.

BVE-38786-1-2-3-4  Magnolia (Mix The Lot - What   Vic rejected
                 Have You Got ?)
BVE-38787-1-2-3  *Ain't That A Grand And Glorious    -
                 Feeling ?

   Acc. by vn/p/g, with Joe Green-d where shown.
                                     New York, June 22, 1927.

BVE-39284-3  Under The Moon (You-oo-oo-oo)        Vic 20787, HMV B-2565
BVE-39285-    I Walked Back From The Buggy Ride   Vic 20822, HMV B-2578
               - dJG

   Acc. by O/Nat Shilkret.           New York, June 27, 1927.

BVE-39297-    I'm Gonna Dance Wit De Guy Wot Brung Vic 20822, HMV B-2578
               Me (w/Billy Murray)

                                     New York, July 7, 1927.

BVE-39633-1-2-3  Herman The German, My Friend     Vic rejected
                 From Berlin (w/Billy Murray)
BVE-39634-1-2  Mister O'Toole (w/Billy Murray)      -

                                     New York, July 8, 1927.

BVE-39637-1-2  Broken Hearted                     Vic rejected

Acc. by O/Leroy Shield.                         New York, August 5, 1927.

BVE-39637-    Broken Hearted                          Vic 20825, HMV B-2590
BVE-39942-1-2-3  Look In The Mirror (And You'll       Rejected
                 See Just Who I Love)
BVE-39943-1-2  Baby Feet Go Pitter Patter ('Cross      -
               My Floor)

Acc. by O/Percival Mackey.                      Small Queen's Hall, London, Dec. 20, 1927.

Bb-12162-1-2  Did You Mean It ?                       HMV rejected
Bb-12163-1-2-3  Just A Memory                          -
Cc-12164-1-2  Private recording                       HMV
Cc-12165-1    Private recording                        -

Acc. by O/Leonard Joy.                          New York, January 7, 1929.

BVE-49620-3  I'll Get By, As Long As I Have You    Vic 21839, HMV B-2991

Acc. by studio orchestra.                       New York, January 11, 1929.

BVE-49057-1-2-3  Won't You Tell Me, Hon (When      Rejected
                 We're Gonna Be One ?) (w/Johnny Marvin)
BVE-49058-2  Ev'rybody Loves You (w/Johnny Marvin) Vic 21848, HMV B-2991

Acc. by O/Leonard Joy.                          New York, January 29, 1929.

BVE-49693-3  Give Your Little Baby Lots Of Lovin'  Vic 21874, HMV B-3014
BVE-49694-1  I'll Never Ask For More                  -            -

Acc. by O/Nat Shilkret.                          New York, April 2, 1929.

BVE-51600-1-2-3  The Things That Were Made For       Vic rejected
                 Love
BVE-51601-1-2-3  I'll Tell The World                  -

Acc. by Phil Baker-pac-v/unknown vn.    New York, April 8, 1929.

BVE-51612-1-2-3-4  My Melody Man                      Vic rejected

Acc. by O/Leonard Joy.                          New York, April 16, 1929.

BVE-51600-4-5-6  The Things That Were Made For       Vic rejected
                 Love
BVE-51601-4-5-6  I'll Tell The World                  -

                                                New York, May 8, 1929.

BVE-51600-7-8  The Things That Were Made For Love  Vic rejected

                                                New York, June 13, 1929.

BVE-53561-1-2-3-4  Please Don't Cut Out My           Rejected
                   Sauerkraut (w/Billy Murray)
BVE-53562-3  Katie, Keep Your Feet On The Ground   Vic 22040
             (w/Billy Murray)

                                                New York, December 26, 1929.

BVE-58140-1-2-3  A Darn Fool Woman Like Me           Vic rejected
BVE-58141-1-2-3  Watching My Dreams Go By             -

                                                New York, June 30, 1930.

BVE-62300-3  Swingin' In A Hammock                   Vic 22469, HMV B-3632
BVE-63101-3  I Love You So Much                       -

New York, August 6, 1930.

BVE-63327-1-2-3  Wasn't It Nice ?                          Vic rejected
BVE-63328-1-2-3  I'll Be Blue, Just Thinking Of You          -
BVE-63329-1-2-3  Under The Moon It's You                     -

  Acc. by O/Nat Shilkret.                  New York, August 20, 1930.

BVE-63327-4  Wasn't It Nice ?                               Vic 22524, HMV B-3690
BVE-63328-4  I'll Be Blue, Just Thinking Of You              -

                                           New York, December 11, 1930.

BVE-64828-1-2-3  He's Not Worth Your Tears                 Vic rejected

                                           New York, December 12, 1930.

BVE-64828-4-5-6  He's Not Worth Your Tears                 Vic rejected
BVE-64829-1-2-3  To Whom It May Concern (w/Johnny            -
                 Marvin)

                                           New York, December 19, 1930.

BVE-64830-1-2  (I Am The Words) You Are The                 Vic rejected
               Melody) (w/Johnny Marvin)
BVE-64831-1-2  Yours And Mine (w/Johnny Marvin)             -

  Acc. by studio orchestra.                London, February 12, 1934.

GB-6556-3  Who Walks In When I Walk Out ?                   Br 01706
GB-6557-1-2-3  Over On The Sunny Side                       Rejected

  Acc. by Harry Jacobson-p.                London, February 20, 1934.

GB-6557-4  Over On The Sunny Side                           Br 01706
GB-6584-1  Aileen Stanley Song Successes - Part 1  Br 01722, Dec M-461
           (Intro. How Do You Do ?/Gonna Get A Girl/My Best Girl/Everybody  Loves
           My Baby/Ain't That A Grand And Glorious Feeling ?/Side By Side)
GB-6585-3  Aileen Stanley Song Successes - Part 2    -                    -
           (Intro. When My Sugar Walks Down The Street/Dum - Dum - Dummy/Somebody
           Stole My Gal/Here Am I, Broken Hearted/Souvenirs)
GB-6586-1-2-3  Ol' Pappy                                    Rejected
GB-6587-1-2-3  Jimmie And Me                                -

  Acc. by O/Nat Shilkret.                  New York, April 5, 1935.

BS-89520-   I'm Livin' In A Great Big Way                   HMV BD-289
BS-89521-   I'm In Love All Over Again                      -
BS-89522-1-2  Music In My Heart                             Rejected
BS-89523-1-2  Life Is A Song (Let's Sing It Together)       -

  Acc. by O/Clifford Greenwood.            London, July 8, 1935.

OEA-2162-1  Rags                                            HMV BD-251
OEA-2163-1  Don't You Ever Fall In Love                     -

  Acc. by O/Ronnie Munro.                  London, July 9, 1937.

OEA-5000-3  I've Got My Love To Keep Me Warm                HMV BD-444
OEA-5401-1-2-3  Never In A Million Years                    Rejected
OEA-5402-1-2-3  The You And Me That Used To Be              -
OEA-5403-3  It Looks Like Rain In Cherry Blossom            HMV BD-444
            Lane

## DOUGLAS  STEVENSON

B. Versailles, Ky., 1882; popular vaudeville singer of the first third of the  century; d. there, December 31, 1934.      New York, May, 1922.

  8948    Songs of Yesterday by Stars of Today    Voc 35010 (part side)

B. Indiana, Pa., May 20, 1909; educated at Princeton U., studied architecture before
   embarking on film career (debut in MURDER MAN, 1935; since then an enormous number
   of memorable films, e.g., ROSE MARIE; BORN TO DANCE; AFTER THE THIN MAN (1936); OF
   HUMAN HEARTS; THE LAST GANGSTER; NAVY BLUE AND GOLD (1937); VIVACIOUS LADY;  SHOP-
   WORN ANGEL; YOU CAN'T TAKE IT WITH YOU; MADE FOR EACH OTHER (1938); ICE FOLLIES OF
   1939; MR. SMITH GOES TO WASHINGTON; DESTRY RIDES AGAIN (1939); THE    PHILADELPHIA
   STORY (1940); ZIEGFELD GIRL (1941); career interrupted by war service, resumed  in
   1946 with IT'S A WONDERFUL LIFE; then CALL NORTHSIDE 777 (1947); ROPE (1948); HAR-
   VEY (1950); NO HIGHWAY (in England); THE GREATEST SHOW ON EARTH (1951); THE  GLENN
   MILLER STORY (1953); THE FAR COUNTRY (1954); STRATEGIC AIR COMMAND; THE  MAN  FROM
   LARAMIE (1955); THE MAN WHO KNEW TOO MUCH (1956); THE SPIRIT OF ST. LOUIS  (1957);
   BELL, BOOK AND CANDLE (1958); ANATOMY OF A MURDER; THE FBI STORY (1959); HOW   THE
   WEST WAS WON (1962); CHEYENNE AUTUMN (1964); DEAR BRIGITTE; SHENANDOAH (1965); THE
   RARE BREED (1966); FIRECREEK (1967); BANDOLERO (1968).

Vocalist with the Princeton Triangle Orchestra. (It is believed that other sides  by
this band were made with James Stewart).New York, October 12, 1931.

170614-2  Day After Day                           Col Personal Recording

## EUGENE  STRATTON

B. Buffalo, N. Y., 1861; r.n. Eugene Ruhlman; began stage career with the Four  Arnold Brothers in the mid-seventies; joined Haverley's Original Mastodon  Minstrels,
   in Chicago, October 21, 1878; came to London with them, opening at Drury Lane   on
   July 31, 1880; joined Moore and Burgess Minstrels in London soon afterwards,stayed
   with them through the 1880s; became known as a first-class "blackface" song—dance
   comedian in the 1890s, making outstanding hits with songs by English writer Leslie
   Stuart; one of the few American minstrel men to record; d. London, September   15,
   1918.

Vocal, acc. by Leslie Stuart (composer)-p.
                                        London, April 7, 1899.

    1863    Is Yer Mammie Always Wid Yer ? (sic)      Ber 2399
    1864 ?  Little Dolly Daydream                     Ber 2384
    1866    The Cake Walk                             Ber 2401
    NOTE:- Matrix 1865 is not by Eugene Stratton.

Acc. by studio orchestra.               London, December 7, 1903.

    4645    My Little Octoroon                        Rejected
    4646    My Little Octoroon                        G&T GC3-2013
    4647    Lily Of Laguna                            Rejected
    4648    The Coon Drum Major                       G&T GC3-2012
    4649    Little Dolly Daydream                     G&T GC3-2008
    4650    I May Be Crazy                            G&T GC3-2011
    5723 ?  Lily Of Laguna                            G&T 2-2415 (7")
    5724    The Coon Drum Major                       G&T 2-2411 (7")
    5725 ?  Little Dolly Daydream                     G&T 2-2451 (7")

                                        London, January 31, 1911.

    4775f   Little Dolly Daydream                     HMV 02377
    4776f   I May Be A Millionaire                    HMV 02391

                                        London, February 1, 1911.

    4777f   Lily Of Laguna                            HMV 02364, C-556
    4778f   I May Be Crazy                            Rejected
    4779f   I May Be Crazy                            HMV 02341, C-556

## THE STREET  SINGER

See Arthur Tracy.

## GLORIA SWANSON

B. 1898; one of the original Mack Sennett bathing beauties, but who became a front-
   rank film actress, successfully making the transition from silents to talkies,and

still makes guest-appearances on TV.  Screen debut in THE ROMANCE OF AN   AMERICAN
DUCHESS (1914); made many Keystone comedies and following silents : DON'T    CHANGE
YOUR HUSBAND and MALE AND FEMALE (1919); THE AFFAIRS OF ANATOL (1921); BLUEBEARD'S
EIGHTH WIFE (1923); THE WAGES OF VIRTUE (1924); MADAME SANS GENE  1925);   UNTAMED
LADY (1926); SADIE THOMPSON (1928); many others; best-known talkies include    THE
TRESPASSER (1929); INDISCREET (1931); MUSIC IN THE AIR (1934); FATHER TAKES A WIFE
(1941); SUNSET BOULEVARD (1950); THREE FOR BEDROOM C (1952); the Italian    NERO'S
MISTRESS (1956).

Vocal, acc. by O/Nat Shilkret.             New York, August 3, 1929.

BVE-55645-2  Love (Your Spell Is Everywhere) (Film  Vic 22079, LPV-538, LSA-3074,
             "The Trespasser")                       RD-7869, HMV B-3168
BVE-55646-   Serenade (Toselli) (Film "The          Vic 22079    -
             Trespasser")

   Acc. by O/? Leroy Shield.                Hollywood, July 25, 1930.

PBVE-54897-1-2  Love Is Like A Song              Vic rejected
PBVE-54898-1-2-3  You're The One                   -
PBVE-54899-1-2-3  Say "Oui," Cherie                -

   Acc. by studio orchestra.               New York, c. April 21, 1931.

E-36721/2  Come To Me (Film "Indiscreet")            Br 6127, 01147
E-36723-   If You Haven't Got Love (Film "Indiscreet") -      -

   Acc. by O/Philip Braham.                London, December 21, 1932.

OB-4374-1  I Love You So Much That I Hate You       HMV B-4357
OB-4375-1  Ich liebe dich, My Dear                     -

## GLADYS SWARTHOUT

B. Deepwater, Mo., 1904; educated High School, Kansas City; awarded degree of Doctor
  of Music, Bush Conservatory, Chicago; stage debut in New York in LA GIOCONDA (Metropolitan Opera House, 1929); also sang there in productions of SADKO; LE PREZIOSE
  RIDICOLE; NORMA; PETER IBBETSON; LA FORZA DEL DESTINO; MIGNON, and CARMEN;   Paramount Pictures wanted her as rival to Jeanette MacDonald (MGM) and Grace Moore(Columbia); she thus appeared in films such as ROSE OF THE RANCHO (with John Boles)and
  GIVE US THIS NIGHT (with Jan Kiepura, both 1936); CHAMPAGNE WALTZ and TO HAVE  AND
  TO HOLD (1937); ROMANCE IN THE DARK (1938); last picture, AMBUSH (1939).

Vocal, acc. by O/Alexander Smallens.       New York, April 3, 1936.

CS-101172-1  Mon coeur s'ouvre a ta voix ("Samson   Vic 14143, HMV DB-2992
             et Dalila" - Saint-Saëns)
CS-101173-1  Amour, viens aider ma faiblesse ("Samson   -          -
             et Dalila" - Saint-Saëns)
CS-101174-1  Pres des remparts de Seville            Vic 14419
             (Seguidilla) ("Carmen" - Bizet)
CS-101175-1  L'amour est un oiseau rebelle (Habanera)   -
             ("Carmen" - Bizet)
CS-101176-1  None But The Lonely Heart (Tchsikovsky)Rejected
CS-101177-1  Pauline's Romance ("Pique Dame"-Suppe)    -
CS-101178-1  I Mean To Say I Love You (Film "Give      -
             Us This Night")

   Acc. by Lester Hodges-p.                New York, April 3, 1936.

BS-101179-1-3  Clouds                           Vic 4318
BS-101180-1  Spenthrift                            -

   Acc. by O/William Daly.                 Hollywood, October 8, 1936.

BS-97882-1  Could I Be In Love ? (Film "Champagne  Vic 4324, HMV DA-1542
            Waltz")
BS-97883-1  Paradise In Waltz Time (Film "Champagne    -          -
            Waltz")

Acc. by Lester Hodges-p.                          New York, January 10, 1940.

CS-046403-    Lascia ch'io pianga ("Rinaldo"-Handel)Vic 16778
CS-046404-    Come Again, Sweet Love (John Dowland)/      -
              Nymphs And Shepherds (Henry Purcell)
CS-046405-    Le Temps des Lilas (Boucher-Chausson) Vic 16779
CS-046406-1   El Majo Discreto (Tonadilla) (Enrique       -
              Granados)/Romanza de Solita ("La Romeria de los Cornudos" - G. Pitta-
              luga)
CS-046407-1   Serenade (Siegfried Sassoon - John     Vic 16780
              Alden Carpenter)
CS-046408-1   My Lagan Love ("Three Traditional           -
              Ulster Airs" - arr. Hamilton Harty)
CS-046409-1   The Kerry Dance (J. L. Molloy)         Vic 16781
CS-046410-1   The Lord's Prayer (Albert Hay Malotte)      -

Acc. by O/Al Goodman, or Lester Hodges-p where shown.
                                                  New York, July 29, 1942.

BS-075486-1-2  Ah Love, But A Day - pLH              Rejected ?
BS-075487-    My Heart Stood Still                   Vic 10-1038
BS-075488-    Begin The Beguine                      Vic 10-1036
BS-075489-    I'll See You Again                     Rejected ?
BS-075490-    Smoke Gets In Your Eyes                Vic 10-1037
BS-075491-    Through The Years                           -
BS-075492-    O Dry Those Tears - pLH                Rejected ?

                                       New York, July 30, 1942.

BS-075495-    Cantiga de Ninas - pLH                 Rejected ?
BS-075496-    None But The Lonely Heart - pLH             -
BS-075497-    Bless This House - pLH                      -

BS-075600-    Give Me One Hour                       Vic 10-1037
BS-075601-    Mother                                 Rejected ?
BS-075602-    Dancing In The Dark                    Vic 10-1037
BS-075603-    The Man I Love                         Vic 10-1038
BS-075604-    It's A Lovely Day Tomorrow             Vic 10-1036

## MARGARET SYLVA

B. Brussels, 1875; r.n. Marguerite Alice Helena Smith; principally an opera soprano,
but her Edison cylinders are of musical comedy material, thus included here; made
Edison records of operatic excerpts. D. Glendale, Calif., February 21, 1957.

Vocal, acc. by studio orchestra.              New York, 1911-1912.

              The Melody Of Love                     Ed 28001
              Love Is Like The Rose (w/Arthur Albro) Ed 28002
              I Will Give You All For Love           Ed 28003
              There Is A Land Of Fancy (w/Carl Haydn) Ed 28004

## HARRY  TALLY

B. Lee County, Va., June 30, 1866; very popular vaudeville singer, both solo and  as
a member of the Empire City Four, with the bass singer of which, Harry Mayo,  made
some records for Edison in addition to the considerable number he made for Columbia
and Victor.  D. Ocean Park, Calif., August 16, 1939.

Vocal, acc. by unknown p.                     New York, c. August, 1902.

932-    Mandy, Won't You Let Me Be Your Beau ?  Col 932

                                       New York, c. November, 1902.

1087-   The Furniture Man                           Col 1087
1088-   Sadie Moore                                 Col 1088

New York, c. June, 1904.

1784-    The Gondolier                            Col 1784

Acc. by studio orchestra.                  New York, July 1, 1904.

A-1549-1-2  Mandy, Won't You Let Me Be Your Beau ? Vic 2936
B-1549-1-2  Mandy, Won't You Let Me Be Your Beau ?   -
A-1550-2    Seminole Indian Song                  Vic 2937
A-1551-1    If I Were Only You                    Vic 2938
B-1551-1    If I were Only You                      -

New York, July 18, 1904.

A-1618-1    Navajo                                Rejected
B-1618-1-2  Navajo                                  -
A-1619-1    Sadie Moore                             -
B-1619-1-2  Sadie Moore                             -
A-1620-1    I'm Going To Live Anyhow Until I Die    -
B-1620-1    I'm Going To Live Anyhow Until I Die  Vic 4060
A-1621-1    My Little Creole Baby                 Vic 2978
B-1621-3    My Little Creole Baby                   -

New York, July 19, 1904.

B-1620-4-5  I'm Going To Live Anyhow Until I Die  Vic 4060
A-1622-1    Kitty Dooley                          Rejected
B-1622-2    Kitty Dooley                          Vic 2977
A-1623-1    My Sweet Magnolia                     Rejected
B-1623-1-2  My Sweet Magnolia                       -
A-1624-1-2  I've Got A Feeling For You            Vic 2956
B-1624-1    I've Got A Feeling For You              -
A-1625-1    Always In The Way                     Rejected

New York, July 20, 1904.

A-1619-2    Sadie Moore                           Rejected
A-1625-2    Always In The Way                       -
B-1625-1    Always In The Way                     Vic 2976, 16099
A-1626-1    All Aboard For Dreamland              Vic 2955
B-1626-1-2  All Aboard For Dreamland                -
A-1627-1    Stella                                Rejected
B-1627-1    Stella                                  -
A-1628-1    Egypt, My Cleopatra                     -
B-1628-1    Egypt, My Cleopatra                   Vic 4148

Acc. by unknown piano.            New York, c. September, 1904.

1853-    Egypt, My Cleopatra                      Col 1853

Acc. by studio orchestra.         New York, c. September, 1904.

1857-    Teasing                                  Col 1857

New York, c. September, 1905.

3277-    Goodbye, Sweet Manhattan Isle            Col 3277, 32812 (cyl.),
                                                  Busy Bee 320 (cyl.)

New York, December 7, 1905.

B-2927-1-2  Silver Heels                          Vic 4579
B-2928-1    Wait Till The Sun Shines, Nellie      Vic 4551 (Canada only)
B-2929-1    My Irish Molly-O                      Vic 4580        -
B-2930-2    Why Don't You Try ?                   Vic 4593        -
B-2931-2    On An Automobile Honeymoon            Vic 4592, 16098

                                   New York, December 8, 1905.

B-2928-3  Wait Till The Sun Shines, Nellie        Vic 4551, 16097
B-2930-3  Why Don't You Try ?                      Vic 4593, 16098
B-2932-1  Fly Away, Birdie, To Heaven              Vic 4618 (Canada only)
B-2932-2  Fly Away, Birdie, To Heaven              -      16099
B-2933-1  Can't You See I'm Lonely ?               Vic 4619
B-2934-1  My Dusky Rose                            Vic 4647 (Canada only)
B-2934-2  My Dusky Rose                            -

                                   New York, June 13, 1906.

C-3462-2  Somewhere (w/Haydn Quartet)              Vic 31548
C-3462-3  Somewhere (w/Haydn Quartet)              -      (Canada only)
B-3463-2  Holding Hands (w/Haydn Quartet)          Vic 4821
B-3464-1  When The Girl You Love Loves You         Vic 4859
B-3464-2  When The Girl You Love Loves You         -      (Canada only)
B-3465-1  A Little Lunch For Two                   Vic 4820
B-3465-2  A Little Lunch For Two                   -      (Canada only)

                                   New York, June 14, 1906.

E-3465-1  A Little Lunch For Two                   Vic 4820
B-3466-1  Alice, Where Art Thou Going ?            Vic 4775 (Canada only)
B-3466-2  Alice, Where Art Thou Going ?            -
C-3467-1  Just One Word Of Consolation             Vic 31549
C-3467-2  Just One Word Of Consolation             -      (Canada only)
C-3468-1-2  Sweet Rose Of Asthore                  Rejected
B-3469-1  The Girl Who Was Meant For Me            Vic 5078 (Canada only)
B-3469-2  The Girl Who Was Meant For Me            -

                                   New York, c. August, 1906.

 3501-   Cheer Up, Mary                            Col 3501

                                   New York, May 7, 1907.

B-4463-1  Deutschland                              Vic 5139 (Canada only)
B-4463-2  Deutschland                              -
E-4463-1  Deutschland                              -      (Canada only)
E-4463-2  Deutschland                              -
B-4464-1  Broncho Buster                           Vic 5224
B-4465-2  Roll Around                              Vic 5130
B-4466-1  A Friend Of Mine Told A Friend Of Mine   Vic 5160, 16221
E-4466-1  A Friend Of Mine Told A Friend Of Mine   -
E-4466-2  A Friend Of Mine Told A Friend Of Mine   -      (Canada only)

                                   New York, July 26, 1907.

B-4715-1  Bye-Bye, Dearie                          Vic 5258 (Canada only)
B-4715-2  Bye-Bye, Dearie                          -
B-4716-2  Sacramento                               Vic 5260, 16156
B-4716-3  Sacramento                               -      (Canada only)
B-4717-1  Ballooning                               Vic 5213
B-4717-2  Ballooning                               -      (Canada only)
B-4718-1-2  Take Me Back To New York Town          Vic 5230

                                   New York, January 22, 1909.

B-6745-2  In Those Good Old Country Days           Vic 16259
B-6746-2  Let's Go Into A Picture Show             Vic 16283
B-6747-1-2  Good Luck, Mary                        Rejected

                                   New York, October 21, 1910.

B-9570-2  My Bonnie Blue Bell                      Vic 16689

                                   New York, November 21, 1910.

 19126-   Come, Josephine, In My Flying Machine    Col A-966

New York, c. September, 1914.

At The Ball, That's All (w/Harry Mayo)    Ed 50238, Amb 2595

New York, c. January, 1915.

When My Ship Comes In (w/Harry Mayo)      Ed 50269

New York, c. May, 1915.

Somebody Knows (w/Harry Mayo)             Ed 50297, Amb 2753

New York, c. July, 1915.

Piney Ridge (w/Harry Mayo)                Ed 50315

New York, c. September, 1916.

I Was Never Nearer Heaven In My Life      Ed 50394, Amb 3012
  (w/Harry Mayo)

## EVA  TANGUAY

B. Marbleton, Quenec, Canada, August 1878; one of the outstandingly great vaudeville
personalities, who by her magnetic personality and showmanship could command  huge
salaries for appearances anywhere in the U.S.A.  She made one silent film in 1917,
WILD GIRL; this title, and that of her most famous song (and the only one she ever
recorded) sum up her extrovert attitude to life; she was frowned on by some  civic
authorities who considered her leg-show and fantastic stage-wear indecent, but she
could caricature herself perfectly as few other artists did.  D. Hollywood,  January 11, 1948.

Vocal, acc. by studio orchestra.          Los Angeles, c. 1922.

I Don't Care                              Nordskog (un-numbered ?),
                                          IRCC 5017, AR 2290, Veritas 107

## JULIUS  TANNEN

American monologist, compere and character-study actor-comedian, noted for his fast-
talk patter; originator of George M. Cohan's famous curtain speech beginning  "My
father thanks you, my mother thanks you....") Very popular in the U.S.A. during the
years between 1914 and 1930, but flopped badly in London; the audiences could  not
appreciate his rapid patter.

Humorous monologues.                      New York, August 11, 1927.

BVE-39964-   Cohen At The Telephone - Part 1    Vic 20921
BVE-39965-   Cohen At The Telephone - Part 2       -

Camden, N. J., November 23, 1927.

BVE-40737-1-2  More Chatter                   Vic rejected

Camden, N. J., November 29, 1927.

BVE-40737-3  More Chatter                     Vic 21115
BVE-40749-1  The Human Chatterbox Plays Golf     -

## TASCOTT

American vaudeville comedian, very popular during the early years of the century.

Vocal, acc. by studio orchestra.          New York, issued as shown in brackets.

    Shame On You                          Ed 9033 (July, 1905)
    You Must Think I'm Santa Claus        Ed 9091 (September, 1905)

B. April 23, 1929; one of the greatest child film-stars, making her debut in  short
films at three, in features soon afterwards, and in star parts at five, beginning
with LITTLE MISS MARKER (1934); this was followed by such memorable films as BABY
TAKE A BOW; STAND UP AND CHEER and BRIGHT EYES (1934); CURLY TOP and THE LITTLEST
REBEL (1935); CAPTAIN JANUARY; DIMPLES; POOR LITTLE RICH GIRL and STOWAWAY (1936);
HEIDI (1937); REBECCA OF SUNNYBROOK FARM (1938); THE LITTLE PRINCESS and SUSANNAH
OF THE MOUNTIES (1939); THE BLUE BIRD (1940); and as a teenager, she starred in a
further series including I'LL BE SEEING YOU (1944); THE BACHELOR AND THE   BOBBY-
SOXER (1947); MR. BELVEDERE GOES TO COLLEGE (1949); now actively engaged in Cali-
fornian politics; awarded special recognition in 1934 "of her outstanding contri-
bution to screen entertainment." She made no commercial records as such, but her
films have supplied soundtrack material for a number of LPs, shown below.

| | |
|---|---|
| On Accounta I Love You (Film "Baby, Take A Bow") (1934) | Fox 3006, TFM-3172, Movie 71012, Top Rank JKR-8003 |
| Baby, Take A Bow (Film "Stand Up And Cheer") (1934) | Fox 3006, TFM-3172, Movie 71012 |
| On The Good Ship Lollipop (Film "Bright Eyes") (1934) | Fox 3006, TFM-3172, 103-2, MFP 1141, Movie 71001, Starline MRS-5086, Top Rank JAR-139, JKR-8003 |
| Animal Crackers In My Soup (Film "Curly Top") (1935) | Fox 3006, 103-2, MFP 1141, Starline MRS-5086, Top Rank JAR-139, JKR-8003 |
| When I Grow Up (Film "Curly Top") (1935) | Fox 3006, TFR-3172, Movie 71012, Starline MRS-5086 |
| Polly Wolly Doodle (Film "The Littlest Rebel") (1935) | Fox 3006, Top Rank JKR-8003 |
| Early Bird (Film "Captain January") (1936) | Fox 3006, MFP 1141 |
| At The Codfish Ball (Film "Captain January") (1936) | Fox 3006, TFM-3172, Movie 71012, Starline MRS-5086 |
| The Right Somebody To Love (Film "Captain January") (1936) | Fox TFM-3172, 103-2, Movie 71012 |
| Sextet from "Lucia di Lammermoor" (w/Guy Kibbee-Slim Summerville) (Film "Captain January") (1936) | MFP 1141 |
| When I'm With You (Film "Poor Little Rich Girl") (1936) | Fox 3006, TFM-3172, Movie 71012 |
| Oh, My Goodness (Film "Poor Little Rich Girl") (1936) | As above plus Starline MRS-5086, Top Rank JKR-8003 |
| You Gotta Eat Your Spinach, Baby (Film "Poor Little Rich Girl") (1936) | Fox 3006, TFM-3172, Movie 71012, Starline MRS-5086 |
| But Definitely (Film "Poor Little Rich Girl") (1936) | Fox 3006, MFP 1141 |
| Picture Me Without You (Film "Dimples") (1936) | MFP 1141, Starline MRS-5086 |
| Hey ! What Did The Blue Jay Say ? (Film "Dimples") (1936) | Fox 103-2 |
| That's What I Want For Christmas (Film "Stowaway") (1936) | Fox 3006, MFP 1141 |
| Goodnight, My Love (Film "Stowaway") (1936) | Fox 3006, 103-2 |
| I Love To Walk In The Rain (Film "Just Around The Corner") (1938) | Fox 3006, MFP 1141, Starline MRS-5086 |
| This Is A Happy Little Ditty (Film "Just Around The Corner") (1938) | Fox 3006, TFM-3172, Movie 71012 |
| Be Optimistic (Film "Little Miss Broadway") (1938) | Fox TFM-3172, Movie 71012 |
| We Should Be Together (w/George Murphy) (Film "Little Miss Broadway") (1938) | MFP 1141, Starline MRS-5086 |
| Sing Me An Old-Fashioned Song (Film "Little Miss Broadway") (1938) | MFP 1141 |
| How Can I Thank You ? (Film "Little Miss Broadway") (1938) | Fox 3006, TFM-3172, Movie 71012 |
| An Old Straw Hat (Film "Rebecca Of Sunnybrook Farm") (1938) | Fox 3006, Top Rank JKR-8003 |
| Come And Get Your Happiness (Film "Rebecca Of Sunnybrook Farm") (1938) | Fox 103-2, MFP 1141 |
| Lay-De-O (Film "The Blue Bird") (1940) | Fox 3006, TFM-3172, Movie 71012 |
| Tra-La-La (w/Charlotte Greenwood-Jack Oakie) (Film "Young People") (1940) | Fox TFM-3172, Movie 71012, MFP 1141, Starline MRS-5086 |

B. Coventry, England, 1847; daughter of well-known actors; stage debut at eight  in
   A WINTER'S TALE; appeared as young actress with various stock organizations, then
   joined Sir Henry Irving's company and remained with this until his death in 1905.
   She became known throughout the English-speaking world as the greatest living interpreter of Shakespeare, and is still regarded as the finest of her time,   long
   after her death on July 21, 1928. All her records are of Shakespearean excerpts.

Dramatic speech, unacc.                        New York, February 21, 1911.

| B-9988-1-2 | Mercy Speech ("The Merchant Of Venice" | Rejected |
| | - Act 4) | |
| C-9989-1 | Potion Scene ("Romeo and Juliet," Act 4) | - |
| B-9990-1 | I Have Brought Claudio ("Much Ado About | Vic 64191 |
| | Nothing," Act 2) | |
| C-9991-1 | Ophelia's Mad Scene - Part 1 ("Hamlet") | Rejected |
| C-9992-1 | Ophelia's Mad Scene - Part 2 ("Hamlet") | Vic 74239 |
| B-9993-1 | Manilius, Hermione And Ladies ("A | Vic 64193 |
| | Winter's Tale," Act 2, Scene 1) | |

New York, February 28, 1911.

| B-9988-3 | Mercy Speech ("The Merchant Of Venice," | Vic 64194, HMV 2-3535 |
| | Act 4) | |
| C-9989-2 | Potion Scene ("Romeo and Juliet," Act 4) | Vic 74240 |
| B-10017-1 | Death Of Falstaff ("Henry V," Act 2, | Rejected |
| | Scene 3) | |

## KAY THOMPSON

B. 1902; studied music as a child, and was a piano prodigy with the St. Louis  Symphony Orchestra at 16; appeared with the Mills Brothers in California in 1929 before they achieved world fame; joined Fred Waring's organization as vocalist  and
   arranger; to MGM, 1942, and became vocal coach for Judy Garland; made vocal score
   for films (BROADWAY RHYTHM; THE HARVEY GIRLS; THE KID FROM BROOKLYN, in which she
   acted; ZIEGFELD FOLLIES); composed for the latter film and NO LEAVE, NO LOVE; she
   also appeared in MANHATTAN MERRY-GO-ROUND, STARS OVER BROADWAY and FUNNY FACE.Al-
   though the labels of her records suggest she was also a bandleader, she was  only
   accompanied by studio musicians.

KAY THOMPSON AND THE BOYS : Vocal, with studio orchestra.
                                        New York, November 11, 1935.

| B-18261-1 | You Let Me Down | Br 7560, Epic SN-6059 |
| B-18262-1 | You Hit The Spot | - |
| B-18263-1 | Out Of Sight, Out Of Mind | Br 7564 |
| B-18264-1 | Don't Mention Love To Me | - |

KAY THOMPSON AND HER ORCHESTRA : As above.
                                        New York, April 13, 1937.

| BS-07785-1 | Carelessly | Vic 25564 |
| BS-07786-1 | There's A Lull In My Life | - |
| BS-07787-1 | It Had To Be You | Vic 25582 |
| BS-07788-1 | Exactly Like You | - |

## CAROLYN  THOMSON

The star of the American original production of THE VAGABOND KING at the Casino,New
   York, September 21, 1925.

Vocal, acc. by O/Leroy Shield, with the Victor Light Opera Company.
                                        New York, December 7, 1925.

BVE-34119-1  Only A Rose ("The Vagabond King")     Vic 19897, HMV B-2426

## LAWRENCE TIBBETT

B. Bakersfield, Calif., 1897; began his career as an actor with Tyrone Powers' Company; learned singing, and was accepted by the Metropolitan Opera Company after a
   single audition; made many records, mostly of operatic and concert music  outside

the scope of this book, but also starred in several films (THE ROGUE SONG and THE
NEW MOON (1930); THE SOUTHERNER and CUBAN LOVE SONG (1930-1931);METROPOLITAN(1935)
and UNDER YOUR SPELL (1937), and only the records he made of songs he sang in them
are listed here. D. 1960.

Vocal, acc. by O/Nat Shilkret.              New York, January 13, 1930.

BVE-58187-1  The Rogue Song (Film "The Rogue Song")Vic 1446, HMV DA-1101
BVE-58188-3  The Narrative (Film "The Rogue Song")      -              -

                                            New York, January 15, 1930.

BVE-58195-2  When I'm Looking At You (Film "The    Vic 1447, HMV DA-1102
               Rogue Song")
BVE-58196-3  The White Dove (Film "The Rogue Song")    -              -

                                            New York, March 5, 1931.

BVE-67492-2  Without A Song (Film "The Southerner")Vic 1507, HMV DA-1206
BVE-67493-2  Life Is A Dream (Film "The Southerner")    -              -

  Acc. by Stuart Willie-p.                  New York, March 6, 1931.

BVE-67494-1  Wanting You (Film "The New Moon")      Vic 1506, HMV DA-1200
BVE-67495-1  Lover, Come Back To Me (Film "The New     -              -
               Moon")

                                            Hollywood, October 26, 1931.

PBS-68327-3  Tramps At Sea (Film "Cuban Love Song")Vic 1550, HMV DA-1251
PBS-68328-2  Cuban Love Song (Film "Cuban Love Song")   -              -

  Acc. by O/? Nat Shilkret.                 New York, October 9, 1935.

CS-95371-2  On The Road To Mandalay (Film            Vic 11877, HMV DB-3036
               "Metropolitan")

## HARRY   TIERNEY

B. Perth Amboy, N. J., May 21, 1894; learned piano and became concert pianist in the
  U. S. A. and Europe before becoming a composer of scores for musical comedies, such
  as WHAT NEXT ? (1917); IRENE (1919); UP SHE GOES and GLORY (1922); KID BOOTS(1923);
  ZIEGFELD FOLLIES OF 1924; RIO RITA (1927); CROSS MY HEART (1928); also individual
  songs such as SAW MILL RIVER ROAD (1923). D. New York, March 22, 1965.

Piano acc. to Dorothy Lee (vocal).          Hollywood, August 11, 1930.

PBVE-1303   My One Ambition Is You                  Vic test

## VESTA TILLEY

B. Worcester, England, May 13, 1864; stage debut at $3\frac{1}{2}$ in Gloucester; at 5 she first
  appeared in male clothes, and from that time on, her act was principally that of a
  male impersonator; London debut at the Royal, Holborn, March 25, 1878; made   many
  successful tours of the U.S.A., appearing first at Tony Pastor's, New York,   April
  16, 1894; also played the title role in MY LADY MOLLY in New York (Daly's,  1904);
  popularized a large number of typical British music-hall songs, played in   pantomime all over the British Isles. D. 1952.

Vocal, acc. by studio orchestra.            London, c. October, 1904.

        Following In Father's Footsteps         Pathe 50210
        The Wise Old Owl                        Pathe 50211
        Algy (The Piccadilly Johnny With The    Pathe 50212
          Little Glass Eye)
        Royal Artillery                         Pathe 50213, 294, 1206
        I'm A Bachelor                          Pathe 50214   -       -

London, issued on dates shown in brackets.

| | | |
|---|---|---|
| I'm Following In Father's Footsteps | Ed 13571 | (March, 1907) |
| The King Of The House Is Baby | Ed 13581 | (April, 1907) |
| Jolly Good Luck To The Girls Who Love The Soldiers | Ed 13583 | (May, 1907) |
| It's Part Of A Policeman's Duty | Ed 13593 | (June, 1907) |
| Algy (The Piccadilly Johnny) | Ed 13603 | (July, 1907) |
| The Royal Artillery | Ed 13620 | (August, 1907) |
| The Seaside Smile | Ed 13624 | (September, 1907) |
| When The Right Girl Comes Along | Ed 13634 | (November, 1907) |
| Following A Fellow With A Face Like Me | Ed 13732 | (April, 1908) |
| I'm The Idol Of The Girls | Ed 13752 | (May, 1908) |

London, c. March, 1910.

Give It To Father                          Amb 12178 (June, 1910)

London, c. December, 1910.

LXO-1110  Jolly Good Luck To The Girl Who Loves   Jumbo 545, Sc 404, Valkyrie 373
          A Soldier
LXO-1111  Come And Be One Of The Midnight Sons        -                            -
          The Girls I Left Behind Me            Jumbo 561
          Sidney's Holidays                        -        Sc 404

London, c. July, 1911.

Introduce Me To The Lady               Jumbo 670
Mont From Monte Carlo                      -

London, c. October, 1913.

LXO-2468  I'll Show You Around Paree            Jumbo 1096
LXO-2469  What Would The Seaside Do Without The     -
          Ladies ?
          Let's Make A Night Of It Tonight     Jumbo 1062
          Aunt Matilda                             -
          The Maiden's Sea Trip                Clm 501
          When A Fellow's In Love                  -

Acc. by O/Albert W. Ketelbey.       London, c. July, 1915.

29751     Jolly Good Luck To The Girl Who Loves A   Re G-7079
          Soldier
29752     The Army Of Today's All Right             -

London, c. February, 1917.

75367     Where Are The Girls Of The Old Brigade ?  Col L-1153
75368     It's A Fine Time For A Soldier (Six Days'   -
          Leave)

London, c. February, 1919.

76384     I've A Bit Of A Blighty One            Col L-1317
76385     Sidney's In Civvies Again                  -

## FRANK TINNEY

B. Philadelphia, Pa., March 29, 1878; blackface comedian very popular on both sides
of the Atlantic, principally in vaudeville, but also appeared in SOMETIME (Vaude-
February 5, 1925) in London; first appeared there in 1913. D. Northport, New York
November 28, 1940.

Humorous monologues.                New York, August 25, 1915.

45966-    Frank Tinney's First Record            Col A-1834, Veritas 107

New York, September 2, 1915.

45980-   Frank Tinney's Second Record              Col A-1854, Veritas 107

London, July, 1924.

A-1067   Hello, Ernest - Part 1                    Col 3490
A-1068   Hello, Ernest - Part 2                    -

A-1096   Hello, Ernest - Part 3                    Col 3491
A-1097   Hello, Ernest - Part 4                    -

## STELLA TOBIN

American vaudeville artist of the "coon-shouting" variety, very popular during   the
   opening years of the century.

Vocal, acc. by studio orchestra.          New York, late 1907.

         Will He Answer "Goo-Goo" ?             Ed 9758
         Tipperary                              Ed 9824
         Daddy's Little Tomboy Girl             Ed 9852

New York, issued July, 1908.

         Love Me Like I Like To Be Loved        Ind 788
         He And She In Vaudeville (w/Steve Porter) Ind 818

Acc. by O/Charles A. Prince.               New York, c. October, 1909.

   4152-   I'm Going To Do What I Please          Col A-737, D&R 3645

## DICK TODD

B. Montreal, Canada, 1914; secured regular radio work on NBC in New York, 1938, with
   Larry Clinton's orchestra, later as soloist; r.n. Arthur Todd (so-described on the
   first two Bluebird records); made some short films; very popular during the   years
   immediately preceding and during World War II as "The Canadian Crosby."

Vocal, acc. by own guitar.                 New York, February 10, 1938.

BS-019644-   Any Old Place Is Lover's Lane (As      BB B-7446
                Long As I'm With You)
BS-019645-1  Thanks For The Memory                  BB B-7434
BS-019646-1  Goodnight, Sweet Dreams, Goodnight     -
BS-019647-1  Love Walked In                         BB B-7446

   Acc. by studio orchestra.               New York, April 28, 1938.

BS-022668-1  Cathedral In The Pines                 Vic 25839
BS-022669-1  As Long As We're Together              Vic 25843
BS-022670-1  The Girl In The Bonnet Of Blue         Vic 25839
BS-022671-1  Ride, Tenderfoot, Ride                 Vic 25843

Vocalist with Larry Clinton and his Orchestra.
                                           New York, June 22, 1938.

BS-023718-1  The Sunny Side Of Things               Vic 25892

Vocal, acc. by O/Larry Clinton.            New York, July 12, 1938.

BS-024022-1  Hi-Yo Silver                           Vic 26003
BS-024023-1  There's A Faraway Look In Your Eye     Vic 26004
BS-024024-1  So Help Me (If I Don't Love You)       -
BS-024025-1  Figaro                                 Vic 26003

Vocalist with Larry Clinton and his Orchestra.
                                           New York, July 16, 1938.

BS-024047-1  Change Partners                        Vic 26010

Vocal, acc. by O/Leonard Joy.          New York, September 14, 1938.

| BS-026881-1 | Someone Thinks Of Someone | Vic 26058 |
| BS-026882-1 | When I Go A-Dreamin' | Vic 26057 |
| BS-026883-1 | Love Doesn't Grow On Trees | Vic 26058 |
| BS-026884-1 | Sixty Seconds Got Together | Vic 26057 |

New York, October 10, 1938.

| BS-027478-1 | Gardenias | BB B-7874 |
| BS-027479-1 | In Ole Oklahoma | - |
| BS-027480-1 | You Look Good To Me | BB B-7888 |
| BS-027481-1 | This Is Madness (To Love Like This) | - |

New York, November 9, 1938.

| BS-028934-1 | When Paw Was Courtin' Maw | BB B-10034 | |
| BS-028935-1 | You're The Only Star (In My Blue Heaven) - | | HMV BD-719 |
| | (w/The Three Reasons - Girls' Trio) | | |
| BS-028936-1 | It Took A Million Years | BB B-10045 | |
| BS-028937-1 | Say It With A Kiss | - | |

New York, December 17, 1938.

| BS-030725- | Deep Purple | BB B-10072, HMV BD-699 |
| BS-030726- | Are You In The Mood For Mischief ? | - |
| BS-030727-1 | Waltz Medley (Gus Edwards Hits) | BB B-10097, HMV BD-750 |
| | (Intro. School Days/I Can't Tell Why I Love You/Sunbonnet Sue) |
| BS-030728-1 | Fox Trot Medley (Gus Edwards Hits) | -              - |
| | (Intro. By The Light Of The Silvery Moon/Tammany/Goodbye, Little Girl, Goodbye) |

New York, February 8, 1939.

| BS-031895-1 | I Get Along Without You Very Well (w/ | BB B-10150, HMV BD-719 |
| | The Three Reasons) | |
| BS-031896-1 | I Promise You (w/The Three Reasons) | - |
| BS-031897-1 | Little Lad (w/The Three Reasons) | BB B-10144 |
| BS-031898-1 | Penny Serenade (w/The Three Reasons) | - |

New York, March 13, 1939.

| BS-032971-1 | Little Sir Echo (w/The Three Reasons) | BB B-10169, HMV BD-699 |
| BS-032972-1 | I Can't Get You Out Of My Mind (w/ | -         HMV BD-705 |
| | The Three Reasons) | |
| BS-032973-1 | At A Little Hot Dog Stand (w/The | BB B-10183 |
| | Three Reasons) | |
| BS-032974-1 | I'm Building A Sailboat Of Dreams | -         HMV BD-705 |
| | (w/The Three Reasons) | |

New York, March 31, 1939.

| BS-035388-1 | Mary's A Grand Old Name | BB B-10198 | |
| BS-035389-1 | Girl Of My Dreams | - | HMV BD-737 |
| BS-035390-1 | You've Got Me Crying Again | BB B-10217 | - |
| BS-035391-1 | Somebody Nobody Knows | - | |

New York, April 24, 1939.

| BS-035782-1 | Why Begin Again ? (w/The Three | BB B-10234, HMV BD-730 |
| | Reasons) | |
| BS-035783-1 | Blue Evening (w/The Three Reasons) | - |
| BS-035784-1 | Gotta Hit That Texas Trail Tonight | BB B-10274 |
| | (w/The Three Reasons) | |

New York, May 1, 1939.

| | | | |
|---|---|---|---|
| BS-036574-1 | Prairie Boy (w/The Three Reasons) | BB B-10274 | |
| BS-036575-1 | A Home In The Clouds (w/The Three Reasons) | BB B-10272 | |
| BS-036576-2 | I Paid For The Lie That I Told You (w/The Three Reasons) | - | HMV BD-730 |

New York, June 16, 1939.

| | | |
|---|---|---|
| BS-037652-1 | Guess I'll Go Back Home (This Summer) (w/The Three Reasons) | BB B-10327 |
| BS-037653-1 | What Goes On Behind Your Eyes ? (w/The Three Reasons) | BB B-10335 |
| BS-037654-1 | Moonlight Serenade (w/The Three Reasons) | BB B-10327, HMV BD-811 |
| BS-037655-1 | A Table In A Corner | BB B-10335 |

New York, July 7, 1939.

| | | |
|---|---|---|
| BS-038235-1 | Time On My Hands | BB B-10374, HMV BD-796 |
| BS-038236-1 | Manhattan | - |
| BS-038237-1 | Drifting Down The River Of Dreams | BB B-10355 |
| BS-038238-2 | Old Mill Wheel | - |

New York, August 17, 1939.

| | | |
|---|---|---|
| BS-041579-1 | Blue Orchids | BB B-10398, HMV BD-779 |
| BS-041580-1 | One Morning In May | BB B-10431, HMV BD-796 |
| BS-041581-1 | Lazy River | - |
| BS-041582-2 | It's A Hundred To One (I'm In Love) | BB B-10398, HMV BD-779 |

New York, September 20, 1939.

| | | | |
|---|---|---|---|
| BS-042706-1 | At Least You Could Say "Hello" | BB B-10435 | |
| BS-042707-1 | Am I Proud ? | - | |
| BS-042708-1 | Sweet Dreams, Sweetheart | BB B-10445 | |
| BS-042709-1 | To You, Sweetheart, Aloha (w/The Three Reasons) | - | HMV BD-912 |

New York, October 24, 1939.

| | | | |
|---|---|---|---|
| BS-043307-1 | It's The Talk Of The Town | BB B-10559 | |
| BS-043308-1 | I Can't Get Started | BB B-10755 | |
| BS-043309-1 | It's A Hap-Hap-Happy Day | BB B-10488, HMV BD-811 | |
| BS-043310-1 | The Creaking Old Mill On The Creek | - | HMV BD-836 |

New York, December 8, 1939.

| | | |
|---|---|---|
| BS-045735-1 | After All | BB B-10538 |
| BS-045736-1 | Angel In Disguise | BB B-10636, HMV BD-854 |
| BS-045737-1 | In Our Little Part Of Town | BB B-10538 |
| BS-045738-1 | The Gaucho Serenade | BB B-10559 |

New York, January 22, 1940.

| | | | |
|---|---|---|---|
| BS-046486-1 | Last Night's Gardenias | BB B-10599 | |
| BS-046487-1 | Saddle Your Dreams | BB B-10596 | |
| BS-046488-1 | The Singing Hills | - | HMV BD-836 |
| BS-046489-1 | Angel | BB B-10599 | |

New York, February 12, 1940.

| | | |
|---|---|---|
| BS-047046-1 | Tiny Old Town | BB B-10621, HMV BD-854 |
| BS-047047-1 | Moments In The Moonlight | BB B-10667 |
| BS-047048-1 | I'll Be Seeing You | BB B-10636 |
| BS-047049-1 | With The Wind And The Rain In Your Hair | BB B-10621 |

New York, March 11, 1940.

| | | |
|---|---|---|
| BS-047099-1 | I'll Be With You In Apple-Blossom Time | BB B-10755 |
| BS-048100-1 | Cecilia | BB B-10677, HMV BD-912 |
| BS-048101-1 | My ! My ! | BB B-10667 |
| BS-048102-1 | Polka Dots And Moonbeams | BB B-10677 |

New York, April 15, 1940.

| | | |
|---|---|---|
| BS-048903-1 | Write A Letter To Your Mother | BB B-10697 |
| BS-048904-1 | Mother Machree | - |
| BS-048905-1 | Devil May Care | BB B-10729, HMV BD-869 |
| BS-048906-1 | Make-Believe Island | - |
| BS-048907-1 | You Can't Brush Me Off (w/Dinah Shore) | BB B-10720 |
| BS-048908-1 | Outside Of That I Love You (w/Dinah Shore) | - |

New York, May 29, 1940.

| | | |
|---|---|---|
| BS-050891-1 | It's All Over Now (I Won't Worry) (w/male trio) | BB B-10769 |
| BS-050892-1 | When The Swallows Come Back To Capistrano (w/male trio) | -           HMV BD-869 |
| BS-050893-1 | All This And Heaven Too | BB B-10789, HMV BD-894 |
| BS-050894-1 | Where Do You Keep Your Heart ? | -          - |

New York, July 1, 1940.

| | | |
|---|---|---|
| BS-051591-1 | Orchids For Remembrance | BB B-10805 |
| BS-051592-1 | Can't Get Indiana Off My Mind | BB B-10822 |
| BS-051593-1 | My Greatest Mistake | - |
| BS-051594-1 | I'm Waiting For Ships That Never Come In | BB B-10805 |

New York, August 6, 1940.

| | | |
|---|---|---|
| BS-054688-1 | We're All Americans (All True Blue) (w/male quartet) | BB B-10840 |
| BS-054689-1 | Sweet Lorraine (w/male quartet) | - |

New York, August 7, 1940.

| | | |
|---|---|---|
| BS-054695-1 | You've Got Your Mother's Big Blue Eyes | BB B-10861 |

New York, October 23, 1940.

| | | |
|---|---|---|
| BS-057020-1 | A Nightingale Sang In Berkeley Square | BB B-10912 |
| BS-057021-1 | Goodnight, Mother | - |
| BS-057022-1 | Dream Valley | BB B-10933 |
| BS-057023-1 | Adi-Adi-Adios | - |

New York, November 14, 1940.

| | | |
|---|---|---|
| BS-057643-1 | Three At A Table For Two | BB B-10968 |
| BS-057644-1 | Along The Santa Fe Trail | BB B-10949, HMV BD-917 |
| BS-057645-1 | Love Of My Life | BB B-10968          - |
| BS-057646-1 | Do You Know Why ? | BB B-10949 |

New York, November 15, 1940.

| | | |
|---|---|---|
| BS-057647-1 | RCA Personal Radio Spot - 50 seconds (sic) | |

New York, January 3, 1941.

| | | |
|---|---|---|
| BS-058736-1 | The Mem'ry Of A Rose | BB B-11024 |
| BS-058737-1 | You Forgot About Me | - |

(continued on page 628)

New York, January 3, 1941 (cont.)

| | | |
|---|---|---|
| BS-058738-1 | Rose Of The Rockies | BB B-11044 |
| BS-058739-1 | When You Said "Goodbye" | - |

New York, March 7, 1941.

| | | |
|---|---|---|
| BS-062741-1 | It Makes No Difference Now | BB B-11142 |
| BS-062742-1 | Worried Mind | - |
| BS-062743-1 | Rushin' Around On Rush Street (w/ The Four Belles) | BB B-11112 |
| BS-062744-1 | Just A Little Bit South Of North Carolina (w/The Four Belles) | BB B-11091 |
| BS-062745-1 | It Was Wonderful Then (And It's Wonderful Now) (w/The Four Belles) | BB B-11112 |
| BS-062746-1 | We Go Well Together (w/The Four Belles) | BB B-11091 |

New York, April 17, 1941.

| | | |
|---|---|---|
| BS-063781-2 | I Wonder What's Become Of Sally ? | BB B-11212 |
| BS-063782-1 | Say It Isn't So | - |
| BS-063783-1 | Together | BB B-11156 |
| BS-063784-1 | Maria Elena | - |

New York, June 9, 1941.

| | | |
|---|---|---|
| BS-065689-1 | A Little Street Where Old Friends Meet | BB B-11195 |
| BS-065690-2 | Wasn't It You ? | - |

New York, July 9, 1941.

| | | |
|---|---|---|
| BS-066800-1 | Glad Rag Doll | BB B-11246 |
| BS-066801-1 | Don't Julia Fool Ya | BB B-11228 |
| BS-066802-1 | In The Middle Of A Dance | BB B-11246 |
| BS-066803-1 | Shepherd Serenade | BB B-11228 |

New York, September 5, 1941.

| | | |
|---|---|---|
| BS-067753-1 | I Don't Want To Set The World On Fire | BB B-11291 |
| BS-067754-1 | Concerto For Two | - |
| BS-067755-1 | Delilah | BB B-11335 |
| BS-067756-1 | Orange Blossom Lane | - |

New York, September 17, 1941.

| | | |
|---|---|---|
| BS-067907-1 | Sweethearts Or Strangers | BB B-11309 |
| BS-067908-1 | The Sun Has Gone Down On Our Love | BB B-11367 |
| BS-067909-1 | It's Your Worry Now | BB B-11309 |
| BS-067910-1 | Pay Me No Mind | BB B-11367 |

New York, November 26, 1941.

| | | |
|---|---|---|
| BS-068367-1 | Tropical Magic | BB B-11387 |
| BS-068368- | 'Tis Autumn | - |
| BS-068369-1 | The White Cliffs Of Dover | BB B-11406 |
| BS-068370-1 | How About You ? | - |

New York, January 11, 1942.

| | | |
|---|---|---|
| BS-068850-1 | Tica-Ti-Tica-Ta | BB B-11451 |
| BS-068851-1 | Dreamsville, Ohio | BB B-11440 |

New York, January 12, 1942.

| | | |
|---|---|---|
| BS-068854-1 | Loretta | BB B-11451 |
| BS-068855-1 | Sing Me A Song Of The Islands | BB B-11440 |

New York, February 19, 1942.

| | | |
|---|---|---|
| BS-071948-1 | I Told You So | BB B-11494 |
| BS-071949-2 | Angeline | BB B-11482 |
| BS-071950-1 | Dear Old Pal Of Mine | - |
| BS-071951-1 | I'm Thinking Tonight Of My Blue Eyes | BB B-11494 |

New York, March 25, 1942.

| | | |
|---|---|---|
| BS-073484-1 | It's Unbelievable | BB B-11531 |
| BS-073485-1 | Someday, Sweetheart | - |

New York, June 4, 1942.

| | | |
|---|---|---|
| BS-075257-1 | My Great-Great-Grandfather | BB B-11557 |
| BS-075258-1 | The Singing Sands Of Alamosa | - |

New York, July 22, 1942.

| | | |
|---|---|---|
| BS-075439-1 | I'm Old-Fashioned | BB B-11577 |
| BS-075440-1 | When The Lights Go On Again (All Over The World) | - |

## THELMA TODD

B. c. 1908; d. mysteriously in 1935; in her short life she impressed her  hilarious
style of humour on audiences who enjoyed MONKEY BUSINESS (1931); HORSE   FEATHERS
(1932); COUNSELLOR AT LAW (1933); MAID IN HOLLYWOOD (1934) and others,  including
some short films.

Vocal, acc. by Leroy Shield-p.          Culver City, Calif., April 27, 1929.

| | | |
|---|---|---|
| BVE-312-1 | Let Me Call You Sweetheart/If I Had You | Vic test |
| BVE-313-1 | Honey (w/Eddie Dunn) | - |

## PINKY TOMLIN

B. Eros, Ark., September 9, 1908; educated at University of Oklahoma, where he led a
dance band; to California, 1934; became singer in night-clubs and theatres; wrote
several songs that became big hits (THE OBJECT OF MY AFFECTION (1934); THE LOVE-
BUG WILL BITE YOU (IF YOU DON'T WATCH OUT) (1937) and LOVE IS ALL (1940),   among
others.

Vocal, acc. by studio orchestra.        Los Angeles, January 10, 1935.

| | | |
|---|---|---|
| LA-317- | A Porter's Love Song (To A Chambermaid) | Br 7377 |

Los Angeles, January 11, 1935.

| | | |
|---|---|---|
| LA-318-A | Sittin' Bull/Shine | Br 7378 |
| LA-319- | He's A Curbstone Cutie (They Call Him Jelly Bean) | Br 7377 |
| LA-320-A | Ragtime Cowboy Joe | Br 7378 |

Acc. by O/Russ Plummer.          Los Angeles, July 8, 1935.

| | | |
|---|---|---|
| LA-383-B | That's What You Think | Br 7502, Dec F-5825 |
| LA-384- | When Work Is Through | Br 7525 |
| LA-385-B | Sweet | Br 7502, Dec F-5825 |
| LA-386- | The Trouble With Me Is You | Br 7525 |

Acc. by O/Cy Feuer.          Los Angeles, December 29, 1935.

| | | |
|---|---|---|
| LA-1084- | I Won't Take No For An Answer | Br 7653 |
| LA-1085- | Barnyard Serenade | - |
| LA-1086- | You Can Depend On Me | Br 7594 |
| LA-1087- | Changing My Ambitions | - |

Los Angeles, August 19, 1936.

| | | |
|---|---|---|
| LA-1152- | Got To Dance My Way To Heaven | Br 7731 |
| LA-1153- | You're Not The Kind | - |
| LA-1154- | I'm Right Back Where I Started | Br 7811 |
| LA-1155- | Tetched In The Haid | Rejected |

Los Angeles, November 19, 1936.

| | | |
|---|---|---|
| LA-1191- | Sittin' On The Edge Of My Chair | Br 7897 |
| LA-1192- | With Love And Kisses | - |

Los Angeles, December 6, 1936.

| | | |
|---|---|---|
| LA-1201- | A Rhyme For Love | Br 7811 |

Acc. by O/Joe Haymes.                New York, March 9, 1937.

| | | |
|---|---|---|
| B-20770- | The Love Bug Will Bite You (If You Don't Watch Out) | Br 7849 |
| B-20771- | I'm Just A Country Boy At Heart | - |

Acc. by O/Cy Feuer.                Los Angeles, January 28, 1938.

| | | |
|---|---|---|
| LA-1564- | Home Town | Br 8082 |
| LA-1565- | My First Impression Of You | Br 8091 |
| LA-1566- | Lost And Found | - |
| LA-1567- | Shenanigans | Br 8082 |

Acc. by O/Harry Sosnik.                Los Angeles, April 25, 1938.

| | | |
|---|---|---|
| DLA-1280-A | The Old Oaken Bucket | Dec 1821, 25333 |
| DLA-1281-A | Smiles | - |
| DLA-1282- | Red Wing | Dec 2187 |
| DLA-1283- | Red River Valley | - |

Los Angeles, August 15, 1938.

| | | |
|---|---|---|
| DLA-1404-A | In Ole Oklahoma (w/The Foursome) | Dec 2014, 25296, Br 02716 |
| DLA-1405-A | Ragtime Cowboy Joe (w/The Foursome) | -      -      - |
| DLA-1406-A | What Are You Doin' Tonight ? | Dec 2018, Br 02906 |
| DLA-1407-A | Rosie The Redskin | -      - |

Acc. by Texas Jim Lewis and his Band.   Los Angeles, December 17, 1940.

| | | |
|---|---|---|
| DLA-2278- | The Object Of My Affection | Dec 3649, 7-1 |
| DLA-2279- | I Did It And I'm Glad | - |
| DLA-2280- | What's The Reason (I'm Not Pleasin' You) | Dec 3811, 25333 |
| DLA-2281- | The Love Bug Will Bite You (If You Don't Watch Out) | - |

## ARTHUR TRACY

B. Philadelphia, Pa.; wanted to be an accountant, but was offered leading role in a Shubert production of BLOSSOM TIME; travelled with this, getting valuable experience for stage and film career; sang with various dance bands, thus reached radio stardom; began film career in THE BIG BROADCAST (1932), coincidentally with huge success of his English version of the Spanish (Cuban) song MARTA; to London, summer of 1935, remained there until 1939, making some films (LIMELIGHT (1936); THE STREET SINGER (1937); FOLLOW YOUR STAR (1938), etc.); returned to London, 1948 to find he was still very much appreciated; although out of show-business since 1950 he still returns to London from time to time, where there is a fan-club operating on a firm basis. Always known as "The Street Singer."

Vocalist with Manolo Castro and his Havana Yacht Club Orchestra.
New York, July 10, 1931.

BS-70119-2  Marta (Rambling Rose Of The Wildwood)  Vic LOC-1010 (vocal part only)
(continued on page 631)

New York, July 10, 1931 (cont.)

BS-70121-1  There's No Other Girl (After Loving   Vic 22768
                You)
BS-70122-1  I'm All Dressed Up With A Broken Heart        -

   Acc. by own piano-accordion.          New York, c. October 9, 1931.

E-37247-A  Marta (Rambling Rose Of The Wildwood)  Br 6216, Pan 25179, Dec F-5608,
                                                    F-6520, 7-3

New York, November 4, 1931.

E-37347-A  Call Me Darling (Call Me Sweetheart,   Br 6216, Pan 25179, Dec F-5608
                Call Me Dear)

   Acc. by Peggy Riat-p, with speech by Kenneth Roberts.
                                New York, November 18, 1931.

BS-70956-1  The Street Singer Unemployment        Vic Special Record
                Record (Intro. Marta/Do You Share ?)

   Acc. by own piano-accordion.          New York, c. December 4, 1931.

E-37443-   Home                                   Br 6227, Pan 25126, Dec F-6802
E-37444-   Save The Last Dance For Me                     -

New York, March 1, 1932.

B-11384-A  Auf Wiedersehen, My Dear               Br 6279, Pan 25206, Dec F-6802
B-11385-A  Candles In The Sky                     Rejected
B-11386-   Kiss Me Goodnight                      Br 6279

New York, April 11, 1932.

B-11686-   When A Pal Bids A Pal Goodbye          Br 6298, Pan 25225
B-11687-   My Mom                                      -            -

New York, July 8, 1932.

B-12039-   My Romance                             Br 6356, Pan 25269
B-12040-A  Masquerade                             Br 6346, 01345
B-12041-   Somewhere In The West                       -      Pan 25282
B-12042-A  As You Desire Me                       Br 6356, 01345

New York, November 14, 1932.

B-12580-A  When The Wandering Boy Comes Home      Br 6482, Dec F-3346
B-12581-   Play, Fiddle, Play                     Br 6433, Dec F-3437
B-12582-A  Take Me In Your Arms (Nothing But A Lie)   -    Dec F-3913
B-12583-A  I Want To Go Home                      Br 6482, Dec F-3346

New York, November 16, 1932.

B-12597-   Out Of The Darkness (You Have Come To  Br 6453, Dec F-3423
                Me)
B-12598-   A Boy And A Girl Were Dancing               -    Dec F-3437
B-12599-   Let's Dance                            Rejected ?
B-12600-A  And So To Bed                                   Dec F-3525
B-12601-   Arm In Arm                                      Dec F-3423

New York, December 8, 1932.

B-12698-A  Dreaming                               Dec F-3337
B-12699-A  Wanderer                                   -

New York, January 10, 1933.

B-12874-A  Funiculi' Funicula'                    Br 6546, Dec F-3462, Pan 25717
B-12875-A  Maria, Mari' !                              -       -           -

New York, February 14, 1933.

| | | | |
|---|---|---|---|
| B-13064-A | Here Lies Love | | Dec F-3495 |
| B-13065- | I Bring A Song | Br 6512, | Dec F-5753 |
| B-13066-A | Farewell To Arms | — | Dec F-3525 |
| B-13067-A | Can't We Meet Again ? (And Let's Be Sweethearts) | | Dec F-3495 |

Acc. by O/Victor Young.          New York, April 20, 1933.

| | | |
|---|---|---|
| B-13269-A | Gypsy Fiddles | Br 6561, Dec F-3577 |
| B-13270-A | In Old Vienna | —       — |

New York, May 5, 1933.

| | | |
|---|---|---|
| B-13301-A | My Gypsy Rhapsody | Br 6579, Dec F-3608 |
| B-13302-B | Reflections In The Water | —       — |
| B-13303-A | An Old, Old Man With An Old, Old Pipe (And An Old, Old Lady Beside Him) | Dec F-3637 |

New York, July 11, 1933.

| | | |
|---|---|---|
| B-13529-A | Sleep, My Darling, Sleep (Within My Arms) | Br 6614, Dec F-3913 |
| B-13530- | Blue Hours | Rejected |
| B-13531-A | Trouble In Paradise | Br 6614, Dec F-3637 |

Acc. by own piano-accordion.     New York, September 27, 1933.

| | | |
|---|---|---|
| B-14090- | Just A Year Ago Tonight | Dec F-3711 |
| B-14091- | The Last Round-Up | — |

Acc. by O/Ray Sinatra.           New York, January 4, 1934.

| | | |
|---|---|---|
| BS-81027- | I'll Have The Last Waltz With Mother | RZ MR-1278 |
| BS-81028- | How Was I To Know ? | RZ MR-1249 |
| BS-81029- | Everything I Have Is Yours | — |
| BS-81030-1 | If I Didn't Care | RZ MR-1278 |

Acc. by own piano-accordion.     New York, March 7, 1934.

| | | |
|---|---|---|
| B-14909-A | Play To Me, Gypsy (The Song I Love) | Dec F-3921 |
| B-14910-A | Home On The Range | — |

New York, March 28, 1934.

| | | |
|---|---|---|
| B-15004- | Let's Fall In Love | Dec F-3960 |
| B-15005- | Little Dutch Mill | — |

San Francisco, June 16, 1934.

| | | |
|---|---|---|
| SF-115- | My Song For You | Dec F-5187 |
| SF-116- | Gypsy Serenade | — |

San Francisco, July 3, 1934.

| | | |
|---|---|---|
| 152617-A | A Lonely Singing Fool | Dec F-5162 |
| 152618-A | Shadows On The Pavement | — |

NOTE:- This is a most unusual instance of a recording made in a Columbia studio by a Brunswick artist expressly for issue in Great Britain - on Decca !

New York, August 20, 1934.

| | | |
|---|---|---|
| 38353-C | Love In Bloom | Dec F-5209, Pan 25688 |
| 38354-A | Rollin' Home | Dec 108 -      — |

New York, September 21, 1934.

| | | |
|---|---|---|
| 38453-A | The Street Singer Medley (Your Favour-ites) - Part 1 (Intro. Marta/Home On The Range/Play To Me, Gypsy) | Dec 295, F-5292, Pan 25702 |

(continued on page 633)

New York, September 21, 1934.

| | | |
|---|---|---|
| 38462-A | The Street Singer Medley (Your Favour-<br>ites) - Part 2 (Intro. Call Me Darling/Masquerade/Auf Wiedersehen,   My<br>Dear) | Dec 295, F-5292, Pan 25702 |
| 38463-A | I Love You Truly | Dec 438, F-5248, F-7318 |
| 38464-B | Just A Poor Street Singer | Dec 108    - |

New York, November 2, 1934.

| | | | |
|---|---|---|---|
| 38942-A | Give Me A Heart To Sing To | | Dec F-5300 |
| 38943-A | (When Your Heart's On Fire) Smoke<br>Gets In Your Eyes | Dec 428    -<br>Pan 25650 | F-7407, |
| 38944- | With Every Breath I Take | | Dec F-5342, Pan 25651 |
| 38945- | June In January | | - |
| 38946-A | Ole Faithful | | Dec F-5294, Pan 25650 |
| 38947-A | Just A-Wearyin' For You | Dec 438,    - | F-6699, F-7318 |

New York, November 19, 1934.

| | | |
|---|---|---|
| 38944- | With Every Breath I Take | Dec rejected ? |

Acc. by own piano-accordion, with vn and celeste.

New York, March 26, 1935.

| | | |
|---|---|---|
| 39461- | Soon | Pan 25708 |
| 39462-A | My Heart Is An Open Book | Dec F-5607 |
| 39463- | It's Easy To Remember | Pan 25728 |
| 39464-A | Lovely To Look At | Dec 428, F-5628 |

New York, June 20, 1935.

| | | |
|---|---|---|
| 39642-A | One Night In Napoli | Dec F-6636 |
| 39643-A | Tell Me That You Love Me | Dec F-5830 |
| 39644-A | Love Me Forever | Dec 601, F-5628 |
| 39645-A | Ninon | Dec F-5607 |

Acc. by studio orchestra.                    London, July 26, 1935.

| | | |
|---|---|---|
| GB-7338-1 | When I Grow Too Old To Dream | Dec F-5624 |
| GB-7339-2 | In A Little Gypsy Tea Room | - |
| GB-7340-1 | Red Sails In The Sunset | Dec F-5661 |
| GB-7341-1 | Leave Me With A Love Song | - |

London, September 22, 1935.

| | | |
|---|---|---|
| GB-7406- | Twenty Miles To Nowhere (w/male<br>quartet) | Dec F-5745 |
| GB-7407- | East Of The Sun (And West Of The Moon) | Dec F-5697 |
| GB-7408- | The Wheel Of The Wagon Is Broken | - |

London, October 2, 1935.

| | | |
|---|---|---|
| GB-7454- | A Little Dash Of Dublin | Dec F-5745 |
| GB-7455- | The Rose In Her Hair | Dec F-5753 |
| GB-7456-1-2 | Cocktails For Two | Rejected |

London, November 1, 1935.

| | | |
|---|---|---|
| GB-7470- | Misty Islands Of The Highlands | Dec F-5713 |
| GB-7471- | It's My Mother's Birthday Today | - |
| GB-7472-1-2 | Stranded (Film "Limelight") | Rejected |
| GB-7473-1-2 | Nirewana (Film "Limelight") | - |

London, November 2, 1935.

| | | |
|---|---|---|
| GA-7474-2 | Eili, Eili | Dec K-826 |
| GB-7475-1-2 | We Were Meant To Meet Again (Film<br>"Limelight") | Rejected |

(continued on page 634)

ARTHUR TRACY (cont.)

London, November 2, 1935 (cont.)

GB-7476-1  Farewell, Sweet Señorita (Film          Dec F-5880
               "Limelight")
GB-7477-1-2  The Whistling Waltz (Film "Limelight")Rejected
GB-7478-   Stay Awhile (Film "Limelight")          Dec F-5882

London, December 15, 1935.

GB-7543-   As Long As Our Hearts Are Young         Dec F-5828
GB-7544-   Solitude                                -        F-6209
GB-7545-2  Trees                                   Dec F-5830, F-6520

London, January 5, 1936.

GB-7472-   Stranded (Film "Limelight")             Dec F-5882
GB-7473-   Nirewana (Film "Limelight")             Dec F-5881
GB-7475-   We Were Meant To Meet Again (Film       -
               "Limelight")
GB-7477-3  The Whistling Waltz (Film "Liemelight") Dec F-5880

London, January 18, 1936.

GB-7616-   Marilou                                 Dec F-5859
GB-7617-   On Treasure Island                      -
GB-7624-1  The Sunset Trail                        Dec F-5862
GB-7625-2  Old Ship O' Mine                        -
     NOTE:- Matrices GB-7618/7623 inclusive are not by Arthur Tracy.

New York, June 23, 1936.

61193-     Robins And Roses                        Dec F-6012
61194-A    All My Life                             Dec F-6013
61195-A    We'll Rest At The End Of The Trail      -
61196-     On The Beach At Bali-Bali               Dec F-6012

London, July 24, 1936.

TB-2325-1  Laughing Irish Eyes                     Dec F-6024
TB-2326-1  The Hills Of Old Wyomin'                -
TA-2327-1  A Chazendel oif Chabos (A Cantor For    Dec K-826
               The Sabbath)

London, September 4, 1936.

TB-2415-2  It's A Sin To Tell A Lie                Dec F-6071
TB-2416-1  When I'm With You                       -

London, October 7, 1936.

TB-2532-1  When The Poppies Bloom Again            Dec F-6138
TB-2533-1  Serenade In The Night                   Dec F-6136
TB-2534-2  South Sea Island Magic                  Dec F-6138
TB-2535-1  Old Sailor                              Dec F-6136

London, November 6, 1936.

TB-2620-1  Did Your Mother Come From Ireland ?     Dec F-6193
TB-2621-2  The Miller's Daughter, Marianne         -

London, December 4, 1936.

TB-2684-1  I'll Sing You A Thousand Love Songs     Dec F-6235
TB-2685-1  The Way You Look Tonight                -
TA-2686-1-2  If I Love Again                       Rejected
                        London, January 12, 1937.
TB-2745-2  In The Chapel In The Moonlight          Dec F-6251
TB-2746-1  I Dream Of San Marino                   -
TB-2747-   So Do I                                 Dec F-6285

London, January 22, 1937.

TB-2779-    Pennies From Heaven                      Dec F-6285

London, March 30, 1937.

TB-2939-1   Harbour Lights                          Dec F-6351
TB-2940-1   Goodnight, My Love                          -          Ecl ECM-2050
TB-2945-2   Halfway To Heaven (Film "The Street     Dec F-6475
            Singer")
TB-2946-1   Street Serenade (Film "The Street Singer") -
NOTE:- Matrices TB-2941/4 inclusive are not by Arthur Tracy.

London, April 8, 1937.

TB-2991-2   Across The Great Divide                 Dec F-6380
TB-2992-1   On The Trail Where The Sun Hangs Low        -

London, May 18, 1937.

TB-3061-1   Delyse                                  Dec F-6402
TB-3062-1   Choir Boy                                   -
TB-3063-    Keep Calling Me Sweetheart              Dec F-6427
TB-3064-1   When The Harvest Moon Is Shining        Dec F-6452

London, June 20, 1937.

TB-3106-    All Alone In Vienna                     Dec F-6427
TB-3113-1   In A Little French Casino               Dec F-6438
TB-3114-1   The Greatest Mistake Of My Life         Dec F-6452
TB-3115-1   Will You Remember ? (Sweetheart)        Dec F-6438
NOTE:- Matrices TB-3107/3112 inclusive are not by Arthur Tracy.

London, July 16, 1937.

TB-3152-1   September In The Rain                    Dec F-6432
TB-3163-1   Broken-Hearted Clown                        -
NOTE:- Matrices TB-3153/3162 inclusive are not by Arthur Tracy.

London, August 31, 1937.

DTB-3208-   Where Are You ?                         Dec F-6463
DTB-3209-   It Looks Like Rain In Cherry Blossom    Dec F-6465
            Lane
DTB-3216-   A Sailboat In The Moonlight             Dec F-6485
DTB-3217-   In An Old Cathedral Town                    -
NOTE:- Matrices DTB-3210/5 inclusive are not by Arthur Tracy.

London, October 7, 1937.

DTB-3244-1  Let Us Be Sweethearts Over Again        Dec F-6495
DTB-3245-2  Shake Hands With A Millionaire              -
DTB-3260-   Moon At Sea                             Dec F-6511
DTB-3261-   You Needn't Have Kept It A Secret           -
NOTE:- Matrices DTB-3246/3259 inclusive are not by Arthur Tracy.

London, October 14, 1937.

DTB-3287-2  My Gypsy Dream Girl (Film "Command      Dec F-6525
            Performance")
DTB-3288-2  Whistling Gypsy (Film "Command          Dec F-6526
            Performance")
DTB-3289-1  Danny Boy (Film "Command Performance")      -
DTB-3290-1  Dance, Gypsy, Dance (Film "Command      Dec F-6525
            Performance")

London, October 15, 1937.

DTB-3293-1  Can I Forget You ?                      Dec F-6564
DTB-3294-1  Sympathy                                Dec F-6572
DTB-3295-1  Mine Alone                              Dec F-6564

London, October 21, 1937.

DTB-3310-1  Was It Rain ?                                   Dec F-6524
DTB-3311-1  Moonlight On The Waterfall                      Dec F-6539
DTB-3312-1  The Little Boy That Santa Claus Forgot            -

Acc. by own piano-accordion, with piano and male voice chorus.
London, October 29, 1937.

DTB-3321-1  Home Town                                        Dec F-6524
DTB-3335-1  Tavern Ditties - Part 1 (Intro.                  Dec F-6538
              After The Ball/Two Lovely Black Eyes/Sweet Adeline)
DTB-3336-1  Tavern Ditties - Part 2 (Intro.                    -
              The Old Oaken Bucket/Sweet Genevieve/Daisy Bell)
NOTE:- Matrices DTB-3322/3334 inclusive are not by Arthur Tracy.

Acc. by small orchestra.              London, November 1, 1937.

DTB-3337-1  Old Pal Of Mine                                  Dec F-6541
DTB-3338-1  Little Old Lady                                    -
DTB-3339-1  Giannina Mia                              Dec F-6572, Ecl ECM-2050

Acc. by O/Peter Yorke.                London, December 14, 1937.

DTB-3444-1  De Lawd Loves His People To Sing        Dec F-6820
              (Film "Follow Your Star")
DTB-3445-1  Laugh, Clown, Laugh ! (Film "Follow          -
              Your Star")
DTB-3446-2  Goldilocks (Film "Follow Your Star")    Dec F-6819
DTB-3447-1  Waltz For Those In Love (Film "Follow        -
              Your Star")

London, December 16, 1937.

DTB-3448-1  Sailing Home                                     Dec F-6581
DTB-3449-1  When The Organ Played "O Promise Me"             Dec F-6699
DTB-3450-1  In The Mission By The Sea                        Dec F-6581
DTB-3451-   Water Lilies In The Moonlight                    Dec F-6612

Acc. by studio orchestra.             New York, December 30, 1937.

63120-      There's A Gold Mine In The Sky          Dec F-6592
63121-      Bei mir bist du schoen (Means That          -
              You're Grand)

New York, January 28, 1938.

63227-      Little Drummer Boy                       Dec F-6611
63228-A     The Girl In The Alice Blue Gown          Dec F-6636
63229-      Home Town                                Rejected

Acc. by small orchestra.              London, August 16, 1938.

DR-2808-    Somebody's Thinking Of You Tonight       Dec F-6730
DR-2809-    My Heaven In The Pines                       -
DR-2850-1   Goodnight, Angel                         Dec F-6761, Ecl ECM-2050
DR-2851-1   I Won't Tell A Soul (I Love You)             -              -
NOTE:- Matrices DR-2810/2849 inclusive are not by Arthur Tracy.

London, October 18, 1938.

DR-2975-1   Little Lady Make-Believe                 Dec F-6818, Ecl ECM-2050
DR-2976-1   The Sweetest Song In The World               -              -
DR-2995-1   Music, Maestro, Please                   Dec F-6863
DR-2996-1   The Red Maple Leaves                         -

London, November 21, 1938.

DR-3091-1   Everyone Must Have A Sweetheart          Dec F-6884
DR-3092-1   There's Rain In My Eyes                      -          Ecl ECM-2050

London, December 22, 1938.

DR-3197-1  Cinderella (Stay In My Arms)         Dec F-6924
DR-3198-1  I'm Singing A Song For The Old Folks      -

London, February 6, 1939.

DR-3263-1  Grandma Said                        Dec F-6949
DR-3264-1  The Umbrella Man                        -

London, February 22, 1939.

DR-3344-1  Two Sleepy People                   Dec F-6979
DR-3345-1  I Shall Always Remember You Smiling     -           Ecl ECM-2050

London, March 21, 1939.

DR-3418-   To Mother, With Love                Dec F-7020
DR-3419-   I Miss You In The Morning               -

London, May 18, 1939.

DR-3586-1  Speak To Me Of Love                 Dec F-7141
DR-3587-1  I'll See You Again                  Dec F-7142
DR-3588-1  Serenade ("Frasquita")              Dec F-7141, Ecl ECM-2050
DR-3589-1  Smilin' Through                     Dec F-7142

London, May 24, 1939.

DR-3596-1  I Paid For The Lue That I Told You  Dec F-7082
DR-3597-1  Au Revoir (But Not Goodbye)             -
DR-3598-1  Love's Last Word Is Spoken          Dec F-7143
DR-3599-1  Roses Of Picardy                        -           Ecl ECM-2050‡

London, May 26, 1939.

DR-3628-1  Ol' Man River                       Dec F-7144, Ecl ECM-2050
DR-3629-1  The Song Of Songs                       -
DR-3630-1  You Are My Heart's Delight          Dec F-7145
DR-3631-1  Ma Curly-Headed Babby                   -

London, June 1, 1939.

DR-3636-1  South Of The Border (Down Mexico Way)  Dec F-7094
DR-3637-1  (I'm Afraid) The Masquerade Is Over     -           Ecl ECM-2050

New York, January 4, 1940.

67024-A  Somewhere In France With You          Dec F-7394
67025-A  I Shall Be Waiting                        -
67026-A  Faithful Forever                      Dec 2967, F-7407
67027-   Marta (Rambling Rose Of The Wildwood)     -    F-6520, Ecl ECM-2050

New York, May 13, 1940.

67716-   Say It (Over Again)                    Dec F-7573
67717-   The Breeze And I                          -

Acc. by O/Victor Young.              Los Angeles, December 26, 1940.

DLA-2298-A  San Antonio Rose                   Dec F-7859, Ecl ECM-2050
DLA-2299-A  Along The Santa Fe Trail           Dec F-7837
DLA-2300-A  I'd Know You Anywhere              Dec F-7859
DLA-2301-A  We Three (My Echo, My Shadow And Me)  Dec F-7835
DLA-2302-A  Arthur Tracy's Message For England  Dec Special Record

Los Angeles, December 31, 1940.

DLA-2316-A  Frenesi                            Dec F-7837
DLA-2317-A  Chapel In The Valley               Dec F-8018
DLA-2318-A  You Forgot About Me                    -
DLA-2319-A  The Last Time I Saw Paris          Dec F-7835

Acc. by small instrumental group.        New York, February 19, 1942.

| | | |
|---|---|---|
| 70360- | The White Cliffs Of Dover | Dec F-8171 |
| 70361- | The Shrine Of St. Cecilia | Dec F-8160 |
| 70362- | Shepherd Serenade | Dec F-8171 |
| 70363- | When The Roses Bloom Again | Dec F-8160 |
| 70364-A-B | Russian Rose | Rejected |

## THE TRIX SISTERS

Helen and Josephine Trix were American vaudeville comediennes who were stars in New York as teenagers and in London as young women long before the "sisters" acts became popular as a fashion in music in the thirties. Helen was born in Newmanstown, Pa., August 21, 1892; Josephine, her younger sister, joined her sometime in the second decade of the twentieth century, and they made their London debut in a C. B. Cochran revue, THE LEAGUE OF NOTIONS (Oxford, January 17, 1921), in which the Dolly Sisters were also appearing (but who never recorded). The Trix Sisters also starred in A TO Z (Prince of Wales's, October 11, 1921), and TRICKS (Apollo, December 22, 1925), to both of which Helen contributed original material. As an act, they were pioneers of British radio, and appeared in several Royal Command Variety Performances. Helen Trix d. New York, November 18, 1951.

HELEN TRIX : Vocal, acc. by studio orchestra.
New York, October 17, 1906.

| | | |
|---|---|---|
| B-3905-1 | Is Marriage A Failure ? (w/Dan W. Quinn) | Vic 4914 |
| B-3906-2 | Fol -De-Iddley-I-Do (w/Dan W. Quinn) | Vic 4959 |
| B-3908-1 | The Bird On Nellie's Hat | Vic 4904 |
| | NOTE:- Matrix B-3907 is by Dan W. Quinn only. | |

New York, November 9, 1906.

| | | |
|---|---|---|
| B-4021-2 | The Next Horse I Ride On | Vic 4946 |
| E-4021-1 | The Next Horse I Ride On | - |
| B-4022-1 | You Can Never Tell From The Label | Rejected |
| E-4022-1 | You Can Never Tell From The Label | - |
| E-4023-2 | Chip O' The Block | Vic 4913 |
| B-4024-1-2 | Scotch And Polly | Rejected |
| B-4029-2 | It Ain't All Honey And It Ain't All Jam | Vic 4986 |
| E-4029-1 | It Ain't All Honey And It Ain't All Jam | - |

The following Edisons were issued in the months shown in brackets.

| | |
|---|---|
| Is Your Mother In, Molly Malone ? | Ed 9365 (October, 1906) |
| The Next Horse I Ride On | Ed 9392 (November, 1906) |
| Chip Of The Block | Ed 9426 (December, 1906) |
| The Bird On Nellie's Hat | Ed 9450 (January, 1907) |
| Whistle It (w/Ed Meeker-Billy Murray) | Ed 9471 (February, 1907) |
| I've Told His Missus All About Him | Ed 9534 (May, 1907) |
| Lulu And Her La-La-La | Ed 9574 (June, 1907) |

The following Indestructible cylinder was issued in March, 1908.

| | |
|---|---|
| Rum-Tiddley-Um-Tum-Tay | Ind 746 |

THE TRIX SISTERS : Vocal duets, acc. by ? George Fishberg-p.
Hayes, Middlesex, February 17, 1921.

| | | |
|---|---|---|
| HO-6089-AE | I Never Worry About The Morning ("The League Of Notions") | HMV rejected |
| HO-6090-AE | I Just Want To Give Myself Away ("The League Of Notions") | - |
| HO-6091-AE | That's How I Knew (That You Were The One For Me) ("The League Of Notions") | - |
| HO-6092-AE | There'll Come A Time ("The League Of Notions") | - |
| HO-6093-AE | Back To London Town ("The League Of Notions") | - |

Hayes, Middlesex, April 15, 1921.

| | | |
|---|---|---|
| Bb-70- | I Never Worry About The Morning ("The League Of Notions") | HMV B-1228 |
| Bb-71- | I Just Want To Give Myself Away ("The League Of Notions") | — |
| Bb-72-2 | That's How I Knew (That You Were The One For Me) ("The League Of Notions") | HMV B-1229 |
| Bb-73-1 | There'll Come A Time ("A To Z") | HMV B-1302 |
| Bb-74-2 | Back To London Town ("The League Of Notions") | HMV B-1229 |

Acc. by George Fishberg-p, or studio O/George W. Byng, as shown.

Hayes, Middlesex, November 23, 1921.

| | | |
|---|---|---|
| Bb-699- | I've Joined The Squirrel Family ("A To Z") - pGF | HMV B-1301 |
| Bb-700- | Noah's Ark ("A To Z") - pGF | HMV B-1327 |
| Bb-701- | Sweet Daddy, I Love You ("A To Z")-pGF | HMV B-1300 |
| Bb-702- | I'm Going Home ("A To Z") - pGF | — |
| Bb-703- | Keep Movin' (w/chorus) ("A To Z") -O/GWB | HMV B-1301 |
| Bb-704-2 | Dapper Dan (w/Jack Buchanan) ("A To Z") - O/GWB | HMV B-1302 |

Acc. by Helen Trix-p, or Josephine Trix-banjoline-ukulele.

London, February, 1925.

| | | |
|---|---|---|
| A-1793 | When You Go Away ("Tricks") | Col 3684 |
| A-1794 | We Don't Give A Darn About Nothin' ("Tricks") | — |
| A-1796 | Sweetie Do ("Tricks") | Col 3685 |
| A-1797 | No One Dances Like My Man (Helen Trix only) ("Tricks") | — |
| | The Georgia Weddin' ("Tricks") | Col 3601 |
| | In Honeysuckle Time | — |
| | Desperate Blues (Helen Trix only) | Col 3686 |
| | Trix's Boodle-Um-Boo (Banjoline acc.) | — |

London, October 27, 1925.

| | | |
|---|---|---|
| WA-2540-1-2 | Yes, Sir ! That's My Baby | Col rejected |
| WA-2541-1-2 | Bam Bam Bamy Shore | — |
| WA-2542-1-2-3 | I Wonder Where My Baby Is Tonight ? | — |
| WA-2543-1-2-3 | My Sweetie Turned Me Down | — |

London, January 30, 1926.

| | | |
|---|---|---|
| WA-2800-1-2 | My International Wedding Day ("Tricks") | Col rejected |
| WA-2801-1-2 | Vanity Fayre | — |

London, February 2, 1926.

| | | |
|---|---|---|
| WA-2808-1 | I Care For Him And He Cares For Her (I Care For Her And She Cares For Me) | Col 3914 |
| WA-2809-1 | I'm Sitting On Top Of The World | Col 3915 |
| WA-2810-2 | Ukulele Lullaby (w/piano and ukulele) | Col 3914 |
| WA-2811-2 | I'm Knee Deep In Daisies | Col 3915 |

New York, September 14, 1926.

| | | |
|---|---|---|
| | Timbuctoo | Vic test (un-numbered) |
| | Ukulele Lullaby | — |
| | Boo-La-Boo | — |

London, April 19, 1928.

| | | |
|---|---|---|
| WA-7270-1-2 | The Grass Grows Greener | Col rejected |
| WA-7271-1-2 | Henry's Made A Lady Out Of Lizzie | — |
| WA-7272-1-2 | Stay Out Of The South | — |
| WA-7273-1-2 | Where Is My Meyer ? | — |

London, September 12, 1928.

| | | |
|---|---|---|
| WA-7273-3 | Where Is My Meyer ? | Col 5043 |
| WA-7802-1 | Ready For The River | - |
| WA-7803-1 | Stay Out Of The South | Col 5031 |
| WA-7804-1 | A Hundred Years From Now | - |

Acc. by Helen Trix-p/Al Bowlly-u.        London, November 6, 1928.

| | | |
|---|---|---|
| WA-8068-2 | Sweet Ukulele Maid | Col 5149 |
| WA-8069-1 | Out Of The Dawn | - |
| WA-8070-1 | I Hope I Don't Meet Molly (On The Day | Col 5183 |
| | I Marry Flo) | |
| WA-8071-1 | My Rock-a-Bye Baby (Helen Trix only) | - |

Bowlly omitted.                          London, January 17, 1929.

| | | |
|---|---|---|
| WA-8354-1-2 | Negro Complaints | Rejected |
| WA-8355-1 | Shout Hallelujah ! 'Cause I'm Home | Col 5236 |
| WA-8356-1 | I'm Crazy Over You | - |
| WA-8357-1-2 | 'Tain't So, Honey, 'Tain't So | Rejected |

Acc. by the Gilt-Edged Four.             London, February 6, 1929.

| | | |
|---|---|---|
| WA-8519-2 | Nagasaki | Col 5300 |
| WA-8520-2 | I'm On The Crest Of A Wave | Col 5349 |
| WA-8521-2 | Pickin' Cotton | - |
| WA-8522-2 | Glad Rag Doll | Col 5300 |

London, March 26, 1929.

| | | |
|---|---|---|
| WA-8354-3 | Negro Complaints (acc. by Helen Trix | Col 5368 |
| | -p/Len Fillis-g only) | |
| WA-8761-1-2 | Carolina Moon | Rejected |
| WA-8762-1 | That's The Good Old Sunny South | Col 5368 |
| WA-8763-2 | Diga Diga Doo (Helen Trix only) | Col 5382 |
| WA-8764-1 | I Must Have That Man (Josephine Trix only) | - |

London, June 20, 1929.

| | | |
|---|---|---|
| WA-9181-1-2-3 | Anything To Hold You, Baby (Helen | Rejected |
| | Trix only) | |
| WA-9182-1-2 | Building A Nest For Mary (Josephine | - |
| | Trix only) | |
| WA-9183-2 | The Hollow Of A Hill | Col 5647 |
| WA-9184-1-2 | I'm Just In The Mood Tonight (Helen | Rejected |
| | Trix only) | |
| WA-9187-1-2 | You Want Lovin' (But I Want Love) | - |
| | (Josephine Trix only) | |
| WA-9188-1-2 | Golden Paradise | - |

NOTE:- Matrices WA-9185/6 are not by either of the Trix Sisters.

London, August 15, 1929.

| | | |
|---|---|---|
| WA-9359-2 | Come On, Baby | Col 5584 |
| WA-9360-2 | S'posin' | - |
| WA-9361-1 | You're My Silver Lining Of Love | Col 5647 |
| WA-9362-1-2 | What've I Done ? | Rejected |

## SOPHIE  TUCKER

B. Boston, Mass., January 13, 1884; debut as a singer in her father's cafe in  Hartford, Conn., 1905; to New York soon afterwards, appearing in cabaret on 40th  St.,
and in a black-face act at the 116th Street Music Hall, December 9, 1906;  various
appearances in vaudeville, then on regular stage in ZIEGFELD FOLLIES OF 1909 (Jardin de Paris, June 14, 1909); many subsequent tours with revue and vaudeville;  to
London, 1922, for debut in ROUND IN FIFTY (Hippodrome); appeared many times  there
in variety, cabaret and revue; starred in EARL CARROLL'S VANITIES (Music Box,  New
York, September, 1924); in FOLLOW A STAR (Winter Garden, London, September 17,1930
with Jack Hulbert); LEAVE IT TO ME (Imperial, New York, November 9, 1938);   HIGH

KICKERS (Broadhurst, New York, October 31, 1941); she made a few films, beginning
with HONKY TONK (1929), and GAY LOVE (1934, in England); BROADWAY MELODY Of 1938;
SENSATIONS OF 1945; r.n. Sophia Abuza, nicknamed "The Last of the Red Hot Mamas";
d. 1966.

Vocal, acc. by studio orchestra.            New York; issued as shown in brackets.

| | |
|---|---|
| That Lovin' Rag | Ed 10360 (June, 1910) |
| My Husband's In The City | Ed 10366 (July, 1910) |
| That Lovin' Two-Step Man | Ed 10411 (October, 1910) |
| Reuben Rag | Ed 10449 (January, 1911) |
| Phoebe Jane | Ed 4M-566 (January, 1911) |
| That Lovin' Soul Kiss | Ed 10493 (June, 1911) |
| Some Of These Days | Ed 4M-691 (July, 1911) |
| Missouri Joe | Ed 4M-716 (August, 1911) |
| Good Morning, Judge | Ed 10529 (January, 1912) |
| Knock Wood | Ed 4M-852 (January, 1912) |

NOTE:- Only the above ten cylinders were issued, but Sophie Tucker made nine two-
minute and five four-minute cylinders in ten sessions for Edison, probably making
some titles in both types.  The dates of these sessions are :- January 5  and 11,
1910; April 26 and 29, 1910; May 2 and 6, 1910; February 7 and 24, 1911; March 2,
1911,  and July 27, 1911.

New York, c. October, 1919.

| | |
|---|---|
| Don't Put A Tax On The Beautiful Girls | AV 12226 |
| You Can't Remember What I Can't Forget | - |

New York, c. January, 1921.

| | |
|---|---|
| Learning | Sophie Tucker 1000 |
| It's All Over Now | - |

New York, March, 1922.

| | | |
|---|---|---|
| 70499-A | Jig Walk | OK 4590 |
| 70500-B | High Brown Blues | OK 4565 |
| 70505-A | Blue Bird, Where Are You ? | OK 4617 |
| 70514-C | She Knows It | OK 4565 |
| 70564-A | Pick Me Up And Lay Me Down In Dear Old Dixieland | OK 4590 |
| 70565-A | Complainin' (It's Human Nature To Complain) | OK 4617 |

New York, March, 1923.

| | | |
|---|---|---|
| 71353-B | Aggravatin' Papa | OK 4817, Col CL-2604 |
| 71354-B | Come On Home | OK 4818   - |
| 71360-A | You've Got To See Mama Ev'ry Night | OK 4817 |
| 71361-A | Seven Or Eleven | OK 4818 |
| 71377-B | Papa, Better Watch Your Step | OK 4839 |
| 71396-B | Vamping Sal | OK 4837 |
| 71397- | Down By The River | - |
| 71422-C | Old King Tut | OK 4839 |

Acc. by small jazz band.            St. Louis or Chicago, January, 1924.

| | | |
|---|---|---|
| 8514-B | I've Got A Cross-Eyed Papa (But He | OK 40068, Par E-5429, E-5430 |
| 8515-B | Hula Lou | - 40129, 14083 - |

Acc. by Ted Shapiro-p.                Chicago, February, 1924.

```
8552-B  Red Hot Mama                          OK 40129. Par E-5428, Col CL-2604
8553-A  Mama Goes Where Paoa Goes (In Yiddish) OK 14083, Par E-5430
8554-A  The One I Love Belongs To Somebody Else OK 40054, Par E-5428
        Twelve O'Clock At Night               -
```

                                      Hayes, Middlesex, November 19, 1925.

```
Bb-7324-1-2  Big Boy                           Rejected
Bb-7325-2  Me And Myself                       HMV B-2223
Bb-7326-1-2  Sob Sister Sadie                  Rejected
Bb-7327-2  Nobody Know What A Red-Head Mama Can HMV B-2223
        Do
```

Acc. by Ted Lewis and his Band.       Chicago, November 23, 1926.

```
142955-2  Some Of These Days                   Col 826-D, 3169-D, 36300, 4269,
                                               FB-2812
```

Acc. by Miff Mole's Molers, with Ted Shapiro-p.
                                      New York, April 11, 1927.

```
80716-B  After You've Gone                     OK 40837, Par R-3353, PMC-7006,
                                               Col CL-2604
80717-C  I Ain't Got Nobody                    OK 40837, Par R-3353, Col CL-2604
```

                                      New York, April 15, 1927.

```
80737-B  One Sweet Letter From You (One Sweet  OK 40813, Par R-3342*,Col CL-2604
        Letter From Home*)
80738-A  Fifty Million Frenchmen Can't Be Wrong As above, plus Col SEG-7766
```

Acc. by Ted Shapiro-p.                Chicago, September 1, 1927.

```
81301-  Blue River                            OK 40895. Par R-3413
```

                                      Chicago, September 2, 1927.

```
81303-B  I Ain't Takin' Orders From No One     OK 41249, Par R-423, Col CL-2604
81304-  There's A Cradle In Caroline           OK 40895, Par R-3413
81305-A  Some Of These Days                    Col CL-2604
```

                                      Chicago, September 3, 1927.

```
81311-C  What'll You Do ? (Orch. acc.)         OK 40921, Par R-3455, Col CL-2604
81314-B  There'll Be Some Changes Made         -            -  PMC-7006 -
```

Acc. by O/Ted Shapiro-p.              New York, March 9, 1928.

```
400137-B  The Man I Love                       OK 41010, Par R-100, R-3181,
                                               Col SEG-7766
400138-C  My Pet                               OK 41010, Par R-100
```

                                      New York, April 16, 1928.

```
400614-A  'Cause I Feel Low Down               OK 41058, Par R-197
400615-B  Oh ! You Have No Idea                -            -
```

                                      London, June 13, 1928.

```
WA-7494-1  Stay Out Of The South               Col 4941, MFP 1164
WA-7495-2  There's Something Spanish In My Eyes  -
```

                                      London, June 15, 1928.

```
WA-7508-2  Virginia (There's A Blue Ridge 'Round Col 4942, MFP 1164
        My Heart)
WA-7509-1  He's Tall, Dark And Handsome (w/Ted   - OK 41249   -
        Shapiro)
```

London, June 20, 1928.

WA-7521-2  My Yiddishe Momme - Part 1 (In English)Col 4962, SEG-7766
WA-7522-2  My Yiddishe Momme - Part 2 (In Yiddish)     -

London, August 28, 1928.

WA-7730-2  I Know That My Baby Is Cheating On Me  Col 4995, MFP 1164
WA-7731-1  Conversational Man                            -        -
WA-7732-2  He Hadn't Up Till Yesterday              Col 5064     -
WA-7733-1  Is He The Boy Friend ?                   Col 5030     -

London, August 30, 1928.

WA-7745-1  Aren't Women Wonderful ?                 Col 5064

London, September 3, 1928.

WA-7774-2  Away Down South In Heaven                Col 5030

Hollywood, March 21, 1929.

PBVE-50549-1-2-3  I Don't Want To Get Thin (Film  Vic rejected
           "Honky Tonk")
PBVE-50550-1-2  I'm Doin' What I'm Doin' For Love     -
           (Film "Honky Tonk")

Hollywood, March 22, 1929.

PBVE-50550-4  I'm Doin' What I'm Doin' For Love  Vic 21993, HMV B-3131
           (Film "Honky Tonk")
PBVE-50555-4  He's A Good Man To Have Around     Vic 21994, LPV-538, LSA-3074,
                                                 RD-7869, HMV B-3132

Hollywood, March 25, 1929.

PBVE-50561-3  I'm The Last Of The Red Hot Mammas  Vic 21994, LCT-1112, BB B-6835,
           (Film "Honky Tonk")                    HMV B-3586

Hollywood, April 1, 1929.

PBVE-50574-4  I'm Feathering A Nest (Film "Honky  Vic 21993, HMV B-3131
           Tonk")
PBVE-50575-3  That's What I Call Sweet Music      Vic 21995, HMV B-3586

  Acc. by Ted Shapiro-p-speech (?)    Hollywood, April 2, 1929.

PBVE-50549-6  I Don't Want To Get Thin (Film     Vic 21995, HMV B-3132
           Honky Tonk")

  Acc. by Ted Shapiro's O/Leonard Joy.  New York, June 27, 1929.

BVE-53590-2  Moanin' Low                         Vic 22049, HMV B-3720

  Acc. by negro jazz band/Leonard Joy.  New York, July 10, 1929.

BVE-55602-2  Some Of These Days                  Vic 22049, BB B-6835, HMV B-3720

  Acc. by O/Ted Shapiro.        London, c. October, 1930.

           I Never Can Think Of The Words     Bcst 5195, BI 4020
              ("Follow A Star")
           Follow A Star ("Follow A Star")        -
           That's Where The South Begins      Bcst 5196
              ("Follow A Star")
           If Your Kisses Can't Hold The Man      -     BI 4020
              You Love ("Follow A Star")

London, November-December, 1930.

| | | |
|---|---|---|
| LO-811 | Washin' The Blues From My Soul | Bcst 5208 |
| LO-812 | That Man Of My Dreams | - |
| Z-1782 | Too Much Lovin' | Bcst 657 (8") |
| Z-1783 | Hollywood Will Never Be The Same | - |

London, January, 1931.

| | | |
|---|---|---|
| LO-839-X | Makin' Wicky Wacky Down In Waikiki | Bcst 3001 |
| LO-840-XX | What Good Am I Without You ? | - |
| Z-1827 | It's A Pleasure | Bcst 674 |
| Z-1828 | Make Yourself At Home | - |

London, April, 1931.

| | | |
|---|---|---|
| LO-949 | My Canary Has Circles Under His Eyes | Bcst 3042 |
| LO-950-XX | Egyptian-Ella | Bcst 3062 |
| LO-951 | On A Little Balcony In Spain | Bcst 3042 |
| | That's How I Feel About You, Sweetheart | Bcst 3062 |

London, May, 1934.

| | | |
|---|---|---|
| CE-6489-1 | That's Something To Be Thankful For | Par R-1869 |
| CE-6490-1 | Sophisticated Lady | Par R-1852 |
| CE-6491-1 | Stay At Home Papa | Par R-1851 |
| CE-6492-2 | Lawd, You Made The Night Too Long | Par R-1869 |
| CE-6493-3 | Louisville Lady | Par R-1851 |
| CE-6494-1 | My Extraordinary Man | Par R-1852 |

London, February 2, 1937.

| | | |
|---|---|---|
| CE-7943-1 | No One Man Is Ever Going To Worry Me | Par F-632, Dec 23033, MFP 1164 |
| CE-7944-1 | Life Begins At Forty | Par F-621, R-3181 -   11047, |
| | | Col SEG-7766 |
| CE-7945-1 | When A Lady Meets A Gentleman Down South | Par F-621, MFP 1164 |
| CE-7946-1 | My People | Par F-632    - |
| CE-7947-1 | Foolin' With The Other Woman's Man | Par F-622    - |
| CE-7948-1 | You'll Have To Swing It | -      - |

Acc. by Harry Sosnik and his Orchestra. Los Angeles, September 21, 1937.

| | | |
|---|---|---|
| DLA-949-A | The Lady Is A Tramp | Dec 1472, DL-4942, 7-2, Br 02893 |
| DLA-950-A | Some Of These Days | -      -  V-Disc 358 - |

## RUDOLPH  VALENTINO

B. Castellaneto, Italy, 1895; emigrated to U.S.A.; worked as gardener's boy, then in a cheap dance hall, afterwards as an exhibition dancer (r.n. Rodolfo Alfonso Raffaelo Pierre Filibert Guglielmi di Valentina d'Antonguolla); teamed with partners (Bonnie Glass, then Joan Sawyer), secured small parts in films (MY OFFICIAL  WIFE, 1914; PATRIA, 1916); then began to be noticed more in ALIMONY and A MARRIED VIRGIN (1918); many small parts until THE FOUR HORSEMEN OF THE APOCALYPSE (1921) made him a star; then followed THE SHEIK (1921); BEYOND THE ROCKS; THE YOUNG RAJAH; BLOOD AND SAND (1922); MONSIEUR BEAUCAIRE; A SAINTED DEVIL and COBRA (1924); THE EAGLE (1925); and his last film, SON OF THE SHEIK. D. New York, August 23, 1926.

Vocal, acc. by studio orchestra.         New York, May 14, 1923.

| | |
|---|---|
| Kashmiri Song (Pale Hands I Loved) | Br 3299 (not issued) |
| El Relicario (In Spanish) | -      Rare Records S-102 |

NOTE:- These, the only records Rudolph Valentino ever made, were coupled as   dubbings on a special memorial record issued without make or number in 1930.

B. Pottstown, Pa., 1880; r.n. William Vandegrift. Famous vaudeville comedian   and
   raconteur.  D. Newport, N. H., November 16, 1952.

Humorous monologues with vocal, acc. by O/Walter B. Rogers.
                                         Camden, N. J., January 27, 1916.

B-17070-1-2  To My Dog  (unacc.)                        Vic rejected
B-17071-1-2-3  Mickey The Pum Pum Man                   -

                                         Camden, N. J., January 28, 1916.

B-17070-3  To My Dog (unacc.)                           Vic 17960
B-17071-6  Mickey The Pum Pum Man                       -

   Acc. by O/Charles A. Prince.          New York, June 16, 1917.

77160-   Have A Heart, Napoleon (w/Peerless            Col A-2307
            Quartet) - Part 1
77161-   Have A Heart, Napoleon (w/Peerless            -
            Quartet) - Part 2

                                         New York, June 27, 1917.

77177-   Mike's The Boy (w/Peerless Quartet)           Col rejected
77178-   O'Grady Was In Line                           -

## VAN  AND  SCHENCK

Very popular vaudeville comedy team, 1915-1930; Joe Schenck b. Brooklyn, New  York,
   1892; d. Detroit, June 28, 1930; they wrote several songs, the most popular being
   ALL SHE'D SAY WAS "UMH-HUM" (1920). After his death, Gus Van continued solo.

Vocal, acc. by studio orchestra.        New York, c. November, 1916.

   2328-2  It's A Long, Long Time Since I've Been  Em 7107 (7")
              Home

   Acc. by O/Eddie King.                 Camden, N. J., December 29, 1916.

B-18892-2  Yaddie Kaddie Kiddie Kaddie Koo              Vic 18220
B-18893-2  That's How You Can Tell They're Irish        -

   Acc. by O/Rosario Bourdon.            New York, March 1, 1917.

B-19328-2  Dance And Grow Thin                         Vic 18258
B-19329-2  For Me And My Gal                           -
B-19330-2  There's Something Nice About The South Vic 18269

                                         New York, March 30, 1917.

B-19538-3  I Don't Think I Need A Job That Bad         Vic 18363
             (Gus Van only)
B-19539-2  Far Away In Honolulu                        Vic 18269
B-19540-1-2  They've Got Me Doing It Too               Rejected

   Acc. by O/Eddie King.                 New York, May 25, 1917.

B-19955-2  Mulberry Rose                               Vic 18318
B-19956-1-2-3  Miss America                            Rejected

                                         New York, July 5, 1917.

B-19956-4-5-6  Miss America                            Rejected
B-20323-2  The Ragtime Volunteers Are Off To War  Vic 18340

                                         New York, July 13, 1917.

B-20337-2  When I'm As Strong As Samson Was (Gus  Vic 18363
             Van only)
B-20338-2  Southern Gals                               Vic 18340

New York, August 17, 1917.

B-20636-1-2-3  The More I See Of Hawaii, The      Rejected
                  Better I Like New York
B-20637-2  I Miss The Old Folks Now               Vic 18429

New York, November 1, 1917.

B-20939-3  I Don't Want To Get Well               Vic 18413

New York, December 28, 1917.

B-21296-1-2-3  The Graveyard Blues                Rejected
B-21297-1-2-3  Hello, America, Hello              -
B-21298-2  In The Land O' Yamo Yamo               Vic 18443
B-21299-1-2-3  Midnight In Dreamy Spain           Rejected

    Acc. by O/Charles A. Prince.       New York, April 16, 1918.

    77771-  Beans, Beans, Beans (Gus Van only)    Col A-2629

New York, May 1, 1918.

    77802-  Ragtime Moses' Old-Time Bamboshay     Col A-2630
    77803-  In The Good Old Irish Way             Col A-2588
    77804-  My Marie                              -

New York, May 3, 1918.

    77808-  Tackin' 'Em Down                      Col A-2570

New York, May 4, 1918.

    77813-  You'll Always Find A Lot Of Sunshine  Col A-2570
               In My Old Kentucky Home

New York, July 31, 1918.

    77974-  I'm Too Tired To Make Love (Gus Van   Col A-2629
               only)
    77975-  They Were All Out Of Step But Jim     Col A-2630

New York, September 27, 1918.

    78084-  Why Do They Call Them Babies (When They Col A-2674
               Mean Grown-Up Ladies ?)
    78085-  When Tony Goes Over The Top           Col A-2665

New York, September 28, 1918.

    78087-  I'm Goin' To Fight My Way Right Back  Col rejected
               To Carolina

New York, October 11, 1918.

    78108-  You'll Find Old Dixieland In France   Col A-2665

New York, October 26, 1918.

    78164-  Non-Essential (Gus Van only)          Col rejected
    78165-  Liberty Bond Magee                    -

New York, April 16, 1919.

    78393-  Oh, How She Can Sing                  Col A-2757

New York, May 20, 1919.

    78440-  Open Up The Golden Gates To Dixieland Col A-2820
               (And Let Me Into Paradise)

New York, June 20, 1919.

| 78518- | Mandy | Col A-2780 |
|        | Mandy | LW 1196 (5") |

New York, September 13, 1919.

| 78648- | Sweet Kisses | Col A-2792 |

New York, October 22, 1919.

| 78750- | Everything Is Rosy Now For Rosie | Col rejected |
| 78751- | Pittsburgh, Pa. (Gus Van only) | - |

New York, November 6, 1919.

| 78800- | When Mariutch Shake-a Da Shimmie Sha Wob | Col rejected |
| 78801- | My Friends Morris And Max (Gus Van only) | - |

New York, April 19, 1920.

| 79128- | All The Boys Love Mary | Col A-2942 |

New York, April 20, 1920.

| 79129- | After You Get What You Want You Don't Want It | Col A-2966 |

New York, June 24, 1920.

| 79306- | You Tell 'Em | Col A-2966 |

New York, June 26, 1920.

| 79312- | I Love The Land Of Old Black Joe | Col A-2976 |

New York, September 17, 1920.

| 79421- | All She'd Say Was "Umh-Hum" ("Ziegfeld Follies of 1920") | Col A-3319 |

New York, September 25, 1920.

| 79433- | In Napoli | Col A-3319 |

New York, September 29, 1920.

| 79438- | I've Got The Blues For My Kentucky Home | Col A-3337 |

New York, November 1, 1920.

| 79494- | Marimba | Col A-3337 |

New York, November 30, 1920.

| 79544- | I Want To Go To The Land Where The Sweet Daddies Grow | Col A-3361, 3035 |
| 79545- | I Used To Love You But It's All Over Now | Rejected |

New York, April 5, 1921.

| 79796- | Sweet Love | Col A-3408 |

New York, April 21, 1921.

| 79806- | Ain't We Got Fun ? | Col A-3412, Re G-7732 |

New York, May 25, 1921.

79860-    Ain't You Coming Out, Malinda ?         Col A-3427

New York, July 22, 1921.

79957-    In The Old Town Hall                    Col A-3461
79958-    Sally, Won't You Come Back ? (Joe        Col A-3478
            Schenck only)
79959-    What's A-Gonna Be Next ?                 Col A-3461

New York, September 9, 1921.

79977-    Siren (Of A Southern Sea)               Col rejected

New York, September 27, 1921.

80003-    Down In Midnight Town                   Rejected
80004-    O'Reilly (I'm Ashamed Of You)           Col A-3490

New York, September 28, 1921.

80008-    Mulberry                                Rejected
80009-    Who's Been Around ?                     Col A-3490

New York, February 27, 1922.

80192-    Carolina Rolling Stone                  Col A-3577
80193-    Virginia Blues                             -

New York, April 17, 1922.

80298-    Sometimes Something Somebody Wants You  Col rejected
            To Do Simply Can't Be Done (Gus Van only)
80299-    When I Start Comparin' Old Erin With You   -
            (Joe Schenck only)

New York, April 19, 1922.

80311-    California                              Col A-3614, Re G-7876
80312-    Sweet Indiana Home                         -

New York, May 12, 1922.

80345-    Pullman Porter Blues (Gus Van only)     Col rejected

New York, June 27, 1922.

80423-    The Yankee Doodle Blues                 Col A-3668
80424-    Dixie Highway                           Rejected

New York, July 18, 1922.

80462-    I'm The Black Sheep Of Dear Old         Col A-3668
            Dixieland

New York, August 11, 1922.

80519-    When You And I Were Young Maggie Blues  Col A-3694
80520-    Early In The Morning                    Rejected

New York, September 18, 1922.

80552-    Carolina In The Morning                 Col A-3712
80553-    I'm Gonna Plant Myself In My Old           -
            Plantation Home

New York, October 3, 1922.

| | | |
|---|---|---|
| 80580- | You Can Have Him, I Don't Want Him,<br>Didn't Love Him Anyhow Blues | Col A-3735 |
| 80581- | All For The Love Of Mike | - |

New York, October 13, 1922.

| | | |
|---|---|---|
| 80605- | Georgia Cabin Door | Col A-3753 |
| 80606- | Kentucky Echoes | - |

New York, November 13, 1922.

| | | |
|---|---|---|
| 80667- | You Tell Her - I Stutter | Col A-3770 |
| 80668- | Away Down East In Maine | - |

New York, November 23, 1922.

| | | |
|---|---|---|
| 80685- | Down In Maryland | Col A-3806 |

New York, January 3, 1923.

| | | |
|---|---|---|
| 80767- | Mississippi Moon | Col A-3806 |

New York, April 17, 1923.

| | | |
|---|---|---|
| 80965- | Beside A Babbling Brook | Col A-3887 |
| 80966- | My Old Ramshackle Shack | - |

New York, May 1, 1923.

| | | |
|---|---|---|
| 80998- | That Red-Head Gal | Col A-3905 |
| 80999- | Trot Along | - |

New York, August 13, 1923.

| | | |
|---|---|---|
| 81175- | Stealing To Virginia | Col A-3981 |
| 81176- | Steamboat Sal | - |

New York, October 5, 1923.

| | | |
|---|---|---|
| 81264- | That Bran' New Gal O' Mine | Col 6-D |
| 81265- | Sittin' In A Corner | - |

New York, November 9, 1923.

| | | |
|---|---|---|
| 81339- | Kaintucky | Col 36-D |
| 81340- | Roamin' To Wyomin' | - |

New York, December 26, 1923.

| | | |
|---|---|---|
| 81437- | If She Was What She Was When She Was<br>Sixteen (Joe Schenck only) | Col 100-D |

New York, January 3, 1924.

| | | |
|---|---|---|
| 81453- | You're In Kentucky, Sure As You're Born | Col 61-D |

New York, February 1, 1924.

| | | |
|---|---|---|
| 81517- | Mindin' My Bus'ness (Gus Van only) | Col 78-D |
| 81518- | Promise Me Eve ything Never Get Anything<br>Blues (Gus Van only) | - |

New York, February 28, 1924.

| | | |
|---|---|---|
| 81591- | Down Where The South Begins | Col 101-D |
| 81592- | Waitin' Around | - |
| 81593- | The One I Love Belongs To Somebody Else<br>(Joe Schenck only) | Col 100-D |

New York, March 28, 1924.

| | | | |
|---|---|---|---|
| 81656- | My Papa Doesn't Two-Time No Time | Col 116-D | |
| 81657- | What's Today Got To Do With Tomorrow ? | - | |

New York, May 23, 1924.

| | | |
|---|---|---|
| 81791- | Shine | Col 149-D |
| 81792- | You Know Me, Alabam' | - |
| 81793- | I Wonder What's Become Of Sally ? (Joe Schenck only) | Col 148-D |
| 81794- | Lena, You're Leaning All Over Me (Gus Van only, acc. by Joe Schenck-p) | - |

New York, July 9, 1924.

| | | |
|---|---|---|
| 81865- | I Must Have An Italian Girl | Col 176-D |
| 81866- | Sister Hasn't Got A Chance Since Mother Hair | - |

New York, August 8, 1924.

| | | |
|---|---|---|
| 81910- | Choo Choo (Gotta Hurry Home) | Col 197-D |
| 81911- | Too Tired | - |

New York, August 29, 1924.

| | | |
|---|---|---|
| 81964- | Spain | Col 207-D |
| 81965- | When I Was The Dandy And You Were The Belle (Joe Schenck only) | Rejected |
| 81966- | Morning (Won't You Ever Come 'Round ?) | Col 207-D |
| 81967- | He Used To Be Called Bad Bill (But He's Sweet William Now) (Gus Van only) | Rejected |

Acc. by Joe Schenck-p.                New York, April 15, 1925.

| | | | |
|---|---|---|---|
| 140528- | Take 'Em To The Door Blues | Col 387-D | |
| 140529- | What Do We Get From Boston ? | Col 352-D | |
| 140530- | Everything Is Hotsy-Totsy Now | - | 3811 |

New York, July 10, 1925.

| | | |
|---|---|---|
| | My Best Gal | Vic test (un-numbered) |
| | Original Two-Time Man | - |
| | Loud-Speakin' Papa (You'd Better Speak Easy To Me) | - |

New York, June 17, 1927.

| | | |
|---|---|---|
| 144287- | Vo-Do-Do-De-O Blues | Col 1071-D |
| 144288- | Ain't That A Grand And Glorious Feeling ? | - |

New York, July 8, 1927.

| | | |
|---|---|---|
| 144451- | Pastafazoola | Col 1092-D |

New York, July 15, 1927.

| | | |
|---|---|---|
| 144374- | Magnolia | Col 1092-D |

New York, October 17, 1927.

| | | |
|---|---|---|
| 144874- | There's A Rickety Rackety Shack | Col 1221-D |

New York, October 18, 1927.

| | | |
|---|---|---|
| 144882- | There Must Be Somebody Else | Col 1162-D |

New York, November 23, 1927.

145232-   Is She My Girl Friend ?                      Col 1221-D

New York, December 7, 1927.

145282-   Away Down South In Heaven                    Col 1302-D
145283-   You Can Tell Her Anything Under The Sun       -
          (When You Get Her Under The Moon)

New York, July 13, 1928.

146637-3  Skadatin-Dee (Just A Funny Sound And A  Col 1492-D, 4984, Veritas 107
          Melody)
146641-2  Get Out And Get Under The Moon                -          -
          NOTE:- Matrices 146638/40 inclusive are not by Van and Schenck.

   Acc. by O/Leonard Joy.              New York, March 11, 1929.

BVE-49776-1-2-3  Dixie Troubadours              Vic rejected
BVE-49777-1-2-3  That's The Good Old Sunny South   -

New York, April 10, 1929.

BVE-51147-3  My Castle In Spain Is A Shack In     Vic 21979, HMV B-3083
             The Lane

   Acc. by O/Nat Shilkret.             New York, April 17, 1929.

BVE-51633-3  That's My Idea Of Heaven              Vic 21979, HMV B-3083

   Acc. by O/Leroy Shield.        Culver City, Calif., October 28, 1929.

PBVE-54483-1-2  Does My Baby Love ?                Rejected
PBVE-54484-1  Dougherty Is The Name               Vic 22352
PBVE-54485-1-2  I Gotta See My Partner (Joe        Rejected
          Schenck only)

Culver City, Calif., October 31, 1929.

PBVE-54486-1-2-3  Ten Mammas (w/The Rounders)      Vic rejected

Culver City, Calif., November 5, 1929.

PBVE-54483-4  Does My Baby Love ?                  Vic 22352

Culver City, Calif., November 6, 1929.

PBVE-54490-1-2-3  Harlem Madness                   Vic rejected
PBVE-54491-1-2-3  Ain't You, Baby ?                  -
PBVE-54492-1-2  There'll Never Be Another Mary       -
          (Joe Schenck only)
PBVE-54493-1-2  He's That Kind Of A Pal              -

   Acc. by O/Leonard Joy.              New York, March 11, 1930.

BVE-59625-1-2-3  He's That Kind Of A Pal (w/Phil  Vic rejected
          Dewey-Leo O'Rourke-Frank Luther) (Joe Schenck only)
BVE-59626-1-2-3  There'll Never Be Another Mary      -
          (Joe Schenck only)

GUS VAN : Vocal, acc. by studio orchestra.
                                New York, February 19, 1931.

10434-   In A Cafe On The Road To Calais           ARC rejected ?

New York, April 7, 1931.

10543-   I've Gotta Heavy Levee Date With Mandy   ARC rejected ?
10544-   Please Don't Cut Out My Sauerkraut         -

                                        New York, June 15, 1931.

10699-    Roll On, Mississippi, Roll On          ARC rejected ?
10700-    When Yuba Plays The Rumba On The Tuba      -

                                        New York, March 17, 1933.

BS-75537-    Shake Hands With A Millionaire      BB B-5015, B-7469, 1839,
                                                 Eld 1903, Sr S-3100
BS-75538-    Two-Buck Tim From Timbuctoo         As above except BB B-7469

    Acc. by O/Eli Oberstein.         New York, April 12, 1933.

BS-75796-1   Oh ! Ya ! Ya !                      BB B-5046, B-7469, Eld 1972
BS-75797-1   We're All Back Together Again, Me And   -              -
             That Old Gang Of Mine

## CLARICE VANCE

B. Louisville, Ky., March 14, 1871; r.n. Clara Ella Black; appeared in farce-comedy
productions in the 1890s; developed her famous style of "coon-shouting" in 1897;
retired from stage work in 1917; d. Napa, Calif., August 24, 1961.

Vocal, acc. by studio orchestra.        New York, issued as shown in brackets.

        Marian                             Ed 9051 (August, 1905)
        Save Your Money 'Cause De Winter Am   Ed 9214 (February, 1906)
        Comin' On

                                        New York, November 9, 1906.

B-4018-1  If Anybody Wants To Meet A Jonah, Shake  Vic 4930
          Hands With Me
B-4019-2  He's A Cousin Of Mine                   Vic 4931

                                        New York, November 13, 1906.

B-4035-1-2-3  Down And Out                         Vic rejected

                                        New York, November 16, 1906.

B-4035-4-5  Down And Out                           Vic rejected

                                        New York, March 26, 1907.

B-4333-1-2  Many The Time                          Rejected
B-4334-1  I'd Rather Two-Step Than Waltz, Bill     Vic 5118
B-4335-1  Yo' Eyes Are Open, But You're Sound      Vic 5119
          Asleep
E-4336-2  Marian                                   Vic 5120 (8")

                                        New York, August 7, 1907.

B-4768-1-2  I'm Wise                               Vic 5253, 17253
B-4769-1-2  That's Where Friendship Ends           Rejected

                                        New York, August 9, 1907.

B-4779-1-3  Handle Me With Care                    Vic 5278
B-4779-2  Handle Me With Care                        -      (Canada only)

                                        New York, January 16, 1908.

B-5024-1  That Friend Of Mine                      Vic 5374
B-5025-1  Common Sense                             Rejected
B-5026-1  I'm Afraid To Come Home In The Dark      Vic 5373
B-5027-1-2  Baby Talk                              Rejected

New York, January 29, 1908.

B-4336-1-2  Marian                              Vic 5120, 16295

New York, January 29, 1909.

B-6757-2  Goodbye To Johnnie                         Vic 5710, 16672
B-6758-2  It Looks To Me Like A Big Night Tonight  Vic 16295
B-6759-2  Love Me Like I Like To Be Loved          Vic 5675, 16802

## CONRAD VEIDT

B. Berlin, Germany, January 22, 1894; son of a doctor, but determined to be an actor
from the time he left school; first engagement in 1913, but the war interrupted his
career, which he resumed in 1917 after his Army discharge; many films in  Germany,
notably THE CABINET OF DR. CALIGARI (1919); WAXWORKS (1924); LUCREZIA BORGIA(1925);
THE STUDENT OF PRAGUE and THE HANDS OF ORLAC (1926); to Hollywood to make  THE BE-
LOVED ROGUE (1927); first German talkies include RASPUTIN (1930) and CONGRESS DAN-
CES (1931); first British film ROME EXPRESS (1932); other British pictures include
THE WANDERING JEW (1933); JEW SUSS (1934); THE PASSING OF THE THIRD FLOOR BACK and
KING OF THE DAMNED (1935); UNDER THE RED ROBE (1936); DARK JOURNEY (1937); THE SPY
IN BLACK (1939); CONTRABAND (1940); to Hollywood for the rest of his career; among
many films he made there are NAZI AGENT and CASABLANCA (1942) and ABOVE  SUSPICION
(1943).  D. 1943. Last German film F.P.1 (1933).

Vocal, acc. by studio orchestra.        Berlin, c. February, 1933.

CE-6001-1  The Airman's Song (w/chorus) (Film      Par R-1482
             "F. P. 1")
128326      Where The Lighthouse Shines Across The Bay  -
NOTE:- The first of the above two sides was probably dubbed from the soundtrack of
the film F. P. 1, in London, hence its English Parlophone matrix serial.

## LUPE VELEZ

B. Mexico, 1909; r.n. Guadelupe Velez de Villalobos; made several short silent films
for Hal Roach between 1924 and 1926; then appeared in THE GAUCHO (1927) and  sound
films such as LADY OF THE PAVEMENTS and THE WOLF SONG (1929); RESURRECTION (1931);
THE HALF-NAKED TRUTH and CUBAN LOVE SONG (1932); PALOOKA, STRICTLY DYNAMITE(1934);
THE GIRL FROM MEXICO (1935); MEXICAN SPITFORE (1939); she committed suicide, December 14, 1944.

Vocal, acc. by studio orchestra.        New York, March 30, 1929.

BVE-51106-1  Mi Amado (Film "The Wolf Song")       Vic 21932, LPV-538, LSA-3074,
                                                    **RD-7869**, Zon 5425
BVE-51107-3  Where Is The Song Of Songs For Me ?   Vic 21932    -

## VESTA VICTORIA

B. Leeds, Yorkshire, England, November 26, 1873; became a leading music-hall  artist
with her perceptive impressions of Cockney life in song, though not herself   one;
played for twenty weeks in New York on top salary in 1907, and made WAITING AT THE
CHURCH an international hit.  D. London, April 7, 1951.

Vocal, acc. by ? Landon Ronald-p.        London, June 24, 1903.

   3951-R  On A Motor Car                           G&T GC-3454
   3952-R  Ching Ching Chinaman                     Rejected
   3953-R  Ching Ching Chinaman                     G&T GC-3453
   3954-R  All The Best                             Rejected
           A Country Girl                           G&T 03003

London, July 16, 1903.

   4043-R  He Calls Me His Own Grace Darling        G&T GC-3488
   5481-R  Riding On A Motor Car                     G&T 3324 (7")
   5482-R  Ching Ching Chinaman                      G&T 3325 (7")
   5483-R  He Calls Me His Own Grace Darling        G&T 3326 (7")
   5484-R  The Country Girl                         G&T 3327 (7")

London, probably July 16, 1903.

'Ackney With The 'Ouses Took Away          G&T 03005

Acc. by unknown piano.              London, c. July, 1903.

| 25123- | All Through Riding On A Motor | Col 25123 |
| 25124- | Ching Ching Chinaman | Col 25124 |
| 25125- | He Calls Me His Own Grace Darling | Col 25125 |
| 25126- | Father, Mother And An Apple | Col 25126 |
| 25127- | The Country Girl | Col 25127 |
| 25128- | 'Ackney With The 'Ouses Took Away | Col 25128 |

London, c. January, 1905.

In The Summertime                          Pathe 50270
The Riding Song                            Pathe 50271

Acc. by studio orchestra.           London, August 31, 1905.

| 1062d | It Didn't Take Long To Come Off | Zon 43039 (7") |
|  | It's All Right In The Summertime | G&T 3380 (7") |
| 2537e | It's All Right In The Summertime | Zon X-43095 |
| 2538e | It Didn't Take Long To Come Off | Zon X-43089 |
| 2539e | The Turkey Girl | Zon X-43094 |
| 2540e | It Ain't All Honey And It Ain't All Jam | Zon X-43090 |

London, c. January, 1906.

It Didn't Take Long To Come Off            Ed 6665
The Turkey Girl                            Ed 6701
My Wife Won't Let Me (Waiting At The       Ed 6792
   Church)

New York, June 17, 1907.

B-4592-1  Poor John                        Vic rejected

New York, June 18, 1907.

| B-4592-2 | Poor John | Rejected |
| B-4594-1 | Man, Man, Man (Girls, You're Thinking Too Much Of The Men) | Vic 5221 |
| B-4595-1 | I've Told His Missus All About Him | Vic 5249, G&T GC-3752 |
| B-4596-1 | Summer Blouses | Rejected |
| B-4597-1 | It Ain't All Honey And It Ain't All Jam | Vic 5251 |
| B-4598-1 | The Artist's Model (It's All Right In The Summertime) | Rejected |
| B-4599-1 | Billie Green | Vic 5184 |
| B-4600-1 | Waiting At The Church | Vic 5182 |
| B-4601-1 | The Next Horse I Ride On | Vic 5181 |

New York, June 20, 1907.

| B-4592-3 | Poor John | Vic 5183 |
| B-4596-2 | Summer Blouses | Vic 5180 |
| B-4606-1 | He Calls Me His Own Grace Darling | Vic 5250 |
| B-4607-1 | Oh Girls, Never Trust A Policeman | Rejected |

New York, July-August, 1907.

I Told His Missus All About Him      Ed 10354 (issued Sept. 12, 1907)

London, October 12, 1911.

| Ab-14270e | Don't Sing The Chorus | Rejected |
| Ab-14271e | Now I Have To Call Him Father | HMV GC-3896 |

London, November 21, 1911.

| | | |
|---|---|---|
| Ab-14524e | Is Anybody Looking For A Widow ? | Rejected |
| Ab-14525e | The Gramophone Song | Zon 761 |
| Ab-14526e | Poor Old Adam | Rejected |
| Ab-14527e | Arcadee | Zon 761 |

London, August 14, 1912.

| | | |
|---|---|---|
| Ab-15469e | Look What Percy's Picked Up In The Park | Rejected |
| Ab-15470e | Look What Percy's Picked Up In The Park | Zon 918 |
| Ab-15471e | Carlo | Zon 960 |
| Ab-15472e | What's Good Enough For Father | - |
| Ab-15473e | It's Easy To Be A Lady | Zon 918 |
| Ab-15474e | It's Easy To Be A Lady | Rejected |

London, November 15, 1912.

| | | |
|---|---|---|
| Ab-16020e | Skating (On The Same Place Every Time) | Zon rejected |
| Ab-16021e | I've Got My Mother's Husband And She's Got Mine | - |
| Ab-16022/3e | Uncle Billy Was A Fireman | - |

London, November 19, 1912.

| | | |
|---|---|---|
| Ab-16041e | His Lordship - My Old Man | Cinch 5431 |
| Ab-16042e | Don't Get Older, If You Please, Ma Dear | Rejected |
| Ab-16043e | Mary Ann, Come In | Cinch 5431 |

London, September 10, 1931.

CAR-787-1   Vesta Victoria - Old-Time Medley,     Re MR-414
            Part 1 (Intro. Waiting At The Church/He Calls Me His Own Grace   Dar-
            ling) (w/The Jolly Old Fellows)
CAR-788-1   Vesta Victoria - Old-Time Medley,       -
            Part 2 (Intro. Now I Have To Call Him Father/Poor John)  (w/The Jolly
            Old Fellows)
CAX-6214-1  Vesta Victoria - Old-Time Medley,     Col DX-290
            Part 1 (Intro. Waiting At The Church/He Calls Me His Own Grace   Dar-
            ling/It's All Right In The Summertime) (w/chorus)
CAX-6215-1  Vesta Victoria - Old-Time Medley,       -
            Part 2 (Intro. Now I Have To Call Him Father/Poor John/Daddy Wouldn't
            Buy Me A Bow-Wow) (w/chorus)

## ESTHER   WALKER

Vaudeville comedienne very popular during the 1920s; appeared in MONTE CRISTO, JR.,
   at the Winter Garden, New York in 1919 and is said to have stolen the show.

Vocal, acc. by the Salon Dance Sextette. New York, c. May, 1919.

I'll Be Your Baby Vampire                   AV 12200

Acc. by O/Joseph Pasternack.          Camden, N. J., July 23, 1919.

B-23089-1-2-3  Sahara (We'll Soon Be Dry Like     Rejected
               You) ("Monte Cristo, Jr.")
B-23090-4  Nobody Knows ( nd Nobody Seems To Care)Vic 18613

Camden, N. J., August 8, 1919.

B-23089-5  Sahara (We'll Soon Be Dry Like You)    Vic 18613
           ("Monte Cristo, Jr.")
B-23090-5-6-7-8  Nobody Knows (And Nobody Seems   Rejected
           To Care)

Camden, N. J., September 26, 1919.

B-23173-3  Blues (My Naughty Sweetie Gives To Me) Vic 18619
B-23174-1  Sweet Kisses                                -

Camden, N. J., November 18, 1919.

B-23480-3  How Sorry You'll Be                     Vic 18657
B-23481-1-2-3  All The Quakers Are Shoulder        Rejected
           Shakers

Camden, N. J., November 20, 1919.

B-23484-1-2-3-4  I'll Dance My Way Right Back To  Vic rejected
           To Dixieland
B-23485-1-2-3  Slow And Easy                         -

  Acc. by O/Rosario Bourdon.         Camden, N. J., May 12, 1920.

B-24107-1-2-3  After You Get What You Want, You  Rejected
           Don't Want It
B-24108-3  Whatcha Gonna Do When There Ain't No  Vic 18680
           Jazz ?

Camden, N. J., May 14, 1920.

B-23485-6  Slow And Easy                          Vic 18680

Camden, N. J., September 29, 1920.

B-24604-1-2-3-4  I Want To Be The Leader Of A     Vic rejected
           Band

  Acc. by O/Joseph Pasternack.       Camden, N. J., September 30, 1920.

B-24604-5-6-7-8  I Want To Be The Leader Of A     ·Vic rejected
           Band
B-24605-1-2-3-4  Nobody To Love                      -
B-24606-1-2-3  You're Just A Little Too Late        -

  Acc. by Rube Bloom-p.              New York, c. December, 1925.

           Five Foot Two, Eyes Of Blue        Br 3008
           What Did I Tell Ya ?                   -

New York, c. January, 1926.

           I Want Somebody To Cheer Me Up     Br 3020
           I Love My Baby (My Baby Loves Me)     -

New York, c. March, 1926.

           I'm In Love With You, That's Why    Br 3110
           Poor Papa (He's Got Nothin' At All)   -
           I'm Lonely Without You (w/Ed Smalle) Br 3113
           As Long As I Have You And You Have Me  -
             (w/Ed Smalle)

New York, c. June, 1926.

E-19501/3  Ya Gotta Know How To Love           Br 3215
E-19507/9  Hard-To-Get Gertie                    -
E-19510/2  Brighten My Days                    Br 3226
E-19513/5  I Don't Want Nobody But You           -

E-19540/3  What Did I Do ? (w/Ed Smalle)       Br 3228
E-19545/6  All I Want To Do (Is To Be With You)  -

New York, c. October, 1926.

| E-20367 | Don't Me Angry With Me (w/male quartet) | Br 3348 |
|---|---|---|
| E-20375 | It Made You Happy When You Made Me Cry | - |
| E-20386 | Whisper - Ssh ! | Br 3349 |
| E-20389/90 | All Alone Monday (w/male quartet) | - |

New York, c. November, 1926.

| E-20796½/8 | Take In The Sun, Hang Out The Moon | Br 3387 |
|---|---|---|
| E-20800/1 | I'm Tellin' The Birds, Tellin' The Bees How I Love You | - |

New York, October, 1927.

| E-24562/4 | Good News | Br 3666 |
|---|---|---|
| E-24566/8 | I Left My Sugar Standing In The Rain | - |
| E-24597/8 | After I've Called You Sweetheart (How Can I Call You Friend ?) | Br 3670, 3674 |
| E-24600/1 | I Ain't That Kind Of A Baby ! | -    - |

## GEORGE W. WALKER

See Bert Williams.

## NANCY WALKER

B. Philadelphia, Pa., 1922; first attracted attention by her work in radio serial, LADY NEXT DOOR; New York stage debut in BEST FOOT FORWARD (Ethel Barrymore, October 1, 1941); to Hollywood to appear in film of the same show, also GIRL CRAZY and BROADWAY RHYTHM; back in New York, she starred in ON THE TOWN (Adelphi, December 28, 1944).

Vocal, acc. by O/Leonard Joy.       New York, November 24, 1941.

| BS-068353-1 | What Do You Think I Am ? ("Best Foot Forward") | BB B-11385 |
|---|---|---|
| BS-068354-1 | Shady Lady Bird ("Best Foot Forward") | BB B-11400 |
| BS-068355-1 | Just A Little Joint With A Juke Box | BB B-11385 |
| BS-068356-1 | Ev'ry Time ("Best Foot Forward") | BB B-11400 |

## POLLY WALKER

B. Chicago, 1908; r.n. Heather Eulalie Walker; stage debut at three in Chicago with her parents in STARLIGHT; also as a child she appeared in films with Gloria Swanson and Wallace Reid; New York debut in vaudeville at the Palace, 1923; first big part in New York (after many tours all over the country) in Ziegfeld's NO FOOLIN' (Globe, June 24, 1926); toured with this as ZIEGFELD FOLLIES OF 1927: back in New York, played Molly Malone (her favourite part) in THE MERRY MALONES (Erlangers, September 26, 1927); this was with George M. Cohan, in whose BILLIE at the same theatre (October 1, 1928) she played the title-role; London debut in LOVELY LADY (Phoenix, February 25, 1932), following this with OUT OF THE BOTTLE (Hippodrome, June 11, 1932); toured Australia in THE MERRY MALONES, and in Hollywood she made films such as HIT THE DECK (1935) and SLEEPLESS NIGHTS.

Vocal, acc. by O/Leonard Joy.       New York, November 9, 1928.

| BVE-48144-1-2-3-4 | Where Were You - Where Was I ? ("Billie") | Vic rejected |
|---|---|---|
| BVE-48145-1-2-3-4 | Billie ("Billie") | - |

New York, November 26, 1928.

| BVE-48144-7 | Where Were You - Where Was I ? ("Billie") | Vic 21799 |
|---|---|---|
| BVE-48145-7 | Billie ("Billie") | - |

Acc. by O/Ray Noble.                         London, July 4, 1932.

OB-3127-2  We've Got The Moon And Sixpence (w/     HMV B-4224
              Clifford Mollison)
OB-3128-3  Put That Down In Writing (w/Clifford         -
              Mollison)

## MARY JANE  WALSH

B. Davenport, Iowa, 1918; New York debut in I'D RATHER BE RIGHT (Alvin, November 2,
   1937); further successes in TOO MANY GIRLS (Imperial, October 28, 1939) and LET'S
   FACE IT (Imperial, October 28, 1941).

Vocal, acc. by studio orchestra.             New York, c. November, 1939.

        I Like To Recognize The Tune ("Too Many  Col 35235
           Girls")
        Love Never Went To College ("Too Many Girls")-
        Give It Back To The Indians ("Too Many    Col 35236
           Girls")
        I Didn't Know What Time It Was ("Too       -
           Many Girls")

                                        New York, c. April, 1940.

        Every Sunday Afternoon                  Col 35477
        It Never Entered My Mind                   -

Acc. by O/Max Meth.                          New York, c. November, 1941.

        Farming ("Let's Face It")                LMS L-343
        I Hate You, Darling ("Let's Face It")       -
        Ace In The Hole ("Let's Face It")        LMS L-344
        Everything I Love ("Let's Face It")         -

## THE WATSON SISTERS

Singing vaudeville act of the 1920s and earlier.

Vocal, acc. by studio orchestra/Charles A. Prince.
                                   New York, November 20, 1916.

47176-   Yaddie Kaddie Kiddie Kaddie Koo          Col rejected

                                   New York, November 21, 1916.

47177-   Way Down In Iowa (I'm Going To Hide      Col rejected
            Away)

                                   New York, August 23, 1917.

77283-   China, We Owe A Lot To You               Col A-2375
77284-   If I Can't Have You All Of The Time,        -
            Then I Don't Want You At All

                                   New York, c. December, 1919.

7167-    Lend Me Jim                              OK 4075
7168-    Never Let No One Man Worry Your Mind        -
            (Fanny Watson only)

Acc. by unknown piano (probably played by one of them).
                                   New York, December 15, 1927.

        Together On Our Trip Abroad           Vic test (un-numbered)

## MABEL  WAYNE

B. Brooklyn, New York, July 16, 1904; studied music in Switzerland; became a singer
   and pianist in vaudeville; gave this career up in 1924 to devote time to  writing

songs, with which she had great success (e.g., IN A LITTLE SPANISH   TOWN   (1926);
RAMONA (1927); CHIQUITA (1928); IT HAPPENED IN MONTEREY (1929); LITTLE MAN, YOU'VE
HAD A BUSY DAY; WHO MADE LITTLE BOY BLUE ? and HIS MAJESTY, THE BABY (1934);  HOME
AGAIN and MALOLA (1935).

Vocal, acc. by own p, w/unknown vn/vc.    London, January 25, 1935.

CAX-7414-1  Some Of My Songs - Part 1 (Intro.        Col DX-672
            In A Little Spanish Town/It Happened In Monterey/Who Made Little   Boy
            Blue ?)                                      -
CAX-7415-1  Some Of My Songs - Part 2 (Intro.
            Little Man, You've Had A Busy Day/Ramona/His Majesty, The Baby)

Piano acc. to Collie Knox-v, with Bert Ambrose-vn.
                                        London, March 8, 1935.

GB-7012-1  Malola
GB-7013-1  Home Again                        Dec F-5481
                                                 -

## CLIFTON WEBB

B. Indianapolis, Ind., November 19, 1893; stage debut at seven in Carnegie Hall, New
   York; appeared there subsequently in a number of juvenile roles; studied painting;
   also grand opera under Victor Maurel, the great French baritone, appearing  at the
   Black Boy Opera House in Boston in December, 1911 in MIGNON, followed by LA TOSCA,
   LA BOHEME, MADAME BUTTERFLY and HANSEL AND GRETEL; New York debut in regular stage
   productions in THE PURPLE ROAD (Liberty, April 7, 1913); other stage successes in-
   clude DANCING AROUND (Winter Garden, October 10, 1914); NOBODY HOME (Princess,Apr.
   20, 1915); VERY GOOD, EDDIE (Princess, December 23, 1915); LOVE O' MIKE (Shubert,
   January 15, 1917); LISTEN, LESTER (Knickerbocker, December 23, 1918); AS YOU WERE,
   playing three roles (Central, January 27, 1920); London debut in THE FUN  OF  THE
   FAYRE (Pavilion, October 17, 1921); remained in London for PHI-PHI (also Pavilion,
   August 16, 1922); returned to New York and starred in MEET THE WIFE (Klaw,November
   26, 1923); SUNNY (New Amsterdam, September 22, 1925); FLYING COLORS (Imperial,Sep-
   tember 15, 1932); AS THOUSANDS CHEER (Music Box, September 30, 1933, which ran for
   400 performances); BLITHE SPIRIT (Morosco, November 5, 1941); also toured with THE
   MAN WHO CAME TO DINNER (1940-1941) and made many films from 1944 until shortly be-
   fore his death in 1966; best-remembered for his portrayal of the part of Lyn  Bel-
   vedere, he appeared in such widely-differing films as LAURA (1944); THE DARK COR-
   NER (1945); THE RAZOR'S EDGE (1946); SITTING PRETTY (1948); MR. BELVEDERE GOES TO
   COLLEGE (1949); CHEAPER BY THE DOZEN and FOR HEAVEN'S SAKE (1950);  MR.  BELVEDERE
   RINGS THE BELL (1951); TITANIC and MR. SCOUTMASTER (1953); THREE COINS  IN  THE
   FOUNTAIN (1954); THE MAN WHO NEVER WAS (1956); BOY ON A DOLPHIN (1957);THE REMARK-
   ABLE MR. PENNYPACKER (1958); SATAN NEVER SLEEPS (1962). R.n. Webb Paremelee  Hol-
   lenbeck.

Vocalist with Leo Reisman and his Orchestra.
                              New York, October 3, 1933.

BS-78071-2  Easter Parade ("As Thousands Cheer")   Vic 24418, HMV BD-122
BS-78072-1  How's Chances ? ("As Thousands Cheer")       -

                              New York, October 11, 1933.

BS-78164-1  Not For All The Rice In China ("As     Vic 24428, LPV-565, HMV B-6524
            Thousands Cheer")

## WEBER AND FIELDS

Joe Weber (1867-1942) and Lew Fields (1867-1941) were the sons of poor Jewish  immi-
   grants, in partnership at nine years of age (!) in New York (minstrel shows); soon
   changed this to "knockabout Dutch" act, using hilariously mangled English;  opened
   the former Broadway Music Hall as Weber and Fields' Theatre in 1895, managed this,
   and appeared there, until 1904; careers then separated, but they were re-united in
   HOKEY-POKEY (44th Street, February 8, 1912) and a silent film, THE BEST OF ENEMIES
   (1915); Joe Weber retired in 1918, Lew Fields opened his own theatre and  acquired
   the Herald Square Theatre; retired 1930; they teamed up again for occasional  performances during the 1930s.

Humorous dialogues.                           New York, March 7, 1912.

  19794-   Etiquette Scene                         Col A-1203

                                              New York, March 14, 1912.

  19814-   Mike And Meyer - Hypnotic Scene         Col A-1159
  19815-   Mike And Meyer - Drinking Scene              -            AR 2290
  19816-   Mike And Meyer - Race Horse Scene       Col A-1203

                                              New York, March 22, 1912.

  19828-   Mike And Meyer - Mosquito Trust         Col A-1168
  19829-   Mike And Meyer - Heinie At College           -

                                              New York, July 9, 1912.

  38129-   Contract Scene                          Col A-1219
  38130-   Stock Exchange Scene                         -

                                              New York, July 16, 1912.

  38137-   Insurance Scene                         Col A-1220
  38138-   Singing Scene                                -

                                              New York, August 26, 1915.

  45970-   The Pool Game                           Col rejected
  45971-   Mike And Meyer Going To War                  -

                                              New York, August 28, 1915.

  45973-   Restaurant Scene                        Col A-1855
  45974-   Trust Scene                                  -

                                              New York, June 14, 1916.

  46834-   The Marriage Market Scene               Col A-2092

                                              New York, June 27, 1916.

  46879-   Baseball Game                           Col A-2092

                                              New York, October 3, 1933.

BS-78075-1  Mike And Meyer At The Fire House-Pt. 1 Rejected
BS-78076-1  Mike And Meyer At The Fire House-Pt. 2      -
BS-78077-1  Mike And Meyer At The Football Game    Vic 24430, LPV-580, LSA-3086
            - Part 1
BS-78078-1  Mike And Meyer At The Football Game         -
            - Part 2

## MILLIE WEITZ

A member of the cast of the hugely successful PINS AND NEEDLES (Labor Stage,November
  27, 1937).

Vocal, acc. by Harold Rome (composer)-Baldwin Bergesen-p.
                                              New York, February 1, 1938.

  63234-A  Nobody Makes A Pass At Me ("Pins And    Dec 23060, Br 02617
            Needles")

## ELISABETH  WELCH

B. New York City, February 27, 1908; formerly a social worker among children in com-
  munity centre; studied stagecraft and made her New York debut in   BLACKBIRDS   OF
  1928; to Paris for an engagement at the Moulin Rouge; returned to New York to play
  in THE NEW YORKERS (Broadway, December 8, 1930); London debut in the revue   DARK
  DOINGS (Leicester Square, June, 1933, in which she played the lead); this was fol-

lowed by NYMPH ERRANT (Adelphi, October 6, 1933); a season in variety at the Pal-
ladium and other theatres; further outstanding successes include GLAMOROUS NIGHT
(Drury Lane, May 2, 1935); LET'S RAISE THE CURTAIN (Victoria Palace,September 28,
1936); IT'S IN THE BAG (Saville, November 4, 1937); NO TIME FOR COMEDY(Haymarket,
March 27, 1941); SKY HIGH (Phoenix, June 4, 1942); to Gibraltar and Malta in Sir
John Gielgud's Company, entertaining troops; after a season in Blackpool,returned
to London to star in ARC DE TRIOMPHE (Phoenix, November 9, 1943); HAPPY AND GLO-
RIOUS (Palladium, October 3, 1944, which ran for 938 performances); film   career
began in 1934 with DEATH AT BROADCASTING HOUSE; also appeared in SONG OF FREEDOM,
SHOW BOAT and BIG FELLA (1936-1937) with Paul Robeson, q.v.; very popular on  BBC
radio in SOFT LIGHTS AND SWEET MUSIC (1933-1935).

Vocalist with Irving Mills and his Hotsy-Totsy Gang.
                                    New York, July 27, 1928.

E-27901-A  Doin' The New Low-Down ("Blackbirds     Br 4014
              of 1928")
E-27902-A  Diga Diga Doo ("Blackbirds of 1928")       -

Vocalist with Maceo Jefferson and his Boys.
                                    Paris, March-April, 1933.

SS-1626-B  Stormy Weather                          Salabert 3360
SS-1627-A  Crying For Love                         Salabert 3372

Vocal, acc. by O/Ray Noble.               London, October 18, 1933.

OB-5136-2  Solomon ("Nymph Errant")                HMV B-8031, MFP 1245

                                    London, November 4, 1933.

2B-5170-3  C. B. Cochran Medley - Part 2 (Intro.  HMV C-2628
              Blackbirds/One Dam Thing After Another/This Year Of Grace) (w/ Edward
              Cooper, compered by Charles B. Cochran)

                                    London, February 20, 1934.

OB-4789-2  Soft Lights And Sweet Music - Part 1    HMV B-8144
              (Intro. Just Like A Melody Out Of The Sky/Soft Lights And Sweet Music/
              When Day Is Done/Darktown Strutters' Ball)
OB-4790-1  Soft Lights And Sweet Music - Part 2       -
              (Intro. So Shy/I'll Never Be The Same)

                                    London, April 14, 1934.

OB-5975-2  Soft Lights And Sweet Music - Part 3    HMV B-8172
              (Intro. Lazy Day/Sweet Sue)
OB-5976-1  Soft Lights And Sweet Music - Part 4       -
              (Intro. Getting Sentimental/The Japanese Sandman/Goodnight, Sweetheart)

  Acc. by Drury Lane Theatre O/Charles Prentice.
                                    London, April 18, 1935.

2EA-1483-  Far Away In Shanty Town ("Glamorous     HMV C-2741
              Night")
2EA-1484-  A Girl I Knew ("Glamorous Night")          -

  Acc. by O/? Clifford Greenwood.       London, May 18, 1936.

OEA-2936-1 I Still Suits Me (w/Paul Robeson)       HMV B-8497, Vic 25376
              (Film "Show Boat")

                                    London, May 20, 1936.

OEA-2937-1 Sleepy River (w/Paul Robeson and        HMV B-8482
              chorus) (Film "Song Of Freedom")

Vocalist with Benny Carter and his Orchestra.
                                    London, mid-June, 1936.
  S-120-2  I Gotta Go                              Voc S-16

Vocalist with Benny Carter and his Swing Quartet.
                          London, June 20, 1936.

S-121-1  When Lights Are Low                  Voc S-16, Br 7853

                          London, October 13, 1936.

S-124-1  Poor Butterfly                        Voc 526
S-125-1  Drop In Next Time You're Passing       Voc 515
S-126-2  The Man I Love                         -
S-127-1  That's How The First Song Was Born    Voc 526

Vocal, acc. by O/Eric Ansell.        London, July 6, 1937.

OEA-5050-1  Harlem In My Heart (Film "Big Fella") HMV B-8608
OEA-5051-1  One Kiss (Film "Big Fella")          -

  Acc. by the New Mayfair Orchestra/Walter Goehr.
                          London, January 20, 1938.

2EA-5987-1  Gershwin Medley - Part 1 (Intro.    HMV C-2991
              I Got Rhythm/My One And Only/Clap Your Hands) (w/Robert Ashley)
2EA-5988-1  Gershwin Medley - Part 2 (Intro.
              The Man I Love/'S Wonderful/Strike Up The Band) (w/Robert Ashley)
2EA-5989-1  Gershwin Medley - Part 3 (Intro.    HMV C-2992
              The Man I Love/Lady, Be Good/Do-Do-Do/Someone To Watch Over Me)(w/Rob-
              ert Ashley)
2EA-5990-1  Gershwin Medley - Part 4 (Intro.    -
              Swanee/That Certain Feeling/Tell Me More/Fascinating Rhythm) (w/Robert
              Ashley)

  Acc. by small orchestra/? George Scott Wood.
                          London, October, 1940.

OEA-8921-1  Much More Lovely                    HMV BD-889
OEA-8922-1  And So Do I                         HMV BD-901
OEA-8923-1  These Foolish Things/A Nightingale Sang  -
              In Berkeley Square
OEA-8924-1  The Nearness Of You                 HMV BD-889

## ORSON WELLES

B. Kenosha, Wis., May 6, 1915; before becoming a prominent actor, producer and  film
and stage director, he was a newspaper correspondent; stage debut at the Gate Theatre, Dublin (JEW SUSS, November, 1931); returned to U.S.A., toured with Katharine
Cornell in Shakespearean and other roles; organized and managed the Woodstock Theatre Festival, Woodstock, Ill., in the summer of 1934; New York stage debut at the
Martin Beck Theatre in ROMEO AND JULIET (December 20, 1934); many other subsequent
appearances in New York; became a Director of the Negro People's Theatre there,and
produced a Negro version of MACBETH (1936); caused notorious panic due to the too-
real quality of his radio production of THE WAR OF THE WORLDS (October, 1938); his
best-known film is his first (CITIZEN KANE, 1941); he has starred in many since,as
this list shows :- JANE EYRE (1943); NAPOLEON (1954); THREE CASES OF MURDER(1955);
MOBY DICK (1956); THE LONG HOT SUMMER (1958); DAVID AND GOLIATH (1959); AUSTERLITZ
(1960); IS PARIS BURNING ? and A MAN FOR ALL SEASONS (1966); OEDIPUS (1967); CATCH
22 and WATERLOO (1970), and many others.

Dramatic speech, with  members  of the Mercury Theatre.
                          New York, March 1, 1938.

XCO-22490-  The Tragedy Of Julius Caesar-Pt. 1   Col set C-10
XCO-22491-  The Tragedy Of Julius Caesar-Pt. 2   -

                          New York, March 11, 1938.

XCO-22562-  The Tragedy Of Julius Caesar-Pt. 3   Col set C-10
XCO-22563-  The Tragedy Of Julius Caesar-Pt. 4   -

New York, March 21, 1938.

| | | |
|---|---|---|
| XCO-22602- | The Tragedy Of Julius Caesar-Pt. 5 | Col set C-10 |
| XCO-22603- | The Tragedy Of Julius Caesar-Pt. 6 | - |
| XCO-22604- | The Tragedy Of Julius Caesar-Pt. 7 | - |
| XCO-22605- | The Tragedy Of Julius Caesar-Pt. 8 | Rejected |

New York, March 25, 1938.

| | | |
|---|---|---|
| XCO-22605- | The Tragedy Of Julius Caesar-Pt. 8 | Col set C-10 |
| XCO-22606- | The Tragedy Of Julius Caesar-Pt. 9 | - |
| XCO-22607- | The Tragedy Of Julius Caesar-Pt. 10 | - |

Location and date unknown; c. 1938.

| | | |
|---|---|---|
| ME-1001/1024 | The Merchant Of Venice | Col set C-6 |
| ME-1025/1044 | Twelfth Night | Col set C-7 |

With Fay Bainter of the Mercury Theatre, and O/Bernard Herrmann. (This is Columbia album set C-33; an abridged edition of ten sides was also issued on Columbia discs 11117-D/11121-D, auto-coupled on 11224-D/11228-D).

Los Angeles, April 17, 1940.

| | | | | |
|---|---|---|---|---|
| LA-2196- | Macbeth - Part 17 | | LA-2198- | Macbeth - Part 18 |
| LA-2197- | Macbeth - Part 8 | | LA-2199- | Macbeth - Part 1 |

Los Angeles, April 18, 1940.

| | | | | |
|---|---|---|---|---|
| LA-2200- | Macbeth - Part 13 | | LA-2201- | Macbeth - Part 12 |

Los Angeles, April 20, 1940.

| | |
|---|---|
| LA-2202- | Macbeth - Part 10 |

Los Angeles, April 23, 1940.

| | | | | |
|---|---|---|---|---|
| LA-2203- | Macbeth - Part 7 | | LA-2204- | Macbeth - Part 4 |

Los Angeles, April 25, 1940.

| | | | | |
|---|---|---|---|---|
| LA-2205- | Macbeth - Part 2 | | LA-2206- | Macbeth - Part 3 |

Los Angeles, April 26, 1940.

| | | | | |
|---|---|---|---|---|
| LA-2208- | Macbeth - Part 5 | | LA-2212- | Macbeth - Part 11 |
| LA-2209- | Macbeth - Part 6 | | LA-2213- | Macbeth - Part 15 |
| LA-2210- | Macbeth - Part 9 | | LA-2214- | Macbeth - Part 16 |
| LA-2211- | Macbeth - Part 14 | | | |

## SCOTT WELSH

See Victor Herbert.

## MAE WEST

B. Brooklyn, N.Y., August 17, 1892; stage debut at five with Hal Clarendon's stock-company at the Gotham Theatre, Brooklyn; appeared with many similar companies in a variety of juvenile roles; several years in vaudeville; appeared in A LA BROADWAY (Folies Bergere, N.Y., September, 1911); considerable success in VERA VIOLETTA at the Winter Garden, November 20, 1911; A WINSOME WIDOW (Moulin Rouge, April 11, 1912) and on tour in vaudeville for the next six years; returned to New York for SOME-TIME (Shubert, October 4, 1918); wrote and appeared in several plays in the 1920s; SEX (Daly's, April 26, 1926); THE WICKED AGE (Daly's, November, 1927); title role in DIAMOND LIL (Royale, April 9, 1928); THE CONSTANT SINNER (Royale, Sept., 1931); CATHERINE WAS GREAT (Shubert, August 2, 1944); achieved world-wide fame, and even some notoriety, from her films, such as NIGHT AFTER NIGHT (1932); I'M NO ANGEL and SHE DONE HIM WRONG (both of which she wrote, 1933); BELLE OF THE NINETIES (1934); KLONDYKE ANNIE and GO WEST, YOUNG MAN (both of which she wrote, 1936); MY LITTLE CHICKADEE (which she co-authored, 1939); her autobiography, GOODNESS HAD NOTHING TO DO WITH IT, was published in 1959; she made a long-playing album of rock-n-roll numbers in her seventies, and in 1970 starred in MYRA BRECKINRIDGE.

Vocal, acc. by studio orchestra.          New York, February 7, 1933.

B-13037-A  I Like A Guy What Takes His Time (Film   Br 6495, 01491, Col CL-2751,
            "She Done Him Wrong")                    Dec 7-1
B-13038-A  Easy Rider (I Wonder Where My Easy        Br 6495, 01491, Col CL-2751,
            Rider's Gone) (Film "She Done Him         Epic SN-6059, Tpl 545
            Wrong")

                                         Los Angeles, October 3, 1933.

LA-33-A  I'm No Angel (Film "I'm No Angel")          Br 6675, 01635, Col CL-2751,
                                                     DB-1804
LA-34-A  I Found A New Way To Go To Town (Film       As above
          "I'm No Angel")

                                         Los Angeles, October 7, 1933.

LA-61-A  They Call Me Sister Honky-Tonk (Film        Br 6676, 01636, Col CL-2751
          "I'm No Angel")
LA-62-A  I Want You-I Need You (Film "I'm No Angel")  -        -        -

Vocalist with Duke Ellington and his Orchestra.
                                         Hollywood, April 23, 1934.

PBS-79181-1  My Old Flame (Film "Murder At The       Vic rejected
              Vanities")

                              ANNA WHEATON

B. Savannah, Ga., 1896; popular musical comedy and revue artist in New York and London during the World War I years (in PUSH AND GO, London Hippodrome, May 10, 1915)
and OH ! BOY (Princess, New York, February 20, 1917).  D. Pasadena, Calif., December 25, 1961.

Vocal, acc. by O/Albert W. Ketelbey.     London, c. June, 1915.

6506     My Snake-Charming Girl (w/Jamieson         Col 560
          Dodds) ("Push And Go")

Acc. by O/Charles A. Prince.             New York, December 23, 1916.

47255-   Drip, Drip, Drip Went The Waterfall        Col A-2261
47256-   Oh ! I Want To Be Good But My Eyes Won't Col A-2288
          Let Me

                                         New York, March 13, 1917.

47417-   'Till The Clouds Roll By (w/James           Col A-2261
          Harrod) ("Oh ! Boy")

                                         New York, March 19, 1917.

47433-   M-I-S-S-I-S-S-I-P-P-I                        Col A-2224, 2851

                                         New York, March 22, 1917.

47437-   I Wonder Why                                Col A-2238

                                         New York, March 23, 1917.

47438-   Rolled Into One ("Oh ! Boy")                Col A-2238

                                         New York, May 11, 1917.

77048-   Constantinople                              Col A-2295

New York, May 16, 1917.

77063-    That Creepy Weepy Feeling (I Loved You   Col A-2276
          The Moment We Met) (w/James Harrod)

New York, June 7, 1917.

77117-    Help, Help ! I'm Sinking              Col A-2295

New York, June 12, 1917.

77138-    How Can Any Girl Be A Good Little      Col A-2338
          Girl ?

## FRANCES  WHITE

Popular American vaudeville comedienne who made a great impression with her partner
   William Rock when they appeared in HITCHY-KOO (Cohan and Harris Theatre, New York
   June 7, 1917); she came to London and appeared in cabaret at the then newly-built
   Kit-Cat Restaurant in 1926.

Vocal, acc. by O/Joseph Pasternack.      Camden, N. J., July 30, 1917.

B-20459-2   Six Times Six Is Thirty-Six        Vic 18357, 45151
B-20460-2   M-I-S-S-I-S-S-I-P-P-I                  -       45133
B-20461-2   I'd Like To Be A Monkey In The Zoo  Vic 45149

Camden, N. J., December 27, 1917.

B-21292-1-2   The Lady Or The Ship (w/William Rock)Vic rejected
B-21293-1-2   Go-Zin-To                            -

  Acc. by the Kit-Cat Band.           Hayes, Middlesex, March 9, 1926.

Bb-8066-1-2   I Love My Baby (My Baby Loves Me)   HMV rejected
Bb-8067-1-2   Nothing Else To Do                   -
Bb-8068-1-2   Then I'll Be Happy                   -
Bb-8069-1-2   M-I-S-S-I-S-S-I-P-P-I                -

## FRED  WHITEHOUSE

B. New York City, June 14, 1895; writer of special material for music publishers for
   twenty years; in vaudeville as "The Phonograph Singer."  D. New York City,June 16,
   1954.

Vocal, acc. by O/Charles A. Prince.     New York, October 21, 1919.

78749-    Since Katie The Waitress Became An      Col rejected
          Aviatress

New York, October 28, 1919.

78761-    Don't Take Advantage Of My Good Nature  Col A-2835

New York, December 23, 1919.

78888-    When My Baby Smiles At Me               Col rejected

New York, c. March, 1920.

68403    Oh By Jingo, Oh By Gee                   Pathe 1300

## JACK  WHITING

B. Philadelphia, Pa., June 22, 1901; originally in secretarial work, but gained some
   stage experience as an amateur; turned professional and had New York debut in  the
   1922 edition of ZIEGFELD'S FOLLIES (New Amsterdam, June 5, 1922); other successful
   shows include AREN'T WE ALL ? (Gaiety, May 21, 1923); STEPPING STONES (Globe, November 6, 1923); ANNIE DEAR (Times Square, November 4, 1924); THE RAMBLERS (Lyric,
   September 20, 1926); HOLD EVERYTHING (Broadhurst, October 10, 1928); HEADS UP (Alvin, November 11, 1929); AMERICA'S SWEETHEART (Broadhurst, February 10, 1931);TAKE

A CHANCE (Apollo, November 26, 1932); London debut in ANYTHING GOES (**Palace,** June
14, 1935); remained in London to star in RISE AND SHINE (Drury Lane, May 7, 1936);
ON YOUR TOES (Palace, February 5, 1937); returned to New York, appeared in HOORAY
FOR WHAT ! (Winter Garden, December 1, 1937); VERY WARM FOR MAY (Alvin,    November
17, 1939); HOLD ON TO YOUR HATS (Shubert, September 11, 1940); toured in    ARSENIC
AND OLD LACE, 1941; THE OVERTONS (Booth, February 6, 1945, then toured with this);
also appeared on vaudeville circuits and in films.

Vocal, acc. by the Palace Theatre Orchestra.
London, July 2, 1935.

| | | | |
|---|---|---|---|
| CAX-7572- | You're The Top (w/Jeanne Aubert) ("Anything Goes") | Col DX-697 | |
| CAX-7573- | All Through The Night ("Anything Goes") | Col DX-698 | (part side) |
| CAX-7574- | In The Ship's Cell/Be Like The Bluebird (w/Sydney Howard) ("Anything Goes) | - | (whole side) |

Acc. by studio orchestra.          London, October 14, 1935.

| | | |
|---|---|---|
| CA-15358-1 | The Girl On The Little Blue Plate | Col FB-1188 |
| CA-15359-1 | The Rose In Her Hair | - |

Acc. by Carroll Gibbons and the Savoy Hotel Orpheans.
London, March 4, 1937.

| | | |
|---|---|---|
| CA-16273-1 | There's A Small Hotel ("On Your Toes") | Col DB-1687 |
| CA-16274-1 | On Your Toes ("On Your Toes") | - |
| CAX-7957-1 | On Your Toes - Selection, Part 1 (Jack Whiting sings a chorus of QUIET NIGHT) | Col DX-773 |
| CAX-7958-1 | On Your Toes - Selection, Part 2 (Jack Whiting sings a chorus of IT'S GOT TO BE LOVE and THE HEART   IS QUICKER THAN THE EYE) | - |

Acc. by George Scott Wood and the Six Swingers.
London, May 8, 1937.

| | | |
|---|---|---|
| CA-16377-1 | The Love Bug Will Bite You (If You Don't Watch Out) | Col FB-1695 |
| CA-16378-1 | Big Boy Blue | - |

## MARSHALL P. WILDER

B. Geneva, N.Y., September 19, 1859; well-known raconteur and vaudeville comedian in
the 1890s and 1900s.  D. St. Paul, Minn., January 1, 1915.

Humorous monologues.               New York, c. September, 1908.

| | |
|---|---|
| A Few Short Stories | Ed 4M-54 |
| Stories About The Baby | Ed 4M-57 |

## BERT  WILLIAMS

B. Nassau, British West Indies, November 12, 1874; began professional career  in the
1890s with Lew Johnson's Minstrels; then joined Martin and Selick's Mastodons at a
considerably higher salary; while in San Francisco, he met George Walker, formed a
partnership with him lasting ten years, in which time they recorded, and  appeared
in London in an all-negro musical comedy (IN DAHOMEY, Shaftesbury, May 16, 1903; a
great hit, it ran for 251 performances).  The end of the partnership in 1909 meant
Bert Williams's appearing in vaudeville solo; he also made several short films,and
one somewhat longer one (A NATURAL BORN GAMBLER, 1916); d. suddenly, March 4,1922.

Vocal, acc. by C. H. H. Booth-p.       New York, October 11, 1901.

| | | |
|---|---|---|
| 987-1 | I Don't Like That Face You Wear (w/ George Walker) | Vic 987 |
| 991-1 | In My Castle On The River Nile | Vic 991 |
| 992-1 | The Phrenologist Coon | Vic 992 |
| 993-1 | Where Was Moses When The Light Went Out? | Vic 993, G&T GC2-2846 |
| 994-1 | All Going Out And Nothing Coming In | Vic 994  (continued on page 667) |

New York, October 11, 1901 (cont.)

995-1-2  Junie (George Walker only)                  Vic 995
996-1    Good Afternoon, Mr. Jenkins (George         Vic 996
         Walker only)
997-1    Good Morning, Carrie (w/George              Vic 997
         Walker)
998-1    The Ghost Of A Coon                         Vic 998
999-1    Her Name's Miss Dinah Fair (George          Vic 999
         Walker only)
NOTE:- Matrices 988/990 inclusive are not by Bert Williams or George Walker.

New York, November 8, 1901.

998-2     The Ghost Of A Coon                        Vic 998
1083-1    The Fortune Telling Man                     Vic 1083
1084-1    My Little Zulu Babe                         Vic 1084
1085-1-2  She's Getting More Like The White          Vic 1085
          Folks Every Day

New York, November 10, 1901.

1086-1-2  My Little Zulu Babe (w/George Walker) Vic 1086
NOTE:- All the above Victor records were made in both 7- and 10-inch form,  except
998 and 1084, which were only made in 10-inch size.  They were also allocated numbers 3609/3619 respectively, but they do not seem to have been catalogued thus.  It
seems, however  that the number 998 was allocated both to THE GHOST OF A COON  and
IF YOU LOVE YOUR BABY, MAKE DEM GOO-GOO EYES, which according to the files, was re-
numbered 3616 (two takes used) and issued thus, but never listed in the catalogue!

Acc. by ? Landon Ronald-p.          London, June 5, 1903.

3851-R/3852-R  The Cake Walk                 G&T rejected
               He'd A Funny Little Way With Him    Zon 42106 (7")

Acc. by unknown piano.              London, c. April, 1904.

          It Wasn't His Turn To Laugh       Col 200986 (cyl., issd. July,1904)
          Bill's Whistle                    Col 201030 (cyl.; issd. Sept.1904)

          Bill's Whistle                    Lambert 5176 (cyl.)
          Whistling Johnnie                 Lambert 5202 (cyl.)

Acc. by studio orchestra.          New York, c. April, 1906.

3410-   Pretty Desdemona (w/George Walker)        Col/Har 3410, Star 2251,
                                                  Rare Records V-210

New York, c. May, 1906.

3423-   Nobody                                    Col 3423, A-302, 33011 (cyl.)

New York, c. June, 1906.

3454-   Here It Comes Again                       Col 3454, 85075 (cyl.), Star 2223

New York, September 29, 1906.

30038-  I've Such A Funny Feeling When I Look   Rejected
        At You
30039-  All In, Out And Down                     Col 30039, A-5031

New York, c. September, 1906.

3504-   Let It Alone ("Abyssinia")               Col 3504, A-305, 33025 (cyl.),
                                                 85086 (cyl.)

3515-   I'm Tired Of Eating In The Restaurants  Col 3515, A-298, 32990 (cyl.)

New York, c. October, 1906.

3536-   He's A Cousin Of Mine                  Col 3536, A-303, A-862,
                                               33053 (cyl.)

New York, c. November, 1906.

3557-   The Mississippi Stoker                 Col 3557, A-801, 85074 (cyl.),
                                               Aretino D-673, Climax X-730

New York, c. November-December, 1906.

3575-   I've Such A Funny Feeling Whem I Look  Col 3575
        At You

New York, c. January, 1907.

3593-   Fare Thee ! On Ma Way ! Jes' Gone      Col 3593, Fairview (un-numbered)

New York, c. June, 1910.

4682-   I'll Lend You Anything                 Col A-915
4683-1  Something You Don't Expect             Col A-929
4684-   Constantly                             Col A-915

New York, c. August, 1910.

4849-1  Play That Barber-Shop Chord            Col A-929

Acc. by O/Charles A. Prince.        New York, January 3, 1913.

36538-  You Can't Do Nothin' Till Martin Gets  Col A-6216
        Here
36539-  How ? Fried !                          -
38525-  My Landlady                            Col A-1289

New York, January 7, 1913.

38539-  Woodman, Spare That Tree               Col A-1321
38540-  Nobody                                 Col A-1289, AR 2290

New York, January 13, 1913.

38553-  Borrow From Me                         Col A-1354

New York, January 14, 1913.

38554-  On The Right Road                      Col A-1354

New York, January 21, 1913.

38576-  I Certainly Was Going Some             Col A-1321

New York, February 4, 1914.

39204-  You Can't Get Away From It             Col A-1504
39205-  The Darktown Poker Club                -

New York, August 2, 1915.

45906-  I'm Neutral                            Col A-1817
45907-  Everybody                              Col A-1909

New York, August 4, 1915.

45911-  Indoor Sports                          Col A-1817

New York, August 7, 1915.

45925-  Samuel                                 Col A-1909

                                    New York, September 7, 1915.

45986-    Hard Times                          Col rejected

                                    New York, September 9, 1915.

46004-1   Purpostus                           Col A-1853
46005-2   Never Mo'                             -
46006-    Eph Calls Up The Boss               Rejected

                                    New York, July 22, 1916.

46944-    The Lee Family                      Col A-2078
46945-    I'm Gone Before I Go                  -

                                    New York, September 14, 1917.

77341-    No Place Like Home                  Col A-2438
77344-    Twenty Years                          -
NOTE:- Nothing is known of what may have been on matrices 77342 and 77343.

                                    New York, August 26, 1918.

78025-3   O Death, Where Is Thy Sting ?       Col A-2652, 35590

                                    New York, August 29, 1918.

78030--   You'll Find Old Dixieland In France   Rejected
78031-2   When I Return                       Col A-2652

                                    New York, February 13, 1919.

78298-3   Oh Lawdy (Something's Done Got Between  Col A-2710
             Ebecaneezer And Me)
78299-2   Bring Back Those Wonderful Days       -        35591

                                    New York, April 4, 1919.

78380-2   Everybody Wants A Key To My Cellar    Col A-2750, 35591

                                    New York, April 16, 1919.

78394-    It's Nobody's Business But My Own     Col A-2750, 35593

                                    New York, April 29, 1919.

78411-    Elder Eatmore's Sermon On Generosity   Col rejected

                                    New York, June 27, 1919.

49643-2   Elder Eatmore's Sermon On Generosity    Col A-6141
             (w/Alex Rogers-Bob Slater-Mary Straine)
49644-    Elder Eatmore's Sermon On Throwing Stones   -

                                    New York, November 24, 1919.

78828-    I'm Sorry I Ain't Got It, You Could   Col A-2877
             Have It If I Had It Blues

                                    New York, December 1, 1919.

78833-1   The Moon Shines On The Moonshine    Col A-2849, 35590, Veritas 107
78833-2   The Moon Shines On The Moonshine      -

                                    New York, December 2, 1919.

78834-    Checkers (It's Your Move Now)       Col A-2877
78835-    Somebody                            Col A-2849

New York, April 18, 1920.

| 79126-3 | Ten Little Bottles | Col A-2941, 3035 |
| 79127-3 | Unlucky Blues | - |

New York, May 6, 1920.

| 79163-1 | Lonesome Alimony Blues | Col A-2979 |
| 79164- | Get Up | Col A-3305 |

New York, June 28, 1920.

| 79318-3 | Save A Little Dram For Me | Col A-2979 |

New York, June 29, 1920.

| 45906- | I'm Neutral | Col A-1817 |

New York, September 7, 1920.

| 79402- | I Want To Know Where Tosti Went When He Said "Goodbye" | Col A-3305 |

New York, October 25, 1920.

| 79484- | You Can't Trust Nobody | Col A-3589, 35593 |

New York, November 12, 1920.

| 79515-1 | Eve Cost Adam Just One Bone | Col A-3339 |
| 79516-3 | You'll Never Need A Doctor No More | - |

New York, December 10, 1920.

| 79566-2 | My Last Dollar | Col A-3356 |
| 79567-2 | I'm Gonna Quit Saturday | - |

New York, July 12, 1921.

| 38525- | My Landlady | Col A-1289 |
| 79934- | 'Tain't No Disgrace To Run When You're Skeered | Rejected |

New York, July 13, 1921.

| 79940- | I Ain't Afraid Of Nuthin' Dat's Alive | Col rejected |

New York, October 24, 1921.

| 80038- | Brother Low Down | Col A-3508, 35592 |

New York, October 28, 1921.

| 80040-2 | Unexpectedly | Col A-3508 |

New York, February 24, 1922.

| 80191- | Not Lately | Col A-3589 |

## FRANCES WILLIAMS

B. St. Paul, Minn., 1903; r.n. Frances Jellineck; stage debut in cabaret in Tait's Restaurant, San Francisco, then after two years, appeared in vaudeville; New York debut in INNOCENT EYES (Winter Garden, May 20, 1924); in the following ten years, she appeared in the following successes :- ARTISTS AND MODELS (Winter Garden, June 24, 1925); THE COCOANUTS (Lyric, December 8, 1925); GEORGE WHITE'S SCANDALS (all at the Apollo, June 14, 1926; July 2, 1928; September 23, 1929); succeeded Gertrude Lawrence in THE INTERNATIONAL REVUE (Majestic, February, 1930); starred in THE NEW YORKERS (Broadway, December 8, 1930); EVERYBODY'S WELCOME (Shubert, October 13, 1931); LIFE BEGINS AT 8.40 (Winter Garden, August 27, 1934); succeeded

Ethel Merman in PANAMA HATTIE (46th Street, December, 1941); many others.

Vocal, acc. by Dave Dreyer-p.              New York, August 28, 1925.

        Yes, Sir ! That's My Baby              Vic test (un-numbered)

   Acc. by own piano.                    New York, July 23, 1928.

BVE-120   What A Night For Spooning/More Than   **Vic** test
        Anybody/I Just Roll Along

   Acc. by studio orchestra.             New York, early August, 1929.

| | | |
|---|---|---|
| E-30595- | It's Unanimous Now | Br 4499 |
| E-30597- | Then You've Never Been Blue | - |
| | | |
| E-30710- | Bottoms Up | Br 4503 |
| E-30711- | Bigger And Better Than Ever | - |

                         New York, January 10, 1933.

| | | |
|---|---|---|
| 265029-1-2 | Underneath The Harlem Moon | Rejected |
| 265030-1-2 | Try A Little Tenderness | - |
| 265031-1 ? | Hey ! Young Fella | Epic L2N-6072 |

                         New York, November 23, 1937.

| | | |
|---|---|---|
| P-22057- | Slightly Indiscreet Song | LMS |
| P-22058- | I Shot The Works | - |
| P-22059- | Tally Ho ! | - |
| P-22060- | Sussie And Lousy Louisa | - |

## WILLIAMS SISTERS

Hannah and Dorothea Williams were well-known  Chicago night-club entertainers  with
Charley Straight's Orchestra at the Rendezvous Cafe (1925-1926) and Ben Pollack's
Californians at the Southmoor Hotel (1926-1927).

Vocalists, acc. by small jazz band (probably members of Ben Pollack's Californians).
                               Chicago, December 15, 1926.

| | | |
|---|---|---|
| BVE-37244-1-2 | I've Grown So Lonesome Thinking Of You | Vic rejected |
| BVE-37245-1-2 | Sunday | - |

Vocalists with Ben Pollack and his Californians.
                               Chicago, December 17, 1926.

| | | |
|---|---|---|
| BVE-37261-2 | He's The Last Word | Vic 20425 |
| BVE-37261-3 | He's The Last Word | X LX-3003, LVA-3003 |

Vocalists, acc. by Wayne Allen-p.       Chicago, December 18, 1926.

| | | |
|---|---|---|
| BVE-37266-3 | Nothing Else Matters Any More | Vic 20452 |
| BVE-37267-2 | Sam, The Old Accordion Man | - |

## NAT M. WILLS

B. Fredericksburg, Va., July 11, 1873; r.n. Edward McGregor; star comedian of   many
FOLLIES shows on Broadway as raconteur; usually billed as "The Happy Tramp"; originated the famous NO NEWS monologue; d. Woodcliff-on-Hudson, N.J., December 9,1917.

Humorous monologues, unacc. unless shown as with orchestra.
                              New York, October 14, 1908.

| | | |
|---|---|---|
| B-6538-1 | No News, or What Killed The Dog | Vic 5612, 17222, HMV 1428 |
| C-6539-2 | The Flag He Loved So Well (w/Orch.) | Vic 31720 |
| B-6540-2 | Are You Sincere ? | Vic 5613 |
| B-6541-2 | B.P.O.E. (Elks' Song) (w/Orch.) | Vic 5614 |
| B-6542-2 | The Old Oaken Bucket | Vic 5659, 16661 |

New York, October 16, 1908.

B-6549-2  Our Boarding House (w/Orch.)                Vic 5616
B-6550-1-2  Hoboken                                   Rejected
   NOTE:- An interesting fact relating to why both takes of the last side above  were
   rejected is given in the Victor recording ledger : B-6550-1 was "broken," but   we
   are not told how; B-6550-2, however, is marked "M. O. Noon whistles recorded."  We
   may ponder on why this title was never re-made, perhaps under more soundproof con-
   ditions !

New York, March 23, 1909.

B-6917-1-2  Rainbow and Sunbonnet Blue                Rejected
C-6918-1  At The Comic Opera                          Vic 35079
B-6919-1  A Traveling Man                             Rejected

New York, March 24, 1909.

B-6919-2  A Traveling Man (w/Orch.)                   Rejected
B-6922-1  Song Of The English Chappie                 Vic 16687
B-6923-1-2  Liberty                                   Rejected

New York, March 25, 1909.

C-6925-1  Hortense At The Skating Rink                Vic rejected
B-6926-1  A Talk On Father                            -

New York, March 26, 1909.

B-6549-3  Our Boarding House (w/Orch.)                Rejected
B-6919-4  A Traveling Man                             Vic 5725
C-6925-2  Hortense At The Skating Rink                Vic 35156
B-6932-1  Jungle Town Parody (Teddy In Africa)        Vic 5695
B-6933-1  Saving Up Coupons For Mother                Vic 5700

New York, March 27, 1909.

C-6934-2  Reformed Love                               Vic 31736
C-6935-1  Hortense At Sea                             Vic 35093

   Acc. by studio orchestra.           New York, April 21, 1909.

           The Flag He Loved So Well                  Ed 4M-176
           Our Boarding House                         Ed 4M-212
           B. P. O. E. (Elks' Song)                   Ed 4M-223, Amb 2320, AR 2290
           Burlesque Opera                            Ed 4M-236, Amb 2099

New York, April 19, 1913.

38797-  Comic Medley Song                             Col A-1352
38798-  Drink Cure                                    -

New York, September 22, 1913.

B-13838-1  New York, What's The Matter With You ?  Vic 17461
              ("Follies of 1913")
B-13839-1  That Ragtime Suffragette ("Follies of    Rejected
              1913")
B-13840-1  If A Table At Rector's Could Talk        Vic 17461
              ("Follies of 1913")
B-13841-1  Too Much Dog                             Rejected
B-13842-1  Parodies On Eight Familiar Songs         Vic 17894
B-13843-1  The Trail Of The Lonesome Pine - Parody  Rejected
B-13844-1  Christian Science (unacc.)               -
C-13845-1  Darky Stories (unacc.)                   -

New York, February 5, 1914.

C-13845-2-3  Darky Stories (unacc.)                  Vic rejected

Acc. by O/Walter B. Rogers.                Camden, N. J., February 10, 1915.

B-13841-2-3  Too Much Dog                          Vic 17768
B-13844-2  Christian Science (unacc.)              Vic 17915
B-13845-2  Darky Stories (unacc.)                  Vic 17768
C-15694-3  Automobile Parody                       Vic 35601
B-15695-1  A Father Of Thirty-Six (unacc.)         Vic 17894

Unacc.                                     New York, March 26, 1915.

39997-  No News, or What Killed The Dog            Col A-1765

                                           New York, March 29, 1915.

45505-  Two Darky Stories (Colored Social Club/ Col A-1765
         The Head Waiter)

                                           New York, c. April, 1917.

        No News, or What Killed The Dog            Em 7171 (7")
        Hortense At The Skating Rink               Em 7193 (7")
        To Europe On A Cattle Boat                 -

## AL H.  (METZ) WILSON

B. March 3, 1968; date of death not known. Noted German-dialect actor of the 1890s-
1900s; appeared in THE IDEA, STRUCK OIL and THE TWENTIETH-CENTURY GIRL, and  from
1900 onwards he ran his own touring company and appeared in its very    successful
productions of THE WATCH ON THE RHINE, A PRINCE OF TATTERS and (in 1905) THE GER-
MAN GYPSY; he was featured in a sketch called METZ IN THE ALPS in 1906-1907,  and
in 1908-1909 in WHEN OLD NEW YORK WAS DUTCH.

Vocal, acc. by studio orchestra.           New York, January 26, 1906.

C-3046-1  The Winding Of The Yarn                  Vic 31498
B-3047-1  In Tyrol                                 Vic 4620, 16096
B-3048-1  Under The Harvest Moon                   Vic 4621    -

                                           New York, April 27, 1906.

B-3343-1-2-3-4  Sleep, Baby, Sleep                 Vic 2560 (take used not kno n)
E-3343-1  Sleep, Baby, Sleep                        -       (8")
B-3344-1  The Cuckoo Song                          Rejected
E-3344-1  The Cuckoo Song                           -
B-3345-1  The Germans' Arrival                     Vic 2561, 17257
E-3345-1  The Germans' Arrival                     Rejected
E-3346-1  Everybody Works But Father (In Germa )    -

                                           New York, November 6, 1907.

B-4906-1  Whispering Breezes                       Vic 5322
C-4907-1  Songs Of Old Fatherland                  Vic 31687
B-4908-1  The Fairest Flower Of All                Rejected ?
B-4909-1  Wilson's Lullaby                         Vic 5563

                                           New York, c. 1916.

        As The Years Roll On                       Pathe 20034
        Mother Mine                                -

## BESSIE WYNN

American vaudeville artist of the opening years of the century.

Vocal, acc. by studio orchestra.           New York, September 23, 1909.

        My Pretty Little Piece Of Dresden China Ed 4M-346

                                    New York, October 6, 1909.

         It's Hard To Find A Real Nice Man          Ed 10278

                                    New York, October 8, 1909.

         Not For Me                                 Ed 10329

                                    New York, July 9, 1910.

         I'd Love To, But I Won't                   Ed 10441

                                    New York, November 18, 1910.

         Title(s) not known                         Ed rejected

## THE  YACHT CLUB BOYS

Messrs. Adler, Kelly, Kern and Mann, using the above group-name after the night-club
in New York where they first appeared, singing their own and other suitably  smart
numbers, were a very popular cabaret act throughout the 1920s and 1930s.

Vocal quartet, acc. by own piano (player not known).
                                    New York, c. July, 1926.

E-19814/5  How Could Red Riding Hood ?          Br 3270
E-19817/8  Every Little While                   -
E-19820/1  Oogel, Oogel, Oo (The Monkey Song)   Br 3269
E-19822/3/4  The Vulgar Boatman                 -

                                    New York, c. December, 1926.

E-20974    Ain't That Too Bad ?                 Br 3405
E-20977    What Will You Think Of Me ?          -

E-20985    Nobody's Baby But Mine               Br 3409
E-20987    Ya Gonna Be Home Tonight ?           -

                                    New York, October, 1927.

E-25191/2  I Fell Head Over Heels In Love       Br 3671
E-25194/5  You Can't Walk Back From An Aeroplane   -

                                    New York, October, 1928.

E-28256-   Do You ? That's All I Want To Know   Br 4113

                                    New York, January, 1929.

E-29016-   The Monte Carlo Song                 Br 4188
E-29017-   I'm Wild About Horns On Automobiles  -
             That Go "Ta-Ta-Ta-Ta"

                                    New York, December 30, 1932.

265025-1-2  Mahatma Gandhi/Shut The Door        Col rejected

                                    New York, January 4, 1933.

265026-1-2  Spain                               Col rejected
265027-1-2  Madman's Lullaby                    -
265028-1-2  We All Love To Sing In The Bath Tub   -

   Acc. by small jazz band.        New York, January 16, 1934.

152688-2  Sing-Sing Isn't Prison Any More    Col 2908-D, DB-1356, FB-1238
152689-2  The Great American Tourist         -          -         -
152690-2  We Own A Salon                     Col 2887-D, DB-1357, FB-1237
152691-1  The Super-Special Picture Of The Year   -     -         -

B. Poland, July 6, 1892; family emigrated to U.S.A., 1897; educated at University of
Michigan, graduated 1913 and for a time was a reporter on THE BUFFALO COURIER; be-
gan writing songs, first published being LONESOME MOON and ALL ABOARD FOR   DIXIE-
LAND (1914); great success, followed these with dozens of others, many in   collab-
oration with Milton Ager (e.g., LOVIN' SAM (1922); OGO POGO; I WONDER WHAT'S   BE-
COME OF SALLY ? (1924); HARD-TO-GET GERTIE (1926); AIN'T SHE SWEET ?; AIN'T THAT A
GRAND AND GLORIOUS FEELING ?; ARE YOU HAPPY ?; IS SHE MY GIRL FRIEND ? (1927);  MY
PET; GLAD RAG DOLL; FOREVER (1928); HAPPY DAYS ARE HERE AGAIN (1929); many others;
wrote the big hit ARE YOU FROM DIXIE ? in 1915; music for RAIN OR SHINE (1927);the
London production FOLLOW A STAR (1930); several ZIEGFELD FOLLIES and GEORGE  WHITE
SCANDALS, film scores; opened his own publishing house.

Vocal, acc. by Dan Dougherty-p.          New York, January 2, 1929.

BVE-160-1  Glad Rag Doll                          Vic test

## MARGARET YOUNG

Began her career as a society entertainer in Detroit, then launched into vaudeville;
very popular from the early 1920s onwards; made some Capitol records in 1949.

Vocal, acc. by O/Rosario Bourdon.          Camden, N. J., March 26, 1920.

B-23783-1  Oh ! By Jingo ! (Oh ! By Gee ! You're   Vic 18666
             The Only Girl For Me)

                                        Camden, N. J., July 2, 1920.

B-24194-1-2-3  'Way Down Barcelona Way (That       Vic rejected
             Diddle-De-Um-Te-Dum)
B-24195-1-2-3  Lonesome Alimony Blues                  -

  Acc. by studio orchestra.              New York, c. February, 1922.

  7617   Maybe You Think You're Fooling, Baby   Br 2253
  7621   High Brown Blues                          -

                                        New York, c. March, 1922.

         Oo-Oo Ernest                          Br 2265
         Oogie-Oogie-Wa-Wa                         -

                                        New York, c. May, 1922.

         Nobody Loves Me Now                    Br 2284
         Stumbling                                 -

                                        New York, c. July, 1922.

         Nobody Lied (When They Said That I     Br 2297
           Cried Over You)
         Oh ! Is She Dumb !                        -

                                        New York, August, 1922.

  8579   'Way Down Yonder In New Orleans        Br 2319
  8583   True Blue Sam                             -

                                        New York, c. October, 1922.

         He Loves It                            Br 2346
         Lovin' Sam (The Sheik Of Alabam')         -
         Jimbo Jambo                           Br 2359
         Tomorrow (I'll Be In My Dixie Home Again)  -

                                        New York, c. November, 1922.

         Don't Think You'll Be Missed          Br 2371
         Whoa, Tillie ! Take Your Time

New York, c. December, 1922.

| | |
|---|---|
| Bad Little Boys Aren't Goody-Good | Br 2386 |
| Counterfeit Bill | - |

New York, c. February-March, 1923.

| | |
|---|---|
| Seven Or Eleven | Br 2413 |
| Wanita | - |

New York, c. June, 1923.

| | |
|---|---|
| Papa, Better Watch Your Step | Br 2459 |
| Somebody's Wrong | - |

New York, c. August, 1923.

| | |
|---|---|
| Stingo Stungo | Br 2475 |
| He May Be Your Good Man Friday (But He's | - |
| Mine On Saturday Night) | |

New York, c. January, 1924.

| | |
|---|---|
| Hula Lou | Br 2583 |
| Dancin' Dan | - |

New York, c. June, 1924.

| | |
|---|---|
| Too Tired | Br 2673 |
| Doodle-Doo-Doo | - |

New York, c. October, 1924.

| | |
|---|---|
| Big Bad Bill (Is Sweet William Now) | Br 2736 |
| Me And The Boy Friend | - |

New York, c. February, 1925.

| | |
|---|---|
| I Ain't Got Nobody To Love | Br 2806 |
| Nobody Knows What A Red-Head Mama Can Do | - |

## MAURICE YVAIN

One of the few French popular music composers to make great and lasting success with
his tunes in the U.S.A. and Great Britain; composed MON HOMME (MY MAN), 1920,which
Fannie Brice (q.v.) made into a huge hit; J'EN AI MARRE (known in America as IT'S
UP TO YOU and in England as I'M FED UP), 1921; AVEC LE SOURIRE (LET'S DANCE THRO'
LIFE), 1921, and others.

Vocal, acc. by own piano.         New York, May 6, 1930.

BVE-1106   Un amant - un mari         Vic test

## ADDITIONS

FRED DUPREZ :         London, c. January, 1922.

| | |
|---|---|
| Brother Bill And Father | Col 893 |
| The Movies | - |

JOE HAYMAN :         London, c. April, 1917.

| | |
|---|---|
| Cohen And The House Boat : Cohen | Col 2779 |
| Phones For It | |
| Cohen And The House Boat : On The Boat | - |
| Cohen, Commercial Traveller (Pts.1-2) | Col 2961 |

J. H. MURRAY : New York, 1922 - Man In The Moon/I'm Only A Pilgrim   Voc 14549